MOON HANDBOOKS®

OREGON

springtime in the
Wallowa Mountains

Anglers from around the world come to test themselves on the North Umpqua River.

MOON HANDBOOKS®

OREGON

SIXTH EDITION

ELIZABETH & MARK MORRIS

AVALON
TRAVEL

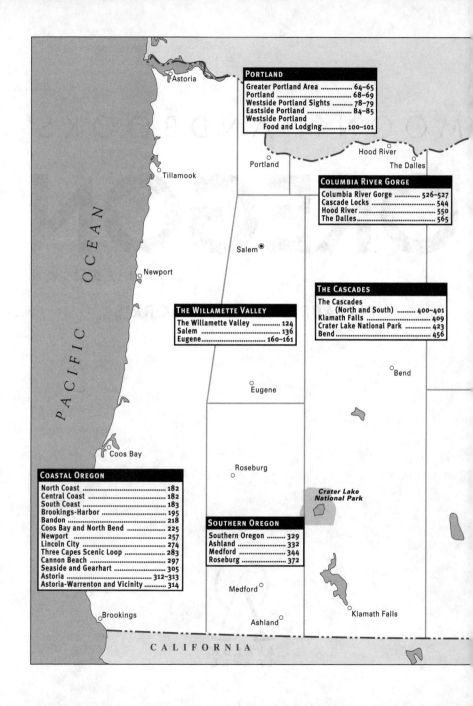

Astoria

Tillamook

PACIFIC OCEAN

Newport

Portland

Hood River

The Dalles

Salem

Eugene

Bend

Coos Bay

Roseburg

Crater Lake National Park

Brookings

Medford

Ashland

Klamath Falls

CALIFORNIA

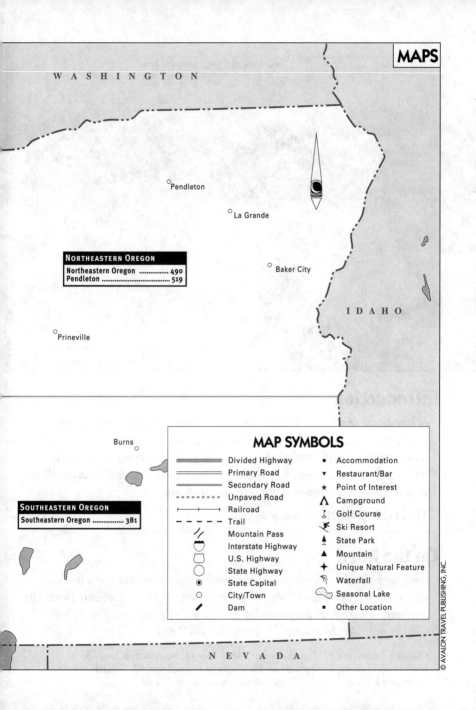

WASHINGTON

Pendleton

La Grande

NORTHEASTERN OREGON

Baker City

IDAHO

Prineville

Burns

SOUTHEASTERN OREGON

MAP SYMBOLS

═══ Divided Highway	• Accommodation
─── Primary Road	▼ Restaurant/Bar
─── Secondary Road	★ Point of Interest
- - - - - Unpaved Road	Λ Campground
├──┼──┤ Railroad	⌡ Golf Course
– – – Trail	⚡ Ski Resort
⁄⁄ Mountain Pass	▲ State Park
Interstate Highway	▲ Mountain
U.S. Highway	✛ Unique Natural Feature
State Highway	↘ Waterfall
◉ State Capital	～ Seasonal Lake
○ City/Town	▪ Other Location
⁄ Dam	

NEVADA

Contents

© MARK MORRIS

Introduction 1

When Lewis and Clark first set eyes on this landscape two centuries ago, they were greeted by sagebrush deserts, dense forests, shimmering lakes and rivers, and pristine snow-covered slopes. Today, Oregon's pioneer spirit still draws adventurous travelers—to hike, boat, fish, ski, climb, and explore cities that match progressive attitudes with small-town charm.

On the Road 31

The biggest problem you'll face when visiting the Beaver State is narrowing down the countless possibilities. Whether employing your Northwest Forest Pass, attending music festivals, or tracing the journey of Lewis and Clark, this chapter provides the practical information you'll need.

Portland 62

Graced with natural waterways and a mild climate, Portland is the state's green, urban core—equal parts cultural center, marketplace, and working metropolis. Smell the roses in Washington Park, go antiquing in Sellwood, shop for kitsch in the hip Hawthorne District, or cozy up with a latte in an independent coffeehouse.

The Willamette Valley 123

Encompassing state capital Salem, bike-friendly Corvallis, and earthy yet sophisticated Eugene, this fertile valley yields intellectuals and utopians along with its harvests of berries and wine grapes.

Coastal Oregon 181

Sandy beaches punctuated with rugged rock formations; wild rivers and broad, lazy estuaries; steep headlands and a wall of forested mountains—nowhere is the meeting of land and sea so dramatic. Linked by an unbroken scenic highway and blessed with a plethora of peaceful B&Bs, the Oregon coastline makes a great escape.

Southern Oregon

Southern Oregon has a reputation for harboring the eccentric. Bigfoot sightings are not uncommon, the Oregon Vortex defies gravity, thousands flock to Ashland for a hearty dose of Shakespeare, and folks get fanatical about rivers— whether fishing the Umpqua or kayaking the Rogue.

Southeastern Oregon

This high-desert region boasts pastel blue skies, geologic marvels, and plenty of elbow room. Spend time at an old-fashioned rodeo, view migrating birds at wildlife refuges, or dig for the Plush "diamond."

The Cascades

The Cascades are one of the world's most magnificent natural playgrounds: More than 160 parks and forests provide easy access to hiking, camping, climbing, and skiing. Hundreds of miles of ski trails crisscross the landscape, the fresh water teems with fish, and a bevy of luxury resorts ensures that you'll rough it in style.

Northeastern Oregon

*You'll hear echoes of the Old West in Northeastern
Oregon—whether you're touring Chief Joseph's
homeland, tracing the steps of the Oregon Trail's eager
pioneers, or floating the winding Snake River. A gondola
ride to the top of Mount Howard is about as fast as life
gets in these parts.*

Columbia River Gorge

*This is the Northwest's primal landscape and weekend
wilderness: towering waterfalls, moss-draped rainforests,
orchards back-dropped by snowcapped volcanoes—all in
a sweeping chasm five miles wide, 80 miles long, and
4,000 feet deep.*

Resources

About the Authors
Mark and Elizabeth Morris

Mark and Elizabeth Morris first became involved in travel writing while working as editors at Moon Publications, when the original Handbook series was produced in two crowded rooms of the publisher's Northern California home. In those days, the text was set an agonizing 13 picas at a time on a clunky old Linotronic typesetter, and laying out a guidebook called for more hot wax than a beauty salon needs in a month.

Mark made the transition from editor-in-chief to travel writer with his first book, *Odyssey Illustrated Guide to Ireland*. Elizabeth took up the post of managing editor at Moon, and worked for a time in Hong Kong at Moon's former affiliate, China Guides.

Mark continued to pursue his passion for coastal destinations by co-authoring *Moon Handbooks Atlantic Canada*. Their love of the Pacific Northwest led Elizabeth and Mark to settle in Portland and begin their extensive explorations of the region. In the early years of the Internet boom, the pair caught the attention of a little Seattle-based company called Microsoft Corp. Mark was hired to manage travel-content development for what would become Expedia.com, a leading online travel website, while Elizabeth became managing editor for Microsoft's popular mapping and route-planning products. Thrilling as 70-hour work weeks and commuting in Seattle traffic were, after seven years Elizabeth and Mark left the software giant to return to the less hectic life of full-time travel writing.

When the opportunity arose to take ownership of *Moon Handbooks Oregon* from their old friend Stuart Warren, Elizabeth and Mark were delighted to accept, and they hope that longtime readers as well as new ones will be pleased with this sixth edition. Oregon is unquestionably one of their two favorite states; the other one, they haven't found yet.

*This book is dedicated to our moms, Suzanne and Beverly.
We couldn't have done it without you.*

Introduction

In the middle of the 19th century, Theodore Winthrop, a novelist and adventurer from New England, made the following observation during his journey to the Oregon Territory:

Our race has never yet come into contact with great mountains as companions of daily life, nor felt that daily development of the finer and more comprehensive senses which these signal facts of nature compel. . . . These Oregon people, in a climate where being is bliss—where every breath is a draught of vivid life—these Oregon people, carrying to a newer and grander New England of the West a full growth of the American Idea . . . will elaborate new systems of thought and life.

What this translates to today is that "these Oregon people" know how to live, and live well. Many modern travelers to the state will tell you that nowhere else in the country has civilization meshed so peacefully with the environment. Progressive land-use policies, preserving vast tracts of irreplaceable land and curbing the blight of suburban sprawl, attest to Oregonians' appreciation of their gemlike coastline, productive farmland, mountain ranges, and other unspoiled landscapes.

As much as the great outdoors, the arts are cherished here; music and dance, theater, and a myriad of visual arts enrich the lives of residents and draw visitors by the multitude. The state also celebrates its historical heritage, ethnic makeup, and rich cuisine in a thousand festivals.

© MARK MORRIS

Hug Point State Park

In short, Oregon remains a place that is still environmentally and socially intact.

Most of these rewards of the good life didn't come easily, though. Just as it took Oregon Trail pioneers many months to cross 2,000 miles of treacherous deserts and forbidding mountain passes to reach the promised land, Oregonians have sacrificed much to blaze trails in the thickets of environmental legislation and jurisprudence. The dilemma of one person's conservation being another's unemployment has been a continuous fact of life here; this debate will undoubtedly continue into the future as Oregon strives to find an equable balance among competing interests.

Inevitably, the outcome will bring more change and perhaps the regrettable passing of a way of life for many. But one fact is clear—if Oregon has erred on the side of conservation, it has at least preserved an increasingly valuable and endangered commodity: its natural resources. The proof is here for you to see.

The Land

GEOGRAPHY

If Oregon were part of a jigsaw puzzle of the United States, it would be a squarish piece with a divot carved out of the center top. To the west is the Pacific Ocean, and some 370 miles of beaches, dunes, and headlands; to the east are the Snake River and Idaho. Up north, much of the boundary between Oregon and Washington is defined by the mighty Columbia River, while southern Oregon lies atop the upper borders of California and Nevada.

If this puzzle also depicted the vertical relief of topographic features, it would show broad rows of mountains dividing the coast from the inland valleys, as well as peaks cutting off western Oregon from the central and eastern parts of the state. East of the highest central range the Columbia Plateau predominates, broken up in the northeast where mountainous features reassert themselves. In the southeast, scattered lakes dot the landscape in the least-mountainous expanse of the state. The Great Basin desert—characterized by rivers that evaporate, peter out, or disappear into underground aquifers—makes up the bottom third of eastern Oregon. Here, the seven-inch annual rainfall of the Alvord Desert seems as if it would be more at home in southeastern California and Nevada than in a state known for blustery rainstorms and lush greenery.

Highs and Lows

Moving west to east, let's consider the major mountain systems, beginning with the Klamath Mountains and the Coast Range. The Klamaths comprise the lower quarter of the state's western barrier to the Pacific; the eastern flank of this range is generally referred to as the Siskiyous. As we move north, the Oregon Coast Range, a younger volcanic range, replaces the Klamaths. The highest peaks in each of these cordilleras barely top 4,000 feet and stand in between narrow coastal plateaus on the west side and the rich agricultural lands of the Willamette and Rogue valleys on the other. Running up the west-central portion of the state is the Cascade Range, which extends from Northern California up to Canada. Five of the dormant volcanoes within Oregon top 10,000 feet above sea level, with Mount Hood the state's highest peak, at 11,239 feet.

Beyond the Cascades' eastern slope, one finds semiarid high-desert conditions contrasting with the Coast Range rainforests and the mild, wet maritime climate that characterizes much of western Oregon. The contrast is repeated in the northeast, where the 10,000-foot crests of the snowcapped Wallowas rise less than 50 miles from the hot, arid floor of Hells Canyon, about 1,300 feet above sea level.

In addition to Hells Canyon, America's biggest hole in the ground (7,900 feet maximum depth), Oregon also boasts the continent's deepest lake: Crater Lake, with a depth of 1,958 feet (according to soundings taken on the lake by the federal government in September 2000).

Last of the Red-Hot Lavas

Each part of the state contains other well-known remnants of Oregon's cataclysmic past. Offshore waters here feature 1,477 islands and islets, the eroded remains of ancient volcanic flows. Lava fields dot the approaches to the High Cascades. East of the range a volcanic plateau supports cinder cones, lava caves, and lava-cast forests in the most varied array of these phenomena outside of Hawaii.

The imposing volcanic cones of the Cascades, most perfectly realized in Mount Hood, and the inundated caldera that is Crater Lake, formed by the implosion of Mount Mazama some 6,600 years ago, are some of the most dramatic reminders of Oregon's volcanic origins. More fascinating evidence can be seen up-close at Newberry National Volcanic Monument, an extensive area south of Bend that encompasses the obsidian fields and lava formations left by massive eruptions. (Incidentally, geologists have cited Newberry on their list of volcanoes in the continental United States most likely to erupt again.) Not far from the Lava Lands Visitor Center in the national monument are the Lava River Cave and Lava Cast Forest—created when lava enveloped living trees 6,000 years ago.

Earthquakes and Tsunamis

Scientists exploring Tillamook County in 1990 unearthed discontinuities in both rock strata and tree rings indicating that the north Oregon coast has experienced major **earthquakes** every several hundred years. They estimate that the next one could come within our lifetimes and be of significant magnitude. In this vein, Japanese scientists maintain that a 9.0 quake struck the Northwest coast in 1700, based on tsunami records indicating that six- to nine-foot-high tidal waves hit Japan's coastline. This date is also consistent with Northwest Native American oral histories and geologic evidence.

These coastal quakes are caused by what geologists call subduction. This process occurs when one of the giant plates that make up the earth's crust slides under another as they collide (see the introduction in the Cascades chapter for more on plate tectonics). In Pacific Northwest coastal regions, this takes place when the Juan de Fuca plate's marine layer is pushed under the

WHAT'S IN A NAME?

One theory of how Oregon got its name derives from a reputed encounter between native peoples and the Spanish mariners who plied West Coast waters in the 17th and 18th centuries. Upon seeing the abalone shell earrings of the coastal Salish, the European sailors are said to have exclaimed, *"Orejon!"* ("What big ears!")—later anglicized to "Oregon." Others point out the similarity between the name of the state and the Spanish locales Aragon and Obregon (in Mexico). Additionally, the word "Oregon" belonged to a Wisconsin tribe who purportedly traded with Columbia River natives during salmon season.

A less fanciful explanation has it that the state's name was inspired by the English word "origin," conjuring the image of the forest primeval. The French word *ouragan* ("hurricane") has also been suggested as the source of the state's name, courtesy of French Canadian fur trappers who became the first permanent white settlers in the region during the early 19th century. In this vein, the reference to the Columbia River as the "Oregan" by some French Canadian voyageurs who came here with the "beaver brigades" of the Northwest and Hudson Bay Companies is another possible etymological ancestor.

It was recently noted that "Oregonon" and "Orenogonia," two Greek words pertaining to mountainous locales, were seen on old navigators' maps marking the area between Northern California and British Columbia. Given that the famous Pacific Northwest explorer Juan de Fuca was actually Greek (born Valerianos) and that many navigators were schooled in Greece, perhaps Oregon's name originated in the Mediterranean.

OREGON WEATHER

City	Jan.	Feb.	Mar.	Apr.	May	June	July	Aug.	Sept.	Oct.	Nov.	Dec.	*A.A.R.
Astoria													
High (° F)	48	51	53	56	60	64	67	68	68	61	53	48	
Low (° F)	37	38	39	41	45	50	53	53	50	44	40	37	
Rain (inches)	9.6	7.9	7.4	4.9	3.3	2.6	1.2	1.2	2.6	5.6	10.5	10.4	67.2
Baker City													
High (° F)	34	42	51	59	67	75	85	85	76	63	45	35	
Low (° F)	17	22	27	31	38	44	48	47	39	30	24	17	
Rain (inches)	0.9	0.6	0.8	0.9	1.4	1.2	0.7	0.9	0.7	0.6	1	1	10.7
Bend													
High (° F)	40	44	51	57	65	73	81	81	72	62	46	40	
Low (° F)	23	25	27	30	36	41	46	46	39	32	28	23	
Rain (inches)	1.8	1.2	2	0.7	0.9	0.8	0.6	0.6	0.5	0.6	1.5	1.8	13
Brookings													
High (° F)	55	56	58	60	63	67	68	68	68	65	58	55	
Low (° F)	42	42	42	44	47	50	52	53	51	48	45	41	
Rain (inches)	11.3	10.1	9.6	5.7	3.6	1.8	0.5	1	1.9	5.2	10.6	12	73.3
Coos Bay													
High (° F)	53	55	55	57	61	64	67	68	67	63	57	53	
Low (° F)	39	41	41	43	47	50	53	53	50	46	43	39	
Rain (inches)	9.5	8.1	7.9	5.2	3.4	1.7	0.5	0.9	1.7	4.6	10.4	10.4	64.3
Eugene													
High (° F)	46	51	56	61	67	73	81	82	77	65	52	46	
Low (° F)	33	35	37	39	43	47	51	51	47	41	37	33	
Rain (inches)	7.7	6.4	5.8	3.7	2.7	1.5	0.6	1	1.5	3.4	8.4	8.3	51
Grants Pass													
High (° F)	47	54	60	66	73	81	89	89	83	70	53	46	
Low (° F)	31	33	34	36	41	45	49	49	43	37	35	31	
Rain (inches)	5	4.4	3.7	2	1.2	0.5	0.4	0.5	0.9	2.1	5.1	5.4	31.2
Klamath Falls													
High (° F)	40	45	51	57	66	74	83	83	76	65	48	40	
Low (° F)	20	25	28	31	36	43	48	46	39	30	25	19	
Rain (inches)	1.7	1.3	1.2	0.8	0.8	0.7	0.3	0.6	0.5	0.8	1.8	1.6	12.1

City	Jan.	Feb.	Mar.	Apr.	May	June	July	Aug.	Sept.	Oct.	Nov.	Dec.	*A.A.R.
Newport													
High (° F)	51	54	55	57	60	63	65	66	65	61	55	51	
Low (° F)	39	39	40	41	45	48	51	51	49	45	42	39	
Rain (inches)	10.3	8.7	7.7	4.9	3.7	2.7	1	1	2.4	5.1	10.7	11.4	69.6
Pendleton													
High (° F)	40	47	55	62	70	79	88	87	77	64	49	40	
Low (° F)	27	31	35	40	46	52	58	57	50	41	34	28	
Rain (inches)	1.5	1.2	1.3	1.1	1.2	0.8	0.4	0.6	0.6	1	1.6	1.5	12.8
Portland													
High (°F)	46	50	56	61	67	73	79	79	74	63	51	46	
Low (° F)	37	39	41	44	49	53	57	58	55	48	42	37	
Rain (inches)	6.2	5.2	4.5	3.1	2.5	1.6	0.8	1	1.9	3.4	6.4	6.8	43.4
Roseburg													
High (° F)	50	55	60	65	71	78	86	86	81	69	56	49	
Low (° F)	35	37	38	41	46	51	55	55	50	44	40	35	
Rain (inches)	5	4.1	3.8	2.8	1.8	0.9	0.4	0.7	1.1	2.3	5.4	5.4	33.7
Salem													
High (° F)	47	51	56	61	67	74	82	82	77	64	52	46	
Low (° F)	33	35	37	39	44	48	52	52	48	41	38	34	
Rain (inches)	5.9	5.1	4.2	2.8	2.1	1.5	0.6	0.7	1.4	3	6.4	6.5	40.2
The Dalles													
High (° F)	41	48	57	65	74	80	88	88	81	67	50	42	
Low (° F)	30	32	37	43	50	56	61	61	52	42	35	30	
Rain (inches)	2.6	1.9	1.2	0.7	0.6	0.4	0.2	0.3	0.5	1	2.2	2.7	14.3

* Average Annual Rainfall

continental North American plate. With virtually every part of the state possessing seismic potential that hasn't been released in many years, the pressure along the fault lines is increasing. The fact that Oregon building codes have not yet acknowledged this became evident in March 1993, when a quake centered 30 miles south of Portland and registering 5.7 on the Richter scale accounted for several million dollars' worth of damage. In September of that year, two Klamath Falls temblors averaging nearly 6.0 on the Richter scale compounded the impression that the earth's internal burners are heating up again. The Klamath Falls quakes were the largest recorded in the state since 1873.

In coastal areas, one of the greatest dangers associated with earthquakes is the possibility of **tsunamis,** popularly (but incorrectly) known as tidal waves. The waves are produced by an offshore quake—even one centered thousands of miles distant. As a tsunami draws closer to the shore, driven by the force of the quake, it takes in preceding waters and builds into a series of waves traveling as fast as 500 miles per hour and reaching as high as 100 feet. Ever since a tsunami unleashed by Alaska's Good Friday quake in 1964 (measured at 14.2 feet high at the mouth of the Umpqua River) resulted in four casualties in Beverly Beach and over a million dollars in damage, local authorities have made seismic preparedness a priority, with a system of warning sirens and evacuation signs pointing the way to higher ground.

The Great Meltdown

However pervasive the effects of seismic activity and volcanism here, they must still share top billing with the last Ice Age in the grand epic of Oregon's topography.

At the height of the most recent major glaciation, the world's oceans were lower by 300–500 feet, North America and Asia were connected by a land bridge across the Bering Strait, and the Oregon coast was miles west of where it is today. The Columbia Gorge extended out past present-day Astoria. As the glaciers melted, the sea rose.

When that glacial epoch's final meltdown 12,000 years ago unleashed water dammed up by thousands of feet of ice, great rivers were spawned and existing channels were enlarged. A particularly large inundation was the Missoula Flood, which began with an ice dam breaking up in what's now Montana. Before it subsided, it carved out the contours of what are now the Columbia River Gorge and the Willamette Valley. Other glacial floodwaters found their outlet westward to the sea, digging out silt-ridden estuaries in the process. Pacific wave action washed this debris back up onto the land, helping to create dunes and beaches.

CLIMATE

The Rain Shadow

Oregon's location equidistant from the equator and the North Pole subjects it to weather from both tropical and polar air flows. This makes for a pattern of changeability in which calm often alternates with storm, and extreme heat and extreme cold seldom last long. Of the world's 10 different climate zones, Oregon experiences seven.

Oregon's weather system is best understood as a series of valley climates separated from each other by mountain ranges which draw precipitation from the eastbound weather systems. Moving west to east, each of these valley zones records progressively lower rainfall levels until one encounters a desert on the eastern side of the state.

It all begins when moisture-laden westerlies off the Pacific slam into the Coast and Klamath Ranges. As the mountains push the clouds higher, they drop their moisture in the form of rain or snow. That's because rising air cools three degrees Fahrenheit for every 1,000 feet of altitude gain, and cooler air can't hold as much moisture as warm air. As a consequence, rainfall at the coast often exceeds 80 inches a year. In parts of the coastal ranges, yearly totals of well over 100 inches aren't uncommon.

By contrast, the Willamette and other inland valleys on the east side of the mountains usually record half that total. However, during 20-year "rainy cycles" caused by what meteorologists call the "Pacific oscillation," the interior regions can see double their normal rainfall.

The rain shadow effect is repeated when the Cascades catch precipitation from eastward-moving cloud masses, wringing the moisture out of the storms; consequently, the eastern side of this range often records annual rainfall totals below 10 inches.

The Coast

Wet but mild, average rainfall on the coast ranges from a low of 64 inches per year in the Coos Bay area to nearly 100 inches around Lincoln City. Just inland from the coastal plateau, though, the mountains tend to be substantially wetter, averaging 150 inches per year. The Pacific Ocean moderates coastal weather year-round, softening the extremes. Spring, summer, and fall generally don't get very hot, with highs generally in the 60s and 70s Fahrenheit, and seldom topping 90°. Winter temperatures only drop to the 40s and 50s, and freezes and snowfall are quite rare occurrences. For additional details on coastal weather and the best times to visit, see the "Climate" section of the Coastal Oregon chapter.

Western Oregon

If there is one constant in western Oregon, it is cloudiness. Portland and the Willamette Valley receive only about 45 percent of maximum potential sunshine; more than 200 days of the year are cloudy and rain falls an average of 150 days. While this might sound bleak, consider that the cloud cover helps moderate the climate by trapping and reflecting the earth's heat. Daily fluctuations in temperature average only 15° F here; the difference between the average temperatures of the warmest month, July, and the coldest one, January, is only about 20° F. Best of all, on average, fewer than 30 days of the year record temperatures below freezing. Thus, the region, despite being on a more northerly latitude than parts of Canada, has a milder climate. Except in mountainous areas, snow usually isn't a force to be reckoned with here. Another surprise is that Portland's average annual rainfall of 40 inches is usually less than totals recorded in New York, Miami, and Chicago.

East of the Cascades, the opinion is, it's so dry in the Oregon desert even the jackrabbits pack canteens. The drysiders will assure you that people in western Oregon don't tan, they rust.

While Portland and the rest of the Willamette Valley share mild climates, with wintertime highs of 45° F and average summertime mercury readings between 65° and 75° F, their weather differences are worth noting. Portland is affected by icy winds coming out of the Columbia River Gorge, originally derived from frigid Rocky Mountain air. At these times, the otherwise mild Portland climate experiences uncharacteristic frosts. Part of Portland's reputation for having a cold climate derives from its location 150 miles farther north than frigid Green Bay, Wisconsin. The warming influence of the Japanese current, however, mitigates the effects of Portland's northerly location.

The rest of the Willamette Valley is affected by temperature inversions. In winter, for example, warm air above the valley walls holds in the colder air below, resulting in enduring, but not endearing, fogs. In the southern valleys, fog helps to counterbalance the region's long dry season: Ashland and Medford sometimes record only half the yearly precipitation of their neighbors to the north, as well as higher winter and summer temperatures. At the same time, these inversions can cause unwelcome pollution to linger.

In much of western Oregon, the day-night differences in temperature are seldom extreme because of cloud cover and vegetation. Both act to keep the air cool and moist during the day and trap heat at night. Still, visitors from the East Coast may be struck by how much more Oregon cools down at night than locales in the mid-Atlantic states.

While it's difficult to predict daily weather patterns in western Oregon, there are definite seasonal climatic shifts here. In winter, arctic and tropical air masses collide over the Pacific, producing much of the state's rain. During the summer the clashes are less frequent. At that time, Oregon weather is more affected by Pacific Ocean temperatures and air pressure differences between inland and coastal areas.

Eastern Oregon

By contrast, the scorching deserts of eastern Oregon can give way to cold temperatures at night. This is because clear skies and a dearth of vegetation facilitate the escape of heat. Consider that on May 2, 1968, the difference between the high and low temperatures at Juniper Lake, north of the Alvord Desert in southeastern Oregon, was 81 degrees.

Mountain areas also experience extreme diurnal temperature fluctuations. Thin mountain air does not filter out ultraviolet radiation as effectively as the denser air at lower elevations, so the sun's force is accentuated at higher elevations. At night, chill spreads quickly through this thin air.

FLORA

With 4,400 known species and varieties, Oregon ranks fourth among U.S. states for plant diversity, including dozens of species found nowhere else.

Trees

The mixed-conifer ecosystem of western Oregon—dense, far-reaching forests of Douglas fir, Sitka spruce, western hemlock, interspersed with bigleaf maple, vine maple, alder—is among the most productive woodlands in the world, boasting such record specimens as the **Doerner fir** in the Coast Range outside Coquille. It's rated the nation's largest Douglas fir by the American Forestry Association based on height (329 feet), diameter (11.5 feet), and crown size.

Indeed, statewide, Oregon has over 40 "champion" trees that have somehow managed to escape the ax and chainsaw, including the record ponderosa pine outside Bend, the world's biggest Sitka spruce off U.S. 26 near Cannon Beach, Oregon's largest Monterey cypress in Brookings, and a bevy of other distinctions.

Telling what's what in these forests, though, can be confusing. Oregon schoolchildren first learn to distinguish between fir, spruce, hemlock, and ponderosa pine by a mnemonic device: The needles of a fir are flat, flexible, and friendly. Spruce needles are square, stiff, and will stick you. Hemlock needles have a hammock-like configuration, and the crown of the tree is curved as though it's tipping its hat. Finally, the ponderosa pine's platelike bark is a distinctive feature.

Tree lovers will also be taken by such arboreal aberrations as southern Oregon's redwood groves and rare myrtle trees (prized by woodworkers and especially woodturners for its distinctive coloring and grain), the huge ponderosa pines in the middle of Christmas Valley desert, and fall color in Portland and Willamette Valley towns from deciduous trees planted by early pioneers. A particularly striking natural display along the McKenzie River mixes red vine maple and sumacs with golden oaks and alders against an evergreen backdrop.

With only seven percent as much rainfall as the Coast Range forests get, 20 million acres of eastern Oregon's desert is largely rabbitbrush, cheatgrass, sagebrush, and juniper. In the John Day backcountry of eastern Oregon, you can find even hedgehog cactus.

Old-Growth Forests

Of the 19 million acres of old growth that once proliferated Oregon and Washington, only 10 percent survive, and portions are always under threat of further destruction by logging. Naturalists describe an old-growth forest as a mixture of trees, some of which must be at least 200 years old, and a supply of snags or standing dead trees, nurse logs, and streams with downed logs. Throughout this book, reference are made to old-growth groves that are noteworthy for size, age, beauty, ecological significance, or ease of access. Of all the old-growth forests mentioned in this volume, **Opal Creek** (see Willamette Valley chapter), recently incorporated into a protected wilderness, most spectacularly embodies all of the above characteristics.

Flowers and Fruits

The state of Oregon has long been associated in the public mind with such sobriquets as the "Emerald Empire" and the "Chlorophyll Com-

BOB RACE

Douglas fir

BOB RACE

Called both California laurel and Oregon myrtle, this tree is technically neither. Crush a leaf to release its distinctive, camphorlike aroma.

monwealth." While giant conifers and a profuse understory of greenery do in fact surround the state's most populous areas, this ecosystem represents only the most visible part of Oregon's bountiful botany. Other worlds exist in between the mist-covered mountains and the deserts.

While not as visually arresting as the evergreens of western Oregon, the state's several varieties of **berries** are no less pervasive. Found mostly from the coast to the mid-Cascades, blackberries favor clearings, burned-over areas, and people's gardens. It also takes root in the woods alongside wild strawberries, salmonberries, thimbleberries, currants, and salal. Within this edible realm, wild food connoisseurs especially seek out the thin-leafed huckleberry found in the Wallowa, Blue, Cascade, and Klamath Ranges. Prime snacking season for all these berries ranges from midsummer to midfall.

Exempt from exploitation but no less prized are the rare plant communities of the Columbia River Gorge and the Klamath/Siskiyou region. A quarter of Oregon's rare and endangered plants are found in the latter area, a portion of which is in the valley of the Illinois River, a designated Wild and Scenic tributary of the Rogue. *Kalmiopsis leachiana,* a rare member of the heath family endemic to southwestern Oregon, even has a wilderness area named after it. The state's botanical communities are considered among the most

diverse on the planet, boasting 800 species (including 14 "endemics") found nowhere else in the world.

Motorists will treasure such springtime floral fantasias (both wild and domesticated) as the dahlias and irises near Canby off I-5; tulips near Woodburn; irises off ORE 213 outside Salem; the Easter lilies along U.S. 101 near Brookings; blue lupines alongside ORE 97 in central Oregon; apple blossoms in the Hood River Valley near the Columbia Gorge; pear blossoms in the Bear Creek Valley near Medford; beargrass, columbines, and Indian paintbrush on Cascades thoroughfares; as well as Scotch broom, rhododendrons, and fireweed along the coast. And on some of the busiest highways in the state, Willamette Valley daffodils pave a springtime yellow brick road through the heart of the Emerald Empire.

Wildflower lovers will notice that in the country east of the Cascades the undergrowth is often more varied than the ground cover in the damp forests on the other side of the mountains. This is because sunny openings in the forest permit room for more species and for plants of different heights. And, in contrast to the white flowers that predominate in the shady forests in western Oregon, "dry-side" wildflowers generally have brighter colors. These blossoms attract color-sensitive pollinators such as bees and butterflies. On the opposite flank of the range, the commonly seen white trillium relies on beetles and ants for propagation, lessening the need for eye-catching pigments.

Mushrooms

Autumn is the season for those who covet wild chanterelle, matsutake, and morel mushrooms, particularly between the first rains and the onset of frosts. The Coast Range from September through November is the prime picking area for chanterelles—a fluted orange or yellow mushroom in the tall second-growth Douglas fir forests. After picking, don't put mushrooms in plastic bags. Use waxed paper or a basket, and leave them uncovered unless it's raining. And, of course, you should be absolutely certain of what you have before you eat wild mushrooms, or any other wild food.

Of late, fungus fever has reached epidemic proportions, largely due to a matsutake mushroom shortage in Japan, where it is prized for medicinal and spiritual qualities as well as a soup garnish. Matsutakes have fetched as much as $500 a pound in Japan, a fact that has precipitated violence in northern Klamath County forests and other areas that were saturated with pickers during the fall harvest. If you plan to sell what you find, you need to purchase a permit from the National Forest Service for a nominal fee.

FAUNA

Oregon's creatures great and small comprise an excitingly diverse group. Oregon's low population density, abundance of wildlife refuges and nature preserves, and biomes running the gamut from rainforest to desert explain this variety. Throughout the state, numerous refuges, such as the **South Slough National Estuarine Research Reserve,** the **Malheur Bird/Wildlife Refuge,** the **Jewell Preserve for Roosevelt Elk,** and the **Finley Bird and Wildlife Preserve** provide safe havens for both feathered and furry friends.

While the dominant animals in each of the state's ecosystems are profiled in the relevant chapters, there are certain species whose ubiquitous presence demands an in-depth treatment.

Small Mammals

Many of the most frequently sighted animals in Oregon are small scavengers. Even in the most urban parts of the state, it's possible to see raccoons, skunks, chipmunks, squirrels, and opossums. Most are frequently encountered in woodsier neighborhoods, often around garbage cans, in parks, and near picnic areas. Urban gardens attract moles and pocket gophers.

West of the Cascades, the dark-colored Townsend's chipmunks are among the most commonly encountered mammals; east of the Cascades, lighter-colored pine chipmunks and golden mantled ground squirrels proliferate in drier interior forests. The latter two look almost alike, but

BANANA SLUGS

You won't go far in the Oregon coast woodlands or underbrush before you encounter the state's best-known invertebrates—and lots of them. There are few places on earth where these snails-out-of-shells grow as large (3–10 inches long) or as numerous. The reason is western Oregon's climate: moister than mist but drier than drizzle. This balance, combined with calcium-poor soil, enables the native banana slug and the more common European black slug to thrive.

The bane of Oregon gardeners, the eight species of nonnative slugs that have established themselves in the Northwest prey on crops and gardens. Native species generally confine themselves to forests, where they feast on indigenous plants. When these critters are not eating vegetation, you'll see them moseying along at a snail's pace on sidewalks or forest trails.

© MARK MORRIS

banana slug, ubiquitous denizen of the forest floor

INTRODUCTION

ANN LONG LARSEN

Townsend's chipmunk

the stripes on the side of the chipmunk's head distinguish them from each other. Expect to see the dark brown, cinnamon-bellied Douglas squirrel on both sides of the Cascades.

Urban jungles, suburbs, and other communities throughout Oregon have seen an infestation of opossums in recent decades. These docile nocturnal marsupials are usually sighted during twilight hours and often as road kills. Brought by a contingent of rural folk from Arkansas as a food source back in the 1930s and '40s, their numbers have increased exponentially. In fact, people are becoming so used to North America's only marsupial that the opossum is taking on a new life as a domesticated household pet. They can't get rabies or distemper because their body temperatures are too low, and their ability to grasp objects with their tail and the presence of opposable thumbs make opossums fascinating to watch. Just catch them when they're awake. These nearly blind fruit and carrion eaters spend most of their lives asleep.

Beavers in the Beaver State

Beavers (*Castor canadensis*), North America's largest rodents, are widespread throughout the state, though they're most commonly sighted in second-growth forests near marshes after sunset. Fall is a good time to spot beavers as they gather food for winter. The beaver has long been Oregon's mascot, and for good reason: it was the beaver that drew brigades of fur trappers and spurred the initial exploration

and settlement of the state. The beaver also merits a special mention for being perhaps the most important animal in Oregon's forest ecosystem. Contrary to popular conception, the abilities of Mother Nature's carpenter extend far beyond the mere destruction of trees to dam a waterway. In fact, the activities associated with lodge construction actually serve to maintain the food chain and the health of the forest.

When a mated pair (beavers mate for life) packs sticks and mud to dam a river or stream, the resulting pool of deeper water in which they build their lodge protects these ungainly creatures from predation. The dam also reduces the stream's current and potential flooding of the lodge. The beavers' chances for survival are aided by their ability to enter the lodge underwater and to stay beneath the surface for as long as 20 minutes. Ear flaps and retractable membranes that protect their eyes enable them to dive comfortably, and a flat paddle-like tail helps them to swim. With a pair of long, sharp middle teeth, beavers are perfectly equipped to cut willow, birch, alder, vine maple, and other trees into sticks of exact specifications and float them to the construction site. If river conditions don't permit a dam spanning two shorelines, beavers will build their lodge into a bank.

The beaver's lodge, together with its pond, foster a fertile web of life. Aged trees killed by the intrusion of a pond into a forest become homes for millions of insects, which provide food for woodpeckers and other birds. Fish, turtles,

ANN LONG LARSEN

beaver

frogs, and snakes soon inhabit the pond and its surrounding environment, and herons, muskrats, otters, and raccoons arrive later as part of the newly emerging ecosystem. Bears, birds of prey, and deer may come to the shore to drink or feed on smaller animals. Fish may feed on mosquito larvae in the still waters. After the beavers have exhausted the nearby food supply and have moved on, the pond may eventually drain and become a fertile meadow and home to yet other creatures.

The presence of beavers has other positive implications for the nearby human population. In early times, pioneers coveted the fertile soil left from a drained beaver pond. Floods and droughts are tempered in the long run by beaver activities; control of soil erosion and reduced numbers of forest fires are other positive byproducts.

ANN LONG LARSEN

Roosevelt elk

Deer, Elk, and Pronghorn

Sportspeople and wildlife enthusiasts alike appreciate Oregon's big-game herds. Big-game habitats differ dramatically from one side of the Cascades to the other, with Roosevelt elk and blacktail deer in the west and Rocky Mountain elk and mule deer east of the Cascades. The Columbian whitetail deer is a seldom-seen, endangered species that populates western Oregon.

Pronghorns reside in the high desert country of southeastern Oregon. The continent's fastest mammal, it is able to sprint at over 60 miles per hour in short bursts. The low brush of the open country east of the Cascades suits the pronghorns' excellent vision, which enables them to spot predators. The most dangerous predator of all is kept at a distance by the boundaries of the Hart Mountain National Antelope Refuge (see "Sights" in the Southeastern Oregon chapter).

Desert Critters

When talking about this desert region, it should first be noted that marine fossils dating back 225 million years were found in eastern Oregon creekbeds. These crustaceans were discovered in present-day Lake County, which today is home to such diverse wildlife as pronghorn and wild mustangs. Because 99 percent of desert animals are nocturnal, it's difficult to see many of them. Nonetheless, their variety and exotic presences should be noted. Horned lizards, kangaroo rats, red-and-black ground snakes, kit foxes, and four-inch-long greenish-yellow hairy scorpions are some of the more interesting denizens of the desert east of the Cascade Mountains. Should you ever have the chance to witness the intelligence of coyotes on the hunt or the nimble-footed bighorn sheep dancing along a precipitous ridge here, you'll never forget it.

Bears

Black bears, *Ursus americanus,* proliferate in remote mountain forests of Oregon. The state's Department of Fish and Wildlife estimates that 14,000–19,000 black bears roam the western Cascades and the Coast Range. Adults average between 200 and 500 pounds and have dark coats. Despite Washington Cascades sightings of the feared grizzly—a species twice the size of the black bear, with three-inch claws, sharper teeth, and a meaner disposition—no encounters have been reported in the Oregon wilderness since 1931.

Black bears shy away from people except when provoked by the scent of food, when cornered or surprised, or upon human intrusion into territory near their cubs. Female bears tend to have a very strong maternal instinct

ANN LONG LARSEN

black bear

move a human limb with one swipe of the paw, so close encounters should be avoided at all costs. To this end, campers should place all food in a sack tied to a rope and suspend it 20 feet or more from the ground.

About every third year, usually in February, the female produces one or two cubs, born blind, helpless, and small enough to fit into teacups. The young stay with her through the first summer and commonly den up with her the following winter.

Other Land Animals

While sightings are rare, the state boasts cougar and wild horse populations. The nocturnal stalking behavior of the cougar and the remoteness of the wild horse habitat in the Great Basin make any encounter with these creatures memorable.

"Kiger" mustangs, descendants of horses that the Spanish conquistadores brought to America centuries ago, are identified by their hooked ears, thin dorsal stripes, two-toned manes, and faint zebra stripes on their legs. Narrow trunks and a short back are other distinguishing physical characteristics. They sometimes can be identified from a distance by the herding instinct bred into them by the Spanish. The kigers constitute a small percentage of the 2,000 wild mustangs in the state.

Birds

Oregon is rapidly gaining a reputation as one of the best birding states. The U.S. Fish and Wildlife Service has established viewpoints for wildlife- and bird-watching at 12 Oregon national wildlife refuges, which are detailed in respective destination chapters.

Seasonal variance in populations throughout the state is often dramatic. Bird-watchers present during the changing of seasons can best appreciate the diversity of the influx. For example, in the winter and summer the outskirts of Klamath Falls become inundated with more bald eagles than anyplace else in the lower 48; other times of year, many of these birds are in Alaska.

Other birds of prey, or raptors, abound all over the state. Northeast of Enterprise and near

that may construe any alien presence as an attack upon their young. Authorities counsel hikers to act aggressively and defend themselves with whatever means possible if a bear is in attack mode or shows signs that it considers a hiker prey. Jump up and down, shout, and wave your arms. It may help to raise your jacket or pack to make yourself appear larger. Bears can run faster than the fastest human on steroids can sprint, and their retractable claws enable black bears to scramble up trees like squirrels. Furthermore, bears tend to give chase when they see something running. However, if attacked by a grizzly (not in a prey situation), you should play dead.

So if you see a bear at a distance, try to stay downwind of it and back away slowly. Remember, bears are omnivorous, eating fruits and greens as readily as meat, but it is worth noting that human flesh has no appeal to them. In fact, some studies suggest that our body scent is abhorrent to bears.

Despite their strong sense of smell, bears possess very poor eyesight, which makes an attack by mistake a possibility, particularly when a human on the run resembles the bear's prey. Bears can re-

Zumwalt are two of the best places to see hawks. Species commonly sighted include the ferruginous, red-tailed, and Swainson's hawks. Rafters in Hells Canyon enjoy a 71-mile stretch of the 1,000-mile Snake River, where golden eagles and peregrine falcons nest. Portlanders driving the Fremont Bridge over the Willamette River also might get to see peregrine falcons. Along I-5 in the Willamette Valley, look for red-tailed hawks on fenceposts, and American kestrels, North America's smallest falcons, sitting on phone wires.

Farther south, turkey buzzards circle the dry areas during the warmer months. Vultures are commonly sighted above the Rogue River. Along the lower Columbia east of Astoria, more than a hundred bald eagles have chosen to winter; in 1989 the Twilight Creek Eagle Sanctuary was established in this estuary. The upper McCord Creek spur of the Elowah Falls Trail (see "Hiking" under Troutdale and Historic Highway Access Routes in the Columbia River Gorge chapter) has a cliffside overlook into a canyon that has been home to a family of osprey for years. In central Oregon, osprey are frequently sighted off the Cascades Lakes Highway south of Bend, nesting atop hollowed-out snags near water (especially Crane Prairie Reservoir).

In terms of sheer numbers and variety, the coast's mudflats at low tide and the tidal estuaries are among the best birding environments. Numerous locations along the coast—including Bandon Marsh, Three Arch Rock near Cape Meares, and South Slough Estuarine Research Reserve near Coos Bay—offer outstanding opportunities for spotting such pelagic species as pelicans, cormorants, guillemots, and puffins, as well as waders such as curlews, sandpipers, and plovers, plus freshwater fowl like various ducks and geese. Rare species such as tufted puffins and the snowy plover enjoy special protection here, along with other types of migratory birds.

Visitors to Sauvie Island near Portland will be treated to an amazing variety of birds. The northern third of this island is a protected wildlife refuge. More than 200 bird species come through here on the Pacific Flyway, feeding in grassy clearings. Look for eagles here on the island's northwest side. Herons, ducks of all sorts, and geese also live on the island.

The best inland locations to take in an array of migratory species are wildlife preserves such as Finley and Malheur, in the southeast portion of the state. Malheur is Oregon's premier bird retreat and stopover point for large groups of Canada and snow geese, whistling swans, and pintail ducks. It's also home to the rare sandhill crane and such fellow travelers as swans, egrets, and herons.

Apart from great flocks of geese, gulls, and other shorebirds, the species most travelers notice are Clark's nutcracker and the large Steller's jay, whose grating voice and dazzling blue plumage often command the most attention. Mountain hikers are bound to share part of their picnic lunch with these birds. At high elevations, the quieter Clark's nutcracker (also known as the "camp robber") will more likely be your guest.

Unfortunately, the western meadowlark, the state bird, has nearly vanished from western Oregon due to loss of habitat, but thanks to natural pasture east of the Cascades you can still hear its distinctive song. Just look for this bird's brown plumage with buff and black markings. The meadowlark also is distinguished by a yellow underside with a black crescent pattern across the breast and white outer tail feathers.

Salmon and Steelhead

In recent decades, dwindling Pacific salmon and steelhead stocks have prompted restrictions on commercial and recreational fishing in order to restore threatened and endangered species throughout the Northwest. Encouraging signs of progress have been seen in the last couple of years, with some rebounding runs, but the jury is certainly still out on the long-term prognosis for many wild anadromous fish. For more information about fish populations and fishing restrictions, see Oregon Department of Fish and Wildlife's website, www.dfw.state.or.us.

Spring and fall are prime times to savor the splendor (as well as the flavor) of the Pacific salmon. During these seasons, some of Oregon's rivers and streams become choked with spawning

SALMON OR STEELHEAD?

Touted as the best-tasting salmon, king or chinook salmon are also the largest species, sometimes weighing in at over 80 pounds. Coho or silver salmon are known among anglers as fiercely fighting fish, despite a weight of just 10–20 pounds. In 1994, the El Niño warming current inhibited coho reproduction enough to bring about a total ban on harvesting this species. That turned around after 2000, when a cautious sport-fishing season reopened in Oregon.

chinook salmon

Chum salmon (known derogatorily as "dog salmon" because Canadian and Alaskan native people thought them worthy only of being fed to their dog teams) are found only in the Miami and Kilchis Rivers, near Tillamook. Two other species, sockeye and pink (or humpback) salmon are not caught south of Washington waters, but you may see them sold in Oregon stores.

coho salmon

Steelhead are sea-run rainbow trout averaging 5–20 pounds whose life-cycle generally resembles that of salmon—save for the fact that steelhead generally survive after spawning and may live to spawn multiple times. Runs of steelhead, often heavily supplemented by hatchery-raised fish, are found in rivers and streams up and down the coast. They provide great—if challenging—sport angling, but are not harvested commercially.

steelhead

fish returning to the site of their conception, where they will mate and die. As with the eruptions of Old Faithful geyser and the return of the swallows to Capistrano, this poignant dance of death affords a look at one of Mother Nature's time clocks.

The salmon's life cycle begins and ends in a freshwater stream. After an upriver journey from the sea of sometimes hundreds of miles, the spawning female deposits 3,000–7,000 eggs in hollows (called redds) she has scooped out of the coarse sand or gravel, where the male fertilizes them. These adult salmon die soon after mating, and their bodies then deteriorate to become part of the food chain for young fish.

Within three to four months, the eggs hatch into alevin, tiny immature fish with their yolk sac still attached. As the alevin exhaust the nutrients in the sac, they enter the fry stage, and begin to resemble very small salmon. The length they remain as fry differs among various species. Chinook fry, for example, immediately start heading for saltwater, whereas coho or silver salmon will remain in their home stream for one to three years before moving downstream.

The salmon are in the smolt stage when they start to enter saltwater. The five- to seven-inch smolts will spend some time in the estuary area of the river or stream, while they feed and adjust to the saltwater.

When it finally enters the ocean, the salmon is considered an adult. Each species varies in the number of years it remains away from its natal stream, foraging sometimes thousands of miles throughout the Pacific. Chinook can spend as many as seven years away from its nesting (and ultimately its resting) place; most other species remain in the salt for two to four years. Theories about how the salmon's miraculous homing instinct works range from electromagnetic impulses in the earth to celestial objects, but one thing has been established with certainty—"the nose knows." When salmon's olfactory orifices were stuffed with cotton and petroleum jelly, they were unable to find their spawning streams. The current belief is that young salmon imprint the odor of their birth stream, enabling them to find their way home years later.

The salmon's traditional predators such as the sea lion, squawfish, harbor seal, black bear, Caspian tern, and herring gull pale in comparison to the threats posed by modern civilization. Everything from pesticides to sewage to nuclear waste has polluted Oregon waters, and until recent mitigation efforts were enacted, dams and hydroelectric turbines threatened to block Oregon's all-important Columbia River spawning route.

History

NATIVE PEOPLES

Early Days

Long before Europeans came to this hemisphere, native peoples thrived for thousands of years in the region of present-day Oregon. A popular theory concerning their origins maintains that their ancestors came over from Asia on a land/ice bridge spanning what is now the Bering Strait. Along with archaeological evidence, shipwrecks of Asian craft on the Pacific coast also support the theory that Native Americans had Eastern Hemisphere contact. This contention has been further substantiated by facial features and dental patterns common to both peoples, as well as isolated correspondences in ritual, music, and dialect.

Despite common ancestry, the tribes on the rain-soaked coast and in the Willamette Valley lived quite differently from those on the drier eastern flank of the Cascade Mountains. Tribes west of the Cascades enjoyed abundant salmon, shellfish, berries, and game. Broad rivers facilitated travel, and thick stands of the finest softwood timber in the world ensured that there was never a dearth of building materials. A mild climate with plentiful food and resources allowed the wet-siders the leisure time to evolve a startlingly complex culture. This was perhaps best evidenced in their artistic endeavors, theatrical pursuits, and in such ceremonial gatherings as the traditional potlatch, where the divesting of one's material wealth was seen as a status symbol. Dentalium and abalone shells, woodpecker feathers, obsidian blades, and hides were especially coveted. Later on, Hudson's Bay blankets were added to this list.

After contact with traders, Chinook, an amalgam of Native American tongues with some French and English thrown in, was the common argot among the diverse tribes that gathered in the Columbia Gorge each year. It was at these powwows that the coast and valley dwellers would come into contact with their poorer cousins east of the Cascades. These dry-siders led a seminomadic existence, following the game and avoiding the climatic extremes of winter and summer in their region. In the southeast desert of the Great Basin, seeds and roots added more protein to their diet. Subsistence needs were thus pushed to the fore in

ANN LONG LARSEN

The Umpqua were among Oregon's first residents.

their cultures while creative and recreational endeavors were limited.

The introduction of horses in the mid-1700s made hunting, especially for large bison, much easier. In contrast to their west-of-the-Cascade counterparts, who lived in 100- by 40-foot longhouses, extended families in the eastern tribes inhabited pit houses when not hunting. The demands of chasing migratory game necessitated caves or crude rock shelters.

Twelve separate nations populated Oregon. Although these were further divided into 80 tribes, the primary allegiance was to the village. The "nation" status referred to language groupings such as Salish and Athabascan. Tribal names such as Calapooya, Alsea, or Shasta Costa were usually derived from a word in the local argot for "The People," or from what a neighboring tribe called "Them." On occasion, European explorers bestowed a name upon the particular native grouping. An example of this was the "Rogue" Native American appellation. According to one theory, this name came from French fur trappers who referred to the troublesome tribe as *"les coquins,"* which was translated as "the rogues." Another theory was that "Rogue" was inspired by the ocher riverbed, described as *rouge* by French

trappers and subsequently misspelled. Across the region, many Native Americans were united in their worship of Spilyai, the coyote demigod. Spilyai, as well as many other figures animal and human, formed the subject of a large body of folk tales that explain the origins of the land in ways that are both entertaining and insightful.

Conflicts with White Settlers

The coming of white settlers meant the usurpation of tribal homelands, exposure to European diseases such as smallpox and diphtheria, and the passing of ancient ways of life. Violent conflicts ensued on a large scale with the influx of settlers seeking missionary work and government land giveaways in the 1830s and '40s. In the 1850s, mining activity in southern Oregon and on the coast incited the Rogue River Indian Wars, adding to the strife brought on by annexation to the United States.

All these events compelled the federal government to send in troops and to eventually set up treaties with Oregon's first inhabitants. The attempts at arbitration in the 1850s added insult to injury. Tribes of different—indeed, often incompatible—backgrounds were rounded up and grouped together haphazardly on reservations, often far from their homelands. In the century that followed, the evils of modern civilization destroyed much of the ecosystem upon which these cultures were based. An especially regrettable result of settlement was the decline of the Columbia River salmon runs due to overfishing, loss of habitat, and pollution. This not only weakened the food chain but treated this spiritual totem of the many tribes along the Columbia as an expendable resource.

For a while, there was an attempt to restore the balance. In 1924, the government accorded citizenship to Native Americans. Ten years later, the Indian Reorganization Act provided for tribal guards and prohibited the sale of land to non-Native Americans. A decade later a court of treaty claims was established. In the 1960s, however, the government, acting on the premise that the Native Americans needed to assimilate into white society, terminated several reservations.

Recent government reparations have accorded

ON THE TRAIL OF THE FIRST OREGONIANS

About five miles south of Warm Springs on U.S. 26, an eye-popping view of Mount Jefferson's snowcapped volcano cone looms across 50 miles of sagebrush. The base of the mountain marks the western extent of the Warm Springs tribe's thousand-square-mile reservation.

You'll find a smaller but equally impressive display of tribal wealth at the **Museum at Warm Springs** (P.O. Box C, Warm Springs 97761, 541/553-3331), located below the viewpoint at the bottom of the Deschutes River Canyon. Audiovisual displays, old photos, and tapes of traditional chants of the Paiute, Warm Springs, and Wasco peoples (descendants of the tribe that greeted Lewis and Clark) are aesthetically arrayed here. Each tribe's distinct culture, along with the thriving social and economic community they collectively formed, constitute the major themes in the Northwest's only tribal museum.

Replicas of a Paiute mat lodge, a Warm Springs tepee, and a Wasco plank house, along with recordings of each tribe's language, underscore the cultural richness and diversity of the area's original inhabitants. The exhibits, culled from a collection of more than 20,000 artifacts, range from primitive prehistoric hand tools to a high-tech push-button-activated Wasco wedding scene. Tribal foodstuffs and art are on sale in the bookstore. The museum is open daily 9 a.m.–5 p.m. except Thanksgiving, Christmas, and New Year's Day. Admission is $7, discounts for seniors and children.

Aficionados of Northwest native lore might want to visit the Museum at Warm Springs as part of a 170-mile tour that includes three other noteworthy exhibit halls. Begin at the **High Desert Museum** (see "Bend" in the Cascades chapter), a 90-minute drive south of Warm Springs on U.S. 97, 10 miles south of Bend. The next stops on our tour are the **Columbia Gorge Discovery Center** and **Wasco County Historical Museum** in The Dalles (see "The Dalles" in the Columbia River Gorge chapter). To get there, continue north on U.S. 26 to ORE 35. Follow ORE 35 to I-84 in Hood River and head east on I-84. Leave the interstate at Exit 82 at The Dalles and follow the signs.

Our final stop is the **Maryhill Museum of Art** (35 Maryhill Museum Dr., near Goldendale, WA, 509/773-3733). Artifacts from Alaska, the Midwest, and the Southwest were unearthed by Dr. Luther Cressman and other archaeologists not far from the museum. To get here, return to I-84 and head a few miles east, crossing over the Columbia past The Dalles Dam via U.S. 197. Once in Washington, turn right (north) on Highway 14. Keep an eye out for the Horsethief Lake State Park sign and the petroglyphs after you arrive on the Columbia's north shore. A little more than 20 miles up the road, near Goldendale, is the museum. It's pretty hard to miss this large French château–style building surrealistically planted on the sparsely vegetated bluff above the Columbia. The museum is open daily 9 a.m.–5 p.m. mid-March–mid-Nov. Admission is $7 adults, $2 ages 6–16.

To do justice to the tribal legacy celebrated at all four museums, it's best to take two or three days to complete this circuit.

---

many native peoples preferential hunting and fishing rights, monetary/land grants, and the restoration of tribal status to certain disenfranchised groups. In Oregon, there are now nine federally recognized tribes and six reservations: Warm Springs, Umatilla, Burns Pauite, Siletz, and Grand Ronde. Nonetheless, most of the 40,000 native people of the region feel they can never regain their birthright. In an attempt to repay this irredeemable debt, Native American gaming came to Oregon in the mid-1990s, and

Native Oregonians now operate eight lucrative casinos in the state.

Archaeological Perspectives

To help measure what we've lost by the passing of the traditional ways, archaeologists have unearthed all manner of native artifacts. One that has evoked considerable controversy is a site found at Fort Rock, east of the Cascades near Bend. Charcoals from a hearth there are thought to be more than 13,000 years old, exceeding earlier estimates of the period of human presence in the region by about 3,500 years. A sandal found at the same site dated at around 10,000 years old had been the previous standard-bearer.

Another significant find is a gallery of 5,000-year-old petroglyphs on the walls of a cave in the foothills just east of the Willamette Valley. The valley itself boasts perhaps the best-known excavation in the state, due to its location on the site of the Oregon Country Fair near Eugene. Relics there have been dated at 8,000–10,000 years of age.

Other recent finds include coastal and Rogue Valley digs where 9,000-year-old artifacts have been unearthed. In 1997, an obsidian flaked in the Clovis style indicates that Ice Age people roamed the Rogue Valley as long as 11,000 years ago. The distinctive grooves in the obsidian mark it as a product of the Clovis big-game hunter culture. In 2002, researchers began excavating a site at Indian Sands, in Samuel H. Boardman State Park north of Brookings, which yielded artifacts dating back more 12,000 years, making it the oldest known site of human activity yet found on the coast.

In 1999, the oldest house in Oregon and possibly the United States was discovered on the shoreline of Paulina Lake. The archaeological significance of this 9,500-year-old site might eventually be rivaled by finds in several Woodburn city parks, 35 miles south of Portland. In the summer of 2000, a human hair was found in 12,000-year-old soils of an ancient wetland, along with animal bones thousands of years old.

Currently, debates over whether ancestors of present-day Oregon's Native American peoples were predated by other ethnicities are raging among experts in the field. These questions were raised by the discovery of Kennewick Man, compelling close examination of DNA in subsequent finds. Kennewick Man, the Northwest's most intact human remains, was found on the Columbia River shoreline in 1996 in Kennewick, Washington, about 160 miles north of Portland. While determination of ethnicity was inconclusive, what appeared to be Caucasian facial features gave impetus to such inquiries. This subject is covered in greater detail in the Columbia River Gorge chapter.

In terms of written history, a manuscript found in a Chinese monastery could have the distinction of being the first written account of a voyage to our continent. A Chinese navigator, Hee-li, was spirited from offshore Cathay waters by a violent storm. According to the tale, both captain and crew survived the storm but were thrown off course during their return voyage by a cockroach lodged underneath a compass needle. Hee-li persisted in following the cockeyed compass in the direction he thought was west, despite sunsets appearing on the opposite horizon. After crossing miles and miles of open ocean, the ship docked in a country of forests towering around a vast inlet, which the mariners explored.

The manuscript, which supposedly dates to 217 B.C., was found 21 centuries later in the archives at Shensi Province by an American missionary to China. In it, a reference to towering trees and red-faced men could well have referred to the Pacific Northwest. In any event, Chinese and Japanese shipwrecks along the Oregon coast have been dated as early as the fifth century A.D. Potsherds and other ceramic artifacts found along the Columbia River also point to early contact with the Orient.

When you look at this evidence, it is clear that while East may be East and West may be West, the two probably *did* meet in the Oregon Country.

EXPLORATION, SETTLEMENT, AND GROWTH

In the 17th and 18th centuries, Spanish, English, and Russian vessels came to offshore waters here in search of a sea route connecting the Atlantic with the Pacific. Accounts differ, but the first sightings of the Oregon coast have been credited to either Juan Cabrillo (in 1543) or the English explorer Sir Francis Drake (in 1579). Other voyagers of note included Spain's Vizcaíno and de Alguilar (in 1603) and Don Bruno de Heceta (in 1775), and England's James Cook and John Meares during the late 1770s, as well as George Vancouver (in 1792). Robert Gray's 1792 voyage

10 miles up the Columbia River estuary was the first American incursion into the area.

In 1996, a front-page story in the *London Times* proclaimed Sir Francis Drake the first European to set foot on the coast (previously Heceta was credited with the first landing) on the basis of an archaeological find in Little Whale Cove south of Depoe Bay. Timbers from a stockade left by Drake, who is known to have beached for repairs, were purportedly found, leading to this speculation. See special topic, "Drake's Lost Harbor," in the Coastal Oregon chapter.

Sea otter and beaver pelts added impetus to the search for a trade route connecting the two oceans. While the Northwest Passage turned out to be a myth, the fur trade became a basis of commerce and contention between European, Asian, and eventually American governments. The pattern was repeated inland when the English beaver brigades eventually moved down from Canada to set up headquarters on the Columbia near present-day Portland.

American Expansion in Oregon

The Americans entered the area when Robert Gray sailed up the Columbia River in 1792. The first American overland excursion into Oregon was made by the Corps of Discovery in 1804–1806. Dispatched by Thomas Jefferson to explore the lands of the Louisiana Purchase and beyond, Captains Meriwether Lewis and William Clark and their party of 30 men and one woman, Sacagawea, trekked across the continent to the mouth of the Columbia, camped south of present-day Astoria during the winter of 1805–1806, and then returned to St. Louis. Lewis and Clark's exploration and mapping of Oregon threw down the gauntlet for future settlement and eventual annexation of the Oregon Territory by the United States. The expedition also initially secured good relations with the Native Americans in the West, thus establishing the preconditions to trade and the missionary influx. In fact, several decades after the coming of the expedition, the Nez Percé tribe sent a delegation to William Clark in St. Louis to ask for "The Book of Heaven," as well as teachers of

Meriwether Lewis

the Word. For more on Lewis and Clark see the Columbia River Gorge chapter.

But before the missionaries came west, there were years of wrangling over America's right to settle in the new territory. The American John Jacob Astor's Pacific Fur Company was a case in point. The mere threat of British gunboats on the Columbia caused the quick departure of Astor's company during the War of 1812. It

William Clark

wasn't until the Convention of 1818 that the country west of the Rockies, south of Russian America, and north of Spanish America was open for use by American citizens as well as British subjects. The following year, the United States and Spain signed a treaty that fixed the present southern border of Oregon. With the Monroe Doctrine in 1824 opposing European expansion in this hemisphere, another blow was struck toward weakening British rule in the Northwest.

During the 1820s, however, the Hudson's Bay Company continued to hold sway over Oregon country by means of Fort Vancouver, on the north shore of the Columbia. More than 500 people settled here under the charismatic leadership of John McLoughlin, who oversaw the planting of crops and the raising of livestock. Despite the establishment of almost half a dozen Hudson's Bay outposts, several factors presaged the inevitable demise of British influence in Oregon. Most obvious was the decline of the fur trade as well as England's difficulty in maintaining her far-flung empire. Less apparent but equally influential was the lack of white females in a land populated predominantly by white trappers and explorers. If the Americans could attract settlers of both genders, they'd be in a position to create an expanding population base that could dominate the region.

The first step in this process was the arrival of the missionaries. In 1834, Methodist soul-seekers led by Jason Lee settled near the Willamette River. Four years later, another mission was started in the eastern Columbia River Gorge. In 1843, Marcus and Narcissa Whitman's missions started up on the upper Columbia in present-day Walla Walla, Washington (until 1853, the Washington area was considered a single entity with Oregon). The missionaries brought alien ways and diseases for which the Native Americans had no immunity. As if this weren't enough to provoke a violent reaction, the Native Americans would soon have their homelands inundated by thousands of settlers lured by government land giveaways.

The Oregon Trail
But it wasn't just the Organic Act's 640 free acres

© MARK MORRIS

A replica of a blockhouse marks the site of Fort Astoria, built in 1811 by John Jacob Astor's men in what would become the town of Astoria.

that each adult white male could claim in the mid-1840s that fueled the march across the frontier. The westward expansion that Americans regarded as their "manifest destiny" leapt to the fore as a ready solution to the problems of the 1830s. During this decade, the country was in its worst depression yet, with land panics, droughts, and an unstable currency. Despite ignorance of western geography and the hardships it held, the Oregon Trail, a 2,000-mile frontier thoroughfare, was viewed with covetous eyes, especially in Missouri. (By 1840, 400,000 settlers had arrived there, tripling the population in 10 years.) Around Independence, Missouri, the trees thinned, the settlements ended, and the Oregon Trail began.

More than 53,000 people traversed the trail between 1840 and 1850 en route to western Oregon. In 1850, the Donation Land Act cut in half the acreage of the Organic Act, reflecting the diminishing availability of real estate. But although a single pioneer man was now entitled to only 320 acres, and single women were excluded from land ownership, as part of a couple they could claim an additional 320 free acres. This promoted marriage and, in turn, families on the western frontier, and helped to fulfill Secretary of State John C. Calhoun's prediction that American families could outbreed the Hudson's Bay Company's bachelor trappers, thus winning the battle of the West in the bedroom.

The Donation Land Act also stipulated that nonwhites could not own any part of the Oregon Territory, enabling the pioneers to seize native people's lands with impunity. The act impeded the growth of towns and industries, too, as large parcels of land were given away to relatively small numbers of people, which kept the population geographically distant from one another. This was one reason why urbanization was slow in coming to the Northwest.

The Applegate Trail

Another route west was the Applegate Trail, pioneered by brothers Lindsay and Jesse Applegate in the mid-1840s. Each had lost sons several years before to drowning on the Columbia River. The treacherous rapids here had initially been the last leg of a journey to the Willamette Valley.

On their return journey to the region, the brothers departed from the established trail when they reached Fort Hall, Idaho. Veering south from the Oregon Trail across northern Nevada's

THE CORPS OF DISCOVERY

For nearly two decades at the end of the 18th century, Thomas Jefferson dreamed of mounting an expedition to explore the virtually unknown North American continent west of the Mississippi River. Like others of his era, Jefferson believed in the existence of the Northwest Passage, a navigable route between the northern Pacific and Atlantic Oceans, the discovery of which could revolutionize trade between the United States and the Orient, and speed the growth (and increase the wealth) of the young republic. In January 1803, President Jefferson finally succeeded in securing funding from Congress to outfit such an ambitious undertaking. Congress granted $2,500, though the eventual cost would top $38,000.

Jefferson invited his secretary, 28-year-old Meriwether Lewis, to lead the expedition, which the president named the Corps of Discovery. Its stated goals would be "to make friends and allies of the far Western Indians while at the same time diverting valuable pelts from the rugged northern routes used by [Great Britain] . . . and bringing the harvest down the Missouri to the Mississippi and thence eastward by a variety of routes." Furthermore, Lewis would be charged with mapping the territory and chronicling the peoples, plants, and animals encountered along the way. Lewis, in turn, asked a former Army comrade, William Clark, to co-captain the expedition with him.

Just two months after Congress approved the request, Jefferson consummated the Louisiana Purchase, an agreement that ceded New Orleans and 820,000 square miles of France's North American territories to the United States, for $15 million dollars—about three cents an acre. Overnight, the area of the United States doubled, and Lewis and Clark's mission assumed even greater importance.

In May 1804, after months of preparation and recruitment, the Corps set off in a large keelboat and two pirogues up the Missouri River, from a base near St. Louis, then the western edge of white civilization. Over the next two years, their route would take them north and west, up the drainages of the Missouri River, across the Rockies, and into the Columbia River system and finally to the Pacific Ocean. The Corps, consisting of 32 men and one woman, the Shoshone Sacagawea, would spend October 1805 to May 1806 in what today are Oregon and Washington, including four wet, miserable months at Fort Clatsop, near Astoria (see "Astoria and Vicinity" in the Coastal Oregon chapter).

Along the way, Lewis and Clark charted some 8,000 miles of territory hitherto unexplored by European Americans and documented 300 species of flora and fauna previously unknown to Western science. Journals kept by Lewis, Clark, and three of their sergeants chronicle their experiences with such vividness they still captivate readers today. The effect their journey had in accelerating westward expansion of the United States across the continent can hardly be overstated.

Black Rock Desert, they traversed the northeast top of California to enter Oregon near present-day Klamath Falls. A southern Oregon gold rush in the 1850s drew thousands across this route.

Early Government and Statehood

There was enough unity among American settlers to organize a provisional government in 1843. Then, in 1848, the federal government decided to accord Oregon territorial status. With migration increasing exponentially from 1843 on, there was little doubt in Congress about Oregon's viability. Still, it took frontiersman Joe Meek to coalesce popular opinion. He had first performed this role in Champoeg, at the northern end of the Willamette Valley, in 1843, when he boomed out the rallying cry for regional confederation, "Who's for a divide?", in order to force a vote on the question of whether to challenge the British claim of sovereignty in the region. Two Canadians, F. X. Matthieu and Etienne Lucier, crossed the line and won the day for the Americans. In equally dramatic fashion, Meek strode into the halls of Congress fresh from the trail in mountain-man regalia to forcefully argue the case for territoriality. Congress granted the petition and Meek accompanied newly appointed territorial governor Joseph Lane to Oregon in the spring of 1849.

The Oregon Territory got off to a rousing start thanks to the California gold rush of 1849. The rush occasioned a housing boom in San Francisco and a need for lumber, and the dramatic population influx created instant markets for the agriculture of the Willamette Valley. Portland was located at the north end of the valley and 110 miles upriver from the Pacific on the Columbia, near the world's largest supply of accessible softwood timber. The young city was in a perfect position to channel goods from the interior to coastal ports. So great was the need in California for food that wheat from eastern Oregon was declared legal tender. The exchange rate started around one dollar a bushel and went as high as six dollars. The economic benefits from the gold rush notwithstanding, Oregon lost two-thirds of its adult male population to gold fever. Many of the emigrants returned when the news

of gold discoveries in southwestern Oregon came out between 1850 and 1860. The resulting influx helped establish the Rogue Valley and coastal population centers.

However, strategic importance and population growth alone do not explain Oregon's becoming the 33rd state in the Union. Shortly before statehood, the Dred Scott decision had become law in 1857. This had the effect of opening the territory to slavery. While slavery didn't lack for adherents in Oregon, the prevailing sentiment was that this controversial institution was neither necessary nor desirable. Because territorial status would be a potential liability to a Union on the mend, the congressional majority saw an especially compelling reason to open its doors to this new member. When nonslavery status was assured, Oregon entered the Union on Valentine's Day, 1859.

Economic Growing Pains

During the years of the Civil War and its aftermath, internal conflicts were the order of the day within the state. By 1861, good Willamette Valley land was becoming scarce, so many farmers moved east of the Cascades to farm wheat. They ran into violent confrontations with Native Americans over land. Between 1862 and 1934, the Homestead Act land giveaways helped fuel these fires of resentment. Miners encroaching on Native American territory around the southern coast eventually flared into the bloody Rogue River Wars (see "History" in the Coastal Oregon chapter), which would lead to the destruction of most of the native peoples of the coast.

In the 1870s, cattlemen came to eastern Oregon, followed by sheep ranchers, and the two groups fought for dominance of the range. Just when it appeared that eastern Oregon land was ripe for agricultural promoters and community planners, the bottom fell out. Overproduction of wheat, uncertain markets, and two severe winters were the culprits. In the early 20th century a population influx created further problems by draining the water table. Thus, the glory that was gold, grass, and grain east of the Cascades was short-lived. Many eastern Oregon towns grew up and flourished for a decade, only to fall back into desert, leaving nary a trace of their existence.

Unlike the downturn east of the Cascades, boom times were ahead for the rest of the state as the 20th century approached. In the 1860s and '70s, Jacksonville to the south became the commercial counterpart to Portland, owing to its proximity to the Rogue Valley and south coast goldfields as well as the California border. During this period, transportation links began to consolidate, in part due to the efforts of stagecoach magnate Ben Holladay. The first stagecoach, steamship, and rail lines moved south from the Columbia River into the Willamette Valley; by the 1880s, Portland was joined to San Francisco and to the east by railroad. Henry Villard was the prime mover in this effort, eventually dominating all commerce in the Northwest by channeling freight and passengers through Portland and along the Columbia. In 1900, Union Pacific magnate James J. Hill picked up where Villard left off. By selling 900,000 acres of timberland to lumber baron Frederic Weyerhaeuser at $6 an acre (with the stipulation that Weyerhaeuser build his mills close by Union Pacific tracks), he hitched the destinies of the region to the iron horse.

Progressive Politics

In the modern era, Oregon also blazed trails in the thicket of governmental legislation and reform. The so-called Oregon system of initiative, referendum, and recall was first conceived in the 1890s, coming to fruition in the first decade of the 1900s. The system has since become an integral part of the democratic process.

In like measure, Oregon's extension of suffrage to women in 1912, a 1921 compulsory education law, and the first large-scale union activity in the country during the 1920s were red-letter events in American history. This tradition of reform continues to this day with Oregon's bottle-deposit policies and progressive land-use statutes. More recently, the Oregon Health Plan has extended health care coverage to the state's working poor by expanding the procedures covered by Medicaid. The plan's costs are controlled by prioritizing various services, an idea that could set the precedent for a future federal health insurance plan.

The 1930s were exciting years in the Northwest. Despite widespread poverty, the foundations of future prosperity were laid during this decade. New Deal programs such as the Works Projects Administration and the Civilian Conservation Corps undertook many projects around the state. Building roads and hydroelectric dams created jobs and improved the quality of life in Oregon, in addition to bolstering the country's defense during wartime. Hydroelectric power from the Bonneville Dam, completed in 1938, enabled Portland's shipyards and aluminum plants to thrive. Low utility rates encouraged more employment and settlement, while the Columbia's irrigation water enhanced agriculture.

World War II

Thanks to Henry Kaiser's mass-production techniques, 10,000 workers were employed in the Portland shipyards. Such well-known "liberty ships" as the *Star of Oregon* were born here, making the state an integral part of the war effort. But in addition to laying the foundations for future growth, the war years in Oregon and their immediate aftermath were full of trials for state residents. Vanport, a city of 18,000 (at one time, 45,000) that grew up in the shadow of Kaiser aluminum plants and the shipyards north of Portland, was washed off the map by a Columbia River flood. Tillamook County forests, which supplied Sitka spruce for airplanes, endured several massive fires that destroyed 500 square miles of trees. Along with these natural disasters, Oregon was the only state among the contiguous 48 to have a military installation (Fort Stevens, near Astoria) shelled by a Japanese submarine, to endure a Japanese bombing mission on the mainland (on Mount Emily, near Brookings), and to suffer civilian casualties when a balloon bomb exploded (near the Gearhart Mountain Wilderness Area in Lake County).

The Modern Era

With the perfection of the chainsaw in the 1940s, the timber industry could take advantage

HOTBED OF BIOREGIONALISM

Oregonians have a well-deserved reputation for embodying the maverick spirit. Oregon's politicians, for example, don't always vote with a party majority, and even the state's motto, "She flies with her own wings," expresses this outlook. In addition, the state holds unofficial status as a haven to social, religious, and cultural groups that eschew convention. Therefore, it is altogether fitting to find here the only serious American secessionist movement outside of the Southern Confederacy.

At various times since the 1850s, the people of Oregon and Northern California have tried to establish a new state. With common interests transcending state boundaries, inhabitants of this region attempted to secede in each of the years 1852–1854. The most recent drive, in 1941, for an independent state named Jefferson (so chosen for that president's vision of America as a self-sufficient agrarian country) was dramatized by a blockade of ORE 99 at the Oregon–California border. The movement got as far as inaugurating an acting governor, but the United States' entry into World War II several days later preempted further action.

Southern Oregon is still a hotbed of bioregional revolt. The 1973 book *Ecotopia,* by Ernest Callenbach, added fuel to the fire by proposing that Northern California break off from the rest of the state to join with Oregon as a single republic based on environmental imperatives. Another bioregional manifesto, *The Nine Nations of North America,* divided the continent into nine bioregions on the basis of their cultural, historical, ethnic, economic, and environmental interests. The region north of San Francisco to Vancouver was identified once again as "Ecotopia."

In recent years the Ashland–Jacksonville area and the surrounding Rogue and Applegate Valleys have carried the torch for bioregionalism, often invoking as a rallying cry the name of the late, great state-that-never-was, Jefferson. With a constituency ranging from survivalists and radical environmentalists to folks just tired of big government and bureaucracy, this activist region coalesces the spirit of Jefferson throughout the state.

To keep up on the politics and patrimony of Jefferson, send for the newsletter of the Siskiyou Regional Education Project (P.O. Box 220, Cave Junction, OR 97523).

of the postwar housing boom. During that decade, the population increased by nearly 50 percent, growing to over 1.5 million. During the 1950s and 1960s, the Army Corps of Engineers carried out a massive program of new dam projects, resulting in construction of The Dalles, John Day, and McNary dams on the main stem of the Columbia and the Oxbow and Brownlee dams on the Snake River. In addition, the flooding on the Willamette was tamed through a series of dams on its major tributary watersheds, the Santiam, the Middle Fork of the Willamette, and the McKenzie.

Politically, the late 1960s and '70s brought environmentally groundbreaking measures spearheaded by Governor Tom McCall. The bottle bill, land-use statutes, and the cleanup of the Willamette River were part of this legacy. In the decades to follow, former Senator Mark Hatfield's national prominence attracted federal monies to the state, funding key projects in transportation, education, research, and tourism.

The 1990s saw the Oregon economy flourish, fueled by the growth of computer hardware and software industries here as well as a real estate market favorable to California retirees. The latter has had sociological ripple effects with many longtime state residents feeling displaced by the transformed economy and living standards. The legalization of gambling and drastic cuts in education have provoked controversy on all sides of the political spectrum. While a retreat from longstanding legislative commitments reflects the demographics of Oregon's new arrivals as well as its changing economic climate, Oregon's physician-assisted suicide bill, extensive vote-by-mail procedures, medical marijuana initiative, and low-cost health insurance program for the indigent (the Oregon Health Plan) have sustained its maverick image.

Economy

Oregon's economy has traditionally followed a boom-bust cycle, but has in recent decades diversified away from its earlier dependence on resource-based industries, forest products in particular. The state's major manufacturing industries today also include high tech, primary and fabricated metals, transportation equipment, and agricultural crops and processing. Important non-manufacturing sectors, which account for five out of seven jobs in the state, include wholesale and retail trade, education, health, and social services, high-tech non-manufacturing jobs (such as software development), tourism. Along with the rest of the country in the early years of the 21st century, Oregon has suffered from the bursting of the high-tech bubble and the subsequent stock market retreat and economic recession.

Currently high tech employs about 24,000 workers statewide, while agriculture and forest products employ about 60,000 and 75,000 workers, respectively. But these numbers tell only part of the story; the scenario for every sector of Oregon's economy should change dramatically in the coming years.

The ripple effects from the decline in timber will affect many aspects of society in the Northwest. Weyerhaeuser, Georgia Pacific, and other wood-products giants are bracing for a reduction in the allowable cut as well as export restrictions. More timber from private holdings, as opposed to government lands, will be harvested, and jobs will shift to the manufacture of secondary wood products such as doors, window frames, laminated beams, and furniture parts. Nonetheless, don't count big timber out. Each year, a handful of timber giants such as Willamette Industries make the top-10 list of Oregon companies. With Clatsop County's Tillamook State Forest reaching maturity after disastrous fires six decades ago, a huge harvest is expected from the northern Coast Range throughout the first decade of the millennium.

In agriculture, specialty products have become the fastest-growing business in Oregon. These products include nursery crops (Monrovia is the nation's largest nursery and Oregon is the number one Christmas tree state) as well as wine grapes, herbs and organic produce, gourmet mushrooms, goat cheese, and other fare prized by "foodies." At the same time, large-scale agribusiness is thriving with the booming food-processing and -packing industries proliferating in the lower Willamette Valley and eastern Oregon.

High-tech industries and tourism are often mentioned as the engines of future economic growth. But high tech is currently experiencing hard times, and no one knows for certain when the climate will change. Meanwhile, the state has begun to invest more money into attracting more tourism dollars. Tourism is a $6.1 billion industry for the state, but more potential remains underutilized. Until recently, Oregon had one of the country's smallest budgets for self-promotion, but state officials are hopeful that more marketing efforts nationally and internationally will pay big dividends. Currently, economists estimate that every dollar invested in tourism marketing yields a five-dollar return in local and state tax revenues—more than $230 million annually. The Lewis and Clark Bicentennial (2003–2006), in particular, is expected to bolster the state's tourism coffers. The latter will augment the influx who come each year to enjoy Oregon's world-class kulturfests and nature on a grand scale.

FOREST PRODUCTS

Until recently, logging and wood products have been the most important industries to Oregon in terms of jobs provided and revenue produced. Despite recent declines, tens of thousands of workers are still employed in logging, sawmills, and paper production, contributing billions of dollars annually to Oregon's gross state product. Oregon is still the leading supplier of wood products in the nation, providing one-fifth of the country's softwood lumber. The logging industry is still vitally important to the state's economy, with primary and secondary wood-processing industries accounting for some $10 billion per year in sales and directly employing some 75,000 workers.

Throughout its history, the Oregon logging industry has been dogged by controversy. In the 1920s, shoddy treatment of workers resulted in the first large-scale unionization in the country and inspired the spadework for the AFL-CIO.

Currently, the forestry and economic practices that are the basis of the industry are being questioned. The National Forest Service administers most of the lands slated for timber harvest and has been scrutinized for what some critics charge are policies not in keeping with healthy forest ecosystems. Some of these purported excesses have been reined in, resulting in the reduction of the allowable cut and devastating losses in employment and revenue. Regardless of the imminent ban on logging in spotted owl habitats and the like, the industry faces a slowdown simply because of the lack of trees to cut. Nonetheless, timber products should continue to be a major force in the state. This becomes clear when we look at "the tale of the tape." Consider that because of these environmental restrictions and shortfalls, Oregon produced 6.2 billion less board feet of timber in 1993 than in 1992. But because lumber wholesale prices rose during this period, Oregon still ranked number one in the country in timber revenues. In the year 2000, Oregon still led the nation in lumber production despite logging cutbacks due to environmental statutes. The latter was due to improved milling techniques. Given projected profits from the harvest of a huge forest that was replanted in the wake of the Tillamook Burn over a half-century ago, this trend should become more pronounced into the next century. Be that as it may, Big Timber will assume a lower profile in the more diversified economy that has come to this state in the last decades.

The new forestry orientation has created job opportunities for tree planters, because the law mandates that for every tree cut on federally owned land, at least nine must be replanted. It has also resulted in gains for private timber owners, significant players in the new Oregon economy.

AGRICULTURE

In the 1930s a Woody Guthrie song extolled the "pastures of plenty" in the Northwest. Seven decades later, the pastures are still plentiful, only more so. Among other crops, Oregon's $3.7 billion agricultural sector (2001 farm and ranch sales) leads the nation in the production of such varied agricultural commodities as filberts, peppermint, blackberries, loganberries, rhubarb, several kinds of grass seed, and Christmas trees. The Willamette Valley boasts the most diversified farming region on the planet; the Bing and maraschino cherries and elephant garlic were developed here, and the valley's legendary fertility inspired tens of thousands of Oregon Trail emigrants.

An oft-heard refrain in pioneer days was "Crops never fail west of the Cascades." The Oregon Trail migration and government land giveaways resulted in the settlement of most of the Willamette's good agricultural land by the mid-1850s. In the 1860s, gold-rush activity put a premium on eastern Oregon's wheat. Later on, alfalfa, sheep, and livestock diversified farmers' options on the dry side of the mountains. Today, this region's food-processing plants have enjoyed a boom, particularly with the potato crop; McDonald's gets most of its spuds for french fries from eastern Oregon, as do several of the leading potato-chip and frozen-food manufacturers. Oregonians themselves look to the east side toward Hermiston for the best melons and potatoes in the state.

The golden age of Oregon agriculture began with the tapping of the Columbia River for irrigation water, enabling large-scale farming to get started. At about the same time, World War II compelled Oregon to develop its own flower-bulb industry instead of relying upon Japan. Today, Oregon is a leader in nursery crops, ornamental flowers, and flower seed production (number three in nursery crops in the United States).

Oregon grows about 200 different commercial commodities, ranking only behind California in crop diversity. Agriculture-related employment accounts for about 140,000 jobs, meaning 1 out of 12 Oregonians is involved in getting food from the farm to market.

Perennial leaders among vegetable crops in the state are onions, sweet corn, potatoes, beets, mint, and snap beans. The top corporate agricultural revenue producers include such giants as Tillamook Cheese, Norpac (the state's largest farmer-owned food processor), and Smith's Frozen Foods (peas, corn, and carrots—the largest private employer in Umatilla County). While beef, nursery stock, hay, grass seed, dairy products, and wheat traditionally have been the leading economic entities in the state's several-billion-dollar farm economy, specialty crops and processing currently enjoy the fastest rates of growth. With changing forestry policies, sales of logs from small, nonindustrial woodlots have rocketed to the top of Oregon's leading revenue producers. In addition, Oregon wineries garner top honors in international competitions, with the bulk of the prizes going to the pinot noir and chardonnay varietals from Yamhill and Washington Counties.

FISHING

Since the first people arrived on these shores 8,000 years or more ago, Oregon's rich coastal waters have provided sustenance and sport. The king of fish here, economically as well as recreationally speaking, is the salmon. The once-abundant fish was a self-replenishing gold mine that enriched the state and fueled the development of coastal towns like Astoria and Gold Beach.

Oregon fish canneries once supplied the world, but the industry peaked in the 1890s, and went into steady decline as fish disappeared. The state's last cannery closed down in 1979. In the modern era, Oregon salmon fisheries grew into a megabusiness, until stocks dramatically declined in the 1990s. The factors are many and complex, and fraught with political tension. In the early days, fish wheels and nets depleted rivers once so choked with spawning fish that a pioneer pitchfork stuck haphazardly into the water would often yield a salmon. Dam construction and pollution joined overfishing to further reduce the catch. Watersheds have been compromised by clearcuts, which increases erosion that clogs spawning streams with silt and mud and reduces shaded riparian environments for the coldwater-loving salmon. Cattle grazing has also impacted spawning areas with collapsed stream banks and polluted water.

In spite of the habitat degradation and other pressures, hope is being restored by the resurgence of salmon and steelhead populations in Oregon waters since the year 2000. In 1997,

White Star Packing Company label, Astoria, 1885

returning Oregon coastal coho salmon numbered an alarmingly low 22,000 fish, which triggered a listing as "threatened" under the Endangered Species Act. Commercial and sport fishing for coho were shut down. Five years later, 268,000 coho returned, and a tentative fishery was reopened, which was expanded again in 2003. The resurgence has been attributed to the return of colder water and upwelling of nutrients, after an absence of several decades. Naysayers point out that most of the returning fish are from hatcheries, with negative implications for the long-term health of the species.

Past salmon shortfalls have spawned alternative ocean fisheries. Bottom fishing for black ling cod and rockfish, together with the harvest of such long-ignored species as hake, whiting, and pollock have increased in proportion to the decline of salmon, flounder, albacore tuna, smelt, and halibut. Growing out of the pollock fishery has been the development of a successful surimi (artificial crab) industry supplying Asian and U.S. markets. Be that as it may, the aggressive harvest of the 55 species of rockfish that are marketed as red snapper brought about catch limits in 2000, giving another signal that fisheries are in transition. Clam, oysters, shrimp, and crab continue to be strong facets of the industry, despite occasional pollution problems.

GOLD AND MINERALS

Although not a major economic force in the modern era, gold mining played a pivotal role in the early growth of towns throughout the state. In the decade following the California gold rush of 1849, thousands of miners came into southern Oregon because of gold finds in the Rogue Valley and on the south coast. The boomtown of Jacksonville was created in 1851 near a gold-bearing creek, and the Applegate Trail became the low-road alternative to the Oregon Trail for cross-country emigrants. Baker, Jacksonville's eastern Oregon counterpart, was located near the main spur of the Oregon Trail. Both places were reputed to be

among the wildest towns west of Chicago during the mid-19th century. In any case, Oregon gold production helped the Union win the Civil War. One stretch of Canyon Creek near Canyon City in the John Day area of eastern Oregon yielded $28 million in gold for Union coffers.

In addition to the Canyon City strike, other activity compounded the impression that 1860 was a golden decade. During that era, gold finds launched Jacksonville as a center of commerce. In addition, gold was reported in the foothills surrounding Cottage Grove, near the southern tip of the Willamette Valley. This latter discovery by James "Bohemia" Johnson (so named because of his heritage) in 1863 lay virtually dormant until the early 20th century, due to insufficient technology to mine the million-dollar deposits.

The Bohemia mining country also generated a story, perhaps apocryphal, that part of Cottage Grove was paved with gold-rich gravel from the Row River. So far, no one has been willing to rip up the streets and check. To the south 150 miles, the "streets of gold" story was rehashed with a new twist during the Depression, when residents unearthed tens of thousands of dollars from old claims in their backyards.

Throughout the state, gold is still in "them thar hills," but its price on the world market has to be high enough to make it financially feasible to extract. Moreover, mining companies wanting to break ground in Oregon need to keep bird-watchers, ranchers, and state regulatory agencies happy. The resistance to proposed cyanide leaching of gold-laden soils in southeathern Oregon during the 1990s is a case in point.

Southwestern Oregon is often touted as the part of the state with the most mineral wealth. The only producing nickel mine and smelter in the United States is still operating in Riddle, a small Douglas County town off of I-5. In addition to gold and nickel, deposits of copper, chromium, platinum, manganese, asbestos, mercury, iron, molybdenum, zinc, coal, and limestone have been mined in the region. South coast offshore oil- and mineral-mining leases have been proposed, but environmental restrictions make such operations more likely off the central coast near Newport.

But when all is said and done, the most mundane minerals and aggregates make the most money. Sand, gravel, and limestone for the manufacture of cement account for half of the revenues in the state's $270-million-a-year mining economy.

On the Road

Outdoor Recreation

When it comes to outdoor recreation, Oregon's cup runneth over, and this bounty is not restricted to any one corner of the state. Whether it's climbing some of the world-class ascents at Smith Rock in central Oregon, hiking between wilderness lodges along the Rogue River Trail, or fishing for steelhead and chinook on the Willamette River in the heart of downtown Portland, Oregonians and out-of-state visitors can take their pick of golden moments. Lovers of life on the wild side will discover that, in Oregon, their greatest problem is narrowing down the countless recreational opportunities.

Ever since Mount Bachelor was selected by *Ski* magazine as one of the country's top five resorts, and no fewer than six state golf courses have been named by *Golf Digest* as among the nation's best, the word has gotten out that Oregon is a pretty special place for outdoor enthusiasts. However, there are still some well-kept secrets: scuba diving off Port Orford; surfing near Cannon Beach and Seaside; mountain biking in the hills near Eugene; the best night skiing in America an hour away from Portland, Eugene, and Medford; hut-to-hut skiing in the Wallowas; hunting game birds and spelunking in eastern Oregon; and hang gliding in the high desert town of Lakeview, to name just a few.

© MARK MORRIS

Manzanita Beach

OREGON HIGHLIGHTS

Portland
- **International Rose Test Garden,** pages 74–75
- **The Pearl District,** page 80
- **Powell's Books,** page 82

The Willamette Valley
- **Breitenbush Hot Springs,** Detroit, page 147
- **Silver Falls State Park,** Sublimity, page 144
- **Wine-tasting,** Yamhill County, pages 127–129

Coastal Oregon
- **Fort Clatsop National Memorial,** Astoria, page 316
- **Oregon Coast Aquarium,** Newport, pages 256–258
- **Oregon Dunes National Recreation Area,** Reedsport, pages 235–236
- **Winter whale-watching,** coastwide, page 192

Southern Oregon
- **Oregon Shakespeare Festival,** Ashland, page 335–336
- **Peter Britt Music Festival,** Jacksonville, page 354
- **Rogue River trips,** pages 359–361

Southeastern Oregon
- **Desert hiking,** pages 385, 391, 393–396
- **Hart Mountain National Antelope Refuge,** near Plush, page 387

- **Malheur National Wildlife Refuge,** near Princeton, pages 393–394
- **Summer Lake birdlife,** page 384

The Cascades
- **Crater Lake,** page 422–427
- **Deschutes and Umpqua Rivers recreation,** pages 431–432, 465–466
- **Mount Hood and Mount Bachelor skiing and hiking,** pages 406–408, 464, 483–484
- **Sunriver Lodge** and **Inn of the Seventh Mountain,** Bend, pages 471, 472

Northeastern Oregon
- **Hells Canyon National Recreation Area backpacking,** page 516
- **Imnaha River trout fishing,** pages 512–513
- **Jetboats on the Snake River,** pages 516–517
- **Mount Howard Gondola,** Wallowa Lake, page 510
- **Pendleton Round-Up,** Pendleton, pages 521–522
- **Wallowa cross-country skiing and hiking,** pages 511–512

Columbia River Gorge
- **Cascade Locks,** pages 543–549
- **Hood River Blossom Festival,** Hood River, page 559
- **Multnomah Falls,** Historic Columbia River Highway, page 540
- **Windsurfing,** Hood River, pages 553–554

USER FEES AND PASSES

In recent years, numerous state and federal parks, national recreation areas, trails, picnic areas, and other facilities have begun charging day-use fees, which are separate from overnight camping fees (the exception to this is camping at rustic campsites in national forests, which is covered by the Northwest Forest Pass). At sites that charge fees, the day-use fee is currently $3 per vehicle at state parks, $5 per vehicle at federal sites. The good news is that the number of state parks charging fees likely will not increase any time soon, as a proposal to add two dozen locations to the list was turned down by the Oregon Parks and Recreation Department in 2003. Visitors can pay for day use at individual sites, or, if you're planning to visit a number of coastal parks or hike the trails on federal lands, you can save money by purchasing one of the passes described below.

Oregon Pacific Coast Passport
The best deal if you plan to visit many state and federal sites along the Oregon coast, this pass covers entrance, day-use, and vehicle parking fees at all state and federal fee sites along the entire

Oregon portion of U.S. 101. It does not cover the cost of camping at state parks, which is a separate fee. It was created to alleviate some of the confusion caused by having to buy different passes at the various federal (Forest Service, National Park Service, Bureau of Land Management) and state (Oregon Parks and Recreation Department) fee sites along the U.S. 101 corridor.

At press time, 17 coastal sites managed by the National Park Service, National Forest Service, Bureau of Land Management (BLM), and Oregon state parks are covered by the Passport, including: Fort Stevens State Park, Ecola State Park, Nehalem Bay State Park, Cape Lookout State Park, Fogarty Creek State Recreation Area, Heceta Head Lighthouse Viewpoint, Honeyman State Park, Shore Acres State Park, Fort Clatsop National Memorial, Oregon Dunes National Recreation Area, Sutton Recreation Area, Cape Perpetua Scenic Area, Sand Lake Recreation Area, Marys Peak Recreation Area, Drift Creek Falls Trail, Yaquina Head Outstanding Natural Area, and Hebo Lake.

Two basic Passports are available depending, on customer needs and preferences. An **Annual Passport,** valid for the calendar year, is $35. A **Five-Day Passport** is $10. Passports may be purchased at welcome centers, ranger stations, national forest headquarters, national memorials, and state park offices. Call 800/551-6949 to purchase by credit card or for directions to a convenient location near you.

State Park Passes

Another option, valid for day-use fees at Oregon's state parks that levy fees (such as Rooster Rock in the Columbia Gorge and the coastal parks listed above), is to buy a one-year ($25) or two-year ($40) State Park Pass. It's available from state park offices, by phone (800/551-6949), and from G.I. Joe's stores and other vendors. See the Oregon State Parks website (www.oregonstateparks.org/dayuse_permit.php) for more details and a complete list of vendors.

Northwest Forest Pass

In response to major reductions in timber harvests and cutbacks in federal money, a revenue shortfall has made it hard to keep up trails and campgrounds at a time when the region's population has put more demand on these facilities. The Northwest Forest Pass ($30, valid for one year) is a vehicle-parking pass for the use of many improved trailheads, picnic areas, boat launches, and interpretive sites in the national forests of Oregon and Washington. Funds generated from pass sales go directly to maintaining and improving the trails, land, and facilities. You will see "Northwest Forest Pass Required" signs posted at participating sites. Fees are collected at kiosks or dispensed by machine. Passes are also available at many local vendors (such as G.I. Joe's, park stores, and chambers of commerce) as well as by phone (800/270-7504). You can also order them online at www.fs.fed.us/r6/feedemo. You can also check this website to find out if a pass is required before you head out.

In contrast to the old fee system, these passes are good all over the Northwest, eliminating the necessity to purchase a separate pass with each entrance to another national forest. This pass covers most National Park Service and Forest Service sites in Oregon and Washington but is not valid for campground fees (with the exception of rustic campsites), concessionaire-operated sites, and Sno-Parks.

A backpacker enjoys the rugged splendor of Hells Canyon National Recreation Area's high country.

ON THE ROAD

© ERIC W. VALENTINE/COURTESY OF WWW.PRAISEPHOTOGRAPHY.COM

Golden Passport Program

Most National Forest Service lands do not charge a fee for use, whereas most National Park Service sites, such as national parks and monuments, do. You can pay an entrance fee at each site or park you visit, or you can participate in the Golden Passport Program, which offers three distinct passports. The annual **Golden Eagle Passport** ($65) allows the owner to use all Forest Service, Park Service, BLM, and U.S. Fish and Wildlife sites, as well as developed day-use sites and recreation areas. The $10 **Golden Age Passport** is a lifetime pass covering entrance fees for U.S. citizens over the age of 62 (proof of age required). Passport holders also get a 50 percent discount at campgrounds, boat launches, and swimming areas. The third pass, the free **Golden Access Passport,** is available only to those who are blind or permanently disabled (check with the forest service for eligibility requirements). It offers the same benefits as the Golden Eagle Pass.

For more details or to purchase a pass, contact the National Forest Foundation (877/465-2727, www.natlforests.org).

CAMPING AND HIKING

Oregon has more state parks than almost any other state, as well as a natural environment suited to all manner of recreational activities.

TOP FIVE HIKES IN OREGON

La Pine State Recreation Area

A boundless 2,333-acre recreation nirvana, this park is chock-full of hiking, biking, and fishing opportunities. Trails are flat and perfect for beginners. The 15 miles of single-track dirt biking trails are reachable from any of the parking lots. This park is a just a few miles off of U.S. 97 in Deschutes County. (See Southeastern Oregon chapter.)

Larch Mountain

One of the wettest places in Oregon, old growth can be found in this extensive ancient forest atop Larch Mountain on the periphery of the Columbia River Gorge. Larch Mountain is 31 miles east of Portland on I-84. At the base of Multnomah Falls, climb Franklin Ridge Trail to the summit for a view of the Cascade volcanoes. Be aware that there's a 4,200-foot elevation gain. (See Columbia River Gorge chapter.)

Oswald West State Park

Most of the mountain, and the prominent headlands of Cape Falcon, are encompassed within the 2,500-acre gem of Oswald West State Park. Several hiking trails weave through the park, including the 13 miles of the Oregon Coast Trail linking Arch Cape to the north with Manzanita. To get there head 10 miles south on U.S. 101 from Cannon Beach to the Cape Falcon Trail parking lot. Start there and head south on Cape Falcon Trail, where you can continue south to Neahanie Mountain or north to Cape Falcon. Excellent coastal views the entire way. (See Coastal Oregon chapter.)

Silver Falls State Park

Ten waterfalls cascade off canyon walls in a forest filled with gargantuan Douglas fir, ferns, and bigleaf and vine maple at this park. The best time to come is during fall foliage season when there are few visitors, just before icy roads and trail closures inhibit travel. To get there, drive 15 miles southeast of Silverton on ORE 214 to get to the park. At the parking area near the South Fork of Silver Creek, start the 7.5-mile Trail of Ten Falls loop through Silver Canyon. (See the Willamette Valley chapter.)

Smith Rock State Park

Majestic spires tower above the Crooked River at this 623-acre state park. Seven miles of well-marked trails follow the Crooked River and wend up the canyon walls to emerge on the ridgetops. Please stay on well-worn paths. To get there, drive nine miles north from Redmond to N.W. Crooked River Drive and head north to the park entrance about 100 yards from the Rockhard Store. Begin your hike here, starting a five-mile loop over Misery Ridge. (See the Cascades chapter.)

With a coastline that is largely owned by the public, the nation's first scenic highway in the Columbia Gorge, and the country's fifth national park at Crater Lake, Oregon has long given voice to a sensitive land-use ethic. Here are some suggestions to help keep Oregon the way it is:

- Stay on the trails to prevent erosion and avoid damage to such fragile vegetation as alpine wildflowers.
- Use established campsites and refrain from digging tent trenches or cutting vegetation.
- Camp several hundred feet from water sources.
- Bring a tool to dig a latrine and make it 4–6 inches deep.
- If you pack it in, pack it out. Leave nothing but footprints.
- Avoid feeding wild animals so you don't inhibit their natural instinct to fend for themselves.

Camping in State Parks

Despite charging the highest camping fees in the West, the coast's state parks are still the most heavily used (per state park acre) in the country—a tribute to their excellence.

Regarding the cost of campgrounds, there's good news and bad news. The bad news is fees at state park campgrounds have gone up in the past few years. The good news is they are not expected to go up much more. Park rates are also subject to change, and some of the less developed, off-the-beaten path parks don't even charge a fee. But for those that do, May 1–Oct. 30 prices average at about the following rates: electrical hookup sites $20; tent sites $16; primitive/overflow sites $9; hiker/biker sites $4–6; yurts $27–42. During the discounted "Discovery Season," Oct. 1–April 30, electrical hookup sites are $16; tent sites are $12; and hiker-biker site and yurt fees remain the same. The extra vehicle charge during either season is $7.

A new addition at state parks, yurts have been added to many campgrounds. Yurts are canvas-walled, wood-floored shelters equipped with fold-up beds, heaters, and lamps; they sleep five.

Half of Oregon's state park campgrounds accept campsite reservations; the other half are first-come, first served. Reservations, however, are accepted for special facilities such as cabins, yurts, and tepees, at

© MARK MORRIS

Yurts, wood-floored circular tents, are an increasingly popular option for overnighters at several state parks.

all state parks that have them. The state park system has a central information hotline (800/551-6949) and a website (www.oregonstateparks.org) where you can get park maps, campground layouts, rates, and other information.

Reservations for state parks can be made by phone via a Reservations Northwest (503/731-3411 in Portland metro area, 800/452-5687 elsewhere). Business hours are Mon.–Fri. 8 A.M.–7 P.M. Online reservations, with a Visa or MasterCard, are handled by a private vendor, ReserveAmerica (www.reserveamerica.com). Reservations may be made from two days up to nine months in advance. In addition to the campsite fee, a $6 processing fee is charged.

If you need to **cancel your reservation** three days or more before your scheduled arrival, call Reservations Northwest at the numbers above. Two or fewer days before your trip, call the park directly to cancel your reservation. Phone numbers for all parks are found on each individual park's web page (www.oregonstateparks.org). Cancellation service fees and requirements for special facilities, such as yurts and cabins, may vary. Your $6 reservation fee is nonrefundable, and a $3 cancellation fee will be charged if you cancel in the last two days.

Camping in National Forests

The National Forest Service maintains hundreds of campsites, trails, and day-use areas in the state's 14 national areas. Refer to the forest service website (www.fs.fed.us/recreation) or one of the specific destination chapters in this guide, for listings.

Campsites are usually much less developed than those at state parks; they generally include a table, a fire grate, and a tent or trailer space. Electric hookups are not available, although most campgrounds have water and vault or flush toilets. Most overnight sites charge a user fee. You may camp a maximum of 14 days out of every 30 on forest service land. Fees are $10–15 for campsites, $5–7 for an extra vehicle. Campsites can be reserved online with a Visa or MasterCard through ReserveAmerica (www.reserveamerica.com).

Outdoor Gear

Oregon is one of the best places to purchase outdoor recreation equipment. First of all, Portland, Bend, and the two college towns of Eugene and Corvallis boast many stores and equipment manufacturers that cater to Oregon's love affair with the outdoors. Although outdoor gear tends to be expensive wherever you buy it, Oregon's comparatively low overhead and lack of sales tax help keep costs down. Look for markdowns on items with "blems" (cosmetic defects), as well as "annex" stores selling the same or closeout items. If you need a high level of sophistication in your gear, chances are you'll find state-of-the-art hardware within the Beaver State.

In this vein, the **Columbia Sportswear Outlet Store** (1323 S.E. Tacoma St., Portland, 503/238-0118) saves you 30–50 percent on the prices you'd pay at their downtown flagship store on S.W. Broadway and Taylor. For rain parkas, fleece vests, and the like, it's hard to beat this local company (one of the most successful outfitters in the United States) for stylish attire that'll keep you warm and dry in the Northwest winter and comfortably cool in summer.

Discount prices are available at **Andy and Bax** (324 S.E. Grand, Portland, 503/234-7538).

Everything from U.S. Army reissue coolers and other G.I. surplus to a wide variety of camping equipment is available here. Specialty items such as Metsker Oregon County maps and whitewater guidebooks are also sold here.

More than a dozen **G.I. Joe's** stores across the state provide competitive prices on outdoor equipment, with sale prices that often undercut their competitors. **REI** (www.rei.com), the popular outfitter, has retail outlets in Portland, Tigard, and Eugene. **Bi-Mart** (www.bimart.com), the

CAMPING CHECKLIST

Don't leave home without these things, or you may be sorry.

- canteen
- clothing in layers of polypropylene, wool, and waterproof-breathable fabrics (such as Gore-Tex), many of which can wick perspiration away from the skin, thus helping you stay dry and warm through damp or sweaty conditions
- compass
- cooking and eating utensils
- cookstove—lightweight and preferably one that can use a variety of fuels
- first-aid kit containing adhesive bandage tape, aloe vera, antibiotics, antiseptic, aspirin, bandages, cold compress, cotton, diarrhea medication, hydrogen peroxide, iodine, ipecac syrup, lip balm, scissors, sterile gauze pads, tongue depressor, tweezers, and two rolls of gauze
- flashlight or lantern
- foam mat or Therm-a-Rest inflatable pad
- freeze-dried food
- insect repellent
- map of area
- nylon twine
- plastic bags
- sunscreen
- Swiss Army knife
- synthetic sleeping bag that can retain up to 85 percent of your body heat, even when soaked
- tent—light, durable, and water-resistant
- waterproof footwear
- water-purification tablets or filter devices
- wooden matches dipped in nail polish or wax (for waterproofing)

discount membership store, has some 50 locations across Oregon and boasts competitive prices on camping, fishing, and other outdoor gear.

FISHING AND HUNTING

Oregon takes a back seat to few other places when it comes to sport fishing and hunting opportunities, with varied shooting and angling possible all over the state. Rules and bag limits for both are subject to frequent change, so get a copy of the **Oregon Department of Fish and Wildlife**'s hunting and fishing regulations, available at the agency office (2501 S.W. 1st Ave., Portland, OR 97207, 503/872-5268), sporting goods stores, some grocery stores (such as Fred Meyer), and other outlets. Better yet, check the website (www.dfw.state.or.us) for the most current information.

The "Outdoors Notebook" in the Thursday sports section of the *Oregonian* is a helpful resource for current conditions, forecasts, and other information. A good supplement to this is the paper's telephone service, Outside Line (503/225-5555, ext. 9010), which updates statewide hunting and fishing reports throughout the week.

Fishing

After years of serious decline, the early years of the 21st century have seen dramatic improvements in the returns of salmon and steelhead, thanks largely to habitat protection, improvements to dams that make them more fish-friendly, and other conservation efforts, as well as cyclical changes in ocean currents and nutrient levels. In 2003, for example, an estimated one million chinook passed through the fish ladders at the Columbia River's Bonneville Dam, the largest run in some 60 years. The rebounding populations have been a boon to anglers, who target salmon offshore as well as in freshwater.

Sturgeon are another extremely popular game fish, weighing into the hundreds of pounds, in the larger rivers, particularly the Columbia and the Umpqua. Off the coast, bottom fishing for rockfish and other species is a year-round activity, depending on the weather. Warm ocean currents bring albacore tuna in August and September,

and halibut are usually available in summer, though the season is variable and is set yearly by the Pacific Fisheries Management Council. Fishing for trout, both wild native cutthroat and rainbows as well as planted hatchery fish, is popular all across the state. Standout areas include the Deschutes River, a blue-ribbon stream noted for its large "redband" rainbow trout, as well as excellent steelhead fishing. Other notable steelhead streams include the coastal Rogue and Umpqua Rivers, as well as the Sandy and Clackamas Rivers, right in Portland's backyard. Smallmouth bass provide excellent sport on the John Day and Umpqua Rivers, and largemouth bass draw anglers to warm-water lakes across the state. These are merely some highlights of what Oregon has to offer. See destination chapters for additional details.

About a thousand fishing guides are licensed in Oregon. Fishing opportunities on your own are almost limitless, but hiring a guide can be money well spent if you're exploring unfamiliar waters or you lack a boat. Major **charter-fishing** centers on the coast include Astoria, Hammond, Warrenton, Garibaldi, Depoe Bay, Newport, Winchester Bay, Charleston, Gold Beach, Bandon, and Brookings. Charter rates vary a bit, but typical prices up and down the coast are as follows: $55–60 for a half day (5–6 hours) of bottom fishing, $100 for a full day; $100 for an eight-hour salmon outing; $175 for 12 hours of tuna fishing; $150 for a 12-hour halibut charter. Inland, expect to pay $150–250 per person per day for guided trips for salmon, steelhead, sturgeon, and other species. Guide and charter services are listed in each destination chapter. Chambers of commerce in each town can also provide extensive listings.

Nonresident **fishing licenses** cost $8 (for one day), $14.50 (two days), $21 (three days), $27.50 (four days, $34.75 (seven days), or $48.50 (full year). Nonresident licenses include Combined Angling Tags (allowing the taking of salmon, sturgeon, steelhead, and halibut). The cost for a one-year license for residents is $20.50 for adults, $6.25 for ages 14–17. A Resident Annual License costs $19.75; a Combined Angling Tag costs $16.50 for adults, $6.50 for minors (under 18).

ON THE ROAD

Hunting

Hunters, too, enjoy a broad range of opportunities throughout Oregon. Shooting for upland game birds—chukar, Hungarian partridge, pheasant, grouse, and quail—can be good to excellent in eastern and central Oregon, the Cascades, and the coastal ranges. The eastern half of the state, as well as the Willamette Valley, Columbia River basin, and coastal areas, offer waterfowl hunting. Wild turkeys, introduced successfully on the eastern side of Mount Hood, have proliferated and are now hunted in almost every county of the state. Bigger game include elk, black bears, cougars, blacktail deer in western Oregon and mule deer in the east. A limited number of special tags are issued also for pronghorn, bighorn sheep, and mountain goats.

The rules governing hunting in the state are more complex and variable than those for fishing. Check the regulations carefully for seasons, restrictions, and bag limits, and, again, consult the Department of Fish and Wildlife's website (www.dfw.state.or.us) for the latest information. An annual hunting license for nonresidents is $58.50, for residents $17.50. In addition, hunters must purchase special tags or stamps to legally hunt for specific game, which can be spendy for out-of-state hunters. For example, a deer tag is $191.50 for nonresidents, $14.50 for residents.

WINDSURFING

Windsurfing conditions near the town of Hood River have made the Columbia River Gorge world famous. Other than the San Francisco Bay Area, no other place in the continental United States boasts summertime air flows as consistently strong as those in the Gorge. Championship events and top competitors have coalesced on the shores of the river here, 60 miles east of Portland. Water temperatures between 55 and 65 degrees and consistent winds that occasionally exceed 40 miles per hour allow sailboarders to "rig up" from spring until fall at the Hood River Marina and Riverfront Park in The Dalles. The great river of the West runs in the opposite direction of the westerly air flows, which can cause large waves to stack up and allow sailboarders to maintain their positions relative to the shore. In short, the area offers the perfect marriage of optimal conditions and scenic beauty.

Some coastal waters, too, are gaining popularity for sailboarders. Floras Lake, near Port Orford, and Pistol River State Park, near Gold Beach, are top destinations. The latter hosts the Pistol River Wave Bash National Windsurfing Competition, each June.

WHITE-WATER ACTIVITIES

Oregon's world-class white-water rafting and kayaking prove that the rain clouds here have a silver lining. With 90,000 river miles in the state and hundreds of outfitters to choose from, however, neophyte rafters have an embarrassment of riches. To help navigate the tricky currents of brochure jargon and select the experience that's right for you, here's a list of rivers to run and questions to ask before going.

The famous **Rogue River** reaches its white-water crescendo at the green forested canyons of the Klamath Mountains in southwestern Oregon, a backdrop for potential sightings of deer, elk, bear, bald eagle, and otters. Come June to September to avoid the rainy season and be spared current fluctuations due to dams upstream. This run is characterized by gentle stretches broken up by abrupt and occasionally severe drop-offs as well as swift currents. In fact, Blossom Bar (where Meryl Streep braved the elements in the movie *The River Wild*) is often cited as one of the state's consummate tests of skill for rafters. The Rogue is ideal for half- and full-day rafting trips, with most outfitters putting in near the town of Merlin and continuing downstream as far as Foster Bar. Water turbulence on the Rogue is often intensified by constricted channels created by huge boulders. Depending on the season, rafters can expect Class II, III, and IV rapids (see "River Rapids Classification" chart), interspersed by deep pools and cascading waterfalls. At day's end, superlative campsites offer repose and the chance to savor your adventures.

Despite the dryness and isolation of Oregon's southeast corner, the **Owyhee River** has become a prime destination for white-water enthusiasts.

COURTESY OF BLM/RON MURPHY

ON THE ROAD

Rafters negotiate rocky Pinball Rapids on the North Umpqua River.

The reasons include the red-rock canyons, lava flows, and sagebrush tablelands that line its course. The 53 miles from Rome to the Owyhee Reservoir have two sections of exceptionally heavy rapids, but the many pools of short, intense white water alternating with easy drifts make for a well-paced trip. Stay alert even along stretches of placid water and such eye-catching diversions as a 10-mile gorge lined by 1,000-foot-high walls and frequented by wild horses and pronghorns, because sharp rocks abound along the Owyhee's course. The best times to come are during May and early June. Before going, check conditions with the Vale BLM District office (541/473-3144, www.or.blm.gov/vale), because the Owyhee can only be run in high snowmelt years. Access to rafting put-in points in this part of the state is greatly facilitated by a four-wheel-drive vehicle.

The **John Day River** in northeastern Oregon offers an even-flowing current as it winds 175 miles through unpopulated rangeland and scenic rock formations. This is the longest free-flowing river in the United States. Below Clarno, the grade gets steep, creating the most treacherous part of the state's longest river (275 miles) within Oregon. The 157-mile section of the John Day that rafters, canoeists, and kayakers come to experience also has falls near the mouth that require a portage. The special charm of this Columbia tributary is the dearth of company you'll have here even during the river-running season of late March through May and then again in November. Just watch out for rattlesnakes along the bank and remember that the siltload in this undammed river reduces it to an unboatable trickle in summer months. Contact the Prineville BLM office (541/416-6700, www.or.blm.gov/prineville) for more information.

Unlike the John Day and the Owyhee Rivers, the **Deschutes rapids** aren't totally dependent on snowmelt. As on the Rogue, river runners enjoy superlative conditions even in the driest of years. As a result, it has become the busiest vacation waterway in the state. The 44 miles between Maupin and the Columbia River contain sage-covered grasslands and wild rocky canyons where you might see bald eagles, pronghorns, and other wildlife. If there's a good run of salmon or steelhead, you might also encounter plenty of fishing boats. Expect most of the thrills and spills near the mouth of this 250-mile river. Heavy winds might also whip up in the final quarter of the journey. This area averages 310 days of sunshine annually, so weather is seldom a problem except for excessively hot summer days. The destination chapters in this book cover more details and more rivers.

Chambers of commerce and phone books are good sources on white-water activities. For example, the Portland Yellow Pages lists four columns of ads under "Rafts and River Trips." Typical outfitter services include gourmet meals, wetsuits or rain gear, and inflatable rafts and kayaks. Should you consult commercial backpacking magazines and newspaper sports and travel sections (also check the "Outdoors" section of the *Oregonian* on Thursday), chances are the blurbs might include adjectives such as "participatory" (i.e., you paddle and perhaps help set up camp) and "deluxe" (i.e., you don't paddle if you don't want to, fancy equipment, and good eats provided). Guided raft trips begin at about $50 for a half-day trip and increase to $200 (and up) a day for longer trips. Groups can get volume discounts.

However, detailed as these listings may be, they mean little without some follow-up. For example, if "gourmet meals" are advertised, find out what they include. To ensure an intimate wilderness experience, ask about the number of people in a raft and how many rafts on the river at one time. Are there any hidden costs such as camping gear rental or added transfer charges? What is the cancellation policy? Another consideration is the training and experience of the guides. Can he or she be expected to give commentary about history, geology, and local color? You might also want to check about the company's willingness to customize its trips to special interests such as photography, birdwatching, or hiking.

SNOW SPORTS

One of the silver linings to Oregon's legendary precipitation is that so much of it falls in the form of snow in the mountains. Mount Hood, for example, has been buried by as much as 100 feet of snow in a single year. That makes a lot of people happy here from late fall through spring and even into summer, as Oregon snowpacks support the longest ski season in the country (at Timberline on Mount Hood), as well as snowboarding, snowmobiling, and snowshoeing.

In addition to hundreds of miles of groomed and backcountry cross-country ski routes, a dozen alpine resorts are concentrated in the northern and central Cascades and in the state's northeast corner. Portlanders have their choice of five developed ski resorts—Mount Hood Ski Bowl, Cooper Spur, Mount Hood Meadows, Timberline, and Summit (the Northwest's oldest ski resort, dating to 1927)—just an hour's drive away on **Mount Hood.** In the central Cascades, there's family-friendly **Hoodoo Ski Bowl** southeast of Salem, **Willamette Pass** southeast of Eugene, and **Mount Bachelor,** the Northwest's largest and most developed ski area, southwest of Bend. At **Mount Bailey,** near Diamond Lake in the southern Cascades, downhillers can experience Snowcat skiing, a more affordable alternative to being dropped off on inaccessible slopes by helicopter. The area also offers extensive cross-country, skating, sledding, and snowmobiling terrain. Near the California border, **Mount Ashland** offers downhill action in southern Oregon, in addition to 100 miles of cross-country trails.

Far from everything, but worth the drive for the fine dry powder of the south-central Oregon desert, is **Warner Canyon Ski Area,** east of Lake-

RIVER RAPIDS CLASSIFICATION

Class I:	Easy, beginner
Class II:	Requires care, intermediate
Class III:	Difficult, experienced
Class IV:	Very difficult, highly skilled
Class V:	Exceedingly difficult, expert only
Class VI:	Unnavigable

view. In the northeast, skiers have their choice of **Anthony Lakes Ski Area,** between Baker City and La Grande, and **Ferguson Ridge Ski Area** and **Salt Creek Summit,** both east of Joseph.

For details on all the above ski areas, see individual destination chapters. For snow reports and other updated information throughout the season, a good source is OnTheSnow.com (www.on-thesnow.com/OR/).

Sno-Park Permits

Between November 15 and April 30, note that for winter sports in many areas, you'll need to purchase a Sno-Park permit to park your vehicle in posted winter recreation areas. Sporting goods stores, ski shops, and DMV offices near the slopes sell them for $15/season, $3/day. Parking in an Oregon Sno-Park without a permit can earn you a $30 fine.

Entertainment and Events

The majority of large crowd-drawing events take place June–Sept., but there are plenty of cool-weather and ongoing activities to keep you entertained throughout the year. The free weekly local magazines are a great source for events and entertainment listings and can be found in most of the larger burgs and college towns. See the "Festivals and Events" special topic in this chapter for a list of the state's most popular fetes, and check out the destination chapters for details on music festivals, theater seasons, rodeos, food fests, and other gatherings.

Oregon loves to celebrate its heritage, as well as its artistic and gastronomic bounty. The following seasonal sampler highlights some of the festivals and celebrations throughout the state.

In spring, two coastal gourmet affairs of note are the Newport Seafood and Wine Festival and the Astoria Crab Feed and Seafood Festival. Also around this time, Florence's Rhododendron Festival and Brookings's Azalea Festival, both on the coast, attract blossom connoisseurs.

If you have kids in tow, take advantage in June of the parades, carnival rides, air shows, and floral splendor of Portland's Rose Festival or the Cannon Beach Sandcastle Festival. You could fill up July and August with such varied musical talents as the new vaudeville acts of the Oregon Country Fair, the gold-record performers at Jacksonville's Peter Britt Music Festival, not to mention the blues icons who appear at the Waterfront Blues Festival in Portland, the West Coast's largest.

During August, festival-goers can toast their appreciation of Oregon at Portland's **Oregon Brewers Festival,** where more than 60 microbreweries are showcased, and the **Annual International Pinot Noir Festival** in McMinnville, attracting master vintners from around the world. Summer festival-hoppers might also want to take in **Da Vinci Days** in Corvallis, uniting the community's scientific and artistic elements, and Portland's **Bite,** featuring the best in food.

In the fall and winter, the leading events west of the Cascades include Mount Angel's **Oktoberfest,** the **Eugene Celebration,** the **Corvallis Fall Festival,** and Thanksgiving open houses in the wine country. At Christmastime the leading events are Albany's **Victorian Parlor tours,** Portland's **Christmas Ships,** and light displays all over the state.

While most of Oregon's celebrations take place west of the Cascades, there are notable exceptions to the rule. Bird-watchers relish the Klamath Basin **Bald Eagle Conference** in February and the springtime **John Scharff Migratory Waterfowl Conference** in Burns. Highbrows can take in the summertime literary festival at **Fishtrap** in the Wallowas or rock out at the **Bend Summer Fest** in central Oregon. Rockhounds flock to summer mineral shows in the central Oregon hamlets of Madras and Prineville. Rodeo fans can whoop and holler at the venerable **Pendleton Roundup** in September. Such celebrations of ethnicity as Portland's **Cinco de Mayo** (one of the largest celebrations of this kind in the nation) and **Scandanavian festivals** in Astoria and Junction City express the state's diversity.

LEWIS AND CLARK BICENTENNIAL EVENTS

Lewis and Clark's Corps of Discovery, consisting of 32 men and one woman, the Shoshone Sacagawea, spent October 1805 to May 1806 in what today are Oregon and Washington. Along the way, Lewis and Clark charted some 8,000 miles of territory and documented 300 species of flora and fauna previously unknown to western science. Two centuries later, the nation has begun to celebrate Lewis and Clark's achievement anew, and the bicentennial has spawned a minor industry in itself. Communities along their historic route will stage re-enactments, exhibits, and other events in commemoration, and Oregon, naturally, is participating wholeheartedly.

While you may have missed the National Lewis and Clark Bicentennial Kick-Off Event in Monticello, Virginia, in January 2003, it's not too late to participate in celebrating the Corps of Discovery's final destination: Oregon. Among 15 bicentennial "Signature Events" scheduled across the country into 2006, "Destination: The Pacific" and subsequent "Wintering Over" events commemorate the four months Lewis and Clark spent near the mouth of the Columbia River in southwestern Washington and northwestern Oregon. The National Park Service's live traveling exhibit, **"Corps of Discovery II,"** will re-create the journey of Lewis and Clark by retracing the original historic trail on the dates chronicled in the journals, 200 years later. This exhibit is slated to be in Oregon October 2005–April 2006. Refer to the NPS website (www.nps.gov/focl) for exact Corps II sites and dates.

As this book goes to press in 2004, plans are still evolving for commemorative events along the Lewis and Clark Trail, which will continue into fall of 2006. In Oregon, events are planned from The Dalles to Cannon Beach. At press time, many event dates, times, and venues have yet to be finalized. Check with the various organizations noted below for updated information.

FESTIVALS AND EVENTS

January
Crustacean Classics, Lincoln City
Whale-watching, coastwide

February
Bald Eagle Conference, Klamath Basin
Portland International Film Festival

March
Original Yachats Arts and Crafts Fair, Yachats
Beachcomber's Festival, Brookings
Dune Mushers Mail Run, Coos Bay and Florence
Inner City Blues Festival, Portland
Whale-watching, coastwide

April
Hood River Blossom Festival, Hood River
Pear Blossom Festival, Medford

May
Boatnik Festival, Grants Pass
Cinco de Mayo, Portland
Rodeo, Christmas Valley

June
Sandcastle Day, Cannon Beach
Rodeo, Sisters
Rose Festival, Portland
Shakespeare Festival "Feast of Will," Ashland

July
Chief Joseph Days, Joseph
Curry County Fair and Rodeo, Gold Beach
Da Vinci Days, Corvallis
International Pinot Noir Celebration, McMinnville
Lincoln County Fair and Rodeo, Newport
Miner's Jubilee, Baker City

Destination: The Pacific

The focus of Oregon's Signature Event, "Destination: The Pacific" (P.O. Box 2005, Astoria 97103, 503/325-8618, www.DestinationThePacific.com) is a week of activities that commemorate the Arrival, the Vote, the Crossing, and the Wintering Over of the Lewis and Clark Expedition on the shores of the Pacific. The Signature Event runs November 23–27, 2005, and kicks off four months of activities that conclude at the end of March 2006, when a special departure celebration takes place.

Break bread with re-enactors and members of Corps of Discovery II at the **Breakfast with the Corps** and a **Commemorative Thanksgiving Dinner** at Station Camp in Chinook, WA, on November 24, 2005.

Also during the Signature Event, live theater will be staged throughout the week at several venues. A country-dance featuring traditional music and a gala at Astoria's historic Liberty Theater to honor the cultures of the Chinook and Clatsop tribes will top off the week. The **Native American Exposition** at the Clatsop Fairgrounds in Astoria November 25–27, will feature Native American art, crafts, foods, and entertainment.

Among the many events to follow are the opening of new trails, including the Fort-To-Sea Trail from Fort Clatsop to Sunset Beach in Oregon and the Lewis and Clark Discovery Trail between Ilwaco and Long Beach in Washington; the official dedication of monuments, such as the Maya Lin Confluence piece at Fort Canby State Park, Ilwaco, WA; boat excursions on the Columbia River to view the route of the expedition's crossing; and a re-dedication of Fort Clatsop.

At Fort Clatsop, along the Washington Discovery Trail, at the Salt Works in Seaside, and along the Lewis and Clark National Historic Trail to the ocean, volunteers will don period clothing and assume personas to act out historically accurate interpretations of members of the Corps of Discovery. The Journey's End National Art Exhibit will feature Lewis and Clark themes. Check the Lewis and Clark Expedition's

ON THE ROAD

Oregon Coast Music Festival, Coos Bay, North Bend, and Charleston
Oregon Country Fair, Eugene
Peter Britt Music Festival, Jacksonville
Subaru Annual Gorge Games, The Gorge
Summer Fest, Bend
Waterfront Blues Festival, Portland

August
Astoria Regatta Week, Astoria
The Bite, Portland
Blackberry Arts Festival, Coos Bay
Oregon Brewers Festival, Portland
Oregon Trail Days and Rendezvous, La Grande

September
Cascade Festival of Music, Bend
Chowder, Brews, and Blues, Florence
Cranberry Festival, Bandon
Fall Festival, Corvallis
Corvallis Kite Festival, Lincoln City

Harney County Fair, Burns
Oregon State Fair, Salem
Pendleton Round-Up, Pendleton

October
Oktoberfest, Mount Angel
Silver Salmon Celebration, Astoria
Yachats Village Mushroom Fest, Yachats

November
Celtic Music Festival, Yachats
Stormy Weather Arts Festival, Cannon Beach
Wine-tasting open houses, Wine Country

December
Christmas ships, Portland
Festival of Lights, Bandon
Holiday lights and open house, Shore Acres State Park, Charleston
Victorian parlor tours, Albany

(www.lewisandclarkcoast.com) or Destination: the Pacific's (www.destinationthepacific.com) websites for specific venues, dates, and times, which are subject to change.

Events and Exhibits Timeline

January–December 2004: "Picturing the Corps of Discovery: The Lewis and Clark Expedition in Oregon Art," at the state capitol, Salem.

2004–summer 2006: "Cargo—Equipment and Supplies of the Lewis and Clark Expedition," at the Columbia Gorge Discovery Center and Museum (5000 Discovery Dr., The Dalles 97058, 541/296-8600, www.gorgediscovery.org), explores the 30 tons of goods the Corps hauled—Native American gifts, arms and accoutrements, medicines, clothing, mathematical instruments, camp equipment and provisions, and transportation.

July 2004: "Oregon, My Oregon," a new permanent exhibit at the Oregon Historical Society (1200 S.W. Park Ave., Portland, 503/222-1741, www.ohs.org), includes a section devoted to the Lewis and Clark Expedition.

September 2004: "Discovering the Rivers of Lewis and Clark," at the Oregon Historical Society, examines water routes followed by Lewis and Clark, and the status of those rivers today.

December 2004: "Before Lewis and Clark: Mapping the Pacific Northwest," another exhibit at the Oregon Historical Society, includes pre-1805 printed works on early exploration and mapping of the Oregon country.

January–June 2005: "People of the River Exhibit," a collaborative project between the Portland Art Museum and the Smithsonian's National Museum of American Indians, focuses on the Native American peoples who lived on the rivers from the mouth of the Snake to the Pacific Ocean, and features a 100-year-old collection of Native American artifacts never before exhibited. At the Portland Art Museum (1219 S.W. Park Ave., Portland, 503/276-4293, www.pam.org).

April 2005–September 2006: "Tribal Lifeways Technology Exhibit," a living history village at Tamástslikt Cultural Institute (72789 Hwy. 331, Pendleton 97801, 541/966-9748, www.tamastslikt.com) illustrates the village setting as the expedition would have seen it.

October 2005–April 2006: "Corps of Discovery II," tentatively scheduled to be in Oregon, retraces the original route.

November 11, 2005–March 11, 2006: National Lewis and Clark Bicentennial Exhibition. Reunited for the first time since 1806, this rare collection of Lewis and Clark artifacts, coordinated through the Missouri Historical Society, will be displayed at the Oregon Historical Society (1200 SW Park Ave., Portland, 503/222-1741, www.ohs.org.

November 24–27, 2005: "Destination: The Pacific." For details on Oregon's Signature Event, see section immediately preceding.

December 2005–March 2006: A variety of activities at and around Fort Clatsop will commemorate the winter the Corps spent here.

March 2006: The Closing Ceremony at Fort Clatsop will commemorate the expedition's departure from the coast and the beginning of their return journey.

Accommodations

Oregon lodging prices are for the most part significantly lower than those of neighboring California and Washington. Nonetheless, accommodations in Portland, parts of the Cascade Range, the coast, and tourist destinations such as Ashland can put a strain on the pocketbook. Fortunately, state park and national forest campgrounds proliferate in many of the most popular areas, offering low-cost overnight lodgings in attractive settings (see "Camping and Hiking," earlier in this chapter).

For extremely popular destinations, such as Cannon Beach and other coastal towns, plan to reserve well in advance during peak times, such as summer weekends and holidays. Lodgings can sell out weeks or months in advance, and you may find yourself with no place to stay if you don't plan ahead. During such times, lodging bargains may be hard to find, as it's a seller's market.

Oregon has no state sales tax, though budget shortfalls could change that in the future. For now, it makes purchases in the state all the more attractive.

"Off-season" specials are a way to beat the crowds and the costs. For example, before Memorial Day and Labor Day room rates on the coast can drop by 25 percent or so, and in winter, even by 50 percent.

While there's no sales tax in Oregon (yet), note that a local lodging tax—ranging 6–12 percent, depending on the locale—will be added to your bill. In addition, a recently implement one percent statewide "transient lodging" tax, dedicated to tourism-promotion efforts, also applies.

HOTELS AND MOTELS

Throughout most of the state, the familiar chain motels and hotels proliferate, each providing a generally consistent experience in its class, ranging from ultra-budget to upscale. In this book, we cover representative chain lodgings, but also try to focus attention on independent or unusual accommodations that have something special to offer in terms of location, ambience, service, or amenities.

BED-AND-BREAKFASTS

These bits o' Britain provide a homey alternative to the typical hotel room. Ashland and the coast lead the country in bed-and-breakfast establishments per capita, but the idea seems to be catching on everywhere in Oregon. And why not? Whether they offer a glass of sherry by a crackling fire to warm up Ashland theater-goers or a huge picture window onto a Pacific storm, these retreats can impart that extra-special personal touch to the best the state has to offer.

If a turn-of-the-century Victorian or an old farmhouse doesn't give a bed-and-breakfast an extra measure of warmth, the camaraderie of the guests and the host family usually will. Most bed-and-breakfasts restrict kids, pets, and smoking in deference to what are often close quarters. Ask in advance about whether children are welcome, and what ages are appropriate. Private baths are also sometimes in short supply. Offsetting any privacy limitations is an included full or continental breakfast. And in Oregon, it has become customary to see homemade jams and breads as well as a complimentary glass of a local wine for a nightcap.

VACATION HOME RENTALS

While B&Bs can add to a romantic weekend on the coast or enjoyment of an Ashland theater excursion thanks to walking distance from the theater and thematic decor, we realize these establishments don't make sense all the time for everyone. This book also lists realty companies in certain locations whose properties afford more privacy. Deals abound thanks to the volume of vacation homes that often sit idle or can accommodate large enough parties to offset a high nightly rate.

The cost-conscious traveler should also keep in mind that there is usually no shortage of large condos and vacation homes along the coast and in resort areas that rent out to large parties who can split costs.

HOSTELS

The final word on beating the high cost of lodging may go to youth hostels (in Ashland, Bandon, Bend, Eugene, Portland, and Seaside), with rates generally $15–20 per night. Oregon is also blessed with dynamic Elderhostel programs featuring educational experiences and low-cost accommodations. The adventuresome senior can choose from a range of offerings such as a Shakespeare theater program in Ashland or a comparative religion class at a retreat center in Sandy. In-state, call 541/552-6677; otherwise contact **Elderhostel** (877/426-8056, www.elderhostel.org) for registration and details.

Food and Drink

OREGON CUISINE

What will the newcomer to Oregon notice most on his or her plate? It all depends on where you happen to be. From the Basque food in southeastern Oregon to Portland's purveyors of A to Z ethnic cuisines, there's no shortage of exotic and satisfying offerings in a state most famous in the public mind for salmon and jumbo pears.

As for humbler fare, jo-jos (refried baked potato spears encased in spices), the patented Gardenburger (Portland's own version of the vegetarian hamburger), and marionberry jams, jellies, and pies are foodstuffs most likely to confound out-of-staters.

The marionberry is a dark maroon berry whose tarter-than-blackberry taste and small seeds make it ideal for dessert fare, especially marionberry ice cream. Higher up on the food chain, world-class Oregon lamb and the seasonally available excellent fresh sturgeon, venison, and game birds are other little-known taste treasures here. The frequent use of locally grown herbs, exotic mushrooms, and organic produce in regional restaurants will also catch your taste buds by surprise. Award-winning dairy products, berry products coveted by gourmet ice-cream makers, and hazelnuts in demand all over the world are other palate-pleasers in Oregon's horn of plenty.

Oregon specialties can be complemented with a world-class pinot noir, gourmet coffee, or microbrew. In addition to quality spirits accompanying your meal, fresh-squeezed juices and old-fashioned root beer (notably Widmer's and Henry Weinhard's) provide quality nonalcoholic refreshments. In short, while there is not a defined substratum of cuisine that is quintessentially Oregon, uniqueness and variety combine here to satisfy even the most sophisticated palate.

Oregon's abundance of fresh produce, seafood, and other indigenous ingredients prompted America's apostle of haute cuisine, James Beard, to extol the restaurants and cooking of his home state. In his autobiography, Delights and Prejudices, he implies that Oregon strawberries, Seaside peas, Dungeness crab, and other local fare are the standards by which he judges culinary staples around the world. This cornucopia is the basis of a regional cuisine emphasizing fresh natural foods cooked lightly to preserve flavor, color, and texture.

Nonetheless, it is possible to have a bad meal in this state. In fact, the quality of the cuisine in some remote eastern Oregon towns is a source of self-deprecating humor for the locals. And as many Yankees will tell you, there is no shortage of bland New England–style clam chowder on the Oregon coast.

Still, it's easy to dine well at an affordable price throughout most of the state. Affordable doesn't have to mean McDonald's, either. Because Oregon abounds in places with genuine ambience and home cooking at a good value, fast-food listings are kept to a minimum in this book. Budget travelers might want to bring their own food to expensive resort environments.

Throughout the state, stores purvey locally made food products, which make excellent gifts. In both the Portland and Eugene airports, for example, mini-malls sell Oregon jams, smoked salmon, hazelnuts, wines, and similar products.

The restaurant recommendations in this book were made with the traveler in mind who would prefer to have some cash left over at the end of a meal to take advantage of a raft trip or a museum. At the same time, we recognize that one of the most pleasurable ways to get to know a locale is at the dinner table. Thus, "justifiable splurges" occasionally supplant "dollar-value" orientation, especially when the locale lends itself to gourmet dining, such as in Ashland, Portland, the coast, and the wine country.

LIQUOR AND MICROBREWERIES

Note Oregon's liquor laws: liquor is sold by the bottle in state-sanctioned liquor stores only, open Mon.–Sat. Beer and wine are also sold in grocery stores and retail outlets. Liquor is sold by the drink in licensed establishments 7 A.M.–2:30 A.M. The minimum drinking age is 21.

Throughout the Northwest one encounters the popular phenomenon of microbreweries and pubs serving their own beers. Oregon has nearly 70 craft breweries, a third of them located in Portland. Technically, the term "microbrewery" in Oregon refers to an establishment that sells beer on the premises in limited quantities—less than 20,000 barrels a year. However, this term connotes more than mere quantitative distinctions. Microbrews are handcrafted beers minus preservatives or chemical additives to enhance head or color. Instead of the rice or corn used by the big

outfits, the micros just use barley, malt, hops, yeast, and water. The end result is a more full-bodied, tastier brew with a distinct personality. The trend is so pervasive in Portland that this metropolis is touted as "the city that made Milwaukee nervous."

The reason Oregon is awash in gourmet suds owes much to the availability of topnotch ingredients—hops, barley, and clear water. Almost a third of the world's hops is produced here in the Northwest. The Willamette Valley alone cultivates more than a dozen varieties. Add Cascade mountain water, malted barley from the Klamath basin, and Hood River–grown yeast cultures and you can see why there are more breweries and brewpubs per capita in Oregon than anywhere else in the United States.

Some big names in the custom brew scene include Portland Brewing Co., whose Mc-Tarnahan's Scottish Ale won a gold medal at the Great American Beer Festival in Denver; Bridgeport Brewing Co., a pioneer on the microbrew circuit which won a prestigious world championship when its India Pale Ale beat out more than 140 competitors in the 2000 Brewing Industry International Awards in London; Full Sail Ale, widely distributed all over the state; McMenamin's Pubs (with numerous brewpubs in western Oregon); Widmer Brewery, whose *hefeweizen* is Oregon's most popular microbrew; Rogue Brewing Company, the Oregon coast's finest and winner of numerous national competitions; and the Deschutes Brewery, whose porters and dark beers are esteemed by connoisseurs.

One of the best opportunities to sample at least some of these fine brews is at the Oregon Brewers Festival, held in Portland in August. (See "Fairs and Festivals," in the Portland chapter, for details.)

Transportation

BY CAR

For the vast majority of visitors (and residents), the automobile is the vehicle of choice for exploring the state. Oregon is blessed with good roads and light traffic on many thoroughfares. Consider that 141,000 miles of roads and 2.3 million registered cars works out to about 16 cars per mile. But before you stomp on the accelerator, keep in mind that the Man is equipped with the latest in radar technology and sometimes lies in wait out in the middle of nowhere.

Legally, you can only open up to 65 mph on sections of I-5 and I-84. The rest of the roads in the state have a 55 mph maximum speed limit. However, most people here seem to cruise at 5–10 (or more) miles above the speed limit and usually appear successful in avoiding trouble with the law. In 2003, the Oregon Transportation Commission began considering a plan to raise the speed limit on some sections of rural interstates, up to 65 mph for trucks and 70 mph for cars, though any changes may take a year or more to implement.

Oregon roads are often depicted in TV automobile commercials—inviting places replete with mountains majesty or cliffside coastal grandeur. The Historic Columbia River Gorge Highway near Vista House and the Thomas Creek Bridge north of Brookings are two prime-time TV ad locations, but there's beauty all over the state. The magnificent scenery prompted the construction of the first paved public road in the state with the Columbia River Highway, constructed 1913–1915. Now known as the Historic Columbia River Gorge Highway, it is rated by AAA among the country's top 10 most scenic roads. The 362 miles of U.S. 101 between Brookings and Astoria, known as the Oregon Coast Scenic Highway, is another internationally renowned drive. Compounding the impression that Oregon is King of the Roads was the designation of the Cascade Lakes Scenic Highway outside of Bend as a scenic byway, chosen by the Scenic American Association for its "exceptional scenic, historic, and recreational value." Oregon currently leads the nation for the highest number of these thoroughfares.

While the roads are beautiful and largely unfettered by rush-hour bottlenecks (with the exception of Portland commuter traffic), the motorist must be sensitive to the weather and pavement conditions. Frequent cloudbursts can cause cars to hydroplane all over the road, thick palls of fog that hang over the Willamette Valley can cause multicar pileups, and the icy mountain roads of the Cascades and eastern Oregon also claim their share of victims.

Another consideration for drivers in Oregon is the fact that the road signs found throughout the state are sometimes less than explicit. Whether it's a turn sign appearing a half block after the fact or directional markers obscured from view by tree limbs, this state seems to have more than its share of unwanted surprises for motorists.

The Oregon Department of Transportation advises on **road conditions** by phone (503/588-2941 in Oregon, 800/977-ODOT out of state) and via the TripCheck website (www.tripcheck.com).

Winter Driving

The first rule to follow when rain, snow, or hail make pavement slick or fog reduces visibility is to slow down. It sounds obvious, but drivers, particularly those unaccustomed to driving in snow, seem to forget this simple safety precaution. From late fall to early spring, expect snow on the Cascade passes and I-5 through the Siskiyous; snow tires and/or chains are often required. More than an inch or so of snow on the ground is uncommon in Portland and the Willamette Valley. Keep in mind that in winter, the roads may be covered with sand and gravel in places because the state does not use salts or other chemicals to melt snow and ice. The ground-up pumice from nearby lava deposits comes in many colors and provides great traction, but it sure can scratch up the paint on your car if you tailgate. Also, give oncoming trucks a wide berth to avoid the sandblasting likely to follow in their wake.

Another thing to remember in the winter Cascades is your **Sno-Park permit.** Without the daily sticker or season pass in your left-hand window, a car left in a Sno-Park area can receive a $30 ticket. This permit is essentially a duty levied by the state to pay for the upkeep of parking and rest areas and for snowplowing in the mountains. Pick these up at a Department of Motor Vehicles office, ski shops, sporting goods stores, and other commercial establishments: $3/day, $7/three consecutive days, and $15/season. They apply to travel November 15–April 15.

Fuel

Gas is readily available on the main western routes, but finding it can be a little trickier on the more remote east side, especially after 5 P.M. Oregon's small-town gas stations are disappearing all over the state due to legislation mandating costly replacements of old gas tanks, which are prone to seepage. In other words, fill up before you leave the city. Another thing to remember is that Oregon is one of the few states that does not have self-service gasoline outlets, one reason that the state has some of the highest gas prices in the country. Another reason is the gas tax levied to help pay for Oregon's roads.

Rentals

Renting a car is no problem, assuming you have a credit card. The rental chains (Avis, Alamo, Budget, Dollar, National, and Thrifty) have outlets in Portland and many other population centers. You can also flip through the Yellow Pages and try to save some bucks with an independent operator. But while *you* may not care how the Rent-a-Dents and Ugly Duckling Rent-a-Cars look, they're not the vehicles of choice to impress your date. Another thing to consider is that the major chains have more service centers to assist you in the event of any mechanical problems. And while it costs a little more, it is always a good idea to make certain you're adequately insured.

BY AIR

It is a simple enough matter getting to and getting around Oregon by air. If there is a break in the weather, the views are breathtaking. The main point of entry is Portland International Airport (PDX), which is serviced by over a dozen airlines. Your travel agent can help you find the best current bargains, and a good weekly overview of the best airfares is printed in the Sunday travel section of the *Oregonian*. Because these "best fares" have multiple changes within the course of the week, they're probably best used in conjunction with an online-booking service, a travel agent, or airline websites.

Horizon Air (800/547-9308, www.horizon-air.com), the commuter-league farm club of Alaska Airlines, connects Portland and a half-dozen small airfields in the state (Bend/Redmond, Eugene/Springfield, Medford, Klamath Falls, North Bend/Coos Bay, and Pendelton) as well as numerous other cities around the western states. Horizon operates commuter prop planes with 10–40 seats. If you are sensitive to loud noises and pressure change, ask for earplugs when you check in for your boarding pass.

BY TRAIN

The Pacific Northwest Corridor, stretching 466 scenic miles between Eugene and Vancouver, B.C., was the fastest growing federally designated high-speed rail corridor in the country in 1999. Thanks to Spanish-made Talgo trains, capable of reaching speeds up to 79 mph, the Cascadia bioregion (Eugene to Vancouver, B.C.) enjoys an efficient and scenic mass-transit link. Three *Cascades* trains make daily round-trips between Portland and Seattle, supplemented by another train from Seattle to Vancouver, B.C. Two trains go from Portland south to Eugene daily. Also leading the charge is the *Coast Starlight,* which runs between L.A. and Seattle with stops in Oregon at Klamath Falls, Chemult, Oakridge, Eugene, Salem, and Portland.

Note that getting a sleeper on the extremely popular *Coast Starlight* requires reservations 5–11 months in advance any time of the year. Those who take this route northbound from California will see why when the train crosses into Oregon. After riding all night from the San Francisco Bay Area, passengers wake up to sunrise over alpine

ON THE ROAD

lakes and the snowcapped Cascades. As the tracks take you higher, you can see thousands of treetops in the foreground of dramatic peaks, especially if you're on the right-hand side of the car. From Cascade Summit, you head down into Eugene along the beautiful McKenzie River. Commentary over the loudspeaker and on the complimentary handbills enhances your sense of place. Farther along, Christmas tree farms, llama ranches, and other pastoral landscapes will also make you glad to forgo the interstate.

The trains on these routes are Superliners. These bilevel trains are replete with such people spaces as full-service dining cars and sightseers' lounges. The wraparound windows in these cars and a smooth ride are conducive to passenger interaction. Gourmet meals in the dining cars recall the good old days of rail travel. Budget travelers should pack their own, but the local bounty of each region on the menu rates at least one justifiable splurge. Microbrews and Oregon pinots can add to the fun.

Such amenities as reclining seats (with leg rests) and a sightseers' lounge with swivel seats by picture windows are added pleasures. Should you be fortunate enough to get a sleeper, they come equipped with air-conditioning, light panels, piped-in music, and vanities. Fresh flowers are an appreciated extra in these units and a parlor car spares folks the hassle of competing with coach passengers for scarce space in the lounge car. Travelers can enjoy books, games, snacks (showcasing regional products), and complimentary wine and cheese in the Pacific Parlor car.

The *Empire Builder,* which connects Portland with Chicago, shows off the Columbia River Gorge to good advantage in ultramodern Superliner coaches. With a trackbed on the Washington side of the Columbia, you get a distant perspective on the waterfalls and mountains across the river. In summer, this train stops in Glacier Park, Montana.

Amtrak also runs bus service in such corridors as Portland to Eugene and Chemult to Bend. The latter service makes accessible Bend's creature comforts and sightseeing to riders of the *Coast Starlight* who disembark in Chemult.

Trains are usually more expensive than buses

but cheaper than planes. However, as with buses, special airfares occasionally undercut Amtrak. Kids aged 2–11 travel half fare; children under two ride free. Other discounts are offered to groups, seniors, people with disabilities, and students. The company also advertises special holiday packages.

For information and reservations, call 800/872-7245, visit the website (www.amtrak.com), or obtain Amtrak's local station number through directory assistance. Individual destination chapters in this book include additional details.

BY BUS

Greyhound, and smaller companies created in the wake of deregulation and Greyhound cost-cutting, have regular connections to most population centers in Oregon. In terms of the consumer experience, all this means is that you might have a bus with a different paint job that uses Greyhound terminals and fare structures. Pierce Pacific Stages, Porter, Valley Retriever, Gray Line, and other smaller companies operate on former Greyhound routes and information about their schedules is available from Greyhound personnel.

If present trends continue, Greyhound itself will soon be operating mostly along I-5 in western Oregon. Because routes are continually being dropped and added, it's imperative to check with Greyhound (800/229-9424, www.greyhound.com) to confirm the most current schedules and routes. The lack of terminals in remote locations is another reason to plan your bus trip carefully. Don't contact local terminals for fare and schedule information.

As for comfort, a ride on an MCI (the bus most commonly used) is both good news and bad news. First, the good news: on the West Coast, buses are usually no more than 10 years old, which means you can enjoy footrests, reclining seats, and air-conditioning. Most folks will also appreciate the fact that smoking is not permitted on mass transit while in Oregon. And, should the bus on your route fill up, the company will put another bus into service. In fact, this

TOURS

While not for everybody, group travel is the fastest-growing aspect of a fast-growing industry. Those inclined to see Oregon by package tour can recline in the air-conditioned comfort of a Mercedes-like motorcoach as it rolls past the many-splendored landscapes of Oregon. A knowledgeable guide gives you the scoop on what you're seeing in addition to building your anticipation for cliffside coastal grandeur, a jetboat ride on the Rogue, or a play at Ashland's Shakespeare Festival. Sound idyllic? If so, touring Oregon by motorcoach could well be the mode of travel for you.

Many of these packages may seem expensive, but if you compare the price of meals, lodgings, and other services to what you'd pay independently, it's a good dollar value for the upscale traveler. In addition to volume discounts, the tour companies provide the services of a guide to spare you the hassles associated with the logistics and practicalities of travel.

Despite the togetherness that comes from sharing a positive experience with others, younger folks can sometimes feel alienated from the predominantly older clientele and/or constraints imposed by a schedule. On the other hand, there is no better way to survey Oregon in style with a limited amount of time.

The advantages of Oregon tour travel are made manifest by looking at the package put together by **Tauck Tours** (276 Post Rd. West, Westport, CT 06880, 800/468-2825). Their itinerary features a loop from Portland, taking in the best of the coast, the Willamette Valley, a jetboat trip on the Rogue River, a Shakespeare play in Ashland, Crater Lake, and a Cascades Mountain resort as well as the Columbia River Gorge. Along the way, four- and five-star hotels and restaurants give you the luxurious repose to savor your experiences. To book a tour or request additional information, contact the companies or see a travel agent.

Tour season in Oregon begins in late May and can run until the end of September. Before or after that, you're playing dice with the weather. In general, during tour season, prepare for warm and pleasant days all over the state, morning coastal fog, and cool mountain nights.

Touring options out of Portland and Bend are covered in the Portland and Cascades chapters, respectively. Foremost in terms of quality and variety are those of **Evergreen Gray Line of Portland** (800/422-7042) and **Wanderlust Tours** of Bend (800/962-2862). Such Gray Line day trips as the Columbia Gorge–Mount Hood Loop and the north coast supplement the company's city tours. Trips to the state's popular events such as the Pendleton Roundup and the Hood River Blossom Festival are also available. Finally, each August, Gray Line usually offers a four-day loop showcasing all the land forms of the state (except for the coast) with special emphasis on Crater Lake. Wanderlust Tours specializes in day trips taking in America's most varied array of volcanic phenomena outside Hawaii, Crater Lake, and other day trips near Bend. The company's ecotourism packages featuring everything from snow camping to old-growth forest ecology are especially recommended. These are geared to the average person's budget. Consult the appropriate destination chapter for more details.

extra departure often runs as an express instead of a local, assuming there's a preponderance of passengers with a common destination.

The bad news is not that bad. Too much air-conditioning in summer and too much heat in winter can be dealt with by dressing accordingly. The unappetizing fare in many of the terminals can be avoided by bringing your own food.

The ticket prices, while usually about twice the cost of driving, are still not out of line. Even though a special airline fare might occasionally undercut the bus on longer interstate routes, for the most part the 'Hound costs less than a flight. Consider too that half-fare discounts are available to kids aged 5–11 and to those with disabilities traveling with an attendant. Discovery Passes, valid for varying combinations of U.S. and Canadian travel, for assorted terms from 7 to 60 days, are another way to save money if you plan to cover a lot of miles. Also keep an eye out for various promotions that feature low-cost long-distance travel, particularly during the summer. The

Ameripass and promotional fares are honored by most of the Greyhound franchises, but all connections should be clarified upon purchase.

A few hints about seating will ensure a smooth trip. The first and last seats on the bus can be a boon or a bane to your traveling comfort, depending on your needs. If a footrest and the ability to recline your seat are important, avoid these locations. The front seats are generally the only seats that lack footrests, and the back ones don't recline. Worse yet, restrooms are in the rear of the coach, which inevitably results in an unpleasant odor on longer trips for those seated close by. Despite these shortcomings, the views out the front windshield are the best to be had, and the back row of three seats offers the most stretching room.

BY BICYCLE

Oregon is user-friendly to bicyclists. With special bike routes in cities such as Eugene, Medford, and Portland, Oregon has given the right of way to cyclists. In the wake of the oil shocks of the 1970s, the Oregon legislature allocated one percent of the state highways budget to develop bike lanes and encourage energy-saving bicyclists. In addition to establishing routes throughout the state with these funds, many special parks were developed with bicycle and foot access specifically in mind. For example, minutes away from Eugene's downtown is the Willamette River Greenway bike-path system, which winds through a string of parks. Oxygen-rich air from the vegetation and the peaceful gurgling of the Willamette make a pleasant change from the fumes and roar of traffic. A decent biker could easily beat a car across town during rush hour using the bicycle network.

A similar respect has been granted to the cyclist on the open road. According to the Oregon *Motor Vehicles Handbook,* a bicycle has the right of

way, which means that cars and trucks are not supposed to run you off the road. Nonetheless, remember that there are always motorists whose concepts of etiquette vis-à-vis bikers were formulated elsewhere. Play it safe out there: wear a helmet and reflective clothing, keep close to the right of the road, and always use a light at night. While most of the drivers will give you a wide berth and slow down if necessary in tight spots, rush hours, traffic patterns, and circumstance can change that.

BOB RACE

The Oregon Department of Transportation (503/986-3556, www.odot.state.or.us/techserv/bikewalk) produces some useful and free resources for cyclists, which can be ordered by phone or online. *The Oregon Bicycling Guide* includes statewide maps of bike trails and routing suggestions as well as listings for rental/repair shops and bike touring groups. Other publications include the *Oregon Coast Bike Route Map* and *Oregon Bicyclist Manual.*

Visas and Officialdom

ENTRY REQUIREMENTS

Entry requirements are subject to change. For current information, see the U.S. Department of State's Bureau of Consular Affairs website (www.travel.state.gov). With the exception of Canadian citizens, all visitors from abroad must be in possession of a valid passport in order to enter the United States. Canadians need only present proof of citizenship, though a passport is recommended. Also required in most cases is a round-trip or return ticket, or proof of sufficient funds during a visit and to afford a return ticket. Visitors from most countries must also have a valid visa for entry.

VISAS

In addition to a valid passport, nationals of most countries must have a visa (valid for 90 days) in order to enter the United States for business,

pleasure, or medical treatment. Exceptions are citizens of the 27 countries currently participating in the Visa Waiver Program, who do not need a visa. They are: Andorra, Australia, Austria, Belgium, Brunei, Denmark, Finland, France, Germany, Iceland, Ireland, Italy, Japan, Liechtenstein, Luxembourg, Monaco, the Netherlands, New Zealand, Norway, Portugal, San Marino, Singapore, Slovenia, Spain, Sweden, Switzerland, and the United Kingdom. In addition, Canadian citizens do not require a visa for entry for pleasure travel; proof of Canadian citizenship (such as a passport), however, is required.

Applicants for visitor visas should generally apply at the American embassy or consulate with jurisdiction over their place of permanent residence. Although visa applicants may apply at any U.S. consular office abroad, it may be more difficult to qualify for the visa outside the country of permanent residence.

ON THE ROAD

Special Interests

TRAVEL WITH CHILDREN

Oregon is a great place to travel with kids, with plenty of attractions and activities to keep them interested. One of the first things travelers by car will notice is the ample number of rest stops, with one every 30–60 miles or so on most major routes. In most towns and cities, public parks offer play structures and open spaces where kids can burn off some energy. In a pinch, many fast-food outlets, such as McDonald's, have indoor play areas (some quite elaborate), that give kids a chance to stretch their legs during a break from the highway. Many Oregon state parks offer excellent recreational opportunities for families such as guided hikes, nature programs, and campfire presentations.

Many B&Bs and other intimate lodgings discourage children. Where possible, we've indicated policies (for and against) in accommodations list-

ings, but it's always a good idea when making a reservation to inquire as to whether the lodging is appropriate for children.

TRAVELERS WITH DISABILITIES

Oregon is generally proactive with regard to providing accessible facilities for persons with disabilities, though there's always room for improvement. The great outdoors and some older buildings (lighthouses, for example), of course, can pose some insurmountable challenges, but many parks and recreation areas work to accommodate visitors with mobility issues. The following agencies can answer questions and provide information about access in Oregon's public lands: the National Forest Service (503/872-2750), the Bureau of Land Management (503/375-5646), U.S. Fish and Wildlife (503/231-6214), and the Oregon Department of Fish and Wildlife (503/229-5403). **Access-Able Travel Source** (P.O. Box 1796, Wheat Ridge, CO 80034, 303/232-2979, www.access-able.com) is another good resource for information on accessible outdoor activities as well as domestic and international travel.

The **Golden Access Passport,** which allows free entry to designated federal recreation areas such as national parks and monuments, BLM lands, and U.S. Fish and Wildlife sites, is available to those who are blind or permanently disabled. The pass is free to qualified applicants. Get details from the National Forest Foundation (877/465-2727, www.natlforests.org).

SENIORS

Elderhostel (877/426-8056, www.elderhostel.org) is a nonprofit organization that offers mature travelers a full spectrum of affordable recreational and cultural experiences all over the world. Dozens of opportunities are usually available in Oregon at any given time, and may include such experiences as natural history

courses on the coast, theater tours and performances at the Ashland Shakespeare Festival, train excursions, field trips to the desert, Columbia River cruises, and much more.

GAY AND LESBIAN TRAVELERS

In Portland, college towns such as Eugene and Corvallis, and most touristed areas, gay and lesbian visitors can expect to find progressive attitudes. In these places there are venues that specifically cater to same-sex couples. Outside of these places, one may find the attitude considerably less open and accepting; in more rural parts of the state, the attitude may be downright hostile. In Portland, a free monthly magazine, *Just Out* (www.justout.com), is a useful resource, providing entertainment and events listings in the area as well as addressing political and social issues. Another useful resource, with some destination and travel-planning information for Oregon (as well as the rest of the world), is Gay.com's travel pages (www.gay.com/travel).

Health and Safety

EMERGENCY SERVICES

Throughout Oregon, **dial 911** for medical, police, or fire emergencies. Isolated rural areas often have separate numbers for all three, and they're listed under "Information and Services" in each section of this book. Then, too, one may always dial 0 to get the operator. Most hospitals offer a 24-hour emergency room. Oregon's larger cities maintain switchboard referral services as well as hospital-sponsored free advice lines. Remember that medical costs are high here, as in the rest of the U.S.; emergency rooms are the most expensive for medical care. However, low-cost inoculation and testing for certain infectious diseases is available through the auspices of county health departments in major cities.

HEALTH HAZARDS

Hypothermia

In this part of the country, anyone who participates in outdoor recreation should be alerted to problems with hypothermia—when your body loses more heat than can be recovered and shock ensues. Eighty-five percent of hiking-related fatalities, for example, are due to hypothermia. In fact, the damp chill of the Northwest climate poses more of a hypothermia threat than do colder climes with low humidity. In other words, it doesn't have to be freezing in order for death from hypothermia to occur; wind and wetness often turn out to be greater risk factors. Remember that a wet human body loses heat 23 times faster than a dry one. Even runners who neglect to dress in layers in the cold fog of western Oregon often contract low-level symptoms during the accelerated cooling-off period following a workout.

Hypothermia sets in when the core temperature of the body drops to 95° F or below. One of the first signs is a diminished ability to think and act rationally. Speech can become slurred, and uncontrollable shivering usually takes place. Stumbling, memory lapses, and drowsiness also tend to characterize the afflicted. Unless the body temperature can be raised several degrees by a knowledgeable helper, cardiac arrhythmia and/or arrest may occur. Getting out of the wind and rain into a dry, warm environment is essential for survival. This might mean placing the victim into a prewarmed sleeping bag, which can be prepared by having a healthy hiker strip and climb into the bag with his or her endangered partner. Ideally, a groundcloth should be used to insulate the sleeping bag from cold surface temperatures. Internal heat can be generated by feeding the victim high-carbohydrate snacks and hot liquids. Placing wrapped heated objects against the victim's body is also a good way to restore body heat. Be careful not to raise body heat too quickly, which could also cause cardiac problems. If body temperature doesn't drop below 90° F, chances for complete recovery are good; with body temperatures between 80° F and 90° F, victims are more likely to suffer some sort of lasting damage. Most victims won't survive a body temperature below 80° F.

Measures you can take to prevent hypothermia include eating a nutritious diet, avoiding overexertion followed by exposure to wet and cold, and dressing warmly in layers of wool and polypropylene. Wool insulates even when wet, and because polypropylene tends to wick moisture away from your skin, it makes a good first layer. Gore-Tex and other waterproof breathable fabrics make for more comfortable rain gear than nylon because they don't become cumbersome and hot in a steady rain. Finally, wear a hat: more radiated heat leaves from the head than from any other part of the body.

Frostbite

Frostbite is not generally a major problem until the combined air and wind-chill temperature falls below 20° F. Outer appendages such as fingers and toes are the most susceptible, with the ears and nose running a close second. Frostbite occurs when blood is redirected out of the limbs to warm vital organs in cold weather, and the exposed parts of the face and peripherals cool very rapidly. Mild frostbite is characterized by extremely pale skin with random splotchiness; in more severe cases, the skin will take on a gray, ashen look and feel numb. At the first signs of suspected frostbite, you should gently warm the afflicted area. In more aggravated cases, immerse hands and feet in warm (108–113° F) water. Do not massage or you risk further skin damage. Warming frostbitten areas against the skin of another person is suitable for less serious frostbite. The warmth of a campfire cannot help once the skin is discolored. As with hypothermia, it's important to avoid exposing the hands and feet to wind and wetness by dressing properly.

Poison Oak

Neither the best intentions nor knowledge from a lifetime in the woods can spare the western Oregon hiker at least one brush with poison oak. In this writer's experience, 90 percent of the afflicted campers knew to look out for the three shiny leaves, but still woke up in the next few days looking like a pepperoni pizza.

Because the plant seems to thrive in hardwood forests, it's a good idea to wear long pants, shirts, and other covering on excursions to this ecosystem. Major infestations of the plant are seldom encountered in the Coast Range. In the fall, the leaves are tinged with red, giving the appearance of Christmas decorations. Unfortunately, this is one gift that keeps giving long after the holidays. Even when the plant is totally denuded in winter, the toxicity of its irritating sap still remains a threat. Whatever the season, fair-skinned people tend to be more prone to severe symptoms. Direct contact is not the only way to get the rash. Someone else's clothing or a pet can transmit the oils; you can even get it by inhaling smoke if the shrub is in a burning pile of brush.

When you know you've been exposed, try to

BOB RACE

poison oak

get your clothes off before the resin permeates your garments. Follow up as soon as possible with a cold bath treated with liberal amounts of baking soda or bleach or a shower with lots of abrasive soap (Fels Naptha or Boraxo). Conventional wisdom counsels against the use of hot water because it opens up the pores and can aggravate the condition. Nonetheless, some people say to apply hot water first to draw out the "itch," followed by cold water to seal up the pores. If this doesn't stop the symptoms, cooling the inflamed area with copious applications of aloe vera or calamine lotion, which draws out the contaminants, is another recourse. Clay is also considered effective in expelling the poison. Cortisone cream is effective at temporarily quelling the intense itching that accompanies a poison oak rash.

Some tree-planters and other forest workers build up their immunity by eating poison-oak honey and drinking milk from goats who graze on the weed. Health-food stores now sell a poison oak extract that, if taken over time prior to exposure, is said to mollify the symptoms. But scientists in Oregon might have come up with the best answer of all. Tec Laboratories

(P.O. Box 1958, Albany 97321, 541/926-4577, www.teclabsinc.com) has developed Tecnu, a cleanser that removes toxic plant oils from the skin, as well as various medications for dealing with the itch, all marketed under the Oak-N-Ivy brand, and available at drugstores throughout the state as well as online.

Giardia

Folk remedies just won't do it for that other hiker headache, "beaver fever." Medically known as giardiasis, this syndrome afflicts those who drink water contaminated by *Giardia lamblia* parasites. Even water from cold, clear streams can be infested by this microorganism, which is spread throughout the backcountry by beavers, muskrats, livestock, and other hikers. Boiling water for 20 minutes (or more at higher elevations) is the most common prevention to spare yourself from endless hours as king or queen of the throne during and after your trip.

Should that prove inconvenient, try better living through chemistry: apply five drops of chlorine, or preferably iodine, to every quart of water and let it sit for a half hour. Also available are water pumps that filter out giardia and other organisms, but they cost about $20 and up. First-Need is a filter/pump device that costs about $80 for a small unit. Potable water is also achieved by purification pills such as Potable Aqua, iodine-based tablets that cost about a nickel each. However, these chemical approaches are less reliable than boiling, and the treated water won't win any awards for flavor, either. Whatever method you choose, try to avoid major rivers or any creek that runs through a meadow as your source of water.

Mosquitoes

Mosquitoes can be a problem particularly in the Cascades, the Willamette Valley, and parts of the Columbia River Gorge. While repellents abound, only those that contain DEET generally have success. Unfortunately, this is a far-from-benign substance that can "peel paint, melt nylon, destroy plastic, wreck wood finishes, and destroy fishing line," according to *Foghorn Outdoors Oregon Camping* author Tom Stienstra (Avalon Travel

Publishing, 2002). Cutter's is a popular brand. While citronella-based products (a natural repellent) are not toxic, they only work for a few hours before reapplication is necessary.

When mosquitoes are present, it's a good idea to wear long pants and shirts to reduce the chance of getting bitten. Otherwise, you may want to stay indoors during prime mosquito time, around dusk.

Ticks

Of approximately 20 species of hard ticks found in Oregon, only four species are commonly found on humans. Of these, the western black-legged tick (also known as the Pacific tick and deer tick) is the only known carrier in the western United States of the bacterium that causes Lyme disease, a debilitating condition you do not want to catch.

First discovered in Lyme, Connecticut, in 1975, Lyme disease is now extant in western Oregon, Washington, and Northern California. The first sign of an infected bite is a circular rash called *erythema chronicum migrans*. It appears within 3–30 days at the site of the bite, and gradually enlarges to several inches in diameter, clearing up at the center while staying red around the edges. The rash may be accompanied by flu-like symptoms, and it spreads all over the body in one out of two cases.

The second stage of the illness affects only about 15 percent of those infected, but the consequences can be severe. Inflammation of the nerves and covering tissues of the spinal cord and brain can often result in headaches, as well as memory loss and concentration problems.

With the world's highest volume of grass seed produced between Salem and Eugene, allergy-susceptible visitors should expect some sneezing, wheezing, and itchy eyes during the June–July pollination season.

The heart can also be affected, resulting in decreased heart function and fainting spells. The last stage occurs weeks to years after the bite. It is characterized by aching joints, and the knees appear to be particularly vulnerable. It is suspected that the illness can also contribute to arthritis in the victim's future.

The good news is that the disease can usually be cured with a 10-day dosage of antibiotics, if caught early. Delay in treatment can lead to serious complications. If you see the telltale red rash days or weeks after your romp in grassy, brushy, or wooded areas, see a doctor.

A prescription for prevention would be to lay the insect repellent on thickly before venturing into potentially infested areas. Also, be sure to check your body and clothing frequently during and after possible exposure. Ticks often may be found attached in the underarms, the groin, behind the knees, and at the nape of the neck.

If you find an attached tick, removed it promptly to reduce the chance of it spreading the bacteria. The experts at Oregon State University recommend that you carefully grasp the tick with tweezers, as close to the skin as possible, and remove it intact by pulling it straight out, steadily and firmly. Don't twist, as this increases the chance of breaking off mouth parts and leaving them embedded in your skin. Some people suggest first coating the tick liberally with Vaseline, which deprives it of oxygen. After a while, the tick will begin to back out and may be easier to remove. Afterward, wash up with soap and water, and apply an antiseptic to the bite area. The same routine applies to pets as well.

Information and Services

TRAVEL INFORMATION

The Oregon Tourism Commission (775 Summer St. N.E., Salem 97310, 800/547-7842, www.traveloregon.com) is an outstanding resource for visitors and residents alike. The state-run organization maintains an exceptionally informative website and produces a number of useful free maps and publications, with extensive listings of lodgings and activities, suggested itineraries, events, and more.

Nine "welcome centers," located near the borders along major routes into the state, are a good first stop for newly arriving visitors. They stock literature and maps on the entire state, though their regional offerings tend to be best represented. These information offices are open Mon.–Sat. 8 a.m.–6 p.m., Sunday 9 a.m.–5 p.m., and daily until 5 p.m. in April and October. Most are open year-round, while the others close for the win-

ter. See the "Visitor Information Sources" special topic in this chapter for contact info for each.

Other useful contacts are the Oregon Parks and Recreation Department (1115 Commercial St. N.E., Salem 97301, 503/378-6305 or 800/551-6949, www.prd.state.or.us); the Bureau of Land Management (333 S.W. 1st Ave., Portland 97204, 503/808-6002, www.or.blm .gov); and the National Forest Service (333 S.W. 1st Ave., Portland, 503/808-2971, www.fs.fed .us/r6/). All offer free information and maps on the specific recreation areas and preserves under their respective auspices.

For members only, AAA Oregon/Idaho (600 S.W. Market St., Portland 97201, 503/222-6734 or 800/452-1643, www.aaaoregon.com) provides free tour guides and high quality, detailed maps of the state, counties, and major towns.

In addition, several regional tourism authorities offer similar information and services for

VISITOR INFORMATION SOURCES

Statewide
Oregon Tourism Commission
775 Summer Street N.E.
Salem, OR 97310
800/547-7842
www.traveloregon.com

Oregon Welcome Centers and Tourism Associations
Astoria Welcome Center
at Astoria-Warrenton Area Chamber of Commerce
111 West Marine Drive
P.O. Box 176
Astoria, OR 97103
503/325-6311

Brookings Welcome Center
(Open mid-April–October)
1650 Highway 101
P.O. Box 6098
Brookings, OR 97415
541/469-4117

Klamath Welcome Center
(Open mid-April–October)
11001 Highway 97 South
Klamath Falls, OR 97603
541/882-7330

Lakeview Welcome Center
at Lake County Chamber of Commerce
126 North E Street
Lakeview, OR 97630
541/947-6040

their corner of Oregon; see "Internet Resources" at the back of this book for a complete listing. Finally, the best sources for local information are the many chambers of commerce and visitor info centers operating in communities across the state. These are listed in the destination chapters.

MAPS

The visitor information offices noted above, and those in the accompanying special topic, are all good sources for free state, regional, and town maps. Some of the best road and city maps available are those produced by AAA, but again, they're offered only to members, which in itself makes membership an investment to consider.

Particularly useful for outdoor recreation is *Oregon Atlas and Gazetteer,* a large-format book of full-color topo maps of the entire state, published by DeLorme (800/569-8332, www.delorme.com). While the scale of the maps is not really suitable for hiking, the book nevertheless does briefly describe about three dozen hikes,

as well as bike routes, scenic drives, and paddling trips. Other useful features include tables and locations of parks and campgrounds, boat launches, and fishing and hunting sites. The book is available in bookstores, sporting goods shops, some grocery stores, and directly from DeLorme.

An Oregon-based mapmaker, **Raven Maps** (541/773-1436 or 800/237-0798, www.ravenmaps.com) is esteemed among the cartographic cognoscenti for its detailed state and regional maps. Based on U.S. Geological Survey maps, these computer-enhanced topographic projections depict vertical relief (by shading) and three-dimensionality. Many of Raven's offerings are large enough to cover a dining-room table, with costs starting around $30. All Raven maps are printed in fade-resistant inks on fine-quality paper and are also available in vinyl-laminated versions suitable for framing.

Trail Maps

Accurate trail and topo maps are worth their weight in gold for hikers, mountain bikers,

ON THE ROAD

North Central Oregon Tourism Promotion Committee
404 West 2nd Street
The Dalles, OR 97058
541/296-2231 or 800/255-3385

Ontario Welcome Center
(Open mid-April–October)
1202 South I-84 North
Ontario, OR 97914
541/889-8569

Regional Visitor Information Center at Oregon City
1726 Washington Street
Oregon City, OR 97045
503/657-9336 ext. 114 or 866/962-5225

Downtown Portland Welcome Center
at Pioneer Courthouse Square
701 S.W. Sixth Avenue, Suite 1
Portland, OR 97204
503/275-8355

Portland Welcome Center at Jubitz
10350 Vancouver Way (Exit 307)
Portland, OR 97217
503/345-0565

Umatilla Welcome Center
(Open mid-April–October)
100 Cline
P.O. Box 1560
Umatilla, OR 97882
541/922-2599

For more visitors information sources, see "Internet Resources" at the back of this book.

anglers, and other outdoorspersons. Oregon maps published by the U.S. Geological Survey can be purchased in bookstores and outdoor stores for about $3 each.

A few hints might help first-time users: First, the fine squiggly lines covering the map are called "contour lines." When you see them close together, expect steep slopes. Conversely, kinder, gentler terrain is indicated by larger spaces between contour lines. By molding a pipe cleaner in the pattern of a trail, then straightening it out and superimposing it on the mileage scale at the bottom of the map, you can find out the distance you'll be covering.

Another good series of maps is put out by Green Trails. Unlike USGS maps, these maps show trail mileage and campsites. Look for them at outdoor stores and ranger stations. In this vein, DeLorme Mapping puts out both an Oregon and Washington *Atlas & Gazeteer* that is unsurpassed in delineating trailheads. It can be purchased in bookstores, some grocery stores, and outdoor stores.

An excellent resource for trail and specialty maps and other outdoor information is **Nature of the Northwest** (800 N.E. Oregon St., Suite 177, Portland, 503/872-2750, www.naturenw.org).

MEDIA

The two largest-circulation dailies in the state come out of the most populous cities, Portland and Eugene. Both the *Oregonian* and the *Eugene Register Guard* have gained a bevy of Pulitzers and other awards. In general, the *Guard* has fewer columns generated by wire services and stringers than does the *Oregonian*. The result is a big-town paper with a charming small-town feel.

The *Oregonian* has several special sections of interest to the traveler. On Thursday, the "Outdoors" section offers a digest of activities for the active traveler—be it hiking trail suggestions, fishing, hunting, and skiing or boating tips. The Wednesday "Science" section might have a geology article explaining part of Oregon's landscape. On Friday, "Arts and Entertainment" outlines a full cultural calendar with news and reviews of movies, plays, concerts, literary readings, gallery openings, and restaurants. The focus is on the Portland metro area, but coverage extends statewide, to some degree. The Sunday edition has a decent "Travel" section that usually contains one or two interesting getaways in the state.

The *Oregonian* is distributed statewide, while the *Guard* is carried in newspaper dispensers as far away as the south coast of Oregon. The editorial content of each paper is mostly middle of the road but can be activist on environmental issues. While this last assessment would be challenged by residents of different parts of this politically diverse state, a more or less equal number of letters to the editor from the extreme right and the extreme left each day indicates a measure of balance.

Alternatives to the big dailies are found in a number of excellent tabloids, including Portland's *Willamette Week,* the *Eugene Weekly,* Astoria's monthly *Hipfish,* and others.

Portland and Eugene also dominate the broadcast media, serving far-flung rural communities by means of electronic translators. What is especially noteworthy throughout the state is tremendous support of listener-subscriber public TV and radio, under the auspices of OPB, Oregon Public Broadcasting (www.opb.org). OPB radio also offers a live stream via its website. Some standout programs of interest to visitors include the long-running "Oregon Field Guide," which explores natural history, outdoor recreation, travel, and environmental issues; and "Oregon Art Beat," which profiles local artists, craftspersons, and performers of all stripes.

Warm Springs Indian Reservation's KWSO 91.9 FM is a progressive country radio station spiced with elders chanting in the morning and topical discussions of native issues by younger tribe members. Other local stations of interest are listed in individual destination chapters.

Even though regional monthlies such as *Northwest Travel* and *Sunset* do not have a strictly Oregon focus, there are usually several destination pieces about the state in each edition of these magazines. *Oregon Coast* magazine confines its coverage to subjects closer to home. All these periodicals can be obtained at newsstands throughout the state. *Oregon Magazine,* a feisty monthly available online (www .oregonmag.com), offers a smorgasbord of articles on state politics, travel, and culture, in addition to viewing national and international issues through an Oregonian lens.

TELEPHONES

Oregon has two area codes. **503** is in use for the greater Portland metropolitan area including Mount Hood and the westerly portion of the Columbia River Gorge, as well as Astoria to Lincoln City on the coast, and Portland to Salem in the Willamette Valley. It's **541** for the rest of the state. Refer to the area code map at the beginning of phone books if you are not sure of the long-distance prefix. Note that in Oregon you must dial the area code, even for local calls. For long-distance calls within the state, dial 1 before the correct area code and then the seven-digit telephone number. For directory assistance dial 1, the appropriate area code for the locale you are searching, and then 555-1212.

Cell phone users should be aware that service in some parts of Oregon—including mountainous regions, the south coast, and the state's eastern areas—can be spotty to nonexistent. You may have to hunt around for that increasingly rare species, the phone booth, to make your call in those cases.

WEBSITES AND INTERNET ACCESS

With the meteoric growth of the Internet, most hotels, visitor attractions, government agencies, and even restaurants now have websites. We've included those websites that can help with planning or that enhance the travel experience.

While large sections of Oregon outside the larger cities and towns aren't the most thoroughly "wired" parts of the world, that's changing fast and you shouldn't have too much trouble getting logged on. Many large hotels and motels now offer rooms with Internet access (sometimes free, sometimes for a nominal fee), as do most libraries. Internet cafés, providing access by the hour, seem to come and go; see specific destination chapters for details.

ON THE ROAD

Portland

In shadows cast by 100-year-old trees and buildings, the new Northwest is taking shape in Portland, Oregon. Amid lush greenery rare in an urban environment, high-tech business ventures, a full cultural calendar, and an activist community are carving out a vibrant image. A latticework of bridges over the Willamette River adds a distinctive profile, while parks, malls, and other people spaces give Portland a heart and a soul. The overall effect is more European than American, where the urban core is equal parts marketplace, cultural forum, and working metropolis.

Such a happy medium is the result of progressive planning and a fortunate birthright. Patterns of growth in this one-time Native American encampment at the confluence of the Willamette and Columbia Rivers were initially shaped by the practical Midwestern values of Oregon Trail pioneers as well as by the sophistication of New England merchants. Rather than the boom-bust development that characterized Seattle and gold-rush San Francisco, Portland was designed to be user-friendly over the long haul. During the modern era, planners added such progressive refinements as extensive mass-transit systems and strict limits on building height and spacing. In this vein, Portland's decades of growth have thankfully preserved the city's aesthetically pleasing and historic architecture. Over time, the place once called "Stumptown" has become the poster child for cities that work.

Another blessing is Portland's auspicious location. Even though it sits 110 miles from the Pacific Ocean on the Columbia River, the city's

Eclectic shops line Hawthorne Boulevard.

port is one of the West Coast leaders in overall tonnage of foreign waterborne cargo and is recognized as the second leading grain export site in the world. Timber and a remarkable diversity of agricultural produce from eastern Oregon, the Columbia River Gorge, and the Willamette Valley also depart the port of Portland, bound for the Pacific Rim. In addition to this commerce on the Columbia, battleships, ocean liners, and other vessels go into dry dock here for repair and renovation.

Portland's waterways are its lifeblood in other ways. Mount Hood's Bull Run watershed supplies some of the purest drinking water anywhere in the United States. The printing, textile, papermaking, and high-tech industries also place a premium on Portland's clean-running aqueous arteries (the area boasts more than 1,100 such companies). Cheap and abundant power from the Willamette and Columbia Rivers' hydro projects has enticed other industries to locate here as well.

The traveler will appreciate Portland's proximity to rural retreats, outdoor recreation, and natural beauty. With scenic Columbia Gorge and year-round skiing on Mount Hood to the east, and Cannon Beach, the "Carmel of the Oregon Coast," to the west, relief from urban stress is little more than an hour away. Other nearby getaways include the wine country and the historic sites of Champoeg and Oregon City. Closer to home, Portland's Forest Park is the largest urban wilderness in the country, and after a visit to Washington Park, you'll know why Portland is nicknamed "Rose City."

The cultural offerings in this city of more than 500,000 are noteworthy for their scope and excellence. Whether it's the wine, cheese, and camaraderie on first-Thursday-of-the-month gallery walks or the smorgasbord of live theater and state-of-the-art concert halls, Portland's music mavens and culture vultures enjoy a full table. In like measure, bibliophiles revel in one of the world's largest bookstores, Powell's, as well as many other outlets for specialty titles and rare editions. The literary set enjoys a full calendar of lectures and readings by prominent visiting authors and local literati such as Ursula Le Guin and Jean Auel. For music lovers, top rock acts regularly hit Portland, while the local pub scene showcases many fine blues and jazz players. The Portland Symphony Orchestra has gained an international reputation through its compact-disc recordings and world tours. The flames of art and knowledge are kept burning at such fine institutions as the Portland Art Museum and the Oregon Museum of Science and Industry. Rounding out this array of cultural offerings are more movie screens, radio stations, bookstores, and dining spots than in any American city of comparable size.

However, all is not rosy in the city of roses. In recent years, Portland has suffered its share of such urban ills as gang violence, escalating real estate prices, and a growing homeless population. Locals will tell you that rush-hour traffic jams on the Banfield Expressway (I-84), the Sunset Highway (ORE 26), and the "Terwilliger Curves" portion of I-5 get worse each year. Despite these problems, Portland's quality of life is still frequently touted by surveys and media as being unsurpassed by few, if any, major American cities. In 2000, *Money* magazine selected Portland the best place to live in the United States. Come now and see Portland in its Golden Age.

HISTORY

Sauvie Island, northwest of the current city limits, was the site of a Native American village whose name inspired William Clark to christen the nearby river the Willamette in 1805. Two decades later, England's establishment of Fort Vancouver across the Columbia brought French trappers into the area, some of whom retired around what would eventually become Portland. The city was officially born when two New Englanders, Pettygrove from Portland, Maine, and Lovejoy from Boston, Massachusetts, flipped a coin at a dinner party to decide who would name the 640-acre claim they co-owned. The state-of-Mainer won and decided in the winter of 1844–1845 to name it after his birthplace. The original claim is located in the vicinity of Southwest Naito Parkway (also known as Front Avenue).

The trade that grew up along the Willamette River and the Tualatin Plank Road south of the

To Vancouver and Seattle

Columbia River

WA OR

14

205

Sand Island

Government Island

Lemon Island

N.E. MARINE DR

N.E. AIRPORT WAY

BYP 30

To Hood River

N.E. HALSEY ST.

N.E. 82ND AVE.

S.E. 82ND AVE.

213

213

COLWOOD NATIONAL GOLF CLUB

PORTLAND INTERNATIONAL AIRPORT

N.E. FREMONT ST.

N.E. SANDY BLVD.

Rose City Golf Course

N.E. 60TH AVE.

Mt. Tabor Park

S.E. DIVISION ST.

S.E. FOSTER RD.

26

SEE "EASTSIDE PORTLAND" MAP

N.E. 57TH AVE.

84

N.E. 42ND AVE.

S.E. 39TH AVE.

REED COLLEGE

N.E. 33RD AVE.

NORTHEAST

N.E. BROADWAY ST.

N.E. KILLINGSWORTH ST.

N.E. ALBERTA ST.

PORTLAND

Hawthorne

SOUTHEAST

N.E. BELMONT ST.

S.E. HAWTHORNE BLVD.

S.E. POWELL BLVD.

S.E. 28TH AVE.

BLVD.

ST.

N.E. COLUMBIA

LOMBARD

N.E. 15TH AVE.

Crystal Springs

N.

99E

PENINSULA PARK AND SUNKEN ROSE GARDENS

MARTIN LUTHER KING JR. BLVD.

LLOYD CENTER

GRAND AVE.

43

N. WILLIAMS AVE.

Ross Island

Tomahawk Island

PORTLAND YACHT CLUB

N. VANCOUVER AVE.

ROSS ISLAND BR.

To Vancouver and Seattle

East Delta Park

N. DENVER AVE.

N. INTERSTATE AVE.

5

30

WESTSIDE

FREMONT BR.

BROADWAY

STEEL BR.

BURNSIDE BR.

MORRISON BR.

HAWTHORNE BR.

5

West Delta Park

N. GREELEY AVE.

N PORTLAND RD.

N. COLUMBIA BLVD.

N. LOMBARD ST.

Willamette River

Swan Island Industrial Park (Port of Portland)

405

WASHINGTON PARK ZOO

SOUTHWEST

Smith Lake

BYP 30

UNIVERSITY OF PORTLAND

N. WILLAMETTE BLVD.

N.W. FRONT AVE.

N.W. YEON AVE.

NORTHWEST

Washington Park

SEE WESTSIDE PORTLAND MAPS

10

Pier Park

N.W. ST. HELENS RD.

Park

Macleay Park

BARNES RD.

8

To Astoria and Sauvie Island

30

Forest Park

SKYLINE

BLVD.

N.W. CORNELL RD.

To Cannon Beach

S.W.

26

To Beaverton

217

N.W.

S.W.

GREATER PORTLAND AREA

PORTLAND

Milwaukie

Sellwood

OAKS AMUSEMENT PARK

LEWIS AND CLARK COLLEGE

SELLWOOD BRIDGE

S.E. TACOMA ST.

S.E. JOHNSON CREEK BLVD.

S.E. 82ND AVE.

205

213

213

224

99E

S.E. MCLOUGHLIN BLVD.

Willamette River

PACIFIC HWY.

43

S.W. TERWILLIGER BLVD.

Tryon Creek State Park

S.W. BOONES FERRY RD.

COUNTRY CLUB RD.

A AVE.

Oswego

Lake Oswego

Lake Oswego

IRON MOUNTAIN BLVD.

LAKE VIEW BLVD.

GROVE ST.

KRUSE WAY

SOUTH SHORE BLVD.

MCVEY AVE.

S.W. ROSEMONT DR.

Mary S. Young State Park

West Linn

Wilderness Park

MELDRUM BAR PARK

CLACKAMETTE PARK

★ MCLOUGHLIN HOUSE NATIONAL HISTORIC SITE

Oregon City

Clackamas

Clackamas River

213

99E

To Molalla

To Canby

S.W. BRYANT RD.

S.W. CHILDS RD.

Tualatin River

205

S.W. STAFFORD RD.

5

Tigard

217

99W

To Newburg

Tualatin

S.W. BOONES FERRY RD.

5

To Salem and Eugene

1.5 mi

1.5 km

0

0

© AVALON TRAVEL PUBLISHING, INC.

PORTLAND'S ECONOMY

With the world's second-most-active grain export port, I-84 and three transcontinental railroads linking the city to the east, and I-5 providing connections north and south, Portland is perfectly located to take advantage of Pacific Rim trade as well as stateside business opportunities. As such, Portland is the second-most-active freight hauling and distribution center on the West Coast.

Portland's early stages of revival picked up steam in the 1970s, turning a city mostly known for rain, roses, and run-down buildings into a showplace of eye-catching art and architecture. In the 1990s, the town made a graceful shift from old-tech timber burg to high-tech metropolis; Portland's economic prosperity over the last several decades seemed to be limitless. In 2000, with more than 1,000 technology companies, from Intel—the largest private sector employer—to Hewlett-Packard, Epson, NEC, and scores of small software firms, onlookers predicted it would be the best-poised U.S. city to make the transition to the new millennium. But with the decline of high tech, Oregon's jobless rate soared to one of the highest in the nation. The slump hit Portland's social services and public schools particularly hard. In 2003, its wounded public schools became the subject of national ridicule in Doonesbury's running comic strip.

City planners are optimistic about the future, so much so that plans are under way for what the Oregonian calls the "boldest, riskiest venture the city has undertaken": a $1.9 billion plan to develop a 31-acre area south of the Ross Island Bridge. The South Waterfront District, as it has been named, aims for a new high in neighborhood design, complete with aerial tram and urban waterfront. It may be a decade in the making, but the city expects that the development will bring 5,000 jobs and provide 2,700 housing units for starters.

city allowed Willamette Valley lumber and produce an outlet to sea trade through Portland's Columbia River port. This was especially important in the mid-19th century, during the California gold rush, when San Francisco needed resources to feed its housing boom. Portland thus transitioned from a sleepy village called Stumptown to the major trade and population center in the state, incorporating in 1851. Another defining event was Portland's selection as the terminus of the Northern Pacific Railroad in 1883, linking the city to the eastern United States.

The single greatest boost to the emergence of Portland as Oregon's leading city, however, was the Lewis and Clark Exposition in 1905. Two to three million people attended this centennial celebration of the famed expedition, establishing the city as the gateway to the Orient for the American business community and paving the way for the dramatic growth that followed. By 1910, Portland had grown to a metropolis of a quarter million people, nearly tripling its population in just five years.

The years between 1905 and 1912 saw the substantial expansion of railroads, farming, and livestock raising east of the Cascades, due in part to Portland's growth as a commercial hub. The shift of America's timber industry from the Great Lakes states to the Northwest also occurred during this period. In response to this deluge of commodities, new wharves and factories were built at the northern end of the Willamette Valley. On the grounds of the original exposition site, northwestern Portland became a center of housing and commerce. City leaders have hopes that the 2003–2006 bicentennial celebration of the Lewis and Clark expedition will once again be an opportunity to showcase the town in a beneficial way. A reprise of the 1905 exposition is slated for 2005.

Development

Portland is a little city with a lot of personality. From the town's inception, civic leaders have made visionary decisions dedicated to maintaining livability and a rich quality of life. In the 1850s, during Portland's first blush of development, town fathers thought to set aside the Park Blocks, a mile-long stretch of greenery, sculpture, and towering trees in the heart of downtown. Throughout its history, the city's desire to be more than just a commercial center has been expressed by the creation of numerous parks and gardens.

In the modern era, measures designed to prevent the blight of its urban core by the automobile have resulted in the best mass transit system in America. Other progressive planning initiatives from the 1970s have become part of the fabric of life here. The elimination of a freeway to give way to Waterfront Park and the creation of Pioneer Square, a European-style piazza in the city center, are two such outgrowths. On the heels of these developments, the "1 percent for art" provision dedicating a portion of any new construction costs to public art became a prototype for similar programs in other cities. A more recent statement of Portland's priorities came with the central library's 1998 multimillion dollar restoration to turn-of-the century elegance. The integration of these decisions provides structure for a town whose character is rural yet urbane, artistic, and green.

Recently, Portland's growth-related stresses have been eased by other innovative decisions such as the extension of the light-rail transit system (MAX) into distant suburbs, citywide recycling, the creation of an inner city street car, and implementation of an urban growth boundary. The idea of the urban growth boundary is to stop leapfrog development across the open countryside by confining the new subdivisions and commercial enterprise to agreed-upon areas. In so doing, it also keeps Willamette Valley farmland from being exploited by real estate interests for quick profit. This embrace of innovation has enabled Portland to place second in the country in *Utne Reader*'s ranking of "enlightened" cities, first among large cities. In the late 1990s, the *New York Times* selected Portland as the only large population center with a chance of weathering the transition into the next century gracefully, thanks to visionary urban planning.

On the downside, limited acreage for expansion created by the urban growth boundary have led to escalating land prices. According to a Harvard University study, new homes here were 44 percent more expensive in 1998 than they were in 1991. And in a city whose inhabitants savor public green spaces and the immediacy of the great outdoors, increased urban density is not necessarily to everyone's liking.

However history will judge Portland's land use planning legacy, travelers will immediately recognize that this is a place to live as well as to sightsee. Visitors come here not for a glimpse of a Golden Gate Bridge or a Space Needle, but rather to enjoy a clean, compact city in the midst of spectacular natural surroundings with enough cultural attractions, dining spots, and shopping opportunities to merit an extended stay.

Sights by Neighborhood

If you're an early planner, before you arrive you might want to contact the Portland Oregon Visitors Assn. (26 S.W. Salmon St., Portland 97204-3299, 877/678-5263, www.travelportland.com) for free maps and their informative Portland Book. In addition to in-depth Portland coverage, coastal and Columbia Gorge highlights are briefly detailed in the latter.

Once you get here, there are a couple of things worth keeping in mind. First, most Portlanders sleep east of the Willamette River. The business district, shopping areas, museums, and theaters west of the Willamette can be reached easily from east-side residential areas by mass transit, car, and MAX line via one of 12 bridges.

Second, familiarizing yourself with directional reference points will help you smoothly navigate the city. The line of demarcation between north and south in addresses is Burnside Street; between east and west it's the Willamette River. These give reference points for the address prefixes southwest, southeast, north, northwest, and northeast. Avenues run north-south and streets run east-west. Almost every downtown address carries a southwest or northwest prefix. For more tips on orienting yourself, see "Getting There" and "Getting Around" later in this chapter.

PORTLAND

PORTLAND

N.E. 33RD AVE.

N.E. COLUMBIA BLVD.

N.E. LOMBARD ST.

N.E.

BYP 30

99E

N.E. KILLINGSWORTH ST.

N.E. ALBERTA ST.

N.E. PRESCOTT ST.

N.E. FREMONT ST.

N.E. 21ST AVE.

N.E. 15TH AVE.

NORTHEAST

N.E. BROADWAY

WEIDLER ST.

N.E.

84 30

I-205 N.E. SANDY BLVD.

E. BURNSIDE ST.

N. WILLIAMS ← AVE.

AVE. →

30

N. VANCOUVER AVE.

N. ALBINA AVE.

5

N. INTERSTATE AVE.

GREELEY AVE.

405

BROADWAY BRIDGE

BURNSIDE BRIDGE

NORTHWEST

N.W. LOVEJOY ST.

N.W. GLISAN ST.

N.W. EVERETT ST.

PGE PARK ★

LEWIS & CLARK

W. BURNSIDE RD.

NORTH

N. LOMBARD ST.

N.

Willamette River

Swan Island

N.W. NICOLAI ST.

N.W. VAUGHN ST.

29TH AVE.

N.W. FRONT AVE.

N.W. YEON AVE.

N.W. ST. HELENS RD.

PITTOCK MANSION ★

Macleay Park

N.W. CORNELL RD.

N. WILLAMETTE BLVD.

← To Sauvie Island

Forest Park

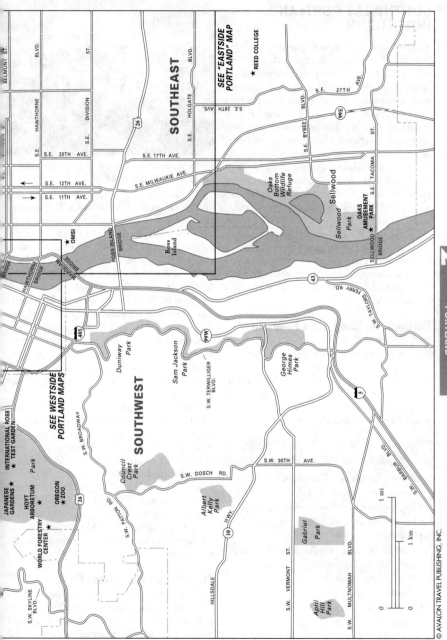

PORTLAND

© AVALON TRAVEL PUBLISHING, INC.

SOUTHWEST PORTLAND: DOWNTOWN

The best introduction to Portland is a walking tour that also takes advantage of the city's excellent mass transit. Despite the convenience of car travel, the flavor of this compact downtown is better appreciated on foot supplemented by bus or bike. Otherwise, Portland's mix of people, parks, and public art is too easy to miss. Moreover, the compact beauty of the city center invites strolling—the downtown area is only some 13 by 26 blocks, and the blocks are half the length (200 feet) of those in most other cities. What's more, downtown is basically flat, letting you log miles on foot relatively painlessly. So for the downtown area, ditch the car, put on your walking shoes, and get a mass transit schedule at the TriMet office at Pioneer Courthouse Square. Yet no matter how fast you move, it's not possible to do all of the different portions of this tour in one day, so slow down and savor each part.

Portland Building, Ira's Fountain, and Public Art

We'll begin our tour below a statue that is said to symbolize the city: Raymond Kaskey's *Portlandia,* which ranks right behind the Statue of Liberty as the world's largest hammered copper sculpture. Located outside Michael Graves's postmodern Portland Building, S.W. 5th Av-

Portland, as seen from the West Hills looking east toward Mount Hood

enue between S.W. Main and S.W. Madison, the golden-hued female figure holding a trident re-creates the Lady of Commerce on the city seal. Locals refer to it as "Queen Kong," and practical jokers from Portland State University sometimes dangle a giant yo-yo from her outstretched finger. Inside the Portland Building on the second floor is the **Metropolitan Center for Public Art** (1120 S.W. 5th Ave.), where you can pick up a brochure annotating a walking tour of the city's murals, fountains, sculptures, statues, and other public art pieces. This profusion of public art comes from the "1 percent for art" program, founded in the early 1980s.

More graphic evocations of the region are rendered by the simulated cascades at **Ira's Fountain,** also known as Forecourt Fountain. To get to the fountain, walk down S.W. 4th Avenue to Clay Street. Walk down the hill (east) to Portland's **Civic Auditorium** (also known as Keller Auditorium; see the theater listing in the "Entertainment" section) at S.W. 3rd and Clay for a full frontal view of the fountain. At the southern end of the Civic Auditorium is Main Street, where a left turn and a two-block stroll takes you to the waterfront.

Tom McCall Waterfront Park

Your introduction to mile-long Tom McCall Waterfront Park begins at **RiverPlace,** an attractive area of restaurants, specialty shops, and boating facilities. The boutiques, brewpubs, and an ornate piazza on the southern edge of this complex overlook the Willamette in the shadow of the Marquam Bridge. It's hard to imagine that 1894 floodwaters were high enough here to totally submerge many of RiverPlace's present-day storefronts. It's equally difficult to conjure hundreds of citizens volunteering to pile sandbags along this part of the waterfront in 1996 to prevent a reprise of the earlier disaster. In any case, you can follow the paved walkway north to a more benign encounter with water at the **Salmon Street Springs Fountain** a few minutes south of RiverPlace bordering Front Avenue/Naito Parkway. This is often the centerpiece of Portland's many festivals and provides a refreshing shower on a hot day. The fountain water's ebb and flow is meant to evoke the rhythms of the city.

If you have any questions about Portland at this point, stop off at Portland Oregon Visitors Association, **POVA** (503/275-9750 or 800/962-3700, www.travelportland.com or www.pova.org), www.pova.org), across Front Avenue (hereafter known as Naito Parkway) from the Salmon Street Springs Fountain. Free maps and sightseeing literature are available here and attendants are on hand to answer questions. A ticket outlet here sells discount theater seats where walk-ins can get half-price day-of-the-show deals. Ticketmaster, Fastixx, and Artistix tickets are also available here.

Tom McCall Waterfront Park is named for the governor credited with helping to reclaim Oregon's rivers. In the early 1970s the park's grassy shore replaced Harbor Drive, a freeway that impeded access to the scenic Willamette River. To go back to the time when the town's destiny was entwined with the Willamette and the Columbia, walk north along the waterfront until you are just south of the Burnside Bridge. Across Naito Parkway at the Ash Street stoplight is the oldest part of town.

The Skidmore Historical District

A block south of the corner of Ash Street and Naito Parkway, the **Oregon Maritime Museum** (113 S.W. Front Ave., 503/224-7724) has photos of the era when sternwheelers plied the rapids

of the Columbia River Gorge that are worth the $4 admission price alone. Also, don't miss the USS *Portland,* the last steam-operated tug on the West Coast. Moored in the harbor across from the museum, like its parent facility it's open Fri.–Sun. 11 A.M.–4 P.M. After the museum go back to Ash Street (look for the historic firehouse) and head west a block. Make a right on S.W. 1st and Ash, and walk along the cobblestones through the Skidmore Historic District. Along with the neighborhood's classic architecture, heritage markers help inspire historical reverie.

A little south of the Burnside Bridge, you'll read that the **Skidmore Fountain** (S.W. 1st Avenue and S.W. Ankeny Street) is named for a man who intended that it provide refreshment for "horses, men, and dogs." Local brewery owner Henry Weinhard offered to fill the fountain with beer for its grand opening, but the city leaders declined, fearing the horses would get drunk. Just south of the fountain, read the Ankeny Block placard on the wall for a good, concise description of Portland's architectural evolution. Despite the spouts and animal troughs, the 1888 bronze-and-granite fountain is still purely decorative. It does serve, however, as a portal to the largest continuously operating open-air handicrafts market in the United States.

Saturday Market (www.saturdaymarket.org) is an outdoor potlatch of homegrown edibles, arts, crafts, and excellent street performers. The market takes place every Saturday and Sunday from March through Christmas Eve in the shadow of the Burnside Bridge. On Saturday the hours are 10 A.M.–5 P.M.; on Sunday the market operates 11 A.M.–4:30 P.M.

The food booths here are a street-grunter's delight. The handicrafts range from exquisite woodwork (at reasonable prices) and feather jewelry to homemade fire-starter kits and juggling toys. What's astonishing is the high quality that's been maintained here for decades. Travelers on a budget should note that prices at food booths drop as closing time approaches.

Across S.W. 1st Avenue and cobblestoned **Ankeny Square** from the Skidmore Fountain is the **New Market Theater,** constructed in 1872 as a theater and a produce market.

A few blocks south of the market (double-back along 1st), the **Failing Building** (235 S.W. 1st Ave. and Oak St.) typifies the influences and use of cast iron so popular during the 1880s. Today it houses McCormick and Schmick's restaurant. Writer Gideon Bosker asserts you can trace the evolution of American architectural style on a stroll through Portland. This is easy to believe if, from the Failing Building, you walk three blocks east to S.W. Front Avenue and turn left to a prime location of elegant restorations. Prior to Portland's era of expressways and bridge building, this whole neighborhood was filled with cast-iron facades and Italianate architecture. Back on 1st Avenue catch the MAX light rail going south to Morrison Street, exiting several blocks west at 5th Avenue close to a more contemporary expression of Portland's mercantile instincts.

Bus and light-rail travel is free throughout much of downtown.

Pioneer Courthouse Square

If you follow Morrison across 5th Avenue you'll be on the north side of Pioneer Courthouse, 555 S.W. Yamhill, the oldest public building in the state, constructed between 1869 and 1873. This landmark is surrounded by statuary with small bronzed beavers, ducks, and sea lions congregating near a series of pools on the north side of the Pioneer Courthouse. On the south side of the courthouse on Yamhill Street, a bear with a fish in its mouth may be seen. The classic contours of this gray granite structure contrast with the blue-tiled, mauve-and-beige tuxedo-patterned facade you saw at the Portland Building. On the first floor of the Hall of Justice is a post office with historic photos on the wall. Period furniture and brass lamps line the hallways on the way to the Ninth Circuit Court of Appeals, located upstairs in room 204. If court is not in session, ask a security guard to let you in, 8:30 A.M.–5 P.M. weekdays, to see the Victorian courtroom. Also, from the cupola atop the courthouse peer out the same window

from which President Rutherford B. Hayes viewed the city in 1880.

One block west, outside the front door of the building, is **Pioneer Courthouse Square,** bordered by Yamhill, Morrison, 6th Avenue, and Broadway, the cultural vortex of the city. On the south side of the square is *Allow Me*, a life-sized statue of a businessman with an umbrella hailing a cab. Also within the amphitheaterlike confines of the square is **Powell's Travel Bookstore** (701 S.W. 6th Ave., at S.W. Yamhill, 503/228-1108). Down the hall are TriMet offices, where mass transit info can be procured and questions answered 9 A.M.–5 P.M. weekdays (or call 503/238-RIDE, www.TriMet.org).

Diagonally across the square is a 25-foot column known as the **weather machine.** Every day at noon the forecast is delivered by one of three creatures: a dragon in stormy weather, a blue heron if it's overcast, or a sun figure. As if that's not enough, the machine also emits a small cloud accompanied by a fanfare while colored lights display temperature and air quality. The redbrick square in summer hosts jazz, folk, and other types of music. On warm spring and summer nights the music and crowds return, augmented by symphony-goers departing the **Portland Center for the Performing Arts** just up Broadway. Casual Northwest attire mingles easily with business suits here.

Should you tire of people-watching, inspect the bricks on the square, each of which bears the name of one of the 50,000 donors who paid $15–30 for the privilege. From the northeast corner of the square gaze up at the white-brick and terra-cotta clock tower of the Jackson Tower on S.W. Yamhill and Broadway, and over at the copper sheathing of the Guild Theater building on 9th and Salmon to experience the glory that was Portland in the early part of this century.

Another part of the Pioneer Courthouse Square experience can be had in the middle of the amphitheater located on the northwest corner of the square. Here you might notice people talking to themselves. If you follow suit, you'll be treated to a perfect echo bouncing back at you.

The South Park Blocks Cultural District

Paralleling Broadway and the square to the east is the South Park Blocks Cultural District, created in 1852. This area is situated in a broad mall lined with trees and statues. Flanking this mall (just south of Salmon and Park) are theaters and museums. On this part of the mall note the four drinking fountains put in by early 20th-century lumber magnate Simon Benson to promote a teetotaling mindset among his workers. Close by is the Italianesque Shemanski Fountain with its *Rebecca at the Well* statue. A decade ago, the city increased the number of brighter period-style lampposts to make this neighborhood inviting after dark. Come to the South Park Blocks in the fall and you can sense Portland's New England heritage. One-hundred-year-old elm trees with their bright yellow leaves line a series of small parks down the middle of the South Park Blocks. These sentinels tower above cast-iron benches, bronze statues, and neatly trimmed lawn fronting the **Portland Art Museum,** the **Portland Center for the Performing Arts,** and the **Oregon Historical Society.** Be sure to check out the murals portraying Lewis and Clark, Sacajawea, fur traders, and Oregon Trail pioneers on the south and west walls of the Historical Center on Main Street. **Portland State University** is at the end of the South Park Blocks.

The **Oregon History Center** (1230 S.W. Park Ave., 503/222-1741) unfurls a pageant of Oregon's patrimony with interactive exhibits, artifacts, paintings, and historical documents relating to early explorers and pioneers as well as vintage photos of native tribes. The extensive collection of photographs, maps, documents, and artifacts from the center's second-floor library is catalogued onto an electronic database linked to the Internet and accessible via research terminals within the exhibit galleries and library. The center's hours are Tues.–Sat. 10 A.M.–5 P.M., Sunday noon–5 P.M., closed Monday. The museum's admission allows patrons to use the photo archives (the best collection of historic Oregon photos in existence) and library, $6 adults, $3 students, and $1.50 ages 6–18. Consult local media outlets to keep up on revolving exhibits here. The Historical Center is likely to be one of the few locales in the country to host a traveling exhibit of Lewis and Clark artifacts for the bicentennial exposition 2003–2006.

Across the street, the **Portland Art Museum** (1219 S.W. Park Ave., 503/226-2811), was designed by famed architect Pietro Belluschi. The Grand Ronde Center for Native Art on the second and third floors can broaden your perspective on Northwest Native Americans. The masks and baskets displayed here are not merely ornamental but are intimate parts of tribal ritual. The totem animals, rendered with loving detail, represent archetypes in native belief systems. Eons-old basalt carvings and 19th-century beaded bags and reed baskets by Columbia River Gorge natives are on the third floor while the second floor highlights Alaskan and western Canadian coastal art. It also displays plateau tribe and meso-American pieces. The Native American art exhibits make a nice lead-in to the pioneering generations of the Portland art scene displayed on the third floor. The fourth floor houses work from the last 40 years of Oregon art. Northwest themes are also breathtakingly displayed in Albert Bierstadt's historic painting of Mount Hood (European and American Collection) and in the century-old photos of Oregon on the basement level.

The Asian art wing is also noteworthy. Four galleries illuminate different eras of Chinese, Japanese, and Korean art. The museum's collection of European masterworks includes Picasso, Monet, Degas, Calder, Brancusi, Stella, and Renoir. Perhaps the museum's most touted acquisitions are Monet's *Water Lilies* and Brancusi's sculpture *The Muse.*

In recent years, blockbuster exhibits such as *The Imperial Tombs of China,* Wyeth's Helga pictures, a Monet retrospective, and *The Splendors of Ancient Egypt* have put this place on the map for art aficionados. Add a recent 60,000-square-foot addition to gallery space, and its clear that the West Coast's oldest art museum has come into its own. Hours are Tues.–Sun. 10 A.M.–5 P.M., open until 9 P.M. the first Thursday of each month. Admission is $7.50 adults with discounts for seniors and students.

Each Memorial Day weekend the median mall of the South Park Blocks in front of the museum hosts the only annual art festival in the country organized by Native Americans. With more than 250 Native American artists exhibiting and selling everything from ceramics to beadwork to basketry and weaving, this is a Northwest regional take on the famed Santa Fe Indian Market in New Mexico. Music, arts demonstrations, ceremonial dances, and a food court featuring frybread tacos, alder-smoked salmon, and other indigenous dishes also make this a worthwhile event. The outdoor marketplace runs Sat.–Sun. 10 A.M.–6 P.M.; there is a $2–5 suggested donation and some cultural events charge admission. For more info call 503/224-8650.

Close by the art museum is a bus stop on the corner of S.W. Jefferson and 10th where you can catch TriMet bus #63, which takes you up into the West Hills to Washington Park. Here, you'll find two world-famous botanical gardens and a highly regarded zoo.

Pioneer Place

Pioneer Place is an attractive upscale shopping atrium. Downstairs is a food court with dozens of quality concession stands purveying an array of cuisines. On the third (topmost) floor is **Todai,** an all-you-can-eat Japanese seafood buffet. Shoppers might also want to note the Pendleton shop (900 S.W. 5th Ave., 503/242-0037), near the corner of 4th and S.W. Salmon. If the famous retailer of quality wool blankets and clothing is too pricey, check out their outlet and factory across the Columbia River in Washougal, Washington.

WASHINGTON PARK

You can get to Washington Park via a TriMet bus or by MAX light rail. Once there you'll find that the hillside is home to the International Rose Test Garden, the Japanese Gardens, and the Oregon Zoo. In addition, you'll find the Portland Children's Museum, the Forest Discovery Center & Museum, the Hoyt Arboretum, the Vietnam Memorial, and nearby, the Pittock Mansion.

International Rose Test Garden

In summer a free shuttle runs from the terminal elevator in the zoo parking lot about a mile down the hill to the Rose Garden. By car from downtown, you can begin your tour of Washington Park by going west on Burnside about a mile past N.W. 23rd and hang a fishhook left at the light onto Tichener. Follow the hill up to Kingston and make a right. Follow Kingston a quarter mile into Washington Park and park at the tennis courts. Just below the tennis courts is the Rose Garden, and the Japanese Gardens sign and access road should be visible up the hill from where you parked. Another way to reach Washington Park is by taking U.S. 26 to the zoo exit. Drive past the zoo and Forest Discovery Center. Make a right and follow the road over the hill and through the woods down to the Rose Garden.

The Rose City's welcome mat is out at this four-acre garden overlooking downtown. With more than 400 species and 10,000 rose plants

International Rose Test Garden

BIRD'S-EYE VIEW

These eye-popping excursions to stunning vistas are best undertaken by car as mass transit is problematic in the West Hills behind the city and at Sauvie Island.

Pittock Mansion

This mansion is frequently featured as the first stop on many bus tour itineraries because of its history, architecture, and an all-encompassing view of the city. Situated at nearly the highest point in the West Hills, 1,000 feet above sea level, this French Renaissance mansion completed in 1914 also stands above the rest of the grand edifices in the city for other reasons. *Oregonian* founder Henry Pittock spared little expense in furnishing his 22-room shack with such accoutrements as modern showers with multiple shower heads, a central cleaning system, room-to-room telephones, and a Turkish smoking room. The "whorl-pattern" wooden floors in some of the public rooms here are a must-see as are the views of the city from the bedrooms upstairs. The antique furniture, access to Forest Park trails, and fair-weather views of the Cascades (Mounts Hood, St. Helens, and Rainier are potentially visible) from the lavishly landscaped back yard also make this place a fixture on many itineraries. It's also a movie location and TV backdrop favorite, including *Imaginary Crimes* (1994) starring Harvey Keitel, as well as *Good Morning America* and several evening magazine shows.

Regular tours are conducted daily except Sunday (1–5 P.M.; 503/823-3624); the grounds are open to the public until dark. The mansion is especially nice to visit when it's bedecked in Christmas finery. Be that as it may, the summer flowers surrounding the structure and the vistas in back of the mansion may well offer the most compelling reasons to come up here. Lunch and afternoon tea are available in the Gate Lodge, the former caretaker's cottage behind the mansion. In the north corner of the Pittock parking lot, a trail leads two miles down to Cornell Road through an old-growth forest.

Mass-transit access from downtown is provided by bus 77 to N.W. Barnes and Burnside Street, at which point you'll have to walk the steep half mile up Pittock Avenue. To get there by car, head west up Burnside past the turnoff to Washington Park. Turn right at the sign for Pittock Mansion onto Pittock Avenue and follow the signs. From here, it's a quarter-mile drive up steep and curving switchbacks.

Council Crest

Considered to be among Portland's preeminent vistas, Council Crest can be enjoyed from atop a butte in a ridgetop neighborhood in the posh West Hills. At 1,073 feet above sea level, this is the highest point within the city limits. Purportedly named during an 1898 National Council of Congregational Churches conference that met here, Council Crest later gained notoriety in its early decades as an amusement park at the end of a streetcar line. Today, Council Crest is home to such Portland luminaries as award-winning film director Gus Van Sant. The bluff looks out on snowcapped volcanoes and 3,000 square miles of territory. As you circle the summit, out to the west the panorama of the Tualatin Valley and Washington County is worth a gander, particularly at sunset. On the eastern side, steps lead up to an observation platform with arrows indicating locations of five Cascades peaks (check out the echo here). Even if they are not visible, the view of downtown and the rest of the city to the east is breathtaking.

To get to Council Crest from Burnside, turn left (south) on Vista (N.W. 23rd), turn left on Greenway, then take the right fork, Council Crest Way, into the park.

The Skyline from Council Crest

From atop Council Crest you'll note the two tallest buildings in the Portland skyline. In case you're wondering which of the two bank towers is the highest, consider the following, then decide upon your frame of reference. The Wells Fargo tower, the whitish building in the center of the city, has 40 stories. Sitting to the north is a big pink structure, the 42-story U.S. Bank tower. Number crunchers might take interest in the fact that the top of the Wells Fargo tower is still a tad higher (despite a shortfall of two stories) when the slope of downtown Portland is taken into account.

continued on next page

PORTLAND

BIRD'S-EYE VIEW (cont'd)

Sauvie Island

Ten miles northwest of Portland at the confluence of the Willamette and Columbia Rivers is the rural enclave of Sauvie Island, a scant 20 minutes from downtown. On clear days here, views of the snowcapped Cascades Range backdrop ocean-going freighters and cruise ships. Visitors enjoy horseback riding, swimming, and U-pick farms plying apples, berries, peaches, pears, nectarines, melons, green beans, corn, zucchini, tomatoes, and pumpkins. A favorite spot for bird-watching, the area sees eagles, great blue herons, geese, and sandhill cranes among the 250 species that pass through on the Pacific Flyway. Wildlife aficionados sight red foxes and black-tailed deer on the island's northern half. In addition, anglers come to Sauvie's lakes and sloughs for panfish and bass, and to the Columbia side for sturgeon, salmon, and steelhead. Bikers come for the 12-mile "hill-less" biking loop. Nearby is **Collins Beach,** a nudist hangout. For more information, call 503/621-3488.

Other seasonal highlights here include watching the Christmas ships (whose colored lights and yule-time decor resemble the most elaborate parade floats imaginable) and swimming at **Walton Beach** at the end of N.W. Reeder Road. Mid-January offers a rare chance to see bald eagles feeding here.

This is Oregon as it was, before Starbucks, gas stations, and souvenir shops. Described by the British Navy and Lewis and Clark as a major outpost of Chinookan culture (see the Columbia River Gorge chapter introduction), in the early 19th century Sauvie drew Euro-American settlers, who came to engage in the extensive trade along the Columbia River and to till the fertile soil.

History buffs and nature lovers can enjoy fall foliage at the **James Y. Bybee House** (Howell Park Rd., 503/222-1741). This 1858 farm, built by Oregon Trail pioneers, is furnished with pieces from that period. If you're not edified by reading Sauvie Island's history dating back to Lewis and Clark, the Bybee House also features a collection of old farming implements and an orchard with 115 species of apples brought by the pioneers. The house is open Sat.–Sun. noon–5 P.M. June–Labor Day.

In late September, the Bybee House is open for the **Wintering In Festival** (see "Fairs and Festivals," later in this chapter). Combining this event with a bike ride through the island's pumpkin patches, yellow-leafed cottonwoods, and river views is a wonderful way to herald the coming season. There is no admission charge to this event, although Sauvie's parking fee might destroy the island-out-of-time ambience. (Pay for parking at Sam's Cracker Barrel Grocery on Sauvie Island Road; turn left after coming off the bridge). Just remember to gas up and hit the ATM beforehand; neither are here. The island is open for day use 4 A.M.–10 P.M.

To reach Sauvie Island, take I-5 north to the Fremont Bridge, then cross the bridge and look for signs to U.S. 30 northwest to St. Helens, Linton, and Sauvie Island.

---

it's the largest rose test garden in the country. "Rose test" refers to the fact that the garden is one of 24 official testing sites for the All American Rose selections, a group of leading commercial rose growers and hybridizers in the United States. The blossoms are at their peak in June, commemorated by the Rose Festival, but even if you're down to the last rose of summer, there's always the view of the city back dropped by (if you're lucky) Mount Hood. The best vantage point for the latter is the east end of the garden along the Queen's Walk, where the names of the festival beauty-contest winners are enshrined (since 1907).

Japanese Gardens

From the Rose Garden head west up the steps that go past the parking lot and tennis courts on the way to the Japanese Gardens, (off Kingston Avenue in Washington Park, 503/223-9233, www.japanesegarden.com). You can walk up the short but steep road that leads to the Japanese Gardens, or hop the free open-air shuttle that climbs up the hill every 10 minutes or so. The Japanese Gardens so moved the Japanese ambassador in 1988 that he pronounced it the most beautiful and authentic landscape of its kind outside Japan. Ponds and bridges, sand and stone,

Japanese Gardens in Washington Park

April cherry blossoms, and a snowcapped Fujiyama-like peak in the distance help East meet West here. This is always an island of tranquility, but connoisseurs will tell you to come during the fall-foliage peak in October; many people in Japan feel gardens such as these are at their best when it's raining. The Japanese Gardens are open every day except Thanksgiving, Christmas, and New Year's Day. Daily guided tours are offered April 15–October 31 at 10:45 A.M. and 2:30 P.M. with the price of admission, $6.50 for adults. Discounts for students and seniors; kids under age 3 get in free.

Oregon Zoo

The Oregon Zoo (4001 S.W. Canyon Rd., 503/226-1561) predates the Rose Garden (1887 versus 1917), and it exerts almost as ubiquitous a presence within the city. The city is justly proud of the zoo's award-winning elephant-breeding program and the nation's largest chimpanzee exhibit. Also noteworthy is a colony of Humboldt penguins from Peru. Whenever possible, animals are kept in enclosures that re-create their natural habitats. An example is the African Grasslands exhibit, a savannalike expanse housing impalas, zebras, giraffes, and a black rhinoceros. Steller Cove showcases gargantuan sea lions, sea otters, tidepools, and other creatures evocative of the state's shoreline. The ersatz coastal caves and simulated blowhole here also hint at the quality of local color exhibits to come.

The zoo features several trains, one of which leaves the park. The Zooliner train (the terminal is on a bluff south of the Rose Garden, but the train can also be boarded in the zoo itself) runs from the Japanese Gardens four miles to the zoo. Passengers must pay for zoo admission before boarding the train, which runs at 40-minute intervals. Figure on 35 minutes for a round-trip. The ride itself is worth your time if only because the Zooliner is a 30-year-old steam engine. But that's not all. The forested ridge defining the route features 112 species of birds, 62 kinds of mammals, and hundreds of plants. During a brief stopover, you may see some peaks of the Cascade Range. The train does not run during the rainy season or when zoo attendance is low. Call the zoo for schedule, 503/226-1561.

There are several food service outlets at the zoo. The major restaurant is the Africafe, which offers a good selection of moderately priced cafeteria food. The chance to dine overlooking a glassed-in aviary is the big attraction, however.

Compounding the impression that it's all happenin' at the zoo are the concerts in the amphitheater (see "Live Music Festivals and Venues" later in this chapter).

The zoo is open 9:30 A.M.–5:30 P.M. April–Memorial Day, 9:30 A.M.–6 P.M. June–Labor Day, and 9:30 A.M.–4 p.m. the rest of the year. Admission is $8.50 for adults, with discounts for seniors and kids 3–11. Because many of the animals are nocturnal, it's usually best to get to the zoo early in the morning.

Children's Museum 2nd Generation (CM2)

Adjacent to the zoo is the Children's Museum (4015 S.W. Canyon Rd., 503/223-6500), which moved to this location in 2001. Activities here are designed for children 6 months old–10 years

PORTLAND

WESTSIDE PORTLAND SIGHTS

N.E. GRAND AVE.

MARTIN LUTHER KING JR. BLVD.

84

5

OREGON CONVENTION CENTER

5

ROSE GARDEN ARENA/ MEMORIAL COLISEUM

BURNSIDE BRIDGE

N. INTERSTATE AVE.

Willamette River

STEEL BRIDGE

MAX

Tom McCall Waterfront Park

N.W. FRONT AVE.

BROADWAY BRIDGE

1ST AVE.

2ND AVE.

SATURDAY MARKET

OLD TOWN

CLASSICAL CHINESE GARDEN

3RD AVE.

S.W. ANKENY ST.

SKIDMORE HISTORIC DISTRICT

OREGON MARITIME MUSEUM

4TH AVE.

CHINATOWN

S.W. PINE ST.

5TH AVE.

CHINATOWN GATES

S.W. OAK ST.

UNION STATION (AMTRAK)

GREYHOUND BUS STATION

6TH AVE.

N.W. GLISAN ST.

N.W. FLANDERS ST.

N.W. EVERETT ST.

N.W. DAVIS ST.

N.W. COUCH ST.

TRANSIT MALL

6TH AVE.

BROADWAY AVE.

N.W. NAITO PKWY

BROADWAY AVE.

POST OFFICE

7TH AVE.

W. BURNSIDE ST.

PARK AVE.

N.W. FRONT AVE.

NORTH PARK BLOCKS

PARK AVE.

N.W. LOVEJOY ST.

N.W. HOYT ST.

PARK AVE.

THE PEARL

8TH AVE.

9TH AVE.

BLITZ-WEINHARD BREWERY

S.W. STARK ST.

10TH AVE.

POWELL'S BOOKS

S.W. WASHINGTON ST.

11TH AVE.

McMENAMINS CRYSTAL BALLROOM

S.W. ALDER ST.

12TH AVE.

13TH AVE.

14TH AVE.

15TH AVE.

405

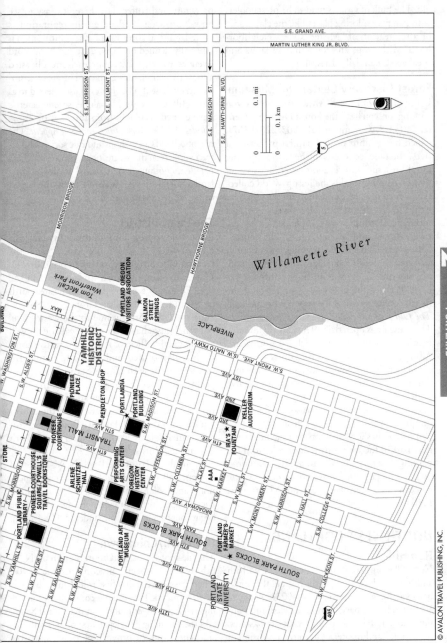

PORTLAND

© AVALON TRAVEL PUBLISHING, INC.

old. The bulk of visitors tend to be preschoolers with parents exploring places like the clay studio or a re-creation of "Mister Rogers Neighborhood" with props and look-alike sweaters and sneakers. Open daily, Tues.–Fri.

Forest Discovery Center and Museum

Up the hill from the MAX elevator in the zoo parking lot, you'll see the Forest Discovery Center (4033 S.W. Canyon Rd., 503/228-1367), which has exhibits on the natural processes of trees, the types of forests in the world, fighting forest fires, silviculture, and timber industry activities. Also featured is the Jessup Wood collection, which displays examples from the 505 trees native to North America. Dioramas, films, and mechanized exhibits are complemented by lectures, shows, and special events. The center's best-known (and after five minutes, most boring) attraction is the 70-foot talking tree. Worth more of your time is the second-floor rainforest exhibit. Perhaps the best way to understand the mixed conifer forests of the region is by taking in *The Old Growth Forest: Treasures in Transition.* The museum is open daily, 9 A.M.–6 P.M. in summer, 10 A.M.–5 P.M. in winter (closed Christmas). Admission is $3.50–4.50 for adults with discounts for children and seniors. Outside the museum are an old-growth stump of impressive girth and a steam engine that began hauling logs in the Coast Range in 1909. Also, don't miss the unique wooden items in the gift shop.

The zoo has a MAX stop that facilitates the next part of the tour. An elevator ride from the parking area can take you to a Civic Stadium–bound train (also known as PGE Stadium) where you can catch a bus that takes you to Northwest Portland's Nob Hill.

NORTHWEST PORTLAND

Nob Hill

Nob Hill is north of Burnside between N.W. 18th and N.W. 27th Avenues. In the heart of the neighborhood, N.W. 21st through N.W. 23rd Avenues, Victorian homes have been remodeled into boutiques to join stylish shopping arcades, bookstores, restaurants, and theaters. Given the profusion of

brewpubs and coffee spots here, it's easy to see how Northwest Portland got its reputation as "latte-land" and "beer-vana." The gentrification is especially defined on N.W. 21st and N.W. 23rd Avenues, where, at last count, each street boasted almost two dozen dining spots. The area encompassed by these thoroughfares is also referred to as Nob Hill. On N.W. 21st alone, several eateries have earned accolades from the likes of *Zagat Guides,* the *New York Times,* and *Bon Appetit.* The neighborhood's artsy shops and café society also attract strollers en masse, creating a people-watcher's paradise. Looming over industrial northwest Portland a mile northwest is **Forest Park,** the largest urban wilderness in the United States.

The Pearl District

If you proceed west down Burnside by vehicle or on foot across the I-405 overpass or catch the Central City Streetcar from the Portland State University campus, you'll find yourself in the Pearl District. It is encompassed in the area north of Burnside to Marshall and from N.W. 8th Avenue to N.W. 15th Avenue to the west. Here, old warehouses have become art galleries as well as studios and offices of Portland's creative community. Renovated buildings and new high-priced condos with Union Station views also proliferate. First-Thursday-of-the-month gallery walks feature hors d'oeuvres and 8 P.M. closing time at neighborhood galleries. On the southern fringe of the Pearl, **Powell's Books** (see "Entertainment" later in this chapter) is on 10th Avenue and Burnside.

From the heart of the Pearl, N.W. 10th and Everett, walk east to Broadway and go five blocks north and look for the tile roof of Union Station backdropped by the Broadway Bridge. From here begin your tour of what Portlanders call Old Town.

Old Town/Chinatown

The tile-roofed clock of **Union Station** on N.W. 6th Avenue has been a beacon since the 1890s, when passenger trains first rolled into the red-brick terminal. This is the second-oldest operating major passenger terminal in the United States, and the oldest big city depot west of St. Louis. Inside, check out the ornate high ceilings, marble floors, and vintage photographs. While Portland has always had a rep as a port city, much of the shipboard cargo arrived or departed behind a locomotive. By the late 19th century it was served by no fewer than three major rail lines. Theory has it that the city decided to build Union Station on top of the lakefront landfill donated by prominent sea captain John Couch rather than have several different depots controlled by the rail lines. Some historians also credit Couch with the selection of Portland's town site, which he favored over the area near present-day Linton, northwest of the city.

If you walk southeast from Union Station to S.W. 4th, you pass through **Chinatown/Old Town,** a compact area of restaurants, galleries, and Asian grocery stores. In 1890 Portland had the largest Chinatown on the West Coast. The Chinese came to work on the railroad and in eastern Oregon gold mines. Back then, opium and gambling dens and houses of negotiable affection proliferated in the neighborhood. Perhaps the most notorious corner of Old Town/Chinatown was S.W. 2nd and Couch, the location of Erickson's Saloon. Here sailors would partake at a bar that stretched 684 feet around. Occasionally, bartenders would conspire with work contractors to drug a seaman's drink. When unconscious, the sailor would then be transported to a waiting ship by means of underground tunnels that extended down to the waterfront, later waking to find himself "hired" and at sea. Rumor has it that a tunnel is being opened up for visitors. Check POVA (877/678-5263, www.travelportland.com, www.pova.org) for details. Shanghaied seamen were not the only ones down on their luck in Portland's rough-and-tumble waterfront. In fact, the term "skid row" is sometimes said to have originated here. This expression came from the "skid roads," paths on which logs were slid downhill to waterfront mills. After logging booms went bust, folks down on their luck would "hit the skids" in these parts of town.

Today, the area puts its best foot forward two blocks west at the Chinatown gates. The gargoyled gate at 4th Avenue and Burnside is always good for a photograph. Notice that the male statue is on the right with a ball under his foot, while the female has a cub under her paw. Also note the red lampposts. These are traditional Portland gaslight posts, but they have street names on them written in Chinese. Acupuncture houses, herbal shops, and traditional groceries keep the old ways alive next to the galleries of Portland's contemporary art scene.

In spring, the cherry blossoms on 5th and Davis become the highlight of Chinatown along with the contemplative repose found at the **Portland Classical Chinese Garden.** This intricate landscape is located on a block bounded by N.W. 2nd and 3rd Avenues and Everett and Flanders Streets. Three hundred tons of cloud-shaped rock and elaborate carvings were imported from China to help shape the hemisphere's largest and most authentic garden of this genre. Decorative pavilions, a teahouse, a large reflecting pool, and other motifs were inspired by gardens in the 2,500-year-old city of Suzhou, the Venice of China. Admission is $7 for adults, $6 for seniors, $5.50 for students, with children under 5 for free. The hours are 9 A.M.–6 P.M. in spring, summer, and fall. After Halloween, winter hours are 10 A.M.–5 P.M. For more info call 503/228-8131 or log on to www.portlandchinesegarden.org.

Overlapping this neighborhood are the museums, galleries, restaurants, shops, and signature architecture of **Old Town** (along with many homeless people). Many of the buildings here date from the 1880s, despite the fact that Portland's beginnings stretch back four decades earlier. This is because an 1872 fire razed much of what was then the commercial district. Cast-iron buildings with Italianate flourishes went up in the wake of the fire. While a large number of these foundry facades were torn down in the 1940s to make way for a Willamette River bridge and a waterfront freeway, a few survive in Old Town and the adjoining **Skidmore Historic District.** (In fact, there are more of these facades here than in any other place in the United States except New York City's Soho district.) While these neighborhoods are adorned with antique street signs, newly touched-up "old brick," and lots of iron and brass to evoke old Portland, such accoutrements aren't

PORTLAND

always necessary to induce historical reverie. There are enough turn-of-the-century white terra-cotta building facades and other period architecture for that. The danger of fires throughout the 19th century compelled the introduction of white terra-cotta in the early 20th century. Old Town runs predominantly north of W. Burnside between Front and 4th Avenues.

Powell's City of Books

Portlanders buy more books per capita than people in most other parts of the country. In bookstore sales per household Portland ranks ahead of New York City. Powell's Books (1005 W. Burnside, 503/228-4651) is not only a Portland institution, it is the largest independent bookstore in the world. Add such accolades as author Susan Sontag calling it "the best bookstore in the English-speaking world" and you can believe tales of famous writers finding books here that were impossible to find elsewhere. Over a million new and used books are housed in a labyrinth of hallways that take up a city block. A helpful staff and maps of the stacks help locate whatever you might be looking for in 50 sections ranging from automobiles to Zen. Hours are Mon.–Sat. 9 A.M.–11 P.M., Sunday 9 A.M.–9 P.M. The Coffee Room, on the west side of the store, sells gourmet coffee drinks, pastries, salads, soups, and snacks. It's a favorite place for singles to make connections. Free parking in the store garage and frequent readings by renowned authors enhance the store's appeal. Browse the website, www.powells.com, to get a sense of what the *Wall Street Journal* called "one of the most innovative and creative enterprises in the country."

Portland Public Library

Other landmarks for bibliophiles include an incredible library, a complete periodical store, and used bookstores specializing in rare editions. **Portland Public Library's central branch** (801 S.W. 10th, 503/223-7201) is an architecturally stunning renovation of a 1913 building designed by Alfred Doyle (architect of the Benson Hotel and U.S. Bank) that houses an accessible (60 percent open stacks) collection of books, CDs, videos, and periodicals.

There's even a Starbucks coffee shop on-site. This is the most used central branch of a public library per capita in the nation. Call for hours.

NORTHEAST PORTLAND
Lloyd Center

Go to any Gresham-bound MAX station in downtown Portland (pick-up points include Skidmore Fountain–Ankeny Square and N.W. 1st Avenue and Davis Street in Old Town). Purchase "one-two" zone tickets and head to Lloyd Center. The world's largest shopping center in 1960, today this mall boasts more than 100 retail outlets; a domed ice-skating rink, **Lloyd Ice Pavilion;** and one of the largest theaters in the city, **Lloyd Cinemas** (4510 N.E. Multnomah, 503/248-6938), with 10 screens and a futuristic neon interior. The vibrant restaurant scene of nearby Broadway also draws people to the area. Despite these attractions, the journey might be better than the destination. The MAX route goes over the Steel Bridge, from which there are great views of the city and river traffic (and on clear days, Mount Hood) as well as the Rose Garden Arena and the spires of the convention center.

The Grotto

The Grotto (N.E. 85th and N.E. Sandy Blvd., 503/254-7371) is a Catholic shrine whose hand-hewn cavern surrounded by lushly landscaped grounds can induce a profound sense of peace, no matter your religious orientation. Within the ivy-covered, fern-lined grotto is an impressive marble pietà. Outside the 30- by 50-foot enclosure, old-growth firs tower over the 110-foot cliff housing the shrine. Roses, camellias, rhododendrons, and azaleas, and a cliffside view of the Columbia River also make this worth the 20-minute pilgrimage from downtown Portland (take TriMet bus #12). The Grotto is open daily 9 A.M.–dusk, and while admission is free, there's a nominal charge to take the elevator to the upper level. This cliffside aerie offers views, floral displays, and walking paths. On clear days, the glass-enclosed meditation room with comfortable chairs facing the river offers perhaps the best long-distance view of Mount St. Helens to be had within the city limits.

SOUTHEAST PORTLAND

Hawthorne District

To get to Hawthorne Boulevard, hop a #14 TriMet bus from S.W. 5th Transit Mall. From Northeast Portland's Halsey Transit Center catch a #75 bus. This line follows S.E. 39th Avenue to the heart of the Hawthorne neighborhood, which stretches from S.E. 17th to S.E. 55th Avenues along Hawthorne Boulevard. Stores purveying records, fine coffees, secondhand clothing, antiques, crafts, and books join cafés and galleries recalling the hip gourmet ghettos of Berkeley, California, and Cambridge, Massachusetts. A dense concentration of these establishments can be found between 32nd and 46th Avenues.

Hawthorne Boulevard was named after a psychiatrist and long-time area resident who oversaw an asylum near Mount Tabor, the neighborhood's eastern terminus. This peak is the country's only extinct volcano within the city limits of a major population center. It has drive-up views of Mount Hood, downtown, and the Willamette Valley. There are also old-growth conifers and brilliant vistas of fall color dotting the Portland cityscape visible from Tabor's upper slopes. If you don't have a car, a #15 Mount Tabor bus (or #14 Hawthorne) will get you close enough to hike the trails to these panoramas. If you're picnicking on the slopes, try Hawthorne Boulevard's best bakery (also voted number one in Seattle), **Grand Central** (2230 S.E. Hawthorne), for baguettes, scones, pies, and cakes.

North of Hawthorne is N.E. Belmont, and south of Hawthorne is S.E. Clinton. Both are heirs-apparent to hip-strip status. Belmont features restaurants, brewpubs, a theater, and espresso bars. On the other side of Hawthorne, the block defined by S.E. 26th and Clinton offers purveyors of antiques and art-house videos.

Oregon Museum of Science and Industry (OMSI)

It's often been said that even though Portland's downtown is west of the Willamette, her future is on the eastern shore. The transfer of the Oregon Museum of Science and Industry's main

campus from Washington Park to the other side of the river paved the way for the Blazer arena project (see "Recreation" later in this chapter) and the exponential growth of restaurants and nightspots here. To get there from I-5, take the exit onto Water Avenue. From the Marquam Bridge, take Exit 300-B. From I-405 and the Hawthorne Bridge, look for brown signs next to the highway directional markers. TriMet's #6 bus picks people up downtown on S.W. Salmon and 5th Avenue and drops them off in front of OMSI. This bus can also be caught at the Oregon Convention Center MAX station.

OMSI (1945 S.E. Water Ave., 503/797-4000) is a hands-on interactive museum where you can pilot a ship from its bridge, gain insight on cardiology from a walk through a giant heart, or coordinate the Gemini space capsule's movements from Mission Control. The showcase of OMSI's new 18.5-acre campus, however, is the Omnimax theater (adults $8.50, $6.50 seniors and kids). Here you can be transported into such exotic locales as a volcano or deep space through the medium of 70-mm film projected onto a four-story-high domed screen. Incredibly vivid acoustics make it possibly the most intense audiovisual experience ever created. Astronomy and laser shows at the Murdock Sky Theater (additional admission) and six exhibit halls containing interactive displays make OMSI the perfect entree into the world of science and technology for all ages and levels of sophistication.

The museum is open daily 9:30 A.M.–7 P.M.; open Tues.–Sun. until 5:30 P.M. in winter.

Crystal Springs Rhododendron Garden

Southeast of downtown near the Reed College campus, distinguished for producing the highest number of Rhodes Scholars in the United States and ranked the finest academic institution in the country in a 1999 **U.S. News and World Report** survey, is the Crystal Springs Rhododendron Garden (S.E. 28th Ave. at Woodstock Blvd., 503/823-3640). Come in April and May to see 600 varieties of rhodies and azaleas on seven acres broken up by an island on a spring-fed lake. Even without the 2,500 species of flowers here, bird-watching

PORTLAND

EASTSIDE PORTLAND

N.E. 57TH AVE.

ZIEN HONG

TILLAMOOK ST.

HALSEY ST.

MAX

N.E. 51ST AVE.

N.E. STANTON ST.

HOLLYWOOD

BRAZEE ST.

N.E. 47TH AVE.

N.E. 41ST AVE.

N.E. 42ND AVE.

Wilshire Park

SHAVER ST.

N.E. 39TH AVE.

N.E. 36TH AVE.

LAURELHURST

GLISAN

SANDY BLVD.

Grant Park

N.E. 33RD AVE.

N.E. 32ND AVE.

VITA CAFE

BERNIE'S SOUTHERN BISTRO

MASON ST.

PRESCOTT ST.

N.E. 28TH AVE.

BROADWAY

N.E.

N.E.

N.E. WASCO ST.

84

30

N.E. 20T

GOLD BOUTIQUE

ALAMEDA

N.E. 17TH AVE.

FREMONT ST.

SISKIYOU ST.

N.E. 21ST AVE.

KNOTT ST.

WHITE HOUSE B&B

CHEZ JOSE

PORTLAND GUEST HOUSE

THOMPSON ST.

IRVINGTON

HANCOCK ST.

COLOSSO RESTAURANT AND TAPAS BAR

KILLINGSWORTH ST.

ALBERTA ST.

N.E. 15TH AVE.

N.E. 12TH AVE.

N.E. 10TH AVE.

Irving Park

TILLAMOOK ST.

MILO'S

PASTINI PASTARIA

LLOYD CENTER

MULTNOMAH ST.

MAX

WEIDLER ST.

N.E.

HOLLADAY ST.

N.E. 7TH AVE.

SAIGON KITCHEN

N.E. MARTIN LUTHER KING JR. BLVD.

N.E. GRAND AVE.

N.E. MALLORY AVE.

N.E. RODNEY AVE.

30

N. SKIDMORE ST.

N.E. SHAVER ST.

N. WILLIAMS AVE.

N. VANCOUVER AVE.

N. INTERSTATE AVE.

BROADWAY BRIDGE

STEEL BRIDGE

N.W. FRONT AVE.

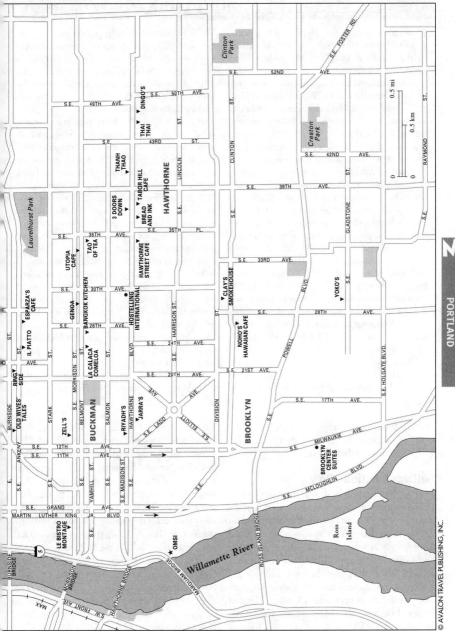

PORTLAND

© AVALON TRAVEL PUBLISHING, INC.

ESCAPE TO WASHINGTON COUNTY

For early settlers, getting the crops to market and to Columbia River ports via Portland necessitated a frontier thoroughfare, the Tualatin Plank Road. Today, a different sort of promised land has grown up around the Plank Road: Washington County. Given the million-dollar deals cut in high-tech boardrooms (Intel, headquartered in Hillsboro, is Oregon's largest employer with 9,000 employees) and the Nike headquarters here, the region between Portland and the Coast Range summit may be more aptly termed "Oregon's tomorrow country."

Equally prominent is Washington County's identity as a retreat from Portland's urban stress. Despite a population glut around Beaverton, most of the county is decidedly rural. You can enjoy a bacchanal 10 minutes from downtown Beaverton at places like **Ponzi Vineyards** (Vandermost Rd., Beaverton, 503/628-1227, www .ponzivineyards.com); hike Coast Range trails a half hour away (contact the **Tillamook State Forest Office** in Forest Grove, 503/357-2191, www.odf.state.or.us); or follow a primrose path through botanical displays and U-pick farms (contact the **Washington County Visitor's Association** in Beaverton, 503/644-5555 or 800/ 537-3149, www.wcva.org).

Other Washington County escapes include the 10-mile bike trail around human-made Hagg Lake, seven miles southwest of Forest Grove (503/359-

5732), and **Pumpkin Ridge golf course** (N. Plains Exit on U.S. 26, 15 miles west of Portland, 503/647-4747, www.pumpkinridge.com), one of *Golf Digest*'s top choices for the best public course in the country. After 18 holes, cool down with microbrews in the homey confines of a 142-year-old estate at McMenanims **Cornelius Pass Roadhouse** (4045 N.W. Cornelius Rd., 503/640-6174) or at one of the world-class wineries in the county. Two tasting rooms of note around Forest Grove are **Montinore** (3663 S.W. Dilley Rd., 503/359-5012, www.montinore .com), whose red and white wines have scored gold medals at the Oregon State Fair, and **Momokawa** (820 Elm St., Forest Grove, 503/357-7056 ext. 233, www.sakeone.com), the Northwest's only producer of premium sake. Brochures annotating vineyard and scenic loops are available at tasting rooms and from the visitor's association.

As anyone who has toured Washington County's award-winning wineries or enjoyed its rural splendor can tell you, the time to visit "tomorrow country" is today. To avoid rush-hour traffic on the Sunset Highway (U.S. 26), follow Burnside Street and Barnes Road out of downtown along a beautiful winding route through the West Hills across the county line. Paradoxically, this itinerary parallels the old Tualatin Plank Road, one of Oregon's preeminent pathways to economic opportunity in the old Oregon Territory 150 years ago.

---

and fall foliage encourage a visit. A $3 admission fee is charged every day except Tuesday and Wednesday, when it's free.

Sellwood Antique Row

Antique hunters will be drawn from downtown to Sellwood in the southeast of Portland. Once a separate city, it annexed itself to Portland in 1890. More than 30 antique stores are spread along 13 blocks with names like Den of Antiquity and Gilt. This shopper's paradise is clustered around S.E. 13th Avenue between Tacoma and Bybee Streets. As with the Hawthorne District, many of the stores open after 11. Most Sellwood stores close Sun. and Mon. From downtown Portland, the #40 bus drops you at 13th and

Tacoma. Another choice is #70 from the Rose Quarter, which stops every two blocks on 13th.

After antiquing, head over to **Sellwood Park** (S.E. 7th Ave. and Sellwood Blvd.). The western extremity of this park sits on a tree-lined bluff above the Willamette. Tennis courts, picnic tables, and access to Oak Bottoms Wildlife Refuge make this park a delight in spring and summer. Below the bluff is **Oak Park,** where a vintage carousel, pool, and roller rink on the Willamette's eastern shore add to the recreational menu. To drive to Oak Park from downtown, take McLoughlin Boulevard south to the Tacoma Street Exit. Take a left (heading west) to 7th Street, turn right on 7th, and then take the first left onto Spokane. Follow the signs to Oak Park.

Sports and Recreation

SPECTATOR SPORTS

Portland is a town more for athletes than devotees of spectator sports. Nonetheless, the two stadiums in the Rose City draw huge crowds.

In a city where NBA basketball borders on obsession (thanks to the Blazers' NBA record for consecutive playoff appearances and the fact that it's the only pro sports team for almost 200 miles), the **Rose Garden Arena** (503/235-8771, www.rosequarter.com) located at the east end of the Broadway Bridge, and its accompanying shops-and-restaurant complex, can be expected to increase the traffic considerably on the Willamette's eastern shore. (If you MAX out to the complex, exit the train at the Rose Quarter transit center.)

The Rose Garden's high seating capacity (20,339) and enhanced views have given Portland an exciting arena for basketball and concerts. The proximity of the Memorial Coliseum and the Oregon Convention Center enables the city to attract world-class athletic events, industrial shows, and conventions.

The Rose Garden's elliptical contours with seating aligned in a gentle grade offers better sightlines than those found in most other arenas in the world. In addition, the large size of the venue relative to the number of seats provides more generous leg room than the knees-in-your-mouth seating arrangement found in your typical sports stadium. State-of-the-art acoustics put the finishing touches on your enjoyment. The arena was nominated as the best new arena concert venue of 1996 by an industry group. Computerized acoustic panels have made this stadium a wonderful place to hear everyone from Garth Brooks to Eric Clapton.

While most **Trail Blazer** seats are reserved for season ticket-holders, some are available at Ticketmaster outlets or through the arena box office. Then, of course, there are always the overpriced offerings of ticket brokers advertised in the *Oregonian* or scalpers who may be found beyond a four-block radius of the Rose Garden. It's best to call the Blazer ticket line (503/231-8000 or 503/797-9600), or write their corporate offices (700 N.E. Multnomah, Ste. 600, Portland 97232) well in advance. You can also log on to www.nba.com/blazers/ to check ticket prices or buy tickets.

The Blazers' former home, the **Memorial Coliseum** (1401 N. Wheeler, 503/235-8771) now hosts the **Winter Hawks,** a hockey team of the Western Hockey League.

HIKING

Portland is famous for more park acreage per capita than any other major American city, with one-twelfth the city's area devoted to public recreational venues. Within these holdings, the city has more urban wilderness than any other municipality in the country. As whole books have been written about these retreats, we will confine ourselves to just a few hikes and refer the reader to the **Portland Audubon Society Bookstore** (5151 N.W. Cornell Rd., 503/292-6855, www.audubonportland.org, just off the MacLeay Park to Pittock Mansion Trail). The bookstore sells maps of more than 200 urban wildlife habitat sites in Portland. Also check out *A Pedestrian's Portland* by Karen and Terry Whitehill (Mountaineers Books, $10.95); the book outlines 40 walks in greater Portland, which the authors divide into six areas.

Without doubt, the part of Portland most conducive to a walk on the wild side is up in the hills behind the Northwest neighborhood. The largest urban wilderness in the country, **Forest Park** is accessible off I-5 (heading north) by taking the Fremont Bridge into Northwest Portland and making a left onto Nicolai Street or Vaughn Street. Turn left onto 27th Avenue and follow it to Thurman Street. Make a right on Thurman and follow it to its end to reach the portal of Forest Park. The paved walkway at the edge of the wilderness has numerous side trails to forested hillsides. Despite scenic beauty, the smells and sounds of Portland's industrial northern extremity can occasionally pierce the tranquility here. Thus, weekends and holidays are recommended for excursions into this preserve. Nonetheless, what other city has a park in which bear, elk, deer, and cougar have been sighted? What other city park has old-growth trees and wild scenic areas? The park is 8.5 miles long, 1.5 miles wide.

A scenic adjunct is **MacLeay Park,** which can be reached via the Forest Park route and a turnoff onto Upshur Road (instead of Thurman), following it to its end. The Audubon Society Headquarters and bookstore is located on Cornell Road a half mile from the trailhead. The gentle uphill trail here follows a deep gully paralleling a creek. (See "Pittock Mansion," under "Washington Park," earlier in this chapter).

Another way to reach MacLeay and Forest Parks is via the 14-mile **Wildwood Trail,** which heads north through the Hoyt Arboretum and Pittock Acres before plunging downhill into the parklands below. The trail begins on Canyon Road near the zoo, OMSI, and Forestry Center. Or you can drive to the **Arboretum Visitor Center** (4000 S.W. Fairview Blvd., 503/288-TREE, www.hoytarboretum.org, open daily 10 A.M.–4 P.M.) or the Pittock Mansion to begin your descent into MacLeay and Forest Parks. The park itself is open daily 6 A.M.–10 P.M.

The gem of Wildwood Trail, the **Hoyt Arboretum** covers 214 acres and seven miles of trails, including a one-mile tour through one of the country's largest collections of conifers. On Saturdays and Sundays Oct.–April at 2 P.M., guided tours highlight foliage season. Prize species include the endangered Brewer's weeping spruce and the dawn redwood. This tree had been considered extinct for five million years until a remote stand was found in China. Hoyt's dawn redwood bore the first cones produced in this hemisphere in 50 million years.

Wildwood Trail is part of a proposed larger network of trails to loop the city. This was originally the brainchild of the Olmsted brothers (of Yosemite Valley and Central Park fame) at the turn of the century. Their proposed 40-mile loop concept has expanded to a 140-mile matrix. Now the goal is to complete a hiking/biking path connecting parks along the Columbia,

Sandy, and Willamette Rivers. To find out more, contact the **Portland Parks and Recreation Department** (503/823-2223, www.portlandparks.org) or pick up a map of the loop at Powell's Travel Bookstore at Pioneer Courthouse Square, 503/228-1108.

On the other end of town, another potential component of the loop beckons urban walkers in search of rural pleasures. Snaking along the east bank of the Willamette River between the Sellwood and Ross Island Bridges, the **Oak Bottoms Wildlife Refuge** is a bird-watcher's paradise. Great blue and green herons find this wetland a prime habitat. In winter, a dozen species of waterfowl can be sighted. Summertime residents include warblers, orioles, swallows, and woodpeckers. Whenever you go, look for wood ducks joining such permanent denizens as beavers and muskrats.

A ridge along Sellwood Boulevard frames Oak Bottoms and offers good views. You can hike into it at the north end of Sellwood Park at S.W. 7th Avenue and Sellwood Boulevard. The parking lot at the 5000 block of S.E. Milwaukie Avenue also offers access. After you descend, a loop trail encircles the wetlands, paralleling the bluff on the east side and following the railroad tracks to the west.

CAMPING

Given the relative proximity of wilderness areas where sleeping under the stars is the norm, Portland hasn't felt the need to be especially camper-friendly. Nonetheless, some nearby retreats rate a mention. In addition to the campgrounds listed below, Champoeg Park, located 25 miles south, also has campsites worthy of consideration (see "A Tour Through History" in the Wilamette Valley chapter).

The **Jantzen Beach RV Park** (1503 N. Hayden Island Dr., Portland 97217, 503/289-7626 or 800/443-7248, www.jantzenbeachrv.com) lets you experience the tranquility of the Columbia shore within walking distance of "civilization." There are 169 sites for RVs of any length. Every imaginable camping amenity exists here, and whatever else you need is minutes away thanks to Jantzen Beach Mall that you'll pass en route. To get there, head north out of downtown about four miles on I-5 and take Exit 308 (if you miss it, you'll cross the Columbia River Bridge into Washington). The off-ramp takes you to Hayden Island Drive. Follow it left and west back toward the freeway underneath a tunnel a half mile to the park. Open year-round, sites go for $26 per night.

For those who enjoy rural serenity within commuting distance of downtown, there's camping in **Milo McIver State Park** (24101 South Entrance Rd., Estacada 97023, 503/630-7150 or 800/551-6949, www.oregonstateparks.org/park_142.php). This retreat, set on the banks of the Collowash River (five miles northwest of Estacada), is 25 miles from downtown Portland, but it seems farther away, particularly when you're gazing at the knockout sunset view of Mount Hood here. To get there, take I-84 east to I-205 south and follow the exit to ORE 224/Estacada. The road forks right at the town of Carver to go 10 miles (look for Springwater Road) to the campground. There are 44 hookup sites, flush toilets, showers, firewood, and a laundry here, as well as fishing for winter steelhead and late-fall salmon. Other recreation includes hiking, horse trails, and a boat ramp. Mount Hood ski slopes are an hour east of the park. Bagby Hot Springs and the trail to it through an old-growth forest are other attractions within an hour's drive off ORE 224. Campground fees are $13 per night with no reservations, and it's open March 15–November 1.

Another camping option about 35 miles east of Portland off I-84 is **Ainsworth State Park** (503/695-2301 or 800/551-6949, www.oregonstateparks.org/park_146.php). Picnic tables, fire rings, flush toilets, and an RV camp enhance a prime location near the trails and waterfalls of the Columbia River Gorge. Nightly rates are $10–16 on a first-come, first-served basis. You can get there via the Columbia River Highway (see the introduction to the Columbia River Gorge chapter) or by taking Exit 35 off I-84 West. Bring earplugs here if you're a light sleeper. Noise from trains, planes, and a freeway might make you forget you're surrounded by the Gorge's spectacular waterfalls and cliffs.

AUDUBON OLD-GROWTH SANCTUARIES

The aforementioned Audubon Bookstore is a good place to get directions to the city's oldest treasures. While the groves of centuries-old trees aren't large, the fact that these 500-year-old gigantic vegetables are minutes away from the downtown core is compelling. The impression of a time machine voyage is reinforced when you consider that of the 19 million acres of old growth that once covered the Northwest, only 10 percent remains. The Audubon Society sponsors Old Growth Walks, generally in mid-November. Recent flood damage threatens the survival of this resource, so take advantage now of the opportunity to see giant Douglas fir and Western red cedar that were alive when Columbus sailed across the ocean.

TENNIS, GOLF, AND WATER RECREATION

Tennis courts, golf courses, public pools, and lakes offering swimming and sailing abound in the Portland area.

Portland Parks and Recreation (503/823-3189, www.portlandparks.org) oversees the city's 115 tennis courts. The best public courts in terms of surface and surrounding environment are located up the hill from the Rose Garden in Washington Park. Use of them is free of charge. To get there from downtown, take Burnside west up the hill. About a mile past N.W. 23rd, hang a sharp left (feels almost like a U-turn) at the light onto Tichner. Take the next right onto Kingston, and proceed for a minute or so to the parking lot adjacent to the tennis courts.

For golfers, Portland has more publicly owned golf courses per capita than any U.S. city. Twenty 18-hole courses are within 20 miles of the city, but only half are public. Two of the three best are Heron Lakes and Eastmoreland. **Heron Lakes** (3500 N. Victory Blvd., 503/289-1818, www.heronlakesgolf.com), designed by Robert Trent Jones, is 15 minutes from downtown. To get there, take Exit 307B off I-5, head south of the expo center, and look for signs. The route here

PORTLAND

BAGBY HOT SPRINGS: A PORTLAND TRADITION

Portlanders have long cherished outings to such nearby retreats as the coast, Mount Hood, and the Columbia River Gorge. There are less well-known but equally esteemed retreats that locals here like to keep to themselves, due to fear of overcrowding. Bagby Hot Springs is one of them, set in a grove of old-growth cedar in Mount Hood National Forest, a 1.5-hour drive from Portland.

Each summer thousands make the pilgrimage to the healing waters here. If you visit in high season, July and August, expect a scene conjuring a latter-day Woodstock Nation on the Ganges. But come weekdays in the cooler months and you're guaranteed a memorable experience dipping into the carved cedar tubs. Nighttime soaking in the 138-degree water on full-moon nights is a special treat year-round (bring a flashlight). At all times be aware that theft is a problem, so lock up your valuables. Your only other concern is snow, as Bagby is high enough in the Cascades to occasionally be inaccessible due to road conditions. The 1.5-mile trail from the parking lot to the pools through an ancient forest is an easy jaunt, and should the clothing-optional policy be inhibiting, there are partitions and smaller pools for a modicum of privacy. Assuming you come at a quiet time, Bagby Hot Springs is proof that the best things in life and in Oregon are free.

To get there, take I-205 from Portland to Exit 224, which will take you through Estacada along the Clackamas River. There are some nice campsites along this waterway (call 503/630-6861 or 877/444-6777 or check out www.reserveusa.com) as well as pretty views en route. The Clackamas is also known for intense white water, dangerous swimming, and good steelhead fishing. Twenty-six miles southeast of Estacada on ORE 224 you'll pass the Ripplebrook Ranger Station. Bagby signs soon appear near the Timothy Lake Junction, where you'll bear right on FS 46, turning right on FS 63 after three miles. Four miles later, turn right onto FS 70 and drive six miles to the parking area.

If you're interested in an extended stay in the area, a half mile west of the Ripplebrook ranger station is Alder Flat, a secluded, no-reservation, no-fee campground, open late April to late September. Set on the banks of the Clackamas, it's reachable by a one-mile hike. At the ranger station, you can also check whether FS 46 is open south to Breitenbush, another of the Northwest's favorite hot springs (see "Salem" in the Willamette Valley chapter). This road is prone to closure from snow and rock slides. The rangers can also tell you how to link up with ORE 26, a road that is also frequently closed in snowy months. Better yet, call the Detroit Ranger station (503/854-3366) beforehand for road and weather conditions.

---

included the floodplain of the Vanport flood that obliterated a whole town in the late 1940s. **Eastmoreland Golf Course** (2425 S.E. Bybee Blvd., 503/775-2900, www.portlandparks.org/ parks/eastmorelandgolf.htm), located near the Crystal Springs Rhododendron Garden, features a driving range. Portland public course fees average around $25 for 18 holes. **Pumpkin Ridge** (U.S. 26, N. Plains Exit, 503/647-4747, www.pumpkinridge.com) was featured on *Golf Magazine's* top 100 places to golf list in 2000. On weekdays, greens fees for their public course, Ghost Creek, are $40–95, $50–120 on weekends.

For information on area lakes and public swimming pools, contact **Portland Parks** (1120 S.W. 5th Ave., Room 502, 503/823-2223, www.portlandparks.org).

ICE SKATING

Skaters can follow in the tracks of Portland personality Tonya Harding and hit the ice at **Lloyd Center** (Weidler St./Multonmah Blvd. between N.E. 13th and N.E. 15th Streets, 503/282-2511, www.lloydcenter.com) and **Clackamas Town Center** (12000 S.E. 82nd Ave., 503/786-6000, www.clackamastowncenter.com). For a couple bucks' skate rental, you too can cut double axles in these practice venues. Call ahead for hours.

RUNNING, WALKING, AND CYCLING

Named the "Best Running Town" in the country in 2003 by Runners World magazine, Portland hosts numerous running and walking events. The well-regarded **Portland Marathon** (503/226-111, www.portlandmarathon.org) and the **Cascade Classic** are two of them. To find out about these and other events, contact the **Oregon Road Runner's Club** (P.O. Box 2115, Gresham 97030, 503/646-7867); they'll be glad to recommend the best places to run. Bipeds in less of a hurry can pick up a free annotated walker's map at Powell's Books (1005 W. Burnside, 503/228-4651).

The website of the City of Portland's Office of Transportation (www.trans.ci.portland.or.us/bicycles/pdxorgs.htm) lists up-to-date information for cyclists. *Getting There by Bike,* published by the government agency Metro, is sold at bike shops and bookstores across town. A major problem is crossing the Willamette River. The Hawthorne and Burnside Bridges are best, although bikes must share sidewalks with pedestrians. Provisions to let bicycles on TriMet buses (bike racks are on board), the MAX, and streetcar

routes will help you get out of the armchair and onto the road. For more information, see TriMet's website (www.trimet.org/guide/bikes.htm) or call their bike hotline, 503/962-7644.

Rent bikes from **Fat Tire Farm** (2714 N.W. Thurman St., 503/222-3276). Repair bikes at the **Bicycle Repair Collective** (4438 S.E. Belmont, 503/233-0564).

In recent years, there has been an increase in covered bike parking, showers, locker space downtown (call the Bicycle Transportation Alliance at 503/226-0676 for info) as well as increased numbers of bike lanes on commuter thoroughfares. Cyclists are currently excited about the 16.8-mile springwater corridor that runs from S.E. Portland through Gresham to Boring. Much of this bike thoroughfare is on reclaimed rail line. Views of Mount Hood abound throughout much of the route. Along the way, easy access to Leach Botanical Gardens, Powell Butte, and other worthy detours are available. Contact **Portland Parks and Recreation** (1120 S.W. 5th Ave., Room 1302, Portland 97204, 503/823-2223).

Cyclists looking for organized 30- to 100-mile rides at a touring pace should hook up with the **Portland Wheelmen Touring Club Hotline** (503/257-PWTC, www.pwtc.com).

Entertainment

THEATER

Portland's concentration of first-rate theater as well as opera, dance, and other kinds of stage productions is fast becoming one of the West Coast's worst-kept secrets. Portland is home to the second oldest art museum and the first symphony in the region, and equal doses of tradition and eclectic dynamism characterize the current offerings.

Headquarters for much of this activity is the **Portland Center for the Performing Arts** (1111 S.W. Broadway, 503/248-4335). Four stages grace this facility: 3,000-seat **Keller Auditorium,** 2,776-seat **Arlene Schnitzer Hall,** 900-seat **Newmark Theater,** and 350-seat **Dolores Winningstad Theater.** Each theater has features suited to different kinds of productions. The Schnitzer Hall is

a sumptuously restored 1928 vaudeville and movie house. The Winningstad is a high-tech Shakespearean courtyard theater with wraparound balconies. The Intermediate is the crown jewel here, with elegant cherry paneling, teal velour upholstery, and a stage as large as the seating area. Keller Auditorium at 3rd and Clay is designed to accommodate larger audiences. On the way to the stage, the aisles are pitched at such an incline that women should think twice about wearing high heels. While lacking the aesthetic flair of the other theaters, the acoustics and vantages of the stage here are top-notch.

In addition to newspaper listings, the following numbers offer information on Portland performing arts: **Oregon Symphony** (503/228-1353 or 800/228-1353, www.orsympony.org);

Oregon Ballet (503/222-5538,888/922-5538, www.obt.org); **Portland Opera** (503/241-1802 or 866/739-6737, www.portlandopera.org).

More than a dozen theatrical troupes make up a significant presence on Portland's cultural scene. **Imago Theatre** (27 S.E. 8th Ave., 503/231-9581, www.imagotheatre.com) is an internationally acclaimed troupe that employs multimedia visuals, masks, puppets, dance, and animation to achieve dramatic resonance. Imago performs in an old Masonic hall that's at once intimate and spacious enough for the ambitious visual effects and movement of this cutting-edge troupe. **Do Jump Extremely Physical Theater** (Echo Theater, S.E. 37th and Hawthorne, 503/231-1232, www.dojump.org), like Imago, wowed New York critics while touring recent innovative productions. Trapeze and other circus arts combine with whimsical choreography here to make social commentary or aesthetic statements that can be appreciated by everyone from children to urban sophisticates.

GALLERIES

More than 30 gallery owners coordinate show openings the first Thursday of every month, many offering complimentary refreshments. Visit the conflagration of galleries in the Pearl District around N.W. 11th, 12th, and Glisan, or the area close by Saturday Market near the Burnside Bridge, which draws the biggest crowds. The Art Museum offers free admission on First Thursdays.

Contact the Portland Oregon Visitors Association, POVA (503/275-9750 or 800/962-3700, www.travelportland.com or www.pova.org) for details about **Last Thursdays,** a similar event at month's end highlighting the nascent dynamic gallery and independent designer district on N.E. Alberta Street. Portland Institute for Contemporary Art (PICA) is also an indispensable resource for art lovers. PICA (503/242-1949, www.pica.org) offers lectures, performances, and exhibitions at many venues throughout the city.

Art in The Pearl showcases the creations of the local artistic community in the city's leading gallery neighborhood in an outdoor street festival with food booths and music. It usually happens the last weekend of August. Call POVA for more info (503/275-9750 or 800/962-3700).

ART THEATERS

Besides venues for music and dancing, Portland has a handful of places that may be termed "art theaters," whose diverse cultural offerings provide some of the most stimulating entertainment in the city. Two of the best are described below.

The **Aladdin Theater** (3017 S.E. Milwaukie Ave., 503/233-1994, www.aladdin-theater.com) is a 1920s burlesque house that has been elegantly gussied up to host an eclectic array of performers such as Laurie Anderson, Buena Vista Social Club, and Arlo Guthrie. This is the city's only nonsmoking concert club.

The **Clinton Street Theater** (2522 S.E. Clinton, 503/238-8899, www.clintonsttheatre.com) is an art house cinema featuring films that generally would not have a market in most other theaters. This might mean the *Rocky Horror Picture Show* every Saturday night or dated propaganda films such as *Reefer Madness.* The foregoing fit right in with such nearby bohemian hangouts as retro-chic **Dot's Cafe** (2521 S.E. Clinton, 503/230-0203; open daily) and hippie-Mex taquería, **La Cruda** (2500 S.E. Clinton, 503/233-0745; open daily) as well as the vintage clothing and furniture stores lining Clinton Street near S.E. 26th.

COMEDY

Music and laughs, they're all here in the Rose City, but in varying degrees. To put it more bluntly, jazz is hot, comedy is usually not. Portland's major comedy club, **Harvey's** (436 N.W. 6th Ave., 503/241-0338, www.harveyscomdyclub.com) might suffer from poor acoustics and a lack of intimacy if you sit in the back, but the talent is there; besides, it's just about the only game in town. The cover charge ranges $10–12. A reasonably priced menu and a full bar are available at this club. A location near Chinatown offers dining alternatives, and proximity to Greyhound and Amtrak make it a convenient destination for travelers.

DANCE CLUBS

Here are a few alternatives where you can dance to something other than Portland's predominant blues and rock.

The best place to dance in the Northwest is **McMenamin's Crystal Ballroom** (1332 W. Burnside, 503/225-0047, www.danceonair.com/crystal). In addition to the usual fare, McMenamin's hosts a Sunday ballroom event (with lessons beginning at 4 P.M.) in a majestic 1914 restored dance hall. In the 1960s Marvin Gaye, James Brown, Etta James, Ike and Tina Turner, the Allman Brothers, and others gave this vintage moveable dance floor a workout. Imagine a dance floor on ball bearings in a Roaring 20s–era dance hall bedecked with artwork and ornate chandeliers, hosting a diverse array (New Wave, ballroom, Latin, blues) of top-flight talent. Here the legacy goes back to Tommy Dorsey and Glen Miller and continues up through Aretha Franklin and the Grateful Dead.

Jubitz Ponderosa Lounge (10205 N. Vancouver Way, 503/345-0300, www.jubitztravelcenter.com) is a place to do your boot-scootin' boogie and Texas two-step to live bands. Just take I-5 north to Exit 307 and veer right on the frontage road onto Vancouver Way.

Reggae fans writhe the night away to live Rasta music at the **Red Sea** (318 S.W. 3rd Ave., 503/241-5450) on Thursday nights. Other nights a DJ plays an eclectic assortment of world beat, ska, and other genres. Open Wed.–Sun. 7 P.M.–2:30 A.M.; $6 cover.

Fernando's Hideaway (824 S.W. 1st Ave., 503/248-4709, www.fernandoshideaway.com), a tapas bar (the food here is good too) near Yamhill Market, offers Latin dancing upstairs in very tight confines. There's usually a small cover ($3–5) and very often women get in free.

CINEMA

The *Oregonian* offers a free 24-hour news and information service called **Oregonian Inside Line** (503/225-5555). Dial FILM (3456), the category prompt to access film listings for all the cinemas in town. In addition, each theater has its own extension, which you can access directly. A complete list of extensions is published in the Sunday "TV Click" section of the *Oregonian*. (See "Media," later in this chapter, for more details.) Adults can expect to pay $7.50 for a movie after 5 P.M. at most Regal movie theaters (www.regalcinemas.com), a chain that controls 85 percent of Portland's movie screens. Prior to that, half-price matinees are in effect. At some theaters, seniors and students enjoy half-price discounts for evening shows.

Downtown Portland offers an array of genre movie houses, such as **Cinema 21** (616 N.W. 21st Ave., 503/223-4515, www.cinema21.com); **Broadway Metroplex** (1000 S.W. Broadway, 503/255-5555, ext. 4607); **Fox Tower 10** (S.W. Park and Taylor, 503/225-5555, ext. 4604); and **Mission Theater** (1624 N.W. Glisan, 503/225-5555, ext. 8832).

The February **Portland International Film Festival** (503/221-1156, www.nwfilm.org), held at Portland Art Museum's Northwest Film Center, showcases foreign and art flicks that serious film-lovers will especially appreciate. The festival also uses the **Regal Fox Theater** for some films. When the festival isn't in session, this classic venue located just southwest of Pioneer Square (near the corner of S.E. Broadway and Yamhill) specializes in independent and alternative films.

In the Northeast, budget art houses (ticket prices range $2–5) include **Hollywood Theatre** (N.E. 41th and Sandy, 503/281-4215, www.hollywoodtheatre.org) and the **Laurelhurst** (N.E. 28th and Burnside, 503/232-5511, www.laurelhursttheater.com). Check the Friday **Oregonian** (or call the newspaper's Inside Line) and **Willamette Week** for reviews and listings.

Courtesy of brewpubmeisters the brothers McMenamin, Portland also features two restored vintage theaters (among other screening facilities) featuring just-past-first-run flicks and 1940s classics (tickets $2–5) along with pub grub and beer. The old couches at the **Mission Theater and Pub** (1624 Glisan, 503/223-4031) and the snack-friendly tables, seatback mug-holders, and armrests in front of you at the neo-Moorish **Bagdad Theater and Pub**

(3710 S.E. Hawthorne, 503/230-0895) make these brewpub/movie house marriages work. For info on what's playing at McMenamin's establishments, check out their website (www .mcmenamins.com).

TOURS

A listing of tours may seem out of place in a guide for independent travelers, but sometimes organized outings provide insights otherwise unavailable.

One such perspective is provided by a harbor cruise on a sternwheeler, a mode of transport that opened up the Willamette a century ago. The 599-passenger *Columbia Gorge* (541/374-8427 or 800/643-1354, www.sternwheeler.com) offers trips in Cascade Locks (see the Columbia River Gorge chapter for info on this as well as cruise ships plying the Columbia) in the region for which it is named. River cruises on the Willamette visit the Willamette greenway, an untouched area south of the city. Downriver trips pass city lights and ships bound for Pacific Rim ports. The *Cascade Queen* departs Riverplace Marina May 1–September 30, 3–5 P.M. Cruises run on weekends with sightseeing packages ($15 adults, $9 children) and brunch cruises at roughly double the sightseeing rate. Dinner cruises for $45/adult, $30/child, are also available.

Willamette Jetboat Excursions (503/231-1532, www.jetboatpdx.com) takes you down to Oregon City's historic Willamette Falls on two-hour tours starting from OMSI. The May–October itineraries are $27 for adults and $17 for kids 4–11 (infants and toddlers go free).

Ecotours of Oregon (3127 S.E. 23rd Ave., Portland 97202, 503/245-1428 or 888/TOURS-33, www.Ecotours-of-Oregon.com) runs tours blending ecological understanding with having a good time. Door-to-door van transport from anywhere in the Portland area, lunch, and commentary are included in itineraries that run $40–63 per person per day (city tours to whale-watching, respectively). Packages focusing on whale-watching, Native American culture, Mount St. Helens, and old-growth trees typify the refreshing focus of this small company. Trips

are usually confined to vans of six with a professional naturalist-historian guide.

Another riverside perspective is available courtesy of the **Willamette Shore Trolley** (311 State St., Lake Oswego 97034, 503/697-7436, www/trainweb/org/oers/wst.htm), an authentic vintage streetcar. The 30-mile round-trip journey between Portland and the southern suburb of Lake Oswego lets you enjoy lush forest and parklands on the west bank of the Willamette that would otherwise be inaccessible. The east bank of the river is clearly visible, as are many interesting homes. Round-trip fare is $9 for adults, $5 for ages 3–12. The trolley operates daily in summer and on weekends during winter. The enclosed heated cars are best appreciated during winter, a season when the leaves are off the trees so views are unobstructed. Tours begin near Naito Parkway and Harbor Place and end up at 311 North State Street in Lake Oswego. A vintage trolley runs at Christmastime in other parts of the city as an adjunct to existing mass transit. Call TriMet for details.

Portland's TriMet (www.TriMet.org) provides vintage trolley service along a two-mile portion of its light-rail system on Sundays May–Jan. Replica trolley cars run between downtown Portland, and the Lloyd District, a "second downtown" office and shopping district across the Willamette River. The vintage cars currently operate on a seasonal schedule, which is subject to change. Dressed in replica uniforms, the conductors interact with passengers in addition to performing traditional duties like announcing stations and operating the doors.

Finally, there is **Gray Line of Portland** (P.O. Box 17306, 21320 N. Suttle, Portland 97217, 503/285-9845 or 800/422-7042). Gray Line in most cities runs competent tours with experienced drivers; Portland's outfit is no exception. In addition to day trips to such locales as Mount Hood, the Oregon Coast, and the Columbia River Gorge, three- and seven-hour city tours depart all year long from Union Station. Half-day trips such as the Multnomah Falls/Columbia Gorge tour (about $40 per person) and full-day trips such as the Mount Hood Loop (about $55 per person) are highly recommended. Skiers will want to inquire about their buses up to Mount Hood Meadows. Free weekly round-trip shuttles to Chinook Winds Casino in Lincoln City on the coast are another interesting offering of this company. While calling to reserve is handy, consider stopping by their downtown offices at the Embassy Suites on 319 S.W. Pine. Not only will you be able to talk directly to a helpful ticket agent, but you can also pick up brochures and a free Portland tour map, an info-filled user-friendly layout of the city. Finally, be aware that Gray Line offers free hotel pick-ups in conjunction with their tours in selected locations.

Events

FAIRS AND FESTIVALS

Cinco de Mayo celebrates the Mexican Revolution and Latino pride at Waterfront Park the first weekend (including Thursday and Friday) in May. This has become the largest celebration of its kind in the country. Mariachis, folk dance exhibitions, a large selection of Mexican food, and fireworks displays are included in the festivities. In a 1997 survey Portland ranked eighth as a city hospitable to Latinos, Oregon's largest ethnic minority. Their presence is evident in the recent proliferation of taquerías, some of which have a presence at the festival. Admission is $6 (adults), kids and seniors $3.

In July, check out the **Multnomah County Fair** (Oak Park in Sellwood, 503/761-7577, www.oregonfairs.org). The prize bulls, cowpokes, and carnival midway remain, but the fair has ventured into the great beyond of multicultural diversity. In the fair's present incarnation you're likely to find an authentic American Indian powwow, Mexican folk ballet, and a photo exhibit featuring well-known professionals. In addition, you can enjoy Latin combos and jazz groups as well as an array of international cuisines alongside the expected country music and cotton candy. (Usual hours Wed.–Sat. noon–11 P.M., Sunday noon–9 P.M. Admission $5–7, discounts for ages 6–12.)

An August festival, **The Bite** (Tom McCall Waterfront Park, 503/657-5382, www.portlandbite.com) lets you sample local culinary specialties of Portland restaurants, with the proceeds going to the Special Olympics. Live music is also featured.

Another palate-pleasing August affair is the **Oregon Brewers Festival** (www.oregonbrewfest .com). Taking place the last full weekend in July in Portland's Tom McCall Waterfront Park, North America's largest gathering of independent brewers showcases the wares of more than 70 breweries. Admission is free but to sample the product of dozens of brewers, you must buy a 14-ounce souvenir mug for $4; two $1 beer tokens are good for a half glass each. According to noted beer expert Michael Jackson, no other cities can compete with the quality and quantity of microbrews put out in Seattle and Portland. A few rounds at the Brewers Festival would tend to make most anyone a believer.

In October, watch the salmon spawn at Oxbow Park in the Sandy River Gorge outside Gresham. Old-growth walks, an eight-kilometer run, a barbecue, and arts and crafts round out this fête. To get there from downtown, take I-84 east to the Wood Village Exit. Turn south on Division and east on Oxbow Parkway, then follow the signs to Oxbow Park. Or, take I-84 to Exit 17, drive east a mile, then make a right on 257th Street and follow it to Division, where the previous directions take effect. There's a vehicle fee and an additional charge for lunch and activities. Festival-goers will tell you that a rainy day seems to encourage salmon-spawning activity. Anglers are kept busy with spawning runs of coho, fall, and spring chinook salmon, and winter and summer steelhead trout. Call 503/248-5050 for more information. Hours are Sat.–Sun. 10:30 A.M.–5 P.M.

The Oregon Historical Society's **Wintering in Festival** (Howell Territorial Park, Sauvie Island, 503/222-1741, www.ohs.org) happens near the

PORTLAND ROSE FESTIVAL

The Portland Rose Festival (503/227-2681, www.rosefestival.org) has been the major wingding here for nine decades. The Rose Queen and her court (chosen from local high school entrants), sailors and prostitutes, and floats from several parades clog Portland's traffic arteries during this 24-day citywide celebration each June. Air shows, a hot-air balloon classic, the Indy World Series car race, and a traditional rose show round out the main attractions. The flier available at Portland Oregon Visitors Association has more information about what is essentially a small town festival done with big town flair. Even if parades and crowds are not your thing, the civic pride here is genuine and appealing. Portlanders camp out along the parade route in the same places year after year, sometimes several days in advance just to catch a coveted glimpse at the floats passing by.

The key to enjoying festival events is avoiding traffic and parking hassles. A $4 TriMet (503/238-7433) entitles the passholder and up to three kids six and under to unlimited rides on MAX or the bus all day long. As for traffic, be especially wary of the waterfront. Such festival features as food booths and carnival rides in Tom McCall Park, as well as military ship displays on the Willamette, draw crowds reminiscent of lemmings to the sea.

Another good reason to come to the waterfront is the chance to see the dragon boat races. These brightly painted ceremonial canoes from China have been taken up in earnest here. With 16 paddlers and a coxswain, teams compete on the Willamette River.

Two of the more colorful offshoots of the June fete are the **Grand Floral Parade** and the **Festival of Flowers** at Pioneer Courthouse Square. In the latter, all manner of colorful blossoms fill the square to overflowing. This bouquet is on display during the first week of the several-week celebration. As for the Grand Floral Parade, this usually begins the Saturday following the opening of the festival. The floats combine the beauty of flowers with high-tech wizardry in aesthetically whimsical creations. You can reserve seats in the Coliseum ahead of time (call for pricing), but save your money and station yourself on an upper floor along the parade route or visit the floats at Oregon Square between Lloyd Center and the Convention Center during the week following the parade. Any lofty perch is sufficient for taking in all the hoopla, drill teams, Rose Queen, and equestrian demonstrations. This procession is the second-largest all-floral parade in the United States.

Gray Line (503/285-9845) features a package that spares you the hassles of parking and traffic, and offers great parade seats and breakfast at the Coliseum, all at a very fair price. Parade route restaurants on Burnside set up tables outside to take in the festivities. The parades and the flower displays prove that in Rose Festivals, as in life, the best things are free.

---

autumnal equinox. Enjoy fresh farm produce, crafts, and music at the restored pioneer homestead (see "Sauvie Island," earlier in this chapter).

HOLIDAY EVENTS

The day after Thanksgiving, a Christmas tree is lit in Pioneer Square and a skating rink installed. Skate rentals are available and a small admission is charged. The best Christmas lights display is on Peacock Lane in southeast Portland near beautiful Laurelhurst Park, 29th and Stark; check at POVA for more details (503/275-9750 or 800/962-3700).

The Christmastime **Grotto's Festival of Lights** (N.E. 85th and Sandy Blvd., 503/254-7371, www.thegrotto.org) includes animated lighting displays, narrated fiber-optic displays, and other illuminated depictions of the life of Christ. Set amid gorgeous surroundings, this is the largest choral festival in the Pacific Northwest and a very special holiday event. Admission is $6.

Finally, a Portland event that's sure to please is the annual parade of **Christmas ships** (www.christmasships.org.htm). Boats with lights creating images of a fire engine, Santa's sleigh, angels, and other fanciful designs parade on the Columbia and the Willamette. Portlanders line waterfront parks and restaurants to enjoy this spectacle, which usually runs for about a week and ends on December 23.

LIVE MUSIC FESTIVALS AND VENUES

Portland is fortunate to have a critical mass of talented musicians. Notable among the tuneful offerings from this community is one of the West Coast's most vibrant jazz and blues scenes, more opportunities to hear classical music than are currently available in Seattle, and plenty of places to suit fans of country, rock, and folk music.

Many nationally known jazz players (such as bassist Ben Wolf and drummer Mel Brown) and blues men (Robert Cray, Paul DeLay, and Curtis Salgado, to name a few) were spawned from this milieu. In addition to fostering homegrown talent, Portland has become a prime stop for touring practitioners of these quintessentially American art forms. Several summertime outdoor festivals offer especially good places to get an earful, along with year-round jazz and blues performed in stadiums, coffeehouses, brewpubs, and dance halls. (See listings in the "Arts and Entertainment" section of the Friday *Oregonian*, www.oregonlive.com/events, and in *Willamette Week*, www.wweek.com.)

The **Inner City Blues Festival** (503/249-5071 www.cascadeblues.org) at the Crystal Ballroom in March throws together the city's best acts in its finest dance venue. Tickets are about $15 each.

The **Waterfront Blues Festival** (503/282-0555, www.waterfrontbluesfest.com) is the largest festival of its kind on the West Coast. It takes place the first weekend in July at Waterfront Park, and many famous artists attend. The $5 admission and donations (two canned-good items) go to the Oregon Food Bank.

During the same period, end of June through mid-July, is **Chamber Music Northwest** (Reed College Commons, 3203 S.E. Woodstock Ave., 503/294-6400, www.cmnw.org), presenting concerts for five weeks nightly except Sunday. Music begins at 8 P.M. and people picnic beforehand. Enjoy strawberry shortcake at intermission. Tickets to this nationally acclaimed series range

$20–38. In addition to the concerts at Reed, performances take place at Catlin Gabel School. To get there from downtown, head west on Burnside. This becomes Barnes Road, where you'll see a sign for the school about five miles west of the Rose Garden turnoff near St. Vincent's Hospital.

The **Mount Hood Jazz Festival** (P.O. Box 696, Gresham 97030, 503/665-2837, www.mthoodjazz.com) is *the* event for jazz and blues connoisseurs. The best artists in the world converge annually the first weekend of August at Mount Hood Community College in Gresham 20 minutes east of downtown Portland. Buying tickets in advance (about $20 per day) through Ticketmaster is advisable due to frequent sellouts. If lawn chairs or picnic-style blankets are not your perch of preference, the covered west grandstand provides protection from the sun as well as offers views of Mount Hood.

For summer outdoor concerts, it's all happening at the **Oregon Zoo** (503/280-2493, www.zoooregon.org/concerts). Crowds spread out on the lawn below the stage to hear first-rate, often big-name talent, usually at a lower price ($9–20) than they would pay elsewhere in the city to see acts of such caliber. Because these events take place in the early evening and are free with zoo admission, it's not uncommon to see throngs of dancing children below the stage.

A higher-priced version of same is enacted at the **Rose Garden Amphitheater** in Washington Park in September. Nationally prominent acts of diverse genres perform in what is probably one of the more scenic and acoustically superior venues in the state. Tickets go on sale at Ticketmaster outlets in late June.

The **Heathman Hotel Lounge** (1009 S.W. Broadway, 503/790-7752, www.heathmanhotel.com) is another quality jazz spot with small plates from a five-star kitchen and prices to match. Nightly jazz with Frenchified Northwest cuisine, at moderate prices, is also a focal point in the art-filled Euro bistro **Brasserie Montmartre** (626 S.W. Park Ave., 503/224-5552; open daily). Drinks and great hors d'oeuvres with live jazz several nights a week can be enjoyed at the Lobby

Court at the **Benson Hotel** (309 S.W. Broadway, 503/228-2000, www.bensonhotel.com) in wood-paneled elegance that harks back to 1913. Blues aficionados will appreciate the array of talent showcased nightly at both **The Candlelight** (2032 S.W. 5th, 503/222-3378, www.candlelightcafebar.com), a gritty, smoky bar near Portland State University, and **Billy Reed's** (2808 N.E. MLK Jr. Blvd., 503/493-8127, www.billyreeds.com), a cavernous bastion of high-class pub grub. Rock fans enjoy **Berbati's** (231 S.W. Ankeny St., 503/248-4579), where great Greek food and music of all genres have made it Portland's leading late-night live music club. Jazz, comedy, and poetry slams take place here. The cover can range $1–20 but averages around $10. These establishments tend to be open daily from 11 A.M.

Accommodations

Portland poses no problem for those seeking accommodations at a good dollar value. Whether it's the luxury of downtown accommodations, the convenience and tradition of Historic Landmark Northeast Portland B&Bs, the best of the country near the best of the city in Sauvie Island guesthouses, or the rock-bottom rates at a Southeast Portland hostel, you can't go wrong. RV travelers and campers are also blessed with some good choices. Even so, travelers of all descriptions need to reserve well in advance for June, July, and August.

The listings below reflect a cross-section of desirable places to stay, organized by type of lodging. For more information on special rates and for online booking, contact the **Portland Oregon Visitors Association (POVA)** (877/678-5263, www.pova.com/visitors/index).

MOTELS
Downtown
It's hard to find rooms downtown below $80 that are clean, safe, and well located, reflecting Portland's recent emergence as an expensive city. Nonetheless, it's still cheaper than Seattle or San Francisco with less traffic and crime.

Days Inn (1414 S.W. 6th Ave., 503/221-1611 or 800/899-0248, www.daysinn.com) is centrally located near Portland State University, downtown shopping, and cultural venues. Amenities range from a heated outdoor pool to free covered parking. There is also a decent on-site restaurant. While nothing special, the rooms, which range $70–130 (the majority of the doubles are below $80), cover the basics well enough to make it a dollarwise downtown lodging.

Southeast Portland
Brooklyn Center Suites (3717 S.E. Milwaukie Ave., 503/231-1858, www.brooklyncentersuites.com) offers two modern spacious rooms with fully equipped kitchens, a queen bed, a direct-dial phone, a color TV, and a bath/shower. Situated in the Historic Brooklyn neighborhood, this Mom 'n' Pop version of a residence inn is perfect for extended stays, thanks to $65/night, $350/week rates. A gift bottle of Oregon wine or microbrew (or a nonalcoholic alternative if requested) greets you upon arrival. This is an especially good choice for parents visiting their Reed College student children or culture vultures wanting to take in such nearby haunts as downtown museums, Sellwood antique stores, and the Aladdin Theatre.

Airport
The expansion of PDX airport has been paralleled by the growth of nearby lodging alternatives, most with free shuttle to and from the airport. Here are a few options.

A 12-minute ride from the airport (by free shuttle) is **Quality Inn** (8247 N.E. Sandy Blvd., 503/256-4111 and 800/424-6423, www.choicehotel.com). Located near The Grotto (old-growth trees and contemplative surroundings—see listing earlier in this chapter) and the Cameo Cafe (see listing later in this chapter), it's a world away from terminal traffic snarls. Better yet, it's halfway between the airport and downtown with easy access via city bus. While the rooms are typical of moderately priced ($80–150) chains, the free breakfast and other amenities make it a good choice.

The **Country Inn** (7025 N.E. Alderwood Rd., 503/255-2700 or 888/987-2700, www.countryinns.com) is a 150-room hotel with a pool, spa, fitness center, and well-appointed rooms for $69–106. A free airport shuttle and breakfast are also available.

Courtyard by Marriott (11550 N.E. Airport Way, 503/252-3200 or 800/321-2211, www.marriott.com), a comparably sized hotel, offers somewhat more modest rooms in the same price range (beginning at $75/double) as well as suites ($125) with microwaves, wet bars, and other appreciated extras. A restaurant, pool, and spa facilities are also on-site. It's three miles east of the airport, with 24-hour free shuttle service to the terminal.

The **Silver Cloud Inn Airport** (11518 Glenn Widing Rd., 503/252-2222 or 800/205-7892, www.silvercloudinn.com) is a more upscale choice with doubles for $91–105. All 100 rooms face a lake, helping you forget the proximity of the terminal and freeways. In-room PC dataports, microwaves and refrigerators, free coffee and continental breakfast, and on-site whirlpool and exercise facilities also rate thumbs up. A courtesy airport shuttle and nearby airport restaurants are also noteworthy.

HOTELS
Downtown

Despite moderate rates, at first glance the **Mallory Hotel** (729 S.W. 15th Ave. at Yamhill, Portland 97295, 503/223-6311 or 800/228-8657, www.malloryhotel.com) suggests a luxury lodging, with a lobby boasting ornate plaster, crystal chandeliers, and an elegant, sky-lit interior. The marble pillars and chandeliers in the dining room (try the German pancakes for breakfast) sustain the four-star facade along with the elaborate jungle motif of the Driftwood Room Lounge. Somehow it all feels very British, especially when it's raining outside. A location on the MAX line not far from the boutiques of the Northwest district and South Park

Blocks cultural attractions also recommend it. With an address like this, the Mallory's free parking is especially appreciated. The smallish, rather plain rooms account for the low rates, around $105 for a double. If you're lucky enough to score a king-sized suites for $165, you'll walk away shaking your head in disbelief at this lodging value.

The **Hotel Lucia** (400 S.W. Broadway, 503/228-7221 or 800/225-1717) is another good buy in a comparable price range. The Hotel Lucia shares a location with hotels that charge double its rate ($125 and up), close by the best of downtown shopping, galleries, and Pioneer Square. Typhoon!, a quality Portland eatery (see "Food," later in this chapter) is on-site, and Powell's Books is a five-minute walk away. There's a lot of street noise near here at night however, so book an upper floor if possible.

The **Four Points Sheraton** (50 S.W. Morrison, 503/221-0711 or 888/627-8263, www.fourpointsportland.com) $99–160) overlooks Waterfront Park and the Willamette River through large windows. Sheraton renovated the guest rooms and lobby here in a stylish, ultramodern motif (they advertise "contemporary lodging with European flair") and the hotel is ideally located for morning joggers, folks who want to visit Saturday Market or shop and dine near Pioneer Square.

The **Paramount Hotel** (808 S.W. Taylor St., 503/223-9900, www.portlandparamount.com) is Portland's newest European-style boutique hotel. Within just a few blocks of MAX, Pioneer Square, department stores, and fine dining, it's city-center location can't be beat. Each of the 154 oversized guest rooms and suites feature granite-finished bathrooms. For those who want to splurge, the Paramount Class rooms feature large terraces and jetted tubs; Grand Suites offer fireplace, wet bar, whirlpool bath, and sweeping views of downtown Portland. The onsite Dragon Fish restaurant serves pan-Asian cuisine, and Café Appassionato provides coffee and light fare for guests. Rates are $164–350.

The **Portland Hilton** (921 S.W. 6th Ave., 503/226-1611, www.portland.hilton.com) has

PORTLAND

WESTSIDE PORTLAND FOOD AND LODGING

N.E. GRAND AVE.

MARTIN LUTHER KING JR. BLVD.

84

5

5

ROSE GARDEN ARENA/ MEMORIAL COLISEUM

N. INTERSTATE AVE.

Willamette River

STEEL BRIDGE

MAX

BROADWAY BRIDGE

N.W. FRONT AVE. (N.W. NAITO PKWY.)

BURNSIDE BRIDGE

Tom McCall Waterfront Park

N.W. FRONT AVE.

1ST AVE.

2ND AVE.

OLD TOWN

CLASSICAL CHINESE GARDENS/ TEAHOUSE

3RD AVE.

FONG CHONG ▶

CHINATOWN

LA PATISSERIE

ALEXIS ▶

SKIDMORE HISTORIC DISTRICT

BERBATI'S

S.W. ANKENY ST.

BIJOU CAFE

S.W. PINE ST.

DAN & LOUIS OYSTER BAR

S.W. OAK ST.

4TH AVE.

5TH AVE.

6TH AVE.

UNION STATION (AMTRAK)

GREYHOUND BUS STATION

BROADWAY AVE.

N.W. GLISAN ST.

N.W. FLANDERS ST.

N.W. EVERETT ST.

N.W. DAVIS ST.

N.W. COUCH ST.

TRANSIT MALL

6TH AVE.

POST OFFICE

7TH AVE.

8TH AVE.

PARK AVE.

NORTH PARK BLOCKS

W. BURNSIDE ST.

9TH AVE.

THE PEARL

CAFE AZUL ▶

BENSON HOTEL

S.W. PARK AVE.

HOTEL LUCIA/ TYPHOON! ●

S.W. STARK ST.

N.W. LOVEJOY ST.

N.W. HOYT ST.

PHO VAN ▶

10TH AVE.

11TH AVE.

12TH AVE.

OBA! ▶

13TH AVE.

14TH AVE.

15TH AVE.

S.W. WASHINGTON ST.

S.W. ALDER ST.

BRIDGEPORT BREW PUB ▶

405

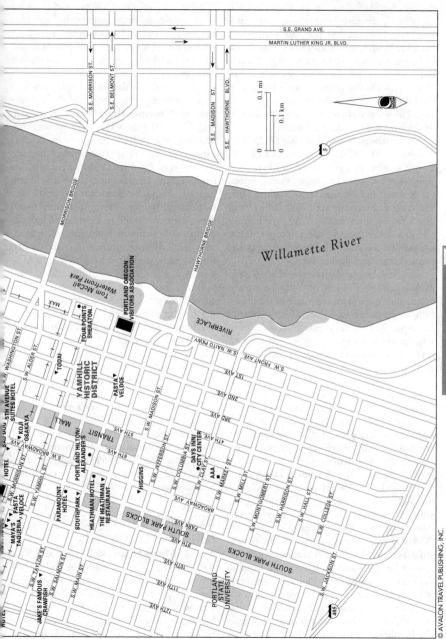

PORTLAND

doubles for $149–185. Business travelers will enjoy newly remodeled rooms, generous corporate rates, frequent flyer plan compatibility, a complete business center, a state-of-the-art health club, and a miracle-working concierge. Alexander's, an exceptional rooftop restaurant (see "Food," later in this chapter), and a location in the heart of the theater district across the street from Niketown are other extras that rate thumbs up with the modern-day road warrior.

The **Northwest Silver Cloud Inn** (2426 N.W. Vaughn St., 503/242-2400) has rates of $89–150. For this price, you get comfy, aesthetic surroundings with such amenities as refrigerators, microwaves, and a location near Portland's best shopping and restaurants in Nob Hill. There's also a fitness room and spa. While the Silver Cloud abuts an industrial district to the north, thankfully, the boutiques and eateries to the south cast a bigger shadow here.

The **5th Avenue Suites Hotel** (506 S.W. Washington, 888/861-9514, www.5thavenuesuites.com) is the latest big player in the luxury hotel sweepstakes. At $119–189 a double, it's less expensive than its downtown upscale counterparts with more spacious rooms and such extras as a complimentary regional wine-tasting every evening in the lobby. A mix of classical and contemporary art and indoor greenery decorate the public rooms, but the plush furnishings in the guest units are what captures most travelers' attention. It is arguably the most central location in town and has an affordable restaurant, the Red Star Grill, emphasizing gourmet interpretations of American food.

The interior of the **Heathman Hotel** (1009 S.W. Broadway, 800/551-0011, heathmanhotel.com) exudes understated Old World elegance with generous use of teak paneling and marble. The public rooms feature art ranging from Andy Warhol to turn-of-the century prints. The location amid theaters and museums has attracted everyone from John Updike, Alice Walker, and Luciano Pavarotti to presidents and foreign dignitaries. While rooms (starting at $139) are usually a little smaller than similarly priced accommodations, the antiques and other room appointments here set the Heathman apart. A first-class restaurant, a

400-film video collection, a library, and afternoon tea are appreciated extras. At night the Heathman bar has jazz, and while it's spendier than many spots in River City, you'd be hard-pressed to find better mixed drinks, appetizers, and atmosphere anywhere else in Oregon.

History buffs and downtown explorers will all find something to appreciate at the lovingly renovated **Governor Hotel** (S.W. 10th at Alder, 503/224-3400 or 800/554-3456, www.govhotel.com). Built in 1909 during one of the city's exponential growth spurts, the old Governor has emerged from its 1990 facelift with its sparkling terra-cotta facade and old-style charm intact. Inside, high ceilings, arts and crafts–style furnishings, and the lobby's sepia-toned mural depicting scenes from the Lewis and Clark Expedition all contribute to the turn-of-the-century sense of taste, proportion, and sanity. Rooms begin at $139, suites at $185. In addition to modern amenities and a central location in a classic setting, you're also paying for appreciated extras. With a bar featuring music most nights of the week (usually jazz), a good restaurant (Jake's Grill), and an excellent health club, the Governor is a good choice for business and pleasure.

In the historic Multnomah Hotel building, Portland's downtown **Embassy Suites** (319 S.W. Pine St., 503/279-9000) is not your run-of-the-mill chain hotel. Priding itself on guest loyalty due to exceptional personalized service, Embassy guests have access to an indoor pool, fitness room, cocktail reception, and complimentary cooked-to-order breakfast. The Portland Steak and Chophouse restaurant is also on the premises. Two bedroom suites run $169–300.

BED-AND-BREAKFASTS
Downtown

The **MacMaster House B&B** (1041 S.W. Vista Ave., 503/223-7362 or 800/774-9523, www.macmaster.com) is located near Washington Park, Northwest shopping, and Council Crest viewpoint. In one of the city's ritziest neighborhoods, the eight rooms in this mansion include two units with private bathroom ($140). The other rooms ($110) share facilities. Some rooms have fireplaces or interesting murals and one has a claw foot tub. The public rooms also have objets d'art and decor that are the essence of Victoriana. Rooms here might fetch a higher price but for a steep flight of steps at the entrance. Nonetheless, the latter are appreciated after the included full breakfast.

Northeast Portland

This neighborhood's bed-and-breakfast options combine easy access to a local restaurant row, moderate rates, and lodgings rich in amenities. Convenient mass transit linkages to downtown and the Norman Rockwellian charm of Northeast Portland's early 20th-century architecture also make this area a good base from which to explore the area.

A good choice in Northeast Portland's "close-in" Irvington neighborhood is the **Portland Guest House** (1720 N.E. 15th, 503/282-1402). The broad tree-shaded avenues of this area and its proximity to excellent restaurants on Broadway alone would mandate mention of this alternative to downtown hotels. While the high-ceilinged Victorian elegance and summer blueberries from the garden for breakfast are enticements to many, it's its room tariff that often closes the deal, $65–95 single, $75–105 double. The owner says there's always quite a run on the single rooms from businesspeople traveling on their own nickel, so be sure to book well in advance. The availability of rooms with private baths and easy access to the bus (lines #8, #9, and #77) are also appreciated.

McMenamin's Kennedy School (5736 N.E. 33rd, 503/249-3983 or 888/249-3983, www .mcmenamins.com/kennedy) is a B&B set in an old elementary school that has been transformed into a complex parlaying a theater, restaurant, and concert venue with the brewpub experience. Madcap mosaics, carvings, and paintings festoon the hallways along with historic photos from the days the building was a citadel of higher learning. The rooms (Sun.–Thurs. $99, Fri.–Sat. $109) are lavishly decorated with art as well as antique furniture. Add a phone, modem, and private bath to such perks as ad-

mission to the movie theater, use of the pool, and breakfast and you can understand why this place is more than just a chance to sleep soundly in a classroom. Be sure to inquire about lodging/dining packages that feature discounts and or extra amenities.

The opulent **White House Bed and Breakfast** (1914 N.E. 22nd, 503/287-7131 or 800/287-7131, www.portlandswhitehouse.com) gives you the presidential treatment. Located just off Broadway near an avenue of shops and restaurants, only 5–10 minutes from Lloyd Center and downtown, this lovingly restored 1912 lumber baron's mansion with Greek columns evocative of its namesake in D.C. has rates ranging $100–179. Beyond the tall mahogany front doors here, hand-painted murals in the huge foyer usher guests into the crystal chandeliered dining room. Antique guest room furnishings and claw foot tubs may sustain the illusion that you're staying in the Lincoln Bedroom, but the innkeeper's baked scones and other goodies at breakfast (sautéed apple French toast) and tea, together with complimentary sherry nightcaps, impart the touch of home.

Sauvie Island

The delights of Portland's backyard are detailed in "Sports and Recreation," earlier in this chapter.

Westlund's River's Edge B&B (22502 N.W. Gillihan Rd., Sauvie Island, 503/621-9856, www.riversedge-bb.com) is a good place to take in the rural grandeur of Sauvie Island, less than a half-hour from downtown Portland. From a picnic area in back, view sunrises and sunsets with Mounts St. Helens and Hood to provide snow-capped accents or watch passing river traffic and Pacific Flyway bird migrations. The B&B itself offers two rooms with shared bath, a kitchenette, and a sitting room for $85. Both rooms can be had for $140. The rate includes a full or continental breakfast (be sure to try the innkeeper's coffeecake).

HOSTELS

The Hawthorne neighborhood's hostel offers proximity to Clinton, Belmont, and Hawthorne "hip strips" as well as area eateries. Folks more inclined to spend their money on cultural pursuits and dining adventures will forsake some comforts and privacy to patronize these lodgings.

Hostelling International (3031 S.E. Hawthorne Blvd., 503/236-3380 or 866/447-3031, www.portlandhostelorg) has rates of $16–19 (dorms beds)and $38–44 (private rooms). Hostellers also like easy access on mass transit. From downtown take #14 down Hawthorne Boulevard; from the airport take #12, then transfer to #5. Kitchen privileges as well as breakfasts and summertime barbecues for a small additional charge are appreciated extras here. Next door, a burger joint, **At the Hop,** seems especially popular with foreign visitors

on a budget (try the patty melt and shakes). Make reservations well in advance for this large, rambling white hostelry in summer due to the influx of folks from other countries. A spacious screened-in back porch provides a cool place to sleep in July and August. It should also be mentioned that a day-use fee of $3 is invoked and some chores are required. In summer, the hostel sometimes organizes van trips to the wine country, Columbia Gorge, the coast, and other getaways.

Another hostel, at 1818 N.W. Glisan (541/241-2783, www.2oregonhostels.com), also offers a location in the stimulating Nob Hill neighborhood as well as such extras as a washing machine and individual rooms ($30–46) if the $18 units don't offer enough privacy.

Food

Portland is second only to San Francisco in the highest number of restaurants per capita in the country. Perhaps more impressive is the fact that you can have a singular dining experience for much less than you'd pay for a gourmet outing in either Seattle or San Francisco. Even the traditionally overpriced, bland food served in many hotel dining rooms can often turn out to be affordable and tasty.

A few peculiarities are worth mentioning. Many dinner places listed here do not serve on Mondays. Portland restaurant coffee will probably be stronger than what you're used to if you aren't from Seattle or San Francisco. You can get away with virtually any mode of dress here in even the most upscale establishments. The recent proliferation of pan-Asian and Mexican taquerías reflects recent immigration trends. What also might surprise newcomers to Portland dining is the large number of places that profile breakfast.

In addition, bus commuters, cyclists, and pedestrians on the go appreciate the variety of street carts (purveying burritos, bento, and the like) in the heart of the bus mall around S.W. 5th and Stark.

The establishments reviewed below reflect neighborhoods that are commonly visited by

travelers on the fly as well as a cross-section of cuisines and price ranges.

BREAKFAST

Portland's most famous breakfast haunt is the **Original Pancake House** (8601 S.W. 24th St., 503/246-9007). This Wed.–Sun. operation has spawned many imitations, but the Original is still the greatest. The restaurant opens at 7 A.M. and closes at 3 P.M., but be there early on weekends. Latecomers should bring a book because waits for seating can be excruciatingly long. Once at the table, the famous apple pancake is a Frisbee-sized cinnamon-laced delight for the growing boy or girl. The menu also features four gourmet omelettes. Despite the 1950s knotty pine walls, expect to pay around $8 for breakfast—not bad for a place James Beard and Art Buchwald once ranked as among the top 10 restaurants in the nation.

Five miles south of the Pancake House is another suburban favorite, moderately priced **Marco's** (7910 S.W. 35th, 503/245-0199) in a cluster of antique shops, boutiques, and cafés known as Multnomah Village. Another outlet is at N.E. 24th and Fremont. Intriguing omelette combinations (try Italian sausage, sweet peppers, tomatoes, onions, herbs, and asiago), wonderful home fries, and a culinary approach that keeps nutritional concerns foremost makes the 12-minute trip by car (Exit 296 off I-5) or 20 minutes by bus (lines #41 and #45) from downtown worth it. After breakfast, go around the corner to **Annie Bloom's** for books, especially regional titles. Later on, come back to Marco's for lunch or dinner, saving room for a multi-ethnic menu that's partial to vegetarians as well as carnivores who prefer their beef from naturally grazed cows. There are also nightly fresh fish specials, Marco's legendary mulligatawny soup each Thursday, imaginative desserts such as coconut mango cheesecake, and an assortment of newspapers and magazines to help you pass time till you're hungry again. In this vein, breakfast is served all day from 7 A.M.

> *Portland is second only to San Francisco in the highest number of restaurants per capita in the country—and your dining experience will be less expensive, too.*

Although lunch is also served at the **Bijou Cafe** (132 S.W. 3rd Ave., 503/222-3187), it has built its reputation on breakfast. While fried cinnamon bread and red snapper or roast beef hash are morning mainstays in this cheery café, ordinary breakfast foods are done perfectly here with the freshest and most nutritious ingredients. Open for breakfast, lunch, and dinner; prices $5–13.

For decades, breakfast at the **Stepping Stone Cafe** (N.W. 24th and Quimby, 503/222-1132) has meant quality eats in the formica-styled confines of a well-kept 1950s hash house. This reinvented corner café serves up tasty, filling breakfasts for prices more commonly seen in Mexican bus stations and Las Vegas casinos than in Portland's trendy Northwest district. The latter contention is made manifest before 9 A.M. with the "birdwatcher's special": two eggs, new potato hash browns, toast, and coffee for $5. Breakfast served every day until 2 P.M.

Dollar value is a term usually not associated with breakfast tabs that can range $9–11, but the **Cameo Cafe** (8111 N.E. Sandy, 503/284-0401) just west of The Grotto near the corner of 82nd and Sandy (and the corner of N.W. 23rd Place and Westover, 503/221-6542) is an exception. Portions and quality here more than justify this description. The homey café is always busy satisfying devotees of its "acre" pancakes (try the strawberry banana) and waffles, "real" home fries, and home-baked multigrain bread. Everything else here bespeaks the restaurant's commitment to excellence, from large jugs of Vermont maple syrup gracing each table to the smiling wait staff who seem able to guess just when you'll need a "warm-up" to your morning coffee. Lunch ($9–11) and dinner ($14–16) offer generous smatterings of Asian and Italian dishes to complement American comfort food.

Northeast Portland's breakfast hot spot is **Milo's** (1325 N.E. Broadway, 503/288-6456). One bite of smoked salmon hash or French toast with spicy sausage and cheddar cheese should explain its popularity. Lunch here boasts salads, sandwiches, and pasta in the same price range as breakfast ($6–8). Open daily for breakfast, lunch, and dinner. (If Milo's is too busy, another popular breakfast place is the Cadillac Cafe, just a few blocks east.)

NORTHWEST CUISINE

Downtown Portland features a wealth of street carts purveying gourmet food as well as a cross-section of restaurants expressing the city's growing sophistication.

To feast the eyes as well as the palate, try **Alexander's** (921 S.W. 6th Ave., 503/226-1611), on the 23rd floor of the Portland Hilton. Views of the snowcapped Cascades backdropping Portland's cityscape and the exquisite presentation of the food can evaporate material concerns such as entrée prices over $26. This is one of Portland's best rooftop restaurants.

At the **Heathman Restaurant** (1001 S.W. Broadway, 503/790-7752 or 800/551-0011), French meets Northwest in a constantly changing menu. Fare ranges from a marinated sea bass salad for lunch to a pistachio-stuffed leg of rabbit for dinner. The creative use of local ingredients can be seen with salmon, which may be served smoked in a hash for breakfast or seared with wasabi bearnaise sauce later in the day. Entrée prices run ($15–25). Open daily for breakfast and lunch; dinner is served 5:30–10 P.M. every night except Monday.

The neighborhood defined by N.W. 21st and N.W. 23rd Avenues boasts the closest thing to a "restaurant row" in Portland. Amid art galleries and boutiques are temples to Northwest cuisine and ethnic food with flair. There are also places serving down-home food that could be appreciated anywhere.

Founded by French-Canadian loggers at the turn of the century, **Besaw's** (N.W. 23rd and Savier, 503/228-2619) is a meat-and-potatoes-meets-brie-and-chablis kind of place, where comfort food shares the menu with dishes prepared with house-smoked salmon, wild mushrooms, and other gourmet ingredients. This orientation is in evidence at breakfast with the prosciutto and egg scramble, lunch with grilled salmon sandwiches, and dinner with pepper-glazed pork with apple chutney and coq au vin. Made-from-scratch desserts such as apple raspberry bread pudding and berry brown Betty can conclude your meal of high-class comfort food at workingperson's prices. Ports, cognacs, well-made Irish coffee, and other after-dinner drinks at Besaw's century-old mahogany bar can make waiting for a table here eminently bearable. Open every day except Monday.

Paley's (1204 N.W. 21st Ave., 503/243-2403) is the quintessential Northwest bistro and, according to many Portlanders, the most enjoyable dining experience in town. This intimate restaurant (16 tables seating maybe 50 people) has a few stalwart dishes backing up the seasonally rotating menu. The latter might include grilled chinook with chanterelles, arugula salad with goat cheese, and other culinary expressions of the region. Entrées run $18–26 and elaborate salads and small plates, $10–12. The front porch of Paley's turn-of-the century Victorian makes outdoor dining on a summer night (and other times of year thanks to radiant heat from overhead lights) a pleasure, particularly for those who find the tight interior inhibiting. Open every night for dinner.

Across the street from Paley's, **Wildwood** (1221 N.W. 21st Ave., 503/248-9663) is another shrine to Northwest cuisine. While entrée prices run high for dishes such as mesquite roasted leg of lamb, such signature starters as skillet roasted Washington mussels in a tomato saffron garlic broth and wood-oven baked sweet onion and bacon pizza let you enjoy lunch or a light dinner for around $10. This warm, inviting space is on the dance card of every visiting "foodie," so make reservations. Open Mon.–Sat. for lunch, Sunday for brunch, nightly for dinner at 5:30 P.M.

The **Bread and Ink** (3610 S.E. Hawthorne, 503/239-4756) is known as *the* gathering place in the Hawthorne neighborhood. For breakfast, an assortment of homemade breads and imaginative omelettes will sustain you. Later on in the week, lunchtime diners line up for a massive burger topped with Gruyere cheese and Bermuda onion and locally esteemed salmon sandwiches. Dinner is a primer on Northwest cuisine—whatever's in season, the freshest ingredients, creatively prepared. Breakfast and lunch can run in the $7–15 range, dinner $15–23. Open daily.

3 Doors Down (1429 S.E. 37th Ave., 503/236-6886), as its name implies, is a few doors away from Hawthorne Boulevard. Dishes such as roasted salmon or halibut with pancetta and chanterelles, and baked steamer clams with garlic and wine, have made the Italian-accented menu here a favorite. This reservationless restaurant is filled to overflowing Tues.–Sat., so get here before 6 P.M. or prepare to wait for a table.

Caprial's Bistro and Wine (7015 S.E. Milwaukie Ave., 503/236-6457) turns out a changing chalkboard menu of visually stunning, complex, creative dishes inspired by Caprial Pence, who oversees this restaurant with the same geniality that characterizes her TV show. Expect to pay around $20 for a dinner entrée and salad. What you're paying for can best be appreciated by Caprial's treatment of salmon. Instead of the tired preparations of this regional staple, you might get it here baked in a chive-breadcrumb crust with sorrel stuffing, topped by a pinch of melted butter and lemon. The nominal corkage fee charged for wine purchased at retail prices is also noteworthy. And if you're as impressed as we were, you can buy Caprial's cookbook on your way out of this spacious yet cozy restaurant. Open for lunch and dinner; closed Sunday and Monday.

SEAFOOD

Dan and Louis Oyster Bar (208 S.W. Ankeny, 503/227-5906) is a 1907 treasure trove of maritime memorabilia and antiques as well as oyster stew made with prized Yaquina Bay oysters. The owner's ancestors helped start the oyster farm on the coast that made these bivalves famous at the turn of the century. You can enjoy this legacy today along with other fresh Oregon seafood (most entrées start at $16). While it ain't exactly cutting-edge cuisine, this restaurant's affordability and decor make it a good choice for family dining. Couple a weekend meal here with a visit to nearby Saturday Market. Open daily for lunch and dinner.

Jake's Famous Crawfish (901 S.W. 12th St., 503/226-1419) is not just famous for those lobsterlike denizens of the Oregon freshwater deep. It is also renowned for the widest-ranging seafood menu in the Northwest and one of the most extensive Oregon wine lists. The largest privately owned fine art collection in the region also graces the mahogany-paneled confines of Jake's. Nevertheless, it's the local crawfish (available May–Sept.) that let the restaurant make a name for itself. Other specialties include clam chowder, smoked salmon and sturgeon, steamed butter clams, spring chinook salmon, bouillabaisse, and the best Irish coffee in town. The menu's entrée prices run $9–27 for lunch and dinner here. Getting reserved seating in this 100-plus-year-old landmark is often difficult, but not enough to deter dozens of reservationless people who might wait more than an hour for a table. Open weekdays for lunch and dinner; weekends dinner only.

McCormick and Schmick's (235 S.W. 1st Ave., 503/224-7522) has venerable roots—it's the offspring of century-old Jake's restaurant and enjoys a location in the historic Failing Building. Despite its bloodline and Victorian digs, this place is inclined to experiment with such avant-garde combinations as Cajun seared rockfish with lime cilantro butter sauce or seafood stir-fry with lemon ginger glaze. More straightforward fare can also be found on this restaurant's extensive menu and "fresh sheet." Expect to pay $13–22 for a full dinner. Open daily.

Huber's (411 S.W. 3rd, 503/228-5686) bills itself as the oldest restaurant in town, dating back to 1879. Spanish coffee served with a flame-juggling flourish and the best turkey dinner in town are claims to fame here, but the draw for many patrons is the chance to dine surrounded by tropical hardwoods, stained glass, and the glory that was Portland in the 19th century. Prices range $7–13 for lunch, $9–20 for dinner.

For dinner in a classic setting, try **Jake's Grill** (Governor Hotel, S.W. 10th and Alder, 503/220-1850 or 800/554-3456; see "Hotels" earlier in this chapter), an offspring of a famous seafood restaurant but with a different emphasis than its patrimony might suggest. Jake's dinner menu is not exclusively pricey steaks, chops, and seafood ($10–25). Expertly prepared, affordable comfort food such as chicken pot pie also shows up on the menu. Open for lunch and dinner; closed Sunday.

Salty's on the Columbia (3839 N.E. Marine Dr., 503/288-4444) is a great choice for Columbia Gorge–bound travelers. The river frontage and fish-on-ice displays that greet you set the mood for a seafood feast. Bills can run high ($30 per person for dinner is common), so save this one for an occasion. Otherwise, lunch prices ($12–16) might fit better into your budget. Many fresh specials supplement the menu; smoked alderwood salmon is a specialty here. When you emerge from the restaurant, fair-weather views of Mount Hood can provide the finishing touch to your dining pleasure. Salty's also runs a free shuttle to and from downtown and many local hotels. Open daily for lunch and dinner; Sunday meals include brunch.

ASIAN

Japanese
Koji Osakaya (several blocks north of Pioneer Square at 606 S.W. Broadway, 503/294-1169,

among several other outlets) is a reliable choice for Japanese food. This outpost of sushi, soba, and teriyaki can accommodate everyone from hard-core devotees of fresh raw fish to the most finicky vegetarian. You can spend $5 on a roll or as much at $20 for assorted sashimi. Close quarters and no reservations occasionally create a wait for a table, but you'll leave satisfied. Open daily for lunch and dinner.

Thai

Typhoon! (400 S.W. Broadway at Hotel Lucia, 503/224-8285, or 2310 N.W. Everett St.; 503/243-7557) has graced the pages of national gourmet magazines and other high profile media. What all the fuss is about is Thai food reflecting the culinary and aesthetic sensibilities of the chef/owner Bo Kline. This is as evident in the boldly colorful decor of its Northwest Everett location and ornate presentation on each plate as it is from one bite of *miang kum*. Inspired by Thai street food, this build-it-yourself dish consists of fresh spinach leaves wrapped around toasted coconut, dried shrimp, shallots, ginger, and Thai chilies, topped with plum sauce. Seafood dishes such as Fish on Fire (halibut flambé with curry sauce) and Bags of Gold (shrimp wontons tied up with chives) also might make you forget pad Thai noodles. Prices range $6–8 for lunch, $9–20 for dinner. Open daily; call each location for hours.

Bangkok Kitchen (2534 S.E. Belmont, 503/236-7349) is the kind of place Portlanders have up their sleeve to catch visiting Thai-food aficionados by surprise. No one would ever guess that behind the walls of a 1950s diner facade, authentic Thai food is served, drenched in hot-sweet fish sauce or a peanut-and-chili-pepper blend that'll make you cry out in both pain and ecstasy. Don't specify "hot" here unless you're still on Novocaine after a dental appointment. Menu items do not usually exceed $8–10. Open daily.

Thanh Thao (4005 S.E. Hawthorne, 503/238-6232) is the favorite of devotees of pan-Asian food. In a vast menu of Vietnamese and Thai specialties, peanut chicken, eggplant in garlic sauce, and barbecue pork rice noodle typify the well-prepared, moderately priced entrées. Open daily for lunch and dinner; closed Sundays.

Thai Thai (4604 S.E. Hawthorne, 503/236-1466) offers some standout dishes at good prices. *Som tum,* a shredded green papaya salad with shrimp, peanuts, tomato, chili, lime juice, and fish sauce, and *tom ka gai,* a coconut milk–based hot sweet soup with choice of meat or tofu, set the standard among Portland Thai places. The rest of the menu at this warm, welcoming family restaurant in the shadow of Mount Tabor has a consistent level of quality with prices between $5–10.

Chinese

While not for the faint of palate, the dim sum at **Fong Chong** (301 N.W. 4th, 503/228-6868) is one of the more exotic low-cost dining adventures in the city. It all begins at 11 A.M. every day, when carts of steaming Cantonese delicacies come whooshing down the aisles. Even if the mumbled explanations of the barely bilingual staff don't translate, the array of crepes and buns stuffed with chicken, shrimp, pork, and other fillings are so varied and cost so little (averaging $3–5) that you can't miss. After 3 P.M. the restaurant reverts to unexciting Cantonese fare. Open daily at 10:30 A.M.

Legin (8001 S.E. Division St., 503/777-2828) is the current challenger to Fong Chong's title as the doyenne of dim sum in Portland. An expansive pink restaurant with fish tanks and large circular tables often filled with Chinese families, it boasts a 300-item menu of Cantonese specialties too exotic for most American tastes, such as shark's fin soup and chicken feet, as well as seasonal seafood specials ($6–8 for lunch and $8–28 for dinner) that are popular with everyone. A sumptuous dim sum repast here (daily 10 A.M.–3 P.M.) will rarely exceed $10. Just arrive early on Sunday if you want to get a table.

Sushi in Portland ranges from elaborate eateries catering to Japanese businessmen to gourmet sections of supermarkets. A good sushi bar for the neophyte is **Yoko's** (2878 S.E. Gladstone, 503/736-9228), located in the Southeast not far from Reed College. This is sushi creatively put together for American palates. At night, dinner entrées supplement the sushi menu. Open daily.

Vietnamese

Although Vietnamese flavors predominate at **Saigon Kitchen** (835 N.E. Broadway, 503/281-3669), Thai dishes such as beef in coconut juice and basil leaves and ginger chicken are highlights. The $6 lunch specials Mon.–Fri. are an especially good value. Dinner combination plates in the $8–10 range might include such uncommon specialties as garlicky salted squid or charcoal chicken rolled up in rice papers with lettuce, mint, cilantro, and peanut sauce. Another outlet is on S.E. Division and 39th Avenue (503/236-2312).

For artfully prepared Vietnamese cuisine served in the trendy Pearl District, try **Pho Van** (1012 N.W. Glisan, 503/248-2172; two other locations). Choose from the typical fare (such as *pho,* a beef noodle soup) or the more unusual (sea bass steamed in banana leaves, for example). Open Mon.–Sat. for lunch and dinner.

The neighborhood between N.E. 50th and N.E. 70th along Sandy Boulevard is the vortex of Portland's Asian business community. Here, at **Zien Hong** (5314 N.E. Sandy Blvd., 503/288-4743) and **Yen Ha** (6820 N.E. Sandy Blvd., 503/287-3698), Vietnamese, Chinese, and Thai influences assert themselves in the cuisine of each kitchen. Extensive menus, low prices, and high quality distinguish both restaurants; both open daily. Several other restaurants nearby are dedicated to *pho.* For just a few bucks, you get a big bowl that's sure to satisfy; other soups and entrées are also offered. **Pho 54** (6852 N.E. Sandy Blvd., 503/281-9674) comes recommended; open daily. Portland's large Vietnamese community has graced the Rose City with some of the best purveyors of this cuisine outside Saigon, so sayeth *New Yorker* food philosopher Calvin Trillin.

MIDDLE EASTERN

Lebanese

Portland is starting to see many quality Middle Eastern restaurants, but we'd like to recommend an "old reliable." **Al Amir** (233 S.W. Stark, 503/274-0010), a long-time dinner favorite, is located on the periphery of Old Town in the dark paneled Gothic elegance of the former home of Portland's archbishop (circa 1879). The fancy digs belie the down-to-earth prices. The menu emphasizes Lebanese specialties, and there's a belly dancer on Friday and Saturday evenings. The lentil soup with plenty of cumin, babaghanoush (an eggplant dip), lamb kebabs, and rich, garlicky hummus are standouts. A mezza plate lets you sample a variety of items including falafel, hummus, babaghanoush, and tabouleh. Open daily for lunch and dinner, except dinner only on Sunday.

Riyadh's (1318 S.E. Hawthorne Blvd., 503/235-1254) home-cooked Lebanese comfort food conjures the offerings at a Middle Eastern bazaar. While the falafel, hummus, and babaghanoush are as good here as we've had anywhere, lesser-known dishes such as kafta (ground beef minced with parsley, onions, cilantro, and spices) and manikish (a cheeseless herbal pizza) deliciously expand gustatory horizons. Despite low prices and generous portions in this small café, leave room for homemade halawa (a ground sesame candy) and first-rate baklava. Open daily for lunch and dinner.

Middle Eastern–Inspired

Garbonzo's (922 N.W. 21st Ave., 503/227-4169) is the place to go for inexpensive late-night Middle Eastern food. Falafel, spinach pie, and other specialties are prepared à la carte or come with such "salads" as hummus and tabouleh. The most expensive item on the menu is lamb kebabs with salads. Open from 11 A.M. till late.

AFRICAN AND INDIAN

Ethiopian

Jarra's (1435 S.E. Hawthorne, 503/230-8990) was Portland's first introduction to Ethiopian food and its mouth-burning stews known as *wat.* This may be the hottest food in the state, but the flavors of lamb, beef, and chicken assert themselves through the peppers. The spongy *enjera* bread that accompanies your meal also manages to soak up some of the heat. Dinner will cost less than $15 here, but be prepared to buy an extra drink to cool off your taste buds. Open Tues.–Sat.

Indian

A small northern Indian restaurant on the corner of 11th Avenue and S.W. Morrison has become the talk of Portland's cost-conscious gourmets. The $7 buffet lunch at **India House** (1038 S.W. Morrison St., 503/274-1017) lets you load up your plate with a variety of vegetable curries, samosas (triangular potato pastries with flaky crust), tandoori chicken, basmati rice, and salads.

swagat (4325 S.W. 109th Ave., Beaverton, 503/626-3000) features southern Indian food with its crepe-like dosas filled with a spicy vegetable curry, crispy tempura-like spinach pakoras, and tasty breads. Vegetarians will appreciate the meatless entrées on the dinner menu here. Despite a lack of ambience in a suburban strip mall and at times overly laid-back service, everyone from high-tech execs to local Indian families patronize this popular restaurant off the Beaverton/Hillsdale highway. Fans of spicy food will especially appreciate lamb or chicken vindaloo here. Downtown swagat fans can partake of spiffier digs at the corner of N.W. 21st and Lovejoy.

EUROPEAN

Italian

Until this decade, Portland was the Bermuda Triangle for lovers of Italian food. Unless you wanted to spend more than $60 per person for a seven-course dinner at **Genoa** (2832 S.E. Belmont, 503/238-1464), the top Italian restaurant in the Northwest according to Zagat and

PORTLAND BY THE SLICE

Pizza styles from Chicago, New York, and other locales are represented in the Pacific Northwest. Expect to pay $2.25 a slice on the average and enjoy a great variety of toppings.

Pizza in Portland means **Escape From New York** (622 N.W. 23rd Ave., 503/227-5423) if you're an East Coast purist who likes foldable crust, copious cheese, and conventional toppings. Open seven days 11:30 A.M.–11 P.M.

If you're not averse to paying a little more for your pizza (from $2.75/slice), head to one of **Pizzicato's** half-dozen outlets around town (two of them at 705 N.W. Alder, 503/226-1007, and 28 N.E. Burnside, 503/236-6045, open daily 11 A.M.–9 P.M.). Exotic toppings such as lamb, sausage, chanterelle and shitake mushrooms, and rock shrimp make a meal out of a slice. For price, selection, an array of organic toppings, and a stimulating campus ambience, **Hot Lips Pizza** (1909 S.W. 6th, 503/224-0311), near Portland State University, is a good choice. Open Mon.–Sat. 11 A.M.–10 P.M. and Sunday noon–8 P.M.

On the eastside, **It's a Beautiful Pizza** (3341 S.E. Belmont, 503/233-5444) has psychedelic decor, live music, and some of the best pies in the city (from $2.50/slice). These also might be the most filling slices around. Open noon–midnight or so.

The **Oasis Café** (37th and Hawthorne, 503/231-0901) may be bare bones in terms of decor, but a seat at the ample window front counter allows you to enjoy not only some of the best pizza in town, but also the best people-watching. Open daily 11 A.M.–11 P.M.

Another place for pizza is the **Bridgeport Brew Pub** (1313 N.W. Marshall St., 503/241-7179). The malt-based pizza crust with olives, chorizo, yellow peppers, and eggplant washed down by Blue Heron or Coho Pacific ale can only be described as quintessential Portland. For $5 you can sample seven distinct beers made by Oregon's first microbrewery. On warm days, the outdoor loading dock that serves as the brewery's "picnic area" feels like a millionaire's patio after the second glass. Open Mon.–Thurs. 11:30 A.M.–11 P.M., Friday and Saturday 11:30–midnight and Sunday 1–9 P.M.

The decor at **Mt. Hood Pizzas** (4611 E. Burnside, 503/622-6465) may be Elvis-inspired, but the pizza names give a nod and a wink to the snowboarder crowd, who used to frequent the former Mount Hood location. If you're not a pizza person, try the sandwiches or burgers. Stop by or order by phone: According to the owner, they've never turned down a delivery request to date.

Gourmet magazine, there was a shortage of first-rate pasta houses geared to the average traveler's budget. Thanks to a resurgence led by **Pazzo** (627 S.W. Washington, 503/228-1515), Italian food has finally carved out a niche. Pazzo's insistence on local fresh produce, meats, and fish has resulted in such creative dishes as smoked salmon ravioli in lemon cream with asparagus. Celebrities in town for a movie shoot and locals in search of something more than just spaghetti and meatballs typify the clientele. Prices ranges $10–16 at lunch, $12–25 at dinner. Great desserts, designer pizzas, and low-priced gourmet take-out items can be found at **Pazzorria Bakery** next door.

Pasta Veloce, a Portland-area chain, serves up quality pasta dishes in the $5–8 range, backed up by moderately priced soups and salads. Two downtown outlets can be found at S.W. Morrison and 10th, 503/916-4388, and at S.W. Salmon and 3rd, 503/223-8200.

Along with the Original Pancake House, the **Old Spaghetti Factory** (0715 S.W. Bancroft St., 503/222-5375) is another locally born national chain. And just as its counterpart has garnered accolades for food transcending the assembly-line stereotype of franchises, the Spaghetti Factory's lush wood paneling, waterfront location, and decent food at amazing prices belies the connotation of the word "chain." Main courses for lunch and dinner run $7–10, a price that will seem unbelievable after one bite of spaghetti with clam sauce, garnished with mizithra cheese (better than parmesan). Finding this place can be difficult but if you head south from downtown on Macadam till the Bancroft turnoff and look for the blue tile roof after you emerge from the tunnel, the only thing to worry about is getting a table in this reservationless bastion of family dining. Open daily for lunch and dinner.

Nob Hill, Portland's culinary version of Little Italy, encompassing the blocks between N.W. 21st and N.W. 23rd Avenues, has almost a half-dozen Italian restaurants. We'll profile two. **Il Fornaio** (115 N.W. 22nd Ave., 503/248-9400) has an ambitious menu that tries to tour the different regions of Italy backed up by an excellent on-site bakery (*il fornaio* means "the oven"). In addition to the pricey dinner menu ($30+ for

antipasti, entrée, dessert, and wine), humbler lunchtime fare can be enjoyed in the same bright, airy setting of brick and wood, white tiles, and white linen. Open daily for lunch and dinner.

Caffe Mingo (807 N.W. 21st Ave., 503/226-4646) has nine entrées that deliciously stretch a dollar and your stomach. In a menu that rotates seasonally, the Northwest mushrooms (or clams) cooked in olive oil, garlic, and lemon then sealed in parchment is a Tuscan appetizer not to be missed. This small, popular trattoria doesn't take reservations so misanthropes beware; even if you get here when the restaurant opens (5 P.M.), you'll still find yourself rubbing elbows (literally) at rustic wooden tables with an interesting cross-section of savvy diners.

Pastini Pastaria (1426 N.E. Broadway, 503/288-4300) features almost two dozen pasta dishes inspired by the friendliness of neighborhood pasterias in Italy. Despite semi-formal touches, pasta dishes rarely exceed $12 here.

Il Piatto (2348 S.E. Ankeny, 503/236-4997) is an intimate and popular neighborhood place with charming faux Tuscan decor. Culinary flights of fancy include dishes such as house-made white bean salad with prosciutto-wrapped prawns. While some entrées may seem overly rich to American palates, you can box up the always-flavorful leftovers for tomorrow's lunch. A multicourse meal with a glass of wine here might run $25.

Gino's Restaurant and Bar (8057 S.E. 13th Ave., 503/233-4613) serves standout pasta dishes in a charming 100-year-old building. The red-checked tablecloths and the Italian-accented dinner menu say trattoria, but lunch-time sandwiches, homemade soups and bread, and salads can satisfy anyone looking for a light midday repast. For dinner, the steamed mussels and clams is the best version of this dish you'll find in Portland. To find Gino's, just look for the sign indicating the Leipzig Tavern, the defunct historic watering hole that previously occupied this building, on the corner of 13th and Spokane. Open daily; dinner only.

For dinner, take the Neapolitan night train to **Assaggio** (7742 S.E. 13th, 503/232-6151), where the adventurous, moderately priced fare (most of the 20 pastas on the menu are under $10) is conducive to sampling multiple dishes. The name of the restaurant refers to this orientation. As such, the best deal for dinner is the choice of three pasta dishes for $12.50 pp. The charmingly rustic decor, pastas prepared with wild mushrooms, fresh pesto, and the like, and affordable high quality Italian wines by the glass pull in the crowds here, so try to arrive before 6 P.M. If you can't, the adjoining wine bar (with great hors d'oeuvres) makes waiting a pleasure. This small restaurant accepts reservations only for parties of six or more. Open for dinner only; closed Sunday and Monday.

French

At **Bistro Casanis** (1639 N.W. Glisan, 503/546-1696) you may encounter actual French patrons, usually a mark of authenticity. For delicious French dishes served in an intimate setting, the $22 prix-fixe menu is a good value with the choice of an appetizer, entrée, and dessert. Open for lunch and dinner Mon.–Fri. and dinner only on Saturday; closed Sunday.

Spanish/Tapas

Colosso Restaurant and Tapas Bar (1932 N.E. Broadway, 503/288-3333) serves small plates of Spanish delicacies ($4–15) and wicked cocktails (especially vodkas/citrus juice concoctions) to facilitate the get-acquainted process for hipsters and other creatures of the night. Desserts are served here as well. Open nightly at 5 P.M.

Mediterranean

SouthPark (on the corner of S.W. Salmon and Park, 503/326-1300), next to the Art Museum and near the Portland Center for the Performing Arts, bills itself as a seafood grill and wine bar, but it is much more. Here, Northwest ingredients stylishly accompany recipes from Spain, Portugal, Italy, Turkey, and Morocco. Begin by choosing one of several shellfish appetizers prior to indulging in paella or paprika-rubbed pork loin chops. Tall windows on the city's theater district, a spectacular wine list, and the buzz of downtown culture vultures give SouthPark an excitingly urbane pulse. Prices range from $8.50 for

tapas up to $18.50 for meatier dishes. Open daily for lunch and dinner.

At the edge of Old Town is a Portland institution. Joie de vivre is in the air when you step into **Alexis** (215 W. Burnside, 503/224-8577), but it's not just the retsina, Greek music, and folk dancing that keep people coming back. This is the best Greek food in Oregon. Appetizers such as calamari or saganaki (fried cheese) might start your meal here. You can spend an evening just ordering appetizers and enjoying the crusty bread, but it would be a shame to forgo such entrées ($9–13) as the moussaka and oregano chicken. On weekends this moderately priced taverna features belly dancing and an atmosphere that'll bring out the Zorba in anyone. Closed Sunday.

MEXICAN/TEX-MEX

The largest ethnic minority population in Oregon is from Mexico, most of whom arrived in the 1990s, a decade that saw the state's Latino population double to more than 91,000. The influx has created the second largest Cinco de Mayo celebration in the country and dozens of Mexican taquerías serving the classic stuff in down-home style.

Chances are you've never had Mexican food like the dishes prepared at **Cafe Azul** (112 N.W. 9th Ave., 503/525-4422). Tinga pie (a chicken and vegetable pastry seasoned with herbs, currants, and smoked chipotle chiles) and cochinita pibil (marinated pork tacos with stringy red onions doused in orange juice) typify what may be best described as gourmet interpretations of peasant fare. Little known ingredients, often indigenous to Central and Southern Mexico, spice up complex moles (a chocolate-based BBQ sauce), stews, and other dishes in a menu that changes with the seasons. Such Northwest takes on this theme as wild mushroom empanada use the regional bounty of fresh produce to full advantage. Reassuringly familiar accompaniments such as cinnamony Mexican hot chocolate, guacamole, and flan may help you get your culinary bearings here, but most of the time only your taste buds will be your guide. Dinner prices can total $25–40 pp here, high for Mexican food, but you won't experience a tastier intro to the flavors of the sun anywhere. Closed Monday.

The most trendy dinner spot in the avant-garde Pearl District is **Oba!** (555 N.W. 12th Ave., 503/228-6161). Upon entering the restaurant's high-ceilinged burgundy and buff-colored confines, a wave of sound hits you that pulsates throughout the several dining rooms and bar here. The animated talk and laughter might be catalyzed by the mango margaritas and over-the-top appetizers such as crispy coconut prawns with jalapeno citrus marinade and seared rare ahi tuna with mango tomatillo salsa. Whether it's melted cheese with spicy sausage from Spain, arepa corncakes from Colombia, Brazilian black bean pork feijoada, or yuca, the starchy tuber ubiquitous throughout equatorial South America, the focus is on Latin cuisine, albeit with New World interpretations. Moderately priced; open nightly for dinner at 5:30 P.M.

A good way to judge a Mexican restaurant is by its chiles rellenos. If a place can make this popular dish with a light, crisp batter so as not to mute the taste of the chile pepper and melted cheese, chances are it can pull off the whole enchilada in fine style. **Chez Jose** (2200 N.E. Broadway, 503/280-9888) passes this test and probably meets any other standard you might use to judge a Mexican restaurant. You'll also enjoy the fact that a sumptuous combination plate here can feed two people for around $10 (main courses range $6–10). Open Mon.–Sat. for lunch and dinner; Sunday, dinner only.

A few blocks off N.E. Burnside you'll find the best Tex-Mex food in the city. Behind the gold-starred blue facade, **Esparza's Cafe** (2725 S.E. Ankeny St., 503/234-7909) welcomes you with mahogany booths and a "Back in the Saddle Again" decor. While other *antojitos* (traditional appetizers and snacks) demonstrate flair, it's the brisket in chile colorado sauce, scrambled huevos rancheros, and diced nopalito cactus lightly dusted with cornmeal that'll evoke El Paso–Juarez for those who have been there. If you haven't, forgo Otis and Aretha on the jukebox for a norteño polka to accompany Esparza's

flavors of the *frontera*. Main course prices range $9–20 for lunch and dinner; open daily.

Dingo's (4612 S.E. Hawthorne, 503/233-3996) is what happens when you cross the hip Hawthorne ghetto with the fish taco stands so popular in Baja. This place gets salmon, tuna, and halibut trimmings from a supplier who purveys the filets to gourmet restaurants. Open every day except Sunday.

A newly emerging hot spot for Mexican food is **La Calaca Comelona** (2304 S.E. Belmont, 503/239-9675). Frida Kahlo–style murals and Day of the Dead puppets festoon the walls here. Instead of just the usual tacos and tostadas, this place includes combination taco platters consisting of several kinds of cooked meats and vegetables served with homemade tortillas. To ease the fire, fresh-squeezed tropical juices are worth a few extra bucks, if you can forgo a bottle of Negra Modelo, any true Mexican beer connoisseur's choice. By the time you leave, you should understand that the restaurant's name ("the hungry skeleton") refers only to the decor. Open daily, except Sunday.

In the Sellwood neighborhood, **Cha-Cha-Cha's** (1605 Bybee, 503/232-0437, with two other locations on Glisan and N.E. Broadway) is a brightly colored Grandma's house serving Mexican dishes at reasonable prices. A great place to take the kids. Open daily.

Somewhat more removed from Antique Row is the **Iron Horse** (6034 Milwaukie Ave., 503/232-1826), a combination neighborhood pub/restaurant with surprisingly decent Mexican/Southwestern food. Along with the moderately priced traditional dishes, try the chicken Belize tostada, flavored with orange, oregano, and cinnamon. Open for lunch and dinner; closed Monday.

Taquerías

Area taquerías have changed the lunchtime habits of many Portlanders. Much of the fuss is about specialties such as *birria* (a shredded goat meat stew) and tacos, and *machaca* burritos containing seasoned, stringy beef with scrambled eggs, tomato, onion, refried beans, and cheese. Carnitas (seasoned fried pork) is another favorite in burritos and tacos. Both *comida Mexicana cognoscenti* and gringos enjoy such south-of-the-border fish plates as *ceviche* (marinated seafood cocktail), *sopa de pescado* (fish soup), and *mojarra* (a whitefish). You'll also find more conventional Mexican dishes (tacos, enchiladas, and chiles rellenos, etc.) at these joints, except the food's better, the portions are larger, and the prices are lower (many items under $3). The funkily charming decor of these places might feature chile wreaths and murals to help transport you to sunnier climes during Portland's wet winter.

Places to get your taquería hit include **La Sirenita** (2817 N.E. Alberta St., 503/335-8283, open 10 A.M.–10 P.M. daily); **La Bonita** (2839 N.E. Alberta St., 503/281-3662, open 11 A.M.–9 P.M. Tues.–Sat, closed Monday); **El Burrito Loco** (3126 N.E. 82nd Ave., 503/252-1343, open 10 A.M.–10 P.M. daily, with outlets in Gresham and North Portland); **El Guerrerense** (1473 N.E. Prescott, 503/281-7168); **Los Tres Hermanos** (a van in a parking lot on S.E. Division between 33rd and 34th); **Chintos** (a van on 9th and S.W. Washington); **Maya's Taquería** (1000 S.W. Morrison, 503/226-1946); **Santa Fe Taquería** (831 N.W. 23rd Ave., 503/220-0406); and **Aztec Willie's** (Broadway and N.E. 15th).

AMERICAN

For more than 50 years, the **Ring Side** (2165 W. Burnside, 503/223-1513) served mainstays of steak and prime rib until menus began making some concessions to the culinary trends of the "heart smart" 1990s. Caesar salad (with a seafood option) as well as grilled salmon and halibut (also consider the lamb chops and chicken livers) now come highly recommended. Epicurean taste trends and health regimens may come and go, but when all is said and done, it's still the plump Walla Walla sweets that put the restaurant's name up in lights. The American Academy of Restaurants rated this place among the top-10 steakhouses in the country, which may explain the high prices.

Both construction workers and suits line up at the counter at the **Foothill Broiler** (33 N.W. 23rd Place, 503/223-0287) to order well-prepared comfort food with no frills at low prices. Caesar salad, Greek salad, gyros, homemade pies, and one of the best hamburgers in the city compel an early arrival to avoid the queue. This is the place to grab a quick bite before hitting Cinema 21 or doing last-minute shopping. Open 7 A.M.–9 P.M. Mon.–Sat.

Large portions of ribs, Hawaiian stir-fry, and a blast of hot-sweet flavors served in a bustling friendly atmosphere have made **Noho's Hawaiian Cafe** (S.E. Clinton and 26th, 503/233-5301) the dining hub of an up-and-coming "hip strip" of antique shops, quirky restaurants, and an avant-garde theater. Huge-portioned entrées averaging $6–10 and occasional live music explain the lines of wait-listed diners that extend out the door on weekend nights. Open daily.

Sayler's Country Kitchen (4655 S.W. Griffith Dr., Beaverton, 503/644-1492) is a solid steak-and-potatoes family restaurant. Unfortunately, it's better known for its 72-ounce top sirloin dinner, which is free if you can finish it, $50 if you can't. After packing 'em in for four decades, Sayler's can be counted on for low prices. Afterward, visit the nearby **Washington County Visitor Center and Convention Bureau** (see the special topic "Escape to Washington County," earlier in this chapter, for additional travel and dining tips). They have a second location at 105019 S.E. Stark, 503/823-6594. Open for dinner, daily.

Cafés

The **Utopia Cafe** (3308 S.E. Belmont, 503/235-7606) began as an espresso shop but now is known as a place to enjoy breakfast, lunch, and dinner. Start the day with brioche French toast, blue corn pancakes, or such scrambled egg fantasies as the Little Italian, made with basil, sun-dried tomatoes, and sour cream. Expect daytime entrées here to range $5–8. Across the street, all-night gourmet market **Zupans** has reasonably priced takeout options. Open daily.

Step into tradition at **Zell's** (1300 S.E. Morrison, 239-0196), a longtime eastside favorite. A late Sunday repast of German pancakes washed down by Zell's excellent Irish coffee is guaranteed to put a spring in your step. Also recommended are the salmon Benedict and any of the blackboard specials. Otherwise, their locally famous Fisherman's Stew can sate the hungriest hiker. Entrées at both meals average $8.

The **Tabor Hill Cafe** (3766 Hawthorne, 503/230-1231) is another dollar-wise Hawthorne mainstay. Berry pancakes and overstuffed omelettes are breakfast highlights while inventive pasta dishes with fish and chicken fill the menu the rest of the day. Expect to pay $7–9 for breakfast and $10–12 for dinner.

For a great meal for less than $7, try **Good Dog, Bad Dog** (708 S.W. Alder, 503/222-3410). The Oregon Smokey is a spicy introduction to Northwest cuisine. Choose from 10 meaty sausages at this budget diner's dream. These are often best enjoyed with a microbrew. Open daily for lunch and early dinner.

The **Hawthorne Street Cafe** (3345 S.E. Hawthorne, 503/232-4982) carries the banner for a neighborhood long known for its bohemian feel and ethnic flair. Therefore, it shouldn't be surprising that this restaurant serves up hearty breakfasts and lunches whose nutritional concerns are reminiscent of the '60s—but with the tastiness of Mediterranean cuisine. Moderate prices and cozy mini-dining rooms in a refurbished old mansion also make this place a winner. The farmer's omelette and eggs Florentine typify the first-rate breakfast fare. In the same price range as breakfast, lunch fare such as grilled chicken sandwich and rock shrimp pasta salad also rate a thumbs up. Open daily.

Deli

Kornblatt's (628 N.W. 23rd, 503/242-0055) may be the only Oregon outpost of Jewish "deli" food that would be recognizable to East Coast transplants jaded from too many Portland-style five-grain bagels. By contrast, Kornblatt's sticks to what works in New York. Here the "Nova" (mild lox) is thin-sliced, the whitefish salad smoky, the kugel (noodle pudding) heavy with cinnamon, the bagels boiled and chewy, and the pickles extra sour. Try corned beef hash served with egg and bagel and cheese blinzes for filling breakfasts. Open daily.

Cajun/Southern

One block away, **Bernie's Southern Bistro** (2904 N.E. Alberta, 503/282-9864) offers a complex medley of Southern recipes (such as boneless buttermilk fried chicken) and award-winning service. The bar menu can't be beat for bargain eats. Open Tues.–Sat.

Le Bistro Montage (301 S.E. Morrison, 503/234-1324) is the salvation of Portland night owls in search of quality cheap eats in an atmosphere that confirms that there's intelligent life in the universe. In addition to such bayou classics as jambalaya (try it with smoked mussels or Andouille sausage), étouffée, and blackened catfish, intriguing variations on macaroni-and-cheese redefine the meaning of budget gourmet. This is a place that charmingly flaunts its view "that the customer is not always right" in everything from its refusal to serve decaf coffee (and only Rainier beer) to the way the Chopin nocturne dinner soundtrack might give way to Nine-Inch Nails and Bob Marley late into the night. Open Mon.–Fri. for lunch and dinner, Saturday and Sunday dinner only. Open till 2 A.M. or later. They don't take reservations or credit cards.

Clay's Smokehouse (2932 S.E. Division, 503/235-4755) serves up smoked meats and fish with aromas of hickory, mesquite, and alderwood. We recommend the cold smoked seafood platter featuring smoked oysters, salmon (the best in town), and catfish. And, as you might expect, there's a selection of microbrews to accompany your repast. Entrées are in the $10–12 range.

Regarding barbecue, the current buzz in Portland is that **Tennessee Red's** (2133 S.E. 11th Ave., 503/231-1710) is the man. Whether you like Texas-style beef brisket or North Carolina pork loin, this small ribs joint operated by an hombre who has cooked for heads of state won't fail to please. The house ribs are brine-marinated, spice-rubbed, and then wood-smoked the way Red learned to do it in Memphis. Red's moderate prices ($5–11) make it easy to savor it all and still have enough left over for a takeout order. Outdoor seating in summer here is a pleasure and on weekends occasionally feature live blues music. Open for lunch and dinner daily.

Dessert

Several streets over, **Papa Haydn** (5829 Milwaukie Ave., 503/232-9440) Portland's doyenne of desserts, dispenses pricey-but-worth-it decadence. Like its larger northwest Portland outlet (701 N.W. 23rd, 503/228-7317), this restaurant also has a menu of well-rendered Northwest cuisine with dinner entrées running $10–18, but its after-dinner creations are the main reason to come. Try the autumn meringue, a chocolate mousse and meringue creation that has become the Portland gold standard for all dessert fantasies. Open for lunch and dinner Mon.–Sat., Sunday for lunch/brunch only.

VEGETARIAN

Leading the resurgence in the Albina neighborhood is a bright, quirky, veggie-friendly place known as the **Vita Cafe** (3024 N.E. Alberta, 503/235-8233). With an easy-on-the-wallet menu that pleases vegans as well as burger-lovers (serving free range and hormone-free beef), and a clientele running the gamut from eastside matrons to spike-haired students, this place embodies the changing character of the neighborhood. Local artists' creations adorn the walls (ask about the neighborhood's last Thursday of the month gallery walk) and all kinds of meat substitutes fill the plates here. Open weeknights until 11 P.M., weekends until midnight.

Old Wives' Tales (1300 E. Burnside, 503/238-0470) is a restaurant whose wholesome multiethnic vegetarian cuisine demonstrates that "moderately priced and nutritious" doesn't have to mean boring. The addition of chicken and fresh seafood, along with beer, wine, and espresso, to the offerings of this onetime "health food" restaurant has enabled it to make the transition to the epicurean tastes of today. The kids' playroom makes for an excellent diversion for child and parent alike. Expect to pay $7 for breakfast and lunch. Dinner entrées run $7.50–16. Open daily.

WATERING HOLES

Brewpubs

Brewpubs are built around microbrews and pub grub with personality. These bastions of brew helped create Portland's identity as "Munich on the Willamette." While excellent establishments abound, Portland's preeminent brewpub meisters are the McMenamin brothers. With dozens of establishments throughout western Oregon, this chain has been a major catalyst to the current popularity of craft beers. The typical McMenamin's pub features imaginative antiques, art, and architecture on a grand scale. Such accoutrements dress up their taverns as well as McMenamin-owned complexes such as Portland's Kennedy School and Troutdale's Edgefield (see "Accommodations" section in Columbia River Gorge chapter) and Portland's Crystal Ballroom (see "Dance Clubs" earlier in this chapter).

A glass or a pitcher of suds may cost a little more at McMenamin's, but the quality and selection make quaffing here a good value. Try the raspberry-flavored Ruby, Strawberry Fields, or the seasonal Kris Kringle (spiked with ginger, cinnamon, and allspice), along with more traditional brews such as India Pale Ale or Terminator Stout. Notable pub grub on the menu includes fish-and-chips and the brewers salad topped with hazelnuts and dressed with their signature Ruby ale raspberry vinaigrette, but the burgers (made with Oregon country beef) have the biggest following.

For more info on locations and music and movie offerings at McMenamin outlets, go to www.McMenamins.com or call 503/249-3983.

The **Widmer Brewery and Gasthaus** (929 N. Russell St., 503/281-3333) is revered by beer lovers throughout the country as the birthplace of Oregon's most popular microbrew, Widmer Hefeweizen, distributed nationally in bottles. The Gasthaus is the place to enjoy this wheat beer straight from the tap, still cloudy with sediment. The elegant back bar and a mix of wood and brick throughout the restaurant impart a feeling of warmth here complementing homestyle German cooking with Northwest ingredients. To get here, follow N.E. Interstate near the Broadway Bridge and Rose Garden Arena a half mile down to the corner of Russell Street. Open Saturday 11 A.M.–1 A.M., Sunday noon–9 P.M., and weekdays 11 A.M.–11 P.M.

Bridgeport's **Hawthorne St. Ale House** (3632 S.E. Hawthorne, 503/233-6540) expands upon the pizza menu of its Northwest Portland outlet with a menu featuring everything from grilled eggplant and fried catfish sandwiches to a killer stout onion soup. These are foods that go splendidly with our personal favorite brew, Blue Heron Ale, which recently won a coveted bronze medal at the Brewing Industry International Awards in London). Open Mon.–Thurs. 11:30 A.M.–11 P.M., Friday and Saturday 11:30 A.M.–midnight, and Sunday 11:30 A.M.–10 P.M.

Taste a bit of Portland at the **Rose and Raindrop Public House** (532 S.E. Grand St.,

SOUTHEAST COFFEEHOUSES

Portland's coffeehouses are a regional take on the Viennese tradition of café society—homes away from home to spend an idle hour reading a paper, gabbing with the "regulars," or writing the great American novel while sipping rich European-style brewed drinks made from whole bean coffee. While Starbucks, Coffee People, Peet's, and Torrefazione pour quality brew throughout Portland, the independent coffeehouses have the kind of ambience that better evokes the Beat era, when these establishments were incubators to a nascent counterculture.

The **Pied Cow** (3244 S.E. Belmont, 503/230-4866) is a coffeehouse set in a striking old Victorian home. Outside, a tree-shaded yard with tables fills up during warm weather. Most of the year, however, the tastefully garish interior with multiple alcoves provides shelter from the storm. Add the Pied Cow selection of espresso drinks and baked treats and you have the perfect setting to revive the grand old art of conversation. Open Tues.–Fri. 4 P.M.–midnight, Saturday and Sunday from noon–midnight.

The **Fresh Pot Cafe** (3723 S.E. Hawthorne, 503/232-8928) is set inside Powell's Bookstore on Hawthorne, so you can peruse prospective purchases while enjoying house-roasted java. At 75 cents a cup with a free refill, this is premium coffee at truck-stop prices. Open Mon.–Thurs. 9 A.M.–10 P.M., Friday and Saturday 9 A.M.–11 P.M., and Sunday 9 A.M.–9 P.M.

As you approach **Rimsky-Korsakoffee House** (707 S.E. 12th Ave., 503/232-2640), the old red house gives no indication (not even a hand-lettered sign bearing its name!) that this is Portland's favorite artsy hangout. Only the lines extending out the door on a crowded weekend might convey that the place is something special. Folks come for mocha fudge cake washed down by espresso drinks, live classical music, and people and ideas in creative ferment. You'll shell out around $6 a person to indulge in dessert (try the raspberry fool) and a cappuccino. The atmosphere of a refined house party reigns here weekdays 7 P.M.–midnight and weekends 7 P.M.–1 A.M. Expect a surprise in the upstairs bathroom.

The coffee lover's holy grail, the perfect cup, could well be found at **Stumptown Roasters** (4525 Division St., 503/230-7797). Fresh-roasted just-ground beans are made into a gourmet elixir with the addition of pure water and the French press. While the decor is nothing fancy, it's a comfy place where couches, a well-stocked magazine rack, and a good sound system compel a diverse clientele to linger. They have a second location on S.E. Belmont.

The latter combination is also in evidence at **Common Grounds** (4321 S.E. Hawthorne, 503/236-4835). Add a reasonably priced menu of light meals and tasty dessert fare washed down by Italian roast Torrefazione coffee and you can understand why this is the Hawthorne neighborhood's most popular coffeehouse. Open Mon.–Fri. 6:30 A.M.–10 P.M., Saturday and Sunday 7 A.M.–10 p.m.

Portland's most aesthetic kaffee klatsch takes place at **Palio** (1996 S.E. Ladd Ave., 503/232-9412), a big-windowed, tiled dessert house located in a tree-lined neighborhood of public gardens and Craftsman bungalows. Come in June to see the nearby Ladd's Addition rose gardens bloom and sip a cup on the outdoor patio. During Portland's dreary winter, the books, board games, and intimate corners complement the rich cakes and espresso here to combat seasonal affective disorder. Mon.–Fri. 7 A.M.–11 P.M., Saturday and Sunday 9 A.M.–11 P.M. The #10 TriMet bus stops in front of this hard-to-find retreat.

PORTLAND

503/238-6996). A large selection of micro-brews, derivative recipes (ale-marinated steel-head), and great pub grub (such happy-hour items as smoked salmon Caesar salad and fried oysters are on a bar menu beginning at $2.25) express the regional bounty amid classic turn-of-the-century decor. Open Mon.–Thurs. 11 A.M.–1 A.M. Saturday 11 A.M.–2 A.M. and Sunday 9 A.M.–1 A.M.

McCormick and Schmick's **Harborside Pilsner Room** (0309 S.W. Montgomery, 503/220-1865) has one of the better happy-hour (4–6P.M. daily) menus as well as some of the best river frontage in the city. It also has 30 microbrews and an outlet of Full Sail Brewery on display behind glass paneled walls. Open Sun.–Thurs. 11 A.M.–10 P.M., Friday and Saturday 11 A.M.–11 P.M.

Teahouses

Although known for its coffee and beer joints, Portland boasts several character-laden teahouses. The rainy clime seems to be conducive to sipping tea while contemplating the nature of life.

The **Tao of Tea** (3430 S.E. Belmont, 503/736-0119) is a feat of architecture and design. Bamboo, reclaimed wood, low tables, and Asian artifacts unite to create an ambience that is immaculately Zen. The teahouse proffers over 100 teas from around the world. Among their most popular are the oolong teas, served in traditional Chinese gung fu earthenware. A diverse food menu complements the tea selections. Our favorites are chana chaval (chickpea curry with rice) and stuffed flatbreads (cauliflower, miso, or potato) served with a side salad and dahl. Open Wed.–Mon. 11 A.M.–11 P.M. and Tuesday 5–11 P.M. The Tao of Tea also operates the **Classical Chinese Teahouse** at Portland's Chinese Gardens (N.W. 2nd and Everett, 503/224-8455). Lauded as the most authentic Chinese teahouse in the United States, the 16th-century style teahouse serves over 30 Chinese teas. Sitting in the teahouse, sipping tea amidst the gardens while gazing upon the reflection of the sky in the opposing pond, it's easy to understand why the teahouse

is called the "Tower of Cosmic Reflections." Open daily 10 A.M.–5 P.M.

Located in the Pearl District, Portland's "little Soho," the **Tea Zone** (50 N.W. 11th, 503/221-2130) offers over 60 loose-leaf teas (many organic) and boasts the largest selection of teapots and accessories in the city. Open Mon.–Wed. 8 A.M.–6 P.M., Thurs.–Fri. 8 A.M.–8 P.M., Saturday 10 A.M.–8 P.M., and Sunday 10 A.M.–6 P.M.

U-PICK AND FARMERS MARKETS

The free *Tri-County Farm Fresh Produce Guide* (18640 N.W. Walker Rd. #1400, Beaverton 97006, 503/725-2101, www.tricountyfarm.org) lists dozens of U-pick outlets and farm-fresh fruit stands in the Clackamas (Washington) and Multnomah County areas. The guide supplies addresses, phone numbers, hours, maps, and the best months to find produce items. Pick one up at Powell's Travel Bookstore at Pioneer Square or at the main store. The **Ripe and Ready Hotline** (503/226-4112, operates April 15 through November) can further help you locate outlets.

U-pick concessions, roadside stands, and farmers markets are often the best and sometimes the only places to find Oregon strawberries, whose ripened-on-the-vine sweetness comes with a fragility that precludes a shelf life in supermarket chains.

Portland Farmer's Market (South Park Blocks near Portland State University and Montgomery Streets, 503/241-0032, www.portlandfarmersmarket.org, Saturday 8:30 A.M.–2 P.M.) features famous local chefs giving cooking demonstrations here in summer months as well as such indigenous produce as Rainier cherries, gourmet wild mushrooms, and elephant garlic. This market operates May through October.

Our favorite weekend outlet for fresh produce, spring through fall, is the **Hollywood Farmer's Market** (located in the bank parking lot on N.E. 44th Ave. and Tillamook, 503/233-3313), just north of Sandy Boulevard and minutes from downtown. It's a smaller affair, but you can still find homemade goat cheese, live music, gourmet wild mushrooms, fresh berries, master gardener consultations, and children's activities. Hours are 8 A.M.–1 P.M. and may change seasonally (the market runs into October).

U-pick aficionados flock to Sauvie Island on the Columbia for peaches, apples, pumpkins, raspberries, and strawberries. This rural retreat is about eight miles from downtown via I-5 north to the Fremont Bridge. After crossing the bridge, go west on Nicolai, looking for U.S. 30 signs to St. Helens, Linnton, and Sauvie Island.

If the pickings are slim, superlative bird-watching and a nudist beach are the island's other claims to fame. If you go straight for 1.5 miles after crossing the Sauvie Island Bridge, you'll see **Kruger's Farm Market** (503/621-3489). The latter supplies **Kruger's Produce** (outlets on NE Weidler and 15th and N.W. 21st and Johnson, www.krugersfarmmarket.com). Here, you can buy first-rate local produce or go the U-pick route. Picnic tables and the affiliated Wildbirds Nursery featuring U-cut flowers add to the appeal.

Information and Services

Portland's visitor-information resources are far-reaching and extensive. Begin at Portland Oregon Visitors Association, **POVA** (26 S.W. Salmon St., Portland 97218, 503/275-8355 or 800/962-3700, www.pova.org). This facility sits across Front Avenue from Waterfront Park's beautiful fountain. Hours are Mon.–Fri. 9 A.M.–5:30 P.M., Saturday 9 A.M.–4 P.M., and Sunday 10 A.M.–2 P.M. In addition to knowledgeable personnel, POVA has the most complete collection of travel-information pamphlets in the state. While Portland is naturally the focus of most of these publications, materials about every part of the state fill the racks here. A discount theater ticket outlet is also available here. The best free maps of the city are available nearby from Powell's at Pioneer Square and from Hertz on the corner of S.W. 6th Avenue and Salmon (503/228-4651).

Media

The *Oregonian* (1320 S.W. Broadway, 503/221-8327), Portland's only daily, is joined by 16 alternative or community papers that circulate around the city. The *Oregonian's* "Arts and Entertainment" section comes out each Friday. The Wednesday "Outdoors" insert covers the state sea level to ski level. Finally, the Oregonian Inside Line (503/225-5555) is a free 24-hour news and information service from the *Oregonian*. Extensions covering restaurants, theaters, cinemas, live music venues, coastal and mountain getaways,

public transport, guided hikes, and the Portland Theatre Alliance exemplify the scope of this service. Look for a full list of extensions in the paper's Sunday "TV Click" section.

Of all the free weeklies, most useful to the traveler is *Willamette Week*. This publication's excellent cultural listings and restaurant reviews make it a valuable resource. It comes out every Wednesday and can be found at cafés, bookstores, and restaurants in the greater Portland area. Also noteworthy, the weekly's personal ads are heavily patronized.

Portland's nearly three dozen radio stations have something for everybody. The AM band features a preponderance of call-in talk shows. The FM band concentrates more on music, though several listener-subscriber stations do their part to revive the grand old art of conversation with interviews and news commentary. KBOO (90.7 FM) features eclectic community-based programming. KOPB (91.5 FM) offers classical music and National Public Radio news shows.

Internet fans will find the Citysearch Portland website (portland.citysearch.com) to be an easy-to-use directory to the community. Restaurants, hotels, and cultural attractions are continually updated and supplemented by graphics and maps. The listings go beyond the usual electronic Yellow Pages format with content-laden blurbs written by savvy locals.

Many of Portland's cafés are wired for easy Internet access. Two of them are **Heaven**

(421 S.W. 10th Ave., 503/243-6152) and **Internet Arena** (1016 S.W. Taylor, 503/224-2718, www.inetarena.com).

The American Automobile Association (AAA) (600 S.W. Market St., 503/222-6734) has a good selection of travel books and maps and is glad to answer questions—whether or not you're a member.

Getting There

BY AIR

Portland International Airport (877/739-4636, www.portlandairportpdx.com) is among America's fastest-growing airports, setting traffic records each month. PDX is served by more than a dozen major airlines, all of which can be accessed from the airport website's list of airlines (www.portlandairportpdx.com/web_pop/SERVING.htm).

Storage facilities at PDX include lockers (C and D concourses) that charge 75 cents a day, and D.J.'s Baggage Service (across the hall from Continental and American baggage claims, 503/281-9464), with nightly rates starting at $2 a suitcase. Lockers can accommodate only smaller items.

Just south and almost under the ramp from the terminal's departure level and just east of Alaska/Horizon luggage carousels is the MAX station. The airport train merges with Eastside MAX at the Gateway Station. The train turns around at S.E. 11th downtown to head back to the airport. Onboard will be luggage racks.

Finally, the Portland Airport is situated a mere 20-minute drive from the western portal of the Columbia River Gorge in Troutdale. With car rental facilities, limo services to Gorge resorts such as Skamania Lodge, and TriMet buses equipped with bicycle racks that can access Troutdale and the Historic Highway, you can be out of the airport and off on an adventure within an hour of landing.

The **PDX Ground Transportation Center,** which is the pick-up area for taxis, town cars, shuttle vans, and other providers, can be found on the west side of the parking garage. Taxis, town cars, Gray Line, and hotel shuttles are located in the center section of the terminal's lower roadway (baggage claim/departure level). The airporter shuttles, TriMet, and airport rental car shuttles and reserved vehicles can be found in the section of the lower roadway closest to the garage.

The **Gray Line Express** (503/285-9845) will take passengers to the Portland Hilton and most downtown hotels in about half an hour's time. It leaves the airport every 45 minutes, from 5 A.M.–midnight. It costs $15 one-way and $22 round-trip (discounts for seniors and children).

TriMet city bus line (Route 12) leaves the airport hourly and goes to the transit mall along

PORTLAND BRIDGES

Of all the metro areas in the United States, Portland is arguably *the* City of Bridges. With a dozen bridges on the Willamette and two on the Columbia, the spans are both numerous and diverse. The three oldest were built prior to World War I. Bridge-ophiles can also revel in the broad array of bridge types presented here that were designed by the preeminent engineers of their day. Many of the Willamette River crossings are illuminated by strategically placed floodlights at night, adding yet another pleasing visual dimension. The **Steel Bridge**'s (1912) two spans can be raised and lowered independently. The **St. John's Bridge** (1931) is the only steel suspension bridge in Portland and one of only three major suspension bridges in Oregon (the other two are across the Crooked River/Lake Billy Chinook).

From the newest bridge, the **Fremont** (constructed in 1973) to the oldest, the **Hawthorne Bridge** (constructed in 1910), downtown bridges are located a third of a mile from each other and are, for the most part, safe and accessible for bicyclists and pedestrians (only the I-5 Marquam and I-405 Fremont Bridges are off-limits to non-motorized vehicles and pedestrians).

S.W. 5th and 6th Avenues. Available from 5:30 A.M.–11:30 P.M. daily, the cost is about a buck. Five taxi companies serve PDX, available 24 hours per day, any day of the week. The ride costs about $28 one-way to downtown.

Airport MAX (www.trimet.org/max/redline/index.htm) enables arriving and departing travelers to take light rail. This Red Line runs from Beaverton Transit Center through downtown Portland to the Portland International Airport (PDX), every 15 minutes during the day. For $1.60, the trip from/to the airport and City Center takes just 38 minutes. MAX's low-floor cars enable passenger to easily roll luggage on board.

To drive to the city from PDX, follow the signs to downtown. This takes you first to I-205

South which then flows into I-84 East. About 10 minutes later, you'll flirt briefly with I-5 South before quickly exiting onto the Morrison Street Bridge. This takes you across the river where the first cross street encountered is S.W. 1st Avenue.

BY CAR

Portland sits on or near the routes of Interstates 5, 405, 205, and 84. I-5 runs from Seattle to San Diego and I-84 goes east to Salt Lake City. I-405 circles downtown Portland to the west and south. I-205 bypasses the city to the east. U.S. 26 heads west to Cannon Beach on the coast and east to the Cascades.

For parking information, see "By Car" under "Getting Around."

Getting Around

In Portland, streets are named and run east and west, avenues are numbered and run north and south, and boulevards exist in the netherworld of thoroughfares that go in many directions. Newcomers should note that the Willamette River delineates east-west address prefixes and Burnside Street, north-south ones. Also, Northwest Portland streets proceed in alphabetical order from Burnside moving north with streets keyed to names of early settlers. Back in midtown, Naito Parkway is, in effect, "Zero Avenue," with numbers going up as you move west away from the river. (Naito Parkway is also called Front Avenue, paralleling the Willamette.) These avenues are all one-way. Traffic along 5th and 6th Avenues is largely restricted to mass transit.

Adding to the confusion, Martin Luther King Boulevard, Portland's main route in town before the Interstates, used to be called Union and the old name survives in some quarters. As it heads south, it becomes McLoughlin Boulevard. Broadway (in effect, 7th Avenue) is Portland's only undefined arterial, having an east-west orientation when it has the prefix N.E.; with the prefix S.W. or when it's just plain Broadway, it runs north-south. No rules of logic seem to apply in the West Hills when it comes to finding your way.

Finally, addresses increase by 100 each block, beginning at the Willamette River for streets and Burnside for avenues. Despite idiosyncrasies, Portland is, for the most part, easily navigable.

BY CAR

The parking situation in Portland has its good news and bad news. Even though parking meters and day parking proliferate in the city, it's often hard to find an empty spot. Even so, the parking sticker kiosks on every block throughout downtown make it easy to pay for parking (credit and debit cards are accepted); the stickers are placed on the driver-side windows. Valid stickers (those with time left on them) can be used at more than one parking place. In addition, many of the parking garages accept merchant validation stamps (on the garage receipt) for free parking. As for parking on the street, parking is free 6 P.M.–8 A.M. on weekdays and all day Sunday.

Two reliable cab companies are **Broadway Cab Company** (503/227-1234) and **Radio Cab** (503/227-1212). Cabs charge about $2 upon pick-up and each additional mile is $1.50. A trip from the airport to downtown runs about $28. It can be difficult to hail a cab here, so it's

PORTLAND

best to give them a call or catch one in front of a hotel.

Finally, keep in mind that gas prices in Portland could well be higher than those in other U.S. cities, as Oregon has no self-service gas stations or oil refineries in the state.

PUBLIC TRANSPORTATION

Begin your orientation to the TriMet bus system at Pioneer Square. The TriMet office (701 S.W. 6th Ave., 503/238-RIDE) is open weekdays 9 A.M.–5 P.M. Information can be obtained from TriMet drivers, hotel front desk clerks and concierges, or any branch of Willamette Savings. Adult fares range from $1.25 (basic fare) to $1.55 (long trips); senior fares are discounted. These fares also apply to the MAX. MAX runs every 15 minutes. Buy tickets from machines at MAX stations before boarding. TriMet buses require exact change, and you can purchase tickets at the TriMet office or aboard the area bus.

Passengers in the downtown area can ride free anywhere in "Fareless Square." This 300-square-block area is defined by I-405 to the south, N.W. Hoyt Street to the north, and the Willamette River to the east. Thirty-one shelters (color-coded by their region) make up Transit Mall. Southbound buses pick up passengers on S.W. 5th Avenue; northbound travelers board on S.W. 6th Avenue.

The first step in setting up your own personalized mass-transit tour is picking up a schedule at one of the TriMet service centers or bus-information racks scattered around town. For the ultimate aid in figuring where you want to go and when, pay $2.50 for a complete TriMet guide, which includes a map (or you can purchase the map alone for $1), schedules, and the lowdown on attractions in various neighborhoods.

Gorge-bound travelers can bypass 17 miles of suburbs by taking MAX light rail from downtown to the Gresham stop. Here catch a #80, #24, or #81 TriMet bus to Troutdale and the western portal of the Historic Highway.

BY BIKE

Portland has long been known as a bicycle-friendly city. Its nationally recognized bicycle program provides a comprehensive, safe bikeway network to increase the number of residents who bicycle to work, on errands, and for exercise or pleasure. To accomplish this, the city has created close to 200 miles of bikeways (bicycle lanes, boulevards, and multi-use trails). As a result, many more folks are riding bicycles. In 1975 about 200 cyclists crossed the Hawthorne Bridge daily by bike; today, it's up to 2,400.

TriMet buses, equipped with bike racks, can accommodate cyclists. For more information check the TriMet website (www.trimet.org/guide/bikes) or contact their 24-hour hotline (503/962-7644). For more general biking info contact the **Office of Transportation Bicycle Program** (503/823-7082, www.trans.ci.portland.or.us/bicycles).

The Willamette Valley

The Willamette Valley is one of the most productive agricultural areas in the world. Annual production includes more than 250 different commodities. The valley boasts national leadership in everything from berry and prune production to grass seed and timber. It has carved an identity as the primary source of such specialty crops as English holly, bearded iris, and lily bulbs. Coveted green beans, the highest-yielding sweet corn in the United States, and domination of world markets in grass seed and hazelnuts compound the impression of pastures of plenty.

With all of this economic prosperity, it is no wonder that Salem is Oregon's seat of power, while Portland, Eugene, and Corvallis are considered the intellectual capitals. The Willamette Valley also happens to be the population center of Oregon, supporting 100 cities and 70 percent of the state's population. (Geographically speaking, Portland is part of the Willamette Valley, but it has its own chapter in this book.)

Between 1970 and 1990, half a million people came here to stay. Another 700,000 new pioneers are projected by the end of the year 2012. The region as a whole, including Portland, accounts for more than 75 percent of the state's residents despite occupying only 11 percent of the area. Nonetheless, one seldom gets the feeling of being in a big metropolis south of Portland, thanks to bike routes, parks, and land-use planning based on environmental imperatives.

This mix of environmental conservation, excellent growing conditions, and culture is probably best exemplified by the phenomenal (almost overnight) success of the winemaking industry here. Best known for the cool-climate wine grapes, Oregon's handcrafted wines are produced in small lots rather than corporate quantities.

tulips in full bloom at the Wooden Shoe Bulb Company

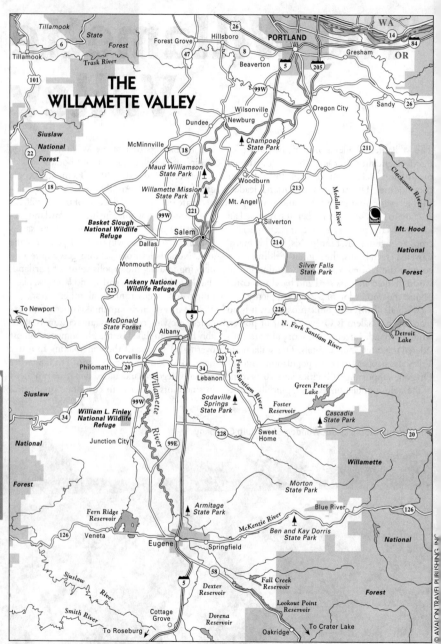

THE WILLAMETTE VALLEY

Despite the small-scale operations, Oregon vintners are giving their French counterparts some serious competition.

THE LAND

Within 50 miles of the fertile Willamette Valley are the Pacific Ocean to the west and the Cascade Mountain Range to the east. At the north end of the Willamette is Portland, and to the south (beyond Eugene) are the Rogue and Umpqua Valleys.

This 25- to 40-mile-wide and 120-mile-long fertile river valley bordered by rainforested mountain ranges was the object of Oregon Trail pioneer dreams. Here the pioneers found a land where crops never failed. Today, 69 percent of the land remains forested, with 22 percent used for agriculture.

The Native Americans who first lived in the area never cultivated the soil or logged, save for burning to provide browse for deer and soils for grasses, roots, and berries. But centuries of fire in the valley had cleared the land of trees and set the stage for the current agricultural colossus. This practice exposed rich alluvial soils deposited by floods thousands of years ago, earth that is ideal for farming.

The first Europeans who came here in the second decade of the 1800s declined to take advantage of the prime farmland, preferring instead to reap easy money from the fur trade. It fell to the Oregon Trail influx in the mid-19th century to break ground for the present-day agricultural success story.

HISTORY

Before the white settlers arrived, the Kalapuya tribe lived in this fertile area for centuries, supplied with endless amounts of game, berries, camas (a lilylike perennial with a sweet bulbous root) and wapato tubers, and fish. Deer, elk, and other game were abundant. All the evidence suggests that the Willamette Valley people had achieved a remarkably stable equilibrium with their environment. The ancestors of these people were most likely the first settlers in the valley.

They lived seasonally, wintering here, in the area for more than 5,000 years. While an estimated 80,000 Kalapuyas once dwelled here, their numbers decreased in the early 19th century due to exposure to diseases brought in by non–Native American explorers and traders.

The first European-Americans arrived in 1812. Working primarily as trappers and food gatherers for the fur-trading companies at Astoria, these early residents built a log dwelling house near the Willamette River, the exact location of which is unknown.

To early white settlers, this place offered a second chance and a stage upon which to play out their most cherished economic, civic, educational, and cultural impulses. One hundred fifty years after the emigrants' epic march across the continent, diversified agriculture, esteemed universities, and cosmopolitan cities fill the Willamette Valley landscape. Covered bridges and historic homes remind us of the taming of the frontier.

The progressive orientation of the 1960s and '70s arose from the Willamette River area's history. Once the river became the transport route for valley produce to Portland en route to gold rush–era San Francisco, prosperity and people coalesced around its shores. A century later, 20 municipalities and more than 600 industrial plants along the river had so befouled the waters that Governor Tom McCall described it as an "open sewer." The next decade's Willamette Greenway legislation put $50 million and the efforts of industry toward a cleanup. The results were the first significant salmon spawning runs in

40 years and a spate of riverfront parks and recreation areas. While much of this progress has been rolled back in the industrial expansion of the last decade, moves are currently underfoot to revive the legacy of earlier years. This should be expedited by the federal Superfund designation of 5.5 miles of the river in and around Portland harbor front.

The Wine Country

Although the vinifera grape thrives throughout the interior valleys of western Oregon from the Columbia River to the California border, what the national media calls the "wine country" usually includes only those vineyards west and southwest of Portland in Yamhill County. This is where the rich soil and long, warm, gentle growing season have created conditions that sustain the largest concentration of vineyards in the Northwest. The slow-cooling fall days engender a complexity in the regional product by inhibiting high sugar concentrations while maintaining the natural acidity of the grape. In summer, Oregon's northern latitude makes for long sunny days without excessive heat, a condition that bodes well for the harvest. These factors combine to produce wines delicate in flavor, low in alcohol, and crisp in finish, despite a tendency toward fruitiness.

A free annual publication, *Oregon Winery Guide* (Oregon Wine Advisory Board, 1200 N.W. Naito Parkway, Ste. 400, Portland 97209, 503/228-8326, www.oregonwine.org), is available at Argyle and Honeywood wineries or from the Oregon Wine Advisory Board, which will ship directly to you. It's a great source for anyone planning to visit vineyards throughout the state.

The following wine country ramble concentrates on what most people are looking for: the pick of the harvest. In Oregon that means Yamhill County pinot noir. This vintage has bested the vaunted red wines of Burgundy in numerous competitions. The fact that the world's leading pinot noir festival is held in Yamhill County's McMinnville each year also reflects the exalted status of this wine-growing region.

Despite this status, tasting rooms in Oregon are often no-frills, makeshift affairs, but can impart a personal touch sometimes lacking from slick, promotion-oriented wineries. Oregon vintners are quick to explain this lack of glitz by saying they prefer to put their money into the product. After a day along the trails of the pinot noir, you'll happily drink to that!

Of all the events in the Yamhill wine country and its counterparts, no fete can boast the world-class status of the **Annual International Pinot Noir Celebration** (P.O. Box 1310, McMinnville 97128, 800/775-4762). More than 60 American and international pinot noir producers are on hand for symposiums, tastings, and winery tours. Meals prepared by internationally known chefs are also a highlight. The three-day event takes place at the end of July on the Linfield College campus in McMinnville. While the cost of registration, $795, is prohibitive for many, tickets to the final tasting can be purchased separately for $125. This epicurean delight takes place on the last day and features a tasting of more than 50 esteemed vintages from around the world. Registration forms go out in February.

While harvest festivals, concerts, and other events effectively complement tasting and touring, a drive through the region from mid-September into early October could well offer the biggest treat for the senses. At this time, the sight of multihued grape leaves creates a festive fall

a Willamette Valley vineyard

feeling, while intoxicating aromas of fermentation fill the air.

Tasting and Touring

Yamhill County wineries and tasting rooms are generally closed in winter and open Memorial Day–Thanksgiving 11 A.M.–5 P.M. During the week of Thanksgiving, most wineries in the region have an open house. In any case, it's always a good idea to call in advance to confirm hours and other details. Blue-and-white signs on ORE 99W and its offshoots help point the way to such pantheons of pinot as Erath, Honeywood, Sokol Blosser, Yamhill Valley, and Amity. All these places have tasting rooms open to the public and accommodate visitors for more of the year than many of their counterparts.

Good wine and good food go together, which explains the creation of some surprisingly sophisticated restaurants and bed-and-breakfasts in this very rural area. Of late, a profusion of espresso shops, art galleries, and other outgrowths of "big city" culture have sprung up alongside the wine country's grange halls and feed stores. Yamhill wine touring has also become popular because downtown Portland sits a mere 30 to 40 miles away from the state's greatest concentration of wineries. Just take I-5 south of the city and go west on ORE 99W, and within 45 minutes you'll find yourself in the midst of filbert orchards and grape stakes. In terms of distance, this might evoke wine-touring routes from San Francisco to the Napa and Sonoma Valleys, but the similarity ends there. Don't expect extensive tours of Oregon wineries and on-site restaurants. Nevertheless, as the Oregon wine country grows in popularity, weekend traffic gets worse every year. Hiring a car and driver or a tour company is becoming an increasingly appealing (and safer) alternative for many wine enthusiasts. See "Information and Transportation" later in this chapter for information on these providers.

YAMHILL COUNTY BACCHANAL

Yamhill County is home to more than 80 wineries and 200 vineyards. As one of the major pinot noir–producing regions in the world, the area's local wineries also produce pinot gris, pinot blanc, chardonnay, Riesling, Gewürztraminer, sparkling wine, sauvignon blanc, cabernet, and merlot.

Newberg

Your Yamhill County bacchanal starts two miles east of Newberg where **Rex Hill Vineyards** (30835 ORE 99W, Newberg 97132, 800/739-4455, www.rexhill.com) highlights pinot noir, pinot gris, chardonnay, and Riesling. Rex Hill won the "2002 Winery of the Year" award twice, given by *Wine & Spirits* magazine. Previous years' pinots also won prestigious awards. Persian rugs, antiques, an ornately carved front door, and a lit fireplace extend a warm welcome to visitors. Try the winery's excellent pinot gris, a varietal you probably won't have the chance to taste outside of Oregon. Open daily 11 A.M.–5 P.M.

After leaving Rex Hill, should your designated driver need a pick-me-up, hit the brakes at **Coffee Cottage** (808 E. Hancock, Newberg, 503/538-5126). In addition to first-rate java and snacks, there's an in-house bookstore and occasional live music on Fridays and Saturdays. Covered-and-heated outdoor seating also recommend this spot.

Dundee

Oregon's best-known and, until recently, greatest-producing winery (35,000 cases annually) is **Erath** (9409 N.E. Worden Hill Rd., Dundee 97115, 503/538-3318, www.erath.com). Its wood-paneled tasting room sits high in the Red Hills of Dundee, where beautiful picnic sites command an imposing view of local vineyards and the Willamette Valley. To get there, go two miles north from the center of Dundee until you see a blue state highway sign marking the turnoff near the junction of ORE 99W and 9th Street. Ninth Street turns into Worden Hill Road, a thoroughfare destined to be lauded as the glory road of Oregon wine, given the legacy of Erath. Appropriately, the road looks out over vistas dominated by grapevines. The tasting room is open daily 11 A.M.–5 P.M.

HISTORY OF THE PINOT NOIR

If you look at a globe, you'll notice that ORE 99 west of Portland shares a latitude in common with the great winemaking regions of the world. Nonetheless, it may well be America's coldest, wettest wine-growing region. While Oregon's Yamhill County (located on the northern cusp of the Willamette Valley) is not yet Burgundy or the Loire Valley of France, its early-ripening grapes, notably the pinot noir and chardonnay, regularly vie with the world's best in international competitions. This began in 1983, when an Oregon pinot noir beat out dozens of French pinot noir burgundies. Yamhill Valley Vineyards came in first, Sokol Blosser second, and Adelsheim third. The French vineyard Domaine Drouhin took fourth, thereafter buying a vineyard in Yamhill County.

The state also gained attention for its truth-in-labeling law, which mandates that the varietal grape named on the bottle must be 90 percent of the pulp used to make the wine in question; other states require just 75 percent. Two wines you'll find here and nowhere else outside Oregon (in the United States) are the Riesling-like Muller-Thurgau (most comparable to Blue Nun) and the chardonnay of the '90s, pinot gris. Finally, keep in mind that 1994 was the banner year for Oregon pinot noir, with 1997 and 1998 also gaining kudos. This vintage has a spicy, fruity, almost zinfandel-like character. Try it with grilled fish and vegetables or even with roast beef.

Maturity of both the vine and the vintner will continue the popularity of the Oregon pinot noir. As the vineyards have aged, so too do the winemakers who have learned how to create better and better wine.

Close by is **Lange Estate Winery and Vineyards** (18380 N.E. Buena Vista Dr., Dundee, 503/538-6476, www.langewinery.com), a good place to try pinot gris. Oregon-style pinot gris is medium-bodied, bright, and acidic, with citrusy overtone—really good with grilled salmon.

An easy stop on 99W is **Duck Pond Cellars** (23145 Hwy. 99W, 503/538-3199, Dundee, www.duckpondcellars.com), which produces wines from both Oregon and Washington states. The tasting room features other gourmet products for sale. Open daily 11 A.M.–5 P.M.

The intersection of Sokol Blosser Lane and ORE 99W sits about two miles west of Dundee. Sokol Blosser Lane leads to a winery of the same name. In addition to its pinot noir, the **Sokol Blosser** (5000 Sokol Blosser Lane, 800/582-6688, www.sokolblosser.com) chardonnay is especially recommended at the tasting room. Robert Parker in *Wine Spectator* raved about the latter varietal here. The vineyard is open daily 11 A.M.–5 P.M. Free tours of the vineyard are given every hour, and an array of Oregon gourmet food products is on sale here. A free brochure explaining viticulture through the seasons and labeled grape plantings are other features visitors may appreciate.

Located in downtown Dundee, the **Argyle Winery** (691 ORE 99W, 503/538-8520, www.argylewinery.com) tasting room is the place to come to sample sparkling wine good enough to have graced the Clintons' White House table. *Wine Spectator* in May 1999 tabbed it the best all-around winery in Oregon. In any case, it is the state's leading producer of sparkling wine in the tradition of French champagne. The Victorian farmhouse tasting room opens daily 11 A.M.–5 P.M.; closed major holidays.

While cruising the wine country around Sokol Blosser and Erath, antique collectors can pull off ORE 99 into the town of Lafayette to visit **Lafayette Schoolhouse Antiques** (748 ORE 99W, 503/864-2720) where Oregon's largest antique display can be found in the old schoolhouse, mill, and auditorium. Imagine 10,000 square feet of antiques spread over three floors in a 1910 building. The mall promises it won't sell reproductions. Open daily 10 A.M.–5 P.M.

McMinnville

The tasting room of **Yamhill Valley Vineyards** (16250 Oldsville Rd., off ORE 18, 503/843-

3100 or 800/825-4845, www.yamhill.com) is set amid an oak grove on a 200-acre estate and features a balcony overlooking the vineyard. This winery's first release, an '83 pinot noir, first distinguished itself at a 1985 tasting of French and Oregon vintages held in New York City. Since the 1980s, the winery has maintained this standard. Open daily 11 A.M.–5 P.M.; closed in winter.

Amity

Another Yamhill County winery is **Amity Vineyards** (18150 Amity Vineyards Rd. S.E., Amity 97101, 503/835-2362 or 888/264-8966, www.amityvinyards.com). The tasting room is located on a 500-foot hill looking out over southern Yamhill County to the Coast Range, making for some beautiful sunset views. Many award-winning varietals are here to sample. Also noteworthy is the state's first chemical-free organic wine. It's open 11:30 A.M.–5:30 P.M. daily; closed Thanksgiving, Christmas, and the month of January.

For something on the sweet side, **Kristin Hill Winery** (3330 S.E. Amity Dayton Hwy., 503/835-0850) welcomes visitors daily March–January noon–5 P.M. or by appointment. Come and taste their specialty, a traditional "Methode Champenoise" (sparkling wine). Pinickers welcome.

Amity wines are also featured at the **Lawrence Gallery** (503/843-3633) in Sheridan, nine miles southwest of McMinnville on ORE 18. Several dozen other Oregon wines are featured here, as well as the work of a multitude of Oregon artists and craftspeople. Five acres of sweeping lawns and gardens surrounding this renovated century-old building make it even more of a reason to stop. Outdoor art pieces proliferate in these elegant landscapes at every turn. The Fresh Palate Cafe is also on-site, open daily for wine-friendly lunches and Sunday brunch.

Not far from Amity is the monastery of the **Brigittine monks** (23300 Walker Lane, Amity 97101, 503/835-8080). Their chocolate truffles and fudge are highly regarded, and rooms are rented for spiritual retreats.

PRACTICALITIES

Accommodations

Given the proximity of Portland, most folks do the wine country as a day trip. Should you care to extend your stay, there are plenty of bed-and-breakfasts to accommodate you.

The **Mattey House** (10221 N.E. Mattey Lane, McMinnville 97128, 503/434-5058, www.matteyhouse.com) combines Old World charm and proximity to wineries. Set in the middle of vineyards and orchards, this 1892 Victorian mansion looks inviting at the end of a day of wine touring. While some of the rooms may be small or lack phones or TVs, you can't beat the Mattey House for coziness and refinement. All rooms have private bathrooms. A homemade breakfast gets your Yamhill bacchanal off to a great start. This fusion of viticulture and Victoriana begins at $105 a night, up to $125 (midsummer weekends). To get there, turn off ORE 99W between McMinnville and Lafayette onto Mattey Lane and drive until you get to a large oak tree near the house.

McMenamin's Hotel Oregon (310 N.E. Evans St. McMinnville, 800/472-8427, www.mcmenamins.com/McHO/) has the spirit of fun, good food and drink, and art-filled restored elegance of the other outposts of the Brothers' M empire. A rooftop outdoor bar, comfy rooms (half with private or shared bath; half with communal bath), and a sumptuous included breakfast make this a winner for $75–125 (depending on the day of the week). For a good dollar value, ask about wine country packages including a tour of vineyards and meals along with bed and board.

Situated off of Highway 18, close to ORE 99W, the **Red Lion Suites McMinnville** (2535 N.E. Cumulus Ave., 503/472-1500, www.westcoasthotels.com) provides modest accommodations at the right price ($94).

Close to McMinnvile, the **Lobenhaus B&B** (6975 N.E. Abbey Rd., Carlton, 97111, 503/864-9173 or 888/339-3375) is a tri-level lodge on 27 acres, with comfortable accommodations and a peaceful atmosphere. Each guestroom has a private bath and a deck overlooking a spring-fed pond. Guests can take advantage of two common living rooms, each with TV and fireplace. The $120 rate includes a full breakfast.

Just up the road from Sokol Blosser, **Wine Country Farm Cellars** (6855 Breyman Orchards Rd., Dayton 97114, 503/864-3446, www.winecountryfarm.com) combines wine growing with bed-and-breakfast accommodations. Watch the pinot noir grow, take a hike, get a massage, or take a horse-drawn buggy ride. Rates are $115–175.

Food

The wine country is home to some of the leading purveyors of gourmet fare in the Northwest. In contrast to the emphasis on budget-conscious choices throughout most of this book, we've selected two wine country eateries that are "justifiable splurges." Given the natural pairings of good wine and good food, to do any less would be a disservice to our readers.

Make reservations well in advance to dine at one of the best Italian restaurants in the state, **Nick's Italian Cafe** (521 3rd St., McMinnville, 503/434-4471). The low-key atmosphere of McMinnville's downtown and the 1950s feel of this one-time soda fountain might at first make you wonder about such an assessment, but any trepidation will be quickly dispelled by the aroma of Nick's hearty fare and a wine list that is both extensive and distinctive. As a host to many wine-country functions, Nick is privy to special releases found nowhere else. The latter are fitting accompaniments to such unique culinary interpretations as lasagna with pine nuts, local mushrooms, and dried tomatoes; green vegetarian spinach ravioli with parmesan; and minestrone with pesto. A five-course, fixed-price dinner goes for about $40 and is highly recommended. Dinner is not served on Monday.

Another unpretentious gem of a restaurant, **Tina's** (760 ORE 99W, Dundee, 503/538-8880) is located even closer to Portland. As you're heading west on ORE 99 look for a small red boxlike structure on the right-hand side of the road alongside the 7-Eleven store across from the Dundee fire station. Tina's uses the freshest Oregon ingredients to create simple yet elegant fare. For budget diners, this place is a justifiable splurge, and big city sophisticates will recognize good dollar value with one bite of the pan-fried oysters with a lemon thyme mayonnaise or grilled rabbit with morel mushrooms. Don't expect menus here. Do expect to find local produce in season along with Willamette Valley lamb, pork, game hen, and rabbit as well as fresh fish from the nearby Pacific. The desserts are out of this world. Entrées range $15–25. Open nightly for dinner.

Just east, where ORE 99 meets 7th Street, is a complex worth visiting. **Your Northwest** (110 S.W. 7th St., 503/554-8101) sells a good selection of indigenous Northwest food and crafts; the venerated **Ponzi Vineyards** has a tasting room (connoisseurs tout its elegant '97 reserve pinot noir); and the **Dundee Bistro** (503/554-1650) is a local favorite (open daily for lunch and dinner). Along with pinot noir that is even talked about in France (with hors d'oeuvres for a small additional charge), Ponzi provides a comfortable wine bar setting.

Red Hills Provincial Dining (276 Hwy. 99W, Dundee 97115, 503/538-8224) is a cozy, charm-filled restaurant, using only the freshest local ingredients to create awarding-winning French- and Italian-inspired food, or so say *Bon Appétit* and *Wine Spectator* magazines. Open for dinner nightly at 5 P.M.

The **Joel Palmer House** (600 Ferry St., Dayton, 503/864-2995, www.joelpalmerhouse.com) is considered one of Oregon's finest historic homes, on both the Oregon and the National Historic Registers. It was originally owned by the aforementioned, who was speaker of the Oregon house of representatives in 1862, and Oregon state senator 1864–1866. Jack and Heidi Czarnecki have turned the Joel Palmer House into a one-of-a-kind restaurant that combines their love of mushroom hunting with fine wine. Open for dinner Tues.–Sat. 5 A.M.–9 P.M. Located at the junction of Highways 221 and 223 (off of Highway 18).

Information and Transportation

An excellent pamphlet and website is available from **Yamhill County Wineries Association**

(P.O. Box 25162, Portland 97298, 503/646-2985, www.yamhillwine.com). Contact the **McMinnville Chamber of Commerce** (417 N. Adams St., McMinnville 97128, 503/538-2014) or the **Newberg Chamber of Commerce** (115 N. Washington, Newberg 97132, 503/538-2014) for winery and accommodations information.

If you prefer to leave the driving and commentary to someone else, the following companies offer tours by bus or car (particularly for parties of four or more): **Adventures in Wine** (P.O. Box 30806, 503/256-5673, www.adventuresinwine.us); **Classic Tours** (503/297-2824 or 800/580-5824); and **Wine Tours Northwest** (503/439-8687). They charge anywhere from $300–500 a day; half-day rates are available.

Several local towncar and limousine services will also drive you to and from Yamhill's finest, charging about $50 per hour, with a two-hour minimum. To name a few: **Eagle Towncar** (503/222-2763); **Excel Limo Service, Inc.** (503/646-5466); and **Five Star Limousine Service** (503/585-8533 or 800/517-9555).

A Tour Through History

CHAMPOEG STATE PARK

Below Yamhill County, just southeast of Newberg on ORE 219, is Champoeg (pronounced "sham-poo-ee" or "cham-poo-ee-eck"), often touted as the birthplace of Oregon. The name means "field of roots" in Chinook, referring to the camas coveted by Native Americans, who boiled it to accompany the traditional salmon feast.

Champoeg State Park commemorates the site of the 1843 vote to break free from British and Hudson's Bay Company rule and establish a pro-American provisional government in the Oregon country. To get there from Portland, drive south on I-5 until you see signs for Exit 278. This exit directs you to a rural route that goes five miles to the park visitors center (503/678-1251). The 568-acre park is equidistant from Portland and Salem along the Willamette River.

The visitors center has exhibits detailing how the Kalapuyas, explorers, French Canadian fur traders, and American settlers lived in the Willamette Valley. It's open daily 9 A.M.–5 P.M., and there is no admission charge. The grounds also contain several historic buildings. Adjacent to the visitors center is the Manson Barn, built in 1862. The Old Butteville jail (1850) and one-room schoolhouse have also been moved to Champoeg to help evoke frontier life. Just west of the park entrance is a replica of the 1852 house of pioneer Robert Newell. Particularly interesting is the second

floor, which showcases Native American artifacts and a collection of inaugural gowns worn by the wives of Oregon governors. The house (503/678-5537) is open Feb.–Nov. Wed.–Sun. noon–5 P.M. Admission is $1.50 for adults, 50 cents for children. The **Pioneer Mother's Museum** replicates the dwellings in the Willamette Valley circa 1850. A collection of guns and muskets 1775–1850 is also on display. Admission is 75 cents. In addition, there's a day-use fee of $3. Besides the historical exhibits, the park also features a botanical garden of native plants and hiking and biking trails.

During July, Thurs.–Sun., the **Champoeg Historical Pageant** (503/678-1649) traces Oregon life from settlement to statehood. The spirited drama entitled *Doc* traces the life of Champoeg founder Robert Newell. Showtime is 7:30 P.M., preceded by history exhibits, music, and a picnic supper 5:30–7:30 P.M. The show takes place at the Champoeg State Park amphitheater under the stars. Admission is $7, seniors $6, and students $5. Recently, this amphitheater has been hosting big-time musical talent during the summer. Rock concerts and other events are listed in the *Oregonian's* "Arts and Entertainment" section.

If you want to extend your stay, **Champooeg State Park** offers six tent sites and 48 sites with RV creature comforts ($14–18). There are also six yurts for rent ($27.50). Call 800/452-5687 for reservations ($6 reservation fee). This year-round

THE WILLAMETTE VALLEY

facility is one of the few out-of-town camp-grounds within easy driving distance (25 miles) of Portland. Add beautiful Willamette River frontage, and you might consider this the consummate budget alternative to a night in the city or a pricey wine-country B&B.

Willamette Mission State Park is also in this area (just look for signs). It is home to one of the world's largest cottonwoods and the charming Wheatland car ferry across the Willamette River.

FRENCH PRAIRIE LOOP

Before leaving Champoeg State Park, pick up a brochure at the visitors center outlining the French Prairie Loop, a 40-mile byway for car and bicycle touring. History buffs, thrift shoppers, and antique aficionados will enjoy the chance to indulge their passions on this drive. French-Canadian trappers settled here in the 1820s and '30s to help the Hudson's Bay Company establish a presence in the Willamette Valley. During the 1849 California gold rush, wheat and produce from this area were shipped to granaries and warehouses in the area of present-day Portland and on to San Francisco.

Churches and buildings dating back to the 19th century have earned **St. Paul,** one of the towns on the loop (ORE 219), National Historic District status. The Northwest's oldest Catholic church, St. Paul's (circa 1846—some parishioners claim ancestral links with the French-Canadian trappers who were Oregon's first permanent white settlers), underwent a million-dollar reconstruction due to the March 26, 1993, earthquake. The church was rebuilt with its original bricks and was reinforced with concrete. Each July 4 weekend, an Oregon tradition takes place here with the highly regarded St. Paul rodeo, fireworks display, and chicken barbecue. Besides staging the rodeo with one of the largest purses in the world, attracting top riders and ropers on the circuit, a highly respected Western art show is on display at the fairgrounds. Call 800/237-5920 for details.

On the east side of the loop, **Aurora,** at the junction of ORE 219 and ORE 99, also enjoys National Historic District status. Oregon's

legacy as a haven for utopian communities began here with a Prussian immigrant, Dr. William Keil. He started up a communal colony for Oregon Trail pioneers, naming the town that grew out of it after his daughter. The Aurora colony fused Christian fundamentalism with collectivist principles, garnering distinction for its thriving farms and the excellence of its handicrafts. Despite Aurora's early success, a smallpox epidemic in 1862 and the coming of the railroad (which undermined Willamette River trade in the next decade) provided the catalysts for the town's demise. Keil himself died in 1877, and the struggling colony disbanded a few years later.

The **Old Aurora Colony Museum** (212 2nd St., Aurora, 503/678-5754) consists of five buildings, including two of the colony's homesteads, the communal wash house, and the farm equipment shed. Admission is $2.50 for adults, $1 for children ages 6 and up, free for kids under 6. The entry fee admits you to a slide show explaining the history of the colony and a tour of the buildings. Each season has different hours of operation; call for times. Items of interest include old tools, a musical instrument collection, and a recording left over from the colony band, as well as quilts and an herb garden.

The museum is easily located by turning east as you enter town. After one block, you'll see the museum, housed in a former ox barn. Sometimes colony descendants are on hand to answer questions or demonstrate historical objects such as an ingenious spinning wheel devised by William Keil. After visiting the museum, you can take an Aurora walking tour (ask for the free pamphlet) of 33 nearby structures such as clapboard and Victorian houses, and antique shops, all clustered along ORE 99E.

OREGON CITY

Farther north from Canby on ORE 99E, the road attractively parallels the Willamette River. Jagged rock bluffs on one side of the highway contrast with the smooth-flowing river framed by stately cottonwood and poplar trees. More variety is added by islands in the channel and the broad expanse of 40-foot **Willamette Falls** in Oregon City. As the terminus of the Oregon Trail and the only seat of American power in the territory until 1852, this town is the site of many firsts. Leading off the list is Oregon City's status as the first incorporated city west of the Rockies. Other claims to fame include the West's first mint, paper mill, and newspaper, and the world's first long-distance electric power transmission system. The Oregon territorial capital also was the site of the state's first Protestant church and Masonic lodge.

Ironically, a representative of British interests in Oregon country is credited with starting Oregon City. John McLoughlin, the Canadian-born chief factor of the Hudson's Bay Company, encouraged French-Canadian trappers to cross the Columbia River from Fort Vancouver and settle here in the northern Willamette Valley, inspiring the name French Prairie. To further the development of this British beachhead, McLoughlin built a flour mill near Willamette Falls in 1832. He moved down to Oregon City himself in the 1840s and became an ardent supporter of American settlers who wanted Oregon to be independent of England and part of the United States.

Oregon City was the first incorporated town west of the Rockies. Other claims to fame include the West's first mint, paper mill, and newspaper, and the world's first long-distance electric power transmission system.

McLoughlin's flour mill set the precedent for other uses of water power here. It also helped attract pioneers who came over the Cascades via the Barlow Road extension of the Oregon Trail. As a result, Oregon City became a manufacturing center. Its river port thrived due to Willamette Falls impeding the movement of merchant ships farther south on the river. Although the development of the railroad and the city of Portland diminished Oregon City's importance, its glory days live on today thanks to National Historic District status. Buildings that date back to the mid-19th century exemplify Queen Anne, Federal, and Italianate architectural styles.

Basalt terraces divide the city into three levels. Downtown is wedged between the river and a 100-foot bluff. A municipal elevator provides transportation between the commercial traffic in the lower part of town and the historic building on the bluff. Years ago, the McLoughlin House was originally situated on the river but later was moved to the heights to make room for "progress."

Museum of the Oregon Territory

Heading north on ORE 99E from Willamette Falls, look for the Tumwater turnoff on the east side of the highway for the Museum of the Oregon Territory (211 Tumwater Dr., Oregon City, 503/655-5574). Gazing south back at the falls from the elevated perspective of the museum parking lot is a fitting prelude to the exhibits. Prior to perusing the diaries, artifacts, and historic photos on the second floor, you'll encounter a time line that correlates world events over thousands of years to the geologic, political, and social growth of Oregon. This imparts a larger perspective to what you'll see in the exhibit hall. Signposts for your journey through the ages include Native American baskets and arrowheads, a horse-drawn carriage, and the world's first kidney dialysis machine (invented locally). The county collection serves as a valuable complement to the End of the Trail Interpretive Center and historic homes just north of here. The admission is $2–4 for adults, with discounts for kids, seniors, and families. Hours are Mon.–Fri. 10 A.M.–5 P.M.; Saturday, Sunday, and holidays 1–5 P.M.

McLoughlin House

Ten minutes north on ORE 99E you'll come to a somewhat-the-worse-for-wear rendition of the old territorial capital city. For a glimpse of the glory that was 19th-century Oregon City, take a right turn off ORE 99E (McLoughlin Boulevard) onto 7th Street and follow it to the base of the cliff. At 7th and Railroad Streets, you'll see an immense gray elevator scaling the

THE WILLAMETTE VALLEY

McLoughlin House in Oregon City

90-foot escarpment (operates Mon.–Sat. 7 A.M.–7 P.M. free of charge) backdropping the lower section of town. Take a left turn when you exit the elevator, and a few minutes' stroll northeast along the cliff top will have you peering across a street at the back yard of an Oregon City landmark.

The McLoughlin House (713 Center St., 503/656-5146, between 7th and 8th Streets) is an impressive clapboard-style home of the "Father of Oregon." To spare it flood damage, the building was moved from its original site near the river to this location. Behind it are steps leading back to the lower section of town. The admission, $2–4 for adults, discounts for seniors and kids, may seem a tad steep to view an unexciting collection of original and period furnishings, but the docent's ghost stories and historical insights can make it all come alive. In addition, the grounds are lovingly landscaped with rhododendrons, azaleas, and roses. The building is open Tues.–Sat. 10 A.M.–4 P.M., Sunday 1–4 P.M., closed holidays and the month of January.

End of the Trail Interpretive Center

The End of the Trail Interpretive Center (1726 Washington St., 503/657-0988) showcases Oregon City's claim as the terminus of the Oregon Trail. This status is also claimed by The Dalles (a city in the Columbia River Gorge). Without belaboring the merits of each claim, it suffices to say that Oregon City was at the end of the Barlow Trail, a spur route over Mount Hood from The Dalles for pioneers understandably leery of the raft trip down the Columbia River. Hours are Mon.–Sat. 9 A.M.–5 P.M., Sunday hours are similar but may vary. The center is closed in January.

This new large-scale interpretive center was built to commemorate the 150th anniversary of the Great Migration of 1843. To get there coming from Portland, take I-205 south to the Park Place Exit, turn south on ORE 213 and follow the signs to Abernethy Green. Organizers have selected an area often identified as the end of the Barlow Road section of the trail to set up these facilities. To find them, just follow Washington Street north to its intersection with Abernethy Road or ask one of the locals for directions to Kelly Field. From I-205, you should be able to see three connected buildings in the shape of giant covered wagons.

Visitors first enter a gallery filled with artifacts from pioneer days displayed in the period setting of a Missouri provisioner's shop. The first building also features storytellers dressed in period clothing explaining the items taken on the trail by the pioneers. The second gallery will showcase a 17-minute presentation on the Oregon Trail, an excellent introduction to the whole state and the modern-day fruition of pioneer dreams. After the video a corridor with displays of Oregon Trail artifacts leads to a gift shop and three-dimensional model of the End of the Oregon Trail. Open Mon.–Sat. 9 A.M.–5 P.M.; admission is $5.50 for adults, $3 for ages 12 and under and 65 and over.

Another way to take in the history of Oregon City and the Oregon Trail is at the pageant held Tues.–Sat. at 8 P.M. at the Interpretive Center's outdoor amphitheater, mid-July through the beginning of August. Tickets are $10 with discounts for seniors, students, children, and families. Call 503/657-0988 or 656-1619 for more information.

John Inskeep Environmental Learning Center

The John Inskeep Environmental Learning Center (Clackamas Community College, 19600 South Molalla Ave., Oregon City 97045, 503/657-6958, ext. 2351), three miles north of Kelly Field on ORE 213, is pioneering efforts of a different sort. The 80-acre environmental-study area showcases alternative technologies and recycling against a backdrop of ponds, trails, and wildlife. Exhibits on aquaculture, birds of prey, and wetlands are included in this environmental education center's portrayal of Oregon's ecosystems. The exhibits are supplemented by one of the largest telescopes in the Northwest (open Wednesday, Friday, and Saturday 7:30–10:30 P.M., $2 admission). Tours and interpretive programs are available at the center on Sunday afternoons. Hours of the entire complex are daily 9 A.M.–dusk with a $2 admission charge.

The center has a special outreach program in February. Each Saturday 3–4:30 P.M. visitors can learn about beavers, spring chinook salmon, herons, waterfowl, and wildlife on the center's 37-foot *Envirotrekker*. This vessel is moored in Oregon City's sportcraft boat marina. For more information, call 503/657-6958, ext. 2351, Tues.–Sat., or consult the *Oregonian*'s "Arts and Entertainment" listings on Friday during February. Adjacent to the Inskeep Environmental Learning Center is the **Home Orchard Society Arboretum,** displaying Oregon's array of fruit-bearing plants.

Salem

The used-car lots and fast-food outlets encountered on the way into Salem off I-5 contrast with the inspiring murals and displays in the capitol. It's comforting to be reminded of Oregon's pioneer tradition and proud legacy of progressive legislation. Close by, the tranquil beauty and stimulating museums of historic Willamette University also provide a break from the carbon-copy drabness of a town dominated by gray buildings housing the state's bureaucracies.

The Kalapuyan name for the locality of Salem was Chemeketa, or "Place of Rest." Connotations of repose were also captured by the Methodist missionary appellation "Salem," an anglicized form of the Arabic *salaam* and the Hebrew *shalom* meaning "peace." The surrounding croplands along with Willamette River transport and waterpower quickly enabled Salem to become the New Jerusalem envisioned by Oregon Trail pioneers. Over the years, the city forged an economic destiny in government, food processing, light manufacturing, and wood products. Today, it has a population of more than 137,000 people.

SIGHTS

Mission Mill Museum

In 1840–1841 the site of the Jason Lee House and Parsonage moved from the Willamette River upstream to Mill Creek, laying the foundations for the present-day cityscape. These structures along with the Boon Home were part of a Methodist mission to the Native Americans. The reconstructed Thomas Kay Woolen Mill (take Exit 253 off I-5), dating back to 1889, is also on the four-acre site of what is now called Mission Mill Museum, (1313 S.E. Mill St., 503/585-7012). Tours led by guides in period costumes begin at 10 A.M., noon, and 2 and 4 P.M. The oldest frame house in the Northwest and water turbines converting fleece into wool fabric are interesting, but those with limited time might prefer to come here just to obtain brochures about the Salem area at the reception area in front.

The museum is open daily 10 A.M.–4:30 P.M. except Thanksgiving, Christmas, and New Year's Day. To gain admission to the historic houses and the mill, adults pay $5, seniors $4.50, students 12–18 $4, and children under 6 get in free. To get to the museum from I-5, exit at

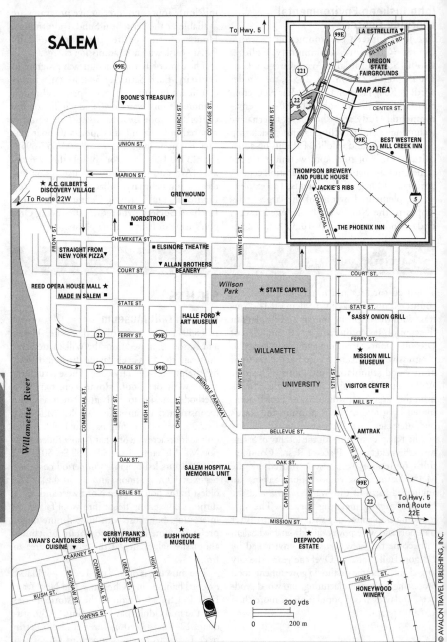

SALEM

To Hwy. 5

99E

BOONE'S TREASURY

CHURCH ST.
COTTAGE ST.
SUMMER ST.
UNION ST.
MARION ST.

★ A.C. GILBERT'S
DISCOVERY VILLAGE
To Route 22W

CENTER ST.

GREYHOUND

NORDSTROM

FRONT ST.
CHEMEKETA ST.

STRAIGHT FROM
NEW YORK PIZZA ▼

COURT ST.

■ ELSINORE THEATRE
▼ ALLAN BROTHERS
BEANERY

WINTER ST.

REED OPERA HOUSE MALL ★
MADE IN SALEM ■

STATE ST.

Willson
Park

★ STATE CAPITOL

COURT ST.

HALLE FORD ★
ART MUSEUM

STATE ST.

▼ SASSY ONION GRILL

22   FERRY ST.   99E

WILLAMETTE

FERRY ST.

★ MISSION MILL
MUSEUM

22   TRADE ST.   99E

UNIVERSITY

VISITOR CENTER ■

Willamette River

COMMERCIAL ST.
LIBERTY ST.
HIGH ST.
CHURCH ST.
PRINGLE PARKWAY
WINTER ST.

MILL ST.

12TH ST.

BELLEVUE ST.

AMTRAK

OAK ST.

OAK ST.

13TH ST.

SALEM HOSPITAL
MEMORIAL UNIT ■

CAPITOL ST.
UNIVERSITY ST.

99E

LESLIE ST.

22

To Hwy. 5
and Route
22E

MISSION ST.

KWAN'S CANTONESE
CUISINE ▼

GERRY FRANK'S
▼ KONDITOREI

BUSH HOUSE ★
MUSEUM

★
DEEPWOOD
ESTATE

KEARNEY ST.

HINES ST.

COMMERCIAL ST.
SAGINAW ST.
LIBERTY ST.
HIGH ST.

★
HONEYWOOD
WINERY

BUSH ST.

OWENS ST.

0   200 yds
0   200 m

Inset map:
99E
LA ESTRELLITA ▼
SILVERTON RD.
221
OREGON
STATE
FAIRGROUNDS
MAP AREA
CENTER ST.
22
99E
22   BEST WESTERN
MILL CREEK INN ●
THOMPSON BREWERY
AND PUBLIC HOUSE
▼ JACKIE'S RIBS
COMMERCIAL ST.
5
● THE PHOENIX INN

© AVALON TRAVEL PUBLISHING, INC.

THE WILLAMETTE VALLEY

ORE 22, go west on Mission Street for two miles to the 13th Street overpass, turn north onto 12th Street, and go west on Mill Street. If you arrive by Amtrak, Mission Mill is within walking distance.

Willamette University

Not far from the museum is Willamette University (900 State St., 503/370-6300), the oldest institution of higher learning west of the Mississippi. It began as the Oregon Institute in 1842, a school that Methodist missionary Jason Lee founded to instill Christian values among the settlers. Over the years, Willamette University has turned out its share of Oregon politicos, including longtime senators Mark Hatfield and Bob Packwood. It also has to be one of the prettiest campuses in the nation.

The campus is one of Salem's many oases of greenery that soften the hard edge of a city dominated by government buildings and nondescript downtown thoroughfares. Campus landscape architecture features a Japanese garden (the Martha Springer Garden, at the southeast corner of campus, also boasts roses, a rock garden, and an English perennial garden), ornate fountains, and a grove of five sequoias six feet in diameter. When you stand in the middle of these redwoods, you should be able to discern a star pattern formed by their canopies, giving rise to the name "star trees." This grove, which sits between the state capitol and Collins Hall (home of the science departments), has beside it an Oregon rock of ages. Found atop Ankeny Hill in Salem, the granite boulder floated down from northeastern Washington on an ice raft during the same Missoula Floods that shaped the Columbia River Gorge eons ago. This glacial erratic stands as a reminder that the Willamette Valley is largely composed of Lake Missoula sediments. In Collins Hall, crystals and exhibits on Oregon glacial activity join an impressive taxidermic array of Oregon wildlife. There's no admission charge and it's open during university hours. Finally, if you're hungry, the food court at the student union, Goudy Commons, is exceptional, reasonably priced, and with enough variety to suit all tastes.

the State Capitol Mall in Salem

State Capitol

If visiting the State Capitol (900 N.E. Court St., 503/986-1388) strikes you as the kind of saccharine excursion best reserved for a first-grade class trip, you're in for a pleasant surprise. The marble halls of Oregon government are adorned with attractive murals, paintings, and sculptures of the seminal events in this state's inspiring history. These incidents are given eloquent voice by on-site tour guides whose commentary is sure to fill in any gaps in your understanding of this pioneer saga. The capitol is located on Court Street between West Summer and East Summer Streets, just north of Willamette University.

Atop the capitol dome is a gold-leafed bronze statue of a bearded, axe-wielding pioneer. Massive marble sculptures flank the main entrance—*Covered Wagons* on the west side and *Lewis and Clark by Sacajawea* on the east. Maps of the Oregon Trail and the route of Lewis and Clark are visible on the backs of the statues. The symbolism is sustained after you enter the double glass doors to the rotunda. Your eyes will immediately be drawn to an eight-foot-diameter bronze state seal, set into the floor, which juxtaposes an eagle in flight, a sailing ship, a covered wagon, and forests. The 33 marble steps beyond the cordoned-off emblem lead up to the House and Senate chambers, and symbolize Oregon's place as the 33rd state to enter the Union. Four large murals adorning

THE WILLAMETTE VALLEY

the rose travertine walls of the rotunda illustrate the settlement and growth of Oregon: Robert Gray sailing into the Columbia estuary in 1792; Lewis and Clark at Celilo Falls in 1805; the first white women to cross the continent being welcomed by Dr. John McLoughlin in 1836; and the first wagon train on the Oregon Trail in 1843. Bronze reliefs and smaller murals symbolic of Oregon's industries also are here. The best part of the capitol is the legislative chambers, up the sweeping marble staircases.

Near the ceiling in the Senate and House chambers are friezes depicting an honor roll of people who influenced the growth and settlement of Oregon. Included are Thomas Jefferson, who sanctioned the Lewis and Clark expedition, and Thomas Condon, native son and naturalist extraordinaire. Also among the names are those of six women, headed by Lewis and Clark's interpreter-guide Sacajawea. The biggest surprise in the array might be John Quincy Adams, who determined the southern boundary of Oregon when he was secretary of state. In both legislative chambers look for forestry, agricultural, and fishing symbols woven into the carpets; murals about the coming of statehood are behind the speakers' rostrums.

Among the many architecturally eye-catching features to be found in the capitol are the rotunda's black marble, the House chamber walls and furnishings of golden oak, black walnut room appointments in the Senate, a walnut-paneled governor's office, and bronze doorknobs inlaid with the state seal throughout the building. There is also a carved myrtlewood table inlaid with a mosaic of the capitol in the reception area outside the governor's suite between the House and the Senate. All this was paid for with part of the $2 million it took to build the capitol in 1938.

If you don't want to roam independently, free half-hour building tours are given on the hour weekdays 9 A.M.–4 P.M. and Saturday 9 A.M.–3 P.M., with a lunch break on all days noon–1 P.M. Sunday tours are given on the hour at noon, 1, 2, and 3 P.M.

A tower at the top of the capitol dome gives a superlative view of the valley and surrounding Cascade peaks, worth the 121-step climb from the fourth floor. It's open Memorial Day–Sept. (but closes when the temperature reaches 90° F) and other times of the year by appointment; call 541/986-1388 for tour information. Also worth a look is the ongoing exhibit of outstanding Oregon artists in the governor's ceremonial office upstairs. Downstairs is a fine gift shop of Oregon-made crafts, food, and other indigenous items. You'll also find a café. On the west side of the building (Court Street entrance) is an indoor visitor information kiosk.

To get to the Oregon State Capitol from I-5, take Exit 253 to ORE 22 West. Take the Willamette University/State Offices Exit and follow the signs for 12th Street/State Offices. Turn left onto Court Street.

State Archives Building

At the entrance to the Capitol Mall on North Summer Street, another softly arched marble building has become a popular destination, but not just for the purposes of soaking in Oregon's pioneer and political traditions. The luxurious interior decor of the new state archives building is viewed by Oregonians as a symbol of bureaucratic extravagance in an era of belt-tightening for everyone else. They come here and glare at $127-a-square-yard carpet covering $180-a-square-yard travertine limestone floors, all illuminated by light fixtures costing $5,000 apiece.

Overpriced adornments notwithstanding, the quilt of Oregon historical scenes on the second floor and other thematic objets d'art are both aesthetically pleasing and inspiring. In this vein, anyone who goes to look at the archives themselves will come away with a special perspective on pioneer history. It's hard not to get chills as you read the scrawled accounts of a meeting of early state leaders, or first-hand descriptions of settler life. Original documents relating to the Oregon Territory as well as the first copy of the state constitution also highlight this paper trail. It's all summed up quite well by the words below a glass mural of the pioneers in the reception area: "To think we came all that way, risked everything, used our bodies as plows, and arrived here with our lives."

Capitol Grounds

At each end of the capitol are parks featuring giant sequoias, magnolias, and camperdown elms. Between the capitol and the state executive building on the corner of Court and Cottage Streets is **Willson Park.** Lush lawns, a gazebo for concerts, and a wide variety of trees, including sequoia, Port Orford cedar, Asian cedar, blue spruce, mountain ash, dogwood, and incense cedar, invite a picnic. Two large multicolored rose gardens bloom through much of the year to garnish your spread, and a trio of bronze beavers make the perfect lunch companions. Also to the west of the building are the beautiful E. M. Waite Memorial Fountain and a replica of the Liberty Bell. To the east is **Capitol Park,** where you can admire Corinthian columns salvaged from the old capitol (destroyed by fire in 1935) and statues of Dr. John McLoughlin, Reverend Jason Lee, and the circuit rider, honoring horseback evangelists to the pioneers during the era of missionary zeal.

The oldest government building in Salem is the **Supreme Court building** (1147 State St.) dating back to 1914. It's located to the east of the capitol on the southern half of the block across Waverly Street, facing State Street and bounded by 12th Street. The building's facade is white terra-cotta, and the marble interior has tile flooring. Visual highlights include an ornate stairwell and a stained-glass skylight in the third-floor courtroom framing a replica of the Oregon state seal. Above all, don't miss the public restrooms. Tastefully appointed in marble, oak, and tile, these facilities were described in *Oregon* magazine as "doing justice to public needs."

South of the legislative building and the campus are some other places that encourage a step back in time. The historic **Deepwood Estate** (1116 S.E. Mission St., 503/363-1825) features tours of an elegant 1894 Queen Anne–style home with hand-carved woodwork, gorgeous stained-glass windows, and a well-marked nature trail. English formal gardens here evoke a more genteel era, and the Pringle Creek Trail's native flora and the public greenhouse's tropical plants have a timeless appeal. Parking is at 12th and Lee Streets near the greenhouse. The Deepwood Estate is open May–Sept., noon–4:30 P.M. every day except

Saturday. Winter hours are Sunday, Monday, Wednesday, and Friday 1–4 P.M.; the grounds are closed on holidays. Admission is $4, with discounts for children and seniors. Sit in Deepwood's pagoda-like gazebo with the scent of boxwood heavy in the air on a spring afternoon and you'll soon forget the hue and cry of political proceedings at the capitol.

Bush House and Park

Bush House Museum (600 Mission St., 503/363-4714) is located in Bush Pasture Park off Mission, High, and Bush Streets. This 1877 Victorian, with many original furnishings, is the former home of pioneer banker and newspaper publisher Asahel Bush, who once wrote about his competitor, "There's not a brothel in the land that would not have been disgraced by the presence of the *Oregonian.*" Even if you're not big on house tours, the Italian marble fireplaces and elegant walnut-and-mahogany staircase are worth a look. The museum is open Sept.–May, Tues.–Sun. 2–5 P.M., and June–Aug., Tues.–Sun. noon–5 P.M. The last tour begins at 4:30 P.M. Adults pay $3, with discounts for students and seniors. The house is part of the 80-acre Bush Pasture Park. Besides being a sylvan retreat for picnickers and sports enthusiasts, the park is home to the **Bush Barn Art Center** (541/581-2228). Located next to the Bush House, this center features two galleries with monthly exhibits. On the grounds you'll also find the Bush Conservatory Greenhouse and rose gardens. The Bush Barn hours are Tues.–Fri. 10 A.M.–5 P.M., Saturday 1–5 P.M. The conservatory is open Mon.–Fri. 8 A.M.–4 P.M., Saturday 2–4:30 P.M. Both have free admission. To get there from I-5 take Exit 253 and drive two miles west on ORE 22 (Mission Street). Turn south on High Street and enter the park on Bush Street, one block south of Madison.

A. C. Gilbert's Discovery Village

If you liked Portland's OMSI and Eugene's Science Center, A. C. Gilbert's Discovery Village (116 N.E. Marion St., 503/371-3631) should sate your inquiring mind or those of your kids. Also housed in this cheerful cluster of restored

Victorians by the Willamette River is the national Toy Hall of Fame. Inspired by A. C. Gilbert, a Salem native whose many inventions included the Gilbert Chemistry Set and the Erector Set, Discovery Village's hands-on expositions incorporate art, music, drama, science, and nature. Whether you're designing a card or bookmark in the craft room, putting on a puppet show, or disassembling a parking meter, the outlets for creativity here are adaptable to any mood or mindset. If you don't have participatory inclinations, you can still enjoy fascinating exhibits like the one dedicated to A. C. Gilbert, whose Olympian athletic exploits and proficiency as a world-class magician were overshadowed by his inventions. As you might expect, even the gift shop here is a winner. Museum hours are Tues.–Sat. 10 A.M.–5 P.M. and Sunday noon–4 P.M. Admission is $4 per person, $3 seniors.

Hallie Ford Museum of Art

The second-largest art museum in the state and part of Willamette University, Hallie Ford Museum (700 State St., 503/370-6875) features Native American baskets and a third-century Buddhist bas-relief from Pakistan. Asian pieces are also prominent here. Contemporary work is exhibited on a rotating basis. Open Tues.–Sat. 10 A.M.–5 P.M., admission $5.

Honeywood Winery

Of the half-dozen local vintners, Honeywood Winery (1350 S.E. Hines St., 503/362-4111) is the oldest and the most easily reached, with a location close to Mission Mill Village. It also bills itself as Oregon's oldest winery, having opened in 1933. Honeywood produces a full line of fruit and varietal wines (its Grande Peach won a Gold Medal at the 1997 state fair, and its raspberry and marionberry took Silver). The winery offers free tasting Mon.–Fri. 9 A.M.–6 P.M., Saturday 10 A.M.–5 P.M., and Sunday 1–5 P.M., all year long. Salem's wine country is largely clustered along ORE 22 (north of the highway) in a region known as the Eola Hills. Ask the folks at the Honeywood tasting room for information.

Reed Opera House Mall

At the corner of Court and Liberty is the Reed Opera House Mall. This one-time venue of minstrel shows and other pioneer cultural activities still retains a brick facade and long windows but has new tenants—the boutiques and restaurants of a tastefully rendered shopping mall. After you admire the restoration, which helped this atrium gain admittance to the National Register of Historic Places, peek inside a shop that does justice to the creative traditions of the frontier. **Made in Salem** (189 N.E. Liberty St., 541/399-8197) is a crafts co-op of four dozen local artisans. Creations made from stained glass, Oregon's exotic woods, and other media are featured, along with artists working on-site. Open Mon.–Thurs. 10 A.M.–6 P.M., Friday 10 A.M.–9 P.M., Sunday noon–3 P.M.

Gardens

Both **Schreiner's Iris Gardens** (3625 N.E. Quinaby Rd., Salem 97305, 503/393-3232) and **Cooley's Gardens** (11553 N.E. Silverton Rd., Silverton 97381, 503/873-5463) bill themselves as the world's largest iris growers. Both claims are correct based on different criteria, but the important thing to remember is that from mid-May through the first week of June these are the places to visit to take in the peak blossom seasons. Schreiner's is seven miles north of Salem next to I-5, and Cooley's is on the way to Silver Falls State Park. Both places can be visited 8 A.M.–dusk.

SPORTS AND RECREATION
Golf

The **Salem Golf Club** (2025 Golf Course Rd., 503/363-6652) is one of the best public courses in the state. Another option is **Santiam Golf Course** (8724 Golf Club Rd., Aumsville, 503/769-3485). If you drive 15 minutes east on ORE 22 (at Exit 12), you can look forward to combining a round of golf with a walk in the country. Low greens fees and a full-service restaurant and bar add to the pleasure. Open seven days. Greens fees are $18–29. The new and highly regarded **Creekside Golf Course** is open

ENCHANTED FOREST

Seven miles south of Salem off I-5 on Exit 248 is the Enchanted Forest (8462 Enchanted Way, Turner 97392, 503/363-3060, www.enchanted-forest.com), one man's answer to Walt Disney. An enterprising Oregonian has single-handedly built a false-front western town, a haunted house, and many more attractions.

In the 1960s Roger Tofte, the father of four young children, realized there was very little for a family to see and do together in Salem. He formulated the idea for a theme park where he could use his creative talents. Though he had very little time or money to make his dream a reality, he was able to purchase the original 20 acres of land off I-5 for $4,000, in monthly payments of $50. In 1964, he began construction.

Finally, in 1971, Tofte officially opened the park. Over the years, Tofte has successfully incorporated three of his children into the business: Susan (co-op-erations officer and artistic director), Mary (co-operations officer and chief financial officer), and Ken (head of attractions development and ride maintenance).

Whether it's the old woman who lived in the shoe, the seven dwarves' cottage, or Alice in Wonderland's rabbit hole, these and other nursery-rhyme and fairy-tale re-creations will get thumbs up from anyone under 99 years of age. One of the most inventive attractions is an old English village, which features a life-sized Geppetto and Pinocchio telling stories punctuated by animated characters popping their heads out of windows.

The park is open daily 9:30 A.M.–6 P.M. March 15–March 31; April weekends only; May–Labor Day daily; September weekends only. Admission is $7.95 for adults, $6.95 for ages 3–12, extra for the bobsled ride and haunted house.

---

to the public Mon.–Fri. Tee times may be reserved up to five days in advance by calling 503/361-0210.

Camping

Many of the Salem area excursions are close to campsites. **Silver Falls State Park** (20024 Silver Falls Hwy., Sublimity 97385, 800/452-5687, www.oregonstateparks.org) lets campers escape the valley's summertime heat. There are 46 tent sites and 47 sites for trailers or motor homes up to 35 feet long. Rates are $12–20. From mid-April to early October this facility operates with electricity, piped water, and picnic tables. Showers, firewood, and a laundry are available. In addition to hiking, swimming, and biking, there are stables near the park's entrance.

On the way to Breitenbush Hot Springs, **Cleator Bend** (Willamette National Forest, ORE 22, Detroit 97360, 503/854-3366, www.fs.fed.us/r6/willamette) offers a campground close enough to the Breitenbush Hot Springs Retreat Center and facilities to permit day use there. Nearby, the Breitenbush River has good fishing. There are nine sites for trailers or motor homes up to 16 feet long, as well as picnic tables and fire grills. Fees are $10 a night from mid-May to late September. On Forest Service Road 46, you'll pass several other campgrounds between ORE 22 and the retreat center.

Cove Creek is a campground located near recreation mecca Detroit Lake. With 63 sites, flush toilets, pay showers ($.25 per minute in quarters only), a boat launch, and other amenities, the $16 nightly fee is well worth it. Campsites are located in a lush second-growth Douglas fir forest against a slope. Because there are no individual RV hookups, dump sites, or phones, Cove Creek is designed more for car campers, backpackers, and outdoor recreationists than people looking for a place to park a rig long-term. The campground is located east of Detroit off Blowout Road. With no reservations, a sign on the highway will announce if the site has reached capacity. For more information, contact the Detroit Ranger Station (503/854-3366).

ENTERTAINMENT AND EVENTS

Salem's recreational mix belies its reputation for being a town dedicated to legislation and little else. Cultural life revolves around the

Pentacle Theatre (P.O. Box 186, Salem 97303, 503/364-7121), located five miles west of downtown Salem. From the government buildings, follow the signs marked "ocean beaches" and "Dallas." Signs on the right-hand side of the highway, at N.W. 52nd Avenue, direct you up the hill and to the theater. This large, attractive wooden building hosts an award-winning eight-play season.

The **Elsinore Theatre** (170 High St., S.E. Salem, 503/375-3574) is a vintage theater and emerging downtown cultural venue. Check the *Statesman Journal* for what's scheduled. Along with the L. B. Day amphitheater at the fairgrounds hosting big-name acts and brewpubs featuring live music, there are summer concerts at Salem Riverfront Park.

Salem is full of studio tours, downtown art tours, and art galleries, as well as theater and musical events (Salem is the Oregon Symphony's home away from home). For arts information and tickets contact the Mid-Valley Arts Council, (189 Liberty St. N.E., Suite 208, 541/364-7474, ticket office 503/370-7469). The Friday *Statesman Journal*'s "Weekend" section also gives complete cultural listings.

The Salem Art Association (600 Mission St., 503/581-2228) puts on the **Salem Art Fair and Festival** the third week of July. This multiday event includes 200 artists, performing arts, food, children's activities, a five-km run, an Oregon authors' table, wine and cheese tasting, and art-technique demonstrations.

The **Oregon State Fair** (2330 N.E. 17th St., 503/947-3247 or 800/833-0011) is an annual celebration held in Salem during the 12 days prior to Labor Day. The fair showcases Oregon agriculture, industries, tourist attractions, natural resources, government, and cultural activities. Big-name entertainment, amusement-park rides, an international photography show, and a horticultural exhibit are also included in this blend of carnival and commerce. The best way to get there off I-5 is via Exits 253 or 258. Admission is $8 for ages 13 and up, $5 for seniors, children under 6 get in free. Parking is $5. Entertainment tickets for musical events will run you an extra $5–15.

This is the largest agricultural fair on the West Coast. It is also host to one of the 10 largest horse shows in the nation. While there's no shortage of worthwhile events, family fun can come with a hefty price tag.

PRACTICALITIES
Accommodations

You won't find many quaint historic inns among Salem's lodging choices, which is dominated by mid-priced chains clustered east of I-5, at Exit 252 south of downtown. The "high-end" choice here is the **Phoenix Inn** (4370 Commercial St., 503/588-9220, www.phoenixinnsuites.com). For $70–154, you get a "mini-suite" with microwave and refrigerator as well as access to exercise and spa facilities. Not far behind is the **Best Western Mill Creek Inn** (3125 Ryan Dr. S.E., 503/585-3332 or 800/346-9659, www.best-western.com/millcreekinn) with large rooms for $86–93. In addition to a range of amenities comparable to those found at the Phoenix Inn, such extras as a free shuttle service to the Salem Airport and Amtrak and an included breakfast at a nearby Denny's are noteworthy.

The **Red Lion** (3301 Market St. N.E., 503/370-7835) in east Salem provides all of the usual amenities, plus an on-site restaurant, and has a pet-friendly policy. Rates run $59–119.

For more choices, log on to www.salemlodging.com.

Food

Salem is blessed with an unusually large number of small Mexican restaurants for a Northwest city this size. Many of these establishments boast regional specialties from the state of Jalisco that cater to the large influx of agricultural workers who've come to the Willamette Valley from northwestern Mexico. Ubiquitous entrées in these places include *carne asada* and *camarones al mojo de ajo. Carne asada* is grilled beefsteak, often tough but flavorful. *Camarones al mojo de ajo* is shrimp coated with garlic and butter. These eateries include **Ixtapa Family Mexican Restaurant** (4405 Liberty Rd. S., 503/371-3781); **Los Arcos Mexican Restau-**

rant (3969 Commercial St. S.E., 503/581-2740); and **Taquería El Padrino** (3545 Portland Rd. N.E., 503/581-4964).

The **Sassy Onion Grill** (1244 State St., 503/378-9180) is the kind of breakfast and lunch place that satisfies a broad-based clientele by covering the traditional bases with enough forays into ethnic cuisine to keep things interesting. Fresh fruit smoothies, delicious oatmeal, pollo poblano, and orange almond chicken demonstrate a range that is very "today." The prices, however, hark back to yesteryear, with sumptuous breakfasts running $5–7 and lunch tabs a buck or two higher.

Coffee-lovers will take note that the top three leading coffee purveyors in Salem (according to a *Statesman Journal* reader poll) are within a couple of blocks of each other on Court Street. The poll-winning **Allan Brothers Beanery** (545 Court St., 503/399-7220) has light breakfasts, homemade pastries (cheesecake is recommended), soups, salads, quiche, spanakopita, and lasagna. All are high quality and less than $5.

Another hangout conducive to conversation is **Boon's Treasury** (888 N.E. Liberty, 503/399-9062). You can down microbrews and enjoy live blues and jazz amid the brick confines of the old treasury building. **Straight from New York Pizza** (233 Liberty St. N.E., 503/581-5863) sells delicious thin-crusted East Coast–style slices for little more than $2.

The Salem branch of the McMenamin's brewpub empire, the **Thompson Brewery and Public House** (3575 S. Liberty Rd., 503/363-7286) offers a casual brewpub meal. The restaurant's pizza, appetizers, burgers, sandwiches, or salads (all less than $10), washed down by McMenamin's ales, beers, or their own Edgefield wines, are guaranteed to please. Set in a charming old house that'll make you forget south Salem's commercial sprawl, the brewery is open Mon.–Sat. 11 A.M.–1 A.M., Sunday noon–midnight.

Everyone knows that a half-hour after you've eaten a large Chinese meal, you're hungry enough for dessert. Perhaps this inspired the location of **Gerry Frank's Konditorei** (310 S.E. Kearney St., 503/585-7070) across from **Kwan's**

Cantonese Cuisine (835 S.E. Commercial, 503/362-7711). These restaurants flank two sides of Commercial Street near its intersection with Kearney, so it's a good bet that many diners have enjoyed Kwan's delicacies, such as steamed salmon or Dungeness crab in black bean sauce, then topped it off with a slice of baklava or Black Forest cake at the Konditorei. In any case, it was Gerry Frank who brought Chef Kwan from Hong Kong to Salem, blessing this corner of Commercial Street with a delicious union of opposites. And while you're downing a second piece of torte at the Konditorei (open till midnight Fri.–Sat.), you can console yourself that the meal you just finished at Kwan's had no MSG and was prepared with organic vegetables (when available) and purified water. Kwan's also has dishes prepared with low-cholesterol emu. Dinner checks at Kwan's seldom exceed $15 per person; lunch is usually less than $6.

Chang's Mongolian Grill (3928 Center St. N.E., 503/373-9779) has been a pan-Asian favorite in Portland for decades. The Salem outlet is based on the same concept, in which diners choose the fixin's for a stir-fry and proceed to a large grill where a chef prepares it to order. The price ($6.75 lunch, $9.95 dinner) also includes dessert.

U-pick farms are a delight from spring through fall in and around Salem. Cherries, strawberries, apples, peaches, plums, and blackberries are some of the bounty available. Early in June, the *Statesman Journal* puts out a list of local outlets in the area (what's available where and when) titled "Oregon Direct Market Association." Fruit stands are listed in this guide as well. Many concessionaires, such as **Bauman Farms** (12989 Howell Prairie Rd., 503/792-3524) offer both self-service harvest and over-the-counter sales. Several dozen agricultural products are available here, ranging from 10 berry varieties to pumpkins. Items such as fresh home-pressed apple cider and holiday gift packs round out the array. To get to Bauman's take ORE 99E one mile south of Woodburn to Howell Prairie Road. Following the signs, go about a half mile to reach the stand.

THE WILLAMETTE VALLEY

Information and Services

The **visitor center** (1313 Mill St., 503/581-4325 or 800/874-7012, www.salemvisitorcenter.com), located in the first building of the Mission Mill complex, has pamphlets and brochures covering Salem and the entire state. It's open Mon.–Fri. 8 A.M.–5 P.M. Ask about the Marion County Historical Society's Heritage Tree program if you're interested in pioneer plantings and trees of great size. For general Willamette Valley information, call 800/526-2256.

The Salem *Statesman Journal* (503/399-6622) is sold throughout the Willamette Valley, central coast, and central Oregon. The newspaper's "Weekend" section features entertainment listings and reviews every Friday that cover the week to come. Although these listings focus on Salem, considerable attention is also given to events throughout the Willamette Valley, central Oregon, and the coast.

Transportation

Salem's State and Center Streets run east-west, while Commercial and Liberty Streets run north-south. East and West Nob Hill Streets run southeast. With a profusion of one-way streets and thoroughfares that end abruptly, it's important to keep your bearings. One helpful frame of reference is supplied by remembering that Commercial Street runs north-south along the Willamette River on the western edge of town.

Salem provides a lot of ways to get in and out of town. The **Greyhound** station (450 N.E. Church St., 503/362-2428) is open daily 6:45 A.M.–8:45 P.M. **Amtrak** (13th and Oak Streets, 503/588-1551 or 800/872-7245) sits across from Willamette University and is close to Mission Mill Museum. If you are looking for a reasonably priced shuttle to or from Portland International Airport that goes almost everywhere north of Eugene in the Willamette Valley, **Valley Shuttle** (800/532-2622) is recommended. The Salem **airport** (503/588-6314) is a few miles east of downtown. A Salem-to-Portland airport shuttle is run by **Hut Limousine Service** (503/363-8059). For short hops to town, there's Salem **A-Cab Taxi Company** (503/763-6969).

Or rent a car at **Enterprise Rent-a-car** (355 Pine St. N.E., 800/325-8007).

Mass-transit bus service in town means **Salem Area Mass Transit (Cherriots)** (216 High St., 503/588-2877 or 503/588-2424). Terminals are in front of the courthouse. Fare is about $1–2, depending on the length of your trip, and originate from High Street. Especially appreciated is the Free Zone. Unlimited free rides are permitted within most of the State Capitol Mall as well as to hundreds of downtown shops and restaurants. The zone is defined by the Willamette River on the west, 12th Street on the east, Union to the north, and Mission to the south.

SILVERTON TO BREITENBUSH

Silver Falls State Park

If this state park (22024 Silver Falls Hwy., Sublimity 97385, 503/873-3495, www.open.org/slvrfall/) were in California instead of the remote foothills east of the Willamette Valley, it would probably be designated a national park and be flooded with visitor facilities and people year-round. Instead, one of Oregon's largest and most spectacular state parks remains relatively quiet except during the summer. At that time, hordes seeking relief from the valley heat head up to this cool enclave of waterfalls, 26 miles northeast of Salem. They come to see 10 major waterfalls 30 to 178 feet in height cascading off canyon walls in a forest filled with gargantuan Douglas fir, ferns, and bigleaf and vine maple. There are also yew, chinquapin, and hemlock trees. The best time to come is during fall foliage season when there are few visitors, just before icy roads and trail closures inhibit travel. Freezing east winds of autumn sometimes make the falls here appear like ice sculptures. In spring, the mid-April blooming of trilliums and yellow wood violets on the canyon bottom is another highlight.

To get here from Salem, drive east on ORE 213, an extension of Silverton Road (easily accessed from the State Fairgrounds), 20 miles to Silverton and follow the signs to the park. Before heading into the park, a stop in Silverton is recommended. This rural town of 6,500 is the home of **Oregon Gardens,** a botanical display that will eventually grow to 250 acres—five times the size of the fabled Butchart Gardens in Victoria, B.C. With a dream team of landscape architects as well as millions of dollars and the state's dynamic nursery industry (the top agricultural entity in 1994) behind them, the gardens will give Silverton another world-class tourist attraction in addition to Silver Falls State Park. A Frank Lloyd Wright–designed home is also an attraction within Oregon Gardens.

While it might take a decade or two to be classed with the world's preeminent botanical displays, the seeds being planted in the hill-and-pond landscape off ORE 213 west of town are already breaking ground in other ways. Silverton is preparing for the anticipated tourism onslaught by launching several new ventures. At the top-drawer **Silver Grille** (206 E. Main, 503/873-4035), the world travels of the deft restaurateurs meet the agricultural bounty of the region (open 5–9 P.M. Mon.–Sat.). A few blocks east of the Silver Grille, Norman Rockwell murals adorn the Masonic Lodge wall. **Macs Place** (201 N. Water St., 503/273-8441) is a hoppin' blues joint, and there's a first-run movie theater at the corner of Water and Main Streets.

The big "do" in Silverton is **Homer Davenport Days,** usually held the first weekend in August, when locals enjoy crafts, food, music, and the spectacle of neighbors racing furniture down Main Street. Davenport was a nationally famous cartoonist in the 1930s and a Silverton favorite son. Most of the action takes place at Coolidge-McClain Park Friday evening and Saturday 10 A.M.–8 P.M. (For information, write to Homer Davenport Days, P.O. Box 781, Silverton 97381, or call 503/873-5211.)

Should you decide to stay in town rather than camp at the park, economical options include the **Nordic Hotel** (310 N. Water St., 503/873-5058) and the **Egg Cup B&B** (11920 Sioux St., 503/873-5497). Both are clean, well located, and inexpensive.

The main drag in town, Water Street (a.k.a. ORE 214, the Silver Creek Falls Highway) heads south out of town toward the park. En route, stop at the chamber of commerce outdoor information kiosk (421 S. Water St., 503/873-5615) to pick up a Silverton directory/map and a park folder. Traveling south and eventually east en route to the park on ORE 214, the road climbs up into gently undulating hills past Christmas tree farms and nursery stock.

A dearth of signs and a distance that seems longer than the posted 15 miles from town will have you second-guessing these directions until you come to the North Falls parking lot. While North Falls is a few miles north of the visitor services and facilities of Silver Creek Falls State Park headquarters at the day-use area, you can park your car at the trailhead here and skip the admission kiosk and shopping-mall-sized parking lot down the road.

Serious hikers will want to take on the seven-mile **Silver Creek Canyon Trail,** which heads down into a fern-lined basalt gully going past all the falls. The profusion of trees and moisture gives the air a special freshness, and when the sun hits some of the 10 falls just right you can see rainbows. A two-car shuttle is recommended if you plan to hike the whole loop. The highlights of this 1930s-vintage Civilian Conservation Corps trail are 177-foot **South Falls** and 136-foot **North Falls.** The opportunity to walk behind these waterfalls attracts a lot of visitors, who follow the trail through a basalt overhang in the cleft of each cliff. Bikers and horseback riders also enjoy specially designated trails in this 8,300-acre paradise.

North Falls and South Falls are easily reached from the North Falls parking lot and the day-use area, respectively, so you don't have to hike the whole loop to see both. To get to the day-use area from North Falls parking lot, drive several miles south up the hill (on ORE 214), stopping after a mile or two to look back at a spectacular view of North Falls. At the day-use area, a $5 per vehicle day-use fee is collected at the entrance to the parking lot. The day-use area features a museum, thick forests with trails, picnic areas,

Springtime wildflowers, stunning fall foliage, and more than 10 waterfalls are a fraction of what Silver Falls State Park has to offer.

THE WILLAMETTE VALLEY

retreat cabins, and the state's largest campground (see "Camping," under Salem "Sports and Recreation," earlier in this chapter).

In the museum, vintage photos from the area's incarnation as a logging site founded by land speculator James "Silver" Smith (so named for his penchant for carrying around a sack of silver dollars) and wildlife exhibits provide a nice introduction. A short distance from the museum is a viewpoint and the trailhead to South Falls. Like the North Falls trail, this too is a steep ascent of about a quarter mile.

If you plan to visit the park from Portland, leave I-5 at Woodburn and follow rural ORE 214 south through Mount Angel and Silverton. From Salem, the ORE 213 routing outlined previously is both efficient and pleasant, but you can also approach the park further south by taking ORE 22 east out of Salem and following the signs northeast to the park from Sublimity. Although longer, this route enables you to do a Salem-to-Silver Creek Falls loop on different roads, taking in more varied landscapes in the process.

Mount Angel

Four miles northwest of Silverton off ORE 214 is a retreat of a different sort. High above the rest of the Willamette Valley is **Mount Angel Abbey.** From miles away, the neo-Gothic outline of St. Mary's steeple beckons the outside world to this monastery; on the way up to the abbey, stop in to enjoy the serenity of the church, established by Father Odematt after his arrival from Europe in 1883 to start a colony of German Catholics.

The Benedictine abbey sits on a 300-foot hill overlooking cropland and Cascade vistas. From the bluff, look northward to Mount Hood, Mount St. Helens, Mount Adams, and, according to locals, Mount Rainier on exceptionally clear days. Further inspiration can be gained from an ancient manuscript library and views of the Willamette Valley southern expanses from the meditation patio of the Retreat House. The abbey's midsummer Bach Festival, frequently sold out, features professional musicians in an idyllic setting; call for tickets months in advance.

Guided tours of the abbey are offered by appointment. Meditative retreats can be arranged

for a minimal fee (write to Mount Angel Abbey Retreat House, St. Benedict 97373, or call 503/845-3045). Although the accommodations are ascetic, the peace of the surroundings and the beauty of the monks' rituals will evaporate your cares no matter your spiritual orientation. Weekend retreats begin Friday at 7:30 P.M. and end on Sunday at 1 P.M.

Mount Angel's other claim to fame is **Oktoberfest,** which takes place in mid-September in the town itself. Over the quarter century of its existence, hundreds of thousands of folks have come to enjoy the *Weingarten,* the beer garden, and the oompah-pah of traditional German music. The biggest ethnic folk festival in the Northwest offers stage shows, art displays, yodeling, and street dancing amid beautiful surroundings. The biggest attraction of all, however, is the food. Stuffed cabbage leaves, strudels, and an array of sausages are the stuff of legend in the Willamette Valley. In this vein, don't miss the Benedictine sisters' coffeecake and the Old World–style farmers market. (For details call 541/845-9440, or write to Oktoberfest, P.O. Box 1054, Mount Angel 97362.)

Bikers relish the foothills and farmland around Mount Angel, which are nearly devoid of traffic. Fall color is exceptional here, and a varied topography ensures an eventful ride whatever the season. Lowland hop fields and filbert orchards give way to Christmas tree farms in the hills. On the way up, pumpkin and berry patches also break up the predominantly grassy terrain. This region is known as well for its crop of red fescue, a type of grass seed grown almost nowhere outside the northern Willamette Valley. Back in Mount Angel, recover from your ride at the excellent restaurant at **Mount Angel Brewing Company** (210 Monroe St., 541/845-9624) in the middle of town. Wash down the hearty fare with homemade root beer.

Nurseries abound in the area as well. If you were to visit the **Wooden Shoe Bulb Company** (33814 S. Meridian Rd., Woodburn 97071, 541/634-2243, www.woodenshoe.com) in late March and early April, it would colorfully illustrate Oregon's rites of spring. And, when the sky is clear, the sight of Mount Hood backdropping the tulip fields is unforgettable. The 17-acre tulip farm is located near Woodburn; take Exit 271 off I-5 (en route to Molalla), turn right at the flashing yellow light onto Meridian Road, and go 1.5 miles. Look for the field ablaze in color on the right. Afterward you can head south through the town of Monitor and reach Mount Angel via a delightful rural route.

Mount Angel's location an hour south of Portland makes it an excellent day trip. Just take the Woodburn Exit 272 off I-5 and follow the blue Silver Falls tour route signs. If you're approaching the Mount Angel Abbey from Salem off I-5, take the Chemawa Exit and follow the signs.

Breitenbush Hot Springs

Salem residents have traditionally taken to the hills via ORE 22 along the North Santiam River to enjoy the fishing and camping at **Detroit Lake** and the skiing at Hoodoo Ski Bowl (see "Skiing the Cascades" in the Cascades chapter). Lately, the traffic to the mountains includes those seeking a different kind of renewal. Breitenbush Hot Springs Retreat and Conference Center (P.O. Box 758, Detroit 97342, 503/854-3314) offers mineral-springs baths, trails forested with old growth, as well as a wide variety of programs aimed at healing body, mind, and spirit.

Whether or not a rustic retreat appeals to you, the peace and beauty of the Breitenbush complex will enchant and edify. Set in the Cascade foothills, this one-time Native American encampment's artesian-flow hot springs have attracted people for healing throughout the ages. The pools, set variously in forest and meadow, have curative effects thanks to 30 freely occurring minerals including the salutary chemical lithium. Music, storytelling, theater, and superb vegetarian cuisine are also part of the experience. Finally, a special sanctuary with a vaulted glass pyramid roof lets you watch the stars or winter storms through the canopy of trees.

The retreat cabins are spartan but sufficient. All have electricity and heat, and most have indoor plumbing. Rates are $90 per person (bring your own bedding or pay $15 extra), including three sumptuous vegetarian meals and use of the facilities and waters. Large tents on platforms are

also available June–Oct. for $45–55 per person. Day-use fees for hot springs and other facilities are $15 for a full day and $8 for a half-day. Individual all-you-can-eat meals for daytime visitors cost $8, and the food is sure to make converts of those who still think of vegetarian fare as "rabbit food." Just bring your own coffee if you're used to one for the road.

Near Breitenbush are such remarkable natural areas as Breitenbush Gorge, Opal Creek, Bull of the Woods, and Jefferson Park; for more information contact the Detroit Ranger Station at 503/854-3366.

On site you'll find the Spotted Owl Trail near the entrance of Breitenbush parking lot. In addition to this and other trails (get maps at the reception desk), sacred sweat-lodge ceremonies conducted by Native Americans are offered free of charge. Pre-registration is required, however, and participants are financially responsible for all other Breitenbush services and facilities used (hot springs and cabins). Write or call Breitenbush for more details and a catalog listing workshops, seminars, speakers, and lodging.

To get to Breitenbush from Salem, take ORE 22 to the town of Detroit. Turn at the gas station—the only one in town—onto Forest Service Road 46. Drive 10 miles to Cleator Bend Campground. Go 100 feet past the campground and take a right over the bridge across Breitenbush River. Follow the signs, taking every left turn after the bridge, to the Breitenbush parking lot.

If Breitenbush is full, the nearby **All Seasons Motel** (ORE 22 and Forest Service Road 46, 503/854-3421) is clean and comfy ($55/double). The ecumenical spirit is on display in the rooms with Eastern holy books alongside Gideon's Bibles. It's not at all inconvenient to drive 15 minutes from here to the retreat center.

Opal Creek

The old-growth forests and emerald pools of Opal Creek were an environmental battleground for years until a land swap with a timber company who owned logging rights here and then the 1996 legislation to establish it as a wilderness. Opal Creek's 31,000-acre watershed has been called the most intact old-growth ecosystem on the West Coast (including a grove of thousand-year-old, 250-foot red cedar).

To get here from Salem, take ORE 22 for 19 miles east to Mehama. At the second flashing yellow light (at the corner with Swiss Village), turn left off ORE 22 onto Little North Fork Santiam River Road past the State Forestry office and go about 15 miles toward the Elkhorn Recreation Area. Stay on this route until Forest Service Road 2209 (mostly gravel) and be sure to veer left, uphill, at the Y intersection. About six miles past the Willamette National Forest sign, a locked gate will bar your car from proceeding farther down Road 2209. Park and follow the trail to a large wooden map displaying various hiking options. Sometimes a box with leaflets also has routing information.

While old-growth trees abound not far from the parking lot, be sure to cross over to the south side of the North Fork of the Little Santiam River (indicated by trailside signs). Here you can take in the placidity of Opal Pool, a small circular translucent aquamarine catch-basin at the base of a cascade that cuts through limestone. Located several miles from the parking lot over gently rolling terrain, Opal Pool is the perfect day-hike destination.

Mount Jefferson

After a soak in the pools at Breitenbush, your muscles will be primed to hike up Mount Jefferson, Oregon's second-highest peak, 10,495 feet above sea level. This snowcapped symmetrical volcanic cone dominates the Oregon Cascades horizon between Mount Hood to the north and the Three Sisters to the south. Unlike Mount Hood, Mount Jefferson is rarely visible to motorists approaching from the west.

Twelve miles east of Detroit on ORE 22 turn left; follow Forest Service Road 2243 (Whitewater Creek Road) 7.5 miles to the Whitewater Creek trailhead. Then it's an easy 4.5-mile hike to Jefferson Park. This is the northern base of the mountain and features a plethora of lakes and wildflowers. The alpine meadows here are full of purple and yellow lupine and red Indian paintbrush in July. On the way up, wild strawberries and red huckleberries can provide a delectable snack. For a special experience during the summer, start the walk after 5 P.M. when there's a full moon and the trail is bathed in soft lunar light.

Above Jefferson Park, the ascent of the dormant volcano's cone is a precarious endeavor and should only be attempted by the best in the business. You'll reach the bottom of Whitewater Glacier at 7,000 feet. Thereafter, climbing routes steepen to 45 degrees and snow and rock ridges destruct upon touch. Near the top, the rocks aren't solid enough to allow the use of ropes or other forms of climbing protection. Climbers must resort to "death moves," particularly because going down is even more dangerous than going up. Even if you head up the more sedate south face, you can expect difficulties due to the instability of the final 400 feet of rock on the pinnacle.

Those who elect not to make the ascent may run into other problems. Sometimes the mosquitoes in Jefferson Park are bloodthirsty enough to pierce thick clothing. On occasion the area is so crowded with day-use visitors and folks trekking the nearby Pacific Crest Trail, this place seems more like a city park than a mountain wilderness. No matter. The sight of Mount Jefferson in alpenglow at sunset or shrouded in moonlight will make you forget the intrusions of humankind or the elements.

Corvallis

The name "Corvallis" refers to the city's pastoral setting in the "Heart of the Valley." But this appellation tells just part of the story. The influence of Oregon State University looms so large here that it might as well be called "College Town, U.S.A." In fact, Cascadia, the quintessential college town in the novel *A New Life*, by the late Oregon State University professor Bernard Malamud, was modeled on Corvallis. Everything from the coffeehouses and used bookstores to the pizza joints and network of biking trails seems to owe its existence to the ivy-covered walls of academe here.

This community was tapped the second-best "micropolitan" city in the country by the *Rating Guide to Life in America's Small Cities* (Prometheus Books), based on environment, economics, education, housing, transportation, sophistication, recreation, public safety, and urban proximity. Beauty, tranquility, and Corvallis's central location in the heart of the valley also recommend it as a base from which to explore the bird sanctuaries, the Coast Range, and nearby historic communities. In town, you'll be struck by the abundance of stately old trees, some dating back to the first pioneers, who arrived in 1847. Streets with wide bike lanes—Corvallis leads Oregon with 8.2 percent of its workforce commuting by bicycle—and scenic routes for cyclists that parallel the Willamette and Mary's Rivers also contribute to the idyllic time warp feeling here. This is especially the case in summer, when many students leave town.

SIGHTS
Campus and Downtown
In springtime, the daffodil-lined approach to Corvallis on ORE 99W is made even more glorious by the Coast Range and its highest mountain, 4,097-foot **Mary's Peak,** to the west over the hay meadows. During much of the winter, rain and fog obscure the summit from view.

Your first stop in town should be the 500-acre campus of **Oregon State University** (OSU), home to 15,200 students (follow the signs to Jefferson or Monroe Streets, 541/737-0123). The parklike campus of this 1868 land-grant institution is the hub of activity in town, with a slew of eateries, bookstores, and craft boutiques on its periphery. Cultural activities on campus include lectures, concerts, theater productions, films, and art exhibits. Many are free and open to the public. Get an activities calendar at no cost by writing to the Office of University Relations, Oregon State University, Corvallis 97331.

Visit OSU from the end of February through mid-March and you can watch ewes giving birth in the lambing barns at the Sheep Center. Visitors are welcome during daylight hours every day except Thursday morning when a class is held there. To get to the center from downtown Corvallis, head west on Harrison Boulevard to the 53rd Street intersection. Continue west through the intersection on N.W. Oak Creek Road. A sign after 1.8 miles will indicate the road to the center; this one-lane road has turnouts allowing you to yield to oncoming traffic.

While the notion of one of these fleecy specimens on a dinner plate might seem akin to eating Bambi, this facility's research has helped establish Oregon lamb as a gourmet product. Thanks to a diet of nutritious grasses indigenous to Northwest soils, Oregon lambs are larger and richer in flavor than their better-publicized New Zealand counterparts. The barns are open every day during daylight hours. While there are no formal guides, student staffers and yellow informational fliers will help answer questions. The sight of a newborn standing and walking a few minutes after birth is amazing to first-time visitors.

The campus also maintains 11,500 acres of woodlands, notably **McDonald Experimental Forest** and **Peavy Arboretum,** entrance eight miles north of Corvallis on ORE 99W, which feature hiking trails as well as the chance to see the rare Fender's blue butterfly. The species had been thought extinct for 50 years until a habitat was discovered here in 1990. This ecosystem serves primarily as a living laboratory for the university's Forestry Department.

Benton County Courthouse, near 4th, 5th, and Monroe, is the oldest functioning courthouse in the lower Willamette Valley. You can't miss its large white clock tower. Also downtown is the **Corvallis Art Center** (7th and Madison Streets, 541/754-1551), located in the renovated 1889 Episcopal church near Central Park. It sells local crafts and hosts weekly lunchtime concerts. Gallery hours are Tues.–Sun. noon–5 P.M.

Houses, Heritage, and Hospitality

A large concentration of historic homes and covered bridges can be found around Corvallis, making it more than just another college town. In addition to the surrounding heritage-conscious communities, artifact collections and pageantry also liven up the historical landscape of Linn and Benton Counties.

Six miles west of Corvallis on ORE 34 is the town of **Philomath,** home to the **Benton County Historical Society** (1101 Main St., Philomath 97370, 541/929-6230). Looms, carriages, printing presses, and other pioneer-history exhibits are mildly diverting here, but the real star is the 1867 Georgian-style brick structure housing the collection. Just look for the imposing building on the right side of the highway as you head toward the coast. Hours are Tues.–Sat. 10 A.M.–4:30 P.M., Sunday 1–4:30 P.M. Admission is free.

Tyee Winery

Located 10 miles off ORE 99W south of Corvallis on the way up into the Coast Range is **Tyee Winery** (26335 Greenberry Rd., Corvallis, 541/753-8754). As such, it can be incorporated into trips to nearby destinations such as Finley Wildlife Refuge, Mary's Peak, or Alsea Falls. Pinot gris, pinot noir, chardonnay, and Gewürztraminer are featured here. Tyee won the 1997 Oregon State Fair's best red wine award. After wine-tasting, you can enjoy a picnic on the grounds of this historic farm site or a 1.5-mile loop to beaver ponds. Open July–Aug. Fri.–Mon. noon–5 P.M., April–June

Saturday and Sunday noon–5 P.M., closed Jan.–March.

Natural Attractions

The pastures of Lebanon and Brownsville east of Corvallis are good places to spot bald eagles. Venture out to the fields (beginning in February) when sheep are lambing to see America's symbol soaring above the newborns. In the winter, grass seed farms outside Albany, Coburg, and Junction City attract tundra swans.

West of Corvallis, two spots have drawn seekers of natural beauty and solitude for many years. Mary's Peak and Alsea Falls are each a short drive from ORE 34, a scenic route to Waldport, which branches off of U.S. 20 southwest of Philomath.

Mary's Peak sits about 12 miles southwest of Corvallis. From I-5, take ORE 20 into Corvallis, then ORE 34 to Philomath. From here it's nine miles west to the road's Coast Range Summit (1,230 feet). A sign north of the highway points the way to a 10-mile drive to the top of the Coast Range's highest peak (4,097 feet) on Forest Service Road 30, the only road on the peak's south side. Along the way, pretty cascades, interesting rock outcroppings, and over-the-shoulder views of the Cascades on the eastern horizon intensify your anticipation of this mountaintop Kalapuyan vision-quest site.

When you get to the parking lot at the end of the road, the view is impressive—but don't stop there. If it's a clear day, take the short walk across the meadows to either of the two summit lookouts for perspectives on Mounts Hood and Jefferson, the Three Sisters to the east (reportedly eight Cascades peaks in total are potentially visible from here), and the Pacific Ocean at the base of the Coast Range to the west. For information contact **Siuslaw National Forest Supervisor's Office** (4077 Research Way, P.O. Box 1148, Corvallis 97333, 541/750-7000).

In the foreground of the Cascades, agricultural plots patchwork the verdant Willamette Valley, site of 70 percent of Oregon's prime farmland. For most of this century, huge smoke plumes rose off the valley floor in August, making it look like a war zone. And it was, in a sense. Despite the lack of shots fired, you're

WILLAMETTE BIRD SANCTUARIES

The federal government established several bird sanctuaries between Salem and Eugene in the mid-1960s because of the encroachment of urbanization and agriculture on the winter habitat of the dusky Canada goose. This species now comes to **Baskett Slough National Wildlife Refuge** (NWR), west of Salem, **Ankeny NWR,** southwest of the capital, and **Finley NWR,** south of Corvallis, each October after summering in Alaska's Copper River Delta. Refuge ecosystems' mesh forest, cropland, and riparian environments attract hummingbirds, swans, geese, sandhill cranes, ducks, egrets, herons, plovers, sandpipers, hawks and other raptors, wrens, woodpeckers, and dozens of other avian ambassadors. Migrating waterfowl begin showing up in the Willamette Valley in mid-October. By mid-March, large numbers of Canada geese, tundra swans, and a variety of ducks descend on the refuge.

The pamphlet **"Birds of Willamette Valley Refuges"** details the best months to bird-watch, frequency of sightings, and locations of hundreds of kinds of birds (available from Refuge Manager, Western Oregon Refuges, 26208 Finley Refuge Rd., Corvallis 97337, 541/757-7236).

To maintain the sanctity of the birds' habitat, the refuges restrict birders by closing some trails in winter; other trails farther from feeding grounds are kept open year-round. A hike that can be enjoyed any time of year is Finley NWR's one-mile **Woodpecker Loop.** A variety of plant communities exists here, due to Kalapuyan field burning followed by pioneer logging and cattle grazing. Its location on the border between the Coast Range and the Willamette Valley also contributes to the diversity. Forests of oak and Douglas fir, and a mixed-deciduous grove, combine with marshes to provide a wide range of habitats. Look for the rare pileated woodpecker in the deciduous forest. The loop's trailhead is reached by taking ORE 99W (from Corvallis) to Refuge Road. Look for the footpath on the right after driving three miles. A drop box has a pamphlet with pictures and information on the birds, wildlife, and plant communities here.

Ankeny NWR is located 12 miles south of Salem off I-5 at Exit 243, and Baskett Slough NWR lies northwest of Rickreall on ORE 22. Visit fall through spring for the best chance to see ducks, geese, swans, and raptors.

In recent years, the proliferation of Canada geese in the lower Willamette Valley has compelled people to question if the refuges have been too successful. Farmers complain that the birds interfere with crops. Currently, state wildlife managers are rethinking the protections accorded to the migratory fowl. After seeing the dwindling numbers of the state bird, the western meadowlark, in the Willamette Valley due to human encroachment, let's hope the powers that be can reach a healthy balance.

looking at what had been, until very recently, an environmental battleground. The state's 275-million-dollar-a-year grass-seed industry burns the fields here in order to kill off such diseases as ergot and nematodes. The fire also eradicates weeds that compete with rye grass and would otherwise have to be sprayed with herbicides. Field burning also recycles nutrients back into the soil.

Nonetheless, the respiratory distress inflicted upon valley residents has compelled several serious attempts to ban the practice. When smoke from grass-seed fields was implicated in a 20-car pileup on I-5 in 1989, the antiburning campaign gained impetus. While farmers have been able to head off opposition by pointing to the agricultural benefits and cost-effectiveness of field burning, they also have been working with opponents to find alternative uses for the straw. There is optimism on both sides that creating new uses for the excess straw, and expanding existing ones, will eventually eliminate the need to burn the fields. Using the straw to fuel power plants, and to make paper, composition firewood, fiberboard, composting materials, kitty litter, and animal feed are some of the possibilities being considered. The last use has already resulted in a 20-million-dollar annual export market with Japan, which uses the baled straw to fatten livestock. In 1997, the Willamette Valley saw the first significant large-scale reductions in field burning in history.

The outlook is not so sanguine for opponents of clear-cutting on the flanks of Mary's Peak. The forest service claims its hands are tied, despite potential damage to the watershed when erosion on denuded slopes spills into streams. The summit, thanks to its status as a federally designated botanical area, remains untouched. A biome unique to the Coast Range exists up here, with such flora as alpine phlox, beargrass, iris, tiger lily, Indian paintbrush, purple lupine, and the blue-green noble fir. Exceptionally large species of this fragrant tree grow on the Meadows Edge Trail. This trail connects to a primitive car-camping area with 16 sites (open March 21–Oct. 31, $4 per night) two miles below the summit. It's part of a nine-mile network of trails around the upper slopes of the mountain.

You'll also find hemlock, fir, and grand fir here. In terms of wildlife, local creeks are home to the unique Mary's Peak salamander, and the surrounding woods host bald eagles, redtail hawks, spotted owls, and Clark's nutcrackers—seldom seen west of the Cascades. There are also squirrels and, very occasionally, black bears. Mary's Peak is a prime viewing spot (when it's clear) in western Oregon for the Perseid meteor shower in August.

Snow, an infrequent visitor to most Coast Range slopes, can often be found here in winter, even at lower elevations. In fact, the road is sometimes impassable without chains from late fall till early spring. A Sno-Park permit is required for day use, Nov. 15–April 15. Contact the Waldport Ranger Station (541/563-3211) for more information.

Farther down ORE 34 is the town of **Alsea.** The adjoining Lobster Valley area drew many

countercultural refugees here in the '70s, a portion of whom have remained to become farmers and craftspeople. The greenness of the valley surrounded by Coast Range foothills recalled the lower alpine regions of Europe enough to inspire the nickname "Little Scotland."

South of here, a paved-over logging road through the tall timbers of the Coast Range can take you back to the Willamette Valley on a remote scenic byway. Look for a sign that says "Alsea Falls, South Fork Road/Monroe." There's also a campground with 16 sites, piped water, pit toilets, picnic tables, and fire rings for $14 per night. You'll follow the Alsea River much of the way until you come to the sloping parking lot near Alsea Falls on the east side of the road. A short trail leads you to a picturesque cascade, ideal for a picnic. The road continues through once-active logging towns into farming country and the Finley Wildlife Refuge south of Corvallis (see the special topic "Willamette Bird Sanctuaries"). From here, ORE 99W goes north to Corvallis or south to Junction City and Eugene.

Camping

Camping in this part of the Willamette Valley can be delightful, especially in late spring and early autumn.

About 14 miles east of Sweet Home off U.S. 20 is **Cascadia State Park,** near the banks of the South Santiam River (for reservations, call 800/452-5687). Rocks here form great swimming holes. A nearby waterfall, a cave with petroglyphs, an old-growth Douglas fir, and a hand pump to draw up mineral water are other appeals. Also along U.S. 20 are superlative boating and fishing on Green Peter and Foster Lake reservoirs. No reservations are required for Cascadia's 25 tent sites and trailer spaces. Such amenities as piped water, flush toilets, and firewood are available, and a store is located within a mile. The campground is open March–late October (sites $10–14).

In Corvallis, your best bet April–late October is **Willamette City Park** (Corvallis City Parks & Recreation Department, 1310 S.W. Avery Park Dr., Corvallis 97339, 541/757-6918).

To get here drive a mile south of the city on ORE 99W, then go a half mile east on S.E. Goodnight Road to the park. For $9 a night, you can enjoy one of the 25 sites for tents and RVs serviced by vault toilets, piped water, and a small outdoor kitchen. If you need civilized comforts, a store, café, and laundry are a mile away. Trails to the nearby Willamette River yield bird-watching and fishing opportunities in this 40-acre park.

ENTERTAINMENT AND EVENTS

The **Peacock Tavern** (125 S.W. 2nd, 541/754-8522, $2 cover) is where Corvallis rocks out to live music Wed.–Sun. Oregon blues stars such as Lloyd Jones, Paul De Lay, and Curtis Salgado perform here. Next door, the Corvallis drama scene coalesces around the **Majestic Theater** (115 S.W. 2nd, 541/757-6977), a 1913 restored vaudeville house. Close by is the excellent **Grass-roots Bookstore.** Culture vultures also enjoy the **OSU International Film Series** (541/737-2450), staged in Gilfillan Auditorium, corner of Orchard Avenue and 26th Street. First-run flicks show at **Ninth Street Cinema World** (1750 9th St., 541/758-7469).

The first full weekend of June, the town of **Lebanon** celebrates its **Strawberry Festival** (104 Park St., Lebanon 97355, 541/258-7164, www.ci.lebanon.or.us/festivalhist). Southeast of Albany off U.S. 20, Lebanon has become famous for its annual *Guinness World Record*–sized strawberry shortcake, the 17,000 pieces of which are dished out at the climax of the event.

The third weekend in June, the 100-year-old **Brownsville Pioneer Picnic** features an old-time fiddlers jamboree and a tug-of-war involving large local teams. Also on the agenda are a parade, carnival, crafts fair, foot race, and tour of historical homes (for information see "Brownsville," later in this chapter). The three-day celebration is held near the spot where a ferry plied the Calapooia in 1846, now part of 10-acre Pioneer Park, located off Main Street at the end of Park Avenue. Each day of the event begins with a wagon-train breakfast.

Albany's **World Championship Timber Carnival** takes place July 1–4. Contact the visitors association (800/526-2256) for more information. Admission is $8 for adults and $6 for children for three days of logging-related competition. While such events as speed-climbing, springboard-chopping, and log-rolling have little place in the increasingly mechanized world of modern timber management, they're still fun to watch.

Two area musical events held each summer are the **Memorial Day Bluegrass Festival** at Airlie Winery north of Corvallis (15305 Dunn Forest Rd., Monmouth 97361, 503/838-6013, www.airliewinery.com) and the **Oregon Jamboree** (P.O. Box 430, Sweet Home 97386, 541/367-8800, www.oregonjamboree.com), Oregon's largest country music event. In years past, Merle Haggard, Wynonna Judd, Dwight Yoakam, Lee Ann Rimes, and other big names have appeared for this early August event, organized to help timber-dependent communities cope economically with the era of limits in Oregon forests.

Da Vinci Days (P.O. Box 1536, Corvallis 97339, 541/757-6363, www.davinci-days.org) held in late July focuses on the creative spirit embodied by the genius for whom the festival is named. Sculpt, play chess on a computer, take part in a drama, or just sit and listen to music, as Corvallis's vibrant artistic and scientific community shares its inspirational bounty. New vaudeville acts and food booths also showcase the region's creativity. Kinetic sculpture races—these must be seen to be believed—lectures by scientists, and interactive exhibits impart an intellectual air to the proceedings. The festival takes place on the Oregon State University campus and in Central Park, between 9th and 11th Streets, beginning 6 P.M. Friday and continuing 10 A.M.–11 P.M. Saturday and 10 A.M.–6 P.M. Sunday. Admission is $8 for adults, $4 for kids. Because festival events are spread out all over town, a car or a bike is necessary to take full advantage of it all.

Of the many events in Corvallis, the premier celebration has to be the **Corvallis Fall Festival** (www.corvallisfallfestival.com). This gathering of exceptional artists and craftspeople is now in its second decade. Nonstop varied entertainment and a block of food concessions, including an Oregon wine garden, provide a backdrop for this hotbed of creative ferment 10 A.M.–6 P.M. the last weekend in September. Contact the chamber of commerce (541/757-1544) for more information about this event that takes place in Central Park, between 6th and 8th, Monroe and Madison. The Corvallis chamber can also update you on an art walk the first Wednesday of each month.

The Oregon State University **basketball** season at Gill Coliseum (26th and Washington, 541/754-2951) is a favorite wintertime activity. Football is played at nearby Reser Stadium; since the arrival of famed coach Dennis Erickson, it's the hottest ticket in town.

PRACTICALITIES
Accommodations
Of the two dozen or so lodging options (mostly chain motels) in Corvallis, the following two are best in their respective price ranges. The **Super 8 Motel** (407 N.W. 2nd St., 541/758-8088), a few blocks from downtown and on the Willamette River, is nothing fancy, but there's a spa and pool, and the price is right at around $70. **Econolodge** (345 N.W. 2nd St., 541/752-9601) has clean rooms for $52 a night.

With a sister location in Reedsport, **Salbasgeon Suites** (1730 N.W. 9th St., 541/753-4320, 800/965-8808, www.salbasgeon.com) is situated in the heart of Corvallis's business district, just a jaunt from dining and shops. Guests have access to the large indoor heated swimming pool, sauna, and a gym as well as in-room high-speed Internet access. Rates run $83–165.

The newly constructed **Hilton Garden Inn** (2500 S.W. Western Blvd., 541/752-5000, 800-HILTONS) has rooms that range from simple to suite ($79–269). At the corner of 26th and Western, this is one of Corvallis' finest accommodations for the business traveler, featuring rooms with large desks, ergonomic chairs, high-speed Internet access, and two dual-line speakerphones with voicemail and data ports.

The **Hanson Country Inn** (795 S.W. Hanson St., 541/752-2919, www.hcinn.com) gives you the feeling you're way out of town though it's actually within walking distance of campus. Antiques, canopy beds, 1920s woodwork, and a book-lined library warm up the interior. On the outside, a hillside overlooking the Hanson farm offers a feeling of tranquility. With private bath and an included breakfast, it's hard to believe the rates are around $150. A two-bedroom cottage, ideal for families, sits behind the main house.

Food
Bombs Away Cafe (2527 Monroe St., 541/757-7221) is an always-filled-to-capacity 65-seat restaurant with colorful murals on the walls and lines of waiting-list hopefuls anxious to sample finger food made with the freshest ingredients and organic produce. Another reason for the queue are the prices, $3–13. Try the duck chichimangas, jalapeño fries, green chili, or chicken tamales. Close by are a strip of pizza places and ethnic restaurants you'd expect to find in a college town.

The **Albany Farmer's Market** (Water and Broadalbin Streets, Albany, open Saturday 9 A.M.–noon, June–Thanksgiving) is a short drive from Corvallis. Enjoy the Willamette Valley's bountiful harvests of corn, fruit, garlic, peppers, or whatever else happens to be in season. Cut flowers are on sale as well as such regional specialties as the mild-tasting, large-cloved elephant garlic, marionberries (a tart hybrid blackberry developed by OSU), and dried jumbo Brooks prunes. Best of all, you're buying direct from the grower at a fraction of supermarket cost. Corvallis also has a farmers market that takes place Saturday 9 A.M.–1 P.M. late May–late October in the City Hall parking lot, at 6th and Monroe. There is also a market held Wednesday 8 A.M.–1 P.M. at the Benton County Fairgrounds (110 S.W. 53rd St.). Look for excellent Alsea Acre Alpine's goat cheese and The Co-op's calzones here along with other regional staples.

Another Albany tradition is **Novak's Hungarian Restaurant** (2306 Heritage Way S.E.,

541/967-9488). Authentic *kolbasz* (a spicy sausage), stuffed cabbage, and chicken paprika exemplify the earthy Eastern European fare served in a family-friendly atmosphere. Lunch and dinner are served Sun.–Fri. At dinner, there's a light menu for $7 and a Hungarian menu for $8–14.

If you're on the go in Albany, the **Two Rivers Mall** (300 W. 2nd St.) features several restaurants. Of these, **Pastabilities** (next door to the Visitor Information office) is recommended, serving moderately priced Italian food, salads, espresso, and dessert.

Back in Corvallis, **Magenta** (1425 N.W. Monroe Ave., Ste. A, 541/758-3494) features a fusion of culinary genres with heavy emphasis on French and Vietnamese and a price range that's ambitious for this college town ($12–23 for entrées). Open daily for lunch and dinner.

Perhaps the best place to provision a picnic is **First Alternative Co-op** (1007 S.E. 3rd, 541/753-3115), which you'll encounter as you come into town via ORE 99W from the south. The organic produce section is a marvel, and the largely volunteer staff can give excellent leads on what's happening in the area.

Another spot for those who place a premium on wholesome fare is **Nearly Normal's** (the violet-tinged bungalow on the corner of Monroe and 15th, 541/753-0791), whose jungle of greenery and mismatched kitschy decor does justice to its name (inspired by a character in a Tom Robbins novel). Low prices ($5–9) and huge helpings reflect the predominantly student clientele, who savor egg and stir-fry dishes, burritos (Mex dishes are big here), and falafel. Patio dining on sunny days is a highlight. Closed Sundays.

The **Gables** (1121 N.W. 9th, 541/752-3364) is full of students and parents on graduation day enjoying prime rib, fresh seafood, rack of lamb, and other traditional standbys. Before the arrival of the heavy artillery, try the elegant chicken bisque as an appetizer. This is the most expensive place in town (entrées $12–30, 25 percent off at the early-bird special), but the understated elegance and venerable cuisine make it perfect for an occasion. To get here, follow Har-

rison to 9th; the restaurant is located a half mile west of ORE 99W.

Thanks to river frontage and a varied menu at once upscale and affordable, **Michael's Landing** (603 N.W. 2nd, 541/754-6141) is one of Corvallis's most popular restaurants. While Italian, Cajun, and Asian flavors occasionally assert themselves here, the menu seldom strays from beef, chicken, and seafood. What does stand out is the finesse of the experienced chef. Dinner prices run $10–24, lunch $7–15. Sunday brunch (10 A.M.–1 P.M.) is well attended thanks to outdoor seating and a variety of entrées. Open for lunch and dinner Mon.Sat., brunch and dinner on Sunday.

Information and Services

The **Corvallis Area Chamber of Commerce** (420 N.W. 2nd, Corvallis 97330, 541/757-1505) has a driving-tour brochure of the area. Better yet, contact the helpful folks at the **Corvallis Visitor's Information Center** (420 N.W. 2nd, Corvallis 97330, 541/757-1544). They can direct you to such locally favorite attractions as a recently renovated covered bridge on the university campus and Avery Park Rose Gardens. The latter boasts floral beauty framed by towering redwoods.

To catch up on local events, read the *Corvallis Gazette Times* (P.O. Box 368, Corvallis 97339, 541/753-2641). KOAC (550 AM) is an excellent public radio station with a top-notch news team and classical music offerings. Serving much of western Oregon, KOAC can be picked up in remote coastal and mountain communities.

Transportation

Greyhound and **Valley Retriever** (153 N.W. 4th, Corvallis, 541/757-1797) operate every day, with routes north, south, and west to the coastal town of Newport. The **Green Tortoise** (800/867-8647) departs the Corvallis/Lebanon Exit 228 on ORE 34 (behind the AM/PM Mini-Mart) for points north at 2 P.M. and points south at 2:30 P.M. Albany's **Greyhound** (108 4th Ave. S.E., 541/926-2711) has service to Klamath Falls and Bend as well as Willamette Valley locations. Albany also hosts an **Amtrak** station (110 W. 10th St., 541/928-0885).

Corvallis Transit (501 Madison, 541/757-6988) operates city buses with a weekday one-way fare of 50 cents. To get back and forth between Corvallis and Albany, catch the **Linn Benton Loop System** buses (541/967-4318) by the university at the corner of 15th Street and Jefferson Avenue; the fare is 85 cents. Buses stop outside Albany's City Hall on Broadway and 2nd.

Corvallis is laid out logically, and it's easy to get anywhere within 15 minutes. With 47 miles of bike trails and 13 miles of paved bike paths, it's not surprising the city has garnered kudos from national media for its commuter-friendly traffic arteries. Recreational bikers sing the praises of the Corvallis-to-Philomath bike path. It begins along the Willamette River in downtown Corvallis and continues eight miles through rural Benton County before ending in Philomath.

ALBANY

Twelve miles east of Corvallis on U.S. 20 is Albany, which has more historic homes than any other city in Oregon. More than 350 Victorian houses bespeak Albany's golden age, 1849 to the early 20th century, when wheat was the primary crop and steamships and railroads exported Willamette Valley produce and flour. In 1910, 28 trains departed this commercial hub daily. The **Albany Visitors Association** (Two Rivers Mall, 300 S.W. 2nd Ave., Albany 97321, 800/526-2256) and an information gazebo at the corner of 8th and Ellsworth Streets have maps and pamphlets about the three historic districts covering 100 blocks here. The visitors association is open daily mid-May–Dec. 31 and Mon.–Sat. Jan.–mid-May. Ask about Christmas trolley tours. While you're here, be sure to get directions to the **Monteith House** (518 W. 2nd Ave., 800/526-2256), the oldest pioneer frame building in Albany, dating to 1849. Also inquire about the **Albany Regional Museum,** whose exhibits on the Kalapuya tribe and Albany's pioneer and Victorian eras provide a good introduction. Taped messages on the radio station 1610 AM can also

update you on events and attractions within a five-mile radius of town.

In their heyday, two Albany residential districts were rivals. The **Hackleman District,** Ellsworth to Madison Streets and 2nd to 8th Avenues, was a working-class neighborhood that at one time featured a furniture factory and a railroad station. These houses are practical but rich in Victorian nuance. The adjoining **Monteith District,** Elm to Ellsworth Street and 2nd to 12th Avenues, was home to wealthy merchants and businessmen; the houses here are grand and opulent.

Also imbued with Willamette Valley history are the area's charming **covered bridges.** These canopied crossings protected the wooden trusses from rain, extending the life of the bridges by several decades. By the late '30s, many of the 300 or so covered bridges in the state had fallen into disrepair or were replaced by modern steel and concrete spans. Statewide, 48 remain, with 30 in the Willamette Valley. A pamphlet available from the Albany Visitors Association lays out a self-guided tour of eight bridges within a 20- to 30-minute drive from the Albany-Corvallis area. All of these fall within an eight-mile radius of Scio, a town 13 miles northeast of Albany on ORE 226.

To get to Scio, head north on I-5 for about 10 or 15 minutes, then take Exit 233 and follow the signs east to ORE 226. Of all the bridges in this loop, don't miss the bright red paint job of the Shimanek Bridge and the creekside splendor of the Larwood Bridge. In Scio itself a small **pioneer museum** (contact the Albany Visitors Association, 800/526-2256, for hours, location, and information) survives on donations. The hodgepodge of Oregon Trail memorabilia, wood carvings, 19th-century newspapers and family heirlooms in this oddly curated assemblage can be more affecting than the slicker, high-tech displays you'll encounter elsewhere in the state. Visitor services in this area are minimal, so take advantage of state rest areas on the interstate and the A&W Root Beer Stand in Scio.

Prime time for a stroll down Albany's memory lane is during the Christmas holiday season. In December (usually the second Sunday), annual old-fashioned **parlor tours** let you revel in eggnog, snapping fires, and frontier hospitality as a guest at a number of Victorian homes. Visitors are welcomed by hostesses at each home and are permitted to walk through the parlor and other open rooms. Entertainment and homemade refreshments are part of the festivities. Tickets are available by calling 800/526-5526 and are $10 for adults, $8 for seniors, free for children 12 and under. Historical district hay-wagon and trolley caroling tours are part of the package and can get you in the holiday spirit.

Exterior house tours led by guides dressed in Gibson girl costumes take place 1–5 P.M. every Sunday in July and August. The **house tours** leave in horse-drawn carriages from the information gazebo and are well worth the admission price for Victoriana fans. Interior tours are available 11 A.M.–5 P.M. the last Saturday in July; admission costs the same as the Christmas parlor tours. Visitors are invited to walk through the gardens and entire interiors of several homes; background anecdotes are supplied by guides. Old-fashioned quilts and dolls complement the tour, as do many people in turn-of-the-century dress strolling the avenues. At all times of the year, more than a dozen antique shops also lure visitors here. A list of these stores is available at the information gazebo. **Flinn's Parlor** (222 1st Ave. W., downtown Historical District, 541/928-5008) has a dinner theater presentation and a well-regarded tour service.

Check www.albanyvisitors.com for more information about Albany events.

BROWNSVILLE

A more down-home version of the pioneer experience awaits in Brownsville. Drive south on ORE 99E (or I-5) and take Exit 216; ORE 228 will take you five miles east into this small town located between the Calapooia River and the Cascade foothills. This 1846 settlement began to prosper in 1862 with a woolen mill and, shortly thereafter, the coming of the railroad. Today, the **Linn County Historical Museum** (101 Park Ave., Brownsville 97327, 541/466-3390) is

located in a turn-of-the-century train depot flanked by freight cars and a circus train. Inside these structures are displays (a barbershop, kitchen, post office, etc.) illustrating the lifestyle of the area's first settlers, the Kalapuya tribe, and local natural history. Kids will especially relish the vintage covered wagon and 50 miniature horse-drawn wagons, sleighs, carriages, and carts. After viewing exhibits, pick up a self-guided tour brochure Mon.–Sat. 11 A.M.–4 P.M., Sunday 1–5 P.M. Donations suggested.

The museum also coordinates wagon-ride interludes into the past. Known as **Carriage Me Back Days,** these excursions reenact daily life from days of old. This pageant takes place the third weekend of April. Check here too about tours of the **Moyer House** (204 N. Main St.), the elegant 1881 Italianate home of a successful mill owner/door manufacturer. The home's high-ceilinged interior features a Carrera marble fireplace, ornate wood trim, hand-painted floral patterns, stencils on the ceilings, and oil-painted outdoor scenes on the upper panels of the bay windows. The 1881 grand piano in the south parlor is another must-see. The distinctive cupola perched atop the roof housing a glass observatory will catch your eye from a distance. Come in June to see the strangely twisted wisteria tree on the front lawn in full bloom.

The Brownsville area has other worthwhile attractions. A **pioneer cemetery** on the east end of Kirk Street shelters the grave of the last known member of the Kalapuya tribe; some headstones here date to 1846, when Brownsville was established. What ended up being Oregon's third-oldest continuously operating settlement began as a ferry stop on the Calapooia River. A collection of rocks, tribal arrowheads, and woodcarvings is housed in an interesting stone structure at the **Living Rock Studio** (911 W. Bishop Way, 541/466-5814). The highlight is the series of colorful Biblical scenes made from thin slabs of rock, but don't miss out on the second-floor logging exhibit. The suggested donation is $2; hours are Tues.–Sat. 10 A.M.–5 P.M.

The state's oldest yearly celebration takes place here in June with the **Pioneer Picnic.** Another event of interest is the **Antique Fair** on the third weekend of August, where food, entertainment, and treasures from old farmsteads are featured. Northeast of Brownsville between Sweet Home and Lebanon is the **Council Tree,** a huge Douglas fir that served as the site of the annual gathering of the Kalapuyas. This 400-year-old tree can be reached by taking ORE 228 to Sweet Home and heading north a few miles on U.S. 20 to Liberty Road, which goes a mile to the turnout.

Northeast of town, the **Quartzville Creek** recreational corridor has gold-panning opportunities. Follow U.S. 20 seven miles and turn left to the access road that goes 27 miles to Quartz Creek. A week's panning here is not likely to produce a quantity large enough to fill a tooth, but the pleasant surroundings and primal thrill of finding "color" in your pan is sure to get you hooked. The Sweet Home area is famous among rockhounds for petrified wood and agates. Finally, Brownsville might evoke a feeling of déjà vu, having provided big-screen backdrops for such films as *Isn't It Shocking, The Flood, The Body,* and *Stand By Me.*

Should you decide to overnight in the Brownsville area, you can get a room for $50–60 at **Pioneer Best Western Lodge** (intersection of I-5 and ORE 228, 800/359-4827).

Eugene

Eugene's location confers many blessings. The Willamette River curves around the northwest quarter of the community, and abundant trees and flowers dot the cityscape. From an elevated perch you can see the Coast and Cascade Ranges beckoning you to beach and mountain playgrounds little more than an hour away.

In town, a world-renowned Bach Festival and other big-time cultural events are showcased in the Hult Center, praised by the *Los Angeles Times* as having the best acoustics on the West Coast. The University of Oregon campus provides another forum for the best in art and academe, while its Hayward Field track has been the site of the U.S. Olympic Trials several times.

Outdoor gatherings such as Saturday Market and the Oregon Country Fair (see special topic under "Events") bring the community together in a potlatch of homegrown edibles, arts, and crafts. But it doesn't take an organized festival to draw the townsfolk outside. Even during persistent winter rains, locals can be seen jogging, bicycling, and gardening.

Because of the sparsely populated hamlets east, west, and south of town, Eugene is a hub for health care and shopping. Visitors from rural Lane County flock to the Eugene/Springfield area on weekends to shop at Valley River Center, see a movie, attend a convention, or simply go "garage saling." This place seems to have more flea markets than just about anywhere!

Of late, the town has been the focus of national media stories about the activist community. Isolated violent confrontations grab most of the recent headlines, obscuring the work of numerous labor, environmental, and human services organizations (more per capita than any city of comparable size) who've labored with quiet effectiveness for several decades. The results can be seen in worker-owned collectives, organic food-buying co-ops, a wheelchair-friendly cityscape, preserved ancient forests, and wetland protection against industrial pollution.

This utopian orientation and community spirit together with the recreational, artistic, and intellectual attractions of this town have drawn retirees who've driven real estate prices up. The emerging high-tech sector also contributes to what one recent survey termed the nation's third least affordable housing market. Many Eugenians' salaries have failed to keep pace with rising home prices, and it's often more profitable for property owners to rent to students than offer their real estate at fair market value.

While visitors need not concern themselves with such matters, Eugene might pose some problems for those with sensitive respiratory systems. This is due to sporadic temperature inversions over the southern Willamette Valley, which is framed by mountain ranges that narrow like a funnel near the town. As a result, the wintertime fog and smoke from woodstoves can sometimes linger, creating air stagnation advisories. In like measure, springtime pollens from ornamentals, trees, and nearby grass-seed fields get trapped here, making this season a challenge for the allergy sufferer. August field burning occasionally causes air quality emergencies as well.

Be that as it may, Eugene belongs on the itinerary of anyone who wants to experience urban sophistication and active pursuits in a beautiful natural setting.

Economy

The pioneers who established Eugene's town site in the mid-1800s were motivated by visions of material prosperity derived from thick forests and fertile soil. Later, Eugene took advantage of its position between the Siuslaw and Willamette Forests to become a center of timber sales after the post–World War II housing boom. For decades thereafter, area mills yielded products ranging from plywood to wood chips and the economy rose and fell with the Forest Service's allowable cut.

These days, Eugene is in the chips again, but this time it's silicon wafer chips for computers. Just a few years ago, the Milken Institute rated this town of just over 142,300 the third-fastest-growing technology center in the country. Such local companies as chipmaker Hyundai (a controversial presence with local environmentalists), Hynix Semiconductor, and software giant Symantec have helped lead the charge, taking advantage of Eugene's proximity to I-5 and its location in between California's Silicon Valley and the Seattle/Portland Silicon Forest. Recruitment of talent is facilitated by the presence of a major university and a high quality of life.

Together with neighboring Springfield's population of 54,000 the region has become the second-largest residential center in the state. Like Eugene, which was once the leading point of origin for domestic timber sales, former milltown

COURTESY OF ED HEATON/CONVENTION & VISITORS ASSOCIATION OF LANE COUNTY OREGON

sunset on Fern Ridge Reservoir, west of Eugene

Springfield has carved out a new identity. As gateway to the scenic McKenzie River National Recreation Area, Springfield is moving away from what had been an almost exclusively resource-based economy. While forest products are still an important part of the mix, they have a lower profile regionwide than they did in previous decades. Nevertheless, the area's resource-based economy is alive and well just outside the Eugene/Springfield area, as evidenced by the King Estate winery (Oregon's largest in terms of capacity), thriving nursery industry, Christmas tree farms, world-leading berry, mint, and filbert croplands, and the world-leading grass-seed industry.

The University of Oregon is the area's second-largest employer and a leading recipient of federal grants. Ripple effects from the campus presence can be seen a few blocks away at one of Oregon's health-care hubs, Sacred Heart Hospital, as well as at the biotech and software companies that have grown up in the shadow of the university.

THE WILLAMETTE VALLEY

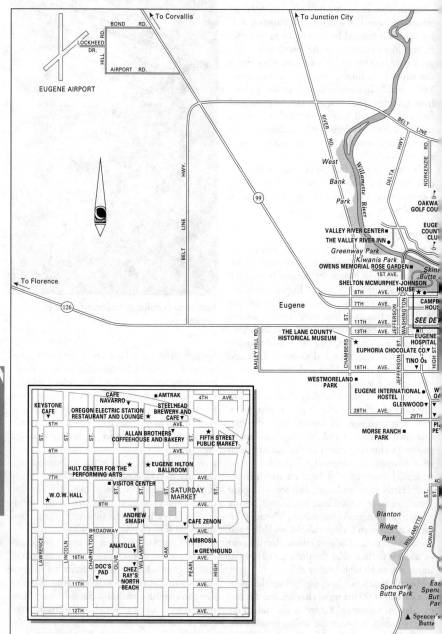

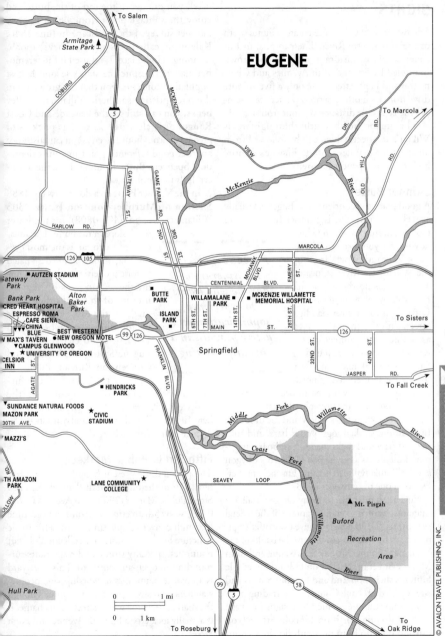

EUGENE

To Salem

Armitage State Park

COBURG RD.

MCKENZIE VIEW DR.

To Marcola

OLD HILL RD.

McKenzie River

GATEWAY ST.

GAME FARM RD.

2ND ST.

3RD ST.

HARLOW RD.

MARCOLA

126 105

Gateway Park

AUTZEN STADIUM

Bank Park

Alton Baker Park

SACRED HEART HOSPITAL

ESPRESSO ROMA

CAFE SIENA

CHINA BLUE

MAX'S TAVERN

BEST WESTERN NEW OREGON MOTEL

CAMPUS GLENWOOD

UNIVERSITY OF OREGON

EXCELSIOR INN

AGATE ST.

HENDRICKS PARK

SUNDANCE NATURAL FOODS

AMAZON PARK

30TH AVE.

MAZZI'S

SOUTH AMAZON PARK

HOLLOW RD.

LANE COMMUNITY COLLEGE

CIVIC STADIUM

BUTTE PARK

WILLAMALANE PARK

ISLAND PARK

5TH ST.

7TH ST.

MAIN ST.

14TH ST.

28TH ST.

CENTENNIAL BLVD.

MOHAWK BLVD.

EMERY ST.

MCKENZIE WILLAMETTE MEMORIAL HOSPITAL

99 126

FRANKLIN BLVD.

Springfield

126

To Sisters

32ND ST.

42ND ST.

JASPER RD.

To Fall Creek

Middle Fork Willamette River

Coast Fork

SEAVEY LOOP

Willamette River

Mt. Pisgah

Buford Recreation Area

Hull Park

0   1 mi

0   1 km

99

5

58

To Roseburg

To Oak Ridge

THE WILLAMETTE VALLEY

© AVALON TRAVEL PUBLISHING, INC.

SIGHTS

The two areas of visitor interest are minutes south of the Willamette River. The campus, in Eugene's southeast quadrant, and the downtown (bounded by 5th and 10th Avenues and Charnelton and High Streets) are only a five-minute drive from each other. Serious walkers can manage the two-mile distance without trouble.

The major north-south thoroughfare is Willamette Street, which can be followed from downtown five miles south to Eugene's favorite hiking haunt, Spencer's Butte.

Skinner Butte

A good place to get oriented in Eugene, visually as well as historically, is Skinner Butte. If you look north from most anywhere downtown you'll see this landmark. A beautiful park fronting the Willamette River is located at the butte's northern base. It's reachable by following the Scenic Drive signs to the river via High Street. This riverfront site served as a dock for pioneer sternwheelers and was where founding father Eugene Skinner ran a ferry service for farmers living north of the river. The town tried to become a major shipping port, but the upper Willamette was uncharted, as well as too shallow and meandering. In addition, sunken logs, gravel bars, and submerged trees and rocks made steamboat navigation difficult. As a result, Ben Holladay's Oregon and California Railroad became Eugene's most effective mode of transport in 1871.

Eugene Skinner, like so many Oregon Trail–era migrants, wanted to take advantage of the federal government's 320-acre land giveaway offer to pioneers, so he staked a claim from the banks of the Willamette to present-day 8th Avenue and from Monroe Street to the river on Hilyard Street. He built his shelter on 2nd and Lincoln Streets and later opened up Lane County's first trading post.

By following the Scenic Drive signs from the park or driving north on Lincoln Street (you can also walk up from the south side in 15 min-

Eugene belongs on the itinerary of anyone who wants to experience sophistication and active pursuits in a beautiful setting.

utes), you can get to the top of the butte and enjoy the vantage point from which Eugene Skinner surveyed the landscape in June 1846. Kalapuyas called this promontory Yapoah, meaning "High Place," and used it for ceremonial dances. Despite the state's second-largest population concentration that has grown up in the once-pristine southern Willamette Valley below, you can still see the Cascade and Coast Ranges on a clear day, as well as pockets of greenery throughout the city. You can also spot another good reference point in your orientation, **Spencer's Butte,** looming above the southern hills four miles away.

In the Skinner Butte area don't miss the 1888 **Shelton McMurphey-Johnson House** (303 Willamette St., 541/484-0808), on the lower south slope of the butte. The aqua-colored Victorian is the most eye-catching of some 2,000 designated historic properties in the city. During the second week of May the interior of this and other landmarks in the east Skinner Butte neighborhood may be toured 1–4 P.M. at no charge (contact Eugene/Springfield Visitors and Convention Bureau, 800/547-5445). At other times, the furnished rooms and historic photos of the Midgeley's mill area of early Eugene are on display here Tuesday, Thursday, and Sunday noon–4 P.M. A small admission is charged.

Fifth Street Public Market

The past and the present happily coexist a few blocks from the butte's south flank at the Fifth Street Public Market (296 E. 5th Ave., 541/484-0383, www.5thstreetmarket.com), an old-time feed mill converted into an atrium. This rustic structure houses an impressive collection of craft boutiques, specialty stores, and restaurants surrounding an open-air courtyard. This courtyard is a favorite haunt of sun worshippers, people-watchers, and street performers. Note: Though the market bears the word "street" in its name, it is actually located on East 5th Avenue and High Street.

For a more down-home version of the public market, head to the area near 8th Avenue and Oak Street each Saturday from the first weekend in April through the second Saturday of November. The **Saturday Market** then moves indoors to the Lane Event Center (13th and Jefferson) to become the Holiday Market from the weekend before Thanksgiving to Christmas Eve (open Saturday and Sunday, some weekdays. The Saturday Market features open-air crafts, street performers, and food booths 10 A.M.–5 P.M. While the latest incarnation of this traditional gathering is not the bargain basement it used to be in the '70s, the good vibes and creative spirit of the community are still in ample evidence.

The small farmers market set up across 8th Avenue from the crafts area has always been a good place to get fresh, inexpensive produce. Open Saturday 9 A.M.–5 P.M. April–Nov. and Tuesday 10 A.M.–4 P.M. April–mid-October. In addition, should the rigors of travel be getting you down, pay a visit to **Green Journey** (541/935-0629). Tucked away toward the rear of the farmers market, these botanical wizards sell ornamentals from all over the world as well as rare and medicinal herbs.

Wineries

Silvan Ridge/Hinman Vineyards (27012 Briggs Hill Rd., 541/345-1945, www.sylvanridge.com) is a perfect place to spend a summer afternoon. The winery, 15 miles southwest of downtown near Crow, is open noon–5 P.M. daily. Drive west on 11th Avenue, turn left on Bertelson Road, then right on Spencer Creek Road. A left down Briggs Hill Road takes you to the tasting room, located on a hillside overlooking a valley. The ride out here is a favorite of the local biking community, who continue on into the Coast Range via Vaughan Road (ask for directions at the winery for the Crow Valley Store that sits opposite Vaughan Road). While at the vineyard, also ask to sample Hinman's award-winning Gewürztraminer if you like wines with a distinctive tang. If available for tasting, the pinot gris is also a connoisseur's delight. Oregon is the only state in the nation to produce this wine, which is especially nice with seafood and has become a cov-

eted addition to wine lists in sophisticated restaurants elsewhere.

LaVelle Vineyards (89697 Sheffler Rd., 541/935-9406, www.lavelle-vineyards.com) makes a wonderful stop on the way out to the coast with a location just off ORE 126 near Elmira. In addition to secluded tables with umbrellas at which to enjoy LaVelle's pinots and Rieslings with your picnic lunch, the works of local artists are on display in the winery itself. A trail to a hillside on the grounds lets you see the snowcapped Three Sisters on a clear day. The winery is also represented by an outlet in the Fifth Street Market.

King Estate (80854 Territorial Rd., 541/942-9874 or 800/884-4441, www.kingestate.com) is set on 820 acres with a state-of-art winery resembling a European chateau. Production focuses on organic pinots and chardonnay. For dining and touring, they are open daily in the summer; winter hours are weekends noon–5 P.M. or by appointment. Reservations are recommended.

Hult Center for the Performing Arts

While you're walking between the two markets, you might look west past the Eugene Hilton and notice another imposing building close by. This is the Hult Center for the Performing Arts (1 Eugene Center, 541/687-5000, on Willamette Street between 6th and 7th Avenues). In addition to its status as a top-flight performance venue, this place is worth a look for aesthetics alone. From the frog and troll statues that greet you at the 6th Avenue entrance to the high-ceilinged interior bedecked with masks, artistic touches abound.

Hult Center talent (with nine resident companies) is showcased beneath interlocking acoustic panels on the domed ceiling and walls of the 2,500-seat **Silva Concert Hall** (which resembles a giant upside-down pastel-colored Easter basket). The **Jacobs Gallery** exhibits local artwork, providing another feast for the eyes. Even the bathroom tile here is done up in a visually pleasing theatrical motif. Free one-hour guided tours are offered every Thursday and Saturday at 1 P.M. or by special arrangement. Call for reservations or make arrangements at the front desk.

THE WILLAMETTE VALLEY

Campus

From downtown head a few blocks south to 13th Avenue then east to the University of Oregon campus (visitor information available at Oregon Hall, Agate and 13th, 541/346-3111), bounded by Franklin Boulevard, 11th and 18th Avenues, and Alder and Moss Streets. With an enrollment around 17,000 students, plus multimillion-dollar federal endowments placing the school in the upper echelon of American university funding, you might be expecting a bureaucratic, impersonal feeling here. Instead, the grounds of the campus are graced by architecturally inviting buildings dating back to the school's creation in the 1870s, as well as 400 varieties of trees. **Deady Hall,** the oldest building on campus, was built in 1876. The quiet and tranquility of the campus are sustained by a ban on vehicular traffic beyond 13th Avenue and Kincaid Street. A free **campus tour** leaves from Oregon Hall weekdays at 10 A.M. and 2 P.M. You're better off, however, just picking up the map and setting your own pace.

If you wander the north part of the University of Oregon complex toward Franklin Boulevard, you'll see majestic and rare trees (including a Chinese dawn redwood) dotting the landscape between the law and journalism schools. Interesting outdoor sculptures also liven up a stroll of the campus.

Museums

A must on any campus tour is the **Museum of Art** (next to the main library, 1430 Johnson Lane, 541/346-3027). The highlight is a second-floor nationally renowned Asian collection (don't miss the jade), but the revolving paintings and photography exhibits on the first floor are also usually worthwhile. Hours are Wed.–Sun. noon–5 P.M. year-round. Admission is free. If you're so inclined, call the museum office about their free one-hour tours. (At press time, the museum is undergoing renovations and is scheduled to re-open in fall 2004.)

Maude Kerns Art Center (1910 15th Ave., 541/345-1571) is near the University of Oregon campus. Set in an old church, this gallery is dedicated to contemporary art of nationally

Deady Hall, the oldest building on the University of Oregon campus, dates back to 1876.

known as well as regionally prominent artists. The center is open Mon.–Fri. 9 A.M.–5 P.M., Sat. 12–5 P.M. Admission is free. This gallery and others downtown are the focal points of a first Friday of the month gallery walk 5:30–8:30 P.M. (contact Lane Arts Council for details, 541/485-2278). These galleries have open houses with food and drink, combining art appreciation with conviviality. Exhibiting artists are on hand to talk about their work. Falling rents downtown have enabled a large concentration of galleries to develop here. Art connoisseurs will also relish beautiful murals in Eugene and all over Lane County.

The nearby **Science Factory** (2300 Leo Harris Parkway, 541/682-7888). The factory's raison d'être is to stimulate scientific understanding and curiosity in everyday life. Permanent exhibits here have an OMSI-like (see "Sights by

Neighborhood" in the Portland chapter) flavor, and are complemented by a new set of scientifically thematic expositions every three months. The Science Factory's hands-on orientation reaches its apex during the summer thanks to these traveling exhibits. Hours are Wed.–Fri. 12 P.M.–5 P.M., Saturday and Sunday noon–5 P.M.; usually closed on the days the U. of O. Ducks play.

The excellent Lane Service District **Planetarium** is connected to the Science Factory. Its 45-minute presentation is highly recommended (call ahead for times and admission prices). The Science Factory/Planetarium complex is reached from I-5 by taking I-105 West to the Coburg Road Exit and following the signs to Autzen Stadium (look for Centennial Boulevard and the Leo Harris Parkway).

Oregon prehistory is showcased in the **Natural History Museum** (1680 E. 15th Ave., 541/346-3024, www.natural-history.uoregon .edu), with artifacts from digs in eastern Oregon and bird and mammal fossils from around the state. A portion of Thomas Condon's fossil collection displays the curiosities culled from the earth by the man known as Oregon's first geologist and the discoverer of the John Day Fossil Beds (see the Northeastern Oregon chapter). There's also a set of sagebrush sandals dated at 9,350 years of age (from the collection of those found by Dr. Luther Cressman), 15-million-year-old shell fossils, and a whale vertebra and mammoth tusks. Other cultures make up the focus of exhibits here. Hours are Tues.–Sun. noon–5 P.M. A small donation is requested. To get there from Hayward Field on Agate Street, go east on 15th and look for a fish sculpture on your right (in front of an attractive wooden building) across the street from the dorms. Pick up the *Trees of Eugene* tour pamphlet at the information desk to annotate a scenic and historic jaunt through Eugene's leafy glades.

The **Lane County Historical Museum** (740 W. 13th Ave., 541/682-4242) can be found next to the fairgrounds. Just look for the steam donkey on the front lawn. There are other 19th-century logging vehicles and period rooms on display. The Oregon Trail exhibits are among the most interesting. Hours are Wed.–Fri. 10 A.M.–4 P.M., Saturday noon–4 P.M. Admission is $2 for adults, $1 seniors, and $.75 for youth.

Next to the Museum of Art is the **University of Oregon Library.** On the second floor, the **Oregon Collection** (541/346-3468) has books and periodicals about the state in open stacks—a great place to plan trips or learn about the region. The nationally famous map library on the first floor can also augment the trip-planning process with its extensive collection of all sorts of maps, its helpful staff, and its well-tuned photocopying machines.

This campus has often been selected by Hollywood to portray the ivy-covered halls of academe, most notably in the comedy *Animal House.* The 1996 production of *Without Limits,* the story of the late famed runner Steve Prefontaine, was also shot on campus and in the surrounding area. In nearby Cottage Grove and Brownsville, *Stand By Me* was filmed about a decade earlier.

Close to the Eugene Airport, the **Oregon Air and Space Museum** (90377 Boeing Rd., 541/ 461-1101, www.oasm.org) has vintage aircraft, artifacts, and displays depicting the history of aviation space. Open Mon.–Sat. noon–4 P.M. Admission is $5.

PARKS
Hendricks Park

Beyond the campus and downtown, the Eugene area has five parks that rank among its preeminent attractions (other parks and recreational areas are covered in "Sports and Recreation," later in this chapter).

About two miles east of the campus on a forested ridgeline is Hendricks Park, home to 850 naturally occurring rhododendrons and azaleas and about 10,000 hybrids. There are several ways to get to the park, the easiest being to turn from Fairmount Boulevard onto Summit Drive. Or take Lane Transit bus 27/Fairmount, disembark at Summit Drive, and hike on up the hill a quarter mile. Two parking lots accommodate cars—one near the picnic area of stoves and tables, the other at the upper entrance on Sunset Boulevard. The rhododendron gardens are in their glory during May, with 15- to 20-foot specimens in shades of pink, red, yellow, and purple. Even though the display declines by late June, it's always a great place to stroll. Gorgeous views of the city can be enjoyed from the west end of the garden, and tree-shaded footpaths lead to benches located in secluded cul-de-sacs on the hillside. Tours are available in April and May on Sunday afternoons; call 541/682-5324 for information.

Owens Memorial Rose Garden

Another floral display is located at the end of Jefferson Street, along the banks of the Willamette River. Walk on the riverside bike path behind the Valley River Inn (ask at the front desk to clarify) and the shops of Valley River Center until you get to the footbridge. On the other side of the river, loop back in the direction of the hotel for about a half mile till you arrive at the rose garden. Thirty varieties of roses peak in June and last until fall. Along with 4,500 roses and magnolia blossoms in spring, tremendous old cherry and oak trees also command attention. To get here from I-5, take I-105 West and take the West Eugene offramp. Turn right at the bottom of the ramp onto Madison and follow it north toward the Willamette River. One block to your right is Jefferson Street and the entrance to the Rose Garden (300 N. Jefferson, 541/682-4824). The park is open daily.

Ridgeline Trail

The South Hills Ridgeline Trail is only minutes from downtown Eugene and offers wildlife-watching opportunities (look for deer, tree frogs, garter snakes, and all kinds of birds) and more species of fern than perhaps any other single spot in Oregon. In addition, old-growth Douglas fir and the lovely and increasingly hard-to-find calypso orchid grow here. The trail is seldom steep and has some spectacular views of the city through clearings. A spur route leads up to the highest point in Eugene, 2,052-foot Spencer's Butte, via a steep and often muddy trail. (If you like seclusion, however, this route might be preferable to the ones outlined in the next paragraph.) The Ridgeline Trail can be reached from several points, including Dillard Road; near the corner of Fox Hollow and Christenson Roads; near Willamette and 52nd; off Blanton Road near 40th; and the Spencer's Butte parking area (see below).

Spencer's Butte

The Spencer's Butte parking lot is nearby. Just drive south on Willamette Street until you see the signs on the left side of the road. According to one legend, the butte was named after a 19th-century English trapper killed by Native American arrows. The Kalapuyans called it Chamate, meaning "Rattlesnake Mountain." An 1848 account (from Batterns DeGuerre's *Ten Years in Oregon*) of the view from the summit reads as follows:

On one hand was the vast chain of Cascade Mountains, Mount Hood looming in solitary grandeur far above its fellows; on the other hand was the Umpqua Mountains, and a little farther on, the coast ridge. Between these lay the whole magnificent panorama of the Willamette Valley, with its ribbon streams and carpetlike verdure.

The view today has all of the above, but there are some differences. Below the north summit you look down on Eugene/Springfield, with Fern Ridge Reservoir in the northwest toward Junction City. Beyond the reservoir you can sometimes see Mary's Peak. Other Cascade Mountains not noted in the previous account but sometimes visible from the butte include Mount Jefferson, Mount Washington, the Three Sisters, and Mount Bachelor. To the southeast, Creswell and the hills around Cottage Grove are visible.

The two main trails to the top vary in difficulty. If you bear left immediately after leaving the parking lot, you'll come to the route known among the locals as The Face. This trail is shorter in distance than its saddleback counterpart but much steeper and littered with boulders and, sometimes, muddy spots. It can be scaled in 40 minutes by anyone in reasonable health.

The main trail is a straight shot from the parking lot, looping up and around the steep hills. These inclines are broken up by flat stretches. Allow about an hour for the ascent. Signs caution against rattlesnakes, falling limbs, and poison oak, the latter being the most likely problem. The three shiny leaves of the notorious plant can be seen in many places along the trail, particularly on the flanks of the summit. A mixed-conifer forest featuring old-growth Douglas fir with an understory of numerous ferns and wildflowers will usher you along. Die-hard hikers equipped with boots or other durable footwear will enjoy "shooting the butte" in the snow. A "snow shoot" leads you up into a winter wonderland with trails wreathed by old-growth fir dusted with snowflakes.

Mount Pisgah

Mount Pisgah (Buford Park, 541/747-3817, www.efn.org/~mtpisgah/) features a mile hike to a marvelous viewpoint and an arboretum on the lower slopes. The arboretum at the end of Seavey Loop Road (plants and bird lists are often available at the visitors center, open weekends) sponsors such events as a fall fair dedicated to area mushrooms and a spring wildflower show and plant sale (dates vary; call ahead). Mount Pisgah can be reached by following E. 30th Avenue from Eugene past Lane Community College to the I-5 interchange. Cross the bridge over the freeway, turn left, and take the next right onto Seavey Loop Road. You'll cross the Coast Fork of the Willamette River and then turn left onto a gravel road (look for the Mount Pisgah signs) that leads to the trailhead; the arboretum is just beyond the parking lot.

The path to the 1,514-foot summit has a dearth of trees, enabling hikers to enjoy vistas of the Willamette Valley on the way up. At the top an unforgettable perspective of the valley in the foreground and the Three Sisters and other Cascade peaks in the distance awaits. A monument is on the summit, honoring author Ken Kesey's son and other members of the ill-fated University of Oregon wrestling team who perished in a van accident (Oregon's most cele-brated author lived two miles to the east in Pleasant Hill). This memorial consists of a sculpture with a relief map depicting the mountains, rivers, towns, and other landmarks in the Eugene area. Supporting the map are three five-sided bronze columns upon which the geologic history of Oregon over the past 200 million years is portrayed, using images of more than 300 fossil specimens.

Those making the climb in August will find blackberry bushes for browsing along the way. If you're perspiring from the climb, when you're back on the valley floor head south of the trail-head to the adjoining **Buford Recreation Area** for a dip in the cool waters of the Willamette River. The banks of the Coast Fork here also have a great profusion of white oak, blackberry bushes, and poison oak.

SPORTS AND RECREATION

Eugene's identity is rooted in its reputation as "Tracktown, U.S.A.," and also in its superlative Parks and Recreation Department. *Self* magazine called the city America's best place to work out, citing Eugene's numerous exercise facilities and playing fields. The article cited the 100 miles of bike paths, backcountry cycling minutes from downtown, and track events. Eugene has the seventh-best network of bike lanes in the country, according to a *Bicycling* magazine survey. Bikes can be taken on Lane Transit District city buses and Amtrak trains. Finally, Eugene was named the second-healthiest place to live in the country by the author of *50 Healthiest Places to Live and Retire in the U.S.* based on the city's bike paths, natural food stores, and abundance of cultural and recreational pursuits.

But wait, there's more. Hiking trails, white-water rafting, golf courses, and other outdoor pursuits are complemented by more sedate activities like wine-tasting, scenic drives, and museums. The following listings scratch the surface of this array. More information can be culled from the Convention and Visitors Association of Lane County, CVALCO (see "Information and Services" later in this chapter).

Water Recreation

Alton Baker Park, along the Willamette, and the **Millrace Canal,** which parallels the river for three or four miles, provide escapes from Eugene's main downtown thoroughfares. The canal is easily accessed from the University of Oregon campus by crossing Franklin Boulevard. Farther west on the Willamette is the **Riverhouse Outdoor Program** office (301 N. Adams St., 541/682-5329), headquarters of the Parks Department outdoor program and a roped-off swimming area. This is the place to rent river craft.

Reservoirs beyond downtown Eugene provide a wide range of recreation. For information contact the U.S. Army Corps Public Information (P.O. Box 2946, Portland 97208-2946). The one closest to town is **Fern Ridge Lake.** Camp, picnic, swim, water-ski, sail, or watch wildlife here. In addition, fishing for crappie, cutthroat trout, largemouth black bass, and catfish is excellent in early spring. This lake was formed when the Long Tom River was dammed in 1941. Its southeast shore was designated a wildlife refuge in 1979.

To reach the lake drive 10 miles west of downtown on W. 11th Avenue (ORE 126) toward Veneta, or take Clear Lake Road off of ORE 99W. Marinas on the south or north shores are especially coveted by sailboaters and sailboarders. The lake is drained in winter to allow for flood control, but the resulting marsh and wildlife refuge host tree frogs, newts, ospreys, rare purple martins (in spring), black-tailed deer, red foxes, beavers, muskrats, minks, pond turtles, and great blue herons. The wildlife area is closed to the public Jan.–March 15 for the protection of wintering birds. Regarding birds, there are 250 species found here including tundra swans, northern harriers, Canada geese, mergansers, and peregrine falcons. Perhaps the most eye-catching are the egrets because of their white plumage and large size. To get here, make a right off ORE 126 onto Territorial Road and look for a sign on the right. This section of Territorial Road is also part of the Old Applegate Trail, the southern counterpart to the Oregon Trail. This trail ended in the Salem area after coming up through Northern California into Oregon.

Dorena Reservoir, 50 minutes south of Eugene, has camping, fishing, and boating. The Army Corps dammed the Row River to create the facility, which can be reached by driving south on I-5 or ORE 99 for 20 miles to Cottage Grove. Then head under the bridge below I-5's Cottage Grove Exit (Exit 174) and pick up Row River Road (this goes up into the mountains, so check snow conditions), which goes eight miles east to Dorena Lake. Several miles up Row River Road, pick up Layng Road and go 1.5 miles to Currin Bridge. Another 1.2 miles south down Layng Road is Mosby Creek Bridge. More covered bridges are close by.

A popular retreat for locals is **Cougar Reservoir and Hot Springs.** From Eugene go 42 miles on ORE 126 to the town of Blue River, then four miles down Forest Service Road 19 (the paved Auferheide Drive) up to the west side of Cougar Reservoir. The springs can be reached by hiking to the end of a short trail; thanks to user fees, they have remained a splendidly kept site. This trail overlooks a steep drop-off, so be careful. The several pools in this tranquil forest setting can be crowded on weekends. Purchase a Forest Service Recreation Pass at the ranger station. Occasional incidents with law enforcement penalizing those without a pass do occur.

Camping

If you're looking for campsites in the covered-bridge country above Cottage Grove try **Baker Bay** (52 tent sites, $16/night, 541/942-7669). Located about 18 miles from Eugene, Baker Bay offers sail- and motorboats for rent. Take I-5 South to Mosby Creek Road (take the Cottage Grove Exit), turn left, then left again on Row River Road, and then take the right fork.

Near the quaint town of Coburg north of Eugene is a **KOA Kampground** (541/343-4832). Take the Coburg Exit off I-5, head west, and you'll find the KOA a mile or so down the road. For $16.20 a night you get a tent site for two people; $23.20 is the charge for a vehicle hookup.

Between the coast and the Oregon Country Fair grounds, **Triangle Lake Park** (541/927-6189) has 23 sites for $10 a night. Proceed 25 miles northwest from the fairgrounds on ORE 126. Take a right onto Territorial Highway, then

OFF THE BEATEN PATH

A long with the well-known hiking areas described in this chapter, the nearby Cascade and Coast Ranges also have some recently developed hidden gems, thanks, paradoxically, to such extractive industries as logging and gravel. The industrial "cat" trails that once cut swaths through these forests are today maintained (and sometimes paved over) by the Forest Service for access to natural wonders. Two such places are Kentucky Falls and a grove of the tallest trees in the Northwest.

Picturesque **Kentucky Falls** is set in an old-growth forest on the upper slopes of the Coast Range. To get here from downtown Eugene, drive 35 miles west on ORE 126 to the Whiteaker Creek Recreation Area on the south side of the road, approximately six miles west of the Walton Store and post office. The route to Kentucky Falls winds through the clear-cut lower slopes of 3,700-foot-high **Roman Nose Mountain.**

From Whiteaker Creek Recreation Area drive one mile south and make a right turn. Then after one mile bear left on Dunn Ridge Road (Forest Service Road 18-8-28). After about seven miles the pavement ends and you'll turn left on Knowles Creek Road; go 2.7 miles. Make a right onto Forest Service Road 23 (gravel) and proceed 1.6 miles until you make a right onto Forest Service Road 919. Continue for 2.6 miles to the Kentucky Falls trailhead, marked by a sign on the left side of the road. An old-growth Douglas fir forest on

gently rolling hills for the first half mile gives way to a steep descent into a lush canyon. The upper falls is visible a little more than a mile down the trail. You'll hear the water before you actually get a full cross section of a broad cascade pouring out from over the rim of this green canyon. On your drive back to ORE 126, retrace your route carefully to avoid veering off on a hair-raising spur route to Mapleton.

A chance to see what may be the **Northwest's tallest trees** is possible northeast of Lowell. This recently discovered grove's 500-year-old Douglas firs average nearly 300 feet in height. The tallest tree has been measured at 322 feet, which places it in the rarefied atmosphere of the giant sequoia. Be sure to take along a forest map from the Lowell Ranger Station (541/937-2129) or the Forest Service headquarters in Eugene (211 E. 7th Ave., 541/465-6517).

To get here from Eugene, take ORE 58 to Lowell. From Lowell, follow Jasper-Lowell Road two miles to the Unity Covered Bridge and turn right onto Big Fall Creek Road. Proceed down Big Fall Creek Road for 11 miles to where it becomes Forest Service Road 18. Turn left onto Forest Service Road 1817 and continue for 10 miles until you reach Forest Service Road 1806, at which point you will turn left. Go down 1806 for three miles and then turn left onto Forest Service Road 427. The trailhead is a half mile down the road on the left side, but park on the right.

a left on ORE 36 to Triangle Lake. You'll find the campsites just after the lake.

Fern Ridge Shores (541/935-2335) is located in a quiet family park 12 miles west of Eugene. Take Jeans Road off ORE 126 near Veneta. Unlike the other previously mentioned sites, Fern Ridge Shores does not accept reservations. Campsites go for $25 per night; hookups are $25.

RVers, Oregon Country Fair-goers, rock concert attendees, and Scandinavian Fair visitors have been taking advantage of **Richardson County Park** (25950 Richardson Park Rd., Junction City, 541/935-2005) on the shores of Fern Ridge Reservoir six miles northwest of Eugene.

The 88 sites with hookups and water can be accessed by taking Clear Lake Road off of ORE 99 to its intersection with Territorial Road. Space availability is on a first-come first-served basis in this shaded campground rich in amenities and recreation. It's open April 15–Oct. 15 and costs $20 per night.

Cottage Grove

In addition, Dorena Reservoir is the gateway to the **Bohemia mining district** (see "Events," later in this chapter), site of old abandoned mines. Check the **Cottage Grove Pioneer Museum** (Birch and H Streets, 541/942-3963) for more

THE WILLAMETTE VALLEY

information on these attractions, or contact the **Cottage Grove Chamber of Commerce** (710 Row River Rd., P.O. Box 487, Cottage Grove 97424, 541/942-2411). The chamber of commerce is located two miles east of the ranger station in Cottage Grove, which has a map of a 70-mile Bohemia driving loop ("Tours of the Golden Past"), as well as updates on snow conditions. Ask also about the 14.1-mile **"rails to trails" loop** that follows the paved-over tracks of an old mining train from Cottage Grove to Culp Creek—perfect for mountain biking, birding, and mushroom hunting (especially after the first fall rains). For more information on this route, contact the Bureau of Land Management, Eugene District (2890 Chad Dr., P.O. Box 10226, Eugene 97440, 541/683-6600).

While you're in the area, the **Cottage Restaurant** (2915 Row River Rd., 541/942-3091) is recommended for homemade soups, vegetarian dishes, fudge pie, and cheesecake. For lunch ($4–6.50), their large salads (try artichoke hearts, Gruyère cheese, and cashews on chicken) and sandwiches are the best in the area. In town, the **Book Mine** (702 Main St., Cottage Grove, 541/942-7414) is one of the best bookstores between Eugene and Ashland.

Sports Facilities and Programs

The University of Oregon and Eugene Parks and Recreation provide the community with a smorgasbord of recreational facilities and programs.

University sport facilities are open to the public year-round for a nominal fee. Covered tennis courts and racquetball courts are found on 15th Avenue, east of the physical education building. There are also gyms, weight rooms, a swimming pool, and more racquetball courts inside the physical education building. Contact the university's recreation desk (103 Gerlinger Hall, 541/346-4113) for more information.

Headquarters for the **University of Oregon Outdoor Program** (541/346-4365, www.uoregon.edu/~opwww) is located in a southeast-corner basement room of the Erb Memorial Union, corner of 13th and University, festooned with maps, photos, and bulletins covering every sport from biking to bungee jumping. The program

sponsors more white-water activities than any other group in town, as well as backpacking trips outside the state to supplement area hikes. Outings are run on a cooperative shared-expense basis with the participants customizing the trip to their needs. In addition to these activities, you can also connect with people on your own through the office exchange bulletin board. The Outdoor Program also loans camping equipment at no charge. In addition, it's an excellent resource center for statewide travel information, with books, maps, pamphlets, and videos about Oregon wilderness locales and outdoor activities.

Especially popular are the pools and fitness centers at **Echo Hollow** (1560 Echo Hollow Rd., 541/682-5525) and **Sheldon** (2445 Willakenzie Rd., 541/682-5314). There is a nominal drop-in user fee, or you can purchase a one-month pass. These fitness centers are equipped with weights and exercise paraphernalia. Consult the Parks and Recreation literature or call for the schedule.

Lane County Ice (Lane County Fairgrounds, 13th and Monroe, Eugene, 541/687-3615) offers ice-skating lessons and open public skating.

There are more than 15 bike sales and repair shops in Eugene's Yellow Pages. Eugene and Springfield together boast 120 miles of on-street bike lanes, limited-access streets, and off-street bikeways. **Collins Cycle Shop** (60 E. 11th, 541/342-4878) enjoys a central location. Here and elsewhere, look for the high-quality bikes, bike equipment, backpacks, and raingear made by the local **Burley Designs** co-op.

Spectator Sports

Each spring, the University of Oregon track team, a perennial contender for the status of best team in the nation, holds meets at **Hayward Field** (Agate and 15th Avenue). This site has also hosted such world-class events as the NCAA Finals and the United States Olympic Trials.

Fall means Duck football at **Autzen Stadium** (Martin Luther King Boulevard on Day Island). To get there, head north on Ferry Street. Just after crossing the Willamette River, take a hard right on Martin Luther King Boulevard. In winter, the townsfolk cram into **MacArthur Court,** a funky anachronism from the 1920s located just south of the physical education building on University Street. Even if you're not a fan, you're bound to get caught up in the frenzied decibels of "quacker backers" who support a team known for its never-say-die attitude.

In summer, the **Eugene Emeralds** play ball at Civic Stadium (2077 Willamette St., 541/342-5367), for honor, glory, and a chance to break into the big leagues. Even if you don't catch a future hall-of-famer on the way up, enjoy the best concession food you'll ever taste at a ballpark.

Golf

Laurelwood Golf Course (2700 Columbia St., Eugene, 541/687-5321 for information, or 541/484-4653 for tee times, www.laurelwood-golf.com) is a city-owned golf course with a 250-yard driving range. Greens fees (around $14) and rentals are reasonable.

Of the many courses in Lane County, **Tokatee** (54947 ORE 126, Blue River, 541/822-3220 or 800/452-6376) is the best. In fact, on several occasions *Golf Digest* rated it among the top 25 courses in the nation, and *Back Nine* rated it the best public course in the Pacific Northwest. To get here, drive 47 miles east of Eugene on the McKenzie Highway (ORE 126). The 18 holes here are set in a mountainous landscape patrolled by elk and other forest creatures in the shadow of the Three Sisters. Greens fees are $26 for 18 holes. It's always a good idea to call ahead for reservations.

Other Activities

Of the many public **tennis** courts throughout Eugene, the best-lit facilities are at the University of Oregon and at 24th and Amazon Parkway near Roosevelt Middle School.

Near the Amazon courts, runners will enjoy the bark-o-mulch trail that follows Amazon Creek in a one-mile loop. This is a good spot to catch such world-class athletes as Mary Slaney and Marie Mutola doing interval training. The best jogging of all, however, is found at the four-mile **Prefontaine Trail** along the Willamette River east of Alton Baker Park. Named after Steve Prefontaine, whose world-record times and finishing kicks used to rock the Hayward Field grandstands before his untimely death in 1975, this soft path meanders along the river not far from the university. Exercise equipment can break up your run on the "par course" section of the Prefontaine Trail. To get here, follow the bike path from Alton Baker Park east toward Springfield.

Another route is the road behind 24-Hour Fitness (1475 Franklin Blvd.), which is closed off to motorized traffic. This leads to the footbridge that takes bikers, hikers, and joggers to the Prefontaine Trail, Willamette River Bike Trail, Autzen Stadium, and other facilities found along the Willamette River Greenway. The **Willamette River Bike Trail,** a six-mile pathway running east/west on both sides of the river, takes in parts of Skinner Butte Park and Alton Baker Park.

If you're more interested in taking to the trails on your trusty steed, head to **C-Bow Arrow Ranch** (33435 Van Duyn Rd., 541/345-5643), located off I-5 at Exit 199, four miles north of Beltline Highway. Trail rides and lessons are also available at **Triangle S Ranch** (541/747-7039).

Some of the best urban **climbing** to be found anywhere is at The Columns, a basalt cliff located on public land against the west side of Skinner Butte in downtown Eugene. Limited parking is available at The Columns, but it's more enjoyable to ride a bike here by following the road rimming the butte. Climbing is free.

ENTERTAINMENT

Keeping up with Eugene's multifaceted entertainment offerings involves previewing the listings put out by two local newspapers, *Eugene Weekly* and the daily *Eugene Register Guard*. Their local event phone line (503/485-2000) allows callers to access the schedules of almost every theater and museum in town. The daily's Friday Arts & Entertainment section is especially recommended. Call the University of Oregon ticket office (541/346-4461) for athletic event information. For more information on what's happening around town, peruse the community bulletin boards at Fifth Street Public Market and Sundance Natural Foods.

Dancing and Music

If you tire of watching other folks in action, the best spot for frenetic dancing in town is the **W.O.W. Hall** (291 W. 8th Ave., 541/687-2746, www.wowhall.org). This old Wobblie (International Workers of the World) meeting hall has remained a monument to Oregon's activist past in labor history. Despite having all the ambience of a junior-high-school gym, it hosts some surprisingly famous rock and blues performers. The W.O.W. bills itself as having the best hardwood dance floor in the Pacific Northwest. In any case, it's probably the most crowded and features an interesting cross section of Eugenians. Beer and wine are served downstairs.

Dancing to live bands at the **Erb Memorial Union Ballroom** (13th and University, 541/346-6000) is a Eugene tradition. Local-guy-who-made-good Robert Cray and other nationally known performers have played here. The dance floor is more spacious than the W.O.W. Hall's but can actually exceed its downtown counterpart in BTUs generated by the mass of writhing bodies.

Concerts frequently take place within the cavernous enclaves of Autzen Stadium, the home field to the Oregon Ducks football team. A good sound system has made it possible for tens of thousands of concert attendees to enjoy such artists as Bob Dylan and U2.

The **Eugene Hilton Ballroom** (66 E. 6th Ave., 541/342-2000, www.hiltoneugene.com) also hosts big names running the gamut of popular music. For more sedate listening, the **Hult Center** (see "Sights," earlier in this chapter) is next door to the Hilton. The Eugene Symphony and other estimable local groups like the Eugene Concert Choir perform here along with a wide-ranging array of headliners from the world of music and comedy. At Christmastime, the Eugene Ballet's *Nutcracker* is always a treat.

Live jazz in the basement of **Jo Frederigo's** (295 E. 5th Ave., 541/343-8488) is made more enjoyable by crayons, paper, and one of their famous Long Island iced teas. Decent Italian food is served upstairs.

Down the block, the **Oregon Electric Station Restaurant and Lounge** (27 E. 5th,

541/485-4444) hosts live jazz and rhythm-and-blues acts. This historic landmark features excellent dinner ($12–45) and lunch ($8–16) entrées, a full bar, a back room with wing chairs, and the ambience of an English club. But you never forget you're in Tracktown U.S.A. thanks to a wall festooned with photos of Alberto Salazar and Steve Prefontaine. Open nightly.

In the same neighborhood, **The Beanery** (152 W. 5th Ave., 541/342-3378) has live folk and blues at night and the same excellent coffee as its Corvallis outlets. This spacious coffeehouse, located in a charming old building across from the Lane County Jail, attracts everyone from off-duty cops to madmen playing speed chess. Home-baked goodies and breakfast, lunch, and dinner entrées (under $10) can be ordered at the counter. Open daily.

Closer to campus is **Taylor's Bar and Grille** (894 E. 13th Ave., 541/344-6174), situated directly opposite the academic buildings and the university bookstore. They have DJs a few nights a week, a dance floor, a big-screen cable hookup, espresso drinks, and a selection of microbrews. In addition, pricey but substantial burgers, sandwiches, soups, and Cajun food ($5–10) will help you bop till you drop. Open daily.

The "in" place to go is **Good Times Cafe and Bar** (375 E. 7th Ave., 541/484-7181), where a $2 cover lets you enjoy Tuesday night blues acts. Out in the Whiteaker neighborhood, **Sam Bond's Garage** (407 Blair Blvd., 541/343-2635) serves live music and microbrews at $3.50/pint and a menu of vegetarian pub grub till dawn; open every day. On the mall in midtown, the **Wild Duck** (169 W. 6th Ave., 541/485-3825) features big-name acts in a more mainstream setting. The Northwest pub fare here is good too, especially the smoked salmon potato pancakes. Meals are usually under $10; cover charge varies, depending on the act.

Theaters

While there's no shortage of movie houses in this town, the real screen gems are usually found at the university (consult the *Oregon Daily Emerald*, the U. of O. student newspaper, distributed free at Fifth Street Market, the University of Oregon

Bookstore, and Sundance Natural Foods) and the **Bijou Theatre** (492 E. 13th Ave., 541/686-2458, www.bijou-cinemas.com). The university series favors cult films and classics (*Yellow Submarine, The Last Wave, The Bicycle Thief, King of Hearts,* etc.) and the inexpensive ticket price helps you forget the oppressiveness of the lecture halls that serve as theaters. For about twice the price, the Bijou is the place to see foreign films, art flicks, and less commercial mainstream movies. Located in an intimate Moorish-style converted church, the Bijou offers great munchies and late-night presentations.

If you want first-run motion pictures, chances are you can find whatever you're looking for at **Movies 12** (Gateway Mall, 2850 Gateway St., Springfield, 541/741-1231).

Cutting-edge theater can be enjoyed at **Lord Leebrick** (540 Charnelton, 541/684-6988).

EVENTS

There is a lot happening in this south Willamette Valley hub of culture and athletics. Several events, however, best impart the flavor of the area.

Oregon Bach Festival

Of all the kulturfests in the Willamette Valley, only one enjoys international acclaim. The Oregon Bach Festival (541/346-5666 and 800/457-1486, www.bachfest.uoregon.edu) takes place over two weeks late June–early July under the baton of famed Bach interpreter Helmuth Rilling from Germany. The *New York Times* once rated the festival the best of its kind in the country, and an influx of renowned visiting opera and symphonic virtuosi guarantees that this will remain the case. More than two dozen separate concerts are featured, with musical styles ranging from the baroque era to the 20th century. The centerpieces of the festival, however, are Bach works such as the *St. Matthew Passion,* numerous cantatas, and the Brandenburg Concertos.

Performances take place in the Hult Center and at the Beall Concert Hall at the University of Oregon Music School. Free events, including "Let's talk with the conductor," miniconcerts, and children's activities also take place at these venues during the festival. Particularly recommended is the festival's Discovery Series: six concertos preceded by a short lecture-demo by Helmuth Rilling. Each 5 P.M. concert features a different Bach church cantata. Free noon concerts in the Hult lobby are also popular. A scheduled series of brunches, lunches, and dinners with the musicians also adds a special touch to the event.

Art and the Vineyard

Appealing to lowbrow and highbrow alike is Art and the Vineyard, which generally takes place over the July 4 weekend in Alton Baker Park. This event brings together art, music, and wine in a tranquil park near the Willamette River. One hundred artists' booths and the offerings of a dozen vineyards frequently grace the affair, along with live music (jazz, country, blues, and folk) and food concessions. An admission is charged to this outdoor celebration of Eugene's cultural richness. Contact CVALCO (800/547-5445) for details.

Other Events

A gallery walk the first Friday of every month lets culture vultures enjoy open house exhibitions all over town. Consult the preceding Sunday *Register Guard* for a complete listing of participating venues.

The university sponsors the **Willamette Valley Folk Festival** (541/686-INFO) in the spring, which has attracted the likes of Tom Paxton and blues harpist James Cotton. Call for a schedule of upcoming concerts. The festival generally takes place behind the student union on the second weekend of May. The event is free but bring cash to enjoy Eugene's amazing array of food vendors.

Music lovers also revel in the city's summer **Concerts in the Parks** festival. A series of free concerts is also held in Alton Baker Park's Cuthbert Amphitheatre mid-July to late August. Nancy Griffith, David Grisman, and Robert Cray typify the national names appearing here. Call 541/687-5000 for tickets and information. Lower profile groups grace Amazon and Westmoreland Parks as well as several other venues throughout the city.

OREGON COUNTRY FAIR

Just after the Bach Festival in mid-July, the Oregon Country Fair takes place as the second major cultural event of the summer. If you've been too busy to follow the growth of the '60s counterculture, put on your paisley and follow an eclectic caravan of hand-painted schoolbuses, Volkswagen Beetles, Volvos, and BMWs to the Oregon Country Fair.

After buying your ticket at the gatehouse, join the crowds of tie-dyed, fringed, and love-beaded fair-goers. Entering, you wander through a kaleidoscope of natural fabrics, graceful ceramics, stained glass, rainbow candles, and thousands of other variously sculpted wares. Machine-manufactured items are simply unavailable. Every aspect of the fair—its 350-plus booths and its participants—is, in a sense, art.

What? Two hours gone by already? You need a cup of espresso and a piece of torte if you're going to make it through this day. Or perhaps you want a **Ritta's** burrito bulging with avocado, salsa, and sprouts. The choices are mouthwatering: Get fried rice, sushi, blazing salads, or even a tofuless tofu burger (100% ground beef), and more.

Overwhelmed by the constant parade of costumed stilt walkers, strolling musicians, winged "country fairies," children in face paint, barebreasted men and women, and other ambient wonders? Not far from any burnout point is a stage.

Shady Grove is a quiet venue for acoustic folk, classical, new age, and other music. The **Daredevil, W. C. Fields,** and **Energy Park** stages host contemporary New Vaudeville stars and other rollicking performers. See the **Royale Famille du Canniveaux** debut a unique musical comedy. Marvel as the **Reduced Shakespeare Company** performs *Romeo and Juliet* backward in one minute flat. Shake your head and mutter as **Up For Grabs** juggles circular saw blades and/or small children.

But wait, there's more. Try **The Circus** with its parade, orchestra, and veteran virtuosos. Ogle snake

---

Contact CVALCO (800/547-5445) for a schedule and more information.

Bohemia Mining Days convenes in mid-July; many of the events take place at re-created Bohemia City on ORE 99. Highlights of the five-day event include the Prospector's Breakfast, gold-panning demonstrations, a half-marathon, a bake-off, a flower show, an ugly-dog contest, and other competitions. Don't miss the Grand Miner's Parade, which happens on Saturday afternoon. Floats, horse teams, drill teams, and color guards make their way from Harrison Avenue to Row River Road with colorful costumes and the kind of enthusiasm last seen around here after turn-of-the-century lucky strikes. A small admission is charged on some days. For information contact the Cottage Grove Chamber of Commerce (710 Row River Rd., P.O. Box 587, Cottage Grove 97424, 541/942-2411).

Outside of Eugene, the annual **Junction City Scandinavian Festival** (Greenwood Street, between 5th and 7th, Junction City) celebrates the town's Danish founders the second weekend in August. Swedish, Finnish, Norwegian, and Icelandic heritage also exert a presence at the festival.

Folk dancing, traditional crafts, and food make up the bulk of the activities. Skits of Hans Christian Andersen folktales are enacted during the four-day event, along with guided hour-long bus tours that take you by Scandinavian pioneer farmsteads. Tour tickets are available at the information windmill for $2.50. Junction City is 12 miles northwest of Eugene off ORE 99. Contact the local chamber of commerce (P.O. Box 3, Junction City 97484, 541/998-6154) for more information. They can also tell you how to get to the mid-March **daffodil drive** on Ferguson Road west of Junction City.

Another summer event outside Eugene is Springfield's **Filbert Festival.** Held at Island Park by the river, this assemblage of food and crafts booths and top music acts is augmented by bungee jumping, a timber sports competition, and Native American cultural displays. To find out more about the mid-August fete, contact the Springfield Chamber of Commerce (541/746-1651).

Autumn is ushered in with the **Eugene Celebration.** This two-week fete in late September includes such events as the mayor's Fine Art Show, readings by Oregon authors at the Hult

charmers and belly dancers at the **Gypsy Stage.** Or dance to the national and international stars of rock 'n' roll, reggae, and alternative music on the **Main Stage.**

Starting to sound less like a hippie fair and more like a well-catered and -established art convention? Don't worry; there's always a sojourn into geo-socio-political-eco-consciousness at **Community Village.** Several booths here and in **Energy Park** teach and demonstrate the latest in new and matured '60s activism and environmental awareness.

Tired already? So are we, but there's a whole year to rest up and reminisce before the next Oregon Country Fair.

This annual fantasyland is staged among the trees east of Noti on ORE 126. The best way to get there without much traffic is to take the free shuttle from the downtown bus station near 11th and Willamette. It goes directly to the wooded fair site near the Long Tom River, 13 miles from Eu-gene. Another shuttle departs from Civic Stadium on Pearl across from South Eugene High School. Bus service usually begins at about 10:30 A.M., with the last departure from the fair site at 7 P.M. Due to the popularity of this event, which attracts more than 50,000 attendees, mandatory advance ticket purchase prior to arrival on-site has been instituted for those taking mass transit. Car access to the fair is open 10 A.M.–6 P.M., but on-site parking is limited. Parking costs $5 at the gate, a couple of bucks less when reserved in advance.

For more information, contact the Oregon Country Fair (P.O. Box 2972, Eugene 97402, 541/343-4298, www.oregoncountryfair.org). Admission is $10–15 (kids 12 and under free, 55 and above half price). Purchase tickets in advance through **Fastixx** (800/992-8499) at the Hult Center, or at the U. of O. Erb Memorial Union. Gates open at 11 A.M. and close at 7 P.M. Dogs, drugs, and video recorders are prohibited.

Center, the Fifth Avenue Jazz Festival, and the coronation of the Slug Queen. Street performers all over town and food booths in the parking lot at 8th Avenue and Willamette also help the community put its best foot forward. For more information, contact Downtown Events Management Inc. (541/681-4108).

ACCOMMODATIONS

A few bed-and-breakfasts and a youth hostel provide the best values for the dollar in town. Seniors, however, can use various discount cards (AARP, etc.) to offset the high prices of such upscale accommodations as the Valley River Inn (which also has special packages at a good value). Otherwise, you have a choice of inexpensive motels on East Broadway and moderately priced ones on Franklin Boulevard. The best bets for the budget traveler are the campsites and rustic digs east of town on the McKenzie River Highway (see "The McKenzie River Highway" in Cascades chapter). As with many Oregon towns, an 8 percent room tax is added to the tariff.

Backpackers passin' thru the big city, prospective students checking out the U, or just about any dollar-wise traveler will appreciate the **Eugene International Hostel** (2352 Willamette St., 541/349-0589). For $16 per night, members ($19 nonmembers) can sleep in the communal rooms with bunk beds or spend $30–40 for a private room. Guests enjoy the hospitality of a spacious historic home with a comfortable living room, large dining area, and patio. With some of Eugene's best food shopping close by, it's possible to take full advantage of excellent kitchen facilities (the kitchen is vegetarian), assuming you can resist the equally compelling area dining. A #24 or #25 city bus goes from downtown to the corner of 24th and Willamette, stopping a few blocks from the hostel. Check in between 5 P.M. and 10 P.M. Check out at 11 A.M. Reservations suggested.

The **Best Western New Oregon Motel** (1655 Franklin Blvd., 541/683-3669) is our choice for visiting parents of U. of O. students or for folks in town to attend a sporting or cultural event. It's located right across the street from the Registration Office and dormitories. Like all Best Westerns, this place offers many amenities (spa, pool, fitness room, racquetball

THE WILLAMETTE VALLEY

court) and well-appointed rooms. Behind the hotel lie Alton Baker Park and a walking and jogging trail along the river. Rates run $70–85.

The **Lorane Valley B&B** (86621 Lorane Hwy., 541/686-0241, www.loranevalley.com) is the perfect blend of best-of-the-country but close-to-the-city. Perched on a grassy knoll overlooking the Lorane Highway, this aerie is just minutes from downtown, with rooms for $80–90. About the only thing that might deter first-time guests is a steep road that looks more treacherous than it is. Peaceful summer nights with cricket lullabies and morning breakfast highlighted by Dutch babies overflowing with whipped cream make this a favorite during the Bach Festival and graduation, so reserve well in advance. If you are bringing small children, please make prior arrangements.

The **Campbell House** (252 Pearl St., 541/343-1119, www.campbellhouse.com) is a 19-room Victorian in the historic east Skinner Butte neighborhood ($92 and up includes breakfast). Proximity to the Fifth Street Market and the river, as well as the sophistication of a European-style pension, makes this antique-filled 1892 gem a good lodging choice.

The upstairs of a popular eatery and just a block from campus, the **Excelsior Inn,** (754 E. 13th Ave., 541/485-1206, www.excelsior.com) offers 14 attractive bed-and-breakfast rooms featuring antiques, cherry furniture, marble tile, and fresh-cut flowers ($79–225, less in winter). Spa rooms are available in the suites, and king or queen beds and computer ports are in every room. Rates include breakfast from the menu.

Ask any local what the best place in town is and the answer will probably be the **Valley River Inn** (1000 Valley River Way, Valley River Center, 541/687-0123, www.valleyriverinn.com). With front and back doorways opening onto Eugene's prime shopping area and the Willamette River, respectively, this upscale hostelry offers modern convenience close to the tranquility of nature. River views, a first-rate restaurant (Sweetwaters; see "Food," below), a crackling fire in the lobby, proximity to riverside hiking and biking, and pool and spa facilities add to the allure. With prices exceeding $200 for river-view rooms ($50 less in winter), we would recommend this first-

class lodging only to business travelers on an expense account if not for the hotel's family packages. For $150–160 per room, a family also receives recreational options.

FOOD

While there are a number of good restaurants in Eugene, you'll probably be more impressed by the staggering array of locally made gourmet products and natural foods available at markets here. As you might have guessed, many of these delectables are foremost chemically free and nutritionally sound. Produce labels in many Eugene specialty food stores intone "fresh," "home grown," and "organic" with the constancy of a mantra, and meat and poultry markets carry products that are rabbinically pure.

Health-Food Stores

Two of the leading purveyors of Eugene cuisine began as hippie health-food stores several decades ago. Today, **Sundance Natural Foods** (748 E. 24th, 541/345-6153) and the **Kiva** (125 W. 11th, 541/342-8666) stock more than just grains, sprouts, and vitamins, and feature some of the best selections of wine and organic produce in the state. Sundance's fresh salad bar and hot buffet is a good deal for anyone who enjoys large helpings of creative healthful entrées for $5. **Friendly Foods** (2757 Friendly, 541/688-3944) and **Wild Oats** (2489 Willamette, 541/345-1014, or 2580 Willakenzie Blvd., 541/334-6382) have expanded the largely vegetarian stock of their hippie forefathers with more meat and takeout items.

Breakfast and American Cafés

The eateries on the campus periphery are a cut above those found in most college towns. Start the day at **Campus Glenwood** (1340 Alder, 541/687-0355) or at the southside **Glenwood** (2588 Willamette St., 541/687-8201), both open daily. The menus offer standard American breakfast fare, with a few entrées deferring to eclectic college-town tastes. What these establishments have in common are large portions in the $5 range.

If your tummy can just handle coffee and a

croissant in the morning and your wallet can yield no more than several dollars, head to **Espresso Roma** (825 E. 13th Ave., 541/484-0878). If hunger pangs should set in, this restaurant has a breakfast special for early arrivals and stuffed croissants and other pastries. Open daily. There is also a delightful outside courtyard that fills up when the rain stops. A few doors down, tasty, inexpensive breakfasts and lunches can be had at **Cafe Siena** (853 E. 13th Ave., 541/344-0300). With menu choices in the $3–6 range, this place is popular with the campus crowd. Homemade soup seems to be a lunchtime staple for regulars here.

Rennie's Landing (1214 Kincaid, 541/687-0600) serves breakfast, gourmet burgers, homemade soups, beer, and wine. Late-night and predawn hours, an outside deck, and a location right across from the U. of O. campus make this a favorite with the campus crowd—particularly after Duck games. Open daily.

Sweetwaters, the elegant restaurant of the Valley River Inn (1000 Valley River Way, 541/687-0123), boasts a riverside outdoor deck that might offer Eugene's most delightful dining experience on a warm summer night. The extensive menu draws largely on regional ingredients assembled creatively to best bring out the flavors of mountain, valley, and coast. Whatever you decide to do, take a sweater—it cools down fast at night. Main courses are $12–20. Sunday brunch here won the local newspaper readers poll as the best in town.

Brewpubs and Fish-n-Chips

Not too far from the campus, the McMenamin brothers have two **brewpubs** (1485 E. 19th. St., 541/242-4025, and 1243 High St., 541/345-4905). Each repeats the successful formula of the establishments discussed in the Portland chapter. The High Street pub is in a comfy converted old house, with a tree-shaded brickwork back patio that makes the perfect hangout on a hot afternoon. Open daily.

Vying with Sweetwaters for Eugene's most scenic restaurant river frontage is **McMenamin's North Bank** (22 Club Rd., 541/343-5622). With an outdoor deck, picturesque windows overlooking the Willamette, and a moderately priced menu ($7–12 for sandwiches and pasta dishes) of quality pub grub featuring everything from eggplant sandwiches to Communication Breakdown Burger, this is the best place to experience how Oregon's preeminent brewpub-meisters have made dining fun. Should wintertime mist obscure river views, you'll appreciate the penchant of the Brothers M for eccentric woodwork and wistful murals. (Open till 1 A.M. Mon–Sat., till 11 P.M. Sunday.)

On the east side of Blair Boulevard on 7th Street across from the places just mentioned is **Full Boat Cafe** (830 W. 7th Ave., 541/484-2722), a fish market with an attached café. The array of fish-n-chips ($6 range) is noteworthy for its freshness and tartar sauces. The attached fish market sells the freshest Dungeness crab in town, excellent smoked salmon, and microbrews. Open daily.

Newman's (1545 Willamette St., 541/344-2371) is a walk-up fish-n-chips window. Here you can get gourmet renditions of salmon, halibut, and cod with chips for $4–6. Closed Sundays.

Italian

In the shadow of the campus is one of the best restaurants in town, the **Excelsior Cafe** (754 E. 13th Ave., 541/485-1206), located in a charming old colonial home. Lunch and dinner are served daily, and Sunday brunch 10A.M.–2P.M., featuring such dishes as fungi omelet and hazelnut pancakes. The Italian menu changes with the seasons, but you can always find "gourmet" pizzas and dinner main courses ($10–26) garnished with such Willamette Valley signature ingredients as goat cheese, elephant garlic, filberts, and Oregon blue cheese. Despite a reputation for fine food, it's the desserts and cozy bar that are the biggest draws here on weeknights.

Up the street from the Excelsior, **Napoli Restaurant and Bakery** (686 E. 13th Ave., 541/485-4552) serves gourmet pizza, soups, pasta, and an array of baked goods and desserts. Southern Italian specialties doused in a piquant tomato sauce, like spinach manicotti and polenta with sausage, stand out here, as do a variety of calzones. This airy plant-filled café with sloping glass walls and classical music is the perfect place to sip espresso and talk; checks rarely exceed $12. Closed Sunday.

Across the street from Cafe Zenon is a spacious two-story Italian restaurant, **Ambrosia** (174 Broadway, 541/342-4141). Antique furnishings and stained glass set the stage for Old World cuisine prepared to suit contemporary tastes. The individual-size gourmet pizzas (cooked slowly in a wood-burning oven), a wonderful squid-in-batter appetizer, and northern Italian specialties will make spaghetti and meatballs seem like old hat here (entrées $10–16). Ambrosia was honored by *Wine Spectator* for having one of the most outstanding wine lists in the country.

Pizza Pete's (2673 Willamette, 541/484-0996) is another Italian place that's particularly popular with the college crowd. Tuesday night the all-you-can-eat spaghetti bash featuring four different sauces and bottomless baskets of garlic bread lines 'em up all evening long. The house record is seven plates of spaghetti. Prices are usually under $10 a plate. Open daily.

The Fifth Street Market may lack a microbrewery, but one block west, the **Steelhead Brewery and Cafe** (199 E. 5th Ave., 541/686-2739) gives suds connoisseurs a nearby place to quaff the city's best local brew. If the results of the 2002 Great American Beer Festival are any indication, this distinction is an understatement. Out of 570 imports and domestic brews in the contest, judges found Steelhead Stout and Steelhead Amber best in their respective categories. The paneled walls, comfortable seating, and quality pub fare are other enticements to pass an hour or two here. The varied menu can include calzones, pizza, burgers, sandwiches, pastas, soups, vegetarian entrées, and calamari plates (main courses $5–9).

Dinner on the outside deck at **Beppe & Gianni's Trattoria** (1646 E. 19th Ave., 541/683-6661) is one of Eugene's coveted summertime dining experiences. The menu features homemade pastas with light northern Italian cream or olive oil based sauces, graced by fresh vegetables, meats, or fish. Meals are around $10–15.

Chances are that many U. of O. alums still remember the status enjoyed by **Track Town Pizza** (1809 Franklin Blvd., 541/484-2799) as the staff of life for late-night cramming sessions. The pies are still served with diverse toppings, fresh ingredients, and rapid delivery.

The same clientele frequent **Sy's New York Pizza** (1211 Alder, 541/686-9598) down the block. Sy would make his mentor, Original Ray's of New York, proud with a by-the-slice operation that lines 'em up at lunch and dinnertime. Deep-dish or regular crust slice prices hover near $3 with an added topping.

Mexican

A quarter mile west of center city is Blair Boulevard and the Whiteaker Neighborhood. In recent years, a budget restaurant row has been developing in what had been a strip of fast-food places and greasy spoons in previous decades. These places are, for the most part, easy on the pocketbook while offering an interesting variety of cuisines.

A few blocks south across 7th Street is a concentration of eateries including **La Tiendita/Taco Loco** (900 Blair Blvd., 541/683-9171), serving up locally renowned tamales and other south-of-the-border specialties adjacent to a store devoted to Latino foodstuffs. Low prices ($7–9), huge portions, and down-home Mexican and El Salvadoran specialties (try the *pupusas*) draw a large takeout clientele at lunch. Closed Sunday. Close by, **Los Jarritos** (764 Blair Blvd., 541/344-0650), operated by a member of the same family, offers similar fare. The **Jade Palace** (906 W. 7th Ave., 541/344-9523) is noteworthy for seafood and vegetarian fare, with buffets offering good dollar value. Closed Monday.

Asian, Indian, and Middle Eastern

Shiki (81 Coburg Rd., 541/343-1936) is located across the Ferry Street Bridge, a few miles north of downtown shortly before the exit for I-105 to Springfield. The classic decor of the restaurant's tatami rooms, 53 kinds of sushi, a varied selection of sake, and such traditional dishes as *shabu shabu* belie the symmetrical western contours of the restaurant's facade, a former Sizzler, located in the Goodwill parking lot. While it'll take at least $15 to feel full here, it's a small price to pay for a first-rate international dining experience. Open Tues.–Sun.

The best buffet in town for quality and affordability is **Taste of India** (2495 Hilyard St.,

541/485-9560). For $8 at lunch and $11 for the Sunday dinner buffet, you get an all-you-can-eat selection of expertly prepared tandoori dishes, breads, and vegetarian selections. Open seven days a week.

Downstairs in the Fifth Street Market, **Casablanca** (296 W. 5th Ave., 541/342-3885) has Middle Eastern cuisine with pita sandwiches, babaghanoush, hummus, and other regional specialties. This is a good place for lunch in the $6 range. Open daily.

In the heart of downtown, **Anatolia** (992 Willamette, 541/343-9661) features Greek and Indian food par excellence. Spicy curries and vindaloo chicken are complemented by *saganaki* (fried cheese), spanakopita (spinach cheese pie), and gyro sandwiches. The best baklava in town with a shot of ouzo or retsina can finish off a richly flavored and moderately priced repast (most expensive dinner entrée, $14). Open for lunch Mon.–Sat. and dinner daily.

A few blocks east is downtown's gourmet gulch. Two places stand out from the pack. **Cafe Zenon** (898 Pearl St., 541/343-3005) has an international menu that is constantly changing. Despite this challenge, the Zenon manages to pull off dishes ranging from Italian to Thai in fine style. The only problems you'll run into are getting in—reservations aren't taken and there's often a wait—and getting out without stopping at the eye-popping dessert display. Breakfast and lunch can be enjoyed here at half the price of dinner ($15–20); open daily. When there's a wait at Cafe Zenon, **Full City Coffee** (842 Pearl St., 541/344-0475), several doors down, can be counted on to sustain you with the best coffee in a town. Famous for its daily grind, this is one of several locations in town.

Several blocks west of the library, **Cafe Soriah** (384 W. 13th Ave., 541/342-4410) is a popular choice for a romantic dinner or weekday business lunch. Both its patio for summer outdoor dining and its bar topped a local restaurant poll for ambience, but the Mediterranean/Middle Eastern cuisine is the real attraction. Moussaka and various dishes featuring chicken and lamb with vegetables sautéed in olive oil stand out here. Dinner entrée prices begin around $10.

A noontime favorite is the combination lunch at **China Blue** (879 E. 13th Ave., 541/343-2832). Sumptuous lunch specials frequently go for less than $5. Indonesian dishes and Sunday dim sum vary the menu. Around the block, **Maple Garden** (1275 Alder St., 541/683-8128) celebrates several decades serving Chinese specialties from different provinces to students (the preferred hangout for the U. of O.'s Asian community). The $5 lunch specials and dinner selections topping out at $9 have huge portions and may be the biggest bang for the buck in town.

> *The 2002 Great American Beer Festival named Steelhead Stout and Steelhead Amber best in their respective categories.*

Dessert

A block south from the Vets Club on the corner of Willamette is **Euphoria Chocolate Co.** (6 W. 17th Ave., 541/343-9223), a chocolatier of national repute. Their Grand Marnier truffle and other confections are sold around town. Come here after holidays and buy the bite-size Santas, hearts, and bunnies at reduced price.

INFORMATION AND SERVICES

A bevy of literature befitting Oregon's second-most-populated town can be obtained from the Convention and Visitors Association of Lane County, **CVALCO,** (115 W. 8th Ave. Suite 190, Eugene 97401, 800/547-5445, www.visitlanecounty.org). The entrance is on Olive Street.

The **Smith Family Bookstore** (768 E. 13th, 541/345-1651, and 525 Willamette St., 541/343-4717) purveys an excellent collection of used books. The **University of Oregon Bookstore** (13th and Kincaid) and the **Bookmark** (865 Olive, 541/484-0512) have the best selection of new titles and periodicals.

Sip N' Surf (99 W. 10th, #119, 503/343-9607, www.sipnsurf.com) provides Internet access, as does the **Web Zone** (296 E. 5th, Ste. 102, 541/434-0442, www.ido.net/webzone/).

Public radio stations are all clustered near the bottom of the FM dial, with KLCC (89.7 FM) the dominant presence. The station's programming ranges from new-wave jazz to blues. It also has a dynamic news department. The University of Oregon station KWAX (90.1 FM), broadcast in eastern Oregon and on the coast, provides continuous classical music. Perhaps the most popular AM station in the area is talk radio KUGN (590 AM).

Eugene Weekly (1251 Lincoln St., 541/484-0519) has the best entertainment listings in Eugene. At the beginning of each season, the magazine's *Chow* edition will point you in the direction of Eugene gourmet restaurants. At all times, environmental articles and reviews by David Johnson are a highlight. This publication is available free at commercial establishments all over town.

TRANSPORTATION

If you're in your own car, remember (1) the campus is in the southeastern part of town; (2) 1st Avenue parallels the Willamette River; and (3) Willamette Street divides the city east and west. The downtown mall, which encompasses the area from 6th through 11th Streets (north to south) and Pearl through Charnelton (east to west), allows through traffic north or south via Olive and Willamette Streets. Navigation is complicated by many one-way roads and dead-ends. Look for alleyways that allow through traffic to avoid getting stuck.

Amtrak (4th and Willamette, 541/344-6265, www.tickets.amtrak.com) offers once-daily service both north to Portland/Seattle and south to Sacramento, Oakland, and Los Angeles on the *Coast Starlight*. There are also several high-speed trains heading north to Portland daily. In addition, Amtrak runs several express buses each day between Portland and Eugene.

Greyhound (9th and Pearl, 800/231-2222) is the other major mode of long-distance public transport. Ten Greyhound buses a day let you head south to San Francisco or north to Portland (two daily) from Eugene. Sample fares from Eugene to Portland are $15 one-way, $25 round-trip. Greyhound also links Eugene with the coast and Bend.

Around town, **Lane Transit District** (541/687-5555, www.ltd.org) has canopied pavilions displaying the bus timetables downtown. The bus mall on 11th and Willamette has pocket-sized schedules. Fares are about $1.50 (children and seniors half price), about a third less on weekends, and half price after 7 P.M. All buses are equipped with bike racks. The **ride board** on the bottom floor of the Erb Memorial Union at the University of Oregon has a list of rides available for those willing to share gas and driving. **Emerald City Taxi** (541/686-2010) is fast, reliable, and reasonably priced.

The **Eugene Airport** (541/682-5430, www.ci.eugene.or.us) is a 20-minute drive northwest from downtown. Just get on the Delta Highway off Washington Street and follow the signs. There is no bus service to the airport. United and United Express (800/241-6522) and Horizon (800/547-9308) all operate flights in and out of Eugene. **OmniShuttle** (541/461-7959, www.omnishuttle.com) provides door-to-door shuttle service to and from Eugene Airport to six geographic zones in Lane County. **Rental car companies** Avis, Budget, Hertz, and Enterprise also have kiosks at the airport.

Coastal Oregon

For most Oregon visitors who travel west of the Coast Range, life's a beach. Despite Pacific temperatures cold enough to render swimming an at-your-own-risk activity, the cliffside ocean vistas, wildlife, beachcombing, and other attractions make the coast the state's number-one regional destination.

Though parts of a seamless whole, sharing a common shoreline and linked by an unbroken scenic highway, each section of the coast possesses a distinct regional flavor and allure that have attracted visitors for centuries—to explore, to exploit, to enjoy, to escape. Feeling far from everything, the south coast is a world apart, a landscape of mountains cloaked by dense evergreen forest, parting to reveal wild rivers and black-sand beaches punctuated with dramatic rock formations. Much of the central coast is "Dune Country," an otherworldly sandscape dotted with lakes and bisected by broad, lazy estuaries. In the north, journey's end for Lewis and Clark, steep headlands break up wide, sandy beaches, extending to the state's far northwestern tip at the mouth of the Columbia River.

THE LAND

The Oregon coast encompasses nearly 400 miles of beaches, rainforest, dunes, high-rise headlands, rocky sea stacks and islands, and tidal pools showcasing marine worlds in miniature. The narrow coastal plateau is hemmed in by the Klamath Mountains in the state's southern quarter and by the Coast Range beginning near Coos Bay in the north, which together form a palisade between the sea and the state's interior. Neither range is particularly high, with their tallest peaks barely topping 4,000 feet. More than a dozen

© MARK MORRIS

Haystack Rock at Cannon Beach

NORTH COAST

Ilwaco
101
401
4
WA
Columbia River
OR
Astoria
Warrenton
30
To Portland
Gearhart
202
Seaside
Tillamook Head
Cannon Beach
26
Elsie
Cape Falcon
53
Nehalem River
Manzanita
Nehalem
To Portland
Wheeler
PACIFIC
Rockaway Beach
OCEAN
Garibaldi
Bay City
Tillamook Bay
Wilson River
Cape Meares
6
Oceanside
Tillamook
Netarts
Cape Lookout
101
Beaver
Hebo
Pacific City
Cloverdale
To Portland
Siuslaw
Neskowin
National
22
Willamina
Cascade Head
Forest
Otis
18
Grand Ronde
Lincoln City
Rose Lodge
To Salem
Salishan
Gleneden Beach
Siletz River
Depoe Bay
Siletz
0   10 mi
0   10 km
Logsden

© AVALON TRAVEL PUBLISHING, INC.

COASTAL OREGON

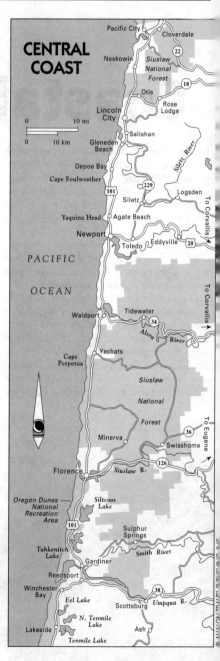

CENTRAL COAST

SOUTH COAST

To Florence
Gardiner
Reedsport
Umpqua R.
38
Winchester
Bay
Eel Lake
Lakeside
N. Tenmile
Lake
Tenmile Lake
Oregon Dunes
National Recreation
Area
101
Allegany
North Bend
Coos Bay
Charleston
Coos
Bay
S. Fork Coos R.
Cape Arago
Sumner
PACIFIC
Coquille
42S
Coquille
Point
Dora
Bandon
Norway
OCEAN
Myrtle Point
42
Bridge
To Roseburg
Langlois
South Fork Coquille R.
Denmark
Powers
Cape
Blanco
Sixes
Port Orford
Siskiyou
National
Forest
River
Ophir
Agness
Rogue
Wedderburn
Illinois River
Gold Beach
Kalmiopsis
Wilderness
101
River
Klamath Mountains
Carpenterville
Chetco
0   10 mi
0   10 km
Brookings
Harbor
OR
CA
To Crescent City

© AVALON TRAVEL PUBLISHING, INC.

major rivers and scores of smaller streams cut through these mountain barriers to the sea. The valleys the rivers follow through the mountains are the same routes traversed now by the east-west highways that link the coast with rest of the state.

With rare exceptions, all beaches in Oregon below mean high tide are owned by the public. This is thanks, largely, to Governor Oswald West, who in 1913 pushed through far-sighted legislation defining Oregon's ocean beaches as public highways (which they in fact were before real roads were built) and thus off-limits to private encroachment. Later, Oregon's Beach Bills of 1967 and 1972 were written to further guarantee public access to the state's gem of a coastline. In recent years, however, certain sections of this "publicly owned" paradise have increasingly become exclusive bailiwicks of the wealthy with gated communities cutting off access to certain beaches.

Black sand, high in iron and other metals, is common on the coast, particularly south of Coos Bay. There was also enough gold in the black sands to spur a flurry of gold-mining activity on the south coast 140 years ago. Scientists have known for decades of the placer deposits of heavy minerals washed ashore on prehistoric beaches thousands of years ago when ocean levels were much lower. These beach sands now lie submerged. Over the years, mining companies have eyed the continental shelf off the south coast for possible exploitation of ilmenite, magnetite, chromite, zircon, garnet, gold, and platinum. Despite a study indicating a significant presence of precious metals in the sands offshore from the Rogue River and Cape Blanco, though, the high costs of mining them discourage such ventures.

Speaking of sand, the central Oregon coast has about 32,000 acres of shimmering white dunes, the largest oceanfront collection in North America and the highest in the world. Some hills top out at over 500 feet high. Oregon's Sahara is located along a 40-mile stretch between Coos Bay and Florence. Buffeted by winds, the dunes are continually on the move; in some places, highways are in danger of being engulfed by the shifting sands.

COASTAL OREGON HIGHLIGHTS

- **Fort Clatsop National Monument,** Astoria, page 316
- **Golfing** at Bandon Dunes Golf Resort and Westin Salishan Golf Links, pages 221, 277
- **Jetboats on the Rogue River,** Gold Beach and vicinity, page 204
- **Old-growth forest hiking,** Cape Meares, Cape Perpetua, Drift Creek Wilderness, Loeb State Park, and other points coastwide, pages 198, 247–248, 253–254, 286
- **Oregon Coast Aquarium,** Newport, pages 256–258
- **Oregon Dunes National Recreation Area,** Reedsport, pages 235–236
- **Salmon, steelhead, and bottom fishing,** coastwide, page 193
- **Winter whale-watching,** coastwide, pages 192, 262, 269, 271

CLIMATE

Oregon's coastal weather can best be summed up as wet and mild. The coast as a whole receives roughly 70 inches of rain yearly on average. Most of that falls from late fall to mid-spring, while May through September are generally fairly dry.

The Lincoln City area tends to record the highest amounts of rain, with nearly 100 inches a year, while locations both north and south are generally less wet by comparison. Inland from the coastal plateau, the Coast and Klamath ranges receive substantially more precipitation. Precipitation averages 150 inches over the coastal mountains; indeed, in the unusually wet winter of 1996–1997, Laurel Mountain in the Coast Range near Lincoln City was drenched with 204 inches, Oregon's record.

The moderating influence of the Pacific Ocean gives the coastal region an unusually mild climate for a state so far north. Even in winter, daytime highs along the coast tend to reach the mid-50s Fahrenheit, while nighttime lows generally drop into the 40s. Spring, summer, and fall see highs in the 60s and into the 70s, with overnight lows staying in the mid-40s to mid-50s.

Summer highs above 90° F are unusual, though the mercury in south-coast locations such as Brookings and Bandon may top 100° F on rare occasions. Midwinter and spring dry spells with 60°-plus temperatures commonly occur.

Any time of year, the coast can be fairly breezy; in winter and spring, particularly, you may encounter proper gales scouring the beach. While that can make for terrific kite flying, picnics aren't quite so much fun at those times. In winter, the winds typically blow from the south and southwest while the gentler summer winds usually come from the northeast.

When to Go

In general, count on good traveling weather mid-April through mid-September, with a preponderance of daytime highs in the 60s. Within this period, there might be enough cloudy days to dismay travelers accustomed to simmering California beaches, but storm-watching is an acquired taste that makes the Oregon coast attractive when the weather turns nasty. An added plus is that when summertime inversions drive temperatures above 100° F east of the Coast Range, the heat draws cooler maritime air to the shore. The mountains often lock in these welcome fronts, though they also can cause coastal fog and overcast conditions to linger. Nonetheless, respite from the characteristic morning fog banks in summer is often only minutes away upriver along one of the many tidal estuaries. As a general rule, September is the most reliable month for clear coastal weather.

Finally, newcomers to the region at any time of year should know that the icy temperatures of the coastal waters (as low as 40–45° F) make the beaches more valued for beachcombing than for swimming. Even in the hottest days of summer, water temperature doesn't exceed 62° F, and hypothermia is an ever-present danger that sometimes kills.

FLORA

The state of Oregon has long been associated in the public mind with such sobriquets as the "Emerald Empire" and the "Chlorophyll Commonwealth." While giant conifers and a profuse understory of greenery do in fact predominate, this ecosystem represents only the most visible part of the Oregon coast's bountiful botany. In addition to Brookings's Azalea Festival and Florence's Rhododendron Festival, coast-bound travelers come to take in such horticultural highlights as the insect-eating Darlingtonia plant, Oregon myrtle trees, and some remaining stands of ancient old-growth forest. Serious botanists might search out the pine mushroom, exclusive to the Oregon dunes and Japan, or probe the Kalmiopsis Wilderness near the south coast, habitat to many rare plants.

Coos Bay marks the boundary between the Mediterranean beach floras found south to California and the sub-arctic species growing north from there into Washington and British Columbia.

Dune, Beach, and Bog

Apart from the spectacular springtime fireworks of rhododendron and azalea blossoms, the Oregon coast doesn't show off its **wildflowers** as boldly as other parts of the state, such as Steens Mountain, the Cascades, and the Wallowas. The flowering plants of beach, dunes, and headlands, rather, tend to be more subtle. Among some of the species found only along the Oregon coast are beach bursage, yellow sand verbena, beach evening-primrose, seashore bluegrass, dune tansy, and silvery phacelia. The best months for viewing wildflowers are usually June and July.

Many coastal travelers will notice **European beachgrass** (*Ammophila arenaria*) covering the sand wherever they go. Originally planted in the 1930s to inhibit dune growth, the thick, rapidly spreading grass worked too well, solidifying into a ridge behind the shoreline, blocking the windblown sand from replenishing the rest of the beach and suppressing native plants. Populations of formerly common natives such as beach morning-glory, yellow abronia, gray beach pea, and American dune-grass are now much diminished. The now-endangered pink sand

U.S. Highway 101, the Main Street of the Oregon coast, is a 363-mile National Scenic Byway that was recently designated an "All-American Road," one of 20 in the country selected for its archaeological, cultural, historic, natural, recreational, and scenic qualities.

verbena, once abundant along the coast from British Columbia to northern California, is restricted to a few locations along central and southern Oregon coast. Herbicides, burning, and tilling have been employed in recent years to remove European beachgrass and restore the dune ecosystem to a more natural state, but progress against the pernicious weed is slow and difficult.

Freshwater wetlands and bogs, created where water is trapped by the sprawling sand dunes along the central coast, provide habitats for some unusual species. Best known among these is the cobra lily (*Darlingtonia californica*), which can be viewed up close at the just north of Florence. Also called Darlingtonia or pitcher plant, this carnivorous bog dweller survives on hapless insects lured into a specialized chamber, where they are trapped and digested. For more information, see "Darlingtonia Botanical Wayside" under "Florence and Vicinity," later in this chapter.

Coastal salt marshes, occurring in the upper intertidal zones of coastal bays and estuaries, have been dramatically reduced due to land "reclamation" projects such as drainage, diking, and other human disturbances. The halophytes

© MARK MORRIS

Oregon dunes landscape, near Florence

ROUTES TO THE COAST

From the Interstate 5 corridor, where most of the state's population is concentrated, 10 main routes will get you to the coast. Most are two-lane state highways for all or part of the journey through rural hinterlands and the coastal mountains.

From Portland, **U.S. 30** runs north through St. Helen's and follows the bottomlands along the south bank of the Columbia River to Astoria, 98 miles to the northwest. If you're coming down from the north on I-5, cross the Columbia from Longview, WA, to Rainier, OR, and continue west on U.S. 30 from there.

Busy **U.S. 26** runs west, then angles northwest, from Portland, through agricultural Washington County and then into the woods of the Clatsop State Forest before joining U.S. 101 between Cannon Beach and Seaside. About 25 miles west of Portland, **ORE 6** branches off from U.S. 26 and follows a roller-coaster course alongside the Wilson River to Tillamook.

A third route from Portland starts with **ORE 99W** and a dozen maddening stop-and-go miles through the strip development of Tigard. After Newburg you emerge into a lovely countryside of vineyards and hazelnut orchards around Dundee. Pick up **ORE 18** for the second half of the trip, which runs past Oregon's number one attraction, the Spirit Mountain Casino in Grande Ronde, before you hit the Coast Highway just north of Lincoln City and another Indian-owned casino, Chinook Winds. Note that the casinos attract more than three million visitors a year, which helps make ORE 18 one of the most dangerous roads to drive in the state.

From Salem, **ORE 22** runs 26 miles to the west and connects with ORE 18 about midway to the coast.

Farther south, **U.S. 20** curves down from Albany through Corvallis and on to Philomath. From there you can continue 46 miles to Newport, or veer southwest on **ORE 34** for a winding 59 miles through a remote section of the Siuslaw National Forest to Waldport.

ORE 126, from Eugene to Florence, is one of the more direct routes, zipping through the flatlands and foothills before throwing you a few curves on the way to the burg of Mapleton, and then hugging the Siuslaw River the last dozen miles.

Near Curtin, south of Cottage Grove, leave I-5 for a brief detour on ORE 99 before catching **ORE 38.** This scenic two-lane—Oregon's "foremost motorcycle road" according to Harley-Davidson—follows the valley of the mighty Umpqua River to Reedsport, about a 57-mile trip. If you're coming from the south on I-5, cut off onto **ORE 138** at Sutherlin to save some miles on this route.

ORE 42 shadows the Coquille River through farm country for much of its course from Roseburg to Coos Bay. Recent improvements to this highway make it possible to get there in under two hours, but it's a longish 87 miles. Motorists should still be aware that this thoroughfare carries more truck traffic than any other interior-to-coast road in Oregon. But weekenders will encounter few trucks and light traffic to impede the enjoyment of the waysides, wineries, and historic buildings. If the southern coast is your destination, branch off on **ORE 42S** at Coquille; from there it's 17 miles to Bandon.

South of Roseburg, if you're partial to pavement there's no good and direct route to the coast. The only option is **U.S. 199** from Grants Pass, skirting the remote eastern edge of the Kalmiopsis Wilderness before dropping into northern California. The highway runs through the awesome giants of Redwoods National Park before hitting the Coast Highway near Crescent City. From there, it's 22 miles north up to Brookings. All told, count on about two hours to travel this roundabout, albeit beautiful, 100-mile route.

(salt-loving plants) that thrive in this specialized environment include pickleweed, saltgrass, fleshy jaumea, salt marsh dodder, arrow-grass, sand spurrey, and seaside plantain. For an excellent introduction to this complex ecosystem, visit the **South Slough National Estuarine Research Reserve,** south of Coos Bay (covered under "Sights" in the Bay Area section, later in this chapter). **Bandon Marsh National Wildlife Refuge** (see "Recreation" under "Bandon," later in this chapter) protects the largest remaining tract of salt marsh within the Coquille River estuary. Major habitats include undisturbed saltmarsh, mudflat, and Sitka spruce and alder riparian communities, which provide resting and feeding areas for migratory waterfowl, shore and wading birds, and raptors.

FAUNA

In the air, on the land, under the water, and in between, opportunities for wildlife viewing abound all along the coast, but standout areas include the state's six coastal national wildlife refuges: Oregon Islands, Cape Meares, and Three Arch Rocks protect important habitat for seabirds, seals, and sea lions among coastal rocks, reefs, islands, and several headland areas, while Nestucca Bay, Siletz Bay, and Bandon Marsh national wildlife refuges preserve estuarine habitats of saltmarsh, wetlands, and woods rich in waterfowl, raptors, fish, and other fauna.

Tidepools

For most visitors, the most fascinating coastal ecosystems in Oregon are the rocky tidepools. These Technicolor windows offer an up-close look at one of the richest—and harshest—environments, the intertidal zone, where pummeling surf, unflinching sun, and the cycle of tides demand tenacity and special adaptation of its inhabitants.

Marine biologists subdivide this natural blender where surf meets shore into three main habitat layers, based on their position relative to tide levels. The **high intertidal zone,** inundated only during the highest tides, is home to creatures that can either move, such as crabs, or are well adapted to tolerate daily desiccation, such as acorn barnacles and finger limpets, chitons, green

Green anemones are common inhabitants of Northwest tidepools, like this one near Yachats.

algae, and limpets. The turbulent **mid-intertidal zone** is covered and uncovered by the tides, usually twice each day. In the upper portion of this zone, California mussels and goose barnacles may thickly blanket the rocks, while ochre sea stars and green sea anemones are common lower down, along with sea lettuce, sea palms, snails, sponges, and whelks. Below that, the **low intertidal zone** is exposed only during the lowest tides. Because it is covered by water most of the time, this zone has the greatest diversity of organisms in the tidal area. Residents include many of the organisms found in the higher zones, as well as sculpins, abalone, and purple sea urchins.

Standout destinations for exploring tidepools include Cape Arago, Cape Perpetua, the Marine Gardens at Devil's Punchbowl, and beaches south and north of Gold Beach—among many other spots. Tidepool explorers should be mindful that, despite the fact that the plants and animals in the tidepools are well adapted to withstand the elements, they and their ecosystem are actually quite fragile, and they're very sensitive to human interference. Avoid stepping on mussels, anemones, and barnacles, and take nothing from the tidepools. In the Oregon Islands National Wildlife Refuge and other specially protected areas, removal or harassment of any living organism may be treated as a misdemeanor punishable by fines.

Birds

One of the most immediately noticeable forms of wildlife at the coast are the birds of sea, shore, and estuary. The abundance and variety of species you may encounter are a large part of the reason that Oregon is rapidly gaining a reputation as one of the best bird-watching states. Seasonal variance in populations is often dramatic, so timing is important.

The **Oregon Islands National Wildlife Refuge,** which comprises all the 1,400-plus offshore islands, reefs, and rocks from Tillamook Head to the California border, is a haven for the largest concentration of nesting seabirds along the West Coast, thanks to the abundance of protected nesting habitat. During the April–August breeding season, seabirds that can be seen here include common murres, pigeon guillemots, rare tufted puffins, Brandt's and pelagic cormorants, and black oystercatchers, along with the ubiquitous western gulls. From June to October, you may spy brown pelicans skimming the waves. Aleutian Canada geese use Table and Haystack rocks during March and early April.

In terms of sheer numbers and variety, the coast's mudflats at low tide and the tidal estuaries also make excellent bird-watching environments. Species to look for on the flats and shorelines include Pacific golden-plovers and pectoral and Baird's sandpipers. The **western snowy plover,** listed as threatened under the Endangered Species Act, gets special protection at the state's nine nesting sites in Curry, Coos, Douglas, and Lane Counties. The small shorebird, which resembles a sandpiper, nests on open sandy beaches above the high-tide line, and is sensitive to disturbance from human foot traffic, vehicles, and unleashed dogs. During the nesting season, mid-March to mid-September, coast visitors may encounter areas posted or roped off to protect snowy plover nests.

Resident and migratory birds commonly spotted on the estuaries and lakes of the coast include common loon, western and horned grebes, great blue heron, American widgeon, greater scaup, common goldeneye, bufflehead, and red-breasted merganser.

Seals, Sea Lions, and Otters

Pacific harbor seals, California sea lions, and Steller sea lions are frequently sighted in Oregon waters. California sea lions are the animals you might have seen in circuses. These 1,000-pound mammals are characterized by their large size and small earflaps,

which seals lack. Unlike seals, they can point their rear flippers forward to give them better mobility on land. Lacking the dense underfur that covers seals, sea lions tend to prefer warmer waters.

Steller sea lions can be seen at the Sea Lion Caves (covered under "Florence and Vicinity," later in this chapter). They also breed on reefs off Gold Beach and Port Orford. The largest sea lion species, males can weigh more than a ton. Their coats tend to be gray rather than black like California sea lions'. They also differ from their California counterparts in that they are comfortable in colder water.

Look for Pacific harbor seals in bays and estuaries up and down the coast, sometimes miles inland. They're nonmigratory, have no earflaps, and can be distinguished from sea lions because they're much smaller (150–300 pounds) and have mottled fur that ranges in color from pale cream to rusty brown.

Another marine mammal that was once common on the Oregon coast, and indeed along the entire Pacific coast from Japan to Mexico, is the **sea otter.** Two centuries of ruthless hunting by Russian, European, and American fur traders, though, nearly eradicated the species entirely. By the time Oregon's last known sea otter was killed, in 1906, the otters had disappeared from British Columbia to central California. Today, the only sea otters living in Oregon are those in the Oregon Zoo and the Oregon Coast Aquarium, but an organization called the Elakha Alliance is working to restore otters to their natural habitat.

Gray Whales

Few sights along the Oregon coast elicit more excitement than that of a surfacing whale. The most common large whale seen from shore along the west coast of North America is the gray whale (*Eschrichtius robustus*). These behemoths can reach 45 feet in length and weigh 35 tons. The sight of a mammal as big as a Greyhound bus erupting from the sea has a way of emptying the mind of mundane concerns. Wreathed in seaweed and sporting barnacles and other parasites on its back, a California gray whale might look more like the hull of an old ship were it not for its expressive eyes.

After decades of hunting had brought them to

the brink of extinction, gray whales gained full protection in 1946 by the International Whaling Commission. In the ensuing years, the population has recovered dramatically. When the gray was removed from the Endangered Species List in 1994, the population was estimated at 23,000, which is thought to be close to its pre-whaling population. Gray whales continue to enjoy protection worldwide, apart from a quota harvested each year along the Siberian coast.

Some gray whales are found off the Oregon coast all year, including an estimated 200–400 during the summer, though they're most visible and numerous when migrating populations pass through Oregon waters on their way south December–February and northward early March through April. This annual journey from the rich feeding grounds of the Bering and Chukchi seas of Alaska to the calving grounds of Mexico amounts to some 10,000 miles, the longest migration of any mammal. Their numbers peak usually during the first week of January, when as many as 30 per hour may pass a given point. By mid-February, most of the whales will have moved on toward their breeding and calving lagoons on the west coast of Baja California.

From early March through April, the juveniles, adult males, and females without calves begin returning northward past the Oregon coast. Mothers and their new calves are the last to leave Mexico and move more slowly, passing Oregon from late April through June. During the spring migration, the whales may pass within just a few hundred yards of coastal headlands, making this a particularly exciting time for whale-watching from any number of vantage points along the coast. Researchers speculate that gray whales stay close to shore as a way to help them navigate.

For details on how, when, and where to observe these magnificent creatures, see "Whale-watching" under "Recreation," later in this chapter.

HISTORY

The First Peoples

No one knows when the first inhabitants took up residence on the Oregon coast, but ongoing research periodically turns up ever-older evidence.

In 2002, archaeologists began excavating a site at Indian Sands, in Samuel H. Boardman State Park north of Brookings, which yielded artifacts dating back more 12,000 years, making it the oldest known site of human activity yet found on the coast. Prior to that discovery, the dig site at Tahkenitch Landing, in the Oregon Dunes near Gardiner, had been the earliest known coastal habitation, dated at 9000–8630 B.C.

By the time the white explorers and settlers came here, Native American culture was a patchwork of languages and cultural traits as diverse as the topography. Most native coastal communities typically included a dozen or more small bands linked by a common dialect. These bands or villages consisted of perhaps an extended family in one or two houses, or a larger grouping under a headman. Linguistic and lifestyle divisions between native communities were reinforced by mountains, an ocean too rough for canoes, and other geographic barriers.

Early Explorers

A major impetus for exploring this coast was the quest for the mythic Northwest Passage—a sea route connecting the Pacific with the Atlantic. While the Northwest Passage turned out to be a myth, the fur trade became a basis of commerce and contention between European, Asian, and eventually American governments. The first American overland excursion into Oregon was made by Lewis and Clark's Corps of Discovery, which crossed the continent from 1804 to 1807. (See the special topic "Corps of Discovery" in the Introduction chapter.)

Rogue River Wars

In the 1850s, a short-lived gold-mining boom in the Rogue River Valley and south coast beaches drew settlers to southern Oregon. It was another gold rush, however, that had the greatest implications for the development of the region. In 1849, the influx of prospectors into California's Sierra Nevada occasioned a housing boom in San Francisco, port of entry to the goldfields. The demand for Coast Range timber and foodstuffs from Oregon's inland agricultural valleys caused downriver Pacific ports such as Astoria and

Newport to flourish. As a result, the coastline of California's friendly neighbor to the north was able to develop the necessary economic base for it to prosper and endure.

Like the tragic story played out all across the continent, however, the coming of white settlers to Oregon meant the usurpation of tribal homelands, exposure to European diseases such as smallpox and diphtheria, and the passing of a way of life. Violent conflicts ensued on a large scale with the influx of settlers and government land giveaways, and the mining activity in southern Oregon and on the coast incited the Rogue River Wars, when the native peoples along the south coast began to fight back. The conflict lasted for six years, during which more than 2,000 Native Americans died.

The hostilities compelled the federal government to send in troops and to eventually set up treaties with Oregon's first inhabitants. In the aftermath of the Rogue Indian Wars in the 1850s, the Chetco, Coquille, Coos, Umpqua, Siuslaw, Alsea, Yaquina, Nestucca, and Tillamook peoples were grouped together with the Rogue River tribes and forced to live on the 1.1-million-acre Siletz Reservation, which reached from Cape Lookout in Tillamook County to near the mouth of the Umpqua River. The culture and heritage of many indigenous peoples were lost forever. More tragic than the watering down of cultural distinctiveness was the huge mortality rate resulting from natives being forcibly "removed" to the reservation. Of the approximately 3,240 natives moved to the reservation in 1857, disease, starvation, and exposure would reduce their number to 1,015 in 1880; by 1900, only 430 coastal Native Americans survived on the reservation.

Over the years, whatever wealth the Siletz tribes had left was stripped as a result of the government's failure to honor a multitude of treaties. The final indignity came in 1951 with the termination of the Siletz Reservation. The divestiture of tribal status meant the loss of health services, educational support, tax exemptions, and other benefits. Predictably, this last in a long line of forced transitions brought about alcoholism and despair in many native peoples. In 1977, Senator Mark Hatfield and Congressman Les AuCoin helped push a bill through Congress for tribal restoration, an effort that spurred economic revitalization through tribal ventures ranging from logging and construction to gaming. The last endeavor has been accompanied by an interest in the old ways and a renewed sense of pride in native identity.

Industry, Exploitation, and Development

The exploitation of Oregon's fishing resources has been an enduring aspect of life in the region for thousands of years. Salmon has always been the most valued species, from prehistory up to modern times. Native Americans on both sides of the Cascades depended upon it, and commercial fishermen have viewed it as a mainstay for more than a century. Canning technology and fishing methods first perfected in Alaska made their way to Oregon in the 1860s, in time to meet the demands of emerging domestic and foreign markets. Canneries crowded the shores of the Columbia at Astoria and all the other major rivers down the coast, and exported thousands of tons of fish yearly until the dwindling supplies finally closed them down.

Logging of coastal and inland forests supplied the sawmills that were established at every port, supplying the building booms of the Northwest and beyond. A brisk coastal trade developed, as steamships plied Oregon ports on busy routes between San Francisco and Seattle. Before roads were finally built through the coastal ranges, transportation between coastal communities and the inland valleys was by river, and sternwheelers moved goods and passengers up and down the Siletz, Yaquina, Umpqua, and other navigable rivers. Popular tourist areas developed in Newport, Seaside, and other towns.

In the latter half of the 19th century, rail lines began to connect the coast to the interior, but it took the development of reliable roads to bring the coast out of its isolation. In 1919, Oregon voters approved construction of a north-south coastal route, first called the Roosevelt Military Highway and later the Oregon Coast Highway. The road was completed in 1932, and the last of a dozen magnificent bridges, designed by Oregon's master bridgebuilder Conde McCullough, were finished in 1936, finally opening up the entire coast to auto travel.

RECREATION

The outdoor appeal of the Oregon coast is unmatched, and the beaches are only the beginning. Hikes through ancient rainforests, excellent fishing for salmon and steelhead, crabbing and clamming in bays and estuaries, white-water jetboat rides, hiking and cycle-touring, surfing, whale-watching, birding, and more are all on the agenda. Below is an overview of recreational opportunities along the coast.

Beachcombing

Among the first things a newcomer to the Oregon coast notices are the huge piles of driftwood on the beach. Closer inspection usually reveals other treasures. Beachcombers particularly value agates and Japanese glass fishing floats. The volume and variety of flotsam and jetsam here come courtesy of the region's unique geography. Much of the driftwood, for instance, originates from logging operations located upriver on the many water-

You never know what you'll find.

ways that empty into the Pacific. In addition, storms, floods, rockslides, and erosion uproot trees that eventually wash up on shore. In addition to driftwood and floats, shells, coral, sand dollars, starfish, and other sea-borne trophies can be best culled from the intertidal zone on south coast beaches. While you may not always come across a perfectly polished agate or a message in a bottle, you'll probably find beachcombing on the Oregon coast to be its own reward.

Japanese **fishing floats** are swept into Oregon waters when the Kuroshio current crosses the Pacific and takes a southerly turn. These balls of green and blue glass sometimes require more than a decade to reach Oregon after breaking free from fishnets thousands of miles across the sea. Though glass floats are rather rare these days, having largely been replaced by plastic and foam, March is the best time to look for them, especially after two-day storms from the northwest, west-southwest, or due west. December through April is the best season to find agates, jaspers, petrified wood, and a variety of fossils. At that time, the gravel bars covered by sand in summer are exposed.

On the southern coast, the Coos Bay sandspit, Bandon's beachfront, the beaches on the western side of Humbug Mountain, and the isolated shorelines of Boardman State Park are choice treasure-hunting spots. Ten Mile Creek south of Yachats and Agate Beach north of Newport are the central coast's best places to look. The more settled and accessible north coast has slimmer pickings due to the larger population of resident beachcombers and the higher visitor influx; the best beachcombing is on the Nehalem, the Netarts, and the Nestucca sandspits.

Consult a **tide chart** any time you anticipate an extended beachcombing excursion (or any other activity on or near the sea). Half a dozen people perish here yearly from being washed off a beach, jetty, or outcropping. Local newspapers usually include tide predictions, and tide charts are usually available from visitors centers, chambers of commerce, and shops. Online, you can get free tide charts for three dozen coastal locations at www.saltwatertides.com. It's also wise to anticipate weather changes, so bring layers.

© MARK MORRIS

Whale-Watching

Whale-watching charters of various kinds are offered along the coast from December into the early spring. By land or by sea, early morning hours are best because winds can whip up whitecaps later in the day, obscuring the signs of surfacing whales. Remember your binoculars and sunglasses. If you go by boat, dress warmly, take precautions against seasickness, and expect to get wet if you go out on deck.

Depoe Bay and Newport are the centers for whale-watching, attracting the majority of the state's whale-watching visitors. Other major ports are Charleston, Winchester, and Garibaldi, but you'll find whale-watching charters operating out of just about all the ports along the coast. Rates range from about $15 to $50 per person for a two- to three-hour tour. See each destination for specific charter companies and details.

You don't need to be on a boat to successfully whale-watch, however. Coastal headlands and beaches provide excellent vantage points (see special topic "Whale Watching Spoken Here," for a list of some of the best sites) from which to spy the gray whales on their journey between Baja California and the Arctic. Just about any coastal location with a view of the sea holds the potential for a whale sighting, but some spots are definitely better than others. Offshore reefs supporting the proliferation of amphipods, the food of the gray whale, are conducive to sightings. Combine the latter with a promontory such as Cape Perpetua or Yaquina Head and you increase your chances even more.

It's possible to spot whales year-round here, as several hundred have taken up permanent or semi-permanent residence in Oregon waters, but whales are far more numerous and your chances of sighting them are far better during their twice-yearly migrations.

WHALE WATCHING SPOKEN HERE

In coordination with the Oregon Parks and Recreation Department, **Whale Watching Spoken Here** (whalespoken.org) is an organization of enthusiastic trained volunteers who staff 28 prime whale-watching sites in Oregon (plus one in Northern California and one in southern Washington). During key weeks of the gray whale migrations, these folks provide information and assist in spotting whales 10 A.M.–1 P.M., Dec. 26–Jan. 2 and through the week of spring break in late March.

The 28 sites, marked by "Whale Watching Spoken Here" signs during Whale Watch Weeks, are among the best vantage points any time of year. From north to south, with their nearest town, they are:

- Ecola State Park (Cannon Beach)
- Neahkahnie Mountain Historic Marker Turnout (Cannon Beach)
- Cape Meares State Scenic Viewpoint (Three Capes Loop)
- Cape Lookout State Park (Three Capes Loop)
- Inn at Spanish Head (Lincoln City)
- Boiler Bay State Scenic Viewpoint (Depoe Bay)
- Depoe Bay Sea Wall
- Rocky Creek State Scenic Viewpoint (Depoe Bay)
- Cape Foulweather (Depoe Bay)
- Devil's Punchbowl State Natural Area (Otter Rock)
- Yaquina Head Lighthouse (Newport)
- Don A. Davis City Kiosk (Nye Beach, Newport)
- Yaquina Bay State Recreation Site (Newport)
- Seal Rock State Recreation Site (Waldport)
- Yachats State Recreation Area (Yachats)
- Devil's Churn Viewpoint (Yachats)
- Cape Perpetua Overlook (Yachats)
- Cape Perpetua Interpretive Center (Yachats)
- Cook's Chasm Turnout (Yachats)
- Sea Lion Caves Turnout (north of Florence)
- Umpqua Lighthouse (Winchester)
- Shore Acres State Park (Charleston)
- Face Rock Wayside State Scenic Viewpoint (Bandon)
- Cape Blanco Lighthouse (Port Orford)
- Battle Rock Wayfinding Point (Port Orford)
- Cape Sebastian (Gold Beach)
- Cape Ferrelo (Brookings)
- Harris Beach State Park (Brookings)

Bicycling

While not for everybody, biking all or part of the Oregon coast is the surest way to get on intimate terms with this spectacular region. Before going, get a free copy of the **Oregon Coast Bike Route Map** (Dept. of Transportation, Salem 97310, www.odot.state.or.us/techserv/bikewalk/ocbr.htm) or from coastal information centers and chambers of commerce. This brochure features strip maps of the route, noting services from Astoria to the California border. With information on campsites, hostels, bike-repair facilities, elevation changes, temperatures, and wind speed, this pamphlet does everything but map the ruts in the road.

Because the prevailing winds in summer are from the northwest, most people cycle south on U.S. 101 to take advantage of a steady tailwind. You'll also be riding on the ocean side of the road with better views and easier access to turnouts, and generally wider bike lanes and shoulders. The entire 370-mile trip (or 380-mile if you include the Three Capes Loop) involves nearly 16,000 feet of elevation change. Most cyclists cover the distance in six to eight days, pedaling an average of 50–65 miles daily.

A number of companies offer pre-planned group bicycle trips, with everything from the bicycle to the meals and lodging included. For example, **Scenic Cycling Adventures** (800/413-8432, www.scenic-cycling.com) offers an eight-day Astoria–Crescent City trip, and a loop trip combining the south coast with the Cascades. **Bicycle Adventures** (206/786-0989 or 800/443-6060, www.bicycleadventures.com) offers several coast packages at a cost of roughly $200/day. **Hidden Trails** (604/323-1141 or 888/9-TRAILS, www.bcranches.com/outdoor/bike/index.htm) offers a fully supported 10-day tour for about $2,500.

Hiking the Oregon Coast Trail

For 362 miles, from the Columbia River to the California border, the Oregon Coast Trail hugs the beaches and headlands, leading hikers into intimate contact with some of the most beautiful landscapes anywhere. Most of the trail runs through public lands, though some portions traverse easements on private parcels and the trail follows the highway and city streets in a number of places. The only coastal long-distance treks separated from U.S. 101 are the 30 miles between Seaside and Manzanita and Bandon and Port Orford. A free trail map and directory are available from the Oregon State Parks information center (800/551-6949, www.oregonstateparks.org). This pamphlet makes it clear where this trail crosses open beaches, forested headlands, the shoulder of the Coast Highway, and even city streets in some towns. Be sure to bring water, particularly on northerly sections of the trail, as much of the trek here is on beachfront away from a potable supply.

Fishing

After years of declining harvests and increasing restrictions, coastal sportfishers have enjoyed some of the best seasons in memory recently, and the near future, at least, looks promising. Runs of spring and fall chinook, coho, and steelhead draw thousand of anglers to the coast each year to enjoy some of the best fishing this side of Alaska. Fleets of charter boats operate out of all the navigable ports on the coast, and there are countless opportunities for do-it-yourselfers from boat, bank, jetty, and pier.

See "Fishing and Hunting" in the On the Road chapter, as well as the destinations covered in this chapter, for additional information.

Crabbing and Clamming

Egalitarian ventures that require a minimum of gear and no license, crabbing and clamming are very popular ways to land a delicious meal. For details check out the Oregon Department of Fish and Wildlife's *Sport Fishing Regulations* booklet and website (www.dfw.state.or.us).

Crabbing just requires a trap, ring, or pot, and some bait (veteran crabbers recommend raw poultry—chicken or turkey backs and necks). Opinions vary as to the best time to crab, but many agree that an incoming tide yields the best catches. Just drop your trap in a likely spot, with a tethered float marking the spot, and haul it up 15–30 minutes later—hopefully full of legal-sized male Dungeness crabs. A handy item to have is a crab caliper, a gauge that measures the minimum-sized crabs you can keep. Bait shops and marinas can instruct you on how to catch dinner. Boats and crab pots are usually available to rent at these places. If boats are unavailable, many harbors have public piers. Some of the best crabbing spots are the estuaries of the Coos, Siuslaw, Yaquina, Tillamook, Netarts, and Nehalem rivers. Bays and estuaries are open for Dungeness year-round; the ocean is open year-round except August 15–Nov. 30.

A spade or small pitchfork are all you need for digging clams on beaches and mudflats, and a bucket to carry away your take. Large gaper clams, cockles, soft-shells, and little-necks are the most common clams found in tidewater areas, while prized razor clams are found on north coast beaches. With the exception of the summer closure for razor clams north of Tillamook Head, the season on shellfish is year-round in Oregon. Low tides, particularly morning minus tides during spring and summer, are the best times for clamming. Mussels are also available for harvest from rocky intertidal areas. Note that all oyster beds are privately owned.

Check the *Sport Fishing Regulations* booklet for catch limits, and before harvesting always inquire locally or contact the Recreational Shellfish Hot Line (503/986-4728) to get current information on shellfish toxins and quarantines.

Brookings-Harbor

If you cross the California-Oregon state border on U.S. 101 in late spring or early summer, the welcome mat of blooming Easter lilies often lines the way into the southern Oregon coast's gateway city of Brookings (pop. 5,725) and its unincorporated bigger neighbor, Harbor (pop. 8,775). While the lilies may not carpet these roadsides so extravagantly during the rest of the year, the coast-bound traveler can still look forward to being greeted by mild temperatures and colorful bouquets, even in winter. Enough 60–70°F days occur during January and February in this south coast "banana belt" town that more than 50 species of flowering plants thrive here—along with retirees, sportsmen, and beachcombers. With two gorgeous state parks virtually part of the city and world-class salmon and steelhead fishing nearby, only the lavish winter rainfall that averages over 73 inches a year can cool the ardor of local outdoor enthusiasts.

Brookings and Harbor sit on a coastal plain overlooking the Pacific six miles north of the California border, split by U.S. 101 (Chetco Avenue) and the Chetco River. Flowing out of the Klamath Mountains east of town, the Chetco drains part of the nearby Siskiyou National Forest and the Kalmiopsis Wilderness, extensive tracts encompassing some of the wildest country in the Lower 48 and renowned for their rare flowers and trees. This area enjoys strict federal protection, safeguarding the northernmost stand of giant redwoods as well as the coveted Port Orford cedar (whose strong but pliable lumber can fetch $10,000 and up for a single tree). The Kalmiopsis Wilderness is named for a unique shrub, the *Kalmiopsis leachiana,* one of the oldest members of the heath family (Ericaceae) that grows nowhere else on earth.

But you don't have to trek miles into the backcountry to enjoy the natural beauty of Brookings and vicinity. Just make your way past the somewhat main drag to Samuel Boardman State Park north of town, where 11 of the most scenic miles of the Oregon coast await you. Or head down to the harbor to embark on a boating expedition, amid some of the safest offshore navigation conditions in the region. In short, Brookings is the perfect place to launch an adventure by land or by sea.

SIGHTS

Camellias bloom at Christmas and the flowering plums add color the next month. Daffodils, grown commercially on the coastal plain south of Brookings, bloom in late January and into February. Magnolia shrubs, some early azaleas, and rhododendrons also bloom in late winter.

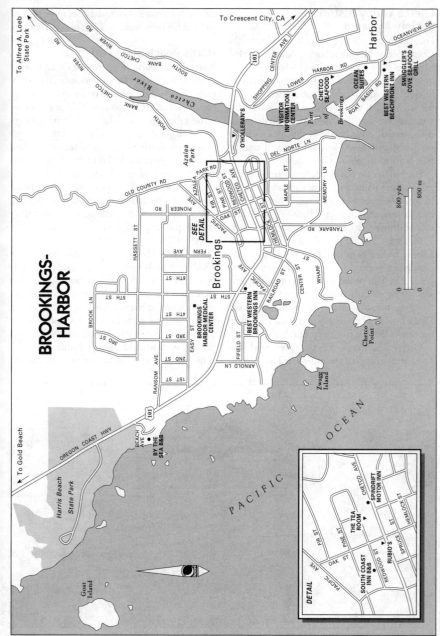

BROOKINGS-HARBOR

To Crescent City, CA

To Alfred A. Loeb State Park

To Gold Beach

CHETCO RIVER RD

NORTH BANK CHETCO RIVER RD

SOUTH BANK CHETCO RIVER RD

Chetco River

Azalea Park

OLD COUNTY RD

Brookings

SHOPPING CENTER AVE

Harbor

OCEANVIEW DR

LOWER HARBOR RD

VISITOR INFORMATION CENTER

Port of Brookings

CHETCO SEAFOOD

BOAT BASIN RD

OCEAN SUITES

BEST WESTERN BEACHFRONT INN

SMUGGLER'S COVE SEAFOOD & GRILL

O'HOLLERAN'S

DEL NORTE LN

AZALEA PARK RD

PIONEER RD

FIR ST

PINE ST

OAK ST

REDWOOD AVE

CHETCO AVE

HEMLOCK ST

MAPLE ST

MEMORY LN

PACIFIC

TANBARK RD

SEE DETAIL

HASSETT ST

FERN AVE

6TH ST

5TH ST

4TH ST

3RD ST

2ND ST

1ST ST

RANSOM AVE

BROOK LN

EASY ST

FIFIELD ST

ARNOLD LN

RAILROAD ST

CENTER ST

WHARF ST

PACIFIC AVE

5TH ST

BROOKINGS HARBOR MEDICAL CENTER

BEST WESTERN BROOKINGS INN

Chetco Point

Zwagg Island

PACIFIC OCEAN

OREGON COAST HWY

BEACH AVE

BY THE SEA B&B

Harris Beach State Park

Goat Island

800 yds

800 m

DETAIL

PACIFIC AVE

FIR ST

OAK ST

PINE ST

REDWOOD ST

SPRUCE ST

HEMLOCK ST

CHETCO AVE

THE TEA ROOM

SPINDRIFT MOTOR INN

RUBIO'S

SOUTH COAST INN B&B

COASTAL OREGON

Chetco Valley Historical Society Museum

Located in the red-and-white Blake House, the Chetco Valley Historical Society Museum (5461 Museum Rd., Brookings, 541/469-6651) sits on a hill overlooking U.S. 101 two miles south of the Chetco River. It's open Tues.–Sat. 2–6 P.M., Sunday noon–6 P.M.; Nov.–mid-May hours are Fri.–Sun. 9 A.M.–5 P.M. A $3 donation is suggested. Built in 1857, the structure was used as a stagecoach way station and trading post before Lincoln was president.

Even if you are not one for museums, several exhibits here stand apart from the traditional collections of pioneer wedding dresses, Native American baskets, and spinning wheels. These include a small trunk that came around Cape Horn in 1706 and a Native American dugout canoe. Should these fail to inspire, a mysterious iron casting of a woman's face might do the trick—especially in light of the speculation that this relic was left by an early undocumented landing on the Oregon coast, perhaps by Sir Francis Drake. Drake has been commonly suggested because of the mask's likeness to Queen Elizabeth.

Oregon's largest Monterey cypress tree is located on the hill near the museum. The 99-foot-tall tree has a trunk circumference of more than 27 feet and has been home to a pair of owls for years.

Harris Beach State Park

You're driving north along the first dozen miles of scenic U.S. 101 in Oregon, but instead of stopping to take out the camera, you're asking yourself, "So, where's the Oregon coast?" It's easy to have second thoughts after a half-hour drive through the "Twilight Zone" of small-town America, with only a few fleeting glimpses of the ocean. And then, at the northern limits of Brookings, across from the State Information Center on U.S. 101, you find your lost picture postcard at Harris Beach State Park. One look at the 24 miles of rock and tide visible from the parking-lot promontory should quell any misgivings.

Harris Beach was named after the Scottish pioneer George Harris, who settled here in the late 1880s to raise sheep and cattle. Besides stunning views, this state park offers many incoming travelers from California their first chance to actually walk on the beach in Oregon. You can begin directly west of the park's campground, where a sandy beach strewn with boulders often becomes flooded with intertidal life and driftwood. The early morning hours, as the waves crash through

the rock gardens of Harris Beach State Park

a small tunnel in a massive rock onto the shoreline, are the best time to look for sponges, umbrella crabs, solitary corals, and starfish.

Offshore, Bird Island (also called Goat Island) is the largest island along the Oregon coast and the state's largest seabird rookery. This outpost of Oregon Islands National Wildlife Sanctuary dispatches squadrons of cormorants, pelicans, tufted puffins, and other waterfowl who divebomb the incoming waves for food.

In addition to beachcombing, you can picnic at tables above the parking lot, loll about in the shallow waters of nearby Harris Creek, or cast the surf for perch.

Mill Beach is the southernmost part of the Harris Beach area. Locals prefer the beach access from downtown, which is easy to miss. To get there, drive toward the ocean on Center Street in downtown Brookings, make a right at the plywood mill, and stop next to a small ballpark. An unimproved road leads to a hillock from which trails take you down to a beach full of driftwood. Residents say that Japanese fishing floats occasionally roll up onto the beach after a storm.

For details on camping, see "Accommodations," later in this section.

Samuel H. Boardman State Scenic Corridor

The stretch of highway from Brookings to Port Orford is known as the "fabulous 50 miles." Some consider the section of coastline just north of Brookings to be the most scenic in Oregon—and one of the most dramatic meetings of rock and tide in the world. The offshore rock formations and winding roadbed hundreds of feet above the surf invite comparison to Europe's Amalfi Drive. This sobriquet is perhaps most apt in the first dozen miles north of Brookings, encompassed by Samuel Boardman State Scenic Corridor. You'll want to have plenty of film and a loose schedule when you make this drive, because you'll find it hard not to pull over again and again, as each photo opportunity seems to out-dazzle the last. Of the 11 named viewpoints that have been cut into the highway's shoulder here, the following are especially recommended (all viewpoints are

marked by signs on the west side of U.S. 101 and are listed in order of appearance).

House Rock was the site of a World War II air-raid sentry tower that sits hundreds of feet above whitecaps pounding the rock-strewn beaches. To the north, you'll see one of the highest cliffs on the coast, Cape Sebastian. A steep, circuitous trail lined with salal (a tart blueberry) goes down to the water. The path begins behind the Samuel Boardman monument on the west end of the parking lot. The sign to the highest viewpoint in Boardman Park is easy to miss, but look for the turnout that precedes House Rock, called Cape Ferrelo (for Cabrillo's navigator, who sailed up much of the West Coast in 1543).

Thomas Creek Bridge, the highest bridge in Oregon (345 feet above the water) as well as the highest north of San Francisco, has been used as a silent star in many TV commercials. A parking lot at the south end of the bridge marks a trailhead down. Do not take the path you see closest to the bridge because it's too steep. At the south end of the lot, the true trail eventually leads down to a view of the bridge on one side and miles of coast on the other. The offshore rock formations here are especially interesting. From here some hikers access the Indian Sands Trail, ending up in pine-rimmed dunes and a sandstone bluff high above the sea.

Two miles down the highway, the **Natural Bridges Cove** sign seems to front just a forested parking lot. However, the paved walkway at the south end of the lot leads to a spectacular overlook. Below, several rock archways frame an azure cove. This feature was created by the collapse of the entrance and exit of a sea cave. A steep, winding trail through giant ferns and towering Sitka spruce and Douglas fir takes you down for a closer look. Thimbleberry (a sweet but seedy raspberry) is sometimes plentiful. Here as in similar forests on the south coast, it's important to stay on the trail. The rainforest-like biome is exceptionally fragile, and the soil erodes easily when the delicate vegetation is damaged.

Natural Bridges's counterpart is near the north end of Boardman Park. A short walk down the hillside trail leads you to the **Arch Rocks** viewpoint to see an immense boomerang-shaped basalt archway about a quarter mile offshore. This site has picnic tables within view of the monolith.

Alfred A. Loeb State Park

Eight miles northeast of Brookings on North Bank Chetco River Road along the Chetco River, Loeb State Park preserves 320 acres of old-growth myrtlewood, the state's largest grove. Many of the aromatic trees here are well over 200 years old. The park is open mid-April–late October.

The .25-mile Riverview Trail passes numerous big trees to connect Loeb Park with the **Redwood Nature Trail.** This trail winds 1.2 miles through the northernmost stands of naturally occurring *Sequoia sempervirens*. This is Oregon's largest redwood grove and contains the state's largest specimens. Within the grove are a number of trees more than 500 years old, measuring 5–8 feet in diameter, towering more than 300 feet above the forest floor. One tree here has a 33-foot girth and is estimated to exceed 800 years in age. When the south coast is foggy and cold on summer mornings, it's often warm and dry in upriver locations such as this one.

For details on camping, see "Accommodations," later in this section.

The Kalmiopsis Wilderness

The lure of untrammeled wilderness attracts intrepid hikers to the Kalmiopsis, despite summer's blazing heat and winter's torrential rains. In addition to enjoying the isolation of Oregon's largest (179,655 acres) and probably least-visited wilderness, they come to take in the pink rhododendron-like blooms of *Kalmiopsis leachiana* (in June) and other rare flowers. The area is also home to such economically valued species as Port Orford cedar and *Cannabis sativa*. The illicit weed is the leading cash crop in the state, and its vigilant protection by growers should inspire extra care for those hiking here during the late fall harvest season. The potential for violence associated with the mushroom harvest here also mandates a measure of caution.

In any case, the forest service prohibits plant collection *of any kind* to preserve the region's special botanical populations. These include the insect-eating Darlingtonia plant and the Brewer's weeping spruce. The forest canopy is composed largely of the more common Douglas fir, canyon live oak, madrone, and chinquapin. Stark peaks top this red-rock forest, whose understory is choked with blueberry, manzanita, and dense chaparral.

Many of the rare species in this wilderness survived the glacial epoch because the glaciers from that era left the area untouched. This, combined with the fact that the area was an ancient offshore island, has enabled the region's singular ecosystem to maintain its integrity through the millennia. You'd think that federal protection, remoteness, and climatic extremes would ensure a sanguine outlook for this ice-age forest, but an active debate still rages over the validity of some logging claims.

In the summer of 2002, the so-called **Biscuit Fire** raged out of control for weeks, ravaging nearly half a million acres of southwestern Oregon, engulfing most of the Siskiyou National Forest and virtually all of the Kalmiopsis Wilderness. This inferno, the nation's largest wildfire of 2002 and the biggest in Oregon for well over a century, destroyed extensive habitat of the endangered northern spotted owl, whose population National Forest Service biologists predict may drop by 20 percent. It will likely be decades before the forest returns to normal. The good news, however, is that flora of the region is well adapted to periodic fires; many of the old-growth trees survived the blaze, and within a few months green sprouts and new growth of many species were reappearing amidst the ashes.

RECREATION

Fishing

Fishing on the Chetco was once one of southern Oregon's best-kept secrets, but the word has gotten out about the river's October run of huge chinook as well as a superlative influx of winter steelhead. And should river traffic become too heavy, the late-summer ocean salmon season out of Brookings may be the best in the Northwest. Boatless anglers can try their luck at the public fishing pier at the harbor and on the south jetty at the mouth of the Chetco. Chinook season generally runs mid-May–mid-September, but that's subject to change so check the regulations.

Various fishing trips for salmon ($75 for 5–6 hours), tuna ($125 for 12 hours), and bottom fishing ($60 for 5–6 hours) can be arranged through **Sporthaven Marina** (16374 Lower Harbor Rd., Brookings 97415, 541/469-3301). In addition to fishing charters, **Tidewind Sportfishing** (16368 Lower Harbor Rd., 541/469-0337) offers **whale-watching** excursions in season.

Camping

Campers should pick up literature on fishing and a Siskiyou Forest Service map at the ranger station in town. In addition to printed matter about Siskiyou and Kalmiopsis trails for hikers, the rangers can tell you where to find some good fishing holes on the nearby Chetco River, noted for its good fall salmon runs and winter steelhead.

Harris Beach State Park (1655 U.S. 101, Brookings, 541/469-2021 or 800/452-5687), two miles north of town, is open all year, but reservations are definitely necessary Memorial Day–Labor Day. Of the 155 total sites ($15–17), 149 are paved (50 electricity only, 36 full hookups), some are shaded, and six are yurts. There is a special camping area for hikers and bicyclists. Picnic tables and fire grills are provided. Flush toilets, electricity, piped-in water, sewer hookups, sanitary service, showers, firewood, laundry, and playground round out the amenities. Whale-watching is particularly good here in January and May, on this piece of beach peppered with basalt outcroppings.

The 320-acre **Alfred A. Loeb State Park** (541/469-2021) is nine miles northeast of Brookings on North Bank Chetco River Road. The park is open mid-April–late October, but camping is allowed only during the summer; no reservations necessary. There are 53 sites for trailers/motor homes (50 feet maximum), a special campground for bicyclists and hikers, and some cabins. Electricity, piped water, and picnic tables are provided; flush toilets and firewood are available. The campground is located in a fragrant, secluded myrtlewood grove on the east bank of the Chetco River. From here, the Riverview Trail takes hikers to the Siskiyou National Forest's Redwood Nature Trail, where nature lovers will marvel at 800-year-old redwood beauties.

Golf

All the press about Bandon Dunes has obscured the development of another great course, **Salmon Run Golf and Wilderness Preserve** (99040 South Bank Chetco River Rd., 541/469-4888). This beautiful 18-hole public links not far from the Kalmiopsis Wilderness was designed with environmentally sensitive imperatives so that numerous wildlife sightings can be enjoyed here long into the future. Whether it's the chance to see salmon (usually after the first rains in November) and steelhead spawning (January), black bears, elk, and wild turkeys, or just the opportunity to play a first-rate course, golfers shouldn't overlook this one. Green fees are $45 for nine holes, $60 for 18, including cart. Beginner and intermediate players may find the Executive 9 ideal. This par-34 course within a course is located on the back nine holes, and measures 1,310 yards. Green fees are $15, including the cart. Your Oregon coastal golf pilgrimage can begin here, then hit Bandon Dunes, Sandpines (Florence), and Salishan (near Lincoln City).

EVENTS

The **Beachcomber's Festival** (800/535-9469), held in late March at the Azalea Middle School, features exhibits, demonstrations, and slide shows as well as an art competition for the best works wrought from indigenous materials such as driftwood, agates, and other beachcomber treasures. To get there, follow Pacific Avenue east of the highway.

The **Azalea Festival** is an unforgettable floral fantasia that takes place each Memorial Day weekend. Among the activities are a parade, flower display, crafts fair, a five-kilometer run, seafood luncheon, and beef barbecue. Much of the activity revolves around Azalea Park. This WPA-built enclave features 20-foot-high azaleas (several hundred years old) and hand-hewn

COASTAL OREGON

myrtlewood picnic tables. Wild cherry and crabapple blooms, wild strawberry blossoms, and purple and red violets round out the bouquet. Butterflies, bees, and birds all seem to concur with locals that this array smells sweetest around graduation time in mid-June. To get there, take Pacific Avenue east of the highway, and turn onto Azalea Park Road.

Like several other Oregon coast towns, Brookings puts the windy weather to good use, with its annual **Southern Oregon Kite Festival** (541/469-2218), held over two days in mid-July. Individuals and teams display their aerial skills at the port of Brookings-Harbor.

Azalea Park is also home to **Nature's Coastal Holiday Light Show** in December, with more than 75,000 lights. The city park is located on the south end of town. The Brookings-Harbor Garden Club and Chamber of Commerce offer garden tours of this park and other gardens. Call the chamber (541/469-3181) for more information on tours and garden-related events.

PRACTICALITIES

Accommodations

If you're weary from your journey to Oregon from California, and want to stop in at the first motel you see, try one of the 30 units at the **Harbor Inn Motel** (15991 U.S. 101 S., 541/469-3194 or 800/469-8444). Small pets allowed. Rates $50–89.

With 35 units and prices at $39–79, the **Spindrift Motor Inn** (1215 Chetco Ave., 541/469-5345 or 800/292-1171) is a good dollar value. Soundproofed walls blunt traffic noise from U.S. 101, and there are ocean views you'd expect to find at higher-priced lodgings.

Up a rung in the $69–110 range, the **Best Western Brookings Inn** (1143 U.S. 101, 541/469-2173 or 800/822-9087) may be about a mile from the ocean, but it's family-friendly with a pool and whirlpool tub, a comfy myrtlewood-paneled lounge, and a very good on-site restaurant. No pets allowed.

For the full oceanfront experience, head south to the town of Harbor. Here, **Best Western Beachfront Inn** (16008 Boat Basin Rd., Harbor,

541/469-7779 or 800/468-4081) offers a window on a colorful port. All units feature private decks, microwaves, and refrigerators. Kitchenettes as well as suites with ocean-view hot tubs and an indoor pool are available. Rates range $79–165, depending upon the season and the room configuration.

The **Pacific Sunset Inn** (1144 Chetco Ave., 541/469-2141 or 800/469-2141) has 40 units right downtown. Rates are $30–85. With just eight units **Ocean Suites** (16045 Lower Harbor Rd., 541/469-4004) rents rooms by the week for $365, or $59 and up for a night. Each comes equipped with full kitchens and living room. No pets allowed.

Bed-and-Breakfasts

A coastal gem one block north of the highway, the **South Coast Inn B&B** (516 Redwood St., Brookings, 541/469-5557 or 800/525-9273, www.scoastin.com) is a 1917 Craftsman building and was once the home of lumber baron William Ward. Designed by famed architect Bernard Maybeck and situated in the heart of old Brookings just blocks away from the beach and shopping, this 4,000-square-foot B&B offers three rooms and a guest cottage that also has a kitchen, at $99–139. All rooms have VCR/TVs (and access to the inn's video library), private bath, and other amenities. An indoor spa with a sauna and hot tub and an included breakfast featuring a health-conscious menu are additional enticements to book space early. Ask the innkeepers about other Maybeck structures in town as well as bicycle/walking treks they conduct June–October.

For a B&B with an ocean view, **By the Sea B&B** (1545 Beach Ave., 541/469-4692 or 877/469-4692, www.brookingsbythesea.com) offers a choice of two rooms, or the lodge room featuring a fishing and hunting decor. A full breakfast is served upstairs in the dining room. Enjoy breakfast and breathtaking ocean views from the stained-glass-topped windows. The house is filled with antiques and the smell of homemade bread. A deluxe continental breakfast is also available, with seasonal fruits and homemade breads, if you prefer to eat in private. On the upper veranda, a spa and a wood-burning fire pot is available for guests' use. Rates are $98–150.

Surrounded by water on three sides, the **Chetco River Inn** (21202 High Prairie Rd., 541/251-0087 or 800/327-2688, $115–135, www.chetcoriverinn) is an intimate alternative. Eighteen miles inland from the coast, the half-hour drive to the inn takes you to the periphery of the Kalmiopsis; once there you feel as if you're in your own private forest. Its location near prime fishing river frontage makes this place especially popular during steelhead season. Swimming holes abound close by and the absence of city lights makes for good stargazing. In addition to an included gourmet breakfast, picnic lunches and dinners are available upon request. The welcome mat here is laid out in the form of thick oriental carpets on floors of green and black marble. Tasteful antiques also decorate this reasonably priced first-class lodging. Rooms are $125–145, including a full country breakfast, with all the coffee, tea, and cookies you can eat. The five rooms plus cottage can easily accommodate up to 14 people in separate beds, or six couples. Children are welcome; cottages are suggested for their comfort. Smoking is limited to outdoors only. No pets allowed.

Food

Brookings has a profusion of family-friendly restaurants that serve large portions at a good dollar value with enough creativity to suit the most finicky eater.

At the north end of town in a small building that gives the appearance of a drive-in is **Rubio's** (1136 Chetco Ave., 541/469-4919), one of the better Mexican places along U.S. 101. This will be apparent upon tasting the house salsa and the chiles rellenos. The house specialty, Seafood à la Rubio, throws together prawns, lingcod, and scallops in a butter, garlic, wine, and jalapeño sauce. Fish tacos, tamales, and margaritas here are also recommended. Rubio's can be spotted on the east side of the highway across from the Flying Gull. Just look for a low-slung wooden building painted yellow with red trim. Inexpensive. Open 11 A.M.–9 P.M. daily.

For a rare ocean-view dining experience in Brookings, try **Smuggler's Cove Seafood & Grill** (16011 Boat Basin Rd., 541/469-6006) serving prime rib and seafood.

In Harbor, **Chetco Seafood** (16182 Lower Harbor Rd., 541/469-9251) serves reasonably priced fresh fish, plus chips in beer batter as good as any on the coast. **Flying Gull Restaurant** (next to the Best Western, 541/469-5700) has a huge menu with one of the largest seafood selections on the Coast, plus certified Black Angus steaks.

Home of Wild River Brewing, **Wild River Pizza** (16279 U.S. 101, Harbor, 541/469-7454) has a menu similar to its outlet in Cave Junction, highlighting crispy crust pizza, salad, and microbrews. Look for it on the east side of the highway about a mile south of the Brookings-Harbor Bridge at the four-way stoplight. While the food is good and inexpensive, this large restaurant tends to fill up with families enjoying the video games and pool tables on weekends. In other words, go elsewhere for an intimate Saturday night dinner.

For prime rib in a low-key lounge atmosphere, head to **O'Holleran's** (1210 Chetco Ave., 541/469-9907) any day of the week 5–10 P.M.

For lighter fare for those heading out to explore, try the **Tea Room** (434 Redwood St., #4, 541/469-7240) for sandwiches, soups, salads, and baked goods; fill your to-go mugs with a nice cuppa the hot stuff.

Information and Transportation

Before you continue north on the country's longest (361 miles) designated scenic highway, U.S. 101, stop off and talk to the friendly folks at the **Oregon Welcome Center** just north of town (1650 U.S. 101, Brookings 97415, 541/469-4117). The facility operates mid-April–October Mon.–Sat. 9 A.M.–5 P.M. It offers brochures covering the coast and the rest of the state. For additional information pertinent to Brookings and environs, the **Brookings-Harbor Chamber of Commerce** (16330 Lower Harbor Rd., Brookings 97415, 541/469-3181 or 800/535-9469, www.brookingsor.com) is located down at the harbor.

Recreational information, including forest and trail maps, is available at the **Chetco Ranger Station** (539 Chetco Ave., Brookings 97415, 541/412-6000). The station's advisories include information on the Siskiyou National Forest and the Kalmiopsis Wilderness. It's open Mon.–Fri. 7:30 A.M.–4:30 P.M. but is closed on holidays. Inquire here about mushroom picking.

Wondering about **offshore weather conditions?** The Coast Guard hotline (541/469-2242) has the answers.

Greyhound (601 Railroad Ave., 541/469-3326), stops twice daily at the corner of Tanbark Road and Railroad Avenue. The fare to Portland is about $40. Curry County's **Coastal Express** buses (in Brookings, call 541/469-6822) run up and down the south coast weekdays only between North Bend and the California border, including local service in Brookings.

Gold Beach and Vicinity

Despite the name Gold Beach, the real riches here are silver, and they swim up the Rogue River in great numbers every year. This town is one part of the coast where the action is definitely away from the ocean. To lure people from Oregon's superlative ocean shores, the Rogue estuary has been bestowed with many blessings. First, it was the gold-laden black sands that were mined in the 1850s and 1860s. While this short-lived boom era gave Gold Beach its name, the arrival of Robert Hume, later known as the Salmon King of the Rogue, had greater historical significance. By the turn of the 20th century, Hume's canneries were shipping some 16,000 cases of salmon a year, and established the river's image as a leading salmon and steelhead stream, a reputation that was later enhanced by outdoorsman Zane Grey in his *Rogue River Feud* and other writings. Over the years, Herbert Hoover, Winston Churchill, Ginger Rogers (who had a home on the Rogue), Clark Gable, Jack London, George Bush, and Jimmy Carter, among other notables, have come here to try their luck. During the last several decades, white-water rafting and jetboat tours focusing on the abundant wildlife, scenic beauty, and fascinating lore of the region have hooked other sectors of the traveling public.

Today, Gold Beach is a town of about 2,100 and the Curry County seat. Besides serving as the south coast tourism hub, a pulp mill and commercial ocean-fishing industry make up the local economy here. The seasonal nature of many local businesses creates serious wintertime unemployment. This fact, combined with torrential rains, drastically reduces the population of Gold Beach from Thanksgiving until spring. Thereafter, the wildflowers and warm weather transform this town into a vacation mecca.

At the north end of town, just before the road gives way to Conde McCullough's elegant Patterson Bridge, the harbor comes into view on the left, full of salmon trawlers, jetboats, pelicans, and seals bobbing up and down. Across the bridge is **Wedderburn,** a baby sister to Gold Beach. Named for the Scottish birthplace of Robert Hume, its major claim to fame is as the home port of the Mailboat, which has been the mail carrier to upriver residents on the Rogue since 1895.

SIGHTS

Museums
At the **Curry County Historical Museum** (920 S. Ellensburg, Gold Beach, 541/247-6113), the local historical society has assembled a small collection of exhibits on Native American and pioneer life, mining in the region's golden age, logging, fishing, and agriculture. It's located at the county fairgrounds at the south edge of town. Particularly interesting are a realistic reconstruction of a miner's cabin, vintage photos, and Native American petroglyphs. Open May 15–Sept. 30, Mon.–Sun. 1–5 P.M.; Oct. 11–May 15, Friday and Saturday noon–4 P.M. Admission is free.

In the harbor area on the west side of U.S. 101, Jerry's Jetboats has assembled the best regional museum on the south coast, the **Rogue**

River Museum (541/247-4571). Centuries of natural and human history are depicted here. In addition to geologic history, photos of pioneer families, arrowheads and other native artifacts, and a taxidermic collage of local critters will round out your introduction to the Rogue Valley. Jerry's river tour clientele will find that perspectives from the museum on the local salmon industry in the 1920s and on early river travel are expanded upon in their jetboat guide's commentary. Museum photos of early river runs, hauling freight, passengers, and mail, also can impart a sense of history to your trip upriver or up the road. It's open 8 A.M. –9 P.M. in summer, till 6 P.M. during the other seasons. Admission is free.

Cape Sebastian

Seven miles south of Gold Beach is Cape Sebastian. This spectacular windswept headland was named by Sebastián Vizcaíno, who plied offshore waters here for Spain in 1602 along with Manuel d'Alguilar. At least 700 feet above the sea, Cape Sebastian is the highest south coast overlook reachable by paved public road. On a clear day, visibility extends 43 miles north to Humbug Mountain, and 50 miles south to California. This is one of the best perches along the south coast for whale-watching. A trail zigzags through beautiful springtime wildflowers down the south side of the cape for about two miles until it reaches the sea. In April and May, Pacific paintbrush, Douglas iris, orchids, and snow queen usher you along. In addition, Cape Sebastian supports a population of large-headed goldfields, a summer-blooming daisylike yellow flower found only in coastal Curry County.

In 1942, a caretaker here heard Japanese voices drifting across the water through the fog. When the mist lifted he looked down from Cape Sebastian trail to see a surfaced submarine. This sighting, together with the Japanese bombing at Brookings and the incendiary balloon spotted over Cape Blanco, sent shock waves up the south coast. But the potential threat remained just that, and local anxiety eventually subsided.

Beaches

The driftwood-strewn strand of **South Beach,** just south of Gold Beach's harbor, is convenient but only so-so. You'll find more exciting stretches both north and south of town. Tidepoolers might

Myers Beach, south of Cape Sebastian

want to stop at the visitors center before heading out and ask for the "Tidepools Are Alive" brochure, with tips and species descriptions. Two miles south, there's easy access to a nice beach and some tidepooling at tiny **Buena Vista State Park,** at the mouth of Hunter Creek. Seven miles south of Gold Beach, there's more tidepooling amid the camera-friendly basalt sea stacks at beautiful **Myers Beach,** part of Pistol River State Park south of Cape Sebastian. The south side of Cape Sebastian and **Pistol River State Park,** a couple of miles farther south, are the only places on the Oregon coast where sailboarders can enjoy wave sailing. The beaches around Pistol River are also productive areas for finding razor clams.

Bailey Beach, north of town between the Rogue River jetty and Otter Point, is another popular spot for razor clamming, and **Nesika Beach,** seven miles from Gold Beach, is another good tidepooling destination.

RECREATION
Jetboat Trips
The best way to take in the mighty Rogue is on a jetboat ride from Gold Beach harbor. Several different companies run this trip, and they all provide comparable service and prices. It's an exciting and interesting look at the varied flora and fauna along the estuary as well as the changing moods of the river. Most of the estimated 50,000 people per year who "do" the Rogue in this way take the 64-mile round-trip cruise. This and the more adventurous 104-mile cruise include a stop for a sumptuous lunch at one of several secluded fishing lodges upriver. The pilots/commentators usually have grown up on the river, and their evocations of the diverse ecosystems and Native American and gold-mining history add greatly to your enjoyment. Bears, otters, seals, and beavers may be sighted en route, and anglers may hold up a big keeper to show off. Ospreys, snowy egrets, eagles, mergansers, and kingfishers are also seen with regularity in this stopover for migratory waterfowl.

In the first part of the journey, idyllic riverside retreats dot the hillsides, breaking up stands of fir and hemlock. Myrtle, madrone, and impressive springtime wildflower groupings also vary the landscape. Both the 64- and 104-mile trips focus on the section of the Rogue protected by the government as a Wild and Scenic River. Only the longer trips take you into the pristine Rogue Wilderness, an area that motor launches from Grants Pass do not reach either. The 13 miles of this wilderness you see from the boat have canyon walls rising 1,500 feet above you. Geologists say that this part of the Klamaths is composed of ancient islands and sea floor that collided with North America. To deal with the rapids upstream, smaller, faster boats are used that skim over the boulders with just six inches of water between hull and rock surface.

The season runs May–October 15. Remember that chill and fog near the mouth of the estuary usually give way to much warmer conditions upstream. These tour outfits have wool blankets available on cold days as well as complimentary hot beverages. Also keep in mind that the upriver lodges can be booked for overnight stays and your trip may be resumed the following day. The following suppliers offer 64- and 104-mile trips; meals are included in the cost of the 104-mile trip (rates range $30–75 for adults, $12–35 for children.)

Just south of the Rogue River Bridge, west of U.S. 101 on Harbor Way, is **Jerry's Rogue River Jetboats** (P.O. Box 1011, Gold Beach 97444, 541/247-4571 or 800/451-3645, www.rogue-jets.com). This heavily patronized company runs trips May–October. Jerry's is noted for personable, well-informed guides. If you forgot a hat to buffer the winds at the mouth of the Rogue, stop in at Jerry's gift shop. While you're there, check out the local jams and critically acclaimed fish prints of local artist Don Jensen.

Rogue River Mailboats (P.O. Box 1165, Gold Beach, 541/247-7033 or 800/458-3511, www.mailboat.com) is located a quarter mile upstream from the north end of the Rogue River bridge. Besides human cargo, this boat also carries sacks of U.S. mail, ensuring a warm welcome in upriver locations.

Fishing

Fishing is a mighty big deal in Gold Beach, which has one of the highest concentrations of professional guides in the state. There's something to fish for just about year-round, but salmon and steelhead are the top quarry. When the spring chinook pour in, April–June, anglers will need to book guided trips well in advance to get a shot at them. Catches peak in May. Summer steelhead and fall-run chinook usually arrive July–September, then it's hatchery coho September–November (sometimes as early as August). In December, the first of the winter steelhead make their appearance and continue into March.

The **Rogue Outdoor Store** (560 N. Ellensburg, Gold Beach, 541/247-7142) is well stocked with fishing, camping, and other gear, and can advise on where, when, and what to fish. Typical rates for guided salmon trips here are $150–200 per person. Contact the Gold Beach Visitor Center (see "Information and Services," later in this section) or the Curry Guide Association (800/775-0886) for a list of over two dozen licensed guides.

Some well-established guides include: Darrell Allen (541/247-2082); Denny Hughson (541/247-2684 or 503/819-1607); Steve Beyerlin (541/247-4138 or 800/348-4138, www .fishoregon.com), for both conventional and fly-fishing; Shaun Carpenter (541/247-2049), conventional and fly-fishing; Helen Burns (541/247-2441 or 541/290-8402, www.helensguideservice.com), one of the few women in a male-dominated club; Ron Smith (541/247-6046 or 800/501-6391); and John Ward (541/247-2866 or 290-2281).

Hiking and Horseback Riding

The 40-mile **Rogue River Trail** offers lodge-to-lodge hiking, which means you need little more in your pack than the essentials. The lodges here are comfortably rustic, serve home-style food in copious portions, and run $150–200 for a double room. They are also comfortably spaced, so extended hiking is seldom a necessity. Call **Rogue Quest** (888/517-1614) if you'd like a guide (about $80/day).

Before you go, check with the Gold Beach Ranger Station on trail conditions and directions to the trailhead. Pick up the western end of the trail 35 miles east of Gold Beach, about one-half mile from Foster Bar, a popular boat landing (see "Camping," immediately following). Park there and walk east and north on the paved road until you see signs on the left marking the Rogue River Trail. Go in spring before the hot weather and enjoy yellow Siskiyou iris and fragrant wild azaleas. The trail ends at Graves Creek, 27 miles northwest of Grants Pass. Be careful of rattlesnakes on the trail.

Hawk's Rest Ranch at Siskiyou West Day Lodge (94667 N. Bank Pistol River Rd., Pistol River, 541/247-6423, www.siskiyouwest.com) offers horseback riding on the beach near the scenic Pistol River, riding lessons, a petting zoo, and other family-oriented attractions.

Camping

Campsites east of town along the Rogue and off U.S. 101 en route to Port Orford provide wonderful spots to bed down for the night. Those taking the road along the Rogue should be alert for oncoming log trucks, raft transport vehicles, and other wide-body vehicles.

Foster Bar Campground (Siskiyou National Forest, Gold Beach Ranger Station, P.O. Box 548, 1225 S. Ellensburg, 541/247-6651) is located 30 miles east of Gold Beach on the south bank of the Rogue. Take Jerry's Flat Road east for 30 miles to the turnoff for Agness. Turn right on Illahe Agness Road and drive three miles to camp. Recently transformed from primitive to developed, campsites here now come equipped with drinking water, toilets, accessible facilities, picnic tables, fire rings, and a boat ramp. First-come first-served; fee is $5 per night. The site is open March–September (but may vary depending on the weather). This is a popular spot from which to embark on an eight-mile inner tube ride to Agness. It's also where rafters pull out, so the parking lot may be jam-packed. The rapids are dangerous, so wear a life jacket. You are also within walking distance of the trailhead of the Rogue River Trail (see "Hiking and Horseback Riding," immediately preceding).

COASTAL FISH RUNS

Note: These dates indicate when fish are expected, *not* necessarily legal seasons; check with the Oregon Department of Fish and Wildlife (www.dfw.state.or.us) for current seasons and restrictions.

	Jan.	Feb.	Mar.	Apr.	May	June	July	Aug.	Sept.	Oct.	Nov.	Dec.
Alsea River and Bay												
Fall chinook										X	X	X
Winter steelhead	X	X	X									X
Sea-run cutthroat trout							X	X	X			
Chetco												
Fall chinook										X	X	X
Winter steelhead	X	X	X									X
Columbia River (lower)												
Spring chinook		X	X	X	X	X						
Summer chinook						X	X					
Fall chinook									X	X	X	
Summer steelhead					X	X	X	X	X	X		
Sturgeon	X	X	X	X	X	X	X			X	X	X
Coho								X	X	X	X	X
Coos Rver												
Fall chinook								X	X	X	X	X
Coho									X	X	X	X

Jan.	Feb.	Mar.	Apr.	May	June	July	Aug.	Sept.	Oct.	Nov.	Dec.

Coquille River

Fall chinook

Jan.	Feb.	Mar.	Apr.	May	June	July	Aug.	Sept.	Oct.	Nov.	Dec.
							X	X	X	X	X

Winter steelhead

Jan.	Feb.	Mar.	Apr.	May	June	July	Aug.	Sept.	Oct.	Nov.	Dec.
X	X	X								X	X

Elk River

Fall chinook

Jan.	Feb.	Mar.	Apr.	May	June	July	Aug.	Sept.	Oct.	Nov.	Dec.
									X	X	X

Winter steelhead

Jan.	Feb.	Mar.	Apr.	May	June	July	Aug.	Sept.	Oct.	Nov.	Dec.
	X	X	X								

Kilchis River

Fall chinook

Jan.	Feb.	Mar.	Apr.	May	June	July	Aug.	Sept.	Oct.	Nov.	Dec.
							X	X	X	X	X

Winter steelhead

Jan.	Feb.	Mar.	Apr.	May	June	July	Aug.	Sept.	Oct.	Nov.	Dec.
X	X	X								X	X

Chum salmon

Jan.	Feb.	Mar.	Apr.	May	June	July	Aug.	Sept.	Oct.	Nov.	Dec.
									X	X	X

Miami River

Fall chinook

Jan.	Feb.	Mar.	Apr.	May	June	July	Aug.	Sept.	Oct.	Nov.	Dec.
							X	X	X	X	X

Winter steelhead

Jan.	Feb.	Mar.	Apr.	May	June	July	Aug.	Sept.	Oct.	Nov.	Dec.
	X	X	X								

Chum salmon

Jan.	Feb.	Mar.	Apr.	May	June	July	Aug.	Sept.	Oct.	Nov.	Dec.
X										X	X

Necanicum River

Fall chinook

Jan.	Feb.	Mar.	Apr.	May	June	July	Aug.	Sept.	Oct.	Nov.	Dec.
								X	X	X	X

Winter steelhead

Jan.	Feb.	Mar.	Apr.	May	June	July	Aug.	Sept.	Oct.	Nov.	Dec.
X	X	X						X	X	X	X

Nehalem River and Bay

Summer chinook

Jan.	Feb.	Mar.	Apr.	May	June	July	Aug.	Sept.	Oct.	Nov.	Dec.
			X	X	X	X	X				

continued on next page

COASTAL OREGON

COASTAL FISH RUNS (cont'd)

	Jan.	Feb.	Mar.	Apr.	May	June	July	Aug.	Sept.	Oct.	Nov.	Dec.
Fall chinook									X	X	X	X
Sturgeon			X	X	X	X	X	X	X	X	X	X
Coho									X	X	X	
Nestucca River												
Spring chinook					X	X	X	X				
Fall chinook									X	X	X	X
Rogue River												
Spring chinook					X	X	X	X	X			
Fall chinook								X	X	X	X	X
Coho								X	X	X	X	X
Summer steelhead				X	X	X	X	X	X	X	X	X
Winter steelhead	X	X	X									X
Siletz River												
Fall chinook								X	X	X	X	X
Steelhead	X	X	X		X	X	X	X	X	X	X	X
Siuslaw River												
Fall chinook								X	X	X	X	X
Winter steelhead	X	X	X		X	X	X	X	X	X	X	X

	Jan.	Feb.	Mar.	Apr.	May	June	July	Aug.	Sept.	Oct.	Nov.	Dec.
Tillamook Bay												
Spring chinook					X	X	X	X				
Fall chinook								X	X	X	X	X
Sturgeon	X	X	X	X	X	X	X	X	X	X	X	X
Coho								X	X	X			
Umpqua River												
Spring chinook					X	X	X	X	X			
Fall chinook								X	X	X	X	X
Coho								X	X	X	X	X
Shad					X	X	X					
Sturgeon		X	X	X			X	X				
Yaquina Bay												
Fall chinook										X	X	X
Sea-run cutthroat trout							X	X	X			

Data adapted from the Oregon Department of Fish and Wildlife

Lobster Creek Campground (contact the Forest Service, 541/247-3600) is nine miles East of Gold Beach via Forest Service Road 33. This $5/night campground is open year-round and has three tent sites, three trailer sites, and one group site with picnic tables, fishing, and flush toilets, but no drinking water. Ask the forest service for directions to the Schrader old-growth trail nearby. It is a gentle one-mile walk through a rare and majestic ecosystem that is under siege in other forests throughout the state. Also nearby is the largest myrtle tree.

Honeybear Campground and RV Resort (P.O. Box 97, 34161 Ophir Rd., Ophir 97464, 541/247-2765 or 800/822-4444, www.honeybearrv.com) is nine miles north of Gold Beach on U.S. 101, then two miles north on Ophir Road, but could just as well be in the Black Forest. The owners have built a large rathskeller with a dance floor. Six nights a week during the summer, there are dances here with traditional German music. Check out their version of October Fest. Locals praise the Honeybear's on-site delicatessen for its homemade German sausage. There are 20 tent and RV sites, picnic tables, flush toilets, hot showers, firewood, a laundromat, and ocean views for $15–25. It's open year-round.

Golf

Cedar Bend Golf Course (P.O. Box 1234, Gold Beach, 541/247-6911) is located in nearby Ophir. Eleven miles north of Gold Beach, pick up Ophir Road off U.S. 101. Follow it to Squaw Valley Road, turn right at the Old Ophir Store, and continue until you see the links. Woods line the fairways, and a winding creek offers a challenge on each of the nine holes. Green fees are $18 for 18 holes, $13 for nine.

EVENTS

The **Wild Rivers Coast Seafood, Art, and Wine Festival** is a two-day event that celebrates wine, fine dining, and arts and crafts of the southern Oregon coast, in mid-May at the Event Center on the Beach (29392 Ellensburg, 541/247-4541).

People line the river for the annual **jetboat races,** which take place in mid-June. Contact Jot's Resort (800/367-5687) or the chamber of commerce for further information.

The **Pistol River Wave Bash National Windsurfing Competition** bring four days of competitive riding to Pistol River State Park each June. For details, contact the Gold Beach Visitor Center (541/247-7526 or 800/525-2334).

In late July or early August, the **Curry County Fair and Rodeo** takes place at the Event Center on the Beach. Highlights include Oregon's largest flower show and a lamb barbecue.

PRACTICALITIES

Accommodations

As in most coastal towns, there is no shortage of places to stay along the main drag, Ellensburg Street (a.k.a. U.S. 101). In fact, Gold Beach offers the largest number and widest range of accommodations on the south coast, with intimate lodges overlooking the Rogue as popular as the oceanfront motels. A discount of 20 percent or more on rooms is usually available during the winter here when 80–90 inches of rain can fall.

Formerly the River Bridge Inn and now a **Motel 6** (1010 Jerry's Flat Rd., 541/247-4533 or 800/759-4533), this inn/motel has modern, comfy river-view rooms for $50–80. Kitchenettes are available, as are spa suites.

Ireland's Rustic Lodge (29330 Ellensburg, 541/247-7718, www.irelendsrusticlodges.com) was started by two women who used to bring meals to the cabins. While this is no longer the case, the touch of home has not been lost. Many of the rooms have fireplaces, knotty-pine interiors, and distinctive decor. Best of all, the grounds are lovingly landscaped with pine trees, flowers, and ocean views. A sandy beach is a short stroll to the west. There are 33 motel lodge units (some with kitchens), seven old but well-kept log cabins (recommended) that sleep up to five, and houses that sleep as many as 11. The rates are $50–80, $95–105 for houses. Ireland's also has an RV park close by the lodge.

Located on the Rogue River's north bank, **Jot's Resort** (94360 Wedderburn Loop, Wedderburn, 541/247-6676 or 800/FOR-JOTS, www.jotsresort.com) can host a full vacation in one compound featuring pool and spa, sports shop, private dock, rental boats, and a restaurant across the street. The rooms here are at a premium in summer when the motorcoach tours come through, leaving other travelers with the less-desirable rooms. Rates range $75–300, so it's best to call for current rates and specials. The Rod 'n' Reel across the street features evening entertainment with low-stakes blackjack, a country music duo, and a big-band dance on weekends.

Tu Tu Tun Resort (96550 N. Bank, 541/247-6664 or 800/864-6357, www.tututun.com) emphasizes the tranquility reinforced by the absence of TV in the rooms (except in the suites and houses). The lodge is located seven miles up the Rogue River from Gold Beach. While there is a TV in the cedar-planked lodge, most guests prefer to take in the view of the river through the floor-to-ceiling windows or enjoy a good book from the lodge's library in front of the massive river rock fireplace. Other appeals include a heated pool and other recreational facilities, beautifully appointed interiors, and delicious meals (served on an inclusive Modified American Plan for about $50 per person May–October; in the off-season, guests are served a continental breakfast only). The rates are $85–290 (lower rates in winter).

Set atop a bluff over the Pacific north of town, the **Inn at Nesika Beach** (33026 Nesika Rd., 541/247-6434) is a three-story neo-Victorian B&B with mind-stopping views, featherbeds, and spas in each of its four rooms. A wraparound porch and an enclosed oceanfront deck also highlight the setting. Breakfast is an event here, served in an elegant dining room facing the ocean. The rates run $130–165 (discounted for two or more nights). They do not accept credit cards or children.

Bed-and-Breakfast

The **Rogue Reef Inn** (30530 Old Coast Rd., 877/234-7333, www.roguereef.com) is just one mile north of the Rogue River and directly overlooks the Rogue Reef and Northwest Rocks. In this contemporary home with four guestrooms (each with private bath), guests walk out onto the three-mile-long stretch of beach which partially intersects the Oregon Coast Trail. The inn is the first home north of the Rogue River north jetty. Rates $85–95 (no credit cards).

Upriver Lodges

Several lodges on the Rogue, some accessible only by boat or via hiking trails, lure visitors deep into the interior. Jetboat trips can drop you off for an overnight or longer stay. Advance reservations are essential.

Accessible by road or jetboat 32 miles inland from the coast, the **Cougar Lane Lodge** (04219 Agness Rd., 541/247-7233) was established in 1949 on the east shore of the Rogue. Spend the night in one of the simple lodge rooms for $45–65, or come for the day to fish (licenses and tackle available at the Cougar Lane store). Dine at the lodge restaurant, overlooking the Rogue, which serves standard American breakfast,

lunch and dinner every day. From here, hike the Rogue or Illinois trails. The Agness RV Park is nearby, for overnight camping.

Also accessible by road and boat, the **Lucas Pioneer Ranch & Fishing Lodge** (03904 Cougar Lane, 541/247-7443) is also 32 miles east of Gold Beach. Cabins here come equipped with cooking and noncooking options and range $45–80. Lunch and dinner are served daily in the lodge—chicken, biscuits, and garden vegetables are standard fare. Reservations are required.

The more remote **Half Moon Bar Lodge** (Box 455, Gold Beach 97444, 541/247-6968 or 888/291-8268, www.halfmoonbarlodge.com) is located in the wild and secluded piece of wilderness, once the site of Native American encampments. Choose from three private cabins or stay in the rustic lodge, which houses a sauna, dining room, and bar. Meals are served family-style and include fresh seasonal garden veggies and fruits. Tour boats take visitors 52 miles upriver; raft down with a white-water guide or fish for steelhead. To get there, hike in 11 miles from Foster Bar along the Rogue River Trail or five miles from Bear Camp near Agness. The lodge can also accommodate small planes on its private airstrip. Call to make arrangements.

Only accessible by helicopter, jetboat, or foot, the **Paradise Lodge** (541/247-6504 or 800/525-2161, www.go-oregon.com) attracts nature enthusiasts interested in the "wildest" experience. Only the meals are scheduled here, where you can take an eco tour, enjoy a sauna, raft or jetboat the rapids, or check out some of the old mining sites in the vicinity. A huge on-site garden provides ingredients for home-cooked meals. Rates are $107 per adult (includes three meals), $77 for kids aged 4–11. Jetboat round-trip rates are $95 per adult and $50 per child.

Food

You can't eat scenery, but Gold Beach restaurants charge you for it anyway. Still, this is one place where the oceanfront and riverside views are often worth the price. Then, too, there's always the option of cheaper restaurants away from port.

COASTAL OREGON

Spring chinook salmon, blackberry pie, and other indigenous specialties taste good anywhere.

Grant's Pancake House (29790 U.S. 101, 541/247-7208) is the breakfast place of choice from the Rogue estuary to California. Filling omelettes, pancakes, waffles, and corned beef hash often make lunch (in the same price range) an afterthought. Nonetheless, locals consider the Thursday clam steak lunch special (breaded East Coast sea clams in a spicy homemade sauce) one of the town's culinary highlights. Open for breakfast and lunch.

Spada's (29174 Ellensburg, 541/247-7732) is one of the few "Chinese" restaurants on the coast. The menu is a mixed bag, however, including many American favorites such as pizza, seafood, and chicken-fried steak. Open daily 11 A.M.–9:30 P.M.

The Nor'Wester (10 Harbor Way, 541/247-2333) is located at the port of Gold Beach, so sometimes you can watch boats unloading your dinner. Not surprisingly, the menu is dominated by seafood, though the wait staff tout the New Zealand lamb chops. What is surprising are such occasional culinary flourishes as chinook salmon broiled under a flame, then covered with a glaze of sake, cayenne, ginger, and soy. Dinner prices top out above $40 for steak and lobster but most entrées are in the $18 range. There are also light (less expensive) dinner options. Open daily for dinner only.

Chives Oceanfront Dining and Lounge (29212 U.S. 101, 541/247-4121, www.chives.net) is the kind of upscale restaurant one might encounter in Marin County but at Oregon prices. (They share a driveway with Gold Beach Resort.) While the menu rotates seasonally, imagine steamer clams in white wine and garlic butter broth or marinated and grilled lamb loin chops with risotto to get an idea of the offerings here. Sophisticated salads and creative sandwiches are also in ample evidence at lunch. Dinner entrées such as king salmon fillet range $15–25. For dessert, the bread pudding with a Jack Daniels sauce is recommended. The restaurant serves lunch and dinner only. Closed in January.

Locals recommend the **Port Hole Cafe** (29975 Harbor Way, 541/247-7411), in the Cannery building at the port with bay and river views, for hearty portions of fish-n-chips, chowder, and homemade pies at decent prices. Open daily 6 A.M.–9 P.M.

Seafood lovers will find some hard choices at the **Chowderhead Restaurant** (29430 Ellensburg, 541/247-0588), which has serves the full range of seafood, plus steaks, soups, and sandwiches. Open for lunch and dinner only.

Information and Transportation

The **Gold Beach Visitor Center** (29279 Ellensburg, Gold Beach 97444, 541/247-7526 or 800/525-2334, www.goldbeach.org) is open Mon.–Fri. 9 A.M.–5 P.M. and Saturday and Sunday 10 A.M.–4 P.M. Their website is excellent and informative, and they'll send you a good, comprehensive information folder upon request. An independently run website, **www.goldbeach.net,** is also packed with detailed tourist information.

The **Gold Beach Ranger District** (29279 Ellensburg, 541/247-3600), offers a free packet on camping and recreation in the district. It's open Mon.–Fri. 7:30 A.M.–5 P.M.

Curry County's **Coastal Express** buses (in Gold Beach, call 541/247-7506) run up and down the south coast weekdays only between North Bend and the California border, including local service in Gold Beach. The **Greyhound station** (29770 Colvin St., 541/247-7246) is a block east of the highway in the north end of town.

Port Orford and Vicinity

In 1850, the U.S. Congress passed the Oregon Donation Land Act, allowing white settlers to file claims on Native American land in western Oregon. This was news, of course, to the tribal nations of the region, who had not been consulted on the decision. William Tichenor, captain of the steamship *Gull,* hoping to exploit the new act, had ambitions to establish an outpost on the coast at what's now Port Orford. When Tichenor observed the hostility of the Quatomah band of the Tututni tribe in the tidewater, he put nine men ashore on an immense rock promontory fronting the beach, due to its suitability as a defensive position. The Native Americans besieged the rock for two weeks, before the whites escaped under cover of night. Tichenor returned with a well-armed party of 70 men, and succeeded in founding his settlement.

From this inauspicious beginning, "Awferd," as the locals call it, established itself as the first townsite on the south coast. Shortly thereafter, the town became the site of the first fort established on the coast during the Rogue River Wars (see "History," earlier in this chapter).

Besides the tragic tribal conflicts, Port Orford has other claims to fame. It is the most westerly incorporated city in the contiguous United States. What's more, *Forbes* magazine has dubbed Port Orford the "sleeper" of the Oregon coast, ready to be awakened due to its "knockout" view. Impressive potential, however, has not yet translated into any great prosperity for the region. Commercial fishing and cedar logging were once the leading revenue producers. In recent years, tourism as well as many eclectic cottage industries have sprung up to supplement the boom/bust, resource-based economy. The outskirts of Port Orford host such diverse undertakings as an escargot farm, llama and sheep ranches, a goat-milk dairy, and commercial berry growers, as well as plots of land devoted to Christmas trees and exotic herbs. Offshore, divers harvest kelp for use as a food supplement and sea urchins to supply the Japanese with a popular aphrodisiac and seafood delicacy. In town, the stunning scenery and low rents probably have played a role in the development of a passel of galleries here, evidencing a nascent artist colony.

SIGHTS

Port Orford has an ocean view from downtown that is arguably the most scenic of any city's on the coast. A waterfront stroll lets you appreciate the cliffs and offshore sea stacks as well as the unusual sight of commercial fishing boats being hoisted by large cranes into and out of the harbor. With only a short jetty on its north side, Port Orford's harbor, the only open-water port in Oregon, is unprotected from southerly swells, so boats can't be safely moored on the water. When not in use, the fleet rest on wheeled, trailer-like dollies near the foot of the pier.

Battle Rock Park

As you come into town on U.S. 101, it's hard to ignore enormous Battle Rock on the shoreline, the site of the 1851 conflict between the local tribes and the first landing party of white settlers. If you can make your way through driftwood and blackberry bushes surrounding its base, you can climb the short trail to the top for a heightened perspective on the rockbound coast that parallels the town. You'll also notice the east-west orientation of the harbor. Once you get to the top of the rock, don't think that the battle is necessarily over. Bracing winds often chill you, and high tides can sometimes render this huge coastal extension an island. The rock is also the focus of a **Fourth of July Jubilee Celebration,** which reenacts the historic battle described above.

Port Orford Heads State Park

Another shoreline scene worth taking in, featuring a striking panorama from north to south, is located up West 9th Street at what the locals call "The Heads," Port Orford Heads State Park. If you go down the cement trail to the tip of the blustery headland, you look south to the mouth of Port Orford's harbor. To the north, many small rocks fill the water, along with boats trolling for salmon or checking crab pots. On clear days visibility extends from Cape Blanco to Humbug Mountain.

Also located here is the historic **Port Orford Lifeboat Station** (541/332-0521), built by the Coast Guard in 1934 to provide rescue service to the southern Oregon coast. After it was decommissioned in 1970, the officer's quarters, the pleasingly proportioned crew barracks, and other outbuildings were converted to a museum depicting the work of the station. A trail leads down to Nellie's Cove, site of the former boathouse and launch ramp. The museum is open April–October, Thurs.–Mon. 10 A.M.–3:30 P.M.

Humbug Mountain

Some people will tell you that 1,756-foot-high Humbug Mountain, six miles south of Port Orford on U.S. 101, is the highest mountain rising directly off the Oregon shoreline. Because the criteria for such a distinction varies as much as the tides, let's just say it's a special place.

There's more than one version of how the peak, formerly called Sugarloaf Mountain, got its name. According to one version, gold miners who were drawn here in the 1850s by tales of gold in the black sands nearby soon discovered that the rumored riches proved to be just "humbug." Perhaps more reliable is the Native American legend that says that if the top of the mountain can be seen, the weather will be good.

Once the site of Native American vision-quests, today Humbug Mountain's shadow falls upon an Edenlike state park campground surrounded by myrtles, alders, and maples. Just north is a breezy black-sand beach. A three-mile trail to the top of Humbug rewards hardy hikers with impressive vistas to the south of Nesika Beach and a chance to see wild rhododendrons 20–25 feet high. Rising above the rhodies and giant ferns are bigleaf maple, Port Orford cedar, and Douglas and grand firs. Access the trail from the campground, or from a trailhead parking area off the highway near the south end of the park. In addition, the **Oregon Coast Trail,** which follows the beach south from Battle Rock, traverses the mountain and leads down its south side to the beach at Rocky Point.

For information on camping, see "Recreation," later in this section.

Prehistoric Gardens

What can we say about this one-of-a-kind roadside attraction, featuring a 25-foot-tall, Formica-green *Tyrannosaurus rex* standing beside the parking lot? Is it kitsch, or is it educational? You decide. In any case, if you've got children in the car, unless they're sleeping or blindfolded you're probably going to have to pull over. Prehistoric Gardens (36848 U.S. 101, Port Orford, 541/332-4463 or 877/332-4463), about 10 miles south of Port Orford, is the creation of E. V. Nelson, a sculptor and self-taught paleontologist who began fabricating life-size dinosaurs here back in 1953, and placing them amidst the lush rainforest on the backside of Humbug Mountain. Paths lead through the ferns, trees, and undergrowth to a towering brontosaurus, triceratops, and 20 other ferro-concrete replicas, painted in a dazzling palette of Fiestaware colors. Open daily 9 A.M.–dusk spring–fall; call for winter hours, which vary. Admission is $7 for adults, ages 11–17 and 65-plus $6, children 3–10 $5.

Cape Blanco State Park, Hughes House

Four miles north of Port Orford, west of U.S. 101, is Cape Blanco, whose remote appendages give you the feeling of being at the edge of the continent—as indeed you are, here at the westernmost point in Oregon. From the vantage of Cape Blanco, dark mountains rise behind you and the eaves of the forest overhang tidewater. Below, driftwood and 100-foot-long bull kelp on slivers of black-sand beach fan out from both sides of this earthy red bluff. The Spaniards who sailed past it in 1603 viewed the cape as being *blanco,* white. It's been theorized that perhaps they were referring to the fossilized shells on the front of the cliff.

With its exposed location, Cape Blanco really takes it on the chin from Pacific storms. The vegetation along the five-mile state park road down to the beach attests to the severity of winter storms in the area. Gales of 100 mph (record winds were clocked at 184 mph) and horizontal sheets of rain have given some of the usually massive Sitka spruces the appearance of bonsai trees. An understory of salmonberry and bracken fern evokes the look of a southeast Alaska forest.

Atop the weathered headland is Oregon's oldest, most westerly, and highest lighthouse in continuous use. Built in 1870, the beacon stands 256 feet above sea level and can be seen some 23 nautical miles out at sea. Cape Blanco Lighthouse also holds the distinction of having Oregon's first female lighthouse keeper, Mabel E. Bretherton, who assumed her duties in 1903. Tours of the facility include the chance to climb the 64 spiraling steps to the top; this is the only operational lighthouse in the state that allows visitors into the lantern room, to view the working Fresnel lens. Tours are offered April–October, Thurs.–Mon. 10 A.M.–3 P.M. A $3 donation is requested. For more information, call 541/332-2207.

Over the years a number of shipwrecks have occurred on the reefs near Cape Blanco, including the *J.A. Chanslor,* an oil tanker that collided with the offshore rocks in 1919, with a loss of 36 lives.

Near Cape Blanco on a side road along the Sixes River is the **Hughes House** (541/332 0248), a restored Victorian home built in 1898 for rancher and county commissioner Patrick Hughes. Owned and operated today by the state of Oregon, the house serves as a museum and repository of antique furnishings. The Hughes House is open April–October, Thurs.–Mon. 10 A.M.–3 P.M. It's also open during the winter holiday season, when punch and cookies are often served the weekend before Christmas.

For information on camping in the state park, see "Recreation."

RECREATION

Beachcombing for agates and fishing floats on nearby beaches and searching for the lost Port Orford meteorite in the surrounding foothills typify the adventures available in the area. The meteorite was found in the 1860s by a government geologist, who estimated its weight at 22,000 tons. Unfortunately, he was unable to relocate the meteorite when he returned for another look.

In the northwest of town, drive west of the highway on 14th or 18th Streets to 90-acre **Garrison Lake** for boating, water-skiing, and fishing for stocked rainbow and cutthroat trout. **Buffington Memorial City Park,** at the end of 14th Street, has a dock for fishing or swimming, plus playing fields, tennis courts, picnic areas, hiking trails, and a horse arena. A half mile north of the lake, look for agates on **Paradise Point Beach.**

The **Elk River,** which empties on the south side of Cape Blanco, and the **Sixes River,** which meets the sea north of the cape, are two popular streams for salmon and steelhead fishing. Chinook and steelhead begin to enter both rivers after the first good rains of fall arrive, usually in November. Private lands limit bank access, with the exception of a good stretch of the Sixes that runs through Cape Blanco State Park. The salmon season runs to the end of the year, steelhead through the following March. **Lamm's Guide Service** (541/440-0558, www.umpquafishingguide.com) runs trips on both rivers.

Between Port Orford and Bandon (just south of Langlois) is **Floras Lake,** which is becoming a mecca for coastal windsurfing. For more information, contact Floras Lake Windsurfing School (P.O. Box 1591, Bandon 97411, 541/347-9205). It's 11 miles north of Port Orford, about four miles west of the highway on Floras Lake Loop Road. On the lake is **Boice Cope County Park,** which has basic tent and RV sites, and a boat ramp. From Floras Lake north to Bandon, the most desolate beachfront on the coast can be found—ideal for beachcombing. Grasses, dunes, and shore pine usher you the third of a mile back to Bandon and chances are good you won't see a soul.

Camping

Humbug Mountain State Park (541/332-6774), six miles south of Port Orford, features 80 tent sites and 30 sites for trailers and motor homes, and wind-protected sites reserved for hikers and bikers. Flush toilets, showers, picnic tables, water, and firewood are available. The regular campsites are $14–16; rates fall by $4 off-season. Hiker/biker sites go for $4 year-round.

Arizona Beach Campground (P.O. Box 621, Gold Beach 97444, 541/332-6491, www.arizonabeachrv.com) is a 70-acre campground close to a beach with lots of driftwood. It has 31 tent sites and almost a hundred RV spaces. You can camp on the beach, in an adjoining meadow, or back in the woods by a tiny stream for $14–20. All the amenities are here, 15 miles north of Gold Beach on U.S. 101, but the closely spaced sites lack privacy. Nonetheless, there are few better places for kids, due to the creek running though the site and the proximity of the Prehistoric Gardens. It's open all year. Holiday reservations only.

Cape Blanco State Park (39745 S. U.S. 101, 541/332-6774 info, 800/452-5687 for cabin reservations) can be reached by driving four miles north of Port Orford on U.S. 101, then heading northwest on the park road that continues five miles beyond to the campground. It features 54 sites (first-come, first-served) for tents ($16), four cabins ($35), trailers and motor homes ($16), a horse camp ($14), and hiker/biker sites ($4); picnic tables, water, and showers are available. For horseback riders, there's a seven-mile trail and a huge open riding area; horses are also allowed on the beach.

PRACTICALITIES
Accommodations
Port Orford is the kind of place where a room with a view will not break your budget. The **Shoreline Motel** (206 6th St., 541/332-2903), across the highway from Battle Rock, has an outstanding view, offers clean rooms, and accommodates pets for $38–58.

Castaway-by-the-Sea (545 W. 5th St., 541/

When it comes to seafood, it's a very short trip from the boat to the plate, with, of course, a short detour through the restaurant's kitchen.

332-4502) features ocean/harbor views from high on a bluff, fireplaces, and housekeeping units, and allows pets; rates are $45–95. The rates on the upper-end lodgings go down significantly in the off-season. It's said that Jack London once stayed in an earlier incarnation of this place.

The **Seacrest Motel** (44 U.S. 101 S., 541/332-3040) features views of coastal cliffs and a garden from a quiet hillside on the east side of the highway. Rates run $57–74.

Home-by-the-Sea (444 Jackson St., 541/332-2855 or 800/480-2144, www.homebythesea.com) includes a full breakfast at rates of $95–105 a night for two. The dramatic hillside view of Battle Rock seascape makes for excellent storm-watching here. Wireless Internet access is available.

Food
In Port Orford, pickings are slim, after massive restaurant closures in the mid-1990s. You're better off waiting to take advantage of Bandon and Gold Beach's array of restaurants.

That said, vegetarian soup and sandwiches ($3–5) can be enjoyed at **Seaweed Natural Food and Grocery** (832 Oregon St., 541/332-3640). More elaborate fare can be had across the street from Battle Rock at **Paula's Bistro** (236 6th St., 541/332-9378), whose menu of pasta, barbecue, and seafood specials ($12–18) and wild decor show ambition and creativity. It also wins by default in "Awferd's" anemic dining scene. Dinner only; closed Monday. **Bartlett's Cafe** (831 Oregon St., 541/332-4175) serves familiar American diner fare for breakfast, lunch, and dinner.

Information and Transportation
Begin your travels here at **Battle Rock Information Center,** open daily on the west side of U.S. 101 (541/332-8055). The people here are especially friendly and helpful. Information is also available online at **www.portorfordoregon.com.**

The **library** (555 W. 20th St.) is open weekdays 8 A.M.–5 P.M.

Greyhound picks up passengers from a convenience store (914 N. Oregon St., 541/332-3181). Two buses go in each direction up and down the coast daily. Curry County's **Coastal Express** buses (in Port Orford, call 541/332-5771) run up and down the south coast weekdays only between North Bend and the California border, including local service in Port Orford.

Bandon

In contrast to the glitzy tourist trappings of some of the larger coastal towns, Bandon-by-the-Sea (pop. 2,900) is characterized by the style and grace of an earlier era. The glory that was Bandon is alive and well in Old Town, a picturesque collection of shops, galleries, restaurants, and historical memorabilia. It's at Bandon that the coast highway finally re-encounters the coast, after long inland stretches of pastureland and forests to the south and north.

While logging, fishing, dairy products, and the harvest of cranberries have been the traditional mainstays of the local economy, in the early part of the 20th century Bandon also enjoyed its first tourism boom. In addition to being a summer retreat from the heat of the Willamette Valley, it was a port of call for thousands of San Francisco–to-Seattle steamship passengers. This era inspired such touristic venues as the Silver Spray dance hall and a natatorium with a saltwater swimming pool. The golden age that began with the advent of large-scale steamship traffic in 1900, however, came to an abrupt end following a devastating fire in 1936, which destroyed most of the town. The blaze was started by the easily ignitable gorse weed, imported from Ireland (as was the town's name) in the mid-1800s. Dramatic descriptions of the townspeople fighting the flames with their backs to the sea earned the incident a citation as one of the top-10 news stories of the year.

The facelift given Old Town decades later, and the subsequent tourist influx, conjured for many the image of the mythical phoenix rising from its ashes to fly again. On the wings of the recovery, Bandon has established itself as a town rooted in the past with its eyes on the future. Today, Bandon is a curious mixture of provincial backwater, destination resort, and new-age artist colony. Backpack-toting travelers from all over the world flock to this town because of its beaches, its cultural and recreational pursuits, and its European-style hostelry. They coexist happily with the large population of retirees, award-winning artisans, and locals who seem to have cornered the market on late-model pickups with gun racks.

SIGHTS

One of the appealing things about Bandon is that most of its attractions are within walking distance of each other. In addition, on the periphery of town is a varied array of things to see and do.

Old Town

Bandon's Old Town, much of which dates from after the 1936 fire, is a half dozen blocks of shops, cafés, and galleries squeezed in between the harbor and the highway. The renovated waterfront invites relaxed strolling, and crabbers and anglers pull in catches right off the city docks. The small commercial fleet based here pursues salmon and tuna offshore.

Throughout Old Town are artists and artisans pursuing their crafts and selling their wares. **2nd Street Gallery** (210 2nd St., 541/347-4133) has a little of everything, from functional and art pottery to blown glass to paintings to sculptures. Open daily 10 A.M.–5:30 P.M. The **New Gallery** (155 Baltimore, 541/347-8221) showcases the work of local jewelers and woodworkers. **Winter River Books and Gallery** (170 2nd St., 541/347-4111) has crystals, objets d'art, and a wide-ranging assortment of travel titles, photo essays, fiction, and tapes that makes this the best bookstore on the south coast.

Close by, the **Bandon Driftwood Museum**

PACIFIC OCEAN

Bullards Beach State Park

COQUILLE RIVER LIGHTHOUSE ★

Sand Dunes

River

To Coos Bay →

MICHIGAN AVE

101

Coquille

COQUILLE RIVER MUSEUM ★

SEA STAR GUESTHOUSE

BANDON FISH MARKET ★

RIVERSIDE DR

1ST ST

CLEVELAND AVE

Table Rock

MADISON AVE

LINCOLN AVE

JETTY RD

OCEAN DR

OLD TOWN

4TH ST

1ST ST

CHICAGO AVE

2ND ST

42S

To Coquille →

Coquille Point

7TH ST

8TH ST

SOUTHERN COOS GENERAL HOSPITAL

8TH ST

9TH ST

11TH ST

VISITOR INFORMATION CENTER

OREGON AVE

ELMIRA AVE

FILLMORE

3RD ST

9TH ST

LEXINGTON AVE

JUNE AVE

BALTIMORE AVE

ALABAMA AVE

OREGON COAST HWY

AVE

City Park

Bandon Beach

SUNSET LODGING ■

FACE ROCK DR

BANDON

BILL

CREEK

RD

Bandon Ocean State Wayside

BEACH LOOP DR

AUCTION BARN RD

ROSA

RD

101

WAVECREST LN

SEA BIRD DR

BEST WESTERN INN AT FACE ROCK ●

SEABIRD LN

GOLF

LINKS RD

0   500 yds
0   500 m

© AVALON TRAVEL PUBLISHING, INC.

BANDON FACE ROCK GOLF COURSE

To Port Orford ↓

and **Art Gallery** (130 Baltimore, 541/347-3719) shows off an interesting collection of natural sculptures, from gnarly root balls to whole tree trunks. It's housed at the Big Wheel General Store, where you'll also find the Fudge Factory (24 flavors of homemade ice cream and butter fudges. Summer hours are Mon.–Sat. 9 A.M.–7 P.M.; Sun. 10 A.M.–6 P.M.; call for winter hours.

Coquille River Museum

This museum, at the corner of U.S. 101 and Fillmore Street (270 Fillmore, 541/347-2164), in Bandon's former city hall, traces the history of the Coquille tribe (pronounced ko-KWELL in native dialect) and its forebears. The chronology continues with the steamers and the railroads that brought in white settlers. One room is devoted to Bandon's unofficial standing as the Cranberry Capital of Oregon. Black-and-white blowups showing women stooping over in the bogs to harvest the ripe berries are captioned with such quips as this politically incorrect classic from an overseer: "I had 25 women picking for me, and I knew every one by her fanny."

Color photos spanning five decades of Cranberry Festival princesses also adorn the walls.

Another room depicts "Bandon's Resort Years, 1900–1931," when the town was called the Playground of the Pacific. The most compelling exhibits in the museum deal with shipwrecks and the fires of 1914 and 1936. Open Mon.–Sat. 10 A.M.–4 P.M., Sunday 10 A.M.–3 P.M.; closed Sunday in winter. Admission is $2 for adults; children are admitted free.

The Beach Loop

U.S. 101 follows an inland path for more than 50 miles between Coos Bay and Port Orford, but you can leave the highway in Bandon and take the four-mile Beach Loop for a lovely seaside detour south of town. Several access roads lead west from the highway to Beach Loop Drive (County Road 29), each about a quarter mile from each other. Most people begin the drive by heading west from Old Town on 1st Street along the Coquille. Another popular approach is from 11th Street, which leads to Coquille Point. The south end of the drive runs through the northern portion of **Bandon State Natural Area,** providing parking, beach access, and picnic tables.

Along the fine stretch of beach are rock formations with such evocative names as Table Rock, Elephant Rock, Garden of the Gods, and Cat and Kittens Rocks. The whole grouping of sea stacks, included within the Oregon Islands National Wildlife Refuge, looks like a surrealist chess set cast upon the waters. The most eye-catching of all is **Face Rock,** Bandon's answer to New Hampshire's lately lamented Old Man of the Mountain. This basalt monolith resembles the face of a woman gazing skyward. A Native American legend says that she was a princess frozen by an evil sea spirit. Look for the Face Rock turnout a quarter mile south of Coquille Point on the Beach Loop.

Half a mile north of Face Rock is the Bandon Face Rock Golf Course, and another mile on is Bandon Beach Riding Stables, which offers beach rides; see "Recreation," later in this section, for details on both. Despite its scenic and recreational attractions, the beaches south of town can be surprisingly deserted. Perhaps this is due to the long, steep trails up from the water along some parts

of the beach. In any case, this dearth of people can make for great beachcombing. Agates, driftwood, and tidepools full of starfish and anemones are commonly encountered here, along with bird-watching opportunities galore. Elephant Rock has a reputation as the Parthenon of puffins, while murres, oystercatchers, and other species proliferate on the other offshore formations.

Bullards Beach State Park

Two miles north of Bandon, bordering the Coquille River estuary and over four miles of beachfront, Bullards Beach State Park (P.O. Box 25, Bandon 97411, information 541/347-2209 or 800/551-6949, reservations 800/452-5687) is a great place to fish, crab, bike, fly a kite, windsurf, picnic, or overnight in the large, sheltered campground. The beach and lighthouse are reached via a scenic three-mile drive paralleling the Coquille River. Look for jasper and agates amidst the heaps of driftwood on the shore. Equestrian trails and horse camping facilities make this a popular destination for riders. The boat ramp gives fishermen, kayakers, and canoeists access to the lower Coquille River and Bandon Marsh National Wildlife Refuge (see "Recreation," later in this section).

The riverside road going out to the Coquille's north jetty takes you through the dunes to the picturesque **Coquille River Lighthouse,** a squat tower with adjacent octagonal quarters. The last lighthouse built on the Oregon coast, it was completed in 1896, then was abandoned in 1939 when the Coast Guard installed an automated light across the river. After years of neglect, the structure was restored in the late 1970s, and is now open throughout the year. Etchings of ships that made it across Bandon's treacherous bar, and some that didn't, greet you as you enter. Volunteers are on duty to staff the gift shop and show you around April–October.

For details on camping at Bullards Beach State Park, see "Camping," later in this section.

West Coast Game Park

Seven miles south of Bandon is the West Coast Game Park (46914 U.S. 101 S., Bandon, 541/347-3106), the self-proclaimed largest wild-animal petting park in the country. There are

© MARK MORRIS

Coquille River Lighthouse, Bullards Beach State Park

450 animals representing 75 different species, including tiger cubs, chimps, camels, zebras, bison, and snow leopards. Along with these exotics you'll also encounter such indigenous species as elk, bears, raccoons, and cougars. Visitors may be surprised to see a lion and tiger caged together, or a fox and a raccoon sharing the same nursery. The park tries raising different species together and often finds that animals can live harmoniously with their natural enemies. Free-roaming animals include deer, peacock, pygmy goats, and llamas. An elk refuge is another popular area of the park.

Even if you're not with a child, the opportunity to pet a pup, a cub, or a kit can bring out the kid in you. The park is open year-round, but call during winter for hours. The park is open daily 9 A.M.–7 P.M. June 15–August, 9 A.M.–5 P.M. the rest of the year. Tickets cost $11 for ages 13 and up, kids $8 for ages 7–12, $5 for ages 2–6, $10 for seniors.

RECREATION
Bandon Marsh National Wildlife Refuge

Bird-watchers flock to the Bandon Marsh National Wildlife Refuge (541/347-3683), especially in the fall, to take in what may be the prime birding site on the coast. The extensive mudflats, especially, attract flocks of shorebirds, including red phalaropes, black-bellied plovers, long-billed curlews, and dunlins, as well as such strays from Asia as Mongolian plovers.

Bandon Marsh lies a short paddle across the river from the state park, or via Riverside Drive, which runs from Bandon to U.S. 101 on the south side of the Coquille River bridge. The refuge protects over 700 precious acres of the Coquille estuary's remaining saltmarsh habitat, along the southeastern side of the river. Migrating birds, waterfowl, bald eagles, California brown pelicans, and other species feast on the rich food sources here.

The refuge and its elevated observation deck are open daily from sunrise to sunset.

Fishing

The Coquille River runs 30 miles from its Siskiyou headwaters before meandering leisurely through Bandon. The north and south jetty are popular spots for perch and rockfish, while the city docks right in Old Town yield catches of perch and crab April–October and smelt July–September. The spring chinook run pales in comparison to those in the Rogue and Chetco to the south, but the fall runs of chinook (beginning September–October) and coho (October–November) are strong and productive. Steelhead usually arrive in November, and the run gathers steam January–February. A boat is necessary for the best steelhead and salmon water, but bank anglers can fish the mouth of Ferry Creek, just off Riverside Drive in Bandon. Fishing guides and gear can be arranged through the **Bandon Bait Shop** (1st and Alabama, 541/347-3905), across from the boat basin. The shop also rents crab rings and other gear, and can point you to productive spots for catching Dungeness crab.

Just off the south end of Beach Loop Drive, 30-acre **Bradley Lake,** protected from ocean winds by high dunes, offers good trout fishing and a boat ramp. Trophy rainbows averaging five pounds, reared at the Bandon Fish Hatchery east of town, are stocked here each spring.

Camping

Bullards Beach State Park (P.O. Box 25, Bandon 97411, information 541/347-2209 or 800/551-6949, reservations 800/452-5687) is a wonderful state park in a great location, between the Coquille River and four miles of beach. The park has 190 campsites, 13 yurts, eight horse-camping sites, and hiker/biker spaces. To get there, drive north of town on U.S. 101 for about a mile; just past the bridge on the west side of the highway is the park entrance. The beach itself is reached via a scenic two-mile drive paralleling the Coquille River. Electricity, picnic tables, and fire grills are provided. You'll also find a store, a café, a laundry, horse riding/camping facilities, an inviting sandy beach, summer evening campfire talks Tues.–Sat., and hiking trails. The fee for camping at Bullards Beach along the Coquille is $16–20 a night. Yurts go for $27.

Golf

Dubbed "Pebble Beach North," **Bandon Dunes Golf Resort** (57744 Round Lake Dr., Bandon 97411, 541/347-4380 or 888/345-6008, www .bandondunesgolf.com) was hailed by *Golf Digest* as the number one new course in 1999 and named the third-best course in the United States by *Golf* magazine, due to its seven holes by the Pacific and unobstructed ocean views from all 18. A second 18-hole course, **Pacific Dunes,** opened here in 2001, and a third course is on the drawing board.

To preserve the natural surroundings along the ocean bluffs, this Scottish links course doesn't allow carts (the only missing amenity here), so you'll have to hire a caddy or schlep your own bag. A luxurious resort (see "Accommodations," later in this section) with Pacific views from a sand dune and a restaurant are also here for those who come to worship in the south coast's Sistine Chapel of golf. It's a mile north of the Coquille River. Green fees for either course, June–September, are $160 for hotel guests, $200 for nonguests; call for rates the rest of the year. Caddie fee is $35 per bag.

Duffers and other mortals may choose instead to tread the equally scenic seaside links two miles

south of town at **Bandon Face Rock Golf Course** (3235 Beach Loop Rd., 541/347-3818), where nine holes will set you back just $10, 18 holes for $16.

Other Activities

On the waterfront in Old Town, **Adventure Kayak** (315 1st St., 541/347-3480), rents kayaks (from $10/hour), teaches classes on a variety of kayak techniques, and offers guided sea-kayak tours of the lower Coquille ecosystem (and farther afield) with a naturalist from $35 for a two- to three-hour paddle. Open daily 10 A.M.–5 P.M. in summer.

Bandon Beach Riding Stables (2640 Beach Loop, 541/347-3423) is four miles south of Face Rock on the Beach Loop. Several beach rides are offered daily, plus sunset rides in the summer. Prices range $30–40 for a 1.5- to two-hour ride. Reservations are advised. Open year-round.

EVENTS

The annual **Wine and Seafood Festival** happens every Memorial Day weekend, at the Community Center in City Park off 11th Street West in Bandon. The free event includes live music, horse-drawn buggy rides, arts and crafts booths, and wine-tasting. The same weekend, competitors in the **Sandcastle Contest** create amazing sculptures out of sand, water, and imagination. This takes place on the beach off Beach Loop Drive at Seabird Lane. Construction starts at 9 A.M.; judging is at 1 P.M. Contact the chamber of commerce (541/347-9619) for details on both events.

A fish fry, kayak and driftboat races, parade, and classic car and motorcycle show are highlights of Bandon's **Fourth of July** celebration; at dusk, fireworks are launched across the Coquille to burst above the river.

The biggest weekend of the year for Bandonians comes the second weekend in September, when the **Cranberry Festival** (541/347-9616) brings everyone together in Old Town for a parade, crafts fair, tours of a cranberry farm, and the Bandon High Cranberry Bowl, when the local football team takes on traditional rival Coquille High.

During the holiday season, the merchants of Old Town and fisherfolk deck their stores and boats with twinkling lights in the traditional **Festival of Lights.** Particularly striking is the Coquille River Lighthouse, lit up across the water like a Christmas tree.

PRACTICALITIES

Accommodations

The expression "You can't go wrong" applies for price, view, cleanliness, and whatever else you're looking for in this town. Bandon bills itself as America's Storm-Watching Capital, and special packages are often available October–March.

A favorite place to stay is the older-but-refurbished **Windermere Motel** (3250 Beach Loop, 541/347-3710). For $68–145, baby-boomers can relive their childhood beach getaways in cedarwood efficiencies or two-story condolike units, situated on a bluff above a windswept beach. Housekeeping facilities and proximity to restaurants (Lord Bennett's) and West Coast Game Park also make this an idea family vacation spot.

Not far away is **Sunset Lodging** (1865 Beach Loop, 541/347-2453 or 800/842-2407, www.sunsetmotel.com). With some units built right into the cliff above a scenic beach, the view here is hard to beat. Whether you're looking for rooms with a kitchen, rooms that accommodate pets, or rooms with a fireplace, there's something here for you in a variety of price ranges ($52–110 for rooms, $165 and up for cabins). A hot tub, indoor pool, on-site laundry, and Lord Bennett's restaurant across the street also recommend this place. Nonetheless, the steep steps down the 80-foot-high bluff to the beach and the popularity of the place might not be to everyone's liking.

The "sleeper" property (for those making a hasty visual appraisal) on the beach loop is **Best Western Inn at Face Rock** (3225 Beach Loop, 541/347-9441 or 800/638-3092). Part of this status has to do with the motel's location near the end of the beach loop across the street from Bandon's coastline and near the nine-hole golf course. Many of the modern, well-appointed rooms have magnificent ocean views. An indoor pool, fitness room, whirlpool, and restaurant also make this an especially good choice for active travelers. In-season, expect to pay $80–205, half that in January. Some suites have fireplaces, kitchenettes, and private patios. There's an on-site restaurant and a short path to the beach.

For avid golfers, the **Lodge at Bandon Dunes** (57744 Round Lake Dr., 888/345-6008, www.bandondunesgolf.com) is a deluxe resort at what is considered one of the country's finest courses. They offer 15 single rooms, four larger single rooms, and two four-bedroom suites. View options vary from golf course and ocean views to dune and surrounding woods. The Lodge is five minutes from Bandon, a mile north of the Coquille, and 30 minutes from the North Bend Airport, which is served by daily flights from Portland. Room and suite rates ($150–900) and green fees ($100–200) are seasonal and subject to change.

Bed-and-Breakfast

The **Sea Star Guesthouse** (375 W. 2nd St., 541/347-9632, www.seastarbandon.com, 541/347-9694 café) has skylights, a natural wood interior, a woodstove, and a harbor-view courtyard. Private, couple, and family rooms are available. The last are more likely found in the four units adjoining (370 1st St.), where you get the feel of a tasteful motel. Guesthouse suites sleep two to six, have private baths, cable TV, queen beds, in-room coffee and tea service, and fireplaces. Rates are $70–105. Private rooms, for two, are a bit less. All units are nonsmoking, and no pets are permitted.

Food

Bandon Boatworks (275 Lincoln Ave. S.W., 541/347-2111) serves delicious traditional breakfast/brunch entrées and fresh seafood and steaks for lunch and dinner. The Boatworks has great views of the Coquille Lighthouse and an intimate lounge with entertainment. The restaurant is closed Monday and often goes into winter hibernation during January and February, so call for reservations or hours.

COASTAL CUISINE

Oregon coast cuisine boasts such delicacies as Dungeness crab, razor clams, Yaquina Bay oysters, and bay shrimp, as well as world-famous salmon. Among nonambulatory shellfish, Oregon's Yaquina Bay oysters are considered gourmet fare. If you want them fresh, avoid the summer months and wait until the weather is cooler. Razor clams are another indigenous shellfish—an acquired taste for many. Once you get past their rubbery consistency, however, you might enjoy this local favorite. Local mussels and albacore tuna near the end of July are also worth a try.

When it comes to fresh fish, you'll notice a variance in price based on how the salmon was caught (or wasn't caught). Troll-caught salmon (usually chinook and coho in Oregon) are landed in the ocean by hook and line, one at a time. This method permits better handling than netted salmon, which are caught in large groups as they come upriver from the ocean to spawn. Thus, you'll pay more for troll salmon, but you can taste the difference. Currently as efforts are undertaken to restore the species in the Northwest, most grocery-store salmon and some in restaurants come from Alaska or fish farms in the Pacific Northwest or Chile. There

are limited stocks of Oregon-caught salmon available, however, and it pays to be sensitive to nuances of harvest and preparation.

Spring chinook salmon (April–May) from the Rogue River estuary seems to be a "can't miss" item for almost everyone. While red snapper would normally also merit such an assessment, this is not always the case in Oregon, due largely to a case of mistaken identity. In contrast to the red snapper found on southern and eastern menus, this Pacific version is a bottomfish. The brown widow rockfish and dozens of other bottomfish species that receive the "red snapper" designation out here have a similar consistency but a more fishy taste than their East Coast counterpart.

© MARK MORRIS

If you want it fresher, you'll have to catch it yourself.

Budget diners and smoked-fish connoisseurs will appreciate the **Bandon Fish Market** (at the boat basin near the intersection of 1st and Chicago, 541/347-4282). Heartier appetites call for the market's excellent fish-n-chips; takeout only. A picnic table outside by the harbor is the place to enjoy it all with a trip across the street to Cranberry Sweets for dessert.

Wheelhouse Seafood Grill (1st and Chicago, 541/347-9331) deep-fries the fish (they also grill and broil) with a beer batter that doesn't mask the taste of the food. Their homemade soup is a spe-

cialty (as is the sirloin steak with prawns), especially the Cioppino Rick, using diverse shellfish and bottomfish in a marinara base. Moderately priced.

South of downtown, **Lord Bennett's** (1695 Beach Loop Dr., 541/347-FOOD) cliffside aerie looks out over the breakers toward Bandon's most dramatic restaurant view. Lunch and dinner do justice to these surroundings with elegantly rendered seafood dishes. Recommended are the bouillabaisse, crab cakes, and blackened ahi. Jazz on selected evenings in the lounge is another nice touch.

Bandon's Cheddar Cheese (800/548-8961), on the east side of U.S. 101 just east of Old Town, was once the second-largest cheese maker in Oregon. The factory, a popular tourist stop known for its huge cheddar bricks, cheese curds, and flavored cheeses, began operation in the early 1900s. Recently purchased by the Tillamook Creamery Association, the location is now an associated retail outlet. There are rumors that Tillamook has plans to create a cheese-making museum on the premises. Visitors can still view the cheese-making video and sample cheeses. The gift store also sells cheesy knick-knacks; open daily 9 A.M.–5:30 P.M.

Five miles south of Bandon, on the east side of U.S. 101, hit the brakes at **Misty Meadows Jams** roadside stand (48053 U.S. 101 S., 541/347-2575) for first-rate jams and jellies, including a variety of products incorporating Bandon cranberries. This family-owned and -operated business has been making delicious concoctions from Oregon-grown fruits since 1970. In addition to preserves, the shop sells olives and fruit-based barbecue sauces, syrups, honey, and salsas. Usually open 8 A.M.–6 P.M.

Information and Transportation
The **Bandon Chamber of Commerce** (300 W. 2nd St., Bandon 97411, 541/347-9616, www .bandon.com), in Old Town, distributes a comprehensive guide and a large annotated pictographic map of the town. Ask them about what they call "the best river fishing and crabbing docks on the coast."

The **Greyhound bus** (800/229-9424) stops at the Sea Star Guesthouse (375 W. 2nd) at 11:05 A.M. for Portland and at 4:30 A.M. and 4:25 P.M. for San Francisco. North- and southbound **Coastal Express** buses (541/469-6822) run three times daily, weekdays only, between North Bend and Brookings, stopping near the north end of Bandon at Ray's Food Place supermarket.

The Bay Area: Charleston, Coos Bay & North Bend

The towns around the harbor of Coos Bay refer to themselves collectively as "the Bay Area." In contrast to its namesake in California, the Oregon version is not exactly the Athens of the coast. Nonetheless, the visitor will be impressed by the area's beautiful beaches, the largest oceanfront dunes in North America, and three wonderfully scenic and historic state parks. Because much of this natural beauty is on the periphery of the industrialized core of the Bay Area, away from U.S. 101, it's easy to miss. All that many motorists see upon entering Coos Bay/North Bend on the Coast Highway are the dockside lumber mills and foreign vessels anchored at the one-time site of the world's largest (and currently, Oregon's second-busiest) lumber port.

The little town of Charleston (pop. 700) to the southwest makes few pretensions of being anything other than what it really is—the third-largest commercial fishing port on the Oregon coast. Four processing plants here can or cold-pack tuna, salmon, crab, oysters, shrimp, and other kinds of seafood. The town might occasionally smell of fish, but the few restaurants and lodgings here are good values. Moreover, a post office, a laundry, and a visitor information center are all conveniently crammed together on the main street, the Cape Arago Highway (County Road 240), and the town is the gateway to a trio of extraordinary state parks: Sunset Bay, Shore Acres, and Cape Arago.

To reach Charleston from points south, take the interesting **Seven Devils Road** from about three miles north of Bandon. This route runs 13 miles alongside beaches, state parks, and an estuarine preserve.

SIGHTS
Coos Art Museum
Located in downtown Coos Bay, the Coos Art Museum (235 Anderson Ave., Coos Bay, 541/267-3901), the Oregon coast's only art museum, features primarily 20th-century and

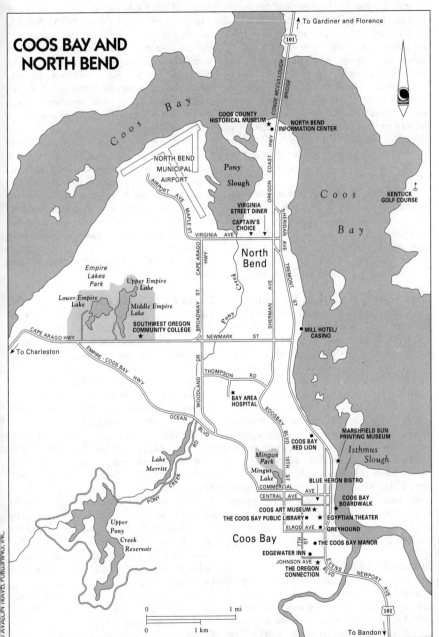

COOS BAY AND NORTH BEND

To Gardiner and Florence

101

Coos Bay

COOS COUNTY
HISTORICAL MUSEUM

NORTH BEND
INFORMATION CENTER

NORTH BEND
MUNICIPAL
AIRPORT

Pony
Slough

Coos

Bay

KENTUCK
GOLF COURSE

VIRGINIA
STREET DINER

CAPTAIN'S
CHOICE

VIRGINIA   AVE

North
Bend

Empire
Lakes
Park

Upper Empire
Lake

Lower Empire
Lake

Middle Empire
Lake

SOUTHWEST OREGON
COMMUNITY COLLEGE

NEWMARK   ST

MILL HOTEL/
CASINO

CAPE ARAGO HWY

To Charleston

EMPIRE - COOS BAY HWY

THOMPSON   RD

BAY AREA
HOSPITAL

OCEAN

COOS BAY
RED LION

MARSHFIELD SUN
PRINTING MUSEUM

Isthmus
Slough

Lake
Merritt

Mingus
Park

Mingus
Lake

BLUE HERON BISTRO

COMMERCIAL

CENTRAL   AVE

COOS BAY
BOARDWALK

COOS ART MUSEUM

THE COOS BAY PUBLIC LIBRARY

EGYPTIAN THEATER

Upper
Pony
Creek
Reservoir

ELROD   AVE

GREYHOUND

Coos Bay

THE COOS BAY MANOR

EDGEWATER INN

JOHNSON AVE

THE OREGON
CONNECTION

NEWPORT   AVE

101

To Bandon

0   1 mi

0   1 km

© AVALON TRAVEL PUBLISHING, INC.

contemporary works by American artists, including pieces by Robert Rauschenberg and Larry Rivers. Etchings, woodcuts, serigraphs, and other prints make up a large part of the permanent collection, which includes several of Janet Turner's richly detailed depictions of birds in natural settings. Other highlights include Kirk Lybecker's photo-realistic watercolors. Don't miss the Prefontaine Room on the second floor of the museum. Photos, trophies, medals, and other memorabilia of this native-son world-class runner illustrate his credo: "I want to make something beautiful when I run."

In addition to the permanent collection, recurring events worth detouring for are the May–June juried show of artists from the western states, and the Maritime Art Exhibit, August–mid-September.

The museum is open Tues.–Fri. 11 A.M.–5 P.M., Saturday 1 P.M.–4 P.M. Free admission.

Coos County Historical Museum

The Coos County Historical Museum (1220 Sherman Ave., North Bend 97459, 541/756-6320, www.cooshistory.org) is located near the south end of the Conde McCullough Bridge, one of several distinctive Depression-era high-wire acts by Oregon's master bridge-builder. The museum houses more than the usual bric-a-brac from earlier eras, thanks largely to the region's heritage as a shipping center. A turn-of-the-century Regina music box, a piano shipped around the Horn, miniature boat models, and a jade Chinese plaque, as well as Coos tribe beadwork and other artifacts make this collection especially memorable. Outside, old-time logging equipment and a 1920s steam train are also worth a look. The museum is open Tues.–Sat. 10 A.M.–4 P.M. and charges $1–2 admission.

Sunset Bay State Park

The Cape Arago Highway west of Charleston leads to some of the most dramatic beaches and interesting state parks on the coast. Among the several beaches on the road to Cape Arago, the strand at Sunset Bay State Park (13030 Cape Arago Hwy., Coos Bay 97420, information 541/888-4902, reservations 800/452-5687) is the big attraction. This is because its sheltered shallow cove, encircled by sandstone bluffs, is warm and calm enough for swimming, a rarity in the Pacific north of Santa Barbara, California. In addition to swimmers, divers, surfers, kayakers, and boaters, many people come here to watch the sunset. Local legend tells that pirates hid out in this well-protected cove.

A four-mile cliffside segment of the Oregon Coast Trail from Sunset Beach south is the best way to appreciate the sea stacks and islands between here and Cape Arago. Good views of Cape Arago Lighthouse across the water can be had along this route. Listen for its unique foghorn. For a shorter hike, follow the signs from the mouth of Big Creek to the viewpoint overlooking Sunset Bay.

For details on camping, see "Camping," later in this section.

Shore Acres State Park

Less than a mile south of Sunset Bay at Shore Acres State Park (541/888-3732), the grandeur of nature is complemented by the hand of man. The park is set on the grounds of lumber magnate and entrepreneur Louis J. Simpson's turn-of-the-century mansion, which began as a summer home in 1906 and grew into a three-story mansion complete with an indoor heated swimming pool and large ballroom.

Originally a Christmas present to his wife, Shore Acres became the showplace of the Oregon coast, with formal and Japanese gardens eventually added to the 743-acre estate. After a 1921 fire, a second, larger (two stories high and 224 feet long) incarnation of Simpson's "shack by the beach" was built. Over the following years the building fell into disrepair, and it and the grounds were ceded to the state in 1942. Because of the high cost of upkeep, the mansion had to be razed, but the gardens have been lovingly maintained.

The gardens here are themselves compelling attractions, but the headland's rim is more dramatic. Perched near the edge of the bluff, on the site formerly occupied the mansion, there

formal gardens at Shore Acres State Park

are decorated with 250,000 colored lights and other holiday touches, daily 4–10 P.M. The gardener's cottage opens and serves free refreshments during this time.

If you bear right and follow the pond's contours toward the ocean, you'll come to a trail. Follow it north for cliffside views of the rock-studded shallows below. Southward, the trail goes downhill to a scene of exceptional beauty. From the vantage point of a small beach, you can watch waves crash into rocks with such force that the white spray appears to hang suspended in the air. Exploring tidepools and caves, as well as springtime swimming in a cove formed by winter storms on the south side of the beach, are pursuits for the active traveler here. In summer, thimbleberries and salal growing along the trail down to the beach can provide sustenance for these activities.

Shore Acres is open year-round 8 A.M.–sunset, with a $3 day-use fee charged per vehicle; the Coast Passport is also valid (see "User Fees and Passes" in the On the Road chapter). The gift shop, near the entrance to garden, is usually open 11 A.M.–4:30 P.M.

Cape Arago State Park

Located 1.25 miles south of Shore Acres, Cape Arago State Park (800/551-6949) lies at the end of the Cape Arago Highway. Locals have made much of the fact that this was a possible landing site of the English explorer Sir Francis Drake in 1579, and have put a plaque here commemorating him.

Beachcombers can make their own discoveries in the numerous tidepools, some of the best on the coast. The south cove trail runs down to a sandy beach and the better tidepools, while the north cove trail leads to more tidepools, good spots for fishing, and views of the colonies of seals and sea lions at Shell Island, including the most northerly breeding colony of enormous elephant seals. Their huge pups, when just a month old, may already weigh 300–400 pounds. Note that the north trail closes March–June to protect seal pups. The picnic tables on the headlands command beautiful ocean panoramas, and are superbly placed

now stands a glass-enclosed observation shelter that makes a perfect vantage point from which to watch for whales, or marvel at the crashing waves. When there's a storm, particularly, the waves really slam into the sandstone reefs and cliffs, hurling up tremendous fountains of spray. It's not uncommon to feel the spray atop the 75-foot promontory. The history of the Simpson family is really the history of the Bay Area, and their story is captioned beneath period photos in the observation gazebo and in the garden in a small enclosure at the west end of the floral displays.

In the seven neatly tended acres of gardens, set back from the sea, the international botanical bounty culled by Simpson clipper ships and schooners is still in its glory, complemented by award-winning roses, rhododendrons, tulips, and azaleas. A restored gardener's cottage with antique furnishings stands at the back of the formal gardens. It's open for special occasions and during the winter holidays. Also in the gardens, note the copper egret sculptures at the pond and the greenhouse for rare plants from warmer climes.

Thanksgiving–New Year's, during the annual **Holiday Lights and Open House,** the gardens

COASTAL OREGON

for whale-watching. The park is free, and open for day use only year-round.

South Slough Estuarine Research Reserve

To many people, an estuary is just a place where you get stuck in the mud. More often than not, however, the interface of fresh- and saltwater represents one of the richest ecosystems on earth, capable of producing five times more plant material than a cornfield of comparable size, while supporting great numbers of fish, birds, and other wildlife. The South Slough of Coos Bay is the largest such web of life on the Oregon coast. The South Slough Estuarine Reserve Interpretive Center (541/888-5558, www.south-sloughestuary.org), on Seven Devils Road, four miles south of Charleston, will help you coordinate a canoe trip through the estuary and offers guided hikes as well.

The center looks out over several estuarine arms of Coos Bay, the largest harbor between San Francisco Bay and the Columbia River. These vital wetlands nurture a vast web of life, which is detailed by the placards captioning the center's exhibits. The coastal ecosystem is presented by the "10-minute trail" in back of the interpretive center. The various conifers and the understory are clearly labeled along the gently sloping half-mile loop. Branch trails lead down toward the water for an up-close view of the estuary itself. Down by the slough, you may see elk grazing in marshy meadows and bald eagles circling above, while *Homo sapiens* harvest oysters and shrimp in these waters of life.

Beginning near the visitors center is the easy, three-mile **estuary study trail,** which follows Hidden Creek from the wooded uplands down the valley to a boardwalk that winds through fresh- and saltwater marshes and leads to several wildlife-observations points.

The center is open daily in summer 8:30 A.M.–4:30 P.M. In the off-season, Sept.–May, it's open weekdays only, same hours. Admission is free.

Myrtlewood

To see an Oregon coast folk art in the making, visit the **Oregon Connection** (1125 South 1st. St., Coos Bay, 541/267-7804), just off U.S. 101 at the south end of Coos Bay. The myrtlewood factory tour shows you how a myrtlewood log gets fashioned into bowls, clocks, tables, and other utensils. No admission is charged for this 25-minute guided run through a working factory. After you're done, the store itself is a delight, with Oregon gourmet foods and crafts supplementing the quality woodwork.

In 1869, the golden spike marking the completion of the nation's first transcontinental railroad was driven into a highly polished myrtlewood tie. Novelist Jack London was so taken by the beauty of the wood's swirling grain that he ordered an entire suite of furniture. Hudson's Bay trappers used myrtlewood leaves to brew tea as a remedy for chills.

During the Depression years, the city of North Bend issued myrtlewood coins after the only bank in town failed. The coins ranged from 50 cents to $10 and are still redeemable—though they are worth far more as collector's items.

Five miles north of North Bend, the **Real Oregon Gift** (3955 U.S. U.S. 101, 541/756-2220) is another large myrtlewood factory and showroom.

Golden and Silver Falls State Park

Two spectacular waterfalls are showcased in this little-known gem of a park located 25 miles northeast of Coos Bay in the Coast Range. Getting to Golden and Silver Falls State Park (800/551-6949) involves driving east of Coos Bay along the Coos River, crossing to its north bank, and continuing along the Millicoma River through the community of Allegany. To find your way from Coos Bay, look for the Allegany/Eastside Exit off U.S. 101. Beyond Allegany, continue up the East Fork of the Millicoma River to its junction with Glenn Creek, which ultimately leads to the park. The narrow, winding gravel roads make this half-hour trip unsuitable for a wide-body vehicle.

You can reach each waterfall by way of two half-mile trails. The 100-foot cataracts lie about a mile apart from one another, and although both are about the same height, each has a distinct character. For most of the year, Silver Falls is more visually arresting because it flows in a near semicircle around a knob near its top. During or just after the winter rains, however, the thunderous sound of Golden Falls makes it the more awe-inspiring of the two. Along the trails, look for the beautifully delicate maidenhair fern.

RECREATION

Fishing

In the fall of 1995, 150,000 spring chinook smolts were released in Coos Bay. In 1997 they returned as mature fish averaging 12–18 pounds, reviving the days of "combat fishing" when hundreds of anglers jostled each other along the bank as they vied for the best fishing spot. These "springers" sometimes exceed 30 pounds and are renowned as an unrivaled dining treat. Also during the last decade, fall chinook and hatchery-reared coho salmon runs have seen healthy increases. Mid-August–November, Isthmus Slough sees a good return of fin-clipped cohos. In saltwater, chinook and coho are found in good numbers within a one- to two-mile radius of the mouth of Coos Bay May through September, though the legal season varies; carefully check the regulations. Remnant striped bass are still occasionally caught in Coos Bay's sloughs and upper tidewater, but their numbers are diminishing.

Coos Bay is also one of the premier areas for crabbing and clamming. The Charleston Fishing Pier is a productive spot for crabs, while the best clamming spots are found along the bay side of the North Spit.

Fishing charters, bay cruises, whale-watching, and the like can be arranged through a number of charter outfits based at the Charleston Boat Basin. **Betty Kay Charters** (541/888-9021 or 800/752-6303, www.bettykaycharters.com) charges typical per-person prices: five hours of rock fishing ($60), five hours of salmon fishing ($80), 12 hours of tuna fishing ($150), 12 hours of halibut fishing ($160); bay cruise, whale-watching, or eco-tours $30. Other operators include **Bob's Sportfishing** (541/888-4241 or 800/628-9633,

www.bobssportfishing.com) and **Fishin's The Mission** (541/297-3474, www.fishinsthemission.com).

Camping

Bastendorff Beach County Park (63379 Bastendorff Beach Rd., Charleston 97420, 541/888-5353) is a conveniently and beautifully located park two miles west of Charleston just off the Cape Arago Highway. It's open for camping year-round, with RV and tent sites for $15–18 (less off-season), as well as cabins ($30) and some hiker/biker sites. Campsites have drinking water, woodstoves, flush toilets, and hot showers (for an extra two bits). Fishing, hiking, and a nice stretch of beach are the recreational attractions, plus there's a good playground for toddlers.

Even though the crowds at **Sunset Bay State Park** (13030 Cape Arago Hwy., Coos Bay 97420, 541/888-4902, reservations 800/452-5687) can make it seem like a trailer park in midsummer, the proximity of Oregon's only major swimming beach on the ocean keeps occupants of the 66 tent sites ($12–16) and 65 trailer sites ($16–20) here happy. The eight yurts go for $27, and primitive hiker/biker sites are $4. Facilities include a laundry and showers, and a boat launch at the north end of the beach. This site, located three miles southwest of Charleston, is popular with fishermen, who can cast into the rocky intertidal area for cabezon and sea bass.

Northwest of the Bay Area—2.5 miles north of the McCullough Bridge—is the Trans-Pacific Parkway, a causeway west across the water leading to Coos Bay's North Spit and the south end of the Oregon Dunes National Recreation Area (NRA), with four Siuslaw National Forest campgrounds and expansive dunes that draw off-road vehicle enthusiasts.

The main **Horsfall Campground** is popular with crowds of noisy all-terrain vehicles and RVs. For more quiet and privacy, continue another mile on Horsfall Beach Road to **Bluebill Lake.** The 18 tent/RV sites are equipped with picnic tables and bathrooms, and the campground is open all year. Ask the campground hosts about area trails and the nearby oyster farm for the ultimate in campfire fare. Close by, **Horsfall Beach Campground** is located in the dunes next to the beach. OHV access and beachcombing are popular activities. Showers are available two miles east at Horsfall Campground. Half a mile away, **Wild Mare Horse Camp** has beach and dune access and a dozen primitive campsites, each with a single or double horse corral. Each of these Siuslaw National Forest campgrounds charges $15 nightly, year-round. Only Horsfall Campground takes reservations (877/444-6777, www.reserveusa.com), May–September.

Golf

There are two public golf courses in the Bay Area. The **Sunset Bay Golf Course** (11001 Cape Arago Hwy., Charleston 97420, 541/888-9301), a nine-holer close to Sunset Bay State Park, has been described as "one of the most interesting courses anywhere" by *Golf Oregon* magazine. Weekend green fees are $19 for 18 holes, $11 for nine. The other is the 18-hole **Kentuck Golf Course,** (675 Golf Course Ln., North Bend 97459, 541/756-4464), across the bay from North Bend along the Kentuck Inlet. Green fees are $16 for 18 holes weekdays, $18 on weekends.

Mill Casino

Occupying the former bayside site of the Weyerhaeuser mill alongside U.S. 101 in North Bend, the Mill Casino (3201 Tremont Ave., North Bend, 541/756-8800 or 800/953-4800, www.themillcasino.com) is operated by the Coquille tribe. Open 24 hours a day, the casino offers blackjack, lots o' slots, poker, and bingo. A large hotel, lounge, and several restaurants (see "Accommodations in North Bend" and "Food in North Bend," later in this section) are on site. Nightly entertainment includes jazz and R&B, while headliners lean toward country performers such as Wynonna and Kenny Rogers.

ENTERTAINMENT AND EVENTS

The **Egyptian Theater** (229 S. Broadway, Coos Bay, 541/267-3456), is a movie house with a pharaonic motif that goes back to the 1920s, when many small towns took to emulating the opulence and foreign intrigue of such big-city movie houses as Graumann's Chinese Theater in Hollywood. Four first-run movies are usually showing here. Across the street, the players of the **On Broadway Theater** (226 S. Broadway, 541/269-2501) stage a changing program of live theater throughout the year, ranging from current Broadway hits to relatively unknown scripts to children's entertainments.

The **Dune Mushers Mail Run** (541/269-0215, www.harborside.com/~mjflcgs/odm/) is an annual noncompetitive endurance dogsled run held the first weekend of March. This is the world's longest organized dry-land run for dogsled teams. Small teams of three to five dogs, and larger teams of five to 10 dogs, haul mushers on wheeled buggies over 70 miles of dunes from North Bend to Florence. The smaller teams start off from Horsfall Beach on Friday, while the larger teams leave the next morning. En route, spectators have opportunities to watch the teams as they pass through Spinreel Park, Winchester Bay, Gardiner, and Florence's South Jetty area, to finish up with a parade through Old Town Florence on Sunday. The "mail" carried by the dog teams are commemorative envelopes, which are sold as souvenirs to support the event.

The first event of note in summer is the **Oregon Coast Music Festival** (P.O. Box 663, Coos Bay 97420, 541/267-0938 or 877/897-9350, www.coosnet.com/music), which runs for two weeks in mid-July and has been going for over 25 years. Coos Bay is the central venue for these south coast classical, jazz, pop, and world music concerts but Bandon, North Bend, Charleston, and other neighboring burgs host some performances as well. Tickets range $5–18.

In late August, the ubiquitous blackberry is celebrated with the **Blackberry Arts Festival** (541/888-1095 or 888-6572). Food and wine-tasting booths, a juried arts and crafts show, and entertainers fill the Coos Bay Mall, Central Avenue, in downtown Coos Bay.

PRACTICALITIES
Accommodations in Charleston
Capt. John's Motel (63360 Kingfisher Dr.,

541/888-4041) is clean and quiet and has some units with kitchenettes. It's within walking distance of fishing, charter boats, clamming, and dock crabbing. Close by is a special fish/shellfish-cleaning station and, with any luck, your dinner. Staying in Charleston also puts you close to state parks and within easy reach of laundry and postal services, as well as offering temperatures that are warmer than Coos Bay in winter and cooler in summer. The rates run $44–77, the studios being on the higher end; reserve well in advance for July and August. Pets okay.

If you'd rather catch your own dinner, the **Plainview Motel** (91904 Cape Arago Hwy., 541/888-5166 or 800/962-2815) provides guests with crab rings and fishing gear. This motel has 12 pet-friendly units, some with kitchens.

Accommodations in Coos Bay

A spendier alternative is the **Coos Bay Red Lion** (1313 N. Bayshore Dr., 541/267-4141 or 800/REDLION). Large rooms with immense beds, thick pile carpet, and everything else in the way of little extras are characteristic of these units. This hotel is also distinguished by its restaurant, one of the best in town, as well as by a lounge with quality entertainment and a happy hour with complimentary hors d'oeuvres. Rates range $65–125. Only 10 minutes from the airport via complimentary shuttle, the hotel is also close to the recreational pursuits described in this chapter.

The **Coos Bay Manor** (955 5th St., 800/269-1224) is the kind of place where a fluffy terry robe and bubble bath sustain the first impressions made by the grand, high-ceilinged colonial-style home and eye-popping river views from the B&B's open-air second-floor breakfast balcony. The five spacious rooms here have their own distinct decor and three have private baths. The rates vary from $80 for a shared bath to $100 for a private bath, less in the winter. Full breakfast.

The bayfront **Edgewater Inn** (275 E. Johnson, 541/267-0423 or 800/233-0423) has loads of perks. With 82 units, many with views and kitchens, guests can take advantage of the fitness and tanning rooms, indoor pool, spa and sauna, and meeting room. A shuttle is also provided. Rates are $75–90.

Accommodations in North Bend

The **Mill Hotel** (3201 Tremont Ave., 541/756-8800 or 800/953-4800, www.themillcasino.com) is located just south of the Mill Casino along the waterfront in a building that once housed a plywood mill. But rather than a milltown ambience this economic development project of the Coquille tribe expresses its owners' patrimony. The exterior of this three-story hotel is the same cedar that tribe members used to build their plank houses, and the fireplace in the lobby is made of Coquille River rocks. The canoe displayed behind the front desk was carved by tribal members and is part of an interpretive display that tells the story of the Coquilles. The well-appointed rooms feature Internet access and views of oceangoing ships. Summer room rates are $109–129 with some suites up to $207. Look for discount deals on these tariffs throughout the year.

Also popular with the casino crowd is the **Ramada Inn** (1503 Virginia Ave., 541/756-3191 or 800/272-6232), just five blocks from U.S. 101. With 96 units and the standard chain hotel amenities, this hotel provides a quiet escape. Rates from $69–100.

Food in Charleston

The **Sea Basket** (63502 Kingfisher Rd., 541/888-5711) typifies the good seafood, fast service, and relatively low prices in these parts. Oysters are especially tasty in this restaurant, with noted breeding farms close by. They are also famous for their Bigman burgers. The fluorescent glare above the cafeteria-style tables frequented by fishermen in work-blackened denims may not count much for atmosphere, but you'll leave satisfied. Open daily for breakfast, lunch, and dinner.

Close by, the **Portside** (63383 Kingfisher Rd., Charleston Boat Basin, 541/888-5544) has won several Silver Spoon Awards from the Diners Club in recent years. Fine dining in Charleston might seem a contradiction in terms, but the chance to select your own lobsters and crabs out of a tank, along with the sight of the fleet unloading other dinners just outside the door, would whet the appetite of any gourmet. Reserve ahead for the Friday night all-you-can-eat seafood buffet at a reasonable price. You may want to pass on the karaoke, depending upon your singing prowess.

Also near the boat basin, on the opposite side of Charleston near the bridge is **Cheryn's.** Specials ($7–20) are broiled fresh chinook in season and fresh Dungeness crab and cheese sandwiches, homemade pies, clam chowder, clam fritters, oyster burgers, and fish-n-chips. Enjoy warm-weather, wind-free dining on the enclosed patio.

Just before the Charleston Bridge, the **Fisherman's Grotto** (541/888-3251) serves all-you-can-eat fish-n-chips seven days a week. If you're an oyster lover, you'll certainly want to visit **Quallman's** (4898 Crown Point Rd., 541/888-3145). Just look for the signs on the north side of the Charleston Bridge on the east side of the highway. Open 10 A.M.–5:30 P.M., it sells fresh high-quality oysters. Several other oyster purveyors make this delicacy available at other Bay Area outlets.

Food in Coos Bay
Even though the **Blue Heron Bistro** (110 W. Commercial, 541/267-3933) is located in the heart of downtown Coos Bay, it evokes dining experiences in San Francisco or Portland. The tile floors, newspapers on library-style posts, and international posters adorning the walls are in keeping with a European-influenced bill of fare. The extensive menu's eclectic array ranges from Greek salad to Cajun-style blackened fish and emphasizes the freshest ingredients (nitrite-free German sausage) and a creative interpretation whenever possible. An impressive list of microbrews and imports as well as Oregon, California, and European wines will complement whatever dish you order. Best of all, for not much more than you'd pay at Denny's, you can enjoy an oasis of refinement in "Timbertown, U.S.A."

Brickstones, the dining room at the Coos Bay Red Lion (1313 N. Bayshore Dr., 541/267-4141, ext. 305), offers extra-thick cuts of prime rib and flambé items prepared tableside that are as much a treat to look at as to taste. This restaurant is an "in" place to eat out, so make reservations. We recommend the smoked prime rib.

For a "Logging Camp Breakfast" locals recommend the **Timber Inn Restaurant** (1001 N. Bayshore Dr., 541/267-4622), where it's served all day long.

Natural food fans converge at **Coos Head Natural Foods** (1960 Sherman, 541/756-7264), serving the largest selection of certified organic produce and food on the south coast.

For a few prime rib–free lunch and dinner options, head over to **Elizabeth's** (274 S. Broadway, 541/266-7708), near the Egyptian Theatre, which features classic American and French cuisine on most nights, with Thai and Indian dishes on select nights. Open for dinner only, closed Sunday.

Food in North Bend
A prime rib special is usually on the menu at the **Mill Casino** (800/953-4800) on the east side of U.S. 101 in North Bend. The restaurant's windows on the bay make the bargain meal of prime rib, salad, vegetables, dessert, and beverage taste even better. Even if you miss the prime rib special, you'll probably appreciate knowing that the restaurant is open 24 hours. The Friday seafood buffet and other buffets throughout the week offer good food in unlimited quantities for less than $10.

A 1950s-style diner serving malts, meatloaf, and burgers, plus an all-day breakfast, the **Virginia Street Diner** (1430 Virginia, 541/756-3475) also provides RVers with easy parking.

For sit-down or takeout seafood, the **Captain's Choice** (1210 Virginia, 541/756-0125) serves enormous pots of clam chowder and oyster stew, but has plenty of "steak and (insert favorite seafood here)" selections for about $10.

If you've had enough of the standard coastal fare, try **Yesterday's Cafe** (1860 Union St., 541/751-0837) for Mediterranean food, including a locally loved lentil soup, in a family-style setting.

Information and Transportation

The **Bay Area Chamber of Commerce** (50 E. Central, Coos Bay 97420, 541/269-0215 or 800/824-8486, www.oregonsbayareachamber .com) is five blocks west of U.S. 101 off Commercial Avenue. It's open Mon.–Fri. 9 A.M.– 7 P.M., weekends 10 A.M.–4 P.M. Sept.–May hours are Mon.–Sat. 9 A.M.–5 P.M. (closed Sunday). Inquire here about tours of the *New Carissa* shipwreck site north of town near Horsfall Dunes.

The **North Bend Information Center** (138 Sherman Ave., North Bend 97459, 541/756-4613) is just south of the McCullough Bridge. It's open Mon.–Fri. 8:30 A.M.–5 P.M., Saturday 10 A.M.–3 P.M., and Sunday 10 A.M.–4 P.M. The center is closed weekends Labor Day–Memorial Day.

The *Coos Bay World* is the largest daily paper on the south coast. In May and August, catch their "Let's Go" section on area getaways.

Recent improvements to ORE 42 make it possible to get to and from Roseburg, 87 miles from Coos Bay, in under two hours. Motorists should still be aware that this thoroughfare carries more truck traffic than any other interior to-coast road in Oregon, but weekenders will usually encounter few trucks and light traffic.

The **Greyhound** bus depot (275 N. Broadway, 541/267-4436) has arrivals from Portland and Lincoln City. Two buses also run between Coos Bay and Eugene. If Greyhound doesn't fit into your plans, consider the North Bend Airport at the north end of town. Horizon Air (800/547-9308) flies between the Bay Area and Portland daily. To get to the airport, follow the signs on the road between Charleston and North Bend.

Public transportation in the Bay Area is limited. **Dial-A-Ride** (541/267-7111) operates on-call daily 8:30 A.M.–4:30 P.M. At press time, the Coos County Area Transit has plans to re-instate regular bus service in North Bend, Coos Bay, and Charleston; call for information. Curry Public Transit's **Coastal Express** buses (541/469-6822) run three times daily, weekdays only, from North Bend and Coos Bay to Brookings, with stops at Bandon, Port Orford, and Gold Beach. The North Bend stop is at the West Pony Village Mall, on Virginia Street, while the bus stops in Coos Bay at the Fred Meyer store on U.S. 101.

Reedsport and Winchester Bay

If you're going fishing or are coming back from a dunes hike, you'll appreciate a hot meal and a clean, low-priced motel room in Reedsport. Otherwise, this town of 5,000 people might seem like a strange mirage of cut-rate motels, taverns, and burger joints in the midst of the Oregon Dunes NRA.

Jedediah Smith explored this country in 1828, after the Hudson's Bay Company's Peter Skene Ogden theorized that the Umpqua River—the largest river between San Francisco Bay and the Columbia—might be the fabled Northwest Passage. It wasn't, of course, but this river is still one of the great fishing streams of the state. Zane Grey avoided writing about it, lavishing the publicity instead upon the Rogue to divert people from his favorite steelhead spots here.

Cargo ships from Scottsburg, a hamlet some 17 miles upriver from Reedsport, supplied San Francisco markets with meat, milk, and produce between 1856 and the early 20th century. In its 1850s heyday, Scottsburg was larger than Portland, with some 5,000 residents, before an 1861 flood destroyed much of the town.

Two miles north of Reedsport, the little burg of Gardiner was created in the wake of a shipwreck. The *Bostonian* (owned by a Mr. Gardiner) was dashed against the rocks at the mouth of the Umpqua in 1856 and from its remnants the first wood-frame structure in this area was built. It was soon joined by other white-painted homes and facilities for a port on the Umpqua. While this "white city by the sea" declined in importance when the highway

COASTAL OREGON

elevated Reedsport to regional hub status, the homes still bear the same color scheme from the earlier era.

Three miles southwest of Reedsport, Salmon Harbor Marina in Winchester Bay (pop. 1,000), a busy port for commercial sport fishing at the mouth of the Umpqua, has given the whole area new life in recent years, following hard times precipitated by the decline in timber revenues.

SIGHTS
Umpqua Discovery Center

In Reedsport's Old Town on the south bank of the river, the Umpqua Discovery Center (409 Riverfront Way, 541/271-4816) interprets the regional human and natural history of this area through multimedia programs, dioramas, scale models, and helpful staff. The boardwalk and observation tower give a good view of the broad lower reaches of the Umpqua. Admission is $5 adults, $2.50 children. Open daily June–Sept. 9 A.M.–5 P.M., 10 A.M.–4 P.M. the rest of the year; closed Thanksgiving, Christmas, and New Year's Day. In summer, free Friday evening concerts are staged here, and the center is the site of the September Tsalila festival (see "Events," later in this section).

Dean Creek Elk Viewing Area

Three miles east of Reedsport, and stretching three miles along the south side of ORE 38, the Dean Creek Elk Viewing Area provides parking areas and viewing platforms for observing the herd of some 120 wild Roosevelt elk that roam this 1,100-acre preserve. The elk move out of the forest to graze the preserve's marshy pastures, sometimes coming quite close to the highway. Oregon's largest land mammal can reach 1,100 pounds at maturity, and the majestic rack on a fully grown bull can spread three feet across. Early mornings and just before dusk are the most promising times to look for them; during hot weather and storms the elk tend to stay within the cover of the woods.

Umpqua Lighthouse State Park

Less than a mile south of Winchester Bay is Umpqua Lighthouse State Park (460 Lighthouse Rd., Winchester Bay, 541/271-4118). Tours (admission $2; information and schedules at 541/271-4631) of the red-capped 1894 lighthouse are offered May–Sept. At other times, you can get a close look at it from the roadside. Adjacent, in a former Coast Guard building, the **visitor center and museum** (541/271-4631) has marine and timber exhibits. Open May–Sept., Wed.–Sat. 10 A.M.–5P.M., Sunday 1–5P.M. Directly opposite the lighthouse, overlooking the mouth of the Umpqua and oceanfront dunes, is a whale-watching platform with a plaque explaining where, when, and what in the world to look for.

Lake Marie, just south near the camping area, has a swimming beach and is stocked with rainbow trout. A one-mile forest trail around the lake makes for an easy hike. A trail from the campground leads to the highest dunes in the United States (elevation 545 feet), west of Clear Lake.

For details on camping at the state park, see "Camping," later in this section.

RECREATION
Fishing

Winchester Bay and the tidewater reaches of the lower Umpqua River comprise Oregon's top coastal sturgeon fishery, and one of the best areas for striped bass, particularly near the mouth of the Smith River, which enters the Umpqua just east of Reedsport. The best action for the Umpqua's spring chinook tends to be inland, below Scottsburg. Fall chinook enter the bay from July through September. Other notable fisheries here are the huge runs of shad, which peak May–June, and smallmouth bass offer action upstream from Reedsport. Crabbing and clamming are also popular and productive pastimes in Winchester Bay and the lower reaches of the river. August–mid-September, tagged crabs are released into the water in and around Winchester Bay, one of them worth a cash prize of $5,000 to whoever catches it.

DUNE COUNTRY

Even though the 47-mile stretch of U.S. 101 between Coos Bay and Florence does not overlook the ocean, your eyes will be drawn constantly westward to the largest and most extensive oceanfront dunes in the world.

How did they come to exist in a coastal topography otherwise dominated by rocky bluffs? A combination of factors created this landscape over the past 12,000 years, but the principal agents are the Coos, Siuslaw, and Umpqua Rivers. The sand and sediment transported to the sea by these waterways are deposited by waves on the flat, shallow beaches. Prevailing westerlies move the particulate matter exposed by the tide eastward up to several yards per year. Over the millennia, the dunes have grown huge, with some topping 500 feet.

Constantly on the move, the shifting sands have engulfed ancient forests, a fact occasionally proven by hikers as they stumble upon the top of an exposed snag. The cross section of sandswept woodlands seen from U.S. 101 demonstrates that this inundation is still occurring. Nonetheless, the motorist gets the impression that the trees are winning the battle, as the dunes are only intermittently visible from the road.

The **Oregon Dunes National Recreation Area** is home to more than 400 species of flora and fauna, but the only dangerous animal within this ecosystem is possibly the American teenager. This species migrates here during summer vacation to enact puberty rites or assault the dunes with a variety of all-terrain vehicles. Of the 31,500 acres within the NRA, nearly half are designated open sand and riding trails for off-highway vehicles such as dune buggies.

Getting Oriented

Reedsport and the nearby fishing village of Winchester Bay have carved out identities as refueling and supply depots for excursions into Oregon's Sahara-by-the-Sea. A great place to start your explorations is the **Oregon Dunes NRA Visitor Information Center** (885 U.S. 101, Reedsport 97467, 541/271-3611, www.fs.fed.us/r6/siuslaw/), at the junction of the Coast Highway and ORE 38. In addition to available information on hiking, camping, and recreation, the Siuslaw Forest Service personnel are very helpful.

Note that a $5 day-use fee is charged per vehicle at most facilities and access points within the Dunes NRA. You can purchase an annual pass at the Dunes Visitor Center for $30.

Because the dunes are difficult to see from the highway in many places, the most commonly asked question in the visitors center is "Where are the dunes?" To answer it for everybody, the National Forest Service opened **Oregon Dunes Overlook** just south of Carter Lake, midway between Florence and Reedsport, at the point where the dunes come closest to U.S. 101. In addition to four levels of railing-enclosed platforms connected by wooden walkways, there are trails down to the sand. It's only about a quarter mile to the dunes and, thereafter, a mile through sand and wetlands to the beach.

You can hike a loop beginning where the sand gives way to willows. Bear right en route to the beach. Once there, walk south 1.5 miles. A wooden post marks where the trail resumes. It then traverses a footbridge going through trees onto sand, completing the loop. If you go in February, this loop has great bird-watching potential. A day-use fee is charged for cars.

Other sites for easy introductions to the dune topography are (from south to north): Spinreel Campground, Umpqua Dunes Trail, Honeyman State Park, and Florence's South Jetty.

Recreation in the Dunes

There are three excellent state parks and a dozen Siuslaw National Forest Campgrounds within the NRA. While joyriding in noisy dune buggies and other off-road vehicles doesn't lack for devotees, the best way to appreciate the interface of ecosystems is on foot. Dunes exceeding 500 feet in height, wetland breeding grounds for animals and waterfowl, evergreen forests, and deserted beaches can be encountered in a march to the sea. Numerous designated hiking trails, ranging from easy half-mile loops to six-mile round-trips, give visitors a chance to star in their own version of *Lawrence of Arabia* as they moonwalk through this earthbound

continued on next page

DUNE COUNTRY (cont'd)

Seas of Tranquility. The soundtrack is provided by the 247 species of birds—along with your heartbeat—as you scale these elephantine anthills. Deserted beaches and secret swimming holes are among the many rewards of the journey.

Prior to setting out, pick up the *Hiking Trails Recreation Opportunity Guide* from the visitors center. This and their other publications will correct the superficial impression that the dunes are just a domain for all-terrain vehicles and campgrounds for day-hikers.

To ensure a bon voyage, it's important to understand this terrain. Carry plenty of water and dress in layers because of hot spots in dune valleys

and ocean breezes at higher elevations. Expect cool summers and wet, mild winters. While rainfall here can average more than 70 inches a year (with 75 percent of it falling March–November), a string of dry, 50–60° days in February is not uncommon. Another surprise is summertime morning fog, brought in by hot weather inland. The fog, together with the inevitable confusion caused by dunes that don't look much different from each other, make a compass necessary. The lack of defined trails also compels such measures as marking your return route in the sand with a stick. Binoculars can help with visual orientation, not to mention the bird-watching opportunities galore.

Charter services operating in the area include: **Reel Fishing Trips** (541/271-3850); **Strike Zone Charters (541/271-9706 or 800/230-5350, www.strikezonecharters.com);** **River's End Guide Service** (541/271-3125, www.umpquafishing.com); and **Jerry Jarmain** (541/271-5583 or 800/653-5583, www.umpqua-river-guide.com).

Dune Access

Some of the most spectacular dunes landscape can be found nine miles south of Reedsport at **Umpqua Dunes,** at North Eel Campground near Lakeside. After you emerge from a quarter-mile hike through coastal evergreen forest, you'll be greeted by dunes 300–400 feet high. It's said that dunes near here can approach 500 feet high and a mile long after a windblown buildup. The views here are most photogenic.

Because a regular trail through the dunes is impossible to maintain, you should only expect to find wooden posts spaced at irregular intervals west of the dunes to guide you to the beach. This trail can also be accessed from the Middle Eel Creek Campground. Look for gray posts about 10 feet high with a blue band at the top marking the trail to the beach, a fairly strenuous five-mile round-trip mostly over soft sand. A shorter and easier one-mile loop trail

leads through woodlands to the dunes for a quick introduction to this landscape.

Lakeside Area

Ten miles south of Reedsport, the sleepy resort town of **Lakeside** hosted visits from Bob Hope, Bing Crosby, and the Ink Spots, among other luminaries, back in its 1930s and '40s heyday. Today, it's still a popular destination, primarily for its proximity to the sprawling, many-armed Tenmile and North Tenmile lakes. These large, shallow lakes offer water-skiing and excellent fishing for stocked rainbow trout and warmwater species, including crappie, yellow perch, bluegill, and lunker largemouth bass up to 10 pounds. A quarter-mile channel connects the two lakes, and a county park on Tenmile Lake has a paved boat ramp, fishing docks, sandy swimming beach, and picnic area.

Camping

Choices abound in this recreation-rich area. Just south of Winchester Bay is **Umpqua Lighthouse State Park** (460 Lighthouse Rd., Winchester Bay, information 541/271-4118, reservations 800/452-5687). The campground alongside Lake Marie has firewood, flush toilets, showers, picnic tables, electricity, and piped water. The 20 RV sites go for $16–20, 24 tent sites for $12–16, two basic yurts for $27, six deluxe yurts (with shower, small kitchen, refrigerator, microwave, TV/VCR) for $45–65, and two rustic cabins for $35. The lake offers fishing, boating, and swimming. Trails from here lead to the highest dunes in the United States (elevation 545 feet), west of Clear Lake.

William A. Tugman State Park (information 541/759-3604, reservations 800/452-5687) is eight miles south of Reedsport, in the heart of Dune Country. This larger campground, with 115 sites, offers a similar range of creature comforts, prices, and recreation opportunities. It sits on the west shore of Eel Lake, east of U.S. 101 across from where the dunes reach their widest extent, two miles to the sea.

Windy Cove Campground (541/271-4138) is a county park with 24 full-hookup sites and four other sites with electricity only. Located on the south side of Salmon Harbor Drive, across from the Winchester Bay marina, it has restrooms, picnic tables, grass, and paved site pads. No reservations taken. It is legal to drive your OHV from this campground directly to the dunes, but it is a couple of miles on the pavement.

About nine miles south of Reedsport, set along Eel Creek near Eel Lake and Tenmile Lake, is **Eel Creek Campground,** a Siuslaw National Forest facility with 51 basic tent and RV sites. Open mid-May–September, reservations (877/444-6777, www.reserveusa.com) are advised. Sites are $15 nightly. The Umpqua Dunes Trail offers access to the dunes and beach.

Eight miles north of Reedsport, the **Tahkenitch Campground** (reservations 877/444-6777, www.reserveusa.com) is another forest service facility, set among ancient Douglas firs and conveniently located near Tahkenitch and other lakes, dunes, and ocean beaches. Open mid-May–September, sites are $15 nightly. A network of trails branches out from here through the dunes, along Tahkenitch, and to the beach.

Another cluster of Siuslaw National Forest campgrounds lies a few miles north; see "Florence and Vicinity," later in this chapter, for details.

Winchester Bay's **Discovery Point Resort** (242 Discovery Point Lane, 541/271-3443, www.discoverypointresort.com) offers dunes enthusiasts dune access and ATV rentals, while providing one- to three-bedroom cabins (sleep up to six) and 60 RV spaces. To get there from Reedsport, head two miles south on U.S. 101 to Winchester Bay; turn right at Pelican Market onto Salmon Harbor Drive. Go one mile, and you'll see Discovery Point Resort on the left. Reservations are highly recommended. RV sites are $18; cabins range $68–98.

EVENTS

Every June, over Father's Day weekend, chainsaw sculptors compete for $10,000 in prizes as they transform pieces of raw western red cedar into grizzly bears, giant salmon, and other rustic works of art during the **Chainsaw Sculpture Championships** (800/247-2155). The event happens at the Rainbow Plaza Old Town Reedsport.

An interesting annual event is **Tsalila** (pronounced sa-LEE-la). Based on the Coos word for "river," this festival (800/247-2155) held the second weekend in September features music, interpretive tours of the Umpqua, alder-baked salmon with squash and corn-on-the-cob dinners, and a traditional tribal village centered around the waterfront at the Umpqua Discovery Center. There's no charge except dinner prices of $10 for adults, $5 for kids.

PRACTICALITIES
Accommodations

Of the half dozen motels that sit along U.S. 101 in Reedsport, the **Fir Grove Motel** (2178 Winchester Ave., 541/271-4848) is slightly less expensive but comparable in comfort (i.e., clean with no frills) to its counterparts. The rooms go for $34–100.

Anchor Bay Inn (1821 Winchester Ave., 541/271-2149 or 800/767-1821) also has clean rooms with one, two, or three beds, family suite, and kitchenettes. Rates are $47 and up; ask for discounts. For a cheaper stay, try the **Economy Inn** (1593 Highway Ave., 541/271-3671 or 800/799-9970) for $30 and up.

If you're interested in this area's ultimate getaway-from-it-all alternative, try the **Salbasgeon Inn of the Umpqua** (45209 ORE 38, Reedsport, 541/271-2025) with nicely appointed rooms on the Umpqua and a romantic location near the elk preserve. This moderately priced ($65–95) lodging should fill the bill. They also have an upscale motel unit managed by Best Western (541/271-4831 or 800/528-1234) in downtown Reedsport, on U.S. 101. By the way, the name was inspired by the region's most popular sport-fishing species: *sal*mon, *bas*s, and stur*geon*.

For $48–70, the **Winchester Bay Motel** (4th and Broadway, Winchester Bay, 541/271-4871 or 800/246-1462) puts you next to the water with all the comfort bases covered. Reserve ahead of time in fishing season.

A few miles north of Reedsport in Gardiner is another lodging with more character than those along motel row for not significantly more money. The **Gardiner Guest House** (401 Front St., 541/271-4005) is located in a cute, tranquil, former paper-mill town that sits close by the confluence of the Smith and Umpqua Rivers. The 1883 home was built by local bigwig and State Senator Albert Reed, for whom Reedsport was named. The recently remodeled home still has the Victorian feel, without lacking in modern conveniences. Choose between a room with the facility down the hall ($55) and a view room with private bath ($75 peak). A large home-cooked breakfast is included in the rate.

Food

There is no shortage of basic but decent places to eat in Reedsport. An example is **Don's Main Street Restaurant** (U.S. 101, 541/271-2032), whose burgers and soup are good enough to get you to Florence. Open daily. After a bite of Umpqua ice cream, however, touted by many to be the best in the state, you might stick around till you're hungry again.

The **Schooner Cafe** (423 Riverfront Way, 541/271-3945), on the boardwalk next door to the Umpqua Discovery Center, has a pleasant riverside patio with a casual atmosphere for a burger, salad, or sandwich.

Another place that rates a special mention is **The Landing** (345 Riverfront Way, 541/271-3328) on the Umpqua near the Umpqua Discovery Center. An *Oregon Coast* magazine readers poll rated the restaurant's steak the best on the south coast. Their oysters, fresh from Umpqua aquaculture in Winchester Bay, are also top-notch. The steak-and-seafood special that appears every so often also has a following. Open daily.

Located in Winchester Bay, **Café Français** (U.S. 101, 541/271-9270) stands out among its fried-fish counterparts, with French country cooking. Specialties include rib lamb chops, baked salmon, escargot (but, of course), and a wine cellar that's stocked with premium vintages. Open for dinner Wed.–Sun. Reservations suggested.

The early morning crowd heads to the conveniently located **Salmon Harbor Cafe** (196 Bayfront Loop, Winchester Bay, 541/271-5523) for home-style breakfast and lunch fare. Open seven days. Just next door, the friendly staff at the **Sportsmen's Cannery and Smokehouse** (Bayfront Loop, Winchester Bay, 541/271-3293) hosts a seafood barbecue smorgasbord that features the catch of the day, oysters, prawns, and all the trimmings. You can also purchase smoked or canned fish; they'll even smoke your catch for you.

Information

The **Oregon Dunes NRA Visitor Information Center** (885 U.S. 101, Reedsport 97467, 541/271-3611, www.fs.fed.us/r6/siuslaw/odnra.htm) and **Reedsport Chamber of Commerce** (541/271-3495 or 800/247-2155, www.reedsportcc.org) share a building at the junction of U.S. 101 and ORE 38. Mid-May–mid-Sept. it's open weekdays 8 A.M.–4:30 P.M., weekends 10 A.M.–4 P.M.; weekdays only the rest of the year.

Florence and Vicinity

"Location, location, and location." This tenet of business success also explains the growing appeal of Florence (pop. 7,000) for retirees and vacationers. Many people who could afford to live almost anywhere choose to do so here between the Oregon Dunes NRA and some of the most beautiful headlands on U.S. 101. The fact that Florence is also situated halfway up Oregon's coastal route and little more than an hour's drive from shopping and culture in Eugene has made it a major beachhead of vacation-home development in the region. A mild climate, a modern health-care facility, award-winning Sandpines Golf Course nearby, and lower housing prices than would be encountered elsewhere in a comparable setting also explain the influx. In recent years, the Florence Events Center has added a cultural dimension to the community calendar.

Florence began shortly after the California gold rush of 1849 put a premium on the lumber and produce shipped out via the Siuslaw River estuary here. Several decades later, the town's name was inspired by a remnant from a French shipwreck that floated ashore, bearing the ship's name, *Florence*. The townspeople either recognized an omen when they saw it or just figured they couldn't come up with anything better.

SIGHTS

If first and last impressions are enduring, Florence is truly blessed. As you enter the city from the south, a graceful bridge over the Siuslaw greets you. Shortly after you leave city limits to the north, U.S. 101 climbs to dizzying heights above the ocean.

The Siuslaw River Bridge is perhaps the most impressive of Conde McCullough's WPA-built spans. The Egyptian obelisks and art deco styling characteristic of other McCullough designs are complemented by the views to the west of the coruscating sand dunes. To the east, the riverside panorama of Florence's Old Town beckons further investigation.

Old Town itself is a tasteful restoration, with all manner of shops and restaurants and an inviting boardwalk along the river. The absence of car traffic is conducive to a pleasant walk after lunch there. Easy access to beach and dunes is offered by South Jetty Road just south of the Siuslaw River Bridge.

Siuslaw Pioneer Museum

To fill yourself in on the early history of Florence and the Siuslaw River valley, and get some notion of Native American and pioneer life, spend an hour or so at the Siuslaw Pioneer Museum (85294 U.S. 101, Florence, 541/997-7884). You'll find it on the south side of the Siuslaw River on the west side of the highway in a converted church. Along with exhibits on early logging and farming, read an account of how the U.S. government double-crossed the Siuslaw tribespeople, who sold their land to the feds and never received the promised recompense. Open year-round Tues.–Sun. 10 A.M.–4 P.M. Adults $2.

Jessie M. Honeyman Memorial State Park

Honeyman State Park, three miles south of Florence, also has a spectacular dunescape and then some. Come here in May when the rhododendrons bloom along the short, sinuous road heading to the parking lot. A short walk west of the lot brings you to a 150-foot-high dune overlooking Cleawox Lake. From the top of this dune, look westward across the expanse of sand, marsh, and remnants of forest at the blue Pacific, some two miles away. A $3 day-use fee applies here, or use the Oregon Coast Passport. For details on camping at this huge state park, see "Camping," later in this section.

Darlingtonia Botanical Wayside

Three miles north up the Coast Highway from Florence, in an area noted for dune access and freshwater lakes, is the Darlingtonia Wayside. In a sylvan grove of spruce and alder are a series of wooden platforms that guide you through a bog

© MARK MORRIS

Darlingtonia Botanical Wayside, north of Florence

where carnivorous *Darlingtonia californica* plants thrive. Shaped like a serpent head, the Darlingtonia is variously referred to as the cobra orchid, cobra lily, or pitcher plant. The sweet smell the plant produces invites insects to crawl through an opening into a chamber.

Inside, thin transparent "windows" allow light to shine inside the chamber, confusing the bug as to where the exit is. As the insect crawls around in search of an escape, downward-pointing hairs within the enclosure inhibit its movement to freedom. Eventually, the weary bug falls to the bottom of the stem, where it is digested. The plant needs the nutrients from the trapped insects to compensate for the lack of sustenance supplied by its small root system. If you still have an appetite after witnessing this carnage, you might want to enjoy lunch at one of the shaded picnic tables here.

Sea Lion Caves

Ten miles north of Florence, you can descend into the world's largest sea cave to observe the only mainland rookery of Steller sea lions (*Eumetopias jubatus*) in the Lower 48. Sea Lion Caves (91560 U.S. 101, 541/547-3111) is home to a herd that averages 200 individuals, though the

numbers change from season to season. These animals occupy the cave during the fall and winter, which are thus the prime visitation times. The Steller sea lions you'll see at those times are cows, yearlings, and immature bulls. In spring and summer, they breed and raise their young on the rock ledges just outside the cave. In addition, California sea lions (*Zalophus californianus*), common all along the Pacific coast, are found at Sea Lion Caves from late fall to early spring.

Enter Sea Lion Caves through the gift shop on U.S. 101. A steep downhill walk reveals stunning perspectives of the coastal cliffs as well as several kinds of gulls and cormorants that nest here. The final leg of the descent is facilitated by an elevator that descends an additional 208 feet. After disembarking the lift into the cave, your eyes adjust to the gloomy subterranean light and you'll see the sea lions on the rock shelves amid the surging water inside the enormous cave. Flash photography is forbidden, so bring high-speed film if you wish to take pictures inside. You have a better chance of seeing these animals inside during fall and winter. A stairway here leads up to a view of Heceta Head Lighthouse through an opening in the cave.

Steller sea lions were referred to as *lobos marinos* (sea wolves) in early Spanish mariners' accounts of their 16th-century West Coast voyages, and their doglike yelps might explain why. You'll notice several shades of color in the herd, which has to do with the progressive lightening of their coats with age. Males sometimes weigh over a ton and dominate the scene here with macho posturings to scare off rivals for harems of as many as two dozen cows. Their protection as an endangered species enrages many fishermen, who claim that the sea lions take a significant bite out of fishing revenues by preying on salmon. In any case, the sight of these huge sea mammals close-up in the cavernous enclaves of their natural habitat should not be missed . . . despite an odor that can be likened to sweat-soaked sneakers.

If you can't observe the animals to your satisfaction in the cave, go a quarter mile north of the concession entrance to the "rockwork" turnout, where the herd sometimes populates the rocky ledges several hundred feet below. It's also a good place to snap a shot of the picturesque Heceta Head Lighthouse across the cove to the north from the turnout.

Sea Lion Caves is open every day except Christmas, 9 A.M.–7 P.M. in summer and 9 A.M.–4 P.M. in winter. Admission is $7 for adults, $4.50 for ages 6–15, and free for kids five and under.

Heceta Head State Scenic Viewpoint and Devil's Elbow

About 11 miles north of Florence, Heceta Head State Scenic Viewpoint is located in a lovely cove at the mouth of Cape Creek, at the base of thousand-foot-high Heceta Head. From here you can get a good look at the graceful arc of Conde McCullough's Cape Creek Bridge, spanning the chasm more than 200 feet above you. Across the cove, photogenic Heceta Head Lighthouse (541/547-3416), completed in 1894, beams the strongest light on the Oregon coast, from a shelf 205 feet up the rocky headland. An easy half-mile trail leads up from the park's picnic and parking area to the tower, which is open for tours daily, March–October, 11 A.M.–5 P.M. Admission is free, but donations aid restoration work here. A little below the lighthouse is **Heceta**

Heceta Head Lighthouse is reputedly the most photographed spot on the Oregon coast.

© MARK MORRIS

House, where the lighthouse keepers used to live. Today, it's a B&B (see "Accommodations," later in this section).

Heceta Head is said to be the most photographed lighthouse in the country; that may be difficult to verify, but it's impossible to quibble with the magnificent sight of the gleaming white tower and outbuildings on the headland, particularly when viewed from a set of highway pullouts just south of the bridge. The vistas from the lighthouse and network of trails on the headland are no less dramatic: see murres, tufted puffins, and other seabirds as well as sea lions on the rock islands below, bald eagles soaring overhead, and, in spring, northbound female gray whales and their calves as they pass close to shore. A trail leading to the north side of Heceta Head offers views to Cape Perpetua, 10 miles to the north.

Just south of Heceta Head is a trail down to the beach at adjoining **Devil's Elbow State Park.** Be conscious of tides here if you climb along the rocks adjoining the beach.

RECREATION
River Cruises

Paddlewheelers along the Siuslaw were part of the two-day Eugene-to-Florence pilgrimage a century ago. Today you can get a taste of that experience aboard the 65-foot sternwheeler *Westward Ho!* (541/997-9691), which leaves from Florence's Old Town docks for a variety of cruises on the river. In addition to the succession of historic sites along the Siuslaw between Florence and Mapleton detailed in the 11 A.M. hour-long cruise, several other daily half-hour cruises at 1 P.M., 2 P.M., and 3 P.M. feature lunch and "lots of music and cool spirits," respectively. On Friday and Saturday there are dinner cruises. Weekday hour-long cruise fares are $12 for adults, $6 for kids under 12; the dinner excursion is $33 per person.

Horseback Riding

Riding across the dunes into the sunset on a trusty steed sounds like a fantasy, but you can do it, too, thanks to **C&M Stables** (90241 U.S. 101, Florence 97439, 541/997-7540). Rates range from $30 to $45 per person for trips of from one to two hours (with discounts for larger parties). The stables are open daily. With beach rides, dune trail excursions, and sunset trips, there's something for everybody. Call for specific times and reservations.

Dune Rides

Another option for those who fear to tread is **Sand Dunes Frontier** (83960 U.S. 101, Florence 97439, 541/997-3544). This company rents vehicles for travel in specially designated areas within the Dunes NRA. Odysseys, small one-person dune buggies, go for $35 per hour and a $50 deposit. You must be strapped in, with a helmet, stay within the marked territory, and be especially careful going uphill. If you lose power on an incline, it's possible to roll over when turning around to go back down. The 20-person dune buggy rides cost $10 for adults, $5 for children 4–11 years old, and kids under five ride for free. A four-seater goes for $45 per hour. Protective goggles are provided, along with a driver. Go in the morning when the sand tends to blow around less.

Siltcoos Lake

Oregon's largest coastal lake, six miles south of Florence, 3,100-acre Siltcoos Lake offers excellent fishing and other recreation. Rainbows are stocked in the spring, and steelhead, salmon (closed to coho fishing), and sea-run cutthroat trout move from the ocean into the lake via the short Siltcoos River in late summer and fall. But the real excitement here is the fishing for warmwater species, which is some of the best in the Northwest. Bluegill, crappie, yellow perch, and brown bullhead action is good through the summer, while fishing for largemouth bass can be good year-round. Access points include several public and private boat ramps on the lake, as well as a wheelchair-accessible fishing pier at Westlake Resort.

In addition, the **Siltcoos River** invites kayakers and canoeists to explore the two-mile stretch between the lake and the sea. Meandering two miles through dunes, forest, and estuary, the Siltcoos is a gentle, Class-I paddle with no white

water or rapids, though there is a small dam midway that must be portaged. Wildlife that you may encounter along the way include mink, raccoons, otters, beaver, and even bears. In the estuary, sea lions and harbor seals are common.

For more information on the Siltcoos area, contact the Oregon Dunes National Recreation Area Visitor Center (541/271-3611) in Reedsport. For details on four Siuslaw National Forest campgrounds sited along the river, see "Camping," immediately following.

Camping

Camping here offers recreational opportunities comparable to those at the Oregon Dunes NRA, with more varied scenery.

Carl G. Washburne State Park (93111 U.S. 101 N., Florence, 541/547-3416 for information, 800/452-5687 for reservations) is popular with Oregonians due to its proximity to beaches, tidepools, Sea Lion Caves, and elk. The eight tent sites and 58 RV sites have such modern conveniences as showers, a laundry, electricity, and piped water. They also have two yurts, which can also be reserved. It's 14 miles north of Florence on U.S. 101 (several miles past Sea Lion Caves), then one mile west on a park road. The fee is $16–20, $5 for hiker and biker spaces, and it's open all year.

In addition, there are nearby forest pathways such as the **Hobbit Trail,** named after the furry-footed characters in J. R. R. Tolkien's works. You'll probably feel like a hobbit when peering up at the high walls woven of roots, peat, and sand that loom above the trail cut deep into the forest floor here. The path winds through dense forest thickets of pine, fir, and rhododendrons down to the beach. Look for the turnout on the right side of the road just over the hill north of the Heceta Head curves on U.S. 101. Ask the park personnel about this and China Creek Trail. You might also ask about a relatively new trail that begins close by that part of U.S. 101 where the Hobbit Trail begins. In three-quarters of an uphill mile, you'll be at Heceta Head Lighthouse.

Three miles south of Florence's McCullough Bridge and on both sides of U.S. 101 is **Hon-**

eyman State Park (84505 U.S. 101 S., 541/
997-3641, reservations 800/452-5687). This
exceedingly popular campground gets very
crowded in the summer—reservations are a
must—but it empties out enough during spring
and autumn to make a stay here worthwhile.
There are 240 tent sites with the basics, a large
number of RV spaces with all the amenities,
and many hiker/biker spots as well (more than
400 sites in total). Rates are $13–21 depending
on the season and type of site. Ask about canoe
rentals here to savor the serenity of Cleawox
Lake. Fishing, swimming, hiking, and dune
buggies are available nearby. In spring, pink
rhodies line the highway and park roads. Advance reservations (800/452-5687) are accepted
Memorial Day–Labor Day.

An ideal place to escape from the summertime coastal crowds is the **North Fork of the
Siuslaw** campground. Chances are you'll see
mostly locals here—if anybody. From Florence
follow ORE 126 about 15 miles to Mapleton
and the junction with ORE 36. The latter road
takes you 13 miles to County Route 5070. Then
it's a short drive to the riverside campsite (or
you can drive the North Fork Siuslaw River
Road from Florence for 14.5 miles). The fee is
$4 between July and early September. Picnic
tables, fire pits, and crawdads are other reasons
to come. Contact the Siuslaw National Forest
Ranger Station (4480 U.S. 101 N., Florence,
541/902-8526) for more information.

Close by is the **Pawn Old Growth Trail**, a
half-mile pathway through several-hundred-
year-old 100-inch-in-diameter, 275-feet-tall
Douglas-fir and hemlock. The trailhead, located at the confluence of the North Fork of
the Siuslaw and Taylor's Creek, is a good place to
see salmon spawning in the fall and observe
water ouzels (also called "dippers"). It follows the
creek and offers interpretive placards along the
way. At one point in the trail visitors walk
through fallen Douglas fir logs 260 inches in
diameter. Placards explain the science of tree
rings. Consult the ranger station in Florence
to get exact directions.

By the way, nearby ORE 36 makes an interesting access road back to the Willamette Valley
if you're not in a hurry. Its circuitous route passes
through Deadwood and ends up in the Junction City area.

Golf

Ocean Dunes Golf Links (3315 Munsel Lake
Rd., 541/997-3232) lets you tee off with sand
dunes (some more than 60 feet tall) as a backdrop. The manicured 18-hole course has a driving range, a full pro shop, and equipment rentals
on site. For the ultimate in golfing by the dunes,
however, try **Sandpines Golf Course** (1050 35th
St., 541/997-1940). This was voted *Golf Digest's*
number one new public course in 1993. To get
there, go west off U.S. 101 on 35th Street. In
May and June rhododendrons line this drive,
which heads into dune country as you move toward the sea. Follow the signs until you see a
water tower not far from the pro shop. Sandpines's layout features fairways lined with Douglas
fir and beach grass on gently undulating terrain.
Coastal winds that kick up in the morning can
figure prominently in your shot selection. Green
fees are $48, carts $26.

ENTERTAINMENT AND EVENTS

Art shows, classical concerts by acclaimed virtuosi (including performances as part of the Ernest
Bloch Music Festival—see Newport "Entertainment and Events," later in this chapter), ballet,
theater, and community events can be enjoyed
within the warm, welcoming, and spacious **Florence Events Center** (715 Quince St., 541/997-
1994 or 888/968-4086, www.eventcenter.org). A
gallery on site displays the works of local artists.

The **Dune Mushers Mail Run** is held the
first weekend of March. On Sunday, the teams
pass through Florence's South Jetty area, to finish
up with a parade through Old Town Florence.
See the Bay Area's "Entertainmnt and Events"
section, earlier in this chapter, for details.

During the third weekend of May, Florence
celebrates the **Rhododendron Festival,** coinciding
with the bloom of these flowers that proliferate
in the area. It's a tradition that goes back to 1908,
when the festival was started as a way to draw attention and commerce to the area. A parade, a

carnival, a flower show, a 5- and 10-km "Rhody Run," and the crowning of Queen Rhododendra are highlights of the festivities. Today, the event attracts more than 15,000 visitors each year. Contact the chamber of commerce (541/997-3128) for more information.

Independence Day celebrations include live outdoor music and a barbecue in Old Town, and a fireworks display over the river.

Chowder, Brews, and Blues (541/997-1994) in late September is a three-day event honoring several things the community relishes. A coastwide clam chowder contest here is a highlight, along with live music and microbrew tasting at the Florence Events Center. Admission is $5–7.

PRACTICALITIES

Accommodations

As just about everywhere else, there are budget motels on the main drag here, but to experience the coast fully, try one of the romantic getaways between Florence and Yachats. Romantic B&Bs abound north of town, covered under "Yachats and Vicinity," later in this chapter.

One of the best bargains in town is the **Lighthouse Inn** (155 U.S. 101, 541/997-3221), a Cape Cod–style two-story motel on the highway close to the bridge and convenient to Old Town. With neatly kept rooms in an untouched 1938 lodging, decorated with bric-a-brac and other homey touches, it may remind you of your grandmother's house. No in-room kitchens, but a common refrigerator and microwave are available for guest use. Most rooms have a queen or king bed; some are considered suites, with two rooms and a connecting bath, which sleep up to five. Ask about the plushest of all, the honeymoon/anniversary suite. Rates are $35 and up.

One block north of Old Town, just across the highway from the Lighthouse Inn, the **Money Saver Motel** (170 U.S. 101 N., 541/997-7131) provides guests with basic affordable rooms in the same price range.

For a river experience, try the **River House Motel** (1202 Bay St., 541/997-3933). Rates start at $69; for river views, guests pay a bit more, starting at $89.

On the south bank of the river, the **Best Western Pier Point Inn** (85625 U.S. 101, 541/997-7191) offers spacious well-appointed rooms, bay views, sand-dune hiking across the street and a good restaurant on site (Lovejoy's fish-n-chips and selection of English ales and microbrews are worth a stop). There is also a beach house for rent along the Siuslaw River that sleeps six. Rates at this large luxury motel run $60–140 off-season. In summer, the rates are $129 and up, double occupancy.

Bed-and-Breakfasts

The **Edwin K B&B** (1155 Bay St., 541/997-8360 or 800/8-EDWINK) has six units with private bath two blocks from Old Town near the Siuslaw River. River views, period antiques, and multicourse breakfasts featuring locally famous soufflés and home-baked breads on fine china have established this gracious 1914 home as Florence's preeminent B&B. Add private baths and whirlpool tubs in some units and a private courtyard and waterfall in back and you'll understand the need to reserve well in advance. Rates are $115–125 (less in winter).

To sample a piece of coastal history in the heart of Old Town, stay at the **Johnson House** (216 Maple St., 541/997-8000 or 800/768-9488), a restored 1890s Victorian furnished with period details throughout, also featuring private bathrooms and a gorgeous flower garden. Touted as the oldest established inn on the coast, the Johnson house is close to shops and restaurants, but you'll want to stick around for their breakfast spread. Rates are $75–125.

About three miles east of town, the **Blue Heron Inn** (6563 ORE 126, Florence, 541/997-4091 or 800/997-7780, www.blue-heroninn .com) is a good choice for amateur ornithologists. River frontage highlighted by a spotting scope might reveal cormorants, herons, bald eagles, and every so often, a tundra swan. Whirlpool tubs, antiques, and a charming home rich in nooks and crannies make the rates ($65–140) a good value. A full breakfast enthusiastically praised by guests is included. A newer media room downstairs entertains guests with rented or in-house videos.

Nine miles north of Florence, and just a short walk from Heceta Head Lighthouse, is **Heceta Light Station B&B** (92072 U.S. 101, 541/547-3696, www.hecetalighthouse.com), built in 1893, where the lighthouse keepers used to live. Today, it's a B&B with antique furnishings and vintage photos, which help re-create the lives of the keepers of the flame. Among the three upstairs bedrooms ($130–230 double), the Mariner's room commands the finest view and is the only room here with private facilities (the other two share a bathroom down the hall). The current caretakers maintain a flock of chickens on the grounds as did the actual lighthouse keepers of yesteryear. Your current hosts keep them as a source of fresh eggs to be used in the included seven-course breakfast, a several-hours affair replete with such dishes as d'Anjou pear with chèvre and Oregon honey and vol-au-vent stuffed with chived eggs and asparagus.

Food

A famous Zen master once said, "If you can make a cup of tea right, you can do anything." The same aphorism seems to apply to clam chowder in coastal restaurants, if three Florence eateries are any indication.

In Old Town, the local **Mo's** (1436 Bay St., 541/997-2185) is the largest outlet of this famed Oregon chowderhouse, and its fresh fish, fast service, fair prices, and Siuslaw River frontage make it this neighborhood's most popular restaurant. Lunch with a cup of chowder might run $6 and bouillabaisse is the most expensive item on the menu. Even if you don't eat here, you might want to stock up on Mo's clam chowder base packaged to go.

Another award-winning chowder as well as an *Oregon Coast* magazine poll winner is the creamy clam-filled concoction made by the **Blue Hen** (1675 U.S. 101, 541/997-3907) at the north end of town. Fourteen finely chopped items go into this orange-specked beige soup. However, as the name and the sign out front

imply, chicken is the mainstay of this small café operating out of a home on the highway. But don't overlook the berry pies. You may be asked to share your table with the interesting cross section of travelers drawn to this Oregon coastal hub. You'll enjoy dining on the outdoor deck in summer. It's open 7 A.M.–8 P.M. daily. Prices run $3–10 for breakfast, $5–10 for lunch, and $7–12 for dinner.

For yet another chowder champ, **Ruby Begonia** (1565 9th St., 541/997-1821) has one of the best seafood chowders on the coast, according to *Sunset* magazine. This golden-hued soup has salmon, halibut, prawns, and clams. The tasty homemade pie and the Mexican entrées add another dimension to the Florence dining scene. They're open daily 8 A.M.–9 P.M.

The **Bridgewater Seafood Restaurant and Oyster Bar** (129 Bay St., Old Town, 541/997-9405) features exotic clam chowder with Indonesian clams, in keeping with a Banana Republic decor, and the only "fine dining" in Old Town. Of course, this also means the highest prices on the waterfront. But to be fair, you're getting what you pay for and then some. The Bridgewater was the recipient of a People's Choice Award for the best clam chowder in town for several years. Fresh fish, often with a Cajun flair, is the star of the menu. Winter through early spring, Wednesdays feature an all-you-can-eat seafood dinner buffet.

For a panoramic river view the whole family can enjoy, the **Bay Bridge** (1150 Bay St., 541/997-7168) has moderately priced steak and seafood as well as pasta and chicken dishes. Open daily.

Traveler's Cove (1362 Bay St., 541/997-6845) manages to combine an import shop and gourmet café under the same roof. The café serves good lunches and is worth a stop for the homemade clam chowder and interesting salads and sandwiches. Fresh Dungeness crab makes an appearance here with crab quiche,

> *Treat yourself to a full fountain service experience at BJ's Ice Cream Parlor (2930 U.S. 101 and 1441 Bay St.), where 48 flavors, ice cream cakes, cheesecakes, gourmet frozen yogurt, and pies complement the cones and cups.*

crab enchiladas, and "crabby" Caesar salad. Best of all, the patio out back provides river views to enjoy along with your meal. A full bar with flavored margaritas might also enhance your appreciation of the river frontage. The café is open 9 A.M.–9 P.M.

The **International C-Food Market** (1498 Bay St., 541/997-9646) gets good word of mouth from locals. This combination restaurant and retail market offers seafood right off the boat. Not only is the freshness of the fish exceptional, but prices are low. The catch of the day and the smoked salmon pizza are both excellent. In September 2000, the ICM won a coast-wide clam chowder competition. Open for lunch and dinner daily.

Scandinavians played a major role in settling the coast. Enjoy some of this tradition at **Synnove's** (2825 U.S. 101, 541/902-9142). Be sure to try such Norwegian specialties as light, delicate halibut and salmon cakes and pan-fried sole. Open for lunch and dinner; closed Monday and Tuesday.

North of town, the **Windward Inn** (3757 U.S. 101, 541/997-8243) rates a special mention. Long a mainstay of the coastal dining scene, the fresh-cut flowers, skylights, and wood-paneled interior have set the stage for memorable repasts for more than half a century. Dinner entrées are typified by such creations as fresh mussels broiled on the half shell with Oregon hazelnuts, Oregon peppered

bacon, and Tillamook cheddar cheese. Open daily.

Another venue that aims to satisfy is the **Firehouse Restaurant** (1263 Bay St., 541/997-2800) serving standard American fare. Dinners include choices such as steak, seafood, pasta, tri-tip. They also have a full bar, which includes a good variety of Northwest microbrews.

The health-conscious crowd head over to **Salmon Berries** (812 Quince, 541/997-3345) to stock up on organic produce, bulk grains, spices, supplements, and the like. Open daily.

Information and Transportation

The **Florence Area Chamber of Commerce** (270 U.S. 101, Florence 97439, 541/997-3128, www.florencechamber.com), is three blocks north of the Siuslaw River Bridge; open 9 A.M.–5 P.M.

The **Siuslaw National Forest Ranger Station** (4480 U.S. 101 N., Florence, 541/902-8526) is located near the BiMart on Florence's main drag. Tune into radio station **KCST,** at 106.9 FM or 1250 AM, for coastal news, weather, and a whole lotta Paul Harvey.

The **Greyhound** (541/902-9076) bus stop, at the 37th Street Laundry (1857-1 37th St., 541/997-5111), sees twice-daily service from two different routes. In addition to two buses coming down from Portland via Lincoln City en route to San Francisco on U.S. 101, there are two buses per day from Eugene.

Yachats and Cape Perpetua

Yachats (pronounced "YAH-hots") is derived from an Alsea word meaning "dark waters at the foot of the mountain." The phrase aptly describes the location of this picturesque resort village of 635 people, clustered on the hillsides and coastal shelf beside the Yachats River mouth in the shadow of Cape Perpetua. Word of mouth has helped to spread the popularity of Yachats as a place for a quiet getaway and a base for enjoying the 2,700-acre Cape Perpetua Scenic Area and nearby beaches.

SIGHTS AND RECREATION

Cape Perpetua

The most notable sight near Yachats, indeed on the whole central coast, is the view from 803-foot-high Cape Perpetua. The name derives from Captain Cook's sighting of the promontory on March 7, 1778, St. Perpetua's Day. It's too bad the British explorer didn't make landfall here to enjoy one of the world's preeminent coastal panoramas. Oregon's highest paved public road this close to the shoreline affords 150 miles of north-to-south visibility from the top of the headland. On a clear day, you can also see 39 miles out to sea.

Prior to hiking the 23 miles of foot trails or driving to the top of the cape, stop off at the **Cape Perpetua Visitor Center** (541/547-3289), three miles south of Yachats on the east side of the highway. A picture window framing a bird's-eye view of rockbound coast, along with exhibits on forestry and marine life, begin your introduction to the region. Cataclysms such as the forest fire of 1846, the monsoons and 138 mph winds unleashed by the 1962 Columbus Day Storm, and 1964 Hurricane Frieda are artfully explained by exhibits. An excellent 15-minute film about Oregon's intertidal biome will also hold your interest.

Personnel at the desk have maps and pamphlets about such trails as Cook's Ridge, Riggin' Slinger, and Giant Spruce, as well as directions for the auto tour to the summit. In addition, they can point the way to tidepools and berry patches. Two naturalist-guided hikes a day are offered to coastal rainforest and tidepools. The center is open 9 A.M.–5 P.M. early May–October, and opens during peak whale-watching weeks from Christmas to New Year's and in late March. Admission is $3 per car. The Pacific Coast Passport, Northwest Forest Pass, and Golden Passports are honored here.

The awe-inspiring 1.5 mile **Saint Perpetua Trail** (from the visitors center) to the cape's summit is of moderate difficulty, gaining 600 feet in elevation. En route, placards explain the role of wind, erosion, and fire in forest succession in this mixed-conifer ecosystem.

At the crest of Cape Perpetua the **Trail of the Whispering Spruce** begins, a quarter-mile loop through the grounds of a former World War II Coast Guard lookout built by the Civilian Conservation Corps in 1933. The southern views from the crest take in the highway and headlands as far as Coos Bay. Halfway along the path, you'll come to a WPA-built rock hut called the West Shelter that makes a lofty perch for whale-watching, one of the best spots on the entire coast. Beyond this ridgetop aerie the curtain of trees parts to reveal fantastic views of the shoreline between Yachats and Cape Foulweather.

The two-mile drive up the cape (where the Whispering Spruce Trailhead can be accessed) is complicated by a not-so-prominent sign on U.S. 101 (mile marker 188.5) indicating the turnoff onto Forest Service Road 55. To begin your auto ascent, drive a hundred yards north on U.S. 101 from the visitors center and look for the steep winding spur road on the right. As you climb, you'll notice large Sitka spruce trees abutting the road. Halfway up, you'll come to a Y in the road. Take a hard left and follow the road another mile to the top of Cape Perpetua. If you miss the left turn and go straight ahead, you'll soon find yourself on a 22-mile loop through the Coast Range to Yachats. Along the way, 18 placards annotate forest ecology.

Another hike from the visitors center goes

down to a geological blowhole (called a "spouting horn"), where sea water is funneled between rocks and explodes into spray. This is the **Captain Cook Trail,** which goes six miles through a dense wind-carved forest and the remains of an old CCC camp under U.S. 101 to an ancient lava deposit on the shore. Given enough wave action, water bubbles up through fissures in the basalt. There are also Native American shell middens built up 300–2,000 years ago in the area.

State Parks, Coastal Waysides

In this part of the coast, state parks and viewpoints abound with attractions. There's so much to see here that keeping your eyes on the road in this heavily traveled section is a challenge.

A mile north of town, **Smelt Sands State Recreation Site** gives access to tidepools and the .75-mile 804 Trail, which follows the rocky shore to a broad, sandy beach to the north. In Yachats, turn west onto 2nd Street to loop around wave-battered **Yachats State Recreation Area,** overlooking Yachats Bay. The route heads north along the ocean, where it becomes Marine Drive. After going through a residential community, it eventually takes an easterly turn to reconnect with U.S. 101.

On the south bank of the Yachats River is a short but beautiful beach loop off U.S. 101 (going south, look for the sign that says "Beach Access"). The road runs between the landscaped grounds of beach houses and resorts on one side and the foamy sea on the other. A wide beach, tidepools, and blowholes on the bank by the river's mouth are a special treat.

Just north of the turnoff for the top of Cape Perpetua (Forest Service Road 55) and U.S. 101 is the turnout for **Devil's Churn,** on the west side of the highway. Here, the tides have cut a deep fissure in a basalt embankment on the shore. You can observe the action from a vertigo-inducing overlook high above, or take the easy, switchbacking trail down to the water's edge. While watching the white-water torrents in this foaming cistern, beware of "sneaker waves," particularly if you venture beyond the boundaries of the **Trail of the Restless Waters.** The highlights here are the spouting horns. All along this stretch of the coast, many trees appear to be leaning away from the ocean as if bent by

Devil's Churn, at the base of Cape Perpetua

© MARK MORRIS

storms. This illusion is caused by salt-laden westerlies drying out and killing the buds on the exposed side of the tree, leaving growth only on the leeward branches. A $3 day-use fee is collected here.

A mile south, **Neptune State Park** has a beautiful beach and is near the 9,300-acre **Cummin's Creek Wilderness** east of U.S. 101. Just north of Neptune Park, Forest Service Road 1050 leads east to the Cummins Creek Trailhead. A half-mile south, gravelly Forest Service Road 1051 can take you to a point where a moderately difficult 2.5-mile hike leads to Cummin's Ridge Trailhead. This pathway has some of the last remaining coastal old-growth Sitka spruce stands. Get maps and detailed directions for these and other area trails at the Cape Perpetua Visitor Center.

Close by, there's a chance to explore tidepools and sometimes observe harbor seals at **Strawberry Hill.** Scenic shorelines can also be found in the next few miles farther south at **Stonesfield Beach State Recreation Site** and **Muriel O. Ponsler State Scenic Viewpoint,** before you arrive at Carl G. Washburne State Park (see "Florence and Vicinity," earlier in this chapter).

Camping

Set along Cape Creek in the Cape Perpetua Scenic Area, the Forest Service's **Cape Perpetua Campground** (reservations 877/444-6777 or www.reserveusa.com) has 38 sites for tent and trailers or motor homes up to 22 feet long. Picnic tables and fire grills are provided. Flush toilets, piped water, and sanitary services are available. The $15 fee applies May–October, when they're open. Reservations are necessary for groups. The forest service rangers put on slide-illustrated campfire talks here and at Tillicum Beach (see Waldport "Camping," later in this chapter) during summer months.

Just south, **Neptune State Park** (800/551-6949) has several free beachfront hiker/biker sites.

EVENTS

This little village seems to be busy with some festival or other event just about every weekend.

For a full schedule, see the local chamber of commerce website (www.yachats.org/events.html). Below are some highlights.

Spring brings two art and crafts festivals to the Yachats Commons (U.S. 101 and W. 4th St.): In late March, the chamber-sponsored **Original Yachats Arts and Crafts Fair** (541/547-3530 or 800/929-0477) exhibits the work of some 75 Pacific Northwest artists and artisans. Admission is free. If you miss that one, come back in late May for **Crafts on the Coast** (541/547-4738 or 541/547-4664).

Yachats pulls out all the stops for the **Fourth of July.** Events include the short and silly La De Da Parade at noon, the Yachats Yamboree (food booths, beer gardens, live music), a farmers market, a musical variety show, and a fireworks show on the bay when darkness falls.

During the Yachats **Smelt Fry,** held the second Saturday of July, up to 750 pounds of this sardinelike fish are served on the grounds of Yachats Commons on 4th Street (just follow the signs to this refurbished schoolhouse). Yachats used to be one of the few places in the world blessed with a run of oceangoing smelt but they have declined drastically due to changing ocean conditions. Nonetheless, the town's traditional "welcome to summer" event has continued thanks to imported Northern California smelt, which augment the local catch. For $8 you get all the deep-fried, delicately flavored smelt (or a sausage plate for $5) you can eat ($3 for children 12 and younger) with side dishes and a beverage. What you're really paying for is a classic small-town festival where you get to rub elbows with a spirited community. More info is available from the chamber of commerce.

The same weekend, the **Yachats Music Festival** takes place several blocks north at the Presbyterian Church (360 W. 7th St.; info at 541/547-3141 or 510/601-6184). Admission is $15 for each performance. The line-up features classical virtuosi and vocalists from the San Francisco Bay Area for evening concerts and a Sunday matinee performance.

A relatively new but popular event here is the **Yachats Village Mushroom Fest** (541/547-3530 or 800/929-0477), held the third weekend in October. Native mushrooms abound in the temperate rainforests of the Cape Perpetua region, and fall is the season to harvest them. The Yachats event was started by Chef John Ullman, who was inspired by similar festivals in Italy. Activities over the weekend include the Friday-night Yachats Rainforest Fungi Feast, mushroom-cooking demonstrations, guided mushroom walks at Cape Perpetua Visitors Center, and the last farmers market of the season.

Another exciting recent addition to the Yachats calendar is the annual **Celtic Music Festival,** held in mid-November. It's a full weekend of concerts and workshops provided by local and visiting musicians. For details, contact the Raindogs shop (162 Beach St., 541/547-3000).

PRACTICALITIES

Accommodations

If you're planning a long stay, check out **Yachats Village Rentals** (541/547-3501), which offers a varied stable of vacation homes ($110–215) for rent. Another option is **Horizon Property Management** (205 U.S. 101, P.O. Box 1047, Waldport 97394, 541/563-5151), which has a list of oceanfront homes that sleep up to 12.

At the beginning of the beach loop (on the south bank of the Yachats River and west of U.S. 101) are the **Shamrock Lodgettes** (105 U.S. 101 S., 541/547-3312 or 800/845-5028). Shamrock's beautiful parklike landscape frames a selection of individual log cabins, redwood units, and deluxe rooms. Stone fireplaces, in-room movies, and ocean or bay views all contribute to a relaxed get-away-from-it-all feeling. The sauna and whirlpool tub on the premises also enhance the "mellowing-out" process. Cabins range $115–150 for two, $131–175 for four, while motel units average $75–110—a small price for peace of mind. The on-site health features a redwood hot tub and sauna. Ask about midwinter specials. Kids okay; pets are allowed in some units.

A short drive farther south, the modern **Yachats Inn** (331 U.S. 101, 541/547-3456 or 888/270-3456, www.yachatsinn.com) is a great place for group retreats or families, with spacious units that are more like well-furnished apartments, all just steps from the beach. The landscaped grounds include an indoor pool, sauna, and teahouse (for large groups, meetings or parties). Rates $51–125.

For those looking for a budget place close to the center of town, try **Rock Park Cottages** (431 W. 2nd, 541/547-3214 or 541/343-4382), adjacent to Yachats State Recreation Area. Consisting of five rustic cottages arranged around a courtyard, Rock Park has to be considered one of the better bargains ($60–115) on the coast. The kitchens are well equipped.

The **Dublin House Motel** (U.S. 101 and 7th Street, 866/922-4287, www.dublinhousemotel.com) offers large guest rooms and ocean views, each with microwaves, refrigerators, coffee makers, and cable TV; some kitchen units are also available. The indoor heated pool is especially nice in the winter months. Rates $45–109.

A little north of the town center, the imposing **Adobe Resort** (155 U.S. 101 N., 541/547-3141 or 800/522-3623) overlooks Smelt Sands Beach. If you appreciate all services in one compound, from dining room to gift shop, the Adobe, $100–120, $245 suite, gets the nod. Pets accepted in some rooms.

For about the same price or even less ($50–130), the smallish rooms of the **Fireside Motel** (U.S. 101, 541/547-3636 or 800/336-3573) offer more than enough amenities. In addition to ocean views, many of the rooms boast such extras as refrigerators and fireplaces. The Fireside also allows pets. Perhaps the most appreciated little touch is the guidebook the management has put together for guest use. It points the way to some of the area's natural attractions, including Smelt Sands and Cape Perpetua. A state park trail behind both properties leads over the rockbound coast to a driftwood-laden beach.

The aptly named **SeeVue** (95590 U.S. 101, 541/547-3227, www.seevue.com) has long been a favorite window on the Pacific for storm- and whale-watchers. This 10-room complex thrives today thanks to an eminently affordable combination of comfort and location, just six miles south of Yachats and three miles south of Cape Perpetua. Assuming you can pull yourself away from watching the waves, there's also prime beachcombing and wildlife-viewing close by. All units here boast Pacific perspectives and thematic decor ($50–85, depending on seasonal availability). There are nonsmoking rooms as well as some housekeeping units. Pets allowed.

For the ultimate in seclusion, the **Oregon House** (94288 U.S. 101, 541/547-3329, www.oregonhouse.com), eight miles south of Yachats, overlooks the Pacific from a bluff and offers guests a reflective phone-free, TV-less atmosphere. Twelve apartments (housed in five different buildings) with baths and kitchens, some with fireplaces and whirlpool tubs, are perfect for groups. In fact, they specialize in groups, but also rent the apartments to individuals. No pets; quiet children okay. Stroll the three acres of gardens or head down the private path to the beach.

Another place where rock and tide get top billing is **Ocean Haven** (94770 U.S. 101, 541/547-3583, www.oceanhaven.com). Located halfway between Florence and Yachats in a section of coast that one travel writer hyped as the "Amalfi Drive of the Americas," this classic beach house has virtually no "motel-type" amenities (no TVs or phones in rooms). Pets (which might spook Coast Range wildlife) and smoking are verboten. This is a peaceful nature-lover's retreat with panoramic views, friendly innkeepers, and a well-stocked library. Rates are $75–120.

Bed-and-Breakfasts

A few classic bed-and-breakfasts south of Yachats rate a mention for those willing to spend a little more for comfort, location, and privacy.

Seven miles south of Yachats, the **Sea Quest Inn** (95354 U.S. 101, 541/547-3782 or 800/341-4878, www.seaq.com) is an antique-filled aerie above the pounding surf. Private entrances and a location adjacent to Ten Mile Creek in this contemporary cedar-and-glass inn make rates above $160 per night well worth it. The "Tis Sweete" is a 1,000-square-foot suite with a king-size canopy bed, a woodburning fireplace, 25-foot-high windows, and wraparound deck all located on a private wing ($350/night, two people). From the fine cognac and wines in the evening, the fruit, scones, and popcorn in the commons, to the chocolates and bottled water in your room, the inn is well stocked with quality goodies catering to your whim and pleasure. Breakfasts are delicacy-laden presentations superior to many hotel fine dining rooms. The wraparound deck affords superlative views of the beach, and telescopes and binoculars are always on hand for spotting whales and other marine life. Many guests return each year, so be sure to book well in advance. Not appropriate for children under 14 years of age.

In the same area and price range are **Ziggurat** (95330 U.S. 101, 541/547-3925), a four-story glass-and-wood pyramid-like structure with an abundance of sunlight and comforts (800-square-foot suites with such extras as a sauna, a baby grand, and a woodstove); and the **Kittiwake** (95368 U.S. 101, 541/547-4470), a sprawling contemporary beachfront home with spectacular views.

Look for all of these inns six miles south of Yachats at mile marker 171 near Ten Mile Creek. At all these establishments you might find such seasonal breakfast fare as local berries and smoked sturgeon. Unlike many of their counterparts elsewhere, most Yachats-area bed-and-breakfasts feature private bathrooms. However, the welcome mat is seldom out for children or pets. Rates are $170 and may require a two-night minimum stay.

Food

Right on the main highway is **La Serre** (2nd and Beach, 541/547-3420). A bright skylit restaurant with lots of plants (La Serre means "the greenhouse") creates an appropriate setting for cuisine that eschews deep-fat frying and embraces whole wheat. This may not suggest gourmet continental fare, but somehow La Serre pulls it off. With entrées running the gamut from strawberry-ricotta crepes to charbroiled steaks, the menu manages to please the Brie-and-chardonnay set as well as their children. The salmon or crabcakes, oven-roasted marinated free-range chicken, Manhattan clam chowder, bouillabaisse, and clam puffs appetizer will sate anyone who just likes good food. For dessert, try the flourless chocolate cake. On chilly evenings, wash it all down with a coffee nudge. Come back Sunday for a memorable breakfast. Main courses can be had for less than $20. Closed Tuesday and the month of January.

On a bluff overlooking Smelt Sands Beach is the glass-enclosed **Adobe Resort** (1555 U.S. 101, 541/547-3141). Two side-by-side semicircular dining rooms, with windows on the crashing surf, are a great place to start the day for breakfast or end it with a romantic evening repast. Ask about the loft, where elevated coastal views provide photo-ops; this is the perfect place to nurse a drink. A Sunday champagne brunch served 9 A.M.–1 P.M. and three meals a day are the real highlights here however. Start the day with one of several seafood omelettes. In the same price range for lunch, we recommend grilled Yaquina Bay oysters. For dinner, the Adobe baked crab pot and various kinds of fettuccine are the ticket.

Right beside the highway, **Joes' Town Center Cafe** (U.S. 101 and 4th St., 541/547-4244) gives the appearance of an old cedar beach house with some modern architectural flourishes. You can sit downstairs near the potbellied stove and bustling counter or upstairs in a windowed loft. On sunny days, kick back on the outside deck. Wherever you plop down, enjoy the full breakfast or lunch, featuring homemade soups and baked goods. Open daily except Wednesday, 8 A.M.–3 P.M.

Elaborate picnic eats are available from the **Yachats Crab and Chowder House** "To Go" shop (131 U.S. 101, 541/547-4132). Pick up fresh half crab and garlic bread, rock cod and halibut fish-n-chips, as well as assorted breads, meats, and cheeses. Along with clam chowder, the restaurant also makes hearty chowders with Dungeness crab or smoked salmon. And remember, wherever you decide to picnic, chances are the view in the restaurant is at least as good and there's usually plenty of seating. Open Mon.–Sat. 11 A.M.–8 P.M.

Known for its chowder, the **Landmark Restaurant** (U.S. 101, 541/547-3215) also has a good selection of fresh fish entrées and some of the most remarkable views on the coast.

Leroy's Blue Whale (541/547-3397), a self-described "family restaurant," can be counted on for low prices for every meal, serving a menu of American food. Culinary flourishes are limited to a smoked salmon and jack cheese omelette for breakfast and dinner-time seafood specials such as squid rings and prawns sautéed in wine and butter. Stays open in January when many of the other eateries in Yachats close early or suspend operation.

The carefully restored **Drift Inn Pub** (U.S. 101, 541/457-4477) offers seafood dishes, crunchy salads, fish-n-chips, and other pub grub in a casual atmosphere.

Information and Transportation

The **Yachats Area Chamber of Commerce** (241 U.S. 101, P.O. Box 728, Yachats 97498, 541/547-3530 or 800/929-0477, www.yachats.org) has a central location on the highway (next to Clark's Market) and a loquacious staff. Ask them about fishing, rockhounding, bird-watching, and beachcombing in the area. Open daily 10 A.M.–4 P.M. March–Sept., Thurs.–Sun. the rest of the year.

The **Central Oregon Coast Association** (541/265-2064 or 800/767-2064, www.coastvisitor.com) maintains a useful website with details on Yachats and the rest of coastal Lincoln County.

The bus stop is also in the parking lot of the Clark's Market complex (U.S. 101 and W. 2nd). Here you can catch **Lincoln County Transit** buses (541/265-4900), which run four times a day, Mon.–Sat., between Yachats and Newport, with a link to Lincoln City.

Waldport

Originally a stronghold of the Alsea tribe, Waldport also has had incarnations as a gold rush town, salmon-canning center, and lumber port. This town of about 2,000, whose name in German means "Forest Port," is pretty quiet today. The chamber of commerce touts Waldport's livability, suggesting that the town's "relative obscurity" has spared it the fate of more crowded tourist hot spots. This may also be explained by a nondescript main drag that gives no hint of surrounding beaches and prime fishing and crabbing spots. A recent influx of retirees has spurred new home building, but this place is still decidedly low-key. For those passing through, Waldport provides a low-cost alternative to the big-name destinations; in Waldport you won't have to fight for a parking spot or make reservations months in advance.

SIGHTS AND RECREATION

Alsea Bay Bridge Historical Interpretive Center

This small museum cum visitors center, operated by the Oregon Parks and Recreation Department and Waldport Chamber of Commerce, stands along the highway on the south side of the river. Exhibits here tell the story of how the sleek 1991 bridge replaced the aging Conde McCullough span across the bay, which has since been demolished. Displays about transportation methods along the central coast since the 1800s, information on the Alsea tribe, and a telescope trained on the seals and waterfowl on the bay are worth a quick stop. In addition, Oregon Parks and Recreation guides lead bridge tours and give clamming and crabbing demonstrations during the summer.

The center (541/563-2002) is open daily in summer, 9 A.M.–5 P.M., Tues.–Sat. 9 A.M.–4 P.M. the rest of the year. Admission is free.

Seal Rock State Recreation Site

Four miles north of town, this park attracts beachcombers and agate-hunters as well as folks who come to explore the tidepools and observe the seals on offshore rocks. The park's name derives from a seal-shaped rock in the cluster of interesting formations in the tidewater. The picnic area is set in a shady area behind the sandy beach. During Christmas and spring breaks, the volunteers of Whale Watching Spoken Here are on hand to help visitors spot passing grays 10 A.M.–1 P.M. The park is open for day use only; call 800/551-6949 for information.

Ona Beach State Park

A couple of miles north of Seal Rock, this beguiling park on the west side of the highway includes a forested picnic area with a quarter-mile trail and a footbridge over Beaver Creek leading to a fine stretch of beach. Day use only; call 800/551-6949 for information.

Drift Creek Wilderness

Seven miles east of Waldport are the nearly 5,800 acres of the Drift Creek Wilderness, which protects the Coast Range's largest remaining stands of old-growth rainforest. Here you can see giant Sitka spruce and western hemlock hundreds of years old, nourished by up to 120 inches of rain per year. These trees are the "climax forest" in the Douglas fir ecosystem. They seldom reach old-growth status because the timber industry tends to replant only fir seedlings after logging operations. There is also perhaps the largest population of spotted owls in the state here, along with bald eagles, Roosevelt elk, and black bear. Drift Creek sustains wild runs of chinook, steelhead, and coho, which come up the Alsea River.

Steep ridges and their drainages as well as small meadows make up the topography, which is accessed via a couple of hiking trails. The trailhead closest to Waldport is the **Harris Ranch Trail**, which descends 1,200 feet in two miles to a meadow near Drift Creek. The local access to Harris Ranch and Horse Creek trails leaves ORE 34 at the Alsea River crossing seven miles east of Waldport. Here, pick up Risely Creek Road (Forest Service Road 3446) and Forest Service

COASTAL OREGON

Road Road 346. The wilderness is administered by the Siuslaw National Forest–Waldport Ranger Station (541/563-3211) which can supply specific directions to the different trailheads into this increasingly rare ecosystem.

Fishing

Waldport's recreational raison d'être is fishing. World-class clamming and Dungeness crabbing in Alsea Bay and the Alsea River's famous salmon, steelhead, and cutthroat trout runs account for a high percentage of visits to the area. Before commercial fishing on the river was shut down in 1957, as much as 137,000 pounds of chinook were netted in a season. The wild fall chinook run remains healthy, and starts up in late August. Catch-and-release for sea-run cutthroats starts in mid-August, while steelhead are in the river December through March. Crabbers without boats can take advantage of the Port of Waldport docks.

Gene-O's Guide Service (P.O. Box 43, Waldport 97374, 541/563-3171) calls on four decades of experience to help you reel in salmon and steelhead. **Dock of the Bay Marina** (1245 N.E. Mill, 541/563-2003) and **Kozy Kove Marina** (9646 Alsea Hwy.) rent and sell crabbing and fishing supplies, and can guide you to the best spots.

Camping

Two excellent campgrounds sit about four miles south of Waldport on U.S. 101 along the beach. **Beachside State Park** (information 541/563-3220 or 800/551-6949, reservations 800/452-5687) is located near a half mile of beach not far from Alsea Bay and Alsea River. This is a paradise for rock fishermen, surfcasters, clammers, and crabbers. For $16–19 a night mid-April–mid-October, there are 50 tent sites, 32 sites for RVs up to 30 feet long, and some hiker/biker sites. Beachside fills up fast, with such amenities as a laundry and hot showers, so reserve early for space Memorial Day–Labor Day.

A half mile down U.S. 101, the forest service has comparable site offerings at **Tillicum Beach** (reservations 877/444-6777 or www.reserveusa

.com). Set right along the ocean, the campground is open all year but requires reservations. For $15 a night you have the full range of creature comforts plus ranger campfire programs in summer. Forest service roads from here access Coast Range fishing streams, which are detailed in a forest service map. You'll also appreciate the strip of vegetation blocking the cool evening winds that whip up off the ocean here.

Should Beachside and Tillicum be filled to overflowing, you might want to set up a base camp in the Coast Range along ORE 34—especially if you have fishing or hiking in the Drift Creek Wilderness in mind. Just go east of Waldport 17 miles on ORE 34 to the Siuslaw National Forest's **Blackberry Campground** (reservations 877/444-6777 or www.reserveusa .com). The 33 sites ($10/night) are open year-round for tents and RVs, most of them on the river. A boat ramp, flush toilets, and piped water are on site. This is a good base for a fishing trip.

PRACTICALITIES

Accommodations

"Cottage" is a word often used to describe accommodations between Yachats and Waldport. It may be a duplex or self-contained cabin, generally by a beach. The prices generally range $70–150 for units with kitchen facilities, fireplaces, and oceanfront locations.

The **Terry-a-While Motel** (7160 S.W. U.S. 101, 541/563-3377, www.terry-a-while.com) has well-appointed rooms that range in style, from modern to vintage, and size (the newer four-plex is ideal for families). Rates are $50–110. The beachfront **Edgewater Cottages** (3978 S.W. U.S. 101, 541/563-2240, www.edgewatercottages.com) come complete with view, full kitchen, and a wood-burning fireplace. Ask about the minimum-stay policy prior to booking; rates are $75–85. For similarly equipped rooms, try the **Cape Cod Cottages** (4150 S.W. U.S. 101, 541/563-2106, www.dreamwater.com). Rates are $69–89.

Formerly the Bayshore Inn, the **Evening Star**

Resort (902 N.W. Bayshore Dr., 541/563-7700 or 877/327-6500, www.eveningstarresort.com) prides itself on great service. Half of the 84 rooms enjoy sweeping views of the bay, bridge, and town, and all are equipped with either one or two queen beds and the usual amenities. There's also a dining room and cocktail lounge, with occasional entertainment, and a fitness room. Rates are $59–150.

The historic **Cliff House** (1450 Adahi Rd., 541/563-2506, www.cliffhouseoregon.com) may appear to be rustic, but its bluff location can't be beat to set a romantic mood. Four rooms, some with whirlpools, are decorated with antiques; even the woodstoves are period. (No pets allowed, and children are best left home with grandma or the sitter.) Rates are $110–225.

Food

Forget fine dining in Waldport. This is an eat 'n' run town. **Grand Central Pizza** (245 S.W. Arrow, 541/563-3232) is a favorite with the locals, across the street from the 76 gas station—you can't miss it. *Oregon Coast* magazine voted this the best pie on the coast. In addition to spaghetti dinners, lasagna, and pizza, the homemade garlic rolls, selection of microbrews, fish-n-chips, and grinder sandwiches are also noteworthy. Best of all, the largest appetites can be sated here for less than $10.

For a hearty breakfast and other meal specials served in a sport-lovers' atmosphere replete with big-screen TV, the **Flounder Inn Tavern** (U.S. 101, 541/563-2266) offers customers lots of pub grub choices, including fish-n-chips and a popular roasted chicken dinner.

Two self-described "family-friendly restaurants" can be counted on for low prices and a varied menu of American food. **Vickie's Big Wheel** (south end of the Alsea Bridge, 541/563-3640) boasts "the best cheeseburger on the coast." **Leroy's Blue Whale** (U.S. 101, 541/563-3445) serves burgers and quick seafood meals. Both places stay open in January when many of the other eateries in nearby Yachats close early or suspend operation.

If you're interested in a unique dining experience, follow ORE 34 farther up the Alsea River for nine miles to a most unlikely site for a good restaurant. Attached to a trailer court and convenience store is the **Kozy Kove Kafe** (9464 ORE 34, Tidewater 97390, 541/528-3251). The dining room and lounge float on a bed of logs by a riverbank and are well placed to observe Australian black swans, elk, salmon jumping in September, and other wildlife. Breakfasts (three-egg omelettes with ingredients such as cajun-smoked salmon and herb cream cheese) are hearty, and lunch and dinner focus on fresh seafood, steak, and prime rib. Clam chowder and strawberry shortcake are recommended accompaniments. Mexican (try the "fajitas with the flame") and Italian entrées add spice to this retreat. Open Wed.–Sun. 9 A.M.–5 P.M.

Yuzen (U.S. 101, Seal Rock, 541/563-4766), five miles north of Waldport, is a Japanese restaurant with an oddly Bavarian facade. Well worth a stop, this country-style Japanese food at moderate-to-expensive prices attracts crowds Tues.–Sun., so avoid peak dining hours. In addition to sushi and miso soup, less well-known fare such as fish noodle soup, *yuza* (pork-minced rock shrimp with vegetables in a dumpling), and *syo-yaki* (a small whole broiled fish encrusted in salt) leave room for new discoveries. To enjoy a high-priced gourmet treat at a moderate price, we recommend sharing an order of *shabu shabu* (paper-thin beef, fresh vegetables, and tofu boiled in a pot and served with three gourmet sauces). With salad and dessert, three people could get away with paying less than $15 apiece. Open for lunch till 2 P.M. and dinner 4–9 P.M.

Information and Transportation

The Walport Chamber of Commerce operates the **visitor center** (P.O. Box 669, Waldport 97394, 541/563-2133, www.pioneer.net/~waldport) in the Alsea Bay Bridge Historical Interpretive Center, just south of the river. Open daily in summer, 9 A.M.–5 P.M., Tues.–Sat. 9 A.M.–4 P.M. the rest of the year.

The **Siuslaw National Forest–Waldport Ranger Station** (1094 S.W. U.S. 101, Waldport

97394, 541/563-3211), can provide information on area camping and hiking, including the trails in the Drift Creek Wilderness.

Waldport gets bus service from **Greyhound (800/231-2222) and Lincoln County Transit** (541/265-4900). Stops are at the Waldport Ranger Station (1094 U.S. 101) and the Waldport Senior Center (265 Elsie Hwy.). The Lincoln County buses run four times a day, Mon.–Sat., between Yachats and Newport.

Newport

In January 1852, a storm grounded the schooner *Juliet* near Yaquina (pronounced yah-KWIN-nah) Bay, where her captain and crew were stranded for two months. When they finally made their way inland to the Willamette Valley, they reported their discovery of an abundance of tiny, sweet-tasting oysters in the bay. Within a decade, commercial oyster farms were established here, the first major impetus to growth and settlement in Newport. The tasty morsels that delighted diners in San Francisco and at New York's Waldorf-Astoria Hotel are almost gone now, but the oyster industry continues in a limited way harvesting introduced species.

The port bustles with the activity of Oregon's largest commercial fishing fleet and second-largest recreational fleet. New factories to process *surimi* (a fish paste popular in Japan) and whiting have provided hundreds of jobs here, and a state-of-the-art aquarium that once housed Keiko the whale (from *Free Willy*) to bring in the tourist dollar. In this vein, new wildlife observation facilities and improved access to tidal pools north of town at Yaquina Head promise to make this park a highlight of the coast. The shops, galleries, and restaurants along Newport's historic Bayfront, together with the Performing Arts Center and quieter charm of Nye Beach, keep up a tourism tradition that goes back to when this town was the "honeymoon capital of Oregon." Today, Newport (pop. 9,960) boasts more oceanfront hotel rooms than any place between San Francisco and Seattle, except perhaps for Lincoln City. This can make for traffic jams on holiday weekends, but it's a small price to pay for proximity to some of the coast's best agate-hunting beaches, cultural programs, and restaurants.

SIGHTS

Oregon State University Hatfield Marine Science Center

Just south of the Yaquina Bay Bridge, head east on the road that parallels the bay to the OSU Hatfield Marine Science Center (Marine Science Drive, Newport 97365, 541/867-0100, http://hmsc.oregonstate.edu). This research and education facility is a low-key but still interesting complement to the very popular Oregon Coast Aquarium, located half a mile south. At the door to greet you is an octopus in an open tank pointing the way to oceanography exhibits and a "hands-on" area where you can experience the feel of starfish, anemones, and other sea creatures. The back hallway has educational dioramas and a theater shows marine-science films throughout the day. If you proceed left from the octopus tank, you'll see tanks with different sea ecosystems. Beyond the walls of the museum, guided field trips (fee charged) explore estuary, beach, and coastal forest habitats at various times of the year (check with the front desk or the website for details). The bookstore has a good selection of nature books, posters, games, and gifts.

The Marine Science Center is open daily 10 A.M.–5 P.M. in summer and Thurs.–Mon. 10 A.M.–4 P.M. the rest of the year. During Whale Watch weeks (Christmas break and spring break), the center temporarily returns to its summer hours. Admission is free, but a $3 donation is suggested to support the center and its programs.

Oregon Coast Aquarium

There are 6,000 miles of water between the Oregon coast and Japan—the largest stretch of open ocean on earth. You can hear *our* side of the story at the Oregon Coast Aquarium (2820 S.E. Ferry Slip Rd., Newport, 541/867-3474, www.aquarium.org), one of the state's most popular attractions.

The aquarium initially featured 40,000 square feet of galleries devoted to wetland communities, near-shore and marine ecosystems, and an environmental center. While it was respected as a top-notch educational facility, it lacked "star power" until the 1996 arrival of Keiko, a 7,720-pound, 32-foot-long orca who starred in *Free Willy.* Understandably, his presence overshadowed four acres of sea lions, sea otters, tidepools, and undersea caves, as well as the largest walk-in seabird aviary in the Americas. Keiko has since been moved to Iceland for re-entry into the wild, but there are still many attractions here to hold your interest.

One of the gems of the aquarium is "Passages of the Deep," a 200-foot-long acrylic tunnel offering 360-degree underwater views in three diverse habitats, from "Orford Reef" to "Halibut Flats" to "Open Sea," where you're surrounded by free-swimming sharks. The "Jewels of the Sea" exhibit showcases several dozen kinds of jellyfish in an almost psychedelic display.

"At the Jetty" is the aquarium's largest permanent indoor exhibit to date. Visitors look through a window into a 35,000-gallon tank to watch white sturgeon and coho and chinook salmon swimming among large basalt boulders that simulate a coastal jetty, such as these anadromous fish in the wild might pass through on their upriver journey to their spawning grounds.

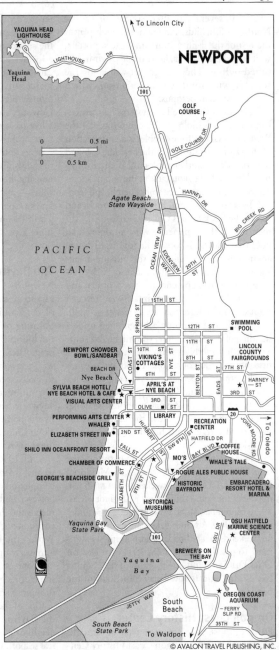

COASTAL OREGON

© AVALON TRAVEL PUBLISHING, INC.

Of the several hundred species of Pacific Northwest fish, birds, and mammals on display in the rest of the facility, don't miss the sea otters, wolf eel, leopard sharks, lion's mane jellyfish, and tufted puffins. The younger set will enjoy the sea cave with simulated wave action, which houses a resident octopus.

Indigenous simulated ecosystems help articulate the region's biology. The centerpiece of the Wetland's Gallery, for example, is a cross section of the salt marsh subject to the periodic ebb and flow of tides. Another ecological niche is illustrated by a 4,730-gallon tank in the Sandy Shores exhibit. Here, you can see smelt, perch, and leopard sharks navigate amid human-made rocks and piers. The Rock Shores Gallery adds another dimension to the experience with an open tidal pool that allows visitors to handle starfish, sea anemones, and the like. In the outside aviary and sea mammal pools, latex molds of rocky outcroppings provide perches for birds, otters, and sea lions (some of these animals were rescued from such debacles as the *Exxon-Valdez* oil spill).

In addition to gaining a heightened understanding of the coast biome, you might also come away with something from the museum shop's first-rate collection of regional books and oceanographic tomes or perhaps a crystal or gemstone. The on-site Mermaid Cafe emphasizes such Oregon fare as Tillamook dairy products, seasonal fruits, and seaood. Outside in the summer, enjoy barbecued burgers and hot dogs and teriyaki shish-kebabs.

The aquarium is open daily year-round (except Christmas Day), 9 A.M.–6 P.M. Memorial Day weekend–Labor Day weekend; 10 A.M.–5 P.M. the rest of the year. Admission is $10.75 for adults, $9.50 for seniors, $6.50 for kids ages 4–13, under four get in free. Advance tickets are recommended on weekends, major holidays, and during the summer. To get there from U.S. 101, turn east on OSU Drive or 32nd Street, south of the Yaquina Bay Bridge, and follow Ferry Slip Road to the parking lot.

Oregon Coast History Center

For a glimpse into the rich past of Lincoln County, stop at the Oregon Coast History Center (545 S.W. 9th St., Newport, 541/265-7509), which incorporates the Log Cabin Museum and the adjacent Queen Anne–style Burrows House, a former boardinghouse built in 1895. It's located a half block east of the chamber of commerce on U.S. 101. The logging, farming, pioneer life, and maritime exhibits (particularly Newport shipwrecks) are interesting, but the Siletz baskets and other Native American artifacts steal the show.

Here you can learn the heartbreaking story of the hardships—forced displacement, inadequate housing, insufficient food, and poor medical facilities—that plagued the diverse tribes that made up the Confederated Siletz Indian Reservation. The museum is open Tues.–Sun. 10 A.M.–5 P.M. June–Sept., 11 A.M.–4 P.M. Oct.–May. Admission is free.

The Bayfront

Newport's Old Town Bayfront District can be easy to miss if you're not alert. At the north end of the Yaquina Bay Bridge, look for the signs pointing off U.S. 101, which lead you down the hill to Bay Boulevard, the Bayfront's main drag. Alternatively, turn southeast off the highway a few blocks north onto Hurbert Street; this runs into Canyon Way, which ends at Bay. On summer weekends, forget about parking anywhere here unless you arrive early. Spots close by the boulevard can often be found, however, along Canyon Way, the hillside access route to downtown.

Until 1936, ferries shuttled people and vehicles to and from Newport's waterfront. With the completion of the Yaquina Bay Bridge that year, however, traffic bypassed the old town area. Commerce and development moved to the highway corridor, and the Bayfront faded in importance. Within the last couple of decades, the pendulum has swung back, and the Bayfront District is now one of Newport's prime attractions, with some of its best restaurants and watering holes, shopping, and tourist facilities.

One of the first things that'll strike you about the Bayfront today is that it's still a working neighborhood, not a sanitized re-creation of a real seaport. Chowderhouses, galleries, and shops stand shoulder to shoulder with fish-processing plants and canneries, and the air is filled with the cries of fishmongers purveying wharfside walkaway cocktails and the harmonious discord of sea lions and harbor seals. On the waterfront, sport anglers step off charter boats with their catches, and vessels laden with everything from wood products to whale-watchers ply the bay. Unfortunately, the severe catch limits and cost of equipment make this less of a working port every year. In deference to the Oregon commercial fisherman and other endangered species, wall murals memorialize fishing boats and whales here on the Bayfront.

Yaquina Bay State Park

In 1871, a lighthouse was built here on a bluff overlooking the mouth of Yaquina Bay, and the lighthouse keeper, his wife, and seven children moved into the two-story wood-frame structure. It soon became apparent, however, that the location was not ideal, as the light could not be seen by ships approaching the harbor from the north. The station was abandoned after just three years, once the nearby light at Yaquina Head was completed. The building was slated for demolition in 1934, when local residents formed the Lincoln

County Historical Society to preserve it. In 1997, the government decided to turn Yaquina Bay's beacon back on.

Today, the handsome restored structure and surrounding grounds make up Yaquina Bay State Park (541/574-3129 or 800/-551-6949), in a beautiful location at the north end of the Yaquina Bay Bridge. The oldest building in Newport, it's the last wooden lighthouse on the Oregon coast. The living quarters, replete with period furnishings, are open daily noon–4 P.M. Admission is free. Be sure to ask the volunteers about the resident ghost here.

From the parking area, you have an excellent photo-op of the bay and the bridge. The park is a good place to have a picnic, or you can descend the trails to the beach and dig for razor clams or hunt for agates and petrified wood.

Nye Beach

The 1890s-era tourism boom that came to Newport's Bayfront spilled over into Nye Beach. In 1891, the city built a wooden sidewalk connecting the two neighborhoods and soon "summer people" were filling the cedar cottages here. In the next century, thanks to an improved river-and-land route from

© MARK MORRIS

COASTAL OREGON

Conde McCullough's elegant 1936 bridge over Yaquina Bay

The keeper's cottage at Yaquina Bay Lighthouse has been restored with 1870s-vintage furnishings.

Corvallis, health faddists (who came for hot seawater baths in the sanatorium) and honeymooners soon joined the mix.

Located a mile north from the Bayfront, to the west of U.S. 101 (look for signs on the highway), this one-time favorite retreat for wealthy Portlanders has undergone a revival in recent years. Rough times and rougher weather had reduced luxurious beach houses here to a cluster of weather-beaten shacks until a performing arts center went up two decades ago. On the heels of the development of this first-rate cultural facility, the conversion of a 1910 hotel into a kind of literary hostel (see special topic "Bedtime Stories" under "Waldport," earlier in this chapter) has encouraged other restorations and plenty of new construction. Culture vultures, beach lovers, and people-watchers now flock to Nye Beach.

Some larger resort and chain hotels have sprung up among the Cape Cod cottages, aging hippies, artists, and friendly fisherfolk, and not everyone is happy about the developments here, as such signs as "The Real Nye Beach—R.I.P." attest. Still, there's plenty of character and charm in this neighborhood, which feels a world away from the Coast Highway commercial strip just a few blocks to the east.

Yaquina Head Outstanding Natural Area

Five miles north of Newport, rocky Yaquina Head juts out to sea. Tools dating back 5,000 years have been unearthed at Yaquina Head. Many were made from elk and deer antler and bone as well as stone. Clam and mussel shells from middens in the area evidence a diet rich in shellfish for the area's ancient inhabitants.

Today, much of the headland is encompassed in the Yaquina Head Outstanding Natural Area (P.O. Box 936, Newport 97365, 541/574-3100), managed by the BLM. "Outstanding" is indeed the word for this place; a visitor could easily spend several hours exploring all the site has to offer.

Yaquina Head Lighthouse, the coast's tallest beacon. In the early 1870s, materials intended for construction of a lighthouse several miles north at Otter Crest were mistakenly delivered here. The 93-foot tower began operation in 1873, replacing the poorly located lighthouse south of here at the mouth of Newport's harbor. Walk up the 114 cast-iron steps for a spectacular panorama of the headland and surrounding coast. The lighthouse is open daily, weather permitting.

Below, an observation deck provides views of seals, sea lions, gray whales, and seabirds. Of the half dozen varieties of pelagic birds that cluster on Colony Rock—a large monolith in the shallows 200 yards offshore—the tufted puffin is the most colorful. It's sometimes called a sea parrot because of its large yellow-orange bill. Puffins arrive here in April and are most visible early in the day on the rock's grassy patches. The most ubiquitous species here are common murres, pigeons guillemots, and cormorants. The murre's white breasts and bellies contrast with their darker bills and elongated backs. The guillemots resemble pigeons with white wing patches and bright red webbed feet. The cormorants look like prehistoric pelicans.

East of the lighthouse, the large Interpretive Center (541/574-3116) features exhibits on local ecosystems, Native American culture, and historical artifacts such as a 19th-century lighthouse keeper's journal. Other highlights include a life-size replica of the Fresnel lens that shines from the top of the nearby lighthouse, a sea cave simulation with a life-size mural of a California gray whale (accompanied by an exhibit detailing its migratory pattern), as well as statues of birds and harbor seals, and information on tidepool inhabitants. The Interpretive Center and gift shop are open daily 10 A.M.–5 P.M. in summer, till 4 P.M. the rest of the year.

Close by, wheelchair-friendly paths give access to tidal pools, augmented by the hand of man, in an abandoned basalt quarry on the south side of the headland. Enjoy sea stars, purple urchins, anemones, and hermit crabs at low tide.

The fee to enter Yaquina Head is $5 per car, which is valid for three days. The Pacific Coast Passport is also valid here.

Beaches

North of town, **Agate Beach** is a broad swath of coastline famed for its agate-hunting opportunities and its views of nearby Yaquina Head. In addition to the semiprecious stones, the contemplative appeal of Agate Beach inspired no less a figure than Ernest Bloch, the noted Swiss composer, who lived here from 1940 until his death in 1959. Famed violinist Yehudi Menuhin spoke of Bloch and the locale thusly: "Agate Beach is a wild forlorn stretch of coastline looking down upon waves

© MARK MORRIS

Yaquina Head Lighthouse

coming in all the way from Asia to break on the shore, a place which suited the grandeur and intensity of Bloch's character." Each summer, the Ernest Bloch Music Festival (see "Entertainment and Events," later in this section) pays tribute to the spirit and music of this man.

Moolack Beach, two miles north of Yaquina Head, is a favorite with kite flyers and agate hunters. Another 1.5 miles north, at **Beverly Beach,** 20-million-year-old fossils have been found in the sandstone cliffs above the shore. Beverly Beach also attracts waders, unique for Oregon's chilly waters. Offshore sandbars temper the waves and the weather so it's not as rough or as cold as many coastal locales. This long stretch of sand (panoramic photos are best taken in from Yaquina Head Lighthouse looking north) is rated among America's 50 best beaches in a list that considers both scenic and recreational appeals.

The beach at **Yaquina Bay State Park,** accessible via a trail from the bluff-top parking area, is a popular spot for clamdigging and agate hunting. Two miles south of the Yaquina Bay Bridge, **South Beach State Park** draws beachcombers, anglers, and picnickers to its miles of broad, sandy beach. The large campground here is the closest available to Newport; see "Camping," later in this section.

COASTAL OREGON

Toledo

Aficionados of antiquities can head east of Newport six miles up the Yaquina River on ORE 20 to Toledo, where "junque" shops abound. This small town's fortunes have risen and fallen with the timber cut. At one time, the world's largest spruce mill was here, but in the era of big timber's swan song, dealers of collectibles have sprouted up to take advantage of coast-bound traffic from the Willamette Valley. Most of the antique shops are located on Main Street. Timber has enjoyed a resurgence here with the mill getting old-growth logs submerged in Yaquina Bay during World War II.

RECREATION

Fishing

Newport is one of the top spots on the coast for charter fishing, and opportunities abound here at the home port of Oregon's second-largest recreational fleet. Bottom fishing (year-round), tuna fishing (Aug.–Oct.), crabbing (year-round), and salmon and halibut fishing (seasonal) are all possible. Typical rates here are $55 for a half day of bottom fishing, $100 for a full day; $100 for an eight-hour salmon outing; $175 for 12 hours of tuna fishing; and $150 for a 12-hour halibut charter.

In addition to a full menu of fishing excursions, most Newport operators also offer whale-watching charters. **Newport Marina Store and Charters** (2212 OSU Dr., South Beach, 541/867-4470 or 877/867-4470, www.newportmarinacharters.com) offers a combination crabbing/fishing trip ($65 for six hours). Two other local operators are **Newport Tradewinds** (653 S.W. Bay Blvd., 541/265-2101 or 800/676-7819, www.newporttradewinds.com); and **Sea Gull Charters, Inc.** (343 S.W. Bay Blvd., 541/265-7441 or 800/865-7441, www.seagullcharters.com).

For those who prefer to take matters into their own hands, the clamming and Dungeness crabbing are superlative in Yaquina Bay. If you haven't done this before, local tackle shops, such as the Newport Marina Store in South Beach, rent crabpots or rings and offer instruction. The best time to dig clams is at an extremely low tide. At that time, look for clammers grabbing up cockles in the shallows of the bay. Tide tables are available from the chamber of commerce and many local businesses.

Whale-Watching

In addition to the fishing charter companies noted above, which all offer whale-watching tours, the best company on the coast in terms of state-of-the-art equipment and natural history interpretation is **Marine Discovery Tours** (345 S.W. Bay Blvd., 800/903-BOAT, www.marinediscovery.com). Whale-, seal-, and bird-watching, an oyster bed tour, estuary and ocean exploration, and a harbor tour, narrated by naturalist guides, exemplify their offerings. Their 65-foot *Discovery* features videocameras that magnify the fascinating interplay between smaller life forms, but the real attractions can be appreciated by the naked eye. Landlubbers will especially relish the full crab pots pulled up from the deep and the resident pod of whales often visible north of Yaquina Bay off Yaquina Head. The two-hour SeaLife tour costs $25 for adults, $20 for ages 13–16, $14 for ages 4–12.

During the prime whale-watching weeks of late December and late March, volunteers from Whale Watching Spoken Here staff the **Don A. Davis City Kiosk** in Nye Beach, to answer questions and help you spot whales.

Camping

The campgrounds at Beverly Beach State Park and South Beach State Park could well be the most popular places of their kind on the Oregon coast. Their proximity to Newport, the absence of other camping in the area, and the special features of each explain their appeal.

Beverly Beach State Park (information 541/265-9278 or 800/452-5687, reservations 800/452-5687) offers 152 tent sites and 127 RV spaces (both $17–21), as well as yurts, set seven miles north of Newport on the east side of the highway in a mossy glade. Across the road is a tunnel leading to a beach. **Devil's Punchbowl** and **Otter Crest** are one and two miles up the highway, respectively. Fees include all amenities; on-site café. Campground is open year-round.

South Beach State Park (information 541/867-4715 or 800/551-6949, reservations 800/452-5687) located just south of the Yaquina Bay Bridge, occupies a long beach with opportunities for fishing, agate hunting, windsurfing (for experts), horseback riding, and hiking. It has the full range of creature comforts, including a laundry. It's open mid-April–late October at $17–21 per night (hiker and biker spaces $5).

Golf

The public course closest to Newport is nine-hole **Agate Beach Golf Course** (4100 North Coast Hwy., 541/265-7331), just north of town. Just the views of Yaquina Head are worth a visit. Open year-round. Green fees are $14 for nine holes, $28 for 18.

ENTERTAINMENT AND EVENTS

Overlooking the sea in Nye Beach, the **Newport Performing Arts Center** (777 W. Olive, 541/265-2787, www.coastarts.org/pac), the coast's largest performance venue, hosts local and national entertainment in the 400-seat Alice Silverman Theatre and the smaller Studio Theatre. At the same address is the **Oregon Coast Council for the Arts,** (541/265-9231 or 888/701-7123, www.coastarts.org), which puts out a free monthly newsletter and has ticket information on the PAC venues. It also has updates on the **Newport Visual Arts Center** (777 N.W. Beach Dr., 541/265-6540), located right above the beach two blocks north at the Nye Beach turnaround. The two floors and two galleries here offer art-education programs and exhibition space for paintings, sculpture, and other works, often with a maritime theme. Runyan Gallery is open Tues.–Sun. 11 A.M.–6 P.M.; Upstairs Gallery is open Tues.–Sat. noon–4 P.M. All exhibits are free.

In addition to its impressive schedule of music, dance, drama, and other arts, the Performing Arts Center screens a series of imported and art films—the ones you probably won't find at the multiplex **Newport Cinema** (5836 North Coast Hwy., 541/265-2111).

In the Bayfront District, Mariner Square (250 S.W. Bay Blvd., 541/265-2206) is a complex of three attractions that mostly appeal to kids: **Ripley's Believe It or Not!, The Waxworks,** and the **Undersea Gardens.** Admission per attraction is $6.95 for adults, $3.95 for children; discounts are offered to hardy souls who want to take in all three.

The biggest bash here (and one of the largest events of its kind in the country) is late February's **Newport Seafood and Wine Festival** (541/265-8801 or 800/262-7844), which features dozens of food booths and scores of Oregon wineries serving up these palate pleasers, along with music and crafts, at the South Beach Marina (across Yaquina Bay from the Bayfront). A huge tent joins the exhibition hall wherein festival-goers wash down delights from the deep with Oregon vintages. Admission runs $6–9, and the event is open only to the 21-and-over crowd.

The second event of note is **Loyalty Days and Sea Fair** (541/265-8801 or 800/262-7844) in early May, featuring sailboat races, a chicken feed, and a parade. What began during the Depression as the Crab Festival, intended to stimulate the market for Dungeness crab, was recast during the depths of the Red Scare of the 1950s as a public expression of patriotism. Although that aspect still undergirds the events, as evidenced by visiting naval vessels, it's really just a big community party stretching over four days, with carnival rides, boat tours, yacht races, bed races, a car show, a parade, and the coronation of the Crab Queen. Admission fee charged.

Each summer, the lectures, recitals, and concerts of the **Ernest Bloch Music Festival** (information 541/765-3142, tickets 541/265-2787, www.coastarts.org/pac) are eagerly anticipated by classical music lovers. The festival usually takes place late June–mid-July, at the Newport Performing Arts Center (777 W. Olive St.), with related performances at other central-coast locales. Along with Bloch's compositions, works by Schubert, Ravel, Saint-Saëns, and other icons of classical music are performed by top musicians in this acoustically superior hall. This event and Lincoln City's Cascade Head Chamber Music Festival are considered the coast's preeminent classical music offerings. Ticket prices range from free to $25.

The **Fourth of July fireworks** display, shot off from the South Beach Marina, is a crowd-pleasing spectacle. Vantage points include Yaquina Bay State Park, the bridge, and the beach. July is also the month for the **Lincoln County Fair and Rodeo** (541/265-6237), held over four days on the third weekend of the month, at the Lincoln County Fairgrounds, on the east side of town a block north of ORE 20.

"Suds & Surf" is the theme of the annual mid-October **Newport Microbrew Festival** (541/265-8801 or 800/262-7844), held at the Rogue Ales Brewery (2320 OSU Dr., Newport, 541/867-3660), at South Beach Marina, just south of the bridge. This event, Oregon's second-largest microbrew festival, brings together 30 of the Northwest's finest craft breweries, complemented by musical entertainment and a variety of food and arts and crafts booths. The festival also features commercial and home-brew competitions. Admission is $6, 21 and over only.

PRACTICALITIES

Accommodations

The **Brown Squirrel Hostel** (44 S.W. Brook St., 541/265-3729) charges $15–20 per night for a room with shared bath and bunk beds (take your sleeping bag). It's one block from the beach.

Viking's Cottages (729 N.W. Coast St., 541/265-2477 or 800/480-2477, www.vikings-oregoncoast.com) has Cape Cod–style cabins with kitchens, recommended for those who want to experience 1920s Nye Beach houses with modern conveniences and kitchens. Most have no phones and only showers—the decks and stairs to the beach are the highlights here. Most go for under $100/night (starting at $70); the large ones rent for $200, sleeping six to eight.

Built in the 1940s, the recently refurbished **Agate Beach Motel** (175 N.W. Gilbert Way, 541/265-8746 or 800/755-5674, www.agate-beachmotel.com) has 10 simple but charming beachfront units overlooking Agate Beach, each

BEDTIME STORIES

The **Sylvia Beach Hotel** (267 N.W. Cliff, 541/265-5428) combines the camaraderie of a hostel with the intimate charm of a bed-and-breakfast. Built in the era when the Corvallis-to-Yaquina Bay train and seven-seater Studebaker touring cars from Portland ferried the summer folks to Nye Beach, its National Historic Landmark designation and literary theme have attracted an enthusiastic following. The 20 guestrooms, named after different authors, are furnished with decor evocative of each respective literary legacy. The Edgar Allen Poe Room, for instance, has a pendulum guillotine blade and stuffed ravens, while the Agatha Christie Room drops such clues as shoes underneath the curtains and capsules marked "poison" in the medicine cabinet.

Most of the rooms ("bestsellers") run $118, with several oceanfront suites ("classics") featuring a fireplace and deck going for $173. "Novels" go for $83. All rates include a full breakfast and reflect double occupancy. At breakfast, you have a choice of entrées and share a table with eight other guests, so misanthropes beware! The fact that no smoking, pets, or radios are allowed on the premises should also be mentioned. Small children are discouraged. If you're looking for a budget room, Sylvia Beach features dormitory bunk beds for $25 per night.

To get there, turn off U.S. 101 onto N.W. 3rd and follow it down to the beach, where N.W. 3rd and Cliff Streets meet. Then look for a large four-story dark green vintage wooden structure with a red roof on a bluff above the surf.

with a private bedroom, kitchen, living room, and sundeck. Drop-ins are welcome, but reservations are recommended. Rates are $85–145.

The perfect Valentine's Day getaway is the **Nye Beach Hotel & Cafe** (219 N.W. Cliff St., 541/265-3334). Here 18 rooms with all the modern amenities (except phones) feature fireplaces as well as willow loveseats on ocean-view balconies ($65 and up). Add whimsical decor evocative of the era when Newport was Oregon's self-proclaimed Honeymoon Capital. The small

The Sylvia Beach Hotel, in Newport Beach's hip Nye Beach district

bistro-café, a bright airy restaurant with a sunset-friendly outside deck, serves creative, multi-ethnic small plates.

Surprisingly, some of the least expensive view rooms in town are available at the **Shilo Inn Oceanfront Resort** (536 S.W. Elizabeth St., 541/265-7701 or 800/222-2244). This chain inn offers 149 standard-equipped rooms, as well as two on-site restaurants and two indoor pools. They are kid- and pet-friendly. Rates are $95–165.

Just down the street is the **Elizabeth Street Inn** (232 S.W. Elizabeth St., 541/265-9400 or 877/265-9400, www.elizabethstreetinn.com) on a bluff overlooking the ocean. All of the rooms in this newer property face the ocean and have private balconies. They come fully equipped with all the modern conveniences. Guests also get a complimentary continental breakfast and have use of the indoor pool, spa, and fitness room. Rates are $99–199.

For comfort, you can't beat the **The Whaler** (155 S.W. Elizabeth St., 541/265-9261 or 800/433-9444, www.whalernewport.com). With 73 rooms—each with a view and some with fireplaces, wetbars, and private balconies—guests are treated to fresh-popped popcorn, pool fa-

cilities, and continental breakfast. Rates start at $109.

The ever-popular **Embarcadero Resort Hotel & Marina** (1000 S.E. Bay Blvd., 541/265-8521 or 800/547-4779, www.embarcadero-resort.com), overlooking Yaquina Bay, has an assortment of suites and townhouses with full kitchen and fireplaces. Off-water studios start at $80.

Bed-and-Breakfast

You may not find any riverboat gamblers aboard the **Newport Belle Bed & Breakfast** (H Dock, Newport Marina, 541/867-6290 or 800/348-1922, www.newportbelle.com), a recently constructed sternwheeler designed as a floating inn, but this 97-foot-long B&B evokes the ambience of the sternwheeler heyday. Choose from five generous staterooms, each with its own personality and private bath. Three of the rooms have queen beds, one has a king, and the family room has a full and a twin. Most have fabulous vistas of the bustling marina and bridge area. In the evening, guests either retire to their staterooms, enjoy the open afterdeck, or socialize in the main salon, where a gourmet breakfast is served every morning. No pets, children, or smoking allowed. Soft-soled shoes required. Rates range $100–145.

Food

This is a town for serious diners—folks who know good food and don't mind paying a tad more for it. It's also the kind of place where wharfside vendors do it on the cheap. June through October, you can pick up the freshest garden produce the area has to offer, plus baked goods, honey, and other delectables, at the Lincoln County Small Farmers' Association's **Saturday Farmers Market**, held in the parking area of the Newport Armory (41 S.W. U.S. 101, 541/574-4040), on the east side of the highway just behind City Hall. It kicks off at 9 A.M.

About seven miles east of the Bayfront, the **Oregon Oyster Farms** (6878 Yaquina Bay Rd., Newport, 541/265-5078) is the only remaining commercial outlet for Yaquina Bay oysters, on sale daily 9 A.M.–5 P.M. Visitors are welcome to

observe the farming and processing of these succulent shellfish. Try oysters on the half-shell, or sample the smoked oysters on a stick. To get there, follow Bay Boulevard east from the Bayfront.

Because you'll probably be spending most of your time at either Nye Beach or the Bayfront, eateries in those neighborhoods highlight this section. The Newport Bayfront is where Mohava Niemi first opened the original **Mo's** (622 S.W. Bay Blvd., 541/265-2979, www.moschowder.com) several decades ago. When word got out about the good food and low prices, Mo's small homey place soon had more business than it could handle. In response to the overflow, **Mo's Annex** (541/265-7512) was created across the street. While both establishments feature such favorites as oyster stew and peanut butter cream pie, the Annex bay window has the best view.

Another solid choice for those who crave fresh seafood is the **Whale's Tale** (452 S.W. Bay Blvd., 541/265-8660). Open daily.

Newport Chowder Bowl (728 N.W. Beach Dr., 541/265-7477) is perfect after a long beach walk. A first-rate salad bar, garlic bread, and award-winning chowder make an excellent lunch. Other lunch/dinner entrées range $5–18.

April's at Nye Beach (749 N.W. 3rd St., 541/265-6855) is a small, stylish café with big Mediterranean flavors close to the Sylvia Beach Hotel. Fish soup and portobello mushrooms in cheese-laden cannelloni are standouts here in a creative menu whose entrées range $12–25. House-made bruschetta and steamed Manila clams are excellent appetizers. For dessert have an eclair dipped in chocolate ganache and topped with slivered almonds. Affordable wines by the glass (around $5) add to one of Newport's best dining experiences. Open Wed.–Sun. for dinner only.

Georgie's Beachside Grill (744 S.W. Elizabeth St., 541/265-9800) in Nye Beach's Hallmark Inn has the best ocean view in town as well as good food. The salmon hash and smoked seafood pasta are highlights. The restaurant also features Cajun (try the catfish or shrimp creole) and Jamaican seafood specials in a dinner menu topping out near $20.

Canyon Way Bookstore and Restaurant (1216 S.W. Canyon Way, 541/265-8319) has been a mainstay of Newport's culinary and cultural scenes for several decades. A combination restaurant, art gallery, clothing boutique, and 20,000-title bookstore, it offers something for everybody. Stay for haute cuisine or carry out homemade quiche, croissants, and espresso. Early-dinner prices halve the later ones, which average $20, for the same order. Menu highlights include prawns Provençale, Yaquina Bay oysters, crabcakes, and a good Oregon-centered wine list. You'll also appreciate extras such as outdoor patio dining and works by local artists adorning the walls.

You don't have to be a guest to have a meal at the **Tables of Content,** the excellent restaurant at the Sylvia Beach Hotel. There's a nice view of the breakers, good company, and it's a good dollar value for creatively prepared Northwest cuisine. Each night features several entrée selections with an appetizer, salad, bread, beverages (alcohol extra), and dessert for less than $20, prix fixe. Diners share tables and are encouraged to break the ice with a game called Two Truths and a Lie, in which they regale each other with several stories, the object being to distinguish which one is true. Reservations mandatory.

Rogue Ales Public House (748 S.W. Bay Blvd., 541/265-3188) is across the Bay in Old Town, serving seafood salads, shrimp melt sandwiches, pizza, fish-n-chips, and seasonal fish dishes. The menu tops out with cioppino. In addition to washing down all the above with renowned Rogue ales, there's Keiko Draft root beer, a creamy concoction laced with honey and vanilla.

Farther east is a wonderful breakfast haunt, the **Coffee House** (156 S.W. Bay Blvd., 541/265-6263). Gourmet pastry and such creative brunch fare as a wild mushroom omelette, crabcakes Florentine, various crepes, and oysters lightly breaded with Japanese panko breadcrumbs are complemented by the best espresso drinks in Newport. The homey confines of this place are a nice escape from the tourist trappings nearby. In fair weather, the outside deck is a relaxing spot for soaking in some rays while you gaze out on the harbor. Breakfast and lunch served daily.

Embarcadero (1000 S.E. Bay Blvd., 541/265-8521) lets you fill up on all the breakfast entrées, fresh seafood, and bubbly you can handle. Count on this place for good service and the freshest fish available. Weekdays, seafood omelettes and frittatas are noteworthy on the breakfast menu. Lunch features a nice selection of salads, sandwiches, and entrées made with the fisherman's fresh catch in roughly the same price range. Otherwise, burgers, sandwiches, and fish-n-chips typify the Mon.–Sat. offerings for lunch. At night, fresh seafood entrées dominate the menu. Reservations are recommended for Sunday brunch between 10 A.M. and 2 P.M. and later for dinner.

Lighthouse Deli (640 U.S. 101 in South Beach, 541/867-6800) has fish-n-chips in a batter that's light enough not to obscure the flavor of fresh salmon, halibut, or cod. If you're looking for a family stop after visiting the Aquarium (just south of the Aquarium turnoff), this is it.

Information and Transportation

The **Greater Newport Chamber of Commerce** (555 S.W. U.S. 101, Newport 97365, 541/265-8801 or 800/541/262-7844, www.newport-chamber.org) has lots of literature and helpful staff. The office is open year-round Mon.–Fri. 8:30 A.M.–5 P.M. June–Sept. it's also open weekends 10 A.M.–4 P.M.

The **Central Oregon Coast Association** (541/265-2064 or 800/767-2064, www.coastvisitor.com) maintains a useful website with details on Newport and the rest of Lincoln County. The City of Newport operates another informative website, **Get to Know Newport** (www.discovernewport.com).

For high-speed Internet access, head to **Oregonfast.net** (428 S.W. U.S. 101, 541/574-1642). They charge $6 per hour.

Greyhound (956 W. 10th St., 541/265-2253) handles long-distance service along U.S. 101. **Valley Retriever** (541/265-2253) buses connect Newport with Corvallis Mon.–Saturday. On weekdays, **Lincoln County Transit** (541/265-4900, www.co.lincoln.or.us/transit/) runs buses four times daily, north to Lincoln City and south to Yachats, with numerous stops en route through Newport. A brochure with schedules and fare info is available in commercial establishments all over town.

The **Newport Municipal Airport** (135 S.E. 84th St., South Beach, 800/424-3655) has sightseeing and charter flights available.

Newport's car-rental agency of choice is **Enterprise Rent a Car** (27 South Coast Hwy., 541/574-1999).

Depoe Bay

In *Blue Highways,* William Least Heat Moon characterized Depoe Bay thusly: "Depoe Bay used to be a picturesque fishing village; now it was just picturesque. The fish houses, but for one seasonal company, were gone, the fleet gone, and in their stead had come sport fishing boats and souvenir ashtray and T-shirt shops."

To be fair, tourists have always come here since the establishment of the town. In fact, for all intents and purposes, the town didn't really exist until the completion of the Roosevelt Highway (U.S. 101) in 1927, which opened the area up to car travelers. Prior to that time, the area had been occupied mainly by a few members of the Siletz Reservation. One of the group, who worked at the U.S. Army depot, called himself Charlie Depot. The town was named after him, eventually taking on the current spelling.

Depoe Bay is in the heart of the so-called Twenty Miracle Miles, describing the attractive stretch of rockbound coast from south of Depoe Bay north up to the broad beaches of Lincoln City. Regardless of what you think of the short commercial strip along the highway here, the scenic appeal of Depoe's location is impossible to ignore. The rocky outer bay, flanked by headlands to the north and south, is pierced by a narrow channel through the basalt cliffs leading to the inner harbor. It's home to an active sport-fishing fleet as well as the whale-watching charters that have earned Depoe Bay its distinction as whale-watching capital of the state.

SIGHTS AND RECREATION

The Bayfront and Harbor

Depoe Bay is situated along a truly beautiful coastline that cannot be fully appreciated from the highway. A quarter-mile-long seawall and promenade invite a stroll. For a panorama of the harbor, continue along the sidewalks across the gracefully arching concrete bridge, designed by Conde McCullough and built in 1927. Other nice perspectives are offered from residential streets west of U.S. 101; try Ellingson Street, south of the bridge, and Sunset Street at the north end of the bay.

Perhaps the most all-encompassing overlook is offered by the glass-enclosed rooftop lookout (open to the public) on top of the **Oregon Coast Aquarium Store,** located right at the harbor entrance. Two "spouting horns," natural blowholes in the rocks north of the harbor entrance, can send plumes of spray 60 feet into the air when the tide and waves are right.

East of the bridge is Depoe Bay's claim to international fame, the world's smallest navigable natural harbor. This distinction is announced by a sign citing its recognition by the *Guinness Book of World Records.* This boat basin is also exceptional because it's a harbor within a harbor. This topography is the result of wave action cutting into the basalt over eons until a 50-foot passageway leading to a six-acre inland lagoon was created. In addition to whale-watching, folks congregate on the bridge between the ocean and the harbor to watch boats maneuver into the enclosure. Depoe Bay's Harbor was scenic enough to be selected as the sight from which Jack Nicholson commandeered a yacht for his mental patient crew in *One Flew Over the Cuckoo's Nest.*

Boiler Bay State Scenic Viewpoint

A half mile north of town is Boiler Bay, so named because of the boiler left from the 1910 wreck of the *J. Marhoffer.* The ship caught fire three miles offshore and drifted into the bay. The remains of the boiler are visible at low tide. This rock-rimmed bay is a favorite spot for rock fishing, birding, and whale-watching. A trail leads down to some excellent tidepools.

© MARK MORRIS

Depoe Bay has the world's smallest navigable natural harbor.

Whale Cove

Half a mile south of Depoe Bay, a picturesque bay has been scooped out of the sandstone bluffs. The tranquility of this calendar-photo-come-to-life is deceptive. There's considerable evidence to suggest that this tiny embayment—and not California's Marin County—was the site of Francis Drake's 1579 landing (see special topic "Drake's Lost Harbor?"), but the jury is still out. During Prohibition, bootleggers used the protected cove as a clandestine port. In the 1980s, a court decision allowing property owners to restrict access to Whale Cove set a precedent undermining public ownership of other Oregon beaches. (More recently, however, this trend was counteracted by another high court decision that prevented a Cannon Beach innkeeper from building on a public beach.)

Rocky Creek State Scenic Viewpoint overlooks Whale Cove. There are picnic tables, and it's a good spot for whale-watching, but there's no access down to the beach.

Otter Crest Loop

The rocky bluffs of this coastal stretch take on an even more dramatic aspect as you leave the highway at the Otter Crest Loop, a winding three-mile section of the old Coast Highway, two miles south of Depoe Bay.

From atop **Cape Foulweather,** the visibility can extend 40 miles on a clear day. The view south to Yaquina Head and its lighthouse is a photographer's fantasy of headlands, coves, and offshore monoliths. Bronze plaques in the parking lot tell of Captain Cook naming the 500-foot-high headland during a bout with storm-tossed seas on March 7, 1778. Comic relief from the coast's parade of historical plaques comes with another tablet bearing the inscription, "On this site in 1897, nothing happened."

The Lookout gift shop on the north side of the promontory is a good place to buy Japanese fishing floats for a few bucks. The million-dollar view from inside the shop is easily one of the most spectacular windows on the ocean to be found anywhere.

Another mile south, in the hamlet of Otter Rock, you'll find another of the Oregon coast's

the view from Cape Foulweather

several diabolically named natural features, the **Devil's Punchbowl.** The urnlike sandstone formation, filled with swirling water, has been sculpted by centuries of waves flooding into what had been a cave until its roof collapsed. The inexorable process continues today, thanks to the ebb and flow of the Pacific through two openings in the wall of the cauldron. A state park viewpoint gives you a ringside seat on this frothy confrontation between rock and tide. When the water recedes, you can see purple sea urchins and starfish in the tidepools of the **Marine Gardens** 100 feet to the north.

To the south of the Punchbowl vantage point are picnic tables and a wooden walkway down to the beach. Close by, in the Otter Rock **Mo's** restaurant, a seat occupied by "The Boss" himself, Bruce Springsteen, on June 11, 1987, is enshrined. Also in Otter Rock, the **Flying Dutchman Winery** (541/765-2553) makes limited batches of hand-crafted wines. It is open daily 11 A.M.–6 P.M. for tastings and tours.

Back on U.S. 101, a mile's drive south brings you to Beverly Beach State Park (see "Newport and Vicinity," earlier in this chapter).

Fishing and Whale-Watching Charters

With the ocean minutes from port here, catching

COASTAL OREGON

DRAKE'S LOST HARBOR?

In 1996, the media exploded with stories raising the possibility that the tiny hamlet of Whale Cove, two miles south of Depoe Bay, could supplant Plymouth Rock as the birthplace of a nation. Rotting timbers from what is theorized to have been a stockade built by Sir Francis Drake in 1579 were unearthed in an area where stories have long circulated that the English privateer made landfall.

Over the years, these notions have been fueled by a number of tantalizing pieces of evidence: an unsigned ship log from Drake's voyage in a museum in England that identified 44 degrees north latitude—the same as Whale Cove—as a landing site; an English shilling dating from 1560 found on the central Oregon coast in 1982; a photo from the 1930s showing a local resident with a distinctly English sword he unearthed; and a ship's cutlass found in Newport in the early 19th century bearing the markings of a 16th-century English arsenal. Moreover, excavations of a nearby Native American village thought to have been buried in the year 1600 turned up brass items, blades, and Venetian beads.

An amateur British historian, Bob Ward, however, makes a compelling case for Whale Cove as the place where Drake spent five weeks in the summer of 1579. In his flagship *Golden Hynde,* the only one of his five-ship fleet to survive the stormy straits around Cape Horn, Drake harassed Spanish settlements throughout Latin America and plundered Spanish ships wherever he met them. Sailing west from Mexico on its return to England via the Cape of Good Hope, the treasure-laden *Golden Hynde* was beset by storms, and Drake had to retreat to land to make repairs. Conventional history has held that he made landfall around San Francisco, most likely on the Marin County coast.

Ward, however, believes that Drake continued his voyage farther north, and sailed into the Strait of Juan de Fuca, thinking he had found the fabled Northwest Passage. Turning around before he realized his mistake, Drake then headed south down the Washington and Oregon coasts, where he found a sandy cove in which to drop anchor and make repairs before the long journey home.

On Drake's return to England after four years at sea, news of his exploits was suppressed. Queen Elizabeth confiscated the logs and charts, and it would be 10 years before an official account of the voyage would be published. In it New Albion, Drake's fabled lost settlement, was described as being around 38 degrees north latitude (in what is now Northern California), in an attempt, Ward believes, to fool the Spanish into thinking the Northwest Passage was much farther south.

After Elizabeth's death in 1603, however, new charts began to appear which placed the landing site much farther north, and early 17th-century charts show a small, shallow bay labeled "Novus Albionis" (New Albion) that is an uncannily accurate depiction of Whale Cove.

Since the initial blizzard of publicity, there has been no final word from the archaeologists and historians involved in corroborating these claims. As most history books have placed New Albion near San Francisco, researchers will not be too quick to claim otherwise without definitive research.

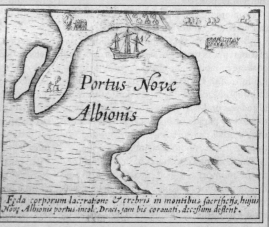

1589 map of Drake's Portus Novae Albionis by Jodocus Hondius—the spitting image of Whale Cove

COASTAL OREGON

a salmon or seeing a whale is possible as soon as you leave the harbor. Most charter operators here offer both fishing and whale-watching excursions. Bottom-fishing trips average around $55 for a five-hour run, salmon fishing about $100 for a seven- or eight-hour day; whale-watching excursions run $15–25 per person per hour.

Dockside Charters (541/765-2545 or 800/733-8915, www.docksidedepoebay.com) offers one-hour trips aboard their 50-foot excursion boat for $15/adult and on 25-foot rigid-hull inflatables for $25/adult. **Tradewinds Charters** (541/765-2345 or 800/445-8730, www.tradewindscharters.com) hosts one- and two-hour trips Dec.–Feb. and March–May. Rates run $15–45/ adult on their fleet of 30- to 52-foot boats and 18-foot Zodiac. A 12-hour tuna charter costs $160. **Zodiac Adventures** (800/571-6463, www.zodiacadventures.com) runs whale-watching tours only, on a 24-foot Zodiac for $25 per person per hour.

EVENTS

The **Depoe Bay Classic Wooden Boat Show, Crab Feed, and Ducky Derby** is held the last weekend in April. Several dozen wooden craft, both restored and newly constructed vessels, ranging from kayaks to skiffs and dinghies to larger fishing boats, are displayed in the harbor and the adjacent Depoe Bay City Park. Rowing races, boat-building workshops, crab races, and other activities are scheduled. The big Crab Feed, held both Saturday and Sunday, 10 A.M.–5 P.M., sees some 1,500 pounds of crab, plus side dishes, devoured at the Community Hall; $14 for a full dinner. The Ducky Derby is a raffle in which you purchase "tickets" in the form of rubber duckies, which race down the harbor's feeder stream vying for prizes. Surprisingly, this event is the only such boat show we know of on the coast, which seems a great shame, given the role boats and ships have played in the history of the Oregon coast. For more information, contact the chamber of commerce.

The **Fleet of Flowers** happens each Memorial Day in the harbor to honor those lost at sea and in military service. More than 20,000 people come to witness a blanket of blossoms cast upon the waters.

The **Depoe Bay Salmon Bake** takes place on the third Saturday of September, 10 A.M.–5 P.M., at Depoe Bay City Park, flanking the rear of the boat basin. Some 3,000 pounds of fresh ocean fish are caught and cooked Native American style on alder stakes over an open fire and served with all the trimmings, to be savored to the accompaniment of live entertainment. Cost is $13–14 per adults, $7–8 children. It always seems to rain on the day of this event, but that's life on the Oregon coast.

PRACTICALITIES
Accommodations

Lodgings in popular Depoe Bay require advance reservations on most weekends and holidays. In a part of the coast brimming with lodging options, we see a need to list those that spectacularly highlight the major reasons to come here.

The **Surfrider Resort** (3115 N.W. U.S. 101, 541/764-2311 or 800/662-2378, www.surfrider-resort.com) is a few miles north of town on picturesque Fogarty Creek's rockbound coast. While it's been around for a while and is not too elaborate, its setting and other appeals mandate a mention. Prices run $69–139 (less in off-season) for oceanfront suites/rooms with decks; some feature whirlpool tubs, kitchens, and fireplaces. A good restaurant, an indoor pool, and midweek specials (two nights with breakfast, $159) also are noteworthy.

The **Inn at Arch Rock** (70 N.W. Sunset St., 800/767-1835, www.innatarchrock.com) comprises a cluster of white clapboard buildings that overlook the bay from their clifftop perch at the north end of town. Thirteen oceanfront rooms run $69–269; three two-bedroom condo units next door sleep six, for $199.

Located about three miles south of Depoe Bay, at one of the most scenic spots in the area (or anywhere on the central coast, for that matter), is the **Inn at Otter Crest** (301 Otter Crest Loop, Otter Rock, 541/765-2111 or 800/452-2101, www.innatottercrest.com), a condo resort perched close to the edge of the sandstone bluffs at the ocean's edge. Rates are $100–139; minimum two-night stay holidays and weekends. The Flying Dutchman dining room (see "Food," immediately following) faces 500-foot Cape Foulweather to the north and is a wonderful place to watch the sunset or scan the sea below for whales.

Gracie's Sea Hag Inn (235 S.E. Bay View Ave., 541/765-2322 or 800/228-0448, www .gracieslanding.com), a small inn overlooking the harbor, affords views of sea otters, ducks, and geese while the whale-watching and fishing boats come and go. All rooms have a harbor view; rates ($89–135) include a hot breakfast. Pets allowed.

The **Channel House** (35 Ellingson St., 541/765-2140 or 800/447-2140, www.channel-house.com) features three rooms and nine spacious suites boasting expansive dramatic views of the ocean, private decks with outdoor whirlpool tubs (in the majority of rooms), fireplaces, plush robes, and other amenities. This bluff-top B&B (there isn't a beach below, just miles of ocean and surrounding cliffs) may not look prepossessing from the outside, but inside the place is all windows and angles. Imagine *Architectural Digest* in a nautical theme. This is the best place in the country to commune with whales, passing boats, winter storms, and the setting sun. The fact that some of the suites can accommodate four people lays out the welcome mat for families (but no pets or young children) or friends and couples traveling together. A continental breakfast with tasty baked goods in an oceanside dining area is included in the rates ($90–260).

Food

Head to the locally popular **Gracie's Sea Hag Restaurant** (58 U.S. 101, 541/765-2734). Their seafood hors d'oeuvres (fried whitefish, scallops, oysters, smoked tuna, and boiled baby shrimp) give ample testimony to their claim that it's "seafood so fresh the ocean hasn't missed it yet." Another popular dish is salmon stuffed with crab and shrimp, baked in wine and herb butter. A lavish salad bar, a Friday night all-you-can-eat seafood buffet, and a recipe for clam chowder feted by the *New York Times* has also generated

local praise. Expect dinner prices in the $11–25 range.

Tidal Raves (279 N.W. U.S. 101, 541/765-2995) boasts the best views in town and a casual ambience. Tidal Raves is open for lunch and dinner with tasty food at moderate prices. In addition to fresh fish and other seafood dishes such as Thai prawns and oyster spinach bisque, the restaurant's pasta specialties are uniformly excellent. The Pasta Rave features crab, shrimp, lingcod, snapper, and more on a bed of linguine with pesto. The Dungeness crab casserole is also noteworthy. For dessert don't miss warm chocolate chunk cookie with Tillamook Vanilla Bean ice cream. Lunch prices are $5–10, dinner $10–18.

The **Spouting Horn** (541/765-2261), overlooking the harbor, serves breakfast, lunch, and dinner. Try their amazing deep-dish blackberry pie. Open Mon. 11:30 A.M.–9 P.M., Wed.–Sun. 8 A.M.–9 P.M.

The **Nautical Nook** (22 Bay St., 541/765-8999), located next door to Tradewinds fishing charters, is a full-service restaurant specializing in humongous burgers as well as seafood, pasta, and pizza. They also have an espresso bar and a beer and wine list. Open daily 6:30 A.M.–9 P.M. (hours may vary due to fishing season). What's unique about this hometown haunt is that they also deliver meals from Otter Rock to Salishan.

The **Flying Dutchman** (301 Otter Crest Loop, Otter Rock, 541/765-2111), located at the Inn at Otter Crest (see "Accommodations," immediately preceding) faces 500-foot-high Cape Foulweather to the north. Classical cuisine is served here at dinnertime, and more reasonably priced sandwiches and salads (less then $10) can be enjoyed at lunch. Breakfast is also served, beginning at 8 A.M., but the real highlight is the evening repast. Dinner favorites include the blackened prime rib and seafood fettuccine. The restaurant's bluffside aerie makes a great place to watch the sunset or look for whales.

Information and Transportation

On the east side of the highway, opposite the seawall, the **Depoe Bay Chamber of Commerce** (70 N.E. U.S. 101, Depoe Bay 97341, 541/765-

2889 or 877/485-8348, www.depoebaycham-ber.org), offers literature about the town and the central coast in general. Open weekdays 11 A.M.–3 P.M., weekends 9 A.M.–4.

The *Depoe Bay Beacon,* a tabloid published twice a month and sold locally for two bits, makes an interesting introduction to local goings-on. The police report will have you shaking your head in wonder.

Three north- and southbound **Greyhound** buses (800/231-2222) hit Depoe Bay each day. The southbound stops at the Fire Hall on U.S. 101 at the north end of town, whereas northbound coaches stop at Whistlestop Market, U.S. 101 and Schoolhouse Road, and Liberty Market (466 N.E. U.S. 101). On weekdays, **Lincoln County Transit** (541/265-4900, www.co.lincoln.or.us/transit/) runs buses four times daily, north to Lincoln City and south to Yachats.

Lincoln City

Back in 1964, five burgs that straddled seven miles of beachfront between Siletz Bay and the Salmon River came together and incorporated as Lincoln City. In commemoration, a 14-foot bronze statue of Abraham Lincoln was donated to the city by an Illinois sculptor. *The Lank Lawyer Reading in His Saddle While His Horse Grazes* originally occupied a city park; Governor Mark Hatfield and actor Raymond Massey, who had portrayed Honest Abe in a 1940 film, attended the dedication. Today the statue stands in a nondescript lot at N.E. 22nd and Quay Avenue. Look for the sign on U.S. 101 near the Dairy Queen pointing the way.

In the following decades, what were discrete towns have grown and melded into an uninterrupted conurbation with a population of about 6,800 (which can balloon to 30,000 on a busy weekend). While the resulting sprawl and "zoned commercial" signs can be maddening at times, the most visited town on the coast must be doing something right. Perhaps it's the proximity to Portland and Salem, or the area's two tribal-run casinos. Perhaps it's the long, broad sandy beach, or the superlative wildlife viewing around Siletz Bay. Or maybe it's the attraction of Devil's Lake State Park, a gem without equal among coastal freshwater playgrounds. Add prime kite-flying, some of the coast's better restaurants, and bibliophilic and antiquing haunts, and it's clear that there's more to the area than the pull of saltwater taffy and outlet malls.

SIGHTS AND RECREATION
The Beach
Lincoln City boasts seven uninterrupted miles of sandy beach, but you have to go looking for most of it. From Siletz Bay north to Road's End State Recreation Area, there are more than a dozen access points. You can head west from U.S. 101 on just about any side street to get there. High coastal bluffs lining the north-central portion of town, though, may mean a climb down (and back up) long flights of stairs cut into the cliff. For something approaching solitude on a crowded day, follow Logan Road west from the highway near the north end of town to **Road's End State Recreation Area**; tidepools and a secluded cove add to the allure. This stretch is popular with sailboarders.

Tidepool explorers should also check out the rock formations at S.W. 11th Street (Canyon Drive Park), N.W. 15th Street, and S.W. 32nd.

The **D River Wayside,** a small park on the beach in more or less the middle of town, is a state park property where you can watch what locals claim is the "world's shortest river" empty into the ocean. Flowing just 120 feet from its source, Devil's Lake, to its mouth at the Pacific, it's short, all right, and despite its unspectacular appearance, was a cause célèbre when *Guinness* withdrew the D's claim to fame in favor of a Montana waterway, the Roe. Local schoolkids rallied to the D's defense with an amended measurement, but the Roe, at a mere 53 feet long, carries the *Guinness* imprimatur as the most

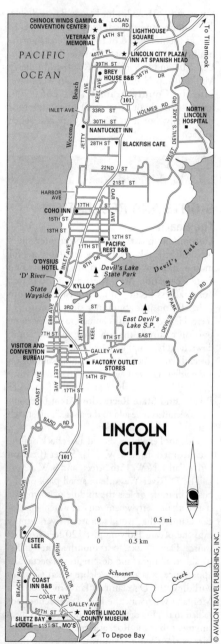

PACIFIC OCEAN

LINCOLN CITY

0   0.5 mi

0   0.5 km

To Tillamook

To Depoe Bay

diminutive stream. (Another bit of geographical trivia, "shortest river" is an unexpectedly hotly contested category, with partisans pushing their contenders in Texas, Arizona, and New Zealand.) In addition to seeing D River flow from "D" Lake into "D" ocean, you can fly a kite on the beach here. It's one of the easier beach-access points, between stretches of high, motel-topped bluffs, so it can get a little crowded here.

Another convenient beach-access point is off S.W. 51st Street at the south end of town, just before **Siletz Bay.** A large parking area here in what's known as the Taft District stands beside the driftwood-strewn shore of the bay, where you can often see a group of harbor seals chasing their dinner or coming in for a closer look at you. It's a short walk to the ocean.

Time was when it was common for storms and currents to wash up that ultimate beachcomber's prize—**glass fishing floats**—on the Oregon coast. Lincoln City improves the beachcomber's odds by distributing over 2,000 glass floats along its beaches October–Memorial Day. Handcrafted by Northwest glass artists, each of the colorful floats is signed and numbered, and placed by volunteers on the beaches above the high-tide line. If you find one, you can call or stop in at the visitors center for a certificate and information about the artist who created it.

Devil's Lake

Devil's Lake, just east of town, is the recreation center of Lincoln City. In addition to windsurfing and hydroplaning, eight species of fish can be caught here, including catfish, yellow perch, crappie, largemouth bass, and trout. Chinese grass carp were introduced to the lake to help control the rampant aquatic weeds. There's also good bird-watching on and around this shallow, 678-acre lake, which attracts flocks of migratory geese, ducks, and other waterfowl. Species to look for include canvasbacks, Canada geese, widgeons, gadwalls, grebes, and mallards. Bald eagles and ospreys also nest in the trees bordering the lake.

The lake takes its name from a local Native American legend. The story tells that when Siletz warriors paddled a canoe across the lake one moonlit night, a tentacled beast erupted from

CASCADE HEAD SCENIC RESEARCH AREA

About 10 miles north of Lincoln City, the 11,890-acre Cascade Head Experimental Forest was set aside in 1934 for scientific study of typical coastal Sitka spruce and western hemlock forests found along the Oregon coast. In 1974, Congress established the 9,670-acre Cascade Head Scenic Research Area, which includes the western half of the forest, several prairie headlands, and the Salmon River estuary. In 1980, the entire area was designated a Biosphere Reserve as part of the United Nations Biosphere Reserve system.

The headlands, reaching as high as 1,800 feet, are unusual for their extensive prairies still dominated by native grasses: red fescue, wild rye, and Pacific reedgrass. The people of the Nechesney tribe, who inhabited the area as long as 12,000 years ago, purposely burned forest tracts around Cascade Head to provide browse for deer and to reduce the possibility of larger, uncontrollable blazes. In contrast to these grasslands, the northern part of the headland is the domain of giant spruces and firs because it catches the brunt of the heavy rainfalls and lingering fogs. Endemic wildflowers include coastal paintbrush, goldenrod, streambank lupine, rare hairy checkermallow, and blue violet, a plant critical to the survival of the Oregon silverspot butterfly, a threatened species found in only six locations. Deer, elk, coyote, snowshoe hare, and the Pacific giant salamander find refuge here, while bald eagles, great horned owls, and peregrine falcons may be seen hunting above the grassy slopes.

On the north side of the Salmon River, turn west from U.S. 101 onto **Three Rocks Road** for a scenic driving detour on the south side of Cascade Head. The paved road curves about 2.5 miles above the wetlands and widening channel of the Salmon River estuary, passes Savage Road, and ends at a parking area and boat launch at Knight County Park. From the park, the road turns to gravel and narrows (not suitable for RVs or trailers) and continues another half mile to its end at a spectacular overlook across the estuary.

Not surprisingly, the area is a mecca for some 6,000 hikers annually and for anglers who target the salmon and steelhead runs on the Salmon River. The **Cascade Head Trail** runs six miles roughly parallel to the highway, with a south trailhead near the intersection of Three Rocks Road and U.S. 101 and a north trailhead at Falls Creek, on U.S. 101 about a mile south of Neskowin. It passes through old-growth forest and offers coastal views near its north end.

A short but brisk hike to the top of the headland on a **Nature Conservancy trail** begins near Knight County Park. Leave your car at the park and walk about a half mile up Savage Road to the trailhead. It's 1.7 miles one way, with a 1,100-foot elevation gain. No dogs or bicycles allowed on the trail.

About three miles north of Three Rocks Road, gravel Cascade Head Road (Forest Service Road 1861), leads four miles west of U.S. 101 to the **Hart's Cove trailhead.** The first part of the trail runs through arching red alder treetops and 250-year-old Sitka spruces with five-foot diameters. The understory of mosses and ferns is nourished by 100-inch rainfalls. Next, the trail emerges into open grasslands. The hilly, five-mile round-trip hike finally leads to an oceanfront meadow overlooking Hart's Cove, where the barking of sea lions might greet you. This trail can be muddy, so boots are recommended to tromp through the rainforest. Note: the trail is closed Jan. 15–July 15.

© MARK MORRIS

Cascade Head and the Salmon River estuary, north of Lincoln City

COASTAL OREGON

the still water and pulled the men under. It's said that boaters today who cross the moon's reflection in the middle of the lake tempt the same fate, but the lake's devil has remained silent for years.

Of the five access points, East Devil's Lake Road off U.S. 101 northeast of town offers a scenic route around the lake's east side before rejoining U.S. 101 near the day-use portion of the state park at the south end of the lake. To reach the camping area of **Devil's Lake State Recreation Area,** take N.E. 6th Drive east from U.S. 101, about a quarter mile north of the D River. The day-use area has a boat ramp, while there's a moorage dock across the lake adjacent to the campground. See "Camping," later in this section.

Mountain bikes, canoes, and paddleboats can be rented at the **Blue Heron Landing** (4006 W. Devil's Lake Rd., Lincoln City 97367, 541/994-4708).

Casinos

One of the biggest draws in town is the **Chinook Winds Casino** (1777 N.W. 44th St., Lincoln City, 541/996-5825 or 888/244-6665, www.chinookwindscasino.com), operated by the Confederated Tribes of Siletz Indians, near the north end of town. In addition to slots, blackjack, poker, keno, bingo, craps, and roulette, the casino has two on-site restaurants and a busy schedule of big-name (or formerly big-name) entertainment. Recent shows, for example, have included the Beach Boys, George Carlin, and Don McLean. Open daily, 24 hours.

About 25 miles east of Lincoln City is the state's number one visitor attraction, **Spirit Mountain Casino** (P.O. Box 39, Grand Ronde 97347, 800/760-7977, http://spiritmountain.com), operated by the Confederated Tribes of Grand Ronde. In 2002, the casino drew 3.3 million people. Games of chance include slots, craps, blackjack, poker, keno, and bingo. It's open every day, 24 hours.

North Lincoln County Historical Museum

This modest museum (4907 S.W. U.S. 101, 541/996-6614) tells the story of this area through

exhibits of old-time logging machinery, homesteading tools, fishing, military life, and Native American history. Check out the early fashion mannequins and a World War II mine that washed ashore. It's open Tues.–Sat. noon–4 P.M. Admission is free.

Camping

Several wilderness retreats are worth noting in the Lincoln City area. One remote escape is at **Van Duzer Wayside,** about 12 miles east of town on ORE 18, which offers a dozen primitive (and free) hiker/biker sites in a beautiful forest near the Salmon River.

More free rustic sites can be found about eight miles north of town and just south of Neskowin. To get there, look for the "Scenic Drive" sign east of U.S. 101 and follow County Road 12 for four miles. From there, travel about 100 yards west on Forest Service Road 12131 and you'll see the campground set along **Neskowin Creek.** To find out about the trails in the surrounding rainforest, contact the Siuslaw National Forest in Hebo (541/392-3161). The campground is open mid-April–mid-October. Bring your own water or water-purification kit. The nearby scenic drive continues up into an area of huge trees captioned by forest service placards explaining the ecology.

More elaborate camping is available at **Devil's Lake State Park** (1452 N.E. 6th St., Lincoln City, information 541/994-2002, reservations 800/452-5687) with 68 tent sites and 32 RV sites with full hookups. Amenities include showers, a café, and a laundry. The fee is $17–21 per night, $29 for yurts, $4 for hiker/biker spaces, mid-April–late October. This campground is just off U.S. 101 at the northeast end of town, between the ocean and Devil's Lake.

Devil's Lake RV Park (4041 N.E. West Devil's Lake Rd., 541/994-3400), near Lakeside Golf, has 80 paved sites with full hookups ($17–21); no tent camping.

Golf and Tennis

At the north end of town, 18-hole **Lakeside Golf Club** (3245 N.E. 50th St., 541/994-8442) charges $30 for a full day, $18 for nine holes.

Serious devotees can head seven miles south to **Westin Salishan Golf Links** (U.S. 101, Gleneden Beach, 541/764-3632 or 800/890-8037) to play the award-winning 18-hole course set in the foothills of the Coast Range and bordered by Siletz Bay and the sea. The green fees for 18 holes are $75–95 May–Oct., $55 the rest of the year, and cart rental is $20. Keep in mind that this is a Scottish-links course, where the roughs are really rough.

Tennis players can enjoy the public outdoor courts at N.W. 28th. These are about half the price at the Salishan (541/764-3633), which averages about $15 per person for a 75-minute set.

ENTERTAINMENT AND EVENTS

Eden Hall

Housed within the renovated Gleneden Brick and Tile Factory, five miles south of Lincoln City in Gleneden Beach, Eden Hall (6645 Gleneden Beach Loop Rd., 541/764-3826 for performance info, 541/764-3825 for restaurant, www.edenhall.com) stages live theater and hosts an impressively eclectic roster of regional and touring musicians. This spacious, airy warehouse has an excellent sound system and is a wonderful place to take in a concert, with an emphasis on jazz, folk, and blues. Enjoy dinner at the adjacent Side Door Café (see "Food," later in this section).

Theater and Movies

Lincoln City's homegrown theater company, **Theatre West** (3536 S.E. U.S. 101, 541/994-5663, www.theatrewest.com), stages a half-dozen productions each year, with an emphasis on comedies, plus musicals and drama.

Catch first-run flicks at the **Bijou Theatre** (1624 N.E. U.S. 101, 541/994-8255), an old-time movie house dating back to the 1930s, making it a rare old survivor around here. The six-screen **Regal Cinemas** (3755 S.E. High School Dr., 541/994-7649), just east of 101 in the south end of town, is its modern competitor.

Festivals

A novel way to shake off the winter doldrums of mid-January is at the **Crustacean Classics,** a three-day weekend event combining a chowder cook-off, wine-tasting, and live crab races. A kids' food-sculpting competition, beverage-serving contest, live music, and crab luncheon add to the fun, held at the Factory Stores at Lincoln City (1500 S.E. East Devil's Lake Rd., 541/996-5000). Admission is $5 per person, or $10 for a family of four.

Lincoln City calls itself the kite capital of the world, pointing to its position midway between the pole and the equator, which gives the area predictable wind patterns. The town holds not one but two kite fiestas at the D River Wayside each year. The spring **Kite Festival** takes place the first weekend in May; the fall festival is held the third weekend in September (541/994-3070 or 800/452-2151, in Oregon). The event is famous for giant spin socks, some as long as 150 feet.

The **Cascade Head Chamber Music Festival** (P.O. Box 605, Lincoln City 97367, 541/994-5333 or 877/994-5333, www.cascadeheadmusic.org) is another Oregon kulturfest that brings together world-class artists in an informal setting. Events are hosted at St. Peter the Fisherman Lutheran Church (1226 S.W. 13th St., 541/994-2007), under the direction of Sergiu Luca, a famed violinist who draws on decades of international experience and the friendship of virtuosi who fly in from all corners of the globe to make music on the Oregon coast. Old World artists such as Beethoven and Brahms as well as contemporary composers are featured in a series of June concerts (usually two a week over several weeks). To order tickets, contact the festival ticket office (541/994-5333), or get them at the gallery in Salishan or the Lincoln City Visitor and Convention Bureau. Tickets run around $15 and may not always be available at the door.

Lincoln City's popular **Sandcastle Building Contest** happens the first Saturday in August, off S.W. 51st, in the historic Taft District alongside Siletz Bay. Call 541/996-3800 for details.

PRACTICALITIES

Accommodations

Of the cheek-by-jowl selection of lodgings in Lincoln City, we're partial to the hotels at the

WESTIN SALISHAN LODGE

When asked to choose *the* place to stay on the Oregon coast, most Oregonians would recommend the Westin Salishan Lodge (7760 N. U.S. 101, Gleneden Beach, 541/764-2371 or 888/SALISHAN, www.salishanlodge.com). Named for a widespread native dialect in the Oregon Territory, this former Westin resort a couple of miles south of Lincoln City is one of a dozen properties in the nation that consistently receives a four-star as well as a five-diamond rating. Almost every year, *Condé Nast Traveler* rates Salishan one of the country's top resorts.

Strictly speaking, the resort is more of a Coast Range mountain lodge than a beach resort. While there are distant Siletz Bay views, most folks quickly learn to appreciate the peace of the forest and golf course here. This paradigm shift is facilitated by art and landscape architecture that convey the vision of John Gray, who built Salishan and such other Northwest properties as Skamania and Sunriver from native materials with respect for the surrounding environment. After making a fortune from the chainsaw business, Gray decided to leave more of a legacy than just stumps.

Even if you don't stay here, the grounds and facilities are worth a look. The art gallery is free and features works by top Oregon artists (also check out master woodcarver Leroy Setziol's bas-relief panels in the dining room). The forested trails behind the golf course (rated among the top 75 in the United States) showcase the rainforested foothills of the Coast Range and the waterfowl near Siletz Bay. Across the street, the Salishan Marketplace features first-rate galleries and a good bookstore, Allegory Books.

The Salishan fetches high prices, $215–365 in summer (as low as $119–295 other times of year for rack rates), attracting well-heeled nature lovers, corporate expense-account clientele, folks enjoying a special occasion, and serious golfers. You'll also find everyday folks and seminar attendees on winter weekend specials at half the summertime rates. Ask about multiday packages for big savings on your room rate.

In addition to the recreational and aesthetic appeal of the resort, the Dining Room (see "Food," later in this section) contributes to Salishan's lofty reputation.

south end of town and near Siletz Bay. While the views are not always expansive, the beachfront isn't as crowded here as it is from the D River north, and you're far from casino traffic. If you want something closer to the gaming tables, there are more than 1,000 other rooms in this town.

The **Ester Lee** (3803 S.W. U.S. 101, 541/996-3606 or 888/996-3606, www.esterlee.com) is a decades-old family motel complex along with some cottages on a bluff above miles of beachfront. All rooms have ocean views and fireplaces and some have kitchens and Jacuzzis. Pets are allowed. It's nothing fancy, but good value for the money. Rates run $46–151, depending on the season and day of the week.

Another pet-friendly place, the **Coho Inn** (1635 N.W. Harbor, 541/994-3684 or 800/848-7006, www.thecohoinn.com) has 50 oceanfront units with fireplaces, kitchens, and continental breakfast. Studios range $60–136; family suites $84–167; extra for pets.

If you've been fantasizing about rolling out of bed, slipping on your robe—coffee in hand—and walking out onto a semi-private stretch of beach, then the **Inn at Spanish Head** (4009 S.W. U.S. 101, 541/996-2161 or 800/452-8127, www.spanishhead.com) may be your best bet. Oregon's only resort hotel right on the beach, the inn takes its place—large and looming—against the backdrop of rugged cliffs. Whether in a suite, studio, or bedroom unit, every room has an ocean view. On-site amenities include Fathoms, the 10th-floor restaurant/bar (see "Food," later in this section), a fireplace lounge, meeting rooms, heated outdoor pool, saunas, spa, and exercise room. Rates start at around $84, with discounts for longer stays.

With five newer units, the **Nantucket Inn** (3135 N.W. Inlet Ave., 541/996-9300, www.thenantucketinn.com) provides guests with oceanfront accommodations just steps from the beach; some rooms come equipped with kitchens,

Jacuzzis, and fireplaces. Continental breakfast is served. Off-season special rates from $99–139.

For a small luxury hotel where golf is not the focus, the **O'dysius Hotel** (120 N.W. Inlet Court, 541/994-4121 or 800/869-8069, www.odysius.com) offers 30 ocean-view units furnished with period antiques. Guests meet in the lobby every afternoon to sample Oregon wine. The hotel accepts pets, provides concierge and massage, and a continental breakfast. Wheelchair accessible. Rates range $149–311.

The **Siletz Bay Lodge** (1012 S.W. 51st St., 541/996-6111 or 888/430-2100, www.siletzbaylodge.com), on the north end of Siletz Bay on a driftwood-strewn beach, is a family-friendly and wheelchair-accessible (with elevators) lodging in a location ideal for bird-watching and viewing seals. About half of the standard rooms have balconies, with delightful views of the bay and the sun going down over Salishan Spit. Spa rooms and spa suites are also available if you happen to be in town for a romantic getaway. Such in-room amenities as microwaves, refrigerators, and coffee makers abound, and a continental breakfast (7–10 A.M.) is included in the rates (summer $79–155; three-night minimum stay on holidays).

Bed-and-Breakfasts

Lincoln City has its share of B&Bs from which to choose. Close to the beach, **Brey House B&B** (3725 N.W. Keel Ave., 541/994-7123, www.breyhouse.com) is one of the oldest B&Bs on the Oregon coast. Shirley Brey has owned the 1940-built three-story Cape Cod–style home with four bedrooms (all private baths and entrances) for 16 years. Be sure to sample their excellent breakfast, which is served in a light-filled room overlooking the ocean. Not appropriate for children. Rates $85–165.

The light and bright **Coast Inn B&B** (4507 S.W. Coast Ave., 541/994-7932 or 888/994-7932, www.oregoncoastinn.com) offers non-smoking guestrooms and a hot breakfast in a sprawling Craftsman-style home located in historic Taft heights, south of Spanish Head. Siletz Bay is a short walk away, as is public beach access. Entirely remodeled in 2001, this home features

comfortable new furnishings and homey decor; rates range $95–125.

Pacific Rest B&B (1611 N.E. 11th St., 541/994-2337) is a newer home with large suites, located on a hillside just above U.S. 101. If you have younger children and want the B&B experience, this is your best bet, as owners Ray and Judy Waetjen welcome the young'uns. Rates $100–175.

The **Salmonberry B&B** has three guest accommodations and is located in a coastal woodland, just a short walk from the southern edges of Siletz Bay. Each individually decorated room has a queen bed, down comforter, sitting area, private bath, and TV/VCR. Room rates ($150–175) include breakfast, complimentary evening wine and cheese, and the unlimited use of all guest spa facilities, including heated indoor swimming pool, sauna, and whirlpool bath.

To rent vacation homes throughout Lincoln County, contact the **Lincoln City Visitor and Convention Bureau** (800/452-2151). Or, try **Pacific Retreats** (3126-A N.E. U.S. 101, 800/473-4833, www.pacificretreats.com), which features a selection of vacation home rentals.

Food

Surprisingly, Lincoln City offers many affordable and palate-pleasing dining options. Some of the best are located near the north end of town. South of the D River (city center), there's a cluster of pricier gourmet eateries that merit special consideration.

Despite a coastal gourmet restaurant row between Depoe Bay and Lincoln City where dinner tabs match those of Portland's upscale restaurants, economical yet tasty options do exist here as exemplified by the **Kernville Steak and Seafood House** (186 Siletz Hwy., Kernville, 541/994-6200). Besides decent food at a good value, this place looks out on the river and surrounding hills through huge picture windows. Blue heron and deer are frequent dinner companions, but the real attractions are the half-dozen nightly seafood specials showcasing fresh-caught shellfish and premium aged beef. Finding this dinner house is tricky because of its inconspicuous facade on the south side of the

COASTAL OREGON

river. Head one mile south of Lincoln City, on the Siletz Highway just east of U.S. 101.

If coastal restaurants are eating a hole in your wallet, there's always tried-and-true **Mo's** (860 S.W. 51st St., 541/996-2535). As usual, count on good clam chowder and full fish dinners as well as superlative views of the water. **Figaro's Pizza** (4095 N.W. Logan Rd., 541/994-4443) offers family dining options such as pizza, lasagna, and salad. Open for lunch and dinner, with reasonable prices.

The best smoked fish in these parts can be had at **Barnacle Bill's Seafood Store** (2174 U.S. 101, 541/994-3022). The smoked sturgeon here is half the price it is on the East Coast, and although it's not thin-sliced New York deli style, it has a more delicate flavor. Look for a little storefront on the east side of the highway in the middle of town.

Kyllo's (1110 N.W. 1st Ct., 541/994-3179) specializes in broiled, sautéed, and baked seafood, plus excellent homemade desserts. The former can be washed down by Oregon microbrews and wines. Seafood dinners are in the $20–30 range, and lunch is often about half that. Locals say they've had good luck with the "specials," which are new and different every night. The restaurant is visible from U.S. 101 as you drive by the D River Wayside. With views of the water on all sides, this restaurant is a good place to linger. Avoid peak dining hours because no reservations are taken.

The reasonable prices at the Salishan Lodge's **Cedar Tree** (see special topic "Westin Salishan Lodge" under "Accommodations," earlier in this section) are a welcome surprise. This casual restaurant might be less elaborate and half the price of Salishan's five-star Dining Room, but its Northwest cuisine comes from the same kitchen. Complete breakfasts won't lighten the wallet too much. For a few pennies more, the hot smoked chinook salmon hash is a highlight. Affordable lunch-time specialties include oyster stew and a Reuben sandwich. For dinner, splurge on the potlatch salmon or an Angus New York strip steak. With a window on Siletz Bay, you don't even have to dress up or make reservations. The Cedar Tree also hosts popular Friday seafood buffets in summer.

At the Salishan's **Dining Room** (800/452-2300) special emphasis is placed on seasonal seafood, game, and other regional delicacies. Dinner here can be quite pricey, but the elegance of the setting, expansive wine list, and creative dishes have long made this a coastal dining destination. Consistently touted as one of the top three restaurants in the state, it has become famous for its creative interpretations of seasonal Northwest delicacies and a 12,000-bottle wine cellar (famous for the world's largest collection of Oregon pinot noir).

A half mile south of Salishan (five miles equidistant from Depoe Bay and Lincoln City) are two other Gleneden Beach eateries with considerable appeal. The **Side Door Cafe** (6675 Gleneden Beach Loop, 541/764-3825) combines a gourmet restaurant with a musical venue. The airy yet cozy-feeling dining room features a menu where rock spring rolls, bouillabaise, and parmesan-encrusted halibut exemplify the menu offerings. The adjoining state-of-the-art Eden Hall theater might feature a Northwest artist with a national reputation, such as jazz singer Nancy King or Portland-based Delta blues artist Kelly Joe Phelps.

The **Bay House** (5911 S.W. U.S. 101, 541/996-3222, www.bayhouserestaurant.com) is a place food critics describe as "intimate" and "elegant." You might also add "expensive." Local gourmets will tell you, however, that the Dungeness crab with artichoke hearts and spinach and the rack of lamb are well worth the price. Oenophiles will want to look at the wine list praised by *Wine Spectator*. The tab at the Bay House is definitely worth it—especially if you're fortunate to be dining in view of the sunset over Siletz Bay. The seasonally changing menu is posted on their website.

Cafe Roma Bookstore and Coffeehouse (1437 N.W. U.S. 101, 541/994-6616) brings an air of refinement to Lincoln City. Fresh home-baked pastries and desserts, fresh-roasted gourmet coffees and espresso drinks, as well as a collection of interesting books make this a wonderful retreat on a cold and drizzly day.

The **Blackfish Cafe** (2733 N.W. U.S. 101, 541/996-1007) also has managed to be included in the shortlist of prime coastal dining destinations. The reason is chef Rob Pounding, whose use of local produce and fresh products enabled Salishan to scale the culinary heights in the previous decade. This orientation is repeated in this beach bistro with a menu that might feature Willamette Valley pork in huckleberry compote and troll-caught chinook salmon with Oregon blue cheese mashed potatoes. In addition to the emphasis on fresh, homegrown, and creative, there is no shortage of humbler fare such as the self-proclaimed "best" clam chowder on the coast and halibut fish-n-chips.

The **Lighthouse Brew Pub** (4157 U.S. 101 North, 541/994-7238) is a welcome rehash of the McMenamin formula so successful in the Willamette Valley. Just look for a lighthouse replica in a parking lot on the northwest side of 101 across from McDonald's. Pizza bread, burgers, sandwiches, and chili can be washed down by McMenamin's own ales or some other quality brew, as well as hard cider and wine. Live music at night is an added plus.

Heading north, **Dory Cove Restaurant** (5819 Logan Rd., 541/994-5180), near Road's End State Park, has prices that are a little higher than Mo's, but the range of broiled seafood entrées (halibut fish-n-chips recommended), chowder, and salmonburger/oysterburger/cheeseburger fantasies make this place an overwhelming favorite with locals. Open daily noon–8 P.M.

If you're en route to the wine country or the Willamette Valley or just want a respite from resort traffic, a place that appeals to everybody is **Otis Cafe** (1259 Salmon River Hwy., 541/994-9560), at the Otis Junction on ORE 18 two miles east of U.S. 101. Here, innovative variations on American road food have been warmly embraced by everyone from local loggers to yuppies (and *New York Times* food critics) stopping off on the drive between Portland and the coast. In September, salmon-fishing devotees can be seen lining up here at 6:30 A.M. Breakfast in this unpretentious café, five miles northeast of Lincoln City, is such an institution that long waits on the porch are the rule on weekend mornings. The reasons why include the thick-crusted molasses bread that comes with many orders,

buttermilk waffles, and their legendary hash browns under melted Rogue Valley white cheddar. A half portion for one dollar less is the equivalent of all-you-can-eat fare, so walk the beach at Neskowin before tackling the unabridged version. Large portions, low prices, and a culinary touch that turns pork chops and rhubarb pie into epicurean delights are in full evidence at lunch and dinner.

Information and Transportation

A little south of the D River, the helpful **Lincoln City Visitor and Convention Bureau** (801 S.W. U.S. 101, 541/994-8378 or 800/452-2151) is open Mon.–Fri. 9 A.M.–5 P.M., Saturday 9 A.M.–5 P.M., and Sunday 10 A.M.–4 P.M. **Driftwood Public Library** (541/996-2277) is in the same municipal complex.

The **Central Oregon Coast Association** (541/265-2064 or 800/767-2064, www.coastvisitor.com) maintains a useful website with details on Lincoln City and the rest of coastal Lincoln County.

The **Traveler's Convenience Center** (660 S.E. U.S. 101), a mile south of the D River, has a coin-operated laundry. The **post office** (541/994-2128) is two blocks east of U.S. 101 on East Devil's Lake Road.

For those who can't resist the urge to surf (the Internet, that is), the **B&B Package Express** (960 S.E. U.S. 101, 541/994-7272), though not technically a cyber café, is a place to get online. They also have fax, copying, and shipping services, and a notary public. Rates are $6 per hour, with a $3 minimum. Open Mon.–Saturday.

Also in town, the **Cyber Garden and Tea House** (1826 N.E. U.S. 101, 541/994-3067) hosts five workstations with DSL connection along with numerous connections for personal laptops. They offer a few other electronic services as well, such as printing, copying, faxing, and scanning. A comfy place with stuffed chairs, they serve coffee, tea, and pastries. Rates runs $9 hourly or $5 per half hour. Open daily.

Lincoln City–bound travelers from Portland (via 99W) and Salem (via ORE 22) pass through the scenic wine and orchard country to connect with ORE 18. This is one of the most dangerous roads to drive in the state, so extra care is called for on this two-laner.

Peak traffic times in Lincoln City can result in 25,000 cars a day crawling through town. As an alternative to rush hour on U.S. 101, you could try detouring on N.E. West Devil's Lake Road or N.E. East Devil's Lake Road, which bypass the worst congestion.

Greyhound (800/231-2222) and **Lincoln County Transit** (541/265-4900, www.co.lincoln.or.us/transit/) buses stop in town. The latter line goes as far south as Yachats; weekday service only, closed major holidays.

For car rentals, contact **Robben Rent a Car** (3244 N.E. U.S. 101). For a list of car-rental agencies on the coast and elsewhere in Oregon, check www.american-car.net/car-rental/OR/.

Three Capes Scenic Loop

The Three Capes Scenic Loop, a 35-mile byway off U.S. 101 between Pacific City and Tillamook, is considered by many to be the preeminent scenic area on the north coast. While the beauty of Capes Kiwanda, Lookout, and Meares certainly justifies leaving the main highway, it would be an overstatement to portray this drive as a thrill-a-minute detour on the order of the south coast's Boardman Park or the central coast's Otter Crest Loop. Instead of fronting the ocean, the road connecting the capes winds mostly through dairy country, small beach towns, and second-growth forest. What's special here are the three capes themselves, and unless you get out of the car and walk on the trails, you'll miss the aesthetic appeal and distinctiveness of each headland's ecosystem. The wave-battered bluffs of Cape Kiwanda, the precipitous overlooks along the Cape Lookout Highway, and the curious Octopus Tree at Cape Meares are the perfect antidotes to the inland towns along U.S. 101. The majority of the Three Capes lodging and dining options are clustered in Pacific City and at the other end in Netarts and Oceanside. In between, it's mostly sand dunes, isolated beaches, rainforest, and pasture.

CAPE KIWANDA

North of Neskowin, U.S. 101 passes through pastoral landscapes befitting Tillamook County's nickname, "The Land of Cheese, Trees, and Ocean Breeze." If you've tasted Tillamook ice cream or award-winning cheddar cheese,

chances are the mere sight of the cows grazing on the lush grasses here will have you thinking about your next meal. The trees and ocean breeze components begin to take form on the Three Capes Scenic Loop turnoff (Brooten Road) about eight miles north of Neskowin. The route leads a couple of miles along Nestucca Bay and the Nestucca River, one of the best salmon and steelhead streams in the state. Strong runs of spring and fall chinook on the Nestucca and the Little Nestucca rivers can yield lunkers above 50 pounds.

As you approach the shore in Pacific City, the sight of **Haystack Rock** will immediately grab your attention. At 327 feet, this sea stack is nearly 100 feet taller than the like-named rock in Cannon Beach. Standing a mile offshore, this monolith has a brooding, enigmatic quality that constantly draws the eye to it. Look closely, and you'll understand why some folks called it Teacup Rock.

The tawny sandstone escarpment of Cape Kiwanda juts a half mile out to sea, framing the north end of the beach. In storm-tossed waters, this cape is the undisputed king of rock and roll if you go by coffee-table books and calendar photos. While other sandstone promontories on the north coast have been ground into sandy beaches by the pounding surf, it's been theorized that Kiwanda has endured thanks to the buffer of Haystack Rock. In any case, hang-gliding aficionados are glad the cape is here. They scale its shoulders and set themselves aloft off the north face to glide above the beach and dunes.

PACIFIC CITY

This small town of about 1,000 at the base of Cape Kiwanda attracts growing numbers of vacationers and retirees, but remains true to its 19th-century origins as a working fishing village. In addition to the knockout seascapes and recreation, if you come here at the right times of day you may be treated to a unique spectacle—the launch or return of the **dory fleet.**

It's a tradition dating back to the 1920s, when gillnetting was banned on the Nestucca River to protect the dwindling salmon runs. To retain their livelihood, commercial fishermen began to haul flat-bottomed, double-ended dories down to the beach on horse-drawn wagons, then rowed out through the surf to fish. These days, trucks and trailers get the boats to and from the beach, and outboard motors have replaced oar power, enabling the dories to get 50 miles out to sea. If you come here around 6 A.M., you can watch them taking off. The fleet's late afternoon return attracts a crowd that comes to see the dory operators skidding their crafts as far as possible up the beach to the waiting boat trailers. Others meet the dories to buy salmon and tuna direct.

In late July, the **Dory Festival** celebrates the area's fleet. The three-day fete includes craft and food booths, a pancake breakfast, a fishing derby, and other activities. Visitors also have the opportunity to ride out through the surf in a dory, for about $10 per person. For more information, call the chamber of commerce (503/965-6161). If you want to join the fishermen other times of

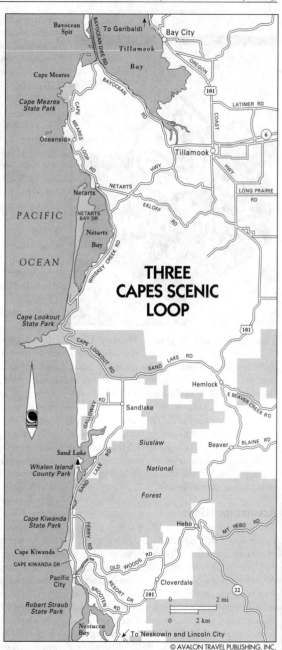

COASTAL OREGON

© MARK MORRIS

year, contact the **Haystack Fishing Club** (888/965-7555), across from the beach near the Inn at Cape Kiwanda, where you can book with Joe Hay, the only licensed dory outfitter in the world. Troll for salmon or lingcod, whale-watch, or just enjoy the ride.

In addition, the Pacific City area is besieged by surfers, who enjoy some of the longest waves on the Oregon coast. **Robert Straub State Park,** just south of town, offers access to Nestucca Bay and to the dunes and a long uninterrupted stretch of beach.

Accommodations

The nicest motel on the Three Capes Loop is the **Inn at Cape Kiwanda** (33105 Cape Kiwanda Dr., Pacific City, 503/965-6366 and 888/965-7001, www.innatcapekiwanda.com). All rooms face a beautiful beach and Cape Kiwanda's giant sand dune. If it's too rainy to go outside, fireplaces and spacious well-appointed rooms make for great storm-watching. Most rooms range $159–299 during summer (prices drop to $109–219 Nov.–April 30); inquire about

special packages that offer discounts on rooms as well as meals at Pelican Brewpub across the road. Whirlpool tub rooms are available here and pets are permitted in some rooms.

Five blocks from the beach, the **Inn at Pacific City** (35215 Brooten Rd., Pacific City 97135, 503/965-6366 or 888/722-2489) is a low-slung, shingle-clad compound where rooms run $78–85 May–October, half that the rest of the year. Across the street, at the **Pacific City Inn** (35280 Brooten Rd., 503/965-6464 or 866/567-3466), rooms fetch $79–95 in summer ($49–65 off-season), with two-room suites for $119–139 in summer. Both of these motels allow pets for an additional $9 nightly.

Food

Our advice is to fill up your tummy in Pacific City before heading north on the sparsely populated Capes Loop. While a few outlets of undistinguished diner food might keep you alive until Oceanside, the other outpost of civilization on the north end of the Loop, the Capes' midsection is more a feast for the eyes.

Los Caporales (35025 Brooten Rd., 503/965-6999) serves up bountiful plates of Mexican food and seafood; the combination plates ($7–10) could feed several people. The restaurant's name refers to foremen at a cattle ranch, perhaps explaining portions fit for wrangler-sized appetites. Open Wed.–Sun. at 11 A.M.

If hanging plants, a piano, and Nestucca River frontage don't make you feel at home, the apple pie and other wholesome fare at the **Riverhouse** (34450 Brooten Rd., Pacific City, 503/965-6722) probably will. The burgers and open-face sandwich combinations are priced on the high side ($9–13) but are the perfect pick-me-ups after a morning of fishing or beachcombing along the Nestucca River estuary. Dinners (most around $20) focus on fish and shellfish. Steamer clams simmered in vermouth make a hearty starter. Or try a salad with the sweet blue cheese dressing, which has enough of a following throughout western Oregon that it's sold in regional supermarkets. Weekends feature the eclectic offerings of live musicians on Saturday night and a wonderful

Sunday brunch. Come early, as seating is limited in this 11-table restaurant.

Close by, at the **Grateful Bread Bakery** (34085 Brooten Rd., 503/965-7337), the challah, carrot cake, marionberry strudel, and other homemade baked goods deserve special mention. The full breakfast menu offers a range of tasty omelettes, served with oven-roasted spuds at great prices. Lunch here might include thin crust New York–style pizza paying homage to the owners' East Coast roots, Tillamook cheese chowder, or dilled shrimp salad sandwich. You can do breakfast or lunch well here for little more than $7. Dinners feature dory-caught cod prepared breaded and grilled or blackened, plus salmon, chicken, and steak. Open Thurs.–Mon. 8 A.M.–8:30 P.M.

A popular and well-known Pacific City hangout is the **Pelican Pub and Brewery** (33180 Cape Kiwanda Dr., Pacific City, 503/965-7007, www.pelicanbrewery.com). Set in a most enviable spot right on the beach opposite Cape Kiwanda and Haystack Rock, this place boasts the best coastal view of any brewpub in Oregon. Halibut fish-n-chips, gourmet pizzas, steamed clams, BBQ pork ribs, and hazelnut-crusted salmon are some of the standouts. The pub's brews, including Tsunami Stout, Dory-man's Dark Ale, India Pelican Ale, and MacPelican's Scottish Style Ale, have garnered stacks of awards.

CAPE LOOKOUT

The scenic route continues north from Pacific City on Cape Drive about six miles to the hamlet of Sandlake. Extensive sand dunes surrounding the Sand Lake estuary here suddenly transition to the rainforested slopes on top of the nearby Cape Lookout. The dunes and beach attract squadrons of dune buggy enthusiasts. Camping is available year-round at Sand Beach Campground (Galloway Road, 877/444-6777), which has basic sites for tenters and RVs. This dramatic area is popular, too, with hikers. **Into The Sunset** (503/965-6326) organizes personalized guided horseback excursions; the "full moon ride" is highly recommended.

A couple miles farther north, look for the large parking area for the 2.5-mile trail to the tip of Cape Lookout. An orientation map at the trailhead details the trail options. Two trails go down to the water's edge, while the trailhead at the northwest corner of the parking lot leads out to land's end. The 2.5-mile-long, one-mile-wide cape juts out from the coast so that hikers feel like they're on the prow of a giant ship suspended 500 feet above the ocean on all sides. Here, more than anywhere else on the Oregon coast, you get the sense of being on the edge of the continent. Giant spruce, western red cedars, and hemlocks surround the gently hilly trail to the tip of the cape. In March, Cape Lookout is a popular vantage point for whale-watching. June through August, a bevy of wildflowers and birds further enhances the rolling terrain en route to the tip of this headland, and in late summer red huckleberries line the path.

Halfway to the overlook, there are views north to Cape Meares over the Netarts sandspit. Even if you settle for a mere 15-minute stroll down the trail, you can look southward beyond Haystack Rock to Cascade Head. Right about where the trees open up, look for a

© MARK MORRIS

bronze plaque commemorating the crash of a World War II plane (with nearly a dozen casualties) embedded into the rock wall bordering the right-hand (north) side of the trail at eye-level. If you're unable to take this hike, there are two unmarked turnouts along the highway between the sand dunes and Cape Lookout parking lot that let you survey the terrain south to Cape Kiwanda.

Cape Lookout State Park

On the north side of the cape is the campground and beach extension of expansive Cape Lookout State Park (13000 Whiskey Creek Rd. West, Tillamook, 503/842-4981 information, 800/452-5687 reservations), which also encompasses the entire cape and the seven-mile-long Netarts Spit within its boundaries. The park has 176 tent sites ($16) and 38 full-hookup sites ($20), as well as 10 yurts ($27), three cabins (with bathrooms, kitchen, TV/VCR, $65), and a hiker/biker camp ($4); discounts apply October–April. Amenities include showers, flush toilets, a laundry, and evening programs. Reservations and deposit are required at this popular campground. Eight miles of hiking trails include a trail beginning at the registration booth leading to a ridge above the ocean. Another trail heads north through a variety of estuarine habitats along a sandspit separating Netarts Bay from the Pacific, a popular site for agate hunters, clammers, and crabbers. There is a $3 day-use fee, which is covered by the Coast Passport.

CAPE MEARES

North from Cape Lookout State Park, the trees along the Three Capes Loop open at a couple of turnouts, offering beguiling views to the north of the seven-mile-long Netarts Spit, Netarts Bay, and Three Arch Rocks just offshore. The road quickly drops down and skirts the shallow bay, which drains and fills with the tides. Netarts Bay and its mudflats are popular with clamdiggers and fishermen crabbers, who can launch boats from Netarts Landing, at the northeast corner of the bay. **Netarts Bay RV Park and Marina** (2260 Bilyeu, Netarts, 503/842-7774)

and **Big Spruce RV Park** (4850 Netarts Hwy. W., 503/842-7443) rent motorboats and crabbing supplies.

NETARTS

Tiny Netarts (pop. about 200) has an enviable location overlooking the bay and the Pacific beyond. Along with nearby Oceanside, it's the closest coastal settlement from Tillamook, and makes for a fine quiet getaway.

The **Terimore** (5105 Crab Ave., Netarts, 503/842-4623 or 800/635-1821) is situated a short walk from the water at the north end of Netarts Bay. Other than some units with fireplaces and kitchens, there are few frills here, but for fair rates you'll find yourself close by the water and within easy driving distance of the Cape Lookout trail and a beach walk away from Roseanna's, the best restaurant on the Capes Loop. Wood-paneled kitchen units with bay and ocean views run $80–100 in summer ($60–80 in winter), while no-view kitchen cottages run $45–75 ($35–60 winter). Ask about special

Netarts Bay, with Three Arch Rocks in the distance

offers in the off-season (Nov.–April). Pets are allowed in some rooms; coin-operated laundry provided.

Happy Camp (P.O. Box 52, 845 Happy Camp Rd., Netarts 97143, 503/842-4012) has 30 tent sites and 38 RV sites. All the amenities are available at $16 a night. Reservations are accepted and it's open all year.

You'll find several lunch and dinner spots to choose from. The view of Cape Lookout is tops at **The Schooner** (2065 Netarts Bay Rd., 503/842-4988), which serves breakfast (starting at 8 A.M.), lunch, and dinner (seafood and steak) daily.

OCEANSIDE

The road between Netarts and Cape Meares heads into the pricey beach-house community of Oceanside (pop. about 250). Many of the homes are built into the cliff overlooking the ocean, Sausalito style. This motif reaches its apex atop Maxwell Point. You can peer several hundred feet down at **Three Arch Rocks Wildlife Refuge,** part-time home to one of the continent's largest and most varied collections of shorebirds. A herd of sea lions also populates this trio of sea stacks from time to time.

While low prices and a window on the water can be found at **Ocean Front Cabins** (1610 Pacific Ave., Oceanside, 503/842-6081 or 888/845-8470), the older, smallish rooms here might at first give some travelers pause. Nonetheless, for as little as $50 (with a kitchenette, $60; two-bed rooms with full kitchens for $75) you'll find yourself literally within a stone's throw of Oceanside's beachcombing and dining highlights.

The aptly named **House on the Hill** (P.O. Box 187, Oceanside 97134, 503/842-6030), also called the Clifftop Inn, is perched on a bluff at Maxwell Point. For $95–185 for standard units, $120–225 for kitchen units, you get the seclusion and cliffside ocean grandeur of this headland. Off-season discounts knock about 25 percent off the rates. Most of the 16 units here are not especially elaborate, but the sweeping view is easily worth whatever you pay for the room. The

office maintains a little museum with sea specimens and newspaper articles about the area as well as a telescope focused on the offshore Three Arch Rocks bird refuge.

Another good lodging option is **Bender Vacation Rental Properties** (503/233-4363), boasting six units with cliffside ocean views, large private decks, and full kitchens (except for one unit). Other amenities include fireplaces, TVs, VCRs, and microwaves. Pets are welcome at most locations. For $70–175/night on a two-night minimum, this is a great deal.

A popular draw for hungry Three Capes travelers, **Roseanna's Oceanside Cafe** (1490 Pacific Ave. N.W., Oceanside, 503/842-7351) garners high marks from just about everyone. At first, the weather-beaten cedar-shake exterior might lead you to expect an old general store, as indeed it was decades ago. Once you're inside, however, the ornate decor leaves little doubt that this place takes its new identity seriously. From an elevated perch above the breakers, you'll be treated to expertly prepared local oysters and fresh salmon. The menu is surprisingly extensive, as is the wine list, but be forewarned—the bills can be high at Roseanna's (around $30 per person for dinner) and the service leisurely, so you might just want to enjoy lunchtime gourmet sandwiches. Better yet, come for blackberry cobbler dessert; order it warm so the Tillamook Vanilla Bean ice cream on top melts down the sides, and watch the waves over a long cup of coffee.

The **Anchor Tavern** (1495 Pacific Ave., Oceanside, 503/842-2041) is a nearby alternative for food by the beach. Along with microbrews, specialties are smoked meats, BBQ ribs, clam chowder, pizza, and burgers. A light meal with a microbrew won't set you back more than $10. Hanging above the bar is a wide-angle photo of Hartford, Connecticut. The four-foot-long picture depicts the kind of urban sprawl that will make you glad you're here.

Oceanside Espresso (1610 Pacific Ave., Oceanside, 503/842-1919) is at the north end of the main drag on a bluff above the beach. While locating gourmet coffee drinks in this part of the coast is about as easy as finding the Holy Grail, this place has even more going for it—windows overlooking the surf in front of the Three Arch Rocks. Light breakfast with fresh-baked pastries, lunchtime homemade soup and sandwiches, and the works of local artists adorning the walls all make a stop worthwhile.

CAPE MEARES SCENIC VIEWPOINT

With stunning views, picnic tables, a newly restored lighthouse, and a uniquely contorted tree a short walk from the parking lot, Cape Meares Scenic Viewpoint is the user-friendliest site on the Three Capes Loop. The park was named for English navigator John Meares, who mapped many points along this coast in a 1788 voyage. The famed **Octopus Tree** is less than a quarter mile up a forested hill. The tentacle-like extensions of this Sitka spruce have also been compared to the arms of a candelabra. Another writer likened this tree to a gargantuan spider in a near-fetal position.

The 10-foot diameter of its base supports five-foot-thick trunks, each of which by itself is large enough to be a single tree. Scientists have propounded several theories for the cause of its unusual shape, including everything from wind and weather to insects damaging the

spruce when it was young. A Native American legend about the spruce contends that it was shaped this way so that the branches could hold the canoes of a chief's dead family. Supposedly, the bodies were buried near the tree. This was a traditional practice among the tribes of the area, who referred to species formed thusly as "council trees."

Beyond the tree you can look back at Oceanside and Three Arch Rocks Refuge. The sweep of Pacific shore and offshore monoliths makes a fitting finale to your sojourn along the Three Capes Loop, but be sure to also stroll the short paved trail down to the lighthouse, which begins at the parking lot and provides dramatic views of an offshore wildlife refuge, Cape Meares Rocks. Bring binoculars to see tufted puffins, pelagic cormorants, seals, and sea lions. The landward portion of the refuge protects rare old-growth evergreens.

The restored interior of **Cape Meares Lighthouse,** built in 1890, is open daily May–Sept., 11 A.M.–4 P.M. This beacon was replaced as a functioning light in 1963 by the automated facility located behind it, and it now houses a gift shop. A free tour is occasionally staffed by volunteers who might tell you about how the lighthouse was built here by mistake, and perhaps offer a peek into the prismatic Fresnel lenses.

Tillamook and the Tillamook Bay Area

Without much sun or surf, what could possibly draw enough visitors to the town of Tillamook (pop. 4,270) to make it one of Oregon's top three tourism attractions? Superficially speaking, tours of a cheese factory and a World War II blimp hangar, in a town flanked by mudflats and rain-soaked dairy country, shouldn't pull in more than a million tourists a year. But they do. As anyone who has driven to Tillamook via the scenic Three Capes Loop or past Neahkahnie Mountain on U.S. 101 can attest, those tasty morsels of jack and cheddar provide the perfect complement to the surrounding region's scenic beauty.

Tillamook County is home to more than 26,000 cows, which easily outnumber the county's human population. They're the foundation of the Tillamook County Creamery Association's famous cheddar cheese and other dairy products, which generate about $85 million in annual sales. Other important contributors to the local economy are fishing and oyster farming.

In 1933, a wildfire devastated forests in the Coast Range east of town in what was the worst disaster in the state's history. The Tillamook Burn raged for four weeks, reducing massive acreage of old growth to rows of charred stumps. The fire pushed a cloud of ash 40,000 feet into the air. Ashfall was recorded 500 miles out to sea and as far east as Yellowstone National Park in Wyoming, while Oregon's upper left edge lived in semidarkness for weeks. Fires in 1939 and 1945 further ravaged the area, leaving a total of 355,000 acres destroyed by the three blazes. More than 72 million seedlings planted by a community reforestation effort in the years that followed have produced an impressive stand of trees in these forests today.

In 1940–1942, partially in response to a Japanese submarine firing on Fort Stevens in Astoria, the U.S. Navy built two blimp hangars south of town, the two largest wooden structures ever built, according to *Guinness*. Of the five naval air stations on the Pacific coast, the Tillamook blimp guard patrolled the waters from Northern California to the San Juan Islands and escorted ships into Puget Sound. While all kinds of blimp stories abound in Tillamook bars, only one wartime encounter has been documented. Recently declassified records confirm that blimps were involved in the sinking of what was believed to be two Japanese submarines off Cape Meares. In late May 1943, two of the high-flying craft, assisted by U.S. Navy subchasers and destroyers, dropped several depth charges on the submarines, which are still lying on the ocean floor.

Until 1946, when the station was decommissioned, naval presence here created a boomtown. Bars and businesses flourished and civilian jobs were easy to come by. After the war years, Tillamook County returned to the economic trinity of "trees, cheese, and ocean breeze" that has sustained the region to the present day.

SIGHTS

Tillamook Cheese Factory

With over a million visitors a year, the Tillamook Cheese Factory (4175 U.S. 101 N., Tillamook, 503/842-4481) is far and away the county's biggest drawing card. The plant welcomes visitors with a reproduction of the *Morningstar,* the schooner that transported locally made butter and cheese in the late 1800s and now adorns the label of every Tillamook product. The quaint vessel symbolizing Tillamook cheesemaking's humble beginnings stands in stark contrast to the technology and sophistication that go into making this world-famous gourmet product today.

Inside the plant, a self-guided tour follows the movement of curds and whey to the "cheddaring table." Whey is drained from the curds, which are then cut and folded. These processes are coordinated by white-uniformed workers in a stadium-sized factory. As you look down on the antiseptic scene from the glassed-in observation area, it's hard to imagine this as the birthplace of many a pizza and grilled-cheese sandwich. Tastes of a few samples, however, prove it's true. Tillamook ice cream has been touted by the *New York Times* as superior to Häagen-Dazs, and their extra premium aged sharp white cheddar was rated by the National Milk Producers in 1997 as the country's best cheese.

User-friendly informational placards and historical displays recount Tillamook Valley's dairy history from 1851, when settlers began importing cows. The problem then was how to ship the milk to San Francisco and Portland. Even though salting butter to preserve it allowed exportation, ships still faced the difficulty of negotiating the treacherous Tillamook bar. In 1894, Peter McIntosh introduced techniques here to make cheddar cheese, whose long shelf life enabled it to be transported overland.

In the early 1900s, the Tillamook County Creamery Association absorbed smaller operations and opened the modern plant in 1949. Today, Tillamook produces tens of millions of pounds of cheese annually, including Monterey jack, Swiss, and multiple variations of their award-winning white cheddar. Pepperoni, butter, cheese soup, milk, and other products are also available. There's a gift shop (more Holstein-themed tchochkes than you've probably dreamed of) and a full-service restaurant, but the big attraction is the ice cream counter. Have a double-scoop chocolate peanut butter cone—worth every penny. The Tillamook Cheese Factory and visitors center is open daily 8 A.M.–8 P.M. in summer and 8 A.M.–6 P.M. Labor Day–mid-June.

Blue Heron French Cheese Company

A quarter-million people a year visit Tillamook County's *second*-most-popular attraction, Blue Heron French Cheese Company (2001 Blue Heron Dr., 503/842-8282), located a mile south of the Tillamook Cheese Factory. Housed in a large white barn, Blue Heron is famous for its Brie, though the cheese is no longer produced on site. In addition to cheeses and other gourmet foods, the shop sells gift baskets, and over 90 varieties of Oregon wines are available in their wine-tasting room. A deli serves lunches of homemade soups and salads. For kids, there's a petting farm with the usual barnyard suspects. Open daily 8 A.M.–8 P.M. in summer, shorter hours the rest of the year.

Tillamook Air Museum

South of town off U.S. 101 you can't possibly miss the enormous Quonset hut–like building east of the highway. The world-class aircraft collection of the Tillamook Air Museum (6030 Hangar Rd., Tillamook, 503/842-1130) is housed in and around Hangar B of the decommissioned Tillamook Naval Air Station. At 1,072 feet long, 206 feet wide, and 192 feet high, it's the largest wooden structure in the world. During World War II, this and another gargantuan hangar on the site (which burned down in 1992) sheltered eight K-class blimps, each 242 feet long.

Inside the seven-acre structure, you can learn about the role the big blimps played during wartime as well as how they are used today. In addition, there's a large collection of World War II fighter planes (many one-of-a-kind models) as well as photos and artifacts from the naval air station days. Be sure to check out the cyclo-crane, a combination blimp/plane/helicopter. This was devised in the 1980s to aid in remote logging operations; it ended up an $8 million bust.

If possible, bring binoculars here to see the interesting latticework of rafters and Navy-uniformed mannequins on the catwalks 20 stories up. To get there from downtown, take U.S. 101 south two miles, make a left at the flashing yellow light, and follow the signs. The museum is open daily 10 A.M.–5 P.M. Admission is $9.50 adults, $8.50 seniors, $5.50 ages 13–17, $2 ages 7–12.

Tillamook County Pioneer Museum

East of the highway in the heart of downtown, Tillamook County Pioneer Museum (2106 2nd St., Tillamook, 503/842-4553) is famous for its taxidermic exhibits as well as memorabilia from pioneer households. Particularly in-

You can't miss the Tillamook Air Museum in massive Hangar B.

triguing are hunks of ancient beeswax with odd inscriptions recovered from near Neahkahnie Mountain (see special topic "Enjoying the Outdoors," later in this section). Old photos are also worth the admission price. The old courtroom on the second floor has one of the best displays of natural history in the state. There are many beautiful dioramas, plus shells, insects, and nest eggs. The Beals Memorial Room houses a famous rock and mineral collection along with fossils.

The main floor and the basement highlight human history with antique kitchen tools, old-time logging equipment, Native American artifacts and basketry, historic modes of conveyance (from stagecoaches to cars), and simulated pioneer households. In short, this is probably Oregon's best pioneer history museum. It's open Mon.–Sat. 8 A.M.–5 P.M., Sunday noon–5 P.M. April–September. Admission is $3, $7 for families, $2 for seniors, and $.50 for ages 12–17.

Oregon Coast Explorer Train

A delightful way to see Tillamook Bay, the beach, Nehalem Bay, and the Nehalem River Valley is on board this excursion train pulled by a gleaming, restored 1910 Heisler Locomotive Works engine. The train makes weekend runs between Tillamook and Mohler (home of the Nehalem Bay Winery) via Bay City, Garibaldi, Rockaway, and Wheeler; fare is $12/adults. The **Nehalem Bay Winery** (34965 ORE 53, Nehalem, 503/368-9463, www.nehalembaywinery.com) offers tastings and sales of its varietals and berry wines (pinot noir, Gewürztraminer, and blackberry). You can tour the grounds here and picnic daily 10 A.M.–6 P.M. or enjoy the tasting room's welcoming milieu.

In addition, the train offers coast supper runs, picnic runs inland Garibaldi to the Salmonberry Canyon Wilderness, Fall Foliage excursions, and special "Santa" trips in December. The main season kicks off in late May and lasts through September, but the Explorer operates a reduced schedule at other times of the year. For details and a schedule, call 503/842-8206, or check the website at www.potb.org/oregoncoastexplorer.htm.

Munson Creek Falls

Seven miles south of Tillamook, a 1.5-mile access road turns east from U.S. 101, leading to the highest waterfall in the Oregon Coast Range. Munson Creek Falls drops 266 feet over mossy cliffs surrounded by an old-growth forest. The very narrow, bumpy dirt road then takes you to the parking lot. A quarter-mile trail leads to the base of the falls, while another, slightly longer trail leads to a higher viewpoint; wooden walkways clinging to the cliff lead to a small viewing platform. This is a spectacle in all seasons, but come in winter when the falls pour down with greater fury. Note that motor homes and trailers cannot get into the park; the lot is too small.

RECREATION
Fishing

Among Oregon anglers, Tillamook County is known for its steelhead and salmon. Motorists along U.S. 101 know that the fall chinook run has arrived when fishing boats cluster outside the Tillamook Bay entrance at Garibaldi. As the season wears on, the fish—affectionately called "hogs" because they sometimes weigh in at more than 50 pounds—make their way inland up the five coastal rivers—the Trask, Wilson, Tillamook, Kilchis, and Miami—that flow into Tillamook Bay. At their peak, the runs create such competition for favorite holes that the process of sparring for them is jocularly referred to as "combat fishing," as fishing boats anchor up gunwale to gunwale to form a fish-stopping palisade called a "hogline." Smokehouses and gas stations dot the outer reaches of the bay to cater to this fall influx.

The **Guide Shop Inc.** (12140 Wilson River Hwy., Tillamook, 503/842-3474) can arrange for a full day of fishing for chinook and silver salmon, steelhead, sturgeon, or trout; rates are about $150 per person, for one to four anglers. Also, see "Garibaldi," later in this section, which is home base for several charter operations.

Golf

Golfers choose between two public courses in Tillamook. About two miles north of town,

ENJOYING THE OUTDOORS

Between Tillamook and Cannon are two excellent places to pitch a tent or park that RV. Whether you stay for just a day or a full week, you can spend your time kayaking, fishing, walking in rainforest, or simply beachcombing. Even searching for buried treasure is an option.

Nehalem Bay State Park

Just south of Manzanita, occupying the entire sandy appendage of Nehalem Spit, is scenic, sprawling **Nehalem Bay Campground** (info 503/368-5943, reservations 800/452-5687), a favorite with beginning sailboarders, bikers, beachcombers, and anglers. To get there, turn south at Bayshore Junction just before U.S. 101 heads east into the town of Nehalem. Sandwiched between the bay and a four-mile beach stretching from Manzanita to the mouth of the Nehalem River are six full-hookup sites and 270 sites with electricity and water that go for $16–20, plus some bargain hiker/biker sites ($4). There are 18 yurts for $27, a horse camp (17 sites with corrals, $12), and even a fly-in camp (six primitive sites) adjacent to the airstrip. A $3 day-use fee applies to noncampers.

Park amenities include evening programs, flush toilets, piped water, and hot showers. Open year-round. As big as this park is, it does fill up in summer, so reservations are recommended (particularly during July and August). Campers here often head over to the **Bunkhouse** (36315 U.S. 101, Nehalem, 503/368-6183), for ample and tasty breakfasts.

Oswald West State Park

Just north of Manzanita, **Neahkahnie Mountain** towers nearly 1,700 feet up from the edge of the sea. U.S. 101 climbs up and over its shoulders, to an elevation of 700 feet, and the vistas from a half-dozen pullouts (highest along the Oregon coast) are spectacular—but do try to keep your eyes on the snaking road until you've parked your car. This stretch of the highway, built by the WPA in the 1930s, was constructed by blasting a roadbed from the rock face and buttressing it with stonework walls on the precarious cliffs. Soaring a thousand feet above, on the east side of the highway, is the peak named for the Tillamook tribe's fire spirit, Neah-Kah-Nie. The faint-hearted or acrophobic certainly couldn't have lasted long on this job. The handiwork of these road builders and masons can be admired at

east of U.S. 101, **Bay Breeze Golf Course** (2325 Latimer Rd., Tillamook, 503/842-1166) charges $10 for nine holes on weekends. Another two miles north, **Alderbrook Golf Course** (7300 Alderbrook Rd., Tillamook, 503/842-6413) charges $24 on weekends for 18 holes.

Other Activities

Besides fishing, the Tillamook State Forest holds plenty of other recreational opportunities. From a distance, the forest seems like a tree plantation, but hidden waterfalls, old railroad trestles from the days of logging trains, and moss-covered oaks in the Salmonberry River Canyon will convince you otherwise. Bird-watchers and mushroom pickers can easily penetrate this thicket thanks to 1,000 miles of maintained roads and old railroad grades.

Two challenging trails off ORE 6, **King Mountain,** 25 miles east of Tillamook, and **Elk Mountain,** 28 miles east of Tillamook, climb through lands affected by the Tillamook Burn, but with scenic views throughout. Thanks to salvage logging in the wake of the disaster and subsequent replanting, myriad trails crisscross forests of Douglas and noble fir, hemlock, and red alder. Pick up the helpful pamphlet *Tillamook Forest Trails* put out by the Oregon Dept. of Forestry, Tillamook District (4907 E. 3rd St., Tillamook 97141, 503/842-2543).

Bird-watchers flock to Tillamook Bay June–November to sight pelicans, sandpipers, tufted puffins, blue herons, and a variety of shorebirds. Prime time is before high tide, but step lively because this waterway was originally called "quicksand bay."

several pullouts, along with the breathtaking vista of Manzanita Beach, Nehalem Spit, and some 17 miles south to Cape Meares.

Most of the mountain, and the prominent headlands of Cape Falcon, are encompassed within the 2,500-acre gem of Oswald West State Park. Several hiking trails weave through the park, including the 13 miles of the Oregon Coast Trail linking Arch Cape to the north with Manzanita. From the main parking lot on the east side of U.S. 101, a half-mile trail follows Short Sand Creek to **Short Sand Beach.** From Short Sand Beach, you can pick up the three-mile old growth–lined Cape Falcon Trail to the highway, or you might want just to linger at Smuggler's Cove, which is a popular spot for surfers year-round. Rainforests of hemlock, cedar, and gigantic Sitka spruce crowd the secluded, boulder-strewn shoreline. At daybreak or dusk, keep an eye out for Roosevelt elk.

A mile south of the main parking lot is the access road to the **Neahkahnie Mountain Summit Trail** on the east side of the highway. It's not well marked; look for a subdivision on the golf course to the west. Drive the gravel road up a quarter mile to the trailhead parking lot and begin a moderately difficult 1.5-mile ascent. Allow about 45 minutes to get to the top. The summit view south to Cape Meares and east to the Nehalem Valley ranks as one of the finest on the coast.

Whether you believe in the stories of lost pirate wealth buried somewhere on Neahkahnie Mountain, there is real treasure today for all who venture here, in the intangible currency of extraordinary natural beauty. The state park bears the name of Governor Oswald West, whose far-sighted 1913 beach bill was instrumental in protecting Oregon's virgin shoreline. That same year, Neahkahnie Mountain was the site of another shipwreck, in somewhat mysterious circumstances.

To camp at Oswald West State Park (800/551-6949), you walk .3 mile from the campers parking lot to 30 primitive campsites in a grove of old-growth conifers backdropped by high cliffs. You can use the wheelbarrows at the parking lot and campground to cart your gear back and forth. Camping is allowed March–October and costs $10–14 a night. There are flush toilets, but this campground is the only state park without electrical hookups.

PRACTICALITIES

Accommodations

Most travelers seem to pass through Tillamook on their way to someplace else, but there are a few lodging choices. **Best Western Inn & Suites** (1722 N. Makinster Rd., Tillamook, 503/842-7599 or 800/299-4817) is close to everything. Rooms have dataports, refrigerator, microwave, iron and ironing board, coffee maker, and cable TV. Amenities include indoor pool, sauna, and hot tub, plus complimentary continental breakfast. Rates are $94–150. **Shilo Inn** (2515 N. Main Ave., Tillamook, 503/842-7971 or 800/222-2244) has standard rooms from $75–129 along with indoor pool, spa, sauna, steam room, and fitness center, and on-site restaurant and lounge. Ask about special discounts.

Food

Tillamook restaurant fare draws on the local bounty from the sea and surrounding farm country. Dungeness crab, bay shrimp, clams, and oysters are indigenous to the area, and a burgeoning number of wine and gourmet outlets throughout Tillamook County can make for a surprisingly interesting taste tour. But the best food is found in the county's smaller towns—Oceanside, Manzanita, Nehalem, and Pacific City. To sample the county's freshest produce, visit the **Tillamook Farmers' Market** in downtown Tillamook. It runs every Saturday, late June–early October, on Laurel Avenue.

Eleven miles south of Tillamook on U.S. 101, near Beaver Road in Hebo, **Bear Creek Artichokes** (503/398-5411) is a large roadside fruit stand purveying the locally grown artichokes as well as an astounding variety of herbs, perennials, and fruit. The cherries, marionberries, blackberries, and plums are recommended, as are the homemade fruit jams, apple dumplings, and scones. While artichokes are a crop not usually seen outside of California, they thrive here. California artichokes traditionally come into Oregon markets March–June, while the 'chokes grown around Tillamook ripen August–October. The Oregon variety is meatier and slightly sweeter. You can buy them here in season, or look for them at farmers markets, Safeway, and Cub Foods.

The **Farmhouse Cafe** at the Tillamook Cheese Factory serves breakfast and lunch; open daily at 8 A.M. The **deli** at the Blue Heron French Cheese Company fixes sandwiches, soups, and salads daily. On the west side of U.S. 101, between the two cheese meccas, lunchtime do-it-yourselfers might check the locally raised and cured meat and smoked salmon at **Debbie D's Sausage Factory** (503/842-2622).

Casual passersby wouldn't figure tiny Bay City, five miles north of Tillamook, as a key stop on a Tillamook County gourmet tour, but those in the know hit the brakes here for excellent seafood, especially oysters. Motoring through Bay City, you'll notice piles of oyster shells on the roadside, destined to be ground into chicken feed. Predictably, local menu entrées with grilled Tillamook Bay oysters are a good bet. The following three places are worth a stop:

Pacific Oyster (5150 Oyster Bay Dr., 503/377-2323) lends credence to this assertion with grilled oysters, or enjoy them smoked, cocktail style, or on the half-shell. Crabcakes, halibut burgers, and clam chowder are also highlights in an extensive menu of fresh seafood. Takeout lunches are in the $6.50–8 range and can be enjoyed outside on the jetty close by interpretive placards that explain this environment.

Downie's Cafe (9320 5th St., Bay City, 503/377-2220) is a greasy-spoon favorite among anglers. Whether it's homemade buttermilk pancakes for breakfast or the famous oysterburger ($6.50) for lunch, you'll leave full and satisfied. Finish off with a slice of homemade pie, especially pumpkin with Tillamook ice cream. To get to Downie's, look for the muraled facade of Artspace Cafe on the east side of U.S. 101 opposite Tillamook Bay. Turn at Artspace onto 5th Street and drive two blocks to its intersection with C Street.

Artspace Cafe and Gallery (U.S. 101 at 5th, 503/377-2782) is another great place for oysters (try the oyster burgers and oysters Italia). There are also fresh fish, chicken, pasta, and vegetarian offerings ($6.25–16.75). Occasional live music, a nice selection of beer, wine, and coffee drinks, paintings by Northwest artists on the walls, and the chance to create your own masterpiece courtesy of tableside crayons and paper all make for a cultural interlude. Open Friday 4–9 P.M., Saturday 11 A.M.–8 P.M., and Sunday 11 A.M.–3 P.M. While you're there, get caught up on Tillamook Bay politics with a copy of the free tabloid **Bay City Slug,** a pugnacious monthly that proudly proclaims itself "The Paper That Hates Progress."

Information

The **Tillamook Chamber of Commerce** (3705 U.S. 101 N., Tillamook 97191, 503/842-7525, www.tillamookchamber.org) is located across the parking lot from the cheese factory. It's open Mon.–Fri. 9 A.M.–5 P.M., Saturday 10A.M.–3 P.M., Sunday 10 A.M.–2 P.M. mid-June–September.

GARIBALDI

Tillamook Bay's commercial fishing fleet is concentrated in this little port town (pop. 970) near the north end of the bay. Garibaldi, named in 1879 by the local postmaster for the Italian patriot, is a fish-processing center: crabs, shrimp, fresh salmon, lingcod, and bottom fish (halibut, cabezon, rockfish, and sea perch) are the specialties here. At the marina, **Bayocean Seafood** (608 Commercial Dr., 503/322-3316) gets it right off the boats, so the selection is both low-priced and fresh. Likewise the crab, fish, and other seafood available next door at **Oregon Gourmet** (606 Commercial Dr., 503/322-2544). If you want it fresher, you'll have to catch it yourself.

And the town's fishing and crabbing piers do attract hordes who want to catch their own. Rent crab traps, kayaks, and other gear at the **Garibaldi Marina** (302 Mooring Basin Rd., 503/322-3312). In addition to dock fishing, guide and charter services offer salmon and halibut fishing, bird-watching, and whale-watching excursions. North of Garibaldi on U.S. 101, the bay entrance is a good place to see brown pelicans, harlequin ducks, oystercatchers, and guillemots. The Miami River marsh, south of town, is a bird-watching paradise at low tide, when ducks and shorebirds hunt for food.

The **Miami River** and **Kilchis River,** which empty into Tillamook Bay south of Garibaldi, get the state's only two significant runs of chum salmon, a species much more common from Washington northward. There's a catch-and-release season for them mid-September–mid-November. Both rivers also get runs of spring chinook and are open for steelhead most of the year.

Several charter companies have offices at the marina. **Troller Charters** (304 Mooring Basin, 503/322-3666) offers fishing excursions (a full day of salmon or halibut fishing for $70) and wildlife-viewing or whale-watching trips ($20 per person). Other outfits include **Garibaldi Charters** (607 Garibaldi Ave., 503/322-0007), and **Siggi G. Ocean Charters** (611 S. Commercial, 503/322-3285).

ROCKAWAY BEACH

This town of 1,200 was established as a summer resort in the 1920s by Portlanders who wanted a coastal getaway. And so it remains today, a quiet spot without much going on besides walks on the seven miles of sandy beach, a **Kite Festival** in mid-May, and an **Arts and Crafts Fair** in mid-August. Shallow **Lake Lytle,** on the east side of the highway, offers spring and early summer fishing for trout, bass, and crappie. The **Visitor Information Center** (503/355-8108), lodged in a bright red caboose in the center of town, can fill you in on other goings-on.

The **Inn on Manhattan Beach** (105 N.W. 23rd Ave., Rockaway Beach, 503/355-2301 or 800/368-6499) is a small, comfortable, beachside motel toward the north end of town, run by the same folks at the Nehalem River Inn. Studios and one- or two-bedroom suites feature jetted spas, plush beds, and French doors opening onto private decks. Some units have kitchenettes. Rates range $79–149 in summer, $49–99 off-season.

The **Inn at Rockaway Beach** (104 S. U.S. 101, 503/355-2400 or 800/265-4291) is a motel in a structure that dates back to 1912, when it was built to house railroad workers. Five one-room units and four two-bedroom suites run $59–89 in summer, $45–65 off-season. Suites, with sitting rooms and kitchenettes, sleep up to seven.

Look to Rockaway's **Beach Pancake and Dinner House** (202 U.S. 101 North, 503/355-2411) for big portions at moderate prices. Locals tout the chicken and dumplings ($7.50). Other features include Mexican dishes, fresh oysters, and breakfast all day ($4.50–13). Open daily at 7 A.M. Photos and paintings by local artists cover the walls at **R and R Espresso & Cafe** (120 U.S. 101 North, 503/355-3315), which opens daily at 6 A.M. for coffee and baked goods; lunch includes salads and panini.

Cannon Beach and Vicinity

In 1846, the USS *Shark* met its end on the Columbia River Bar. The ship broke apart, and a section of deck bearing a small cannon and an iron capstan drifted south, finally washing ashore south of the current city limits at Arch Cape. And so this town got its name, which it adopted in 1922. Replicas of the hardware now stand near that spot, while the originals are preserved at the Cannon Beach Historical Society Museum.

In 1873, stagecoach and railroad tycoon Ben Holladay helped create Oregon's first coastal tourist mecca, Seaside, while ignoring its attractive neighbor in the shadow of Haystack Rock. In the 20th century, Cannon Beach evolved into a bohemian alternative to the hustle and bustle of the family-oriented resort scene to the north. Before the recent era of development, this place was a quaint backwater attracting laid-back artists, summer-home residents, and the overflow from pricier digs in Seaside.

Today, the low-key charm and atmosphere conducive to artistic expression are threatened by a massive visitor influx and price increases. While such vital signs as a first-rate theater, a good bookstore, cheek-by-jowl art galleries, and fine restaurants are still in ample evidence, your view of them from the other side of the street might be blocked by a convoy of Winnebagos.

In *Travels With Charlie,* John Steinbeck bemoaned how present-day Carmel, California, would be eschewed by the very people who gave the town the appealing sobriquet of "artist colony." This same thing could well happen to the Carmel of the Oregon coast, Cannon Beach, unless the growth that began in 1980 slows. Within a decade, the number of motel rooms here has doubled, as has the number of visitors on a busy weekend (now averaging 10,000–12,000).

Nonetheless, the broad, three-mile stretch of beach dominated by the impressive monolith of Haystack Rock still provides a contemplative experience—although you might have to walk a half mile from your parking place to get to it.

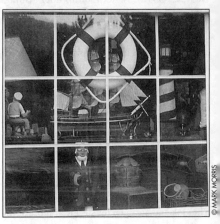

nautical notions: Cannon Beach shop window

© MARK MORRIS

And if you're patient and resourceful enough to find a space for your wheels, the finest gallery-hopping, crafts, and shopping on the coast await. The city is small enough for strolling, only 1.3 miles long, and its location removed from U.S. 101 spares it the kind of blight seen on the main drags of other coastal tourist towns.

Wood shingles and understated earth tones dominate the architecture of tastefully rendered galleries, bookstores, and bistros. Throngs of walkers along Hemlock Street, the main drag, also distinguish this burg from the typical coastal strip town whose heart and soul have been pierced by U.S. 101. You have to go clear to the north end of Cannon Beach to find a gas station, and even then you're liable to bypass its stone-cottage facade.

SIGHTS AND RECREATION
South of Cannon Beach

A few miles north of Oswald West State Park's main parking lot is the Arch Cape Tunnel, cut right through the mountain. This marks the end of the state park but not the beauty. As you head north, views of **Hug Point State Park** and pris-

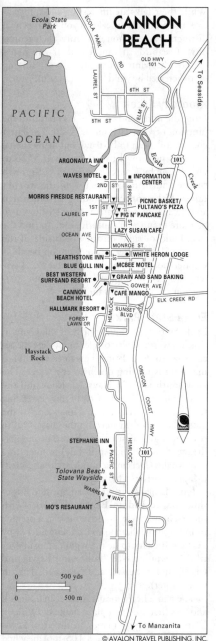

CANNON BEACH

Ecola State Park

ECOLA PARK RD

OLD HWY 101

To Seaside

LAUREL ST

6TH ST

ELM ST

5TH ST

PACIFIC OCEAN

Ecola Creek

101

ARGONAUTA INN

WAVES MOTEL

2ND ST

SPRUCE ST

INFORMATION CENTER

MORRIS FIRESIDE RESTAURANT

1ST ST

PICNIC BASKET/ FULTANO'S PIZZA

PIG N' PANCAKE

LAUREL ST

LAZY SUSAN CAFÉ

OCEAN AVE

MONROE ST

HEARTHSTONE INN

WHITE HERON LODGE

BLUE GULL INN

MCBEE MOTEL

BEST WESTERN SURFSAND RESORT

GRAIN AND SAND BAKING

GOWER AVE

CAFÉ MANGO

CANNON BEACH HOTEL

ELK CREEK RD

HALLMARK RESORT

HEMLOCK

SUNSET BLVD

FOREST LAWN DR

Haystack Rock

OREGON COAST HWY

STEPHANIE INN

PACIFIC ST

HEMLOCK

101

Tolovana Beach State Wayside

WARREN WAY

MO'S RESAURANT

ST

0   500 yds

0   500 m

To Manzanita

© AVALON TRAVEL PUBLISHING, INC.

tine beaches will have you ready to pull over. In summer, this can be a good escape from the crowds at Cannon Beach. Time your visit to coincide with low tide, when all manner of marine life in tidal pools will be exposed. Also at low tide, you may see remains of an 800-foot-long, Model T–sized road blasted into the base of Hug Point, an early precursor to U.S. 101. The cliffs are gouged with caves and crevasses that also invite exploring, but be mindful of the tides so you don't find yourself stranded. Hug Point got its name in the days when stagecoaches used the beach as highways; they had to dash between the waves, hugging the jutting headland to get around.

Another three miles north is **Tolovana Beach Wayside.** Picnic facilities and the view of Haystack Rock aren't the only reasons to come here. This is an excellent base from which to walk south down to Hug Point or north one mile into Cannon Beach.

Haystack Rock

As you get closer to town, Haystack Rock looms larger. This is the third-highest sea stack in the world, measuring 235 feet high. As part of the Oregon Islands National Wildlife Refuge, it has wilderness status, and is off-limits to climbing. Puffins and other seabirds nest on its steep faces, and intertidal organisms thrive in the tide pools around the base. The surrounding tidepools, within a radius of 300 yards from the base of the monolith, are designated a "marine garden"; it's open to exploration, but with strict no-collecting (of anything) and no-harassment (of any living organisms) protections in effect. Flanking the mountain are two rock formations known as the Needles. These spires had two other counterparts at the turn of the 20th century that have gradually been leveled by weathering and erosion. Old-timers will tell you that a trail to the top of Haystack was dynamited by the government in 1968 to keep people off this bird rookery. It also reduced the number of intrepid hikers trapped on the rock at high tide.

The **Haystack Rock Awareness Program** (503/436-1581, www.haystackrock.org), June–August, sponsors free interpretive programs.

ART GALLERIES

Cannon Beach has long attracted artists and artisans, and here art lovers and purchasers will find nearly two dozen outlets for their work. Most of the Cannon Beach galleries and boutiques are concentrated along Hemlock Street, where you can hardly swing a Winsor & Newton No. 12 hogbristle brush without hitting one. Not surprisingly, the seashore itself is the subject and inspiration of many works you'll see here, with Haystack Rock frequently depicted in various media. Cannon Beach Information Center has a guide to all the galleries in town, or you can just stroll and discover them for yourself. A few we like:

The **Cannon Beach Gallery** (1064 S. Hemlock, 503/436-0744) features the works of local and Northwest artists in changing monthly exhibits. **DragonFire Interactive Studio & Gallery** (123 S. Hemlock, 503/436-1533) is a teaching studio, offering weekend classes on various media. Throughout the summer, everyone is invited to come and express his or her creativity, tipple some wine, and listen to live music at the Saturday-night "Paint Party," hosted by local artists 6–10 P.M.

At the north end of town, **White Bird Gallery** (251 N. Hemlock, 503/436-2681), founded in 1971 and one of Cannon Beach's oldest galleries, casts a wide net with paintings, sculpture, prints, photography, glass, ceramics, and jewelry. Next door in Heather's Court, the **Artists Gallerie** (271 N. Hemlock St. #3, 503/436-0336) is a working studio showing the works of four painters whose styles range from realist to pure abstraction. Also at Heather's Court, the **Uffelman Gallery** (503/436-2404) showcases the strikingly modern still lifes of Jeff Uffelman, which transform such mundane ingredients as a handful of peapods or peeled cucumbers into mesmerizing images. **Valley Bronze** (186 N. Hemlock, 503/436-2118) shows sculptures cast at the world-famous foundry in Joseph, Oregon, as well as paintings and diverse works from other prominent artists.

While these talks are interesting and informative, the beach also speaks to you with its own distinctive voices. You can't miss the cacophony of seabirds at sunset and, if you listen closely, the winter phenomenon of "singing sands" created by wind blowing over the beach.

Klootchy Creek

From the north end of town, it's not far to the junction of U.S. 101 and U.S. 26. The latter goes 80 miles east to Portland, but many coastal travelers just travel two miles on U.S. 26 to visit Klootchy Creek Park. In an old-growth spruce and fir forest you'll find the **world's tallest Sitka spruce.** Standing 216 feet high and 52 feet in circumference, it's believed to be more than seven centuries old. To find the tree, look for signs on the north side of the highway shortly after leaving Cannon Beach. A wooden boardwalk protects the tree's root system and lets you approach the tree while sparing you the muddy terrain.

Ecola State Park

Ecola State Park is just north of the Cannon Beach townsite. Thick conifer forests line the access road to Ecola Point. This forested cliff has many trails leading down to the water. The view south takes in Haystack Rock and the overlapping peaks of the Coast Range extending to Neahkahnie Mountain. This is one of the most photographed views on the coast. Out to sea, the sight of sea lions basking on surf-drenched rocks (mid-April–July) or migrating gray whales (December and March) and orcas (May) are seasonal highlights.

From Ecola Point, trails lead north to horseshoe-shaped **Indian Beach,** a favorite with surfers. Some prefer to drive there as a prelude to hiking up Tillamook Head, considered by Lewis and Clark to be the region's most beautiful viewpoint (see "Following Lewis and Clark" under "Seaside and Gearhart," later in this chapter).

The name Ecola means "whale" in Chinook and was first used as a place-name by William Clark, referring to a creek in the area. Lewis and Clark journals note a 105-foot beached

looking south from Ecola State Park

whale found somewhere within present-day Ecola Park's southern border, Crescent Beach. This area represents the southernmost extent of Lewis and Clark's coastal Oregon travels.

There is a $3 day-use fee at the park. The Oregon Coast Annual Pass and Oregon Coast 5-Day Pass are also honored.

Cannon Beach History Center

Permanent exhibits at the small Cannon Beach History Center (corner of Spruce and Sunset, 503/436-9301, open Wed.–Sat. 1–5 P.M.) chronicle the town's timeline, from prehistory to the modern expansion of tourism and recreation. The original, eponymous cannon from the ill-fated *Shark* is also on display here. Admission $1–2.

Horseback Riding

Sea Ranch Stables (415 Old U.S. 101, 503/436-2815), at the north entrance to Cannon Beach off U.S. 101, rents horses 9 A.M.–5 P.M. for beach rides mid-May–Labor Day. Horses are allowed on the beach anywhere along the coast using public access points. Sea Ranch offers a number of one- to two-hour guided rides, including night rides on the beach.

Mountain Biking

Mike's Bike Shop, 248 N. Spruce St., Cannon Beach, 503/436-1266, has rentals for $3–6 per hour. Mike's specializes in mountain bikes, which can also be returned at a Warrenton outlet. You'll also find three-wheel beach-cycles for rent at the north end of town. These are fun for zipping up and down the hard-packed sand when the tide is out.

Hiking

Another reason to head east from Cannon Beach is the hike up 3,283-foot **Saddle Mountain.** To get to the trailhead, take U.S. 26 from its junction with U.S. 101 for 10 miles and turn left on the prominently indicated Saddle Mountain Road. Although it's paved, this road is not suitable for RVs or wide-bodied vehicles. After seven twisting miles, you'll come to the trailhead of the highest peak in this part of the Coast Range. The trail itself is steep and gains more than 1,600 feet in 2.5 miles. Wet conditions can make the going difficult (allow four hours round-trip) and the scenery en route is not always exceptional, but the view from the top is worth it.

On a clear day, hikers can see some 50 miles

COASTAL OREGON

of the Oregon and Washington coastlines, including the Columbia River. Also possible are spectacular views of Mounts Rainier, St. Helens, and Hood, and, unfortunately, miles of clearcuts. If you go May–August you'll be treated to a wildflower display that'll surprise you. On the upper part of the trail, plant species that pushed south from Alaska and Canada during the last Ice Age thrive. The cool, moist climate here keeps them from dying out as they did at lower elevations. Some early blooms include pink coast fawn lily, monkeyflower, wild rose, wood violet, bleeding heart, oxalis, Indian paintbrush, and trillium. Cable handrails provide safety on the narrow final quarter-mile trail to the summit.

Camping

For easier access to Cannon Beach's natural wonders, camping offers nature at a bargain price. Although camping is not permitted on the beach or in Cannon Beach city parks, there are plenty of options for RV, tent, and outdoor enthusiasts.

The **Sea Ranch RV Park** (415 Old U.S. 101, 503/436-2815, www.cannon-beach.net/searanch) has grassy sites nestled among the trees, also home to horses, ducks, rabbits, and raccoons. Open year-round with both full and partial hookups for RVs, campsites include a picnic table and fire ring (firewood sold on the premises), access to restrooms with hot showers—all just three blocks from the beach and downtown. Sites run $20–30, depending on the number of people. Cabins are also available for $65. Pets are welcome, but must be on a leash. Reservations recommended.

For a more pampered experience, check out the **RV Resort at Cannon Beach** (345 Elk Creek Rd., 503/436-2231 or 800/847-2231, www.cbrv-resort.com). Open year-round, with 100 full hookups, indoor pool and spa, free cable TV, on-site convenience store, Laundromat, restrooms, and meeting room. This resort features a Saturday night weenie roast during the summer months. Call for rates.

The family-run **Wright's for Camping** (334 Reservoir Rd., 503/436-2347, www.wrightsfor-camping.com) has quite a history. During the 1930s, the Wrights came from Portland to camp in this area. Then in 1946, Pop Wright bought 10 acres in Cannon Beach from a friend. After running a successful construction company in town, Wright and his wife turned their 10-acre site into a campground. Choose from 19 sites with picnic tables, restrooms, laundry, and fire rings. Wheelchair accessible; leashed pets okay. Rates run $18 and up.

ENTERTAINMENT AND EVENTS

Going strong for over 30 years, the **Coaster Theatre Playhouse** (108 N. Hemlock, Cannon Beach, 503/436-1242, http://coastertheatre.com) stages a varied bill of musicals, dramas, mysteries, comedies, concerts, and other productions. It's open year-round, in a building that started in the 1920s as a skating rink cum silent-movie house. Tickets run $14–16.

The **Puffin Kite Festival,** one of several kite events held on the coast, takes advantage of late April's blustery winds. Individuals and teams demonstrate flying techniques and compete for prizes, and for kids there's a treasure hunt, sandcastle building, and face painting. The festival is held just north of Haystack Rock, in front of the Surfsand Resort, which sponsors the event.

The half dozen or so other sand-sculpting contests that take place on the Oregon coast pale in comparison to Cannon Beach's annual **Sandcastle Day** (503/436-2623), which usually coincides with the lowest-tide Saturday in June. In 1964, a tsunami washed out a bridge, and the isolated residents of Cannon Beach organized the first contest as a way to amuse their children. Now in its fifth decade, this is the state's oldest and most prestigious competition of its kind. Tens of thousands of spectators show up to watch a thousand-plus competitors fashion their sculptures with the aid of buckets, shovels, squirt guns, and any natural material found on the beach. The resulting sculptures are often amazingly complex and inventive. Recent winners included Egyptian pyramids and a gigantic sea turtle. Building begins in the early morning; winners are announced at noon. The American Legion serves up a big breakfast buffet at 1216 S. Hemlock, open to all. The event is free to spectators, but entrants pay a fee.

Beginning in July, the city park (Spruce and 2nd Streets) hosts **Concerts in the Park,** a series of jazz, rhythm and blues, and popular music, Sunday afternoons at the bandstand 2–4 P.M. Well-chosen jazz and folk acts frequently grace the **Bald Eagle Coffee House** (1287 S. Hemlock, 503/436-0522) on weekends.

In July and August, the well-regarded **Haystack Summer Program in the Arts** (503/464-4812, www.haystack.pdx.edu) offers classes and workshops in painting, music, gardening, and writing, including the annual Pacific Northwest Children's Book Conference. In addition, evening readings, art exhibits, and lectures are open to the public.

For a weekend in early November, writers, singers, composers, painters, and sculptors take over the town for the **Stormy Weather Arts Festival** (503/436-2623). Events include music on the streets, plays, a Saturday afternoon Art Walk, and the Quick Draw in which artists have one hour to paint, complete, and frame a piece while the audience watches. The art is then sold by auction.

PRACTICALITIES
Accommodations
If you're not willing to acquire a taste for storm-watching, do not reserve Cannon Beach lodgings mid-January–early March. Much of the 80 inches of annual precipitation falls during this period. Should high room rates or crowds on weekends other times of the year be a deterrent, remember that Cannon Beach is only an hour and a half from Portland, perfect for a day trip.

Several local property management companies offer a large selection of furnished rentals ranging from grand oceanfront homes to quaint secluded cottages. **Cannon Beach Property Management** (3188 S. Hemlock, 503/436-2021 or 877/386-3402) allows visitors to virtually tour its list of homes (www.cbpm.com), as does **Cannon Beach Vacation Rentals** (P.O. Box 723, 866/436-0940, www.visitcb.com). Rates for both range $65–400.

About a one-minute walk to the beach, with friendly management and a great vibe, the **Blue Gull Inn** (632 S. Hemlock, 503/436-2714 or 800/507-2714) offers a choice between a beach house or less expensive motel units. These come with housekeeping facilities. The modern cottages have in-room whirlpool tubs, fireplaces, and full kitchens. Cottages for larger groups are also available. On site are a sauna and laundry room. Rates range $79–170.

The **McBee Motel** (888 S. Hemlock, 503/436-0247) is less elaborate and less expensive ($39–130) but close enough to town and far enough from traffic to merit consideration. McBee accepts pets in its homey cottages.

For a homey atmosphere, try the **Argonauta Inn** or the **The Waves Motel** (both located at 188 W. 2nd St., 503/436-2205 or 800/822-2468, www.thewavesmotel.com). The Argonauta is made up of four houses in the middle of downtown, and has five furnished units just 150 feet from the beach. A cluster of six buildings makes up The Waves, with units to fit the needs of families, couples, or larger groups. Rates for both range $79–359.

Built in the 1920s, the nine-gabled **Wave Crest Motel** (4008 S. Hemlock, 503/436-2842) is a pet- and smoke-free European-style hotel that caters to adults who have no interest in cable TV but share a penchant for sing-alongs around the piano, a good book, witty conversation, and old-fashioned card games. Coffee, tea, and pastries are served in the morning. Some rooms have private bathrooms; others share. Rates are $40–75 year-round.

For a family-oriented beachfront lodge try **Sea Sprite Guest Lodgings** (P.O. Box 933, Cannon Beach, 97110, 503/436-2266 or 866/828-1050, www.seasprite.com). Just south of Haystack Rock, with kitchens, TV, and spectacular views, it's not surprising this place commands $73–300 rates during the regular season. What *is* surprising is the off-season discount of up to 40 percent, Nov.–April Sun.–Thursday. These family-style beach cabins are a throwback to the Oregon coast of an earlier era. Inside you'll find such homey touches as fireplaces, games, books, periodicals, and rockers. Choose from one of six oceanfront cabins, which hold up to two, six, or eight. To get there, take the Beach Loop (Hemlock Street) south of town and turn west at Nebesna Street.

The **Cannon Beach Hotel** (1116 Hemlock, 503/436-1392) is a converted 1910 loggers' boardinghouse with 30 rooms and a small café and restaurant on the premises. Continental breakfasts are included in the $50–190 rates. The most expensive rooms have fireplaces, whirlpools, and partial ocean views. Meals are available in the restaurant adjacent to the lobby, and lunch and dinner can be enjoyed here apart from the lodging package. As with all Cannon Beach accommodations, be sure to reserve well in advance.

Need to stretch your legs? Window shopping on Hemlock Street is a prime activity in Cannon Beach.

The **Best Western Surfsand Resort** (Oceanfront and Gower Streets, 503/436-2274 or 800/547-6100) offers a great combination of location and amenities in Cannon Beach. Lodging options run the gamut from spacious oceanfront rooms, many with such features as kitchens, fireplaces, and spas (in addition to use of the Cannon Beach Athletic Club and an indoor pool and spa) to houses in the Coast Range. Such comforts and conveniences come with a price (rooms begin at $160), but Cannon Beach is one town whose many charms rate a deluxe treatment like this one.

Just a few minutes' walk from downtown, **Ecola Creek Lodge** (208 E. 5th St., 503/436-2776 or 800/873-2749, www.cannonbeachlodge .com) is a Cape Cod–style inn with 22 unique units set within four buildings. Special features include stained glass, lawns, fountains, flower gardens, and a lily pond. Major renovation of the property was completed in January 2000. Les Shirley Park and Ecola Creek separate the lodge from the beach. Rates range $80–199.

The oceanfront **Hallmark Resort** (1400 S. Hemlock, 503/436-1566 or 888/448-4449, www.hallmarkinns.com) boasts romantic views of Haystock Rock. With convention and meeting facilities, a pool and on-site massage available, this is a service-oriented resort geared to accommodate couples, families, and large groups. In-room fireplaces add a romantic touch. Rates run $59–349.

For a more private experience and just steps from the ocean, the **White Heron Lodge** (356 N. Spruce, 503/436-2205 or 800/822-2468) comprises two fully furnished oceanfront Victorian-style homes, both of which sleep up to four. Each of the suites looks directly out to the Pacific. Wide sandy beaches and spacious front lawns make it a great location for families, especially those with small children. Located on a residential dead-end street, the lodge is only one block from the village. Rates are $169–199.

In Cannon Beach the two-bedroom B&B called the **Tern Inn** (3663 S. Hemlock, 503/436-528) is close enough to the beach for good views. Private baths, private entrances, and full breakfasts with home-baked goodies go for $125–175 a night. Reserve a month in advance.

Food

As you might expect, eating out can get expensive here. You can keep prices down at the **Mariner Market** (139 N. Hemlock, 503/436-2442), an antique-filled grocery that's fully stocked with fresh meat, fruit, and vegetables. They carry organic produce and natural food products as well as a deli with fast-food takeout items. Open 9 A.M.–9 P.M. In the fishing business for more than 25 years, **Ecola Seafoods** (208 N. Spruce, 503/436-9130) features fresh-catch Dungeness crab and bay shrimp cocktails, as well as a decent clam chowder. Or sample their smoked salmon and fish-n-chips. You'll find it across from the public parking lots and restrooms.

Bill's Tavern (188 N. Hemlock St., 503/436-2202), once a legendary watering hole, is now a more traditional remodeled brewhouse. While some pine for the original establishment's homier decor, they come for the best in-house brews in town. Sweet thick onion rings, greasy but good fries, one-third-pound burgers, sautéed prawns, and grilled oysters are the bill of fare.

Try the wood-paneled, skylit **Lazy Susan Cafe** (126 N. Hemlock, 503/436-2816) for anytime breakfast (eggs with a side of bread pudding),

COASTAL OREGON

lunch (sandwiches and salads), and light dinner (hot seafood salad). There's also the fresh fish catch of the day and pizza. Head over to the **Lazy Susan Grill & Scoop** (156 N. Hemlock) for lunch or to wash it all down with espresso or a soda fountain concoction at this spacious family-friendly establishment. Open till 5 P.M. (8 P.M. on weekends).

Cafe Mango (1235 S. Hemlock, 503/436-2393) is another breakfast/lunch mainstay, locally famous for such dishes as Amish oatcake waffles, blueberry cornmeal pancakes, frittatas, bagels and lox, and creative omelettes. Such Mexican dishes as pozole soup, chilaquiles, and a breakfast burrito stuffed with homemade refried beans and eggs are also winners in this homey restaurant. Fresh fruit smoothies, homemade ketchup and jam, as well as extensive vegetarian options with organic ingredients also explain Mango's cult status. Open daily 7:30 A.M.–2:30 P.M.

Morris' Fireside Restaurant (207 N. Hemlock, 503/436-2917) is an attractive log building where pot roasts, steak, and seafood are featured along with "logger" breakfasts. Portions are large, and prices are moderate. Open daily 8 A.M.–3 P.M.

The local **Pig 'N Pancake** (223 S. Hemlock, 503/436-2851) has large picture windows overlooking a leafy ravine. Open daily for breakfast and lunch, offering 35 varieties of breakfast (including homemade pancakes) served anytime. For lunch, try the soups, chowder, or halibut fish-n-chips.

Fultano's Pizza (200 N. Hemlock, 503/436-9717) sits unobtrusively near the corner of 2nd and Hemlock on your way to the beach. If you're hungry, aromas of fresh cheese, garlic, and free-baked dough will draw you inside this brick enclave.

Finally, there are several good bakeries in town, but **Grain and Sand Baking** (1064 Hemlock, 503/436-0120) rates the nod if you're looking for a lunch with cosmopolitan flair. With first-rate coffee and fresh juices to wash down muffins, scones, and inexpensively priced light meals (black bean empanadas, homemade lasagna, portobello mushroom quiche, and homemade soups typify the offerings) and an adjoining gallery devoted to local artists, this is a special spot. Best of all, you're close enough to Haystack Rock for a picnic.

Hankering for some authentic West Coast chowder? Head to **Dooger's Seafood and Grill** (1371 S. Hemlock, 503/436-2225, www.cannon-beach.net/doogers/) for award-winning seafood, or order up one of their famous "Chowder Kits." For $12, plus shipping, the kit includes a 51-ounce can of clams, five ounces of potatoes, and all the spices. All you need do is add water and cream. You can even order it online. Dooger's is open for breakfast, lunch, and dinner. Entrées range $11–16.

Whether or not you're staying at the **Stephanie Inn** (2740 S. Pacific, 503/436-2221 or 800/633-3466), you are welcome to join guests in the dining room for a four-course prix-fixe dinner featuring innovative Northwest cuisine. The atmosphere boasts mountain views, open wood beams, and river-rock fireplace. Due to "cozy" seating, reserve well ahead of time. Expensive.

Mo's at Tolovana (195 Warren Way, 503/436-1111), next to Tolovana Park, boasts a restaurant site once selected by *Pacific Northwest* magazine as having "the most romantic view on the Oregon coast." Add this to Mo's reliable formula of fresh fish and rich clam chowder at very reasonable prices in a family-friendly atmosphere and you can't miss.

Information and Transportation

The chamber of commerce operates the **Cannon Beach Information Center** (201 E. 2nd, Cannon Beach 97110, 503/436-2623, www.cannonbeach.org), open Mon.–Sat. 11 A.M.–5 P.M., Sunday 10 A.M.–4 P.M. This facility is near the public restrooms (2nd and Spruce) and basketball and tennis courts.

From U.S. 101, there's a choice of four entrances to the beach loop (also known as U.S. 101 Alternate, a section of the old Oregon Coast Highway) to take you into town. As you wade into the town's shops, galleries, and restaurants, the beach loop becomes Hemlock Street, the main drag.

Sunset Empire Transportation District operates

COASTAL OREGON

The Bus, which serves Cannon Beach, Seaside, Astoria-Warrenton, and points in between. For schedule and fare info, call 503/861-7433. The free **Cannon Beach Shuttle** runs every half-hour on a 6.5-mile loop, from Les Shirley Park on the north end of town to Tolovana Park. It operates daily 10 A.M.–6 P.M., with extended summer hours.

Parking can be hard to come by, especially on weekends, but you'll find public lots south of town at Tolovana Park, and in town at Hemlock at 1st Street and on 2nd Street.

Seaside and Gearhart

Seaside is Oregon's quintessential, and oldest, family beach resort. The beach is long and flat, sheltered by a scenic headland, with lifeguards on duty during the summer months, beachside playground equipment, and the West Coast's only boardwalk north of Santa Cruz, California. Ice cream parlors, game arcades, eateries, and gift shops crowd shoulder to shoulder along the main drag, Broadway. The aroma of cotton candy and french fries lend a heady incense to the salt air, and the clatter of bumper cars and other amusements can induce sensory overload. Atlantic City it's not, thank goodness, but on a crowded summer day the resort evokes the feeling of a carnival midway by the sea. During spring break, when Northwest high school and college students arrive, the population of 6,200 can quadruple almost overnight.

South of town, the presence of clammers and waders in the shallows, and surfers negotiating the swells, also recalls the liveliness of a southern California or Atlantic shorefront instead of the remote peacefulness of many Oregon beaches. East Coast visitors often liken Cannon Beach to Provincetown, and Seaside to Coney Island—prior to their declines as destination resorts. Neighboring Gearhart, a mainly residential community (pop. 995) just to the north, has a few lodgings away from the bustle of Seaside, as well as a venerable 18-hole golf course.

Located along the Necanicum River, in the shadow of majestic Tillamook Head, Seaside has attracted tourists since the early 1870s, when transportation magnate Ben Holladay sensed the potential of a resort hotel near the water. But better transportation was needed to get customers to the place. At that time, the way to get to Seaside was first by boat from Portland down the Columbia River to Skipanon (now Warrenton), and from there by carriage south to Seaside. To speed the connection, Holladay constructed a railroad line from Skipanon to Seaside.

To escape Portland's summer heat, families would make the boat and railroad journey to spend their summer in Seaside. Most men would go back to Portland to work during the week, returning to the coast on Friday to visit the family. Every weekend the families would gather at the

In early spring, trilliums bloom in shaded forest groves.

railroad station to greet him, then see him off again for his trip back to Portland. It wasn't long before the train became known as the "Daddy Train." As roads between Portland and the coast were constructed, the car took over, and the railroad carried its last dad in 1939.

Prior to becoming the state's first coastal resort, Seaside's fame as the end of the Lewis and Clark Trail made it a national landmark. In recent years, the town has become more than just a retreat for Portland families. Oregon's apostle of haute cuisine, the late James Beard, used to hold a celebrated cooking class here each summer. This opened the door for writers' retreats, art classes, and business conventions. If these occasions or a family outing should bring you to Seaside, you'll enjoy the spirit of fun if you don't mind plenty of company on summer weekends.

SIGHTS

The Prom and Broadway

Sightseeing in Seaside means bustling up and down Broadway and strolling leisurely along the Prom. This two-mile-long boardwalk, extending from Avenue U north to 12th Avenue, was constructed in 1921 to replace the rotten planks from a wooden walkway built in 1908 and to protect ocean properties from the waves. A pleasant walk alongside the beach, it offers good vantages from which to contemplate the sand, surf, and massive contours of 1,200-foot-high Tillamook Head to the south.

Midway along the Prom is the **Turnaround,** a concrete and brick

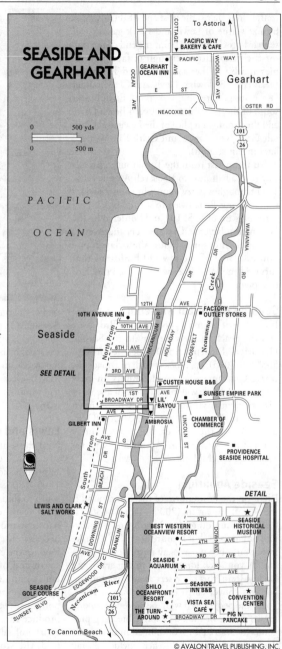

© AVALON TRAVEL PUBLISHING, INC.

COASTAL OREGON

traffic circle that is the west end of Broadway. A bronze statue of Lewis and Clark gazing ever seaward proclaims this point the end of the trail for their expedition, though in fact they explored a bit farther south, beyond Tillamook Head (see "Following Lewis and Clark" under "Recreation," later in this section). Eight blocks south of the Turnaround, between Beach Drive and the Prom is a replica of the Lewis and Clark salt cairn (see "Lewis and Clark Salt Works," later in this section).

Running east from the Turnaround, Broadway runs a half mile to Roosevelt Avenue (U.S. 101) through a dizzy gamut of tourist attractions. Along Broadway, in a four-block area running west of U.S. 101 and bordered by the Necanicum River and 1st Avenue, and Avenue A, you'll find some fancy Victorian frame houses, some of the few old buildings that survived the 1912 fire that destroyed much of the town.

Seaside Historical Museum

If you tire of having a good time on Broadway and the beach, make your way to the Seaside Historical Museum (570 Necanicum Dr., 503/738-7065), six blocks north of Broadway, where Clatsop artifacts and exhibits on early tourism in Seaside will impart more of a sense of history than anything else in town. It's open Mon.–Sat. 10 A.M.–4 P.M. late March–Oct., noon–3 P.M. the rest of the year; Sunday noon–3 P.M. year-round. Admission is $2 for adults, $1 for children.

Seaside Aquarium

Right on the Prom north of the Turnaround is the Seaside Aquarium (200 N. Prom, 503/738-6211). It's not quite the Oregon Coast Aquarium in Newport, but if you're not going to make it that far south it's an okay introduction to sea life for young children. Back in the era of the Daddy Train, this place served as a natatorium, but was converted to its current use in 1937. Today the pool is filled with the raucously barking results of one of the best captive-breeding programs for seals in the world. In addition, a hundred species of marine life here include 20-ray

end of the trail: Lewis and Clark statue at Seaside's Turnaround

sea stars, crabs, ferocious-looking wolf eels and moray eels, and octopus. Open daily 9 A.M.–5 P.M. March–Oct., Wed.–Sun. 9 A.M.–5 P.M. in winter. Admission for ages 6–13 is $3, ages 14 and up is $6.

Lewis and Clark Salt Works

Near the south end of the Prom are the reconstructed salt works of Lewis and Clark. While camped at Fort Clatsop during the winter of 1805–1806, the captains sent a detachment south to find a place suitable for rendering salt from seawater. Their supply was nearly exhausted, and the precious commodity was a necessity for preserving and seasoning their food on the expedition's return journey. At the south end of present-day Seaside, five men built a cairn-like stone oven near a settlement of the Clatsop and Killamox tribes, and set about boiling seawater nonstop for seven weeks to produce three and a half bushels (about 112 quarts) of salt for the trip back east. Truth be told, the stone oven isn't much to look at, but for Lewis and Clark buffs this is an important site, and will host historical reenactments and other events during the 2005–2006 bicentennial.

RECREATION
Following Lewis and Clark

From the south end of Seaside you can walk in the footsteps of Lewis and Clark on an exhilarating hike over **Tillamook Head.** In January 1806, neighboring Native Americans told of a beached whale lying several miles south of their encampment. William Clark and a few companions, including Sacagawea, set off in an attempt to find it and trade for blubber and whale oil, which fueled the expedition's lanterns. Climbing Tillamook Head from the north, the party crested the promontory. Clark was moved enough by the view to later write about it in his journal:

> *I beheld the grandest and most pleasing prospect which my eyes ever surveyed. Immediately in front of us is the ocean breaking in fury. To this boisterous scene the Columbia with its tributaries and studded on both sides with the Chinook and Clatsop villages forms a charming contrast, while beneath our feet are stretched the rich prairies.*

They eventually found the whale, south of Tillamook Head. Ecola Point and State Park here are named for it, after the Chinook word for "whale," *ecola* or *ekkoli.* By the time Clark arrived, however, the whale had been reduced to little more than a skeleton by the industrious Tillamooks, who used every part of the beast they could harvest. Clark measured the leviathan at 105 feet, which, if accurate, could only mean it was blue whale, the largest animal on earth and an extraordinary windfall for the Native Americans. He found the Tillamooks busily engaged in boiling the blubber in a large wooden trough by means of hot stones. The oil, when extracted, was stored in bladders. He had to bargain hard for a share, and wrote this of the negotiations:

> *The Tillamooks, although they possessed large quantities of this blubber and oil, were so penurious that they disposed of it with great reluctance, and in small quantities only; insomuch that my utmost exertions, aided by the party, with the small stock of merchandise I had taken with me, were not able to procure more blubber than about 300 pounds and a few gallons of oil. Small as this stock is, I prize it highly; and thank Providence for directing the whale to us; and think Him much more kind to us than He was to Jonah having sent this monster to be swallowed by us, instead of swallowing of us, as Jonah's did.*

Today, you can experience the view that so impressed Clark on the **Tillamook Head National Recreation Trail,** which runs seven miles through Ecola State Park. Prior to setting out, you could arrange to have a friend drive down to **Indian Beach** to pick you up at the end of this three- to five-hour trek. Or you can be picked up another mile south at the Ecola Point parking lot. To get to the trailhead, drive to the south end of Seaside to Avenue U past the golf course to Edgewood Street and turn left; continue until you reach the parking lot at the end of the road.

Nearby is an area known as **the cove,** frequented by surfers (prevailing winds favor winter surfing rather than summer) and fisherfolk. As you head up the forested trail on the north side of Tillamook Head, you can look back over the Seaside townsite. In about 20 minutes, you'll be gazing down at the ocean from cliffs 1,000 feet above. A few hours later, you'll hike down onto Indian Beach, arriving near the restrooms.

Fish and Wildlife

Just because you're smack-dab in the middle of a family resort town doesn't mean you can't enjoy some of nature's bounty; anglers can reel in trout, salmon, and steelhead from the Necanicum River right in the center of downtown. The **12th Avenue Bridge** is a popular spot for fishing and crabbing. **Cullaby Lake,** on the east side of U.S. 101

about four miles north of Gearhart, offers fishing for crappies, bluegills, perch, catfish, and largemouth bass. At 88 acres, Cullaby is the largest of the many lakes on the Clatsop Plains. Two parks on the lake, **Carnahan Park** and **Cullaby Lake County Park,** have boat ramps, picnic areas, and other facilities. Cullaby is the only practical place to water-ski in the area.

A half mile west of the highway, **Sunset Beach Park** on Neacoxie Lake (also known as Sunset Lake) has a boat ramp, picnic tables, and a playground. Anglers come for warmwater fish species, plus rainbow trout stocked in the spring.

Bird-watchers revel in **Necanicum Estuary Park,** 1900 block of N. Holladay across the street from Seaside High School. Local students have built a viewing platform, stairs to the beach, a boardwalk, and interpretive signs. Great blue and green herons and numerous migratory bird species flock to the grassy marshes and slow tidal waters near the mouth of the Necanicum River. Occasionally, Roosevelt elk, black-tailed deer, river otters, beavers, minks, and muskrats can also be sighted.

Water Sports

Despite the lifeguard on duty in summer, swimming at Seaside's beach isn't the most comfortable unless you're used to the North Sea. Gearhart boasts a quieter beach than Seaside's, though the water's every bit as cool. Warm-blooded swimmers can head to the pool and spa at **Sunset Empire Park** (1140 E. Broadway, Seaside, 503/738-3311), open daily. At Quatat Park, beside the Necanicum River in downtown Seaside, you can rent **kayaks, canoes, and pedal boats** for exploring the waterway.

The surfing venues north of Tillamook Head, Indian Basin, near Short Sands Beach in Oswald West State Park and in Manzanita can be enjoyed with surfboard and equipment rentals from **Cleanline Surf Shop** (719 1st Ave., Seaside, 503/738-7888). The shop rents Boogieboards and surfboards, as well as wetsuits, boots, and flippers.

Golf

Golfers can escape to public courses south of Seaside and north in the small town of Gearhart. At **Seaside Golf Course** (451 Ave. U, 503/738-5261), green fees are $9–10 for nine holes. The British links-style course at **Gearhart Golf Links** (Marion Street, 503/738-3538) was established in 1882, making it one of the oldest on the West Coast. Green fees are $35 for the 18-hole course. The **Highlands at Gearhart** (1 Highland Rd., Gearhart, 503/738-5248) is another public nine-hole course, with ocean views from most holes; $18 for 18 holes.

ENTERTAINMENT AND EVENTS

Seaside predates any other town on the Oregon coast as a place built with good times in mind. A zoo and racetrack were among Seaside's first structures. Saturday afternoons, Quatat Park hosts **free concerts** downtown. **Cannes Cinema** (U.S. 101 at 12th Avenue) is a five-screen multiplex showing the usual fare.

The annual **Oregon Dixieland Jubilee** (800/394-3303, www.jazzseaside.com) takes place at the end of February. This event has been gaining momentum for more than 20 years, and appeals to fans of Dixieland and traditional jazz. The town celebrates **July Fourth** with a parade, a picnic and social at the Seaside Museum, and a big fireworks show on the beach.

In early September, the **Hot Rod Happenin'** (503/717-1914) and **Roadster Show** (800/394-3303) bring classic cars from all over to downtown and the Civic and Convention Center (1st Avenue at Necanicum). The third week in September, the **Seaside Sand Sculpture and Beach Festival** is good fun.

PRACTICALITIES

Accommodations

Whatever your price range, you'll have to reserve ahead for a room in Seaside during the summer, weekends, and holidays (especially spring break). If you do, chances are you'll be able to find the specs you're looking for, given the area's array of lodgings (more than three dozen motels, a few B&Bs, and many vacation rentals); if you don't, come prepared to camp. The Seaside Visitors Bureau's helpful website provides comprehensive listings (www.seasideor.com). A good option for families and groups might be one of the several dozen vacation rentals. Check with the Seaside Visitors Bureau, or contact one of the rental agencies: **Oceanside Vacation Rental** (503/738-7767 or 800/840-7764); **D. B. Rentals** (503/717-9516 or 800/203-1681); or **Northwind Property Management** (503/738-5532 or 800/488-3301).

The cheapest place in town is the **Seaside International Hostel** (930 N. Holladay, 503/738-7911 or 800/909-4776). Unlike the other hostels, it doesn't close down during the day, there's an espresso bar and the Necanicum River runs through the backyard. Close by is the Necanicum Estuary Park described later in this chapter. There are shared rooms with four to six bunks and private rooms for $16–59 a night. To get there from U.S. 101, make a left at the city center sign, turn on Holladay, and continue north. When you get to 9th Avenue look for the hostel on the left. There's no curfew here.

Motel 6 (2369 S. Roosevelt, 503/738-6269), on U.S. 101 about a half mile south of Broadway, has doubles for around $59. The **Comfort Inn** (545 Broadway Ave., Seaside, 503/738-3011), is right on the Necanicum River. Rooms feature fireplaces, spa baths, microwave, fridge, and balconies overlooking the river. Rates are $75–140.

Gearhart offers a respite from the bustle of Seaside. The **Gearhart Ocean Inn** (67 N. Cottage St., 503/738-7373) charges $49–109 (but offers off-season specials Oct.–April) for your choice of 11 New England–style wooden cottages with comforters, wicker chairs, throw rugs, and a location close to the beach. The two-story deluxe units have kitchens and hardwood floors. Pets are allowed in some units. This spruced-up old motor court is one of the best values on the North Coast.

The **Shilo Oceanfront Resort** (30 N. Prom, 503/738-9571 or 800/222-2244), is right by the Prom turnaround and is a justifiable splurge for the oceanfront rooms that have balconies, fireplaces, and kitchenettes. A restaurant with windows on the water (good Sunday brunch) and an ocean-view spa/pool/health club make it worth the $100-plus nightly rate. The lounge features DJ music. **Best Western Oceanview Resort** (414 N. Prom, 503/738-3264 or 800/234-8439) is another large hotel/motel right on the beach. Amenities include on-site restaurant and lounge, heated pool and spa; the majority of rooms face the ocean. Rates run $71–205.

Bed-and-Breakfasts

While motels dominate the lodging scene in Seaside, a few B&Bs offer an alternative. Our top award for creativity goes to the **Seaside Inn B&B** (581 S. Prom, 503/319-3300 or 800/772-7766). This four-story, shingle-sided structure stands right on the beach, with its north gable skewered by a clock tower. Each of the 15 guestrooms is decorated in a unique theme. The queen bed in the '50–'60s Rock & Roll room, for example, is incorporated into the tail end of a '59 Oldsmobile ($115–189). Other themes include the Bubble Room ($120–199), Sports Corner ($110–185), and the Clock Tower Suite ($160–295). Most have a spectacular ocean view.

The **Gilbert Inn** (341 Beach Dr., 503/738-9770 or 800/410-9770) is a well-preserved 1892 Queen Anne, located just a block south of Broadway and a block from the beach. Period furnishings adorn the 10 guestrooms, which all have private bath, down comforters, and other nice touches. The third-floor "Garret" sleeps up to four in a queen and two twin beds, with ocean views from the dormer window. Rates range $105–125 May–September (15–20 percent less off-season), including full breakfast.

North of Broadway, the **10th Avenue Inn** (125 10th Ave., 503/738-0643 or 800/745-2378) is a comfortable 1908 home built just a few steps from the beach. In the parlor, a baby grand piano, guitar, and other instruments are available for musically inclined guests. The three guestrooms have king-sized beds, attached baths, TVs, and small refrigerators. Rates run $89–129.

Next door and operated by the same folks is the **Doll House,** a sweet two-bedroom cottage (ideal for four adults plus two or three children) with full kitchen and a deck with barbecue grill. It goes for $800/week in summer (minimum week's rental), $150 per night off-season (two-night minimum).

Food

While a stroll down Broadway might have you thinking that cotton candy, corn dogs, and saltwater taffy are the staples of Seaside cuisine, several eateries here can satisfy taste and nutrition as well as the broad-based clientele of this beach town.

For breakfast, the Swedish pancakes and crab-and-cheese omelettes at **Pig 'N Pancake** (323 Broadway, 503/738-7243) are tops. If you're seriously hungry try the Frisbee-sized cinnamon rolls. At last count, you could choose from 33 different breakfast variations at this place. You can count on this local chain (with outlets in Astoria and Cannon Beach) for three solid meals every day of the week.

The Stand (109 N. Holladay, 503/738-6592) features the satisfying and inexpensive Mexican fare that you'd find on the streetcart *loncherias* of Guadalajara. The carnitas taco is a mouthful of seasoned pork only exceeded perhaps by its beefy counterpart, the carne asada taco. The chili verde burrito as well as enchiladas, tamales, and other specialties can be enjoyed in the tiled confines of the restaurant.

The **Vista Sea Cafe** (150 Broadway, 503/738-8108) is known for pizza with ingredients such as artichokes, feta, chorizo, and pesto, plus topnotch clam chowder with homemade beer bread. Its location one block from the Turnaround makes it especially convenient.

Dooger's (505 Broadway, 503/738-3773), which also has an outlet in Cannon Beach, has won acclaim for its clam chowder. Local clams and oysters, fresh Dungeness crab legs, sautéed shrimp, and marionberry cobbler are also the basis of Dooger's do-good reputation. The **Bell Buoy of Seaside** (1800 Holladay, 503/738-6354) is a seafood market that makes an excellent razor clam chowder. Much of their seafood is brought in by their own fleet, and they'll pack for overnight shipping.

A rarity in these parts, **Lil' Bayou** (20 N. Holladay Dr., 503/717-0624) dishes up authentic muffulettas, jambalaya, blackened catfish, gumbo, and a host of other cajun and creole standards, right down to side dishes of collard greens, at reasonable prices. Lunch entrées run $5–8, while most dinners are $12–15, topping out at $19.95 for an 18-ounce New York strip steak with Jack Daniel's sauce. Finish off with a slice of sweet potato pecan pie or Aunt B's cheesecake. Oooweeee.

Seaside's toniest dinner house is probably **Ambrosia** (210 S. Holladay, 503/738-7199). A good way to kick off your meal is with a selection from their martini menu, which offers a dozen variations on the standard. The N'Awlins, made with pepper vodka and jalapeño-stuffed olives, is an eye-opener. Entrées include fish, chicken, pork, and duck dishes, and pastas incorporating crab, shrimp, and clams; prices range $13–22, though the couple of beef choices are stiffly priced at $25–27.

Should the ambience of Seaside on a holiday weekend pall, try the **Pacific Way Bakery and Cafe** in Gearhart (601 Pacific Way, 503/738-0245). Gearhart is the area where famed food writer James Beard was raised. Beard himself would probably give Pacific Way's croissants five stars, so flaky and buttery are these breakfast mainstays. They take center stage again at lunch, providing the foundations for delectable sandwich fillings. Particularly recommended are the smoked salmon and cream cheese with thin-sliced red onion on croissant, the cioppino, and Caesar salad. Pasta, crusty pizzas, and seafood dishes (including thick seafood stew) as well as crepes also pop up at lunch and dinnertime. Ribeye steak and local razor clams are other frequent dinnertime highlights in the surprisingly urbane little café hidden behind a rustic old storefront.

Information and Transportation

The **Seaside Chamber of Commerce and Visitors Bureau** (7 N. Roosevelt St., Seaside 97138, 503/738-6391 or 800/444-6740, www

.seasidechamber.com) is open daily from 8 A.M.–5 P.M.

Seaside is very walkable, but for $2 you can ride around town on the brightly painted **Seaside Street Car,** which runs hourly. Sunset Empire Transportation District also operates **The Bus,** which serves Cannon Beach, Seaside, Astoria-Warrenton, and points in between. For schedule and fare info, call 503/861-7433.

Seaside's **Digital Design** (111 Broadway, Ste. 3, 503/717-8350) is a cyber café featuring coffee and espresso along with Internet connections ($5/hour) and digital printing. Open daily.

Astoria and Vicinity

With its river and ocean access and abundance of natural resources, Astoria was long a traditional meeting place for the Native American tribes of this region. These features continue to lure travelers seeking prime recreational opportunities to this historic seaport town.

Many visitors are aware of Astoria's legacy as the oldest permanent U.S. settlement west of the Rockies; its glory days are preserved by museums, historical exhibits, and pastel-colored Victorian homes weathered by the sea air. Hollywood has chosen Astoria's picturesque neighborhoods to simulate an idealized all-American city on close to a dozen occasions.

Such idealization often creates the expectation of a Williamsburg of the West, where the portrayal of history and heritage is a focal point of the local identity. The reality of modern-day Astoria, however, is more accurately captured in a locally popular bumper sticker that defiantly proclaims, "We Ain't Quaint!"

The preserved pioneer past and attractive Victorian homes may soften the rough edges of a once-bustling port that has seen better days, but not enough to let anyone mistake blue-collar Astoria for an ersatz tourist town. The decommissioning of the U.S. Naval station after World War II, the decline in the logging and fishing industries, and the closure of several dozen canneries on the waterfront have had lasting effects on this town of 10,000 people. Empty storefronts here tell

Want some company on your north coast drive? Set your dial to KMUN (91.9 in Astoria and Seaside, 89.5 in Cannon Beach) for community-based programming featuring folk, classical, jazz, and rock music, plus public affairs, literature readings, children's stories, and news.

the story of a resource-based economy bruised by progress, but there's plenty of pluck left in this old dowager, and her best years may be yet to come.

Astoria hath many charms: Historic buildings downtown are undergoing restoration, cruise ships are calling, fine restaurants are multiplying, a lively music and arts scene is thriving, and there's new life along the waterfront, anchored by the excellent Columbia River Maritime Museum.

The waters surrounding Astoria define the town as much as the steep hills it's built on. Along its northern side, the mighty Columbia, four miles wide, is a mega-highway carrying a steady flow of traffic, from small pleasure boats to massive cargo ships a quarter mile long. Soaring high over the river is an engineering marvel that's impossible to miss from most locations in town. At just over four miles long, the Astoria-Megler Bridge, completed in 1966, is the longest bridge in Oregon and the longest bridge of its type (cantilever through truss) in the world. On Astoria's south side, the Young's River, flowing down from the Coast Range, broadens into Young's Bay, separating Astoria from its neighbor Warrenton (pop. 4,040) to the west.

A few miles to the northwest, the Columbia River finally meets the Pacific, 1,243 miles from its headwaters in British Columbia. Where the tremendous outflow (average 118 million gallons per minute) of the River of the West encounters the ocean tides, conditions can be treacherous, and the sometimes monstrous waves around the bar have claimed more than 2,000 vessels over the years. This rivermouth could well be the biggest widow-maker on the high seas, earning it the title Graveyard of the Pacific. Lewis and Clark referred to it as "that seven-shouldered horror" in a journal entry from the winter of 1805–1806.

SIGHTS

Astoria Column

The best introduction to Astoria and environs is undoubtedly the 360-degree panorama from atop the 125-foot-tall Astoria Column on Coxcomb Hill, the highest point in town. Patterned after the Trajan Column in Rome, the reinforced-concrete tower was built in 1926 as a joint project of the Great Northern Railroad and the descendants of John Jacob Astor to commemorate the westward sweep of discovery and migration. The sgraffito frieze spiraling up the exterior illustrates Robert Gray's 1792 discovery of the Columbia River, the establishment of American claims to the Northwest Territory, the arrival of the Great Northern Railway, and other scenes of Northwest history. The vista from the surrounding hilltop park is impressive enough, but for the ultimate experience, the climb up 164 steps to the tower's top is worth the effort.

Before ascending, get oriented with the annotated bronze relief map in front of the column, which notes the distances and directions to such landmarks near and far. From this vantage point, you can see across the rooftops of the town, the Astoria Bridge, giant freighters gliding up and down the Columbia, and a long sweep of the Washington shore. To the northwest are the Columbia Bar and Cape Disappointment. On clear days, look northeast to Mount St. Helens and to Mount Hood on the far eastern horizon. Looking over Young's Bay south and west of Astoria, the Clatsop Plains extend to Tillamook Head and Saddleback Mountain.

Get to the Astoria Column from downtown by following 16th Street south (uphill) to Jerome

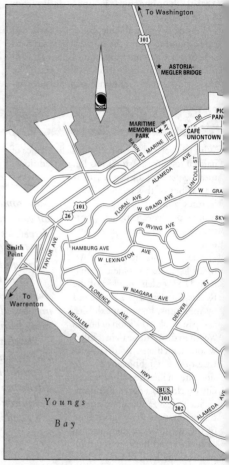

Avenue. Turn west (right) one block and continue up 15th Street to the park entrance on Coxcomb Drive. Open daily dawn–dusk; call 503/325-2963 for further info. A $1 parking fee is requested at the visitors center.

On the Waterfront

While most of Astoria's waterfront is lined with warehouses, industry, and docks, the **6th Street Riverpark** and River Walk will get you front-row views of the river. The park is a local favorite from which to watch ships from the sheltered

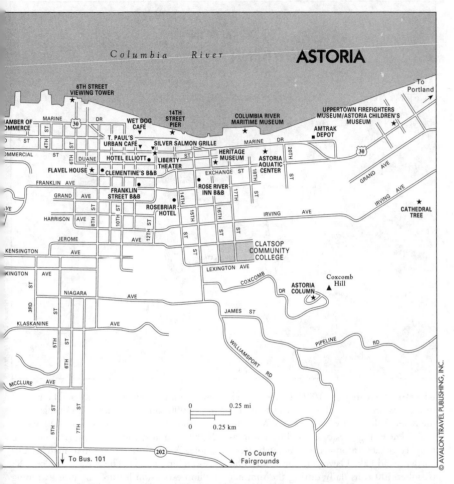

observation platform and to fish for Columbia River salmon. The Lewis and Clark Bicentennial headquarters is here; placards around the park display information about the Lewis and Clark Expedition and the area's Chinook natives.

Walk east from Pier 6, past the fish-packing plants, for an interesting if malodorous and noisy (thanks to the sea lions) perspective on what is still a working commercial fishing port. The 11th Street Pier has been developed with a restaurant and shops, and the 14th Street Pier and 17th Street Dock are two other convenient access points for watching cargo ships, sea lions, and fishing boats.

The **River Walk** provides riverside passage for pedestrians and cyclists along a three-mile stretch between the Port of Astoria and the community of Alderbrook. Eventually, the path will extend another two miles eastward to Tongue Point, and west past the Port of Astoria to Smith Point.

An excellent way to cover some of the same ground, accompanied by color commentary on sights and local history, is by taking a 40-minute ride on Old Number 300, the **Astoria**

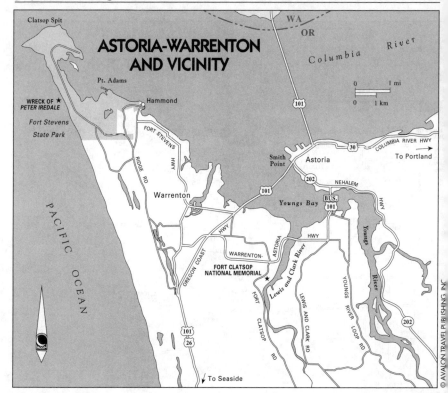

ASTORIA-WARRENTON AND VICINITY

Riverfront Trolley (503/325-6311), which runs on Astoria's original train tracks alongside the River Walk as far east as the East Mooring Basin. The lovingly restored 1913 trolley originally served San Antonio, and later ran between Portland and Lake Oswego in the 1980s. Old Number 300 runs daily during the summer 3 P.M.–9 P.M. weekdays, noon–9 P.M. Fri.–Sunday. Off-season, it operates weekends only, until dark. During heavy rains, the antique trolley may stay put in its newly constructed barn. It costs $1 to ride the trolley as long as you stay on board; the $2 All-Day Fare lets you get on and off as often as you like.

Columbia River Maritime Museum

On the waterfront a few blocks east of downtown Astoria, the Columbia River Maritime Museum (1792 Marine Dr., 503/325-2323, www.crmm.org) is hard to miss. The roof of the 44,000-square-foot museum simulates the curvature of cresting waves, and the gigantic 25,000-pound anchor out front is also hard to ignore. What's inside more than matches this eye-catching facade. The museum's recent $5 million expansion features an award-winning film about the region's maritime history and includes displays on the Coast Guard, salmon fishing, tugboats, and canneries of Astoria. Floor-to-ceiling windows in the Great Hall allow visitors to watch the river traffic in comfort.

The eras when tribal canoes plied the Columbia, Lewis and Clark camped on its shores, and dramatic shipwrecks occurred on its bar are recounted with scale models, exquisitely detailed miniatures of ships, paintings, artifacts. The most dramatic exhibit is of a 44-foot U.S.

Coast Guard motor lifeboat, poised precariously on a wave in a life-size re-creation of a rescue on the Columbia River Bar. The chance to walk the bridge of a World War II destroyer, steer a tugboat, or tie a cleat hitch and other useful knots imparts a hands-on aspect to the experience. Local lighthouses, the evolution of boat design, and harpoons are the focus of other exhibits here. There are also some artifacts from the *Peter Iredale* and other ships that have met their ends on the Oregon coast. Scrimshaw, fishing and cannery memorabilia, a small watercolor of the harbor by a crewmember on Robert Gray's 1792 voyage of discovery, and sea charts dating as far back as 1587 also highlight your visit.

Your ticket also lets you board the 128-foot Lightship *Columbia,* now permanently berthed alongside the museum building. This vessel served as a floating lighthouse, marking the entrance to the mouth of the river and helping many ships navigate the dangerous waters. After almost three decades of service it was replaced in 1979 by an unstaffed 42-foot-high navigational buoy.

The museum is open daily 9:30 A.M.–5 P.M. (closed Thanksgiving and Christmas). Admission for adults is $8, seniors $7, ages 6–17 $4, and children under six get in free. The gift shop has a great collection of books on Astoria's history as well as other maritime topics.

Heritage Museum and Research Library

The Clatsop County Historical Society operates the Heritage Museum (1618 Exchange St., 503/325-2203). Housed in the handsome neoclassical building that was originally Astoria's city hall, it has several galleries filled with antiquities, tools, vintage photographs, and archives chronicling various aspects of life in Clatsop County. The museum's new centerpiece exhibit concentrates on the culture of the local Clatsop and Chinook tribes, from before European contact to the present day. Other exhibits highlight the natural history, geology, early immigrants and settlers in the region, the development of commerce in such enterprises as fishing, fish packing, logging, and lumber. The research library has recently expanded and is open to the public. The Heritage Museum is open daily May–Sept. 10 A.M.–5 P.M., and charges $4 for adults, $2.50 for seniors, and $2 for children 6–12.

Flavel House Museum

Captain George Flavel, Astoria's first millionaire, amassed a fortune in the mid-19th century through his Columbia Bar piloting monopoly, and later expanded his empire through shipping, banking, and real estate. Between 1884 and 1886, he had a home built in the center of Astoria, overlooking the Columbia River, where he retired with his wife and two daughters. From its fourth-story cupola, Flavel could watch the comings and goings of his sailing fleet. Although the captain died in 1893, members of the family lived in the house until 1933. The amazing story of the Flavel family was depicted in colorful detail by Calvin Trillin in a February 1993 issue of the *New Yorker.*

The 25,000-pound anchor from a U.S. Navy battleship outside the Columbia River Maritime Museum dwarfs a young visitor.

When the Clatsop County Historical Society assumed stewardship in 1951, the mansion was slated for demolition, to be paved over as a parking lot for the adjacent courthouse. Fortunately, thanks to the efforts of the historical society and many volunteers, the house still stands today, at the corner of 8th Street and Duane. The splendidly extravagant Queen Anne mansion reflects the rich style and elegance of the late Victorian era and the lives of Astoria's most prominent family. Known locally as "the house with the red roof," it has withstood more than a century of storms off the Columbia River estuary. This landmark for incoming ships is now the foremost monument to Astoria's golden age as the leading port in the Northwest.

The property encompasses a full city block. With its intricate woodwork inside and out, period furnishings, and art, along with its extravagantly rendered gables, cornices, and porches, the Flavel House ranks with the Carson Mansion in Eureka, California, as a Victorian showplace. The 14-foot ceilings, Persian rugs, and an array of imported tiles are upstaged only by the fireplaces framed in exotic hardwoods in every room. The recently restored Carriage House is now an orientation center for visitors, with exhibits, an interpretive video, and museum store.

The Flavel House Museum (441 8th St., 503/325-2203), is open daily from 10 A.M.–5 P.M. May–Sept. and 11 A.M.–4 P.M. Oct.–April. Visitors should stop first at the Carriage House to purchase tickets: $5 for adults, $4 for seniors/students, $2 for ages 6–17, children five and younger free.

Twilight Creek Eagle Sanctuary/ Lewis and Clark National Wildlife Refuge

Six miles east of Astoria in the Burnside area is the Twilight Creek Eagle Sanctuary. To get there, drive east on U.S. 30 and turn left at Burnside. Another left a half mile later takes you to the viewing platform, which overlooks the 35,000 acres of mudflats, tidal marshes, and islands (which Lewis and Clark called "Seal Islands") of the Lewis and Clark National Wildlife Refuge. Bald eagles live here year-round, with 30–35 active nest sites. The area provides wintering and resting habitat for waterfowl (including an estimated 1,000 tundra swans in winter), shorebirds, and songbirds. Beavers, raccoons, weasels, mink, muskrats, and river otters live on the islands; harbor seals and California sea lions feed in the rich estuary waters and use the sandbars and mudflats as haul-out sites at low tides.

Fort Clatsop National Memorial

On November 7, 1805, after a journey of nearly 19 months and 4,000 miles, the Lewis and Clark expedition thought they had at last reached their destination, the Pacific Ocean. "Ocian in View! O! the joy," wrote William Clark in his journal. Alas, they were close, but from the Washington side of the Columbia River they had mistaken its broad mouth for the sea itself. Hindered by waves and foul weather, it would take nearly another week before they actually beheld the Pacific. They explored farther west, to Cape Disappointment, and spent 10 uncomfortable days exposed to the elements on the north shore of the Columbia, then decided to move south for a more suitable location to pass the coming winter.

They chose a thickly forested rise alongside the Netul River (now the Lewis and Clark River), a few miles south of present-day Astoria, for their campsite. There the Corps of Discovery quickly set about felling trees and building two parallel rows of cabins, joined by a gated palisade. The finished compound measured about 50 feet square. The party of 33 people, including one African American, a Native American woman, and her baby, moved into the seven small rooms on Christmas Eve, and named their stockade Fort Clatsop for the nearby tribe.

The winter of 1805–1806 was one of the worst on record—cold, wet, rainy, and generally miserable. Of the 106 days spent at the site, it rained on all but 12. The January 18, 1806, journal entry of expedition member Private Joseph Whitehouse was typical of the comments recorded during the stay: "It rained hard all last night, & still continued the same this morning. It continued Raining during the whole of this day."

While at Fort Clatsop, the men stored up meat and other supplies, sewed moccasins and new garments, and traded with local tribes, all the while coping with the constant damp, illness and injuries, and merciless plagues of fleas. As soon as the weather permitted, on March 23, 1806, they finally departed on their homeward journey to St. Louis.

Within a few years, the elements had erased all traces of Fort Clatsop, and its exact location was lost. In 1955, local history buffs took their best guess and built a replica of the fort, based on the notes and sketches of Captain Clark. In 1999, an anthropologist discovered a 148-year-old map identifying the location of Lewis and Clark's winter encampment, and as it turns out the modern reproduction is sited very close to the original.

Today, in addition to the log replica of the fort, a well-equipped visitors center, museum, and other attractions make Fort Clatsop National Memorial a must stop for anyone interested in this pivotal chapter of American history. The expedition's story is nicely narrated here with displays, artifacts, slides, and films, but the summertime "living history" reenactments are the main reason to come. Paths lead through the grove of old-growth Sitka spruce, with interpretive placards identifying native plants. A short walk from the fort leads to the riverside, where dugout canoes are modeled on those used by the corps while in this area.

The winter of 1805–1806 put a premium on wilderness survival skills, some of which are exhibited here by rangers in costume, daily 9 A.M.–5:30 P.M. Memorial Day–Labor Day. You can see the tanning of hides, making of buckskin clothing and moccasins, and the molding of tallow candles and lead bullets. In addition, visitors may occasionally participate in the construction of a dugout canoe or try their luck at starting a fire by striking flint on steel. For a taste of what Lewis and Clark and their party experienced here, a visit on a cold, wet, wintry day, when every branch and leaf is dripping with rain, is an opportunity to better appreciate their fortitude.

This 125-acre park sits six miles southwest of Astoria and three miles east of U.S. 101 on the Lewis and Clark River. To get there from Astoria, take Marine Drive and head west across Young's Bay to Warrenton. On the other side of the bay look for signs for the Fort Clatsop turnoff. Then turn left off the Coast Highway and follow the direction markers to Fort Clatsop National Memorial (92343 Fort Clatsop Rd., Astoria 97103, 503/861-2471, www.nps.gov/focl).

Admission at press time was $3 per person or $5 per car, good for seven days' admission, but entrance fees will probably rise during the 2004–2006 bicentennial observations. The Oregon Coast Annual Pass and Oregon Coast 5-Day Pass are honored here. Park officials expect that the annual quarter-million visitors will increase by up to 70 percent during the bicentennial. A new, larger parking lot is being built .75 mile from the visitors center; trails and shuttles will connect the two. Plans are also in the works to add a kayak and canoe landing at the lot. Once that lot fills, visitors will have to board special shuttle buses in Astoria, Warrenton, Fort Stevens, Seaside, and Cannon Beach. For details, contact the park or the Sunset Empire Transportation District (503/861-RIDE or 800/776-6406, www.ridethebus.org), which operates The Bus. Park entrance will include the cost of the ride.

Gates to the memorial are open 8 A.M.–6 P.M. during the summer season and 8 A.M.–5 P.M. the rest of the year. Open every day except Christmas.

Fort Stevens State Park

Ten miles west of Astoria, at the far northwest corner of the state, this Civil War–era outpost was one of three military installations (the others were Forts Canby and Columbia in Washington) built to safeguard the mouth of the Columbia River. Established shortly before the Confederates surrendered on April 9, 1865, Fort Stevens served for 84 years, until just after the end of World War II. Today, the remaining fortifications and other buildings are preserved along with 3,700 acres of woodland, lakes, wetlands, miles of sand beaches, and three miles of Columbia River frontage.

sleeping quarters at Fort Clatsop

The fort's creation was not the only outgrowth of the Civil War on the West Coast. The year before, Lincoln had founded the city of Port Angeles, Washington, for "lighthouse purposes." Given the subsequent creation of Fort Stevens shortly thereafter, it's a logical assumption that "lighthouse purposes" also meant watching out for Confederate ships and the British, whom the Union feared would ally with the South. The remote northwest Oregon coast may seem a world away from the bloody battles of the Civil War, until you consider that the last shots of the conflict were fired even farther away, in the Bering Strait. On June 5, 1865, the *Shenandoah* attacked a fleet of Yankee whalers, because the Confederate skipper was unaware of the Appomattox treaty, which had ended the war two months before.

Though Fort Stevens did not see action in the Civil War, it sustained an attack in a later conflict. On June 21, 1942, a Japanese submarine fired 17 shells on the gun emplacements at Battery Russell, making it the only U.S. fortification in the 48 states to be bombed by a foreign power since the War of 1812. No damage was incurred, and the Army didn't return fire. Shortly after World War II, the fort

was deactivated and the armaments were removed.

Today, the site features a memorial rose garden, a Military Museum with old photos, weapons exhibits, and maps, as well as seven different batteries (fortifications) and other structures left over from almost a century of service. Climbing to the commander's station for a scenic view of the Columbia River and South Jetty are popular visitor activities. The massive gun batteries, built of weathered gray concrete and rusting iron, eerily silent amid the thick woodlands, also invite exploration; small children should be closely supervised, as there are steep stairways, high ledges, and other hazards.

During the summer months, guided tours of the underground Battery Mishler ($2) and a narrated tour of the fort's 37 acres on a two-ton U.S. Army truck ($2.50) are also available. The summer programs include Civil War reenactments and archaeological digs; consult the visitors center for schedules.

Nine miles of bike trails and six miles of hiking trails link the historic area to the rest of the park and provide access to Battery Russell and the 1906 wreck of the British schooner *Peter Iredale* (see special topic "Buried in the Sand"). You can also bike to the campground one mile south of the Military Museum.

Parking is available at four lots about a mile apart from one another at the foot of the dunes. The beach runs north to the Columbia River, where excellent surf fishing, bird-watching, and a view of the mouth of the river await. South of the campground (east of the *Peter Iredale*) there's a self-guided nature trail around part of the two-mile shoreline of **Coffenbury Lake.** The lake also has two swimming beaches with bathhouses and fishing for trout and perch.

To get there from U.S. 101, drive west on Harbor Street through Warrenton on Route 104 (Ft. Stevens Highway) to the suburb of Hammond, and follow the signs to Fort Stevens Historic Area and Military Museum (503/861-1671 or 800/551-6949). The fort's hours are daily 10 A.M.–6 P.M. Memorial Day–Labor Day, and Wed.–Sun. 10 A.M.–4 P.M. the rest of the year. Except for the tours, museum admission is free.

© MARK MORRIS

BURIED IN THE SAND

Of the hundreds of ships wrecked on the Oregon coast over the centuries, one of the best known is the British schooner *Peter Iredale*. This 278-foot four-master, fashioned of steel plates on an iron frame, was built in Liverpool in 1890. She came to her untimely end on the beach south of Clatsop Spit on October 25, 1906. En route from Mexico to pick up a load of wheat on the Columbia River, the vessel ran aground during high seas and a northwesterly squall. All hands were rescued and, with little damage to the hull, hopes initially ran high that the ship could be towed back to sea and salvaged. That effort proved fruitless, and eventually the ship was written off as a total loss. Today, nearly a century later, the remains of her rusting skeleton protruding from the sands of Fort Stevens State Park are a familiar sight to most who have traveled the north coast. Signs within Fort Stevens State Park lead the way to the parking area close to the wreck.

COURTESY OF MARK SIMON/IMAGE PERFECT & DESIGN

the *Peter Iredale* on November 13, 1906, two weeks after the wreck . . .

© MARK MORRIS

. . . and in 2004

COASTAL OREGON

There is a $3 parking fee, which is covered by the Oregon Coast Annual Pass and Oregon Coast 5-Day Pass.

For details on camping, see "Camping," later in this section.

RECREATION
Fishing Charters
More than any other industry, commercial fishing has dominated Astoria throughout its history. Salmon canneries lined the waterfront at the turn of the century. Albacore and longline shark fishing put dinner on the table in the 1930s and 1940s. In the modern era, commercial fishing has turned to sole, rockfish, flounder, and other bottom fish. If it's not enough to watch these commercial operations from the dock, try joining a charter.

Tiki Charters (503/325-7818, www.tikicharters.com) will take you out for salmon and sturgeon. Trips depart from the West Mooring Basin in Astoria. River tours are also available. Given the retail price of fresh salmon, you could theoretically pay for a charter trip by landing a single fish. **Gale Force Guides** (Warrenton, 503/861-1494), takes sport anglers fishing for salmon in either salt- or freshwater, depending on the season. On your own, go after trout, bass, catfish, steelhead, and sturgeon in freshwater lakes, streams, and rivers. Lingcod, rockfish, surfperch, or other bottom fish can be pursued at sea, off jetties, or along ocean beaches.

Hiking
An in-town hike that's not too strenuous begins at 28th Street and Irving, meandering up the hill to the Astoria Column. If you drive to the trailhead, park along 28th. It's about a one-mile walk to the top. En route is the **Cathedral Tree**, an old-growth fir with a sort of Gothic arch formed at its roots.

The **Oregon Coast Trail** starts (or ends) at Clatsop Spit, at the north end of Fort Stevens State Park. The most northerly stretch extends south along the beach for 14 miles to Gearhart. It's a flat, easy walk, and your journey could well be highlighted by a sighting of the endangered silver-spot butterfly. The species frequents just six sites, including four in Oregon; Clatsop County is one of them. The endangered status of the creature protects it by law, and has stopped developers from building resorts on coastal meadows and dunes north of Gearhart. Look for a small orange butterfly with silvery spots on the undersides of its wings.

You also might encounter cars on the beach. This section of shoreline is, inexplicably, the longest stretch of coastline open to motor vehicles in Oregon. Call the State Parks and Recreation Division (800/551-6949) for an up-to-date report on trail conditions before starting out.

Fort Stevens State Park has nine miles of hiking trails, through woods, wetlands, and dunes. One popular hike here is the two-mile loop around **Coffenbury Lake.**

Camping
Families flock to **Fort Stevens State Park** (800/452-5687 for reservations). With 253 tent sites, 343 RV sites, and a special area for walk-in campers and bicyclists, the campground is the largest in the state park system. With the park's amenities and other attractions, this is the perfect base camp from which to take advantage of the region. Just be sure to avoid spring break (around March 23–29) if you wish to be spared the rites of spring enacted here by Oregon teenagers. Rates are $17–22. Yurts can be had here for $29, hiker-biker sites for $4. The park is open year-round.

Across the road, **Astoria Warrenton Seaside KOA** (1100 N.W. Ridge Rd., Hammond, 503/861-2606 or 800/562-8506) has 310 sites, with 54 cabins. Summer rates (April–Sept.) are $25.95–33.95 for basic tent sites; up to $39.95–49.95 for deluxe RV sites with all hookups; $45.95–55.95 for one-room cabins (sleep six); $55.95–65.95 for two-room cabins (sleep six). Prices drop about 10 percent the rest of the year. Amenities include indoor pool and hot tub, game room, mini golf, and bike rentals.

ENTERTAINMENT
For the lowdown on all the happenings in and around Astoria, get your hands on a copy of *Hip-*

fish, Astoria's spirited monthly tabloid distributed free all over town.

Astor Street Opry Company

Astoria's long-running *Shanghaied in Astoria,* which is based on the town's dubious distinction as a notorious shanghai port during the late 1800s, is a good old-fashioned melodrama. Chase scenes, bar fights, and a liberal sprinkling of Scandinavian jokes will have you laughing, in between applauding the hero and booing the villain. Performed with gusto by the Astor Street Opry Company, the show has been going on for two decades. Shows Thurs.–Sat. evenings mid-July–mid-Sept., in the converted Old Finnish Meat Market building (279 W. Marine Dr., 503/325-6104). Tickets are $8–16, available at the door.

Liberty Theater

The handsome Liberty Theater (www.liberty-theater.org), whose colonnaded facades along Commercial and 12th Streets converge at the corner box office, is a vibrant symbol of Astoria's ongoing rejuvenation. The ornate Mediterranean-style building in the heart of downtown began its life in 1925 as a venue for silent films, vaudeville acts, and lectures. The theater continued as a first-run movie house, but after decades of neglect this grande dame was showing her age badly, and it looked as though the Liberty would eventually meet the sad fate of so many fine old movie palaces. Happily, though, a nonprofit organization undertook efforts to restore the theater to its original elegance and equip it to be a state-of-the-art performing arts center. Work is ongoing, but already the Liberty hosts concerts, recitals, theater, and other events.

River Theater

This local cultural treasure is located underneath the Astoria Bridge. Every April since 1998, the nonprofit River Theater (230 W. Marine Dr., 503/325-7487, www.rivertheater.com) stages a new edition of its original "Simple Salmon" sketch comedy series. Part writing competition, part theatrical production, the cast acts out sketches submitted by the public, and the audience votes for their favorites. Open mic readings, dinner theater, live community-radio (KMUN) broadcasts, and plays from Shakespeare to Ionesco fill out the changing bill of fare. In addition, the River hosts an impressively eclectic lineup of local and touring musicians, covering most of the bases with Celtic, bluegrass, folk, blues, and jazz, with pop, punk, rock, and gospel tossed in for good measure. Check their website or *Hipfish* for scheduled events.

Movies

Adjacent to the Columbian Cafe, the Columbian Theatre (corner of 11th and Marine, 503/325-3516) screens the big movies you may have missed a month before in their first run. Dine on beer, wine, pizza, and other munchies while you watch. Shows nightly at 7 P.M.; $3 general admission, $2 seniors and kids.

Astoria Gateway Cinema (1875 Marine Dr., 503/338-6575) is a modern movie multiplex, showing the usual stuff, where you can pass an afternoon trying to forget the interminable winter rains here.

Bookstores

Several bookstores in town invite serious browsing, buying, and intellectual stimulation. **Kneedeep in Books** (1052 Commercial St., 503/325-9722) specializes in used books and remainders, as well as new books. On the next block, **Godfather's Books and Espresso** (1108 Commercial, 503/325-8143) sells a mix of new and used books, and has a case full of excellent antique maps and prints depicting the Columbia River and north coast. The espresso bar is a good place to dry out on a rainy afternoon and catch up on local gossip. **Lucy's Books** (348 12th St., 503/325-4210) is a small but big-hearted locally owned bookshop with an emphasis on Northwest regional subjects. Owner Laura Snyder hosts readings by local and visiting writers, and publishes an entertaining quarterly newsletter and book reviews.

EVENTS

Modeled after Elko, Nevada's popular Cowboy Poets Gathering, the **Fisher Poets Gathering** provides a forum in which men and women involved in the fishing and other maritime industries share their poems, stories, songs, and artwork in a convivial seaport setting. Inaugurated in 1998, the annual February event draws writers and artists from up and down the Pacific coast and farther afield for readings, art shows, concerts, book-signings, workshops, films, silent auction, and other activities at pubs, galleries, theaters, and other venues around town. Participation isn't limited to fisherfolk, but extends to anyone with a connection to maritime activity, and themes range from the rigors (and humor) of life on the water to environmental issues. Admission is by donation ($5), at the ticket booth of the Columbian Theater (11th and Marine Drive). For more details and full schedule, check the Clatsop Community College website (www.clatsopcollege.com/fisherpoets).

The **Astoria-Warrenton Crab and Seafood Festival** (503/325-6311 or 800/875-6807), held the last weekend in April at the Clatsop County Fairgrounds, is a hugely popular event that brings in crowds from miles around. Scores of booths feature a cornucopia of seafood and other eats, regional beers and Oregon wines, and arts and crafts. Activities include continuous entertainment, crab races, a petting zoo, and kids' activities. A traditional crab dinner caps off the evening. Admission is $5–7 for adults, $3 for those over 62 and $1 for kids 12 and under. Hours are Friday 4–9 P.M., Saturday 10 A.M.–8 P.M., and Sunday 11 A.M.–4 P.M. To get to the fairgrounds from Astoria, take ORE 202 4.5 miles to Walluski Loop Road and watch for signs. Parking is limited at the fairgrounds. Frequent shuttle service takes folks between the fairgrounds, Park & Ride lots, the Port of Astoria, and local hotels and campgrounds.

The legacy of the thousands of Scandinavians who arrived to work in area mills and canneries in the late 19th and early 20th centuries is still strong in Astoria, with public steam baths, *lutefisk, smorrebrod* platters, and church services in Finnish. Today, the biggest event in town is the **Scandinavian Midsummer Festival** (P.O. Box 7, Astoria 97103, 503/325-6311), which usually takes place the third weekend of June,

Friday through Sunday. Local Danes, Finns, Icelanders, Norwegians, and Swedes come together to celebrate their heritage. Costumed participants dance around a flowered midsummer pole (a fertility rite), burn a bonfire to destroy evil spirits, and have tugs-of-war pitting Scandinavian nationalities against each other. Food, dancing, crafts, and a parade bring the whole town out to the Clatsop County Fairgrounds on Walluski Loop Road just off ORE 202. Admission is $6 for adults and $2 for children over six.

A tradition since 1894, **Astoria Regatta Week** is considered the Pacific Northwest's longest-running festival. Held on the waterfront in early August, the five-day event kicks off with the regatta queen's coronation and reception. Attractions include live entertainment, a grand land parade, historic home tours, ship tours and boat rides, sailboat and dragon boat races, a classic car show, a salmon barbecue, arts and crafts, food booths, a beer garden, and a twilight boat parade. For details and schedule, contact the Astoria Regatta Association (P.O. Box 24, Astoria 97103, www.astoriaregatta.org).

If you miss the spring crab festival, get a second shot in mid-October at the **Silver Salmon Celebration,** held at the foot of Basin Street, near Astoria's West End Mooring Basin. Get fresh salmon right off the boat and enjoy seafood delicacies, beer- and wine-tasting, arts and crafts, live music, and lots of activities for little ones. For more information, contact the Astoria-Warrenton Area Chamber of Commerce (503/325-6311).

ACCOMMODATIONS
Hotels
Built as a private Georgian-style residence in 1902, then converted to use as a convent in the 1950s, the elegant **Rosebriar Hotel** (636 14th St., Astoria, 503/325-7427 or 800/482-0224, www.rosebriar.net) was renovated into a small, comfortable hotel in the early 1990s. Set on a quiet neighborhood street a few blocks uphill from the Maritime Museum, the large bowfront windows of the parlor/lobby and many of the upstairs rooms command a sweeping view of

the town and river below. Original woodwork, tastefully understated decor and furnishings, and cordial service make a stay here quite pleasant. For $59–169 nightly (double occupancy), you have a choice of three rooms with baths or seven without (facilities down the hall). Discounts offered for three-night stays; call or check the website for packages and other specials. A full breakfast is also included. The recently opened Captain's Suite ($249) includes a kitchenette, large master bath, soaking tub overlooking the Columbia, and a sitting room with fireplace. The 1885 carriage-house cottage adjacent to the main hotel has its own kitchen, plus fireplace, whirlpool tub, and private patio. The Rosebriar is one of Astoria's most popular lodgings, so it's a good idea to reserve at least a week and a half in advance during summer.

After a $4.3 million, two-year renovation, the **Hotel Elliott** (357 12th St., 877/378-1924, www.hotelelliott.com) reinvented itself in 2003 as a tiny boutique hotel in the heart of downtown Astoria. The Elliott first opened in 1924, and its current incarnation preserved much of the original charm of its Craftsman-era details, including the mahogany-clad lobby, hand-crafted cabinetry, wood and marble fireplaces and stone floors in all bathrooms, plus such 21st-century mod-cons as high-speed Internet access and big-screen TVs. The hotel's 21 standard rooms and six suites run $105–275 nightly. Five premium suites include the five-room Presidential Suite ($650) with access to a rooftop garden. An original banner painted across the hotel's north side proudly proclaims: Hotel Elliott—Wonderful Beds. The new Elliott has made a point of living up to this claim, with goose-down pillows, luxurious 440-count Egyptian-cotton sheets, featherbeds, and top-of-the-line mattresses to ensure a memorable slumber.

Motels

You'll find about a dozen motels to choose from in and around Astoria, most of them located along U.S. 30, otherwise known as Marine Drive, in the northwest section of town. Most are fairly similar, and don't have the charm that the town's B&Bs offer (see below), but they're generally a bit less expensive and are reasonably close to downtown.

At the west end of town, the **Best Western Astoria Inn** (555 Hamburg St., 503/325-2205 or 800/621-0641) has 73 rooms in a five-story structure overlooking Young's Bay. Facilities include indoor pool, sauna, hot tubs, and laundry. Standard rooms run $63–169.

The **Crest Motel** (5366 Leif Erickson Dr./U.S. 30, 503/325-3141 or 800/421-3141) offers cliffside river views, a coin-operated laundry, and a whirlpool set in a gazebo overlooking the river. View rooms run $81–115 and are worth the extra money; standard rooms sans view are $62–84. Lower rates apply in off-season, and discounts are available for AAA members and seniors. About a half mile closer to town, **Comfort Suites** (3420 Leif Erickson Dr./U.S. 30, 503/325-2000) has river-view rooms with microwave, fridge, and free HBO; continental breakfast is served from 6–10 A.M. Facilities include a heated pool, spa, sauna, exercise room, and laundry. Rates range $69–139.

The sprawling **Red Lion** (400 Industry, 503/325-7373 or 800/RED-LION) is located right at the Mooring Basin Marina, just off Marina Drive. Motel units seem a bit worse for wear, but you can't get any closer to the river, and view rooms have a front-row seat on the passing ship traffic. Standard rooms run $59–99; the Romantic Getaway to Astoria package ($109–119) includes view room, champagne, and dinner for two in the on-site Seafare Restaurant (see "Food," later in this section).

Bed-and-Breakfasts

With its wealth of large, elegant Victorians, it's not surprising that Astoria has more B&Bs than any other town on the Oregon coast. The historic former homes of merchants, politicians, sea captains, and salmon canners number among them.

A block east of the Rosebriar Hotel, the **Rose River Inn B&B** (1510 Franklin Ave., 503/325-7175), offers two river-view suites ($120–130) and two guestrooms ($85–110) in a large, cheerfully painted Victorian, decorated with European antiques and art and surrounded by a neatly tended garden. Each room includes a clawfoot tub, and the River Suite also has a Finnish sauna. Road-weary travelers should consider a massage from innkeeper Kati, a licensed massage therapist from Helsinki.

Franklin Street Bed and Breakfast (1140 Franklin St., 503/325-4314, www.franklin-st-station-bb.com) is a grand, four-story Victorian built in 1900. Six rooms and suites, five with private bath, and queen beds accommodate up to 14 guests. The view from the fourth-floor Starlight Suite is unmatched, and there's even a telescope for up-close ship spotting. The Hide-Away Suite has its own kitchen, dining area, living room, and private entry. Rich woodwork and local art are appreciated extras. It's within easy walking distance of downtown and a breakfast is included in the rates ($80–135). A minimum two-night stay is required on weekends, and 10-day advance reservations have become necessary due to the popularity of this place.

Clementine's Bed and Breakfast (847 Exchange St., 800/521-6801, www.clementines-bb.com), a handsome two-story home built in the Italianate style in 1888, stands in good company across the street from the Flavel House, and is itself on Astoria's Historic Homes Walking Tour. From the gardens around the house come the fresh flowers that accent the guestrooms and common areas, as do the herbs that spice the delicious gourmet breakfasts. There are five rooms in the main house with rates ranging $85–150. All rooms include feather beds and private baths; upper-story rooms have private balconies with river views.

In addition, two spacious, sunny suites are available in the Moose Temple Lodge, adjacent to the main house, for $150–155. Built in 1850, this is the oldest extant building in Astoria; it was the Moose Temple from 1900 to 1940 and later served as a Mormon church. Renovated with skylights, wood floors, and fireplaces, small kitchens, and several beds, these are ideal for families or groups. Pets are welcome. September–May, Clementine's offers packages combining cooking classes with one- or two-night stays. Courses include bread- and pastry-making and theme classes such as "A Weekend in Provence." Clementine's requires a two-night minimum stay

on weekends mid-May–mid-Oct. and on holiday weekends. Single-night stays are fine the rest of the year, and discounts are available off-season.

FOOD

Over the past several years, Astoria has developed a reputation for excellent dining at fair prices, with a number of restaurants standing out for their creative and consistently delicious fare. Espresso fans will also be pleased to know that there are no fewer than 20 outlets for the stuff in town, with hole-in-the-wall cafés seemingly down every side street. Part of the fun is finding them.

From Mother's Day to early October, follow local tradition and stroll leisurely up and down 12th Street, between Marine Drive and Duane Street, where vendors offer farm-fresh produce, crafts, and specialty foods. **Astoria's Sunday Market** is held each Sunday 10 A.M.–3 P.M.

For do-it-your-selfers, visit **Josephson's Smokehouse** (106 Marine Dr., 503/325-2190, www.josephsons.com). Established in 1920 and set in a falsefront clapboard building near the waterfront, Oregon's most esteemed purveyor of gourmet smoked fish produces Scandinavian cold-smoked salmon without dyes or preservatives. Josephson's caters to mail-order clientele and fine restaurants that serve the product upon arrival. You can buy direct here at a cheaper (but not cheap) price than the mail-order rates. Pickled salmon, salmon jerky, sturgeon caviar, crab, oysters, and a variety of alder-smoked and canned fish are also sold here. On typically foggy days here in midwinter, there's nothing finer than a cup of very thick Josephson's clam chowder.

Casual Fare

As widely appreciated as it is small, the **Columbian Cafe** (1114 Marine Dr., 503/325-2233) is where the meatless '60s meet cutting-edge Northwest cuisine. The good selection of pasta entrées, crepes, and fresh catch of the day are all expertly prepared and moderately priced. The chef here is also famous for Uriah's St. Diablo jelly, which comes in garlic, jalapeño, and red-pepper flavors. These jellies are available here and sold throughout the state. You may also enjoy the free-flowing political repartee with the staff and regulars in this cramped (several booths and a lunch counter) but friendly place. Breakfast is a highlight here. Dinners run $10–20, with most lunch and breakfasts $4–8. Open Mon.–Fri. 8 A.M.–2 P.M., weekends 9 A.M. to 2 P.M.; dinner hours are Wed.–Sat. from 5 P.M. till they're done.

Adjacent are the Columbian Theatre, which shows second-run flicks which you can enjoy with beer, wine, and pizza, and the VooDoo Room, one of Astoria's most active live music clubs.

A state travel magazine has named the **Ship Inn** (1 Second St., 503/325-0033) the best pub in Oregon, and another regional publication gave it a thumbs-up for its seafood and business lunches ($6–14). Despite its unprepossessing exterior, the Ship is popular with locals and visitors who appreciate good fish-n-chips, cheese plates, Cornish pasties, and other English specialties such as steak-and-kidney pie and bangers and mash, and imported brews. A welcoming fire, great waterfront views, and live music, including jazz and bluegrass, also provide conviviality here.

In a beautifully restored 1892 Victorian on the hillside above the town, the **Home Spirit Bakery** (1585 Exchange St., 503/325-6846) is a special find that's quickly become a local favorite. The bakery and café, open Tues.–Sat. 9 A.M.–3:30 P.M., sells highly esteemed sourdough loaves and flaky pastries, and lunches focused on quiche (asparagus is yummy, $4.95), salads, and sandwiches made with their own croissants ($5.50). Dinner, served Thurs.–Sat. 5:30–8 P.M., is a prix-fixe affair ($21). Salads and starters might include roasted peppers, fiddleheads, capers, and olives on garden lettuces with potato and leek tart; entrée choices could be farro risotto with roasted asparagus and spring vegetables, black-wattle fish pie, raspberry chicken, or pork loin stuffed with feta cheese and winter greens. Finish up with homemade sorbet, Key lime pie, or tiramisu. Reservations are recommended.

"Eat well, laugh often, and love much" is the motto that neatly sums up the vibe at the easygoing **T. Paul's Urban Cafe** (1119 Commercial St., 503/338-5133). The menu of hip diner food with fresh Northwest twists includes towering turkey sandwiches, bay shrimp ceviche, Caribbean jerk quesadilla, prawn pasta, and clam chowder. Coffee drinks, beer, and wine are served. Open Mon.–Thurs. 9 A.M.–9 P.M., Friday and Saturday 9 A.M.–11 P.M.

Astoria's only brewpub, the **Wet Dog Cafe** (144 11th St., 503/325-6975), is home to the Pacific Rim Brewery, maker of eight hand-crafted microbrews, ranging from the golden Pacific Pale Ale to the full-bodied Sow Your Wild Oatmeal Stout. There's also a full bar. The café is housed in a cavernous remodeled former waterfront warehouse, with good views out the big windows. Food is basic pub grub: fish-n-chips, burgers, pizzas, sandwiches, and salads, with all-you-can-eat ribs on Fridays. Happy hour specials and children's menu are available. The Dog is quiet at weekday lunchtimes, but Thursday–Saturday nights get rowdy, when there's live music. Open Mon.–Fri. 11 A.M.–11 P.M., Friday and Saturday 11 A.M.–2 A.M. Kitchen closes at 9 P.M.

A good choice for families with kids, the Astoria outlet of **Pig 'N Pancake** (146 W. Bond St., 503/325-3144) of this small north-coast chain (others are in Seaside and Cannon Beach) excels at big, filling breakfasts at reasonable prices ($3.95–9.95). Their specialty is homemade pancakes and waffles, available in a dozen variations, including potato pancakes, Swedish (thin, crispy pancakes with lingonberries), pecan-filled, and of course pigs in a blanket. Lunch relies mainly on sandwiches (with some seafood twists such as Dungeness crab on an English muffin, topped with melted cheese), chowder, and salads, while dinners branch out with pasta, stir-fry, prime rib, and halibut and salmon served grilled, broiled, or steamed. Open daily 6 A.M.–10 P.M.

Gourmet
In the days when transportation here was mostly by water, Astoria's neighborhoods developed unique personalities. One of these was Uniontown, located west of the present downtown, where Scandinavian fishermen and longshoremen hung out near the fish-processing plants. Underneath the Astoria Bridge in this waterfront

district, **Cafe Uniontown** (218 W. Marine Dr., 503/323-8708) boasts an upscale menu with such seasonal offerings as raspberry hazelnut chicken breast; oven-roasted lobster tail; portobella, ricotta, and garlic ravioli; and bacon-wrapped filet mignon. Special requests can be accommodated. Wednesday is Rib Night, when $14.95 buys you all you can eat. Live music on weekends could be bluegrass or jazz piano. Check out the 1907-vintage bar in the restaurant's lounge, where weekend songfests can end your evening on a high note. It's open Tues.–Fri. for lunch and Tues.–Sun. for dinner.

For a bit of a splurge, local seafood aficionados recommend the **Silver Salmon Grille** (1185 Commercial St., 503/338-6640) for fine dining in an atmosphere that's somewhat formal but not starchy. Attractive murals of the eponymous fish adorn the walls inside and out, and salmon takes pride of place on the dinner menu as well, in a variety of preparations that are fresh and cooked to a T. Additional seafood items such as butter-grilled razor clams, several beef choices such as London broil, pork and chicken, and pasta dishes fill out the extensive menu, with prices falling in the $15–24 range. A selection of Northwest microbrews and a wine favoring Oregon and French vintages nicely complements the entrées. The lunch menu reprises many of the dinner selections for $8.95–13.95, along with filling sandwiches and burgers for $5.95–9.95. Open daily at 11 A.M.

In a century-old converted cannery building on Pier 6, **Gunderson's Cannery Cafe** (1 Sixth St., 503/325-8642) seats you as close to the waterfront as you can get without a boat. This 13-table mauve and pink restaurant serves up an innovative bill of fare that's popular with locals and knowledgeable out-of-towners. Whether you have crabcakes in red pepper pesto or pecan-crusted halibut, leave room for the desserts you'll pass in the display case at the entrance. The lunch menu features a halibut burger, generous Caesar salads, pizzas on homemade focaccia crust, and what many consider to be Astoria's best clam chowder. Prices range $5–12 at lunch, $9.50–25 for dinner. Winter hours are Tues.–Sat. 11 A.M.–8 P.M., Sunday

9 A.M.–6 P.M.; summer hours start in June and are Mon.–Sat. 11 A.M.–8:30 P.M., Sunday 9 A.M. for breakfast and brunch. Outdoor seating usually starts in March.

INFORMATION AND TRANSPORTATION

The **Astoria Chamber of Commerce** (111 W. Marine Dr., 503/325-6311 or 800/875-6807, www.oldoregon.com) operates the Oregon Welcome Center at its offices, providing a plethora of brochures and maps for visitors to Astoria and other destinations on the north Oregon coast. They will send you a free guidebook with plenty of handy info (write to P.O. Box 176, Astoria 97103, or order online). Open daily 8 A.M.–6 P.M.; Oct.–April hours are Mon.–Fri. 9 A.M.–5 P.M.

With 10,000 people, Astoria is the largest city and the media hub of the north coast. The local newspaper, the *Daily Astorian,* is sold around town and is worth a look if only to get the editorial slant of Steve Forrester. This former Washington correspondent's witty commentary on events local, regional, and national pulls no punches. The *North Coast Times Eagle* is a politically activist monthly that holds forth on coastal issues. It's sold around town and at Powell's Books in Portland. The free monthly *Hipfish* is a publication in the great tradition of the alternative press of the '60s. Whether you agree with their take on regional politics or not, the thoughtful, lively articles and complete entertainment listings will enhance your visit to the North Coast.

Amtrak Thruway Motorcoach Service runs daily between the north coast and Portland Union Station. Board the coach in Astoria at the MiniMart (95 W. Marine Dr.). Departure from Astoria is at 8 A.M.; arrival in Portland, 10:15 A.M. Depart Portland at 6 P.M.; arrive in Astoria at 8:15 P.M. The bus stops upon request at Seaside, Warrenton, and Gearhart. For information and reservations, call 800/USA-RAIL or check the Amtrak website (www.amtrak.com).

In 2003, Amtrak initiated train service between Portland and Astoria for the first time in

© MARK MORRIS

The 4.1-mile-long Astoria–Megler Bridge links Oregon and Washington.

living memory, with the **_Lewis & Clark Explorer_**. Late May–early September, the excursion train departs Linnton Station in Northwest Portland (get there by bus from downtown's Union Station at 7:30) Fri.–Mon. at 7:50 A.M., follows the scenic route along the Columbia on the water-level Burlington Northern tracks, and arrives at Astoria's old train depot on 20th Street off Marine Drive at 11:50 A.M. The train departs Astoria at 4:50 P.M., arriving in Portland at 8:50 P.M. One-way tickets are $24 general, $20 for seniors. Contact Amtrak (see above) for reservations and more details. As part of the Lewis and Clark Bicentennial, this special train is slated to run summers through 2005, though Oregon's budget woes at press time could derail those plans.

Getting around Astoria can have its pitfalls for the unsuspecting. Potentially troublesome for visitors are the steep hills and the city's layout of seemingly random one-way streets. Holidays and summer weekends bring heavy traffic along U.S. 30, a.k.a. Leif Erickson Drive (east end of town) and Marine Drive (center and west), Astoria's major traffic artery. In light of the this, you might consider the following alternatives.

For visitors willing to let go of their cars for a while, the Sunset Empire Transportation District, better known as **The Bus** (503/861-RIDE or 800/776-6406, www.ridethebus.org), provides reasonably frequent transportation around Astoria, and along the coast from Warrenton (including Fort Stevens State Park and Fort Clatsop) to Cannon Beach. Most routes are served every 40–60 minutes, Mon.–Saturday.

COASTAL OREGON

Southern Oregon

South of the Willamette Valley and west of the Cascades is a corridor of the state most residents call southern Oregon. To be more precise, this label refers to cities along I-5 below Cottage Grove as well as towns in the shadow of the Siskiyou Mountains' eastern flank. What the Coast Range is to the Willamette Valley, the Siskiyous's rugged V-shaped canyons, wild rivers, and serpentine rock formations are to southern Oregon. The outstanding features of this region include world-class kulturfests, the biggest chunk of remaining wilderness on the Pacific coast, and California retirees who've come in search of cheap real estate and more sun than they'll see anywhere else west of the Cascades.

Recently, attention has been focused on the northern part of the Siskiyou range and its 440,000 acres of old-growth Douglas fir. Many timber company contracts to clear-cut these trees are being contested by environmental groups. The environmentalists claim the forest represents one of the world's most botanically diverse regions—with eight different soil types and more living matter per hectare than any other forest on the planet. As always, timber companies see the trees as a renewable resource and argue that logging would create minimal damage to the ecosystem.

The region is no stranger to activism and unconventionality in general. From back-to-the-land idealists to hard-core survivalists, southern Oregon has attracted all stripes. Added to this eclectic mix are more than 100 high-tech companies (the "Silicon Orchard"), white-water rafters, anglers, and culture vultures who flock to

Applegate Valley, near Jacksonville

© LEIGH BHADY

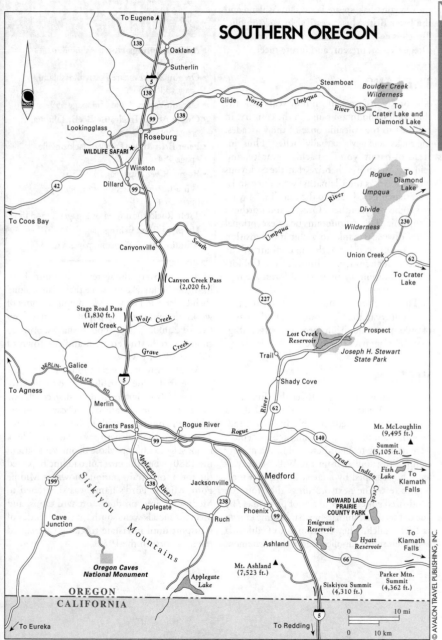

SOUTHERN OREGON

To Eugene

138
Oakland
Sutherlin
5
138
Steamboat
Glide
North
Umpqua
River
138
Boulder Creek
Wilderness
To
Crater Lake and
Diamond Lake

99
138
Lookingglass
Roseburg
WILDLIFE SAFARI
Winston
Rogue-
Umpqua
To
Diamond
Lake

42
Dillard
99
Umpqua
Divide
Wilderness
230

To Coos Bay

Canyonville
South
Union Creek
62
To Crater
Lake

Canyon Creek Pass
(2,020 ft.)
227

Stage Road Pass
(1,830 ft.)
Wolf Creek
Wolf Creek
Lost Creek
Reservoir
Prospect

Grave
Creek
Trail
Joseph H. Stewart
State Park

MERLIN-
GALICE
Galice
5
RD
Shady Cove

To Agness
Merlin
62

Grants Pass
Rogue River
Rogue
River
140
Mt. McLoughlin
(9,495 ft.)

99
Summit
(5,105 ft.)

199
Applegate
River
238
Jacksonville
Medford
Dead
Indian
Fish
Lake
To
Klamath
Falls

Siskiyou
Mountains
Applegate
238
Ruch
Phoenix
99
HOWARD
PRAIRIE
LAKE
COUNTY PARK
To
Klamath
Falls

Cave
Junction
Emigrant
Reservoir
Hyatt
Reservoir

Ashland
66
Parker Mtn.
Summit
(4,362 ft.)

Oregon Caves
National Monument
Applegate
Lake
Mt. Ashland
(7,523 ft.)

OREGON
CALIFORNIA
Siskiyou Summit
(4,310 ft.)
0   10 mi
0   10 km

To Eureka
To Redding
5

© AVALON TRAVEL PUBLISHING, INC.

the Oregon Shakespeare Festival in Ashland and the Peter Britt Music Festival in Jacksonville. Travelers enjoy this dynamic region, too, where Oregon's past, present, and future meet.

THE LAND

The Siskiyous are 130 million years old, the third oldest mountain range in the country. In contrast to the volcanic ooze of the Cascades, the rocks here never actually melted. Thus, instead of basalt, you find schist, granite, and feldspar. Scientists theorize that the Siskiyous (also known as the Klamaths) were once an island that annexed itself to the coastline of what was to become southern Oregon and northern California. These mountains boast exceptional floral diversity thanks to a climatic transition zone influenced by both the cool air of the Northwest and warmer, drier air from California. In addition, many types of forest are represented here.

The huge area of unexplored, unmapped backcountry in the Siskiyous adds to their aura of mystique, as do the numerous reports of Bigfoot sightings over the years.

HISTORY

It was gold on the Rogue River that first drew European-Americans to this territory inhabited by the Rogue (Takelma) tribe. In early 1852, two itinerant prospectors, Cluggage and Poole, were returning to a northern California mining camp with supplies from the Willamette Valley. They camped by a creek in the area for a night's rest. The next morning, they found a good-sized gold nugget in a hoof print made by one of their pack animals in what became known as Rich Gulch. They continued to California with their miner supplies, but in the excitement

of their discovery, the secret slipped out. They hurriedly backtracked to stake their claims along Rich Gulch and Daisy Creek. Within a matter of weeks, the mining camp population grew from two to 2,000. Tents, wooden shacks, and log cabins were hastily erected, and the town of Table Rock City was born.

Around this time settlers following the Applegate Trail, a southern alternative to the Oregon Trail, also migrated here. A stagecoach line in the 1870s and a railroad a decade later established commerce with California markets. The seat of the prosperity was Jacksonville, a major stagecoach stop whose boom went bust in the 1880s when the new railroad line bypassed the town for a train station known as Middle Ford. Middle Ford's name was shortened to Medford. Forest products, orchard crops, and precious metals went south on these modes of transport until interstate trucking supplanted the iron horse in the 1930s.

Ashland

With the exceptions of Stratford-upon-Avon and its Shakespeare productions, and Oberammergau, Germany, and its passion play, few towns are as closely identified with theater as Ashland is. Tickets to the renowned Oregon Shakespeare Festival are the coin of the realm here, with contemporary classics and off-off-Broadway joining productions by the Bard. You immediately sense this is not just another timber town from the Tudor-style McDonalds, vintage Victorians, and high property values ($283,000 for a four-bedroom in 2004). The newcomer will also be struck by the dearth of neon and obtrusive signs in this town of 19,500.

Ashland . . . stay four days, see four plays.

Blessed with a bucolic setting between the Siskiyous and the Cascades, Ashland embodies the spirit of the Chautauqua movement of a century ago, which dedicated itself to bringing culture to the rural hinterlands. Up until the 1930s, however, entertainment in these parts mostly consisted of traveling vaudeville shows that visited the Ashland/Jacksonville area to cheer up the residents of a gold-rush country in decline.

Then Southern Oregon University started up the Shakespeare Festival under the direction of Professor Angus Bowmer. Such noted thespians as George Peppard, Stacy Keach, and William Hurt graced Ashland's stages early in their careers, and the festival has garnered its share of Tony awards and other accolades. Today, the Oregon Shakespeare Festival is the largest classic repertory theater in the country and enjoys the largest audience of any kind of theater in the United States. Annual attendance generally exceeds 350,000.

Ashland's tourist economy is also sustained by its auspicious location roughly equidistant to Portland and San Francisco. Closer to home, day trips to Crater Lake, Rogue River country, and the southern Oregon coast have joined the tradition of "stay four days, see four plays" as a major part of Ashland's appeal.

SIGHTS
Lithia Park

Ashland's centerpiece is 100-acre Lithia Park. Recognized as a National Historic Site, the park was designed by John McLaren, landscape architect of San Francisco's Golden Gate Park. It's set along Ashland Creek where the Takelmas camped and the region's first flour mill was created. Ashland, Ohio, natives built the mill here in 1854, originally calling it Mill Creek. (Some scholars suggest Ashland was named after the birthplace of Henry Clay, Ashland, Kentucky.) The park was also the site of Ashland's Chautauqua.

The park owes its existence to Jesse Winburne, who made a fortune from New York subway advertising and tried to develop a spa around Ashland's Lithia Springs, which he said rivaled the venerated waters of Saratoga Springs, New York. Although the spa never caught on due to the Depression, Winburne was nevertheless instrumental in landscaping Lithia Park with one of the most varied collections of trees and shrubs of any park in the state. Winburne was also responsible for piping the famous Lithia water to the plaza fountains so all might enjoy its beneficial minerals. While many visitors find this slightly sulfurous, effervescent water a bit hard to swallow, many locals have acquired a taste for Ashland's acerbic answer to Perrier and happily chugalug it down.

A walk along Winburne Way's beautiful tree-shaded trail is a must on any itinerary here. This footpath and a scenic drive through the park start west of the Lithia Fountain. Redwoods, Port Orford cedar, and other species line the drive, which takes you along Ashland Creek to the base of the Siskiyous.

The hub of the park in the summer is the bandshell, where concerts, ballets, and silent movies are shown. Children love to play at the playgrounds or feed the ducks in the ponds.

SOUTHERN OREGON

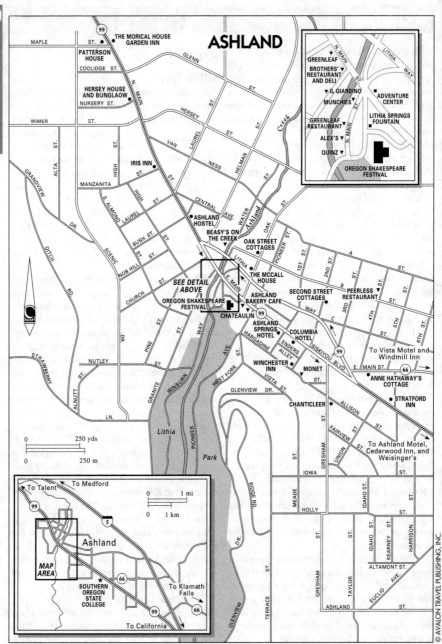

ASHLAND

MAPLE ST.

THE MORICAL HOUSE GARDEN INN

PATTERSON HOUSE

COOLIDGE ST.

GLENN ST.

HERSEY HOUSE AND BUNGLAOW

NURSERY ST.

WIMER ST.

N. MAIN ST.

HERSEY ST.

IRIS INN

MANZANITA ST.

VAN NESS

LAUREL ST.

HELMAN ST.

Creek

CENTRAL AVE.

WATER ST.

ASHLAND HOSTEL

BEASY'S ON THE CREEK

OAK STREET COTTAGES

OAK ST.

PIONEER ST.

1ST ST.

2ND ST.

A ST.

THE MCCALL HOUSE

SEE DETAIL ABOVE

OREGON SHAKESPEARE FESTIVAL

LITHIA

E. MAIN

ASHLAND BAKERY CAFE

SECOND STREET COTTAGES

B ST.

PEERLESS RESTAURANT

3RD ST.

4TH ST.

5TH ST.

6TH ST.

CHATEAULIN

99

C ST.

WAY

ASHLAND SPRINGS HOTEL

COLUMBIA HOTEL

ENDERS ALLEY

SISKIYOU BLVD.

99

To Vista Motel and Windmill Inn

NUTLEY ST.

WINCHESTER INN

HARGADINE ST.

MONET

E. MAIN ST.

66

ANNE HATHAWAY'S COTTAGE

GLENVIEW DR.

VISTA ST.

CHANTICLEER

ALLISON ST.

STRATFORD INN

Lithia Park

GRESHAM ST.

FAIRVIEW ST.

UNION ST.

To Ashland Motel, Cedarwood Inn, and Weisinger's

0   250 yds
0   250 m

IOWA ST.

MEADE ST.

HOLLY ST.

IDAHO ST.

IDAHO ST.

RIDGE RD.

IDAHO ST.

KEARNEY ST.

HARRISON ST.

ALTAMONT ST.

GRESHAM ST.

TAYLOR ST.

EUCLID AVE.

ASHLAND ST.

Detail (inset, upper right)

N. MAIN ST.

LITHIA WAY

GREENLEAF

BROTHERS' RESTAURANT AND DELI

IL GIARDINO

MUNCHIES

ADVENTURE CENTER

LITHIA SPRINGS FOUNTAIN

GREENLEAF RESTAURANT

ALEX'S

QUINZ

N. MAIN ST.

OREGON SHAKESPEARE FESTIVAL

Lower inset

To Talent

To Medford

99

5

0   1 mi
0   1 km

Ashland

MAP AREA

SOUTHERN OREGON STATE COLLEGE

66

GLENVIEW DR.

TERRACE ST.

To Klamath Falls

66

99

To California

© AVALON TRAVEL PUBLISHING, INC.

Big kids enjoy tennis, volleyball, horseshoes, or traversing one of the many trails in the park. Every Tuesday on Water Street next to Ashland Creek the **Farmer's Market** is held. Rogue Valley farmers, craftspeople, and ranchers sell arts and crafts, fruit and produce, and dried flowers.

Pick up the *Woodland Trail* guide at the plaza's visitors center kiosk. The gentle mile-long loop takes you from the plaza past a beautiful Japanese garden to the upper duck pond where mallards, wood ducks, and the endangered western pond turtle can be seen on the pond's island. A highlight for bird-watchers is in winter when there are 100–200 wood ducks here and ouzels that dive below the surface of Ashland Creek for fish.

Museums and Galleries

The **Hanson Howard Gallery** (82 N. Main, 541/488-2562, wwwhhgallery.com) features monthly exhibits of contemporary artists in a bright, airy corner shop at the north end of downtown. Closed Monday. The **Foray Gallery** (500 A St., 541/482-2917) is an artist-owned enterprise that features an eclectic collection of sculpture, paintings, fiber arts, printmaking, and jewelry. It's located in a thriving commercial strip by the railroad tracks. Closed Sunday and Monday.

Schneider Museum of Art (Southern Oregon State College campus, 541/482-6245) features contemporary art by national and international artists. Hours are Tues.–Sat. 11 A.M.–5 P.M. Ashland is also home to the **Science Works** (1500 Main St., near Walker Street, 541/482-6767, www.scienceworksmuseum.org), a hands-on museum that offers interactive exhibits, live performances, and activities Saturday and Sunday 10 A.M.–4 p.m. (hours and days vary depending on the season). Admission is $7.50 adults, $5 ages 2–12, under two free.

SPORTS AND RECREATION

Skiing

Perched high atop the Siskiyou range and straddling the California-Oregon border is 7,523-foot **Mount Ashland** (541/482-2897, www.mtashland.com). To get here, take the Mount Ashland Exit off I-5 and follow the road four miles up to the complex.

While Mount Ashland is 15 miles from downtown Ashland by road, it's only eight miles away by Nordic ski trail. Skiers of all levels enjoy the 23 different runs, 100 miles of cross-country trails, and breathtaking vistas. The vertical drop here is 1,150 feet. An average of 325 inches of snow falls on the mountain, making it possible to ski Thanksgiving through Easter. Daily lift rates ($14–43) vary depending on the lift; lower rates are available for seniors and youth (ages 9–17); children under eight ski free. Ski at night for $20. Don't forget to purchase your Oregon Sno-Park permit.

Spring and fall are good times to visit Ashland, as accommodation rates are lower than during the peak summer tourist season. Many proprietors include free Mount Ashland lift tickets with the price of the room. Check with the Southern Oregon Reservation Center (see Ashland "Information and Services," later in this chapter) about available ski packages. After the snow has melted, the walk to the top of Mount Ashland is an easy one, with good views of the Siskiyous and 14,162-foot Mount Shasta in California. It's prudent to bring along a sweater even in warm weather, as it can get fairly windy.

Adventure Center

The Adventure Center (40 N. Main St., 541/488-2819 or 800/444-2819, www.raftingtours.com) offers half-day, full-day, and multiday fishing, rafting, and cycle trips for any size party. The cost of the rafting trips includes gear (wetsuits, splash jackets, booties, etc.), guides, and transport from Ashland. Half-day trips ($70) include a snack and run 9 A.M.–1 P.M. or 1–5 P.M. The longer whitewater picnic trip ($120) includes lunch and runs 9:30 A.M.–4 P.M. Rated one of the best floats in southern Oregon, the upper Klamath River trip ($135) generally runs 7:30 A.M.–5:30 P.M. and includes all meals.

The **Bear Creek Bike and Nature Trail** crisscrosses through town before going down the valley to Medford along Bear Creek. If you like to ride a bike but are not big on pedaling, contact the Adventure Center for information about their Mount Ashland downhill bike cruise. This half-day morning or picnic-lunch ride descends 4,000 feet on 16 miles of quiet paved roads through the countryside to Emigrant Reservoir. The three-hour morning cruise ($65) departs at 8 A.M. and includes fruit, pastries, and drinks. The four-hour picnic cruise ($69) departs at 11 A.M. and includes a great lunch in a beautiful mountain glade. Bicycles, safety equipment, round-trip transfer from Ashland, and an experienced guide are provided. All you have to do is steer! The Adventure Center also rents mountain bikes by the hour or by the day; the fee includes helmet, lock, and maps.

Mountain Biking

One of the more popular local bike rides is the **Lithia Loop Mountain Bike Route.** The 28-mile ride is strenuous, gaining 3,000 feet in elevation the first six miles. Caution is in order the last seven miles of descent. To avoid the steep ups and downs, you can drive up to the top and ride the fairly level 15-mile stretch. The Lithia Loop is mostly within the Ashland watershed, the source of the city's water supply, and it may be closed during midsummer and fall.

The **Siskiyou Crest Mountain Bike Route** begins at the Mount Ashland ski area parking lot. The 31-mile round-trip ranges from moderate to difficult and affords incredible views of Mount Shasta. The route ends at Dutchman Peak, where you'll find one of the few cupola-style fire lookouts left in the Pacific Northwest. This particular lookout was built in 1927. Please note, bicycles are not allowed on the nearby Pacific Crest Trail.

The **Ashland Ranger District** (645 Washington St., Ashland 97520, 541/482-3333) can provide directions and additional information about these and other mountain bike trails in the area.

Horseback Riding

Graduate from a two-wheeled coast to a four-legged gallop with **Mountain Gate Stables** (4399 ORE 66, Ashland, 541/482-8873, www.mountaingatestables.com), which offers many

horseback-riding packages starting at $30. To get there, take Ashland Street (ORE 66) two miles east of the Ashland Hills Inn. Short trail rides take in scenic views of the mountains and valleys; longer rides, deep into the woods of the Greentree Mountains, include saddlebag lunches prepared by the Greentree Restaurant. And in the event of inclement weather, you can always practice your walk, trot, and canter in the arena.

About a half hour from Ashland up ORE 66 is **Greensprings Box R Ranch** (16799 ORE 66, 541/482-1873), where you can ride the historic Applegate Trail and many other wilderness trails that wend through this beautiful mountainous area. While their rates may be a little higher than nearby counterparts ($35–50 for one- to two-hour rides), the scenery makes it well worth it. As you traverse the old-growth forests and mountain meadows, there are opportunities to view deer, elk, eagles, osprey, bears, cougars, and even wild horses. Three-hour dinner rides and the all-day ride are timed to take maximum advantage of the animals coming out at dusk. Customized overnight trips (3–10 days) include everything but sleeping bag and personal gear. Most of the camps are set up near a mountain lake or stream with time for fishing, hiking, or just plain relaxing. Winter attractions include sleigh rides with hot drinks and a campfire. Call ahead for reservations and trip departure times. Log ranch houses are also available at the Box R, fully equipped with kitchen, washer/dryer, and two bedrooms per unit. With rates from $110–160, they are good lodging options for families or larger groups (8–16).

Equipment and Golf

Rent outdoor recreation equipment at reasonable rates from **Ashland Mountain Supply** (31 N. Main St., 541/488-2749, www.ashlandmountainsupply.com).

A few miles outside of Ashland on ORE 66 is **Oak Knoll Golf Course** (3070 ORE 66, 541/378-0344, www.oakknollgolfcourse.com). Get into the swing of things before the play; at $13 for nine holes and $24 for 18 holes, even if you triple bogey, you can't miss. For weekend rates, add a dollar or two to the greens fee.

Water Activities

Jackson Hot Springs (2253 ORE 99, 541/482-3776) is two miles north of Ashland on the old highway and has a naturally heated public swimming pool as well as private mineral baths.

Meyer Memorial Pool (Hunter Park, Summit Street, Ashland, 541/488-0313) includes a wading pool for infants and toddlers under age five, as well as a large swimming pool for grown-ups. Open summer season.

Six miles east of Ashland on ORE 66 is **Emigrant Reservoir** (541/776-7001). In addition to water-skiing, sailing, fishing, and swimming, there is a 270-foot twin flume waterslide open Mon.–Thurs. 10 A.M.–7 P.M., Fri.–Sun. 10 A.M.–8 P.M.

A half hour east of Ashland on Dead Indian Road is **Howard Prairie Lake Resort** (P.O. Box 4709, Medford 97501, 541/482-1979, www.howardprairieresort.com). Tucked away in the Cascade Mountains at 4,500 feet and surrounded by tall pines and fir trees, this six-mile-long lake peppered with small islands is noted for its runs of rainbow trout. The resort marina offers boat rentals ($40 half day, $50 full day) and everything else you may need (including friendly advice about where the fish are biting) to land some supper. A general store, restaurant, lodging, and 250-acre campground are also found at this retreat.

ENTERTAINMENT AND EVENTS

Oregon Shakespeare Festival

While Lithia Park is the heart of Ashland, Shakespeare is the soul of this community. The festival began when Angus Bowmer, an English professor at Ashland College, decided to celebrate Independence Day weekend in 1935 with a Shakespeare production. The city fathers were so unsure of the reception they asked him to allow boxing matches on the stage during the day prior to the performance. By the time he retired as artistic director of the festival in 1971, his Fourth of July dream had grown into an internationally acclaimed drama company with

Oregon Shakespeare Festival in Ashland

three theaters, one named in his honor. Over the last 60 years, more than four million people have purchased tickets to the event. Today, the festival contributes over $24 million annually to the local economy.

The three festival theaters are located at the southeast end of Lithia Park. Take the Shakespeare steps up the small hill by the Lithia water fountains to get to the complex known as the Festival Courtyard. The **Elizabethan Theatre,** built on the site of Ashland's Chautauqua Dome, was modeled after the Fortune Theatre of London, circa 1600. This outdoor summer-only theater, the largest of the three, is primarily the domain of the Bard. While Shakespeare under the stars is incredibly romantic (I knew she would be my wife after we saw the play together—true story), it can also get very cold after sunset in the spring and fall. In summer, even on 100° days, it's not uncommon for it to cool down to the low 60s after intermission. Dress warmly and consider investing a few bucks in the rental lap blankets and pillows for extra comfort. Curtain-times run 8–8:30 P.M. with most shows ending around 11 P.M. This theater closes by mid-October and the festival itself ends October 30.

The second-largest playhouse is the 600-seat **Angus Bowmer.** This indoor complex has excellent acoustics, computerized sound and lighting, and nary a bad seat in the house. The echoes of Shakespeare's immortal poetry fill this hall during the wetter winter months when the outdoor stage is closed. Finally, the 150-seat **New Theatre** is the actor's and director's theater, where modern works and experimental productions are the norm. This theater is small enough to stage plays that might be overwhelmed by a larger venue.

Getting tickets to the Oregon Shakespeare Festival (15 S. Pioneer St., P.O. Box 158, Ashland 97520, 541/482-4331, www.orshakes.org) is as much a part of the show as the performance. Due to tremendous popularity, seats sell out months in advance, especially for the comedies. All seats are reserved, with the best up front (but not too close) commanding top dollar and prices decreasing for seats farther from the stage. Ticket prices range $14–63 for the Elizabethan and Angus Bowmer Theatres and $26–53 for the New Theatre. Children under age six are not permitted. Once tickets are purchased, there are no refunds. Call the box office for performance times, dates, and ticket availability. Open Tues.–Sun. 9:30 A.M.–performance time, Monday 9:30 A.M.–5 P.M.; closed most holidays.

If you are unable to get advance tickets, your best bet is to show up at the Shakespeare Plaza an hour or two before the show with a sign stating what show you want to see. If you are lucky, you will score tickets from someone with extras. Avoid bidding wars with other would-be theater-goers, as ticket scalping is frowned upon here. Otherwise, be at the ticket window at 6 P.M.; any available seats will be released at that time. There are usually standing-room-only tickets ($12) if all else fails. And remember, there is no late seating at any of the theaters.

Finally, catch the free **Green Show** before the play. It begins at 7:15 P.M. (6:45 P.M. in September) on the plaza outside the Elizabethan Theatre and features elaborately costumed dancers, jugglers, and medieval musicians. Humorous asides, flirtatious Renaissance dancing, magic tricks, and other high jinks help liven things up. Although every aspect of the show has been researched for authenticity, there is a whimsical air to the proceedings making it accessible to everyone. The Green Show serves as an appetizer to the main course, often relating directly to the show it precedes in the Elizabethan Theatre. It ends at 7:30 P.M. with a second show at 7:45 P.M. in a small stage to the rear of the Elizabethan Theatre. A 32-page *Guide to the Green*

Show sells for about two bucks at the Tudor Guild booth, detailing the historical antecedents of the show's instruments, music, dances, and scripts.

Other Acts in Town

Shakespeare isn't the only act in town. Some of the other local companies include the **artattack theater ensemble** (310 Oak St., 541/482-6505, www.artattacktheater.com), producing big city premiers and innovative renderings; **Oregon Cabaret Theatre** (1st and Hargadine, 541/488-2902, www.oregoncabaret.com) with musical reviews in a club setting; and **Southern Oregon State College** productions. Ashland is also home to the **Ballet Rogue,** Southern Oregon's only professional company, which gives many summer performances. The **Ashland Visitor Information Center** (541/482-3486) has complete information on all the goings-on, as does the Southern Oregon Reservation Center (541/488-1011 or 800/547-8052).

A few miles north of Ashland is the town of Talent. Here, the **Actor's Theatre** (Main Street and Talent Avenue, 541/535-5250, www.attalent.org) features Broadway musicals and intimate plays in a 110-seat playhouse.

Nightlife

Allann Brothers (1602 Ashland St., 541/488-0700) is a cozy coffeehouse with live music Friday and Saturday nights. Gourmet coffee drinks, soups and sandwiches, and fine desserts are available. **Evo's Java and Tea House** (376 E. Main St., 541/488-3581) occasionally features late-night jazz and blues. Kat Wok (62 E. Main St., 541/482-0787), a pan-Asian restaurant, sushi bar, and night club, is the only venue where hip hop and funk join r&b and jazz on the dance floor. For cocktails in an intimate setting overlooking the plaza, try **Alex's** (35 N. Main St., 541/482-8818). The **Bull's Eye Bistro** (212 E. Main St., 541/488-1700) serves light meals and features live entertainment on the weekends.

Wine-Tasting

The climate of southern Oregon is ideal for many Bordeaux varietals such as cabernet sauvignon, sauvignon blanc, and merlot. The country cottage tasting room at **Ashland Vineyards** (2275 E. Main St., 541/488-0088 or 866/4-WINENET) gives you the opportunity to sample the local product. Open 11 A.M.–5 P.M. daily except Monday (by appointment only Jan.–Feb.); winery tours, a picnic area, and wine for sale are also offered.

Nearby is **Weisinger's Vineyard** (3150 Siskiyou Blvd., 541/488-5989 or 800/551-WINE). The vineyard, which has received national and international awards, produces cabernet sauvignon, Gewürztraminer, pinot noir, chardonnay, sauvignon blanc, and Italian varietals. Perched upon a knoll, the view of the valley, vineyard, and surrounding mountains from the tasting room heightens the experience. In addition to wines, visitors may purchase deli foods, soft drinks, and gifts. A beehive displayed in the tasting room is set up so you can see the queen and her subjects hard at work. Open daily 11 A.M.–5 P.M. May–Sept., Wed.–Sun. 11 A.M.–5 P.M. Oct.–April.

Events

The **Ashland Independent Film Fest** (541/488-3823) is five-day affair held in April, during which filmmaker and audience get to know one another. The **Rogue Valley Growers and Crafters Market** (under the Lithia Street/Siskiyou Boulevard overpass a half-block north of the plaza) takes place May–October on Tuesdays 8:30 A.M.–1:30 P.M.

The **Feast of Will** celebrates the opening of the Shakespeare Festival. It usually takes place mid-June at Lithia Park. Contact the box office for tickets to this bacchanal. In July and August, the Ballet Rogue presents **Ballet in the Park** (541/535-4112) in Lithia Park. Call for dates and times.

ACCOMMODATIONS

Motels

Ashland's high cost of living is reflected in the rack rates of the town's accommodations. Nonetheless, there's generally something to be found to meet the needs of most every budget. A few small ma 'n pa motels still remain offering time-warp rates, among them **Vista Motel** (535 Clover Ln.,

541/482-4423 or 888/672-5290) with rooms for $35–48, and **Ashland Motel** (1145 Siskiyou Blvd., 541/482-2561 or 800/460-8858), $42–70.

Moderately priced rooms with the accoutrements to befit their tariffs include **Cedarwood Inn** (1801 Siskiyou Blvd., 541/488-2000 or 800/547-4141, www.brodeur-inns.com), $56–148; **La Quinta Inn** (434 Valley View Rd., 541/482-6932 or 800/527-1133, www.hotels-west.com), $60–120; and **Windmill Inn** (2525 Ashland St., 541/482-8310 or 800/547-4747, www.windmillinns.com), $60–150. Most of these properties accept pets, have pools, and include a continental breakfast.

A clean and meticulously maintained, privately owned and operated premium motel is the **Stratford Inn** (555 Siskiyou Blvd., 541/488-2151 or 800/547-4741, www.stratforninnashland.com), $80–150, located just five blocks from the theaters with reserved parking for guests. All rooms have a micro fridge, and a couple of kitchen suites are available. Free laundry services, free ski lockers during ski season, elaborate continental breakfast, and an indoor pool and Jacuzzi all contribute to the inn's high occupancy rate.

Hotels

The **Ashland Springs Hotel** (212 E. Main St., 541/488-1700 or 800/325-4000, www.ashlandspringshotel.com) on the corner of 1st and Main (a block from the Elizabethan Theater) is a first-class historic hotel. Dating back to 1925, when it was considered a skyscraper showplace, it's the tallest building between San Francisco and Portland. It languished in obscurity for decades until its multimillion dollar restoration a few years back.

This 70-room, nine-story hotel evokes the grandeur of the past. The lobby boasts an original terrazzo floor and lavish rugs amid copious indoor greenery. Afternoon tea is served on the mezzanine under old-style ceiling fans. Elfinwood, the wood-paneled on-site restaurant, boasts whimsical drawings of elves and gnomes on the walls, and an antique Parisian bar backdropped by terra cotta depictions of theatrical themes. A grand ballroom, a bar in which parlor games and musical entertainment may be enjoyed, as well as English gardens add more touches evocative of another era. Luxuriously appointed guestrooms boast oversized windows highlighting nice views. Room rates are $89–209.

A dollar-wise choice in this high-priced town is the **Columbia Hotel** (262 1/2 E. Main St., 541/482-3726 or 800/718-2530, www.columbiahotel.com). This well-kept 1910 with a grand piano in the lobby has 24 rooms running from $50–110. Rooms at their sister property, **The Palm** (1065 Siskiyou Blvd., 877/482-2635, www.palmcottages.com) go for $49–125.

Bed-and-Breakfasts

The warm traditions of England are represented in Ashland not only by the Oregon Shakespeare Festival but also by the town's numerous bed-and-breakfasts, the most of any locale in the state (as well as the most per capita in the country). Although they cost a bit more than motel units, you get much more for your money. In addition to such extras as fresh flowers in your room, antique brass beds with down comforters, and complimentary evening aperitifs, hearty morning meals are usually included. The high price of many of these establishments can sometimes be split between couples traveling together. Another plus is that most of these inns are within easy walking distance of the theaters.

Because bed-and-breakfasts are small as well as popular, most innkeepers suggest reserving at least a year in advance. June–September visits usually require a two-night minimum stay. Off-season rates are 10–30 per cent less than peak.

The **Ashland B&B Clearinghouse** (541/488-0338 or 800/588-0338, www.bbclearinghouse.com) offers one-call reservations for more than 50 bed-and-breakfasts, 14 houses, and 4 old hotels—a total of over 1,000 possible rooms. Ask for their free Ashland guide. Open Mon.–Sat. 9 A.M.–9 P.M. The **Oregon B&B Guild** (800/983-4667, www.bandbashland.com) can help you find quality lodgings in Ashland and can even assist with B&B reservations throughout the state. You can also log on to **www.ashland-bed-breakfast.com**.

Chanticleer (120 Gresham, 541/482-1919 or 800/898-1950) rules the roost with five romantic rooms ($85–195) replete with fluffy comforters and private baths. Their gourmet breakfasts are the talk of Ashland. Round-the-clock refrigerator rights, complimentary wines and sherry, and a full cookie jar on the kitchen counter help keep you wined and dined throughout your stay. Massage treatments ($60/hour) further sustain the feeling of being pampered. Corporate rates and perks like private room phone lines with personal answering machines, discounted shuttle transfers to and from Medford International Airport, and even secretarial services can make your stay here a working vacation.

The six rooms of **Anne Hathaway's Cottage** (586 E. Main St., 541/488-1050 or 800/643-4434, www.ashlandBandB.com), $75–145, four blocks from the theaters, boast fresh-cut flowers, down comforters, firm beds, and private baths. The two-room J.T. Currie Suite can comfortably accommodate four, and is good for families.

The **Hersey House and Bungalow** (451 N. Main St., 541/482-4563 or 888/343-7739, www.herseyhouse.com), $75–150, is an elegantly restored Victorian with antique furniture and private baths. The bungalow is a separate guest cottage that includes a fully equipped kitchen, living room, and two bedrooms making it well-suited for families and groups up to six. Room rates depend upon season and number of guests and include a continental breakfast.

The **Iris Inn** (59 Manzanita, 541/488-2286 or 800/460-7650, www.irisinnbb.com), $65–145, is a cheerful Victorian with a fitting decor located four blocks from the theaters. Full breakfast in the morning, cold drinks during the day, and wine and sherry at night add to the classical atmosphere. After a walk through the Iris gardens, you'll probably agree with Shakespeare: "of all the flowers, methinks a rose is the finest."

The **McCall House** (153 Oak St., 541/482-9296 or 800/808-9749, www.mccallhouse.com), $100–225, is a restored Italianate built in 1883 by Ashland pioneer John McCall. A National Historic Landmark, this nine-room inn is a block from restaurants, shops, theaters, and Lithia Park. Delectable fresh baked goodies with juice or tea are served each afternoon. The Carriage House offers two beds, a kitchenette, and a private phone.

The **Morical House Garden Inn** (668 N. Main St., 541/482-2254 or 800/208-0960), $112–214, is a restored seven-room 1880s farmhouse and newer guesthouse with three luxury suites, each with a picture-postcard view of Grizzly Mountain and the Siskiyou foothills. Wooden floors, stained-glass windows, and antiques sustain the "good old days" theme despite no shortage of modern conveniences. The two acres of gardens provide organic produce for breakfast in season, as well as a wide variety of herbs and flowers. Many species of birds and butterflies are attracted to the gardens, which are tastefully accented by a waterfall and stream meandering through the grounds. Given all this, it's sometimes hard to remember that you are only a few blocks away from downtown theaters and shopping.

Two blocks south of the theaters is the critically acclaimed **Winchester Country Inn** (35 S. 2nd St., 541/488-1113 or 800/972-4991, www.winchesterinn.com), $110–225, offering 18 rooms with personality and private baths. The individual attentiveness of the staff of 35 recalls a traditional English country inn. Bay windows, private balconies, and exquisite English gardens add further distinction to this nonsmoking establishment. Exotic gourmet delicacies are featured at breakfast, and dinner and Sunday brunch is available in the full-service dining room (see "Fine Dining," later in this section). Visit the website to check out their changing special packages.

Families and couples traveling together will appreciate the space and privacy of the **Oak Street Cottages** (171 Oak St., 541/488-3778, www.oakstreetcottages.com), $210–280. Located a block from Lithia Park and the theaters, each cottage has a full service kitchen, dining room, and large living room. Enjoy eating outside on your own private patio equipped with a picnic table and barbecue. These units can comfortably accommodate 6–10 people. A second option would be **Second Street Cottages** (138 N. 2nd St., 541/488-0888 or 877/488-0898, www.2sc.com), $185. Featuring two cottages

MT. ASHLAND INN

Skiers, hikers, and anyone who wants to savor views of Mounts McLoughlin and Shasta from the snug confines of a three-story cedar lodge will appreciate Mt. Ashland Inn (Box 9444, 550 Mt. Ashland Rd., Ashland 97520, 541/482-8707 or 800/830-8707, www.mtashlandinn.com). Flourishes such as stained glass, oriental rugs, an ornate fireplace, and Windsor chairs impart a cozy charm.

The Mt. McLoughlin suite ($180) affords views of Shasta out one window and McLoughlin out the other. Sky Lakes Suite ($200) offers another knockout vista as well as a whirlpool tub for two with a rock waterfall, river rock gas fireplace, microwave, refrigerator, and other luxurious amenities. Four other rooms are also available, the lowest going for $135–160 per night. Paul Bunyan–esque breakfasts emphasizing locally produced foodstuffs fuel hikes and cross-country ski trips on the nearby Pacific Crest Trail. Complimentary cross-country skis, snowshoes, sleds, and mountain bikes are available for hotel guests. In addition, the inn's 7,500-foot elevation makes for excellent stargazing from its comfortable deck.

each with two bedrooms and fully equipped kitchens just two blocks from downtown, it's almost too good to be true.

If you want to keep your canine or feline companion with you, consider the pet-friendly **Patterson House** (639 N. Main St., 541/482-9171 or 888/482-9171, www.patterson-house.com), $70–125. Lest you think lodging our furry friends makes for a menagerie, only mature, well-behaved animals are welcome by prior arrangement. Parents with infants can also find sanctuary here, another rarity in the B&B world. This spacious 1910 Craftsman home offers four tastefully apportioned air-conditioned rooms with private bath. A healthy vegetarian breakfast further adds to this establishment's uniqueness.

Finally, saving the best for last, you'll bathe in naturally occurring hot spring water at the **Lithia Springs Inn** (2165 W. Jackson Rd., 541/482-7128 or 800/482-7128, www.ashlandinn.com), $85–385. Located a couple of miles from downtown, it's close enough for access to Ashland culture, yet far enough away for some real peace and quiet. Seven acres of working gardens provide fresh food and flowers for breakfasts and decoration. Their 3,000-book library has all kinds of interesting tomes, and a secret bookcase in the living room hides an entrance to another room. Twelve of the 14 rooms have whirlpools fed from the hot springs. There are eight cottage suites, two theme suites, and four regular rooms available for guests to enjoy. Most of the one- and two-room cottages adjacent to the lodge feature a fireplace, refrigerator, wet bar, and double Jacuzzi. Be sure to book well in advance to take advantage of this unique property.

Hostels

Offering 35 beds and family rooms, the **Ashland Hostel** (150 N. Main St., 541/482-9217, www.ashlandhostel.com) is a two-story 1902 house near the Pacific Crest Trail, only three blocks from the Elizabethan Theater and Lithia Park, and two blocks from the Greyhound station. Reservations are absolutely essential, especially March–October. Family/couple rooms are available, $20–47. The hostel also has a coin-op laundry.

Ashland is famous for having one of the more dynamic Elderhostel programs in the country. Seniors bed down at Southern Oregon State dorms and take Shakespeare classes at the university to enhance their appreciation of the plays. To find out about the offerings of this hostel as well as the programs of its counterparts in Sandy near Mount Hood, Corvallis, and Lakeview, contact **Elderhostel** (75 Federal St., Boston, MA 02110-1941, 617/426-8056 or 541/552-6677) or log on to www.sou.edu/housing/elderhostel for more information.

FOOD

Ashland's creative talents are not just confined to theatrical pursuits. Some of Oregon's better restaurants can be found around Main Street. Even the humbler fare served in Ashland's unpretentious cafés and burger joints can be memorable. The city has a five percent restaurant tax, a surcharge seen nowhere else in the Beaver State except Lincoln City.

Breakfast and American Cafés

Close to the Lithia Fountain, the **Ashland Bakery Cafe** (38 E. Main St., 503/482-2117) is a low-cost alternative to the array of haute cuisine on this block. For $5–10, enjoy high-quality breakfasts, sandwiches, and main courses. Whether it's smoked salmon and cream cheese on a bagel, a tofu scramble, or fresh-baked pastry, you can't go wrong. Open daily for breakfast and lunch; dinner is served Wed.–Sunday.

The second-floor patio at the **Greenleaf Restaurant** (49 N. Main St., 541/482-2808) makes a wonderful spot to enjoy an evening snack. Healthful fare with Mediterranean flair ($6–12), espresso, and a good selection of desserts pull in the evening crowds, just as the omelettes, frittatas, and fruit smoothies attract devotees of healthy breakfasts ($6–10).

Grizzly Peak Roasting Company (11 N. 1st, 541/488-4883), open 7 A.M.–8 P.M., has the freshest java in town, roasted daily on site. Eggs Italiano are a house specialty. Add in cheese and other options and stuff it into a fresh croissant, and you have one of the best-tasting and economical breakfasts in town.

New York meets the Northwest at **Brothers' Restaurant and Deli** (95 N. Main St., 541/482-9671), another popular local hangout for breakfast ($6–10), Specializing in gourmet soup and sandwiches, Brothers' is open for breakfast, lunch, and dinner.

Mexican

At **Munchies** (64 N. Main St., 541/488-2967), the food is made mostly from scratch and has no MSG or lard. They make their own vegetarian refried beans and offer five different vegetarian specials, all for under $9. The eatery also serves a mean set of burgers. Open daily for breakfast, lunch, and dinner.

Eclectic

Alex's (35 N. Main St., 541/482-8818) serves lunch ($5–15) and dinner ($12–20), highlighting regional ingredients on a changing menu.

For lunch, you can't go wrong with the Dungeness crab quesadilla, chicken pine nut dumplings, or Cajun fish tacos. Dinner favorites include rack of lamb. Arrive early at this temple to elegant but inexpensive cuisine to get one of the three tables on the balcony above the street.

Pangea (272 E. Main St., 541/552-1630) is a creative sandwich/salad emporium featuring hormone-free and free-range meats, and organic coffee and produce. Whether it's a Cleopatra salad or a wrap, the preparations are light, flavorful, and reasonably priced. This place is perfect for a quick meal before the show on a hot midsummer night.

Omars (1380 Siskiyou Blvd., 541/482-1281), Ashland's oldest restaurant (mastodon bones were found when excavating for the restaurant in 1946), is noted for its seafood. You'll also be impressed by the restaurant's chicken Dijon, steaks, and moderate prices ($10–30). The map on the back of the takeout menu is better than the ones supplied by governmental agencies. Open Mon.–Fri. for lunch and dinner; dinner only on Saturday and Sunday. Winter hours may vary.

Finally, we like the concept at **Quinz** (29 N. Main St., 541/488-5937). Instead of the structured meal format where each individual is inclined to consume exclusively from his or her own plate, Quinz features small plates and shareables, so that everyone can sample a bit of everything. This makes for a more sociable milieu for enjoying upscale ($5–15) casual dining. Foods of Greece, Spain, Italy, and the Pacific Northwest are all represented here, and an outstanding selection of wines by the glass complements the menu. Moroccan lamb meatballs with almonds in a cumin-coriander tomato sauce or a plate of grilled prawns with spinach and feta won't set you back more than $8, tastefully proving that less is more. Open daily in the summer months; winter hours vary.

The **Back Porch Barbecue** (92 N. Main St., 541/482-4131) lives up to its name. In addition to chicken, ribs, and the like ($8–18), live music on summer weekends, and tables outside the building along the creek round out the cookout motif. Open daily for lunch and dinner.

Italian

The food at **Il Giardino** (5 Granite St., 541/488-0816) is as Italian as the Vespa scooter parked in the foyer. No American-style spaghetti and meatballs here, just tried-and-true Italian food by a *paesano* chef. The rolled eggplant stuffed with goat cheese is one haymaker of an appetizer and their pasta dishes (most around $10) bring Old World taste back home. A half dozen seafood entrées come with salad made from fresh organic greens. Daily specials are also always a good bet as is a wine list well suited to all palates and pocketbooks. Seating is limited, so reservations are highly recommended. Open daily for dinner.

Geppetto's (345 E. Main St., 541/482-1138) is the place to go for Italian cuisine. Nothing fancy, just real food prepared and served by real people at real prices ($8–20). This Ashland institution offers some deliciously wild concoctions, such as cheese wontons with homemade salsa. Open daily.

Health Food

One of the best alternative groceries in southern Oregon is the **Ashland Community Food Co-op** (237 N. 1st, 541/482-2237). Open Mon.–Sat. 8 A.M.–9 P.M., and Sunday 9 A.M.–9 P.M., a great variety of organic produce and organic bulk foods can be found here.

Fine Dining

The **Winchester Inn** (35 S. 2nd St., 541/488-1113 or 800/972-4991) is not only a renowned B&B but a first-rate dinner-house as well. The Victorian National Historic Landmark dining room may look out on an English garden with a gazebo, but modern sensibilities permeate a menu that changes seasonally (dinner entrées $15–26, brunch $8–13). Their *teng-da* beef, an Indochinese filet mignon in a marinade of soy, lemon, horseradish, black pepper, and anise, is a permanent fixture. Open for Sunday brunch and dinner every night.

As with the Winchester Inn, the **Peerless Restaurant** (265 4th St., 541/488-6067 or 800/460-8758) is set in a picturesque B&B (the garden is spectacular, so dine alfresco if possible).

The appetizer list on the summer menu trumpets the restaurant's fresh-and-homegrown orientation. The extensive, seasonally rotating entrée menu of Northwest cuisine with global influences might contain braised Oregon rabbit, hot alder-smoked king salmon, and a sashimi dish. Whether you choose an inexpensive bistro dinner, an entrée ranging in price from $16–30, or a multicourse dinner for $65, you will be totally satisfied—especially if you finish with one of their soufflés or handmade chocolates.

Across the street, **Monet** (36 S. 2nd, 541/482-1339) is an excellent choice for upscale ($20–30) French cuisine that's a bit lighter on the sauces for American palates. The French-born and -trained chef/owner imparts an impressionistic flair to the restaurant's culinary delights. Classical music, white tablecloths, and paintings from local artists further enhance the mood. Fresh herbs for dinner come from the garden adjacent to the outdoor patio where patrons can enjoy a memorable meal during the warmer months. Seating is limited, and reservations are recommended. Open for dinner Tues.–Saturday.

Beasy's on the Creek (51 Water St., 541/488-5009) brings to Ashland a fusion of Texan and Mediterranean flavors. While the fresh fish and center cut steaks are the main draw ($13–25), the pasta dishes are also winners. But whatever the entrée, be sure to ask for some of Bud's Black Seafood Gumbo. A warm interior of brass and mahogany, a good wine list, and organic Mexican coffee with dessert put on the finishing touches to an elegant dinner presentation. Outdoor seating overlooking Ashland Creek is available during the warmer months. Open for dinner daily.

Chateaulin (150 E. Main St., 541/482-2264, www.chateaulin.com) looks the most Shakespearean, with its dark wooden interior and lighted stained glass behind the bar. Traditional French and nouvelle cuisines ($15–30 for dinner) are offered from a weekly menu. Chateaulin's bistro menu averages half the cost of their regular offerings. Whether it's crepes stuffed with portobello mushrooms, spinach, goat cheese, and garlic or escargot served with country pâté, the bistro fare here manages to fuse a medley of delicate flavors. If you can't decide, go for the prix-fixe dinner ($29). Beginning nightly at 5:30, this menu offering (which changes weekly) features a three-course dinner and two courses of specially chosen wine. Chateaulin's adjoining gourmet food and wine shop also offers custom picnic lunch baskets (order 24 hours in advance). If you go there after the play for one of their 25 specialty coffee drinks, be careful what you say about the performance—Hamlet or Falstaff may show up wearing blue jeans. Dinner served every night except Monday.

INFORMATION AND SERVICES

Ashland Visitor Information Center (110 E. Main St., Ashland 97520, 541/482-3486, www.ashlandchamber.com) offers brochures, play schedules, and other up-to-date information on happenings. Another excellent source of information is the **Southern Oregon Reservation Center** (P.O. Box 477, Ashland 97520, 541/488-1011 or 800/547-8052, www.sorc.com). This agency specializes in arranging Shakespearean vacation packages with quality lodging, choice seats for performances in all three theaters, and other tour and entertainment extras.

The **Oregon Welcome Center** offers travel information on the whole state. Traveling on I-5, take Exit 14. At the stop sign, turn left onto Ashland Street. Go over the freeway overpass and get into the left-hand turn lane and turn left onto Washington Street. The center is located at the Ashland Ranger District. Watch for "Tourism Information" signs.

Evo's Java House (376 E. Main St., 541/482-2261) provides Internet access.

TRANSPORTATION

Greyhound (91 Oak St., 541/482-2516) serves Ashland with a handful of daily north- and southbound departures. Local connections between Medford and Ashland are possible through **Rogue Valley Transportation** (541/779-2877, www.rvtd.org). Pick up a bus schedule at area businesses or libraries, or online. Contact **Ski Ashland** (P.O. Box 220, Ashland 97520, 541/482-2897) for information on the

Mount Ashland daily bus to and from Medford and Ashland. Twenty-four-hour taxi service is available from **Ashland Taxi** (541/890-8080). United Express and Horizon Air fly into Medford-Jackson airport, 15 miles north of town. Amtrak has a station 70 miles east of Klamath Falls and 75 miles south at Dunsmuir, California.

Medford

Today, along with a resource-based economy revolving around agriculture and timber products, Medford is becoming established as a retirement center. Proximity to Ashland's culture, Rogue Valley recreation, and Cascade getaways, as well as rainfall totals half those recorded in the Willamette Valley, are some of the enticements. Unfortunately, if the current population of 63,000 grows much larger, the already poor air quality here will become worse. Already smog alerts brought on by heat and inversions have some folks calling the city "Dreadford."

Call it what you will, but for cost of living, proximity to mountains and coast, and employment opportunities, many folks consider Medford the best place to live in southern Oregon.

SIGHTS

Table Rocks

About 10 miles northeast of Medford are two eye-catching basaltic buttes, Upper and Lower Table Rock. They are composed of sandstone with erosion-resistant lava caps deposited during a massive Cascade eruption about four to five million years ago. Over the years, wind and water have undercut the sandstone. Stripped of their underpinnings, the heavy basalt on top of the eroded sandstone is pulled down by gravity, creating the nearly vertical slabs that we see today.

The Table Rocks were the site of a decisive battle in the first of a series of Rogue Indian wars in the 1850s. Major Philip Kearny, who later went on to distinguish himself as the great one-armed Civil War general, was successful in routing the Native Americans from this seemingly impervious stronghold. A peace treaty was signed here soon afterward by the Rogue (Takelma)

tribe and the American government. For a time, this area was also part of the Table Rock Indian Reservation, but the reservation status was terminated shortly thereafter.

For nearly a century, the Table Rocks were the domain of vultures and rattlesnakes until the **Lower Table Rock Preserve** was established in 1979. This 1,890-acre preserve is near the westernmost butte, which towers 800 feet above the surrounding valley floor. Established by the

JACKSON AND PERKINS

Medford is home not only to fruit megacorporation Harry and David, but also to the world's largest private rose grower. The history of Jackson and Perkins (1310 Center Dr., 800/292-4769) began in 1872 on the East Coast, where the company first began wholesaling nursery stock. Their mail-order business started at the 1939 World's Fair in New York. Many customers who had ordered roses appreciated having them shipped and requested the same service the following year. From this nucleus, the reputation quickly spread, and orders for the company's roses came in from all over the country.

Jackson and Perkins moved to California's San Joaquin Valley in 1966 to take advantage of the 262-day growing season. The roses are now raised in California, then harvested and sent to the Medford plant where they are prepared for nationwide shipment.

The company's annual catalogues offer bulbs, seeds, and plants of all kinds, as well as their award-winning roses. Take a walk down the primrose path of their 43,000-square-foot Test and Display Garden (next to the warehouse on ORE 99) May–October to enjoy the colorful sights and sweet smells of the floral displays.

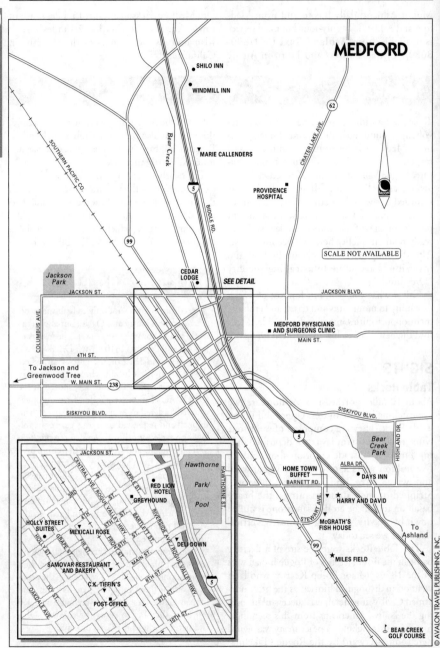

MEDFORD

SHILO INN
WINDMILL INN
MARIE CALLENDERS
PROVIDENCE HOSPITAL
Bear Creek
SOUTHERN PACIFIC CO.
CRATER LAKE AVE.
BIDDLE RD.
SCALE NOT AVAILABLE
CEDAR LODGE
SEE DETAIL
Jackson Park
JACKSON ST.
JACKSON BLVD.
MEDFORD PHYSICIANS AND SURGEONS CLINIC
COLUMBUS AVE.
4TH ST.
MAIN ST.
To Jackson and Greenwood Tree
W. MAIN ST.
SISKIYOU BLVD.
SISKIYOU BLVD.
Bear Creek Park
HIGHLAND DR.
ALBA DR.
DAYS INN
HOME TOWN BUFFET
BARNETT RD.
HARRY AND DAVID
STEWART AVE.
McGRATH'S FISH HOUSE
To Ashland
MILES FIELD
BEAR CREEK GOLF COURSE

JACKSON ST.
CENTRAL AVE./ROGUE VALLEY HWY.
RED LION HOTEL
GREYHOUND
Hawthorne Park/Pool
HAWTHORNE ST.
3RD
APPLE ST.
5TH ST.
BARTLETT ST.
RIVERSIDE AVE./ROGUE VALLEY HWY.
HOLLY STREET SUITES
HOLLY ST.
4TH ST.
GRAPE ST.
FIR ST.
6TH ST.
7TH ST.
MEXICALI ROSE
DELI DOWN
MAIN ST.
IVY ST.
SAMOVAR RESTAURANT AND BAKERY
OAKDALE AVE.
C.K. TIFFIN'S
8TH ST.
POST OFFICE
9TH ST.
10TH ST.
5

© AVALON TRAVEL PUBLISHING, INC.

Nature Conservancy and later turned over to the government, the preserve protects an area of special biologic, geologic, historic, and scenic value. Pacific madrone, white oak, manzanita, and ponderosa pine grow on the flank of the mountain, while the crown is covered with grasses and wildflowers. Newcomers to the region will be especially taken by the madrone trees. This glossy-leafed evergreen has a "skin" that peels in warm weather to reveal a smooth, coppery orange bark. It's found mostly in the Northwest and was noted by early explorers as fuel for long, slow, hot-burning fires.

Park checklists show that more than 140 kinds of plants reside here, including dwarf meadow foam, which grows no place else on earth. One reason is that water doesn't readily percolate through the lava. Small vernal ponds collect on top of the butte, nurturing the wildflowers that flourish in early spring. The wildflower display reaches its zenith in April. A dozen species of flowers cover the rock-strewn flats with bright yellows and vivid purples.

Hikers who take the two-mile trail to the top of horseshoe-shaped Lower Table Rock are in for a treat. Be on the lookout for batches of pale lavender fawn lilies peeking out from underneath the shelter of the scraggly scrub oaks on the way up the mountain. You'll want to walk over to the cliff's edge, which will take you past some of the "mima mounds" or "patterned ground" that distinguishes the surface of the butte. How the mounds were formed is a matter of scientific debate. Some scientists believe they represent centuries of work by rodents, others think they are accumulated silt deposits, while still others maintain they were created by the action of the wind. However they got there, the mounds are the only soil banks on the mountain that support grasses, which are unable to grow on the lava. Lichens and mosses manage to grow on the lava, however, painting the dull black basalt with luxuriant greens and fluorescent yellows during the wetter months.

The trail up Upper Table Rock is a little over a mile but much steeper than the Lower Table Rock trail. Clay clings to the slopes of Upper Table Rock, making the going both sticky and slippery during the wet season. The trail affords wonderful vistas of the Rogue River and Sams Valley to the north. Two benches along the way are good places to stop and rest, savor the view, and scrape the heavy clay off your shoes.

The trail reaches the top of the butte on the far eastern side. The ponds up here are smaller and fewer than those on Lower Table Rock, but the mima mounds are more clearly defined. Upper Table Rock also shows less wear and tear from human activity, and the flower show is just as spectacular. Long black strips of hexagonal basalt look as though they were formed by tanks marching across the butte while the lava was cooling. You'll find that this irregular, knobby surface is difficult to walk on, but the colorful mosses and lichens love it. Also look for the tiny bouquets of grass widows, lovely purple flowers that dangle on long, graceful stalks. The odd-looking building off to the west is a navigation device maintained by the Federal Aviation Administration. It's easy to get disoriented out here, with hundreds of acres to explore. The point where the trail heads back down the mountain is marked by two large trees, a ponderosa pine and a Douglas fir, accompanied by a smaller cedar.

To get to the Table Rocks, take ORE 62 northeast out of Medford. Take the Central Point Exit (Exit 33) east about one mile to Table Rock Road, and turn north (left). Continue 7.6 miles, passing Tou Velle State Park. Turn east (right) and continue approximately one mile to the signed parking lot, which will be on your left. The trail to the top of Upper Table Rock begins there. There are some basic campground-style toilets at the trailhead. The **BLM** (3040 Biddle Rd., 541/770-2200) has additional information on the Table Rocks.

Harry and David

For those not inclined to shell out $30 (the mail-order price) for a gift box of 6 Royal Riviera pears, come to the south part of Medford where Harry and David (1314 Center Dr., Medford 97501, 541/776-2277, www.harryanddavid.com), the nation's leading purveyor of mail-order fruit, has a store. From November till Christmas, no catalogue concern of any kind in the country ships more weekly packages. This success is reflected in the spacious new digs that replaced the company's old country store during the early nineties. Strolling through the aisles, you can enjoy samples of products. The fruit-stand section of the store offers farm-fresh fruit and vegetables. You can also find rejects from Harry and David's Fruit-of-the-Month Club that are nearly as good as the mail-order fruit but are too small or blemished to meet their high-quality standards. It's worth noting that less than half the fruit the company grows is good enough to be included in their fruit baskets.

The gourmet-foods section features their complete line of freshly made baked goods, smoked meats and fish, and cheeses. Again, be on the lookout for products with slight imperfections that go for a fraction of the cost listed in the store catalogue. The jams and fruit spreads in particular are less expensive here.

Harry and David took over their family's Bear Creek Orchards in 1914. Bear Creek Orchards was recognized for the size and quality of its pears, which were shipped to the grand hotels of Europe. But the lucrative export market of this company collapsed during the Depression, so the brothers decided to sell their fruit by mail. To establish a new reputation domestically, they headed for both seaboards. Each brother carried sample gift boxes of fruit, which they personally delivered to high-rollers like David Sarnoff, Walter Chrysler, Leland Stanford, and Alfred P. Sloan. Their first foray was an immediate success, and their mail-order business was born in 1934. The turning point came in 1936 when *Fortune* featured a full-page ad run by the brothers. This was followed up by similar spreads in other national media, usually depicting an American Gothic–style photo of the brothers in front of the product. With this higher profile came a decision by the brothers to change their last name from Rosenberg to Holmes in the 1950s, in reaction to the trial of alleged Russian spies, Julius and Ethel Rosenberg. Shortly after the name change took effect, they died within a few years of each other.

Today, the company is owned by the Japanese behemoth Yamanouchi Pharmaceutical, which has built stores coast-to-coast. While other changes abound, ranging from an Internet presence to a shift in the company's demographic target market (from seniors to baby-boomers), Harry and David still grows all its fruit within a 15-mile radius of the Medford store.

For visitors unable to make it south from the Portland area, there is an outlet store just outside the city. Heading east, take Troutdale Exit 17 off I-84 to 257th Avenue, then make a quick right, followed by a quick left into the Columbia Outlet Mall, and look for it on the west side of the complex.

Rising Sun Farms

Another local food producer to make it big on the national circuit is **Rising Sun Farms** (5126 S. Pacific Hwy., Phoenix, 800/888-0795, www.risingsunfarms.com). The flavors of the Pacific Northwest are represented in their cheese tortas, vinaigrettes, marinades, and mustards. Good "emergency food" can be found in the form of their pestos. Made from core ingredients of organically grown basil, extra virgin olive oil, almonds, and sea salt, their half dozen varieties can turn a motel hotplate meal into a fine dining experience. Open Mon.–Friday.

Grist for the Mill

About 15 minutes away from Medford on ORE 62 is Oregon's last original water-powered grist mill that's still in operation, the **Butte Creek Mill** (P.O. Box 561, 402 Royal, Eagle Point 97524, 541/826-3531). To get here, take ORE 62 about 10 miles north to Eagle Point and follow the signs to the mill. Built in 1872, the foundation pillars were hand-hewn with an axe, and wooden pegs and square nails hold up the rest of the structure. The two 1,400-pound millstones were quarried in France and assembled in Illinois. From there, they were shipped around the Horn and then transported over the mountains by wagon. Genuine stone-ground products are available in the mill shop, including 12 kinds of flours, four kinds of meal, four cracked grains, six cereals, four mixes (pancake, waffle, cornbread, and biscuit), and other grain products. A variety of health-food products rounds out the nutritious collection of edibles here. Open Mon.–Sat. 9 A.M.–5 P.M. (except major holidays).

Adjacent to the mill is the **Oregon General Store Museum.** This museum is a re-creation of a typical late-1800s general store. Home remedies, giant coffee grinders, pickle barrels, and other common goods of the day are exhibited. A working music box, antiques and collectibles, and old advertising signs add to the decor. Open Saturday 11 A.M.–4 P.M., donations are eagerly accepted.

Just down the street from the mill is the **Lost Creek Covered Bridge.** The 39-foot-long bridge was built in 1919 and exhibits a queen post truss design with a shingle roof and flying buttress braces. The rough wooden floor is composed of diagonal planks. Lost Creek was so named because, during its thousand-foot drop in elevation over a distance of two miles, it disappears beneath a lava flow for a while before resurfacing again. The bridge is closed to vehicular traffic, but you can get a good picture of it by walking across it to the east side of Lost Creek.

Ridin' the Rails

Just about anyone who likes trains will enjoy **Medford Railroad Park** (on Berrydale Avenue off Table Rock Road, 541/770-4586 or 541/779-7979), a few blocks from the Rogue Valley Mall. The park features miniature steam trains that run the second and fourth Sundays of each month, April–October, 11 A.M.–3 P.M. Locomotives and other railway equipment are faithful reproductions of full-size trains, except that one inch here equals a foot in the real world. Coal, wood, oil, and propane fire the steam boilers that propel the trains around a mile-long track. Passengers are carried in small cars across bridges and culverts, and over a small grade. Full-size cars, cabooses, a hopper car, and locomotives are also on display. Admission is free.

Crater Rock Museum

In 1952, Delmar Smith held a meeting in his home for a local mineral society. More than 50 years later, he gives tours of the Crater Rock Museum (2002 Scenic Ave., Central Point, 541/664-1355, www.craterrock.com), created

mostly by the efforts of the Roxy Ann Gem and Mineral Society. While small in size, the museum offers a selection large in scope. Showcased is an impressive array of gems, minerals, fossilized rock, petrified wood, agates, crystals, and moss agates—many of them collected in Oregon. Many examples of the state rock, the thunder egg, and the state gem, the Oregon sunstone, are also prominently displayed. The museum also boasts an excellent early Native American artifacts collection, many of the pieces found in the Rogue Valley. Of note are the tribal effigies, small fired-clay figurines. The building also houses a library with over 450 geology reference books, and the gift shop has maps and directions to good rockhounding sites. Open Tuesday, Thursday, and Saturday 10 A.M.–4 P.M. Admission is free, donations accepted.

To get here from the south, take I-5 Exit 32 and go west on Pine Street to ORE 99. Head north on 99 to Scenic Avenue, where you will make a right (east). Proceed down Scenic Avenue and you will see the museum. If coming from the north, take I-5 Exit 35 and go south on ORE 99 until you get to Scenic Avenue, where you will take a left (east). From either direction, look for the signs and the flashing yellow caution light in the middle of ORE 99 that marks Scenic Avenue.

SPORTS AND RECREATION
Golf

Near Miles Field is **Bear Creek Golf Course** (2325 South Pacific Hwy., 541/773-1822). This is a compact nine-hole course that's both a challenge and a bargain at $10 a round. If you would rather go for a regulation-sized course, **Cedar Links Golf Course** (3144 Cedar Links Dr., 541/773-4373), in northeastern Medford, has 18 holes waiting for you. To get there, take ORE 62 north toward White City. Turn right on Delta Waters Road, right again on Springbrook Road, and then left on Cedar Links Drive. The greens fee is $15 for nine holes and $22 for 18 holes; add a dollar or two more on weekends.

Once rated among the top-10 public-access

THE LEGENDS OF ONE-EYED CHARLIE AND BLACK BART

It has been a century since southern Oregon has heard the pounding hooves and grinding axles of an approaching Portland-to-Sacramento stagecoach, but the West's first organized interstate transportation system hasn't been forgotten. Such stage line stopovers as Wolf Creek Tavern, north of Grants Pass, and Jacksonville, west of Medford, have been commemorated with National Historic Landmark and National Historic District status. In addition to these evocations of the era, the stories of two romantic figures, One-Eyed Charlie and Black Bart, help to evoke a time when the Wild West lived up to its name.

One-Eyed Charlie was a stagecoach driver, a job that commanded considerable respect back in 19th-century Oregon. A look at the roadbeds of such wagon-route remnants as I-5 between Grants Pass and Roseburg, and ORE 238 north of Jacksonville, might help you to understand why. Ruthless highwaymen, conflicts with Native Americans, and inclement weather plagued these frontier thoroughfares. Even without such hazards, bouncing along for days on a buckboard carriage, sans shock absorbers and air-conditioning, required considerable fortitude.

Of all the men on the Oregon-to-California line, One-Eyed Charlie was the driver of choice whenever Wells Fargo needed to transport valuable cargo. Despite a salty vocabulary, an opinionated demeanor, and a rough appearance, all of which might have rankled some passengers, no one was better at handling the horses or dealing with adversity.

When the stage would roll into Portland or Sacramento, One-Eyed Charlie would collect his paycheck and disappear for a few days. It was said that he was a heavy drinker and gambler during his sojourns deep into the seamy frontier underworld. When it came time to make the next trip through, however, he'd be back at the helm, sober and cantankerous as ever.

Inevitably, One-Eyed Charlie's hard-drivin', hard-drinkin' life caught up with him, and he shuffled off this mortal coil. When the coroner was preparing the body for burial, he made a surprising discovery. One-Eyed Charlie was really One-Eyed Charlene! Shock waves reverberated up and down the West Coast at the realization that a woman had been best at what was considered exclusively a man's domain. But the real kicker was that she had voted in the 1860 and 1864 presidential elections for Abraham Lincoln, over half a century before women could legally vote! As the voting records have been lost, legal scholars have been unable to prove or debunk the persistent legend of One-Eyed Charlie.

Another personality from the stagecoach era, the outlaw Black Bart has also become part of Western folklore. Between 1875 and his capture in 1883, he robbed 28 stagecoaches of their gold shipments. Known as the Gentleman Bandit due to his polite treatment of passengers, Black Bart had a penchant for verse. One of his finer efforts read:

I've labored hard and long for bread,
for honor and for riches.

But on my corns too long you've tread,
you fine-haired sons of bitches.

Let come what will, I'll try it on, my
condition can't be worse.

And if there's money in that box, tis
money in my purse.

But the Gentleman Bandit's chivalrous ways proved to be his undoing. A handkerchief much like one he offered to the ladies when he helped them off the stage was found at the scene of a robbery. The initials "CB" were embroidered on its corner and it was traced by its laundry mark to San Francisco. The owner was identified as Charles Bolton, an employee of Wells Fargo Bank. This explained why Black Bart was able to know the arrival time of gold shipments. After completing four years of a six-year sentence at San Quentin, Charles Bolton was released for good behavior. He disappeared shortly thereafter, but will forever be remembered as the Gentleman Bandit for his refinement and the fact that he never shot anyone.

courses by *Golf* magazine, **Eagle Point Golf Course** (100 Eagle Point Dr., Eagle Point 97524, 541/826-8225, www.eaglepointgolf .com) is arguably the finest course in the Rogue River Valley. Designed by Robert Trent Jones II, this 175-acre collection of golf holes boasts enough character to challenge beginners and experts alike. Impressive views of Mount McLoughlin and Table Rocks add to the experience. Greens fees are $68 to walk and $78 to ride. Carts, clubs, and shoes are available for rent here.

Swimming

When the summer mercury heats up into the 90s, it's time to cool off in one of Medford's several public swimming pools. **Jackson Pool** (815 Summit, 541/770-4586) is a popular family place to get wet. In addition to the 100-foot-long waterslide, a concession stand sells ice cream, soft drinks, and other snacks. The swimming season starts June 11 and runs into early September. An open recreational swim is held Mon.–Wed. 1–3 P.M. and also on Friday. Thursday evening is reserved for family swims, 7:30–9:15 P.M. A small admission is charged. **Hawthorne Pool** (505 E. Main St., 541/770-4586) features an open swim Sun.–Fri. 1–3 P.M. and 3:30–5:30 P.M.

Biking and Jogging

Bear Creek, which runs through the city, attracts joggers, bikers, and walkers. These groups also indulge their passions along the Old Stage Road (especially heading into or leaving Jacksonville). For bicycle rentals try **Siskiyou Cyclery** (1259 Siskiyou Blvd., 541/482-1997, www.siskiyoucyclery.com).

Medford's Bear Creek Park is a recreation mecca. Kids love the majestic castle playground, and sports enthusiasts revel in acres of open space. To get there from I-5 take Exit 27 off I-5 at the Barnett Road–Jacksonville interchange. Go east on Barnett Road, and turn left on Highland Drive. The park's main entrance is located next to the fire station on Siskiyou Boulevard near the corner of Highland and Siskiyou. It's open 6:30 A.M.–10:30 P.M.

ENTERTAINMENT AND EVENTS

Jackson County Fair

The Jackson County Fair is held at the county fairgrounds just north of town the third weekend of July. Frequent shuttle-bus departures provided by **Rogue Valley Transportation** (3200 Crater Lake Ave., Medford, 541/799-2988) relieve you of fighting the crowds for limited parking spaces. The buses leave from downtown Medford, Poplar Square, Crater High School, and other points around town. The trip back from the fair is free, and the shuttles run approximately every 15 minutes. Cowboys, ranchers, and farmers all come with their families for fun and top-name entertainment. Country music seems to dominate the stage, with performers like Ricky Skaggs, Waylon Jennings, and Charley Pride drawling out their tunes. If the kids are going to spend the day at the midway, consider purchasing their ride tickets in advance and saving 50 percent off the regular "one price for all rides" (except Saturday). Check with the Southern Oregon Reservation Center (541/488-1011 or 800/547-8052) for pre-sale ticket outlets.

Pear Blossom Festival

The Pear Blossom Festival takes place the second weekend of April with arts and crafts exhibits, a parade, and a 10-km run. The real attraction is the panorama of the orchards in bloom against the backdrop of snowcapped Mount McLoughlin. The parade and run take place downtown, and festivities continue at Alba Park with more than 100 booths of arts and crafts, food, music and children's activities. The fair continues till 4 P.M.

Shopping

You can find many brand-name items at 20–70 percent off retail price at the **Pear Tree Factory Stores** (I-5 Exit 24, 205 Fern Valley Rd., 541/535-1194). Twenty different companies offer a wide range of goods from clothing, accessories, and sportswear to books and housewares. The huge on-site diner serves pretty good food.

From May–October the Medford Shopping Center on Stevens Street hosts the **Rogue Valley Growers and Crafters Market** (P.O. Box 4041, Medford 97501). This open-air market features fresh produce (much of it organic), plants, fresh-cut and dried flowers, baked goods and specialty foods, and locally handcrafted items.

You can find the wares of over 400 artists and craftspeople at the **Crafters Market** (1233 Court St., 541/779-4667), a kind of outlet store and clearinghouse for artisans. Country and Americana motif crafts, dried and silk flowers, quilts, jewelry, furniture, woodwork, stained glass, clothing, ceramics, and many one-of-a-kind originals are all for sale at artist-direct prices. Open weekdays 10 A.M.–6 P.M., Saturday 10 A.M.–5 P.M., and Sunday noon–4 P.M.

ACCOMMODATIONS

Motels and Hotels

Medford has no shortage of motel rooms, most of them clustered near the interstate exits. The old adage "you get what you pay for" usually applies, especially in the case of motel rooms. Some budget choices include **Cedar Lodge** (518 N. Riverside, 541/773-7361 or 800/282-3419), $50–60; **Days Inn** (850 Alba Dr., 541/779-6730 or 800/329-7466), $45–65; and **Pear Tree Motel** (300 Pear Tree Ln., 541/535-4445 or 800/645-7332, www.peartreemotel.com), $60–95.

If you don't want to spend the rest of the trip in the penalty box, pop for the extra bucks and keep peace in the family with a hotel upgrade. **Red Lion Hotel** (200 N. Riverside, 541/779-5811 or 800/RED-LION, www.redlion.com), $80–95; **Rogue Regency Inn** (2345 ORE 62, 541/770-1234 or 800/535-5805, www.rogueregency.com), $95–210; **Shilo Inn** (2111 Biddle Rd., 541/770-5151 or 800/222-2244, www.shiloinns.com), $80–100; and **Windmill Inn** (1950 Biddle Rd., 541/779-0050 or 800/547-4747, www.windmillinns.com), $80–90, are good choices. Most of these superior category properties have pools, accept pets, and offer extras that will help make for a soft landing.

Bed-and-Breakfasts

A romantic bed-and-breakfast with a parklike ambience is the **Greenwood Tree** (3045 Bellinger Ln., 541/776-0000 or 800/766-8099, www.greenwoodtree.com). The rooms and suites ($115–160) have private baths and are decorated with antiques, Persian rugs, and fabric art collections. A lavish breakfast and afternoon tea served in the parlor, on the porch, or out in the garden, as well as chocolate truffles on your pillow at night, further enhance the atmosphere. Outside this hand-hewn and -pegged building dating back to the Civil War, you'll find a willow swing in a three-story barn, a hammock suspended between enormous 300-year-old oaks, and a gazebo beneath shady apple trees overlooking the rose garden.

Holly Street Suites (304 Holly St., 541/779-4716) has three historic structures boasting antiques and Victorian woodwork. The five-room Waverly cottage is a turn-of-the-century showplace coupling red cedar and gold-leaf carvings with modern conveniences. One bedroom features a king-sized canopy bed, while the other has a double bed. The Holly House has two suites accessed by private entrances as well as kitchen and dining rooms with such refinements as an African mahogany wet bar and an antique wood cook stove, king- and queen-sized beds, and room service breakfast. Rates range from $65–95; additional guests are $10 each. Reservations are advised, and the Waverly Cottage has a two-day minimum-stay requirement on weekends and holidays.

FOOD

"Dagwood-style" sandwiches can be found at **Zach's Deli** (1310 F Center Dr., 541/779-8272). Open daily. If your taste buds are set for border food, **Mexicali Rose** (corner of 4th and Fir, 17 W. 4th St., 541/779-4289) can satisfy your cravings. Large dinners replete with rice and beans (be sure to ask for the special black beans) range $7–12. The Super Nachos are a perfect complement to the list of Latin American import beers or giant margaritas on the menu.

A great place for families is **Home Town Buffet** (1299 Center Dr., 541/770-6779). You'll find large spreads of fruits and veggies, salads, hot entrées, and fresh-baked muffins and desserts at a price you can afford. Breakfast is $7, lunch $8, and dinner runs $9. Discounts for children 2–10 are 45 cents per year of age for lunch and 50 cents per year of age for dinner. The restaurant started out here in Medford and has now reached national prominence with more than 50 outlets. Open for lunch and dinner Mon.–Fri. and breakfast, lunch, and dinner Saturday and Sunday.

A good spot for breakfast or lunch downtown is **C.K. Tiffin's** (226 E. Main, 541/779-0480). Their health-conscious menu, $5–10, includes several vegetarian items like garden-burgers, tostadas, burritos, and chili. Soups, salads, sandwiches, and some specialty items are also featured at very reasonable prices. Open Mon.–Fri. 7 A.M.–3 P.M.

For a break from the ordinary, head to **Samovar Restaurant and Bakery** (101 E. Main, 541/779-4967) for some traditional Russian and Middle Eastern cuisine. The *samovar,* a Russian teapot, is the symbol of hospitality and friendship, and this establishment provides a fitting bridge between our two cultures. The owners came to Oregon from Russia. Their pastries are from secret family recipes passed down from generation to generation. Jennia, a medical doctor, uses her expertise to prepare healthy, nutritionally balanced foods using natural ingredients. *Blinichiki* (Russian-style blintzes), *golubtei* (stuffed cabbage), and *piroshki* (small meat or cheese pies) are just a few of the delectables on the menu here. Open for breakfast and lunch Tues.–Sat. 11 A.M.–2:30 P.M., for dinner ($7–17) 5–9 P.M.

A favorite with loggers and truckers, **Withams** (2339 Biddle Rd., 541/772-9307) has inexpensive daily lunch and dinner specials that include soup or salad. The food's pretty good, and the price is right, even though you might think you're on the set for *Convoy.* Open 24 hours a day.

You'll find a good selection of seafood at **McGrath's Fish House** (68 E. Stewart Ave., 541/732-1732), a successful regional chain that has outlets scattered throughout the Pacific Northwest. There are several good appetizers on the menu here you could make a meal out of, like the crab and artichoke dip, the Sicilian prawn quesadilla, or the combo of sampler baskets. Their seafood, meat, and pasta entrées ($9–17) are all generously portioned, replete with your choice of two sides and tangy sourdough bread. Ask for the marionberry cobbler for dessert, served warm with French vanilla ice cream dripping down the sides.

In nearby Talent is the **Arbor House** (103 W. Wagner St., 541/535-6817), which boasts an eclectic menu with everything from fresh seafood and great Indian curries to German sauerbraten. A multigenerational family-run operation, Arbor House offers an uncommon meal in a loving setting that is sure to please. Call ahead for reservations, as space is limited. Open for dinner; closed Monday.

Another option in Talent is **New Sammy's Cowboy Bistro** (2210 S. Pacific Hwy., 541/535-2779); bring cash (no credit cards) and plan ahead (way ahead). With only six tables, New Sammy's fills up fast. Don't be put off by the exterior (gas station upgrade) or the interior decor (Pee Wee Herman's playhouse); the restaurant uses only organically grown food, and everything is homemade. Open Thurs.–Sun., dinners cost $30–40 per person including wine and dessert. Order the chef's special, sit back, and get ready for some great, unusual combinations. No sign, but there's a neon star on the roof, and a parking lot full of Mercedes and BMWs. Reservations recommended.

INFORMATION AND TRANSPORTATION

The **Medford Visitors and Convention Bureau** (101 E. 8th St., 541/779-4847 or 800/469-6307, www.visitmedford.org) has all kinds of useful maps, directories, and information for the asking. The office is open Mon.–Fri. 9 A.M.–5 P.M.

A half dozen buses dock daily at the **Greyhound** station (212 Barnett Rd., 541/779-2103). **Rogue Valley Transportation** (3200

Crater Lake Ave., 541/799-2988) provides connections to Jacksonville, Phoenix, White City, Talent, and Ashland. Most buses depart Medford at 6th and Barnett, Mon.–Fri. 8 A.M.–5 P.M., Saturday 9 A.M.–5 P.M., no service Sunday. Linkages to Eagle Point and White City are courtesy of **Cascade Bus Lines** (541/664-4801); the schedule fluctuates. **Courtesy Yellow Cab** (541/772-6288) has 24-hour service in the Medford area. A wheelchair van, senior-citizen dis-

counts, and special rates on airport transfers are all available on request.

Medford/Jackson County Airport (800/882-7488, www.co.jackson.or.us), the air hub for southern Oregon, is served by America West, Skywest, United, Horizon, and other carriers. Three rental-car agencies are at the airport: **Budget** (541/773-0488), **Avis** (541/773-3003 or 800/831-2847), and **Hertz** (541/773-4293 or 800/654-3131).

Jacksonville

Oregon's pioneer past is tastefully preserved in Jacksonville. Located five miles west of Medford and cradled in the foothills of the Siskiyou Mountains, this small town of 2,400 residents retains an atmosphere of tranquil isolation. With more than 100 original wooden and brick buildings dating back to the 1850s, it was the first designated National Historic Landmark District in Oregon and the third of eight such sites in the nation.

Named in honor of President Andrew Jackson and the town's namesake county, Jacksonville was surveyed in September 1851 into 200-foot-square blocks. Then as now, California and Oregon Streets were the hubs of Jacksonville business and social life. But the city's tightly packed wooden structures proved to be especially prone to fire. Between 1873 and 1884, three major fires reduced most of the original buildings to ash. These harsh experiences prompted merchants to use brick in the construction of a second generation of buildings, and the practice was furthered by an 1878 city ordinance requiring brick construction. Most of the building blocks were made and fired locally. To protect them from the elements and the damp season, the porous bricks were painted; cast-iron window shutters and door frames further reinforced the structures.

Boomtown Jacksonville was the first and largest town in the region and was selected as the county seat. It was even nominated and briefly considered for the state capital. The prominence of Jacksonville was made mani-

fest with the 1883 erection of a 60-foot-high courthouse with 14-inch-thick walls. But like the gold finds that quickly dwindled, Jacksonville's exuberance faded when the Oregon and California Railroad bypassed the town in the early 1880s in favor of nearby Medford. Businesses were quick to move east to greet the coming of the iron horse, and Jacksonville's stature as a trading center diminished. By the time the county seat was moved to Medford in 1925, Jacksonville's heady days had long since vanished.

During the Depression, families with low incomes took up residence in the town's derelict buildings, taking advantage of the cheap rents. Gold mining enjoyed a brief comeback, with residents digging shafts and tunnels in backyards, but it was not enough to revive the derailed economy. However, the following decades saw a gradual resurgence of interest in Jacksonville's gold-rush heritage. The Southern Oregon Historical Society was created after World War II, and individuals began to care for the many unaltered late-1880s buildings and restore them to their former glory. The **Beekman Bank** was one of the first structures to be spruced up, and the prominent **United States Hotel** was rehabilitated in 1964. The restoration movement was rewarded when the National Park Service designated Jacksonville a National Historic Landmark in 1966.

Today, Jacksonville paints a memorable picture of a western town with its historic buildings, excellent museum, and beautiful pioneer cemetery. In addition, a renowned music festival, colorful pageants, and rich local folklore all pay tribute to Jacksonville's golden age.

SIGHTS

Jacksonville Museum of Southern Oregon History

A good place to start your explorations is at the museum (C and 5th Streets). This imposing two-story brick-and-stone Italianate building, completed in 1883, served as the county administration building until 1925, when the county seat was moved to Medford. Nowadays, in addition to pioneer artifacts, a mock-up of pioneer photographer Peter Britt's studio, and interesting old pictures, the museum also has a good walking-tour map of the other historical sites in the city. Admission is $4. The stucco building next door to the courthouse used to be the county jail, but serves today as the children's museum. Kids of all ages will enjoy hands-on play with old-fashioned toys. A small bookstore, the History Store, is located here as well, specializing in local and regional historical publications. Open Wed.–Sat. 11 A.M.–4 P.M.

Historic C. C. Beekman House Living History Program

At the Beekman House (corner of California and Laurelwood Streets) costumed interpreters will introduce you to the friends and family of pioneer banker Cornelius Beekman. The 20-minute guided tours ($4 adults) charmingly set the time machine in motion.

Mansion by Mail

The **Jeremiah Nunan House** (635 N. Oregon St.), also known as the Catalogue House because it was ordered from Knoxville, Tennessee, by a wealthy merchant, is a Queen Anne–style house even tour-weary guidebook writers would recommend. Located just east of town, this 1892 three-story mansion features immense bird's-eye maple doors and 23 stained-glass windows. The $7,792 house, complete with wallpaper and carpets, was shipped in 14 box cars and assembled in six months. Drive or stroll by for a look at the exterior; unfortunately, they no longer give guided tours.

Peter Britt Gardens

Peter Britt came to Jacksonville not long after gold was discovered in Rich Gulch in 1851. After trying his hand at prospecting, he redirected his efforts toward painting and photography. The latter turned out to be his specialty, and for nearly 50 years he photographed the people, places, and events of southern Oregon (Britt was the first person to photograph Crater Lake). He also incorporated new photographic techniques and equipment in his studio as they developed. You'll find his ambrotypes, daguerreotypes, stereographs, and tintypes on display at the Jacksonville Museum of Southern Oregon History.

The Swiss-born Peter Britt was also an accomplished horticulturalist and among the first vintners in southern Oregon. In addition to experimenting with several varieties of fruit and nut trees to see which grew best in the Rogue River Valley, he kept the first weather data records of the region. Another testimonial to his love of plants is the giant redwood tree on the western edge of the Britt Gardens, South 1st and West Pine Streets, which he planted 130 years ago to commemorate the birth of his first child, Emil.

His house was a beautifully detailed Gothic revival home that was built in 1860 and then enlarged in the 1880s. Unfortunately, it was destroyed by fires in 1957 and 1960 and can now be remembered only through photographs. The stone-and-mortar wall visible today marks the site of the original foundation. Some of the remaining plantings are part of the original gardens, and many others were lovingly cultivated in 1976 by Robert Lovinger, a landscape architecture professor from the University of Oregon. The Peter Britt Music Festival was held on the grounds of the estate from 1962 until 1978, when the new Britt Pavilion was built just south of Britt's house.

A short half-mile hike begins 15 yards uphill from the Emil Britt redwood tree. A fairly level path follows the abandoned irrigation ditch that used to divert water from Jackson Creek to the Britt property. Soon you will notice Jackson Creek below the trail, as well as several overgrown sections of a nearly forgotten logging railroad bed. This is a particularly nice walk in the spring when the wildflowers are in bloom and the mosses and ferns are green.

Wine-Tasting

About eight miles southwest of Jacksonville in the Applegate Valley is **Valley View Winery** (1000 Upper Applegate Rd., 541/899-8468 or 800/781-WINE, www.valleyviewwinery.com). While the microclimate and the soil types allow for a great diversity of grape varieties, Valley View concentrates mainly on cabernet sauvignon, merlot, and chardonnay. They must be doing something right, because their Barrel Select bottlings have graced U.S. Presidents' tables, and their award-winning wines are found in many restaurants and wine shops throughout Oregon. Call ahead to confirm hours, which change with the season.

For a taste of some of the Pacific Northwest's best, head for the **Gary West Tasting Room** (690 N. 5th, 541/899-1829, www.garywest.com). Here you can sample fine food and wine for free. After the tastings, you'll have a better idea of what to choose from in their store. Oregon wines, hickory-smoked meats and jerky, and cheeses are some of the goodies you'll want to take home with you. The tasting room packs special Britt Festival picnic baskets, too.

EVENTS

Peter Britt Music Festival

On a grassy hillside amid majestic ponderosa pines near the Britt homesite, a small classical music festival began in 1962. Over 40 years later, the scope of the **Britt Festival** (541/773-6077 or 800/88-BRITT, www.brittfest.org) has broadened into a musical smorgasbord encompassing such diverse styles as jazz, folk, country, bluegrass, rock, and dance, in addition to the original classical repertoire. B.B. King, k.d. lang, the

DOUGLAS COUNTY

A good look at just about any local mountainside tells the story of Douglas County. For years, the economy here has revolved around *Pseudotsuga menziessi* ("false hemlock"), the Douglas fir. Named after David Douglas of the English Botanical Society, who visited Oregon in the 1820s to research Northwest flora and fauna, the Douglas fir accounts for the county's perpetually high timber-production levels. This distinction has earned the county the nickname "Lumberjack County."

After all of this fanfare, you probably think that Douglas County is named after David Douglas, right? Wrong! It's really named after Illinois Senator Steven A. Douglas, who gained fame for debating Abraham Lincoln in 1858 on the "peculiar institution" of slavery. Although Lincoln lost the senatorial election to Douglas, the debates helped Lincoln gain national prominence and polarized the issue, which James Madison called "a firestorm in the night."

Douglas's fame out West, however, was due more to his ardent advocacy of Oregon statehood in Congress. It was no small honor to choose his name to grace this county where stagecoaches passed en route to Jacksonville gold country, where California-bound steamships plied the Umpqua, and where Oregon's most esteemed pioneer family, the Applegates, chose to settle.

Doobie Brothers, Jean-Pierre Rampal, and Joshua Redman are just a few of the big-name artists who have performed here over the years.

The festival runs from the last week of June through the first week of September; most of the nearly 40 concerts occur in August. Tickets range from $20–35 for general admission, but some concerts can run as high as $150. Reserved seats run $5 more than general admission. Concert-goers often bring along blankets, small lawn chairs (allowed only in designated areas), wine, and a picnic supper to enjoy along with entertainment on balmy summer evenings. Be sure to order your tickets well in advance to avoid having to stand outside. Like the Oregon Shakespeare Festival, the shows sell out months in advance, especially for the well-known performers.

Pioneer Days

The Wild West returns to Jacksonville in mid-June with the annual Pioneer Days. A parade in old-time regalia down the main street of town kicks off the party. Following the parade, a street fair featuring arts, crafts, and food booths is held along California Street for the rest of the day. A street dance follows in the afternoon with live music, as well as an old-time fiddlers' performance. Children's games and activities are also scheduled for the afternoon. One of the most popular is the haystack search, in which tots grub around in the straw for more than $200 in hidden currency. Later in the day another fun annual event called the Ugly Legs Contest takes place. Contestants wear paper sacks over their heads so they are judged solely on how bad their legs look. Mud, sandals, worn-out sneakers, and other cosmetic touches are allowed. Other special events are also planned for seniors, and bingo games are held all day long. Call the chamber of commerce (541/889-8118) for details.

PRACTICALITIES

Accommodations

The majority of lodgings in Jacksonville are of the B&B variety. If this isn't your style, you do have one option. The **Stage Lodge** (830 N. 5th St., 541/899-3953 or 800/253-8254, www.stagelodge.com) was designed using the original architecture familiar to historic stage stops along the stage route from Sacramento to Portland. The rooms ($88–165) are clean and comfy.

The **Jacksonville Inn** (175 E. California St., 541/899-1900 or 800/321-9344, www.jacksonvilleinn.com), $115–275 (breakfast included), lies in the heart of the commercial historic district. In addition to eight air-conditioned rooms furnished with restored antiques and private baths,

the inn also offers three deluxe cottages replete with antiques, fireplace, king canopied beds, fruit, and champagne. The inn has an excellent dining room (see "Food," immediately following). Access to mountain bikes to explore the area is included in the room rate. Reservations are highly recommended, especially during the summer.

A block down California Street is the **McCully House Inn** (240 E. California St., 541/899-1942 or 800/367-1942, www.mccullyhouseinn.com), $95–125. Built in 1861 in the classical revival style, this mansion has four beautifully decorated bedrooms with private baths. European and American antiques, oriental rugs, delicate lace curtains, and a magnificent square grand piano (tuned a half step lower than today's A-440) add to the historical ambience. A full "country continental" breakfast is included.

> *Boasting nearly 40 summertime concerts, the Britt Festival has something for every musical taste.*

The **Touvelle House** (455 N. Oregon St., 541/899-3938 or 800/846-3992, www.touvellehouse.com) offers five rooms and one suite (all with private baths) for $130–165. Each room has its own theme and features touches like antiques, handmade quilts, and tasteful interior decorations. Out back by the carriage house is a heated swimming pool and spa. Common areas include a library and a large living room. A full, three-course breakfast is included, and other goodies like fruit and cookies are available for snacking anytime.

The **Orth House** (105 W. Main St., 541/899-8665 or 800/700-7301, www.orthbnb.com), $135–250, was built in 1880 and is listed in the National Register of Historic Homes. Large rooms with claw-foot tubs and period furnishings help to recall a bygone era with the benefit of modern air-conditioning. Full country breakfast and treats are included.

Food

The **Jacksonville Inn** (175 E. California St., 541/899-1900 800/321-9344, www.jacksonvilleinn.com) is consistently rated one of the top restaurants in Oregon by the food press. While the gold-rich mortar sparkles in the walls of the dining room and lounge, the menu is what offers real treasures. Steaks, seafood, and specialties of the inn like veal, duck, and prime rib are among the offerings in a Victorian atmosphere of red brick and velvet. Vegetarian dishes are also available. The five-course dinner featuring stuffed hazelnut chicken is frequently touted as a gourmet's dream meal. A connoisseur's wine cellar of over 700 vintages further enhances your dining experience. Expensive. Open Tues.–Sat. for lunch and dinner, Monday for dinner, and Sunday for brunch and dinner; reservations are suggested.

The **Bella Union Restaurant and Saloon** (170 W. California St., 541/899-1770) is another popular spot. Soups, salads, sandwiches, chicken, steaks, pasta, and pizza are some of the items ($6–15) you'll find on the menu here. Vegetarians have many choices to choose from as well. When the weather is right, the patio behind the restaurant is a pleasant place to eat lunch or enjoy a beer. Picnic baskets are also available, a good choice if going to a Britt festival concert. Be sure to call in your order by 2 P.M. Open daily for lunch and dinner.

Mexican food in downtown Jacksonville can be found at **La Fiesta** (150 S. Oregon St., 541/899-4450, www.chilimanserrano.com). Located in the Orth building, built in 1872, this place is noted for its large portions of gourmet south-of-the-border fare and vegetarian selections. Arrive early to claim one of the half dozen or so tables on the balcony. Open daily for lunch ($5–9) and dinner ($8–16).

MacLevin's Jewish Deli and Restaurant (150 W. California St., 541/899-1251) prepares deli sandwiches made on homemade sourdough rye that taste good enough to transport you momentarily back to the Lower East Side. Their chicken soup with matzo balls rivals Aunt Gail's secret family recipe, and the *Mazel tov* (chicken liver and eggs), cheese blintzes, and latkes (potato pancakes) are other traditional

Jewish fare that also get good grades. The sourdough buttermilk pancakes are unique and flavorful. Eight varieties of bread using organic flour and grains whenever possible are baked fresh daily. A collection of cookies, muffins, and desserts rounds out the selection of baked goods. Best of all, the people here are warm and friendly. Open daily 8 A.M.– 4 P.M.

For the best Thai food in the valley, head for the **Thai House Restaurant** (215 W. California St., 541/899-3585). Dozens of chicken, seafood, curry, noodle, and rice entrées span the spectrum of Far Eastern tastes. Their most popular dish is pad thai, and the pineapple fried rice with shrimp, chicken, cashews, pineapple, and raisins is also a winner. The 21 lunch selections go for about $6, while dinners range $7–12. Open for lunch and dinner Tues.–Fri., Saturday and Sunday for dinner only.

Lighter fare can be procured from **Pony Espresso** (545 N. 5th St., 541/899-3757), which features a full-service espresso bar as well as sandwiches, pizza, quiche, and other light lunch items ($4–7). The nachos here come with the works, and, when combined with one of their caffeinated concoctions, are perfect for an afternoon pick-me-up. Open daily.

Farmers Market

The **Jacksonville Farmer's Market** (N. 5th and C Streets) takes place 9 A.M.–2 P.M. on Saturday from May–October. Look for local peaches and nectarines in the summer, apples and pears in the fall.

Information

The **Jacksonville Chamber of Commerce** (P.O. Box 33, 185 N. Oregon St., Jacksonville 97530, 541/899-8118, www.jacksonvilleoregon.org), open daily 10 A.M.–5 P.M., has the scoop on events and activities.

Drivers, note that the 25-mph speed limit on the main street through town is strictly enforced.

Grants Pass

The banner across the main thoroughfare in town proudly proclaims: "It's the Climate." But while the 30-inches-a-year precipitation average and 52°F yearly mean temperature might seem desirable, the true allure of Grants Pass is the mighty Rogue River, which flows through the heart of this community. More than 25 outfitters in Grants Pass and the surrounding villages of Rogue River and Merlin specialize in fishing, float, and jetboat trips. Numerous riverside lodges, accessible by car, river, or footpath, yield remote relaxation in the shadow of the nearby Klamath-Siskiyou Wilderness.

It was the climate that attracted back-to-the-land refugees of the '60s to nearby Takilma, a planned utopian community. More recently, survivalists, in expectation of nuclear Armageddon, have established a network of shelters in the area. They believe that forests filled with game and foraging opportunities coupled with prevailing winds that will keep radioactive fallout away will improve their odds. . . . Good luck!

The climate is also responsible for the once-thick forests in the surrounding mountains, a timber source for the numerous mills which in turn provided many jobs. However, decades of over-cutting by the lumber companies has dramatically diminished the supply of sawtimber, resulting in mill shutdowns and high unemployment rates. In response, the economic base gradually shifted away from wood products to concentrate on the area's natural beauty, recreational opportunities, and, of course, benign weather.

SIGHTS

Downtown Restoration

At first glance, the downtown main drag in Grants Pass has an old-town feel with a kitschy 1960s facade. Fortunately, it is just that, a facade; the town plans to peel away the layers of siding to reveal the original (albeit dilapidated) turn-of-the-century architecture. In fact, a two-block area in Grants Pass is currently undergoing

a restoration, part of the city's attempt to reconstruct the main street. The re-facing also includes new curbs, trees, old-style streetlights, and brick accents on sidewalks and crosswalks.

Palmerton Arboretum

Six miles down ORE 99 in the town of Rogue River is the Palmerton Arboretum. Originally a five-acre nursery, the arboretum features plant specimens from around the globe, including Japanese pines and Mediterranean cedars in addition to redwoods and other trees native to the Northwest. A real treat in the spring, the ornamental arboretum offers over 40 species of mature trees complemented by several kinds of azaleas and rhododendrons. Admission is free. While you're there, be sure to see **Skevington's Crossing,** a 200-foot-high swinging suspension bridge over

old farmstead near Grants Pass

THERE'S GOLD IN THEM THAR HILLS!

Geologists estimate that the prospectors of the 1850s and commercial mining operations that followed found only 25 percent of Oregon's potential take. With the wild gyrations of the timber-dependent economy, and gold fetching several hundred dollars a troy ounce, it's no wonder that many out-of-work loggers and other people have taken to gold panning in the waterways of southern Oregon.

Almost all streams in Coos, Curry, Douglas, and Jackson Counties are good sources of color. "Color" refers to the flecks and bright chips of metal sometimes called gold dust; larger odd-shaped lumps of gold are nuggets. The gold originally comes from veins in the mountains, where it is washed out by winter weather. Spring floods and heavy rains carry the gold downstream. The density of gold causes it to settle in obstructions (like moss), in quiet water behind boulders, or at the base of waterfalls. These deposits of gold can vary from fine gold flecks to a bonanza of nuggets.

But before you head for the hills, you will need some basic equipment. Specially designed gold pans with flaring sides three to four inches deep are available at many hardware stores. Widths range from six inches to two feet; pick one that is comfortable for you to handle. Keep in mind that a pan full of water and gravel can get pretty heavy! Your pan must also be "blued" be-fore panning, otherwise the layer of oil on it will stick to the gold and cause the stuff to float out with the other lighter materials. Heat the pan on your stove until it is a deep blue color and the oils are burned off. Other useful tools include tweezers, a small vial or two, a trowel, and a small shovel or pick.

Panning takes finesse, but with practice it quickly becomes easier. Put some dirt from a likely location in your pan with some water. Pick out the larger pieces of rock and gravel or squeeze out the moss and discard. Gently swirl the pan around from side to side. This causes the gold to sink to the bottom, making it possible to scoop out more gravel from the top. Tilt the pan at a slight angle, and the gold will fall to the bottom of the lower edge. Remember that gold is 19 times heavier than water and also heavier than most other minerals contained in the gravel of streams.

Continue to dip, shake, and remove sand until you have only a small amount left. This is the stage where you have to be extra cautious not to wash away your gold. When you have taken out as much sand as possible, you will have (if you hit pay dirt) small strands of black sand and gold in your pan. Extract the color with tweezers, grab a beer, and start the process all over again. With some work and a little luck, you'll soon be singing the old refrain, "We're in the money!"

Evans Creek that connects the arboretum to Anna Classick city park.

The Caveman

It's hard to miss the 18-foot-high statue near the north Grants Pass Exit 58 off of I-5. Sporting a simulated mammoth-skin, a dinosaur bone club, and looking like he just strode in off the set of the *Flintstones,* the Caveman been the official welcome to Grants Pass since 1972. Spawned by a semi-notorious local civic group called the Oregon Cavemen, who also parade around in skins, drink saber-toothed tiger "blood," and eat raw meat during their secret initiation rites, the Caveman cost $18,000 to build. While many locals have lambasted the city's mascot as portraying a backward, redneck image for Grant's Pass, it's worth noting that over a dozen businesses and the local high school have proudly embraced the Caveman symbol.

Wildlife Images Rehabilitation and Education Center

Originally a rehab station for injured birds of prey, Wildlife Images (11845 Lower River Rd., 541-476-0222, www.wildlifeimages.org) has expanded into an outreach program to aid all kinds of injured or orphaned wildlife as well as to educate the public. Bears, cougars, raccoons, and many other indigenous creatures have been helped by this organization. Once the animals are well enough to survive in the wild, they are released. Guided tours (by reservation only at 11 A.M. and 1 P.M. daily) allow groups to view the wildlife currently at the facility. Admission is free, but this nonprofit organization relies upon donations to continue its important work. To get here from 6th Street downtown, head south, turn right onto G Street, continue to Upper River Road, and then onto Lower River Road.

Oregon Vortex

About 10 miles south of Grants Pass on I-5 is the House of Mystery at the Oregon Vortex (4303 Sardine Creek Rd., Gold Hill 97528, 541/855-1543, www.oregonvortex.com). Called the "Forbidden Ground" by the Rogue tribe because the place spooked their horses, it is actually a repelling magnetic field where objects tend to move away from their center of alignment and lean in funny directions. For example, a ball at the end of a string does not hang straight up and down, and people seem taller when viewed from one side of the field as opposed to the other. Visitors may bring balls, levels, cameras, or any other instrument they wish to test the vortex for themselves. Guided tours through the house built on this curious site are $8 for adults, $6 for children ages 6–11. Open March 1–Oct. 15 9 A.M.–4:45 P.M., except on Sunday and sometimes Thursday.

SPORTS AND RECREATION
Rafting on the Rogue River

There are about as many ways to enjoy the Rogue as there are critters in and around it. Some people prefer the excitement and challenge of maneuvering their own craft down the treacherous rapids. Oar rafts (which a guide rows for you), paddle rafts (which you paddle yourself), and one-person inflatable kayaks are the most widely used boats for this sort of river exploration. The 40-mile section downstream from Graves Creek is open only to nonmotorized vessels, and river traffic is strictly regulated by the National Forest Service. For more information, stop at the Rand Visitor Center (4335 Galice Rd., Merlin 97534, 541/479-3735).

The limited float permits (25 issued daily) are prized by rafters around the world, as the Rogue not only has some of the best white water in America but also guarantees a first-rate wilderness adventure. And yet, it can be a civilized wilderness. Hot showers, comfortable beds, and sumptuous meals at several of the river lodges tucked away in remote quarters of this famous waterway welcome boaters after a day's voyage. Excellent camping facilities are available for those who want to experience nature directly.

Many outfitters can be found off I-5 Exit 61 toward Merlin and Galice just north of Grants Pass. Rafters hit Class III and IV rapids a little before Galice and for 35 miles thereafter, the stiffest white water encountered on the Rogue. **Adventure Center** (P.O. Box 611, Ashland 97520, 541/482-5139, www.raftingtours.com) has half-, full-, and multiday trips on oar or paddle rafts. Their adventures range from the mild to the wild.

Galice Resort and Store Raft Trips (11744 Galice Rd., Merlin 97532, 541/476-3818, www.galice.com) offers full-day raft or inflatable-kayak trips as well as river craft rentals. Many outfitters include a meal and/or overnight stay here. Lodging accommodations range from primitive cabins to a house with full-service kitchen ($95). A real bargain for large parties is renting out their entire eight-room lodge (sleeps 12), fireplace, hot tub, and kitchen for only $575 per night.

Another river retreat with attractive packages is **Morrison's Rogue River Lodge** (8500 Galice Rd., Merlin, 541/476-3825 or 800/826-1963, www.morrisonslodge.com or www.rogueriver-raft.com), located about 16 miles from Grants Pass. Everything from one-day floats and excursions to two- to four-day trips is available; see their excellent website for further details. The longer excursions include either stays at other river lodges or camping along the great green Rogue. Transportation back to Morrison's is included, or your car can be shuttled downriver to meet you at the end of the trip. You can spend extra time at Morrison's before or after your trip with their American Plan lodging package, which includes breakfast, dinner, and room for $110–165.

Noah's River Adventures (53 N. Main, Ashland 97520, 800/858-2811, www.noahsrafting.com) has been providing quality rafting and fishing trips since 1974. They have half-day and one- to four-day excursions that vary from exciting white-water rafting highs to kinder, gentler floats. From late March–early October, they depart Ashland for the Rogue three times daily, and a round-trip transfer from your lodging is included in the price. See the website for rates and package details.

Orange Torpedo Trips (P.O. Box 1111-S, Grants Pass 97526, 541/479-5061 or 800/635-2925, www.orangetorpedo.com) has half-day and one- to three-day raft or inflatable-kayak (also affectionately known as "orange torpedoes" because of their color and shape) adventures. They also offer a unique VIP two-day package that combines the best on the river: jetboat tour, wagon ride, gourmet dining, lodging, wildlife park, and float trip all rolled into one.

River Adventure Float Trips (P.O. Box 841, Grants Pass 97526, 541/476-6493) has summer raft and fall fishing trips that vary from a half day to several days. **River Trips Unlimited, Inc.** (4140 Dry Creek Rd., Medford 97504, 541/779-3798 or 800/460-3865, www.raftingtrips.com) has been guiding trips on the Rogue for over 35 years. They have one- to four-day raft, Tahiti, or summer-run steelhead fishing trips that include meals and overnight stays at some of the river lodges. See website for additional info. **Rogue River Raft Trips** (8500 Galice Rd., Merlin 97532, 541/476-3825 or 800/826-1963, www.rogueriverraft.com) also offers a multitude of modes and packages to enjoy the river wild.

Rogue/Klamath River Adventures (P.O. Box 4295, Medford 97501, 541/779-3708 or 800/231-0769, www.rogueklamath.com) has one- to three-day white-water rafting and inflatable-kayak trips that give you the option of camping out under the stars or roughing it in style at a river lodge. **Ferron Fun Trips** (P.O. Box 585, Merlin 97532, 541/474-2201 or 800/402-2201, www.roguefuntrips.com) has put together a variety of packages reflecting the Rogue's diversity. In addition to guided rafting, fishing, and white-water trips, they offer a mountain bike adventure above the Rogue on Bear Camp Mountain; an excursion to the working Last Chance Mine, where you get a chance to pan for gold; and a two-day wildlife expedition that combines hiking with rafting the Rogue. Boat rentals are available here, too.

White Water Warehouse (625 Storker Ave., Corvallis, 541/758-3150 or 800/214-0579, www.whitewaterwarehouse.com) has a full summer schedule of three- and four-day rafting and kayaking river trips. Some trips are specifically designed as white-water kayak instructional trips, and this is one lab class that you'll always look forward to attending. See their website for more details.

For more information on scenic fishing and white-water rafting trips, contact the **Rogue River Guides Association** (P.O. Box 792, Medford 97501, 541/772-5194, www.rogueriverguides.com), the previously mentioned Rand Visitor Center, or the **Visitors Information Center** (1995 N.W. Vine St., Grants Pass 97526, 800/547-5927, www.visitgrantspass .org). These information outlets can also supply tips on riverside hiking. The Rogue trails out of Grants Pass aren't as remote as their Gold Beach counterparts, and litter can sometimes mar the route. Nonetheless, the fall color in certain areas along the Rogue, and a profusion of swimming and fishing holes, can add a special dimension to your hike.

Jetboating on the Rogue River

You don't have to risk life and limb in a fancy inner tube to see the Rogue: several local companies offer jetboat tours. On a jetboat, powerful engines suck in hundreds of gallons of water a minute and shoot it out the back of the boat through a narrow nozzle, generating the necessary thrust for navigation. With no propeller to hit rocks and other obstacles, these 20-ton machines can carry 40 or more passengers in water only six inches deep. This makes the jetboat an ideal way to enjoy the beauty of the Rogue while keeping your feet dry. Finally, many outfitters charter drift boats to secret fishing holes for anglers to try their luck landing supper.

THE CHRISTMAS FLOOD OF 1964

Passing through the serene Rogue River Valley today, little can be seen of the ravages of the Christmas Flood of 1964. The autumn of that fateful year seemed to augur the coming of a peaceful winter in Rogue country. With the white snow on the mountains and a ring around the harvest moon, the only thing that seemed missing was ol' Saint Nick himself, riding through the night sky.

But then the rains came—slowly at first. Then little by little, almost imperceptibly, the downpour transformed into a deluge. The warm rains quickly melted the snowpack, and the swollen streams spurred the foaming Rogue on its course to the sea. Logjams and abnormally high tides contributed to record-high water levels. Whole towns had to be evacuated from the onslaught of water. Many families saw their hopes and dreams wash away, victims of the impartial hand of nature.

The inundation was not confined to the Rogue, as the killer storm turned almost every western Oregon river into a frighteningly efficient destroyer. Governor Hatfield declared the region a disaster area. The damage statewide was in the millions of dollars, and many lives were lost by the time the muddy waters receded a week later. To avert a similar catastrophe in the future, the Army Corps of Engineers constructed Lost Creek Reservoir on the upper Rogue not long afterwards.

While time has healed the effects of the flood, you can still find high-water marks here and there in the valley. Tacked high up on trees and bridges, perched over 54 feet above the now placid waters of the Rogue, they serve as a silent reminder of the magnitude of this great disaster. Unfortunately, the February 1997 floods made the memory of the earlier flood a little too real for the many people who have settled along the Rogue in the last few decades.

Hellgate Excursions (953 S.E. 7th, Grants Pass 97526, 541/479-7204 or 800/648-4874, www.hellgate.com) is the premier jetboat operator on this end of the river. Their trips begin at the dock of the Riverside Inn (971 S.E. 6th St., Grants Pass) and proceed downriver through the forested Siskiyou foothills. En route, black-tailed deer, ospreys, and great blue herons are commonly seen. If you're lucky, a bald eagle or black bear might also be sighted. The scenic highlight is the deep-walled Hellgate Canyon, where you'll look upon what are believed to be the oldest rocks in the state. The rugged beauty here provided the backdrop for John Wayne and Katherine Hepburn in *Rooster Cogburn*. Trips including a champagne brunch ($38 for adults, $23 for kids ages 4–11) and a weekday lunch of barbecued chicken and ribs ($43 for adults, kids $29) at a wilderness lodge are two popular offerings. Another option is the white-water adventure trip that goes beyond Hellgate; adults $47, kids $31 (lunch is available but not included). Finally, you can also forgo lunch on the river and just see the canyon for $27, children ages 4–11 $17. These excursions run May 1–Sept. 30 and feature commentary by your pilot, who knows every eddy in the river. Be sure to call ahead for reservations, as space on all of their runs books up fast.

Fishing on the Rogue River

The upper Rogue River is renowned for one of the world's best late-winter steelhead fisheries. Numerous highways and backroads offer easy access to 155 miles of well-ramped river between Lost Creek Reservoir east of Medford and Galice west of Grants Pass. With fall and spring chinook runs and other forms of river recreation, it's no accident that the Rogue Valley is home to the world's top three aluminum and fiberglass drift boat manufacturers. Add rafters, kayakers, and plenty of bank anglers, and you can understand why peak salmon or steelhead season is sometimes described as "combat fishing." Contact southern Oregon visitor information outlets for rules, regulations, and leads on outfitters.

Biking

The place to go for mountain bike rentals and information on area bike trails is **BikeKraft**

ROGUE VALLEY MOREL PICKING

Gourmet mushroom picking can be a fun pastime and/or a money-making proposition in various parts of Oregon. Here in the Rogue Valley, morels, a cone-shaped fungus with deeply crenulated caps and short hollow stems, are one of several coveted varieties that fare especially well. The fact that they're easily identifiable, fry up great in omelettes, and come out in spring makes them especially popular among residents. Although usually found in forested areas such as the foothill below Mount McLoughlin, morels also can be harvested from backyard orchards in Rogue Valley fruit country.

The combination of night temperatures above freezing, high humidity, and daytime temps of 46–60°F is optimum to bring this fungus to fruit. They often pop up in the wake of forest fires or in landscapes disturbed by logging and road building. If it's warm, these mushrooms can be found in late March. When spring conditions hit the lower slopes of the Cascades in the months to follow, pickers usually aren't far behind, in pursuit of what many consider to be the most savory mushroom of all.

(1448 Williams Hwy., 541/476-4935, www.bikekraft.com). They rent mountain bikes by the day or half day. If you want to go on an extended trip, for a few days or a week, they can outfit you. Car racks and trailers are also available for rent. A cash deposit is required. Other helpful resources are the **Siskiyou National Forest Service** (P.O. Box 440, 200 N.E. Greenfield Rd., Grants Pass 97526, 541/479-5301) and the **BLM** (P.O. Box 1047, Medford 97501, 541/770-2200).

Camping

Many fine campgrounds are found along the banks of the Rogue River near Grants Pass. The privately owned and operated RV parks in the KOA genre tend to be more expensive than their public counterparts but offer more amenities like swimming pools, laundries, and other conveniences. **RiverPark RV Resort** (2956 Rogue River Hwy., Grants Pass, 541/479-0046 or 800/677-8857, www.riverparkrvresort.com), $25, boasts a tennis/basketball court, hot showers, laundry facilities, and 700 feet of Rogue River footage to enjoy. Near Tom Pearce Park and the Rogue River is **Moon Mountain RV Resort** (3298 Pearce Park Rd., Grants Pass, 541/479-1145, www.moonmountainrv.com), $20, another well-maintained property offering 50 RV sites with power and propane hookups. About halfway between Cave Junction and Grants Pass is **Redwood Highway KOA** (13370 U.S. 199, Wilderville 97543, 541/476-6508 or 800/562-7566, www.koa-kampgrounds.com), $20–40, which has everything you would expect from a KOA.

The four county parks listed below cost $20 for hookup sites, $15 for tent sites. Contact the **Josephine County Parks Department** (Rogue River 97537, 541/474-5285, www.co.josephine.or.us/parks) for reservations and additional information.

Indian Mary Park is the showcase of Josephine County parks. To get here, go about eight miles east of Merlin on the Merlin-Galice Road. Located on the banks of the Rogue River, this campground has 89 sites, several with sewer hookups and utilities, as well as showers, flush toilets, and piped water. A boat ramp, beautiful hiking trails, a playground, and one of the best beaches on the Rogue make this one of the most popular county campgrounds on the river.

Griffen Park is a smaller campground with 24 sites for tents and trailers. To get here, take the Redwood Highway (U.S. 199) to Riverbanks Road, then turn onto Griffen Road and follow it about five miles to where it meets the Rogue. The park has a boat ramp, showers, flush toilets, piped water, and RV dumping facilities.

Schroeder Park is another complete campground near town. Located on Schroeder Lane off Redwood Avenue, the park has 31 sites, some with hookups and utilities. Showers, flush toilets, and a boat ramp make this a favorite spot for fishing enthusiasts. In addition to a picnic area and an excellent swimming hole, a rope tied to a huge cottonwood on the opposite bank of the river near the park is waiting for any swingers who like to make a big splash.

Whitehorse Park is six miles west of Grants Pass on Upper River Road. Purchased by the county in 1958 from the Rogue Rovers Trail Club, this park has 44 campsites, many with hookups and utilities. Showers, piped water, lighting, and good hiking trails developed by the previous owners are found here. The river channel shifted away from the park in the wake of the Christmas flood of 1964, but it's only about a half-mile walk to a fine beach on the Rogue.

The only state park in the area is the **Valley of the Rogue** (3792 N. River Rd., Gold Hill, 541/582-1118 or 800/452-5687, www.oregonstateparks.org/park_109.php). Located about halfway between Medford and Grants Pass off I-5, the park is set along the banks of its namesake river. The Rogue supports year-round salmon and spring steelhead runs. There are 98 sites for trailers and motor homes, and 21 tent sites, but this place fills up fast, so reservations are recommended during the warmer months. This is also one of the few inland parks that rents yurts, $35–50. Hookups, utilities, showers, laundry, and some wheelchair-accessible facilities round out the amenities here.

Golf

About 15 minutes north of Grants Pass is **Red Mountain Golf Course** (324 Mountain Green Ln., 541/479-2297). This small but challenging executive course of 2,245 yards is a bargain to play. Greens fee is $8 for nine holes, $12 for 18, and $15 for all day Mon.–Fri.; add a dollar for weekends.

ENTERTAINMENT AND EVENTS
Boatnik Festival

The Boatnik Festival starts on Memorial Day weekend at Riverside Park in Grants Pass. A carnival, parade, and softball tournament are featured, but the top event is the white-water boat races. Over two dozen modified speedboats and jetboats compete in a 46-mile course on the Rogue River. Warm-ups begin on Memorial

Day morning, followed by the race at 1 P.M. The competition starts at the boat docks in Riverside Park.

Grants Pass Downs

Horse-racing aficionados will appreciate Grants Pass Downs (www.jocofair.com/racing.asp). The season opens Memorial Day weekend with races on weekends through the Fourth of July. Place your bets on your favorite steeds to place, win, or show; $2 minimum. The cash-sell betting is all computerized, allowing for more exotic bets like the quiniela and the trifecta. The latter are "wheel" bets, in which you get to choose one of every possible combination of two or three horses to win. Admission $2. Even if you're not the betting sort, it's a kick watching the horses thunder around the bend and down the home stretch. The season is May 18–early July, every Saturday and Sunday. Post time is at 1 P.M. with Friday post time at 5 P.M. at the Josephine County Fairgrounds.

Rooster-Crowing Contest

The nearby city of **Rogue River,** southeast of Grants Pass on I-5, has something to crow about. On the last day of June, the Rogue River Rooster Crow is held at the Rogue River Elementary School grounds, beginning with a parade and followed by live music and entertainment. A street fair featuring arts, crafts, and food is also set up on the premises. But the big event takes place early in the afternoon. Farmers from all over Oregon and northern California bring their roosters to strut their stuff and sing out songs to the enthusiastic crowds. A fowl tradition since 1953, the rooster to crow the most times in his allotted time period wins the prize for his proud owner.

Josephine County Fair

The Josephine County Fair normally takes place in mid-August at the fairgrounds in Grants Pass. In addition to the usual fair attractions such as the carnival, concessions, and 4-H livestock, entertainers like Three Dog Night perform for enthusiastic crowds. A popular annual competition held here is the four-wheel tractor pull, in which souped-up farm vehicles attempt to drag a bull-dozer (with its blade down) 100 yards as fast as possible.

PRACTICALITIES
Accommodations
You'll find most motel accommodations clustered around the two Grants Pass I-5 exits. Economy choices include **Royal View Motel** (110 N.E. Morgan Ln., 541/479-5381), $40–60; **Budget Inn** (1253 N.E. 6th, 541/479-2952), $45–60; **Knights' Inn** (104 S.E. 7th, 541/479-5595 or 800/826-6835), $50–65; and **Motel 6** (1800 N.E. 7th, 541/474-1331), $45–70.

There are plenty of midrange hotel chain choices, and most of them have pools, allow pets, and include breakfast. Several such options are **Comfort Inn** (1889 N.E. 6th, 541/479-8301), $55–70; **Best Western Grants Pass** (111 N.E. Agness Ave., 541/476-1117, www.bestwestern-inn.com), $80–100; **Best Western Inn at the Rogue** (8959 Rogue River Hwy., 541/582-2200 or 800/238-0700), $75–150; **La Quinta Inn** (243 N.E. Morgan Ln., 541/472-1808 or 800/531-5900, www.laquinta.com), $75–90; and **Shilo Inn** (1880 N.E. 6th, 541/479-8391), $65–80.

One of the premium sites in town is **Weasku Inn** (5560 Rogue River Hwy., 541/471-8000 or 800/4-WEASKU, www.weasku.com), $125–300, a venerable river lodge that was the secret retreat of Clark Gable, Walt Disney, Carole Lombard, and other entertainment figures. Only 17 guestrooms are available, ranging from lodge rooms and suites to an A-frame cabin. All look out on the Rogue River and are clean, well apportioned, and comfortable. A deluxe continental breakfast is served, as is evening wine and cheese.

With 174 rooms on the Rogue, the **Riverside Inn Resort** (971 S.E. 6th, 541/476-6873 or 800/334-4567, www.riverside-inn.com), $125–325, is the largest hotel on the river. Two swimming pools, two hot tubs, a 24-hour coffee shop, and a day spa provide luxury in a style you can easily get accustomed to. The Hellgate jet-boat excursion boat docks are just below the hotel.

Bed-and-Breakfasts
Situated about 20 minutes outside of Grants Pass and well within the wild and scenic section of the Rogue River is the **Doubletree Ranch** (6000 Abegg Rd., Merlin, 541/476-0120, doubletree-ranch.com). Originally homesteaded 100 years ago, this 160-acre, four-generation working ranch offers cabins for $85–125 with breakfast included. The rugged beauty of the grounds served as the set for the film *Spirit of the Eagle*.

You'll find the look and feel of the British Isles at the gabled **Ivy House** (139 S.W. I St., 541/474-7363). Anglophiles are sure to appreciate the full English breakfast, replete with bangers and a sturdy cup of tea (or coffee if you must). Fine rooms (with private bath) in this 1908 brick home feature touches like down quilts, lace curtains, and the traditional morning tea and biscuits in bed. Afternoon tea, including biscuits, jam tarts, crumpets, sausage rolls, and fresh scones, is available. Luncheons can also be arranged featuring the usual British fare. Room rates ($70–95) are quite reasonable for the experience; advance reservations are required.

About 15 minutes north of town a couple of miles off I-5 Exit 66 is **Flery Manor** (2000 Jumpoff Joe Creek Rd., 541/476-3591, www.flerymanor.com), $85–175. Canopied beds, unique furnishings, and a quiet secluded setting give this country manor a genteel air. All rooms have nice little touches like plush robes, fresh flowers, and morning coffee and tea service. The breakfast features a health-conscious menu. With a private balcony, double Jacuzzi, and fireplace, the Moonlight Suite is the right prescription for a romantic hideaway and is well worth the $175/night rate. Reservations are a must.

Tucked away in the quiet ponderosa of the Rogue River Valley about 15 minutes from Grants Pass is the lovely **Pine Meadow Inn** (1000 Crow Rd., Merlin, 541/471-6277 or 800/554-0806, www.pinemeadowinn.com), $95–130. This large country home atop a wooded knoll was designed and built specifically as a B&B. You'll be sure to enjoy the extra sound-proofing and oversized private bathrooms in each of the four large sunny bedrooms. Downstairs,

French doors open out to the backyard herb and English cutting gardens landscaped with a koi pond and waterfall. The wraparound porch has inviting wicker chairs to relax in while enjoying morning coffee or evening tea with a book from the extensive library. Beneath the pines a hot tub awaits. After your stay here, you'll understand exactly why Meryl Streep wanted to rent the entire house for the summer when *The River Wild* was being filmed on the Rogue.

Not to be confused with Pine Meadow Inn is the **Ponderosa Pine Inn** (907 Stringer Gap Rd., Grants Pass 97527, 541/474-4933 or 866/299-7463, www.ponderosapineinn.com), $80. Only two rooms are available in this bright and cheery country retreat, which was completed in 2000. It is located about 15 minutes from downtown Grants Pass; see the inn's website for map and directions.

Food

Although it's not the gourmet capital of Oregon, Grants Pass is a town where many travelers pull in for a bite. Its proximity to Rogue River recreation and fishing, together with a wide range of reasonably priced dining options, explain its popularity.

R-Haus (2140 Rogue River Hwy., 541/474-3335), a local favorite dinner spot, is a formal dining room in a turn-of-the-century house. Basic fare includes steak, seafood, and pasta ($13–20). Open daily. The servers dress in Victorian style at **Yankee Pot Roast** (720 N.W. 6th, 541/476-0551). Light dinners are around $9, other dinner selections range $11–18. Slow-cooked pot roast simmering in heavy gravy might be the star of the menu, but don't overlook the halibut, homemade soup, and biscuits. Pies made with local berries make a spectacular dessert. Open Wed.–Sunday.

The menu at **China Hut** (1434 N.W. 6th, 541/476-3441) features interesting entrées such as vegetarian *chow yuk,* Mandarin pineapple duck, and *ma po* tofu. You'll need a big appetite to finish their large portions. Lunch specials run $5–8, dinner specials $6–12. Open daily. The **Hong Kong** (820 N.W. 6th, 541/476-4244) restaurant has a takeout family-pack dinner that,

at around $14 for two, is one of the best deals in town. Closed Sundays. **Pongsri's** (1571 N.E. 6th, 541/955-1662) is a Thai restaurant (with some Chinese dishes) hidden away in a nondescript shopping mall near the Visitor Center. You'd never guess it, but you'll find exotic dishes such as *tom ka gai* (a coconut cream soup flavored with ginger-like galangka root) and nearly two dozen vegetarian dishes on the menu here. Lunch specials for $6 pull in the locals, and entrées range $6–12. Open Mon.–Saturday.

Aficionados of the old-time soda fountain will appreciate the **Grants Pass Pharmacy** (414 S.W. 6th St., 541/476-4262). Decent sandwiches ($5) and phosphate drinks for a quarter are featured here. Local old-timers meet here every afternoon, and it's the kids' first stop after school. **Herb's La Casita** (515 S.E. Rogue River Hwy., 541/476-1313) has a little bit of everything, featuring a full menu of Mexican and American dishes and entertainment ranging from karaoke to dancing.

The **Wild River Brewing and Pizza Company** (corner of E and Mill Streets, 541/471-RIVR) is the sister of the Cave Junction outlet and features wood-fired pizza ($16–24 for a large), pastas, burgers, and sandwiches as well as a full-service espresso bar. All breads used for sandwiches are baked on the premises. If you're only there for the beer, five brews are offered year-round and are complemented by four seasonal ones. One of the best ways to sample the local product is via the $1.50 taster glasses. Free brewery tours are also offered. Open daily from 11 A.M. until closing.

Another place to find a great selection of microbrews on tap is at the **Laughing Clam** (121 S.W. G St., 541/479-1110). This nonsmoking eatery and alehouse is kid-friendly, and you can bring the family up until 9 P.M. The moderately priced menu ($5–15) offers a wide range of salads, sandwiches, pastas, and burgers in addition to well-rounded dinner offerings. Several meatless items are featured in all categories. Their appetizers break away from the ordinary pub grub. One example is the onion anemones, sweet Northwest deep-fried onions dipped in beer batter and accompanied by chili mayonnaise. They look kind of like flowers when you get them, putting ordinary onion rings to shame. Oregon wines are featured exclusively here, so check out the house wine specials to taste some of the best in the state. Open daily for lunch and dinner.

A popular place for a weekday buffet or Sunday brunch is **The Brewery** (509 S.W. G St., 541/479-9850). They don't try to make a whole bunch of different things here, but just concentrate on doing some things very well. Salads and sandwiches go for $6–8, and dinners range from $10–20, with frequent specials offered daily. Set in a brewery building built in 1886, the place is dripping with historical ambience. A half dozen quality microbrews are available on draught. Open daily for lunch and dinner except Monday and Saturday, when it's dinner only.

A railroad theme predominates at the **Train Depot** ((577 N.E. F St., 541/471-4800); open daily for breakfast ($4–7), lunch ($5–7), and dinner ($7–10). Thick Belgian waffles have a distinct malt taste to them, complementing a mountain of fresh strawberries and whipped cream. Their hash browns come with many different optional toppings, such as cheese, veggies, green chilies, and even poached egg with Hollandaise sauce. Large portions of home-style cooking served in a bright, full-of-windows building make this place a winner.

If you're in the area Fri.–Sun., take a few moments to drive one exit north of town to Merlin, to visit the **Cake Shop** (215 Galice Rd., Merlin, 541/479-0188). Here, fifth-generation German bakers, using family recipes that date back 150 years, have been producing baked goods that have graced the tables of Presidents Kennedy, Johnson, Nixon, and Reagan, as well as other celebrities. Their breads are excellent, and the hot sheepherder bread and sourdough German rye are chewy, crusty, handmade hearth-baked breads that have the flavor to match the heavenly aroma that pervades the store. One caterer in San Diego regularly flies up in her private airplane, fills it up with bread, and heads back south to use the bread exclusively at her functions. The folks who run the place are getting on in years, so take the time to stop and enjoy this Oregon institution while the opportunity still presents itself. Open Fri.–Sun. from 9 A.M. till they're sold out.

Sunshine Natural Foods (128 S.W. H St., Grants Pass, 541/474-5044) has a café and market catering to those seeking sustenance that's fresh, homegrown, and organic. The soup and salad bar at lunch is always a winner in the $6 range. Open daily except Sunday.

Farmers markets are an Oregon tradition, particularly in the southern part of the state. Grants Pass is said to have the largest one of all, boasting produce, crafts, prepared foods, and strolling entertainers at 4th and F Streets. For more information, contact Growers Market (P.O. Box 576, Grants Pass 97526, 541/476-5375, www.growersmarket.org). It's open Saturday 9 A.M.–1 P.M. mid-March–Thanksgiving, and also on Wednesday at the same times, and runs June–September at Riverside Park.

Information and Transportation

The **Grants Pass/Josephine County Visitor Information Center/Chamber of Commerce** (1995 N.W. Vine, Grants Pass 97526, 541/476-7717 or 800/547-5927, www.visitgrantspass.com) is open 8 A.M.–5 P.M. daily in summer, weekdays in winter.

Greyhound (460 N.E. Agness Ave., 541/476-4513) offers access to the I-5 corridor and the coast.

CAVE JUNCTION
Oregon Caves

About 30 miles southwest of Grants Pass are the Oregon Caves (541/592-3400, www.nps.gov/orca). Take U.S. 199 to Cave Junction, then wind your way 20 miles up ORE 46 (a beautiful old-growth Douglas fir forest lining the road might help divert the faint-of-heart from the nail-biting turns). The last 13 miles of this trip are especially exciting. Remember that there are few turnouts of sufficient size to enable a large vehicle to reverse direction.

The cave itself—as there is really only one, which opens onto successive caverns—was formed over the eons by the action of water. As rain and snowmelt seeped through cracks and fissures in the rock above the cave and percolated down into the underlying limestone, huge sections of the limestone became saturated and collapsed—much as a sand castle too close to the sea always caves in. When the water table eventually lowered, these pockets were drained of water and the process of cave decoration began.

First, the limestone was dissolved by the water and carried in solution into the cave. When the water evaporated, it left behind a microscopic layer of calcite. This process was repeated countless times, gradually creating the beautiful formations visible today. When the minerals are deposited on the ceiling, a stalactite begins to form. Limestone-laden water that evaporates on the floor might leave behind a stalagmite. When a stalactite and a stalagmite meet, they become a column. Other cave sculptures you'll see include helicites, hell-bent formations that twist and turn in crazy directions; draperies, looking just like their household namesakes but cast in stone instead of cloth; and soda straws, stalactites that are hollow in the center like a straw, carrying mineral-rich drops of moisture to their tips.

Discovered in 1874, the Oregon Caves attract thousands of visitors annually. During the Depression, walkways and turnoffs were built to make the cave more accessible. Unfortunately, tons of waste rock and rubble were stashed into nooks and crannies in the cave, instead of being transported out. This had the ironic effect of obscuring the very formations intended for display. However, the National Park Service started to remove the artificial debris in 1985, exposing the natural formations once again. Little by little, the cave is returning to the way it looked before the "improvements" began.

The River Styx, another victim of Depression-era meddling, is enjoying a similar resurrection. This stream used to run through the cave but was diverted into pipes to aid trail and tunnel construction. The pipes ended up buried beneath tons of pulverized rock, and now the Park Service is hard at work undoing the work of humans to let the stream flow where Nature intended.

Tours of the cave are conducted year-round by National Park Service interpreters. Their presentations are both informative and entertaining, and you will leave the cave with a better understanding of its natural, geologic, and human history. A recent discovery in an unexplored part of the caverns was a grizzly bear fossil believed to be over 40,000 years old. Admission is $7.50 for adults, $5 for children ages 6–11. Children younger than six must pass ability requirements (e.g., walking up many stairs for a total vertical climb of 218 feet) and stand a minimum of 42 inches tall to gain entry. The tour (limited to 16 persons) takes a little over an hour and requires some uphill walking. Good walking shoes and warm clothing are recommended. It may be warm and toasty outside, but the cave maintains a fairly consistent year-round temperature of 41°F. Passageways can be narrow, ceilings low, and the footing slippery. During summer you can wait in line up to an hour to go on a tour, and fewer tours are offered October–April. Call ahead for tour times.

Wine-Tasting

You can sample some of the local product at **Foris Vineyards** (654 Kendall Rd., 541/592-3752, www.foriswine.com) and **Bear Creek Winery** (6220 ORE 46, 541/592-3977, www.bridgeviewwine.com/bearcreek). Both wineries offer tours and tastings 11 A.M.–5 P.M. year-round, although their operating hours tend to be reduced in winter (Bear Creek is open weekends only). Bear Creek Winery is on the way to the Oregon Caves. You can combine a lunch at their picnic grounds along with a tasting after your foray into the bowels of the earth.

Camping

Near the Oregon Caves, camping is available at **Grayback** (Illinois Valley Ranger District, 26568 Redwood Hwy., Cave Junction 97523, 541/592-4000, www.fs.fed.us.r6.siskiyou), 12 miles from Cave Junction on ORE 46. There are 25 tent sites and 16 vehicular sites close to Sucker Creek. Electricity and piped water are provided, with a store, laundry, and showers within a mile. Closer to the caves is **Cave Creek** (same address as Grayback's); just take ORE 46 four miles south of the caves to Forest Service Road 4032. Piped water and pit toilets are provided, and showers are available five miles away. You'll also find a ranger station and informative campfire programs here on summer evenings. Both campgrounds charge $15.

Accommodations

The six-story **Oregon Caves Lodge** (P.O. Box 128, Cave Junction 97523, 541/592-3400) offers food and accommodations May 1–Oct. 31. Located about 50 miles west of Grants Pass on U.S. 199, the château stands at an elevation of 4,000 feet. Built in 1934, this artistically rustic building blends in with the forest and moss-covered marble ledges. Indigenous wood and stone permeate this building so that you never lose a sense of where you are. The rooms feature views of Cave Creek canyon, waterfalls, or the Oregon Caves entrance. Rates range $75–125 per night for two to four people. Special "lovers' retreat" weekend packages including discount dinners and cave admissions are also available, but make reservations early, as the number of packages is limited. For a more unique experience, we recommend the sixth floor. The rooms might be smaller, but they have more character and extend out at odd angles from this uniquely configured building. The Pendleton blankets, tall painted chairs, and wooden bed frames add to the historical nuance.

The château has been nicknamed the "Marble Halls of Oregon," and you can see the huge marble fireplace in the fourth-floor lobby for yourself while you thaw out after your spelunking expedition. The food at the château is surprisingly good (breakfast $3–7, lunch $5–8, dinner main courses $8–20), and having Cave Creek running through the center of the dining room definitely adds to the unique atmosphere. Downstairs, the old-fashioned 1930s-style soda fountain dishes up the classic American fare of burgers, fries, and shakes. Open daily.

For a nice after-dinner hike, take a walk down the Big Tree trail, so named for a huge Douglas fir estimated to be more than 1,000 years old. With a circumference of 38 feet, seven inches, it is among the largest standing trees in Oregon. The three-mile round-trip wends its way through virgin forest that has tan oak, canyon live oak, Pacific madrone, chinquapin, and manzanita, as well as Douglas fir and ponderosa pine. The hike is not that difficult, and the solitude and views of the surrounding mountains are as inspiring as the Big Tree. For a shorter jaunt that's just under a mile, try the Cliff Nature Trail. Placards will help you identify the plant life as you traverse the mossy cliffs, and there are also some good vistas of the Siskiyou Mountains.

Approximately 20 miles north of Grants Pass on I-5 in Wolf Creek is the Pacific Northwest's oldest continuously operated hostelry, the **Wolf Creek Inn,** (100 Front St., Wolf Creek, 541/866-2474, www.wolfcreekinn.com). Originally a hotel for the California and Oregon Stagecoach Line, this historic property built in 1883 is now owned by the state and operated as a hotel and restaurant (see "Food," immediately following). Legend has it that President Rutherford B. Hayes visited the tavern in the late 1880s and One-Eyed Charlie (see the special topic earlier in this chapter) used to chew the fat in the dining room. You can also view the small room where author Jack London stayed and wrote part of his famous novel, *The End of the Story.* The staff wears early 19th-century clothing in keeping with the ambience of this famous roadhouse.

Wolf Creek's boardinghouse had its heyday when it was a halfway house on the Portland-Sacramento stagecoach route, but it continues to serve road-weary travelers with rooms that range from $60 to $125 (room tax and continental breakfast included). The period furniture imparts atmosphere, while the beds and private baths are modern enough to be comfortable. Travelers might also find it useful to know that the Wolf Creek General Store (I-5 Exit 76) is open 24 hours.

Three miles east of Wolf Creek is the 1890s-era ghost town of Golden. You'll note two churches (no saloon) in a town built upon dreams spawned by a nearby strike that ultimately yielded 1.5 million dollars.

Fordson Home Hostel (250 Robinson Rd., Cave Junction 97523, 541/592-3203) is located about 10 miles from Oregon Caves. A remarkable collection of antique farm equipment, one of the world's largest Douglas firs, strangely con-

BED-AND-BREAKFAST IN THE TREES

Located in Takilma near Cave Junction, **Out 'n About Treehouse Institute and Treesort** (300 Page Creek Rd., Cave Junction 97523, 541/598-2208 or 800/200-5484, www.treehouses.com) is a unique lodging option that's worth driving a bit out of your way from the Oregon Caves. After all, how many bed-and-breakfasts do you find in a treehouse?

This comfortable rural retreat blends the whimsy of the '60s with 21st-century creature comforts. The well-appointed rooms are bolted to a hundred-year-old white oak, 18 feet above the ground. Should you have misgivings about the structural integrity of these accommodations, be advised that the innkeeper gathered nearly 11,000 pounds of his friends to stand on the several units simultaneously—35 times the weight requirements of the local code. Those desiring a more down-to-earth lodging option can stay in a peeled-fir cabin with a

cozy woodstove. For the deluxe treatment, reserve a 300-square-foot structure built of redwood and Douglas fir that features a sink, tub, fridge, queen-sized futon, loft, and 200-square-foot deck with mountain views. The "treepee," a tee pee done up in Out 'n About style, is always popular with the kids.

Horseback trail rides, trips to the best Illinois River swimming holes, and white-water rafting trips can be arranged through the management. Or, swim in the river that runs through the property. Rates range $90–160 (two-night minimum stay) and include a continental breakfast. Pets are allowed on prior approval only; inquire when making your "treeservation." Your stay here will help you better understand treehouses, treeology, and treeminology, and, like many other guests, you may well leave a "treemusketeer." Tours of Out 'n About run April–October and cost $4 for adults and $2 for children under 13.

torted trees in a natural vortex (water runs uphill, people can't stand up straight), and Bigfoot sightings reported in the area add intrigue to your stay here. If you need more than mystique, there are bicycles available for guests, swimming in a nearby river, freshly prepared homegrown organic vegetables, and a nearby winery. There are also laundry facilities, RV hookups, and a camping area, $2. This HI hostel is located seven miles from Cave Junction on country roads. Reservations are required (space is limited), and young children and pets are not allowed in this budget lodging in the $15 range. Students, backpackers, and bicyclists are eligible for a discount of $2 at the hostel, as well as a discount of $2 at the Oregon Caves.

Camping is available nearby at **Caves Creek Campground** (www.nps.gov/orca/pphtml/camping.html), $18 per night.

Food

Down by the Oregon Caves is **Miller's Wild River Deli and Brewery** (249 U.S. 199 N., Cave Junction, 541/592-3556). Pizza dough, sandwich rolls, and croissants are made from scratch and then topped or stuffed with fresh

ingredients. A salad bar, soup, and Southern-style fried chicken round out the menu (meals range $6–13). Enjoy their handcrafted European-style beers and ales along with their beer-battered potato chips and onion rings. Open daily.

The restaurant at **Wolf Creek Inn** (100 Front St., Wolf Creek, 541/866-2474, www.wolfcreekinn.com) serves hamburgers, hot dogs, and grilled-cheese sandwiches mainly to keep the kids happy, but top billing on the menu goes to Northwest cuisine. The innkeeper incorporates home-smoked meats and produce fresh from the gardens to express the regional bounty. Lunch ($5–9), dinner ($6–17), and Sunday brunch are served. The restaurant is open daily in the high season; closed Monday and Tuesday Oct.–May.

Beyond Cave Junction

Should you care to explore the Illinois River Valley and U.S. 199 beyond Cave Junction, contact the **Illinois River Valley Cooperative Visitor Center** (201 Cave Hwy., Cave Junction 97525, 541/592-2631), open daily 9 A.M. to 4 P.M. You can also consult **Siskiyou National Forest Illinois**

Valley Ranger Station (26568 Redwood Hwy., Cave Junction 97525, 541/592-2166).

Botany buffs will especially want to get the lowdown on the Kalmiopsis Wilderness (see the Coastal Oregon chapter), the redwoods located in California's Smith River drainage, and the fall harvest of chanterelle, morel, and matsutake mushrooms. If you're seeking relief from the summertime heat in the local's favorite swimming hole, get directions to "the Forks," where the east and west forks of the Illinois River meet. The confluence can be accessed a mile south of Cave Junction at Illinois River State Park. Wine fanciers should get directions to Foris, Siskiyou, and Bridgeview Vineyards. Outdoor recreationists will appreciate information on everything from fishing in Lake Selmac and rafting the challenging Illinois River to horse-packing and hiking in the surrounding Siskiyous.

After you cross the California border about 20 miles southwest of Cave Junction, the road begins to wind its way through the Smith River Canyon. This is Redwood Country, and the combination of the wild blue-green Smith River (the only major river on the West Coast that runs unimpeded by dams from the mountains to the sea) and the oldest, largest living things known to humankind make this drive a thrill a minute.

To get to the southern Oregon coast via this route, allow several hours to get to Brookings. Wintertime rainfall that can average over 100 inches annually and the never-ending summertime procession of slow-moving vehicles and the existence of slides on this mostly two-lane highway are other inconveniences. As such, it's worth pulling off the road in **Jedediah Smith National Park** on the California side of U.S. 197 (an extension of U.S. 199). There is a day-use fee of a few dollars to get into the park. Proceed directly down to the picnic area along the banks of the Smith River and park your car. There you will find picnic tables (a great place for lunch) and restrooms. Best of all, there is an excellent nature trail beginning there that loops through the grove. A pamphlet can be procured for a quarter (on the honor system—have some class and ante up) that elaborates upon the natural features delineated by numbered markers along the trail.

Feel how your footsteps make no sound, so thick is the forest floor from hundreds of years of redwood needles and cones. Be sure to see the myrtlewood trees along the trail, as well as the giant root wads from fallen redwoods. Surprisingly, these towering giants have no single tap root, but instead many shallow roots that radiate out in all directions, interlocking with their brethren for protection from stormy weather. It takes only 15–25 minutes to walk the loop, which provides an outstanding experience for children.

Merlin, Galice, and Big Pine

About an hour outside of Grants Pass is the tallest ponderosa pine in the world. Standing a whopping 246 feet high and sporting a 57-inch diameter, **Big Pine** lives up to its name with an estimated volume of 12,500 board feet of wood. This 300-year-old giant lives in a grove of large pines, cedars, and Douglas firs at **Big Pine Campground** (Galice Ranger District, 541/471-6500, www.fs.fed.us/r6/siskiyou).

To get here, take the Merlin Exit off I-5 just north of Grants Pass if you're traveling south, or Exit 61 if you're traveling north, and proceed toward Galice (this Merlin-Galice Road goes 100 windy miles to Gold Beach on the coast). Just beyond Morrison's Lodge, a luxurious getaway on the Rogue River, turn left onto Taylor Creek Road 25. Big Pine Campground is about 10 miles farther. Another routing option is via U.S. 199. About 20 miles south of Grants Pass on U.S. 199, take Onion Creek Road on the north side of the highway and follow it 20 miles to Big Pine.

The campground features 12 picnic sites and 14 campsites. Picnic tables, fire rings, and vault toilets are provided. Water is available from a hand pump between campsites seven and nine. A small playground and primitive softball diamond are tastefully incorporated into the grounds. Many trails take hikers to Big Pine and beyond for a short hike or an all-day adventure. A lazy creek meanders through the area, with alders, hazelnuts, and an array of colorful wildflowers growing along its banks. Deer and other wildlife are frequently spotted grazing in the fragrant meadows nearby. Foragers can pick their fill of blackberries in July and August. Cost is $16–22 a night.

Roseburg

Many people passing through the Roseburg area might quickly dismiss it as a rural backwater. A closer look, however, reveals many more interesting layers beneath the mill-town veneer. While about half of the folks here rely upon the woods as a workplace (and this fact is reflected in the no-nonsense cafés and businesses meeting their needs), growing pockets of refinement are found in between the pickup trucks and lumber mills. An award-winning museum, Oregon's only drive-through zoo, and some fine restaurants are a few examples of culture in the hinterland.

And yet, the true allure of Roseburg is not really in town, but in the surrounding countryside. The Mediterranean climate of the Umpqua Valley has proven ideal for producing world-class wines and contributes to wonderful wine-tasting tours. The beautiful North Umpqua River to the east offers rafting, camping, hiking, and fishing. In addition to catching trout, salmon, and bass, anglers come from all over to enjoy one of the world's last rivers with a native run of summer steelhead. Numerous waterfalls along the river and the frothy white water make the Native American word Umpqua ("Thunder Water") an appropriate name. And if you are really interested in a closer look at a lumber mill, you can visit the world's largest particleboard plant.

In short, there's more here than a hasty visual appraisal would suggest, and it's worth more time than it takes to top off a tank of gas and wolf down a hamburger. Check it out—you'll be glad you did.

SIGHTS

Douglas County Museum of History and Natural History

This nationally acclaimed museum (123 Museum Dr., 541/957-7007, www.co.Douglas.or.us/museum/) is located at the Douglas County Fairgrounds (Exit 123 off I-5). Its four wings feature exhibits that range from a million-year-old saber-toothed tiger to 19th-century steam-logging equipment. Eight-thousand-year-old Native American artifacts, a re-creation of the 1882 Dillard Oregon and California Railroad depot, an imaginative forest-industry exhibit, and an extensive collection of historical photos make your visit both entertaining and educational. Open Mon.–Fri. 9 A.M.–5 P.M., Saturday 10 A.M.–5 P.M., and Sunday noon–5 P.M. Admission is $3.50 for adults, $1 for kids. The on-site Lavola Bakken research library is open Mon.–Fri. 1 P.M.–4:30 P.M. The museum also hosts children's programming held the second Saturday of each month.

Gardens

The **Lotus Knight Memorial Gardens** are in Riverside Park. Located between Oak and Washington Streets on the banks of the South Umpqua River, these gardens are a feast for the eyes with colorful azaleas and rhododendrons in the spring. Open daily 5 A.M.–10 P.M.

South of Roseburg about 15 minutes, near the town of Myrtle Creek, is **Beneschoen Gardens,** with a good collection of rhododendrons, azaleas, azalea-dendrons, and other rare and unusual plants. Over 150 varieties of azaleas are featured here. Peak blooms for both parks occur late April–early May.

Winchester Fish Ladder

The Winchester Fish Ladder is just off I-5 at Exit 129 on the north bank of the North Umpqua River. Here visitors can watch salmon and steelhead in their native environment as they swim by the viewing window at Winchester Dam. The North Umpqua and the Columbia are the only rivers in Oregon that offer this attraction. Spring chinook and summer steelhead migrate upriver May–August, and coho, fall chinook, and more summer steelhead swim on by September–November. December–May, winter steelhead is the primary species seen going through the fish ladders and on past the window. The Umpqua River offers the largest variety of game fish in Oregon.

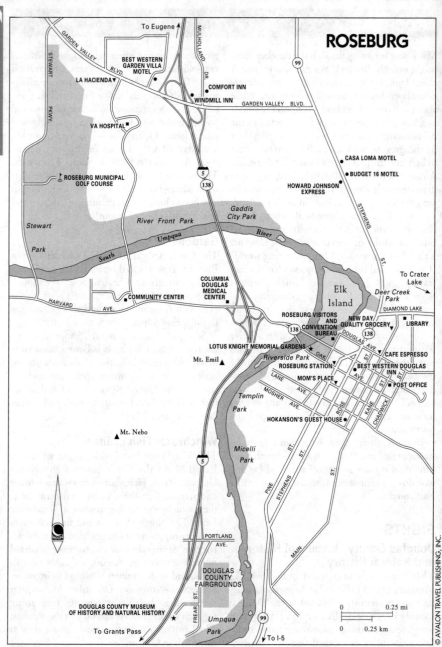

ROSEBURG

To Eugene

BEST WESTERN GARDEN VILLA MOTEL

LA HACIENDA

COMFORT INN

WINDMILL INN

GARDEN VALLEY BLVD.

VA HOSPITAL

CASA LOMA MOTEL

BUDGET 16 MOTEL

HOWARD JOHNSON EXPRESS

ROSEBURG MUNICIPAL GOLF COURSE

Gaddis City Park

River Front Park

Umpqua River

South

To Crater Lake

Stewart Park

Elk Island

Deer Creek Park

DIAMOND LAKE

COLUMBIA DOUGLAS MEDICAL CENTER

HARVARD AVE.

COMMUNITY CENTER

ROSEBURG VISITORS AND CONVENTION BUREAU

NEW DAY QUALITY GROCERY

LIBRARY

DOUGLAS AVE.

CAFE ESPRESSO

LOTUS KNIGHT MEMORIAL GARDENS

Mt. Emil

Riverside Park

ROSEBURG STATION

BEST WESTERN DOUGLAS INN

MOM'S PLACE

POST OFFICE

LANE

MOSHER AVE.

Templin Park

HOKANSON'S GUEST HOUSE

Mt. Nebo

Micelli Park

PORTLAND AVE.

DOUGLAS COUNTY FAIRGROUNDS

DOUGLAS COUNTY MUSEUM OF HISTORY AND NATURAL HISTORY

To Grants Pass

Umpqua Park

To I-5

0   0.25 mi

0   0.25 km

THE GOATS OF MOUNT NEBO

There's a saying that only a dude or a fool will predict the weather. But the folks here in Roseburg were once able to tell with 93 percent accuracy if it was going to rain. Their system was simple enough. A basalt mountain called Mount Nebo that rises up from the west bank of the South Umpqua River near downtown had been home to a herd of goats for as long as anyone could remember. When the goats came down from the top of Mount Nebo, that meant it was going to rain.

In the early 1960s, Mother Nature's barometer had to make way for the wheels of progress. Road-building crews blasted out huge chunks of Mount Nebo to make room for I-5. The goats endured this incursion into their domain and still managed to faithfully make their pilgrimage down from the mountaintop when inclement weather was imminent. But about two decades later, highway engineers decided the freeway entrance at the base of Mount Nebo was dangerous and needed more work. So in 1977, men and machines once again assaulted the goats' territory.

This time, the citizenry of Roseburg came together to protect their weather soothsayers. They circulated petitions to "save our goats" and sent them to Salem with an emotional plea to the governor to halt the construction, but to no avail. With their turf dynamited into oblivion and the gentle grassy glade turned into a steep cliff, the goats departed for points unknown. For years, Mount Nebo survived in the form of an ugly rock escarpment echoing with the 24-hour roar of traffic, while the plaintive bleating of the goats of Mount Nebo was only a fading memory.

In 1997, prison laborers terraced a half-mile path up the mountain and planted over 1,000 brilliant red roses donated by Medford's Jackson and Perkins (this project was inspired by local initiative and contributions of the citizens of Roseburg). Expect Mount Nebo to blossom from springtime to the first frost. Many citizens here feel that this mountain of roses will help restore some of the civic pride and local color that was lost along with the goats of Mount Nebo.

Mill Tour

The world's largest particleboard plant, **Roseburg Forest Products** (541/679-3311, ext. 392, www.rfpco.com), south of Roseburg in nearby **Dillard,** offers tours by appointment only (24-hour advance notice required) Wednesday and Friday at 1:30 P.M. This plant runs around the clock, seven days a week, producing this versatile building material. You'll see the entire process, from wood chip to finished product, accompanied by a cacophony of bells and whistles. The tour lasts approximately two hours, with some uphill walking and stair climbing. No open-toe shoes or high heels are allowed. Visitors must be at least 10 years of age. Contact the Roseburg Visitors and Convention Bureau for information on other local mill tours. As you drive down I-5 outside of town you'll be able to see piles of Roseburg Forest Products lumber on the east side of the highway; the size of these piles bespeaks this company's one-time status as the largest privately held for-profit Oregon-owned and headquartered company.

Wildlife Safari

Tucked away in a 600-acre wooded valley is Wildlife Safari (Safari Road, Winston 97496, 541/679-6761 or 800/355-4848, www.wildlife-safari.org), Oregon's drive-through zoo. To get here, take Exit 119 off I-5 and follow ORE 42 for four miles. Turn right on Lookingglass Road and right again on Safari Road. Admission is $14.50 adults, $11.50 seniors, and $8.50 kids ages 4–12. Open 9 A.M.–5 P.M. every day except Christmas; the park may stay open later in summer but closes at dusk regardless of the season.

Once inside the park gates, the brightly colored birds and exotic game animals transport you to other lands, with an oddly appropriate Oregon backdrop. Be that as it may, every possible step has been taken at Wildlife Safari to re-create African and North American animal-life zones. Lest this conjure the image of lions, tigers, and bears eating Bambi and company for supper before your very eyes, these critters are kept apart from their natural prey. Similar precautions are taken with humans. People must remain inside their vehicles except in designated areas, and windows and sunroofs must be kept closed in the big cats' and bears' areas.

The first loop takes you to see the tigers and cheetahs. These giant felines loll lazily about or catch catnaps in the tall grass. The next link takes you through the heart of "Africa," where the deer and the antelope play. Wildebeests, zebras, and other creatures scamper freely about, seemingly oblivious to the slow parade of cars and people watching them. Elephants, rhinoceroses, and other African big game are also represented here. Soon you are in "North America." Bears, bighorn sheep, pronghorns, moose, and buffalo are just a few of the animals that live down in the valley. Perhaps the most popular attraction is the petting zoo, where children get "hands-on" experience. When the weather is good, you can take a memorable ride on the camel or the elephant.

With 600 animals including America's largest (and cutest) collection of cheetah cubs, this is one safari that appeals to all ages. Speaking of cheetahs, this is one of the few places where they are successfully bred in captivity. After your "safari," pull into the White Rhino restaurant, serving good food within view of lions, giraffes, and white rhinos.

Wineries

Several wineries in the Roseburg vicinity offer tasting rooms and tours. The dry, Mediterranean climate and rich variety of soils in the area are ideal for chardonnay, pinot noir, Gewürztraminer, Riesling, zinfandel, and cabernet sauvignon varietals. A good wine-tour pamphlet with a fine map showing the location of the wineries is available from the Roseburg Visitors and Convention Bureau.

Hillcrest Vineyard (240 Vineyard Ln., 541/673-3709 or 800/736-3709), in business since 1963, is one of the oldest vineyards in Oregon. Their first batch was a humble 240 gallons, but production has since grown to over 20,000 gallons annually. The winery is noted primarily for its Rieslings but also produces cabernet sauvignon, pinot noir, and small quantities of other varieties. Open 11 A.M.–5 P.M. daily.

Callahan Ridge Winery (340 Busenbark Ln.,

541/673-7901 or 888/946-3487, www.callahanridge.com) is open daily 11:30 A.M.–5 P.M. for tastings, tours, and sales. They offer a very dry Gewürztraminer, white zinfandel, and white Riesling, as well as barrel-aged chardonnay and a late-harvest Gewürztraminer. Established in 1979, this winery currently produces about 20,000 cases annually. The tasting room hours are open daily 11 A.M.–6 P.M., April–October.

Down the road from Davidson Winery is **Girardet Wine Cellars** (895 Reston Rd., 541/679-7252, www.girardetwine.com). Philippe Girardet, from a town at the headwaters of the Rhine River in Switzerland, brings European wine-blending techniques to Oregon. This process produces unique chardonnay, pinot noir, cabernet sauvignon, and Riesling wines. Tastings, tours, and sales daily 11–5 P.M. April–Oct., 11–4 P.M. Nov.–March. The winery is closed Dec. 20–Jan. 30 and major holidays.

The **Henry Winery** (687 Hubbard Creek Rd., Umpqua 97486, 541/459-5120 or 800/782-2686, www.henryestate.com) has produced a string of award-winning varietals from chardonnay, Gewürztraminer, and pinot noir grapes. Newcomers to their outstanding lineup include pinot noir blanc and Muller-Thurgau. In addition to tasting and tours daily 11 A.M.–5 P.M., lunch at shaded picnic tables near the vineyard and the Umpqua River can heighten your enjoyment of the fruit of the vine. The third weekend in August is the Henry Goes Wine gala, which you won't want to miss if in the region; see website for info.

La Garza Cellars (491 Winery Ln., 541/679-9654, www.lagarza.com) can be reached by taking Exit 119 (south of Roseburg). Take a left about 100 feet past the first stoplight onto Winery Lane, and continue until you get to the vineyard. Winery tours and a gourmet restaurant are enhanced by beautiful surroundings. Open daily 11 A.M.–5 P.M. May–Sept.; best to call first during the off-season.

SPORTS AND RECREATION

The Umpqua River system is home to a dozen species of popular eating fish that range from the big chinook salmon to the tiny silver smelt. Visit the Oregon Department of Fish and Wildlife website (www.dfw.state.or.us) for additional information on the Umpqua. The following overview will help you decide where and when to go and what to take to land some supper.

Fishing for Chinook Salmon

Spring chinook enter the North Umpqua River March–June, work their way upstream during July and August, and spawn September–October. You'll need a stout rod, sturdy reel, drifting eggs or sand shrimp for bait, and some type of spinner.

Fall chinook are mainly found in the warmer South Umpqua River. Their migration starts in midsummer and peaks in September when the rains increase water flow and lower the river's temperature. Bait and tackle for fall chinook fishing are pretty much the same as spring chinook gear.

Fishing for Steelhead

The best fishing for summer steelhead on the North Umpqua is June–October; the fish spawn January–March. This fish averages only six–eight pounds, but it will make you think you are trying to reel in a chinook by the way it struggles. Fly-fishing for summer steelhead is extremely popular—so much so that the 31-mile stretch from Rock Creek upriver to Soda Springs is for fly-angling only. Elsewhere on the North

Umpqua, spin-casting with drift eggs, plugs, lures, or shrimp is allowed. There are no summer steelhead on the South Umpqua because there are no deep pools for them during the hot summer months.

Winter steelhead are found in both the North and South Umpqua Rivers. They begin their migration upriver in November, so December and January are the best fishing months. The fish spawn February–April. The success of the winter steelhead runs is in great part determined by the weather, which affects important variables like water temperature, level, and color. Generally speaking, if it's cold and wet (but not too wet), the fishing tends to be better. This makes it important to dress warmly in appropriate rain gear so you don't turn as blue as the fish you're trying to catch.

Fishing for Coho and Sockeye Salmon

Coho, alias "silvers," are found throughout the Umpqua River system. The coho life cycle lasts about three years. Each spends its first year in freshwater, heads for the ocean to spend one to two years, and then returns to freshwater to spawn. The adults weigh an average of seven pounds each. At this writing, the status of this fishery is in question.

Far more rare in the Umpqua River system are crimson sockeye. These river denizens usually weigh about 10 pounds; eggs are the preferred bait. Possessing more oil than the chinook, the sockeye is regarded as the number-one salmon for quality and flavor.

Fishing for Rainbow Trout

You'll find this brightly speckled fish in nearly all rivers and streams of the Umpqua River system where the water is relatively cool and gravel bars clean. They don't like warm water and avoid the lower South Umpqua and Cow Creek for this reason. Rainbows do like the riffles at the entry or exit of pools. This is the most common game fish in the water, mainly because the rivers, lakes, and streams of the Umpqua are routinely seeded with over 100,000 legal-size (eight inches or

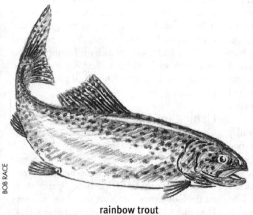

BOB RACE

rainbow trout

longer) rainbows. The fishing season opens in April, with the best fishing in early summer when the fish are actively feeding. The best baits are salmon eggs, worms, or small flies; lures can also be used with success. The most popular tackle is spin-casting gear with a light leader.

Fishing for Brown and Brook Trout

In the rapids of the upper North Umpqua you'll find browns, particularly around Soda Springs. Browns seem to like faster-moving water than rainbows. The average size is about a foot long, but sometimes 20-inchers are landed. Midsummer is the best time to fish for browns. Worms and salmon eggs prove effective, but the best lure is one that resembles a small fish.

High in the icy blue upper reaches of the North Umpqua is a small population of brook trout. The adult brook averages about six inches, which is also the legal minimum size, so light tackle is best. Mid- to late summer is when the brook trout are biting, and they go for eggs and worms.

Fishing for Smallmouth, Largemouth, and Striped Bass

The smallmouth is the most numerous of the three bass species commonly found in the Umpqua River system. The largest concentration of them is near Elkton, and they average between one and two pounds. The best time to fish for this species is when the water warms up to a high 50s–low 60s temperature range during spring and summer. Spinning gear with three-pound test line and a four-inch plastic worm are the most popular, with smaller deep-diving plugs right behind. So plentiful are smallmouth bass on the Umpqua that the river has its own set of guidelines that are more generous than the regulations governing other Oregon waterways. You are allowed 12 bass a day with no more than five that exceed 17 inches in length.

Largemouth bass are found mainly in valley lakes and reservoirs. These fish average two pounds, with some big ones now and then tipping the scales at four pounds. The bait, tackle, and regulations are the same as for smallmouth. The key difference is that anglers should have a boat to keep moving with the school.

Anglers from around the world come to test themselves on the North Umpqua River.

COURTESY OF GREG MORGAN/BLM

Striped bass are found in the main Umpqua and seem to roam back and forth from brackish to sweet water continuously. The striped bass is the largest of the bass species found here, and the Umpqua has produced some world-record catches of the fish over the years. You'll need a boat to fish for "stripers," as the guides call them, as well as a stout rod, 20- to 30-pound test line, and a variety of bait. Minnow or eel imitations are good for trolling, herring or smelt for bottom fishing, and hooks or plugs for surface casting.

Fishing for Shad and Smelt

Commercial fishing interests have been fishing for shad in the Umpqua River since the 1920s. Since 1964, about 60,000 shad a year have been taken from the Umpqua. Shad eggs, or roe, are considered a delicacy, particularly on the East Coast. Smelt are found on the lower Umpqua near Reedsport around Dean Creek.

They have no set timetable for their migrations. Smelt are usually caught with a small mesh net.

Camping

Armacher County Park (541/672-4901), $11–20, is five miles north of town off I-5 on Exit 129. Situated on the North Umpqua, the park has 10 tent sites and 20 RV/trailer sites with full hookups. A bathhouse and picnic area are also found here. **Twin Rivers Vacation Park** (433 Rivers Forks Rd., 541/673-3811), $17–25, is six miles out of town (via I-5, take Exit 125), where the north and south forks of the Umpqua converge. Water, electricity, waste disposal, showers, and a coin-op laundry are available at this 85-site park. **Fairgrounds RV Park** (210 Frear St., 541/440-4505), $20–25, has 50 hookups, water, and a drive-through dump station. **U-Haul RV Center** (1182 N.E. Stephens, 541/672-6864) has a dumping station for self-contained vehicles.

Other Activities

Stewart Park Golf Course (1005 Stewart Park Dr., Roseburg 97470, 541/672-4592) charges $15 for nine holes, $23 for 18 holes; add on a few extra dollars on weekends. In addition to power carts, a lighted driving range, and rental golf clubs, a complete pro shop offers lessons and any peripherals you may need.

Tennis buffs will find free courts at the Douglas County Fairgrounds, Roseburg High School, and Umpqua Community College. Twelve lighted courts are located at Stewart Park (541/673-8650) off Stewart Parkway, but they charge fees and require reservations. Stewart Park also offers nature trails and wildlife viewing. The **YMCA** (541/440-9622), also located in Stewart Park, has racquetball and basketball courts as well as an indoor swimming pool. Umpqua Community College (541/440-4600, ext. 686) has a pool that's open to the public during the summer 1–4 P.M. and 7–9 P.M.

> *To see the works of local, regional, and Northwest artists, visit the Umpqua Valley Arts Center (1624 W. Harvard, 541/672-2532). Two galleries, open daily, feature monthly rotating exhibits.*

Roseburg also has two bowling alleys and two movie theater complexes.

EVENTS

Roseburg's big event is the **Douglas County Fair,** held annually at the fairgrounds the second week of August. Besides the usual assortment of 4-H prize bulls, Mom's marmalade, and Grandma's-secret-recipe apple pie, the bright lights of the midway rides, food booths, and horse and stock-car races add to the festive atmosphere. In the afternoon, big-name singers entertain the crowds with toe-tapping country music. While it's seven days of fun, and well worth seeing if you're in the neighborhood, high temperatures compel an early start. In September, a wine, art, and cheese fest attracts vintners, artisans, and food booths. Contact the Roseburg Visitors and Convention Bureau (800/444-9584) for specifics.

Stewart Park hosts free Tuesday-evening concerts during the summer **Music on the Halfshell** (www .halfshell.org) series, featuring such urbane entertainers as David Grisman and B.B. King. The park's bandstand is located near the banks of the South Umpqua. The **Land of Umpqua Festival** is also held in Stewart Park. The July event celebrates the region's food, wine, and art. Contact the Roseburg Visitors and Convention Bureau (800/444-9584) for details on these festivals.

In December, the **Umpqua Valley Festival of Lights** (800/444-9584, www.umpquafestival-oflights.com) is noteworthy for fanciful creations (including an eight-foot-high waving Santa and a 36-foot-high American flag) and the sheer size of the display.

PRACTICALITIES
Accommodations

There are over a thousand motel rooms for rent in Roseburg, and this competition keeps rates surprisingly low for what Roseburg has to offer.

Budget travelers can bunk down at **Budget 16 Motel** (1067 N.E. Stephens, 541/673-5556) or **Casa Loma Motel** (1107 N.E. Stephens, 541/673-5569) for $40–50/night.

The following chains are all midrange in price ($50–70), amenities, and cleanliness standards: **Comfort Inn** (1539 Mulholland Dr., 541/957-1100 or 800/228-5160); **Best Western Douglas Inn** (511 S.E. Stephens, 541/673-6625 or 877/368-4466, www.bestwesternoregon.com); **Best Western Garden Villa Motel** (760 N.W. Garden Valley Blvd., 541/672-1601 or 800/547-3446); and **Howard Johnson Express** (978 N.E. Stephens, 541/673-5082, www.hojo.com).

For luxury accommodations with laundry, restaurant/lounge, and pool, where pets are permitted, head for the **Windmill Inn** (1450 N.W. Mulholland Dr., 541/673-0901 or 800/547-4747, www.windmillinns.com), $70–100.

The Gothic Revival–style **Hokanson's Guest House** (848 S.E. Jackson St., 541/672-2632), $60–90, was built in 1882 on land once owned by Aaron Rose, the founder of Roseburg. The building is listed in the National Register of Historic Places, and each of its bedrooms has a private bath with a claw-foot tub and period furnishings. Hokanson's Hi-Ho Restaurant is five blocks away.

Food

Roseburg is not exactly the fine-dining capital of Oregon. Most of the folks here are more interested in getting a big plate of food than titillating their palates. Since there is no shortage of fast-food joints, greasy spoons, and truck-driver restaurants, let's focus instead on a few unique options in town.

The **Douglas County Farmers Market** (541/672-9380) takes place April 12–Oct. 25. Located in the parking lot of Roseburg Valley Mall on Stewart Parkway and Garden Valley Boulevard, it's a great place to sample fresh flavors each Saturday 9 A.M.–1 P.M.

A highly regarded Tex-Mex establishment is **La Hacienda** (940 N.W. Garden Valley Blvd., 541/672-5330). You'll know the place when you see it. In front of the cream-colored stucco building with green and orange stripes are tall arches of typical Spanish design. The food inside is equally inviting. In addition to the usual assortment of tacos, tostadas, and tamales, you'll find tasty shrimp and chicken fajitas, combination dinners, and seafood dishes. La Hacienda also features a wide selection of Mexican beers to enhance your lunch ($5–10) or dinner ($7–15). Open daily.

You'll find good deli sandwiches at **Between the Buns** (214 S.E. Jackson, 541/672-0342). "Dagwood-style" sandwiches piled way too high with fillings come at a low price that makes them easy to swallow. Open Mon.–Sat. 10 A.M.–5 P.M.; call the night before to order a picnic lunch.

Brutke's Wagon Wheel (227 N.W. Garden Valley Blvd., 541/672-7555) is the place to go for prime rib. The chef's prime rib recipe dates back 30 years and accounts for more than a third of the food sales at the restaurant. But if you don't fit the beefeater's shoes, chicken and "heart-smart" entrées are also featured on the menu. The restaurant has a colorful, homey atmosphere. You might see loggers in flannel shirts and jeans while other folks sport more formal attire. It's not uncommon for couples to come here for a special occasion and families to drop in for a good, wholesome meal. Open Mon.–Fri. for lunch and dinner, Saturday and Sunday for dinner only.

Cafe Espresso (corner of Douglas and Jackson, 368 S.E. Jackson, 541/672-1859) has a bright, many-checkered decor and a varied lunch menu. Daily specials ($4–7) like quiche and lasagna washed down by cups of premium brew are especially appreciated in a town low on good coffeehouses. Open Mon.–Sat. for breakfast and lunch.

McMenamin's has set up a class act here at **Roseburg Station** (700 S.E. Sheridan St., 541/672-1934). The 1912 Southern Pacific Station was purchased and restored preserving original features like the 16-foot-high ceiling, tongue-and-groove Douglas fir wainscoting, and marble molding. Historical photos and art further recount the depot's storied past. Quality food and microbrews in a setting suitable for family further enhance the appeal. Open daily for lunch and dinner.

New Day Quality Grocery (210 S.E. Jackson, 541/672-0275) has organic produce, bulk foods and herbs, spices, and teas. Open Mon.–Fri.

9:30 A.M.–6:30 P.M., Saturday 9:30 A.M.–5 P.M. Closed Sunday.

Information and Transportation

The **Roseburg Visitors and Convention Bureau** (410 S.E. Spruce St., 541/672-9731 or 800/444-9584, www.visitroseburg.com) has all kinds of useful information free for the taking. One particularly useful pamphlet is a driver's guide to historic places. Although the courteous staff offer decent travel-planning suggestions, they are tight-lipped when it comes to specific recommendations on food and lodging.

MegaByte Internet Cafe (962 W. Harvard Ave., 541/957-8970, www.megabyteinc.com) provides Internet access.

The **Greyhound/Trailways** bus depot (835 S.E. Stephens, 541/673-5326) is open weekdays 7:30 A.M.–6:30 P.M., Saturday 8 A.M.–5 P.M. Routes connect Roseburg with California, the Willamette Valley, Washington, and the Oregon coast. The **Green Tortoise** (800/867-8647) departs from the Tom Tom restaurant (just off I-5 Exit 125) at 11:15 A.M. Sunday and Thursday for northbound destinations, and at 5:15 P.M. Monday and Friday headed south. Be sure to call in advance to arrange for a "flag stop."

Roseburg Sunshine Taxi Express (541/672-2888) can chauffeur you around the city.

OAKLAND

Many travelers drive by the exit marked Oakland on I-5 joking that maybe they made a wrong turn somewhere and ended up in California. But the curious who venture a few miles off the freeway to explore this National Historic Landmark discover that *this* Oakland is an interesting voyage into Oregon's past. Established in the 1850s, this hamlet today gives little indication of the caprices of fate and fortune it has experienced in its 145-year history. Oakland is noteworthy for leftover touches of refinement from its golden age, which seem almost incongruous against its present-day small-town facade. You may recognize Main Street Oakland if you saw the movie *Fire in the Sky.*

Oakland was a stopover point for the main stagecoach line linking Portland and Sacramento until the Oregon and California Railroad came to town in 1872. With these two transportation linkages, Oakland thrived as a trading center for outlying hop fields and prune orchards. In the early 1900s, millions of pounds of dried prunes were shipped all over the world from Oakland. In the 1920s and '30s, raising turkeys became the prominent industry in the area, and Oakland became the leading turkey-shipping center in the western United States. From the '40s through the '60s, the lumber industry dominated the local economy. Today, livestock ranching, farming, and tourism are the economic mainstays.

While not as built-up as its counterpart restoration farther south in Jacksonville, Oakland still provides a good place to pull off the interstate and reflect on the passage of years in a one-time boomtown turned rural hamlet.

Old Town Oakland is a good place to start your tour, because this is where it all began. An excellent free history and walking-tour pamphlet is available at the city hall (117 3rd St.). The original wooden buildings were destroyed by fires in the 1890s, and most of the brick and stone structures in the historical district date back to this era of reconstruction. There are many antique stores, art galleries, and curio shops to browse through as well. The **Oakland Museum** (136 Locust) is worth visiting. The exhibit in the back re-creates Oakland during its boom times. Open daily 1–4:30 P.M., closed on holidays. Admission is free.

The **Lamplighter Inn** (126 Locust, 541/459-4938), open for lunch and dinner, serves basic American food like omelettes, sandwiches, and burgers for $4–7. The lounge in the back of the restaurant is the hot spot in town, where locals come to tilt glasses and play video poker. Fancier fare is found across the street at **Tolly's** (115 Locust, 541/459-3796), "where sodas flow and friendships grow." Lunch is served 10 A.M.–6 P.M. and features deli and croissant sandwiches as well as creative entrées and salads. Elaborate gourmet dinners ($8–17) are served 5:30–9P.M. and are complemented by a fine wine list and mellow piano music. Be sure to save some room for the homemade desserts. Open for breakfast, lunch, and dinner Tues.–Sunday.

Southeastern Oregon

The Great Basin high desert that sprawls across southeastern Oregon occupies three very large, lonely counties: Lake (8,340 square miles), Harney (10,281 square miles), and Malheur (9,925 square miles), as well as a small portion of Deschutes County. Equivalent in area to New England minus Maine, the entire high desert region shelters fewer than 45,000 people, most of whom live near Ontario or Vale near the Idaho border.

Lake County has some of the most intriguing geological formations in the Northwest. Evidence of the cataclysmic forces that shaped the Columbia Plateau and the Great Basin are on display in this starkly beautiful part of the state. Fractures in the ground and wave patterns left by ancient lakes on the flanks of mountains are some of the fingerprints left here by the hand of nature.

The sagebrush, rimrock, and grassy plains of Harney County, one of the least populated areas in the Lower 48, are shared by only 7,400 inhabitants. With an average elevation of 4,000 feet, this northern edge of the Great Basin has a short growing season, a yearly snowfall of 36 inches, and clear skies at least 250 days per year. The main industries are logging, milling, and cattle ranching, with farming limited to hardy grains and hay. An index of the sparse population density here is the fact that Harney County has one of the few public boarding schools in the United States. Students reside in dorms on campus because most come from ranches located many miles from town.

Malheur County, to the north and east, is covered in the Northeastern Oregon chapter.

Steens Mountain

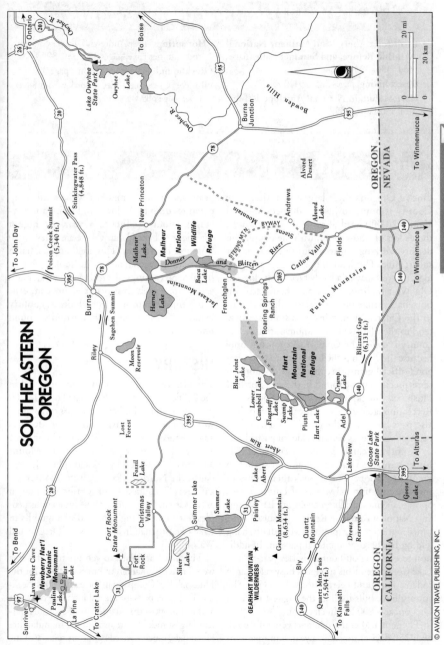

© AVALON TRAVEL PUBLISHING, INC.

SOUTHEASTERN OREGON HIGHLIGHTS

- **Birdlife at Abert Rim, Malheur National Wildlife Refuge,** and **Summer Lake,** pages 384, 386, 393–394
- **Desert hiking,** pages 385, 391, 393–396
- **Hart Mountain National Antelope Refuge,** near Plush, page 387
- **Hot springs,** near Andrews, Lakeview, Plush, and Summer Lake, pages 384, 386, 396
- **Rockhounding,** Harney County, page 397
- **Rodeos,** Christmas Valley, Lakeview, and Silver Lake, page 389

Lake County

One of Oregon's three largest counties, Lake County is home to just 7,500 people—and about 120,000 head of cattle. In other words, there's lots of elbow room, with the population density working out to about one person per square mile. This land of open spaces and geologic marvels spawns a hardy breed that clings to Old West traditions. Cowboys herd cattle on horseback, itinerant prospectors dig for color in the Quartz Mountains, and homesteaders tend to their farms in the remote outback. The county is called the Gem of Oregon not only because the region is the best place to find Oregon's official gemstone, the Plush diamond, a semi-precious stone found in the area north of Plush (see "Rockhounding" under Sports and Recreation later in this chapter). The moniker also pays homage to the gemlike beauty of the county's wide vistas beneath skies of pastel blue.

Visitors can climb the ancient citadel of Fort Rock, camp along a high mountain stream in Fremont National Forest, soak their bones in the soothing mineral waters of Hunter's Hot Springs, or enjoy wildlife viewing at Hart Mountain National Antelope Refuge. Because of the varied vertical topography and wind drafts, hang gliding has become the local passion. In addition to enjoying outdoor activities year-round, Lake County residents support a busy calendar of rodeos, fairs, and celebrations. Lakeview, the county hub, bills itself as the highest town in Oregon, at 4,800 feet in elevation.

The semiarid climate here is generally cool, with 250 days of sunshine a year. Summer temperatures stay in the mid-80s, while winter temperatures drop to the low 30s. Precipitation averages about 16 inches a year. At higher elevations in Lake County, there are as few as 20 frost-free days a year. This area can be a harsh land with little tolerance for the foolish, so take sensible precautions like toting extra water and gas. Despite a low density of creature comforts, you'll enjoy exploring this high desert country loaded to its sandy brim with wonders found nowhere else.

HISTORY

The history of human occupation here and in the Pacific Northwest has been dated back 13,200 years through Dr. Luther Cressman's exploratory work at Fort Rock Cave. Early desert dwellers who roamed the Great Basin in search of game and food witnessed the eruption of Mount Mazama 6,000–8,000 years ago. Their descendants, the Northern Paiutes, were also hunter-gatherers. This Lake County tribe was known as the Groundhog Eaters. These indigenous peoples left more petroglyphs and pictographs in Lake County than in all the rest of Oregon and Washington.

The first Europeans to venture into the area were French-Canadian trappers working for the Hudson's Bay Company in the early 1800s. Seeking out beaver pelts for the fashion trade back east and in Europe—the guard hairs of North America's largest rodent were used in the manufacture of felt hats, much coveted by the aristocracy of the time—these trappers were eventually joined by American mountain men. It wasn't until 1825 that Peter Skene Ogden, chief trader for the Hudson's Bay Company, made an "official" tour of the area when he sensed the threat of an American incursion. John Frémont and a party guided by Kit Carson marched through here in 1843, naming Summer and Abert Lakes.

The journals kept during these expeditions noted broad valleys with grasses "belly-high to a horse." This information attracted a new cast of players to the Great Basin: the cattle and sheep barons. With the passage of the Homestead Act in 1862, homesteaders moved in and started up more modest spreads. The white influx resulted in frequent tensions with the original occupants, which often culminated in bloodletting on both sides. But after the Bannock-Paiute uprising in 1878, the local natives were herded up and banished to a reservation.

In the growth spurt that followed, the town of Lakeview was chartered, in 1889; it burned to the ground in 1900 and was rebuilt with brick and corrugated-iron roofs. Other hopeful hamlets with names like Arrow, Buffalo, and Loma Vista sprang up around the county, thanks to a reactivated Federal Homestead Act in 1909 that sanctioned 320 free acres per settler. Many of these tiny burgs dried up and blew away after the 1918–1920 drought. However, larger communities like Lakeview, Paisley, and Summer Lake held on. With the advent of refrigerated railroad cars, big ranchers prospered, selling beef to our "hamburger nation." Local farmers figured out how to irrigate and cultivate this ornery land, and those tough enough to survive eventually came to terms with life on the dry side.

COURTESY OF OREGON TOURISM COMMISSION

Fort Rock is visible from miles away.

SIGHTS

Starting at the junction of U.S. 97 and ORE 31 at La Pine, many sites described in the following itinerary are annotated in the BLM's "Christmas Valley" publication, available from the BLM Lakeview office (1301 S. G St., Lakeview 97630, 541/947-2177), and in a forest service brochure available from the Fort Rock Ranger District (1230 N.E. 3rd, Ste. A-262, Bend 97701, 541/383-4700, www.fs.fed.us/r6/centraloregon).

A high-clearance vehicle is indispensable in this region if you value your oil pan. At La Pine on U.S. 97, stock up on provisions for your travels into the Great Basin. Seventy miles east, another opportunity for refueling and supply exists at Christmas Valley, a complex of alfalfa farms, a kitty litter factory, and mobile homes spread out over the sagebrush. With several restaurants, two filling stations, two food markets, cut-rate motels, and a golf course near a human-made lake, Christmas Valley makes a good base of operations for area exploration.

La Pine State Recreation Area

Located in Deschutes County, this boundless recreation nirvana lies just a few miles off of U.S. 97. Visitors come to the 2,333-acre park to picnic, camp, mountain bike, and fish the Fall River; it is so vast visitors rarely see one another. The 15 miles of single-track dirt biking trails are, for the most part, flat and perfect for beginners. Bikes can be rented at Bend and Sunriver cycle shops (see the Cascades chapter for listings). The park's 137 campsites ($9–17) and five cabins ($37) can be reserved (800/551-6949). Visit www.oregonstateparks.org for more information about this wonderful area.

Lost Forest

An unusual sight in this area is located 10 miles northeast of Christmas Valley on a rough but passable BLM road. A 9,000-acre stand of ponderosa pines intermixed with the largest juniper trees in Oregon is all that is left of an ancient grove that dates back thousands of years. Surprisingly, studies of tree rings show that this area has received only nine inches of rain a year for the last 600 years, half the amount normally needed to sustain growth of ponderosa pines. But here, a layer of pumicelike soil beneath the surface traps and retains enough moisture to allow the trees to draw water up through shorter-than-usual root systems.

This island of green is 40 miles away from the nearest forest, accentuating the isolation and solitude of these stately sentinels. Many of the junipers here are over a thousand years old. On hot summer days, this place is a welcome source of shade. Any time of year, the sound of the desert wind through the trees can stir contemplation. The final three-mile stretch of the approach to Lost Forest requires high vehicle clearance. To reach the area, drive eight miles east of the Christmas Valley post office, go eight miles north, and then eight miles east. The forest borders the largest inland sand dunes in the state. During warm weather months, check yourself for ticks before leaving here.

Summer Lake

Summer Lake lies 15 miles beyond Silver Lake. En route to Summer Lake on ORE 31, pull into **Picture Rock Turnout.** Take the trail 80 feet to the southeast. Behind the tallest rock is a pictograph. In the town of Summer Lake, the old **Harris School** is worth a picture. This classic one-room schoolhouse, complete with bell tower, is straight out of *Little House on the Prairie.*

The highway also passes through the **Summer Lake Wildlife Area** (53447 ORE 31, Summer Lake 97640, 541/943-3152, www.dfw.state.or.us), home to 170 species of migratory birds. Spring is the best time to see snow geese, avocets, black-necked stilts, and snowy plovers. An eight-mile wildlife-viewing trail around the lake is a recommended diversion at mile marker 70. Pick up a bird checklist from Oregon Fish and Wildlife.

Summer Lake Hot Springs (877/492-8554, www.summerlakehotsprings.com), six miles north of Paisley on the southern tip of Summer Lake, is a private operation open seven days a week 8 A.M.–9 P.M. A dip in the concrete pool costs $5 for people six and over, free to children under six. This hot spring resort has campsites on a bluff above the lake.

The region surrounding Summer Lake (541/943-3931) sits at the interface of desert and mixed conifer forest. Abundant wildlife, geological wonders, Native American sites, and historic structures beckon further investigation. The 20-mile-long and 10-mile-wide lake is surrounded by the mountains of the Fremont National Forest and Winter Ridge.

A good base for exploration is the **Summer Lake Inn** (31501 ORE 31, Summer Lake 97640, 541/943-3983 or 800/261-2778). Situated along the shore of the lake, this reconstructed pioneer homestead is paneled with a variety of wood. The feeling of warmth is enhanced by innkeeper Darrell Seven, whose flair for interior decorating, gourmet cooking, and local storytelling compels a stay here as much as the beautiful outdoor environment does. Guestroom views of the lake and the surrounding 8,000-foot mountains will stimulate dreams of your next day's activities. Amenities include a sauna, hot tub, and activities such as world-class bird-watching, cross-country skiing, fly-fishing, rockhounding, and candlelight dining. The inn is 110 miles from Bend and 65 miles north of Lakeview. Rates are $105–265; $10 per child under 18 per day. The more expensive rates are for self-contained cabins with Jacuzzis and skylights. Gourmet breakfasts and dinners (Wed.–Sat.) can be enjoyed for about $15.

The 1940s-era accommodations of the **Lodge at Summer Lake** (53460 Highway 31, Summer Lake, 97640, 541/943-3994, www.thelodgeatsummerlake.com) feature seven motel units ($56–72) and vacation rentals ($92) that sleep up to six. Rates are lower in the winter. There is an on-site restaurant.

CRACKS AND CAVES

Southeast of Bend, near Christmas Valley, lies a concentration of interesting geological features off ORE 31, which you can pick up off U.S. 97 (near La Pine). One of the more unusual of these oddities is **Hole-in-the-Ground.** Although this 300-foot-deep indentation looks like a meteor crater, scientists believe molten lava came into contact with water here, causing a massive explosion that quarried out a 7.5-mile-diameter crater. We estimate the total area to be about 280 acres. Astronauts came here in 1966 to experience the lunarlike terrain.

To find this unusual and awesome sight from U.S. 97, drive 22 miles southeast on ORE 31; turn left at the Hole-in-the-Ground sign. Drive 3.1 miles to the next sign. Turn right and go 1.1 mile to the final sign. Turn left and go .2 mile to the rim of the Hole.

About five miles farther down the road from the turnoff to Hole-in-the-Ground on ORE 31 is **Fort Rock Cave** (a.k.a. Sandal Cave, www.fortrockmuseum.com/cave), a formation that was carved by wave action against what was once a basalt island in an immense lake. In 1938 anthropologist Luther Cressman discovered over 70 ancient sandals woven from sagebrush in the 50-foot-deep cave. Dated at almost 10,000 years old, the sandals are the oldest human artifacts found in the Northwest and the oldest known surviving footwear on earth.

A mile east of the cave is **Fort Rock State Park** (800/551-6949, www.oregonstateparks.org/park_40.php), which towers 400 feet above the sagebrush plains. At the base of this tuff ring is an area of wave erosion cut by a long-disappeared lake. Fall and winter here offer wildlife-viewing par excellence; large herds of mule deer can be seen mid-November–mid-April, and pronghorn range over the alfalfa fields year-round. Many birds nest in the rocks, and golden eagles, hawks, kestrels, and peregrine falcons soar overhead. The state park offers trails and amenities for climbers and sightseers.

The nearby town of Fort Rock has an old-time flavor that has been accentuated by the recent restoration of homestead cabins in a pioneer village at the **Fort Rock Valley Historical Homestead Museum** (541/576-2251, www.fortrockmuseum.com), open Fri.–Sun. 9 A.M.–dusk.

An interesting journey down into the bowels of the earth is offered at **Derrick Cave,** located 22 miles north of Fort Rock. This large lava tube is a half mile long, with rooms up to 40 feet wide and 60 feet high. During the Cuban missile crisis of 1962, the cave was turned into a fallout shelter. Metal doors were installed and provisions for 1,000 people were stockpiled. The supplies were later plundered by vandals and the cave's civil-defense status was eventually dropped.

If you drive eight dusty miles (the last mile a teeth-chattering ride) north of Christmas Valley on a rough BLM road that begins one mile east of town, you'll come to another break in terra firma that'll pique your imagination. **Crack-in-the-Ground** (www.fortrockmuseum.com/crack1.htm) is about two miles long, 10–15 feet wide, and up to 70 feet deep. On hot days, it's nice and cool within this chasm. In fact, the crack is so deep that sometimes cold winter air gets trapped within and ice is preserved into summer. According to geologists, this dramatic fissure has been open for at least 1,000 years; the opening was once larger but lava from nearby volcanoes filled it in to its present dimensions. A BLM picnic area is at one end of this curious landmark.

Five miles northwest of Crack-in-the-Ground (on rough BLM Road 6109C) is **Green Mountain Campground** and fire lookout, which sits high above the previously mentioned Derrick Cave site. This primitive campground (large enough for three cars but without water or toilets) sits atop a small cinder cone overlooking hundreds of square miles of high desert, lava beds, and forest from 5,190 feet above sea level. In addition to Christmas Valley and Fort Rock Valley, you'll see snowcapped Diamond Peak 70 miles to the west and Wagontire Mountain 50 miles east.

Paisley

A few miles south of the lake is the town of Paisley. The **Paisley Ranger Compound** features several structures built by the Civilian Conservation Corps during the Depression. Check out the pine dugout canoe carved by CCC workers for forest service personnel. Trout fishing on the Chewaucan River and deer hunting also draw folks here. Perhaps Paisley's major claim to fame is the ZX Ranch, the nation's largest at over 1.3 million acres. The ranch property is 137 miles long and 64 miles wide.

If you're getting hungry, inexpensive eateries in Paisley can satisfy your cravings. The **Homestead Restaurant** (331 ORE 31, Paisley 97636, 541/943-3187) is the full-service establishment in the locale, serving breakfast, lunch, and dinner daily. The soup du jour with a sandwich makes a good lunch, and be sure to save room for the homemade cobbler. The local watering hole, **Pioneer Saloon** (327 Main St., 541/943-3289) doubles as a family restaurant. Pizza, steaks, and Mexican food are among the offerings on the menu.

If you need to stay over, the **Miles Motel** (1302 Fremont, 541/943-3148) has clean rooms for $32.

Lakeview

The "big city" of the county (pop. 2,500) is Lakeview, located 142 miles south of La Pine on ORE 31, 96 miles east of Klamath Falls on ORE 140 and 139 miles to Burns on ORE 395.

The **Schminck Memorial Museum** (128 S.E. Lakeview, 541/947-3134) has over 5,000 antiques assembled by the Oregon chapter of the Daughters of the American Revolution. It's open Tues.–Sat. 1–4 P.M. or by appointment, and charges $2 admission.

If you're in the mood for something different, cruise 15 miles south of Lakeview on U.S. 395 past New Pine Creek to Modoc County, California, to get to **Stringer's** (530/946-4112, www.stringersorchard.com). In addition to fine gifts, they claim to produce the world's only wild-plum wine and jam. Open daily.

Look for hang gliders coming off 2,000-foot Black Cap Hill above the east side of Lakeview

May–October. This town's fault blocks and winds have made Lakeview a center for this activity among enthusiasts.

At **Hunter's Hot Springs Resort** (P.O. Box 268, Lakeview 97630, 541/947-4242 or 800/858-8266, www.huntersresort.com), on U.S. 395 north of town, you can swim for a small fee or watch Old Perpetual, one of two Oregon geysers, go off in a pond. Call for rates and reservations.

Abert Rim

Fifteen miles north of Lakeview on U.S. 395 is the Abert Rim, the highest fault escarpment in the United States. The rim rises 2,000 feet above Lake Abert. This unusual body of water has no outlet and is rich in brine shrimp, which attract countless waterfowl and shorebirds. As at Summer Lake, fall is prime bird-watching season; expect thousands of plovers and other shorebirds. Due to its high alkalinity, it is hazardous to swim in the lake.

Below Abert Rim along the east shore of Lake Abert, the slope is covered with boulders, some of which sport petroglyphs. Several are located right off the highway near the geological marker. Forest service roads lead through the North Warner Mountains to BLM trails up the back side of Abert Rim; obtain routing information on these obscure byways from the Lakeview Ranger Station (U.S. 395 N, Lakeview 97360, 541/947-3334). Though reaching the rim requires an arduous journey down bumpy back roads and a steep hike up the mountain, the view from the top is spectacular. Just watch for rattlesnakes in the rocks.

Gearhart Mountain Wilderness Area

About 40 miles west of Lakeview off of ORE 140 is the 22,000-acre roadless Gearhart Mountain Wilderness Area. Accessible only on foot or horseback, two major trails take adventurers into a challenging outdoor environment.

Gearhart Trail (#100) incorporates 12 of the area's 16 miles of improved trails. This trail runs from **Lookout Rock** in the southeast corner of the wilderness, up over the mountain, down to **Blue Lake,** and to a trailhead on North

Creek. The **Boulder Springs Trail** (#100A) runs from the west side of the wilderness to a junction with the other trail a half mile from the mountain summit. For maps and more information, contact the forest service ranger stations in Lakeview, Paisley, or Silver Lake (U.S. 395 N, Lakeview 97360, 541/947-3334).

While you're in the neighborhood, you might want to visit the **Mitchell Monument,** on ORE 140 between the wilderness area and Bly, which commemorates a tragedy that occurred on May 5, 1945. Reverend Archie Mitchell and his wife were escorting five children on a picnic near Corral Creek when one of the kids discovered a bomb dropped by an incendiary balloon. Unfortunately, the child triggered the bomb, and all but the good reverend were killed. This is the only recorded incident of World War II fatalities in the 48 contiguous states. Balloon bombs came down all over the western states, but only Oregon recorded civilian deaths due to their detonation. The balloons were released in hopes of setting fire to Oregon forests.

Hart Mountain National Antelope Refuge

At the far eastern end of the county is a wildlife refuge that stretches across a high plateau rising above Warner Lakes. To get here from Adel, the first town east of Lakeview on ORE 140, go northeast 29 miles to Plush and take the road to the refuge headquarters. The ranger station (541/947-3334) has information.

In summer, hundreds of these agile tan-and-white animals occasionally gather at sunset along the dirt road south of the refuge. The refuge is also home to bighorn sheep, mule deer, 213 species of birds, and many small mammals. A dunk in the hot springs a short distance from the station is highly recommended to loosen the stiffness from bouncing down the dirt roads to get here. A campground is near the hot springs. The refuge is also a popular place for rockhounds searching for agates, fire opals, crystals, and sunstones. Check with the chamber of commerce (126 N. E St., Lakeview 97630, 541/947-6040, www.lake-countychamber.org) or the ranger at Hart Mountain for more information.

Despite the name of the preserve, you won't find any antelope here. In fact, there are no wild antelope in North America—only pronghorn. Because these animals shed the outer sheaths of their horns each year, they differ from their Asian and African counterparts, which have permanent horns. Male pronghorn have prongs, protrusions extending from their sheaths, to further distinguish them from antelope. The lingering misnomer was bestowed on these Oregon animals by Lewis and Clark. At any rate, many scientists believe that pronghorn could be the world's fastest land mammals over a long distance, barely edging out the cheetah on distances exceeding 1,000 yards. It's said they can cruise at more than 35 miles per hour, maintain 60 mph for half a mile, and reach 70 mph in short bursts.

Fossil Lake

Fossil Lake is two miles east of Christmas Valley (www.christmasvalley.org). During wetter times thousands of years ago, this was a watering hole for camels, enormous beavers, flamingos, mammoths,

KAREN McKINLEY

pronghorn

and miniature horses. It was once part of a much larger body of water in the Fort Rock basin that was perhaps 40 miles wide and 200 feet deep. The water and animals disappeared when the climate changed, but their fossilized remains are still unearthed by paleontologists on sanctioned digs. Be aware that it is illegal to remove *any* fossils from the beds without proper authorization. Unfortunately, unscrupulous profiteers have been looting these timeless treasures from the lake and other fossil-rich sites in eastern Oregon. Be sure to notify the authorities immediately if you see any suspicious characters pilfering these valuable relics.

SPORTS AND RECREATION

In Town

The **Lakeridge Golf Course** (ORE 140, Lakeview, 541/947-3855) has a nine-hole golf course with a pro shop, a putting green, lessons, and cart rentals. **Christmas Valley Golf Course** (Christmas Valley, 541/576-2333) is another nine-holer next to a 130-acre artificial lake. It's served by a pro shop in the nearby Christmas Valley Lodge. The restaurant is the only full-service dining room in these parts. Even if you're not a golfer, visit the lake at sunset to hear frogs croaking loud enough to be mistaken for a plane taking off at an airport runway.

On Friday, Saturday, and Sunday, the **Lakeview Showhouse** (22 F St., Lakeview, 541/947-2023) shows feature films for $5 adults, $3.50 seniors, discounts for kids.

The forest service maintains an informative website (www.fs.fed.us/r6/fremont/rog.htm) that lists a plethora of recreational opportunities in this area.

Fishing

With a name like Lake County, you'd be right to think that fishing holes are plentiful here. Known for excellent trout fishing in the mountainous

Thousands of years ago, this area was home to camels, flamingos, mammoths, miniature horses, and several-hundred-pound beavers. The animals disappeared when the climate changed, but their fossilized remains are still unearthed by paleontologists on sanctioned digs.

areas, the region is also gaining a reputation for bass, crappie, catfish, and other warm-water fishing. **Crump, Flagstaff, Anderson,** and **Campbell Lakes** in eastern Lake County provide the hottest action for crappie.

Friday Reservoir, located between Adel and Plush, is stocked with Lahontan cutthroat trout, and **Rock Creek,** which flows out of the Hart Mountain National Antelope Refuge, has red-banded trout. Off U.S. 395 in western Lake County, **Goose Lake,** half in California, half in Oregon, is also home to the native red-banded trout, but it's hard to fish for this unique subspecies in the shallow water. **Drews Reservoir,** 25 miles west of Lakeview on ORE 140, offers excellent fishing for channel catfish—some as large as 10 pounds. In the northern section of the county, **Thompson Valley Reservoir,** reached by driving south from Silver Lake on County Road 4–12, has yielded large rainbows. The **Chewaucan River,** which flows into Abert Lake, is heavily stocked with trout.

Skiing

Winter sports play a major role in Lake County's recreational schedule. **Warner Canyon Ski Area** (541/947-5001, www.fed.us/r6/fremont/rogs/warncan.htm), seven miles east of Lakeview on ORE 140, can accommodate almost any level of Alpine or Nordic skier, with 14 runs and three miles of cross-country trails. Thanks to a mile-high base elevation and the dry southeastern Oregon climate, excellent dry powder conditions are common. The area has a day lodge near the base of the hill with a snack bar that serves breakfast and lunch. The season may start as early as mid-December and run through the end of March. During this time the hill is open Thursday and Friday 1–4 P.M., Saturday and Sunday 10 A.M.–4 P.M. Lift tickets are just $20 a day. Rent skis at **M&D Ski** (118 N. L St., 541/947-4862).

Rockhounding

Rockhounding is a popular hobby in Lake County. Best known for its abundance of sunstones (also known as aventurine or Plush diamonds), the area has jasper, agates, petrified wood, fire opal, wonder stones, thunder eggs, and obsidian as well. To get to the sunstone-hunting grounds, go east on ORE 140 to the Plush junction and turn north. Another spot for rockhounding can be reached by taking Hogback Road just north of the upper section of the Abert Rim; the Hogback junction is about 50 miles north of Lakeview on U.S. 395. For more information visit the **High Desert Rock Shop** (244 N. M St., Lakeview).

Camping

Junipers Reservoir RV Resort (541/947-2050, www.junipersrv.com) is 10 miles west of Lakeview on ORE 140. The charge is $25. This private reservoir with campgrounds is situated on a working cattle ranch that's open May 1–Oct. 15, depending on the weather. Designated as one of six private wildlife-viewing areas in the state, a visit to this spread offers an excellent chance to view longhorn cattle, deer, eagles, ospreys, and coyotes.

Goose Lake Campground is a large facility 15 miles south of Lakeview on U.S. 395. The campground has tent sites, RV hookups, and a boat launch on the shore of the huge lake. The charge is $25. **Corral Creek Campground** is a good headquarters for an exploration of the Gearhart Mountain Wilderness, an area of high meadows, cliffs, and worn-down volcanoes. To get to the campsite turn off ORE 140 at Quartz Mountain, 24 miles west of Lakeview, and drive north on Forest Service Road 3600. **Wildlife Refuge Campground** is on the Ana River just north of Summer Lake on ORE 31. Bird-watchers like to camp here and walk the dikes of Summer Lake looking for waterfowl and swamp mammals.

ENTERTAINMENT AND EVENTS

Many of the earliest pioneers in Lake County were Irish immigrants who worked as sheep-herders, some of whom turned to cattle ranching. To celebrate St. Patrick's Day, the Lakeview Chamber holds **Irish Days** with a parade led by the Grand Leprechaun, usually the town's oldest Irishman. Other popular events are the potato stick races and the cow-chip fling.

The **Christmas Valley Rodeo** runs the last weekend in May. Local cowboys and cowgirls compete in bareback riding, roping, and races. The following weekend is the **Silver Lake Rodeo** with more of the same. During the last weekend in June, the **Lake County Junior Rodeo** is held at the Lake County Fairgrounds in Lakeview. Finally, the fall **Lake County Round-Up** and fair held Labor Day weekend at the county fairgrounds includes a carnival, parade, a barbecue, a buckaroo breakfast, and the annual rodeo. Call the Christmas Valley Chamber (541/576-2166) for more information.

The U.S. Hang-gliding National Championships were held in Lakeview in 1993. Lakeview's **hang-gliding festival** takes place in July each year, the area's biggest event, with recreational pilots, barbecues, fireworks, and biking and running races.

The community of Paisley prides itself on having some of the largest mosquitoes in the state. To raise funds for controlling these pests, the town stages the **Mosquito Festival** in late July. The action includes a parade, a raft race, a turkey shoot, and the crowning of Ms. Quito. You'll also enjoy the relief provided by Paisley's oasis of greenery in the midst of the surrounding sagebrush desert.

Around Christmastime people flock to Christmas Valley's little blue post office to request a timely postal cancellation (done by hand with large franking symbols). Collectors send a letter addressed to themselves with a request for a December 24 or 25 cancellation. Such noel niceties can be obtained by addressing an envelope to Christmas Valley 97641 and enclosing instructions.

In case you're interested, this nondescript alfalfa-farming town got its picturesque name by accident. Southeast of here, John C. Frémont spent Christmas at a lake during one of his mid-19th-century treks and called it Christmas Lake.

A turn-of-the-century mapmaker mistakenly affixed this name to a lake adjacent to the present-day town site, which also took on the merry moniker.

PRACTICALITIES
Accommodations

In Christmas Valley, you'll see the office of the **Desert Inn** (541/576-2262) in a large double-wide structure. Check out the owner's rock collection, then rent a room for $30. Not far away in the same price range is **Lakeside Terrace Motel** (541/576-2309) with a large artificial lake in back and an on-site restaurant; rooms for $34. For something a bit homier on a 100-acre range, head 12 miles east of Christmas Valley to the **Outback B&B** (92946 Christmas Valley Hwy., 541/420-5229) with two rooms from which to choose. You can board your pooch at the kennel here. A full country breakfast is included in the $65 rate.

In Lakeview, the **Best Western Skyline Motor Lodge** (414 N. G St., 541/947-2194) has a pool and hot tub as well as spacious, well-appointed rooms. Rates run $48–68. Just north of Lakeview, **Hunter's Hot Springs Resort** (U.S. 395, 541/947-4282) has basic motel rooms for $55–65 as well as an RV park and restaurant (see "Food," immediately following).

Food

Like most parts of the sagebrush side of Oregon, Lake County isn't known for its cuisine. Be prepared for basic American food with an emphasis on hearty, home-cooked meals. Here's a list of eateries that will refuel your tank.

The **Christmas Valley Lodge** (Christmas Valley Road, 541/576-2333) is connected to Lakeside Terrace Motel (see "Accommodations," immediately preceding) by the town's golf course. It is the only restaurant in town. Denver omelettes for breakfast and steak for dinner ($8–15) typify the fare.

In Lakeview, the **Eagles Nest** (117 N. E St., 541/947-4824) serves a varied menu in a warm, welcoming atmosphere. The reasonably priced prime rib here is testimony to the quality of Oregon beef. Open daily. **Plush West** (9 N. F St., 541/947-2353) features steak, lamb, and seafood ($12–20). It's open for dinner only, from 4 P.M. Wed.–Saturday. **Safeway** (244 N. F St., 541/947-2324) is a good place to stock up on groceries prior to heading out for your adventure.

Just north of Lakeview, **Geyser Grill** at Hunter's Hot Springs Resort (U.S. 395) offers hearty American fare, with dinner entrées $8–15. Open daily.

Transportation

Buses depart twice a day from the **Red Ball Stage Lines Depot** (619 Center St., Lakeview, 541/884-6460) for Klamath Falls and other connecting points. The depot is open 9–11 A.M. for the 9:15 departure (10 A.M. on Saturday), and 4:15–5:15 P.M. for the 5:05 departure. Public **airports** are located in Lakeview, Paisley, Christmas Valley, and Alkali Lake, with private and government strips at Silver Lake, Fort Rock, Adel, and Wagontire. There are no regular commercial flights, but **Goose Lake Aviation** (541/947-4222 or 541/947-3592) provides air-taxi service and an air ambulance at the Lakeview field.

Harney County

For travelers to Harney County, the towns of Burns, Hines, and a few wide spots along U.S. 20 hold few points of interest—just places to refuel your rig and yourself. But off the main thoroughfares traversing the southeastern portion of the state are recreational retreats worthy of closer investigation. The Malheur Wildlife Refuge is nationally recognized as one of the best birdwatching sites in the country; the Steens Mountain Recreation Area is also famous for its stunning scenery; and the Ochoco and Malheur National Forests are renowned for their fishing, boating, camping, backpacking, and hiking opportunities.

HISTORY

Oregon's high desert county was first inhabited by the Bannock, Northern Paiute, and Shoshone tribes. When French-Canadian trappers arrived in the area, they were promptly ripped off by the natives. After losing horses and supplies, the trappers named the nearby river "Malheur" ("Unhappiness" or "Misfortune"). The surrounding region's alkali flats and parched hills also suggest this moniker.

Explorer Peter Skene Ogden scouted the area in 1826 while leading a fur brigade for the Hudson's Bay Company. He wasn't impressed with the region as a place for settlers, but the Idaho gold rush of 1860 brought prospectors through the area on their way to the gold fields, and they told stories of rich grasslands, plentiful water, and broad forests.

Pony soldiers under the command of General William Harney explored the region in 1848 and again in 1858, opening up southeastern Oregon to settlement. The most noted military adventure was the construction of a wagon road built between Harney County and Eugene. The leader of this work party, Enoch Steen, gave his name to Steens Mountain.

In 1878, 2,000 Bannocks, fed up with their loss of territory and poor treatment, took to the warpath. Troops from forts all over the West were sent to fight the natives in a war that dragged on until 1880.

The town of **Burns,** named after the Scottish poet Robert Burns, was founded on January 22, 1884. By 1889 it had a population of 250, which has since grown to over 3,000. A significant boost to the town's economy came in 1924 when a rail line reached Burns. Its sister city, **Hines,** was incorporated in 1930. Named after Chicago lumberman Edward Hines, this town of 1,400 residents is primarily a bedroom community for Burns.

SIGHTS AND RECREATION

Sagehen Hill Nature Trail

The Sagehen Hill Nature Trail is 16 miles west of Burns at the Sagehen rest stop on U.S. 20. This half-mile nature trail has 11 stations on a route that takes you around Sagehen Hill through sagebrush, bitterbrush, and western juniper. Other plants found along the way include lupine, larkspur, owl clover, and yellowbell. The lucky visitor in early May might also catch the sage grouse courtship ritual. The male will display his plumage and make clucking noises to attract the attention of the females. The puffed-up necks and bobbing heads of these feathered philanderers are something to see. If these creatures are not visible, the views of Steens Mountain (elevation 9,733 feet) to the southeast will make the hike worthwhile.

Harney County Museum

The Harney County Museum (18 W. D St., Burns 97720, 541/573-5618, www.burnsmuseum.com) started its career as a brewery and then became a laundry and a wrecking yard. Local pioneer families have donated quilts, furniture, a complete kitchen, a wagon shed, and machinery to the museum. Of special interest are artifacts from Pete French's ranch. The museum is open April–Sept., Tues.–Sat. 9 A.M.–5 P.M. Admission is $4 adults, $6 for a family, and $1 for children.

THE CATTLE KINGS OF EASTERN OREGON

Cattle barons, those early-day entrepreneurs who ran the huge livestock operations of the 19th century, have typically been portrayed as imperious characters in old Westerns. A look at the lives of three eastern Oregon cattle kings—John Devine, Pete French, and Bill Brown—paints a fuller picture.

John Devine came to Oregon in 1868 and started snapping up land by the simple method of squatting on it. He grabbed U.S. government land, tribal territory, and acreage ostensibly owned by road companies, which he quickly covered with vast herds of cattle. Part of his holding included the Alvord and the Whitehorse Ranches on the east side of the Steens. After the devastating winter of 1889–1890, during which he lost 75 percent of his stock, Devine's fortunes plummeted. He was bought out by another cattle baron, Henry Miller, and held on to only the Whitehorse Ranch until his death in 1901 at the age of 62.

Another rancher whose fate is still debated in this arid country is Pete French, an arrogant, forceful man with a bushy mustache that gave him the appearance of Wyatt Earp. Born in Red Bluff, California, in 1849, French moved to Oregon in 1873 to manage the stock ranch of Dr. Hugh Glenn in the Donner and Blitzen Valley. French married the boss's daughter, and after Glenn was murdered by his bookkeeper, French built the French-Glenn Livestock Company into one of the largest spreads in the West. At its peak, the ranch had 100,000 acres on which roamed 30,000 head of cattle and 3,000 horses. Five hundred miles of barbed wire defined this empire stretching from the Donner and Blitzen River to Harney Lake.

While he was developing the P Ranch, French earned the enmity of hundreds of local homesteaders, many of whom were evicted from their squatters' shacks. One of his enemies, homesteader Ed Oliver, rode up to French one day and shot him dead. Oliver was arrested but later acquitted by a jury of settlers.

Bill Brown was a more popular and certainly more eccentric rancher than Pete French. His Gap Ranch, headquartered a few miles east of Hampton, halfway between Brothers and Riley, was at its largest 38,000 acres spread throughout four counties. Bill Brown didn't start out rich and he died penniless. In between he earned and lost a number of fortunes.

His first enterprise was running a flock of 400 sheep. During that era he was so hard up he had only one sock, which he switched from one foot to the other every day. Brown added horses to his holdings with such zeal that by World War I he owned 25,000 head, many of which he sold to the U.S. Cavalry. After the war, and with the advent of mass production of automobiles, Brown lost his shirt and his land.

Many stories have been told about this balding six-footer with a square jaw and a mild manner. He never cussed, drank, or gambled, unless his faith in his store customers could be considered gambling. The operator of a shop, Brown was seldom behind the counter, relying instead on the honesty of his customers, who were asked to toss their cash in a cigar box. Another quirk was Brown's legendary habit of writing checks on anything available, from tomato-can labels to wooden slats. Local bankers had no problem cashing the "checks" for Brown's hired help or suppliers.

Diamond Craters

Diamond Craters have been described by scientists as the most diverse basaltic volcanic features in the United States. To tour these unique formations, drive 55 miles south of Burns on ORE 205 until you reach the Diamond junction. Turn left and begin a 40-mile route ending at New Princeton on ORE 78. On the way you'll see why this area is called "Oregon's Geologic Gem."

There are craters, domes, lava flows, and pits that give an outstanding visual lesson on volcanism. To aid your self-guided tour, pick up the "Diamond Craters" brochure at the BLM office in Hines.

Round Barn

While on the road to New Princeton, stop at the Round Barn, a historic structure built by rancher Pete French to break his saddle horses. Located 20 miles northeast of Diamond, the barn is 100 feet in diameter with a 60-foot circular lava-rock corral inside. Twelve tall juniper poles support a roof covered with 50,000 shingles. Hundreds of cowpokes have carved their initials in the posts of this famous corral.

Malheur National Wildlife Refuge

Malheur and Harney Lakes, fed by the mountain snow runoff filling the Blitzen and Silvies Rivers, have been major avian nesting and migration stopovers since prehistoric times. The contrast between the stark, dry basin land, with its red sandstone monoliths and mesas, and the lush green marshes is startling. These vast marshes (the longest freshwater marsh in the western United States), meadows, and riparian areas surrounded by the eastern Oregon desert attract thousands of birds and hundreds of bird-watchers. The refuge is dominated by three fluctuating lakes—Malheur, Mud, and Harney. These are nourished by a scant eight inches of rain a year. Log on to www.r1.fws.gov/malheur/recreation for more information.

Refuge officials say that 250 species have been counted within its boundaries. Prime bird-watching times are spring and fall. Late spring is an especially good time to visit, before summer's scorching heat and mosquito invasion. In the spring, the flocks come from the Great Basin south of the refuge. They generally nest for several months here and then head north to Canada. In March, the first Malheur arrivals include Canada and snow geese, and in the vast Malheur Marsh, swans, mallards, and other ducks. Also look for sandhill cranes in the wet meadows. Great horned owls and golden eagles are two other early arrivals. Shorebirds are followed by warblers, sparrows, and other songbirds in spring. Red-tailed hawks can be seen swooping over the sage-covered prairies throughout spring, summer, and fall. In the late spring, ponds and canals at Malheur occasionally host the trumpeter swan, a majestic bird with a seven-foot wingspan. This is one of the few places where you can observe this endangered species nesting. Flocks of pelicans

are a summertime spectacle worth catching. See them before they head south to Mexico in the fall.

August–October is another prime time, when birders might see a hundred species. At this time, lucky visitors might see the magnificent snow goose. Another fall arrival is the wood thrush, graced with one of the most beautiful songs in the bird kingdom. Another September–October highlight is the concentration of greater sandhill cranes, Canada geese, and mallard ducks foraging on Blitzen Valley grain fields. The first two weeks of September are particularly nice because hunting season has yet to begin and the aspens have turned golden.

Beyond the barrackslike Malheur Field Station, where students study desert ecology and wildlife, is a gravel road. If you follow the signs you'll come to the refuge headquarters in a grove of cottonwoods looking out over the huge expanse of Malheur Lake. Here you can pick up maps for the self-guided auto tour of the refuge. A short distance downhill is a small museum where more than 250 bird specimens are beautifully arrayed. Also of interest is the charming park on the edge of the lake.

While the absolute numbers of birds at Malheur are not as great as they are at the Klamath Lakes or along the Oregon coast, the variety here is unsurpassed anywhere in the area. Among birders, however, it is the "accidental list" of 55 infrequently sighted species that makes this preserve special. Many of these "exotics" are sighted nowhere else in the region. A total of 312 different species has been sighted here over the last century.

In the late 1800s, settlers enjoyed unrestricted hunting here, and at the turn of the century hunters killed thousands of swans, egrets, herons, and grebes for feathers for the millinery trade. In 1908, President Theodore Roosevelt put a stop to the slaughter by protecting the area as a bird sanctuary. The Blitzen Valley and P Ranch were added to the refuge in 1935. Today, 185,000 acres are protected.

To get to the refuge drive 25 miles south from Burns on ORE 205 and then nine miles east on the county road to Princeton. The last six miles to the refuge headquarters are gravel surfaced. For general information on Malheur, call 541/493-2612. For details and reservations on dorm rooms or trailers within the refuge, contact the Malheur Field Station (HC 72, P.O. Box 260, Princeton 97721, 541/493-2629, www.malhearfieldstation.org). These Spartan accommodations range $18–60. You'll likely share a restroom, and it's necessary to bring your own bedding and a towel. Cafeteria-style meals are available here. Reserve a room in advance to avoid driving 35 miles to Burns for bed and board.

Frenchglen

Named for famous rancher Pete French and his wealthy father-in-law, Dr. Hugh Glenn, the town of Frenchglen was originally known as P Station and was part of the nearby P Ranch. Today, this historic community with its hotel, store, corral, and post office remains essentially the same as it was 50 years ago. To get here, drive about 60 miles south on ORE 205 from Burns.

Steens Mountain

Steens Mountain, named after Major Enoch Steen, an Army officer assigned the task of building a military road through Harney County, is one of the great scenic wonders of Oregon. A 30-mile fault block, the mountain rises straight up from the Alvord Desert to a row of glacial peaks. On the western side, huge gorges carved out by glaciers a million years ago descend to a gentle slope drained by the Donner and Blitzen River, which flows into Malheur Lake.

Steens Mountain has five vegetation zones ranging from tall sage to alpine tundra. The best way to see the transition is to drive the **Steens Mountain Byway** out of Frenchglen to the top of Steens Mountain. This is the highest road in Oregon, rising 9,000 feet in elevation. The first 15 miles of the road are gravel and the last nine miles are dirt. The latter portion is not recommended for low-slung passenger cars.

Starting and ending at Frenchglen, the route up Steens Mountain, sans significant tree cover save for some beautiful aspens, evokes Alaskan

COURTESY OF OREGON TOURISM COMMISSION

Steens Mountain

alpine tundra. Multicolored low-to-the-ground wildflowers and a vast spaciousness give the feeling of being on top of the world. This impression is accentuated by standing in snow while you look 5,000 feet straight down into the sunscorched Alvord Desert, which records just seven inches of rain annually. Steens Mountain is the highest point in the Great Basin. Below, the Alvord Desert is the "truest" desert landform in Oregon.

The first four miles of the trek lead across the Malheur Wildlife Refuge and up to the foothills of Steens Mountain. **Page Springs,** the first campground on the route, is a popular spot offering campsites along the bank of the Donner and Blitzen River. Approximately 13 miles beyond Page Springs is **Lily Lake,** a good place for a picnic. This shallow lake has an abundance of water lilies, frogs, songbirds, and waterfowl.

After Lily Lake, you really start to climb up the mountain to **Fish Lake, Jackman Park** (both with campsites), and viewpoints of Kiger Gorge and the East Rim. **Kiger Gorge** is a spectacular example of a wide, U-shaped path left by a glacier. Blanketed in meadow grasses, quaking aspen, cottonwood, and mountain mahogany at lower elevations, tiny tundra-like flowers proliferate on the 8,000-foot viewpoint. For more information on camping or recreation on these lands, contact the BLM (541/573-4400, www.or.blm.gov/Burns) or log on to www.harneycounty.com/camping.

The **East Rim** is a dramatic example of earth-shifting in prehistoric epochs. The lava layers that cap the mountain are thousands of feet thick, formed 15 million years ago when lava erupted from cracks in the ground. Several million years later, the Steens Mountain fault block began to lift along a fault below the east rim. The fault block tilted to the west, forming the gentler slope that stretches to the Malheur Lake Basin. At the summit (9,670 feet) you can see the corners of four states on a clear day—California, Nevada, Oregon, and Idaho.

A good time to visit is August–mid-September—Indian summer. Nights are cold but daytime temperatures are more pleasant than those of summertime scorchers. Later in the fall, red bushes and yellow aspens attract photographers. Some of the aspens are located at Whorehouse Meadow and are indirectly responsible for its name. Lonely shepherds would scratch love notes and erotica in the tree bark, pining away for a visit from the horse-drawn bordellos that serviced these parts. Wildlife-viewing highlights include bighorn sheep, seen around the East Rim viewpoint in summer; hummingbirds, often observed at high elevations; and hawks, which can be spotted anywhere, anytime here, especially from the ridge above Fish Lake.

The area has off-highway vehicle restrictions to protect the environment. Five gates controlling access to the Steens are located at various elevations and are opened as road and weather conditions permit. Normally, the Steens Byway is not open until mid- to late July and is closed by snow in October or November. Gas is available only in Burns, Frenchglen, and Fields. Take reasonable precautions when driving the loop: sudden storms, lightning, flash floods, and extreme road conditions can be hazardous to travelers. The loop returns to ORE 205 about 10 miles south of Frenchglen.

Catlow Valley/Alvord Desert Loop

Another equally ambitious loop is the drive around Steens Mountain along the Catlow Rim and Alvord Desert and back to Burns. Starting at Burns, head south on ORE 205 through the Malheur Wildlife Refuge, past Frenchglen, and up over the divide into the Catlow Valley, which was once a massive inland lake. A side trip to the ghost town of **Blitzen** starts at a right turn (to the west) four miles south of the Steens Mountain Byway.

This eight-mile jaunt will take you to the ruins of a little town (a half dozen dilapidated buildings) founded in the late 1800s. Blitzen was named after the Donner and Blitzen River, which flows nearby. *Donner und Blitzen* is German for "thunder and lightning," the label given this stream by Captain George Curry, who tried to cross it during a fierce thunderstorm.

The next point of interest on the loop is

Roaring Springs Ranch, tucked under the west rim of Steens Mountain. Originally homesteaded by Tom Wall, the ranch was sold to Pete French and subsequently developed into the largest cattle operation in the county. The dramatic backdrop, well-kept classic ranch building, and the surrounding meadows make Roaring Springs Ranch an ideal Western movie set.

After driving 33 miles through the Catlow Valley you'll come to **Fields,** the largest community on the east side of Steens. Homesteaded by Charles Field, the town was established as a supply station in 1881. Fields now has a gas station, store, café, and motel. The café next to the tiny motel and store here serves great milkshakes. A root beer shake made with hard ice cream flavored with bananas or Oreos tastes great on a hot summer day. Fields' original stone cabin is across the road.

From Fields head north into the Alvord Desert, site of the dry Alvord Lake and the Alvord Ranch. Along the way you'll pass through **Andrews,** a small community at the edge of the alkali flats. Another stop worthy of attention, particularly if you're in need of revitalization after your travels, is **Alvord Hot Springs,** a few miles north of Andrews. This rustic spa is recognizable by its corrugated-steel shack on the east side of the road. Two pools of hot mineral water piped in from spring runoff will cook your bones and soak away your aches and pains at no charge.

The road continues until it connects with ORE 78, which leads back to Burns or south to Burns Junction. The panorama of the east side of Steens Mountain alone is worthy of a trip, but views of the Pueblo Mountains to the south and the Great Basin country to the east are also impressive.

Mickey Hot Springs

A little six- to eight-foot jet of 200°F water on the north end of an ancient dry lake bed is often visible in the spring in the Alvord Desert. Consult the BLM in Hines (541/573-4400, www.or.blm.gov) for directions. This site east of the Steens is fenced to protect the fragile "plumbing system" of the only counterpart to Old Perpetual, a geyser near Lakeview. Also within the 20-acre complex are hot pools, steam vents, and the only mud pot in Oregon.

Oard's Free Museum

Oard's Free Museum (541/493-2535) is located 23 miles east of Burns on U.S. 20. The museum has antique guns, clocks, barbed wire, spinning wheels, and dolls as well as native artifacts, including a Yakima chief's regalia. Open daily 7 A.M.–8 P.M.

Paiute Reservation

If you want a livelier encounter with Native American culture, visit the Burns Paiute Reservation. Contact the tribal headquarters first for information (HC-71, 100 Pa' Si' Go St., Burns 97720, 541/573-2088).

Golf

Harney County's "Oasis in the Desert" is the nine-hole **Valley Golf Club** (345 Burns–Hines Hwy., Burns 97720, 541/573-6251). This challenging course is open to the public, but clubhouse facilities are reserved for members and guests.

the Alvord Desert, seen from Steens Mountain

Rockhounding

Harney County is rockhound country. Each year, thousands of enthusiasts flock to this far-flung corner of the state to collect fossils, agates, jasper, obsidian, and thunder eggs. The **Stinking Water Mountains,** 30 miles east of Burns, are a good source of gemstones and petrified wood. Thunder eggs can be dug up four miles south of Oard's Museum on U.S. 20 after getting permission from the Don Robbins family. Contact them through the museum (541/493-2535).

Warm Springs Reservoir, just east of the Stinking Water Mountains, is popular with agate hunters. **Charlie Creek** and **Radar,** west and north of Burns, respectively, produce black, banded, and brown obsidians. Be sure to collect only your limit—be a rockhound, not a rockhog. Also keep in mind that it is illegal to take arrowheads and other artifacts from public lands.

Fishing

Rainbow and red-banded trout occur naturally in most streams in this area, and many lakes and rivers are also stocked. Good fishing is available on the Donner and Blitzen and Malheur Rivers, Emigrant Creek, Chickahominy Reservoir, Delintment Lake, and Yellowjacket Lake. Krumbo Reservoir on the Malheur Wildlife Refuge is a good bet for trout or largemouth bass.

Camping

There are three high-elevation campgrounds along the Steens Mountain Loop Road. No reservations are accepted and sites are $4 per vehicle per night. For more info, contact the BLM (HC74-12533, U.S. 20 W., Burns 97738, 541/573-4400, www.or.blm.gov). As for summertime Steens weather, the 100°F temperatures in the high desert give way to 50–80°F daytime temperatures atop the mountain. Nonetheless, be aware that the summit can see severe thunderstorms and lightning, and at night, the mercury can drop below freezing, even on days with high noontime temperatures.

Page Springs, four miles southeast of Frenchglen, is open all year. Close to the Malheur Wildlife Refuge, the campground is a good head-quarters for bird-watching, fishing, hiking, and sightseeing. **Fish Lake** is 17 miles east of Frenchglen and open July 1–Nov. 15. The namesake lake is stocked with eastern brook, cutthroat, and rainbow trout. Aspens surround the campsites, which have toilets, well water, and firepits; firewood is included in the campsite fee. Climb up on the ridge above the canpground to watch hawks here. **Jackman Park,** three miles east of Fish Lake, is particularly popular with backpackers, who use it as a takeoff point. It has six sites with toilets and potable water.

A couple of campgrounds to the north of Burns up in the Malheur National Forest are **Yellowjacket** and **Idlewild.** Yellowjacket is on the shore of Yellowjacket Lake, 30 miles northwest of Burns on Forest Service Road 2170. Be sure to keep your food under wraps, especially meats, if you want to avoid being visited by the namesake hosts of the lake. Idlewild is 17 miles north of Burns on U.S. 395. There is no charge for overnighting in either spot, but don't expect amenities either.

Another alternative is the **Steens Mountain Resort** (North Loop Road, Frenchglen, 800/542-3765, www.steensmountainresort.com), located above Page Springs BLM campsites on the Blitzen River. Views of the surrounding gorges are spectacular and there are more amenities than at the BLM facility, including a small store, laundry, dumping facilities, and a public phone. Reservations are recommended and sites are $12–20 for the 99 sites accommodating RVs, trailers, and tents. There are also five cabins that rent for $60–75.

ENTERTAINMENT AND EVENTS

In mid-April, the **John Scharff Migratory Waterfowl Conference** (541/573-2636, www.harneycounty.com/birdfest.htm) held in Burns celebrates the spring return of waterbirds to the region with lectures, movies, slides, and guided bird-watching tours. Burns is also the site of **Obsidian Days,** in mid-June, and the **High Desert Hot Air Balloon Rally** at Burns Union High School the last weekend in June, when the sky is filled with lighter-than-air ships. First-run flicks can be enjoyed in Burns at **Desert Community Theatre** (68 Broadway, 541/573-4220).

Centered in Frenchglen, **Steens Mountain Days,** in early August, includes a 10-km run along the Steens rim, a sagebrush roping contest, a barbecue, a street dance, and a beer garden.

Harney County, once the trapping territory of mountain men like Peter Skene Ogden and Joe Meek, has two blackpowder clubs that relive those days with a yearly **Blackpowder Shoot and Rendezvous** (541/573-2636), held in September. The **Steens Mountain Men** hold their shoot in September and the **Harney Free Trappers** hold theirs in June. These rendezvous attract colorful gatherings of folks in buckskin, talkin', shootin', lyin', and renewing friendships from "afore last winter."

During the first week of September, Burns hosts the **Harney County Fair** (541/573-6166) an old-fashioned county fair featuring a rodeo, 4-H competitions, and exhibits on canning, wine- and beer-making, and leatherworking. At 4,140 feet in elevation, Burns is sometimes dusted with snow during the fair.

PRACTICALITIES

Accommodations

If you're seeking shelter in Burns, you'll find that the properties here are generally inexpensive, have air-conditioning to help you beat the heat, and allow you to bring the family dog along, too.

The **Silver Spur Motel** (789 N. Broadway, Burns 97720, 541/573-2077 or 800/400-2077) offers nonsmoking rooms, a fitness room, a complimentary continental breakfast, and rates of $60–90. You get treated like a king at the **Best Inn** (999 Oregon Ave., Burns 97720, 541/573-1700, www.bestinn.com). Enjoy the tennis courts, two swimming pools, and a decent restaurant (for Burns) without paying a king's ransom. Rates range $55–65. The **Days Inn Ponderosa Motel** (977 W. Monroe, Burns 97720, 541/573-2047 or 800/303-2047) features a swimming pool, nonsmoking rooms, and large, spacious rooms for $50–65.

In Frenchglen, the **Frenchglen Hotel** (c/o John Ross, 39184 Hwy. 205, Frenchglen 97736, 541/493-2825), 60 miles south of Burns on ORE 205, is an excellent place to stay while visiting Steens Mountain or Malheur Wildlife Refuge. Built in 1914 as a stage stopover, the hotel has eight smallish rooms (with shared bath down the hall) for $63–65 and employs ranch cooks who are ready to fix you a family-style breakfast, lunch, or dinner. Breakfast here ($4–8) is a nice prelude to driving to the top of Steens Mountain. The evening repast runs $10–20, and you must be there at 6:30 P.M. Their Better Than Sex chocolate cake is aptly named. Watching thunderstorms sweep across Steens Mountain from the hotel's screened-in porch can provide after-dinner entertainment. The hotel's season runs March–November.

Next door at Frenchglen Mercantile groceries, Southwest Native American art, books, and a mélange of other items are offered. The attached Buckaroo Room features good moderately priced meals (such as Basque chicken) and microbrews. A post office and a BLM information kiosk are also in the Frenchglen complex.

Food

The culinary highlight of Burns is coffee in the deli at the **Safeway** on Monroe Street. In other words, B.Y.O. food here. A little west of Burns, a sign in Hines proclaims "Worst Foods of The World-70's Prices." To be blunt, we think it's worth waiting till you get to Frenchglen to eat. The Frenchglen Hotel and the Buckaroo Room in back of the Frenchglen Mercantile both serve food that's tasty and affordable.

Information and Services

For general information on the region, contact the **Harney County Chamber of Commerce** (18 W. D St., Burns 97720, 541/573-2636). For information on recreation, stop by the **Bureau of Land Management** office (12533 U.S. 20 W., Hines 97738, 541/573-5241). The **Emigrant Creek Ranger District** is also nearby (265 U.S. 20, Hines 97738, 541/573-4300).

The Cascades

The Cascades comprise one of the most magnificent natural playgrounds in the world. This collage of green forest and black basalt outcroppings is topped by extinct volcano cones covered with snow. Plenty of lakes, rivers, and waterfalls provide a pleasing contrast to the earth tones here.

In addition, six national forests, six federal wilderness areas, and Oregon's only national park, Crater Lake, are found in the Oregon Cascades. Add to this list the bevy of luxury resorts, nine developed ski areas, hundreds of miles of cross-country skiing and snowmobiling trails, as well as numerous waterways teeming with fish, and you have all the accoutrements for roughing it in style.

THE LAND

What fault scarps are to the California landscape, lava fields and snowcapped volcano cones are to Oregon. While remnants of the state's not-so-distant volcanic past abound, the most impressive and dramatic examples are found in the High Cascades, a chain of icy peaks stretching from Northern California to British Columbia.

hiking on Mount Hood

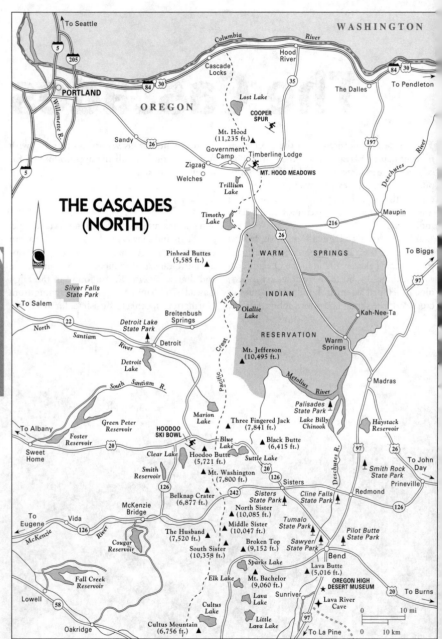

THE CASCADES (NORTH)

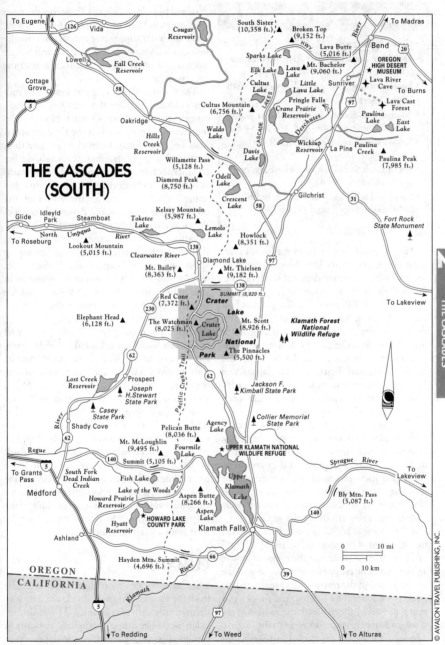

THE CASCADES (SOUTH)

To Eugene
126
Vida

Lowell

Fall Creek Reservoir

Cottage Grove

5

58

Oakridge

Cougar Reservoir

South Sister (10,358 ft.)

Broken Top (9,152 ft.)

Sparks Lake

Elk Lake

Lava Lake

Mt. Bachelor (9,060 ft.)

Little Lava Lake

Cultus Lake

Lava Butte (5,016 ft.)

Bend

20

To Madras

OREGON HIGH DESERT MUSEUM

Sunriver

Lava River Cave

To Burns

Lava Cast Forest

Cultus Mountain (6,756 ft.)

Waldo Lake

Crane Prairie Reservoir

97

Paulina Lake

East Lake

Hills Creek Reservoir

Willamette Pass (5,128 ft.)

Davis Lake

Wickiup Reservoir

La Pine

Paulina Creek

Paulina Peak (7,985 ft.)

Diamond Peak (8,750 ft.)

Odell Lake

Crescent Lake

Gilchrist

31

Glide
Idleyld Park
Steamboat

Kelsay Mountain (5,987 ft.)

Toketee Lake

Lemolo Lake

58

Fort Rock State Monument

North Umpqua River

To Roseburg

Lookout Mountain (5,015 ft.)

Clearwater River

Howlock (8,351 ft.)

Diamond Lake

97

138

Mt. Bailey (8,363 ft.)

Mt. Thielsen (9,182 ft.)

138

SUMMIT (5,920 ft.)

To Lakeview

230

Red Cone (7,372 ft.)

Crater

Lake

Elephant Head (6,128 ft.)

The Watchman (8,025 ft.)

Crater Lake

Mt. Scott (8,926 ft.)

Klamath Forest National Wildlife Refuge

62

National

Park

The Pinnacles (5,500 ft.)

Lost Creek Reservoir

Prospect

Joseph H. Stewart State Park

Casey State Park

62

Jackson F. Kimball State Park

Shady Cove

Pelican Butte (8,036 ft.)

Agency Lake

Collier Memorial State Park

Rogue

River

62

Mt. McLoughlin (9,495 ft.)

Fourmile Lake

UPPER KLAMATH NATIONAL WILDLIFE REFUGE

Sprague River

To Lakeview

To Grants Pass

5

140

Summit (5,105 ft.)

Fish Lake

Upper Klamath Lake

Medford

South Fork Dead Indian Creek

Lake of the Woods

Bly Mtn. Pass (5,087 ft.)

Howard Prairie Reservoir

Aspen Butte (8,266 ft.)

To Lakeview

HOWARD LAKE COUNTY PARK

Aspen Lake

140

Hyatt Reservoir

Klamath Falls

Ashland

Hayden Mtn. Summit (4,696 ft.)

66

River

39

OREGON

CALIFORNIA

Klamath

0   10 mi

0   10 km

5

97

To Redding

To Weed

To Alturas

MOON

THE CASCADES

CASCADES HIGHLIGHTS

The Oregon Cascades lie in the heart of this great range, and many have been named after former military commanders and heads of state. Given their stature and commanding presences, Mounts Hood, Jefferson, and Washington bear such distinction. Mount Hood (11,235 feet) is the tallest in the state, and many others top out at over 10,000 feet. Oregon's peaks are part of the great Ring of Fire which encircles the Pacific and includes Cotopaxi (Ecuador), Fuji (Japan), and Krakatoa (Indonesia), as well as the Cascades' notorious sister volcanoes, Lassen (California) and St. Helens (Washington).

They are linked by the theory of continental drift and plate tectonics. According to the theory, land masses force the ocean floor to slip underneath the continental plate. This creates heat-generating friction, causing rocks to melt. The resulting hot, soupy subterranean mass feeds inland volcanoes with magma and molten rock, 20-plus miles beneath the earth's surface.

When water is added to this hellish brew, the melting point of the rocks is lowered by 1,000°F or more. Water also acts as the major explosive agent of volcanic eruptions, primarily due to the steam created in the reaction. Eventually, the vapors can no longer be confined, and the plugged vent is pierced by the tremendous pressures of the steam and other gases produced from the magma. The lighter materials are ejected first—ash, cin-

ders, and pyroclastic debris. Oftentimes the earth spits up mouthfuls of its fiery interior as well. Once the water supply is spent, the lava usually becomes too viscous to flow, and the vent is once again sealed up by the cooling rock to start the process anew.

The Cascade Range is approximately 25 million years old, perhaps the youngest mountain range in the contiguous 48 states. However, geologists are uncertain when the Cascade volcanoes began to form. Guesstimates date their formation at several million years ago, during the Pleistocene epoch. And while the mountains appear to be dormant, keep in mind that nature's clock is unpredictable. Although the odds of Oregon becoming a Pompeii in our lifetime seem remote, the recent worldwide increase in earthquakes and volcanic eruptions suggests that the earth's internal burners are heating up again, and one of Oregon's slumbering giants may awaken soon. One group of geologists in late 1996 included Newberry Volcano outside Bend on their list of volcanoes in the continental United States most likely to erupt.

There are four major types of volcanoes, and all of them are found in the Cascades. Cinder cones, like Lava Butte and Black Butte, are formed by the explosive ejection of ash and particles of lava; they rarely exceed 1,200 feet in height. Shield volcanoes, like Mount Washington and Three Fingered Jack, form gently sloping domes that tend to be wider than they are high. Erosion is responsible for their present ragged-edged appearance. Plug-dome volcanoes, like Beacon Rock in the Columbia River Gorge, are the result of lava cooling until it's too thick to flow beyond the vent, creating a massive dome. Finally, there are composite volcanoes, making up the bulk of the majestic Cascades, which are formed layer by layer from ash, cinders, and lava.

CLIMATE

The Cascades, never more than 100 to 150 miles from the Pacific, effectively divide the state into dramatically different biomes. The moisture-laden westerlies dump prodigious amounts of precipitation on western Cascade slopes, up to

150 inches a year in some locations. Having thus purged themselves, the clouds then pass over the east side of the range, retaining what little moisture they have left. While the wet-siders are busy picking the moss out from between their toes and enduring the seemingly endless succession of rainy days, the dry-siders enjoy an average of 200 days of sunshine and about 12 inches of precipitation a year.

When it's not raining in the Cascades, it's usually snowing. Willamette Pass, for example, gets an average of 300 inches of snow a year. Crater Lake, often the coldest place in the Cascades, has recorded a chilly -21°F and averages 44 feet annual snowfall. Mount Hood has experienced over 100 feet of snowfall in a single year. The snow nourishes glaciers on the major peaks left over from the last ice age, 11,000 years ago, and feeds rivers, lakes, and streams with summer runoff as well. The snowpack also makes for some of the finest skiing in the Northwest.

Lest you think folks living on the western Cascades' flanks are confined to their log cabins all year by the lavish amounts of precipitation, the good news is that the weather is pleasant and dry most of the summer and into the early fall. Summer temperatures also usher in conditions favorable for a variety of outdoor pursuits. The flip side of the benign weather is that it brings higher numbers of visitors and dry, tinderbox conditions to the forest. Such dry conditions, along with frequent thunderstorms, makes forest fires a recurring seasonal menace.

FLORA AND FAUNA

Flora

The wet western slopes of the Cascades are dominated by the state tree, the Douglas fir. This towering evergreen requires abundant moisture and plenty of sunshine. The drier east side is composed mostly of ponderosa and lodgepole pine forests. The trees often meet with almost no transition zone, because the changes in rainfall are so marked on Cascade summits. However, in southern Oregon, where precipitation levels are generally lower, pine trees have stolen over the

ANN LONG LARSEN

western hemlock branch and cone

crest into the Klamath, Rogue, and Umpqua River basins.

Fires and humans can have more effect on the natural balance of a forest than fluctuations in weather. The changes in ground cover, shade, and soil make conditions more favorable for one species of tree over others. The aggressive Oregon oak is one such example, an easily established tree that can quickly challenge the kingdom of the Douglas fir. The oak's reign, however, is often cut short by the bitter cold, deep snow, and dry summers. Eventually, the Douglas fir is able to usurp the oak and regain its former rule over the forest.

The lodgepole pine is the primary benefactor in the southern Cascades, where frequent summer lightning storms take their annual toll on other species. The tough little cones of this tree endure fires and other adversities such as climatic extremes and barren soils, sprouting when favorable conditions return. The tree colonizes an area rapidly, growing up straight, true, and fine. As their name implies, these forthright trees were often used in the construction of lodges by Native Americans and pioneers. But the lodgepole pine usually meets the same fate as the Oregon oak, sooner or later choked out by the larger and longer-lived climax species like Douglas fir, cedar, balsam fir, Engelmann spruce, white pine, and hemlock.

And the lodgepole pine is not entirely free of competition for turf in the wake of a fire. Oftentimes low brush quickly moves in, firmly establishing its territorial dominance over young pine

THE CASCADES

seedlings. The tenacious manzanita, sticky laurel, and varieties of ceanothus, currants, and other miscellaneous shrubs generically labeled as buckbrush or snowbrush are the predominant examples of this type of chaparral.

Wild rhododendrons, dogwoods, and myriad wildflowers are the smile of spring in the Cascades as Old Man Winter releases his frozen grip upon the land. Summer foragers can find blackberries, huckleberries, and salmonberries, as well as many exotic types of mushrooms, in the damp recesses of the forest. Fall color from hardwoods is limited on Cascade slopes. Bright splashes of gold are provided by ash, aspen, cottonwood, tamarack, and bigleaf maple, but the heavy hitters are the brilliantly colored Douglas and vine maples. The vine maples in particular can make the otherwise lackluster fall foliage of the Cascades come alive with vivid reds and yellows.

Fauna

The Cascades are Oregon's forest primeval. The black bear, wolf, mountain lion, lynx, and bobcat compete with each other as well as with humans in the hunt for beavers, deer, elk (wapiti), and snowshoe hares. The smaller predators such as foxes, weasels, and martens prey upon chipmunks, squirrels, porcupines, and rats. Other commonly encountered forest creatures include the coyote, raccoon, and skunk. A half-dozen species of bats add to the diversity of mammals present in the Cascades. Indeed, this is where the wild things are.

The mountains are also home to a wide range of amphibians and reptiles. Generally speaking, most amphibians, such as frogs and salamanders, are found in cool and damp habitats west of the Cascades, whereas their cold-blooded reptilian fellow travelers (especially the lizard) prefer the warm and dry eastern flank. However, there always seem to be exceptions to every rule. Several of these critters are found on both sides of the Cascades, seemingly oblivious to the inherent climatic discrepancies.

The most widespread example of Cascade herpetology is the Pacific tree frog, *Hyla regilla.* It has been found on both sides of the range at elevations up to 7,000 feet. One secret to the frog's success is its versatility in using available breeding water for egg laying and larval development. While many mountain pools are strictly temporary or seasonal, they nonetheless allow enough time for the rapid growth and subsequent proliferation of the species. Also, the frogs are able to adapt to their terrestrial existence.

During the dry summer months, tree frogs absorb moisture from the night air through their skin. The moisture is collected in their bladder and then excreted through the skin during the day to keep the frog cool. Furthermore, the frogs seem to have enough sense to take refuge during extreme weather conditions in abandoned rodent burrows or rock or log crevices and sit it out.

A handful of other species of frogs and toads also hop around the Cascades. If you are camping near a Cascade lake in the summer, you may be surprised at how loudly the frogs croak at night. While this deep-throated chorus may leave some campers tossing and turning on their air mattresses, others will undoubtedly rest assured that the frogs are also busy consuming an inordinate number of insects, especially the pesky mosquito.

Visitors to the high country come upon many a giant Pacific salamander in mountain waterways. Common in high to low elevations, the timing of their metamorphosis into adults coincides with the seasonal fluctuations of their home stream. In addition to the Pacific giant, six other species of salamanders also call the Cascades home.

Reptiles prefer to slink around the warmer and drier east side. Over a dozen species of snakes and lizards are common to the Cascades. The most dangerous member of the family is *Crotalus viridis,* the western rattlesnake. Able to strike with blinding quickness and inject potentially lethal amounts of venom into its victim, this diamond-headed snake should be avoided at all costs. They like to sun themselves in warm, open spots and can be difficult to spot until you step on them, as they tend to coil up. Listen for the telltale rattle of the snake's tail and give them a wide berth. Baby rattlers, while smaller than the adults, are just as deadly, and more dangerous to wilderness adventurers because their rattles have not

WILLAMETTE NATIONAL FOREST

In the middle of Oregon's Cascade Range is the Willamette National Forest (Supervisor's Office, 211 E. 17th, Eugene 97440, 541/687-6521). Encompassing over 1.6 million acres of land stretching from the Mount Jefferson area east of Salem to the Calapooya Mountains northeast of Roseburg, this enormous forest is about the size of New Jersey.

Eight wilderness areas take up one-quarter of its land, and seven major Cascade peaks lie within its boundaries. In addition to three national recreation trails (Fall Creek, McKenzie River, and South Breitenbush Gorge) and the famed Pacific Crest Trail, over 1,300 miles of developed trails weave throughout Willamette National Forest.

Recreational opportunities abound. Two developed ski areas, Willamette Pass and Hoodoo Ski Bowl, serve schussers. Near each ski park are snowmobile areas, at Waldo Lake and Big Lake, respectively. Cross-country skiing is also available on many of the National Forest Service roads and trails.

Precipitation in the Willamette National Forest ranges 40–150 inches a year, providing the Willamette and McKenzie Rivers with excellent conditions for white-water rafting, drift-boat fishing, canoeing, and kayaking. Dozens of lakes and reservoirs round out the boating picture with sailing, rowing, and water-skiing. Anglers can try their luck catching dinner in one of the forest's many lakes, rivers, and streams. Big-game hunters can stalk black bear, Roosevelt elk, and deer (blacktailed deer west of the Cascades, mule deer east).

And yet this playground in the woods is also the workplace for a significant percentage of the population in the six counties that occupy the Willamette National Forest. The area is usually the top timber producer of all 159 national forests in the United States. Supplying approximately 8 percent of the total cut on National Forest Service lands in the country, the Willamette National Forest generates over $130 million annually in timber receipts. In addition to providing a steady source of employment for thousands of people, the timber industry provides revenues to local coffers to help fund public schools and roads.

Besides the Douglas fir, another Willamette Forest tree has become a source of revenue. The discovery that the Pacific yew tree yields taxol, effective against some kinds of cancer, has focused the eyes of the country here. Just look for a small twisted tree with sparse dark needles, moss-laden branches, peeling reddish bark, and sprouting burls in damp, shady areas. From April to the fall, a small red berrylike growth decorates yew branches. Birds and deer love them but they're poisonous to humans. The fact that the yew thrives in the shade of an old-growth forest has thrust this species into the middle of debates over the importance of preserving the biodiversity of this ecosystem.

Four major highways lead to the Willamette National Forest: ORE 58 (the Willamette Highway), ORE 126 (the McKenzie River Highway), U.S. 20 (the Cascadia Highway), and ORE 22 (the Santiam Highway). Whichever route you choose, William Cullen Bryant's words should apply: "Go forth, under the open sky, and list to Nature's teachings . . . the hills rock-ribbed and ancient as the sun—the vales stretching in pensive quietness between; the venerable woods— rivers that move in majesty, and the contiguous woods where rolls the Oregon."

THE CASCADES

yet developed enough to make any noise. And while you may be tempted to smash a rattlesnake to smithereens with a handy rock or tree branch, keep in mind that these reptiles effectively police the exponential growth of rodent populations.

The Cascades have over 70 species of birds, ranging from the great horned owl to the hummingbird. The successional stages of forest management in the mountains play an important role in the habitat and territory of many species. When an area is first logged over, the grasses and small shrubs that grow soon afterward are favorite haunts of the state bird, the western meadowlark. The mountain quail prefers thicker brush and small trees, the second phase of forest regeneration. The mixed deciduous woods that comprise the next stage make the ideal habitat for warblers. Finally, when the conifers have once again become the climax species of the forest, sharp-shinned hawks will move in. Thus, changes in habitats often increase certain species of birds at the expense of others.

SKIING THE CASCADES

The Cascades are a haven for winter sports that range from alpine and Nordic skiing to snowmobiling, snowboarding, and snowshoeing. There are nine developed ski areas and hundreds of miles of backcountry trails for these wintertime recreational pursuits. And while other ski areas in Colorado, Idaho, and California have been hard-hit by drought, Oregon is still blessed with an abundant annual snowpack that makes for nearly year-round skiing.

It is no wonder that ski pros like Billy Kidd and the famous Mahre brothers hold racing camps in Oregon, or that the Cascades are the official training ground for the U.S. Olympic Ski Team. While the Cascades lack the mystique of the Rockies, the greater challenge here is due to the variability of conditions. Other advantages of Oregon skiing include proximity to major cities and the longest season in the country.

Wherever you ski here, purchasing a **Sno-Park permit** is necessary. AAA and most ski shops near the slopes sell them for $15/season, $7/three days, $3/day. Mount Hood venues are served by equipment rental shops in Hood River and Sandy.

From Portland you can hear road- and ski-condition reports on KINK 102 FM at 6:30 A.M., 7:30 A.M., and 12:15 P.M. Mon.–Fri., Dec.–March. Log on to www.tripcheck.com or call 800/977-ODOT for road conditions and traveler advisory information.

Mount Hood

In addition to being the state's highest mountain, Mount Hood also boasts the most ski areas, five in all. A popular destination for families and beginners is **Cooper Spur** (P.O. Box 977, Hood River 97032, 541/352-7803, www.cooperspur.com). Located on the northeastern flank of the mountain, 24 miles south of Hood River on ORE 35, it occasionally offers protection from storms and prevailing westerlies, yet has more than enough snow for a good time and is af-

fordable. (Depending on weather conditions, it may not be open.) You can also find out about the Cloud Cap auto tour, an 11-mile scenic loop in the area. Nordic skiers appreciate the Tilly Jane Trail here.

Also on the east side is **Mount Hood Meadows** (P.O. Box 470, Mount Hood 97028, 503/287-5438, ext. 182, or 800/754-4663, www.ski-hood.com), the peak's largest ski area. Night skiing is also popular here. Ten miles from Government Camp on ORE 35, hundreds of acres of groomed slopes and seven double chairlifts, plus one triple and one quad, ensure plenty of room for all, though this place is so popular at times you might have to wait. The construction of a new four-seat chairlift should ease congestion on the two-mile-long access road from Oregon 35 to the ski area.

It's often sunny here on the east slope of the mountain when on the west side it's snowing and raining (call 503/227-SNOW for snow report and hours of operation). For mass transit from Portland, call **Bus/lift** (503/287-5438), or purchase tickets through G.I. Joe Ticketmaster (503/790-2787). Round-trip bus fare is $25; lift tickets and bus fare are $49. Massive construction projects over the past few years partially explain Oregon's highest-priced lift tickets here.

Across ORE 35 from the Mount Hood Mead-

Glaciers cover the upper reaches of Mount Hood year-round.

ows turnoff, Teacup Lake offers the best **cross-country skiing** in the state, maintained by a club that requests a small donation. Enhancing your enjoyment of these east-side-of-the-mountain ski venues are low-priced ski/lodging packages at nearby Hood River on I-84. On the east side of Mount Hood, you'll also find the best mountain biking in the state at Surveyor's Ridge trail (see "Hood River" in the Columbia River Gorge chapter). To get there take Forest Service Road 44 east off ORE 35.

The only noncommercial developed sliding hill in the Mount Hood National Forest is at Little John Sno-Park, located nine miles north of Mount Hood Meadows on ORE 35.

Mount Hood SkiBowl

SkiBowl (ORE 35, Government Camp 97028, 503/658-4385, www.skibowl.com) is only 53 miles away from metropolitan Portland on U.S. 26 and features the most extensive night skiing in the country. The upper bowl also has some of the most challenging skiing/snowboarding to be found on the mountain. Within the complex are summer venues for bungee jumping, an alpine slide, and mountain biking and much more.

Across from the Summit Ski Area parking lot (see "Timberline," immediately following), on the south side of U.S. 26, is a secondary access road to SkiBowl. It makes a wonderful 1.5-mile cross-country beginner's trail.

Timberline Ski Area

The undisputed king of the mountain is **Timberline Ski Area** (Timberline Lodge 97028, 503/622-7979 or 800/547-1406). Located 60 miles east of Portland on U.S. 26, the skiing starts where the trees end. To get here, go east of Government Camp on U.S. 26 and take Forest Service Road 50 for six miles.

With the highest vertical drop of any ski area in Oregon (3,600 feet) as well as the highest elevation accessible by chairlift (8,600 feet), 60 percent of Timberline's ski runs are in the intermediate-level category. Given this terrain, it should come as no surprise that the U.S. Olympic Ski Team trains here on Palmer Glacier during the summer months. Timberline has the

longest ski season in the nation. Recent improvements to the Palmer Chairlift have made this experience better than ever.

Attractive midweek ski packages include lodging at the hall of the mountain king, **Timberline Lodge** (503/231-7979 information, 503/222-2211 snow report, www.timberlinelodge.com). This National Historic Site was built in the 1930s as a Works Progress Administration project. Billed as the most magnificent wooden structure ever built, the lodge features fine dining and a heated outdoor swimming pool.

Here, at 6,000 feet, the frequently wet snow known as "Cascades concrete" in other locales is less sloppy. While it's not as light as powder, the 31 runs are so well groomed that Timberline snow is easily navigable. The chairlifts (six in winter, two in summer) are mostly obscured by trees or topography, so you get a feeling of intimacy with the natural surroundings when you're schussing downhill. You can go up two lifts, enjoying a nearly two-mile-long run that drops 2,500 feet vertically.

Though the first fresh snow usually comes in November or December, several years ago there were flurries on the Fourth of July, underscoring Timberline's claim of offering some of the only lift-serviced summer skiing in the United States. Skiers can pay around $39 for a one-day lift ticket ($32 in the off-season) at Timberline. The two summer chairs run daily through Labor Day.

The upper Palmer lift, highest on the mountain, is open only late spring through fall, when conditions are safe for skiing on the Palmer glacier. The Magic Mile chair, directly below the Palmer, is open to the 7,000-foot level for sightseers as well as skiers. The price for nonskiing sightseers is about 20 percent of what skiers pay for lift tickets.

The G.I.-sponsored Timberline Ski Bus costs $25 for the round-trip ride; packages include round-trip transportation and lift ticket for the day. Tickets can be purchased through Ticketmaster. All buses arrive at Timberline at 8:30 A.M. and depart at 4 P.M. Buses run weekends and holidays late Nov.–late March. Consult www.timberlinelodge.com for pickup/drop-off locations.

A mile south of the Timberline turnoff on

U.S. 26 is **Summit Ski Area** (503/272-0256), the place for families, beginners, and people who just like to play in the snow. You can ski on beginners' slopes or rent an inner tube to barrel down the gently sloping surrounding hills. Several other good sliding hills are close by. To get to Summit, drive through the town of Government Camp off U.S. 26. Beyond the stores and concessions you'll see a large parking lot on the left side of the road with a structure housing a burger joint and equipment rental.

Remember that summer temperatures on Mount Hood can vary from below freezing to 90°F. Along with sunscreen, dark glasses, and other warm-weather gear, bring layered ski apparel to adapt to varied conditions.

Hoodoo Ski Bowl

The state's oldest ski area, **Hoodoo Ski Bowl** (P.O. Box 20, ORE 20, Sisters 97759, 541/822-3799, www.hoodoo.com) has the additional distinction of also being the least expensive. Located between Salem and Bend on ORE 20, this family-oriented resort is evenly divided into beginner, intermediate, and advanced terrain and also offers night skiing. Hours are Tues.–Sun. 9 A.M.–4 P.M.; night skiing Wed.–Sun. 4–10 P.M. For updated operating hours and snow report, call 541/345-7416 from Eugene, 541/585-8081 from Salem, 541/752-8887 from Corvallis.

For information on cross-country skiing from Sno-Park areas, contact the **Sisters Ranger District** (Deschutes National Forest, Sisters 97759, 541/549-2111) or the **McKenzie Ranger District** (Willamette National Forest, McKenzie Bridge 97413, 541/822-3381).

Willamette Pass

Willamette Pass (1899 Willamette St., Ste. 1, Eugene 97401, 800/444-5030, www.willamettepass.com), 69 miles southeast of Eugene on ORE 58, has some of the most challenging runs in the state as well as a multitude of beginner and intermediate trails. You'll find some of the steepest runs here, unlike the open chutes or powder bowls at other ski areas. Since Willamette Pass plows its own parking lot, you will not need a Sno-Park permit here. Hours before Jan. 1 are Wed.–Sun. 9 A.M.–4 P.M.; after Jan. 1, Wed.–Sat. 9 A.M.–9 P.M., Sunday 9 A.M.–4 P.M. Call 541/345-SNOW for the ski report.

Mount Bachelor

The Northwest's largest and most complete ski area is **Mount Bachelor** (P.O. Box 1031, Bend 97709, 541/382-2607 information, 541/382-7888 hours and snow report, www.mtbachelor.com). Located 22 miles southwest of Bend on Century Drive, 12 ski lifts, including five high-speed quads, and trails that range from beginner to expert, make for some of the most popular skiing in the state. This is the winter training grounds for the U.S. Olympic Ski Team. *Ski* magazine ranks Mount Bachelor among the top five ski resorts in North America.

With a top elevation over 9,000 feet and steady northwest air flow, skiing here can run well into the summer months. However, avoid skiing here after 1 P.M. in May and June, when conditions become slushy. If you must ski then, choose the west-side snowfields, which hold up better in the late afternoon light. Finally, while there may not be enough snow in summer to ski, you can still ride the chairlift to the peak of this volcano for an unsurpassed view of the surrounding countryside.

Mount Bailey

Limited to just 12 skiers a day, Mount Bailey Snowcat Skiing (Diamond Lake Resort, Diamond Lake 97731, 800/733-7593) is a unique backcountry adventure for the experienced skier. Located north of Crater Lake on ORE 138, Mount Bailey does not have crowds and lines but does have virgin slopes of powder and dynamite scenery. Snowcat skiing tours begin at 7 A.M., by reservation only. Diamond Lake Resort is southern Oregon's most complete winter resort, with downhill and cross-country skiing, skating, sledding, and snowmobiling.

Klamath Falls

"One person's conservation is another's unemployment." This bromide underscores life in Klamath County, which has endured some of the highest unemployment rates and lowest per-capita incomes in the state, largely due to cutbacks in logging. Similarly, the ongoing tug-of-war between farmers and fish—a drama playing out all over the West—brought the area national notoriety in September 2002. In a year of low rainfall, warm temperatures, and an unusually large run of chinook salmon, some 34,000 spawning salmon and other fish died in the Klamath River, due to water diversions to Klamath Basin farms. The diminished river flow forced crowded salmon into warm, sluggish pools, where disease erupted and quickly spread with deadly consequences.

Klamath Falls, or "K Falls" as locals call it, is

THE CASCADES

© AVALON TRAVEL PUBLISHING, INC.

the county's population hub, with nearly 21,000 people in the city limits and an additional 40,000 population in the surrounding urban growth boundary. It's used to hard times after witnessing the decline of its previous economic base, the railroads. In an attempt to build a viable future, the Salt Caves Dam Project was proposed on the Klamath River.

This hydropower project was cancelled after a decade of legal battles over its alleged negative effects on fish populations. The latter paralleled the restrictions put on the ponderosa pine logging (at one time, Klamath Falls milled the most in the United States). Just when it seemed that Klamath Falls was doomed to economic oblivion, help came from unexpected quarters. High-tech and secondary-wood-product companies relocated here, and the development of Klamath Lake's blue-green algae, a high-protein food source, into a multimillion dollar business gave a boost to sagging spirits and fortunes (see special topic on the subject). The establishment of the Klamath Tribes Casino, 22 miles north of Klamath Falls at U.S. 97 (ORE 62 junction), is also viewed as a potential economic impetus.

The biggest hopes for the future here center on K Falls as a place to live. Interest in Klamath Falls as a retirement community was sparked by an American Chamber of Commerce poll in the early '90s showing that the cost of living here was the lowest among western cities surveyed. Another incentive for relocating is a dry climate with more than 290 days of sunshine, cold but not damp winters (less cold and rainy than Bend).

In town, three interesting museums shine lights on different aspects of local history and culture. But the real draw of Klamath Falls is out in the surrounding countryside, which is a paradise for the outdoorsperson. The native trout of Klamath Lake and the nearby Wood and Williamson Rivers are legendary (average size 21 inches). There's world-class white-water rafting on the upper Klamath River, with several hair-raising rapids topping Class IV. But most of all it's the Klamath Basin National Wildlife refuges, a complex of six lake and wetland units stretching into California, that draw visitors—and lots of birds—to the area. The refuges host the largest concentration of

BLUE-GREEN ALGAE

Discovered in Upper Klamath Lake by Harvard graduate Daryl J. Kollman, blue-green algae (*Aphanizomenon flosaquae*) has been touted by **Cell-Tech** (a leading manufacturer of this product) to have more chlorophyll and protein than any other edible organism known to man. Cell-Tech harvests blue-green algae from Upper Klamath Lake and processes it within an hour, using low temperature techniques that help preserve minerals, amino acids, and valuable enzymes. The lake itself is rich in natural nutrients and low in toxins, producing an algae superior to those grown in a human-made controlled environment. While the research on blue-green algae is incomplete, preliminary data suggest that it may enhance mental clarity, improve digestion and elimination, strengthen the immune system, and increase and sustain energy levels.

To arrange a visit of the Cell-Tech plant, call 800/800-1300 and ask for the public relations department; open Mon.–Fri. 6 A.M.–6 P.M.

Not far west of Klamath Falls off of ORE 140 West is **Mares Eggs Springs.** This shallow pond, about an acre in size, is one of the few places on earth where *Nostoc amlissimum gard* (also known as "mares eggs") grow. This blue-green unicellular algae is actually groups of minute cells that are joined together in chains by a gelatinous substance, forming a spherical colony in a rusty green sac. When the colony, or mares egg, reaches maturity, it breaks up into small fragments that in turn form new colonies. The mares eggs found in this locale can range in size from a pinhead to an extra-large potato.

Nostoc thrive here in the cold, clear water. Snowmelt and icy springs feed this pond, and temperatures never exceed 40°F. Mares eggs have also been called witch's butter, star jelly, and spittle of the stars. They are considered a delicacy in China and Japan.

To get to Mares Eggs Springs, take ORE 140 West to the first paved road past the Rocky Point turnoff, marked "To Fort Klamath." Turn right and go past a marsh to a wooded area. The pond is on the right and marked by a sign, but look carefully because it can be easy to miss if you are not paying attention.

bald eagles (up to 500 in winter), the most in the United States outside of Alaska, as well as more than 400 other bird species.

SIGHTS
Favell Museum

A fine collection of Native American artifacts and western art is found at the Favell Museum (125 W. Main St., Klamath Falls 97601, 541/882-9996 or 800/762-9096, www.favell-museum.com). Here you'll find beautiful displays of tribal stonework, bone and shellwork, beadwork, quilts, basketry, pottery, and Northwest coast carvings as well as a collection of over 60,000 mounted arrowheads. Another attraction is the collection of miniature working firearms, ranging from Gatling guns to inch-long Colt 45s, displayed in the museum's walk-in vault.

If artifacts aren't your bag, you're bound to appreciate one of the best collections of western art in the state. Oils, acrylics, and watercolors are featured, as well as bronzes, dioramas, photography, taxidermy, and woodcarvings. The gift shop and art gallery specialize in limited-edition prints and original western art. Open Wed.–Sat. 9:30 A.M.–5:30 P.M. Admission is $4 for adults, $3 for seniors, $2 for ages 6–16, kids under six get in free.

Baldwin Hotel Museum

Travel back in time to the early 1900s thanks to the Baldwin Hotel (31 Main St., 541/883-4207), adorned with original fixtures and furnishings—the legacy of a talented female photographer whose father built the place. A video presentation in the lobby complements guided tours ($4 adults, $3 seniors and students, kids five and under free) of digs once occupied by Presidents Teddy Roosevelt, Taft, and Wilson. It's open Tues.–Sat. 10 A.M.–3:30 P.M., June–September.

Klamath County Museum

A good background on the region can be gained from a visit to the Klamath County Museum (1451 Main St., 541/883-4208). The natural-history section has exhibits on fossils, geology, minerals, and indigenous wildlife of the Klamath Basin. The exploration and settlement area depicts the hardships of pioneer life and the events leading to the Modoc Indian War. The general history section takes you through the World Wars and up memory lane to the present.

Those who really want to revel in local history can make an appointment to pore through the museum's research library, which includes one of the largest regional collections of primary sources on Captain Jack and the Modoc Indian War.

During the summer, a restored 1906 trolley will give you free transportation from the Klamath County Museum to the Favell Museum and the historic Baldwin Hotel. The Klamath County Museum is open daily 9 A.M.–5 P.M. Admission is $3 for adults, $2 seniors and students, $1 kids ages 5–12.

Collier Memorial State Park

About 30 miles north of Klamath Falls on U.S. 97 is Collier Memorial State Park (541/783-2471 or 800/551-6949). Donated to the state in 1945 by Alfred and Andrew Collier as a memorial to their parents, this 146-acre park documents the history of logging's technological improvements (there is no charge for these day-use facilities).

The first building at the south end of the parking lot in the park's Pioneer Village is the logger's homestead cabin, stocked with a wide variety of tools and artifacts on display inside. Near the homestead cabin is the blacksmith shed, representative of the type of shop found in early logging camps. The next building houses an assortment of logging machinery including log wagons with wheels made of cross-cut sections of logs bound in iron, and chain-drive trucks with hard rubber tires. Also on display are steam-propelled devices including tractors, a narrow-gauge locomotive, and a one-person handcart.

Don't miss the 200+-foot-long, 16-foot-wide **Clatsop Fir,** a fallen tree that was mature when Columbus landed in the New World. The tree could supply enough wood for several four-bedroom homes. For better or worse, it's probably the largest Douglas fir ever cut.

Across from the museum are 18 tent sites and

THE KLAMATH RECLAMATION PROJECT

One hundred years ago, about 185,000 acres of the Klamath Basin consisted of shallow lakes and marshes. These wetlands used to be a fall stopover for over six million waterfowl migrating south for the winter. In addition to the wide variety of birds winging their way through the territory, large concentrations of marsh birds, such as pelicans, cormorants, egrets, and herons resided here as well. The fertile web of life created by the wetlands further supported a host of other animals like mink, otter, beaver, deer, bear, and elk. Lunker trout and other fish grew fat in the nutrient-rich waters, providing an abundant food source for the largest concentration of osprey and bald eagles in the contiguous United States.

But our national bird didn't get to rule the roost for long. Many people believed that keeping the wetlands in their natural state was a waste of space. In 1905, the U.S. Bureau of Reclamation began to pull the plug on many of the lakes and marshes here with the initiation of the Klamath Reclamation Project.

Fortunately, some of the basin's original habitat

has been protected as national wildlife refuges that are managed by the **U.S. Fish and Wildlife Service** (400 Hill Rd. W., Tule Lake, CA 96134, 530/667-2231). There are currently six such refuges, three in Oregon and three more just across the state line in California. Coniferous forests, grassy meadows, marshes, open water, sagebrush and juniper grasslands, and cliffs and rocky slopes are some of the habitats found in the refuges. This variety of terrain and vegetation supports an abundant population of wildlife; refuge wildlife checklists show 411 different species present at the refuges.

Late summer and early fall are the best times to observe waterfowl migrations. Starting in mid-September with the arrival of pintails and white-fronted geese, the numbers of ducks and geese swell to more than one million by early November. Canada, Ross's, and snow geese, mallards, green-winged teals, and tundra swans are some of the other major migratory species represented. August and September are also good times to view marsh birds, which generally move out of the basin by late October.

50 spaces with full hookups. Reservations are not necessary for camping, but space for the day-use area can be reserved with Reservations Northwest (800/452-5687). The park is open April 15–Oct. 29, and the campground fee is $14–19. A nature trail and fishing spot are nearby.

Bear Valley National Wildlife Refuge

December–February, the Klamath Basin is home to the largest wintering concentration of **bald eagles** in the lower 48 states. The thousands of winter waterfowl that reside here provide a plentiful food source for these raptors. By January, 700 to 800 eagles from as far north as southeastern Alaska's Chilkat River, Saskatchewan, and the Northwest Territories congregate here. While bald eagles can and do take live birds, they feed primarily on waterfowl that have died from hunting injuries, diseases like fowl cholera, or natural causes.

In addition to a readily available food supply, the eagles require night-roosting areas. The Bear

Valley National Wildlife Refuge (between Keno and Worden) has mature stands of timber that can support up to 300 eagles a night. The eagles prefer trees on northeastern slopes that protect them from the cold southwest and westerly winds. However, the eagles *don't* like it when people bother them. Hence, the roosting areas are closed early November–March 30.

The good news is that there are still ample viewing opportunities of our national bird, especially when it is very cold. Contact the Fish and Wildlife office for the latest information on the best eagle-watching locations. A good sighting can be had driving to Bear Valley at sunrise. To get there, drive one mile south of Worden on U.S. 97. Turn right on Keno Worden Road after the grain silos, cross the railroad tracks, and take an immediate left on the gravel road. Travel for about a mile and pull off the road. From here you can sometimes see up to 100 bald eagles soar from their roosts at the top of the ridge to their daytime feeding area on the refuge to the east. Bring binoculars, warm clothing, and a camera with a telephoto lens.

A world-renowned event, the **Klamath Basin Bald Eagle Conference** is held in February with lectures. The highlight is a pre-dawn field trip to the nearby Bear Valley roost. (For more information, write to Klamath Basin Eagle Conference, 4647 Miller Island Rd., Klamath Falls 97603.)

Get a free map and bald-eagle brochure by sending a stamped, self-addressed envelope to: Klamath Basin National Wildlife Refuges, 4009 Hill Rd., Tule Lake, CA 96134 (530/667-2231). Ask them to include information on local accommodations and restaurants. The nearest motels are in Merrill, Oregon, or Tule Lake and Dorris, both across the border in California.

Klamath Marsh National Wildlife Refuge

March–May is when **waterfowl and shorebirds** stop over in the basin on their way north to their breeding grounds in Alaska and Canada. They rest and fatten up during the spring to build the necessary strength and body fat to carry them through their long migration. May–July is the nesting season for thousands of marsh birds and waterfowl. The Klamath Marsh National Wildlife Refuge (north of Klamath Falls off U.S. 97) is a good place during spring to observe sandhill cranes, shorebirds, waterfowl, and raptors.

The summer months are ideal for taking the self-guided auto tour routes and canoe trails. Descriptive leaflets are available for both attractions from the refuge office. Among the most prolific waterfowl and marsh bird areas in the Northwest, over 25,000 ducks, 2,600 Canada geese, and thousands of marsh and shorebirds are raised here each year. You may also see American white pelicans, *Pelecanus erythrorhynchos,* at the Upper Klamath National Wildlife Refuge during the summer.

Tule Lake and Lower Klamath refuges are open during daylight hours. Overnight camping is not permitted at any of the refuges.

THE CASCADES

COURTESY OF TUPPER ANSEL BLAKE AND UNITED STATES FISH AND WILDLIFE SERVICE

Ross's geese take flight at Lower Klamath National Wildlife Refuge, which also hosts flocks of white-fronted, Canada, and snow geese.

BOB RACE

bald eagle

Entertainment

The region's cultural hub is the **Ross Ragland Theater** (218 N. 7th, Klamath Falls, 541/884-5483, www.rrtheater.org). In addition to the Klamath Symphony and other community organizations, country stars, internationally acclaimed guest artists, and touring Broadway troupes grace the stage of this 800-seat auditorium. Call the theater or check the daily *Herald & News* to see what's scheduled.

SPORTS AND RECREATION

With all the lakes, rivers, and mountains in the region, there's no shortage of fishing, rafting, golfing, and other recreational opportunities. Here's a short list of some local attractions.

Fishing

Three local guides can get you outfitted and on the water angling for the elusive big one. **Free Spirit Guide Service** (Klamath Falls, 541/884-3222); **Lynn Hescock** (Klamath Falls, 541/783-2548); and **Darren Roe Guide Service** (4849 Summers Ln., Klamath Falls, 541/884-3825 or 877/943-5700) all offer trips on the Klamath Lakes and the nearby Wood and Willamson Rivers, both noted for their runs of wild trout. Rates for all three outfitters are roughly the same; half-day trips for one or two people average $250, full-day trips $350 for one person. Contact the outfitter for reservation deposit policies. Also, check www.theguideline.com for more Oregon guide listings.

Boating

One way to get out onto Oregon's largest lake is to rent a sailboat or take a chartered tour through **Meridian Sail Center** (Pelican Marina, Dock C, 928 Front St., 541/884-5869). Tours cost $40 per person, or $175 for a private charter trip. Sailboat rentals are $40 half day, $70 full day. Sailing instruction is also available. Call ahead for the sailing report and to make reservations. **Klamath Lake Touring Company** (541/883-4622, www.klamathbelle.com) offers paddle-wheeler lake tours, for similiar rates, that emphasize the natural history, geography, and native peoples of the area.

Rafting

Just under an hour west of Klamath Falls is what's known as Hell's Corner of the Upper Klamath River. May–October, one- or two-day adventures through this remote, secluded canyon are offered by **Cascade River Runners** (P.O. Box 86, Klamath Falls 97601, 541/883-6340 fax/phone). With several Class IV+ rapids, the Upper Klamath provides some of the best spring and summer rafting in the state. Day trips ($125 adult, $100 youth) take on 18 miles of white water, and two-day campout voyages charge through 24 miles of unforgettable turbulence. Call for reservations and additional trip information; ask about group discounts.

You can also arrange a raft trip in the Klamath Falls region through Ashland's **Adventure Center** (40 N. Main St., Ashland 97520, 800/444-2819, www.raftingtours.com). They also do fishing and biking trips. Rates for rafting depend on the river, but range from $70 for a half day on the Rogue to $450 for three days on the Klamath.

Camping

Most of the campgrounds you'll find in the vicinity of Klamath Falls are privately owned. These facilities cater mostly to RVs with electric, water, and sewer hookups, as well as other creature comforts like swimming pools, laundries, and recreational halls. These properties also tend to be in prime locations, which accounts for rates that are steeper than those of their public counterparts. Fortunately, there are several places to pitch a tent in both types of parks without having to deal with a 40-foot-long mobile home parked right next to your sleeping bag.

On the north end of Upper Klamath Lake adjacent to the Upper Klamath National Wildlife Refuge lies **Harriman Springs Resort and Marina** (Harriman Route, Box 79, Klamath Falls 97601, 541/356-2331). The campground features six tent and 12 RV sites with hookups. Flush toilets, showers, firewood, and a laundry are also available. Tent sites are $14; RV sites are $18. Open year-round. To get there, go 27 miles northwest of Klamath Falls on ORE 140W and take a right onto Rocky Point Road. Proceed another two miles and you will see the resort on the right.

Another mile down Rocky Point Road is **Rocky Point Resort** (28121 Rocky Point Rd., Klamath Falls 97601, 541/356-2287, www.rocky-pointoregon.com), also in close proximity to the Upper Klamath National Wildlife Refuge. This resort has five tent and 28 RV sites with hookups and rustic cabins. Flush toilets, showers, firewood, a laundry, a recreation hall, and other summer-camp trappings are available. Open April–mid-November, the camp charges $14 per night. Ask about canoe rentals for trips on the Upper Klamath Canoe Trail. For more information about the trail, contact the **U.S. Fish and Wildlife Service** (Klamath Basin National Wildlife Refuge, P.O. Box 74, Tule Lake, CA 96134, 530/667-2231).

Several other campgrounds are also found on Upper Klamath Lake. Although a fire in 2003 caused minor damage, the best deal around is still **Hagelstein Park** (County Parks Dept., Klamath Falls 97601, 541/883-5371). The park can accommodate five tent campers and five RVs in sites that feature picnic tables and fire grills, with flush toilets and water nearby. In addition to being the only campground on the east shore of the lake, it's the least expensive campground in the area. Open April–late November, reservations are advisable in this small park. To get there, head north of Klamath Falls for 12 miles and look for the signs on the left side of the road.

Approximately seven miles farther north of Mallard Campground on U.S. 97 is **KOA Klamath Falls** (3435 Shasta Way, Klamath Falls 97601, 541/884-4644). Set along the shore of Upper Klamath Lake, the park features 18 tent and 73 RV sites with hookups. In true KOA style, flush toilets, showers, a pool, laundry, recreation hall, and other amenities are available. Open all year, $24–29 per night; $42 for cabin accommodations.

Golf

There are several area courses open to the public. **Harbor Links** (601 Harbor Isle Blvd., 541/882-0609) and **Shield Crest** (3151 Shieldcrest Dr., 541/884-1493) both offer 9- and 18-hole courses with greens fees in the $25–45 range. Rental golf clubs are also available at these two establishments for about $10. Smaller 9-hole **Round Lake** (4000 Round Lake Rd., 541/884-2520) is a bargain at $9 for 9 holes, $15 for 18 holes.

PRACTICALITIES
Accommodations

Klamath Falls has long been considered the crossroads of southeastern Oregon. John C. Fremont led mapping expeditions for the U.S. government in 1843 and 1846, blazing the way for settlers to arrive via the Applegate Trail. With the arrival of the railroad decades later, Klamath Falls's status in southeastern Oregon also grew. The development of U.S. 97, ORE 140, and ORE 66 in the 20th century infused additional growth to the city.

However, most people over the years just stopped for food and shelter, and then pushed on to where ever they were headed. Though word has recently gotten out that the region offers much more than a pit stop, you can still find quality accommodations at reasonable rates that continue to meet the needs of the traveling public at the crossroads of southeastern Oregon.

Lodging here is fairly inexpensive by Oregon standards, but the lower rates of motels don't necessarily mean lower standards of quality. Travelers on a budget will appreciate **Maverick Motel** (1220 Main St., 541/882-6688 or 800/404-6690), $39–59, and **Cimarron Motor Inn** (3060 S. 6th, 541/882-4601 or 800/742-2648), $65–95, for the pool and continental breakfast, and for allowing pets.

Mid-range properties are the domain of the chains. **Best Western Olympic Inn** (2627 S. 6th, 541/882-9665 or 800/600-9665), $89–119; **Holiday Inn Express** (2500 S. 6th, 541/884-9999 or 800/465-4329, www.basshotels.com); **Quality Inn & Suites** (100 Main St., 541/882-4666 or 888/762-2466), $79–114; and **Red Lion Inn** (3612 S. 6th, 541/882-8864 or 800/RED LION), $79–99, all feature the pool, continental breakfast, and other upgrades expected. The latter two accept pets.

The **Boarding House Inn B&B** (1800 Esplanade Ave., Klamath Falls, 541/883-8584) remains true to its heritage as a boarding house for railroad workers, but with many modern refinements. The period furnishings and fixtures of a half century ago recall a visit to grandmother's house, and at a price she would undoubtedly approve. The two guestrooms ($68) come with walk-in closets, full kitchens, and private bath. The two suites ($78) offer the same amenities plus a larger kitchen and living room. Breakfast is yet another highlight here, as the owner was trained at the California Culinary Academy in San Francisco, and he produces elaborate meal presentations worthy of a five-star rating. Exceptional dinners are also served. It's no wonder that rooms book fast; advance reservations are always necessary.

Ten minutes from town on the south shore of Upper Klamath Lake adjacent to 400-acre Moore Park is **Thompson's B&B** (1420 Wild Plum Ct., 541/882-7938). Their location on the lake and a huge deck overlooking the water make it an ideal place to spot all manner of wildlife. They've been in the business for nearly two decades, and know how to take care of people right. From the commons room stocked with goodies (popcorn, candy, drinks), microwave, and refrigerator to the full American breakfast, everything here is geared to please the guests. Rooms are $85–105. Payment in cash or check only, $25 deposit required, 48-hour cancellation notice policy. Nearby **Meridan Sails** (541/884-5869), at the marina a block away, rents boats for $70/half day.

On the eastern section of the Crater Lake Highway (ORE 62) about a half hour from Crater Lake is **Sun Pass Ranch** (52125 ORE 62, Box 499, Fort Klamath 97626-0499, 541/381-2259 or 541/892-0991). This combo B&B/guest ranch is located in the heart of what some locals call the Sky Lakes Wilderness. Close by the ranch, a wide variety of wildlife can easily be spotted. To help you get to see all those wild critters out there, they offer mountain bike rentals, backcountry pack trips with horses, and even hiking expeditions with llamas. Fishing, rafting, and canoeing are also among the offerings. Room rates are $75–85 double occupancy, $10/extra person; reservations required.

Decent one- and two-bedroom cabins ($70–109) with fully equipped kitchen, private bath, and outdoor barbecue are featured at **Rocky Point Resort** (28124 Rocky Point Rd., 541/356-2287, www.rockypointoregon.com). Guestrooms in the lodge are also available, $65; cabins are $89; tent sites are $16 for two people. You can rent everything from a kayak to a whaler at their marina to explore the waters of Klamath Lake. A restaurant is on site too. Call ahead for advance deposit information and room availability.

The **Running Y Ranch Resort** (5500 Running Y Rd., 541/850-5500 or 888/850-0275, www.runningy.com) offers the total Klamath Basin package experience. Deluxe rooms at the lodge run $119–270 with two- or three-bedroom townhomes for $224–279 per night. Schatzie's on the Green features Northwest and German cuisine and the resort coffee shop offers hearty breakfasts and lunch with a premium on freshly made items. The Y's Arnold Palmer–designed golf course, recently rated by *Golf Di-*

gest as the best new public course in America, costs $65 for 18 holes.

Equestrian pursuits are available April–October; $17 per half hour, $27 per hour, and $37 per hour and a half; a half day costs $75–125 per person depending upon the number of riders. Bike rentals at the Y's Sports Center run $12.50 per hour or $45 per day. Many guests enjoy paddling along ancient Native American canoe routes to one of the Basin's seven bird sanctuaries; call 541/891-0417 for details. Numerous nature hikes and other activities abound. In short, this resort serves up the finest the region has to offer.

Food

Klamath Falls is a small, unpretentious town. Despite being the second-largest city east of the Cascades, Klamath Falls offers few opportunities for gourmet grub. Locals suggest that visitors come here for the birds, not necessarily for the food. Fowl jokes aside, sandwiched in between the obligatory fast-food joints are a flock of noteworthy eating establishments.

For something special in the moderate to expensive range, try **Fiorella Italian Ristorante** (6139 Summers, 541/882-1878). Open for dinner Tues.–Sat., the restaurant specializes in pasticcio (Venetian-style lasagna). Seafood and vegetarian meals are also found on the menu, as well as imported beers and wines.

If you're in the mood for Chinese food, head right for **Wong's** (421 Main St., 541/884-6578). In addition to an assortment of reasonably priced Chinese combination dinners and vegetarian dishes, you can also find American-style steak and seafood here. **King Wah** (2765 Pershing Way, 541/882-0489), specializing in Cantonese cuisine and thick-cut steaks, is another option for Asian fare. Both are open daily for lunch and dinner.

For a meal you're sure to remember, try **Wong's Mongolian Grill** (610 Main, 541/884-6863). Here, you get to be the chef, only you don't do the cooking. More than a dozen veggies, chicken, beef, and shrimp are presented salad bar style. Grab a plate ($10 all-you-can-eat), choose your ingredients, and then top it off with one of 10 different freshly made sauces (peanut, ginger,

teriyaki, etc.). Present your custom arrangement to the cooks, and they will grill it up for you to perfection. Eighteen microbrews are available on tap, and there's also a dance floor that occasionally features live bands. All of this makes the grill one of Klamath Falls' hot spots. Open Mon.–Sat. for lunch and dinner; closed Sunday.

Open Tues.–Sat. for dinner only, the more upscale **Chez Nous** (3927 S. 6th, 541/883-8719) offers continental cuisine, steak, pasta, and seafood, along with an extensive wine list. The food is excellent, the ambience classy. All entrées are served as full-course meals (with soup, salad, potato or rice, vegetables, and bread included). This is the place in town to go to impress your date, but be prepared to pay for it.

When it comes to pizza in Klamath Falls, the locals swear by **McPherson's Old Town Pizza Company** (722 Main, 541/884-8858, and 6200 S. 6th, 541/883-2918). Pizzas come in four sizes, from individual to large, and with three kinds of crusts (thick, thin, or pan), but it is the thin-crust pizza that accounts for over 75 percent of their sales. You'll find one of the best lunch buffet deals in town here; it includes pizza, chicken (regular or barbecue), lasagna, spuds, soups, desserts, and a huge salad bar. Open daily 11 A.M.–10 P.M.

For steak, chicken, and pasta dishes, **Aftershock** (at the Epicenter, 541/273-0700) and **John and Lori's Steak and Country** (205 Main St., 541/883-3910) are local favorites.

Information and Transportation

Over 2.2 million acres of Klamath County is publicly owned. The **Klamath Ranger District Office** (1936 California Ave., Klamath Falls, 541/885-3400) can give or send you outdoor recreational information on the Winema National Forest and other surrounding natural areas of interest. The **Bureau of Land Management** (2795 Anderson Ave., #25, Klamath Falls, 541/883-6916) can also be of assistance in this regard.

You'll find the **Oregon Welcome Center** located on U.S. 97 about halfway between Klamath Falls and the California–Oregon border. They have a broad collection of brochures and information about locales all over the state.

THE CASCADES

The **Klamath County Tourism Department** (507 Main St., Klamath Falls, 541/884-0666 or 800/445-6728), can provide an excellent pamphlet on the self-guided loop tour. Look for this visitors center in Veteran's Park, just off U.S. 97 at the entrance to the city.

Amtrak (S. Spring and Oak Streets, 541/884-2822) can connect you with northern and southern destinations via the *Coast Starlight*. **Greyhound** (1200 Klamath Ave., 541/882-4616) can also take you to California and the Willamette Valley. The **Klamath Falls airport** is serviced by **United Express** (800/241-6522) and **Horizon** (541/884-3331).

Crater Lake Highway

Many locals who live near the Crater Lake Highway sport bumper stickers on their vehicles that read, "I Survived Highway 62." The challenges of successfully navigating this precipitous and circuitous thoroughfare, with its horrific winter weather and slow-moving summer crowds, help give it a killer reputation. Snow can sometimes get deep enough on the upper reaches that 15-foot-high snow poles lining the roadbed are rendered useless in helping the snowplows navigate. In these cases, the crews can only locate the road by means of a radio transmitter, embedded in steel cable, which emits a signal.

Even so, there always seems to be traffic on this winding conduit between Crater Lake and southern Oregon. This isn't surprising when you consider the scenic appeals of the Rogue River and Cascade Mountains. Add excellent fishing on the Rogue below Oregon's largest fish hatchery, Cole Rivers, along with the swimming, boating, and rafting opportunities, and you too will be taking to the hills along Highway 62.

The following contact information can help plan your foray into the Rogue River National Forest: **Prospect Ranger Station** (541/498-2531), **Rogue River National Forest Service** (Medford, 541/858-2200), and the **Oregon Tourism Commission** (www.traveloregon.com). The last can send you a helpful publication entitled *Off the Beaten Freeway: A Guide to Oregon's Scenic Byways* that has some useful tips on this region as well as the rest of the state.

SPORTS AND RECREATION
Hiking
Many choice hikes are found along the 50-mile stretch of the Rogue River Trail from Lost Creek Lake to the river's source at Boundary Springs just inside Crater Lake National Park. Tall waterfalls, deep gushing gorges, and a natural bridge are all easily accessible. Those interested in more than just a short walk from the parking lot to the viewpoint can design hikes of 2 to 18 miles with or without an overnight stay. Travelers with two cars can arrange shuttles to avoid having to double back.

Mill Creek Falls: One of the more scenic recreation spots is owned by Boise Cascade, a timber conglomerate. Boise Cascade has constructed a botanically marked nature trail system through its land to a series of three waterfalls in an impressive, rock-choked section of the Rogue River called the Avenue of the Giant Boulders. To give you an idea of how spectacular this deep and narrow gorge strewn with volcanic monoliths is, the Avenue of the Giant Boulders was actually lit up during the 1920s.

The largest of the three waterfalls is Mill Creek Falls, which plunges 173 feet down into the river. Signs along the highway and Mill Creek Drive (formerly the old Crater Lake Highway), a scenic loop out of the community of **Prospect,** direct visitors to the trailhead. Boise Cascade has also posted a large map that further details the trail routes. The trail is short but steep. Wear shoes you don't mind getting wet and that have good traction, as you may have to scramble over some of the boulders and wade through some small ponds along the way.

Takelma Gorge: A particularly wild section of the river is found at Takelma Gorge. Located one mile from River Bridge Campground on the upper Rogue River, the trail offers vistas of sharp, foaming bends in the river with logs jammed in at crazy angles on the rocks, and ferns growing in the mist of the waterfalls. Although the river's course is rugged, the grade on the trail is an easy one.

Natural Bridge: Even if you're in a hurry, you should take 15 minutes to get out of your car and stretch your legs at the Natural Bridge. Located a quarter mile from Natural Bridge Campground, a mile west of Union Creek on ORE 62, here the Rogue River drops into a lava tube and disappears from sight, only to emerge later a little way downstream. A short paved path takes you to a human-made bridge that fords this unique section of the river. Several placards along the way explain the formation of the Natural Bridge and other points of interest.

Rogue River Gorge: Just outside of **Union Creek** on ORE 62 is the spectacular Rogue River Gorge. The narrowest point on the river, the action of the water has carved out a deep chasm in the rock. A short trail with several well-placed overlooks follows the rim of the gorge. Green mossy walls, logjams, and a frothy torrent of water are all clearly visible from the trail. Informative placards discuss curiosities like the living stump and the potholes carved in the lava rock by pebbles and the action of the water.

National Creek Falls: Another short hike for hurried motorists is National Creek Falls. An easy half-mile walk down a trail bordered by magnificent Douglas firs leads to this tumultuous cascade. To get here, take ORE 230 to Forest Service Road 6530. Follow the road until you reach the trailhead marked by a sign.

Boundary Springs: A two-mile hike down a cool and shady trail takes you to the source of the mighty Rogue River—Boundary Springs. Situated just inside Crater Lake National Park, it's a great place for a picnic. About a mile down the path from the trailhead, hang a left at the fork to get to Boundary Springs. Once at the springs, you'll discover small cataracts rising out of the jumbled volcanic rock that's densely covered with moss and other vegetation. Despite the temptation to get a closer look, the vegetation here is extremely fragile, so please refrain from walking on the moss. To get here, take ORE 230 north

from ORE 62 to the crater rim viewpoint, where parking can be found on the left-hand side of the road.

In the fall, take ORE 62 from Medford and turn east onto ORE 140 to enjoy the golden hues of larch and aspen. En route, you might stop at Fish Lake or Lake of the Woods resorts. From here you can take scenic Westside Road to Fort Klamath. Crater Lake lies a scant six miles from here.

Fishing

The fish runs on the Rogue River are second in size only to the ones on the Columbia. Nearly three million fish are reared and released into the Rogue from the Cole Rivers Fish Hatchery, located 153 miles from the mouth of the Rogue. Close to a half million salmon and steelhead are caught annually on the Rogue. The following guide services can provide you with all you need to land your own catch: **McKenzie Outfitters** (820/704-5145) or **River Trips Unlimited** (541/779-3798).

Rafting

Noah's White Water (541/488-2811) offers guided trips on the upper Rogue, but you can also do the mild, 10-mile section of the upper Rogue River from the hatchery back to town by yourself. It takes about a half day to float downstream, and many people like to enjoy a picnic along the way. **Rogue Rafting Co.** (Shady Cove, across from Shady Cove Park, 541/878-2585) and **Ragin Water Raft** (21873 ORE 62, Shady Cove, 541/878-4000) can get you set up. Equipment ranging from inflatable kayaks, tahitis, water guns, and various-sized rafts that can accommodate up to 12 people are available. Life vests, paddles, and a shuttle service from Shady Cove up to Cole Rivers Fish Hatchery are provided at no extra charge. Rogue Rafting Co. can even outfit you with an ice chest and dry bags to carry your riverbank feast.

Camping

For those who like roughing it in style with all of the amenities in their RVs, a couple of well-maintained trailer parks in the Rogue country can accommodate large vehicles. **Fly-Casters Campground and Trailer Park** (P.O. Box 1170, Shady Cove 97539, 541/878-2749, $15–21) and **Shady Trails RV Park and Campground** (P.O. Box 1299, Shady Cove 97539, 541/878-2206, $16–$20) are both located about 23 miles north of Medford on ORE 62. Situated on the banks of the Rogue River, these parks feature hookups and picnic tables. Flush toilets, bottled gas, gray wastewater disposal, and showers are also available. A grocery store and restaurants are in the nearby town of **Shady Cove.** Both of these parks are good home bases for RV owners who like to fish and hike.

Five miles below Lost Creek Lake on ORE 62 at 1,476 feet in elevation is **Rogue Elk County Park** (Jackson County Parks and Recreation, 10 South Oakdale, Medford 97501, 541/776-7001). This campground features 37 sites for tents and RVs (28 feet maximum) with picnic tables and fire grills. Piped water, showers and flush toilets are also on the premises. Open mid-April–mid-October, the camp fee is $16 per night, $18 for sites with electricity and water hookups. The kids will enjoy swimming in Elk Creek, which, in addition to being adjacent to the campground, is warmer and safer than the Rogue. A playground adds to the fun.

Along the shore of Lost Creek Lake is **Joseph Stewart State Park** (35251 ORE 62, Trail 97541, 541/560-3334). Here you'll find 50 tent and 151 RV sites (40 feet maximum). Electricity, dump station, fire grills, and picnic tables are provided. Flush toilets, water, gray wastewater disposal services, showers, and firewood are also available. Bike paths, a beach, and barbecue grills make this a family-friendly locale. Boat-launching facilities for Lost Creek Lake are located nearby. Open March–October, the fee is $16–22 per night. Eight miles of hiking trails and bike paths crisscross the park. Lost Creek Lake also has a marina, beach, and boat rentals.

If you want to get away from the highway, head for **Abbott Creek** (Rogue National Forest, Prospect Ranger Station, Prospect 97536, 541/560-3623). One of the few backwoods camps in the area that has potable water, it's

seven miles northeast of the town of Prospect on ORE 62 and three miles down Forest Service Road 68. Situated at the confluence of Abbott and Woodruff Creeks and not far from the upper Rogue River, this campground has 25 tent and RV sites (22 feet maximum) with picnic tables and fire grills. Hand-pumped water and vault toilets are also available. Open late May–October, the camp charges $10 per night for the first vehicle and $5 for each thereafter.

Set along the bank of Union Creek where it merges with the upper Rogue River is **Union Creek** (Rogue National Forest, Prospect Ranger Station, Prospect 97536, 541/560-3623). Located 11 miles northeast of Prospect, you'll find 78 tent and RV sites (16 feet maximum) with picnic tables, fire grills, piped water, and vault toilets. Open late May–October, the fee is $14 per night. Many fine hikes on the Rogue River Trail (see "Hiking," earlier in this section) are within close proximity of the campground.

A half mile past Union Creek Campground on ORE 62 is **Farewell Bend** (Rogue National Forest, Prospect Ranger Station, Prospect 97536, 541/560-3623). Located near the junction of ORE 62 and ORE 230, the camp has 61 tent and RV sites (22 feet maximum) with picnic tables and fire grills. Piped water and flush toilets are also within the campground boundaries. Open late May–early September, the fee is $14 per night. This campground is situated along the banks of the upper Rogue near the Rogue River Gorge (see "Hiking," earlier in this section).

A nice little campground tucked off the highway yet fairly close to the Rogue River and Crater Lake National Park is **Huckleberry Campground** (Rogue National Forest, Prospect Ranger Station, Prospect 97536, 541/560-3623). To get here, go about 18 miles northeast of Prospect on ORE 62 and then four miles down Forest Service Road 60. There you'll find 25 tent and RV sites (21 feet maximum) with picnic tables and fire grills. Water and vault toilets are also available. Open late May–October (weather permitting), the campground is free of charge (14-day maximum stay). This campground is at an elevation of 5,400 feet, so be sure to have the proper gear to ensure a comfortable visit (see "Camping and Hiking" under "Outdoor Recreation" in the On the Road chapter).

PRACTICALITIES
Accommodations

The accommodations you'll find on ORE 62 are rustic and simple, catering mainly to anglers and lovers of the great outdoors. The abundance of excellent campgrounds and RV parks also explains the dearth of lodgings.

Rooms at the **Maple Leaf Motel** (20717 ORE 62, Shady Cove, 541/878-2169) come equipped with microwave, toaster oven, small fridge, cable TV, and a picnic and barbecue area to grill the day's catch or some burgers if the fish weren't biting. Rates start at $34 ($7 for each additional person). The **Royal Coachman Motel** (21906 ORE 62, Shady Cove, 541/878-2481) has kitchenettes, cable TV, and HBO for $44–64 per night. The more expensive rooms with decks overlook the river.

The **Prospect Hotel and Motel** (391 Mill Creek Rd., Prospect 97536, 541/560-3664 or 800/944-6490, www.prospecthotel.com) gives you a choice between something old and something new. The hotel, built in 1889 and listed on the National Register of Historic Places, has several small but comfortable rooms with bath. The rooms are named after local residents and famous people who have stayed at the hotel, including Zane Grey, Teddy Roosevelt, and Jack London. Because the hotel is small and old, no children, smoking, or pets are permitted. Rates are $80–145. The adjacent motel features clean, spacious, and modern units that range $60–85, with some kitchenettes available. You can smoke and bring the kids and family dog along, too.

Not far away from Prospect on the Crater Lake Highway is the **Union Creek Resort** (Prospect, 541/560-3565, www.unioncreekoregon.com). Built in the early 1930s, the Union Creek is listed on the National Register of Historic Places. Open year-round, it has rooms

Union Creek Resort, built by the Civilian Conservation Corps in the 1930s

available in your choice of the original lodge, cabins, or housekeeping cabins. The lodge rooms ($40–50), paneled in knotty pine, have washbasins in them; guests all share the bathrooms down the hall. The stone fireplace in the lobby is built of opalized wood from Lakeview, Oregon. The sleeping cabins with bath range $55–65. The housekeeping cabins sleep up to 10 and come with bath and kitchen; they range $65–145. The **Union Creek Country Store,** located at the resort, carries groceries and other essential items. Fishing licenses and Sno-Park permits can also be purchased here.

Food

ORE 62 parallels an old stagecoach road between Fort Klamath and the Rogue Valley. While the ruts in the road are gone, the tradition of frontier hospitality lives on in the establishments along this much-traveled mountain pass.

The finest restaurant on this section of the Rogue River is **Beldi's** (541/878-2010). From the cloth napkins to the crystal wineglasses, you're assured a first-class dinner from start to finish, with moderate prices. The dining room is perched on a bluff overlooking the river, further enhancing the visual appeal of the meal presentation. Be sure to call ahead for reservations. Open for dinner only; closed Monday.

About halfway between Medford and Crater Lake in the vicinity of Prospect are a few eateries worth mention. For moderately priced standard American grub, the **Prospect Cafe and Lounge** (311 Mill Creek Dr., Prospect, 541/560-3641) is open daily for breakfast, lunch, and dinner. The dinner house at the **Prospect Hotel** (391 Mill Creek Rd., Prospect, 541/560-3664) is also recommended. This fine establishment serves breakfast, lunch, and dinner Memorial Day–Labor Day and Sunday brunch on weekends. One very special treat you can enjoy year-round here is huckleberry pie.

Beckie's (Union Creek Resort, 56484 ORE 62, 541/560-3565 or 866/560-3565) is an intimate place to stop for a bite to eat. One half of the building is an old log cabin; the other half is a modern design with plenty of windows. Breakfast comes with all the trimmings. The lunch menu features sandwiches and burgers. Dinners include chicken, pork, or steak entrées. Open daily till 9 P.M. in the summer; winter hours, Mon.–Fri. lunch only.

Crater Lake

High in the Cascades lies the crown jewel of Oregon, Crater Lake. America's deepest lake (1,943 feet) glimmers like a polished sapphire in a setting created by a volcano that blew its top and collapsed thousands of years ago. Crater Lake's extraordinary hues are produced by the depth and clarity of the water and its ability to absorb all the colors of the spectrum except the shortest light waves, blue and violet, which are scattered skyward. Kodak used to send their apologies along with customers' photographs of Crater Lake—they thought they had goofed on the processing, so unbelievable is the blue of the water.

In addition to a 33-mile rim drive around the main attraction, Oregon's only national park, established in 1902, also features 210 campsites, dozens of hiking trails, and boat tours on the lake itself. Admission to the park is $10 per car, or $5 per bicycle. Before you start carrying on about the rate, just be glad that Congress didn't sell the park to Disneyland to lessen the National Debt.

If you're seeing Crater Lake for the first time, drive into the area from the north for the most dramatic perspective. After crossing through a pumice desert you climb up to higher elevations overlooking the lake. In contrast to this subdued approach, the blueness and size of the lake can hit with a suddenness that stops all thought. On a clear day, you can peer south across Crater Lake and discern the snowy eminence of Mount Shasta over 100 miles away in California.

THE LAND

Geologically speaking, the name Crater Lake is a misnomer. Technically, Crater Lake lies in a

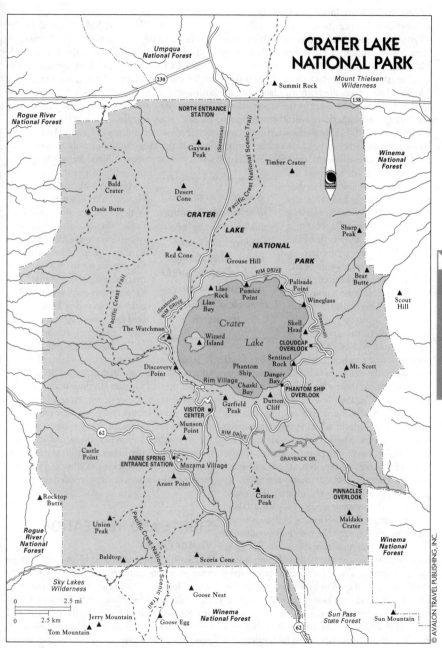

CRATER LAKE NATIONAL PARK

THE CASCADES

caldera, which is produced when the center of a volcano caves in upon itself; in this case, the cataclysm occurred 6,600 years ago with the destruction of formerly 12,000-foot-high Mount Mazama.

Klamath Native American legend has it that Mount Mazama was the home of Llao, King of the Underworld. The chief of the world above was Skell, who sometimes would stand upon Mount Shasta, 100 miles to the south. A fierce battle between these two gods took place, a time marked by great explosions, thunder, and lightning. Burning ash fell from the sky, igniting the forest, and molten rivers of lava gushed 35 miles down the mountainside, burying Native American villages. For a week the night sky was lit by the flames of the great confrontation.

The story climaxes with Skell's destruction of Llao's throne, as the mountain collapsed upon itself and sealed Llao beneath the surface, never again to frighten the Native Americans and destroy their homes. Although the lake became serene and beautiful as the caldera filled with water, the Klamaths believed that only punishment awaited those who foolishly gazed upon the sacred battleground of the gods.

The aftereffects of this great eruption can still be seen. Huge drifts of ash and pumice hundreds of feet deep were deposited over a wide area—up to 80 miles away. The pumice deserts to the north of the lake and the deep, ashen canyons to the south are the most dramatic examples. So thick and widespread is the pumice that water percolates through too rapidly for plants to survive, creating reddish pockets of bleakness in the otherwise green forest. The eerie gray hoodoos in the southern canyons were created by hot gases bubbling up through the ash, hardening it into rocklike towers. These formations have withstood centuries of erosion by water that has long since washed away the loosely packed ash, creating the steep canyons visible today.

Wizard Island, a large cinder cone that rises 760 feet above the surface of the lake, offers evidence of volcanic activity since the caldera's formation. The **Phantom Ship,** located in the southeastern corner, is a much older feature.

The lake is confined by walls of multicolored lava that rise 500–2,000 feet above the water. Although Crater Lake is fed entirely by snow and rain, the lake does contain small amount of saline from surrounding rocks. But the salty water is replaced by pure rain and snow as the saltwater is dissolved away. And yet the level of the lake fluctuates only one to three feet a year, as evaporation and seepage keep it remarkably constant.

Another surprise is that while Crater Lake often records the coldest temperatures in the Cascades, the lake itself has only frozen over once since records have been kept. The surface of the lake can warm up to the 60°F mark during the summer. The deeper water stays around 38°F, although scientists have discovered hot spots 1,400 feet below the lake's surface that are 66°.

Rainbow trout and kokanee (a landlocked salmon) were introduced to the lake many years ago by humans. The rainbow can get up to 25 inches (feeding mainly on the kokanee); the kokanee do not exceed 15 inches. Some types of mosses and green algae grow more than 400 feet below the lake's surface, a world record for these freshwater species. Another distinction was Crater Lake's selection as the purest lake in the world by scientists who, in 1997, determined the water's clarity extended down 142 feet.

> *Kodak used to send their apologies along with customers' photographs of Crater Lake—they thought they had goofed on the processing, so unbelievable is the blue of the water.*

SIGHTS AND RECREATION

Visitor Center

The visitor center is located below Rim Village near park headquarters and is a good place to start. Open year-round except Christmas day, the center provides information, maps, and publications, as well as backcountry permits and first aid. If the lake is socked in by lousy weather, you can see it anyway: excellent films about

THE SNOWS OF CRATER LAKE

Crater Lake is famed for massive snow accumulation. Drifts frequently close roads until the beginning of July. Annual deposits of 50 feet are common, and the average accumulation is 533 inches. If this fails to impress, consider some of the following Crater Lake snow jobs.

In the winter of 1950, the lake saw the most snow ever recorded in the state during a calendar year: 903 inches. The most snow to fall in 12 consecutive months fell here between April 1948 and March 1949, a grand total of 931 inches. The most snow that ever fell on an Oregon locale in one storm, 119 inches, occurred here March 16–25, 1975. The most snow ever recorded in Oregon in one month, 313 inches, fell at Crater Lake in 1950. Some years, a snowplow could be seen clearing off the roof of Crater Lake Lodge. In this vein, the 33-inch total racked up on November 17, 1994, is among the state's highest one-day accumulations.

Anticipation of the foregoing generally manifests in 15-foot-high snow poles going up along ORE 62 in September to mark the route for snow-clearing vehicles that often see action as early as October. When the drifts get high enough, two D7 Caterpillar bulldozers clear the way for rotary snowplows. Often, the only way to find the road is by a radio transmitter device embedded in steel cable on the ground.

Lest these facts deter winter travelers, consider the upside. Only 50,000 people, 10 percent of the park's yearly total, come to the park during the six-month winter season. Those who make the pilgrimage will tell you that seeing the lake wearing its snowy cloak is unforgettable. And on winter weekends, a free 90-minute ranger-led snowshoe hike (with park-provided gear) provides an opportunity to experience the solitude and beauty otherwise available only to cross-country skiers and snowmobilers. Contact the National Park Service for details on these hikes and road/weather conditions (541/594-3000, www.nps.gov/crla).

Crater Lake are shown in the center's theater every half hour and by special arrangement. For information about weather and activities at Crater Lake, log on to www.nps.gov/crla or call 541/594-3000.

The original visitor center is on the rim. A rock stairway behind the small building leads to Sinnott Memorial and one of the best views of the lake. It is perched on a rock outcropping, where accompanying interpretive placards help you identify the surrounding formations as well as flora and fauna. As you drive north from Rim Village you'll notice brown earth a few miles later, having spread out from the last major eruption.

Boat Tours

There are over 100 miles of hiking trails in the park, yet only one leads down to the lake itself. This is because the 1.1-mile-long **Cleetwood Trail** is the only part of the caldera's steep, avalanche-prone slope safe enough for passage. The trail drops 700 feet in elevation and is recommended only for those in good physical condition. There is no alternative transportation to Cleetwood Cove dock, located at the end of the trail, where the Crater Lake **boat tours** (541/830-8700), begin. These narrated excursions depart on the hour 10 A.M.–4:30 P.M. late June–mid-September (call for prices, as they change frequently; discounts for children under 12 and free for kids under 18 months). Allow one hour from Rim Village to drive 12 miles and to hike down to the boat's departure point. Dress warmly because it's cooler on the lake than on terra firma.

In addition to cruising around the lake and giving you a close look at the Phantom Ship and other geologic oddities, the tour includes a 10-minute stop on Wizard Island. Passengers electing to hike the steep, one-mile spiral path to the top of the island volcano can catch a later boat back to the dock. However, keep in mind that boats have limited space, which means your return trip could be as late as 5 P.M., depending upon availability. And while it's a great place for a picnic, please be careful to leave this unique island in an unspoiled condition for future visitors. Allow three hours for the whole experience. It

THE CASCADES

takes one hour to reach the point of embarkation and two hours for the tour itself. Tickets are sold at the dock on a first-come first-served basis.

Hiking

July and August are the most popular months. Colorful flowers and mild weather greet the summer throngs. One of the best places to view the mid-July flora is on the **Castle Crest Wildflower Trail.** The trailhead to this .5-mile loop trail is a half mile from the park headquarters. Stop there for directions to the trailhead as well as a self-guiding trail booklet that will tell you about the ponderosa pine, Shasta red fir, mountain hemlock, lodgepole pine, and rabbit brush along the trail. Wildlife in the area include elk, deer, foxes, pikas, marmots, and a variety of birds. Peak wildflower season is usually around the last two weeks of July.

A suitable challenge of brawn and breath is the **Garfield Peak Trail.** The trailhead to this imposing ridge is just east of Crater Lake Lodge. It is a steep climb up the 1.7-mile-long trail, but the wildflower displays of phlox, Indian paintbrush, and lupine, as well as frequent sightings of eagles and hawks, give ample opportunity for you to stop and catch your breath. The highlight of the hike is atop Garfield Peak, which provides a spectacular view of Crater Lake 1,888 feet below.

When snow buries the area in the wintertime, services and activities are cut to a minimum. However, many cross-country skiers, snowshoe enthusiasts, and winter campers enjoy this solitude. Park rangers lead snowshoe hikes (weather permitting) at 1 P.M. weekends, daily during Christmas week. Ski and snowshoe rentals are available at Rim Village.

Winter trekkers should be aware that there are no groomed cross-country trails. Thus, it's imperative to inquire about trail, avalanche, road, and weather conditions at the visitors center (open 8:30 A.M.–4:30 P.M. daily). Circumnavigating the lake, which is visited by frequent snowstorms, takes two to three days, even in good weather. Only skilled winter hikers should attempt this 33-mile route that requires a com-

pass and maps to traverse unmarked routes and avalanche paths.

Prior to setting out on any extended journey, pick up a permit and some free advice at the visitors center. You might also inquire about a hike to the top of **Mount Scott** (8,926 feet), the highest peak in the area. Lake views and perspectives on 12 Cascade peaks are potential rewards at the end of the 2.5-mile trek.

There are no overnight accommodations in the area mid-October–June (and you are not allowed to sleep in your vehicle), necessitating a long drive out of the park for any creature comforts.

Camping

Mazama Campground, eight miles south of the rim, has 200 sites, restrooms with showers, and a dump station. It's open early June–mid-October. Sites are $14.75 for tents, $15.75 for RVs. **Lost Creek Campground,** located on the eastern section of Rim Drive, has 16 sites, water, and pit toilets. Neither campground has hookups. Lost Creek opens in mid-July and closes mid-September. Contact the park superintendent (541/594-3100) for more information. Foot traffic in the backcountry is light, so you can set up camp wherever you like in the remote areas surrounding Crater Lake.

PRACTICALITIES
Accommodations and Food

One of the nicest things about 183,180-acre Crater Lake National Park is that it's not very developed. The services are concentrated on the southern edge of the lake at **Rim Village;** lodgings are open May–September only. May 19–October 14, accommodations in the park at **Mazama Cabins** (541/830-8700) are found next to Mazama Campground. Each room features two queen beds and a bath, and two are designed for wheelchair access. Be sure to call ahead for reservations.

But you can still get a hot meal at the **Cafeteria** and the **Watchman Deli Lounge.** The Cafeteria is open all year, serving traditional breakfasts, with lunch and dinner offerings including a salad bar, cook-to-order entrées, and deli sandwiches. The Watchman Deli Lounge is located upstairs above the Cafeteria and is open from noon to 11 P.M., mid-June–Labor Day. The menu includes hamburgers, deli sandwiches, pizza, and snacks, as well as microbrews, espresso, wine, and spirits. There are also surprisingly good entrées, not unlike those you'd find in a full-service restaurant. Service can be slow, but the great view from the second-floor window makes up for it. Even though it's called a lounge, families are always welcome. The adjoining gift shop is stocked with postcards and knickknacks. A small grocery section there sells various foodstuffs and beverages in case you've run out of peanut butter and beer.

In 1995, the **Crater Lake Lodge** (P.O. Box 97, Crater Lake 97604, 541/830-8700, www.craterlake.com) reopened (open May–Sept.) to full capacity—71 rooms—after years of restoration. The lodge is situated on the rim south of the Sinnott Overlook and is hewn of indigenous wood and stone. The massive lobby boasts a picture window on the lake and has a decor echoing back to its 1915 origins. The stone fireplace is large enough to walk into and serves as a gathering spot on chilly evenings. Many of the rooms have expansive views of the lake below. Others face out toward upper Klamath Lake and Mount Shasta, 150 miles away in California.

Amid all the amenities of a first-class national park hotel, it's nice to be reminded of the past by such touches as antique wallpaper and old-fashioned bathtubs (rooms 401 and 201 offer views of the lake from claw-foot tubs). Rates are $110–145 for one or two people; loft suites spanning two floors for four people are $180. This marriage of past and present in such a prime location has proven so popular that it's imperative to reserve many months in advance. The 72-seat dining room, $20–25 for gourmet Northwest cuisine in a classic setting, gives preference to reservations made by hotel guests.

Transportation

The only year-round access to Crater Lake is from the south via ORE 62. To reach Crater Lake from Grants Pass, head for Gold Hall and take ORE 234 until it meets ORE 62. As you head up ORE 62 you might spot roadside snow poles in anticipation of the onset of winter. This highway makes a horseshoe bend through the Cascades, starting at Medford and ending 20 miles north of Klamath Falls. The northern route via ORE 138 (Roseburg to U.S. 97, south of Beaver Marsh) is usually closed by snow mid-October–July. The tremendous snowfall also closes 33-mile-long Rim Drive, although portions are opened when conditions permit. Rim Drive is generally opened to motorists around the same time as the northern entrance to the park.

The quickest route from Portland is I-5 to Eugene; ORE 58 east across Cascades to U.S. 97 south. At Chiloquin, take ORE 62 through Fort Klamath into the south entrance of the park.

Umpqua Highway

One of the great escapes into the Cascade Mountains is via the Umpqua Highway. This road runs along the part of the Umpqua River coveted by Zane Grey and Clark Gable as well as legions of less ballyhooed nimrods during steelhead season. The North Umpqua is a premier fishing river full of trout and salmon as well as a source of excitement for white-water rafters who shoot the rapids. Numerous waterfalls, including Watson Falls, feed this great waterway and are found close to the road. Tall timbers line the road through the Umpqua National Forest, and many fine campgrounds are situated within its confines. Mountain lakes like Toketee Reservoir, Lemolo Lake, and Diamond Lake offer boating and other recreational opportunities. The Umpqua National Forest also boasts challenging yet accessible mountain trails up the flanks of Mount Bailey (8,363 feet) and Mount Thielsen (9,182 feet). And when snow carpets the landscape in winter, you can go cross-country skiing, snowmobiling, and snowcat skiing on Mount Bailey free from the crowds at other winter sports areas.

This place is still so wild primarily because of the rugged terrain. The first road was built in the 1920s, a crude dirt trail that ran from Roseburg to Steamboat. Travelers of the day who wanted to get to the Diamond Lake Lodge spent three days traversing this road by car, then had to journey another 20 miles on horseback to reach their final destination. The North Umpqua Road was expanded to Copeland Creek by the Civilian Conservation Corps during the Depression, but the trips to Diamond and Crater Lakes were still limited to a trailwise few.

It wasn't until the late 1950s, when President Dwight D. Eisenhower pushed for development of the nation's interstate freeways and state highways, that road improvement began in earnest. Douglas County responded to the president's call by allocating $2.76 million toward federal matching funds to construct the Umpqua Highway. The all-weather thoroughfare was completed in the summer of 1964, opening up the North Umpqua basin to timber interests, sportspeople, and tourists.

The economy of Douglas County feeds upon the timber of the Umpqua National Forest. Approximately three-fourths of all workers in the county are directly or indirectly dependent on the timber industry. Timber receipts from federal lands generate $60 million annually for county coffers, providing money for roads, schools, and other services. But with over a quarter-million truckloads of logs rolling out of the Umpqua National Forest each year, it's no wonder that the timber boom is going bust. The dwindling supply of trees, after 25 years of unabated cutting and huge cutbacks in the allowable harvest of old-growth timber due to endangered species like the spotted owl, means that the lumberjack county is in for a major transition in the near future.

The good news is that many unspoiled areas were spared the lumberman's axe and are easily accessible to the traveler. Come and enjoy a beautiful green section of the Oregon Cascades on a road less traveled.

SIGHTS

Colliding Rivers

Just off of ORE 138 on the west side of the town of **Glide** is the site of the colliding rivers. The Wild and Umpqua Rivers meet head-on in a bowl of green serpentine. The best times to view this spectacle are after winter storms and when spring runoff is high. If the water is low, check out the high-water mark from the Christmas Flood of 1964. Water levels from that great inundation were lapping at the parking lot, a chilling reminder that *umpqua* means "thundering water" in Chinook.

Waterfalls

Visitors can get an unusual perspective of **Grotto Falls** because there's a trail in back of this 100-foot cascade. If you venture behind the shimmering water, watch your step because the moss-covered rocks are very slippery. To get here, take ORE 138 for 18 miles east of Roseburg to Glide. Follow Little River Road to the Coolwater Campground, and you'll find the turnoff to Forest Service Road 2703 nearby. Take it for five miles until you reach the junction of Forest Service Road 2703-150. Proceed down Forest Service Road 2703-150 for another two miles until you reach the trailhead. It's only a short hike in to view Grotto Falls.

About 10 miles west of the town of **Steamboat** is 50-foot-high **Susan Creek Falls** whose trailhead sits off ORE 138 near the Susan Creek picnic area. A one-mile trail winds through a rainforestlike setting to the falls. The cascade is bordered on three sides by green mossy rock walls that never see the light of the sun and stay

Fall Creek Falls, with tiers of 35–50 feet, is one of more than a dozen waterfalls along the Rogue–Umpqua Scenic Byway.

COURTESY OF BLM/GREG MORGAN

wet 365 days a year. Another quarter mile up the trail are the **Indian Mounds.** One of the rites of manhood for Umpqua boys was to fast and pile up stones in hopes of being granted a vision or spiritual powers. Also called the Vision Quest Site, the site still holds stacks of moss-covered stones in an area protected by a fence.

Four miles west of Susan Creek Falls is **Fall Creek Falls.** Look for the trailhead off of ORE 138 at Fall Creek. A good walk for families with young children and for older people, the mild one-mile trail goes around and through slabs of bedrock. Halfway up the trail is a lush area called **Job's Garden.** Stay on the Fall Creek Trail and in another half mile you'll come to the falls. It's a double falls with each tier 35 to 50 feet in height. Back at Job's Garden, you may care to explore the Job's Garden Trail, which leads to the base of columnar basalt outcroppings.

During fish-migration season, it's fun to venture off of ORE 138 at Steamboat and go up Steamboat Creek Road 38 to see the fish battle two small waterfalls. The first, **Little Falls,** is a mile up the road. It's always exciting to see the fish miraculously wriggle their way up this 10-foot cascade. Four miles farther down Steamboat Creek Road is **Steamboat Falls.** A viewpoint showcases this 30-foot falls, but not as many fish try to swim up this one because of the fish ladders nearby.

Back on ORE 138 about three miles east of Steamboat is **Jack Falls.** Look for the trailhead sign and follow the trail along the brushy bank of Jack Creek to a series of three closely grouped falls ranging 20–70 feet in height.

Two big waterfalls are another 19 miles down ORE 138 near the Toketee Ranger Station. To get to **Toketee Falls,** follow Forest Service Road 34 at the west entrance of the ranger station, cross the first bridge, and turn left. There you'll find the trailhead and a parking area. The half-mile trail ends at a double waterfall with a combined height of over 150 feet. The word *toketee* means "graceful" in the tribal dialect, and after viewing the water plunge over the sheer wall of basalt you'll probably agree it's aptly named.

Double back to ORE 138 and take Forest

THE CASCADES

Service Road 37 near the east entrance of the Toketee Ranger Station. This road will take you to the trailhead of **Watson Falls,** a 272-foot-high flume of water. A moderate half-mile trail climbs through tall stands of Douglas fir and western hemlock and is complemented by an understory of green salal, Oregon grape, and ferns. A bridge spans the canyon just below the falls, giving outstanding views of this towering cascade. The cool spray that billows up to the bridge always feels good on a hot day after the hike uphill.

Another falls worth a visit is **Lemolo Falls.** *Lemolo* is a Chinook word meaning "wild and untamed," and you'll see that this is the case with this thunderous 100-foot waterfall. To get here, take Lemolo Lake Road off of ORE 138, then follow Forest Service Roads 2610 and 2610-600 and look for the trailhead sign. The trail is a gentle one-mile path that drops down into the North Umpqua Canyon and passes several small waterfalls on the way to Lemolo Falls.

Umpqua Hot Springs

The Umpqua Hot Springs is mostly unknown and far enough from civilized haunts not to be overused, yet it's accessible enough for those in the know to enjoy. The springs have been developed with wooden pools and a crude lean-to shelter. It's best to go midweek, as weekends tend to attract more visitors, forcing you to wait your turn for a soak.

To get here, go north from the Toketee Ranger Station and turn right onto County Road 34, just past the Pacific Power and Light buildings. Proceed down 34 past Toketee Lake about six miles. When you cross the bridge over Deer Creek, which is clearly signed, you will be a little less than a half mile from the turnoff. The turnoff is Thorn Prairie Road to the right that goes a mile and ends at a small parking area. Please note that in wet weather this road may be impassable, and it is not recommended for low-slung cars in any season. From the parking area, it's a half mile down the blocked road to the hot springs trailhead and another half mile to the pool.

SPORTS AND RECREATION

Hiking

Over 570 miles of trails crisscross the one-million-acre **Umpqua National Forest,** with elevations that range 1,000–9,000 feet. There are hikes to please families and mountain climbers alike. Wildlife and wildflowers, mountain lakes and mountain peaks, old-growth forest and alpine meadows are some of the attractions visitors see along the way.

If you're camping along the North Umpqua River, many pleasant day hikes are possible on the **North Umpqua Trail.** Beginning near the town of Glide, this thoroughfare parallels the North Umpqua River for most of its 79 miles. Divided into 11 segments from over 3 to just under 16 miles in length, the trail leads high into the Cascades and connects with the Pacific Crest Trail as well as many campgrounds. ORE 138 affords many access points to the trail. Check with the Umpqua National Forest Ranger Station, Diamond Lake Ranger District (HC 60, P.O. Box 101, Idleyld Park 97447, 541/498-2531), for a map and brochure to plan your expedition along this beautiful walkway.

One segment of the North Umpqua Trail is the one-mile **Panther Trail.** This gentle hike begins near Steamboat at the parking lot of the former ranger station. Many wildflowers are seen late April–early June on the way up to the old fish hatchery. One flower to look for is the bright red snow plant, *Sarcodes sanguinea,* which grows beneath Douglas firs and sugar pine trees. Also called the carmine snowflower or snow lily, the snow plant is classified as a saprophyte, a plant that contains no chlorophyll and derives nourishment from decayed materials. Growing 8 to 24 inches in height, the plant has red flowers crowded at the crown of the stem.

A five-mile hike that ranges from easy to moderate is found on the south slope of 8,363-foot **Mount Bailey.** Bring plenty of water and good, sturdy hiking shoes because the last half mile of the ascent is steep, with many sharp rocks. To get to the trailhead, take ORE 138 to the north entrance of Diamond Lake. Turn off onto Forest Service Road 4795 and follow it five miles to the junction of Forest Service Road 4795-300. Proceed down 4795-300 another mile until you see the trail marker.

The easy two-mile **Diamond Lake Loop** takes hikers through a mix of lodgepole pine and true fir to Lake Creek, Diamond Lake's only outlet. There are many views of Mount Bailey along the way, as well as some private coves ideal for a swim on hot days. But while the grade is easy, keep in mind that the elevation is nearly a mile high and pace yourself accordingly. To get to the loop, take Forest Service Road 4795 off of ORE 138 on the north entrance to Diamond Lake and look for the trailhead sign on the west side of the road.

For those who like to climb mountains for reasons other than just because they are there, the **Mount Thielsen Trail** offers a million-dollar view from the top of the mountain. This four-mile moderate-to-difficult trail winds to the top of Mount Thielsen's spire-pointed 9,182-foot-high volcanic peak.

Bring along water and quick-energy snacks; hiking boots are also recommended due to the sharp volcanic rocks that could easily damage ordinary shoes. Extra care should be taken getting up and down the last 200 feet, since the rocks weaken from ice and erosion during the winter and are prone to crumbling underfoot. If you make it to the top, be sure to enter your name in the climbing register found there. Then take a look at the view, which stretches from Mount Shasta to Mount Hood, and forget all the silly preoccupations that plague us mortals. You'll find the trailhead on the east side of ORE 138 one mile north of the junction of ORE 230.

Fishing

The North Umpqua has several distinctions. First, it is known as one of the most difficult North American rivers to fish. No boats are permitted from 15 miles in either direction of Steamboat, and no bait or spinners are allowed either. This puts a premium on skillful fly-fishing. You can wade on in and poke around for the best fishing holes on the North Umpqua, one of the few rivers with a summer run of native steelhead—or better yet, hire a guide.

One of the decisions fishing-guide shoppers have to make is to choose from Gary, Larry, or Jerry. **Gary's Guide Service (607 Fawn Dr., Roseburg 97470, 541/672-2460)** has been in the fishing business for over 20 years and can teach you tried-and-true secrets of the trade. Licensed, bonded, and insured, Gary provides all the equipment for fly- or drift-fishing for salmon and steelhead on the North Umpqua.

Larry's Guide Service (12736 N. Umpqua Hwy., Roseburg 97470, 541/673-3099 or 800/763-6277 pin number 8406, www.oregon guides.com) can help you get out on the river year-round to fish for salmon, steelhead, and striped bass. The driftboats are large and heated; bait, tackle, and safety equipment are all provided. Rates are $150/seat for full-day trips; call ahead for reservations and additional information.

Jerry's Guide Service (3526 N.E. Hughes St., Roseburg 97470, 541/672-8324) echoes Gary's and Larry's offerings. Jerry Phelps, a teacher, naturalist, and guide with a master of science degree, offers an educational and entertaining fishing experience. Jerry's rates also run $150/seat and include lunch.

Bill Conners Guide Service (P.O. Box 575, Glide 97443, 541/496-0309) offers trips on the North Umpqua River for winter steelhead Jan.–April, for chinook salmon May–June and Sept.–Oct., and for summer steelhead June–October. He uses drift boats and gives you a choice of fly-, bait, or lure fishing. Call ahead for rates and reservations.

Brian Jones' **Muddler Enterprises** (622 S.E. 5th St., Bend 97702, 541/496-3037, www.muddlerenterprises.com) specializes in the North Umpqua's 30-plus miles of fly-angling pools and runs.

Rafting

It's no secret that the fishing is excellent on the North Umpqua River. And yet, recently "discovered," the river is only now gaining popularity with white-water rafters and kayakers. But fishing and floating are not always compatible, so guidelines for boaters and rafters have been established by the Bureau of Land Management and the Umpqua National Forest.

The area around Steamboat has the most restrictions, mainly because of the heavy fishing in the area that boaters would disturb. Be sure to check with the forest service (541/672-6601) prior to setting out, to make sure you are making a legal trip. A good way to get started rafting and avoid the hassle of rules, regulations, and gear is to go along with an experienced white-water guide. These leaders provide the safety equipment, the boats, and the expertise; all you have to do is paddle. There are, however, a few things to know before you go.

Don't bother to bring a camera; your hands will be too busy paddling to have time to take pictures. Besides, keeping a camera dry in a raft is not an easy task and often requires special protective equipment. Short pants are preferable, because a little water can be easily brushed off skin, whereas soaked jeans will make you cold and miserable for the duration of your voyage. Ponchos can keep water off your upper body, but they breathe poorly—which means your perspiration will soak you nearly as completely as any souse hole (exhilarating pools of foaming water that can be dangerous because of their strong eddies). Leave the Gucci sandals at home and wear a pair of worn-out sneakers you don't care about. There always seems to be a bit of water in the bottom of the boat, and shoes are always required for safety reasons. Finally, a hat and liberal layers of sunscreen are recommended to protect your skin from the ravages of the mountain sun.

In addition to rafting, inflatable kayak trips are offered by outfitters. Inflatables are easier for the neophyte to handle than the hardshell type, though these craft expose you to more chills and spills. Whatever your mode of floating the river, expect more than a dozen Class III or IV rapids, and plenty of Class IIs, as well as old-growth trees and osprey nests. Best of all, this world-class river is still relatively undiscovered. Spring and summer are the best times to enjoy the North Umpqua, although it's boatable year-round. Boaters are allowed on the river between 10 A.M. and 6 P.M. only, leaving the morning and evening for fish.

North Umpqua Outfitters (222 Oakview Dr., Roseburg 97470, 541/673-4599, www.nuorafting.com) offers raft, kayak, and drift-boat trips. Three-hour raft trips are $75 per person; five-hour raft trips with lunch are $95 per person. This company operates the North Umpqua Kayak School, which gives classes on how to paddle safely, to roll and handle surfing waves, and to survive souse holes. Half- and full-day kayak lessons include all necessary equipment. Half- and full-day drift-boat trips are available for those who like to troll their fishing line in the water on their way downstream. They also rent boats, rafts, kayaks, and the appropriate accoutrements. Their brochure is available at the Roseburg Visitors and Convention Bureau (401 S.E. Spruce St., 541/672-9731 or 800/444-9584). Other outfitters are the **Adventure Center** (541/482-2897, Ashland) and **Orange Torpedo Trips** (209 Merlin Rd., Merlin 97532, 800/635-2925, www.orangetorpedo.com).

You can combine rafting and mountain biking with **Oregon Ridge and River Excursions** (P.O. Box 495, Glide, 541/496-3333 or 888/454-9696, www.umpquarivers.com). Their popular two- or three-day trips take mountain bikes down the trail along the North Umpqua River and feature white-water paddle rafting, too. They also offer raft and kayak packages as well as guesthouse accommodations. Snacks, great outdoor cooking, and comfortable camping are provided. Call for rates and reservations.

Mount Bailey Snowcat Skiing

Located 80 miles east of Roseburg off of ORE 138 in the central Cascades is Mount Bailey. According to **Mount Bailey Snowcat Skiiing** (216 Aspen Lane, Diamond Lake 97731, 541/793-3348 or 800/446-4555, www.mountbailey.com), a group of hardcore skiers, they know where the best runs are to be had. Snowcats transport no more than 12 skiers up the mountain from Diamond Lake Resort to the summit of this 8,363-foot peak. Experienced guides then lead small groups down routes that best suit the abilities of each group. The skiing is challenging and should be attempted only by advanced skiers. Open bowls, steep chutes, and tree-lined glaciers are some of the types of terrain encountered during the 3,000-foot drop in elevation back to the resort.

The prices may also seem steep at up to $220 a day, but it's worth it given the pristine beauty of the area, dearth of crowds, and superlative skiing. You can save some money with the Powder Pass—six days of skiing for the price of five. Other attractive packages include overnight lodging in fireside cabins at Diamond Lake Resort as well as an "alpine lunch" of breads, meats, cheeses, vegetables, homemade pie, and coffee served up on the mountain. Only a limited number of skiers can be booked, so be sure to call ahead for reservations.

Tubing and Snowboarding

If you fit the bunny hill category, you might enjoy inner-tubing or snowboarding near Diamond Lake Resort (800/733-7593, www.diamondlake.net). A rope tow takes "tubers" to the top of the hill daily 9 A.M.–5 P.M. for nonstop thrills and spills on the way back down. The hill has a ticket system similar to other ski lifts, with full-day, half-day, and two-hour passes available. The tubing and snowboarding hill is located at the Hilltop Shop. The $8 entry fee includes inner tube, tow rope, and cable clip. Uphill tows are 50 cents. You can also buy tow ticket packages: 10 tickets for $5; 20 tickets for $8; and 50 tickets for $20.

Cross-Country Skiing

Over 56 miles of designated Nordic trails are found in the Diamond and Lemolo Lakes area along the upper reaches of ORE 138. The trails range in elevation from 4,200 feet to over 8,000 feet at the top of Mount Bailey. Some of the trails are groomed, and all of them are clearly marked by blue trail signs. Contact the **Umpqua National Forest** (Diamond Lake Ranger District, HC 60, P.O. Box 101, Idleyld Park 97447, 541/498-2531) to request maps and information on these trails.

The Diamond Lake Resort (800/733-7593) has equipment, waxes, and rentals, and is open daily 8 A.M.–5 P.M. It costs $17 per day for a rental package including skis, boots, and poles. Lessons are also available. A great option to cross-country buffs is to take a snowcat from Diamond Lake to the north rim of Crater Lake for

cross-country skiing in Upper Rogue country, near Mount McLoughlin

$90 per person. You have the option to ski the 10 miles back to Diamond Lake (mostly downhill) with a guide or ride back on the snowcat for an additional $60.

Snowmobiling

Approximately 133 miles of designated motorized snow trails are concentrated around the Lemolo and Diamond Lakes area. The trails are usually open in late November, when snow accumulations permit, and range from 4,000 to over 8,000 feet in elevation. Many of these trails are groomed on a regular basis, and all are clearly marked by orange trail signs and diamond-shaped trail blazes pegged up on trees above the snowline. Contact Umpqua National Forest (see "Cross-country Skiing," immediately preceding) for maps and additional information.

One of the more exotic runs is into Crater Lake National Park. Snowmobiles and ATVs (all-terrain vehicles) must register at the north entrance of the park and stay on the road. The trail climbs up about 10 miles from the park gates to the north rim of the lake. Be aware that the mountain weather here can change suddenly, creating dangerous subzero temperatures and whiteout conditions. Also, watch for Nordic skiers and other people sometimes found on motorized-vehicle trails.

If you've ever wanted to ride on one of these motorized snow broncs, then this is the way to go. Each person is furnished with his or her own snowmobile and fuel. A half dozen tours are available ranging from $50 for the 1.5-hour 17-mile ride around Diamond Lake to $150 for the eight-hour, 100-mile trip to Crescent Lake. The most popular trip is to the Crater Lake rim. It costs $95 and takes three hours to cover the 50 miles of snowbound terrain. The tour makes a lunch stop at South Shore Azza. Make your reservations at the **Diamond Lake Resort Hilltop Shop** (800/733-7593, ext. 231). The lodge also offers a great room and snowmobile package; for about $100, it includes a room for the night and two snowmobiles for three hours. Call the lodge for prices.

Little River Camping

If the thought of a campground with good shade trees and a waterfall with a swimming hole sounds idyllic, head for **Cavitt Creek Falls** (Bureau of Land Management, 777 N.W. Garden Valley Blvd., Roseburg 97470, 541/672-4491). To get there, head east of Roseburg on ORE 138 to Glide, take Little Creek Road (County Road 17) for seven miles, then continue three miles down Cavitt Creek Road. Ten campsites with picnic tables and fire grills are provided, with piped water, vaulted toilets, and firewood available on the premises. Open May to late October, Cavitt Creek runs $8 per night.

Another campsite five miles up Little River Road is **Wolf Creek** (North Umpqua Ranger District, 18782 ORE 138, Glide 97443, 541/496-3532), which features eight sites for tents and RVs (30 feet maximum) and three tent-only sites. Picnic tables, fire grills, vault toilets, and piped water are provided. Open mid-May–late October, the fee is $8 per night. The grounds also have a group picnic site with a pavilion sheltering 14 picnic tables, plus barbecue grills, flush toilets, and chlorinated water. This facility is booked on a reservation-only basis for $80 per day. A softball field, horseshoe pits, and swimming in the Little River make this a fine place for family get-togethers.

An easy way to keep your cool is at **Coolwater** (North Umpqua Ranger District, 18782 ORE 138, Glide 97443, 541/496-3532). Seven tent and RV sites (24 feet maximum) with picnic tables and fire grills are available; vault toilets and well water from a hand pump are also on the grounds. Open mid-May–late October, the campground is $5 per site. To get here, follow Little River Road 15 miles out of Glide. There are many good hiking trails nearby, including **Grotto Falls, Wolf Creek Nature Trail** and **Wolf Creek Falls Trail.**

One of the best deals on the Little River is at **White Creek** (North Umpqua Ranger District, 18782 N. Umpqua Hwy., Glide 97443, 541/496-3532). Open mid-May–late September, this small four-site campground accommodates tents and RVs for $5 per site. Picnic tables and fire grills are provided, and piped water and vault toilets are available. Situated on the confluence of White Creek and Little River, a good beach and shallow water provide excellent swimming for children. The only catch to this oasis of tranquility is that your stay is limited to two weeks at a time. To get here, take Little Creek Road 17 miles to Red Butte Road and proceed a mile down Red Butte Road to the campground.

Tucked away at an elevation of 3,200 feet on the upper reaches of the Little River is **Lake in the Woods** (North Umpqua Ranger District, 18782 ORE 138, Glide 97443, 541/496-3532). Here you'll find 11 sites for tents and RVs (16 feet maximum), with picnic tables, fire grills, vault toilets, and hand-pumped water. Open June–late October, the camp charges $8 per night. Set along the shore of four-acre, human-made Little Lake in the Woods, motorized craft are not permitted in this eight-foot-deep pond. Two good hikes nearby are to **Hemlock Falls** and **Yakso Falls.** To get here, head 20 miles up Little River Road to where the pavement ends; proceed another seven miles until you reach the campground.

North Umpqua River Camping
Set along the bank of the North Umpqua River 15 miles east of Roseburg on ORE 138 is **Whistler's Bend** (P.O. Box 800, Winchester 97495, 541/673-4863). Picnic tables and fire grills are provided at this county park, as are piped water, flush toilets, and showers. No reservations are necessary, and the fee is $12 per night. The fishing is good here, and even though it's fairly close to town, it doesn't usually get too crowded.

About 30 miles east of ORE 138 is **Susan Creek** (Bureau of Land Management, 777 N.W. Garden Valley Blvd., Roseburg 97470, 541/672-4491). This campground has 31 tent and RV sites (20 feet maximum) with picnic tables and fire grills. Flush toilets, piped water, and firewood are also available. Open May–late October, the fee is $11 per night. Situated in a grove of old-growth Douglas fir and sugar pine next to the North Umpqua River, the campground is enhanced by the presence of a fine beach and swimming hole as well.

Within easy access to great fishing (fly-angling only), rafting, and hiking, **Bogus Creek** (North Umpqua Ranger District, 18782 N. Umpqua Hwy., Glide 97443, 541/496-3532) offers you the real thing. Here you'll find five tent sites and 10 tent and RV sites (30 feet maximum) with picnic tables and fire grills. Flush toilets, iodinated water, and gray wastewater sumps are available. Open May 1–Oct. 31, the fee is $9 per night. As the campground is a major launching point for white-water expeditions and within a few miles of Fall Creek Falls and Job's Garden Geological Area (see "Waterfalls," earlier in this section), it's hard to beat the feeling here.

About 38 miles east of Roseburg on ORE 138 near Steamboat is **Canton Creek** (North Umpqua Ranger District, 18782 N. Umpqua Hwy., Glide 97443, 541/496-3532). Take Steamboat Creek Road off ORE 138 and proceed 400 yards to the campground. This campground features 12 sites for tents and RVs (22 feet maximum) with the standard picnic tables and fire grills, plus piped water, flush toilets, and gray wastewater sumps. Open mid-May–late October, Canton Creek costs $7 per night. Close to good fly-fishing on the North Umpqua, this site gets surprisingly little use.

Horseshoe Bend (North Umpqua Ranger District, 18782 N. Umpqua Hwy., Glide 97443, 541/496-3532) is 10 miles east of Steamboat. There are 34 sites for tents and RVs (35 feet maximum) with picnic tables and fire grills. Flush toilets, piped water, gray wastewater sumps, a laundry, and a general store are also available. Open mid-May–late September, the fee is $11 per night. Located in the middle of a big bend of the North Umpqua covered with old-growth Douglas firs and sugar pines, this is a popular base camp for rafting and fishing enthusiasts.

Diamond Lake Camping
Several campgrounds are in the vicinity of beautiful 5,200-foot-high Diamond Lake; boating, fishing, swimming, bicycling, and hiking are among the popular recreational options here. The trout fishing is particularly good in the early summer, and there are also excellent hikes into the

THE CASCADES

Mount Thielsen Wilderness, Crater Lake National Park, and Mount Bailey areas. While no reservations are technically necessary, these campgrounds can fill up fast, so it's always a good idea to book a space ahead of time. For the campgrounds listed below, contact Diamond Lake Ranger District (HC 60, P.O. Box 101, Idleyld Park 97447, 541/498-2531).

Though ORE 138 twists and turns most of the 80 miles from Roseburg to Diamond Lake, many people head straight for **Broken Arrow.** This 142-site campground with standard picnic tables and fire grills has plenty of room for tents and RVs (30 feet maximum); flush toilets, piped water, and gray wastewater sumps are available. Open early May–late September, the fee is $9–22 per night, depending upon the site. Premium lakeshore sites command top dollar. Diamond Lake and Broken Arrow both accept reservations. Call 877/444-6777 or reserve your space online at www.reserve.com/nrrs/or.

The next campground bears the name of its raison d'être, **Diamond Lake.** Here you'll find 160 campsites for tents and RVs (22 feet maximum) with picnic tables and fire grills. Piped water, flush toilets, and firewood are also available. Open May 15–Oct. 31, the fee is $10–20 per night. Numerous hiking trails lead from the campground, including the Pacific Crest National Scenic Trail. Boat docks, launching facilities, and rentals are nearby at Diamond Lake Lodge.

On the east shore of Diamond Lake is **Thielsen View.** It features 60 tent and RV sites (30 feet maximum) with picnic tables and fire grills. Piped water, vault toilets, gray wastewater sumps, and a boat ramp are also available. It's open late May–late September, and the fee ranges $9–14 per night, depending upon the site. As the name implies, this campground has picturesque views of Mount Thielsen.

PRACTICALITIES

Accommodations

The number of lodgings on the North Umpqua is limited to a few properties that range from rustic quarters to full-service resorts. The abundance of campgrounds and wilderness getaways accessible via the Umpqua Highway partially explains the dearth of motel units. In short, most people come here to get close to nature's teachings and leave the trappings of civilization behind. However, if the weather takes a turn for the worse or you'd rather rough it in style, you have several options that will give you shelter from the storm.

Near Idleyld Park is the **North Umpqua Resort** (P.O. Box 177, Idleyld Park 97447, 541/496-0149). Situated on ORE 138 along the north bank of the Umpqua, the place is not fancy, but it is at least clean. The rooms range $29–85, and good fishing can be had from the private bank of the property on the river. About four miles east of Idleyld Park is the **Dogwood Motel** (HC 60, P.O. Box 19, Idleyld Park 97447, 541/496-3403). Here you'll find clean modern units with or without kitchenettes located on tidy, well-kept grounds. Room rates range $45–70.

Near the summit of the Cascade Mountains about 75 miles east of Roseburg and 13 miles from Diamond Lake is **Lemolo Lake Resort** (2610 Birds Point Rd., Idleyld Park 97447, 541/643-0750, www.lemololake.com). Formed by a Pacific Power and Light dam, Lemolo Lake has German brown trout, as well as kokanee salmon, eastern brook trout, and rainbow trout. The lake is sheltered from wind by gently sloping ridges, and there are many coves and sandy beaches along the 8.3 miles of shoreline. Waterskiing is permitted on the lake. Boats and canoes can be rented, and many miles of snowmobiling and cross-country skiing trails are nearby.

The resort itself has cabins, both housekeeping and standard, and rooms available. Each Swiss-chalet housekeeping cabin is equipped with a furnished kitchen, bathroom with shower, and wood-burning stove. They can sleep up to six and they cost $109–155 per night. The Swiss-chalet standard cabins (with bathroom but no kitchen) sleep six in two double and two single beds for $100–120. Large lodge rooms go for $80–95 and small rooms, $60–75.

Diamond Lake Resort (Diamond Lake, 541/793-3333 or 800/733-7593, www.diamondlake.net) offers lodgings, restaurants, groceries, a service station, a laundry, and showers. Two-bedroom cabins rent for $150–225; rooms ($79) and studios ($90) are less. Lodgings here are popular as base camps for a Crater Lake excursion. This is a rustic mountain resort with enough modern amenities to suit the tenderfoot all four seasons. Mountain bikes, paddle boats, kayaks, canoes, and fishing boats as well as an equestrian center keep you out of the modest accommodations and busy enjoying the spectacular location.

The **Steelhead Run** (23049 U.S. 138, Glide, 541/496-0563 or 800/348-0563, www.steelheadrun.com) is a luxurious ranch-style B&B home situated on the banks of the North Umpqua. Enjoy a full country breakfast or a steelhead dinner in the dinning room with outstanding river views. There's a great swimming hole too. Tariffs are $68–98 for one of the three available rooms, $125–150 for the apartment with kitchen (no breakfast, but pets permitted upon prior approval). Even if you don't stay here, stop by and see their art gallery, which boasts a good collection of western and wildlife art.

The **Steamboat Inn** (42705 N. Umpqua Hwy., Steamboat, 541/498-2230 or 800/840-8825, www.thesteamboatinn.com) is the premier dining and accommodations property on the North Umpqua, situated in the middle of a stretch of 31 miles of fly-fishing turf. The inn's rooms and cabins are extremely popular, so reservations are a must. It's an ideal getaway from civilization, near the hiking trails, waterfalls, and fishing holes for which the Umpqua is famous. The $145–265 room rate is the best investment in peace of mind that you can make. The inn serves breakfast, lunch and dinner to guests; nonguests may also dine (see "Food," immediately following). Closed January and February; other winter months, weekends only.

Food

If you've got a craving for some junk food and just a few dollars to spare, the **Colliding Rivers Drive-In** (19162 ORE 138, Glide, 541/496-3631) can satisfy you. Nothing fancy: burgers, chicken, and spuds.

Munchies (20142 ORE 138, Glide, 541/496-3112) features reasonably priced Mexican food made mostly from scratch with no lard or MSG. They make their own vegetarian refried beans and offer eight vegetarian specials on the menu. The large burrito will fill you up in a hurry. Burgers, sandwiches, and breakfasts served all day can be found here, as can homemade pie. Open seven days a week 8 A.M.–9 P.M.

Make a reservation at the **Steamboat Inn** (42705 N. Umpqua Hwy., Steamboat 97447, 541/498-2230 or 800/840-8825, www.thesteamboatinn.com) to dine with hotel guests on main dishes of beef, fish, poultry, lamb, or pork, served with fresh vegetables and homemade bread. Choose from a wide selection of Oregon wines. Each meal is topped off with a sweet finish. The chef can also accommodate any food allergies, strong dislikes, and vegetarian diets. The Evening Dinner ($40) and Winemaker's Dinner ($75) are served nightly during the summer and on weekends the rest of the year. Reservations recommended.

Oakridge

Halfway between Eugene and the Cascades's summit on ORE 58 lies the town of Oakridge. Originally a Southern Pacific railway stop called Hazeldel, Oakridge changed its name in 1912 to fit the topography. It's also known as the Gateway City to the National Forest. Lumber, secondary wood products (furniture, toys, etc.), recreation, and tourism support this small community (pop. 4,000) tucked away in a foothill valley of the Cascades. The surrounding Willamette National Forest turns out billions of board feet of lumber each year, but it still retains some of the finest wilderness areas in Oregon.

There are over 100 lakes and streams near here, waiting for just about any nimrod to pull out his or her quota of rainbow, German brown, cutthroat, and Dolly Varden trout from the cool waters. A short drive from town are Waldo Lake and Diamond Peak Wilderness Area, as well as summer sailing and water-skiing at Odell Lake. Winter sport enthusiasts can find excellent downhill skiing at Willamette Pass, which features 18 runs, four chairlifts, a rope tow, and a day lodge. There are plenty of beautiful trails available for Nordic skiers too. If you like to fish, hike, camp, sail, ski, mountain bike, or just hang out in the woods, it's all only minutes away from Oakridge. (For information on hiring a fishing or rafting guide for this area, see "Rafting and Fishing" under "McKenzie River Highway," later in this chapter.)

SIGHTS

Westfir Covered Bridge

A short distance out of Oakridge on the Aufderheide National Scenic Byway is the Westfir Covered Bridge. This bright red span has the distinction of being the longest covered bridge in Oregon (180 feet) as well as the tallest covered bridge west of the Mississippi. Furthermore, it is likely that it is also the heaviest span of any wood construction bridge due to its Howe trusses, extension rods, and cords. You can see what remains of the Hines Company mill on the opposite side of the bridge; in its heyday it employed 750 people and operated around the clock. You can get a good picture of the bridge from the road as you approach the town of Westfir.

Salt Creek Falls

About 20 miles southeast of Oakridge, just west of Willamette Pass on the way to Odell Lake on ORE 58, is Oregon's second-highest waterfall, Salt Creek Falls. You'll find the pullout on the south side of the highway. The short walk to the viewing area of the 286-foot-high cascade provides a great photo opportunity. Trails access both the top and the bottom of the falls for those interested in taking a closer look at this raw display of hydropower. Restrooms and a picnic area, all wheelchair accessible, are available at the falls. There are also interpretive placards along the trail to supplement the information kiosk. This waterfall is considered the headwaters of the Willamette River.

Hot Springs

McCredie Hot Springs is found 10 miles southeast of Oakridge on ORE 58 near mile marker 45. A short walk down to Salt Creek brings you to a small hot spring adjacent to the river. This location allows the visitor to enjoy the rush of simultaneously hot and cold water. Depending on how you position yourself, you can take a bath at any temperature you choose. There are plans to develop McCredie Hot Springs into a resort, so it is recommended you partake of this experience while it's still in its natural state.

Another primitive hot springs in the area is **Meditation Pool** (Wall Creek). It's really more like a warm spring, as the water ranges from about 90–104°F, depending upon weather conditions. It's a short easy hike in, and the soak is worth the effort. To get there, turn north onto Rose Street from ORE 58 in Oakridge. Turn right onto 1st Street, proceed east, and 1st Street will eventually become Forest Service Road 24 paralleling Salmon Creek. About 10 miles out of Oakridge, look for Forest Service Road 1934 on the left (north) side of the road. Approximately a half mile down Forest Service Road 1934 you'll see a trailhead sign (the kind with no name, only two figures hiking) on the west (left) side of the road. Follow the path along Wall Creek about a third of a mile up to the creekside pool. East of Oakridge on ORE 58 on the south side of the highway is Greenwater rest area, a beautiful place to take in the laid-back charm of the upper Willamette River.

HIKING AND CAMPING

Fall Creek National Recreation Trail

The Fall Creek National Recreation Trail is about 30 miles southeast of Eugene. To get there, take ORE 58 about 15 miles to Lowell, then go north for two miles to the covered bridge at Unity Junction. Take a right onto Forest Service Road 18 (Fall Creek Road), and stay to the left of the reservoir. Follow the road for 11 miles to Dolly Varden Campground, where the trail starts.

The 14-mile-long Fall Creek Trail is ideal for short day hikes or longer expeditions; several national forest entry/exit points crop up along the way. Another plus is the low elevation of the trail, which makes it accessible year-round. Strolling through the wilderness, you will pass many deep pools, white-water rapids, and over a dozen small streams. Giant Douglas firs, bigleaf maples, vine maples, dogwoods, and red alders are some of the predominant vegetation you'll see along the way. In the spring, visitors are treated to shooting stars, trillium, bleeding heart, and other vibrant wildflowers.

There are five campgrounds en route and three other spur trails that merge into the Fall Creek Trail. **Bedrock Campground** is a particularly popular spot for swimming. Those without a fear of heights can jump off the bridge into the deep waters of the creek 40 feet below, or perhaps attempt a dive off of the adjacent rock escarpment.

Larison Creek Trail

The Larison Creek Trail (Trail 3646) is less than 10 minutes from Oakridge. To get here, take ORE 58 to Oakridge. Turn onto Kitson Springs County Road and proceed for a half mile. Turn right on Forest Service Road 21 and follow it three miles to the trailhead, which you'll find on the right side of the road.

Multicolored mosses cover the valley floor, and its walls simulate a brush-stroked backdrop to stands of old-growth fir. Further contrast is supplied by waterfalls and swimming holes. The mild grade and low elevation of this trail make it accessible year-round.

Tufti Creek Trail

Another good hike close to Oakridge is the Tufti Creek Trail (Trail 3624). To get here, take ORE 58 to Oakridge. Turn onto Kitson Springs County Road and proceed for about a mile. Turn left onto Forest Service Road 23 and follow it for six miles. This will take you along the northeast bank of Hills Creek Lake and on past Kitson Hot Springs (which is also worthy of investigation). Look for the trailhead sign on the right, about a mile past the hot springs.

This short and friendly half-mile trail winds through large Douglas firs and cedars and overlooks Hills Creek Gorge. There are many small waterfalls and deep swimming holes along the way. This trail is also accessible year-round.

Waldo Lake Wilderness

The Waldo Lake Wilderness is a 37,000-acre gem 70 miles southeast of Eugene via ORE 58 (take Forest Service Road 5897 before the Willamette Pass turnoff to go 10 miles to the lake). The centerpiece of this alpine paradise is 10-square-mile Waldo Lake (the third largest in Oregon), whose waters were once rated the purest in the country in a nationwide study of 30 lakes. In 1997, however, Crater Lake got the number one spot as the purest lake in the world with 142-feet visibility. Regardless, peer down into the green translucent depths of this 420-foot-deep lake to see rocky reefs and fish 50–100 feet below.

Canoeing, sailing, trout fishing, and windsurfing (no motorized craft allowed) on the lake complement hiking and cross-country skiing to give you different ways to experience the lake

THE CASCADES

and surrounding region. Add wildlife-watching highlighted by the early September rutting season of Roosevelt elk and you'll quickly understand why Waldo Lake is a favorite with Cascades connoisseurs. The 22-mile loop trail around the lake is popular with mountain bikers and backpackers, and day hikes on the south end edify less diehard recreationists.

To best savor it all, visit the area between late August and mid-October to avoid a plague of summer mosquitoes and early winter snowfall. Whenever you go, expect a lack of crowds, views of 8,744-foot Diamond Peak in the distance, as well as first-rate trails and campgrounds. There's even one forest service campground, **Rhododendron Island** that is accessed only by boat.

While the Rigdon Lakes hike and the Waldo Lake campgrounds in this chapter are a good introduction to this magical realm, there are many more great spots out there waiting to be enjoyed. Your best source for maps, information, and recreational tips is the **Middle Fork Ranger Station** (46375 ORE 58, Westfir 97492, 541/782-2291).

Rigdon Lakes

A more ambitious hike is up to Rigdon Lakes (Trails 3590 and 3583). To get there, follow ORE 58 for 24 miles southeast of Oakridge. Take a left on Forest Service Road 5897. Follow it 10 miles to North Waldo Campground; the trailhead is to the right of the restrooms. This three-mile walk starts at North Waldo Lake Campground on Trail 3590. The trail is mild and scenic, paralleling the north shore of Waldo Lake for about two miles until the Rigdon Trail junction (Trail 3583). Head north (turn right) at the trail intersection for another mile to get to the first of the three Rigdon lakes, which has several peninsulas that are ideal for a picnic and several small islands that might tempt swimmers who don't mind cold water. A hike afterward to the top of Rigdon Butte is highly recommended. You will have to bushwack, as there is no clear trail, but it is not a difficult climb if you follow the saddle of the ridge. From this vantage point, you can see all three Rigdon Lakes as well as many other nearby Cascade landmarks. If you

want to take a closer look at the two other Rigdon Lakes, they're only another mile or so down Trail 3583 from the first lake.

Camping

Blue Pool Campground (Oakridge Ranger Station, 46375 ORE 58, Westfir 97492, 541/782-2291), on the banks of Salt Creek, is 10 miles from Oakridge on ORE 58. During the summer, water is available for flush toilets and general use. Each of the 18 sites features a picnic table and a fireplace grill. It costs $12 for a family per site, or $20 for two families on one site. A Golden Age passport grants the holder a 50 percent discount.

Six miles west of Oakridge on the banks of the Willamette River and not too far from Lookout Point Lake is **Black Canyon Campground.** Open May–late October, there are 72 sites for tents, trailers, or motor homes up to 40 feet long for $14 a night. Picnic tables and fireplace grills are standard; piped water, firewood, and vault toilets are also available. Boat docks and launching facilities are nearby on the south end of Lookout Point Lake. For additional information, write to Willamette National Forest (46375 ORE 58, Westfir 97492, 541/782-2291).

There are two very nice campgrounds up at Waldo Lake called **Shadow Bay** and **North Waldo.** To get there, take ORE 58 for 24 miles southeast of Oakridge. Take a left on Forest Service Road 5897. It is five miles to Forest Service Road 5896, which takes you to Shadow Bay, and 10 miles down Forest Service Road 5897 to North Waldo. Both campgrounds charge $14.

Since there are 150 campsites between the two campgrounds, this usually ensures enough views of this mile-high lake for everyone to enjoy. Open June–late September, the fee is $14 a night. Boat docks and launching facilities are available, plus good sailing and fishing at Waldo. Many trails lead to small backcountry lakes from here; this is a good place to establish a base camp. Contact the Oakridge Ranger District for additional information.

If you want to get away from the traffic of ORE 58 and don't mind bouncing down forest service roads for over half an hour, you might consider **Blair Lake Campground** (Willamette National Forest, 46375 ORE 58, Westfir 97492, 541/782-2291). To get to Blair Lake, head east out of Oakridge on County Route 149 for one mile. Turn left onto Forest Service Road 24 and go eight miles until you hit Forest Service Road 1934. It's another seven miles down Forest Service Road 1934 to Blair Lake.

On the shore of little Blair Lake, a picturesque setting at 4,800 feet with seven tent sites awaits the determined explorer. Open June–mid-October, the fee is $6 per night, no reservations necessary. Picnic tables and fireplace grills are provided, with piped water, firewood, and pit toilets available. Boat docks are nearby, but no motorized craft are permitted on the lake.

PRACTICALITIES

Accommodations

There are some reasonable lodging options in the area. The **Arbor Inn** (48229 ORE 58, 541/782-2611 or 800/505-9047), $32–42, is a small, clean motel with microwaves and refrigerators in all rooms; some kitchenettes are also available. Pets are allowed here on prior approval. The **Best Western Oakridge Inn** (47433 ORE 58, 541/782-2212 or 800/528-1234), which has 30 large, spacious, clean rooms with pool, hot tub, and HBO, ranges $60–105 during the June 1–Oct. 30 summer season. Winter rates are about $5 less.

Odell Lake, 30 miles southeast of Oakridge on ORE 58, deserves a special mention. There are two resorts, several summer homes, and five campgrounds around this 3,582-acre lake. Located in a deep glacial trough, the lake probably filled with water about 11,000 years ago when a terminal moraine blocked the drainage of Odell Creek. Due to the depth of the lake and the nearly perpetual west-to-east winds that blow through Willamette Pass, the water averages a cold 39°F. Those breezes, however, help to keep the pesky mosquitoes and other obnoxious insects away and make for some of the best sailing in the Cascades.

The premier property on Odell Lake is the **Odell Lake Lodge** (P.O. Box 72, Crescent Lake 97425, 541/433-2540, www.odelllakeresort.com). To get there, take the East Odell Exit off of ORE 58 and follow the road a couple of miles. The hotel rooms range $50–64 a night, with the cabins going for $85–150. Skiers may want to take advantage of large cabin 12, which comfortably houses as many as 16 people for $240 a night. Since the lodge is extremely popular, reservations are strongly recommended, as much as a year in advance for weekends.

Moorages are available for rent, as are canoes, powerboats, and sailboats. The lodge has a complete tackle shop to help outfit you to catch the kokanee and mackinaw that inhabit the icy waters, and rental equipment is also available if you didn't bring your own. The restaurant at the lodge will cook your bounty for you and serve it along with soup or salad, potatoes, vegetables, and bread. The lodge also maintains its own system of trails, which provide good biking in the summer and cross-country skiing in the winter. The owners of the resort have put together an area map to guide you to various waterfalls. Bikes and ski equipment can be rented from the lodge. In addition to these outdoor pursuits, basketball, volleyball, badminton, and horseshoes round out the fun. Tots and toddlers will enjoy the sandbox, the toy library, and the swings.

Across the lake from the lodge is **Shelter Cove Resort** (W. Odell Lake Rd., Cascade Summit, 541/433-2548, www.sheltercoveresort.com), which features eight cabins complete with kitchens ($75–195), 69 campsites with picnic tables and electricity ($15–30), and 65 moorages (moorage $10 or free with cabin rental) in the marina. The General Store handles everything from groceries, tackle, and boat rentals to Sno-Park permits and fishing/hunting licenses. The September to October displays of Odell Lake's landlocked salmon spawning are unforgettable. Contact the Rigdon Ranger Station (541/782-2283) to reserve Warner Mountain Lookout, the 14-by-14-foot fire lookout cabin atop the 240-foot tower. At 5,800-feet elevation it has views of Diamond Peak, Three Sisters, and Mount Bachelor. It rents for $40 per night mid-November–mid-May, when not being used as a fire lookout.

In the former office building of Hines Lumber Company in Westfir across the street from the covered bridge is the **Westfir Lodge** (47365 1st St., Westfir, 541/782-3103, www.westfir-lodge.com). The building has been tastefully converted into seven guestrooms with English-style bathrooms (each room has its own private bath, but it's across the hall from the bedroom). The house is full of curious Asian antiques, and the pantry used to be the company vault. A full breakfast (try the English bangers, a mild sausage) is included in the rate, which is $65 for a single, $90 for double occupancy.

Food

Sandwiched in between the roller rink (where the tri-state competition is annually held) and the bowling alley is **Village Cafe** (47961 ORE 58, 541/782-4550). Standard American cuisine is the order of the day. Nothing terribly fancy, but nothing that terrible either. Open daily for breakfast, lunch, and dinner.

Latecomers or early risers should remember that the **Sportsman Cafe** (48127 ORE 58, 541/782-2051) is open daily at 7:30 A.M. and closes any time between 9:30 P.M. and 2:30 A.M. This is where you can hear many a fish story about the day's catch or the big one that got away. If the fish weren't biting, you can still find something good on the menu to get your hooks into. Dinners come with salad, fries, and toast. If you're in the mood for a home-cooked meal, try **Manning's Cafe** (47460 ORE 58, 541/782-4520), the local coffee shop with prototypical coffee shop fare that's open daily for breakfast, lunch, and dinner.

If you like Mexican food, be sure to take in **Rosalina's Mexican Fine Dining** (47720 School St., Oakridge, 541/782-5589) for lunch or dinner when exploring the Willamette National Forest. Tucked away in Oakridge a block off of ORE 58 (behind the Dairy Queen), it seems an unlikely location for a culinary treasure. But once you step inside, you'll immediately notice hundreds of photos tacked up all over the walls of guests who have enjoyed Rosalina's special birthday treatment (sorry, can't tell—it's a surprise!).

Chile rellenos set the gold standard for Mexican restaurants, and at Rosalina's they are absolutely exquisite. The batter is light, fluffy and not greasy. Only fresh Anaheim chilies, roasted and peeled on site, are used. Add Tillamook Monterey Jack cheese and a delicate tomato sauce, and you will agree with us that every bite salutes you. Moderately priced, but worth it. Open 11 A.M.–10 P.M. daily.

Information and Services

The **chamber of commerce** (44284 ORE 58, Oakridge 97463, 541/782-4146) offers a wide assortment of information on the area.

Additional information on biking, hiking, camping, and the Aufderheide National Scenic Byway (see "McKenzie River Highway," immediately following) can be obtained from the **Middle Fork Ranger Station** (46375 ORE 58, Westfir, 541/782-2291). Oakridge also hosts a mountain bike festival called the **Fat Tire Festival** (541/782-4146) usually held the fourth weekend of July. Guided mountain bike tours and one or more races challenge all skill levels. Live entertainment and a barbecue dinner provide the finishing touches for this popular rally.

McKenzie River Highway

The best way to get to this scenic road from the Willamette Valley is to take I-105 east from I-5 near Eugene. Take a left at the end of the interstate near the outskirts of Springfield and you will be on the McKenzie River Highway. There are four lanes for a couple of miles, and this is one of your best chances to ease by any slow-moving vehicles. However, beware of the highway patrol on the road here—it's easy to end up with a ticket!

In any case, just past where the four lanes merge into two, the McKenzie River Recreation Area begins. For the next 60 miles, you will not see any major population centers, as most of the towns consist of little more than a post office. However, you will see beautiful views of the blue-green McKenzie River with heavily forested mountains, frothy waterfalls, jet-black lava beds, and snow-capped peaks as a backdrop. The river was named for Donald McKenzie, a member of Astor Pacific Company, who explored the region in 1812.

The first 15 miles of the McKenzie River Highway pass through many fruit and nut orchards (primarily apples, cherries, and filberts), Christmas-tree farms, and berry patches (blueberry, raspberry, and marionberry). McKenzie River farmers enjoy plentiful water supplies from the McKenzie diversion canal, as well as fertile soils and a mild climate. Walterville is located in the middle of this agricultural section of the McKenzie Recreation Area.

The Leaburg Dam on the right signals your entry into the middle section of the McKenzie, where there are many vacation homes. A total of six dams on the McKenzie provide power, irrigation, and what the Army Corps of Engineers calls "fish enhancement." A favorite haunt of fishing enthusiasts, the mellow waters of the middle McKenzie teem with trout, steelhead, and salmon. You'll notice many driftboats parked in driveways. These boats have bows at both ends to prevent water inundation from either front or back. Mild white-water rafting and driftboat fishing are popular here, and there are many local guides and outfitters ready to help you float your expeditions.

The Willamette National Forest boundary is near Blue River. Huge, old-growth Douglas firs usher the clear blue waters of the McKenzie through the mountains. The McKenzie River National Recreation Trail and many of its counterparts also feature waterfalls, mountain lakes, or lava formations a short trek from the road. In addition to the myriad recreational opportunities, hot springs, quality accommodations, fine dining, and a dearth of crowds give you the southern Cascades at their finest.

SIGHTS

Proxy Falls

To get to Proxy Falls, follow the old McKenzie Pass (ORE 242) from the new McKenzie Pass (ORE 126) for 10 miles. Look for a small hiker-symbol sign on the right-hand side of the road. This is the only marker for the trail to a spectacular pair of waterfalls, Upper and Lower Proxy Falls.

It's an easy half-mile walk to Upper Proxy, an A-plus trail. The trail goes through a lava field and lush forest that changes with the season. There are giant rhododendrons that bloom in late spring, tart huckleberries in summer, and brilliant red foliage from the vine maples in the fall. Take a left at the first fork in the trail. This will take you to Upper Proxy Falls. A particularly good view of the falls can be found near the giant Douglas fir at the base of the pool.

Now that you've seen Upper Proxy Falls from the bottom up, check out Lower Proxy Falls from the top down. Go back to the fork in the trail and take a left. In less than a half mile, you will suddenly be on a ridge looking across a valley at Lower Proxy Falls. A good time to photograph both of these falls is around midday, when the sun's angle best illuminates the water.

Dee Wright Observatory

The Dee Wright Observatory (57600 McKenzie River Hwy., 541/822-3381, on ORE 242), closed in winter, at the first sign on snow, is about halfway between ORE 126 and Sisters. Built in the early '30s as a Civilian Conservation Corps

THE CASCADES

project, it was christened after the building's supervisor, who died prior to its completion. The tower windows line up with views of Mount Jefferson, Mount Washington, and two of the Three Sisters, as well as the eight-mile-long, half-mile-wide lava flow that bubbled out of nearby Yapoah a little less than 3,000 years ago. On a clear day, you can even see the tip of Mount Hood.

The .5-mile Lava River Trail next to the observatory offers a fine foray into the surrounding hills of rolling black rock. In addition to helpfully placed and concise interpretive placards explaining the lava formations, the trail is wheelchair-accessible. But while the walk is easy enough, the 5,300-foot elevation can sometimes make it seem a little more difficult. Note that on ORE 242, the vehicle length is restricted to a 35-foot maximum.

Koosah Falls

This cascade is about 20 miles from McKenzie Bridge on ORE 126. The visitor facilities here provide wheelchair access and excellent views of this impressive 70-foot-high falls on the McKenzie. The blue water bounces and bubbles over and through a basalt formation that flowed into the McKenzie thousands of years ago. If you look carefully, you can see many small springs flowing from crevices at the base of the falls. The blue water may have inspired the name Koosah, which comes from the Chinook word for sky.

Sahalie Falls

Another beautiful waterfall is only a half mile farther east on ORE 126 from Koosah Falls. (From McKenzie Bridge, travel east on ORE 126 to Road 2672. Follow Road 2672 to Forest Service Road 655. Follow Forest Service Road 655 to Sahalie Falls Day Use Area.) On the trail from Koosah Falls, giant cedar and fir trees line the path. It is only a few yards from the parking lot to the viewpoints of the falls. Also the result of a lava dam from the Cascade Range's not-so-distant volcanic past, here the river tumbles 100 feet into a green canyon. These are the highest falls on the McKenzie River—*sahalie* means "high" in the Chinook dialect. It's said that this

waterfall churns out the highest volume of water of any falls in the state.

Anyone who might want to take a shower is welcome to hike the slippery, unimproved trail to the base of the roaring cascade. Most people, however, are content to enjoy the view from benches and observation posts along the paved path. The Disney movie *Homeward Bound* featured these waterfalls in a scene portraying a family cat being swept over the top.

Sawyer's Cave

This ice cave is on the right just past the junction of ORE 126 and U.S. 20, near mile marker 72. You'll need a flashlight and a sweater to explore Sawyer's Cave; watch your head and watch your step. Classified as a lava tube, it's the result of a lava flow that cooled faster on the top and sides, forming a crust. Underneath, the hotter lava continued to drain downhill, leaving the lava tube behind. There are also small stalactites hanging down from the ceilings, formed from lava drippings. The basalt rock is a poor heat conductor, and like a natural refrigerator it keeps the coolness of winter and night inside the cave. Ice can be found on the floor of the cave during the hottest summer months.

Aufderheide National Scenic Byway

One of the nation's first 50 National Scenic Byways, the 58-mile Aufderheide Drive links ORE 126 to ORE 58. You'll find the Auferheide turnoff (Forest Service Road 19) at mile marker 45.9 about five miles east of Blue River. The road winds along the south fork of the McKenzie River, crests over the pass, and then follows the north fork of the middle fork of Willamette River down to Oakridge and ORE 58. Sights along the way include the Delta Old-Growth Grove Nature Trail, Terwilliger (Cougar) hot springs, the spectacular Willamette River Gorge, and the Westfir covered bridge.

Terwilliger (Cougar) Hot Springs

If you'd like to try a hot springs in a natural setting, head for Terwilliger Hot Springs, located in a forested canyon at the end of a .25-mile trail. Hot water bubbles up out of the earth at

116°F and flows down through a series of log and stone pools, each one a few degrees cooler than the previous one. A series of access steps and railings have also been built to help you get to the various soaking ponds. The local custom is optional clothing, so don't be surprised to see people parading around in their birthday suits.

To get there, take the Aufderheide Drive from ORE 126 up toward Cougar Reservoir. The trailhead for the hot springs on the west (right) side of the road is marked by a sign just past milepost seven. You can park in a large lot on the east side of the road about a tenth of a mile past the trailhead (alongside the reservoir). Parking alongside the road is prohibited (and enforced) from sunset to sunrise one mile from the trailhead. The hike is a quarter of a mile to the hot springs. A $3 per-person day-use fee is required, which has enabled this place to be well maintained. Northwest Forest Pass holders' entrance is free. Pay for it at the ranger station or at Harbick's store.

The several pools in this tranquil forest setting can be overcrowded on weekends. This hot spring offers one of the nicest soaking experiences we are aware of in the United States. As with all of the more remote and wild hot springs, take a friend. These places can attract an unsavory crowd.

HIKING

McKenzie River National Recreation Trail

The McKenzie River National Recreation Trail (3507) runs for 26.5 miles. It starts just outside the small town of McKenzie Bridge and goes to the Old Santiam Wagon Road, about three miles from the junction of ORE 126 and U.S. 20. But don't let that scare you. There are enough access points to let you design treks of three, five, eight, or more miles along this beautiful trail. It is hard to say which section of the footpath is the best, as each portion has its own peculiar charms; the following highlights give you a sample of what to expect.

Start at the top of the McKenzie River Trail at the Old Santiam Wagon Road. Completed in the early 1860s, this was the first link of the route from the mid-Willamette Valley to central

and eastern Oregon. Way stations were established a day's journey apart to assist the pioneers along their weary way. While most of these primitive establishments are no more, some of the historic buildings have survived and are still used today by packers. There isn't much left of the Old Santiam Wagon Road either, as much of it was destroyed with the construction of ORE 126. However, a seven-mile stretch remains from ORE 126 through the rugged lava country to the Pacific Crest Trail. A short walk on this former road to the promised land helps you to appreciate both the hardiness of the pioneers and the comforts of modern travel.

From the Old Santiam Wagon Road, the McKenzie River Trail surveys many remarkable volcanic formations. Lava flows over the last few thousand years have built dams, created waterfalls, and even buried the river altogether. At the northern end of Clear Lake, you can see the remains of an ancient forest preserved for nearly 3,000 years in the lake's cool waters. When nearby Sand Mountain erupted, the lava dammed up the McKenzie River and created Clear Lake. Koosah and Sahalie Falls were also created by lava dams, and the view of these white-water cascades from the McKenzie River Trail is much different than the version accessible from the highway. Another interesting sight is the Tamolitch Valley, where the McKenzie gradually sinks beneath the porous lava, disappearing altogether until it reemerges three miles later at cobalt-colored Tamolitch Pool. This area is accessible only on the National Recreation Trail.

If at all possible, arrange your McKenzie outing with friends and take two cars. This way you can have a car stationed at the beginning and ending segments of your hike, and thus avoid doubling back. Also keep in mind that hikes starting at the upper end of the trail take advantage of the descending elevation. Mountain bikes are allowed on all sections of the McKenzie River Trail.

Delta Old-Growth Grove Nature Trail

You'll find this half-mile loop trail on the west side of the Aufderheide Byway not far from ORE

126. This is an excellent opportunity to explore an old-growth ecosystem. In addition to 650-year-old conifers, you'll observe other layers of life from shrubs and ground-cover plants to fish, mammals, birds, and amphibians. Many plant species are clearly marked along the trail of this living laboratory and are explained in detail in a pamphlet called "Delta Old-Growth Grove, Ancient Provider," available from the National Forest Service.

Robinson Lake Trail

The .25-mile Robinson Lake Trail takes you to a heart-shaped lake with some fishing and swimming. To get here, turn off ORE 126 onto Robinson Lake Road. Be on the lookout for logging trucks and rocks on the gravel road. Follow the signs marked Forest Service Road 2664. At the unmarked junction, drive straight onto the red pumice road (Forest Service Road 2664), and continue until you reach the parking lot. It takes about 10 minutes to drive the four miles in. The easy hiking trail is in good condition; the left fork takes you to the center shore of Robinson Lake. The shallow lake warms up considerably during the summer, making a swim all the more inviting.

RAFTING

McKenzie River Adventures (P.O. Box 567, Sisters 97759, 541/822-3806 evening phone calls) has half-, full-, and two-day white-water rafting trips May–September. The half-day (four-hour) trip (lunch included) is $55 per person, $40 per child; the full-day (six-hour) trip (lunch included) is $85 per person, $55 per child. The cruises range from seven to 18 miles and take in some Class II and III rapids. Reservations are recommended.

Jim's Oregon Whitewater (56324 ORE 126, McKenzie Bridge 97413, 541/822-6003 or 800/254-JIMS, www.raft2fish.com) charters white-water rafts April–September and fly-fishing driftboats April–October. The half-day white-water rafting trip (lunch included) costs $52 per person, the full-day (lunch included) is $80 per person, and the two-day overnighter (meals included) is $280 per person. There's a four-adult

minimum for rafts trips. For those interested in some serious fly-fishing, it's $300–370 per boat (1–2 people) per day. Price includes all gear and tackle; you'll need to provide Oregon fishing license and tags, food, and beverage. Reservations are recommended.

Destination Wilderness (Box 1965, Sisters, 800/423-8868, www.widlernesstrips.com) floats the McKenzie March–October. Half-day trips are $55 adults, $45 kids; full-day $85 adults, $65 kids; and two-day $280 adults, and $220 kids. Half- and full-day tours are also offered by **Sun Country Tours** (531 S.W. 13th, Bend, 541/382-6277 or 800/770-2161, www.suncountrytours .com). Transportation to and from Black Butte Ranch is included; $70 per person for a half day; $95 adults, $85 kids for all day.

Larger parties interested in a mellow float on the McKenzie might want to consider a pontoon float with **Helfrich Outfitters** (37855 Shanandoah Loop, Springfield, 800/507-9889, www.helfrichoutfitter.com). These large crafts, which can be described as catamarans without the sail, offer a smoother ride than their smaller inflatable counterparts. The price for a full-day trip is $75 per person and includes lunch at one of the riverside lodges. Reservations are required. Helfrich also offers three- and four-day raft trips as well as fishing and hunting trips.

Oregon Whitewater Adventures (39620 Deerhorn Rd., Springfield, 541/746-5422 or 800/820-RAFT, www.oregonwhitewater.com) offers guided half-day trips (no lunch) for $50, full-day trips for $75, and a two-day overnighter for $215. All necessary gear and transportation back to your car are included. Group discounts are also available.

FISHING

Sure it's crowded, but scenic beauty and the chance to bag a five-trout limit lines 'em up on one of the state's best trout streams. Unless you can get a driftboat, access is limited. On weekends, driftboats and rafters vie for space. You can cast worms or spinners, though you're better off using flies when you're fishing off a boat for rainbows April–October. Consult the **Oregon**

Guides and Packers Directory for guides (531 S.W. 13th St., Bend 97702, 541/617-2876 or 800/747-9552, www.ogpa.org). The best pools tend to be west of Blue River, but it's harder to get to them because of private landholdings. Be sure to check for rules and regulations before you go fishing; the Dept. of Fish and Wildlife, 503/947-6000 or www.dfw.state.or.us/, can give you the information you need.

CAMPING

The following campgrounds are under the jurisdiction of the Willamette National Forest, McKenzie Ranger District (McKenzie Bridge 97413, info 541/822-3381, reservations 877/444-6777 or www.reserveusa.com). Many of these campsites connect with the beautiful McKenzie River National Recreation Trail. The fishing is also quite good on the McKenzie and the many lakes and reservoirs within this bailiwick. Its prime location halfway between Eugene and Bend also helps make the area a popular vacation spot during the summer, so advance reservations must be made at least five days in advance.

A half mile west of McKenzie Bridge on ORE 126 is **McKenzie Bridge Campground.** As the name implies, this 20-site multiuse park is along the banks of its namesake river. The fee is $12 a night. Piped well water, vault toilets, and a boat launch are provided. East of McKenzie Bridge about three miles on ORE 126 is **Paradise Campground.** Although there are 64 tent/RV (up to 40 feet) campsites, flush and vault toilets, and piped water, only half of the sites are in premium riverside locations. The summer trout fishing here can be very good, and the fireplace grills and wooden tables make it easy to cook and eat a fresh-caught meal. Welcome to paradise! The fee is $14 a night and reservations are recommended.

Olallie Campground is 11 miles outside of McKenzie Bridge on ORE 126 and has 17 multiuse sites. Olallie is situated on the banks of the McKenzie River; boating, fishing, and hiking are some of the nearby attractions. Piped water, vault toilets, and picnic tables are provided. The

fee is $12 a night. A couple miles past Olallie on ORE 126 is **Trailbridge Campground** (located on the north shore of Trailbridge Reservoir). Piped water, vault and flush toilets, and picnic tables are provided at this 26-site multiuse campground. Boat docks are close by, and the reservoir is noted for its good trout fishing. This campground is first-come, first-served (and not on the reservation system); $6 for single vehicle. Open June–October.

Another ideal campground for boating enthusiasts is **Lake's End** on nearby Smith Reservoir. One of the few boat-in campgrounds in Oregon, this park can only be reached via a two-mile sail across the lake. To get here, take ORE 126 for 12 miles northeast of McKenzie Bridge and turn left and follow Forest Service Road 730 to two miles to the south end of the reservoir. Boat across to the north shore for camping. Be sure to take along plenty of water, because the campground does not provide any. You will, however, find picnic tables, vault toilets, and plenty of peace and quiet away from the cars and traffic of the other mainstream parks. There is no fee for this escape from the ordinary. Open May 9–Sept. 30; no fee or reservations. Pit toilets.

On the south shore of Clear Lake, 19 miles northeast of McKenzie Bridge on ORE 126, is **Coldwater Cove Campground.** Piped water, vault toilets, and picnic tables are provided at this 35-site multiuse park. The fee is $14 a night. Open end of May to mid-October. **Clearlake Resort** (13000 ORE 20, Sisters 97759, 541/258-3729 message line) is adjacent to the campground and has a store, a summer-only café, and cabins, as well as boat docks, launches, and rentals. Keep in mind that small electric fishing-boat motors are the only mechanical means of propulsion allowed here by the Forest Service. Closes at the end of September; walk-ins are allowed during the winter. Reservations required during the busy summer months can be made by writing to the address above and sending a self-addressed stamped envelope.

A handful of campgrounds dot ORE 242, the old McKenzie Pass, but only **Alder Springs** (four miles east of McKenzie Bridge and another nine miles east on ORE 242) has piped

THE CASCADES

water. This remote campground has six tent sites with tables and fire rings; no drinking water. First-come, first-served; open May–end of September. Also on ORE 242 is privately owned **Camp Yale** (58980 ORE 242, McKenzie Bridge, 541/822-3961). Open all year; 14 full hookups (water, sewer line, and electricity) for $20; no tent sites. Modern restrooms with hot water showers are on site. Camp Yale also offers the only public dump station between Springfield and Sisters.

OTHER ACTIVITIES

Golf

If you like to play golf, you should plan your vacation around a visit to **Tokatee Golf Club** (54947 ORE 126, Blue River, 541/822-3220 or 800/452-6376, www.tokatee.com). Consistently rated among the top 25 courses in America by *Golf Digest,* Tokatee is a marriage of golf and wilderness beauty that creates a unique and satisfying experience. Good for all levels of experience; every hole has its own challenge. No houses are on the fairways to obstruct the knockout views of the forested mountains and the Three Sisters Wilderness. Open February–mid-November. Greens fees are $21 for nine holes, $39 for 18.

Mountain Biking

In the upper sections of the McKenzie, most of the usable trails gain elevation rapidly due to the steep terrain and make for very challenging biking. The most popular route is the **McKenzie River Trail.** Contact the McKenzie River Ranger District (503/822-3381) for detailed information. Bike rentals ($10 a day) and additional information are also available from McKenzie Bridge Store (91837 Taylor Rd., McKenzie Bridge, 541/822-3221).

PRACTICALITIES

Accommodations

Sleepy Hollow Motel (54791 ORE 126, Blue River 97413, 541/822-3805) is located within walking distance of one of the finest public golf courses in the country, Tokatee. This property is open April 1–Oct. 20. The motel has 14 air-conditioned units that range $60–70 $5 each additional person. Reservations are recommended.

The **Cedarwood Lodge** (56535 McKenzie Hwy./ORE 126, McKenzie Bridge 97413, 541/822-3351, www.cedarwoodlodge.com) is tucked away in a grove of old cedars just outside the town of McKenzie Bridge. The lodge has nine vacation housekeeping cottages that feature fully equipped kitchens, bathrooms (with showers), fireplaces (wood provided), and portable barbecues. Rates vary from $85 to $125 for two people, depending on the cabin and the season, $7.50 each additional person. Minimum three-day advance reservations are required July–September and holidays. This is our favorite place here, particularly those units with decks on the river.

The historic **Log Cabin Inn** (ORE 126, McKenzie Bridge 97413, 541/822-3432 or 800/355-3432, www.logcabininn.com) was built in 1906, and President Hoover, Clark Gable, and the Duke of Windsor are among the many notables who have stayed here over the years. With its homey decor, wraparound porch, and cedar-paneled dining hall, the Log Cabin Inn would make a wonderful label on a bottle of maple syrup. Upstairs from the dining room a gift shop featuring antiques and classic toys is worth a gander as is the interesting cross-section of notables in the guest book. There are also nine guest cottages, each one boasting a fireplace, a porch, and a view of the McKenzie River. For $5 per person, the inn will bring a continental breakfast to your cabin for you to enjoy along with the scenery. The Log Cabin's restaurant features game and salmon. Room rates range $90–110 double occupancy. A riverfront tepee (sleeps six) goes for just $45. Reservations required. The inn is located at milepost 51 near the intersection of ORE 126 and ORE 242.

Belknap Lodge and Hot Springs (P.O. Box 1, McKenzie Bridge 97413, 541/822-3512) offers rooms, cabins, and camping. The lodge rooms range $100–200 per couple, $10 each additional person. In the lodge rooms you can

Belknap Lodge

enjoy the hot spring water in the privacy of your own tub. The five cabins range $60–190, $5 each additional person. Camping sites are $20 per site per day, or $30 per person per week. The main attraction on the property is Belknap Springs. The water (which contains 26 different minerals) is gently filtered piping hot into a swimming pool on the south bank of the McKenzie. The property is clean, the scenery is beautiful, and the price is right. For $5, you can use the mineral pool facilities, just what the doctor ordered to ease the aching muscles from that killer hike or the ski marathon. But don't wait too long to fill this prescription—the pool closes at 9 P.M. If you forget your towel, you can rent one.

Both **Heaven's Gate Cottages** (50055 ORE 126, Vida, 541/822-3214) and **Woodland Cottages** (52560 ORE 126, Blue River, 541/822-3597) offer housekeeping cabins right on the McKenzie. Though the cabins at either place are sandwiched between the highway and the river, the unspoiled riverside view more than compensates for the traffic (which drops off considerably by nightfall). One Heaven's Gate cabin called Blue Moon is right over a good fishing hole and nightlights illuminate the rapids for your contemplation. A fireplace adds an additional romantic touch. Woodland Cottages also feature large sun decks on each cabin that are ideal for appreciating the tran-

quility of the river. Their cabins accommodate two to four occupants, and one unit will sleep six. Both establishments' cabins may be old, small, and semi-rustic, but their riverside location helps overcome a multitude of sins. Rates run $65–90.

You know when you cross over the McKenzie on the 165-foot-long Goodpasture Covered Bridge (circa 1938), the most photographed bridge in Oregon, that you're headed for someplace interesting. A great place for families, including pets, and those who want to get away from the noise of the McKenzie highway is the **Wayfarer Resort** (46725 Goodpasture Rd., Vida, 541/896-3613 www.wayfarerresort.com), featuring over a dozen cabins on the McKenzie and glacier-fed Marten Creek, $90–250 per night. Accommodating one to six people, the cabins have porches with barbecues overlooking the water, full kitchens, and lots of wood paneling. Two larger units, the Homestead and the Octagon, can sleep eight and are fully equipped with all the amenities. The Octagon features a deluxe kitchen, wet bar, washer/dryer, and whirlpool tub. Children can enjoy fishing privileges in the resort's private trout pond, while the folks play on the all-weather tennis court. All guests are welcome to supplement their menus with pickin's from the Wayfarer's organic gardens and berry patch. In the summer, advance reservations are a must for this popular retreat.

Food

About 15 minutes up the road near McKenzie Bridge is the **Rustic Skillet** (54771 ORE 126, McKenzie Bridge, 541/822-3400). Open for breakfast, lunch, and dinner, it can be likened to a fancy truck stop—just good ol' American food. Lest this sound like damning with faint praise we should add the menu is diverse for its genre. Kids (young and old alike) will enjoy a complimentary round of miniature golf with their meal.

If you're in the mood for a good lunch or dinner served with a generous helping of historical ambience, head for the **Log Cabin Inn** (see "Accommodations," immediately preceding). Built in 1906, the inn's cedar-paneled dining room

THE CASCADES

reflects the soft hues of a different era. Elaborate salads and sandwiches cost around $7 and are served with potato salad. Dinners range $7–20 and feature salmon and game dishes with all the trimmings.

Information and Transportation

Additional information on attractions and services can be acquired from the **McKenzie River Chamber of Commerce** (P.O. Box 1117, Leaburg 97489, 541/896-3330 or 800/318-8819). Wilderness permits, camping, hiking, and mountain biking information are available the **McKenzie River Ranger District** (57600 McKenzie Hwy., McKenzie Bridge, 541/822-3381). The **National Forest Service** has information about trails and nature walks in the region; write U.S. Forest Service, Willamette

District, P.O. Box 10607, Eugene 97401. You can also contact the **Bend Chamber of Commerce** (777 N.W. Wall St., 541/382-3221, www.bendchamber.org) for their McKenzie-Santiam brochure.

The best way for car-less travelers to get to the McKenzie National Recreation Trail from Eugene is via **Lane Transit District** (541/687-5555, www.ltd.org). Their route 91 bus starts at downtown Eugene and heads up the McKenzie River Highway, making a three-hour round-trip for only $2.50. The bus is equipped to carry a couple of mountain bikes. The terminus point is the McKenzie River Ranger Station at McKenzie Bridge. On weekdays the bus makes two round-trips in the morning and two in the afternoon; on Saturday and Sunday there's one morning and one afternoon trip.

Sisters

Sisters was established in 1888 when nearby Camp Polk, a short-lived military outpost established along Squaw Creek, was dismantled. Following abandonment of the camp, the site was homesteaded in 1870 by Samuel M. Hindman, who subsequently operated a store and post office. Sisters is named after its backdrop to the south, the Three Sisters. These 10,000+-foot-high peaks were the last major obstacle for the pioneers to circumnavigate on their journey to the fertile Willamette Valley. The emigrants named the mountains after some of the virtues that helped propel them through the hardships of the frontier: faith, hope, and charity. Over the years, no one could agree upon exactly which mountain was named what, so the Oregon legislature settled the dispute by labeling the mountains as the North, Middle, and South Sisters respectively.

In any case, while most of the Old Santiam Wagon Road has long since been replaced by asphalt and forest overgrowth, the 19th-century flavor has been preserved in the town of Sisters. Wooden boardwalks, 1880s-style storefronts, and plenty of good old-fashioned western hospitality grace this small town of about 1,000.

Some people are quick to lambast the thematic zoning ordinances of Sisters as cheap gimmicks to lure tourists, while others seem to enjoy the lovingly re-created ambience.

As well as being a food, fuel, and lodging stop, Sisters is also a jumping-off point for a wealth of outdoor activities. Skiing at Hoodoo Ski Bowl, fly-fishing and rafting on the Metolius River, and backpacking into the great Three Sisters Wilderness are just a few of the popular local pursuits. Nearby luxury resorts such as Black Butte Ranch, an annual rodeo a nationally famous quilting event, and North America's largest llama ranch add to the appeal of this vintage-1888 village.

SIGHTS AND RECREATION
Dick Patterson's Arabian Ranch

Dick Patterson's Arabian Ranch (15425 U.S. 20, Sisters 97759, 541/549-3831) is located just outside the city limits. In addition to a large herd of these fine-looking horses, the ranch is also home for over 500 llamas. These critters are used as pack animals on expeditions into the mountains, as well as for pets and wool pro-

Sparks Lake, backdropped by South Sister

duction. Sheep ranchers in particular like to have a llama or two around their livestock because predators such as wolves and coyotes abhor their scent. The Pattersons do not give guided tours of the ranch. However, they will try to accommodate people who would like to visit and see the animals, provided they call ahead and make an appointment.

Llama Treks

It's easy to fall in love with llamas. Their regal manner, soft dark eyes, and gentleness engender an immediate connection. In addition, outfitters who rent them out for guided trips (or solos) point out that their padded feet hardly leave a trace on the trail. Two area outfitters, **Last Camp Llamas** (4555 N.W. Pershall Way, Redmond 97756, 541/548-6828) and **Oregon Llamas** (P.O. Box 6, Camp Sherman, 541/382-5028, www.packllama.com) make their animals available for about $50 a day with a minimum of two llamas. Remember to procure a forest

service permit for overnights in the Three Sisters, Mount Washington, and Mount Jefferson Wildernesses (site of the 2003 B&B Complex fire that destroyed more than 91,000 acres) if you elect to go by yourself. These permits (obtainable from ranger stations) specify grazing etiquette for your animals. An orientation class offered by the outfitter for those traveling independently will review such procedures before you hit the trail.

Metolius River

About 10 miles from Sisters is the second-largest tributary of the Deschutes River, the Metolius. To get here, take the Camp Sherman Highway off of U.S. 20 five miles west of Sisters. This road will take you around Black Butte. On the north face of this steep, evergreen-covered cinder cone lies the source of the Metolius. A quarter-mile trail takes you to a railing where you can see the water bubbling out of the ground.

Known simply as "the Spring," the water wells

up out of the earth at a constant 48°F. The warm, spring-fed waters of the upper Metolius are ideal for insect egg and larval development, which in turn provides an abundant food source for rainbow, brown, brook, and bull trout, kokanee salmon, and whitefish. Consequently, some of the best fly-fishing in the state is found on the upper Metolius. This was no secret to the Native Americans. The name Metolius derives from the Indian word for "floating fish," because of the dead salmon carcasses found in the river after spawning. A beautiful riverside trail follows the Metolius as it meanders through the ponderosa trees past many excellent fishing holes. Drift boats are used to tackle the harder-to-reach places along this 25-mile-long waterway.

Other streams merge with the Metolius, lowering the water temperature to an average of 35°F. While the fishing isn't as good as in the warmer upper reaches, the white-water rafting is actually better downstream. The increased water volume coupled with steeper flow gradients provide plenty of exciting rapids for river-runners to splash around in. The Metolius was designated a National Wild and Scenic River in 1988, creating a 4,600-acre corridor within the unique 86,000-acre Metolius Conservation Area.

Five miles downstream from Camp Sherman (seven miles from the Head of the Metolius Trail) is the Wizard Falls Fish Hatchery. Open every day for visitors. Over two and a half million fish, including Atlantic salmon, brook and rainbow trout, and kokanee salmon, are raised here annually. This hatchery is the only place in the state that stocks Atlantic salmon, which migrate to Hosmer Lake.

Hoodoo Ski Bowl

A little more than a half hour west of Sisters on ORE 126 is one of Oregon's most family-oriented skiing areas, Hoodoo Ski Bowl (541/822-3799). Generally operating from Thanksgiving to Easter (snow conditions permitting), it's open Sun., Mon., Tues., Thurs. 9 A.M.–4 P.M.; Fri. and Sat. 9 A.M.– 10 P.M. Hoodoo features 17 ski runs serviced by three chairlifts and a rope tow. The maximum vertical drop is 1,035 feet, and the runs are fairly evenly divided between advanced, intermediate, and beginner levels of difficulty. The rates at this 55-year-old ski bowl are equally attractive. Adult all-day passes are $35, seniors (65 and over) $26, and children under six accompanied by a paying adult ski free. The rates on the rope tow are $9 per day. The SnowPhone (541/822-3337) has the latest information on weather and snow conditions, or check the skycam (www.hoodoo.com).

For accommodations near Hoodoo, see www.hoodoo.com/lodging.htm.

Camping

A handful of campgrounds open only in summer are near Sisters on the old McKenzie Highway, ORE 242. **Cold Springs Campground** is $12 and just five miles west of town on ORE 242. This campground, 3,400 feet in elevation, has 23 sites for tents and small trailers (22 feet maximum). Picnic tables, fire grills, pit toilets, and water are provided. It's a pretty spot, near the source of Trout Creek. Six miles farther down the road is **Whispering Pine Campground.** No fees are charged at this primitive campground with six tent sites, mainly because there is no water available. Another six miles up the pass at 5,200 feet is **Lava Camp Lake Campground.** Two tent sites and 10 RV sites (22 feet maximum) are available at this rustic campground. There is no fee, but there's also no water. The main allure is its close proximity to the Pacific Crest Trail and the Three Sisters Wilderness.

Information about these campgrounds is available from Sisters Ranger Station (541/549-7700, www.fs.fed.us/r6/centraloregon).

Events

The annual **Sisters Rodeo** (800/827-7522) opens the second weekend of June. In addition to the normal assortment of calf-roping and bronco-bucking, country dances, a buckaroo breakfast, and a 10-km Stampede Run round out the fun. A quilter's fair takes place each summer that can attract over 20,000 in a weekend. Also noteworthy is the annual **Sisters Folk Festival,** held in early September. This even attracts some of the biggest names in blues and folk. Contact the Sisters Chamber of Commerce (P.O. Box 476, Sisters 97759, 541/549-0251, www.sisterscham-ber.com) for the schedule of events.

PRACTICALITIES

Lodges and Resorts

Sisters Motor Lodge (600 W. Cascade, Sisters 97759, 541/549-2551) is within easy walking distance of the shops and boutiques of Sisters. Bedrooms with kitchenettes go for $89–145 a night, and you can bring the dog along, too. The **Best Western Ponderosa Lodge** (505 ORE 20, P.O. Box 218, Sisters 97759, 541/549-1234 or 800/528-1234) is a new, ranch-style resort motel. Rooms ($80–125) feature private balconies with views of the mountains and the adjacent Deschutes National Forest, as well as dial-direct phones and cable TV. Other amenities include a spa, heated pool, and free continental breakfast.

Lake Creek Lodge (Sisters 97759, 541/595-6331 or 800/797-6331, www.lakecreeklodge.com) is located in the nearby Metolius Recreation Area. This full-service resort has individual houses and cottages that range $130–355 depending upon the unit and number of people. Tennis, swimming, and fishing are some of the many activities available here. Dinner is served family-style in the pine-paneled main lodge and features a different entrée each day, complemented by homemade breads, salads, and desserts. The establishment caters especially well to families; pets are allowed on prior approval only.

Another Metolius retreat can be found at **Cold Springs Resort** (Cold Springs Resort Lane, HCR 1270, Camp Sherman 97730, 541/595-6271, www.coldsprings-resort.com.) Open mid-April–mid-October, the cabins here ($110–145) feature naturally pure artesian well water. A footbridge across the Metolius connects the resort to Camp Sherman, where groceries, a church, and a café are within easy walking distance. Pets are allowed here for $5 per night but must be kept on a leash at all times and never left unattended.

The **Metolius River Lodge** (P.O. Box 110, Camp Sherman 97730, 541/595-6290 or 800/595-6290, www.metoliusriverlodges.com) is a 12-unit complex featuring six pine-paneled cabins.

The latter vary in price ($79–150), depending on room configuration and accoutrements. The most coveted pair have decks extending over the river, and the majority have fireplaces. The price includes continental breakfast brought to your door and all the firewood you need.

Wedged in between giant ponderosa pines and the banks of the Metolius are the 12 elegant cabins of the **Metolius River Resort** (P.O. Box 1210, Camp Sherman, 541/595-6281 or 800/81-TROUT, www.metolius-river-resort.com). These beautiful wooden structures, built in 1992, are bright and airy with lots of windows. The cabins are two stories high with more than 900 square feet of living space and comfortably sleep 4–6 people. Featuring a fully equipped modern kitchen, full bath, river rock fireplace (stocked with all the firewood you'll need), and a riverview deck, it's a bargain at $180–195 per night double occupancy (additional person $10 extra). Reservations made well in advance are a must if you want to stay here. You'll find the resort behind the Kokanee Cafe.

Bed-and-Breakfasts

Near the Sisters airport, the **Conklin House** (69013 Camp Polk Rd., Sisters, 541/549-0123 or 800/549-4262, www.conklinguesthouse.com) has a country decor and old-fashioned warmth that spells "welcome home" to the visitor. Relax by the pool, fish in the trout ponds, barbecue on the back porch, or even catch up on some laundry during your stay. Rooms include private baths and are $90–150. All rooms include a full country breakfast, and complimentary refreshments are served in the evening.

A lovely place to enjoy Sisters is at the **Blue Spruce** (444 S. Spruce, 541/549-9644 or 888/328-9644, www.bluesprucebandb.com). Designed and built from the ground up as a B&B, the four rooms here all have their own theme. All bathrooms have a towel warmer, shower, and two-person whirlpool tub. Rooms are clean, bright, big, well-apportioned, and all come equipped with a fridge stocked with complimentary water and sodas. Throw in laundry facilities for guests and a great country breakfast, and it's clear that their $125/night rate is a good value.

English riding style is the forte of **Catalyst Farms** (17045 Farthing Ln., 541/548-7000 or 800/422-5622). The complex features two vacation rentals: an immense white house ($500–700 per night) and a smaller farmhouse ($125–300). The complex also includes an indoor horseback riding arena. It would take a whole chapter to extoll the wonders of this place—everything is top drawer. It suffices to say that a stay here has all the makings of great lifetime memories. See website for all the details. Hope to see you back at the ranch.

Food

The **Depot Deli** (250 W. Cascade, 541/549-2572) serves creative, reasonably priced fare in a re-creation of an old train station. Breakfast is highlighted by multi-ingredient omelettes and scrambles and espresso drinks. For lunch, homemade soups, sandwiches, burgers, and salads will fill you up for $4–7. The outdoor deck is a nice place to escape Sisters's shop-till-you-drop ambience. Open daily.

The **Gallery Restaurant** (230 W. Cascade, 541/549-2631) offers chuckwagon dinners that range $7–16. Surprisingly tasteful paintings on Old West themes, along with flintlocks and other ancient armaments, pay homage to the area's pioneer past. Many eastern Oregonians will tell you that **Papandrea** (325 S.W. Hood and 442 E. Cascade, 541/549-6081) makes the best pizza in the state. While such claims are highly subjective, outlets in Bend and Oregon City attest to this small chain's dedicated following.

There are plenty of pizza joints in town: **Coyote Creek** (497 ORE 20 W., 541/549-9514) open for breakfast, lunch and dinner servers standard American fare with pastas, pizzas, and prime rib. **Martoli's Pizza Inc.** (220 W. Cascade, 541/549-8356) makes a great pie, open daily for lunch and dinner.

The hot spot in town is undoubtedly the **Hotel Sisters and Bronco Billy Saloon** (190 E. Cascade, 541/549-7427). Built in 1912, the upstairs rooms of this historical structure have been refurbished into intimate mini-dining rooms. Barbecued ribs are the specialty of the house, but you can also find fresh seafood, steaks, chicken dishes, and Mexican fare here ($9–20). In one corner of the building, on the other side of the western-style saloon doors, is Bronco Billy's. This funky watering hole must look much the same as it did 80 years ago. A racy painting that used to grace the local brothel is proudly displayed behind the bar, and cowboy hats on most heads complete the picture of a town whose Old West ambience gets better with age. For the price of a beer, you can get one of the local Stetson-hatted good ol' boys to tell you the inside scoop on where to go and what to do in this neck of the woods. Open daily for lunch and dinner.

In nearby Camp Sherman, a special treat awaits at the **Kokanee Cafe** (541/595-6420). Open Tues.–Sun. 5–9 P.M., they feature an excellent variety of expertly prepared chicken, pasta, steak, seafood, and fish entrées. Burgers and grilled cheese sandwiches are offered if the kids don't go for the good stuff. Their special salad made with loads of organic greens is alone worth the trip. Dinners range $17–24 for entrées; burgers and smaller plates are around $10–12. Dinner reservations are crucial during the summer and fishing season, given the small size of the building. The Kokanee is generally open April–November. During this time, the restaurant rents out two rooms upstairs for around $65.

Information and Services

Detailed information about the geology, natural history, wildlife, wilderness areas, and numerous recreational opportunities in the Metolius Recreation Area can be obtained by calling the **Sisters Ranger Station** (541/549-2111). More information is available from the **Sisters Chamber of Commerce** (541/549-0251).

Bend

Since 1980, Deschutes County has been the state's fastest-growing population center. The last twenty years have seen its population jump from 42,400 to over 100,000 with projections for it to double again over the next two decades. The hub of it all, Bend has also seen its population double during this period, to over 60,000 people. This increase is largely due to area hiking trails, fishing streams, golf courses, white-water runs, and ski slopes.

Proximity to all this recreation has made the city of Bend Oregon's leading destination for the active traveler. While the resulting increase in traffic and prices can sometimes make you forget you're in Oregon, Bend's outskirts between the eastern flank of the Cascades and the desert provide respite from what the locals call "Californication." The boom in real estate can be understood by a look at the numbers. The average price for a three-bedroom, two-bath house was $120,000 in 1991. That same house now boasts an average market value closer to $200,000. Not surprisingly, *Money* magazine tapped this city as one of 10 places in the United States where home values could be expected to appreciate significantly over time.

Compounding this impression was Bend's number two ranking in the May 2000 issue of *Modern Maturity's* list of America's best small cities in which to live. During this same month, kudos came from *Money* magazine's number one ranking of Bend as a place to retire in the Pacific Northwest. Thanks to sunshine 250 days a year and a dry climate that makes the average winter low of 27°F feel warmer than 40°F temperatures in the wet Willamette Valley, this town has become particularly attractive to Southern California retirees.

Kudos notwithstanding, Bend faces an uncertain future. Zoning and planning efforts are still playing catch-up and fears of "Los Angelization" run rampant. Bend is the largest Oregon city without mass transit and the increasing sprawl and dependence on the car here can only increase. The sense of community needed to counter these trends from undermining Bend's quality of life has been lacking due to many second homes that sit unoccupied and a flood of new arrivals with urban sensibilities.

The seeds of growth were planted several decades ago when a onetime military encampment a dozen miles south of town was transformed into the Sunriver Resort community. Black Butte Ranch, the Inn of the Seventh Mountain, and other destination resorts soon followed. South of the city is some of the best skiing in the state on Mount Bachelor; to the north, world-class rock-climbing routes at Smith Rock State Park and famed fishing holes on the Metolius River await. Add Cascade hiking, Deschutes River rafting and fishing, and other nearby locales for rockhounding, golf (two dozen courses with a half dozen that rank among the nation's best), horseback riding, and water sports, and you'll understand why Deschutes County has been Oregon's leading engine of population growth over the last several decades.

SIGHTS

Drake Park

The Deschutes River has a dam and diversion channel just above downtown Bend. It provides valuable irrigation water for the farmers and ranchers of the dry but fertile plateau to the north, and creates a placid stretch of water called Mirror Pond that is home to Canada geese, ducks, and other wildlife. Drake Park is on the east bank of this greenbelt and is a nice place to relax, have a quiet lunch, or maybe toss a Frisbee around.

However, you had better be careful where you step, as the birds leave behind numerous land mines. The folks living in those nice houses on the west bank of Mirror Pond got tired of scraping the guano off of their shoes, but unfortunately for them, they were legally unable to do anything against their fowl neighbors due to the birds' protected status.

THE CASCADES

BEND

To Swallow Ridge B&B
and Bend Kampground

To Tumalo State Park

Detail map (SEE DETAIL):

GREENWOOD AVE.

HIGH TIDES ▼
DESCHUTES BREWERY AND PUBLIC HOUSE ▼
ALPENGLOW CAFE ▼
YOKO'S JAPANESE RESTAURANT ▼

GIUSEPPE'S
RISTORANTE ▼

OREGON AVE.

ON THE ROCKS ▼
GREAT
▼ HARVEST
BREAD CO.

D&D ▼
BAR & GRILL

SUPER
BURRITO ▼

MINNESOTA AVE.

TOOMIE'S ▼

CAFE
SANTÉ ▼

▼ PIZZA MONDO

FRANKLIN AVE. DESCHUTES
▼ COUNTY LIBRARY

Deschutes River

Parking

Parking

BROOKS ST.

WALL ST.

BOND ST.

Main map:

EMPIRE AVE.

CHAMBER
OF COMMERCE ■
● RODEWAY INN

RIVERHOUSE RESORT ●
HAMPTON INN

BOYD ACRES RD.

BUTLER MARKET RD.

DIVISION ST.

STUDIO RD.

20
97

0   0.5 mi
0   0.5 km

BEND RIVERSIDE MOTEL ●

REVERE AVE.

● RED LION NORTH
■ RANGER STATION

NEFF RD.

● THE COUNTRY INN THE CITY

PORTLAND AVE.

NEWPORT AVE.

SEE DETAIL

LARA HOUSE ●
● SATHER
HOUSE

Drake
Park

GALVESTON AVE.

WALL ST.

BUS.
20
GREYHOUND

BUS.
97

Pilot Butte
State Park

8TH ST.

GREENWOOD AVE.

ERNESTO'S ITALIAN ▼
■ RED LION SOUTH
● BEST WESTERN INN

FRANKLIN AVE.

20

14TH ST.

BOND ST.

MILL INN B&B ●

BEAR CREEK RD.

CASCADE HOSTEL ●

SIMPSON AVE.

COLORADO AVE.

9TH ST.

15TH ST.

SONOMA LODGE ●

● HONG KONG RESTAURANT AND LOUNGE

WILSON AVE.

97

● WESTWARD HO MOTEL

CENTURY DR.

Deschutes River

REED MARKET RD.

BROSTERHOUS RD.

To Best Western
Entrada Lodge

To Crown Villa →

© AVALON TRAVEL PUBLISHING, INC.

They came up with a rather ingenious solution to the geese and their offensive droppings. The residents chipped in $1,500 to buy a pair of swans from Queen Elizabeth's Royal Swannery in England. Since geese and swans do not get along, the citizens reasoned that the blue-blooded swans would chase away the common Canada geese. While the geese are still here, you will notice that they tend to congregate in Drake Park, while the swans have a decided preference for the private estates. This part of Bend has a refreshing neighborhood feel with older homes surrounded by lawns and trees, providng respite from downtown sprawl.

Pilot Butte

On the east side of town is Pilot Butte. A road spirals its way up to the top of this 511-foot-high volcanic remnant. Locals enjoy a fitness regime of following a trail to the top. You can enjoy a sweeping view of nine snowcapped Cascade peaks and their green forests. It is also pretty at night, with the twinkling lights of the city below and the stars above. Full moons are especially awesome, illuminating the ghostly forms of the mountains in icy, light-blue silhouettes. The scent of juniper and sage adds to the visual splendor.

Pine Mountain Observatory

Another peak experience worth investigating is the Pine Mountain Observatory (541/382-8331, guernsey.uoregon.edu/) located about 40 miles east of Bend on U.S. 20. Take the road out of Millican to the top of 6,395-foot-high Pine Mountain to reach the installation. Three Cassegrain telescopes with 15-, 24-, and 32-inch mirrors are used by University of Oregon professors and students to unlock the secrets of the universe. On this 6,300-foot mountain the friendly astronomers will often allow visitors an intriguing peek at the neighboring stars and planets. Call ahead for information and weather conditions before making the trip. Generally, the public visits after April on Fri. and Sat. evenings. Wear warm clothes and take a flashlight. A donation of $3 per person is suggested.

A Mountain of Glass

Farther down U.S. 20 you ease into the Great Basin desert and such attractions as the Sagehen Nature Trail (see "Sights" under "Burns and Vicinity" in the Southeastern Oregon chapter), located 70 miles from the Pine Mountain Observatory turnoff, and the Glass Buttes. Located 36 miles past the observatory, the latter attraction is one of the world's largest obsidian outcroppings, a mountain of volcanic glass, gently rising 2,000 feet above the surrounding countryside. The **Bureau of Land Management** (3050 N.E. 3rd St., P.O. Box 550, Prineville 97754, 541/416-6700, www.blm.org) can provide you with additional information. From here the next big town is Burns, 55 miles to the east.

Newberry National Volcanic Monument

This national monument enshrines the obsidian fields, deep mountain lakes, and lava formations left in the wake of a massive series of eruptions. While lacking the visual impact of Crater Lake, this preserve is more accessible and less crowded than its southern Cascade counterpart. Beyond Newberry Crater itself, the monument extends north 25 miles along a volcanic fracture zone to Lava Butte. A 1981 U.S. Geological Survey probe drilled into the caldera floor found temperatures of 510°F, the highest recorded in an inactive Cascade volcano.

For more information on all the geologic features encompassed in the area between Newberry Crater and the Lava Butte, contact Deschutes National Forest (1645 ORE 20 E., Bend 97701, 541/383-5300); Lava Land Visitor Center (58201 S. U.S. 97, Bend 97707, 541/593-2421); and Newberry National Volcanic Monument (Fort Rock Ranger District, Suite A 262, Bend 97701, 541/388-5667, www.fs.fed.us/r6/central oregon).

Lava Lands Visitor Center, Lava Butte

About 11 miles south of Bend on U.S. 97 are the Lava Lands Visitor Center (541/593-2421) and Lava Butte. The center has some interpretive exhibits that explain the region's volcanic history, as well as a small but good selection of local

THE CASCADES

geology books and an assortment of free pamphlets on local attractions; their bulletin board has the latest activities and goings-on posted. Guided walks that provide a good introduction to the lava lands are offered here during the summer. Open 9 A.M.–5 P.M. daily from late April–early October.

After your orientation, cruise on up to the top of 500-foot-high Lava Butte, located just behind the visitors center. During the summer, you must take the shuttle, which leaves the parking lot every half hour; adults $1.50, children $1. The rest of the year you can take your own vehicle to the summit, although the road is not recommended for trailers and RVs.

The observation platform on top of this fire lookout (established in 1928) offers the best viewpoint. Be sure to talk with the resident lookout and have him or her explain how to work the Osborne fire finder. Nearly a mile above sea level, the butte affords a commanding panorama of the Cascade Range. On a clear day you can see most of the major peaks, with Mounts Jefferson and Hood looming prominently on the northern horizon. These snow-capped turrets backdrop a 10-square-mile lava field.

You can venture out into this eerie landscape by taking the trail that starts from the visitors center and makes its way to the Phil Brogan lookout. From July–August on Saturday evenings, a park naturalist gives an hour and a half presentation on top of Lava Butte. After sunset, the forest takes on a different character as the creatures of the night make their presences known. As darkness continues to envelope the area and celestial objects come into view, the emphasis shifts to a tour of the constellations and planets. Be sure to call ahead for starting times of this excellent attraction for families.

A short trail circumnavigates the 150-foot-deep crater on Lava Butte and is complemented by informative placards that help you interpret this otherworldly environment. From the trail you can see how the lava flow from the butte changed the course of the Deschutes River. You can also see the *kipukas,* small islands of green trees surrounded by a sea of black lava. Along the trail, look for some of what geologists call splatter. You'll know it when you see it, because it looks exactly like what it sounds like. Pick up a couple of red pumice rocks for the children, who will be fascinated by the way the stones float in the bathtub.

Lava River Cave

About 12 miles south of Bend on U.S. 97 and one mile south of Lava Butte is Oregon's longest known lava tube, the Lava River Cave (541/593-2421). Open from mid-May–mid-October, admission is $3 adults, $2 ages 13–17, and lantern rentals (available at the Lava Lands Visitor Center) are also $3. The cave is a cool 40°F year-round, so dress warmly. Since the walking surface is uneven, flat shoes are recommended. Bring a flashlight to guide you through this lava tube or rent one at the entrance for $1 (lanterns come recommended—no batteries to die out one mile deep in darkness). The trail is an easy 2.4-mile round-trip from the parking lot.

The first chamber you enter is called the Collapsed Corridor. Volcanic rocks that fell from the roof and walls lie in jumbled piles. Freezing water in cracks pries a few rocks loose each winter, which is why the cave is usually closed during the cold months. Stairs take you out of the Collapsed Corridor into a large void called Echo Hall. Here the ceiling reaches 58 feet high and the cave is 50 feet wide. Conversations return from the opposite side of the hall as eerie noises in the dark. The lateral markings you see etched on the walls here show the various levels of past volcanic flows.

At Low Bridge Lane, watch your head because the ceiling dips down to five feet. Look for the "lavacicles" in this and other areas of the cave. (This term comes from a geologist's 1923 publication on the cave called *The Lava River Tunnel.*) Two kinds of them are found here: The hollow cylindrical "soda straws" were formed by escaping gases, and the other cone-shaped formations were created by remelted lava dripping down from the ceiling.

The next curiosity you'll come across is a cave inside the cave, the Two Tube Tunnel. Two tubes running for 95 feet intermittently connect. The smaller tube was formed when the level of the lava flow dropped and the cooling lava created a second roof and tube inside the existing cave.

The terrain changes again in the Sand Gardens. Rain and snowmelt carry volcanic ash down through cracks and openings in the cave and deposit them here. The process continues today with the nearly constant dripping water carving out spires and pinnacles in the sand. These formations take hundreds of years to grow, so please stay behind the fenced-off area. The sand gets thicker and thicker until it completely blocks off the lava tube, forcing an abrupt about-face. The walk back to the light of the sun affords a different perspective on this remarkable natural attraction.

It is important to avoid littering the cave, collecting samples, or doing anything else to mar this national treasure. Don't light flares, paper, or cigarettes, because the fumes kill off insects, a food source for the cave's bat population. Roosting bats should not be disturbed, because waking them from hibernation results in certain death for these winged mammals. Incidentally, bat droppings support this cavernous ecosystem, and others; bat guano is harvested commercially and used for detoxifying wastes, improving detergents, and producing antibiotics. Bats can catch hundreds of mosquitoes within an hour, and are also important pollinators. There are nearly 50 species of bats living in North America, and if left alone, they pose little threat to humans. In short, "leave nothing but footprints, take nothing but pictures, and kill nothing but time."

A couple miles south of Lava River Cave is the **Lava Cast Forest.** Take U.S. 97 and go nine miles on the cinder road (Forest Service Road 9720). From there, follow a self-guided trail through an unreal world created when lava enveloped the trees 6,000 years ago. The lava hardened, leaving behind a mold of the once living trees, much like how the eruption of Pompeii left casts of residents from that famous eruption in Italy.

Benham Falls

Four miles down Forest Service Road 9702 from the Lava Lands Visitor Center is Benham Falls. Give other cars a wide berth and plenty of following distance, as the road's pumice and fine dust are hard on paint jobs and engines. The road leads to a small picnic area in a grove of giant ponderosa pines on the bank of the Deschutes River. With tables, pit toilets, fire grills, and plenty of shade, this is a nice place for a picnic. Be sure to tote your own fluids, though, because there is no water. Day use only, no fees and no camping.

The hike to the falls is an easy one-mile jaunt downstream. Take the footbridge across the river, and enjoy your stroll past a spectacular section of untamed white water. While the water in the Deschutes is much too cold and dangerous for a swim (except perhaps on very hot days), it's always ideal for soaking your feet a little after you've completed your hike. Benham Falls was created when magma from Lava Butte splashed over the side, flowing five miles to the Deschutes. When the molten rock collided with the icy water, the churning rapids and crashing waterfall were created here.

Cascades Lakes Highway

The Cascades Lakes Highway (a.k.a. Century Drive or ORE 46) is an 89-mile drive leading to more than half a dozen lakes in the shadow of the snowcapped Cascades. These lakes feature boating, fishing, and other water sports. Hiking, bird-watching, biking, skiing, and camping also attract people. From downtown, drive west off of U.S. 97 south onto Franklin, which becomes Galveston, to Century Drive (14th Street). Turn left one mile from downtown. The route is well-marked and the road climbs in elevation for a significant portion of the drive.

If you just want a gourmet taste of this realm, we recommend a shortened version of the loop. The following tour can be enjoyed in several hours, even allowing for several stops. By contrast, driving the entire loop necessitates a whole day with only limited time spent out of the car.

Begin by taking U.S. 97 south 13 miles to the Sunriver cut-off. Shortly after making a right turn, you'll come to a fork where you'll go left. (You might first want to procure a map at the Sunriver Lodge concierge desk by driving straight a quarter mile to the main lodge, then doubling back to the fork.) This left fork begins a loop that'll take you through Sunriver property and the Deschutes Forest to the first stop of Little Lava Lake. The drive to the lake is about 10 miles. The Deschutes River begins its 252-mile course to the Columbia from here. A gorgeous view of the South Sister looms to the northwest, and cabins, a store, and a boat ramp provide the creature comforts. Despite the view of the mountain from the store's porch, in the summer your attention could be diverted by the humming-birds who flock to a hanging feeder.

To get to Lava Lake from Forest Route 45 to ORE 372 to the shores of Elk Lake, a favorite of windsurfers and sailors. The year-round cabins at **Elk Lake Resort** (Box 789, Bend, 541/480-7228, www.elklakeresort.com; $35–250) are also popular, as are pictures taken from the lake's beach picnic grounds on the southernmost tip of shoreline. Here you have the full length of Elk Lake before you, back-dropped by the South Sister Mountains and Mount Bachelor. During the snowbound months of winter, access to Elk Lake is by snowmobile, snow-cat van, or dogsled (really!) to a world of groomed cross-country ski and snowshoe trails amidst spectacular alpine scenery.

Not far away, the red volcanic cinder highway contrasts with the black lava flows en route to aqua-tinted Devil's Lake. From the northern end of this lake, on the other side of the highway, you'll find Devil's Pile, a conglomeration of lava flows and volcanic glass where *Apollo 11* astronauts reportedly culled a rock to deposit on the lunar surface. The road winds around to the Mount Bachelor Summit ski lifts (see special topic "Mount Bachelor Summit Chairlift," later in this section). From the deck in front of the sport shop/cafeteria complex, you can see the Three Sisters and Broken Top in a view reminiscent of the Swiss Alps.

You might want to hike the short trail to Todd Lake (see "Camping" under "Sports and Recreation," later in this section); canoe Sparks Lake in the shadow of Broken Top and South Sister; or visit the Ray Atkeson Memorial, dedicated to Oregon's "photographer laureate." All are located between Devil's Pile and the ski lifts. From

Mount Bachelor it's a 15-minute drive back to Sunriver.

High Desert Museum

Six miles south of Bend is the High Desert Museum (59800 U.S. 97 S., Bend 97702, 541/382-4754, www.highdesert.org). If a quick look at the rave reviews in their guest book doesn't immediately convince you that you're in the right place, confirmation is sure to come as you prowl the corridors and outdoor off-the-trail exhibits. This award-winning center for natural resources, native animals, and cultural history of the inter-mountain, western high desert is well worth the price of admission (adults $8.50, seniors $7.50, children ages 6–12 $4, and kids under five free).

Along the many trails that wind through the 150-acre facility, visitors can observe river otters at play, porcupines sticking it to each other, and

a taste of old-fashioned chores at the High Desert Museum

birds of prey dispassionately watching over the whole scene. Replicas of a sheepherder's cabin, a settler's cabin, forestry displays, and other historical interpretations are also along the museum walkways. Open 9 A.M.–5 P.M. daily.

Inside the museum's main building, unique exhibits, slide and movie shows, galleries, and pioneer history demonstrations are presented. The "desertarium" is a special delight full of native plants and populated by 37 small critters whose nocturnal lifestyles often keep them from view in the wild. Bats, lizards, mice, toads, snakes, and owls reveal that the desert is more alive than its superficially barren landscape might suggest.

The **Earle A. Chiles Center** exhibit on the Spirit of the West features eight "you are there" life-sized dioramas. This walk through time begins 8,000 years ago beside a still marsh and takes you to a fur brigade camp, into the depths of a gold mine, and down Main Street of a boisterous frontier town.

The **Spirit of the West Gallery** has representative arts and artifacts of the early American West, as well as tools, clothing, and other personal belongings from the 19th century. The Bounds collection of Native American artifacts and the Hall of Plateau Heritage balance out the museum's coverage of the peoples of the high desert, while the Changing Forest exhibit addresses old-growth life cycles and other issues of forest ecology. Also of interest is the newly opened **Birds of Prey Center.** The **Henry J. Casey Hall of Plateau Heritage,** an 8,000-square-foot venue, showcases the Doris Swayze Bounds Native American artifact collection as well as other Native Americana.

As you might gather, the scope and interactive nature of this facility make it appealing for people who don't usually like museums. With the addition of the Silver Stage Trading gift shop and the Rimrock Cafe, the museum offers visitors a worthwhile diversion outside of Bend. Hours are 9 A.M.–5 P.M. daily, closed Thanksgiving, Christmas, and New Year's Day.

Newberry Volcano

Lava Butte is one of over 400 cinder cones in a family of over 1,000 other smaller volcanoes that together comprise Newberry Volcano. This vast shield volcano covers 500 square miles. In the five-mile-diameter caldera of this mountain, which blew its top 1,300 years ago, lie two alpine lakes called Paulina and East Lakes.

Composed of rocks ranging from basalt to rhyolite, the black obsidian flow that's found at Newberry Volcano has been the source of raw material for Native American spearpoints, arrowheads, and hide scrapers for thousands of years. Prized by the original inhabitants of the area, the obsidian tools were also highly valued by other tribal nations and were a medium of exchange for blankets, firearms, and other possessions at the Taos Fair in New Mexico. These tools and other barterings helped to spread Newberry Volcano obsidian all across the West and into Canada and Mexico.

Centuries later, NASA sent astronauts to walk on the volcano's pumice-dusted surface in preparation for landing on the moon. Additional interest came when a 9,500-year-old circular structure called a "wickiup" was excavated at Paulina Lake in 1992. If you are curious about other archaeological findings in the area and would like to "dig" looking for prehistoric artifacts, contact the **Archaeological Society of Central Oregon** (c/o Central Oregon Environmental Center, P.O. Box 8146, Bend 97708).

Paulina and East Lakes

South from Bend 27 miles on U.S. 97 is the turnoff to Paulina and East Lakes. The 16-mile paved but ragged County Road 21 twists and turns its way up to the lakes in the caldera of Newberry Crater. Several campgrounds and two resorts are located along the shores of these lakes, which are noted for their excellent trout fishing. Be sure to take the four-mile drive (summer only) to the top of 7,985-foot-high Paulina Peak, the highest point along the jagged edge of Newberry Crater, on Forest Service Road 500. Towering 1,500 feet over the lakes in Newberry Crater, the peak also allows a perspective on the forest, obsidian fields, and basalt flows in the surrounding area. To the far west, a palisade of snow-clad Cascade peaks runs the length of the horizon.

Fishing in the area is said to be best in the fall. In Lake Paulina, fisherfolk can troll for kokanee, a gourmet's delight, as well as brown and rainbow trout. Paulina's twin, East Lake, features a fall run of German brown trout that move out of the depths to spawn in shoreline shallows. The Oregon state record German brown trout was caught here in 1993, weighing in at a hair over 27 pounds.

Paulina Lake Resort (P.O. Box 95, La Pine 97739, 541/536-2240) books up early with a dozen three-bedroom log cabins going for $100–175 a night. Hearty lunches and dinners ($4–15) can be had in the resort's log-paneled dining room. Boat rentals and a general store are also on-site. During winter, the resort is open to snowmobilers, giving access to over 330,000 acres of designated snowmobile areas.

East Lake Resort (541/536-2230) offers 16 cabins with housekeeping facilities for $50–145 per night. A snack bar, general store, and boat rentals are on-site, and the nearby RV park has a laundry, public showers, and pay phones. Each year, 225,000 trout are planted in East Lake, and in 1990, Atlantic salmon were introduced here. The cold water and abundant freshwater shrimp make for excellent-tasting fish. Camping is also available; contact the Bend Ranger Station for details. Paulina Resort is open in the summer for fishing and December–March for cross-country skiing and snowmobiling. East Lake Resort is open mid-May–mid-October.

TOURS

A great way to explore central Oregon in depth is through **Wanderlust Tours** (143 S.W. Cleveland Ave., Bend, 541/389-8359 or 800/962-2862, www.wanderlusttours.com), where the focus is on the area's geology, history, flora, fauna, and local issues. Day trips to Crater Lake, the lava lands, the Deschutes River, and the Cascades Lakes Highway are featured. Your guide, Dave Nissen, knows the area as well as anyone in the state, and the small groups (14-passenger van), creative itineraries, and an informal atmosphere merit a hearty recommendation. Dave's ecotourism packages have rated special notice in

Oregon media, and it's clear that he runs the best tour company east of the Cascades. Especially noteworthy is the fact that Wanderlust offers Crater Lake trips ($75 per person, minimum eight passengers).

As no public transportation exists to what is frequently suggested as the eighth wonder of the world, this itinerary takes on special significance. An array of hikes and adventures that focus on the mountain-to-desert variety of central Oregon are also offered ($32–60). Snowshoe tours and snow camping ($35–345) are available in winter, and special moonlight trips can be arranged too. All-day trips include lunch; vegetarian meals available upon request. Call or write for a brochure; reservations are advised.

Cycling Tour

If you like to bike but would rather have gravity do all of the work, consider the **Paulina Plunge with High Cascade Descent** (Box 8782, Bend 97708, 541/389-0562 or 800/296-0562, www.paulinaplunge.com). They provide quality 15- and 18-speed mountain bikes, helmets, experienced guides, and the shuttle transfer from Bend and back. The action starts at Paulina Lake, where you begin your coast down forested trails alongside Paulina Creek. You'll pass by 50 waterfalls on your 3,000-foot descent, as well as abundant wildlife and varied vegetation. Three short nature hikes are necessary to experience the waterfalls and natural waterslides that make this trip famous. A deli-style lunch for $5 extra (vegetarian meals available upon request) and numerous opportunities for photography and fishing round out the fun. The tour costs $50 per person. Large groups of more than 10 people can receive discounts if they book trips in advance. You may bring your own bike, but this will not afford you a discount from the tour price. This popular trip is offered June–October.

SPORTS AND RECREATION

There are a lot of ways to see the area, and some of the best ways are with the help of a few pieces of equipment. Didn't bring your own? No problem. For the "ride of your life" **Central Ore-**

gon **Adventures** (56898 Enterprise Dr., Sunriver 97707, 541/788-8887, www.coadventures.biz) provides high-end snomobile, ATV, wave-runner, scooter and canoe equipment rentals as well as shuttle service for canoers to and from the Deschutes. See their website for prices and details.

For skis, boots, poles, and snowboards, **Bend Ski and Board Sport** (1009 N.W. Galveston, 541/389-4667 or 877/BEND-SKI, www.bendskiandboard.com) can get you outfitted. Clothing, kids' skis, car racks, stunt kites, and many other accessories are also available here. For snowmobiles, **Pauline Tours** (53750 U.S. 97, La Pine, 541/536-2214) can help you prepare for an arctic express adventure with both rentals and tours. Snowmobile maps and other information can be procured from the **Oregon State Snowmobile Association** (Box 435, La Pine 97739, 541/536-3668 or 888/567-SNOW, www.oregonsnow.org).

Hiking and Mountain Biking

The area in and around Bend boasts a rich network of hiking and mountain biking trails, ranging from short, barrier-free interpretive walks in town to strenuous wilderness treks. Snow can lock up many of the trails until as late as June or July, so you'll want to inquire locally before heading out fall through spring. The offices of the **Deschutes National Forest** (1645 ORE 20 E., Bend 97701, 541/383-5300, www.fs.fed.us/r6/centraloregon) and the **Ochoco National Forest** (3160 N.E. 3rd St., Prineville 97754, 541/416-6500, www.fs.fed.us/r6/centraloregon) can offer details; their shared website is an excellent resource of trail information, including maps. Note that parking at most trailheads in the national forests requires a Northwest Forest Pass (see "User Fees and Passes" in the On the Road chapter for details).

For mountain bikers, the **Central Oregon Trail Alliance** (1293 N.W. Wall #72, Bend 97701, www.cotamtb.org) is a good resource. This volunteer group works with the NFS, BLM, and other land managers to enhance mountain biking in and around Bend. Their website describes area trails and shows current conditions. Some short hikes are described under "Sights," earlier in this chapter.

Running 9.1 miles (one-way) through riverside pine forests and lava flows, the **Deschutes River Trail** is a very popular set of three parallel trails—one each dedicated to hikers, bikes, and horseback riders—beginning about seven miles southwest of Bend. To get there, follow Century Drive southwest, then turn south onto Forest Road 41 (Conklin Road), from which there are several access points to the trails, at Meadow, Lava Island, Big Eddy, Aspen, Dillon, Slough, Benham West, and Benham Falls day-use areas. Traffic on the hiking trail closest to Bend can be especially heavy. The season is spring to fall, though most of the trails may remain open in winter during years of low snowfall. A Northwest Forest pass is required for parking, and dogs must be leashed. Four trail sections—at Big Eddy Rapids, Dillon Falls, Benham Falls West, and Benham Falls Picnic Area—are **wheelchair accessible.** They're surfaced with crushed gravel and are of intermediate difficulty level.

About five miles west of town, **Shevlin Park** lures both hikers and mountain bikers with an easy five-mile loop through the pines along the Tumalo Creek gorge and along a ridge burned in the Awbrey Hall fire of August 1990. It's open year-round, with no parking or access fees. Several picnic areas offer quiet spots for lunch. To get there, follow Greenwood Avenue west from U.S. 97 in Bend; Greenwood changes its name to Newport Avenue after a few blocks, then changes again to Shevlin Road as it angles to the northwest.

Another trail close to town that's very popular with mountain bikers is **Phil's Trail,** an eight-mile segment of a larger network of eponymous bike trails (Kent's, Paul's, Jimmy's, etc.—named for the riders who established or popularized them) among the canyon and butte country just west of Bend. Difficulty is generally easy to moderate, with some steep climbs to challenge your lower gears the farther west you ride. To get to the trailhead, head 2.5 miles west on Skyliners Road, then turn left on the first paved road to the south and travel .5 mile. A little farther west, Roads 4610 and 300 also intersect the network. A Northwest Forest Pass is required for parking.

Farther afield, Mount Bachelor beckons hikers in the summer and fall to walk the four-mile **Mount Bachelor Summit Trail** to the mountain's top. This is one of the easiest and safest routes to the top of any Cascade peak, requiring no climbing skills or equipment. An even easier way to reach the top is via the chairlift (see special topic later in this chapter), which runs during the off-season.

To get to the trailhead, follow signs for the upper (east) parking lot at the ski area. The trail begins at the western end of the lot, and climbs to a forested ridge on the mountain's northeastern side, to the upper station of the first section of the ski lift. From there, the trail climbs steeply through the timberline area and continues up to a talus ridge leading to the mountain station of the second lift segment. It's a short hike from this lift station to the summit.

Plaques stationed at viewpoints along the way identify lakes and mountains visible from this 9,000-foot elevation, including Diamond Peak to the south, and the Three Sisters, Broken Top, and Mount Jefferson, and sometimes even Mount Hood, 100 miles away, to the north. The hike involves an elevation gain of 2,600 feet; average hikers should allow two–three hours one-way. Mountain bikes are not recommended on the trail.

Horseback Riding

Several public stables in the vicinity of Bend offer horseback rides that satisfy everyone from the dude to the experienced equestrian. Whether it be a mild-mannered pony for young children or a lively steed for the wannabe buckaroos, you'll find appropriate mounts and trail rides for all ages and skill levels.

Black Butte Stables (P.O. Box 8000, Black Butte 97759-8000, 541/595-2061 or 800/452-7455, www.blackbutteranch.com) at Black Butte Ranch has several packages that take you down trails in the shadow of the Three Sisters.

The Big Meadow pony ride for children (two to six years of age) is $7 for 15 minutes and $12 for a half hour. For safety purposes, one adult per pony is required. The one-hour Big Loop trail ride costs $30; the 90-minute Gobblers Knob ride costs $40; the two-hour Hole-in-the-Wall Gang ride costs $50; and the four-hour Reata Trail ride (for experienced riders only) costs $90. The full-day Black Butte Posse ride costs $150. Given a couple days' advance notice, the proprietors will provide breakfast or a barbecue at the end of the one- and two-hour rides. Reservations are suggested for the short rides and are required for the half-day, full-day, and meal rides. Riding lessons are also available.

Five miles west of Redmond at the Eagle Crest Resort is **Eagle Crest Equestrian Center** (P.O. Box 1194, Redmond 97756, 541/504-9799, www.eagle-crest.com). The 15-minute kids' pony ride costs $7 and the half-hour ride costs $12. Their one-hour trail ride takes you along the river and through the junipers and sagebrush of the high desert and costs $30. Wagon rides, cookout rides, and riding lessons are also available. The venerable **Inn of the Seventh Mountain** (18575 S.W. Century Dr., Bend, 541/382-8711, www.7thmtn.com) offers horseback rides along the Deschutes River and adjacent Deschutes National Forest. The rates are $27 for one hour, $30 for one and a half hours, and $35 for two-hour rides.

About 15 miles south of Bend on U.S. 97 at Sunriver Resort is **Saddleback Stables** (22777 Crestview Ln., Bend 97702, 541/593-6995, www.sunriverresort.com). The 15-minute pony ride costs $7. A good ride for beginners is the half-hour Bald Eagle Loop, $16, which goes along the Deschutes River. The one-hour frontier ride ($26) takes in views of the Deschutes River, wildlife, and wildflowers. The two-hour Ramsey Ride ($41) ride climbs to a panoramic viewpoint overlooking the resort. For those who want to do some serious riding, you can create your own ride (three hours minimum) into the Deschutes National Forest for $50 for the first two hours, then $15 per additional hour. Private lessons and surrey, covered wagon, and sleigh (winter only) rides are also available.

Fishing

With over 100 mountain lakes and the Deschutes River within an hour's drive of Bend, your piscatorial pleasures will be satisfied in central Oregon. The high lakes offer rainbow, brown, and brook trout as well as landlocked Atlantic and coho salmon. The Deschutes River is famed for its red-sided rainbow trout and summer steelhead. You will need appropriate fishing gear like chest waders, rod 'n reel, and fishing license/steelhead tags. All gear and permits are available locally.

A full-service pro shop with everything for the fly fisher is the **Fly Box** (1293 S.E. 3rd St., Bend 97701, 541/388-3330). Custom-tied flies and a full selection of fly-tying tools and materials provide you with the goodies to keep the fish biting. Fly-fishing classes, fishing guide services, and equipment sales, rentals, and repairs can also be found here.

High Desert Drifter (1710 N.E. Hollow Tree Ln., Bend 97701, 541/389-0607) also offers guided fly-fishing float trips on the Deschutes River. They offer multi- and full-day trips that include all meals. Call for rates.

Families are catered to by **Garrison's Fishing Service** (Box 4113, Sunriver 97707, 541/593-8394, www.garrisonguide.com), which features pontoon boats with padded swivel chairs that cruise the lakes and rivers of Central Oregon looking for the big ones. Full-day rates are $175 for the first person, and $75 for each additional individual in your party.

Deschutes River Outfitters (61115 U.S. 97 S., Bend 97702, 541/388-8191 or 888/315-7272, www.deschutesoutfitters.com) features float trips, lake walk-in trips, and steelhead fishing trips that can be customized into single-day or multiday excursions. They have so many different packages and rates that it's best to refer you to their outstanding website for specifics.

While the name **Numb-butt Fly Company** (380 N. Hwy. 26, Madras 97741, 888/248-8309, www.numbbutt.com) may conjure up a less than flattering image, rest assured that their

seasoned guides will heighten your fishing experience. Day trips, walk-in trips, and fly-fishing lessons are all available; see website for rates and availability.

All of these outfitters require completion of a trip application form and a deposit. It's always a good idea to plan your reservations well in advance, especially during the fall fishing season.

Rafting

The Deschutes River offers some of the finest white water in central Oregon. The numerous lava flows have diverted the river to create tumultuous rapids that attract raft, kayak, and canoe enthusiasts. From short rafting trips to multiday adventures, you'll find many options available to enjoy the exciting Deschutes River. You will need swimwear, footwear, sunblock, and sunglasses for all rafting trips. It's also advisable to have a set of dry clothes handy at the end of the voyage.

The **Inn of the Seventh Mountain** (18575 Century Dr., Bend 97701, 541/389-2722 or 800/452-6810, www.7thmtn.com) offers a short two-hour raft trip, $37 adults, $32 children, down a three-mile section of the Deschutes that takes in some Class I–IV rapids. With names like Pinball Alley and the Souse Hole, you can be assured of a good ride! Transfer between the inn and the river is included.

Rapid River Rafters (1151 Centennial Ct. #5, Bend 97702, 541/382-1514 or 800/962-3327, www.rapidriverrafters.com) offers a series of full- and multiday packages on the Deschutes River. The one-day trip, ($85–90) takes in 17 miles of the river from Harpham Flat to Lone Pine. A hearty lunch is included. The two-day trip ($250) floats 44 miles of exciting white water from Trout Creek to Sandy Beach. The three-day trip ($350) runs 55 miles from Warm Springs to Sandy Beach. On all of the multiday trips, the camping and meal preparations at pleasant riverside locations are taken care of by your veteran guides. Season runs from late April to early October, and camping equipment is available for rent if you don't have your own.

Sun Country Tours (531 S.W. 13th St.,

Bend 97702, 541/382-6277 or 800/770-2161, www.suncountrytours.com) is based at the Sunriver Resort. Their two-hour, three-mile Big Eddy Thriller takes in Class I–IV rapids on the Deschutes River and costs $40 per person. The full-day trip ($95 adults, $85 children) runs 13 miles through a dozen minor rapids and seven major ones including Wapinitia, Train Hole, and Oak Springs. A hearty barbecue lunch is included. Multiday packages 29–55 miles in length are also available. The two-day trip costs $250 and the three-day costs $350. All meals on multiday trips are included, and the transfer from Sunriver to Maupin is also part of the day-trip packages. See their website for additional info on McKenzie, Owyhee, and North Umpqua river adventures.

If you would rather shoot the rapids on your own, you can rent canoes, kayaks, and rafts from **Bend Whitewater Supply** (1244 1/2 N.E. 2nd St., Bend 97701, 541/389-7191, www.bendoutdoor.com). This locally owned and operated full-service recreation store can provide you with everything necessary for a safe and enjoyable white-water experience. Bend Whitewater Supply also offers canoe and kayak lessons for the "never ever before" who have never tried it, as well as for advanced paddlers who want to learn more "rodeo style" and technique. One-day float trips on the lower Deschutes, McKenaie, or North Umpqua River are $85 for the paddle trip, or $85 for the "row your own" float. Trips, including transportation, permits, and meals, cost $200 for two days and $295 for three days.

Ouzel Outfitters (Box 827, Bend 97709, 541/385-5947 or 800/788-7238, www.oregon-rafting.com) offers a full-day trip ($90) on the Lower Deschutes out of Maupin. See their website for other offerings throughout the state, including the McKenzie and North Umpqua Rivers.

Camping

With the Three Sisters Wilderness and the Deschutes National Forest flanking the western edges of Bend, there are many wonderful spots to enjoy camping out under the stars. But for those who want to stay within a two-mile radius of civilization, three decent RV parks can be found near Bend. **Bend Keystone** (305 N.E. Burnside, Bend 97701, 541/382-2335), $20; **Crown Villa** (60801 Brosterhous, Bend 97701, 541/388-1131), $39; and **Bend Kampground** (63615 U.S. 97 N., Bend 97701, 541/382-7738 or 800/713-5333), $18–28, offer all of the major amenities. However, while a swimming pool, recreation room, and cable TV hookups are pleasant enough, they can ultimately take the spotlight away from the main attraction: Around Bend, nature is the star.

Tumalo State Park (62976 O.B. Riley Rd., Bend, 541/388-6055 or 800/551-6949, www.prd.state.or.us), $13–17 tents, $21 hookups, and $29 yurts, provides a middle ground between the rugged wilderness and tamed RV parks. Located five miles northwest of Bend off of U.S. 20 along the banks of the Deschutes River, 58 tent sites and 23 sites for RVs up to 35 feet long are available here. Showers, flush toilets, hookups, utilities, and a laundry are also accessible. Open mid-April to late October.

A more secluded setting is **Tumalo Falls** (Deschutes National Forest, 1645 ORE 20 E., Bend 97701, 541/383-5300). Located 16 miles west of town down Forest Service Roads 4601 and 4603, this small campground is situated along Tumalo Creek. Many fine hiking trails are in the area, including a short one to 97-foot-high Tumalo Falls. The volume of white water here is an impressive spectacle. However, campground facilities are primitive—pit toilets and no water.

Another exceptionally beautiful but equally rustic National Forest Service campground is **Todd Lake;** contact the Forest Service for more information. To get here, take Century Drive toward Mount Bachelor. About a mile or two past the ski area, take the first Forest Service Road on the right. While this road eventually arrives at Sisters, it is not recommended for passenger cars. However, you will have to venture less than a mile on a well-maintained section to reach the parking area for Todd Lake. It's a short walk up the trail to the campsites at this 6,200-foot-high alpine lake. While tables, fire grills, and pit toilets are provided, you will need to pack in your own water and supplies, as no vehicles are allowed. It's a good thing, because the drone of a Winnebago generator into the wee hours of the night would definitely detract from the grandeur of this pristine spot. You'll find good swimming and wading on the sandy shoal on the south end of the lake, and you can't miss the captivating views of Broken Top to the north.

Heading north from Bend, outdoor recreationists needn't put away their gear. Between Redmond and Madras is a park that offers hiking, boating, fishing, water-skiing, and birdwatching. **Cove Palisades State Park** (541/546-3412 or 800/551-6949, www.oregonstateparks.org/park_32.php) is located 14 miles southwest of Madras, off U.S. 97. Towering cliffs, Cascade vistas, gnarled junipers, and Lake Billy Chinook with its 72-mile shoreline create a stunning backdrop for outdoor activities. The lake was created when Round Butte Dam backed up the waters of the Deschutes, Metolius, and Crooked Rivers. Two overnight campgrounds offer all the amenities: Deschutes Camp has 82 full-hookup sites and 92 tent sites; the Crooked River camp, perched right on the canyon rim, has 93 sites with electricity and water. Campsites are available May–Oct. and cost $17–22; reserve sites through Oregon State Parks—this is an extremely popular campground.

Farther away from the city is **Lapine State Park** (P.O. Box 5309, Bend 97708, 541/536-2071 or 800/452-5687, www.oregonstateparks.org/park_44.php). Look for a sign on the west side of the highway marking the three-mile-long entrance road located eight miles north of Lapine off U.S. 97. With 14 campsites, swimming, canoeing, and trout fishing, this place fills early on a first-come, first-served basis. This area also has one of the taller ponderosa pines in Oregon (191 feet) and close proximity to the Cascade Lakes Drive, the High Desert Museum, and an array of volcanic phenomena. Open from mid-April to late October depending upon snowfall, this park offers such amenities as flush toilets, firewood, showers, and a laundry. Fees run $13–17 for full-hookup sites, $29 for yurts, and $37 for cabins.

Bird-Watching

About an hour and a half south of Bend near Fort Rock is **Cabin Lake Campground** (Deschutes National Forest, 541/383-5300, www.fs.fed.us/r6/centraloregon) an exceptional spot for viewing a wide variety of birds and wildlife. There is no lake at Cabin Lake, but the forest service has built two small ponds that blend in with the natural surroundings. Permanent wildlife-viewing blinds made of logs, built and donated by the Portland Audubon Society, are adjacent to this small, 12-site campground, and give close visual access to these ponds. In fact, the blinds are so close that binoculars aren't really needed.

Since there is little water in this 3,000-foot-high meeting of desert and mountain biomes, both mountain and desert birds are regularly attracted, usually in large quantities. The red crossbill, a member of the finch family that is increasingly rare, is a regular visitor to this avian oasis. The pinyon jap is another fairly uncommon bird that can be seen here with frequency. Woodpeckers, including Lewis' woodpecker, the common flicker, the white-headed woodpecker, and the hairy woodpecker are also often sighted here. Park checklists show the California quail, bluebirds, chickadees, flycatchers, sparrows, warblers, and the Western tanager making appearances, too. Best viewing times are in the morning, but birds can usually be seen all day long.

Another place popular with birders is Crane Prairie on the Cascades Lakes Highway. This is a breeding ground for osprey who nest in the snags surrounding the water.

Dog Sledding

A unique opportunity is available through **Oregon Trail of Dreams** (541/382-2442 or 800/829-2442, www.sleddogrides.com) to ride in an Iditarod sled behind a team of trained huskies through the spectacular winter scenery of the central Cascades. This is actually a winter training camp for professional sled dog teams preparing to run in the Iditarod and Yukon Quest races, which are both over 1,000 miles long and take nearly two weeks to complete. Many of these huskies were featured in Disney's movie *Iron Will*.

While here in Oregon, they run seven days a week regardless of weather. As such, you will also need to be appropriately dressed as conditions dictate to undertake a dog sled ride.

A good introduction is the standard trip ($60 adults, $30 children under 80 pounds), which includes an hour and a half of orientation and trail time as well as the chance to help care for and feed the dogs after the trip. Kids (at least three years old, up to 80 pounds) love the 10-minute ride ($10) that's offered daily. Serious husky fans can circumnavigate Mount Bachelor on the five-hour, 26-mile-long Marathon trip ($350 per 350 pounds, adults only).

The beginning of all rides starts with an atmosphere of excitement and anticipation. The dogs are pumped up with enthusiasm and ready to run, and the mushers make their last checks of the equipment and harnesses. When the word is finally given to start, hold on tight. Snow flies everywhere as the huskies madly paw their way down the trail, their happy howls echoing through the forest, as you soak it all up in the wake of their exhilaration. Later on, the dogs settle into their rhythm, and the ride becomes more serene, giving you time to enjoy the majestic vistas of Broken Top, the Three Sisters, and Mount Bachelor. It's similar to a snowmobile ride without all the noise, and it's one of those once-in-a-lifetime opportunities that's well worth taking. Reservations are required, and advance booking is recommended.

MOUNT BACHELOR SUMMIT CHAIRLIFT

Even when ski season is over, Mount Bachelor Summit Chairlift (541/382-2442 in Oregon or 800/829-2442, www.mtbachelor.com) and the Sunrise Lodge Lift are in operation. The view from the top of 9,065 foot Mount Bachelor takes in many of the Cascade lakes and peaks. The lift runs 10 A.M.–4 P.M. daily, Memorial to Labor Day and costs $10 adults, $5 children ages 7–12. Try to time your journey to the top with the ranger talks offered at 11:30 A.M. and 2:30 P.M. seven days a week. Lunch is served daily in the mid-mountain Pine Marten Lodge 10 A.M.–4 P.M. Mountain bike rentals are available from the Mount Bachelor Ski and Sport shop at West Village. Bikes are allowed on the cross-country trails, but not on the chairlift.

The peak's natural history is conveyed by a three-mile trail where white bark pine and pumice grape-fern grow. The purplish fern is found in only four other alpine plant communities in Oregon, most notably in the pumice desert on the northwest side of Crater Lake. You can get to Sunrise Lodge and Lift via the Cascades Lakes Highway (see "Sights," earlier in this chapter). Many consider the perspective from Mount Bachelor's 9,065-foot summit to be the finest alpine view in the state.

Llama Trekking

Central Oregon is the heart of the state's thriving llama industry. Here are a couple of ranchers who welcome visitors to see this interesting creature up close.

Oregon Llamas (61702 Teal Rd., Bend 97701, 541/595-2088 or 888/PAC-LAMA, www.packllama.com) takes you to the next level of llama appreciation, out there in the wild open spaces of the West. Offering a plethora of fully catered and guided five-day llama treks in the Three Sisters and Jefferson Wilderness Areas for $150 per day, your two-toed companions will escort you deep into the backcountry, often without the benefit of a trail. It's nice having someone else carrying the bulk of the gear and dealing with the meals and camping details, leaving you free to enjoy the wonder of the wilderness without all the work.

Rancho Paraiso Llamase (19345 Dusty Loop, Bend, 541/388-7333) will be happy to show you around. Please show these ranchers courtesy by contacting them before visiting.

Golf

Central Oregon has recently gained recognition for world-class golfing. And no wonder. With a dozen courses and six more slated for construction, this region of the state offers just about every kind of golf challenge. The warm, sunny days, cool evenings, and spectacular mountain scenery make every shot a memorable one.

Two well-groomed courses, **Big Meadow** and **Glaze Meadow,** are found at Black Butte Ranch (541/595-1500 or 800/399-2322, www.blackbutteranch.com). Big Meadow is more open and forgiving, while Glaze Meadow demands precise shots. Both have tall trees and lush fairways from tee to green. This course was recently named by *Golf Digest* as one of Oregon's top 10 golf courses. Greens fees are $26–36 for nine holes and $42–65 for 18 holes. Reservations for weekdays must be made at least one day in advance, while weekend bookings must be made no later than the Monday before.

Crooked River Ranch (541/923-6343 or 800/833-3197, www.crookedriverranch.com) a nine-hole par-32 course, is wide open with few trees, but that doesn't detract from the challenge or the scenic vistas. Rates are $15–17 for nine holes and $25–30 for 18 holes. Weekend reservations must be made by Thursday.

A blend of open and tight holes can be found on the popular course at **Eagle Crest Resort** (541/923-4653, www.eagle-crest.com). The two nine-hole segments of this par-72 course differ in character. The first set allows you to swing away, while the second places a premium on club and shot selection. The stand of 1,000-year-old junipers in mid-fairway and excellent greens add to the challenge and enjoyment. The greens fees for registered guests are $24–34 for nine holes and $45–65 for 18 holes. Weekend reservations must be made by Thursday.

Eighteen new holes opened up recently near the **Inn of the Seventh Mountain at Widgi Creek** (18707 Century Dr., Bend 97702, 541/382-4449, www.widgi.com). Designed by Robert Muir Graves, the course's strategically placed trees, lakes, and sand traps have already given this place the reputation as the "mean green" golf course of central Oregon. The 18 holes here are mentioned in the same breath as Sunriver's

North Course and Black Butte's Glaze Meadows—good company indeed. The greens fees are $25–50 for nine holes, $40–75 for 18 holes.

A true desert course found in Redmond that requires shot accuracy is the **Juniper Golf Club** (541/548-3121, www.junipergolf.com). This is an 18-hole par-72 course that snakes through the juniper and lava of the high desert. The prevailing winds and abundance of rocks off of the fairway challenge the golfer's shot-making abilities. Rates are $15–20 for nine holes and $25–35 for 18 holes. Reservations are required at least one day in advance.

Three distinct 18-hole courses are found at **Sunriver Resort** (541/593-4402 or 800/801-8765, www.sunriver-resort.com) 15 miles south of Bend on U.S. 97. The South Course is long, with fast greens that require a soft touch. The North Course, the premier course in the area, has been rated among the top 25 in the country and is the site of the annual Oregon Open. Water, abundant bunkers, and constricted approaches to the greens make club selection and shot accuracy very important. The new Crosswater course is touted by the management as the best course north of Pebble Beach. In 2000, it was honored as one of *Golf Digest's* top 100 courses in the United States. You must be a resort guest or member to play on it. The greens fees for twilight (nine holes) are $45–55 and $80–90 for 18 on the north/south course, while the exclusive crosswater course ranges $100–135.

A nearby, more economical championship golf course alternative would be **Quail Run** (541/536-1303 or 800/895-4653). Sand traps, ponds, and tree-lined fairways challenge golfers of all levels without seriously challenging their pocketbooks. Greens fees are $20 for nine holes, and $35 for 18.

Located three miles outside of nearby Sisters, **Aspen Lakes** (541/549-GOLF, www.aspen-lakes.com) offers 27 holes in the shadow of the Three Sisters. Bent-grass fairways and distinct volcanic red cinder bunkers add to the stunning

> *Warm Springs Indian Reservation's KWSO (91.9 FM) features an intriguing blend of progressive country music, morning chants by tribal elders, and discussions of issues concerning Native Americans.*

mountain vistas. Greens fees are $20–25 for nine holes and $40–56 for 18; reservations are always a good idea.

Juniper Aquatic and Fitness Center

One of the finest aquatic and fitness centers east of the Cascades is found at Juniper Aquatic and Fitness Center (800 N.E. 6th St., Bend 97701, 541/389-7665). Part of the Bend Metro Park and Recreation District, the center is located in 20-acre Juniper Park and features two indoor pools and a large 40-yard outdoor pool providing plenty of space for splashing around. Serious swimmers can enjoy frequent lap swims and adults-only swim times daily. An aerobics room, weight room, jogging trail, and tennis court offer other exercise options. A sauna and whirlpool tub provide you with yet another way to sweat it out. Call ahead to see what's on the schedule for the day's activities.

ENTERTAINMENT AND EVENTS

Crooked River Dinner Train

The **Crooked River Dinner Train** (4075 O'Neil Rd., Redmond 97756, 541/548-8630, www.crookedriverrailroad.com) shows off the broad vistas of central Oregon's high desert as well as the state's indigenous delicacies and local wines. The 2.5-hour, 38-mile route through the Ochoco River Valley goes from Redmond to Prineville, offering Sunday champagne brunches, murder mystery theater, and western theme dinners from mid-June till October. Call for prices and schedule updates. This deluxe service can cost more than $65 per person. Office hours Mon.–Saturday.

Events

The **Bend Summer Fest** brings out food booths, Oregon wine and microbrews, art exhibits, and live music all in one big block party the second weekend in July. Contact the Bend Visitors Information Bureau (541/382-8048, www.visit-bend.com) for more details.

The **Cascade Festival of Music** (www.cascademusic.org) is held in late summer on the banks of the Deschutes River in Drake Park. In addition to world-class performances of classical, pop, and jazz in the pavilion tent, children's concerts, music workshops, and strolling minstrels round out the pageant. Tickets and information are available through the Cascade Festival of Music office (541/383-2202 or 888/545-7435); tickets $15–30.

The **Sunriver Music and Arts Festival,** (www.sunrivermusic.org), held in the magnificent log-and-stone structure called the Great Hall at Sunriver Resort, has been pleasing capacity crowds since the festival's inception in 1977. The five-concert series features top performers from around the world. Highlights include the gala pops concert and the gourmet dinner as well as four traditional classical concerts and two children's concerts. Tickets and information are available through the Sunriver Music Festival office (541/593-1084 or 541/593-9310).

ACCOMMODATIONS

Motels

Bend has exploded into the largest full-fledged resort town in the state. On holidays or ski weekends, it's hard to find a decent room if you don't have reservations, and it's bound to get worse. Nonetheless, a profusion of cut-rate motels just off the main drag makes it possible to put a roof over your head without putting a dent in your pocketbook.

You'll find a few Rt. 66 transplants with some of the lowest rates **Sonoma Lodge** (450 S.E. 3rd, 541/382-4891), $40–60; **Westward Ho Motel** (904 S.E. U.S. 97, 541/382-2111 or 800/999-8143), $40–54; and **Rodeway Inn** (3705 U.S. 97 N., 541/382-2211 or 800/507-2211), $45–70. Good dollar value is found at **Bend Riverside Motel** (1565 N.W. Hill St., 541/389-2363 or 800/284-2363), offering rooms from $60–120 per night. Some of their suites overlook the river and have fireplaces and kitchens. The **Riverhouse Resort** (3075 U.S. 97 N., 541/389-3111 or 800/547-3928), $70–90, is good enough for Tauck Tours to occasionally include on their prestigous Oregon Tour motorcoach vacation. Across the street, **Hampton Inn** (15 N.E. Butler Market Rd., 541/388-4114 or 800/HAMPTON), $70–100, always delivers a large, clean room, accepts pets, and includes a continental breakfast.

Both of the Best Westerns, **Best Western Entrada Lodge** (19221 Century Dr., 541/382-4080 or 800/528-1234) and **Best Western Inn** (721 N.E. 3rd, 541/382-1515 or 800/528-1234, www.bestwestern.com) run $70–120/night, have pools, allow pets, and feed you in the morning. The pair of Red Lions, **Red Lion South** (849 N.E. 3rd, 541/382-8384 or 800/RED LION), $70–110, and **Red Lion North** (1415 N.E. 3rd, 541/382-7011 or 800/RED LION, www.redlion.com), $70–115, give you huge rooms, a pool, breakfast, and Showtime. **Shilo Inn** (3105 O.B. Riley Rd., 541/389-9600 or 800/222-2244), $90–150, is yet another suitable upgrade with many amenities. For a more comprehensive list of motels, see the website www.visitbend.org.

Central Oregon Resorts

There are several premier resorts in Deschutes County that have helped transform it from a primarily agricultural area to the Aspen of the Northwest. Golf, horseback riding, tennis, swimming, biking/jogging/hiking trails, saunas, and hot tubs grace these all-year playgrounds, along with first-rate lodgings and restaurants. Ski packages and other special offers are also available at each establishment. While all of them feature recreation amid pleasant surroundings, subtle distinctions among these resorts bear mention.

Located 31 miles west of Bend on U.S. 20, **Black Butte Ranch** (P.O. Box 8000, Black Butte Ranch 97759, 541/595-6211 or 800/452-7455, www.blackbutteranch.com) sits on the plain of the seven peaks. Ponderosa pines, lush meadows, and aspen-lined streams round out the metaphor of mountains' majesty. Over 16 miles of trails thread through the 1,800 acres of forested grounds. Accommodations include deluxe hotel-type bedrooms, one- to three-bedroom condominium suites, and resort homes. Rates for these digs range $100–375. A nationally rated golf course, bike trails, tennis courts, and other facilities also explain why this resort has won the *Family Circle* "Resort of the Year" award twice. In January 1997, Black Butte was voted to the prestigious "gold list" of *Condé Nast's* top hotels and resorts of the world.

Eagle Crest Resort (P.O. Box 1215, Redmond 97756, 541/923-2453 or 800/682-4786, www.eagle-crest.com) is five miles west of Redmond. This relative newcomer to the central Oregon resort scene offers hotel rooms, two-bedroom suites, and condos in the $80–360 range. The terrain and vegetation are representative of the high desert, and backdropped by views of eight Cascade peaks. Ask about ski and golf packages. This is a low-key, family-oriented place.

Another great place for families is the **Inn of the Seventh Mountain** (18575 S.W. Century Dr., Bend 97709, 541/382-8711 or 800/452-6810, www.seventhmountain.com). It is located five miles outside of Bend on Century Drive in the Deschutes National Forest. Bedroom units, fireside studios, and condos are available in the $75–270 range. Their outstanding recreation department plugs the kids into nonstop fun, leaving the parents free to enjoy grown-up pursuits. Ice skating, cross-country skiing, and snowmobile trips are available during the winter months, and rafting, swimming, tennis, golf, horseback riding, and more are offered during the summer. Ask about their ski, rafting, or golf packages.

A location close by the Deschutes River recommends the inn as a base for rafting (see "Sports and Recreation," earlier in this section) and one of the prettiest fall bike rides in Oregon. The whitecaps of the blue Deschutes River and the strewn black lava rock accompany you on the 8.5-mile jaunt to Benham Falls. Add three waterfalls, volcano views, meadows, lava fields, and sage brush flats and you can imagine the visual intoxication of the ride. To get to the starting point, go five miles west of Bend on Century Drive. Turn south just before the golf course at a sign pointing to Meadow picnic area, then drive on a gravel road one mile to a parking area by the Deschutes River.

Yet another place to bring the family is **Kah-Nee-Ta Resort** (P.O. Box K, Warm Springs 97761, 541/553-1112 or 800/554-4786, www.kah-nee-taresort.com). Located at the bottom of a canyon about a dozen miles off U.S. 26 from the town of Warm Springs, Kah-Nee-Ta basks in 300 days of sunshine a year. The 1,000-foot elevation and 12-inch annual rainfall enable golfers to play its championship course year-round. It's

THE CASCADES

even snow-free in February. Owned by the Confederated Tribes of Warm Springs, this arrow-shaped hotel is the centerpiece of the 600,000-acre reservation, which includes a working ranch and wild horses.

Lodging possibilities include authentic tepees from $72; hotel rooms, suites, and cottages range $150–300. The hot mineral baths and spring-fed Olympic-sized swimming pool are among the highlights here. There are also bike rentals, tennis, horseback riding, and hiking. Such native-inspired dishes as salmon cooked outside in the traditional way (with roots and wild herbs) and bird-in-clay (a game hen stewing in its own juices inside a clay mold) also impart a unique flavor to a vacation here. There is a gaming resort on site as well. Day vistors can take advantage of Kah-Nee-Ta's venerated hot spring pool and baths (included in overnight room rate) for $8. The kids are sure to enjoy the 140-foot water slide ($2 for the whole day).

The Northwest's most complete resort, **Sunriver Lodge** (P.O. Box 3609, Sunriver 97707, 800/547-3922), not only has proximity to Mount Bachelor skiing, Deschutes River canoeing/white-water rafting, and hiking/horse trails in the Deschutes National Forest but also boasts golf courses, pools, tennis courts, and 30 miles of biking routes. An on-site astronomical observatory and nature center, which features live animal displays and botanical gardens, together with Sunriver's shopping mall, compound the impression of a recreation mecca with something for everybody.

Larger parties will find the spacious lodge suites to be well worth the $119–450 asking price. Each of these units features a floor-to-ceiling fireplace, a fully equipped kitchen, a sleeping loft, and tall picture windows that open onto a patio. During the summer, complimentary bicycles and a two-hour float down the Deschutes in a canoe are included with room rental. In previous years, this resort won *Family Circle*'s Resort of the Year award.

Condo rentals, $175–275, at Sunriver that sleep from four to ten people are available through **Mountain Resort Properties** (541/593-8685 or 800/346-6337, www.mtresort.com). All units have a fully equipped kitchen, linens, washer/dryer, TV, barbecue, and telephone as well as access to swimming and tennis at Sunriver. Since these are privately owned units, other amenities like VCR, hot tub, sauna, and bicycles will vary. Most of these condos do not allow pets or smoking, but there are a couple of exceptions; inquire when making reservations.

Tucked away in a small valley nine miles west of Bend is **Rock Springs Guest Ranch** (64201 Tyler Rd., Bend, 541/382-1957 or 800/225-3833, www.rocksprings.com). Summer guests here stay by the week (Sat.–Sat.) on the American Plan, where all meals, lodging, horseback riding, and other ranch activities are included in one flat rate; $2,400 adults, $1,485 ages 6–16, $1,235 ages 3–5. Only 50 guests are allowed per week, ensuring a high degree of personal service. Food is ample and delicious, and those with special dietary preferences will be accommodated adequately. Cookies, fruit, and beverages are always available for guests in the lodge dining room. Guests get their own cabins that are clean and well furnished.

A proactive recreation program supervised by well-qualified counselors keeps the kids on the go all day long with croquet, badminton, volleyball, basketball, and horseback riding. The horseback riding program is outstanding, and is the forte of the ranch. Riders are matched up with steeds appropriate to their level, and enjoy rides catered to all levels of experience that grow more challenging as the week progresses. After a day in the saddle, it's great to relax in their spa to work out the kinks. If your family likes to horse around, this is the place to do it.

Bed-and-Breakfasts

Close to downtown Bend, Drake Park, and Mirror Pond is **Lara House** (640 N.W. Congress, 541/388-4064 or 800/766-4064, www.larahouse.com), $95–150. This large three-story house was built in 1910 and features six large bedrooms with private bath. All rooms are furnished with antiques and reflect individual grace and charm. A delicious homemade breakfast is served in the bright solarium overlooking the colorful gardens and Drake Park. A large hot tub helps loosen aching muscles after a long day skiing, hiking, or other outdoor sports. Call ahead for reservations.

Also located in close proximity to Drake Park is the **Sather House** (7 N.W. Tumalo, Bend 97701, 541/388-1065 or 888/388-1065, www.moriah.com/sather), $90–126. Cheery quilts and comforters, antiques, afternoon tea, and satisfying breakfasts ensure that your stay here will be memorable.

Originally an early 1900s hotel and boarding house, the **Mill Inn B&B** (642 N.W. Colorado, Bend, 541/389-9198 or 877/748-1200, www.millinn.com), $60–90, was extensively remodeled in 1990 into a contemporary 10-bedroom inn. Most of the rooms feature private baths, and some room sets adjoin to accommodate families (the Locker Room has four bunks, a bargain at $20/person). All rates include a full breakfast, and ski and golf packages are available. Add access to a washer/dryer, refrigerator, and hot tub, and you'll understand why advance booking is a necessity here.

Two other B&Bs in country-like settings in Bend are **The Country Inn The City** (1776 N.E. 8th St., 541/385-7639), $75, and the **Gazebo** (21679 Obsidian Ave., 541/389-7202) $65. Both of these properties feature a full breakfast; call for reservations and directions. About 15 minutes outside of town on the banks of the Deschutes River is **Swallow Ridge Bed & Breakfast** (65711 Twin Bridges Rd., Bend 97701, 541/389-1913, www.teleport.com/~bluesky), $50–70. Perched atop the building, every window affords a view of either mountain or stream along with generous doses of peace and quiet. Instead of breakfast, you're given all the fixings and a kitchen, and the rest is up to you. Located on a working llama ranch, this B&B lets guests help to feed the animals in the evenings—a bonus to many a city slicker.

FOOD

Around Bend

The scenery around Bend feeds the soul, and restaurants here do the rest. While area restaurants run the gamut from fast-food franchises to ele-

gant dinner houses, many travelers also want something in between those extremes. Some alternatives for every budget are listed below.

Beef and Brew (Bend River Mall, 541/388-4646) is a good dinner house, $8–17, for choice beef, seafood, and a tall cool one. Reservations are recommended. Open daily for dinner. For a low-cost, low-fat, low-cholesterol vegetarian breakfast or lunch with many organic items available, **Cafe Santé** (718 N.W. Franklin, 541/383-3530) is the place to go. Even simple foods like soup and salad are highlights here. Open Mon.–Friday.

Decent Chinese cuisine is found at the **Hong Kong Restaurant and Lounge** (580 S.E. 3rd, 541/389-8880). A wide selection of Cantonese, Szechuan and American food, as well as many vegetarian and health-food dishes, are prepared here (for under $10). Open daily for lunch and dinner.

For some of the largest portions in central Oregon, head down to **Jake's Diner** (61260 U.S. 97 S., 541/382-0118). Hearty breakfasts are served here 24 hours a day, and the tasty giant cinnamon rolls are a treat. Truckers everywhere in the West sing the praises of this place. Nonetheless, lunch and dinner might disappoint you if you're expecting anything other than basic food. Another U.S. 97 shrine to road food is **Dandy's Burgers** (1334 U.S. 97, 541/382-6141).

Ernesto's ItaliFan (1203 N.E. 3rd St., 541/389-7274) has a good reputation with the locals. Situated in an old church and designed with an open kitchen, the dinner entrées range $8–16. Suffice it to say that, mamma mia, you'll find a favorite dish on the menu here. Their moderately priced seafood dishes are available for take out, in tray-size dishes ideal for feeding the gang back at the condo. Open for lunch and dinner Mon.–Fri.; dinner only on weekends.

The **Pine Tavern Restaurant** (967 N.W. Brooks St., 541/382-5581) has been in business since 1919, so they must be doing something right. The restaurant is located in a garden setting overlooking Mirror Pond, and ponderosa pines coming up through the floor enhance the interior ambience. Fresh mountain trout, prime rib, lamb, and hot sourdough scones with honey butter are among the many specialties ($10–25).

Reservations are recommended. Open daily; dinner only on Sunday.

Finally, you'll find the **Grayhawk Inn** (18575 Century Dr., 541/382-8711), at the Inn of the Seventh Mountain. Dinner entrées range $12–25 and feature some vegetarian items on the menu. House specialties take advantage of bountiful and delicious regional ingredients. One such dish is house-made fettuccini tossed with Oregon bay shrimp and hazelnut pesto with Hood River pears. Select the perfect accompaniment to your meal from their vast assortment of Pacific Northwest wines and brews.

Downtown

There are many fine restaurants catering to a wide variety of tastes all within walking distance of each other in the heart of Bend; look for a particularly high concentration near the 900 block of Bond Street, west of U.S. 97. Here's a brief survey of some of what's cookin' downtown.

The place to go for breakfast and lunch is the **Alpenglow Cafe** (1040 N.W. Bond, 541/383-7676). Just about everything here is made on the premises; no canned products are used for anything. They make their own breads, muffins, buns, rolls, and pasta, and use fresh and local Oregon staples whenever possible. A summer seasonal favorite is the berry-stuffed French toast, extra-thick slices of the restaurant's own special bread filled with fresh blueberries or raspberries. Open 7 A.M.–2 P.M., this small but bright establishment fills up fast with patrons in the know.

Budget gourmets hit the **Taco Stand** (221 N.W. Hill St., 541/382-0494), where you can have a filling burrito for around two bucks. There are also chiles rellenos, enchiladas, red snapper burritos, and chile verde. Just look for the line of customers on Hill Street just off of Division. Closed Sundays.

Another good place for cheap eats is **Super Burrito** (118 N.W. Minnesota, 541/317-1384). It's a small "hole in the wall" with only a few tables, which are usually occupied. Their menu highlights large burritos for around $3 with many choices of fillings. The El Super is one of their most popular burritos, overstuffed with chile rel-leno, steak piccado, beans, and their own Mexican avocado sauce. Their food is quick and tasty, but not fast food.

Yoko's Japanese Restaurant (1028 N.W. Bond St., 541/382-2999, and 2670 N.E. ORE 20, 541/382-3300) is Bend's preeminent Japanese restaurant and sushi bar. While the teriyaki, tempura, and sukiyaki dinners are prepared to suit American tastes, it's not uncommon to see Japanese visitors here enjoying their native cuisine. When the popular Japanese TV show *From Oregon With Love* was being filmed in central Oregon, this is where the production crews would eat most of their meals. Dinners range $8–13, and their sushi rolls cost $4–7. Open for lunch and dinner every day, except Sunday; winter hours may vary.

Giuseppe's Ristorante (932 N.W. Bond St., 541/389-8899) brings the taste of northern Italy to Bend. A clean, family style restaurant that is well-rounded and well-known in Central Oregon. All entrées ($14–20) come with a vegetable, a side of spaghetti on polenta, and choice of soup, salad, or minestrone. Their most popular dish is Sambuca di Gamberi, tiger prawns sauteed with pancetta, mushrooms, spinach, and garlic and glazed with sambuca. A good wine list and full service bar known for generous portions complement the food.

Bend also boasts central Oregon's first brewery and brewpub, **Deschutes Brewery and Public House** (1044 N.W. Bond St., 541/382-9242). This is the place to come and relax with fresh, handcrafted ales and better-than-average pub food ($3–10). There are vegetarian burgers, sandwiches, and black bean chili among the offerings. Check the specials board to see which ones of the over 5,000 rotating items are being featured that evening. Large viewing windows in the pub enable you to watch next month's batch being concocted in the brewery. Open daily for lunch and dinner.

A family-oriented atmosphere is found at **On the Rocks** (125 N.W. Oregon Ave., 541/382-5654). This nonsmoking, kid-friendly place caters well to all ages. A wide selection of American pub fare ($6–9) that should please everyone is available, and healthy, party-portion sized dishes make sure no one leaves hungry. Open for lunch and dinner daily; winter hours may vary.

High Tides (1045 N.W. Bond, 541/389-5244) is the child of restaurant Tidal Raves in Depoe Bay, which brings a renowned legacy of cooking experience to central Oregon. This Bend incarnation features more creative versions of upscale seafood entrées ($10–20), and the chef will gladly customize gourmet vegetarian dishes to your liking. Wines, microbrews, gourmet sodas, an espresso cart, and not-too-sweet desserts round out the offerings. Open Mon.–Sat. for lunch and dinner, closed Sunday; reservations are accepted.

Another option is **Pizza Mondo** (811 N.W. Wall St., 541/330-9093), producing Bend's finest hand-tossed, stone-baked pies. Customers gladly pay $17.50 for pies like the Maui Wowie, with Canadian bacon, pineapple, and crushed Macadamia nuts. Dynamite calzones and a mean Caesar salad that would give Brutus pause add to their diverse selections. Pizza is also available by the slice. Open for lunch and dinner seven days a week.

You can find 111 Thai dishes at **Toomie's** (119 N.W. Minnesota, 541/388-5590). Open for lunch ($6–8) and dinner ($7–18), this restaurant serves a wide variety of rice, noodle, curry, chicken, seafood, pork, beef, and vegetarian dishes. Be forewarned that when they say "look out!" about hot and spicy dishes, they mean it. Open Mon.–Fri. for lunch; dinner Thurs.–Sunday.

The Meadows, in Sunriver Resort's main lodge (541/593-3740), is an attractive restaurant with a western theme. Views of Mount Bachelor backdropping the golf gourse go well with a dinner menu emphasizing game dishes in the $17–30 range. Breakfast and lunch options run half this price. Open every day.

INFORMATION AND SERVICES

Cascades East is a free publication distributed at various locations in the region. Natural attractions, restaurants, outdoor recreation, and nightlife are well covered, though with an eye toward promotion more than objectivity. For additional information on the Bend area, the **chamber of commerce** (63085 U.S. 97 N., 541/382-3221 or 800/905-2363, www.bend-chamber.org) is open Mon.–Thurs. 9 A.M.–5 P.M., Friday 8 A.M.–6 P.M. And, the **Bend Visitor and Convention Bureau** (541/382-8048) is open Mon.–Friday.

The Bend and Fort Rock **Ranger Station** (1230 N.E. 3rd St., 541/383-4000, www.fs.fed.or .us/r6/centraloregon) is the place to go for permits and information on the vast array of lands in central Oregon managed by the Forest Service. **Café Internet** (133 S.W. Century Dr., Ste. 204, 541/318-8802, cafeInternet@bendcable.com) provides Internet access.

TRANSPORTATION
By Air
With about a dozen flights to/from Portland and several to/from San Francisco daily, access to central Oregon has improved dramatically in the last decade. The air hub of this section of the state is Redmond Air Center (Redmond 97756, 541/504-7200), located 16 miles north of Bend on U.S. 97. **Alaska/Horizon Airlines** (800/426-0333, www.alaskaair.com) has nonstop jet flights out of L.A. and Seattle; **Horizon Air** (800/547-9308), services the region from Portland and Seattle; and **United Express** (800/241-6522) provides flights to and from Portland and San Francisco. Taxi, limo, and bus transfers connect the traveler to Bend at nominal costs. The terminal has interesting displays on central Oregon attractions. Interactive media and audiovisual aids can even teach locals about their home region.

By Bus
Greyhound (1068 N.W. Bond St., 541/382-2151, www.greyhound.com) is open Mon.–Fri. 8 A.M.–5 P.M., Saturday and Sunday 8:30 A.M.–2:30 P.M. and 8 P.M.–10 P.M., and every other evening 8:30–9:45 P.M. Bus service connects Bend with Klamath Falls to the south and Biggs, Maupin, and The Dalles to the north. The **Central Oregon Breeze Shuttle** (541/389-7469 or 800/847-0157, www.cobreeze.com) serves Bend

to and from Portland International Airport. It's reasonably priced (around $40 one-way; $73 round-trip) and offers pick-ups and drop-offs at downtown hotels. **Redmond Airport Shuttle** (541/382-1687 or 888/664-8449) offers door-to-door service to and from the Redmond airport and to and from the Chemult Amtrak station. A free **ski shuttle** run by Mount Bachelor (541/382-2442) links downtown Bend to West Village on the mountain. **Yellow Cab** (541/382-3311) can always haul you around if you need a ride. There is no inner-city bus service.

By Train

The closest you can get to Bend via Amtrak (800/872-7245, www.amtrak.com) is Chemult, 60 miles to the south on U.S. 97. Amtrak will assist you in scheduling your transfer to Bend.

By Car

The automobile is still the vehicle of choice for exploring this quadrant of the state. Highways 97 and 20 converge on Bend, much as the Native American trails and pioneer wagon roads did 150 years ago when this outpost on the Deschutes was called Farewell Bend. Portland is three hours away via U.S. 97 and U.S. 26, Salem is two hours away via U.S. 20 and ORE 22, and Eugene is two hours away via U.S. 20 and ORE 126. Crater Lake National Park is about two hours south down U.S. 97. There are also many loops worth investigating, like the Cascade Lakes Highway, Newberry Crater, and the Lava Lands, as well as other touring corridors.

At press time, the new Bend Parkway was almost completed. This road parallels Division Street and enables traffic to move more quickly through the city. Nonetheless, expect some disruption in traffic flow because 3rd Street (U.S. 97) always seems to be glutted during peak travel times, so plan accordingly.

You can rent a car for around $40 per day with 50 free miles daily from **Hertz** (1057 S.E. 3rd St., Bend, 541/382-1711, Redmond Airport 541/923-1411, or Sunriver 541/593-1221, ext. 418) and **Budget** (2060 U.S. 20 E., Bend, 541/923-0699).

NORTH OF BEND

North of the Bend-Redmond area, the juniper-and-sage-lined roadsides and the fields of mint and wheat stand in welcome contrast to the malled-over main drags of central Oregon's biggest urban complex. The 500-foot-deep Crooked River Gorge, 15 miles south of Madras off U.S. 97 at Ogden Scenic Wayside, and snowcapped vistas of Oregon's two highest mountains to the northeast (Mounts Hood and Jefferson) add further variety to the topography.

Petersen's Rock Garden

What began as one man's flight of fancy over the years has metamorphosed into a full-fledged rock fantasy. Petersen, a Danish immigrant farmer, created four acres of intricately detailed miniature castles, towers, and bridges made of agate, jasper, obsidian, malachite, petrified wood, and thunder eggs. There are also the Statue of Liberty, the American flag, and many other compositions hewn out of natural rock.

This rock garden to end all rock gardens, Petersen's (7930 S.W. 77th St., Redmond 97756, 541/382-5574), is open 365 days a year 9 A.M.–\7 P.M. (or till dusk in winter). To get here, take Gift Road off of U.S. 97 seven miles south of Redmond and 10 miles north of Bend. Follow the signs; it's only three miles off the highway. There is a very nice museum and gift shop in the rear of the complex featuring many types of rocks, crystals, fossils, and semiprecious gemstones. In the back of the museum is the Fluorescent Room, where little castles made of zinc, tungsten, uranium, and manganese glow in the dark. Free-roaming peacocks, chickens, and ducks are here to remind you that this was once a working farm. The staff will help direct rockhounds to promising sites in the vicinity to further their own collections. Admission is $3 for adults, $1.50 for children 6–16.

Smith Rock State Park

The majestic spires towering above the Crooked River north of Redmond on U.S. 97 are part of this 623-acre state park. Named after a soldier who fell to his death off of the highest promontory (3,230 feet) in the configuration, the park is a popular retreat for hikers, rock climbers, and casual visitors. Seven miles of well-marked trails follow the Crooked River and wend up the canyon walls to emerge on the ridgetops. Because the area is delicate and extremely sensitive to erosion, it's important not to blaze any trails because they may leave visible scars for years. Picnic tables, drinking water, and restrooms can be found near the parking area. The more adventurous can camp out in the park's primitive walk-in camping area for $3 a night. It's located near the park entrance about 100 yards from the Rockhard Store, 9297 N.E. Crooked River Dr., Terrebonne. The campground includes showers and sanitary facilities.

While it's not exactly Yosemite, some of the climbing routes at Smith Rock are as difficult and challenging as any you'll find in the United States. Most of the mountain's 17-million-year-old volcanic rock is soft and crumbly, making descents extra challenging. Chocks, nuts, friends, and other clean-climbing equipment and techniques are encouraged to reduce damage to the rock. On certain routes where these methods would prove impractical, permanent anchors have been placed. Climbers should use these fixed bolts (after testing them first for safety, of course) to minimize impact on the rock face. *Oregon Rock: A Climber's Guide,* by Jeff Thomas, includes listings of all the routes at Smith Rock that do not require mounting of additional fixed protection.

Climbers should never disturb birds of prey and their young in the lofty aeries. Finally, pack plenty of water. The Crooked River is contaminated with chemicals from nearby farmlands and isn't suitable for drinking. Discussions are currently underway to build a destination resort in the area. Needless to say, this is a controversial proposition.

For more down-to-earth concerns, we recommend **La Siesta Mexican Restaurant** (8320 U.S. 97, Terrebonne, 541/548-4848). Located on the south side of town in a nondescript crackerbox of a structure, this climber's eatery of choice features such hard-to-find south-of-the-border specialties as *nopales,* chorizo, and mole sauce.

Moderate prices and dishes made from scratch make this an oasis in the culinary wastes of the high desert. Open daily.

Warm Springs Indian Reservation

The past lives on as more than a memory at the Warm Springs Indian Reservation (www.warmsprings.com), which straddles U.S. 26. Within this 600,000 acre bailiwick, you can see the age-old practice of dip-net fishing on the Deschutes, as well as the richest collection of tribal artifacts in the country at a 27,000-square-foot museum. Along with these touches of tradition, the reservation is the embodiment of the modern-day American dream, successfully operating a dam, a resort hotel, and a lumber mill. It's interesting to note that the employees of these enterprises are the descendants of the same Native Americans who greeted Lewis and Clark on the Columbia in 1805, as well as such Deschutes explorers as Peter Skene Ogden (in 1826), John Fremont, and Kit Carson (both in 1843).

A quarter mile south of the Warm Springs Museum, pull into the restaurant just off of U.S. 26 on the west side of the highway. Here you can down some Native American tacos (fry bread) and a piece of wild huckleberry pie while picking up some tribal gossip in the Warm Springs newspaper. Across the lot is a trading post selling craft items made by the confederated tribes.

Richardson's Recreational Ranch

If you're a rockhound, you'll want to visit Richardson's Recreational Ranch, Gateway Rt., Box 440, Madras 97741, 541/475-2680. This family-owned and -operated enterprise has extensive rock beds loaded with thunder eggs, moss agates, jaspers, jasper-agate, Oregon sunset, and rainbow agates. If you want to chip agates out of one of the many exposed ledges on the ranch, you will need to brings chisels, wedges, and other necessary hard-rock mining tools. Once you've completed your dig, you drop your rocks off at the office and pay for them by the pound. And if you don't care for dirt under your fingernails, you can always find rocks for sale from all over the world in the ranch's rock shop.

The motto here is "fun for everyone," and you're sure to meet many interesting "Rocky fellers" back at the ranch. To get there, take U.S. 97 north of Madras for 11 miles and turn right at the sign near mile marker 81. Follow the road for three miles to the ranch office.

Rajneeshpuram

Throughout its history, north-central Oregon's topographic variety has been paralleled by the diversity of the human landscape here.

The name Madras evokes the mystic East. While this central Oregon town has no such ties, it would have been hard to tell anyone that in the early 1980s. Between 1981 and 1984 the population base of ranchers and farmers was augmented by thousands of red-clad disciples of Indian guru Bhagwan Shree Rajneesh. A 175,000-acre ranch was bought for the faithful near Antelope, a tiny community 30 miles northeast of Madras.

Although the commune demonstrated agricultural and architectural ingenuity, it was the Bhagwan's fleet of 96 Rolls Royces that got the headlines. When the Rajneeshees recruited homeless people to stuff the ballot box in local elections and then sent them away shortly thereafter, they compounded the bad first impression Oregonians had of their new neighbors. Before long, adverse publicity over the community's arsenal of combat weapons and their stated intent to use them alerted authorities to a potential threat. The Rajneeshees turned out to be more of a threat to themselves, with the Bhagwan's second-in-command implicated in everything from plots to murder the guru to the embezzlement of millions. Shortly before the dissolution of Rancho Rajneesh, the guru himself was deported because his vow of silence was inconsistent with a teaching visa. Today, the ranch is being converted into a Christian youth camp.

Shaniko

A half hour northeast of Madras is the ghost town of Shaniko (www.shaniko.com). In its day, Shaniko was the largest wool-shipping center in the United States. The Columbia Southern railroad transported wool, sheep, cattle, gold, and people deep into the remote Oregon outback, and the city at the terminus prospered. Boomtown Shaniko had 13 saloons, stores, hotels, a schoolhouse, and a city hall. But when the railroad's main line was diverted to the Deschutes River, Shaniko's prominence quickly faded.

Today you can still see many old buildings in Shaniko. The water tower provides a remarkable display of the jerry-rigged but nonetheless efficient water-distribution system. The three-room Shaniko schoolhouse (built in 1901) and City Hall, featuring the Constable's office and the jail, are also still standing. If you'd like to overnight here, the moderately priced **Shaniko Historic Hotel** (Shaniko 97057, 541/489-3441 or 800/483-3441) has been restored and combines the ambience of the past with modern comforts.

Mount Hood

Oregon's highest and best-known mountain, Mount Hood (or "Wy'East," as the region's Native Americans knew it) rises 11,239 feet above sea level less than an hour's drive from Portland, and dominates the city's eastern horizon in clear weather. Like Japan's Mount Fuji, California's Shasta, and Washington's Rainier, Adams, and St. Helens, Hood is a composite volcano (or stratovolcano), a steep-sided conical mountain built up of layers of lava and ash over the millennia.

Mount Hood was formed about 500,000 years ago, and has since erupted repeatedly, most recently during two periods over the last 1,500 years. Centuries before the first white explorers entered the region, native tribes of the Pacific Northwest witnessed the mountain's eruptions, and the retelling of the events became tribal lore handed down over generations. According to one legend, Wy'East and Pahto were sons of the Great Spirit, Sahale, who both fell in love with a beautiful maiden named Loowit. She was unable to choose between the two of them, and the braves fought bitterly to win her affection, laying waste to forests and villages in the process. In his anger at the destruction, Sahale tranformed the three into mighty mountains: Loowit became Mount St. Helens, Pahto Mount Adams, and to the south, Wy'East became Mount Hood.

The first white men reported seeing the mountain in 1792, when British Navy Lt. William E. Broughton viewed it from the Columbia River near the mouth of the Willamette River. Broughton named the peak after the British Navy's Admiral Samuel Hood (who would never see the mountain himself).

Hood's latest volcanic episode ended in the 1790s, just prior to the arrival of Lewis and Clark in 1805. On October 18, 1805, William Clark sighted Mount Hood, and made this laconic entry in his journal: "Saw a mountain bearing S.W. conocal form Covered with Snow." They named the peak "Timm Mountain" (after the Native American name for the falls area near The Dalles), before they learned that it had al-

ready been named by the British. As the Corps of Discovery passed farther down the Columbia, they encountered a wide, shallow river still clogged with sediment from the recent eruptions, and named it the Quicksand River. Today, it's the Sandy River, which flows some 50 miles from the flanks of Mount Hood. About forty years later, Oregon Trail pioneers opened the Barlow Road on the south side of Hood, the first wagon trail over the Cascades, leading down to the Willamette Valley.

Since recordkeeping began in the 1820s, no significant volcanic activity has been noted, though in 1859, 1865, and 1903 observers noted the venting of steam, accompanied by red glows or "flames." Though the mountain is quiet, volcanologists keep a careful watch on Hood.

Today, the mountain is the breathtaking centerpiece of the Mount Hood National Forest, which embraces 1,067,043 acres of natural beauty and recreational opportunities right in Portland's backyard. Five downhill ski resorts and numerous cross-country trail systems, 1,200 miles of hiking trails, dozens of jewel-like alpine lakes, and more than 80 campgrounds are just the beginning.

SIGHTS

The **Philip Foster Farm and Homestead** (29912 S.E. ORE 211, Eagle Creek, 503/637-6324, is the end of the historic Barlow Road, the place that greeted the emigrants after crossing Mount Hood en route to the Willamette Valley. Just pick up ORE 211 off ORE 26 in Sandy and head south for six miles to Eagle Creek. This working historical farm features a home, an antique barn, a blacksmith shop filled with period artifacts, and pioneer gardens of flowers, herbs, and vegetables. There is also an apple orchard containing varieties from the pioneer era. Visitors can have hands-on experience grinding corn, building log cabins, and partaking of other chores typical of the pioneers. The Pioneer Store features Northwest food, crafts, and history-oriented items. A lilac dating back to 1843 is also of

Philip Foster Farm and Homestead, the end of the Barlow Road

interest here. Shady picnic tables make this site ideal for a family outing. Admission is free, but donations are appreciated. Hours are Fri.–Sun. 11–4 P.M. mid-June–September.

Another highlight off ORE 26 to Mount Hood is **Cascade Streamwatch** (part of a .75-mile interpretive trail that lets you witness the salmon life cycle in a special way. Located 39 miles east of Portland and two miles west of the Mount Hood Information Center on the south side of the highway in the BLM's Wildwood Recreation corridor near Welches, it's easy to reach. When you pull off the highway, a heritage marker at the first parking lot shares info about the Barlow Road, the final leg of the Oregon Trail, which went through these woods. Several miles down the road is the Wildwood Wetland Trail/Cascades Streamwatch parking lot, where a ticket dispenser will take your $3 day-use fee. Not far from the restroom is the gently rolling Wildwood Wetland Trail. It goes through a beautiful second-growth mixed conifer forest along the Salmon River to several Cascades Streamwatch viewing windows built into the shoreline embankment. While fish-viewing windows can be enjoyed at several other Northwest dams and hatcheries, the chance to get a subterranean perspective on the salmon pilgrimage in a natural environment is unique. Trailside fish carvings and sculptures and information placards on forest ecology and salmon spawning enhance the experience.

The 33-mile **Salmon River** is the only river in the lower 48 states protected as a National Wild and Scenic River for its entire length—from its headwaters on Mount Hood to its confluence with the Sandy River near Brightwood. The Wetlands Trail is a fitting introduction to this special riparian ecosystem. Add fire grills and picnic tables in these idyllic surroundings, and you can easily spend several hours here, in the home of such species as the giant Pacific salamander, red-legged frog, and coho salmon. While spring and fall spawning seasons are optimum to see the coho, it's possible to see fish at most times of the year. For more information, call the BLM at 503/375-5646.

CLIMBING

Mount Hood (11,239 feet), the highest mountain in Oregon, has the additional distinction of being the second-most-climbed glacier-covered peak in the world. Nicknamed the Fujiyama of

America, Mount Hood offers hikes that cater to everyone, from beginners to advanced climbers. Another similarity to its Japanese counterpart is that there are only about two months out of the year that are safe for climbing, from May to mid-July. (Many mountaineers feel that the safe climbing season terminates at the end of July.)

Since the summer heat brings on the threat of avalanche danger and falling rock hazards, the time of day of your departure is just as important as the time of year. Most expeditions depart in the wee hours of the morning when the snow is firm and rock danger is lessened. Though you won't get as much sleep, you will be able to enjoy beautiful sunrise scenery as you venture to the top of the world—in Oregon, that is.

There are a few short and easy hikes from Timberline Lodge that require basic day-hiking equipment—hiking boots, water, snacks, sunglasses, sunscreen, and warm, waterproof clothing (since the weather can change rapidly, even in midsummer). Those intent upon reaching the top of the mountain, however, had best go prepared. In addition to the previously mentioned supplies, an ice axe, crampons and extra straps, extra clothing and food, a first-aid kit, at least a quart of water, a CB radio, a topographic map and compass, and a 120-foot rope are necessary. Your boots should be waterproof and well insulated, because the final 3,000 feet in elevation is over glaciers and snowfields. Wool is one of the best fabrics for keeping warm; wool socks (take an extra pair for emergency mittens), mittens, hat, sweater, and pants will keep you warm even when wet. A warm, water-resistant jacket is also a good idea. Remember that this peak breeds clouds and storms, although most accidents occur in warmer weather when the ice and snow are unstable. Summer snow conditions, the 50-degree slope of the final 2,000 feet, and the tiring effects of the climb have contributed to the deaths of at least 10 people over the years.

While the climb looks like only a few miles on the map, it takes 10–15 hours to make the trip from Timberline Lodge to the top and back. The four primary routes up Mount Hood—Hogsback, Mazama, Wyeast, and Castle Crags—are all *technical* climbs; there is no hiking trail to the summit. Having the right equipment means little if you don't know how to use it. It takes a minimum of three people to compose a safe party (many solo adventurers here have ended up decomposing), and you should have a competent and experienced leader in command. Always register at the lodge before climbing and check out when you return.

Most climbing deaths and injuries are avoidable. Dangers like falling ice, rock, and snow, gaping crevasses, and the temperamental mountain weather can all be surmounted with planning, preparedness, and common sense. The ultimate safety device became available several years ago. For $5 (for three days), climbers can rent a one- by two-inch transmitter at several Portland-area mountain shops. It gives off a signal that will enable search and rescue teams to find you. Be one of the hundreds of thousands of happy hikers who have successfully reached the summit and back, not another unfortunate statistic claimed by Old Man Mountain. Before you go, be sure to register at Timberline's Wyeast Day Lodge for Oregon's most popular alpine challenge. For information on climbing guides (as well as Alpine and Nordic ski instructors), contact the **Timberline Lodge** (Sea to Summit Outdoor Adventures, 503/622-7979 or 503/286-9333).

Hogsback

The most common route up Mount Hood is from the south side, beginning at Timberline Lodge. Once you've driven to the 6,000-foot level, only about 5,000 feet of vertical gain to the summit remain. The south-face route takes climbers up the "Miracle Mile" from the lodge to the top of Palmer ski lift, passing Silcox Warming Hut along the way. As you near the peak, you can pick up the route known as Hogsback.

Of the four routes to the summit departing from Timberline Lodge, Hogsback is the most climbed. A good trip for beginners, the climb takes an average 10 to 12 hours round-trip. The first mile ascends 1,000 feet and ends at the **Silcox Warming Hut.** Built in 1939, this rustic stone-and-timber shelter used to house the upper terminal of the original Magic Mile chairlift.

THAR SHE BLOWS!

Although Mount St. Helens's 1980 eruption garnered that Washington volcano more notoriety than its Oregon counterpart enjoys, Mount Hood is nonetheless a slumbering giant that occasionally snores loudly.

Lewis and Clark apparently missed the last eruption by just a few years, according to a carbon-dated four- to six-inch layer of ash found on the southwest flank of the mountain. It has been suggested that their difficulty in crossing the Sandy River in Troutdale on November 3, 1805, might have been caused by mudflows (lahars) that washed down from this eruption. In 1835, missionary Samuel Parker cited Native American reports of "smoke and fire" on the mountain. Local newspapers reported activity in 1853, 1854, 1859, and 1865; the year 1907 also saw some activity.

More recently, sporadic climber reports of sulfur smells up to a mile away from the source at Crater Rock, 700 feet south of the summit, also suggest volcanic potential. And after 65 quakes in five days and 445 quakes recorded in July 1980 following Mount St. Helens's eruption, authorities evacuated campsites and placed seismic monitoring equipment to keep tabs on the volcano. Dozens of small quakes around the mountain over several days in both February 1998 and January 1999 (including a flurry of tremors exceeding 3.0 that paralleled similar events in 1989 and 1990) also caused trepidation. The 20th anniversary of Mount St. Helens's May 18 eruption was marked by a 2.3 earthquake on Mount Hood. The strongest earthquake in decades occurred in June 2002 at a magnitude of 4.5; hundreds of aftershocks followed.

While Old Man Mountain still appears to be sleeping, the Portland Office of Emergency Management has drafted contingency plans for worst-case scenarios. Portland is located far enough away to be out of range of most volcanic debris, but its water source would be cut off. Portland relies upon the bountiful Bull Run watershed located on Mount Hood, and ash and mudflows from a major eruption would

have devastating effects upon the city's water supply. Giant mudflows into the Columbia River present another threat; they could precipitate downstream flooding. A recent report (see vulcan.wr.usgs.gov) says that the several thousand people living in the river valleys within 22 miles of the volcano could be inundated within an hour of an eruption. Landslides of superheated rock called pyroclastic flow, moving as fast as 90 mph, are another threat.

The federal government has also gotten involved by developing complex evacuation plans for the foothill communities of Sandy, Troutdale, and Hood River. The residents may be lucky enough to escape with their hides intact, but the lush fields and well-groomed orchards on the northeastern side of the mountain would very likely be blanketed with ash and debris and sound the death knell to the local way of life. The loss of this major agricultural resource would have statewide repercussions.

The timber industry would also be hard hit by a major eruption. In addition to thousands of square miles of stumpage destroyed by mud, ash, and lava flows, scientists suggest that there would be a high probability of forest fires as well. Like the fruit growers of the Hood River Valley, the region's loggers would be hard-pressed to eke out a living from the charred ground should the mountain ever blow.

The good news is that the after-effects of a volcanic eruption soften with time. In the wake of the Mount St. Helens's blast, insects, vegetation, and wildlife returned to the area within a year or two. Farmers in eastern Washington who saw their crops destroyed in 1980 enjoyed bumper yields within a decade due to the soil's increased fertility. Falling ash creates a sterile growth medium, but a few years of erosion from Northwest winter precipitation can create a nutrient-rich mix. In fact, volcanic debris can supply such soil-enriching chemicals as calcium, phosphorous, sulfur, and potassium to an ecosystem. Be that as it may, many locals look to the mountain with dread and wonder if it will soon be Mount Hood's turn to roar.

This was the second chairlift built in the country, the first to use steel towers, and the nation's oldest operating chairlift until it was discontinued in 1962. Silcox is now a dorm-style lodging unit with all of the amenities. Call **Timberline Sales** (503/622-0756 in Portland, 800/547-1406 elsewhere) for more information.

The trail continues up Palmer Glacier and onto White River Glacier. You climb up the glacier between Crater Rock and the Steel Cliffs and soon reach the saddle above Crater Rock. From here you stay on the saddle and head for the chute that leads to the summit. **Mazama** is a variation on Hogsback and is a good route for your second climb. You cross the saddle above Crater Rock and reach the summit going up the chute on the far left of the rock outcroppings.

Wyeast

An intermediate route for experienced climbers is Wyeast, which averages 12–14 hours round-trip. About a half mile above Silcox Warming Hut, you cross over White River Glacier and reach the saddle of the Steel Cliffs. From there you follow the saddle up to the top. It doesn't go over as much snow, but the rocks on the ridge of the Steel Cliffs are dangerous and require expertise.

Castle Crags

Castle Crags offers an advanced route for experienced climbers. Because this trail goes over Illumination Rock and the Hot Rocks, climbers must go when the ice and rock are solid January through April. Adding to the dangers of bona fide rock-climbing is the ever-present threat of winter weather. Disorienting whiteout conditions, frigid cold, and wicked gale-force winds compound the hardships already imposed by the grueling trail. This 12- to 14-hour round-trip should only be attempted by serious climbers when the weather conditions are right.

Buried Forest Overlook

If the snowbound summit is not for you, an easier one-mile round-trip hike is the Buried Forest Overlook. This overlook provides a dramatic view of the White River Canyon, where a thick forest was buried during one of the mountain's

major eruptive periods about 200–250 years ago. Superheated gases blew down giant trees like matchsticks, and in the next instant, all was buried underneath a mixture of water, ash, and mud. The erosional forces of wind and water have since exposed the remains of the Buried Forest. To get here, follow one of the trails behind Timberline Lodge up the mountain about a quarter mile until you reach the Pacific Crest National Scenic Trail. Turn east (right) onto the Pacific Crest Trail and follow it another quarter mile or so to the overlook. Hood's north face, steep and rock-strewn, is for more accomplished climbers.

HIKING

Hikes in the **Zigzag Ranger District** (70220 U.S. 26 E., Zigzag 97049, 541/666-0704 or 503/622-3191 from Portland) are an excellent introduction to the wealth of recreation options in the Mount Hood National Forest off U.S. 26. Whether you're driving the whole Mount Hood Loop (U.S. 26 to ORE 35 to I-84) or just looking for a nice day trip from the Portland area, the Zigzag District's relatively low elevation and spectacular views of the state's highest mountain can be enjoyed by neophyte hikers or trailwise veterans.

Coming from Portland, take I-84 to the Wood Village Exit and follow the Mount Hood Loop signs to U.S. 26. En route to the trailheads, U.S. 26 is often lined with vehicles during winter ski weekends and summer vacation, with less traffic during the best hiking seasons, spring and fall.

The first stop you'll want to make is at the **Mount Hood Information Center** (65000 U.S. 26 E., Welches 97067, 541/622-4822 or 888/622-4822), located in Mount Hood Village Resort on the south side of the highway. This facility will help you get your bearings, with a wealth of pamphlets and an information desk. Pick up the free forest service flier "Mount Hood Hikes" here or a few miles up the road at the Zigzag Ranger Station.

Ramona Falls Trail

Of the 15 trails outlined in the Zigzag District, we've chosen one hike as a maiden voyage into

THE CASCADES

this magical realm. Our criteria include ease of hiking, proximity to Portland, and aesthetic appeal. Unfortunately, the latter qualities have also made the Ramona Falls Trail perhaps the most traveled wilderness byway on the mountain. With judicious planning, however, you can avoid peak-use times. To reach Ramona Falls drive 18 miles east of Sandy on U.S. 26 to Lolo Pass Road, close by the ranger station. This route (Route 18) heads north from the Zigzag store, eventually leading up to Lost Lake, whose views of Mount Hood have graced many a postcard.

Instead of going all the way to the lake, you will want to go five miles up Lolo Pass Road to Forest Service Road 1825. From here, you'll take the road about four miles to its end. Once you've parked, all you need to do is follow the trail paralleling the Sandy River. In a little more than a mile you'll come to a seasonal bridge over the river with a pretty view of Mount Hood. On the other side of the river, Trail 797 will get you to Ramona Falls in about two miles. The grade of the slope is gentle throughout, and while much of the trail isn't especially scenic (except for a bridge over the Sandy River, June rhododendrons, and views of Mount Hood), Ramona Falls itself makes it all worthwhile.

Imagine a multitude of cascades coursing over a 100-foot-high, 50-foot-wide series of basalt outcroppings. This weeping wall is set in a grove of gargantuan Douglas firs. The spray beneath this canopy of trees can drop the temperature 20°F, making the place a popular retreat on hot summer days. In the winter the trail makes a great cross-country ski run. In warmer times of the year, Ramona Falls is a popular equestrian trail.

McNeil Point Shelter

Next, we'd like to recommend a hike to the McNeil Point Shelter. A map and consultation, both available at the Mount Hood Information Center, are essential for this one, given some tricky trail nuances. With a trailhead not far from Ramona Falls, this will be a nice follow-up to your maiden voyage. To get there, follow the directions in the camping section to McNeil Campground, veering right on Forest Service Road 1828. Proceed 13

miles until you reach the Top Spur Trailhead #785. A half mile up the hiking trail, take a right on the Pacific Crest Trail and keep right continuing up the trail to a four-way intersection. Gorgeous views of Mount Hood and a spectacular June wildflower display will greet you.

The remaining three miles contain some twists and turns that need cartographic clarification from the Forest Service. Your reward will be breathtaking above-timberline views of the Mount Hood National Forest. This excursion is four miles each way and tame enough for weekend warriors. Just start early enough to give yourself sufficient daylight. In addition to Zigzag-area jaunts, you could spend a year hiking all the trails in the several other ranger districts around the mountain, as described by the pamphlet.

Timberline Trail

More ambitious trekkers will take on the 40-mile Timberline Trail, a three- to five-day backpack usually begun at Timberline Lodge. If you undertake this loop, you'll finish up back at the lodge to cool off in the showers or swimming pool. While the alpine meadows on the Timberline Trail are beautiful, consult the rangers to see if water in the half-dozen creeks passed en route is too high during the June and July snowmelt seasons.

With almost two dozen trails branching off the Timberline, opportunities for shorter day-trip loop hikes abound. Most of the main trail follows the base of the mountain near timberline at elevations of 5,000 to 7,000 feet. On the northwest side, however, it drops to 3,000 feet and merges with the Pacific Crest Trail. This means that there's snow on the trail for most of the year. Make the trip in the fall to avoid the crowds; in July and August the mountain meadows are ablaze with wildflowers.

Backpackers must camp at least 200 feet from water and 100 feet from any trail, mountain meadow, or obvious viewpoint.

CAMPING

Set along the banks of the Salmon River is **Green Canyon** (Zigzag Ranger District, 65000 U.S.

the Salmon River on the flanks of Mount Hood

26 E., Welches 97049, 503/622-3191). Here you'll find 15 campsites for tents and RVs (22 feet maximum), with picnic tables and fire grills, piped water, pit toilets, and firewood available seasonally. Green Canyon is open May–mid- to late-September, and the fee is $14 per night, depending upon the site. No reservations, so arrive early. Nearby is a trail that goes through the old-growth forests lining the Salmon River and past several waterfalls. A store and a café are about five miles away.

To get there, go to Zigzag on U.S. 26 and take Salmon River Road (2618) four miles to the campground. Superlative hiking is close by. Trail #742 is accessible at a point two miles down Forest Service Road #2618 prior to reaching the campground, and again from the lower end of a gravel parking lot two miles past the campground. The trail leading off to the left at the end of the parking lot is a very easy hike accessing old-growth fir and cedar. The Salmon River Gorge, with many waterfalls, volcanic plugs, and forested cliffs, is accessed by a trail several hundred feet above the river. In fall, enjoy red and gold maples; year-round, giant cedars and firs dominate.

Near the replica of the Barlow Road Tollgate is **Tollgate Campground.** Set along the banks of the Zigzag River, this campground has 15 tent sites (16 maximum RV length). Open from late May to midseptember, the campground costs $14 per night. Because it's close to the Mount Hood Wilderness and many hiking trails, it's so popular that finding a campsite here without a reservation on a summer weekend is next to impossible. Take U.S. 26 one mile past Rhododendron to get here. Reserve by calling 877/444-6777. It costs $10 to make a reservation.

Situated on the Clear Fork of the Sandy River, **McNeil Campground** has a good view of Mount Hood. The campground has 34 sites for tents and RVs (22 feet maximum) with picnic tables and fire grills, vault toilets, and firewood are also available. Open May–late September, McNeil charges $12 and up per night. (First come, first served; no reservations.) To reach the campground, turn onto Lolo Pass Road (County Route 18) at Zigzag and follow it for four miles. Turn right onto Forest Service Road 1825 and follow signs to the campground, about a mile farther. For a beautiful drive, go back to Lolo Pass Road and make a right, heading over the pass 25 miles to Dee. It takes about an hour if you drive straight there, but allow another 15 minutes for photo stops from Lost Lake, located on a spur road. Lolo Pass Road's gravel surface sees a fair number of log trucks during the week, so be careful. From Dee it takes 25 minutes to reach I-84 to loop back to Portland. No reservations accepted.

A popular place for a night out in the woods is **Camp Creek.** This campground has 25 sites for tents and RVs (22 feet maximum), with piped water, picnic tables, and fire grills. Vault toilets and firewood are also available. Open from late May to late September, Camp Creek charges $14 and up per night. Situated along Camp Creek not far from the Zigzag River, the campground has double campsites that two parties can share. To get here, go three miles east of Rhododendron on U.S. 26 and turn south to the campground. Reserve by calling 877/444-6777. It costs $10 to make a reservation.

About a mile down the road from Timberline Lodge is **Alpine.** The high-elevation setting here lives up to its name, with snow remaining on the ground until late in the summer during heavy snow years. There are 16 campsites for tents plus piped water, picnic tables, and fire grills. Alpine is open July to late September, and the fee is $14 per night. In addition to summer skiing up at Mount Hood, the Pacific Crest Trail passes by very close to the camp. No reservations accepted.

Near the junction of U.S. 26 and ORE 35 is **Still Creek.** Here you'll find 27 sites for tents and RVs (16 feet maximum), with picnic tables and fire grills. Piped water, pit toilets, and firewood are also available. Open from mid-June to late September, Still Creek costs $14 per night. The campground has many large trees and good fishing and is close to a pioneer cemetery and Trillium Lake. To reach this spot, drive past Government Camp to Forest Service Road 2650. Reserve by calling 877/444-6777.

A good place for a base camp for those who like to canoe is at **Trillium Lake.** At only 60 miles from Portland, the lake is a great place for city kids. If they're 13 years and under, they don't need a fishing license and may keep up to 10 fish per day. Crayfish also prowl the lake bottom awaiting capture. Families also appreciate the opportunity to cruise the lake in a canoe or some other nonmotorized craft. At night, a new amphitheater hosts campfire programs and nature talks. There are 57 sites for tents and RVs (40 feet maximum), with picnic tables and fire grills. Piped water and flush toilets were installed recently; boat docking and launching facilities are nearby, but no motorized craft are permitted on the lake. The campground is open from late May to late September and costs $14–26 per night, depending upon the site. To get here, take U.S. 26 two miles southeast of Government Camp, then turn right onto Forest Service Road 2656. Proceed for one mile to the campground. Reserve by calling 877/444-6777.

A spot that offers good fishing, swimming, and windsurfing is **Clear Lake** (Bear Springs Ranger District, Route 1, Box 222, Maupin 97037, 541/328-6211). Here you'll find 28 tent and RV sites (32 feet maximum) with picnic tables and fire grills. Piped water, vault toilets, and firewood are also available. Clear Lake is open late May to early September, and the fee is $14 per night. Boat docking and launching facilities are nearby, and motorized craft are allowed on the lake. To get there, go nine miles southwest of Government Camp on U.S. 26, then one mile south on Forest Service Road 449 to the campground. Reserve by calling 877/444-6777.

A midsized county park called **Toll Bridge** (7360 Toll Bridge, Parkdale 97041, 541/352-6300) is located 18 miles south of Hood River on ORE 35. This campground has 18 tent and 20 RV (20 feet maximum) sites with electricity, piped water, sewer hookups, and picnic tables. Flush toilets, showers, firewood, a recreation hall, and a playground are also featured. Open April–Nov. (and weekends during the off-season, weather permitting); $13–20 per night. Set along the banks of the Hood River, this campground includes bike trails, hiking trails, and tennis courts.

Nottingham and Sherwood (15 and 11 miles south of Parkdale, respectively). Both are open from Memorial Day to Labor Day and include basic amenities. Fees for each are $14 per night. Both are located on the east fork of the Hood River and offer good hiking. Contact the Hood Ranger District (6780 ORE 35, Parkdale 97401; 541/666-0701 in Portland). No reservations accepted.

If you're taking the back road to Breitenbush, you can bed down in what *Sunset* magazine rated one of the top ten campgrounds in the west, **Timothy Lakes** (reservations 800/280-2267 or information 800/622-3360). Although this version of the forest primeval doesn't have RV hookups, you'll find 1,270 sites with water, picnic tables, vault toilets, and fire rings. Leashed pets are permitted as are mountain bikes. We prefer Timothy Lakes to Trillium and Lost Lake because it can support more campsites, imparting a sense of seclusion. Of the five campgrounds here, **Hoodview** is the most scenic ($14–16). To get there, take U.S. 26 about 39 miles past Sandy. Turn south onto Forest Service Road 42 and proceed for nine miles until you reach Forest Service Road 57. Go west on 57 for a couple of miles and you'll see signs for the campground.

PRACTICALITIES

Accommodations

Since Mount Hood is only an hour away from Portland, most people return to the city instead of staying at one of the commercial properties on the loop.

Cabins are a cost-effective way for groups of three or more to stay in beautiful surroundings near hiking trails, ski slopes, and other outdoor recreation. **Cascade Property Management** (24403 E. Welches Rd., Ste. 104, 503/622-5688 or 800/635-5417, www.mthoodrentals.com), in Portland, posts dozens of enticing offerings on their website. Imagine soaking on a deckside hot tub gazing up at Mount Hood, then bedding down under a skylight revealing a starry sky. These cabins come with all the amenities you'd find in a hotel room and then some (firewood and kitchen implements included). Rates vary with the season and the size of the unit. A typical summer rate for a 1,500-square-foot unit with several bedrooms sleeping six might be $280 per night. Rates go as low as $220 for small units and as high as $500 for larger (2,500 sq. ft.) cabins sleeping more than a dozen people. Many of these cabins enjoy secluded locations and the rental office provides discounted lift tickets to several Mount Hood ski areas. Look for

the rental office just west of the Hoodland shopping center.

Mount Hood Village (65000 E. Hwy 26, Welches, 800/255-3069) is another good value. Close by the Forest Service Info Center and bookstore as well as the Ramona Falls trailhead, Cascade Streamwatch, and the Rendez-vous Cafe, this cluster of wooden cabins also has access to the Salmon River. On-site there's a fitness room, and the Courtyard Cafe serving reasonably priced and tasty breakfasts and lunches. Choose between basic "cabins in the woods" sleeping four ($75 per night) and large "vacation cottages" with features like hot tubs and saunas (beginning at $135). While this complex does not have the seclusion and feeling of privacy found in the offerings by Cascade Property Management, Mount Hood Village is a good choice for families.

Food

It doesn't really matter what you've been up to on the mountain. Whether you've been skiing, hiking, climbing, or biking, the end result is usually the same by the time you get down the hill. You're hungry. The Mount Hood corridor is blessed with a selection of eateries that fit most any mood and pocketbook. From fast food on the fly to leisurely dining, it's all here on the loop between Sandy and Government Camp.

The **Armadillo Crossing** (38781 Pioneer Blvd., Sandy, 503/668-6740) serves authentic Mexican entrées daily for dinner.

One mile west of Zigzag on U.S. 26 in Welches is **The Inn Between** (503/622-5400) open for lunch and dinner. Here you can tour the taps (a dozen draft beers are available) and enjoy a steak cooked just the way you like it (because you can supervise how it's cooked yourself). If you've got a beef against red meat, the inn can prepare a feast to suit even the most discriminating of vegetarian palates. Seafood specialties, teriyaki chicken, and gourmet sandwiches are also among the many offerings. For lighter appetites, a variety of salads and delicious homemade soups are available. If you're only here for the large selection of microbrews.

Follow U.S. 26 to the west end of Government Camp and you'll find the **Mount Hood**

Brewing Company (503/272-0102). Sandwiches, pasta, chili, and design-your-own pizza (all generally priced $8–12) can be washed down by microbrews (try their own oatmeal stout), espresso drinks, and local wines. Also in town is the **Huckleberry Inn** (Government Gamp, Oregon Business Loop, 503/272-3325) which deserves mention if only for its 24-hour, seven-days-a-week restaurant and, you guessed it, wild huckleberry pie. The inn's $143-per-person dormitory rooms (sleep 14) also provide welcome respite for rained-out campers on a budget.

The Resort at the Mountain has two dining choices: the main restaurant **Tartan's** (open daily for the summer season) on the east side of the property closes at end of October, when they shift from high to low season. The salads, seafood items, and meat dishes (especially the pepper bacon) at the Resort at the Mountain's Sunday brunch ($20), served year-round at the main resort building, alone would justify mention of this local favorite (68010 E. Fairway Ave., Welches, 503/622-3101). Add reasonable prices and a lush setting in the foothills of Mount Hood, and you have the ingredients for one of the state's best Sunday repasts. To get there, turn right off ORE 26 just west of the Hoodland Shopping Center and follow the signs.

Despite its location abutting ORE 26, the **Rendezvous Grill and Tap Room** (67149 E. ORE 26, Welches, 503/622-6837) is easy for eastbound travelers to miss in the heavy tree cover on the north (left) side of the highway. Once inside, the alpine motif and friendly hosts set a mood appropriate to the surroundings. As for the menu, the chef imbues the ever-changing bill-of-fare with seasonal flourishes showcasing fresh regional produce and seafood. Whatever the season, expect to see such signature dishes as rigatoni topped with alder-smoked chicken, toasted hazelnuts, dried cranberries, and fresh spinach, all in a champagne cream sauce. And if you're just in for a burger, fries, and a microbrew, count on a good, honest meal with such optional dipping sauces as red-pepper pesto. The chanterelles might come from the surrounding forests, and the pasta and bread might come from Portland's Grand Central Bakery, but the desserts are straight from heaven. Moderately prices; open daily.

Information and Services
The **Mount Hood Information Center** (P.O. Box 819, 65000 E. Hwy. 26, Welches 97067, 503/622-4822) can provide information about local places of interest.

Northeastern Oregon

Oregon's northeastern corner offers plenty of places to escape from the modern world. Many of the small towns here have no traffic lights or cellular phone service. A handmade sign in one Wallowa County town still greets visitors with: "Deer and Elk Skins, Buy or Trade."

What a daunting sight this rugged but beautiful country must have been to the pioneers on the Oregon Trail, as they crossed the Snake River near Ontario. Their first sight of Oregon would have been Hells Canyon, carved out by the Snake River, the deepest river-carved gorge in the world, averaging 6,600 feet in depth. To the west, they could see the Wallowas (one of the West's oldest mountain ranges), topped by 10,004-foot Matterhorn and 9,933-foot Saca-jawea Peaks. The mountains' two million acres extend east from La Grande past the Snake River into western Idaho. The character and tenacity of those pioneers who chose Oregon over California can be glimpsed today in the sunburned, wind-creased faces of the sagebrush citizens who live in this still-wild corner of the West.

For jaw-dropping scenic grandeur and outdoor recreation, the area is hard to top. The magnificent Wallowas easily invoke comparisons to the Swiss Alps. A 67-mile stretch of the Snake at the bottom of Hells Canyon is now one of the nation's protected Wild and Scenic Rivers. And while it remains primarily rural ranch country, the area is becoming an increasingly popular haven for artists, sculptors, and writers.

the Wallowas

NORTHEASTERN OREGON

To Toppenish

To Portland

97

14

206

Biggs

Arlington

19

Condon

218

John Day Fossil
Beds National
Monument
Clarno Unit

Antelope

197

To Madras

Painted

John

Day

Fossil

River

Hills

Stein's
Pillar

Ochoco Summit
(4,720 ft.)

26

Ochoco Lake
State Park

Prineville

126

To
Bend

Paulina

Crooked

River

Prineville
Reservoir
State Park

To The
Dalles

Columbia

River

30

84

Umatilla

395

82

To Spokane

207

Hermiston

730

12

Milton-
Freewater

Walla
Walla

12

11

Pendleton

COLD SPRINGS
NATIONAL WILDLIFE
REFUGE

McKay Creek
Reservoir

Emigrant
Springs
State Park

Lehman Hot
Springs

244

395

John Day Fossil Beds
National Monument
Sheep Rock Unit

19

John Day Fossil Beds
National Monument
Painted Hills Unit

Fossil

26

Madras

To Lewiston

WASHINGTON

OREGON

Ronde

River

3

Elgin

La
Grande

237

203

North Powder

Haines

Baker
City

Sumpter

Granite

ELKHORN DRIVE
NATIONAL SCENIC
BYWAY

7

7

245

Phillips
Reservoir

Dixie Pass
(5,280 ft.)

John
Day

River

Canyon City

STRAWBERRY MOUNTAIN
WILDERNESS

Strawberry Mountain
(9,038 ft.)

Prairie City

Blue Mountain
Hot Springs

26

395

To Burns

Grande

Wallowa

River

Wallowa

Wallowa

Enterprise

Joseph

Wallowa Lake

Mt. Howard
(8,200 ft.)

Matterhorn
(10,004 ft.)

Chief Joseph
Mountain

Eagle Cap (9,685 ft.)

Thief Valley
Reservoir

Halfway

86

30

IDAHO

Snake

River

Imnaha

River

Hells

Canyon

National

Recreation

Area

National

Imnaha

To Boise

84

Farewell Bend
State Park

Ontario

Vale

20

26

To Burns

20 mi

20 km

0

0

© AVALON TRAVEL PUBLISHING, INC.

NORTHEASTERN OREGON HIGHLIGHTS

- **Hells Canyon National Recreation Area,** near Enterprise, pages 515–517
- **Imnaha River trout fishing,** near Imnaha, pages 512–513
- **Jetboats on the Snake River,** Hells Canyon, pages 516–517
- **Mount Howard Gondola,** Wallowa Lake, page 510
- **Pendleton Round-Up,** Pendleton, pages 521–522
- **Wallowa cross-country skiing and hiking,** near Joseph, pages 511–512

U.S. 26: Prineville to Sumpter

Prineville, the geographic center of Oregon, is a fitting starting point for this route across the north-central section of the state. It's the oldest incorporated town in central Oregon and the first encounter with what feels like the "Old West" for those heading east from Bend. A thriving community and the seat of Crook County, Prineville has a population of 8,150, gets a meager 10 inches of rain a year, and relies on agriculture, wood products, and tourism for its economy.

The Stetson-hatted citizens and sagebrush-dotted landscape contrast sharply with Bend's resort-town atmosphere. Coming from the west, you drop down from tall bluffs into the Crooked River Valley and, nearing the city, cruise through hills dotted with juniper. White-and-black magpies dart in front of your car, and red-winged blackbirds observe your passing from their fenceposts.

Prineville is also known as the Gateway to the Ochocos, a heavily wooded mountain range that runs east-west for 50 miles. One of Oregon's least-known recreational areas, the Ochocos are still ruggedly pristine. Beyond these mountains stretches the long valley of the John Day River. Also in the vicinity are the famous John Day Fossil Beds, the historic gold-mining camps of Canyon City and Sumpter, and the Strawberry Mountain Wilderness.

Just as the fossil beds provide a cross section of the earth's history, a trip down U.S. 26 will give you a feel for the leather-tough countryside of central-eastern Oregon and the people who settled here: the second-generation pioneers from the Willamette Valley, the Basques, Scots, and Irish from the old countries, and the Chinese who came to pick over the tailings left by gold miners in a hurry. Their combined heritage is here for the finding, along with night skies unobscured by city lights and diverse wildlife roaming the surrounding plains and forests.

HISTORY
The Ochocos
The Ochoco country, named after a Paiute word for willows, was heavily populated by natives who lived off a bounty of deer, elk, fish, and camas roots. The first significant passage of Europeans other than trappers through the area was the Lost Wagon Train of 1845. Led by Stephen Meek, brother of the Oregon Territory spokesman Joe Meek, the pioneers were seeking a route to the Willamette Valley easier than the arduous trek over the Blue Mountains.

Instead, they found hardship, starvation, thirst, and death on a tortuous journey through the deserts of Malheur and Harney Counties and along the rugged ridges of the Ochoco Mountains. Their hardships finally ended when they found the Crooked River and followed it north to The Dalles. Somewhere during the trek, members of the party scooped up gold nuggets and kept them in a blue bucket. Though the legend of the Blue Bucket Mine has since captivated Oregon history buffs, its actual site has never been found.

In 1860, Major Enoch Steen led an expedition through the region, which resulted in a

NORTHEASTERN OREGON

number of geographic features being named after him, including Steens Mountain and Stein's Pillar. Eight years later, Barney Prine built a blacksmith shop, a store, and a saloon near the bank of Ochoco Creek; the outpost grew into the city of Prineville, the only town in 10,000 square miles. It was settled by the sons of the pioneers who had come west on wagon trains. It was their turn to carve out a life from the wilds.

At the turn of the century, cinnabar, the raw ore in which mercury is found, was discovered in the Ochocos, resulting in an influx of miners. About the same time, a range war broke out between the cattlemen and sheepherders. Groups like the Ezee Sheep Shooters and the Crook County Sheep Shooters Association bragged that they had slaughtered 8,000–10,000 sheep in 1905 alone. Incensed by this lawlessness, the citizens of Oregon moved to stop the killing; still, troubles continued for cattle and sheep ranchers and farmers. Harsh winters took their toll on livestock, and the hope that the plains would be receptive to wheat farming was unrealized.

During World War I, many homesteaders gave up and moved to the cities to work for the war effort. In 1917, Prineville made a decision that wound up boosting the local economy. The town built a railroad to Redmond, linking its line with the Union Pacific. Used primarily to haul ponderosa pine logs, the railroad remains the only city-owned railroad still in operation in the United States. In the 1950s a new industry was added to the mainstays of logging, ranching, and farming. Gemstones of high quality were discovered in the Ochocos, prompting a rockhound/tourism boom that continues to this day.

One peculiar historical note of interest: For most of its 11-decade existence, Crook County was a bellwether county, giving the majority of its vote to the winner of every presidential race. However, the county lost its distinction as the nation's last election-eve litmus test when it chose George Bush over Bill Clinton in 1992.

John Day Region

A string of communities runs east from Prineville

that includes Mitchell, Dayville, Mt. Vernon, John Day, Canyon City, and Prairie City. The early history of this stretch of the John Day Valley centers around the discovery of gold in 1862. According to most estimates, $26 million in gold was taken out of the Strawberry Mountain Wilderness. At the peak of the gold rush, Whiskey Flat, later called Canyon City, was populated by 5,000 miners, which made it larger than Portland at the time. Thousands of Chinese immigrated to the area to work the tailings, or leftovers, from the mines. Their history is well articulated by the docents at the Kam Wah Chung and Company Museum in John Day.

One of the more colorful denizens of Canyon City was the celebrated poet Joaquin Miller, who served as the first elected judge in Grant County. Known as the "Byron of Oregon," this dashing figure dressed like Buffalo Bill and orated his florid sonnets to a baffled audience of miners.

Lastly, the area generated an irony common in history: John Day, the man whose name was attached to a river, a valley, and a town, never saw any of them. A hunter from Virginia, Day was hired to provide meat for the Pacific Fur Company expedition led by Wilson Price Hunt. Thirty miles east of The Dalles, near what was then known as the Mau Hau River, Day and another mountain man were attacked by Native Americans and left naked and injured. The river soon became known as Day's River; mapmakers later changed it to the John Day River.

Today, this sparsely settled land of rimrock, ponderosa pine forests, wild horse herds, rattlesnakes, juniper, and sagebrush has some of the state's least known but most interesting attractions including the Kam Wah Chung and Company Museum, the Painted Hills, and the John Day Fossil Beds.

PRINEVILLE

Driving into Prineville, the three-story white Crook County Courthouse clocktower catches your attention. Built in 1909, it suggests the existence of other architectural monuments. However, the town is still the refueling and supply stop for ranchers and farmers it has always been.

After you leave Prineville, the Old West ambience becomes even more pronounced.

A good place to begin your travels in Ochoco country is at the **A.R. Bowman Museum** (246 N. Main St., Prineville 97754, 541/447-3715, www.bowmanmuseum.org), open Mon.–Fri. 10 A.M.–5 P.M., Saturday 11 P.M.–4 P.M. This museum's two floors of exhibits and displays are a notch above most small-town historical museums. Fans of the Old West will enjoy the tack room with saddles, halters, and woolly chaps. Rockhounds will be delighted with the displays of Blue Mountain picture jasper, thunder eggs, and fossils. Other classic displays include a moonshine still, a country store, an upstairs parlor of the early 1900s, and a campfire setup with a graniteware coffee pot and a pound of Bull Durham tobacco.

The 310-acre **Prineville Reservoir,** 17 miles south of Prineville on ORE 27, was built for irrigation and flood control. A popular year-round boating and fishing lake, it is famous for its huge bass. **Ochoco Lake,** six miles east of Prineville on U.S. 26, is a favorite recreational spot for locals, with year-round fishing, boating, and camping (see "Camping," immediately following).

A popular Prineville get-together is the **Annual Prineville Rockhound Show and Powwow** (P.O. Box 671, Prineville 97754, 541/447-6304), held in mid-June. The powwow attracts prospectors and rockhounds from all over the country.

The first week in July is the time and Prineville is the site for the **Crooked River Roundup,** with pari-mutuel horse racing. There's also a **Crooked River Dinner Train** (541/548-8630), and the chamber puts on the **Fourth of July Breakfast and Splash and Dash.** Check with the **Prineville–Crook County Chamber of Commerce** (390 N. Fairview St., P.O. Box 546, Prineville 97754, 541/447-6304) for details on it and other area attractions.

Camping

For good campsites in the Ochocos, take Ochoco Creek Road approximately 10 miles east of Ochoco Lake. Choices include **Ochoco Camp, Walton Lake,** where you can fish, boat, or hike

the trail to Round Mountain, **Wildwood,** and **Ochoco Divide.** Open mid-April–late October, these campgrounds charge $10 per night. While on this loop, stop at the mining ghost town of **Mayflower.** Founded in 1873, the community was active until 1925. A stamp mill is still visible.

The Ochoco's majestic stands of juniper and ponderosa pine are still one of the state's best-kept secrets. Driving ORE 27 through the basalt canyons of the Crooked River canyon is another nearby natural attraction. Contact the Ochoco Ranger Station (541/416-6500) for more information on the area.

Accommodations

The **Rustlers Inn Motel** (960 W. 3rd, Prineville 97754, 541/447-4185) was designed in the Old West style. Art by local artists and antique furniture grace the rooms. Rates start at $40 for a single and $52 for a double. The **Prineville Reservoir Resort** (HC 78, Box 1300, Prineville 97754, 541/447-7468) is on the shoreline of Prineville Reservoir, 17 miles southeast of Prineville on the Paulina Highway (ORE 27). This resort offers motel accommodations with kitchenettes starting at $75 for a double. Camping units go for $19. The resort also rents fishing boats, paddleboats, and motors.

Those driving U.S. 26 to the Painted Hills, Prineville to Mitchell, will enjoy comfort and moderate prices ($45 and up) at the **Executive Inn** (1050 E. 3rd, Prineville, 541/447-4152, www.executiveinnonline.com), east of downtown. Housekeeping units and air-conditioning are just two of the amenities here. The large multiroom family unit is recommended as a base for a family weekend visit to the Painted Hills as motel accommodations in Mitchell are limited.

Food

If you get hungry while in Prineville, try the folksy and inexpensive **Barr's Cafe** (887 N. Main, 541/447-5897). It's open 5 A.M.–10 P.M., with breakfast served all day. The top-of-the-line restaurant in town is **Club Pioneer** (1851 E. 3rd St., 541/447-6177), with reasonably priced steaks, burgers, and even seafood. **Ranchero**

(964 N.W. 3rd St., 541/316-0103) is one of two locations (the other in Bend) with a great selection of south-of-the-border specialities, in the moderate price range. The **Cinnabar Pizzaria** (123 E. 3rd St., 541/447-3880) serves up pizza and salad. You'll find the ubiquitous Western motif in a building built on the site of the Jackson Hotel, which burned in 1922, and the Prineville Hotel, which went up in flames in 1966.

EAST OF PRINEVILLE

Outside town, the country east of Prineville shifts from juniper flats to pine ridges. One landmark that stands out is **Stein's Pillar,** a 300-foot monolith that rises like a rocky forefinger out of the pines. To get to this impressive column of stone, take the Mill Creek Road at Ochoco Lake, six miles east of Prineville. Stein's Pillar will be on your right. The scenic route back to Prineville from the Mill Creek Wilderness on McKay Road takes you by some exquisite meadows and clear mountain streams.

Another worthwhile place to visit is the **Lookout Mountain Special Management Area** (541/416-6500). Located in the Ochocos, it's a unique biosphere with 28 plant communities, one of the finest stands of ponderosa pines in

---

ROCKHOUNDING

The Ochocos are prime rockhound territory, with free public collecting areas operated by the Rockhound Pow-Wow Association. Two good sites are off of U.S. 26. **Whistler Springs** is between mile markers 49 and 50. Turn left on Forest Service Road 27 for about six miles, then turn right onto Forest Service Road 500 and follow it to the springs. The collection area is near the campground. **White Fir Springs** is a good spot for jasper-filled thunder eggs. To get there, drive to mile marker 41, turn left on Forest Service Road 3350, and follow it five miles to the diggings. For more information on rockhounding and where to dig, contact **Elkins Gem Stones** (833 S. Main St., Prineville, 541/447-5547).

---

the state, lots of elk and deer, a wild mustang herd, and creeks full of rainbow and brook trout. A seven-mile trail starts near the Ochoco Ranger Station 22 miles east of Prineville on Forest Service Road 22 at the campground picnic area, and ends at the summit of Lookout Mountain, from which 11 major peaks are visible. June is the time to see one of the best wildflower displays in the state.

Friends of Lookout, a coalition of environmental and recreational groups, invites you to visit the area and lend your support to efforts to secure legislation protecting this unique habitat. To get there, drive 15.3 miles east from Prineville on U.S. 26, and bear right at the sign for the ranger station.

JOHN DAY FOSSIL BEDS NATIONAL MONUMENT

The next sights as you travel east are among the most prominent tourist stops in eastern Oregon. In the 1860s, self-taught geologist Thomas Condon discovered what is now known as the John Day Fossil Beds. These archives of stone provide a paleontological record of the 40+ million years and five geologic epochs of life on this planet.

The days of 50-ton brontosaurs and 50-foot-long crocodiles, as well as delicate ferns and flowers, are captured in the rock formations of the three beds, easily visited in a day's excursion. This is the richest concentration of prehistoric mammalian and plant fossils in the world. More than 120 species have been identified here, documenting a period dating from the extinction of the dinosaurs to the beginning of the last great ice age.

This 14,000-acre monument is divided into three areas: the Sheep Rock unit, located about 40 miles west of John Day; the Painted Hills unit, another 45 miles farther west; and the Clarno unit, located northwest of the other units, about 20 miles from the town of Fossil.

The Painted Hills

The first stop, the Painted Hills, is 50 miles east of Prineville on a spur road off U.S. 26. Turn left at the sign outside Mitchell and go six miles along Bridge Creek to the site. Stop first at the visitors center to get oriented and fill your canteen. Continuing on, you'll soon notice the startling, deep red colors of the hills, complemented by pink, gold, buff, bronze, and black. Although the view from the road is impressive, you really have to get out and hike the trails to literally get the picture.

The half-mile **Painted Hills Overlook Trail** provides a view of mineral-bearing clays exposed by erosion. Near the junction with the road and the preceding trail is the 1.5-mile **Carroll Rim Trail,** with a spectacular all-encompassing view of the Painted Hills. The **High Desert Trail** is a three-mile loop into the desert for those seeking the quiet and the solitude of the big empty. Enjoy deep yellows, browns, and reds thanks to the multihued volcanic debris that piled up centuries ago.

But the most vivid colors of all are found at the **Painted Cove Trail.** Viewing the red mounds up close is a highlight. A printed trail guide is available at the trailhead. Close by, the **Leaf Hill Trail** will lead you to remnants of a 30-million-year-old hardwood forest. Walking on the hill itself is prohibited, but take a look at the exhibit describing how our knowledge of Oregon's most ancient forests emanated from studies of this area. It's common knowledge among wildflower buffs that the springtime display here is exceptional.

The Clarno Formations

The next beds, the Clarno Formations, are the oldest and northernmost of the three units comprising the national monument. To get to them, take ORE 207 north of Mitchell Service Creek, then ORE 19 to Fossil and ORE 218 to Clarno. Fossil is situated 45 miles north of the Painted Hills, 20 miles from the Clarno unit. You might want to stop in this little town to collect fossils and petrified wood since it's prohibited within the monument. Ask the locals to point the way to the high school. A hill behind the high school contains crumbled shale that bears imprints of leaves from an ancient forest.

After passing through Fossil, the Clarno Formations are 18 miles farther west. Picnic facilities, drinking water, and restrooms are available. The **Clarno Arch Trail** leads you into the formations at the base of the Eroded Palisades, the Petrified Logs, and the Clarno Arch. The Clarno unit's petrified mudslides is one of the few places in the world where stems of ancient plants, as well as their leaves, seeds, and nuts, are preserved in the same location. Fossilized imprints of palm, gingko, and magnolia leaves culled from volcanic mudflows point to a subtropical forest capable of supporting flowering trees.

While the Clarno Formations are the least visually dramatic unit within the monument, they retain a special fascination for paleontologists. Given that even five-million-year-old fossil beds are considered rare, the 40 million years of diverse plant and animal life that existed 5–45 million years ago takes on greater significance.

A scenic little side loop through the ghost town of **Twickenham** will take you through a canyon with sandstone meadows. Follow the signs through this little wayside where the banded cliffs are so close you can almost reach out and touch them.

Sheep Rock Unit

The third area of the John Day beds, the Sheep Rock unit, can be reached by driving back down ORE 19 to Service Creek, where you turn east and follow the John Day River to **Spray** and **Kimberly**—the latter famous for its cherry season in late June—and then south for 20 miles. If you're coming from the Painted Hills, just head to U.S. 26 and continue about 60 miles east to its junction with ORE 19. This road will lead you into the Sheep Rock unit. The **Sheep Rock Overlook Trail** wends through this area.

Another 2.3 miles along ORE 19 will bring you to the **Cant Ranch Visitor Center** (local headquarters for the National Park Service), which maintains the John Day Fossil Beds National Monument. Of the exhibits in the front room, the fossils from the Clarno nutbeds are especially worth attention. Booklets and informational pamphlets supplement the rangers' interpretive talks. You might also want to visit the small structure in the backyard where scientists extract fossil specimens from stone.

Two fascinating trails several miles north of here are the **Island in Time Trail** and the **Blue Basin Trail.** In certain places the ground at Blue Basin is cobalt blue and the creek water is green.

Camping

The John Day Fossil Beds National Monument **administrative office** (420 W. Main, John Day 97845, 541/987-2333, www.nps.gov/joda) has information on natural history and places to camp. For further information on camping in the area contact the **Grant County Chamber of Commerce** (281 W. Main, John Day 97845, 541/575-0547) and request their pamphlet "Selected Local Campgrounds of Grant County." Information about other campgrounds near the John Day Fossil Beds is posted on the bulletin board near the Cant Ranch parking lot. Also, see their website for maps and information on camping.

Of the few campsites available, the most comfortable for Sheep Rock visitors is **Clyde Holliday State Park** (c/o John Day Office of Oregon State Parks, Main St., John Day 97845, 541/923-4453 or 800/452-5687 for reservations). In addition to shaded hookups for $17 and hiker/biker sites for $5 near the John Day River, the park offers films and evening presentations about the fossil beds and other area natural attractions. The park is located off U.S. 26 between the towns of John Day and Mt. Vernon. And if you've been on the trail too long, the **John Day Trailer Park** (660 W. Main, John Day, 541/575-1557) has a laundry and shower to get you ready for the next adventure. Hours are 7 A.M.—9 P.M.

If you're looking to camp near the Clarno unit, the nearest public campground is **Shelton State Wayside,** 10 miles southeast of Fossil on ORE 19.

Accommodations and Food

The **Sonshine B&B** (210 N.W. Canton St., John Day, 541/575-1827) offers two air-conditioned rooms with comfy queen beds and a shared bath, across from Kam Wah Chung. For the same money ($60–70) you'd pay at one of the generic downtown motels, you can enjoy the foregoing with a delicious home-cooked break-fast. A traditional approach to beefsteak is favored by the **Grubsteak Mining Company** (149 E. Main St., John Day, 541/575-1970). Lunch menu items are under $10; dinners can range up to $35.

Another good base of operations is the **Fish House** (110 Franklin, Dayville, 541/987-2124 or 888/286-FISH, www.fishhouseinn.com). This bed-and-breakfast is located six miles west of the fossil beds in a small town with a historical grocery, the century-old Dayville Mercantile on U.S. 26. These pleasant digs are decorated with antique farm tools and fishing gear and go for $50–65. A country breakfast is included. Not far from the bed-and-breakfast is a restaurant, the **Dayville Diggins.** If you plan to drive to Fossil and beyond from here, top off your tank near the Mini Mart, a short jaunt to the east.

Heading northwest to Fossil in summer, you'll be grateful to see fruit stands selling cherries on a long, hot desolate drive through the tan wavy hills of eastern Oregon. If you're looking to stay near the Clarno unit of the Fossil Beds, visitors also have an invitation to "sleep in a fossil bed" at **Bridge Creek Flora Inn** (828 Main St., Fossil 97830, 541/763-2355, www.fossilinn.com). Rates are $60–75 (including an excellent breakfast) for what is definitely the best place in this town of 400 people. This Victorian is near public fossil-digging beds and features rooms with private as well as shared baths. Hidden between the wheat fields and alfalfa, Fossil has no stoplights but it does have a café, a tavern, and a market. There is also the **Fossil Motel and Trailer Park** (541/763-4075). Rates run $30–40.

Should you be visiting Clarno from The Dalles, the 90-minute drive southeast is another long, hot, dusty drive. Along the way, bullet-ridden road signs are belied by residents giving friendly waves to passing vehicles on the highway, maybe because the only other signs of human presence after the small towns of Wasco and Condon here are an occasional steel windmill and grain silos. If you need to stay overnight, the **Condon Motel** (216 N. Washington St., 541/384-2181) has cool, clean, pet-friendly rooms for $42–50, close to nearby fishing, golf, and other recreation.

KAM WAH CHUNG AND COMPANY MUSEUM

A must stop in the town of John Day, the Kam Wah Chung and Company Museum (250 N.W. Canton; call City Hall 541/575-0028 for info) is located near the city park and pool. It's open May–Oct., Mon.–Sat. 9 A.M.—noon and 1–5 P.M., Sunday 1–5 P.M. Admission is $4 for adults, $3 for seniors, and free for children. In addition to the herbal remedies arrayed in cigar boxes labeled with Chinese calligraphy, there are vintage photos, old tools, furnishings, and other artifacts. Even the labels on the old canned goods are fascinating.

This was the center of Chinese life in the John Day area, serving as a general store and pharmacy with over 500 herbs. People came from hundreds of miles away for the herbal remedies of Doc Hay, who lived here. The building also served in more limited capacities as an assay office, fortune teller's studio, and Taoist shrine.

It began as a trading post on The Dalles Military Road in 1866. The influx of Chinese to the area during the gold rush brought about the outpost's evolution into a center for Asian medicine, trade, and spirituality in 1887, when it was purchased by two Chinese apothecaries. It remained a gath-

ering place for the Chinese community in eastern Oregon until the early 1940s. While it admirably fulfilled this role, the opium-blackened walls, bootleg whiskey, and gambling paraphernalia here evidence the less salutary aspects of the Kam Wah Chung lifestyle. At the time of the 1879 census, eastern Oregon had 960 East Coast emigrants and 2,468 Chinese, proof that the current museum is not an arcane exhibit but rather a significant window on the past. In fact, in 1983, scholars from China came to categorize the herbs and religious objects here.

It's the little touches in the faithfully restored building that stay with you. First your eye will be drawn to the metal shutters and outside wooden staircase on this rough stone edifice. Inside, there's a locked and barred herb cage where Ing Hay prepared medicine and where gold dust was weighed. A Taoist shrine graces the room where groceries and opium were dispensed. Finally, the meat cleaver by Doc Hay's bed bespeaks the fear and despair of Chinese life here near the turn of the century. For more information, read *The Chinese Doctor of John Day* by Jerry Barlow and Christine Richardson (Binford and Mort, 1979).

Close by the Painted Hills in Mitchell, situated on a shady hillside, the kid- and pet-friendly **Skyhook Hotel** (U.S. 26, 541/462-3569) has rooms with kitchen facilities in the $45–55 range.

The **Historic Oregon Hotel** (104 E. Main, 541/462-3027) sustains the time machine effect. Several hotels have been on this site since the 1800s, with the current incarnation dating back to 1938. The historic photos in the lobby recount the latter along with three catastrophic floods that have hit this town. Choose between distinctively decorated rooms (some with shared bath) and a set of duplexes in back with rates that range $30–55. A continental breakfast is included.

Close by, the **Little Pine Café** (100 E. Main, 541/462-3733) serves home-cooking at prices evocative of yesteryear. Open daily for breakfast, lunch, and dinner. Another low-budget dining alternative in this genre is the **Bridge Creek Café**

(541/462-3434), located on the west side of Mitchell just past the turnoff from U.S. 26 to the Painted Hills. Open daily.

East of John Day

Another repository of local history is the **Grant County Historical Museum** (541/575-0509) in Canyon City, a couple of miles south of John Day on U.S. 395. The museum is open June 1–Sept. 30, Mon.–Sat. 10 A.M.–5 P.M., Sunday 1–4 P.M. Centered in the heart of Oregon's mining and ranching country, the facility's wealth of memorabilia depicts the early days of Grant County and includes an extensive rock collection plus Chinese and Native American items.

If you're in Canyon City in midsummer, a great festival is **'62 Days,** which celebrates the local discovery of gold in 1862 with a medicine-wagon show, can-can girls, and a reenactment of the opening of historic Sel's Brewery. Contact the

Grant County Chamber (541/575-0547) for more information.

Thirteen miles east of John Day you come to **Prairie City,** currently undergoing a transition into a tourist town similar to Sisters in central Oregon. The **Dewitt Museum** (Bridge Street, Prairie City 97869, 541/820-3598, www.grantcounty.cc) is housed in the old western terminus of the Sumpter Valley Railroad, which operated between Baker City and Prairie City from 1909 until 1947. The depot was restored in 1979 and today has 10 rooms full of artifacts from Grant County's early days. Open May 15–Oct. 15, Thurs.–Sat. 10 A.M.–3 P.M.

If you're hungry, try the **Bird House Cafe** (201 W. Main St., 541/575-1143) for down-home grub and reasonable prices. **Gee's Restaurant** (241 W. Main St., 541/575-2714) serves better-than-expected Chinese American fare.

STRAWBERRY MOUNTAIN WILDERNESS

The Strawberry Mountain Wilderness, a pocket mountain range southeast of John Day, offers a good system of trails, seven lakes, volcanic rock formations, and, if you're lucky, glimpses of bighorn sheep. Set up your base camp at **Strawberry Campground,** eight miles south of Prairie City on County Route 60, then two miles west on Forest Service Road 6001. Open June–mid-October, Strawberry's fees are $7 per night. The campground is next to Strawberry Creek and is the trailhead for jaunts to Strawberry Lake, Strawberry Falls, and Strawberry Mountain. As you might guess, chances are good that you'll find some wild berries along the way!

If your travels find you in this neighborhood in winter, try the groomed snowmobile and cross-country ski trails, which run from the Austin House in Bates (at the junction of U.S. 26 and ORE 7) to Sumpter, a distance of 23 miles. For more information on the trails, contact the Austin House roadhouse (P.O. Box 8, U.S. 26, Bates 97817).

For information on Strawberry Mountain hiking, contact the Prairie City Ranger District at the Malheur National Forest office (P.O. Box 337,

Prairie City 97869, 541/820-3311). Ask about the 11-mile loop circumnavigating 9,000-foot Strawberry Mountain.

SUMPTER AND VICINITY

While not an official museum, the ghost town of **Whitney,** located 12 miles up ORE 7 from its junction with U.S. 26 (about 15 miles east of Prairie City), has a story to tell to those who visit its ruins. Whitney was the terminus for stage lines to the mining and cattle towns of Unity, Bridgeport, and Malheur City. Now abandoned buildings are all that remain of this bustling community of the early 1900s. An interpretive sign just off ORE 7 explains the local history.

Traveling north of Whitney, you come to the **Sumpter Valley Wildlife Area,** a 158-acre site located between Phillips Reservoir and Sumpter on ORE 7. Canada geese, ring-necked ducks, bitterns, and Virginia rails can be seen in the wetlands and gravel dredge remains along the Powder River.

A few miles north of the refuge is Sumpter, a gold-mining town in the Elkhorn Mountains. To get to the historic little town, turn off U.S. 26 at Austin and drive 22 miles on ORE 7 through the Sumpter Valley. The first settlers here were five Southerners who built a stone cabin and christened it Fort Sumter after the South Carolina garrison that was shelled in April of 1861, signaling the start of the Civil War. In 1883, the U.S. Post Office rejected the name, so locals changed it by dropping the "Fort" and adding a "p." The heyday of gold mining in the area was 1900–1905, when over 3,000 miners worked the hard-rock mines and dredged the Powder River. By 1905, most of the gold was gone, but dredging continued until 1954.

Sumpter Valley Dredge Park (541/894-2486 or 800/551-6949) offers trails, wildlife-viewing areas, and railroad displays. With the possible exception of the dredge in Fox, Alaska, this is the longest and most accessible gold dredge in the country. In addition to this park, abandoned digs, mining equipment, and overgrown cemeteries mark a triangular ghost-town loop here along ORE 7, U.S. 26, and I-84.

Another area attraction is the **Sumpter Valley**

Railroad Excursion (P.O. Box 389, Baker City 97814, 541/894-2268, www.svry.com). Passengers ride in two observation cars pulled by a wood-burning, narrow-gauge steam engine originally used to haul logs and ore in addition to passengers. A restored 1920 car and an 1890 caboose are also part of the train. The seven-mile run from Phillips Reservoir to Sumpter costs $9 for adults, $6.50 for children under 16, $20 per family. The railroad is open from Memorial Day weekend to the last weekend in September with four runs daily at 10 A.M., noon, 2 P.M., and 4 P.M. Call or write to find out about special moonlight rides featuring live entertainment and hobo stew. Construction of a depot within Sumpter Valley Dredge State Park, complete with museum and auditorium, is in the planning stages. The railroad will make a 1.5-mile loop around the dredge.

On Memorial Day, July Fourth, and Labor Day weekend, folks head to the fairgrounds for the **Sumpter Flea Market** (P.O. Box 513, Sumpter 97877, 800/523-1235). Collectibles, crafts, and food are arrayed in a beautiful mountain setting. This event is legendary among Oregon's bargain hunters.

If you have a car full of hungry children, you might want to fill them up in the **Elkhorn Saloon and Family Restaurant** (541/894-2244), in Sumpter. They serve large pizzas at low prices.

When you're ready to leave Sumpter, you have three travel options. You can retrace your route back to U.S. 26 and continue east to Vale and Ontario or head west toward U.S. 97 and Bend. A second possibility is to drive 19 miles east on ORE 7 to ORE 245, and then north nine miles to Baker City.

The third choice, the **Elkhorn Drive National Scenic Byway,** takes you northwest from Sumpter through the gold-mining territory to Granite, across the north fork of the John Day, past Anthony Lake, and on to Baker City. Because much of this road is above 5,000 feet in elevation, the loop is open only a few months of the year. The portion south of Anthony Lakes and north of Granite is closed by snow from early November through June or early July. The Elkhorn Byway climbs higher than any other paved road in Oregon (7,392 feet), after passing North Fork John Day Campground and the junction with Blue Mountains Scenic Byway. The craggy granite peaks of the northern Elkhorns—several higher than 8,000 feet—are near this area. Call the ranger district (541/523-4476) for more information and road conditions.

Of all the locales in the region, back-road and ghost-town connoisseurs might want to stop and take a gander at the remains of **Granite** (population 22), Oregon's smallest incorporated town. With its false-fronted buildings of unpainted, splintered boards, Granite a true "ghost town." Hard as it is to believe, this place once had four saloons, a 50-room hotel, several smaller hotels, a boardinghouse, a church, and a wooden jail. Founded in 1862, its mining legacy sustained the town through the 1930s. The need for miners in defense industries at that time compelled President Roosevelt to shut down the mines. Today, people are moving back despite the lack of police or phone service. Instead, regional ties are maintained by visits to the Granite store where miners, retirees, and other residents keep the ghost alive.

NORTHEASTERN OREGON

Along the Old Oregon Trail

The pioneer trek along the Oregon Trail, a tide of migration starting in 1841 and lasting over 20 years, is one of this country's great epochs, celebrated in novels, films, books, and songs. It is among the largest voluntary human migrations ever recorded.

The wagon trains started in Independence, Missouri, as soon as the spring grass was green. Then the race was on to get across the far mountains before the winter snows. Although the first few hundred miles were easy traveling across the plains, the hardships were not long in coming. Contrary to the stereotype of hostile Native Americans being a major cause of casualties, cholera was by far the leading cause of death on the 2,000-mile journey that became known as "The Longest Graveyard." Some historians estimate at least 30,000 immigrants had died on the Oregon Trail by 1859. This would amount to an average of one unmarked grave for every 100 yards between Independence and Oregon City.

By some estimates, over 300,000 people made the trek from the Midwest to Oregon between 1841 and the turn of the century. In 1843, some 900 immigrants traveled the Oregon Trail, a number that swelled to 17,500 just 10 years later. When it was all over, about 50,000 pioneers followed the trail to the end and settled in Oregon Country—present-day Oregon, Washington, and Idaho. But these numbers tell only part of the story.

At Fort Hall in eastern Idaho, there was a fork in the trail and a sign that read "To Oregon." It was here that the pioneers had to make a key decision. They could head south to California and the gold fields shining with the promise of instant wealth, or they could continue west to Oregon, where the fertile Willamette Valley offered its own allure as a New Jerusalem for serious farmers and homesteaders. Some older Oregonians can recall a childhood version of the story, which claimed that the California road was marked by a pile of gold-painted rocks, in contrast to the "To Oregon" sign. The implication was that people who could read—or who were more interested in domestic pursuits than adventure—would head to Oregon. While this intepretation is not seri-

cattle country: Baker Valley pastureland below the Elkhorn Mountains, near Baker City

ously accepted by historians, it remains a source of good-natured humor between the two states.

Located midway between Portland and Salt Lake City in Oregon's far east, Ontario is where "Oregon's day begins." It's the biggest city in Malheur County, with a population of 9,750. Ontario ships over five percent of the nation's onions and provides a good portion of the sweet russet potatoes used for french fries. Other local crops include sugar beets, peppermint, grains, and ornamental flowers. This abundance derives from a location on the fertile plain at the junction of the Snake and Malheur Rivers.

Baker City, set in a valley between the Wallowas and the Blue Mountains, is the jumping-off spot for Hells Canyon, the deepest gorge in the world. Ranchers still drive their herds down the highways here, and folks wave howdy to passersby. It's a friendly place that has held on to its pioneer spirit.

La Grande is located in the Grande Ronde Valley, which the indigenous peoples called Copi Copi ("Valley of Peace"). Home of Eastern Oregon State College, La Grande enjoys a brisk economy based on beef ranching, wheat farming, and timber. Tourism is on the rise as well. In addition to being the gateway to Wallowa Lake and the northern flank of the Wallowa Range, the region has a rich history, which is detailed at a new forest service visitor area along a section of trail in the Blue Mountains between Pendleton and La Grande on I-84.

HISTORY

Ontario, the town at the beginning of the Oregon section of the Oregon Trail, began as a cattle-shipping depot. The 1883 completion of the Oregon Short Line Railroad connected it to the Union Pacific and markets in the east. In 1939, reservoirs began irrigating the Snake River Valley, turning it into a rich agricultural region.

During World War II, relocation centers for Japanese Americans, whose only "crime" was their ancestry, were built here. Stripped of their rights by a single executive order signed by President Roosevelt, about 5,000 Americans of Japanese descent were forced to liquidate their

property and move into prisonlike barracks in remote sections of the West. This serious breach of constitutional freedoms remains one of the saddest chapters in American history. It's also worth noting that many of these unjustly incarcerated pariahs fought in Europe in some of the most decorated units in the American armed forces.

In any case, a good percentage of the internees stayed in the area and now are well represented in the local business and agricultural communities. As in the Columbia Gorge, Japanese surnames grace many a ranch or farmstead in eastern Oregon. An influx of Hispanic migrant workers who came to work the crops in the 1950s and '60s also stayed to start new lives, adding yet another ethnic flavor to a cultural stew that already contained Paiutes and Basques. All of the above is celebrated in the **Four Rivers Cultural Center** (888/211-1222) at Treasure Valley Community College, at the junction of I-84 (ORE 20, U.S. 26, and Idaho 95), featuring a museum, theater, convention center, and formal Japanese garden.

Baker City, the next major town up the line, was named after Colonel Edward Baker, Oregon's first senator, Union general in the Civil War, and a one-time law partner of Abraham Lincoln. Baker City got its charter in 1874 and soon became known as the "Queen City," for all roads led to this commercial center. In 1861, it became the hub of the eastern Oregon gold rush and its population swelled to 6,600, making it bigger than Boise. Stop by the U.S. National Bank here and check out the 80.4-ounce **Armstrong gold nugget,** found in 1913. It's a remnant from the days when this wealthy, raucous frontier boomtown was the biggest and most important in the region. It boasted the finest hotel between Salt Lake City and Portland and even had a high school, the second in the Pacific Northwest.

Pioneer cattleman Herman Oliver recalls his visits to Baker City as a young boy. He remembers the trolley car that ran the length of Main Street for a nickel. When the conductor reached the end of the line, he pulled a pin holding the horse and led the animal to the other end of the trolley and hooked it up for the return trip. Today, this frontier-era cattle, lumber, and gold-mining crossroads recaptures its 120 years of history with stone and brick buildings, many of which date from 1880–1915. Local historians say the town's architectural styles include Italianate, classic revival, Victorian, and Carpenter Gothic. East of town, along ORE 7 and its off-shoots, ghost towns like Granite and McEwen give new meaning to Gertrude Stein's description of another place: "There's no there there." The route, which follows the twisty contours of the Powder River, is particularly pretty when the deciduous trees take on fall hues.

La Grande, the third city on the Oregon Trail, is in a valley where the Nez Percé once gathered for their summer encampments until the Oregon Trail cut through their territory. More than a few of the pioneers were impressed with the possibilities of the Grande Ronde country. They stayed to build a town that became the market center for a broad stretch of wheat and grass-seed farms. Lumber from the Blue Mountains and livestock that fattened easily on lush fields of tall grass also helped the Oregon Trail pioneers' dreams come true. Located alongside the Grande Ronde River (which flows into the Snake), this town is where I-84 hooks up with ORE 82, the road to the Wallowas.

SIGHTS
Vale and Oregon Trail Sites
Vale, the seat of Malheur County, is located on the Malheur River at the spot where the wagons crossed the river, 28 miles west of Ontario on U.S. 20/26. If you're intrigued by the drama of the pioneers, this little town offers an abundance of historical insight as well as evocative murals of historical scenes. On your visit to Vale, look north to **Malheur Butte** at mile marker 254. This long-extinct volcano was used as a lookout point by Native Americans watching for the wagon trains. The next historical site is **Malheur Crossing,** on the east edge of Vale. The pioneers stopped here to take advantage of natural hot water from underground thermal springs to bathe and do their laundry.

The **Keeney Pass Oregon Trail Historic Site,** on the southern outskirts of Vale, has a display of the deep ruts cut into the earth by ironclad wagon wheels. This exhibit marks the most-used route of the wagon trains as they passed through the Snake River Valley on their way to Baker Valley to the north. From the top of this pass you can see the route of a whole day's journey on the trail to Oregon, 150 years ago. Ponder the fact that one pioneer in 10 died on this arduous transcontinental trek as you gaze out at the Snake River crossing near Old Fort Boise to the southeast. In June and July, Indian paintbrush and penstemon add a dash of color to the sagebrush and rabbitbrush that surround the ruts in the trail. Another site of interest is the **Stone House,** one block east of the Courthouse on Main Street. Built in 1872, it replaced a mud hut way station on the trail.

Oregon Trail Interpretive Center
Six miles east of Baker City is the 23,000-square-foot Oregon Trail Interpretive Center (P.O. Box 854, Baker City 97814, 541/523-6391). The center is open summer–early fall 9 A.M.–6 P.M., Nov. 1–March 31 9 A.M.–4 P.M. Admission is $5, $3.50 for seniors and children.

The museum is perched atop Flagstaff Hill overlooking a picturesque section of this famous frontier thoroughfare. The exhibit halls are arranged to simulate the route and experiences of pioneers on the 547-mile section of the trail within state borders. While there are impressive artifacts as well as thought-provoking historic photos and video presentations, don't think of this as another passive viewing experience. The life-sized dioramas of Oregon Trail scenes, accompanied by taped renditions of immigrant voices and wagon wheels, make you feel like part of the great migration.

Theatrical entertainment, living-history exhibits, paintings, and aptly chosen pioneer diary entries recount the crossing of the Blue Mountains and the Cascades, or rafting down the Columbia into the Willamette Valley. The museum's interpretive loop articulates the immigrant's state of mind—whether it's awe giving way to boredom across the Oregon prairie, emotional duress on a perilous river crossing, or relief while adjusting to settlement at journey's end. Attention is given also to the pioneers' effect on Native American lands and cultures.

Outside the museum, your historical reverie is sustained by living-history exhibits and the chance to stand in the actual ruts left behind by pioneer wagons at **Virtue Flat,** a two-mile walk from the center. Here, surrounded by the 10,000-foot Elkhorn Mountains to the west, the Blues to the south, and the craggy Eagle Cap to the northeast, the "land at Eden's gate" becomes more than just another florid phrase from a pioneer diary.

Prior to departing the Oregon Trail Interpretive Center, check out the raised relief map of northeastern Oregon. Besides getting the lay of the land, you can call up information on area attractions by pushing a button.

Oregon Trail Regional Museum

The Oregon Trail Regional Museum (Campbell and Grove Streets, Baker City 97814, 541/523-9308) is open daily 9 A.M.–4 P.M. May–October. It's located across from Geiser Pollman Park, and admission is by donation. In addition to exhibits depicting the great migration, the museum houses an extensive collection of seashells and corals as well as one of the most comprehensive exhibits of rocks, minerals, and stones in the country.

Crossroads Creative and Performing Arts Center

Crossroads Creative and Performing Arts Center (2020 Auburn Ave., Baker City 97814, 541/523-5369) is in the old Carnegie Library. It has monthly exhibits, a gift shop, and an Arts and Crafts Fair held July 17–19.

Eastern Oregon Museum

The Eastern Oregon Museum (3rd and School, Haines 97833, 541/856-3233) is open daily 9 A.M.–5 P.M. May 18–Labor Day. It has an outstanding collection of farming, mining, and pioneer artifacts. Afterwards, hit the **Haines Steakhouse** for dinner.

Hot Lake Mineral Hot Springs

Hot Lake Mineral Hot Springs was considered "Big Medicine" by the western tribes that camped near its healing waters. In 1810, Astor Pacific Fur Company trappers described elk crowding around this spring. Thereafter, the lake, located five miles east of La Grande on ORE 203, became a popular spot for explorers and emigrants. In 1864, Samuel Newhart built a hotel and bathhouse here. A hospital was added at the turn of the century, and it soon became known as the Mayo Clinic of the West, a polite euphemism for one of the Northwest's first "fat farms." During that era, the healing waters were thought to give relief from arthritis and rheumatism. The resort is not currently in operation.

North Powder Elk

North Powder Elkhorn Wildlife Management Area is a winter elk feeding station open for visits (by permit) Dec. 1–April 15. Viewing is also possible from nearby county roads in late afternoon and evening. To get here, drive west 10 miles from Exit 285 off I-84. Viewpoints are one mile south of the headquarters on River Road and two miles north of headquarters on Tucker Flat Road. These Rocky Mountain elk are somewhat smaller than the Roosevelt elk commonly seen on the west side of the Cascades. Call **T&T Wildlife Tours** (541/856-3356, www.tnthorsemanship.com) for information on tours to this area.

Elgin Opera House

This 1912 restored two-story brick house with perfect acoustics hosts movies, plays, live theater, and other entertainment. First-run flicks are shown Friday, Saturday, and Sunday. Call 541/437-3456 for event listings. To get here, take ORE 82 17 miles northeast of La Grande.

Deadman's Pass

Deadman's Pass, at Exit 228 on I-84, led emigrants out of the Blue Mountains into the Umatilla Valley. This was the last big hump they had to cross before the raft trip down the Columbia. The name comes from three incidents during the Bannock Indian War of 1878 in which seven men were killed. Look for a sign directing you up a trail to a sampling of still-visible wagon ruts.

Ladd Marsh Nature Trail

Bird-watchers will enjoy the chance to observe more than 32 species of ducks, geese, swans, and other birds, six miles southwest of La Grande along Foothill Road. Take Exit 268 from I-84. This is one of the largest remaining wetlands in northeastern Oregon.

Blue Mountain Crossing

If you take Exit 248 off I-84 west of La Grande, you'll come to several trailheads located near restrooms and a covered shelter. Here are some of the nation's best-preserved tracks of the Old Emigrant Road. Colorful ceramic panels depict the pioneers' struggle through the tall tress and over the rugged Blue Mountains. Your walk along these shady trails will be enhanced when you consider that over 90 percent of the 2,170-mile route has been destroyed by human activity in the guise of progress. The interpretive center is open during daylight hours (follow the gravel roads about three miles toward the hamlet of Kamela).

In downtown La Grande, Birnie Park on the south side of town was an area used for wagon encampments before Oregon Trail pioneers crossed the Blue Mountains. The park, located on B Avenue and Bekeler, is decorated with an abstract pioneer art memorial and a life-size wrought-iron pioneer play wagon.

ENTERTAINMENT AND EVENTS

Like every town in America, each town on our route has a special festivity in which the locals whoop it up in their own way. La Grande's major celebrations of the year are the **Blue Mountain Days** in late June, which features a parade, rodeo, and motorcycle rally, and the **Oregon Trail Days and Rendezvous** in mid-August.

The **Vale Rodeo** is a four-day fete that takes place July 1–4. It's highlighted by the **Suicide Race,** an event held at nearby Vale Butte in which cowboys race their horses off a steep slope into the arena. Haines, a wide spot on ORE 30 between

According to local wags, the geographical center of the United States—including Hawaii and Alaska—is 12 miles north of Medical Springs, where ORE 203 meets Catherine Creek.

Baker City and North Powder, celebrates the Fourth of July with a competition to name the oldest working cowhand in the Northwest. If you think you qualify, call 541-856-3211.

The **Obon Odori Festival** celebrating Ontario's Japanese heritage is held the third week in July at the Buddhist temple. On the schedule are tours of the temple, a dinner featuring Asian cuisine, arts-and-crafts displays, and an evening of dancing with audience participation. Also held the third week in July, the **Miner's Jubilee** is the big wingding in Baker City. On the bill are a fiddle festival, arts-and-crafts fair, bed and raft races, a cowbelles' breakfast, and the World Championship Porcupine Sprint Race.

SPORTS AND RECREATION

The country through which the Oregon Trail passes is filled with recreational choices. **Ontario-Shadow Butte Golf Course** (541/889-9022) is an 18-hole municipal course with pro shop and lounge, two miles west of Ontario. **Bully Creek Reservoir,** 30 minutes west of Ontario near the small town of Vale, has boat-launch facilities, picnic and camping areas, swimming, and water-skiing. The fishing includes crappie, bass, trout, and perch.

The Grande Ronde is one of Oregon's least known quality rafting experiences to out-of-staters. **Tilden River Tours** (541/437-9270) takes you into the spectacular enclaves of the Grande Ronde River canyon south of Elgin (en route to the Snake) on a trip you'll never forget. Anglers will want to try their luck at Red Bridge State Park on ORE 244. Check first with Oregon Fish and Wildlife officials about regulations governing endangered steelhead and salmon.

Anthony Lakes Ski Area (541/856-3277, www.anthonylakes.com) is between Baker City and La Grande, 18 miles west of North Powder and Haines on I-84. Open the day after Thanksgiving–mid-April, daily 9 A.M.–4 P.M., this ski resort offers a chairlift, Nordic trail system, day lodge, ski shop, and ski lessons. All-day tickets are $28 adults, children under 13 and seniors pay $22, ages 7–12 $15. This is Oregon's first and highest (7,000 feet) ski area. It offers pristine dry powder and a family-oriented environment.

Camping

Of the many campsites in the Wallowa-Whitman National Forest, here are four of the best. **Grande Ronde Lake Campground** along the shore of the lake has all the amenities and good trout fishing as a bonus. The fee is $9 per night. To get here drive 17 miles northwest of Haines on ORE 411, then eight miles west on Forest Service Road 73. The camp is a half mile northwest on Forest Service Road 43.

Sherwood Forest Campground is a small site on the banks of the Grande Ronde River. There is no fee for this campground, which is open late May–late November. Drive nine miles northwest of La Grande on I-84 (Exit 252), then 13 miles southwest on ORE 244. This road meanders along the river and its valley, where ponderosa pine and aspen are broken up by meadows and farmland. From there, drive six miles south on Forest Service Road 51.

After camping, you might want to follow ORE 244 up to **Lehman Hot Springs** (541/427-3015) and thereafter to its junction with U.S. 395. En route you'll pass through Ukiah, often Oregon's coldest place. Therefore, we advise a soak in Lehman Hot Springs prior to arrival in this little mountain town. Each of the three chambers in Lehman's giant swimming pool is calibrated to an increasing degree of hotness, with the hottest level being scorching. This area used to be a historic gathering place for the Nez Percé. Call 800/848-9969 for more information on this drive as well as other activities in the Wallowa-Whitman Forest.

A third site, **Hilgard Junction State Park,** is also on the Grande Ronde River, at the foot of the Blue Mountains. Fees for this 18-site (no hookups) campground are $5 per night. To get here drive eight miles west of La Grande on I-84 to Starkey Road. Popular during deer- and elk-hunting seasons, this campground is on the original route of the Oregon Trail. This site above

the steep slopes of the Grand Ronde Valley gave the pioneers pause. Information placards detail how their wagons maneuvered over this precipitous terrain.

The fourth site is **Emigrant Springs State Park** (541/983-2277 or 800/551-6949), a large facility with flush toilets, a laundry, and a playground, right off I-84 near the Umatilla Indian Reservation between Pendleton and La Grande. The fee is $12 per night. This park has a display on the Oregon Trail and is a good spot to stop while traveling on the interstate, thanks to its laundry, showers, piped water, and other amenities. There are 33 tent sites and 18 fuel hookups in a wooded area.

PRACTICALITIES
Accommodations

These lodgings, ranging from affordable to fancy, should make your trek along the Oregon Trail far more comfortable than it would have been 150 years ago. Baker City is the hub, with 11 motels (455 rooms), two bed-and-breakfasts, and three RV parks. Closer to the high end of the scale is the **Geiser Grand Hotel** (1996 Main St., Baker City, 541/523-1899 or 888/434-7374, www.geisergrand.com), the showplace of Oregon's gold country in 1889. At $89–109 per night with breakfast amid Viennese chandeliers, mahogany columns, and a stained-glass skylight 40 feet above the dining room, you'll feel like you've made a lucky strike. Add 10-foot-high windows in guestrooms looking on the Blue Mountains and reasonably priced meals, and you might want to extend your stay.

The **Sunridge Inn** (1 Sunridge Lane, 97814, 541/523-6444, www.bestwestern.com), with heated pool and private patios, is Baker City's luxury motel with rates of $69–90. The pet- and kid-friendly **Trail Motel** (2815 10th St., Baker City 97814, 541/523-4646) is a more economical choice, with rates of $45–58. If you don't feel like dining in their restaurant, you can whip up something in your own kitchen. The **El Dorado Inn** (695 Campbell St., Baker City 97814, 541/523-6494) is a bargain at $40–70. Amenities include an indoor pool and whirlpool tub. To get here, take the city center exit off I-84. The hotel is conveniently located near the Greyhound station and the Baker City Visitor and Convention Bureau.

In La Grande, **Stang Manor** (1612 Walnut, La Grande 97850, 541/963-2400, www.stangmanor.com) is a Georgian colonial mansion built by a timber baron. Period furniture and stunning woodwork, large individually decorated rooms, and views of the mountains make this a steal at $98–115. Each of the four rooms has a bath. Other appreciated features are the cozy dining room fireplace, bikes available to guests, and home-cooked delicacies for breakfast. Not appropriate for children under age 10.

Eleven miles southeast of La Grande on ORE 203, the nine-unit **Union Hotel** (326 N. Main, Union 97883, 541/562-6135, www.theunionhotel.com) will take you back to another era, with a room and bath for $40–89. The three-story 1921 brick hotel has a tile floor and Old West–themed rooms. The town of Union boasts architecture from its heyday as a gold rush boomtown and the county seat. The town museum has a great exhibit entitled "Cowboys Then and Now." If you're bringing the kids, consider a room with trundle beds.

Food

Not too many recommendations on this route, but here are a few worth tucking in your napkin for. In La Grande, **Mamacita's** (110 Depot St., 541/963-6223) serves tasty Mexican food at low prices (less than $10 for hefty combination platters). The Guadalajara tostada and *arroz con pollo* are particularly good values. A bit more upscale, with prices to match, the **Ten Depot Street** (10 Depot St., 541/963-8766) might be a harbinger of things to come. Such interesting plates as teriyaki tofu, Oregon-raised lamb chops, and a delicious salmon pâté will evoke bistros west of the Cascades. Dinner can sometimes run over $20 here in this converted old Mason's Lodge. Open Mon.–Sat. 5–10 P.M. A lot of people will tell you that the state's best fast food is available at **Nells In 'n' Out** (1704 Adams Ave., 541/963-5733). Creative variations on shakes and floats, hand-curled french fries, and a full array of burgers are highlights.

Ten miles north of Baker City is the well-regarded **Haines Steakhouse** (ORE 30, 541/856-3639). Open Wed.–Mon. for dinner, the tab will run $15–20 per person, but it's worth it. Antiques and cowboy Americana decorate the restaurant, enhancing what may be described as first-rate chuckwagon fare.

Information and Transportation

Useful information to aid your explorations along the Oregon Trail is available from several chambers of commerce, including the **Malheur County Chamber of Commerce** (173 S.W. 1st St., Ontario 97914, 541/889-8012, www.malheur.org); **Vale County Chamber of Commerce** (272 N. Main, Vale 97918, 541/473-3800, www.valeoregon.org); **Union County Tourism** (102 Elm St., La Grande 97850, 541/963-8588 or 800/848-9969); and **La Grande–Union County Chamber of Commerce** (102 Elm St., La Grande 97850, 800/848-9969). Better yet, contact the **Baker County Chamber and Visitor Center** (490 Campbell St., Baker City 97814, 541/523-3356 or 800/523-1235, www.visitbaker.com) or call the **Eastern Oregon/Oregon Trail information line** (800/332-1843).

The *Baker City Herald* (P.O. Box 807, Baker City 97814) publishes a good annual travel guide to the local area. It's available free at area museums and tourist facilities. **DotCom Computers Inc.** (1403 Adams Ave., 541/963-1234, www.dotcomcomp.net) provides Internet access.

There is very little public transit in this land of large distances and small populations. Here's what is available: **Greyhound** has a terminal in Baker City (515 Campbell, 541/523-5011). If you need wheels, rent a rig from **Tamarack Ford** (541/963-2161). **Columbia Bus Company** (1901 Jefferson, La Grande 97850, 541/963-6119) has a bus charter service. **La Grande Aviation** (Route 2, Box 2546, La Grande 97850, 541/963-6572) will fly you where you want to go.

The Wallowas

Ask most Oregonians who have been there and they will tell you that the Wallowa Range is one place in Oregon "you gotta see—you just gotta." Come now, before the word gets out about this backpackers' paradise where snowcapped, Teton-like spires and blue-green glacial lakes are still relatively unvisited.

The Eagle Cap Wilderness Area—with 17 of the state's 29 mountains over 9,000 feet and 50 glacial lakes sprinkled throughout 300,000 acres—is a recreational area that should figure prominently in your travel plans. Campers and cross-country skiers are regularly treated to glimpses of bighorn sheep, mountain goats, elk, and mule deer, as well as snow-streaked granite and limestone peaks rising above meadows dotted with an artist's palette of wildflowers. But you don't have to go far into the backcountry to get away from it all here.

The Wallowa Valley is formed by the drainages of the Wallowa, Minam, and Grande Ronde Rivers. It is backdropped by a half moon–shaped range, 80 miles long and 25 miles at its widest. These peaks soar 5,000 feet above Wallowa County farmlands. The traditional eastern Oregon triad of timber, farming, and cattle ranching fuels the area's economy. Tourism will soon replace timber due to recent cutbacks at area mills. The town of Enterprise is the commercial center of it all, while Joseph is the hub of a growing arts community and the gateway to Wallowa Lake, a recreational haven at the end of the road.

Despite abundant precipitation, the Wallowas and the Cascades block consistent snow accumulation from hitting the Wallowa Valley, hub of its skiing and tourism business. As a result, the leading destination, Joseph, and nearby Wallowa Lake, have been spared the high prices and overcrowding endemic to western ski resorts with spectacular natural settings.

Instead of upscale condos and Bavarian-style ski chalets, 19th-century farmhouses dot the landscape. Instead of turtlenecked jet-setters, cowboy-hatted ranchers and farmers mix freely with local merchants and a cluster of renowned artists who have settled here. While a few entrepreneurs bemoan missing out on the ski-resort economy, townsfolk and visitors alike appreciate this remote, down-to-earth piece of the Old West. Locals will tell you to come in September when pleasant weather and smaller crowds showcase the region at its best.

After a visit to this larger-than-life countryside, it is easy to see how it sustained the proud and indomitable Nez Percé, the native people who once roamed its river canyons, glacial basins, and grassy hills. The air here has a soft sweetness, and a surprising degree of epicurean refinement awaits the discerning visitor.

The Land

The Wallowas are the wettest place east of the Cascades. The higher reaches of the range may get 60 inches of precipitation annually. These upper elevations crest in the **Eagle Cap Wilderness Area** and descend gradually to the south toward Baker City. This is why you sometimes hear Eagle Cap's peaks referred to as the hub of the range and the various ridges, spokes splaying outward in a wagonwheel pattern. Seashells in limestone and greenstone outcroppings attest to the range's age, some 200 million years.

It's theorized that these mountains were once part of tropical islands in the mid-Pacific. Due to continental drift, the range attached itself to an ancient coastline, much like the Klamaths did in southern Oregon. A different link has been established with the Austrian Alps since the Wallowas contain similar fossilized corals, mollusks, algae, and sponges.

HISTORY

The Wallowa Valley, set apart by deep river canyons and mountain ranges, is the ancestral home of the Nez Percé, a tribe known for its horse-raising skills and fierce independence. These regal people, astride their spotted Appaloosas, first encountered Europeans when mountain men wandered onto their land. Lewis and Clark believed that the tribe's generosity with food saved their lives. The tribe's willingness to feed and care for the Bonneville Party, which had struggled up out of the Snake River Canyon in 1834, reinforced their reputation for honor and largesse. Later, however, when a dry spell in the Grande Ronde Valley to the south prompted homesteaders to give the Wallowas a try, native and white cultures clashed.

One source of tension was the settlers' permitting their hogs to trample the camas fields where the natives came to gather food. The U.S.

CHIEF JOSEPH

Known by his people as In-mut-too-yah-lat-lat ("Thunder coming up over the land from the water"), Chief Joseph was best known for his brave resistance to the government's attempts to force his tribe onto a reservation. A nation that spread from Idaho to northern Washington, the Nez Percé had peacefully coexisted with European Americans after the Lewis and Clark expedition; indeed, the tribe had given the newcomers much-needed horses. Joseph had spent much of his early childhood at a mission maintained by Christian missionaries.

But with the incursion of miners and settlers, and because of misunderstandings surrounding the annexation of Native American land through a series of treaties never signed by Chief Joseph, tension increased to the breaking point. White disregard of native property spurred some rash young Nez Percé to retaliate. The ensuing 11-week conflict, during which the Nez Percé engaged 10 separate U.S. military commands in 13 battles (the majority of which the Nez Percé won), guaranteed Chief Joseph's fame as a brilliant military tactician. However, after many hardships including starvation and many lost lives, Chief Joseph surrendered to Generals Miles and Howard on October 5, 1877, only 50 miles from the sanctuary of the Canadian border.

In 1879, Chief Joseph spoke to the Department of Indian Affairs in Washington, D.C., detailing the broken promises of the government, the suffering of his people, and the unjust treatment of the Native Americans by white society, saying:

I have heard talk and talk, but nothing is done. Good words do not last long unless they amount to something. Words do not pay for my dead people. They do not pay for my country, now overrun by white men. They do not protect my father's grave. They do not pay for all my horses and cattle. Good words will not give me back my children. I only ask of the government to be treated as all other men are treated.

Chief Joseph appealed repeatedly to the federal authorities to return the Nez Percé to the land of their ancestors, but to no avail. In 1885, he and many of his band were sent to a reservation in Washington, where, as the presiding doctor was heard to have said, he died of a broken heart.

Chief Joseph

government attempted to resolve the situation by creating a seven-million-acre reservation in 1855, but reneged on the land treaty five years later when gold was discovered in the Wallowas. This breach initiated an era of bad feelings during which various drafts of different treaties generated confusion and distrust.

The settlers later successfully lobbied the government to evict the natives, which led to the Nez Percé War of 1877. Chief Joseph and his people fought a running battle that covered 1,700 miles and ended with their surrender in the Bear's Paw Mountains, 50 miles from the Montana–Canada border. In the mid-1990s the government welcomed the tribe back to the area with land for ceremonies, housing, and an interpretive center.

The phrase "To the victors go the spoils" evokes the life on the frontier once the Nez Percé had been evicted from the Wallowa Valley. The toughest of the settlers endured the winters, droughts, and other hardships in this remote region. One bachelor, in an attempt to ease his loneliness, sent the following note to a friend in Missouri: "Send at once C.O.D. a good-looking maid or widow, 30 years or under. Widow with a few children preferred."

In 1908, a passenger train steamed into Wallowa on a newly laid track from Elgin, expanding a route that had previously seen only horses and wagons. Not much has changed since those early days. The people of the Wallowa Valley believe that they inhabit paradise, and they seem to enjoy sharing it with visitors drawn by its natural beauty and vivid history.

SIGHTS

Enterprise

If you have an afternoon to spare, the Wallowa County Centennial Committee has organized a **walking tour** for you. Stop by the chamber of commerce booth in the Enterprise Mall and pick up their brochure. It has descriptions and locations of many of the historic buildings in the area, like the Wallowa County Courthouse, the Enterprise Hotel, the Oddfellows Hall, and a number of private homes. After an hour of edification and exercise, take a break at the **Bookloft-Skylight Gallery** (107 E. Main, 541/426-3351), just across the street from the county courthouse. Open every day except Sunday. This gathering spot for artists and community activists sells best-sellers and local-history books and offers monthly shows of guest artists, as well as freshly brewed coffee and home-baked cookies.

Joseph

Cruising farther into the valley, you reach the lively community of Joseph (elev. 4,150 ft.), named after the famous Nez Percé chief. The town's 1,054 residents populate the north end of Wallowa Lake, which is cradled at its southern tip by the Eagle Cap Wilderness area. The old-timey charm of Joseph's false-fronted buildings with the Wallowas for a backdrop make it seem more than 335 miles away from Portland.

A must-stop for history buffs is the **Wallowa County Museum** (110 Main St., 541/432-6095). Built in 1888, the museum building has served as a newspaper office, a private hospital, a meeting hall, and a bank (ironically, one of the crooks who robbed the bank later became its president). Its current incarnation as a museum started in 1960. The theme of the museum is Wallowa history, including displays of pioneer life and the Nez Percé. Open from the last weekend in May to the third weekend in September, hours are daily 10 A.M.–5 P.M. Donations accepted.

Joseph is also the center of a blossoming art community in the Wallowas. Galleries here and in Enterprise showcase watercolor and oil

downtown Joseph

paintings, sculpture, pottery, and photographs. Take a walk down Main Street and you'll find a number of art galleries and antique stores. On the west end of town, world-famous bronzes by David Lee Manuel as well as Native American artifacts, John Wayne mementos, and Civil War memorabilia fill the attractive log confines of the **Manuel Museum** (400 N. Main St., 541/432-7235), also known as the Nez Percé Crossing Museum. Admission is $6, $5 seniors, $3 children under 10. Closed Sunday. **Valley Bronze** (18 Main St., 541/432-7445) displays works from the second largest bronze foundry in the country. Daily tours ($5) of their Alder Street foundry are offered.

Wallowa Lake

The brightest gem in the Wallowas setting is Wallowa Lake, which at 5,000 feet in elevation is the highest large body of water in eastern Oregon. This classic moraine-held glacial lake is a few miles south of Joseph on ORE 82 at the east end of the Wallowa Valley. The lake is ringed with lodges, amusement rides, a large state park with an overnight campground, packhorse corrals, boat launches, and marinas. It is also home to the **Wallowa Lake Monster,** a creature with a gentle disposition and a length varying 30 to 100 feet, depending on the sighting. Reports of the critter go back several centuries to Native American tales and are also the current focus of the Monster Observation and Preservation Society (MOPS).

Around the lake you'll find cottonwood, larch, spruce, and fir. Located a half mile from Joseph, the lake is bordered on one side by peaks of the Eagle Cap Wilderness and on the other by rolling farmland that novelist Ethan Canin says "might have given Monet the inspiration for his palette." Be that as it may, exercise caution before you dive in for a swim. Invitingly clear, the lake waters here are extremely cold and should not be experienced until August (and not much thereafter). Try

Thirty miles north of Wallowa Lake on ORE 3 is Joseph Canyon Viewpoint, overlooking the canyon that served as a winter homeland for the Nez Percé. In 1997, a lot of land in this area passed back into Nez Percé hands.

the beach in the county park at the northern end of the lake.

Despite the grandeur, the Wallowa Lake entry to the region might occasion initial misgivings due to the somewhat carnival-like ambience here, replete with go-karts and other entertainment for the kids. Such trepidation can be erased by a ride up the **Mount Howard Gondola** (544/432-5331, www.wallowlaketramway.com). Open during the summer 10 A.M.–5 P.M., the gondola route is the steepest and longest in North America, lifting passengers up 3,700 feet, from the edge of Wallowa Lake to the 8,200-foot summit of Mount Howard. As the lift floats upward, the pastureland and wheat field views near Wallowa Lake give way to forests of lodgepole pine, tamarack, and quaking aspen. On top, stay on the trails through the fragile alpine tundra so as not to damage the tiny and rare plants here.

The 15-minute trip in the closed gondola car costs $19 for adults, and $12 for children under 10. It operates daily June–Aug., and half days in May and September. The ride ends at a snack bar and gift shop on top of the peak. But forget about the snacks, knickknacks, and trinkets; the best reason for taking the trip is the view of 26 mountain peaks, including the Wallowa Range, Snake River country, and Idaho's Seven Devils area. The eight peaks of Eagle Cap Wilderness are mirrored in the lake below, and the gorges of the Snake and Imnaha Rivers stretch to the east.

Wallowa Mountain Loop Road

This scenic, 54-mile drive into Hells Canyon Country begins with the Joseph–Imnaha Highway through farms and canyons. Turn south on Wallowa Mountain Loop Road to the Imnaha River, then ascend into alpine forests along Dry Creek Road to Halfway. You'll come out on the south flank of the Wallowas where *Paint Your Wagon* was filmed in the '60s and Disney's *Home-*

Chief Joseph Mountain, seen from the Wallowa Valley

ward Bound was shot in the early '90s. Turn east for a shoreline view of Snake River Canyon and Hells Canyon at Oxbow (Hells Canyon and Brownlee Dams). This fully paved route can serve as a shortcut to Baker City and Boise in summer.

SPORTS AND RECREATION
Hiking and Camping

Most Eagle Cap Wilderness Area trails are long and steep, and most alpine lakes are at least five miles from a trailhead, so opportunities for easy day hikes are few. Camping is the best way to enjoy the area. Before heading out, pick up the Eagle Cap map from a forest service office or at local sporting goods stores. Higher elevations are usually free from snow by July 1.

If your budget allows for a guided adventure into the Wallowa wilds, here are two excellent services. The **Eagle Cap Wilderness Pack Station** (Route 1, Box 416, Joseph, 541/432-4145, www.eaglecapwildernesspackstation.com) has rides that cost as little as $20 for short trips to

lakes and streams in the Eagle Cap high country, or as much as $750 for deluxe excursions to Hells Canyon or along the Imnaha River. Ask about their "drop" trips, where horses and mules carry people and supplies to a lake, then leave and return at an appointed time. Expect to pay $275 per person for a camping trip done in such a manner.

Wallowa Llamas (Route 1, Box 84, Halfway 97834, 541/742-2661, www.neoregon.com/wallowallamas) offers a unique way to venture into the wilderness. One surefooted, even-tempered llama will carry 20 pounds of your gear; you carry the rest. The outfit offers trips to Hells Canyon, Imnaha Falls, Eagle Meadows, and across the rugged Wallowas. The expeditions are designed for those with some backpacking experience or anyone in reasonably good shape. Excursions average $300–700 for multiday excursions.

Camping out in the Wallowa Valley and the Eagle Cap Wilderness can be as easy as pulling off ORE 82 just 15 miles east of Elgin and pitching your tent at **Minam State Recreation Area** ($5–8), or as rigorous as using one of the following three campsites as a jumping-off point for backpacking into the high country.

Boundary Campsite is five miles south of Wallowa on County Route 515, then two miles south on Forest Service Road 163. There's no fee for this site set along the banks of Bear Creek, but there's also no water. A trailhead provides access to the dazzling grandeur of the Eagle Cap basin.

The next campsite/trailhead is **Two Pan,** one of the most popular gateways into the Wallowas. To get here, head south from Lostine on County Route 551 for seven miles and down Forest Service Road 5202 for 11 miles. This is a rough and rocky washboard grade, so take your time. Firewood and vault toilets are available; there are no fees or water. Trails leave Two Pan for the Lostine River Valley and the glacial lakes at the base of Eagle Cap.

The third campsite is **Hurricane Creek,** three miles southwest of Joseph on Forest Service Road 8205. There's no charge for overnight camping, and piped water and firewood are available. The

Hurricane Creek trailhead leads to a hike along the east slope of the Hurricane Divide past Sacajawea Peak and the Matterhorn to the glacial lakes basin. An ambitious trek would start at Two Pan and end at Hurricane Creek. The lake basin area south of Joseph can get crowded, especially on July and August weekends.

Wallowa State Park campground (Wallowa Lake, Route 1, Box 323, Joseph 97846, reservations 800/452-5687, information 541/432-4185, www.oregonstateparks.org), set amid big, old ponderosa pines, is one of 13 Oregon campgrounds that operate on a reservation system (see "Camping and Hiking" under "Outdoor Recreation" in the On the Road chapter); reserve seven months in advance or you're outta luck. Lake views, large campsites (89 tent and 121 RV sites), clean bathhouses, and covered kitchen shelters make it worth the $17–21 nightly fee; yurt rentals for $29 and deluxe cabins for $58–79 also available. A marina, a sports field, and the cultural diversions of nearby Joseph also recommend an early reservation. As one of six outstanding Far West parks chosen by *National Geographic,* this site is not what you'd call a secret hideaway.

Call the Wallowa Visitor's Center (541/426-5546) for more information about these camping areas.

Wildlife-Watching

Two wildlife-viewing areas await you as you sweep down into the Wallowa Valley. The **Spring Branch Wildlife Area,** a woodland marsh, is two miles east of Wallowa on ORE 82, on the north side where the road leaves the Wallowa River. The eight-acre viewing area, managed by the Oregon Department of Fish and Wildlife, has beaver dams and lots of waterfowl, including the black tern, an insect-eating bird found in eastern Oregon marshes. The **Enterprise Wildlife Area** is two miles west of Enterprise off ORE 82. To get there, turn south on Fish Hatchery Road to this 32-acre site located just before the fish hatchery. Walk down the dike that goes through a grove of trees to view marsh wrens, snipe, mink, beavers, and muskrats.

Skiing

The recreational delights of the Wallowas are not reserved for summer only. The skiing in this alpine wonderland can be excellent, despite the lack of consistency in snowfalls here. **Ferguson Ridge Ski Area** (541/426-3493) is a good example. To arrive, drive east from Joseph about five miles on the Wallowa Loop Highway, then follow signs south on Tucker Down Road. This small facility has a rope tow and T-bar that climb from a 5,100-foot base to 5,800-foot-high Ferguson Ridge. Lift tickets are $12 a day; children under 13 pay $8. It's open 10 A.M.–4 P.M. weekends and holidays. The light eastern Oregon powder here, when there's enough of it, makes for good skiing. Nordic skiers can try a one-mile loop trail or take an eight-mile marked and packed route to Salt Creek Summit.

Another popular spot is **Salt Creek Summit,** about 20 miles southeast of Joseph on Wallowa Loop Highway. The facility has five miles of marked but ungroomed ski trails and a plowed snow park. A European approach to a skiing adventure is a tour of **Wallowa Alpine Huts** (P.O. Box 762, Joseph 97846, 800/545-5537, www.wallowahuts.com). Three-day, two-night hut-to-hut tours of the Eagle Cap Wilderness are priced in the $365 range. Skiers making the seven-mile trek only have to carry personal gear; bedding and meals are provided, along with woodstoves and saunas at the huts. Also available are lessons, helicopter skiing, and telemark camps.

For cross-country skiers, the **Sacajawea Park Cross-Country Ski Trail** challenges the ambitious. Take Hurricane Creek Road west from Joseph to the Hurricane Creek trailhead. This cross-country ski route will take you up into a basin on the northeast side of Sacajawea Peak. After two steep miles through the forest, the trail opens up into a clear area with a view of the surrounding glacial peaks.

Fishing

Fishing in the high country is a matter of choosing your favorite game fish. You can catch trout and steelhead in the streams that flow out of the ice-capped mountains, or bass, crappie, and sturgeon in the **Snake River.** According to experts, the **Imnaha River** is one of the best late-season fishing streams in the Pacific Northwest.

Wallowa Lake is stocked with huge, accommodating trout. You can commonly see 21-inch rainbows pulled out on worm hooks. Less frequently, you call reel in kokanee (landlocked salmon) and mackinaws. Fly-fishers are referred to Eagle Cap Fishing Guides (800/940-3688). Rates for two are $350/day.

Horseback Riding

On the Imnaha River 14 miles south of Imnaha is **Diamond W Ranch** (Route 1, Box 466, Imnaha 97842, 541/577-3157). They have horses for hire; rates are $25 per person for two hours, $50 for a half day, and $75 for a full day.

ENTERTAINMENT AND EVENTS

Most of the local celebrations here revolve around cowboys, Native Americans, and the arts community. The **Wallowa Valley Festival of the Arts** held at the Joseph Civic Center happens during the third week of April. Along with awards for Northwest artists, there are wine-tasting parties, a silent auction, and a quick-draw competition. A recent addition to the festivities is a reading by cowboy poets.

The tiny town of **Lostine** celebrates the **Fourth of July** with artists, craftspeople, and collectors peddling their wares in the Lostine Sidewalk Flea Market Friday 6–9 P.M. and Saturday noon–9 P.M.

The **Wallowa County Fiddlers' Contest** brings fiddlers from throughout the Northwest to mix it up with music, good grub, and the spirit of the pioneer days. Held in Enterprise on the third weekend in July, the contest is a treat for both the performers and their appreciative audiences.

Held in late July, **Chief Joseph Days** (541/432-1015, www.chiefjosephdays.com) is a week-long festival in Joseph that features dances, a carnival, a Grand Parade, a ranch-style breakfast, and a three-day rodeo, one of the largest in the Northwest. Also in Joseph, **Bronze, Blues, and Brews** (800/585-4121) takes place in Au-

Chief Joseph Days

gust, featuring big-name musical talent, gallery and foundry open houses, and locally brewed beer.

Hells Canyon Mule Days (www.equidreams .net/hellscanyonmuledays/), held the second weekend after Labor Day at the Enterprise Fairgrounds, is where pack-animal fanciers can get their kicks. The action includes mule races, a parade, a speed mule-shoeing contest, and endurance races.

Alpenfest (800/585-4121) is a three-day festival held the third weekend after Labor Day in Edelweiss Hall next to the tramway at Wallowa Lake. This gala is a return to the old country and all that's Bavarian, sending echoes into the mountains with music, alpenhorn blowing, and yodeling competitions. Dancing, sailboat racing, and a bounty of Northern European cuisine are also featured.

At various times throughout the year, Joseph

hosts a low-key but talent-laden literary gathering known as **Fishtrap** (P.O. Box 38, Enterprise 97828, 541/426-3623, www.fishtrap.org) in an old Methodist meetinghouse. Authors writing in different genres attend; past participants have included William Kittredge, Ursula LeGuin, Ivan Doig, Sandra Scofield, and Terry Tempest Williams. Writers of all levels come to read their works and discuss social issues. The weekend Winter Fishtrap costs $260–400 depending on housing arrangements; food is included. The five-day workshop in the summer of 2003 cost $285, plus $35/day for room and board. The weekend "Gathering" goes for $160–200, meals included. Fishtrap also offers workshops in mid-September and October, such as an all-day seminar on writing illustrating children's books and an intensive memoir workshop.

PRACTICALITIES

Accommodations

The following lodgings in the Wallowas reflect the special flavor of this unique outback. Locals consider Labor day to mid-October the most beautiful time here.

The **Flying Arrow Resort** (59782 Wallowa Lake Hwy., Joseph 97846, 541/432-2951, www.flyarrowresort.com) has not only a great name, but also a swimming pool, hot tub, chocolate shop, bookstore, and village market. Rates range $85–168. This place is kid- and pet-friendly.

Another accommodation near Joseph is **Eagle Cap Chalets** (Route 1, Box 419, Wallowa Lake Highway, Joseph 97846, 541/432-4704, www.eaglechalets.com). Tucked into the pines near the tram, this cluster of cabins and condos has all you need to visit Wallowa Lake in comfort and style. Rates run $52–95 for a double and $100–145 for two or three bedrooms.

In town, for lodging with fair prices ($32–52), and such little touches as flower baskets and decorative prints, try the **Indian Lodge** (201 S. Main St., Joseph 97846, 541/432-2651 or 888/286-5484).

A couple of hostelries on the shore of Wallowa Lake are good bets for those who want

comfort rather than campouts. The **Wallowa Lake Lodge** (P.O. Box 1, Joseph 97846, 541/432-9821, www.wallowalakelodge.com) is a renovated 1923 hunting lodge on the south shore with a room for two in the $80 range in winter and $95 in summer. Eight cabins with fireplaces and kitchens start at $75 in winter and $145 in summer. Despite their considerable charm, some of the 22 rooms recall the closet-sized dimensions of a cruise-ship stateroom. The Nordic center is a five-minute walk away; store and gas station on site. There's a dearth of twin-bed rooms in the main lodge, so reserve early if that's a consideration. **Matterhorn Swiss Village** (Route 1, Box 350, Joseph 97846, 541/432-4071 or 800/891-2551, www.matterhornswissvillage.com) has rates from $48 to $125. In keeping with the notion that the Wallowas are the Switzerland of America, this facility has six "Swiss" cottages with names like the Alpenhof and Berghof.

Of the several B&Bs in the area, **Trouthaven** (618141 Lakeshore Dr., 541/432-2221) best captures the feeling of being in a blissful time warp here. The rustic cabins begin at $76 and sit on the western shore of the lake—perfect for a family vacation. Open May 1–Sept. 14. **Strawberry Wilderness B&B** (406 W. Wallowa Ave., Joseph 97846, 541/432-3125) is both lodging and art gallery set in a newer log home perfect for the whole family, with facilities for horses. Rates run $65>\#208>95. Open year-round.

Food

Like most frontier outposts in the American West, the Wallowa Valley has lots of standard takeout joints and few eateries worth a special stop. However, the following restaurants will not only keep you going during your visit but give you a few tasty surprises as well.

Terminal Gravity Brewing (803 School St., Enterprise, 541/426-0158) serves as the region's brewpub and multi-ethnic restaurant, open Tues.–Sat. 3–9 P.M. Located in an idyllic poplar grove by a creek, it has also become a hub for frontier vaudeville and offbeat entertainment. The menu is basic but the nightly special can feature Italian, Moroccan, Mexican, and Middle Eastern food, averaging $15 for dinner.

Close to Wallowa Lake, **Vali's Alpine Delicatessen** (541/432-5691) features a different dinner menu each day featuring German and Hungarian specialties. Seatings are at 6 and 8 P.M.; reservations are recommended. Dinners are in the $15 range. Open Tues.–Sun. in summer, weekends only in winter.

Information and Services
The **Wallowa County Chamber of Commerce** (P.O. Box 427A, 107 S.W. 1st St., Enterprise 97828, 541/426-4622, www.wallowacountychamber.com) has a booth in the Enterprise Mall with a full complement of brochures, maps, and other information on the area. Before arrival, give them a call (800/585-4121). The **Wallowa Lake Tourist Commission** (P.O. Box 853, Dept. V, Joseph 97846) is another good source of information. The *Wallowa County Chieftain* (106 N.W. 1st, Enterprise, 541/426-4567) is the area's main newspaper.

Given that two-thirds of the county hereabouts is federal land contained in the Eagle Cap Wilderness, the Wallowa-Whitman National Forest, and the Hells Canyon National Recreation Area, it's a good idea to visit the **Wallowa Information Center** (541/426-5546), a half mile west of Enterprise. There are exhibits highlighting forests, geology, and wildlife, as well as an observation deck with views of meadows, farms, and mountains. The center is open Mon.–Sat. 8 A.M.–5 P.M. in the summer months, with fewer winter hours.

Transportation
The main road into the valley, ORE 821 through the Minam Gorge, has been divided, easing the six-hour drive from Portland. **Moffit Brothers Transportation** (Lostine, 541/569-2284) makes a daily round-trip between La Grande and Wallowa Lake for $18 (one-way). **Wallowa Valley Stage** (541/432-3531) leaves from Paul's Chevron in Joseph. Don't worry about finding this gas station; it's the only one in town.

Spence Air Service (P.O. Box 217, Enterprise, 541/426-3288) is listed in the *Oregon Pilot's Guide* under air service and is available for charter flights. Another option is to take a Horizon flight to Lewiston, Idaho, and rent a car for the 85-mile drive west; you eventually hook up with ORE 3. Or fly into Pendleton, 120 miles away by car.

Hells Canyon

In 1975, Congress established the **Hells Canyon National Recreation Area** (P.O. Box 490, Enterprise 97828, 541/426-5546, www.fs.fed.us/hellscanyon), comprising 650,000 acres of stunning vistas, archaeological sites with petroglyphs, and native ruins, as well as a mighty river thundering through rugged canyon lands. For a 40-mile stretch between Oregon and Idaho, the canyon averages just 10 miles in width, contrasting with its 5,500–6,100-foot depth along the same stretch. It's a hard place to get to, so be sure you check the local weather and road conditions before visiting the area. Also, it's a good idea to pack a snakebite kit. There are rattlesnakes in this country!

The interior of Hells Canyon is a rugged wilderness framed by basalt cliffs. From Idaho's Seven Devils Wilderness to the Snake River in Hells Canyon you'll find areas that replicate most of North America's ecological zones. Cheatgrass, primroses, sunflowers, and prickly pear cactus are included in the canyon's varied botany. Bear, elk, mule deer, bighorn sheep, eagles, otters, and chukhar partridges are frequently seen here. Several outfitters can steer you to the canyon's pictographs, which some sources place at 10,000 years of age. In addition to Chief Joseph and his Nez Percé tribe, the area was also occupied by miners and pioneers, as turn-of-the-century log cabins and shacks attest.

There are several ways to get to Hells Canyon from Oregon. The first route is easiest and on paved roads. From Baker City take ORE 86 for 50 miles east to **Halfway.** Stop here to stock up on groceries and gas, continue on ORE 86 another 16 miles to Oxbow Dam, and then another 20 miles to Hells Canyon Dam. A visitors center is located on the Idaho side of this dam, adjacent to where rafts put in on the Snake River. This site affords a spectacular view of the canyon. Another paved approach is via ORE 82 through the Wallowa Valley to Enterprise, Joseph, and Imnaha. From Imnaha, one of the most isolated towns in America, take a rough, albeit recently improved road for 24 miles to Hat Point Lookout. Once you get there you'll be convinced that the all-encompassing view was worth the hassle.

The Snake River was rated America's most endangered river by American Rivers, a conservation group, in its 2000 annual report. This designation was largely due to depleted salmon stocks. Coho have become extinct and four other species here are currently threatened or endangered. Average annual runs of 100,000 fish during the 1960s have shrunk to 3,000. The latter corresponds chronologically to the construction of four Snake River Dams. The possibility of a causal connection between salmon decline and these dams is discussed in the Columbia River Gorge chapter. In any case, the National Marine Fisheries Service will not render a decision on breaching the dams until 2005 at the earliest. Environmentalists say this may be too late.

SPORTS AND RECREATION

Before your trip into Hells Canyon, consider what the authors of *Hiking the Great Northwest* (Seattle: The Mountaineers, 1998) have to say about hiking here: "Hells Canyon is definitely not paradise. Summer temperatures soar above 100°, rattlesnakes abound, and . . . despite the river, drinkable water can be hard to find." Ticks and poison oak can be problems here, too. Black widow and brown recluse spiders constitute the biggest danger, however. Nonetheless, more than 900 miles of trails await hikers and backpackers. Major trails are maintained but others are difficult to follow.

Of the 12 campgrounds on the Oregon side of Hells Canyon, we recommend the following

Hells Canyon National Recreation Area

three. **Lake Fork Campground,** 18 miles northeast of Halfway on Forest Service Road 39, has 10 sites with drinking water, and the fishing is good at nearby Fish Lake. **Indian Crossing,** located 45 miles southeast of Joseph on Forest Service Road 3960, has drinking water as well as a trailhead for backpacking into the Eagle Cap Wilderness. On the northern end of the recreational area, **Buckhorn Springs** is 43 miles northeast of Enterprise and features a great view, spring water, and berry-picking in season.

Outfitters

Canyon Outfitters (P.O. Box 893, Halfway 97834, 541/742-4110) offers hiking day trips through Hells Canyon. Boats parallel your hike, allowing you to float when you're tired of walking, or when the trail strays from scenic sections along the river. Expect gourmet food and a lot of local color shared around the campfire at day's end. Trips begin at a Halfway bed-and-breakfast, where Canyon Outfitters provides transport to the launch point 40 miles below the Hells Canyon Dam. Four days later you're at Pittsburg Landing. Trips are offered late April–early May for $800 per person. The hosts will also arrange trips out of the canyon ranging from horseback to airplane.

For water sports, spring and fall are the best seasons. Those interested in jetboat trips should remember that the forest service has limited jetboat use on the Snake River to four days a week during peak season. This was done for the safety of rafters. Call the Hells Canyon NRA (541/426-5546) for more information.

Beamers Hells Canyon Tours (800/522-6966, www.hellscanyontours.com) offers jet-boat tours, fishing trips, cruises, and overnight trips to lodges in Hells Canyon, daily May–September and on weekends March, April, and October. For a list of additional outfitters, call the National Forest Service (509/758-0616).

Fishing for trout, catfish, smallmouth bass, and, if you're lucky, 100-year-old sturgeon can add to the pleasure of a raft trip. You might also enjoy swimming in 68°F water. Trips last three to five days, putting in at Hells Canyon Dam or Dug Bar. Try to go either before May 27 or after September 15 to avoid the crowds. Hire a good guide to deal with rough rapids; the Snake River has sections with Class V white water.

PRACTICALITIES
Accommodations
The town of Halfway (pop. 345), a few miles from the Idaho border, is a popular way station for Hells Canyon–bound travelers. The town agreed to change its name to Half.com as part of a Philadelphia high-tech firm's promotion, in exchange for financial incentives and free Internet service. Given the volatility of the Nasdaq, we've decided to stick with the town's original name.

Birch Leaf Guesthouse (Route 1, Box 91, Halfway 97834, 541/742-2990) is a turn-of-the-century farmhouse on 42 acres at the foot of the Wallowa Mountains. Rates begin at $70 and include an organic country breakfast. To get to this place, take Forest Service Road 413 north; at Jimtown Store take the east fork in the road. The birding here is exceptional. A resident excursion planner will help you schedule your recreational activities. Particularly recommended is a loop taking in the Oregon Trail Visitor Center at Baker City, and McGraw Point, the only paved Hells Canyon overlook from Halfway, en route north to Joseph. From McGraw Point, reachable by Forest Service Roads 39 and 3465, you can see the Snake River Canyon, the Seven Devils Range, and the McGraw Canyon. Snow impedes access in November.

Reasonably priced rooms ($52–90) can be had at the **Halfway Hotel** (170 S. Main, Halfway 97834, 541/742-5722). Some have kitchenettes; all are close to gas, food, and shops.

The **Pine Valley Lodge/Halfway Supper Club** (163 N. Main St., Halfway 97834, 541/742-2027, www.pvlodge.com) is one place in town that goes all the way. Candlelit haute cuisine in an 1891 church and eiderdown bedding set the local standard for bed and board. The eight units here run $65–120. Rates include a deluxe continental breakfast.

Food
If you're on your own, it would be prudent to pack a few picnic items. Restaurants are few and far between in this country. Nonetheless, the previously mentioned Halfway Supper Club and its bakery offshoot, the **Maybe Baby Bakery** are highly recommended.

NORTHEASTERN OREGON

Pendleton

The title of Sam Shepard's play *True West* is an appropriate moniker for this prairie outpost. People are really at home on the range here, leaving the city streets pretty quiet until a mid-September rodeo draws cowboys, cowgirls, and wannabes from all over the West. The transformation of Pendleton from a refueling and supply stop for surrounding ranchers to "party central" takes place in September during the Round-Up, with brewtaps going full tilt and streets filled with tourists in straw cowboy hats and bright new bandanas. When you're done whooping it up with the local good ol' boys, a town rich in history and memory awaits.

With a population of 15,000, Pendleton is one of the largest towns in eastern Oregon. It's an economic force thanks to vast wheat fields (Umatilla County ranks fifth in the nation in wheat production), rows of green peas, famous woolen mills, and tourism from the Pendleton Round-Up. The climate is mild and dry, with an average temperature of 51°F and annual rainfall of 13 inches. Locals joke that this is where summer spends the winter. Located on I-84 equidistant from Portland, Seattle, Spokane, and Boise (a little over 200 miles from each), Pendleton sits pretty much by itself in the midst of wide-open spaces. Residents like it that way.

HISTORY

Pendleton, originally called Goodwin's Station, is situated two miles downriver from the Oregon Trail's crossing at Emigrant Springs State Park. The ancient homeland of the Umatilla tribe, the area was visited by Lewis and Clark in 1805 and John Jacob Astor's American Fur Company in 1812. No Europeans established roots until 1843, when Methodist missionaries led by Dr. Marcus Whitman brought a thousand settlers and 1,300 cattle to the region.

The town itself, named after Senator George Hunt Pendleton, was founded in 1868 and incorporated in 1880. At that time, Pendleton consisted of a hotel and five houses. But it grew through the late 1880s into a ripsnorting cattle and farming center with 18 houses of negotiable affection and 32 saloons. It quickly gained the reputation of being the town that couldn't be tamed. The feistiness of the citizens was demonstrated by the theft of the county seal and records from Umatilla Landing, thus making Pendleton the county seat.

SIGHTS

Backdropped by the Blue Mountains to the east and wheat fields to the west, Pendleton's downtown is pierced by the Umatilla River. Two interstates pass through the city (I-84 and I-395). ORE 30 becomes Court Avenue (one-way westbound) and Dorion Avenue (one-way eastbound) in town. Be aware that the stretch of I-84 above Pendleton known as Cabbage Hill is treacherous to drive during icy winters. In addition to the slickness of the surface, sudden blizzards and high winds can result in white-out conditions.

Round-Up Hall of Fame

The Round-Up Hall of Fame (13th and S.W. Court Avenue), open 10 A.M.–5 P.M. daily during the summer, can be found under the south grandstand area at the Round-Up Stadium. The history of America's biggest rodeo is depicted in photos of past champions and famous bucking broncos along with displays of artifacts. The star of the show is a stuffed horse named War Paint. Admission is free and guided tours are available. The Pendleton Round-Up itself costs $11–17 and takes place over four days in September (see "Sports and Recreation," later in this section).

Pendleton Woolen Mills

Next to the Pendleton Round-Up, the town is best known for the Pendleton Woolen Mills (1307 S.E. Court Pl., P.O. Box 969, Pendleton 97801, 541/276-6911), where they make those immortal plaid shirts. After shearing, the wool goes to a scouring mill in Portland where it's graded, sorted, and washed. Then the dried wool

PENDLETON

To Airport and Boardman

EASTERN OREGON STATE HOSPITAL

Umatilla River

To La Grande

To John Day

BALL PARK

FALLEN FIELD

18TH ST.

ROUNDUP GROUNDS ★

ROY RALEY PARK ★

THE HEALTH NUTS ▼

CARDEN AVE.

FURNISH AVE.

DESPAIN AVE.

BAILEY ST.

5TH ST.

7TH ST.

10TH ST.

PIONEER PARK

COURT ST.

DORION AVE.

EMIGRANT ST.

FRAZER ST.

17TH ST.

16TH ST.

BYERS AVE.

AVE.

PARKER HOUSE ■

RAINBOW BAR & GRILL ■

CIMMIYOTTI'S ▼

WORKING GIRLS HOTEL ■

CIRCLE S ▼

RAPHAEL'S ▼

POST OFFICE ■

PENDLETON CHAMBER VISITOR BUREAU ■

PENDLETON UNDERGROUND TOURS ★

GREAT PACIFIC WINE & COFFEE COMPANY ■

MAIN ST.

AVE.

ISAAC

6TH ST.

ROUND-UP HALL OF FAME ★

COURT PL.

17TH ST.

ST. ANTHONY'S HOSPITAL

COURT

PENDLETON COMMUNITY HOSPITAL ■

NYE AVE.

30TH ST.

25TH ST.

PERKINS AVE.

0   0.5 mi

0   0.5 km

NORTHEASTERN OREGON

© AVALON TRAVEL PUBLISHING, INC.

returns to the Pendleton mill for dyeing, carding, spinning, rewinding, and weaving.

The business began over in the Willamette Valley in Brownsville when Thomas Kay, a Yorkshire man whose family was in the woolen business in England, started a weaving mill. His descendant, Clarence Bishop, founded the Pendleton facility. Production began in 1909 with Native American–style blankets, which are still going strong, along with men's and women's sportswear.

Pendleton produces several different labels. The all-wool "Pendleton" blankets are the most extensively marketed to the public. The "Beaver State" blankets are made with a pure fleece wool filling and are heavier, with more intricate designs than the Pendletons; they're also more expensive. The "Cayuse Blanket" is a lower-priced version of the "Beaver State." Pendleton carved its lucrative niche by copying traditional designs for blankets used by Native Americans in Arizona and New Mexico. It introduced Western-style woolen shirts in the 1920s.

Tours run Mon.–Fri. at 9 A.M., 11 A.M., 1:30 P.M., and 3 P.M. Large groups are asked to make an appointment. To get to the mills on I-84 going east, take Exit 207 through Pendleton on Dorion. Do not cross the viaduct, but turn left and proceed four blocks.

Umatilla County Historical Society Museum

In 1881 the Oregon–Washington Railway and Navigation Company, a subsidiary of the Union Pacific Railroad, constructed the northern branch of its transcontinental railroad through northeastern Oregon, and Pendleton served as an important stop on the route. By 1910, Pendleton had become the second-largest city in eastern Oregon, meriting a new railroad depot.

The building (P.O. Box 253, 108 S.W. Frazer, Pendleton 97801, 541/276-0012), an adaptation of the California Mission style, boasts multipaneled windows, decorative brickwork, and wide, flaring eaves. The depot no longer serves railroad passengers but instead houses the mu-

TAMASTSLIKT CULTURAL INSTITUTE

Providing a much-needed balance to the saga of Oregon pioneer migration, the Confederated Tribes of the Umatilla Reservation just outside town have put together the Tamastslikt museum. To get here go several miles east on I-84, then take Exit 216 and drive north for one mile.

The 45,000-square-foot museum describes the effects European-American settlement had on the original inhabitants. Exhibits depict tribal life prior to the pioneers' arrival; the impact of the horse (brought to North America by Europeans) on native peoples; and an Oregon Trail retrospective from the point of view of the Cayuse, Umatilla, and Walla Walla tribes.

The trail, which passed through the current reservation site, created such long-term environmental problems as diminished salmon runs and deforestation in the Blue Mountains. White settlement also brought chicken pox and measles to native communities, while the railroad that paralleled the trail introduced tobacco, syphilis, and tu-

berculosis. Today, nuclear wastes are transported along I-84, paralleling the ruts where prairie schooners once traveled.

In addition to human historical perspectives, an inquiry into the future looks at once-flourishing animal and plant populations that are now extinct, as well as the deleterious effects of newly introduced "exotics" from Europe and Asia. The interpretive center adds a living encampment, interpretive trails, and an outdoor amphitheater. Sharing this 640-acre site at the base of the Blue Mountains is a gaming resort, golf course, RV park, motel, and restaurant.

Admission is $7 for adults, $5 for seniors 55 and over as well as students. It's hard to find the cultural center amid the adjoining gaming facilities, so call ahead. Open daily 9 A.M.–5 P.M. The Pendleton Chamber of Commerce Visitors and Convention Bureau (541/276-7411, www.pendleton-oregon.org) or the **Wildhorse Gaming Center** (800 /654-WILD) has more information.

seum's collection of Oregon Trail pioneer and Native American artifacts. Gold miners, sheep ranchers, and moonshiners are also given attention here in well-captured displays. Particularly interesting is a depiction of native blanket styles used to communicate anger, courtship, and other nonverbal messages enhancing social interaction. (At press time, 2004, the museum was closed for renovations.)

Tours

One of the area's liveliest attractions is **Pendleton Underground Tours** (P.O. Box 1072, 37 S.W. Emigrant Ave., Pendleton 97801, 541/276-0730 or 800/226-6398, www.pendleton-undergroundtours.com). This visit to the wild and woolly days of the Old West takes you through the tunnels underneath the historic district. At one time a series of 90 passageways, originally dug as freight tunnels by Chinese workers who weren't allowed to walk above ground, crisscrossed beneath the downtown area. During the Prohibition era, bootleggers, gamblers, opium dealers, and Chinese railroad laborers frequented the businesses that developed here.

The tour starts at S.W. 1st and Emigrant and continues to the old Shamrock Cardroom, filled with the bouncy sounds of honky-tonk music, where bartenders were once paid with gold dust. From there, it's on to Hop Sing's laundry and bathhouse (a Prohibition speakeasy with secret escapes and a dank opium den), and the Empire Meat Company, complete with mannequins. The tour finishes in the well-preserved Cozy Rooms Bordello. After this event you'll understand how the old town of 3,000 once supported 32 saloons and 18 bordellos.

Open Mon.–Sat. 9 A.M.–5 P.M., Tuesday 9 A.M.–noon, closed Sunday. Admission is $10. Tours run 45 minutes; reservations are recommended. To get here from I-84, take Exit 209 and turn north into Pendleton. Continue up Emigrant Avenue to S.W. 1st Street.

A good place to learn more about the local scene is **Armchair Books** (39 S.W. Dorion, 541/276-7323), which specializes in regional titles and authors. The store offers a good se-

lection of titles concerning Native Americans. Open Mon.–Sat. 9:30 A.M.–5:30 P.M.

Those interested in Umatilla and Cayuse art should visit the **Collectors Gallery** (223 S.E. Court, 541/276-6697) across from the post office. Open Mon.–Sat. 10 A.M.–5 P.M.

Murals

Pendleton is graced by wall murals on commercial establishments and government buildings. Check out the one on the north wall of Albertson's market, across S.W. Court Avenue from the Round-Up Station. Depicted is a wagon train emerging from the Blue Mountains, closely watched by Native Americans on horseback. On Main and S.W. Emigrant is an 1880s street scene, and Frontier Auto Parts' back wall features a tableau of wagons and Native Americans against a Blue Mountain backdrop.

SPORTS AND RECREATION

Lots of sun is conducive to such outdoor activities as golf at **Pendleton Country Club** (541/278-1739), seven miles south of town on U.S. 395, and boating and water-skiing on **McKay Reservoir** (541/922-3232), near the country club. In a little over an hour, fishing enthusiasts can head north and arrive at the Columbia River for salmon, steelhead, and bass, or try the area's reservoirs for bluegills, bass, and catfish. The **River Parkway,** a paved strip paralleling the Umatilla River through much of downtown Pendleton, is recommended for walkers and bikers.

During the winter months, skiing is on tap up at **Spout Springs,** one of the oldest ski resorts in the Northwest. To get here, drive north on ORE 11 to Weston, turn east on ORE 204, and travel a few miles past Tollgate to the ski area. Located 40 miles northeast of Pendleton, it is rumored to hold on to its dry powder longer than any other ski area in the state.

Rodeo Events

In 1910, Pendleton farmers and ranchers got together to celebrate the end of the wheat harvest. This was the first year of the **Pendleton**

NORTHEASTERN OREGON

Round-Up (P.O. Box 609, Pendleton 97801, 541/276-2553, www.pendletonroundup.com). The annual event now draws 45,000 rodeo fans in the grand tradition started by legendary rodeo stars like Jackson Sundown and Yakima Canutt.

Usually held in mid-September at Raley Park, the fun event begins with the **Westward Ho Historical Parade** that brings together covered wagons, mule teams, buggies, and hundreds of Native Americans in full regalia. The **Happy Canyon Pageant** portrays Native American culture, the arrival of the emigrants, clashes between the two groups, and the birth of a frontier town. The Round-Up features such classic competitions as bulldogging, calf-roping, and wild-horse races Wed.–Saturday. Kids will enjoy Western-theme carnival rides on Main Street.

A **tepee encampment** of hundreds of tribes (Umatilla, Cayuse, Warm Springs, Blackfoot, and Nez Percé) on the Round-Up grounds and the **cowboy breakfast** of ham, eggs, flapjacks, and coffee served Wed.–Sat. at 6 A.M. in Stillman Park exemplify the traditions here that take the Old West beyond the rodeo ring.

The Round-Up is staged primarily by 1,600 unpaid volunteers. With over $2 million flooding into local coffers during the festivities, it's no surprise that local schools and government offices close during the pageant. Tickets for each day run $11–17, depending on location.

PRACTICALITIES

Accommodations

The cost for lodging in this town is reasonable. Despite the view of the Blue Mountains from several chain motels perched on a hill above town just off the interstate, travelers seeking the Old West might do better with the B&B recommendations below. The price range is about the same, and this is one place where skipping HBO can yield surprising benefits.

If you show up at rodeo time without a reservation or unprepared to pay double the room rate, you might be out of luck. The chamber of commerce has a list of private homes that rent for a little less than a motel room, but they are normally booked well in advance. If you bring a

tent, camping is usually available in schoolyards and other special sites set up for the several days of the Round-up. There are always the 100 guestrooms at the **Wildhorse Resort Hotel and Casino** (72779 ORE 331, 800/654-9453, www.wildhorseresort.com) located four miles from town off I-84, Exit 216. Rates are $65–175, averaging around $80. Aside from nice views of the countryside, however, this is mostly a gambler's getaway.

A tonic to modern life is a stay at the **Bar M Ranch** (58440 Bar M Ln., Adams 97810, 541/566-3381 or 888/824-3381, www.ranchweb.com/barm), 31 miles northeast of Pendleton on ORE 11. Built on the site of the historic Bingham Springs Resort, the ranch lies at the base of the Blue Mountains in the Umatilla National Forest. A stable of 50 horses, a natural warm springs, a recreation barn, and eight rooms in a hand-hewn log house let you rough it in style. Rates are $1,150 per person per week, which includes horse rides, meals, and all amenities.

Southeast of Pendleton at **Emigrant Springs Campground** (Oregon State Parks, 541/983-2277), runs a lodge with two separate cabins open year-round. Rates are $14 per night.

The **Parker House** (311 N. Main, 800/700-8581, www.parkerhousebnb.com) pays homage to early 20th-century elegance with oriental rugs and original silk wall coverings. A comfy porch, a backyard garden, and a fire blazing in the dining room while you enjoy creative breakfast fare might offer incentive to linger awhile. Rooms at both establishments run $75–95.

Food

During Round-Up, Main Street is cordoned off for fast food, fiddling, and fairground souvenirs. The rest of the year Pendleton offers frontier hospitality at the following places. The **Rainbow Bar and Grill** (209 S. Main, 541/276-4120) is a famous saloon/restaurant for rodeo fans and local buckaroos. The Rainbow serves passable American diner food, which you shouldn't pass up, if only for local color. Prices range $5–15. Open daily 6–2 A.M.

Cimmiyotti's (137 Main, 541/276-4314) is a dark, cozy spot evoking an Old West bordello that has both American and Italian cuisine (main courses $10–18). The **Great Pacific Wine and Coffee Co.** (403 S. Main, 541/276-1350) offers evidence that "hip" has come to Pendleton. They feature imported cheeses, desserts, croissant sandwiches ($5–8), microbrews and the area's largest wine selection, an espresso bar, and gourmet products. Live music is presented on weekends. Open Mon.–Sat. 8:30 A.M.–8 P.M.

The **Health Nuts** (1700 S.W. Court Pl., 541/276-2251) is an oasis of natural foods with a complete selection of whole grains, nuts, yogurt, and organic vegetables in season. Open every day except Saturday.

In an elegant older home across from City Hall, enjoy upscale dining at **Raphael's** (233 S.E. 4th, 541/276-8500). As you savor salmon wrapped in spinach topped by huckleberry puree, venison marsala, or smoked prime rib, a visual feast of Native American art will further engage your senses. You'll spend more than $20 per person for a memorable repast.

Information and Transportation

The **Pendleton Chamber of Commerce Visitor and Convention Bureau** (501 S. Main, Pendleton 97801, 541/276-7411 or 800/547-8911) can steer you to local sights and special events. A self-guided walking-tour map of the historic downtown district is helpful. The tour starts at the corner of Main and Frazer and takes in many historic buildings.

Pendleton Airport (2016 Airport Rd., 541/567-3694), located 3.5 miles west of town center, is served by **Horizon Air** (800/547-9308). **Greyhound** (320 Court Ave., 541/276-1551) and **Mid Columbia Bus Co.** (541/276-5621) offer charters and transportation.

Columbia River Gorge

To native tribes, the Gorge was the great gathering place. To Lewis and Clark and Oregon Trail pioneers, it was the gateway to the Pacific. To first-time visitors, it's the Northwest they've always imagined: towering waterfalls, moss-draped rainforests, and orchard country backdropped by snowcapped volcanoes.

While most visitors confine themselves to the cliffs and dense woodlands at the western end of the Gorge, a surprise awaits the newcomer venturing farther east. Halfway through this cleft in the Cascades, the greenery parts to reveal tawny grasslands and sage-covered deserts under an endless sky. This 80-mile long, five-mile wide, 4,000-foot-deep chasm has as much variety in climate, topography, and vegetation as terra firma can muster.

Visitors can revel in a cornucopia of attractions: the world's largest concentration of high waterfalls, one of the planet's most diverse botanical communities, and a wide spectrum of recreational opportunities that includes skiing, fishing, hiking, rock climbing, windsurfing, and much more—all in the same day.

Reliable summer westerly winds help make the Gorge at Hood River one of the world's top sailboarding destinations.

© MARK MORRIS

Unfortunately, this recipe for a peak travel experience is no secret. As weekend wilderness to the state's largest urban area, the strains on the Columbia River Gorge are palpable. The added impacts of 70,000 full-time residents and pollution have made the Gorge an environmental battleground. In 1997 the Columbia River was added to the list of the country's most endangered watersheds. In addition, many of the Northwest's debates over land use, timber practices, salmon preservation, and other environmental issues rage fiercely here.

THE LAND

If there's one word to describe the forces that created the Columbia River Gorge, it's *cataclysmic*. Volcanic activity, flooding, and landslides have sculpted the present-day contours of this fjord-like border between Oregon and Washington. While eons-old mud and lava flows are visible throughout the Gorge, and ancient avalanche scars still mar the land, there is a dearth of visual clues about the primary agent of landscape alteration here: floods of biblical proportions. Scientists estimate there were at least 40 such inundations between 12,000 and 19,000 years ago.

Geologists believe that glacial erratics—massive rocks not indigenous to the Gorge—were trans-

COURTESY OF THE COLUMBIA RIVER GORGE VISITORS ASSOCIATION

The Columbia River Gorge is a popular getaway for Portlanders.

ported to the region from the area of the present-day Canadian border encased in waterborne icebergs. During the last Ice Age, a 2,000-foot wall of ice formed Lake Missoula, a vast inland sea in what's now northern Idaho and western Montana. The collapse of the ice dam some 15,000 years ago released a wall of water that steamrolled westward at 60 miles an hour. These torrents entered the eastern Gorge at depths exceeding 1,000 feet. The floodwaters submerged what is now Portland and then surged 120 miles south, depositing rich alluvial sediments in the Willamette Valley.

Columbia River

The 1,243-mile Columbia River has its primary headwaters at Lake Columbia in British Columbia, from where it flows south and west from Canada's Kootenay Range. Glacial runoff, snowmelt, and such impressive tributaries as the Deschutes and Snake Rivers guarantee a fairly consistent flow year-round. At peak flows, the river pumps a quarter-million cubic feet of water per second into the Pacific Ocean after draining 259,000 square miles, an area larger than France.

Flow peaks in spring and early summer, coinciding with the region's irrigation needs. Another leading use of the river is hydropower. The Columbia River Basin is the most hydroelectrically developed river system in the world, with more than 400 dams in place throughout the mainstem and tributaries. As a result,

COLUMBIA RIVER GORGE

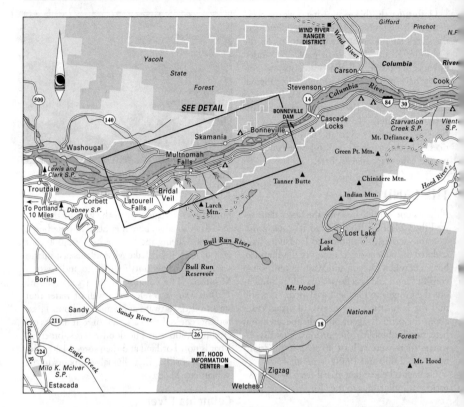

the current incarnation of the Columbia is a stark contrast to the white water that filled its channel before the dams were built. Back in that era, spawning salmon had to jump over several sets of roiling cascades, and shipping was a hazardous enterprise. Floods were commonplace; the flood of 1894, for example, inundated Hood River and The Dalles. Though the Columbia no longer exerts so pervasive an influence on the topography here, it still is more powerful than any river in North America except the Mississippi.

CLIMATE

The disparity between the wet western Gorge and the dryness of its eastern end can be best understood within the larger context of re-

gional precipitation patterns. The Cascade summits can wring more than 200 inches of rain yearly from eastward-moving cloud masses, yet cactus grows less than 50 air miles away in the eastern Gorge. A transition zone beginning a few miles east of Hood River shows an annual precipitation disparity of 19 inches within a dozen miles.

Given these contrasts, it's not surprising that the convergence of weather systems at mid-Gorge often results in meteorological bedlam. In fact, Bonneville Dam recorded the state's one-day record for snowfall, 39 inches, in January 1980. Strong, reliable westerlies make the Gorge a windsurfing paradise. (See "Windsurfing" in the Hood River section, later in this chapter.)

West of the Cascades, winter lows seldom

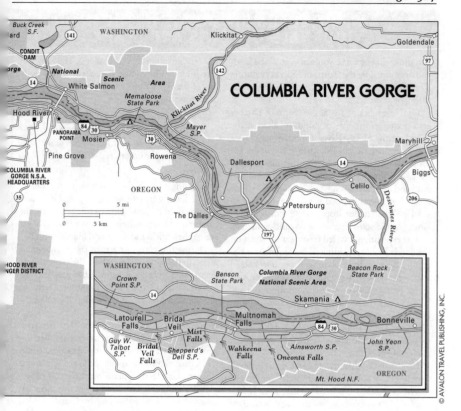

dip below freezing. A notable exception to this happens when frigid winds originating in the Rockies blow through the Gorge in winter. The eastern Gorge experiences more dramatic temperature variations than the western Gorge's more maritime conditions. Wintertime lows below 20°F and summertime highs over 90°F are not uncommon east the Cascades. Hood River has average summer daytime highs of 66°F and average winter lows of 33°F.

For wind and weather conditions in the Gorge, call 541/386-3300. Windsurfers can find out about conditions at www.windance.com.

FLORA

The variety in climate and habitats is paralleled by a diversity of plantlife—more than 800 varieties of trees, shrubs, and wildflowers, including 14 endemics, species found nowhere else in the world.

Transitions East to West

As you drive I-84 from west to east in the Gorge you'll see mixed conifer ecosystems with Douglas fir and western hemlock between Portland and Hood River. Deciduous bigleaf maples and stands of alder also assert themselves among the conifers.

Riparian environments in the Gorge are dominated by willow and black cottonwood. A lush understory of ferns covers the lower reaches of western Gorge waterfalls. Thimbleberry (a species of wild raspberry) and blackberry are also common during late summer.

Pockets of white oak and ponderosa pine

THE COLUMBIA GORGE IN THE JOURNALS OF LEWIS AND CLARK

In the course of a day, you can visit all the landmarks noted by the Corps of Discovery during 17 days in the winter of 1805 and 12 days in the spring of 1806.

On November 3, 1805, the Corps of Discovery's march to the sea temporarily halted at the mouth of the **Sandy River** at present-day Lewis and Clark State Park in Troutdale. It was in this approximate location that Meriwether Lewis noted the river's current threw out "emence quantities of sand and is very shallow. Clark attempted to wade across but found the bed was a very bad quicksand." The incident inspired the name "Sandy River," but in actuality there is no quicksand here.

The expedition traveled upstream 1.5 miles on the Sandy before returning to make camp on Diamond Island in the Columbia River, now known as Government Island. This island is now crossed by the present-day I-205 bridge, northeast of Portland. Noting the presence of more game and timber for fuel in the western Gorge than east of the Cascades, Lewis and Clark considered this region a "good wintering place" before their eventual choice of Fort Clatsop on the coast.

Besides the availability of resources for survival, the Gorge's western portal had special significance for the expedition. Their arrival here in early November 1805 marked the first time in thousands of miles the Corps of Discovery had reached an area documented by previous explorers, the 1792 Vancouver Expedition. By combining the routes charted by the British navy west of the Sandy River with the transcontinental route followed by the Corps of Discovery east of this waterway, the United States could be mapped for the first time from sea to shining sea.

An observation on November 3, 1805, by Private Joseph Whitehouse suggests that this juncture of the expedition's journey was auspicious for other reasons:

Towards evening we met Several Indians in a canoe who were going up the River. They Signed to us that in two Sleeps we Should See the Ocean vessels and white people.

Heading east on their homeward journey in April 1806 the expedition camped the better part of a week on a "handsome prairie" opposite the Sandy to make some "selestial observations, to examine the Quicksand River and kill some meat."

During this time, three men canoed about six miles up the Sandy. Meanwhile, the captains had determined from local natives that they had bypassed a major Columbia tributary en route to their present location at the western portal of the Gorge. According to the *Journals,* the natives also communicated to the explorers that the river drained an "open plain of great extent." Accompanied by seven men and a Native American guide, Clark backtracked to explore the lower Willamette River, making landfall in the northern part of present-day Portland. The discovery of this tributary, called the Multnomah River by Clark, planted seeds for future exploration and settlement in the Willamette Valley, Oregon's current center of population, agriculture, and commerce.

Beacon Rock, the 848-foot core of an ancient volcano, is another prominent topographic feature described by Lewis and Clark. It first becomes visible to eastbound Historic Highway travelers at Portland Women's Forum State Park in Corbett,

begin to show up east of Bonneville Dam. Just outside Mosier, this oak "savanna" dominates the landscape until sagebrush, rabbitbush, cheatgrass, and other chaparral define the beginning of the semiarid desert east of the Cascades Range.

Wildflowers

Fourteen unique wildflower species, some of them survivors from the Ice Age, are found among plants that typically thrive in a Rocky Mountain sub-alpine biome. Thirty-one plants usually encountered at 4,000 feet above sea level are found in the Columbia Gorge at elevations of just 1,600 feet, thriving in the damp, cold air that gets trapped in the shadow of the cliffs. For a list of the Gorge's 14 endemics, their habitat, time of bloom, and locations in the Gorge,

Oregon. This bell jar–shaped mound of basalt appears on the distant Washington shoreline across a 20-mile sweep of river. It is the world's second-highest freestanding monolith behind Gibraltar. Beacon Rock's name is commonly thought to have derived from its visibility, but on October 31, 1805, Clark noted:

a remarkable high detached rock stands in a bottom on the starboard side near the lower part of this island about 800 feet high and 400 paces around we call the Beaten rock.

Not until the homeward journey in April 1806 did the *Journals* refer to it by its current name. On April 6, Lewis observed that:

it is only in the fall of the year when the river is low that the tides are persceptable as high at the beacon rock.

It should be mentioned that tidal fluctuations were also observed near Beacon Rock in the fall of the previous year. At that time, the presence of what the *Journals* mistakenly referred to as "sea otters" (in actuality, seals) also gave strong indications that the Pacific was close enough to exert influences on the Gorge's ecosystem.

Other *Journals* landmarks that Historic Highway and I-84 travelers can enjoy are **Mist Falls** and **Multnomah Falls,** noted but not named in April 1806 entries. Mist Falls is best seen from I-84's Exit 30 turnoff across Benson Lake. This gossamer cascade wafts down a rock face 500 feet high till it's obscured from view by the trees. Sometimes its filmy runoff is not opaque enough to be clearly visible from the interstate, so have binoculars ready. On the Columbia River Highway itself, the turnout on the south side of the road at the eastern end of Benson Lake (look for a yellow sign that says "25 mph," with a squiggly line indicating a winding road) lines up well enough with Mist Falls to offer a closer, but not better vantage point.

Multnomah Falls can be seen from I-84's Exit 31 and the Historic Highway about a mile east of Mist Falls. The superlatives Lewis and Clark used to describe Multnomah Falls echo the adjectives in guidebooks today:

we passed several beautifull casscades which fell from a great height over the Stupendous rocks which closes the river on both sides nearly, except for a small bottom on the South side in which our hunters were encamped. The most remarkable of these casscades falls about 300 feet perpendicularly over a solid rock into a narrow bottom of the river on the south side. it is a large creek situated about 5 miles above our encampment of the last evening. Several smaller streams fall from a much greater hight, and in their decent become a perfect mist which collecting on the rocks below again become visible and decend a second time in the same manner before they reach the base of the rocks.

The dramatic topography the explorers described in *The Journals of Lewis and Clark,* as well as accounts of their own undaunted courage, remain to inspire modern-day Gorge travelers.

check out the National Forest Service website (www.fs.fed.us/r6/columbia/).

FAUNA

The archaeological record indicates that saber-toothed cats, giant beavers, grizzly bear, mastodons, ancient horses, and camels once roamed parts of the Gorge. In 1805, Lewis and Clark noted a Columbia practically overflowing with salmon near The Dalles and Wishram, and complained of an inability to sleep in the western Gorge due to the cacophony of birds in the area. While the wilderness that supported the numbers and variety of these species has largely disappeared, you'd still be hard-pressed to find another region this close to a major urban area with rattlesnake, spotted owl,

COLUMBIA RIVER GORGE

BIGFOOT

One of the secrets the Columbia Gorge might share if it could talk would be the whereabouts of the abominable snowman, a.k.a. Bigfoot or Sasquatch. Indian tribes of the region regarded this creature as a fact of life and celebrated its presence in art and ritual.

Whether it exists outside the mind or not, the King Kong of the Northwest forests has attracted to the region everyone from hunters and academics to curiosity seekers and *National Enquirer* reporters. Although the notion of a half-man, half-ape eluding human capture seems implausible at first, a brief look at some of the evidence might convince you otherwise.

As recently as the winter of 1991, reports from a remote area of the Blue Mountains (the chief drainage of which is the Columbia River) spoke of more than 60 miles of tracks left in the snow by a large five-toed creature. Scientists on the scene were of the opinion that the pattern of the prints and the gait could not have been fake. A similar conclusion was reached in 1982 about a plaster cast of footprints taken from the same mountain range. A Washington State University professor detected humanlike whorls on the toe portions of the prints, which he said showed that the tracks had to have been made by a large hominid.

Reports and evidence of actual encounters abound in Northwest annals, compelling the U.S. Army Corps of Engineers to list the animal as an indigenous species, accompanied by a detailed anatomical description. Skamania County, whose southern border is the Columbia River shoreline, declared the harming of these creatures a gross misdemeanor punishable by a year in jail and a $1,000 fine.

The unwavering belief of Bigfoot adherents among the scientific community and the native insistence that it's a living entity have naturally met with skepticism. But considering that stories about black-and-white bears roaming the alpine hinterlands of China persisted for centuries until the 1936 discovery of pandas, there could be something new under the sun in the 21st century.

cougar, bald eagle, black bear, seal, pika, Roosevelt elk, and other species. Wildlife viewing opportunities are noted in the destinations covered in this chapter.

Living Fossils

Two living fossils, the mountain beaver and the white sturgeon, also exist in this watershed. The mountain beaver (called a "boomer" by locals), is a primitive species of rat that resembles a beaver minus the flat tail. It's thought to resemble its forebears from 65 million years ago. The white sturgeon, a creature that can measure more than 20 feet and weigh over 1,000 pounds, has not changed structurally in 200 million years. (See "Bonneville Dam," which contains a sturgeon hatchery, later in this chapter.)

Salmon

The Columbia Basin chinook salmon run consisted of less than a million fish for much of the 1990s, though the numbers have been spiking upwards since 2000. By contrast, an estimated 10–16 million Columbia River salmon were caught by Native Americans annually in the 1800s. During the 1880s, 55 canneries operated on the Columbia, employing such new technologies such as the salmon wheel, a Ferris wheel–like scooping device that extracted salmon from the river in such large numbers that the wheels were banned in the first decades of the 20th century. Thereafter, perhaps the greatest scourges of salmon populations here were introduced: the hydroelectric dam and hatchery system.

While hundreds of millions of dollars have been spent on research and efforts to mitigate the ill effects posed by the dams, salmon populations generally continue to decline. Polls continually confirm that a large majority of Pacific Northwest residents want to restore the salmon runs, even if financial and other sacrifices are involved. It's as if there is a shared realization echoing the traditional Native American belief—after the salmon, we're next.

HISTORY

First Peoples of the Gorge

Archaeological findings date native presence in the Gorge to some 10,000 years ago. When Lewis and Clark first came through the Columbia River Gorge in 1805, they found a gathering of the tribes near present-day Wishram, Washington, whose numbers and variety surpassed any other native trading center on the continent.

The region hosted indigenous peoples from as far away as Alaska and the Great Lakes, who would come for barter fairs during salmon fishing season. Gambling, races, and potlatches (parties where individuals gave away possessions to gain status) supplemented trade and fishing.

Lewis and Clark encountered evidence of foreign contact on the Columbia from such disparate sources as a Chinook tribal chieftain with red hair and Gorge natives with swords, coins, Hudson's Bay blankets, and other European and Asian goods. Certain artifacts suggest trade with natives from as far away as present-day Missouri and the southwestern United States. Not surprisingly, Chinookan currency consisted of shells from Vancouver Island and blankets crafted by the English Hudson's Bay Company rather than indigenous articles.

Native American Decline

Tribes were moved to reservations outside the Gorge as a result of treaties enacted in 1855 and or the flooding of ceremonial fishing sites at Celilo by The Dalles Dam in 1957. Native aquiescence to the 1855 agreements came after measles and smallpox epidemics reduced their population to a small fraction of the 13,500 natives counted in the region in 1811. While the arrival of settlers on the Oregon Trail brought about some isolated conflicts with Gorge tribes, far more damaging to the long-term survival of native culture here was the destruction of their dietary staples.

The complex and sophisticated culture of Gorge tribes can be appreciated today at the several acclaimed Gorge interpretive centers, where you'll find artifacts, oral histories, photos, and other exhibits. Most petroglyphs, pictographs, cemeteries, and other indigenous cultural landmarks have been largely destroyed by construction or buried beneath reservoirs.

Euro-American Settlement

Most published accounts credit the discovery of the Columbia River to a Captain Robert Gray. He crossed over the treacherous bar of the river's estuary and sailed 13 miles upriver in 1792, claiming the waterway for the United States and naming it after his ship, the *Columbia Rediviva*.

Later in the same year, English explorer George Vancouver dispatched Lt. William Broughton upstream from the river's mouth. He reached an area five miles east of the Sandy and Washougal Rivers. Along the way, he named some of the Cascade Range volcanoes after members of the British naval command (Hood and Rainier). He also threw down the gauntlet for British claims to the Pacific Northwest that persisted well into the next century. Lewis and Clark's expedition, passing through the Gorge 13 years later, accelerated American designs on the region. In 1848, Congress established the Oregon Territory, the first formal territory west of the Rockies. (See "History" in the Introduction chapter for more information.)

Columbia River Highway

In 1911, Samuel Hill, a wealthy, eccentric railroad lawyer, began promoting an idea for a Columbia River Highway, and found supporters in the Portland business community who were swept up in the fervor stirred up by the national Good Roads campaign of the time. This movement supported the construction of paved highways with scenic qualities to foster tourism.

When the first Model T rolled off Henry Ford's assembly line in 1913, Hill's dream began to take form. Timber magnate and hotelier Simon Benson coordinated the project's fiscal management and promotion, and mill-owner John Yeon volunteered as roadmaster of the work crews. Samuel Lancaster, a visionary Tennessee engineer recruited by Hill, added the artistic inspiration for what came to be known as "a poem in stone."

This would not only be the Northwest's first paved public road but one of the defining events in the growth of modern American tourism. Scores of middle-class Portland families in their Model Ts took to the hills above the Columbia on this architecturally aesthetic thoroughfare following the 1915 completion of this highway's first section. After the stretch between Troutdale and The Dalles was completed in 1922, it was dubbed "king of roads" by the *Illustrated London News.*

Service stations, roadside rest stops, motor courts (later called "motels"), and resort hotels that catered to the motorized carriage trade developed here, contributing to the Gorge's economic growth. Of the several dozen roadhouses that lined this highway 1915–1960, only a few structures remain today. A new interstate was constructed in the 1950s and 1960s that made Gorge travel faster, but the charm of the earlier era was lost.

Fortunately, the "king of roads" experienced a renaissance in the 1980s. Political activists, volunteers, government agencies, and federal legislation provided the spadework for the preservation of the Historic Columbia River Highway, the first federally designated scenic highway in the United States. Thanks to its inclusion on the National Register of Historic Places (the only road on the list) as well as listings as an All-American Road, National Scenic Byway, National Heritage Road, and National Historic Landmark, the restoration is becoming a reality.

Plans are afoot to restore most of the route between Troutdale and The Dalles by 2010. Currently, the old highway's sections from Troutdale to Ainsworth State Park and Mosier to The Dalles attract millions of motorists annually. Other segments of the old road are being rebuilt with attention to architectural nuance and potential recreational and interpretive uses. The reconstructed Mosier Twin Tunnels east of Hood River as well as restored sections between Cascades Locks and Eagle Creek and in the Bonneville-to-Tanner Creek corridor exemplify how parts of the highway have been rededicated as hiker-biker trails.

Dams

The introduction of the car wasn't the only event with profound implications for tourism, commerce, and ecology. Beginning with Bonneville in 1938, the construction of the great dams on the Columbia changed the course of one the world's mightiest rivers and the way of life in the Gorge forever. Bonneville and Grand Coulee supplied power for the war effort with such beneficiaries as Kaiser shipyards and Boeing.

Today, Northwest businesses and residents still benefit from the cheap hydropower but at the possible cost of the greatest salmon runs ever known. Besides billions of dollars worth of pollution-free renewable energy at the lowest cost in the western United States, other Bonneville byproducts include 370 miles of lucrative inland shipping, irrigation water for agriculture, and perfect windsurfing conditions.

TRANSPORTATION

For most of the previous century, when people went to the Gorge it usually meant a day's outing by car from Portland to Multnomah Falls. While that short getaway is still popular, the scope of the typical excursion has increased dramatically. Travelers with a historical and cultural bent are joining hikers and bikers to explore the region in-depth. At the same time, the Columbia River has become the fastest-growing domestic cruise destination in the lower 48 states.

By Car

The automobile remains the vehicle of choice for visitors. I-84 through the Gorge has enough eye candy to engage even the most stalwart backroad enthusiast. On this river-level drive you can pass waterfalls, windsurfers, sagebrush, native fishing platforms, Oregon Trail wagon ruts, and topographic features named by Lewis and Clark. To avoid the interstate's high-speed traffic, you have the option of several points of entry onto the Historic Columbia River Highway.

If you only have a day to tour the Gorge by car, a five-hour itinerary looping the Oregon and Washington shorelines is suggested. Such a trip might include a visit to Vista House, photo-ops at several waterfalls on the Historic Columbia River Highway, as well as a museum stop (Maryhill Museum or one of the interpretive centers in Stevenson and The Dalles as well as Bonneville Dam fish-viewing windows/sturgeon hatchery). Another popular one-day excursion from Portland is the Mount Hood Loop, which goes through the Columbia River Gorge after circumnavigating the mountain.

By Bike

The prospect of biking from Troutdale to The Dalles on the Historic Highway by the end of this decade has bicyclists excited. Currently, the several hikers/bikers-only sections of this highway, detailed in this chapter, are whetting this anticipation.

It's possible to take bikes on Portland's TriMet (503/238-RIDE, www.tri-met.org) out to the Gorge, eliminating 17 miles through traffic-filled suburbs. Buses go to Troutdale (the beginning of the Gorge) from Gresham, a town reachable from downtown Portland on bike-friendly MAX light rail. They drop you at the Columbia Gorge Outlet Mall just north of the Historic Highway (pedal a quarter mile south on 257th Avenue and turn left at the stoplight).

Bicyclists seeking the best the Gorge has to offer within a day's ride on a paved surface can take advantage of the first or last sections of the Historic Columbia River Highway using a two-car shuttle. Your two-pedal voyage into this realm should begin at Crown Point's Vista House and end about 10 miles later at the Multnomah Falls NFS visitors center. Along the way, a half-dozen waterfalls coming off the huge basalt cliffs let you experience the kind of vistas inadequately enshrined in calendar art and coffee-table books. Another bike-and-car shuttle showcases more of the Historic Highway between Hood River and The Dalles.

Cruises

Thanks to a revival of interest in Lewis and Clark's journey, Columbia cruises are more popular than ever. Most cruises embark from Portland, taking in the mouth of the river, the Gorge, and the Snake. Some companies also take in the Willamette River or an ocean voyage up into Canada. Most of these small cruise ships carry 150–180 people and guarantee view rooms. Itineraries range 4–14 nights. These are high-end packages (several thousand dollars a week, double occupancy) but are good value nonetheless. The well-appointed ships boast gourmet meals and ideal sightlines on the shipping locks and dam facilities. Add expert commentary by qualified interpreters and you have a trip to remember.

Cruise West (800/888-9378) has a 1,000-mile itinerary with three small cruise ships, departing Portland in April, May, September, and October. This company is part of Alaska Sightseeing–Cruise West, a company started by Chuck West, architect of the highly regarded Holland America–Westours programs in Alaska, in response to client requests for a more intimate group travel experience.

Special Expeditions (800/762-0003) has become synonymous with quality in cruise travel. Sven Lindblad packages trips with groups small enough to guarantee individualized attention from an attentive crew on state-of-the-art craft. In addition to luxury, these cruises offer an in-depth dunk into the human and natural history of the region thanks to visiting authors, historians, and professors. Cruises run May and October.

American West Steamboat (800/234-1232) is currently the most popular company on the river. Their paddlewheelers generally don't go faster than 10–15 miles an hour, a pace more conducive to appreciating the scenery. In addition, the *Queen of the West* also has the most extensive on-board entertainment and longest season.

The **Columbia Queen** (800/457-3619) has one of the more ambitious shore excursion schedules of the ships on the river as well as the shipboard amenities that made its parent company, Delta Queen, famous. These sternwheeler cruises run spring through fall on eight-night 1,000-mile cruises.

For day trips on a sternwheeler, October–mid-June, call **Sternwheeler Columbia Gorge**, in Cascade Locks (541/374-8427). Each cruise concentrates on a different aspect of Gorge heritage (Lewis and Clark, Oregon Trail, etc.) with brunch/dinner packages on weekends at prices comparable to their Portland offerings (see "Tours" in the Portland chapter).

INFORMATION AND SERVICES

Consult the destination sections in this chapter for local ranger station contact information, or go right to the source: the **Columbia River Gorge Scenic Area** (902 Wasco Ave., Ste. 200, Hood River 97031, 541/386-2333, www.fs.fed .us/r6/columbia).

Each year, the excellent *Gorge Guide* comes out with news, reviews, and other perspectives on the region. Available throughout the Gorge, it can also be purchased at many media outlets in Portland and Vancouver. It is sometimes distributed free at visitors centers.

The Forest Service's primary walk-in sales outlet for Oregon topographical maps is Nature of the Northwest (800 N.E. Oregon St., Room 177, Portland, 503/731-4444). Its *Trails of the Columbia River Gorge* map can be found here along with other renderings of the region.

The Gorge's one-stop Internet shop is **www .gorge.net,** which has resources on everything from recreation to fine dining.

Troutdale

Troutdale, where the western portal of the Columbia River Gorge meets the northern Willamette Valley, has taken advantage of its auspicious location since pioneer days. Even before the townsite was established in 1854, the area was an important crossroads en route to hundreds of free acres of tillable paradise—each pioneer's reward for a 2,000-mile walk. To this end, Oregon Trail emigrants either resumed their raft trip down the Columbia here after portaging the white water in the Gorge's midsection or turned inland at the mouth of the Sandy River.

In the next century, oil was discovered here, and Troutdale's agricultural bounty gave overland and steamship transport a short-lived high profile here. While incarnations as a railway hub, smelt-fishing mecca, and the self-proclaimed "celery capital of the world" have also come and gone, this town has plied the Columbia River Highway tourist trade since the second decade of the 20th century.

Such ambitions are still evident in downtown Troutdale's four blocks of nouveau pioneer-style storefronts housing galleries and boutiques. The western edge of town is marked by an outlet mall, a cut-rate motel colony, and a popular 38-acre resort and recreation complex, McMenamin's Edgefield. Much of this development occurred in the last decade, enabling Troutdale to reclaim some of the Gorge gateway status it temporarily lost after a section of the new freeway bypassed the town in the 1960s.

Drive four miles on I-84 past town to the "Corbett curves" (Exit 22 off I-84) to access the prettiest part of the Historic Columbia River Highway, between Portland Women's Forum State Park and the waterfalls.

TROUTDALE AND HISTORIC HIGHWAY ACCESS ROUTES

Historically minded travelers heading east on I-84 should take Exit 18 (the second Troutdale exit) to Lewis and Clark State Park. Besides the intrepid explorers, many other notables have visited here. A heritage marker just past the Sandy River Bridge a short distance south and east on the Historic Highway describes the Vancouver Expedition's exploration of the Sandy's mouth in 1792 on the first European visit to the Gorge. President Herbert Hoover, who spent much of his boyhood in Oregon, is said to have come to the Sandy to enjoy the now-sporadic smelt runs as well the still thriving steelhead fishery.

Smelt were also important to native peoples. Lewis and Clark referred to them as anchovies, a fish harvested by Indians and used for food, oil, and when dried, as candles. Such uses were commonplace among native peoples from Oregon to Alaska. The smelt's decline around 1960 from the Sandy is likely a byproduct of the altered ecosystem of the Columbia and its tributaries. Dams and other human activities have changed flow, water temperature, and the makeup of riparian plant and animal species here; siltation and pollution have also been suggested as culprits. Maynard C. Drawson, author of the self-published *Treasures of the Oregon Country* theorizes that a landfill created during the construction of I-84 changed the flow of the Sandy at its mouth, adversely impacting smelt runs.

In town, the turn-of-the-century **Harlow House** (726 E. Historic Columbia River Hwy., 503/661-2164) deserves mention not only as the home of the Troutdale's founding family, but as a place where what remained of the Gorge native culture sustained its death blow. Along with the trout ponds that town father Captain John Harlow kept here that inspired the town's name, he also had a pond with carp. During an 1880s Sandy River flood, the carp escaped and bred enough to destroy the wapato growing in the shallows of the Columbia throughout most of the Gorge. This starchy tuber, along with camas bulbs, was a staple for Chinookan peoples of the region. After the decimation of this vital food source, the already beleaguered population dwindled to extinction.

Today, the turn-of-the-century white clapboard farmhouse shows off period furniture and other artifacts. It's open Sept. Wed.–Sat. 10 A.M.–4 P.M. and Sunday 1–4 P.M. Admission is $4. The **Rail Depot Museum** (473 E. Historic Columbia River Hwy., 503/661-2164) has the same hours, featuring exhibits that go back to the Union Pacific's 1913 establishment of this terminal site.

Besides Exit 18 off I-84, another way to get on the highway is to take Exit 17 off the interstate followed by a right on 257th Avenue. Just past the outlet mall on your left pick up the Historic Highway by heading east (left) at the light and follow the highway through town.

A more circuitous but interesting route is to bypass the turn onto the Historic Highway through town and take a left at the next light onto Cherry Park Lane. After a mile, turn right a quarter mile past the Troutdale Post Office and go 1.6 miles down the hill to Stark Street. After a left on Stark, the sight of subdivisions gobbling up orchard country is supplanted by forested Cascade foothills and stone retaining walls built by His-

toric Highway artisans. While this part of Stark Street was one of the original entries to the old road from Portland, it assumed a lower profile when more direct routes became available with the completion of I-84 in the 1960s. Nonetheless, connoisseurs of the Historic Highway's masonry have always enjoyed this alternate access. The next display of such craftsmanship happens 10 miles east at the arched railings near Crown Point on the Historic Highway itself.

At the end of Stark Street just before a bridge over the Sandy River, you'll come to the site of the 1912 headquarters of the Portland Auto Club on the east side of the highway. After crossing the bridge you enter the National Scenic Area; the 85 miles between here and the Deschutes River defines the scenic area boundaries in Oregon. This jurisdiction was established to balance area residents' rights to property and making a living with the region's aesthetic, ecological, recreational, cultural, and historical resources.

In about a half mile, just before Dabney State Park, where there are restrooms and river access, you'll find restored mile-marker posts from the old highway. The first one you see is marked 17, reflecting the mileage from Portland on the old route. Because these mileposts no longer apply to the different access routes to the Historic Highway, readers should use the reference system described below.

The Historic Highway from Sandy River Bridge (Mile 0) to Multnomah Falls (Mile 18)

We've designated the Sandy River Bridge as "ground zero" in this book's mile-by-mile delineation of the first section of the Historic Highway. Located a couple of miles west of the Stark Street Bridge, it is most directly accessed by Exit 18 off I-84. After crossing the bridge, the forested foothills of the Sandy River Gorge replace downtown boutiques and the whooshing river mutes the drone of interstate traffic. The next 20 miles traverse historic bridges and stonework, lush orchard country, rainforested slot canyons, more than a half-dozen large waterfalls, and cliffside views of the Columbia River Gorge. The attractions between Corbett and Horsetail Falls

COLUMBIA RIVER GORGE

explain why both the American Automobile Association and Rand McNally rate the Historic Highway as one of the top 10 scenic roads in the country.

Roadside Observations

As the highway climbs uphill east out of the Sandy River Gorge, detours through Silverdale and Corbett occasionally yield some small town treasures. Area residents stage an old-fashioned July Fourth parade with whimsical homemade floats and classic cars followed by bake-offs, cakewalks, and spelling bees along with the inevitable fireworks.

For those interested in the most direct route to highway sightseeing highlights, bear right at Springdale (mile 3.8), and follow Crown Point signs thereafter; .2 mile later, bear left at the intersection with Hurlburt Road. Several miles up the road, the Corbett Country Market (mile 7.5) sells everything from chicken strips and microwave burritos to locally made jams and smoked salmon. There's also the only gas pump until Cascades Locks, 13 miles east. During the era of Columbia River steamboats (late 1850s to the 1920s), potatoes were grown here in the bluffs above the Columbia and transported down to Corbett Landing's docks below.

Portland Women's Forum State Scenic Viewpoint (Mile 8.5)

The view east from Chanticleer Point here is the first cliffside panorama of the Columbia and its gorge that most travelers experience on the highway. It is a sight that graces many thematic postcards and calendar photos. This classic tableau features Crown Point's domed Vista House jutting out on an escarpment about a mile to the east, giving human scale to the cleft in the Cascades 725 feet below. This same perspective on the Columbia (minus the domed observatory) from the now-defunct Chanticleer Hotel in 1913 inspired Sam Hill, Samuel Lancaster, John Yeon, and other prominent men to cast the final vote to build the Columbia River Highway.

Behind a barrier on the western side of the Portland Women's Forum parking lot is a remnant of a 1912 access road that brought Chanticleer Hotel visitors here on a hair-raising ride from the Rooster Rock train station near the shoreline. After a fire destroyed the hotel in 1930, the point was annexed to the holdings of Julius Meier, a prominent Portland department store owner who also became governor of Oregon. Travelers pass his former estate, Menucha (Hebrew for "waters of life"), now a retreat center, on the highway west of here. In 1956, the Portland Women's Forum purchased Chanticleer Point and donated it to the state park system six years later. Other notable purchases by the Women's Forum during this decade included land bordering waterfalls that had been slated for logging. The state scenic viewpoint here was named for the group to honor such activism.

If the highway from Troutdale is too slow or too removed from views of the Columbia, quicker access to the scenic viewpoint and the spectacular Historic Highway views thereafter is provided by Exit 22 (Corbett) off I-84. After passing Corbett Station, a boarded-up roadhouse, make a right to climb the hill. You'll climb a steep curvy mile-long rise (not recommended for large RVs or trailers) and bear left at the top of the hill in Corbett. You'll have two occasions to veer right off this road, but keep left. The expanses of agricultural land eventually give way to river views beginning with Portland Women's Forum. This state park also is a prime place to experience the Gorge winds at their gustiest.

If you wish to get more intimate with the river prior to climbing the hill onto the highway, Exit 22 off I-84 also provides one of the few chances to drive down to the water's edge in this part of the Gorge. Just make a left turn instead of a right as you reach the top of the exit ramp.

From the Women's Forum to Multnomah Falls, readers should note mile references carefully, because geographical features and state parks don't have street addresses, making some of them easy to bypass.

Larch Mountain Turnoff (Mile 9.1)

If you veer right on the road marked "Larch Mountain" at the Y intersection (mile 9.1) with the highway, you'll go 14 miles to an overlook featuring views of the snowcapped Cascades as well as of the Columbia all the way west to Portland. There are also picnic tables and trailheads to the Gorge below, with gorgeous beargrass blossoms in June. Later, huckleberries in August and mushrooms after the first rains await foragers. Also of interest are old-growth fir in the area. Despite this botanical bounty, there's not a larch tree in sight—this species grows east of the Cascades.

To enjoy one of Oregon's classic sunsets, head to the northeast corner of the Larch Mountain parking lot around dusk and follow a gently rolling quarter-mile paved path through forests of old-growth noble fir. The trail's last 100 yards involve a steep climb up to an outcropping. This is **Sherrard Point,** one of the country's preeminent alpine views. To the east, across miles of treetops, is Mount Hood. To the south is Mount Jefferson's symmetrical cone. To the north, Mounts St. Helens, Rainier, and Adams are visible. To the west, the Columbia River becomes bathed in reddish glow during sunset. With the coming of nightfall, the lights of Portland become accentuated in the darkness.

The full moon rising over Mount Hood is also spectacular from this vantage point. However, keep in mind that for several months in winter, the road to the Sherrard Point trailhead is sometimes roadblocked four miles away. This is motivated by concern over snowy, icy conditions in the sloping parking lot. Call the Scenic Area at 541/386-2333 for updates.

An ambitious hike involving a car shuttle between trailheads lets you trek from Larch Mountain down to Multnomah Falls Lodge. This trail drops 4,000 feet in 6.8 miles. To reach the descent route from Larch Mountain viewpoint, retrace your steps along the path back toward the parking lot. At about halfway, veer right up the spur trail that crests on a hill. From this hilltop head west a short distance toward a picnic area where the trail down to the Gorge begins.

Crown Point and Vista House (Mile 9.9)

Driving the interstate, you might notice the distinctive outline of an octagonal structure on a high bluff in the western Gorge. This is the **Vista House Visitor Center at Crown Point**

Vista House Visitor Center, perched on a basalt bluff 733 feet above the Columbia River

(mile 9.9), 733 feet above the Columbia. Construction began in 1916 when the Columbia River Highway was formally dedicated. The occasion was marked when Woodrow Wilson pressed a button in the White House, which electronically unfurled "Old Glory" at the flat circular dirt area that was to become the visitors center. In deference to Prohibition, the event was toasted with loganberry juice as black sedans chugged along the highway to just east of Eagle Creek, the highway's easternmost extent until the 1922 completion of the entire route to The Dalles.

Vista House was completed two years after the highway's official dedication. The outside observation deck up the steps from the main rotunda showcases 30 miles of the Columbia River Gorge. A plaque outside pays homage to Samuel Lancaster for the "poetry and drama" the highway embodies. Photos of the various stages of the road's construction are displayed in the main rotunda, as are wildflower cuttings of the region's endemic plants. Vista House is undergoing renovation, and the regular hours of 9 A.M.–6 P.M. daily, April–October, may vary; call ahead to confirm. The info desk is usually staffed by friendly and knowledgeable volunteer Friends of Vista House (503/695-2230, www.vistahouse.com).

Crown Point was originally called Thor's Crown by Edgar Lazarus, architect of Vista House. This promontory began as a basalt flow 14.5 million years ago when lava filled a canyon of the ancestral Columbia River.

COLUMBIA RIVER GORGE

Figure Eight Loops

The highway between Crown Point and Latourell Falls drops 600 feet in elevation in several miles. As you wend your way downhill from Vista House, it becomes apparent that Lancaster softened the grade of the road here by means of switchbacks. With a grade never exceeding 5 percent and a curve radii of not less than 100 feet, this section presents little problem for modern vehicles, but it challenged period cars and trucks during the highway's first decades. During construction, Scottish stone cutters and Italian masons sometimes hung suspended on ropes, singing while they worked on the precipitous, circuitous roadbed.

Latourell Falls (Mile 12)

Latourell Falls is the first of a half-dozen roadside falls seen by motorists. When the highway was built, special care was taken to ensure the bridge crossing Latourell Creek provided a good view of the falls. Nonetheless, be sure to take the paved 150-yard trail from the parking lot to the base of this 249-foot cataract. Here, the shade and cooling spray create a microclimate for fleabane, a delicate bluish member of the aster family, and other flowers normally common to alpine biomes. The filmy tendrils of water against the columnar basalt formations on the cliffs make Latourell a favorite with photographers. Foragers appreciate maidenhair fern and thimbleberries but not enough to denude the slope.

Another trailhead begins in the middle of the parking lot and climbs around and above the falls, though bushes obscure the overhang from which the water descends when you're looking down from the top. You'll probably be more inclined to stop after 50 yards and take in the distant perspective of Latourell from across the canyon. Latourell Creek flows from the falls underneath the highway bridge toward Guy Talbot State Park with picnic tables shaded by an ancient forest.

The Gorge boasts the largest concentration of roadside waterfalls in North America and the largest cluster of high waterfalls anywhere, including Multnomah Falls (620 feet) and Wahkeena Falls (242 feet).

Close by is the town of Latourell, during the 1880s the social hub for loggers and Joseph Latourell's millworkers, who would kick up their heels at the community dance hall. By the turn of the century, saloons, a house of negotiable affection, and a billiard hall were also serving sternwheeler and train passengers. In 1915 Latourell Villa carried on the tradition, serving lunches, dinner, and locally distilled spirits. Tourism grew with the highway, and the town prospered during the postwar heyday of Oregon's resource-based economy.

The decline of lumber and fishing, along with the construction of I-84, transformed Latourell into a peaceful small town with turn-of-the-century structures. You can drive into this bucolic postcard from the past by turning left (north) a quarter mile west of the ornate highway bridge leading to Latourell Falls parking lot.

Shepperd's Dell (Mile 13.3)

Shepperd's Dell is named for a settler who retreated here for spiritual renewal because of the lack of good roads to a nearby church. This lush forested canyon cut by a waterfall is one of the visual highlights of the Gorge despite the fact that little of this splendor is apparent from the road. An 80-yard paved sloping walkway descends from a bridge (and a parking lot east of it) whose intricate architecture can be appreciated with a glance over your shoulder. Chances are, however, your gaze will be riveted on Shepperd's Dell Fall coursing down out of the forest to plummet sharply over a precipice.

Some historians speculate that Lewis and Clark's journals made reference to the area between Shepperd's Dell and Rooster Rock in April 4 and April 6, 1806, entries describing the Corps of Discovery's hunting grounds.

Bishop's Cap (Mile 13.4)

Bishop's Cap embodies the highway engineering genius of Samuel Lancaster. Here, the base of a basalt outcropping was undercut as little as possible to accommodate traffic. Locals call this altered formation "mushroom rock" due to the simulation of a stem connecting to a mushroom cap. The same motif is repeated around the bend. More highway architecture is visible here with dry masonry walls and stone guardrails.

Bridal Veil Falls State Park (Mile 15)

Another legacy from the past can be experienced at the 1926-era Bridal Veil Lodge across from the state park. This establishment, along with the Columbia Gorge Hotel west of Hood River, are the only operating lodgings from the heyday of the Columbia River Highway. (See Troutdale "Accommodations" and the special topic, "Columbia Gorge Hotel," under Hood River, for more information.)

Across from Bridal Veil Lodge are the falls for which the state park is named, reachable by a trailhead at the east end of the parking lot. A short two-thirds of a mile round-trip hike takes you to the observation platform at the base of this voluminously gushing bi-level cascade.

Bridal Veil Falls State Park is also the trailhead for the 33.5-mile **Gorge Trail 400.** Between here and Wyeth, this largely level trail takes in the Gorge's highest waterfalls as well as newly opened sections of the old Columbia River Highway that are closed to vehicular traffic.

In addition to tree-shaded picnic tables and restrooms open all year, the park features the largest camas patch in the Columbia River Gorge. Camas and wapato were the leading Native American food staples. The camas bulb looks like an onion and tastes very sweet after it is slowly baked. Please leave the camas alone, out of respect for a traditional food source as well as for your own safety—camas with white flowers are poisonous, a fact that is not always established when the bulb is being harvested.

If you're here in April, look for patches of blue along the short **Overlook Trail** to the Pillars of Hercules, a pair of giant basalt monoliths below the railing backdropped by I-84 and the Columbia River. These formations are also called

Spilyai's children, after the Native American coyote demi-god. According to legend, Spilyai transformed his wife into Latourell Falls and his children into these volcanic formations to keep them from leaving him. Overlook Trail is about 20 yards west of the Bridal Veil Falls trailhead.

Bridal Veil Post Office

Industrial logging began in the Gorge in the Bridal Veil Falls area. A town was named for the Bridal Veil Lumber Company, one of several in the area. With implements like the "misery whip" (the two-man crosscut saw) and horse teams for transporting fallen logs over steep slopes, the hardiness of early timber workers was the stuff of legend. Eventually, a log flume was built that brought Douglas fir, hemlock, noble fir, and cedar down from Larch Mountain first to a paper mill, then to a sawmill. In 1940 several hundred people lived in the area, thanks largely to the timber economy. A fire caused the population to decline here two years later. However, the mill's legacy extended four more decades providing lumber for Hood River's fruit boxes and Kraft cheese boxes as well as construction materials for the postwar housing boom.

That era is long gone, but the Bridal Veil Post Office shack (97010), the country's second smallest, still survives. Drive down the hill from the state park and make a left turn heading west, bypassing the freeway entrance ramp (if you're heading east from Portland on I-84 look for Exit 28). On a bluff overlooking I-84 and the Columbia River, look for a building that has also enjoyed incarnations as a first aid station, a saw-filer's workshop, and a rock collector's storage shed.

The original post office had been located close by in a general store near the railroad tracks until 1942. Reportedly, more than 80,000 people have been coming here yearly over the last decade to send out mail. Given the remoteness of this postal station, it's a safe bet many visit solely to imprint their letters and wedding invitations with Bridal Veil's unique and romantic postmark. Visitors also enjoy coming here to gab with the locals and pick up travel tips.

Wahkeena Falls (Mile 17.4)

The name means "most beautiful," and this 242-foot series of cascades that descends in staircase fashion to the parking lot is certainly a contender. To the right of the small footbridge abutting the road is a three-fifths-mile trailhead to upper Wahkeenah Falls. Follow this largely paved trail to a bench just beyond the falls that affords views of both upper and lower cascades. Higher up are panoramic vistas of the Columbia River and Gorge and the ridgeline pathway connecting Wahkeenah to Multnomah. This trail is especially striking in October, when the cottonwoods and the bigleaf and vine maples sport colorful fall foliage.

A picnic area is north of the Historic Highway across from the falls. At this writing, the wooden staircase to the Perdition trail, a spur trail to high elevations, had not been replaced after earlier fires and mudslides.

Multnomah Falls (Mile 18)

At 620 feet, Multnomah is the second-highest continuously running waterfall in the country. This huge cascade pours down from the heights with an authority worthy of the prominent Native American chief for whom it is named.

The half-mile-long uphill trail to the bridge should be attempted by anyone capable of a small amount of exertion. Here you can bathe in the cool mists of the upper falls and appreciate the power of Multnomah's billowy flumes. The more intrepid can reach the top of the falls and beyond, but the view from the parking lot should be edifying. Placards detailing forest canopies and their understories at different elevations and other aspects of the ecosystem are on display in the first 100 yards of the trail. On the way up keep an eye out for such indigenous species as the Larch Mountain salamander and Howell's daisy. If you hear a whistle at higher elevations, it might be a pika.

Look for the image of an Native American woman's face on the rock behind the falls. Legend (disavowed by Native American sources) has it that she threw herself over the falls as a sacrifice to head off an epidemic. Now when the breeze blows through the water, a silvery stream separates from the upper falls, framing the maiden's form as a token of the spirits' acceptance of her gesture. While some of the falls in the surrounding area emanate from creeks fed by melting snows on Larch Mountain, Multnomah is primarily spring-fed, enabling it to run year-round. Between one and two million visitors yearly make Multnomah Falls the most visited natural attraction in the state.

The falls area also has a snack bar as well as **Multnomah Falls Lodge** (503/695-2376, www .multnomahfallslodge.com). A magnificent structure, the lodge was built eight decades ago and is today operated by a private concessionaire under the supervision of the National Forest Service. The day lodge is open daily 8 A.M.– 9 p.m. and has an on-site restaurant but no overnight accommodations. In 1915 Simon Benson bought much of the area around Multnomah and Wahkeenah Falls from the Union Pacific railroad and donated it to Portland City Parks. Today both falls are managed by the National Forest Service.

OUTDOOR RECREATION

Hiking

There are many wonderful hikes along the Historic Highway. In addition to those described below, check out the National Forest Service's **Short Hiking Loops** map, available free at the Multnomah Falls Visitor Center.

Up from the Ashes—Angel's Rest Hike

In early October 1991, massive fires engulfed portions of the Mount Hood National Forest off the Historic Highway. At the time, it was feared that massive erosion from the devastation of the trees and the understory would do in the network of trails in and around the route of the waterfalls. But, as you will see, this cloud had a silver lining.

For a good perspective on the fire as well as a great view of the gorge, Angel's Rest Trail #415 is recommended. To get there off I-84 take eastbound Exit 28 and follow the exit road a quarter mile to its junction with the Historic Highway. At this point hang a sharp right as if you were going to head up the hill toward Crown Point, but pull over into the parking area on the north side of the highway instead. The trailhead is on the south side of the road.

The steep 2.3-mile path to the top of this rocky outcropping gains 1,600 feet and takes you from an unburned forest through vigorous new brush growth beneath live evergreens with singed bark. The latter gives way to charred conifers as you near the summit. Scientists hope these snags and new openings in the forest can breed more biodiversity in the ecosystem. At any rate, the lack of foliage on the branches of burnt trees has opened new vistas of the Columbia Gorge below.

From the top you can enjoy a balcony-seat view overlooking the action. The stage in this case juts out over the Columbia River with sweeping views toward Portland; to the northeast the snowcapped carapace of the Washington Cascades plays peekaboo behind a series of smaller ridges.

Wahkeena-Multnomah Loop

This is a hike of about five miles with panoramic river views, perspectives on four waterfalls, and ancient forests.

To get to Wahkeena Falls, drive I-84 to Exit 28, Bridal Veil Falls. Several miles later you'll come to the falls parking area and trailhead. If you take the trail to the right of the bridge, in about a mile you'll come to Fairy Falls, so named for its ethereal quality. Just past Fairy Falls leave trail #420 for Vista Point Trail #419 to see panoramas from 1,600 feet above the river. There's also a revealing look at the singed trunks left over from the fires of October 1991. Old-growth Douglas fir ushers you through higher elevations on this trail.

Rejoin trail #420 a mile east of where #419 began. Once you get past the first 1.5 miles of this trail's initial steep ascent, the rest of the route is of moderate difficulty. As you begin your descent, you might become confused by a lack of signs at the junction of #420 and the Larch Mountain Trail. Hang a sharp left on #441 to head west and down along Multnomah Creek. At the rear of this gorge is pretty Ecola

Falls. There are several other cascades along the route.

When you hit the blacktopped section of #441, you can either hang a left to enjoy views from the top of the falls a short distance away or make a direct ascent. In any case, at the end of the hike, we recommend dinner at the Bridal Veil Lodge (see "Food," later in this section). After dinner, hike back on trail #442 above the Historic Highway (a.k.a. U.S. 30) to the Wahkeena Falls parking area.

Elowah Falls/McCord Creek Trails

To avoid the crowds while taking in spectacularly varied gorge landscapes, try Elowah Falls/Upper McCord Creek Trails.

From Portland, take I-84 past Multnomah Falls east to Exit 35, Ainsworth State Park. As you come off the access road you'll have a choice of left turns. Take Frontage Road with signs for Dodson. The latter may also be accessed by the Historic Highway after driving five miles east of Multnomah Falls. Drive about two miles to the small parking lot of John Yeon State Park, named for one of the major benefactors of the Columbia River Highway. In the western corner of the lot is the trailhead. Follow it a half mile up the hill. When you reach a junction of two trails, turn right for Upper McCord Creek and left for Elowah Falls.

The Upper McCord Creek trail leads to a mossy glade framing a creek at the top of a waterfall just under a mile from the junction. En route, the trail narrows to a ledge blasted out of a cliff. From behind a railing, gaze hundreds of feet down at the Columbia in the foreground of 12,306-foot Mount Adams. Across the gully, layered basalt strata indicate successive lava flows. This is a good place to look for osprey riding the thermals before they dive down to the Columbia for a fish. The trail continues to a view of dual cascades descending the rockface. These are the feeder streams of Elowah Falls. A short while later, recline on the shady banks of Upper McCord Creek.

Retrace your steps to where the trail forks and descend a half mile from the junction to Elowah Falls. This several-hundred-foot-high feathery cascade is set in a steep rock amphitheater amid hues of green that conjure the verdant lushness of Hawaii.

Swimming

Swimming at **Glen Otto Park** on the west side of the Sandy River Bridge can be precarious due to cold water and swift currents. In the last decade, more than a half-dozen drownings have occurred here. Look for lifeguards here in late spring through summer before diving in. The city government is contemplating requiring swimmers to wear lifejackets here.

Swimming is safe at historic and scenic **Rooster Rock State Park,** Exit 25 off of I-84 near Troutdale. A $3 parking charge is levied on each car. West of the parking area is the monolith for which the park is named. According to some sources, Lewis and Clark labeled the cucumber-shaped promontory on November 2, 1805. Playing fields and a gazebo front a sandy beach on the banks of the Columbia here. The water in the roped-in swimming area is shallow but refreshing. A mile or so east is one of the only nude beaches officially sanctioned by the state (the other one, near downtown Portland, is Collins Beach on Sauvie Island). Scenes from the 1994 movie *Maverick* starring Mel Gibson, Jody Foster, and James Garner were shot near here.

PRACTICALITIES

Accommodations

Motel 6 (1610 N.W. Frontage Rd., Troutdale, 503/665-2254) covers the basics with rooms around $40–60 (lower rates in winter). As you're easing onto the offramp of I-84's Exit 17, just look up to your right to find it. There is a pool and easy access to downtown Portland (15 miles west) and an outlet mall and fast food restaurants a mile or two east. Best of all, you're near the Troutdale access to the Historic Highway.

For a special escape we recommend **Bridal Veil Lodge** (P.O. Box 10, Bridal Veil, 503/695-2333, www.bridalveillodge.com). The lodge, across the road from Bridal Veil Falls State Park, is the last surviving accommodations from the "roadhouse" era on this part of the Historic Co-

lumbia River Highway; the knotty pine walls, antique quilts, and historic photos set the mood. Hospitality is second nature to the innkeepers, as their family has served travelers since 1926. You can stay in the main lodge where you share a bath down the hall or in the cottage rooms. The guest cottage boasts open-beam ceilings, sky windows, and private baths. This is a great place to stay with kids if you are visiting Portland because you're only a half-hour drive from the city but surrounded by the grandeur of the Gorge. Rooms run $85 double, breakfast included.

Imagine a 38-acre estate featuring a restaurant, hotel, brewery, winery and tasting room, movie theater, and golf course amid lavish gardens and artwork at every turn. That's **McMenamin's Edgefield** (2126 S.W. Halsey, Troutdale, 503/669-8610 or 800/669-8610, www.mcmenamins.com). Oregon's preeminent brewpubmeisters have transformed what had been the County Poor Farm and later a convalescent home into a good base from which to explore the Gorge or Portland. This is truly the best of the country near the best of the city. This range extends to lodging styles. You can choose between hotel rooms charmingly decorated with artwork and antiques for $85 (with shared bath) or for $125 (with private bath) or book a hostel bed for $20. Rates include a full breakfast in all rooms, except hostel.

Food

Tad's Chicken 'n' Dumplins (1325 E. Historic Columbia River Hwy., 503/666-5337) is one of the first places you'll pass after crossing the bridge to leave downtown Troutdale. Its classic weather-beaten roadhouse facade has graced this highway since the 1930s. If you decide to forego the restaurant's namesake dish, try the decent fried oysters, fried chicken, steak, or salmon. It's good ol' American food that'll taste even better with drinks on the porch overlooking the Sandy River. Dinner entrées run $11–22.

In Springdale, coffee and pastry at **Mom's Garden Bakery** (32030 Historic Columbia River Hwy., 503/695-3285) is highly recommended. Quiche of the day with soup and salad, breakfast specials, and turkey or roast beef sandwiches for lunch are supported by first-rate cinnamon buns and other home-baked goods and espresso. Inexpensive. Closed Sunday and Monday.

Service can be uneven at the dining room at **Multnomah Falls Lodge** (503/695-2376, www.multnomahfallslodge.com), but the food is surprisingly good when the kitchen isn't over-whelmed. A cheery solarium adjacent to the wood-and-stone dining room makes a casually elegant setting to begin or end a day of hik-ing. If it's cold, however, stay in the main din-ing room near the fireplace to enjoy the paintings and vintage photos of Columbia Gorge scenes. On warm days the outside patio is delightful and if you crane your neck you can see the falls. Particularly recommended is the mini loaf of home-baked wheat bread and

soup for lunch and the steak, seafood, and chicken main courses for dinner. To get there, take I-84 to Exit 28 (Bridal Veil exit) and con-tinue east for three more miles on Historic Co-lumbia River Highway.

Information and Services
The **Multnomah Falls Information Center** (P.O. Box 68, Bridal Veil 97019, 503/695-2372) has a ranger and volunteers on duty year-round to recommend campgrounds and hikes. Ask here about such nearby jaunts as Horsetail Falls, Triple Falls, and Oneonta Gorge (the lat-ter is where a stream cuts through nearly 200 feet of basalt a mile east of Multnomah Falls). Be sure to request the *Short Hiking Loops Near Multnomah Falls* map for a visual depiction of this network of trails. The center is open daily 9 P.M.–5 P.M.

Cascade Locks

The sleepy appearance of modern-day Cascade Locks belies its historical significance. The town is perched on a small bluff between the river and I-84, and its services and creature comforts are mostly confined to its main drag, Wa-Na-Pa Street. Before the shipping locks that inspired the burg's utilitarian name were constructed in 1896 to help steamboats navigate around haz-ardous rapids, most boats had to be portaged overland.

Two events that took place outside the city limits, however, gained the town a permanent place in history books. The first of these claims to fame may not have existed at all, but many rep-utable scientists now believe that an ancient nat-ural bridge once spanned the Columbia's mile-wide channel. According to native oral histories, this formation was destroyed by lava flows from the eruption of two nearby volcanoes. What are believed to be geologic remnants of this event lie just upstream from a modern structure called the Bridge of the Gods in honor of the Native Amer-ican landmark. The span was raised in 1938 to compensate for a heightened river level due to the Bonneville Dam.

The second event, the construction of the Bonneville Dam in the late '30s, inaugurated boom times in the area. The dam created 48-mile Lake Bonneville, which submerged the ship-ping locks. Today you can see Native American dip-net fishermen by the 1896 locks site in the town's riverfront Marine Park. Look for natives selling whole fresh salmon and other species late August into September, weekends 10 A.M. to dusk. Bring waxed paper and or a cooler with ice to help the fish keep till you're back in camp. Call 888/BUY-1855 for more information. Sales are cash only.

Boom times are gone now, but this little town with a dazzling river view and down-to-earth people is a refreshing change of pace from the big city to the west and the burgeoning tourist scene to the east. Reasonably priced food and lodging, a historical museum, the Bonneville Dam, and sternwheeler tours together with su-perlative hiking trails nearby also make for a nice stopover, as long as you don't come during winter. Most of the 75-inch annual precipitation falls at that time, along with ice storms and gale-force winds. Two funnel clouds were even

CASCADE LOCKS

Columbia River

WASHINGTON
OREGON

Thunder Island

(14)

CASCADE LOCKS
MARINE PARK ★ ★

CASCADE LOCKS
HISTORICAL MUSEUM ★

UNION PACIFIC R.R.

Dry Creek

FOREST LN.

KOA
KAMPGROUND

BRIDGE OF THE GODS
(TOLL)

BEST WESTERN
COLUMBIA
RIVER INN

EAST WIND
ICE CREAM ▾

POST OFFICE

REGULATOR ST.

ONEONTA ST.

WA-NA-PA ST.

(30)

84

CHARBURGER
(30)

WASCO ST.

VENTURE ST.

CASCADE INN/
SCANDINAVIAN MOTOR
LODGE

0   0.25 mi

0   0.25 km

© AVALON TRAVEL PUBLISHING, INC.

sighted outside of town during the Columbus Day storm of 1962.

Such violent weather has its benefits, however. The rains fostered the growth of massive Douglas fir trees near here that fed the once-thriving timber industry. Nowadays, the winds account for the Columbia Gorge's status as the windsurfing capital of the world, and the tourist economy's ripple effects are starting to be felt in Cascade Locks.

SIGHTS

Bonneville Dam

The Bonneville Dam (write: Public Information, U.S. Army Corps of Engineers, P.O. Box 2946, Portland 97208) can be reached via Exit 40 off I-84. The signs lead you under the interstate through a tunnel to the site of the complex, Bradford Island. En route to the visitors center you drive over a retractable bridge above the modern shipping locks. On the other side are the powerhouse and turbine room. Downriver is the second-largest exposed monolith in the world (Gibraltar is first). This 848-foot lava promontory abutting the shoreline is known as **Beacon Rock,** a moniker bestowed by Lewis and Clark.

Beyond the generating facilities is a bridge, underneath which is the fish-diversion canal. These fish-ways cause back eddies and guide the salmon, shad, steelhead, and other species past turbine blades. You'll want to stop for a brief

look at the spillways of the 500-foot-wide Bonneville Dam, especially if they're open.

While Bonneville isn't anywhere near the largest or the most powerful dam on the river, it was the first project on the leading hydroelectric waterway in the world. Along with its potential for generating 40 percent of America's power needs, the Columbia's storage of irrigation water and its dam-related recreation sites make the river the most valuable resource in the Northwest—too valuable to be diverted for drinking water in Southern California, despite pleas from Los Angeles politicians. In 2001, however, Bonneville power helped forestall rolling blackouts in parts of Northern California.

Benefits notwithstanding, the downside of damming is graphically illustrated by the sight of Native American fishermen enacting a weary

Bonneville Dam

pantomime of their forefathers by the Bonneville spillways. The **visitor center** (503/374-8820) is open 9 A.M.–5 P.M. year-round. Ask the Army Corps of Engineers personnel at the reception desk about tours of the power-generating facilities and about public campgrounds, boat ramps, swimming, and picnic areas.

The reception area has exhibits on dam operations, pioneer and navigation history on the Columbia, and fish migration. A long elevator ride takes you down to the fish-viewing windows, where the sight of lamprey eels—which accompany the mid-May and mid-September salmon runs—and the fish-counting procedures are particularly fascinating. The fish-counting practice helps determine catch limits on the popular species. Outside the facility there's access to an overlook above the fish ladders. A walkway back to the parking lot is decorated with gorgeous roses from spring into fall.

Retrace your route back to the mainland from Bradford Island and turn right, following the signs to the **fish hatchery.** This facility is open daily 7:30 A.M.–5 P.M. Visit during spawning season (May and September) to see the salmon make their way upriver. At this time, head to the west end of the hatchery, where steps lead down to a series of canals and holding pens. So great is the zeal of these fish to spawn that they occasionally leap more than a foot out of the water.

Inside the building you can see the beginnings of a process that produces the largest number of salmon fry in the state. Here fish culturists sort the fish and extract the bright red salmon roe from the females. These eggs are taken to the windowed incubation building, where you can view trays holding millions of eggs that will eventually hatch into salmon. Once these fry grow into fingerlings, they are moved to outdoor pools where they live until being released into the Columbia River by way of the Tanner Creek canal. The whole process is annotated by placards above the windows inside the incubation building.

The salmon and trout ponds and the floral displays are worth your attention at certain times of the year, but the sturgeon pools to the rear of the visitors center are always something to see.

SINGING ABOUT THE GORGE

Woody Guthrie penned no fewer than 26 tunes here during the spring of 1941. The federal government hired the singer (for $266.60) to write songs to help sell the public on the Bonneville Dam's goal of harnessing the river for irrigation, flood control, and cheap electricity. Out of this effort came such standards as "Roll on Columbia" ("your power is turning our darkness to dawn") and "Pastures of Plenty." Guthrie's signature themes of social justice and environmental grandeur are an enduring legacy that adds to the mythic quality of the Columbia River Gorge.

Bonneville is the nation's only white sturgeon hatchery and the government has made this facility user-friendly. In addition to the pool housing several sturgeon, the glass-enclosed home of "Herman the Sturgeon" offers a window on a 60-year-old eight-foot-long 500-pound fish. Along with this exceptional visual perspective, statistics on size, age, and habits of sturgeon as well as on the evolution of the Columbia's sturgeon fishery are provided.

Biologists say the Columbia River white sturgeon, with bony plates instead of scales, has remained unchanged for 200 million years. Despite being the largest freshwater species in North America, this river-bottom scavenger was largely ignored until the gourmet feeding frenzy of the last two decades put a premium on domestic sources of caviar. When *New York Times* food columnist Craig Claiborne pronounced the Columbia's product superior to that of the Caspian Sea several decades ago, its notoriety was established and catch limits were brought back. The Bonneville Dam visitors center and fish hatchery are both free of charge.

Cascade Locks Marine Park

Down by the river is the Cascade Locks Marine Park (Exit 44 off I-84 East). Look for it on your left going east on Wa-Na-Pa Street; just follow the signs. Here the sternwheeler *Columbia Gorge* (reservations: 541/374-8427 or 800/643-1354, www.sternwheeler.com) makes it possible to ride up the river in the style of a century ago. River legends and scenic splendor accompany you on a two-hour narrated cruise. There are several interesting packages of varying themes and duration. This 145-foot, 330-ton replica carries 599 passengers on three decks. The two-hour sightseeing cruise times vary; ask the sales department for schedules. The fare is $15 per person. An outdoor deck, an inside galley (brunch cruises offered), and competent narration have made these trips popular for years. Dinner and brunch cruises are also available on weekends.

Port of Cascade Locks (541/374-8619, www.portofcascadelocks.org) also houses the ticket office as well as an information center and gift shop, which sells an excellent local hiking trails map. Historical photos of early sternwheelers and $1 showers for hikers also make this facility particularly worthwhile.

About a quarter mile west of the visitors center, **Cascade Locks Historical Museum** (P.O. Box 307, Cascade Locks 97014, 503/374-8535) is housed in an old lockkeeper's residence and exhibits Native American artifacts and pioneer memorabilia. Information about the fish wheel, a paddlewheel-like contraption that conveyor-belted salmon out of the river and into a pen is especially fascinating. This diabolical device was perfected in Oregon in the early 20th century and was so successful at denuding the Columbia of fish that it was outlawed. The museum is open seven days a week May–September. Outside the museum is the diminutive Oregon Pony, the first steam locomotive on the Pacific coast. Its maiden voyage dates back to 1862 when it replaced the 4.5-mile portage with a rail route around the Cascades.

Take a walk over to the old locks. Begun in 1878 to circumnavigate the steep gradient of the river, they were completed in 1896. By the time the Cascade shipping locks were completed, however, river traffic had unfortunately decreased due to cargo being sent by train, so the effects of altering the river flow here were negligible.

HIKING

The following hikes require a Northwest Forest Pass or day pass (see "User Fees and Passes" in the On the Road chapter).

Wahclella Falls and Old Highway Hiker-Biker Trail

The best short hike in the Gorge that doesn't involve significant elevation gain is the walk along Tanner Creek to Wahclella Falls. After a mile of walking you've reached the terminus of the canyon framing the creek. En route, the gently hilly pathway shows off this pretty steep-walled arroyo to great advantage, but the destination is better than the journey.

In a scene evocative of a Japanese brush stroke painting, a waterfall pours down dramatically at canyon's end, seen to best advantage from a bridge over the creek. While the trail on the other side of the river is worthwhile, it doesn't loop all the way back to the parking lot so you'll have to retrace your steps. From I-84 eastbound, reach the trailhead by taking the Bonneville Dam Exit (Exit 40) and making a right at the bottom of the exit ramp into a small parking lot (instead of a left under the tunnel to Bonneville Dam).

From this same parking lot you may access a resuscitated portion of the Columbia River Highway by heading east. However, with lanes barely wide enough to accommodate a golf cart you'll have to leave the car behind. The state decided to re-pave this section of the old road for hikers and bikers, recreating the arched guardrails, bridges, viaducts, and tunnels between here and Cascades Locks to join the surviving ones. In addition to the ornate stonework, the curving, undulating roadbed blasted out of the mountainside before 1920 offers unsurpassed views.

While the Historic Highway parallels the interstate, its elevated perspective on the river and surrounding architectural artistry are a refreshing change of pace from the modern thoroughfare. The highlight of the route is a reproduction of the Toothrock Viaduct annotated by plaques and heritage markers. After exiting this section of the highway via a stairway into the parking lot of the Eagle Creek Fish Hatchery, head east a short distance to the second leg of this hiker-biker trail. The Eagle Creek–to–Cascades Lock section is highlighted by a pretty waterfall at the beginning and a well-rendered tunnel near the end. The distance between Bonneville and Cascades Locks is around four miles.

Eagle Creek Trail

Because the Eagle Creek Trail is highly recommended by a lot of people, try to avoid peak-use times such as summer weekends. This trail begins at Eagle Creek Campground (see "Camping" below) and goes 14 miles to Wahtum Lake, where it intersects the Pacific Crest Trail. Along the trail are seven waterfalls, one of which features a perspective from behind the cascade itself.

Ideally, this is a two-day backpacking trip, but if you prefer a day-trip, consider Eagle Creek Trail #440 about two miles to Punchbowl Falls. It can be reached from the Eagle Creek Campground via Exit 41 off I-84. Fifteen minutes west of this exit is Exit 44 for Cascade Locks. The four-mile round-trip to the falls is an easy hike. If you can, come in February when tourists are scarce and stream flow is high.

From Punchbowl Falls continue 1.5 miles to High Bridge. Tall trees, spring wildflowers, basalt outcroppings, and nice views into Eagle Creek's white-water cleft make the journey almost as compelling as the destination. High Bridge is 80 feet above this particularly beautiful section of the creek. The trail continues on the other side of the Gorge several more miles to 100-foot-high Tunnel Falls, where you can walk through a tunnel behind the falls.

Wildflowers spring up in April and linger on into August in the higher elevations. To locate such Columbia Gorge endemics as Oregon fleabane and Howell's daisy, bring along Russ Jolley's *Wildflowers of the Columbia*. Many of these one-of-a-kinds are species left over from a previous glacial period that have adapted because of the shade and moisture on the south side of the Gorge. Almost two dozen varieties of fern, trillium, beargrass, yellow arnica, penstemon, monkeyflower, and devil's club are among the more common species here. This hike is 13

miles round-trip and is best undertaken on a weekday in spring to catch the blooms and avoid the crowds.

As a prelude to hiking Eagle Creek or one of several other trails in the area, you might want to wander an informative interpretive loop of less than a mile. Just cross the footbridge on the approach road to the Eagle Creek Trailhead over to the other side of the river. After crossing the bridge, follow the markers that describe the region's mixed-conifer forest at various elevations. At trail's end, you might want to take on the steep two-mile trail to Wauna Point. While this trail isn't as visually arresting as other area jaunts, the view of the Columbia River and Gorge at the summit makes the effort worthwhile.

CAMPING

There's no shortage of options for campers in this area. Keep in mind the western Gorge is Portland's backyard and can be very crowded, so avoid peak times whenever possible. In addition to first-come, first-served Ainsworth State Park (see "Camping" in the Portland chapter) several other sites are worth considering. These have been chosen on the basis of location (e.g., near attractions or a prime trailhead) or for special amenities.

While the **Eagle Creek Campground** (541/ 386-2333) can be noisy and crowded, it's an ideal base camp for hiking as it's close to several trailheads. Reservations are accepted only for groups at this, the first campground ever created by the National Forest Service, in the 1930s. There are sites for tents and RVs up to 22 feet long, with picnic tables, fire grills, flush toilets, and sanitary services available. It's located between Bonneville Dam and Cascade Locks off I-84 and is open mid-May to October. The fee is $10. At the seven-mile point of the Eagle Creek Trail (see "Hiking," earlier in this section), there's a primitive free campground, but it fills up on summer weekends.

Herman Horse Camp (541/386-2333) is a half mile east of Cascade Locks, near the Pacific Crest Trail, and a half mile from Herman Creek. A full array of services including a laundry, a store, a café, and showers are within two miles, supplementing the seven tent and RV sites. Piped water, fire grills, picnic tables, and stock-handling facilities are also welcome additions here. It's open mid-May to October, with no reservations and a fee of $8. There are trails here for hiking and horse-packing. Other attractions include the historic Forest Work Center and nearby rock walls, where visitors can admire the handiwork of the Civilian Conservation Corps. There's also a trail leading to Wyeth Campground, a favorite of sailboarders.

Cascade Locks Marine Park (P.O. Box 307, Cascade Locks 97014, 541/374-8619, www .sternwheeler.com) has campsites close to the center of town. The museum and the sternwheeler are housed in the complex. Whatever amenities are not available on site are within walking distance. It's open all year and the fee is $15. No reservations.

Finally, two miles east of town near the banks of the Columbia is the Cascade Locks **KOA Kampground** (841 N.W. Forest Ln., Cascade Locks 97014, information 541/374-8668, reservations 800/KOA-8698). Open February–November 30, this private campground features the basics plus a spa (hot tub/sauna), hot showers, and a heated swimming pool for $20 per tent site, $24–28 for RVs, and $3 each extra person. Kamping Kabins—one room (queen bed and a bunk bed) or two room (queen bed and two sets of bunks)—rent for $40 and $48 per night, respectively (bring your own linens, pillows, towels, sleeping bag, etc.). Kabins fill up quickly, especially on weekends, so reserve well in advance. To get there, take U.S. 30 east from town, and turn left onto Forest Lane. Proceed 1.2 miles down and you'll see the Kampground on the left.

EVENTS

The last weekend in June, the sternwheeler *Columbia Gorge* is welcomed back to Cascade Locks. Free rides on the boat, dozens of food and craft booths, a salmon bake, and races bring out the community in force.

July Fourth fireworks here are ranked among the state's best displays. The multicolored explosions are set off on Thunder Island below the Bridge of the Gods over the Columbia River. Watch from the city park where the Volunteer Fire Department puts on a high-quality salmon bake.

Better yet, book **Cascade Sternwheeler**'s package (including dinner) to take in the fireworks from aboard the riverboat. A DJ spins tasteful renditions of patriotic songs amid the rockets' red glare. For reservations, further information, or for help in creating your own special event, contact them at 800/643-1354 or check their website at www.sternwheeler.com.

PRACTICALITIES
Accommodations
This town of 1,095 people features several inexpensive motels but with camping and numerous lodging alternatives close by, let's focus on a place that shows off the river.

If the best view of the Columbia from a hotel room is important to you, then you'll pay $79–139, $64–120 in winter, at the **Best Western Columbia River Inn** (735 Wa-Na-Pa St., 541/374-8777 or 800/595-7108, www.cascadelocks.net/services). Don't worry about train noise here thanks to effective soundproofing of the hotel walls. Some high-end rooms have hot tubs and all rooms have microwaves and refrigerators. Many rooms also have balconies. You can get a "mountain view" room for $79 in summer, but that would be tantamount to being in Bordeaux and forgoing the wine. In addition to views, there's a health club with a whirlpool, pool, and exercise facilities. With the Charburger next door and the Marine Park down the street, this property has an excellent location.

Food
Forget health food and haute cuisine until you get to Hood River. In Cascade Locks, you get down-home country cookin'—and lots of it—at a decent price.

The **Charburger** (745 Wa-Na-Pa St., 541/ 374-8477) is near the Bridge of the Gods at the beginning of town. This is a great place if you're on the go and don't want to spend a fortune for a quick bite. In addition to an extensive salad bar and a bakery, there is a cafeteria line specializing in "home-baked" (and it tastes that way) chicken, omelettes cooked to order, and other wholesome but unexotic dishes at low prices.

East Wind Ice Cream (located between the Charburger and Marine Park) is a traditional stop for families on a Columbia River Gorge Sunday drive.

The **Salmon Row Pub** (corner of Wa-Na-Pa and Regulator Streets, 541/374-8511) is a small dark brewpub whose smoked salmon chowder, pizza, and sandwiches fill you up on the cheap.

Information and Services

In addition to the Marine Park Visitors Center, the **Port of Cascade Locks Tourism Committee** (P.O. Box 355, Cascade Locks 97014, 541/374-8619) can provide help. The **state police** can be reached at 800/452-8573.

Hood River

In the past, Hood River was known to the traveling public primarily as the start of a scenic drive through the orchard country beneath the snowcapped backdrop of Mount Hood, Oregon's highest peak. Since the early '80s, however, well-heeled adherents of windsurfing have transformed this town into an outdoor recreation mecca. Instead of just the traditional dependence on cherries, apples, peaches, and pears, Hood River now rakes in tens of millions of dollars annually from the presence of "boardheads."

The fury of the winds derives from the heat of the eastern desert drawing in the Pacific westerlies. The confining contours of the Gorge dam up these air masses and precipitate their gusty release. Many local business owners are familiar with the "20-knot clause," permitting their

workers time off to "catch a blow" when the winds are "nukin'" at this speed.

Bounded by picturesque orchard country and the Columbia River with the snowcapped volcanoes serving as distant backdrops, this town of 6,000 enjoys a magnificent setting. The main thoroughfare, Oak Street (which becomes Cascade Street as you head west) is set on a plateau between the riverfront marine park to the north and streets running up the Cascade foothills to the south. New brick facades dress up old storefronts, and casual attire and sandals predominate.

History

Dr. Herbert Krieger, curator of the Smithsonian Institution, came here in 1934 to excavate alongside a stream that once ran between 13th, Oak, and State Streets. Arrowheads and artifacts told of native presence here, but the discovery of 30 ash pits of the type found in Chinook tepees indicated that at one time there had been a village in the area of present-day downtown Hood River. Another dig in Mosier a few miles east of Hood River unearthed an ancient cemetery. Many coins of diverse origin were found here, probably taken by the natives in trade. The latter included Chinese coins, possibly from Warrendale cannery workers. There were also Roman coins and a token from the Northwest Fur Trading Company predating this enterprise's early 19th-century presence in Astoria. Finally, Russian flag standards also pointed to a rich legacy of Columbia River barter.

COURTESY OF LARRY GEDDIS/OREGON TOURISM COMMISSION

pear orchard near Hood River

COLUMBIA RIVER GORGE

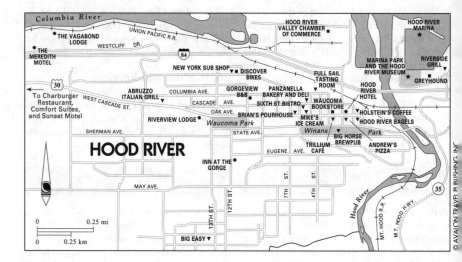

Pioneers began to build farms in the Hood River Valley after the land giveaways of the Donation Land Act of 1850. The rich volcanic soil, glacier water, and mild climate here provided an impetus for agriculture. In 1855 the Coe family came to establish the first post office and planted orchards in the area of present-day 11th and State streets. Five years later a sawmill was built in the Hood River Valley. At that time, the first census showed that only 70 people lived in the area. The region's first large-scale commercial orchard was established in 1876 specializing in Newtown pippin apples.

In the next decade, rail lines enabled strawberries from the area to gain renown in New York. Similar prominence was soon accorded Hood River pears and apples in other large cities. Pears took over the produce business when a killer frost devastated local apple orchards here in 1919 and the commercial strawberry crop here was wiped out forever by a fungus in the 1930s. Today, the valley is considered the U.S. leader in winter pears and ranks first in production of Anjou pears. Today 75 percent of the crop is devoted to pears, with apples, cherries, and peaches marketed in smaller quantities.

While the completion of the Columbia River Highway and the Columbia Gorge Hotel in the 1920s gave birth to tourism here, it wasn't until the early 1980s, when windsurfing became popular, that the leisure economy became a focal point of the local identity. On days when sailboarders can't "rig up," many take to the hills on mountain bikes or hit the slopes at nearby Mount Hood, enlarging the appeal of the town as a mecca for outdoor recreationists. By the spring of 1997 an estimated 35 companies with sailboarding ties—board and sail makers, designers of harnesses and clothing—made Hood River their base.

SIGHTS
Scenic Views
The scenic highlights of Hood River are the orchards during the end of the April Blossom Festival and the leaves during color season in October (See "Events," later in this section).

For a view of the Hood River Valley that does justice to these events, drive to the east end of town and turn right on ORE 35. Head south till you see the sign for Panorama Point. After a left turn, head south about a mile on East Side Road and make a left on a road that'll take you to the top of a knoll with views south and west that do justice to the name Panorama Point.

Vistas here afford a distant perspective on the orchards below Mount Hood that have forever served as a visual archetype of the Pacific Northwest.

As you gaze at this "America the Beautiful" postcard-come-to-life, try to imagine an ancestral Columbia River flowing south through the Hood River Valley passing under the site of what would become Mount Hood. Geologists tell us that this original channel of the river predated the formation of the Cascades. Tens of millions of years ago this waterway flowed down to the area of present-day Salem, then seacoast. In other incarnations, the scene before you was buried beneath glacial debris and volcanic ash that descended the slopes of Mount Hood. In short, it's important to realize that the present-day Hood River Valley is but an eye-blink in geologic time, and that the forces that created it are in temporary remission.

About 15 miles west of Hood River off I-84 is Mitchell Point Overlook, a bluff facing west over a large expanse of the Gorge. This area had been part of the old highway, famous for its tunnel of many vistas. While the tunnel is no more, the parking lot views here can be accessed from Hood River by going west on I-84 and departing the interstate via Exit 56 to loop back on I-84 eastbound a few miles.

Closer to town, another Gorge photo-op awaits at Ruthton Point, a small picnic area just off I-84 on Exit 62, Westcliff Drive. This area sits a few miles west of town, a half mile beyond the Columbia Gorge Hotel, on the river side of the westbound freeway. Across the river are views of Underwood Mountain, a one-time volcano now covered in orchards, vineyards, and expensive "view lots."

Downtown Sights

To learn the history of the region, drive back to the junction of State Street and ORE 35, then turn left (north) and cross I-84 toward the river. At the intersection turn left and follow the signs to Marina Park and the **Hood River Museum** (300 E. Port Marina Dr., 541/386-6772). To get there off I-84, take Exit 64 and follow the signs.

Exhibits trace life in the Hood River Valley from prehistoric times to the founding of the first pioneer settlement in 1854. Thereafter, the area's development as a renowned fruit-growing center is emphasized. Native American stone artifacts, beadwork and basketry, pioneer quilts, and a Victorian parlor set the time machine in motion. The contributions of the local Finnish and Japanese communities, along with World War I memorabilia, introduce the first half of the 20th century. Photos and implements related to fruit harvesting and packing methods round out the historical collections on the first floor. Antique logging equipment, dolls, and remnants of a presentation by local schoolchildren for the Lewis and Clark Exposition in 1905 are also on display.

The museum is open April–Aug. daily 10 A.M.– 4 P.M., Sunday noon–4 P.M.; Sept.–Oct. daily noon–4 P.M. Other months, it's open Monday and Tuesday by appointment. Admission is free but donations are appreciated.

Lovers of antiquity are advised to pick up the self-guided *Hood River Historic District Tour* pamphlet at the chamber of commerce (at the Hood River Expo Center, Portway Ave., 541/386-2000 or 800/366-3530). In addition to 19th-century pioneer homes, the tour includes a National Historic Landmark Train Station at the base of 13th Street.

The **International Museum of Carousel Art** (304 Oak St., 541/387-4622, www.carousel-museum.com) boasts the world's largest and most complete collection of antique carousel art. Most examples of this turn-of-century genre have been lost, taken out of circulation, or broken. A working carousel will soon be added to the biggest carousel tiger in the world and a functioning antique Wurlitzer organ. Hours are Saturday 10 A.M.–4 P.M., Sunday noon–4 P.M. April–October. Admission is $5 adults, $4 seniors, $3 children.

South of Town Sights

Driving south on ORE 35 to the Parkdale exits, be sure to visit the **Hutson Museum** (Parkdale, 541/352-6808). Native American artifacts, pioneer hand tools, and one of the better rock collections in the Northwest make it worthwhile. A nominal admission is charged. Afterward, take advantage of the nearby fruit stands between spring and fall. Here (or in town), you can also hop aboard the Mount Hood Railroad (see "Downtown Sights," immediately preceding).

Also near Parkdale is a series of **lava beds.** From ORE 35 south, go right at the Mount Hood Country Store on Baseline Road en route to Parkdale, then right on Lava Bed Drive. The beds are located a mile west of town. Surprisingly, this lava did not emanate from the slopes of the mountain. Instead it came from a vent more than three miles south and west of town. This flow is thought to be several thousand years old, a fraction of the 30-million-year-old volcanic legacy of the Gorge.

The 25-mile drive to **Lost Lake** begins on 13th Street, which changes names (ORE 281, Tucker Road, and Dee Highway) on its way up the flanks of Mount Hood. About 12 miles from downtown, take a right at the Dee Lumber Mill, where a green Lost Lake sign points the way. From here, bear left and follow the signs.

The lake offers hiking trails, fishing, rowboat rentals, and a small store. There are also campsites and cabins. The cabins range $45–100, with the high-end unit sleeping 6–8. Call 503/386-6366 at least two weeks in advance to reserve campsites and cabins. Come prepared; the closest fuel is in Parkdale.

Late August huckleberry season is a highlight here, but the weather and diminished crowds in September are preferable. In July and August, the rangers have campfire programs on Saturday night. The Lakeshore Trail features a .5-mile long boardwalk through an old-growth cedar grove. You'll enter the old-growth grove two miles into the trail, passing eight-foot thick cedars. Pick up a map with natural history captions that correspond to numbered posts along the route.

The best way to get up close and personal with Mount Hood is with a visit to **Cloud Cap.** There is a beautiful old lodge up here (which is closed) and the entrance to the Mount Hood Wilderness on the north side of the volcano. To get there take ORE 35 24 miles south of Hood River to Cooper Spur Road. Drive past the ski area until you come to Cloud Cap at the end of a 10-mile twisting gravel road. The road is passable only in summer months due to snow at that altitude. From here, hardy adventurers can rub elbows with glaciers, walking up Cooper Spur (a side ridge of Mount Hood) without climbing gear in late summer, to almost 8,600 feet above sea level.

THE FRUIT LOOP

This 45-mile stretch of meandering highway and back roads directs area visitors to some of the richest farmland and most breathtaking scenery in the state—along the Hood River with Mount Hood the backdrop to it all. Vineyards, orchards, farm stands, and country stores dot the decade-old route that crisscrosses over the river, beckoning visitors to picnic, tour, or taste-test the fresh produce.

The route is popular year-round, but folks can sample some of the season's ripest pears, apples, pumpkins, and gourds September–November; tomatoes, corn, peaches, and herbs abound in August and September; and farm-fresh berries and apricots ripen June–August. Bike trails follow the routes in some places. Contact the Hood River Chamber of Commerce (www.hoodriver.org) or consult www.hoodriver-fruitloop.com for the Fruit Loop map and a list of participating farms and country stores.

A few precautions: Parking can be a problem, so farmers ask that you not block other visitors' egress, driveways, or farm vehicles. Fortunately, parking lots usually afford ample space, as they can accommodate larger vehicles, buses, and RVs. Farmers and concessionaires also ask that you leave the family pooch at home as he or she may disturb resident pets or farm animals.

Rowena Crest

The highlight of the continuation of the Historic Columbia River Highway is Rowena Crest. You can get there by heading east on I-84 from Hood River several miles, exiting the freeway at Exit 69, and following directions given under "By Bike," earlier in this chapter.

Rowena Crest, on the Historic Columbia River Gorge Highway west of The Dalles

Almost nowhere else can you see both the dry eastern and wetter western faces of the Columbia River Gorge with such clarity and distinction. The dark Columbia River basalt cliffs are derived from massive lava flows 15 million years ago. The terracing of the region was due to the action of the Missoula Floods upon Columbia Plateau fault scarps. More information on the geology and ecosystem is available from a free pamphlet in the drop box on the north side of the highway, courtesy of the **Tom McCall Nature Preserve.** This 2,300-acre sanctuary on part of Rowena Crest was created by the Nature Conservancy and has trails on the hillsides that are open to the public.

These cliffs represented the beginning of the last hurdle facing Willamette Valley–bound Oregon Trail pioneers. After Rowena, the Gorge cliffs rose up so high that the pioneers were forced to either build rafts and float the then-hazardous rapids on the river, or to follow the Barlow Trail around the south flank of Mount Hood.

Today, Tom McCall Nature Preserve is the site of a mid-May pilgrimage by wildflower lovers. Because the preserve lies in the transition zone between the wet west and the dry east, four endemics and several hundred species flourish here. Included in the spring display are yellow wild sunflowers, purple blooms of shooting stars, scarlet Indian paintbrush, and blue-flowered camas. While the flowers are enticing, be careful of ticks and poison oak. And of course, as with any nature preserve or public park, love the flowers but leave them behind for the next person to enjoy.

ACTIVITIES AND RECREATION
Windsurfing

No serious discussion of important windsurfing locales can avoid acknowledging the Columbia Gorge's reigning status as a world capital of the sport. Hood River is *the* center of the windsurfing scene in terms of sailing sites, related businesses, and the sport's unique subculture. In fact, the meteoric rise of windsurfing in the early and mid-1980s transformed this formerly sleepy rural community into a vibrant, hipster-jock haven. It catapulted Hood River onto the international scene, as evidenced by the whimsical bumper stickers around town bearing the legend "Paris, Tokyo, Rome, Hood River." Blessed by a propitious mix of geography, climate, and river currents, the Gorge was discovered as a place with strong, very reliable summer westerlies (winds going west to east), countered by the strong, westbound Columbia River current.

Actually, three of the top-rated sites for advanced sailors (and for fans) are actually located in Washington. Doug's Beach, the Hatchery, and Swell City are just across the Hood River Bridge.

Three distinct windsurf beaches are within the Hood River city limits. The **Hood River Marina Sailpark** is the largest and most developed of the three. The Port of Hood River has completed a series of improvements such that the site has more amenities than any other windsurf launch in the Gorge. These include bathrooms with showers, food concessions, picnic area, grassy lawn for rigging, an exercise course, and a great family swimming beach area with sheltered, shallow water for tykes. And, as the name implies, you'll find the largest boat marina with boat launches here. Beware of shallow

sandbars off the shore, and the boats entering and exiting the marina. Due to the offerings here (including ample, close-by parking), this can be one of the most crowded sites around.

The well-known **Rhonda Smith Windsurfing School** (541/386-9463) offers rentals for $25 for half day, $30–40 for a full day, and $150–200 per week, depending on the equipment and location. Lessons, including equipment, start at $20 per hour. A private launch area and rescue service round out the package. To get there, take Exit 64 off I-84, then follow the signs to the Marina.

The **Event Site,** a newer and somewhat smaller site, is located to the west of the Hood River's confluence with the Columbia. Major events, including well-known competitions, occur here. It has a lawn for rigging and a small bleacher for spectators. This, plus its convenient location to downtown, make this an ideal spot for spectators. It provides quicker access to deeper water than the Marina, but it can also be quite crowded at times. Chemical toilets and water are available on site. The Event Site is located off Exit 63, or at the north end of Second Street.

Several windsurfing schools (listed below) located in The Hook, named for the shape of the artificial berm built some years back to create a protected harbor, provide instruction in the gentle basin, an ideal location for beginners; once you're out in the main channel, winds can be strong. Other than chemical toilets, amenities are scarce in this area. Instead of a beach, the shore is largely steep and rocky, and the dirt road in later summer can get a bit dusty. Conditions are quite variable, particularly as some places are in a wind shadow caused by nearby Wells Island, a sensitive wildlife area vulnerable to prolonged human exposure. The views to the west (and hence, the sunsets) are just grand.

Access to the Hook is at the west end of Portway, the paved road that first takes you to the Event Site. All three in-town sites charge a day-use fee. Call the Port of Hood River (541/386-1645) for more info.

About eight miles west of town, **Viento State Park** offers good river access for sailing in a beautiful, natural setting. The park has a campground, picnic area, restrooms, and water. Spectators won't have a lot of room, but the wind and wave action can get spicy here. Viento is served by Exit 56 off I-84.

In the opposite direction, six miles east of Hood River, you'll find the **Rock Creek** launch site in Mosier. Amenities are sparse, but include chemical toilets. The river is wide here, and the chop can get high. You can reach Rock Creek off I-84, Exit 69. At the top of the ramp, hang a right, then your first left on Rock Creek Road. The site's on your right just past the dry creekbed.

For information about windsurfing, wind, and weather, call 541/387-WIND (-9463) or pick up a copy of *Northwest Sailboard* (P.O. Box 918, Hood River 97031), available all over town.

The following schools in Hood River cater to beginners: **Big Winds** (541/386-6088); **Front St. Sailboards** (541/386-40440; **Gorge Surf Club** (541/386-5434); and **Hood River Windsurfing** (541/386-5787). Most of these academies of aerodynamics offer lessons through mid-October.

Regarding fall windsurfing, adepts will tell you it's the best. It's less crowded, the water's warm, and winds are lighter at school sites. It easier to find parking and rigging space at launching areas, and there's a quality of light upon the water with enough clear days to add aesthetic appeal. Best of all for beginners is the availability of individualized instruction during fall. While conditions are generally good at most locations along the river during the season, the best places are said to be in the east end of the gorge, notably around Three Mile Canyon and other launch sites in the Arlington, Oregon, and Roosevelt, Washington, areas.

Other Water Sports

The **Hood River Marina** offers an excellent family swim area and boat marina, and also has personal watercraft rentals. **The Hook** offers a nice area (when the winds and windsurfers are absent) for some gentle canoeing or kayaking. (For information on both, see "Windsurfing," immediately preceding).

Koberg Beach State Park, one mile east of

town off I-84, but accessible from westbound lanes only, offers a sandy swim beach in a pretty setting. Be warned, however, the drop-off is steep and not safe for little kids or weak swimmers.

Fishing

The area offers two different types of fishing. You can go for trout in several beautiful small mountain lakes, most of which are west and south of the Hood River Valley. Notable among the latter are Wahtum, Rainy, and North Lakes, all about 45 minutes west of town on good gravel roads. Then too, there is the previously detailed Lost Lake, whose heavy visitation might detract from its desirability during some seasons. Pick up licenses in any Hood River sport shop.

The other option is fishing the Hood River itself, or the Columbia. The former has good trout fishing and both of them have good seasonal steelhead/salmon fishing. The Hood River can be accessed from the county parks covered under "Camping," later in this section. Call the **Gorge Fly Shop** (541/386-6977) for information. For a guide, call **Gorge Flyfishing Expeditions** (541/354-2286). **Phoenix Pharms** (just off ORE 35, 10 miles south of town, 541/386-7770) is a stocked rainbow trout pond where the kids are guaranteed to reel in a big one.

Golf

Two courses are in the area. Offering great views of Mount Hood is the relatively new and popular **Indian Creek Country Club** (3605 Brookside Dr., 541/386-3009). A little farther from town is **Hood River Golf** (1850 Country Club Rd., Hood River, 541/386-3009). It has nine holes (a bit hillier than Indian Creek) and beautiful views of Mount Hood, Mount Adams, elk, and geese. It's open daylight to dark. Come in fall if only to see the spectacular foliage.

Wine-Tasting

Tasting and tours are offered at the **Hood River Vineyard** (4693 Westwood Dr., Hood River 97031, 541/386-7772), open 11 A.M.–5 P.M. daily. The microclimate here is similar to that which produces Germany's Rhine wines. In addition to the Rieslings, chardonnays, Gewürz-traminers, and other white-wine varietals produced here, the area is famous for fruit wines and award-winning pinot noir. Sweet wines, such as Anjou pear, marionberry, and zinfandel are done with great flair.

The cabernet sauvignon from **Flerchinger Vineyard** (4200 Post Canyon Dr., 800/516-8710) took "best of show" at the prestigious Newport Seafood and Wine competition. The winery also produces chardonnay, Riesling, and merlot. Open daily 11 A.M.–5 P.M. Flerchinger Vineyard is a little tricky to find. As for Hood River Vineyard, take Exit 62. Turn right on Country Club Road, which heads west for a brief time right after exiting the freeway. A left onto Post Canyon Drive takes you south to the winery.

Art

The **Columbia Art Gallery** (207 2nd St., 541/386-4512) features works by local artists in exhibits that change monthly. This community-sponsored nonprofit gallery is open Fri.–Mon. noon–5P.M. and weekdays 10 A.M.–5 P.M.

Rail Tours

Train buffs will be delighted to ride the **Mount Hood Railroad** (541/386-3556 or 800/872-4661, www.mthoodrr.com), which goes from the old railroad depot behind the Hood River Hotel (see "Accommodations," later in this section) through the scenic Hood River Valley to its terminus in Parkdale, seemingly at the very base of Mount Hood, due to the volcano's immensity and proximity. Riders sit in a lovingly restored enclosed Pullman coach. Also featured are an antique concession car and, of course, the obligatory red caboose. The standard ride takes about four hours round-trip, including a stop in Parkdale. The railroad also features dinner and brunch trains, and many special event rides, such as the Fruit Blossom Special in April and Christmas Tree Trains, bedecked with carolers and other holiday trimmings. The main season is April–October. Fares for the regular excursion train are $23, with a discount for seniors and $15 for kids under 12.

Air Tours

Scenic Flights Northwest (541/386-1099) offers a 45-minute Gorge flyover for $45 per person. **Air Columbia** (541/490-1779) offers helicopter flights during the Blossom Festival and by appointment. These tours require a two-person minimum and $125 for a 55-minute trip to Beacon Rock and Portland Airport or Mount Hood and Timberline Lodge. For more information on scenic flights, call the Port of Hood River (they operate the airport) at 541/386-1645.

Skiing

Off ORE 35 on the east side of Mount Hood is **Cooper Spur** (541/352-7803). Day and night skiing and cross-country skiing are offered. Low prices ($8–12) and a laid-back atmosphere make this place a favorite with families and beginners. For more on Mount Hood skiing and info on cross-country skiing, see "Skiing in the Cascades" in the Cascades chapter.

Historic Columbia River Highway Trail

This five-mile long segment of the **Historic Columbia River Highway** is a must-see. It provides a great walking and biking experience (car traffic is verboten), with the spectacular engineering feat of the re-opened **Mosier Twin Tunnels** in the middle. Carved out of solid basalt and adorned with artful masonry work, the highway has become famous for the tunnels. They are about a mile from the trail's east end and 600 feet above the river. To start on the east end, take Exit 69 off I-84, turn right off the ramp, then take your first left on Rock Creek Road. Go under the railroad and continue for less than a mile. The parking area is on your left; the highway segment begins across the road.

This segment of the old road was closed in 1953, after years of serious rockfall problems at the tunnel's west portal and the construction of the river grade highway. The State of Oregon has constructed a special rockfall shelter to protect recreationists from the hazard. The trail also features restored original stone masonry work in several places, besides the tunnels. The trailhead parking areas on either end are both called the Mark O. Hatfield Trailhead, just east and west versions. This reflects the instrumental role the influential ex-Senator had in securing federal funding to make this dream a reality.

Access to the west-side parking area is gained from downtown Hood River by going to the State Street and ORE 35 junction, then heading up the hill on Old Columbia River Drive. This road actually is the Historic Columbia River Highway (officially numbered as U.S. 30). The west end has a small visitor contact/information building, with restrooms.

Going west to east lets a hiker, in a mere five miles, witness a rapid climate/vegetation transition zone rarely encountered in such a short distance. Starting on the Hood River side, the highway winds its way through lush, towering Douglas fir groves. By the time you reach the east side of the tunnels by Mosier, you're in a dry oak savannah-grassland ecosystem.

About halfway down the trail, a short interpretive loop trail has been developed, rewarding hikers with stunning views of this varied and beautiful piece of the Gorge. Also, rockhounds will marvel at the dramatic precipice located across the river in Washington, visible from the east end. Locally called "Coyote Wall" it's technically part of a big syncline/anticline system in the area.

Hiking and Mountain Biking in the Gorge

While the most famous Gorge hikes tend to cluster around the west end waterfall area, the Hood River environs has its fair share of great trails for fat tires and two feet. Several of these trails are right on the Gorge, eight miles west of town, accessible via the Viento Park Exit off I-84 (Exit 56). All three are on the south side of the highway.

The **Starvation Creek to Viento Trail** is the shortest and by far the easiest of the three. Actually a restored segment of an abandoned segment of the Historic Columbia River Highway, this mostly paved path runs a little over a mile each way. It offers some decent Gorge views but will be of more interest to history buffs who want to retrace extant remnants of the old highway. This trail also provides access to the other two trails in the area.

Both the **Mount Defiance Trail** (Trail 413) and **Starvation Ridge Trail** (Trail 414) used to be accessible through the Starvation Creek rest stop exit of the highway, which is now closed. So walk the Starvation to Viento Trail, then look for signs for either of the other trails once you get to the west side of the rest stop. Both trails eventually head for the same place, converging high above the Gorge just below the top of Mount Defiance. Being the highest point on the Gorge proper at 4,960 feet, Mount Defiance presents a strenuous workout for anyone up for the challenge.

Either route rewards you with spectacular views of the Gorge, as well as old-growth woods and pristine Warren Lake. The Starvation Ridge is somewhat steeper than the Mount Defiance Trail. This long loop is about 12 miles round-trip. A short, two-mile loop is also possible, by following Trail 413 for a mile, then heading east (left) onto Trail 414. This eventually takes you back to the highway where you started. These trails are really best for hikers only, due to steepness and narrowness.

The **Wygant Trail** is reached off the eastbound-only Exit 58 off I-84, at Mitchell Point. Go right (west) at the top of the ramp, then follow the road heading west. This eventually becomes the trail and follows the old route of the Historic Highway for a stretch. The trail eventually winds its way for almost four miles to the top of Wygant Peak, at 2,214 feet. Along the way, you'll pass through some native Oregon white oak groves, mixed conifer forests, and some openings with lovely views.

Just west of town there's a network of old gravel and dirt roads that local **mountain bikers** love. Post Canyon Road starts out as a typical paved rural road, with houses scattered along each side. Shortly after its start at Country Club Road, the pavement ends and the fat tire fun begins. Several side roads branch off from Post Canyon into the Cascade foothills. You can ride for a long time without seeing any buildings, but you will, no doubt, encounter some clear-cuts and other logged areas, so don't expect pristine forests. Also, be forewarned: the road is at times used by groups of motorbikers, so stay alert.

To get there, take Exit 62 off I-84, turn right at the top of the ramp, then take an immediate right onto Country Club Road. Follow this road about a mile as it bends to the south, then head right into the well-signed Post Canyon.

Mount Hood National Forest Trails

There are many beautiful trails in this national forest, which surrounds the Hood River Valley on three sides. Most are to the south, on the way to Mount Hood. The **East Fork Trail** offers an easy, but very scenic amble along the swift, glacial-fed East Fork of the Hood River. Accessed from either the Robin Hood or Sherwood Campgrounds along ORE 35, it is great on foot or mountain bike. It's about four miles between the two campgrounds, and the trail continues beyond (north) of the Sherwood Campground.

Tamanawas Falls Trail takes off from the East Fork Trail, just about a half mile north of that campground. A short but steeper hike, this trail is uphill all the way to the reward: beautiful Tamanawas Falls.

Surveyor's Ridge Trail (Trail 688) traverses the ridgeline on the east side of the upper Hood River Valley for 17 miles. It offers some great Mount Hood and valley views and is especially fun for mountain bikers. Pick the brains of friendly staff at **Discover Bikes** (1020 Wasco St., Ste. E., 503/386-4820) for equipment and other ideas. The trailhead is off of Forest Service Road 17, which intersects ORE 35 about 11 miles south of Hood River and just past the big lumber mill to the left of the highway.

Another popular trail with mountain bikers is the **Dog River Trail.** This 6.2-mile, sometimes steep trail can be reached at either end off ORE 35. The southern (higher) approach is at the Pollallie Campground. The trail parallels the Hood (previously named "Dog") River.

Perhaps the best place to experience the transition from western alpine conifer forest to interior high desert is **Lookout Mountain** in the Badger Creek Wilderness. This aptly named 6,525-foot peak is the second highest in the Mount Hood National Forest. To get there look for Road 44 (the Dufur cutoff). It comes up a bit south of Cooper Spur Road on the east side of the highway, not far from Robin Hood Campground. Follow it to Forest Service Road 4410, marked by a sign after a hilly five-mile drive. This route takes you to a parking area opposite the trailhead to High Prairie Trail (Trail 493). Remember that there are no signs most of the six miles on Road 4410 to the trailhead, but if you bear left at the outset and ignore all secondary roads, you'll eventually see a sign indicating the final sharp left turn to the trailhead parking area.

The 20-minute walk to the top on Trail 493 takes you to the former site of an old fire spotter's cabin. Directly west looms Mount Hood. Turn 180 degrees and you face the sagebrush and wheat fields of eastern Oregon. To the south, there's the Three Sisters and Broken Top. West and north of those peaks, Mount Jefferson's tricorn hat rises up. The body of water to the southwest is Badger Lake. To the north, views of Mounts Adams, St. Helens, and Rainier (on a clear day) will have you reeling with visual intoxication.

On most days you can expect cool, windy weather, and there are yellow jackets in August and early September. As with any hike in Oregon, be sure to wear bright colors during hunting season. On the way down, several unsigned spur trails loop back to Trail 493. As long as you keep moving downhill north and west, you'll get back to your car.

Windsurfing and vineyard-hopping complement nearby Columbia Gorge hiking and auto touring, as well as Mount Hood skiing. Regarding the latter, the "Gorge Route" from Portland (I-84 and ORE 35) to Mount Hood ski slopes is becoming a popular and scenic alternative to the more direct but traffic-laden U.S. 26. Hood River ski shops offer discounts on rentals to sweeten the deal.

Camping

Hood River County runs three parks with campgrounds in the Hood River Valley.

Tucker Park (2440 Dee Highway, 541/386-4477) is only four miles from town, in a lovely spot along the banks of the gurgling, boulder-strewn Hood River. It's the most developed of the three county parks, with a store, restaurant, laundry, and ice machine just four miles away

in town. It has 14 RV sites with water and electricity ($14), and 80 tent sites ($13).

Tollbridge Park (ORE 35, 541/387-6888) is also set along the Hood River but in the upper valley. It's 17 miles south of Hood River. It offers showers and two grocery stores a short distance away. Full hookup sites are $15, $14 for water/electric, and $13 for tent sites.

Routson Park (off ORE 35, 541/387-6888) sits along a roaring stretch of the Hood River's East Fork, at the gateway to the Mount Hood National Forest. It provides a more rustic setting higher in the mountains, only 25 minutes from town. For the 20 campsites, amenities are more sparse (flush toilets and drinking water available), and trailers are not recommended. Only $5 per site.

Oregon State Parks offers two full-service campgrounds right on the Columbia Gorge. **Viento State Park** is eight miles west of Hood River on the river side of I-84 (800/551-6949 or 800/452-5687). From mid-April to late October, you'll pay $14–16 for one of the 57 sites with water and electric, or $10–16 to pitch your tent at the other 18 sites. Viento also offers direct recreational access to the mighty Columbia.

Memaloose State Park (11 miles east of Hood River on I-84, 800/452-5687) is accessible from westbound lanes of I-84 only. On the Columbia with limited river access, the park offers 43 full hookup sites and 67 tent spaces, showers, and an RV dump station. Sites are $12–20. It's only fair to mention that both of these campgrounds are not far from a main freight train line; in other words, expect to hear the trains go by, even at night.

The private **Sunset RV Park and Campground** (in town at 2300 West Cascade, 541/386-6098), with a laundry on the premises, has hookups sites for 21 RVs.

There are several nice but semiprimitive forest service campgrounds in the Mount Hood National Forest, which surrounds the valley on three sides. All are in pleasant settings. Call the Hood River Ranger Station for information (6780 ORE 35, 541/352-6002). Some of the forest service campgrounds within 45 minutes of town are

Sherwood, Nottingham, both on ORE 35, and Lost Lake, Wahtum Lake, and Laurence Lake. The latter three campgrounds are in the mountains west of the valley.

EVENTS

The most popular events in Hood River County highlight windsurfing and the seasons of blossom, harvest, and foliage in the orchards.

The third weekend in April **Hood River Blossom Festival** (Hood River Chamber of Commerce, 541/386-2000 or 800/366-3530) celebrates breathtaking views of the valley's orchards in bloom. Arts and crafts, dinners, and the seasonal opening of the Mount Hood Railroad also can be enjoyed.

In July, the **Subaru Gorge Games** (541/386-7774, www.gorgegames.com) take place in diverse locales throughout the region. This is an outdoor Olympics of "extreme sports" including windsurfing, mountain biking, kayaking, snowboarding, kitesailing, a l0-km run, rock climbing, and other activities. Top musical acts, street concerts downtown, special sports clinics, and family events round out this nationally televised event.

In July of 2003 the first annual **Hoodfest Music Festival** (541/386-2000 or 800/366-3530) made its debut in Hood River. Fans of blues and rock listen to national acts at the county fairgrounds in Odell.

The fall counterpart to the spring Blossom Festival is the **Hood River Valley Harvest Fest** (541/386-2000 or 800/366-3530). On the second or third weekend in October, the valley welcomes visitors for two days of entertainment, crafts, fresh locally grown produce, and colorful foliage. The apples and pears are ripe, and admission is free. Hood River is the winter pear (Anjou) capital of the world and produces Bartletts, comice, bosc, and other varieties at different times of the year. Cherries, peaches, and apples round out this horn of plenty. Newton pippin apples are another renowned Hood River product. The 15,000 acres of orchards are still the leading economic factor in the county, with Diamond Packing the leading pear shipper in the United States.

ENTERTAINMENT

While not a mecca for after-hours entertainment, Hood River does have a few good offerings in this department. The **Skylight Theater and Pub** (107 Oak St., 541/386-4888), located in the back of Andrew's Pizza, brings first-run Hollywood movies and the occasional art film to downtown. It includes bar service and is really a part of Andrew's, which means you can devour a steaming slice and a frosty mug of ale while viewing a flick.

Hood River and environs has spawned its own mini-microbrew scene, with three establishments brewing and selling their own suds. The most famous is the **Full Sail Tasting Room** (506 Columbia, 541/386-2247), offering beautiful river views with its renowned suds. Hours are noon–9 P.M. daily. The **Big Horse Brew Pub** (115 State St., 541/386-4411), in addition to selling several varieties of its homemade beer (the India Pale Ale is recommended), also serves up a full menu of lunch and dinner items at pub prices. Tucked away in the upper valley, in the heart of tiny Parkdale, is the charming **Elliot Glacier Public House** (4945 Baseline Rd., 541/352-1022). They make great beers, such as a Scottish ale and ample-bodied porter, and also serve some dinner items, with nightly specials. It's the perfect place to stare at the awesome view of nearby Mount Hood while you wet your whistle.

For live music, keep your eye on downtown posterboards for the occasional excellent live shows (mostly regional/national blues acts) periodically playing in the ballroom of the Hood River Hotel.

ACCOMMODATIONS
Motels

Finding a room in Hood River in the summer isn't easy, and the rates reflect it. Nevertheless, the area has a surprising variety of good, relatively reasonable (under $80/night) places to stay. All prices listed here are summer rates; remember to add an 8 percent room tax within the city of Hood River.

The west side is as close as Hood River gets to generic strip development, being the newest commercial area in town. Having said that, there are several decent places to stay here. Some even have lovely Gorge views. Two motels on the far west end of town and just off Exit 62 of the freeway offer perhaps the nicest Gorge views (not counting the nearby Columbia Gorge Hotel, of course).

The **Meredith Motel** (4300 Westcliff Dr., 541/386-1515) has Eisenhower-era furnishings as well as panoramas from most rooms. The only drawback, for light sleepers, is its proximity to the freeway. The **Vagabond Lodge** (4070 Westcliff Dr., 541/386-2992) has lovely landscaped grounds with a playground for kids, and is a bit more set back from the highway. It is also right next to the Charburger, a basic family-fare type restaurant, with cheap but filling breakfasts. Both motels are in the $50–80 range and are two miles from downtown.

Two other relatively new hotels are located on the main drag (West Cascade Street, on the west side), about a mile from downtown. **Comfort Suites** (2625 W. Cascade, 541/308-1000) is the newest and fanciest. To balance out its rather uncharming location, it offers immaculate rooms and amenities such as a pool/spa and some suites with kitchens. Rooms range $80–140. The **Sunset Motel** (2300 W. Cascade, 541/386-6098) offers a good budget option, with rooms from $45–70. It also operates a small RV park on the premises (see "Camping," earlier in this section). Both of these places are walking distance to Cascade Commons, Hood River's new shopping center.

Riverview Lodge (1505 Oak St., 541/386-8719, www.riverviewforyou.com) has some suites with kitchens, plus a pool. Rooms run $70–125.

Hotels

In the heart of downtown is the **Hood River Hotel** (102 Oak St., 541/386-1900 or 800/386-1859, www.hoodriverhotel.com), an impeccably restored turn-of-the-century hotel with a first-rate restaurant (Pasquale's Ristorante, see "Food," later in this section). Most of the rooms go for $69–169, with a few that are more reasonable and a few higher-priced suites with kitchens. Special vacation packages are also featured. The oak-paneled, high-ceilinged lobby,

with cozy fireplace and adjoining lounge/restaurant, is particularly inviting. Some rooms facing the river are exposed to periodic train noise that's not likely to bother anyone except light sleepers. All in all, "the Hotel" (as locals call it) is a nexus of activity and the most charming in-town digs to be found.

If being on the river is essential to you, **Best Western's Hood River Inn** (1108 E. Marina Way, 541/386-2200 or 800/828-7873, www.hoodriverinn.com) is the only place in town to boast direct river frontage and even a small private beach. Its location, however, next to fast food places off Exit 64 and isolated from downtown, is less than ideal. Nonetheless, the rooms ($80–189) provide great opportunities to watch sailboarders, and there's a lounge and decent restaurant on the premises (Riverside Grill, see "Food," later in this section). Best of all, however, are the heated outdoor pool and spa.

Bed-and-Breakfasts

Three quaint B&Bs are located in the leafy old neighborhood near the historic center. **The Inn at the Gorge** (1113 Eugene St., 541/386-4429, www.innatthegorge.com) is a 1908 Victorian that can be summed up thusly: a sailboarder hangout in a classy B&B. Offerings here include group and off-season rates as well as a complete kitchen in three of the four rooms. Even if you're not a "boardhead," the large and tasty breakfast served would be reason enough to give this place a look. Rates run $85–135.

Also catering to sailboarders, the **Gorgeview Bed and Breakfast** (1009 Columbia, 541/386-5770) is located in a historic house with a great porch view and a hot tub. Rooms are quite affordable at $65–85.

Spectacular views from every window are found at **Beryl House Bed and Breakfast** (4079 Barrett Dr., 541/386-5567, www.berylhouse.com). This 1910 farmhouse is only four miles from town in the midst of fruit orchards below Mount Hood, and it's not surprising to find a hearty farm breakfast awaiting you each morning. Rates run $80–95. Guests benefit from the innkeeper's expertise on local restaurants and windsurfing.

The **Old Parkdale Inn** (4932 Baseline Rd.,

COLUMBIA GORGE HOTEL

This hotel is a lovingly rendered homage to the Jazz Age of the Roaring Twenties, when it was graced by visits from Presidents Coolidge and Roosevelt, Rudolph Valentino, Clara Bow, and the big bands. Built in 1921 by lumber magnate Simon Benson, the Columbia Gorge Hotel (4000 Westcliff Dr., Hood River, 541/386-5566 or 800/345-1921, www.columbiagorgehotel.com) has been called the "Waldorf of the West" for its neo-Moorish facade, glittering chandeliers, and 207-foot waterfall on the grounds. Large wing chairs around the fireplace and fresh-cut bouquets in the dining room also bespeak the hotel's enduring refinement. To get there, take Exit 62 off I-84 and drive over the bridge to the north side of the highway and follow Westcliff Drive west.

Spacious rooms with heavy wooden beams, brass beds, fluffed-up pillows, and period furniture clearly demonstrate what was meant by the "good ol' days." The readers of *Condé Nast Traveler* agree, ranking the inn among the top 500 hotels in the world. Rates are high ($170–299, less in winter), but a more romantic retreat would be hard to come by.

The dining room looks east at the Columbia rolling toward the hotel from out of the mountains and west toward sunset alpenglow. Local mushrooms, fruits, and wild game as well as Columbia River salmon and sturgeon are featured prominently here. The "world-famous farm breakfast" can't be beat. Imagine four courses running the gamut of American breakfast food served with such theatrical flourishes as "honey from the sky"—Hood River Valley apple blossom honey poured from a height of several feet above the table onto hot, fresh-baked biscuits. This symbolizes the 207-foot-high Wah Gwin Gwin ("Rushing Water") Falls that descend the precipice in back of the hotel. As they say at the hotel, "You don't just get a choice—you get it all."

Parkdale, 541/352-5551) has three rooms, two of which are spacious suites. The tab runs $110 ($125 for the suites), but the breakfast is gourmet-quality and the peaceful village will satisfy those looking for an escape from the rat race. The gardens, full kitchens, mountain views, and private baths are also appreciated.

The **Mount Hood Hamlet Bed & Breakfast** (6741 ORE 35, 541/352-3574 or 800/407-0570, www.mthoodhamlet.com) has good Mount Hood views, full breakfasts, and a nice mix of modern conveniences and a historic feel for $110–140.

The **Panorama Lodge** (2290 Old Dalles Dr., 541/387-2687 or 888/403-2687, www.panoramalodge.com) is nestled in the wooded hills on the east side of the Hood River Valley. Its five rooms, most with Mount Hood views, go for $50–100 and come with a tasty breakfast.

FOOD

Hood River's status as the premier windsurfing town in North America and a tourist mecca has brought sophisticated tastes and higher prices. No other small town in the Gorge (or the Pacific Northwest, for that matter) can boast such a roster of fine restaurants, not to mention gourmet coffee and options for vegetarians. There aren't too many towns of a few thousand souls anywhere in the world with their own coffer roaster (Hood River Coffee Co.), wineries (Flerchinger, Hood River), microbreweries (Full Sail/White Cap, Big Horse, and Eliot Glacier), and some of the finest fruit in the world. The only thing to keep in mind is that most restaurants here close early (by big city standards), so plan accordingly.

In the parking lot between 5th and 6th Streets and Cascade and Columbia is the **Saturday Farmer's Market** featuring local craft and food booths along with live music. Call the chamber of commerce for more info. Just up the street on 5th is **Panzanella's Bakery and Deli,** serving delicious bread, baked daily, and scrumptious premade deli sandwiches (on fresh bread).

The brightest spot in Hood River's dining scene is **Brian's Pourhouse** (606 Oak St.,

541/387-4344). No place can match Brian's for sheer culinary creativity. This is borne out by the constant stream of repeat customers; Brian's has become a local hangout for the under-40, outdoor-sport-oriented crowd. The chef offers inventive dishes that combine the best of traditional Asian, European, and nouvelle elements, always with a fresh flair. Besides the great regular menu, daily specials are featured. Treat yourself to one of several outstanding appetizers before your main course. All this can be had for relatively reasonable prices.

Pasquale's Ristorante (in the Hood River Hotel at 102 Oak St., 541/386-1900 or 800/386-1859) offers Italian and Northwest cuisine, with some outdoor seating. In a similar price range and genre, the recently opened **North Oak Brasserie** (113 3rd St., 541/387-2310) rounds out downtown's Italian offerings. Besides a solid repertoire of regional Italian entrées, the Brasserie features delectable appetizers, such as grilled goat cheese and roasted garlic. The roasted garlic and brie soup is the house specialty, and serious oenophiles will be drawn here to sample the finest wine collection in town. Open daily for dinner. The **Sixth Street Bistro** (6th and Cascade, 541/386-5737) has a good selection of microbrews on tap and an eclectic menu featuring fresh Northwest and locally grown organic ingredients. Lunch and dinner prices are moderately priced, and kids are welcome.

On "The Heights" (the plateau forming the start of the lower Hood River Valley, a few hundred feet above downtown) you'll find **The Mesquitery** (1219 12th Street, 541/386-2002), where wood-smoke and barbecue flavors issue a wake-up call to your taste buds for lunch (Mon., Wed., and Fri.) or dinner (daily). You'll find the best ribs in town here, not to mention steaks, fish, and many other dishes. Prices run anywhere from moderate to expensive for dinner, depending on how many "sides" you tack on to the main course.

Two other highly recommended restaurants are ensconced at opposite ends of town. To make a special occasion of your evening, try **Stonehedge Garden** (3405 W. Cascade, 541/386-

3940), located in a historic house in a romantic wooded setting on the west end of town. Stonehedge specializes in classic renditions of aged beef, fresh seafood, and fine wines. A must-try dessert is the bread pudding. The setting and quality justify the higher prices. If you're coming from Exit 62 off I-84, look for it just past the gas station across the road. Follow the signs on the right up the dirt road about a mile.

East of downtown, in the Best Western Hood River Inn, is the **Riverside Grill** (1108 E. Marina Way, 541/386-2200). From the restaurant's riverside perch along the Columbia diners can enjoy a fine view while relishing the Northwest cuisine. The prices are moderate to expensive for dinners; they are about half that for breakfast and lunch. The inn is located on the north (river) side of I-84, just off Exit 64.

A cluster of informal but good deli/lunch/coffee places is located along Oak Street in the downtown area. **Andrew's Pizza and Bakery** (104 Oak St., 541/386-1448), easily wins our vote for best pizza in the Gorge. East Coast transplants will especially appreciate the thin-crusted triangles, so reminiscent of the Big Apple's. Lots of extravagant toppings are available, as well as microbrews and great coffee. Open daily. In the back of Andrew's is the Skylight Theater (see "Entertainment," earlier in this section). Down the street one block is **Holstein's Coffee Company** (12 Oak St., 541/386-4115), probably the best straight-up java joint around. Walk across the street for a darn good bagel with one of seven types of cream cheese or other accompaniments at **Hood River Bagel Company** (13 Oak St., 541/386-2123). A few blocks uphill (walk off those calories), **Mike's Ice Cream** (504 Oak St.) serves up great ice cream and shakes April–October; especially noteworthy, when available, is the incomparably delicious huckleberry shake.

The **Trillium Cafe** (207 Oak St., 541/386-1996) is a good option for a wholesome downtown lunch at a reasonable price. They feature delicious quiches on Sunday. Not far from downtown, the **New York City Sub Shop** (1020B Wasco St., 541/386-5144) makes giant sub sandwiches which, true to East Coast tradition, are amply stuffed with piquant ingredients and very reasonably priced. You are guaranteed to leave satisfied.

For sojourners wandering through the valley to admire the pastoral beauty of the orchards or Mount Hood views, **Santacroce's Italian Restaurant** (4780 ORE 35, 541/354-2511) will satisfy your hunger with good, basic Italian food and pizza. Open Wed.–Sun. for dinner only, prices here are moderate. In the lower valley there's **Clubhouse Restaurant** (at the Hood River Golf Course, 1850 Country Club Rd., 541/386-5022), serving American and German cuisine at reasonable prices.

INFORMATION AND SERVICES

The **Hood River County Chamber of Commerce** (at the Hood River Expo Center, Portway Ave., 541/386-2000 or 800/366-3530) has an extensive array of maps, pamphlets, and other information about the area. They also have a huge, 3-D model of the Gorge terrain that is an excellent way to orient you to local geography. Take Exit 63 off I-84 and head north (toward the river), following the signs to the Expo Center. Another source of local visitor information, although limited to outdoor recreation, is the **National Forest Service Scenic Area Office** (902 Wasco Ave., 541/386-2333). To get there, head down 7th Street until it winds around to the left, becoming Wasco Avenue, then follow the signs.

Downtown you'll find the **U.S. Post Office** (408 Cascade, between 4th and 5th Streets). Just two blocks up the street is the **Hood River Police Department** (3rd and Cascade, 541/386-2121). There are public restrooms a block away at the old City Hall (211 2nd St.). **Hood River Memorial Hospital** (13th and May, 541/386-7889) is open 24 hours a day with a physician-staffed emergency room.

Greyhound serves Hood River, stopping at the Port of Hood River office (600 E. Marina Way, 541/386-1212). Also at the same location is **Columbia Area Transit** (541/386-4202), providing van and special bus service, but not offering regularly scheduled routes in town. **Hood River Taxi and Transportation** (1107 Wilson St., 541/386-2255) provides taxi service in and around the city, using just one cab, around the clock except 3 A.M. to 7 A.M. on Saturday. **Blue Star Columbia Gorge Airporter** (800/247-2272) offers airport shuttle service between Hood River and Portland International Airport. The one-stop travel agency that can line you up with home rentals, airline reservations, windsurfing rentals/lessons, and bed-and-breakfasts is **Gorge Central Reservation Service** (220 Eugene St., 541/386-6109).

Two Laundromats are available in town. **West Side Laundromat** (1911 W. Cascade St., 541/386-5650), with extra-large-capacity machines, is across the street from Safeway. The **Heights Laundromat** (1771 12th St., 541/386-3050) is in the Hood River Shopping Center a mile south of downtown.

Radio station KMCQ (104.5 FM) has wind readings 7:20 A.M.–9:50 A.M. at half-hour intervals. Local ski and road reports are also available on this station and on KIHR (105.5 FM), the Hood River station.

Two **Bank of America** branches (115 Oak St. and 115 E. Fourth St.) and Rosauers Supermarket (1867 12th St.) have walk-up **ATMs. Cybertime-cafe** (3708 W. 7th, 541/296-8598) provides **Internet access.**

COLUMBIA RIVER GORGE

The Dalles

It hits you shortly after leaving Hood River. Verdant forests give way to scrub oak, which transitions to sage and the grasslands of eastern Oregon. You've come to The Dalles, a place Lewis and Clark in 1805 called the "Trading Mart of the Northwest." Instead of seeing a Native American potlatch on the Columbia, however, the modern visitor will see 10,000 souls living in the industrial hub of the Gorge. One also sees now-defunct aluminum plants and once-thriving timber mills by the river.

These days, The Dalles focuses on historical tourism as well as an emerging red wine grape industry and already thriving cherry-growing agriculture. A complete perspective on Oregon history as well as rural renewal is impossible without a day trip here.

The Dalles downtown is awash in bits of Oregon's past—the Oregon Trail Marker, the stunning 1897 old St. Peters Landmark, and the historic Baldwin Saloon. Explore the old Fort Dalles grounds and the Fort Dalles Museum, housed in the original surgeon's quarters from the days when the fort was active. Another early landmark, Pulpit Rock, still stands in the middle of 12th Street, just as it did in the 1800s when the Methodist ministers preached to the native populations and settlers. Learn more about Native Americans by viewing Indian baskets, carvings and crafts on display in a massive collection at Maryhill Museum of Art, located across the Columbia River in Washington. While visiting the museum, see Stonehenge, the nation's first memorial to World War I soldiers. Enjoy the work of local artists at The Dalles Art Center located in the historic Carnegie Library.

Shortly after you enter town on Exit 82 (City Center exit), stop off at the **chamber of commerce** (corner of 2nd and Portland Streets, 404 W. 2nd St., 800/255-3385) and pick up their pamphlets, *The Dalles: Historic Gateway to the Columbia Gorge* and *Walking Tours to Historic Homes and Buildings.* Take a gander at the restored Wasco County Courthouse next door, which was moved from its original location. This court presided over much of the country west of the Rockies in the mid-1800s. The following overview in conjunction with these publications can annotate your day trip here. As the walking tour showcases churches, homes, and government buildings built between 1859 and 1929, let's look at those parts of town whose history dates back before that time. Our itinerary will conform to historical chronology.

SIGHTS AND RECREATION
Seufert Park
Although the visitors center is at the west end of The Dalles, begin your travels six miles east of town off I-84 on Exit 87 with the Seufert Park interpretive center, staging area for the free train that tours The Dalles Dam. (For information on this complex, call 541/296-6616 or 800/255-3385).

The train and tour take about an hour and run April 14–June 4, Wed.–Sun. 10 A.M.–5 P.M. with the last train departing at 4 P.M. June 5– to Sept. 3, hours are 9 A.M.–6 P.M. with the last train departing at 5 P.M. Tours run on the half-hour.

On the trip, be on the lookout for displays of petroglyphs unearthed during construction. You'll immediately notice that the dam's longest arm runs parallel to, rather than across, the river. This is because the trough through which the Columbia runs here is so narrow that there wouldn't be room for navigation locks, generators, fish ladders, and spillways with a conventional design.

In addition to detailing the workings of the world's fourth-largest hydroelectric project (largest dam on the lower Columbia), displays and commentary recount the historical importance of this location as a gathering place and gateway for native peoples and pioneer travelers. Just upstream from here was Celilo Falls, where Native Americans armed with spears and dip nets pursued salmon for centuries. Today native fishermen sell salmon for low prices on certain weekends in

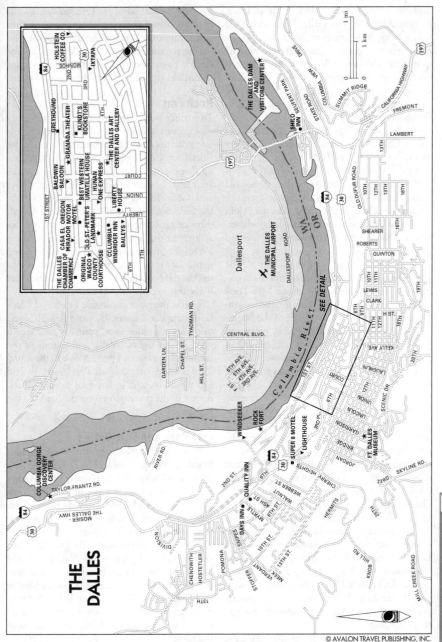

THE DALLES

COLUMBIA RIVER GORGE

© AVALON TRAVEL PUBLISHING, INC.

September. Call 888/BUY-1855 for more information. Although The Dalles Dam ended the fishing frenzy by submerging the falls in 1957, reminders in the form of artifacts and customs recall its spiritual and mercantile significance in the native tradition. Photos portraying Native Americans spreading their 20-foot-long dip nets from precarious platforms above the falls will also help the imagination.

Finally, you might be treated to this same sight on the Columbia today, albeit with lower water and reduced catch levels. If you can be in this area the first weekend of April, the Visitor Information Bureau can direct you to where the age-old native ritual of welcoming the first salmon upstream takes place. The public is welcome to join the Native Americans for frybread, huckleberries, and salmon cooked over an open fire and served with boiled roots and venison.

The Celilo Village is 12 miles east of The Dalles on a shelf at the foot of a bluff overlooking I-84. Just take the Celilo exit off I-84. Look for the ceremonial lodge a short distance southwest of the exit. This was the site of the Native American fishing village described by Lewis and Clark. It went into decline with the coming of the dams, particularly The Dalles project. Today, it's cut off from the river by railroad tracks and the freeway.

Not surprisingly, the Seufert Park interpretive center's emphasis is on the coming of the white settlers. The arrival of Lewis and Clark was the seminal event in defining another role for the river-transportation for westbound travelers in the Oregon country. French voyagers who had passed through at the behest of fur-trapping concerns called these waters near Celilo Falls La Grande Dalle de la Columbia ("The Big Trough of the Columbia"). From this point, the river was not considered safely navigable. As time went on, the area and the town became known as The Dalles. Oregon Trail emigrants loaded their wagons onto boats after portaging them overland around La Grande Dalle. These portages were later abetted by the first railroad tracks in Oregon, constructed by the Oregon Steamship Navigation Company.

Thus, the region near the modern dam site has been a focal point for Oregon native civilizations as well as for a pioneer transportation and trade route. Today, the dam itself is the northern terminus of the world's largest hydroelectric power system. Several other important landmarks are located at the other end of town.

Rock Fort

To further stimulate your reverie of the early explorers and for the sake of historical chronology, your next stop might be Lewis and Clark's Rock Fort. Coming from downtown, take Exit 83 (West 6th Street), turn left and then make your first right onto Webber Street to the port area. Go a mile on Webber and make a right at the UPS building on West 1st Street. As you drive east past the warehouses, several signs reassure you that you'll be at the dynamic duo's overnight bivouac shortly. The undeveloped gravel lot surrounded by big stones overlooking the river contrasts with the warehouses and billboards nearby.

Unlike the more impressive Lewis and Clark landmarks like Rooster Rock and Beacon Rock, this site calls more upon your imagination to ward off the sights, smells, and sounds of the surrounding industrial park. A visit to the mural "Lewis and Clark at Rock Fort" (401 E. 2nd St.) should help fill in any gaps in your visualization of the two explorers on the banks of the Columbia.

City Park and Fort Dalles

For another less-than-thrilling walk on hallowed ground, proceed to The Dalles City Park at 6th and Union Streets. Pioneer Ezra Meeker placed a marker on this site in 1906 to commemorate the end of the original Oregon Trail. In 1845 Samuel Barlow opened the first overland route to the Willamette Valley here, extending the initial route. Barlow Road aficionados should pick up the National Forest Service brochure to guide them over much of this pioneer thoroughfare. The **Dalles Visitor and Convention Bureau** (800/225-3385) puts out a driving-tour pamphlet that also outlines how to traverse the northernmost portions of the route.

In this park you'll also note the Victor Trevitt House. An interesting postscript on this pioneer printer and politico is supplied at the Memaloose rest stop halfway between The Dalles and Hood River on the west side of I-84. Behind the restroom overlooking Memaloose Island on the Columbia is a historical placard mentioning that Trevitt's grave was put on the island among native burial sites at his own request, so high was his esteem for his red brothers. "Memaloose" means "to die" in Chinook, and this island experienced a death of sorts a half-century ago. At the time, water backed up by the Bonneville Dam submerged this sacred site, reducing it to its current half-acre size. Given the decimation of the Native American population and the salmon runs, this event can be viewed as adding insult to injury.

As the final prelude to the walking tour, visit Fort Dalles at 15th and Garrison Streets (for information write: City of The Dalles Museum Commission, P.O. Box 806, The Dalles 97058, 541/296-4547). Unlike the preceding points of interest, there's an actual structure here housing memorabilia. Hours are daily 10 A.M.–5 P.M. March–Oct.; Nov.–Feb., Monday, Thursday, Friday noon–4 P.M., and Saturday 10 A.M.–4 P.M. Coming from the west take Exit 83 off I-84, go east on 6th to Trevitt and follow the signs. Admission is $3 adults, discounts for children and seniors.

The Surgeon's Quarters, dating back to 1856, serves as a museum for armaments, period furniture, and other pioneer items as well as Native American artifacts. In 1850, Fort Dalles was established in response to the massacre of missionaries Dr. Marcus and Narcissa Whitman. The Whitmans had attempted to impose Euro-American ways on the Native Americans with unfortunate results.

For instance, the natives could not understand the concept of private property and felt that Whitman's whipping of those who inadvertently took what they considered to be communal property

A visit to the restored Moorish-style Granada Theater lets you enjoy music and movies in a theater that dates back to vaudeville days.

was unduly harsh. The last straw occurred when a measles vaccine Whitman administered cured the white children but killed the native children. The Native Americans were further confused and understandably angry when they were told that their children's deaths were due to a lack of immunity. Their violent retaliation incited Congress to establish the only military post between Fort Vancouver and the Rockies. The Surgeon's Quarters is the one remaining part of this complex. This is Oregon's oldest historic museum, dating back to 1905.

Several years later, the establishment of Wasco County in 1859 made The Dalles the seat of a 130,000-square-mile bailiwick stretching from the Cascades to the Rocky Mountains. This was the largest county ever formed in the United States.

Now you're ready to take the walking tour described in the pamphlet, with an understanding of the rich heritage of this gateway to the Gorge and the Oregon Country.

Columbia Gorge Discovery Center and Wasco County Historical Museum

To the Native Americans, it was the great gathering place. To Lewis and Clark and the Oregon Trail pioneers, it was the only pass traversing the Cascades Range at sea level. To connoisseurs of the Pacific Northwest's rich historical mosaic and varied landscapes, the Columbia River Gorge is a journey to the source.

The **Columbia Gorge Discovery Center and Wasco County Historical Museum** (5000 Discovery Dr. N., Crates Point, three miles west of The Dalles, ORE 30, 541/296-8600) coalesce the rich historical, geological, biological, and cultural legacies of this region. The Discovery Center addresses the region as a whole, articulating a 40-million-year time line with scale models and videos (as well as simulated "hands-on" experiences) that begins with the cataclysms that created the Gorge on through its native occupation, to the coming of the pioneers and subsequent domination by Euro-Americans.

COLUMBIA RIVER GORGE

Along the way, native plants and animals are given attention along with such diverse activities as road building, orchards, and windsurfing. A decent cafeteria is located on site. A short walk away, the Wasco County Historical Museum reviews 10,000 years of Native American life, early explorers, and industry.

Situated on a bluff above the Columbia on ORE 30, the museums are accessed via Exit 82 off I-84. After turning right onto ORE 30, follow a winding road to the parking lot. Both exhibit halls are open 9 A.M.–5 P.M. daily. A single fee admits you to both venues ($6.50 adults, $5.50 seniors, $3 ages 6–16).

Murals

Historical murals are appearing in many towns with Oregon Trail heritage, and The Dalles is no exception. *Decision at Dalles,* by Don Crook, shows pioneers setting out on the Columbia River route to the Willamette Valley. Look for this 70-foot-high mural at the corner of 2nd and Federal Streets. *Lewis and Clark at Fort Rock,* by Robert Thomas, can be found at 401 E. 2nd Street on the side of Tony's Town and Country Clothing. *The Dalles: Trade Center for 10,000,* by Roger Cooke, is a third mural nearby depicting the gathering of the tribes along the Columbia described by Lewis and Clark. More murals are projected for this town so rich in history and memory.

Windsurfing

Besides its historical significance, The Dalles is gaining a reputation as the best place in the Gorge to learn windsurfing. The bowl-like contours of Riverfront Park mute the power of the winds while isolating the area from the Columbia's stiff current and keeping the waves down. With wind currents that always seem to blow you back toward shore, beginning sailboarders can venture out with a greater feeling of security here than elsewhere in the area.

Other Activities

A visit to the restored Moorish-style **Granada Theater** (223 E. 2nd St., 541/298-4710, www.thegranada.org) lets you enjoy music and movies

in a theater that dates back to vaudeville days. Later, it was the first theater west of the Rockies equipped for talkies.

Sorosis Park serves as a backyard for the locals to enjoy tennis, picnic areas, and just plain beautiful views. To get there, take Trevitt Street south and follow the signs.

PRACTICALITIES

Accommodations and Food

For quaint historic lodgings, you have to head out of town. Take Highway 14 east and cross the river to get to Lyle, Washington. There you'll find a splendid historic railway hotel called the **Lyle Hotel and Restaurant** (100 7th St., Lyle, 509/365-5953, www.lylehotel.com). Rooms are about $70.

Otherwise, for those who elect to stay over in The Dalles, there are several chain-hotel/motels from which to choose. The **Comfort Inn** (351 Lone Pine Dr., 541/298-2800) is one of them and just a short distance to downtown. Rooms come equipped with microwaves and coffee makers. Rates are $85–120. Kids stay free. **Columbia Windrider Inn** (200 W. 4th, 541/296-2607, www.windriderinn.com) is recommended for outdoorsy folks. The primary guest is the sailboarder or outdoor-sports enthusiast who may stay for more than a few nights. It's set up more like hostel, with all of the amenities you'd have in your own home. The innkeeper can offer windsurfing tips and point the way to other outdoor attractions. Prices are an incredible value, ranging $45–60. Discounts for extended stays. More elaborate quarters can be found at **Liberty House B&B** (514 Liberty St., 541/298-5292). Rates range $65–75.

After visiting St. Peters Church, the century-old Gothic revival landmark, you can smooth your reentry into the 21st century by grabbing a bite in the shadow of history at the **Baldwin Saloon** (1st and Court Streets, 541/296-5666). This 1876 building (it was a restaurant then, too) is a repository of turn-of-the-century oil paintings adorning the brick walls. The 18-foot mahogany bar and the pendulum clock also ensure a historical reverie. Try the fresh oysters (pan-fried), smoked salmon mousse, breads, and desserts here. Prices are moderate.

Information and Transportation

Additional information on this area can be had by contacting 800/98-GORGE or www.crgva.org. **Klindt's Booksellers** (315 E. 2nd St., 541/296-3355) represents another bit of history in The Dalles. Established in 1870, it is the oldest book-store in Oregon, complete with original wood floors, a high ceiling, and oak and plate-glass display cases.

Columbia Gorge Express is a shuttle bus service providing transportation through the Columbia River Gorge in both Oregon and Washington (102 Oak St., Hood River 97031, 541/386-3594 or 888/386-6822, www.columbiagorgeexpress.com).

Resources

Suggested Reading

In addition to the titles cited in the text, Oregon-bound travelers would do well to acquaint themselves with these books. We advise readers to search for out-of-print books at www.powells.com.

Atlases

Dicken, Samuel. *The Making of Oregon.* Portland: Oregon Historical Society, 1979. Addressing the human history, economics, and topography of each part of the state, Dicken's publications make Oregon's cultural and geological landscapes come alive.

Dicken, Samuel. *Oregon Divided.* Portland: Oregon Historical Society, 1982.

MacArthur, Lewis. *Oregon Geographic Names.* Portland: Oregon Historical Society, 2003. This text might be physically weighty, but its alphabetic historical rundown of place names makes for light and informative reading.

Coastal Oregon

Gibbs, James A. *Shipwrecks of the Pacific Coast.* Portland: Binford and Mort, 1989. Endlessly fascinating and frequently heartbreaking reading from a master of Northwest maritime lore. Covers all known shipwrecks off the coasts of Oregon, Washington, and California.

Henderson, Bonnie. *Exploring the Wild Oregon Coast.* Seattle: Mountaineers Books, 1994. Primarily a hiking guide, covering a number of lesser-known but rewarding hikes, and enriched with an abundance of information on flora and fauna.

Morris, Elizabeth and Mark. *Moon Handbooks Coastal Oregon.* Emeryville: Avalon Travel Publishing, 2004. An expanded and more de-

tailed version of the Coastal Oregon chapter in this book.

O'Donnell, Terence. *Cannon Beach: A Place by the Sea.* Portland: Oregon Historical Society, 1996. A highly personal historical evocation of life in Cannon Beach and environs.

Ostertag, Rhonda, and George Ostertag. *75 Hikes in Oregon's Coast Range and Siskiyous.* Seattle: Mountaineers Books, 2003. A well-chosen selection of hikes along the length of the coastal ranges covers a broad variety of terrain and difficulty levels. Detailed trail descriptions and maps make this guide particularly useful.

Paulson, Dennis. *Shorebirds of the Pacific Northwest.* Seattle: University of Washington Press, 2003. For the specialist rather than the generalist, there is no better book than this richly detailed guide for distinguishing an avocet from a stilt, a plover from a curlew, and identifying any of the dozens of other species found near the water's edge.

Puterbaugh, Parke, and Alan Bisbort. *Life is a Beach.* New York: McGraw-Hill Book Company, 1988. There are many good books on the coast, but the only one we've found that goes beyond conventional guidebooks was written by out-of-staters. These East Coast residents and former *Rolling Stone* writers portray Oregon's western edge with humor, insight, and graceful prose.

Williams, Paul. *Oregon Coast Hikes.* Seattle: Mountaineers Books, 1985. A good regional hiking guide.

Eastern Oregon

Jackman, E. R., and R. A. Long. *The Oregon Desert.* Caldwell, ID: Caxton Press, 2003.

Jackman, E. R., John Scharff, and Charles Conkling (photographer). *Steens Mountain in Oregon's High Desert Country.* Caldwell, ID: Caxton Press, 2003. These two works are the classics for eastern Oregon. Within the volumes, history and local color fill in the east side of the state's wide-open spaces.

Fiction

Kesey, Ken. *The Last Go Round.* New York: Viking, 1994. The original prankster's latest Oregon-oriented effort is recommended reading for anyone seeking a little texture about the Pendleton Round-Up. Old photos and background information impart a sense of history, and the tensions among a white, a black, and a Nez Percé contestant during the 1911 rodeo will hold your interest.

Kesey, Ken. *Sometimes a Great Notion.* New York: Viking, 1964. This book is a fictional portrayal of what Mark Twain called the "westering spirit."

General Interest

Adams, Melvin. *Netting the Sun.* Pullman, WA: Washington State University Press, 2001. Born and raised in eastern Oregon, Adams's passion for Oregon's high desert informs this collection of haunting and beautifully written essays.

Douglas, William O. *Of Men and Mountains.* San Francisco: Chronicle Books, 1985. The final chapters of the late Supreme Court Justice's autobiography provide some redolent descriptions of life in Oregon. Particularly evocative are his descriptions of the Wallowas.

Egan, Timothy. *The Good Rain.* New York: Alfred A. Knopf, 1990. Egan brings the practiced eye of a *New York Times* correspondent to towns along the Columbia and other parts of Oregon and Washington caught in the transition from a resource-based economy. The historical perspectives of a 19th-century diarist's entries underscore his descriptions of local color and contemporary issues.

Hadlow, Robert W. *Elegant Arches, Soaring Spans: C. B. McCullough, Oregon's Master Bridge Builder.* Corvallis, OR: Oregon State University Press, 2003. Covers the beautiful dozen bridges designed by McCullough between the two World Wars, which he called "jeweled clasps in a wonderful string of pearls."

Jewell, Judy. *Oregon.* New York: Fodor's Compass American Guides, 1998. Read this guide before traveling to the state to complement *Moon Handbooks Oregon* as your on-the-road reference. Beautiful color photos and insightful travel tips liven up this literary rendition of Oregon's greatest hits.

Metzler, Ken. *The Best of Oregon.* Portland: Timber Press, 1986. A loving look at the state by a longtime Oregon journalist and University of Oregon professor.

Nelson, Sharlene, and Ted Nelson (contributor). *Umbrella Guide to Oregon Lighthouses.* Kenmore, WA: Epicenter Press, 2003. Tells the stories of 11 Oregon coast lighthouses, as well as beacons on the Columbia and Willamette Rivers. A good reference for anyone curious about these romantic aids to navigation.

Thoele, Michael. *Footprints Across Oregon.* Portland: Graphic Arts Center Publishing Co., 1988. Based on anecdotes about every-day folks, this is recommended reading for anyone wanting insight into the flesh and blood of Oregon.

Tisdale, Sallie. *Stepping Westward.* New York: Holt and Co., 1991. The award-winning essayist deftly blends fact and fancy. In her treatment of the past, present, and future of the Northwest, the Portland author emphasizes a native worldview.

Guidebooks

Barringer, Jody, and Ruth Berkowitz. *Kidding Around the Gorge*. Hood River, OR: Gorgebooks, 2003. A kid-tested list of activities for and places to take children in the Columbia River Gorge, with easy-to-follow driving directions.

Bell, Mimi. *Offbeat Oregon*. San Francisco: Chronicle Books, 1983. Charming essays about travel in all four corners of the state will get you out of the armchair and onto the road.

Fanselow, Julie. *Traveling the Lewis and Clark Trail*. Helena, MT: Falcon Publishing, 2003. This guidebook for the modern-day explorer acquaints readers with what to see and do along Lewis and Clark's celebrated route from Illinois to Oregon.

Fanselow, Julie. *Traveling the Oregon Trail*. Guilford, CT: Globe Pequot Press, 2001. The adventures continue with Fanselow's scenic and informative guide to the present-day Oregon Trail.

Friedman, Ralph. *Oregon for the Curious*. Caldwell, ID: Caxton Ltd., 1972. Friedman is Oregon's King of the Road. Of his half-dozen books, this one is the most recommended. It still is the best mile-by-mile description of the state ever done.

Garren, John. *Oregon River Tours*. Portland: Garren Publishing, 2003. Detailed maps and charts make this an indispensable tool for anyone braving Oregon's white water.

Mainwaring, William L. *Exploring Oregon's Central and Southern Cascades*. Salem, OR: West Ridge Press, 1979.

Mainwaring, William L. *Exploring the Oregon Coast*. Salem, OR: West Ridge Press, 1985.

Mainwaring, William L. *Exploring the Mt. Hood Loop*. Salem, OR: West Ridge Press, 1992. Main-

waring's texts provide excellent supplements to *Moon Handbooks Oregon* by covering activities, hiking, camping, history, and local color.

Nix, Nell. *Out and About: Portland with Kids*. Portland: Sasquatch Books, 2002. A must-have for those exploring Portland with children.

Samson, Karl. *Frommer's Great Outdoor Guide to Oregon and Washington*. New York: Macmillan Travel, 1998. This text gets our highest recommendation for launching an adventure by land or by sea.

Whitehill, Karen, and Terry Whitehill. *A Pedestrian's Portland: Forty Walks in Portland Area Parks and Neighborhoods*. Seattle: Mountaineers Books, 1989. A wonderful guide for exploring the Rose City on foot.

History

Ambrose, Stephen. *Undaunted Courage*. New York, Touchstone Press: 1996. A classic book on the country's seminal voyage of discovery, the Lewis and Clark expedition. It gives a historical context to the explorers' journals in an entertaining, enlightening way. Read this before taking on The Journals of Lewis and Clark themselves. The latter work is available through many different publishers, but the antiquated grammar and archaic English make it difficult reading.

Barlow, Jerry, and Christine Richardson. *The Chinese Doctor of John Day*. Portland: Binford and Mort, 1979. Chronicles Chinese life in Oregon at the turn of the 20th century.

Beckham, Steven Dow, and Robert M. Reynolds (photographer). *Lewis & Clark from the Rockies to the Pacific*. Portland: Graphic Arts Center Publishing Co., 2002. Focusing on the second half of the expedition's outward-bound journey, this gorgeously illustrated and insightful book covers Lewis and Clark's trying months spent camped in the rainy woodlands of the north Oregon coast.

Crawford, P. W. *The Overland Journey to Oregon.* North Plains, OR: Soap Creek Enterprises, 1997. An autobiographical sketch written by one of Oregon's founding fathers, and the first settler on the Cowlitz River, Peter Crawford. This historical text chronicles his 1847 journey from Indiana to Oregon.

Federal Writers' Project (editor). *WPA Guide to Oregon.* The granddaddy of them all, this 1941 guide is the primary inspiration for *Moon Handbooks Oregon.* The product of dozens of authors working in the Federal Writers' Project, this post-Depression guidebook still sets the standard for thorough coverage and vivid description. Although much of the information is dated, its rundown of pioneer history and glimpses of early 20th-century Oregon make it a valuable tool for any modern traveler. Available in many public libraries.

Friedman, Ralph. *In Search of Western Oregon.* Caldwell, ID: Caxton Press, 1991. A fascinating read, packed with anecdotes, folklore, historical details, and more, all told in Friedman's engaging style.

Oregon Secretary of State (editor). *Oregon Blue Book.* Salem, OR: State of Oregon, 2003. Published biannually by the state of Oregon, this volume provides the best concise history of Oregon. Given its heft and cost (around $30), we recommend a perusal in a library.

O'Donnell, Terrence. *Portland: An Informal History and Guide.* Portland: Oregon Historical Society, 1964. This work by a noted scholar should disabuse you of the notion that history is boring.

Smith, Landon. *The Essential Lewis and Clark.* New York, Ecco Press, 2000. Covers information similar to the dynamic duo's journals, yet provides a much easier read.

Natural History

Alt, David, and Donald W. Hyndman. *Roadside Geology of Oregon.* Missoula, MT: Mountain Press Publishing Company, 2003. Part of the fine Roadside Geology Series, the coast chapters describe, in layman's language, the geologic forces that shaped the region.

Evanich, Joseph E., Jr. *Birders Guide to Oregon.* Portland: Audubon Society of Portland, June 2003. A good all-around guide to the state's birdlife, with a useful breakdown of specific coastal locations and details on what species to watch for and when.

Jolley, Russ. *Wildflowers of the Columbia.* Portland: Oregon Historical Society Press, 1988. An exhaustive study of Oregon's plant species, identifying 744 of the Columbia Gorge's more than 800 species of flowering shrubs and wildflowers.

Laskin, David. *Rains All the Time.* Seattle: Sasquatch Press, 1998. A fascinating inquiry into the region's rainforest-to-desert diversity.

Littlefield, Caroll D. *Birds of Malheur Refuge.* Corvallis, OR: Oregon State University Press, 1990. Recommended for serious birders.

Paulson, Dennis. *Shorebirds of the Pacific Northwest.* Seattle: University of Washington Press, 2003. Contains detailed birding information on the region.

Pojar, Jim, and Andy MacKinnon (editors). *Plants of the Pacific Northwest Coast: Washington, Oregon, British Columbia, and Alaska.* Edmonton, AB: Lone Pine Publishing, 2003. A highly regarded guide to the flora of the entire Northwest region, illustrated with excellent photos.

Sept, J. Duane. *The Beachcomber's Guide to Seashore Life in the Pacific Northwest.* Vancouver, BC: Harbour Publishing Company Limited, 2003. This ideal guide for the casual and curious observer aids in understanding the intertidal zone and in identifying more than 270 species encountered there, including crabs, clams and other mollusks, seaweeds, sea stars, sea anemones, and more.

Suggested Reading

Wallace, David Rains. *The Klamath Knot.* San Francisco: Sierra Club Books, 1984. An excellent book on the natural history of southern Oregon.

Willamette Kayak and Canoe Club (editor). *The Soggy Sneakers Guide to Oregon Rivers.* Corvallis, OR: Willamette Kayak and Canoe Club, 1982. An indispensable guide to Oregon's rivers, replete with maps, class ratings, gradient listings, river lengths, and best seasons to visit.

Yuskavitch, James. *Oregon Wildlife Viewing Guide.* Helena, MT: Falcon Press, 1994. An excellent resource that lists wildlife sites and nearby accommodations. All proceeds from the book go to wildlife site maintenance and publications put out by Defenders of Wildlife.

Photo Essays

Atkeson, Ray. *Oregon I.* Portland: Graphic Arts Center Publishing Co., 1968.

Atkeson, Ray. *Oregon II.* Portland: Graphic Arts Center Publishing Co., 1974.

Atkeson, Ray. *Oregon III.* Portland: Graphic Arts Center Publishing Co., 2003. Atkeson's tomes are the preeminent coffee-table books of Oregon photos. Now available in paperback.

Hoy, Mark. *Backroads of Oregon.* Helena, MT: American Geographic Publishing, 1988. Beautifully photographed, evocative text.

McPhee, Marnie. *Western Oregon: A Portrait of the Land and Its People.* New York: Random House, 2003. Excellent color photos make the westside's landscape and cultural geography come alive.

Environment

Callenbach, Ernest. *Ecotopia.* New York: Bantam, 1983. The author argues that Northern California should break off from the rest of the state to join Oregon as a single republic named "Ecotopia."

Garreau, Joel. *The Nine Nations of North America.* New York: Simon and Schuster, 1986. Another bioregional manifesto, *Nine Nations* divides the continent into nine bioregions on the basis of their cultural, historical, ethnic, economic, and environmental interests.

Seideman, David. *Showdown at Opal Creek.* New York: Carrol and Graf Publishers, 1993. Environmental conflicts among the old-growth forests of Opal Creek are detailed in this fascinating work.

Hiking and Camping Guides

Spring, Ira, and Harvey Manning. *Hiking Guide to the Great Northwest.* Seattle: Mountaineers Books, 1991. Covers a multitude of trails and nature areas.

Stienstra, Tom. *Foghorn Outdoors Oregon Camping.* Emeryville, CA: Avalon Travel Publishing, 2002. Details more than 700 campgrounds across the state, with an excellent selection on the coast. Rich with tips on gear, safety, and other topics.

Sullivan, William L. *Exploring Oregon's Wild Areas.* Seattle: Mountaineers Books, 1988. Undoubtedly the best of its genre, this well-organized book outlines activities for hikers, backpackers, climbers, cross-country skiers, and saddlers. Geology and botany are also addressed.

Wood, Wendell. *A Walking Guide to Oregon's Ancient Forests.* Portland: Oregon Natural Resources Council, 1992. The title says it all. If this guide doesn't motivate you to get outside and enjoy Oregon's splendor, nothing will.

Wuerthner, George. *Oregon's Wilderness Areas.* Englewood, CO: Westcliffe Publishers, Inc., 2002. A fervent and thorough guide to Oregon's 40 wilderness areas. Includes maps, photographs, and day hike suggestions.

Internet Resources

Statewide Information and Services

For more visitor information, see special topic "Visitor Information Sources" in the On the Road chapter.

All Oregon
www.all-oregon.com/
A directory with links to over 5,000 Oregon websites including real estate, wineries, and the Oregon Trail.

Oregon Tourism Commission
www.traveloregon.com

Travel Oregon
www.traveloregon.com
A useful website with information about lodging, recreation opportunities, and a statewide calendar of events.

Regional Information and Services

Central Oregon Coast Association
www.orcoast.com/coca
P.O. Box 2094
313 S.W. 2nd Street, Suite B
Newport, OR 97365
541/265-2064 or 800/767-2064

Central Oregon Visitors Association
www.covisitors.com
63085 N. Hwy. 97, Suite 107
Bend, OR 97701
541/389-8799 or 800/800-8334

Clackamas County Tourism Development Council
www.clackamas-oregon.com
P.O. Box 182
621 High Street
Oregon City, OR 97045
503/655-5511 or 800/647-3843

Columbia River Gorge Visitor's Association
www.crgva.org
404 W. 2nd Street
The Dalles, OR 97058
541/296-2231 or 800-98GORGE

Convention & Visitors Association of Lane County
www.visitlanecounty.org
P.O. Box 10286
115 W. 8th, Suite 190
Eugene, OR 97440
541/484-5307 or 800/547-5445

Convention & Visitors Bureau of Washington County
www.wcva.org
5075 S.W. Griffith Drive, #120
Beaverton, OR 97005
503/644-5555 or 800/537-3149

Eastern Oregon Visitors Association/Oregon Trail Marketing Coalition
www.eova.com
www.otmc.org
P.O. Box 1087
Baker City, OR 97814
541/523-9200 or 800/332-1843

Northwest Oregon Tourism Alliance
www.travelportland.com
26 S.W. Salmon, Box S5
Portland, OR 97204
503/222-2223 or 800/962-3700

Oregon Coast Visitors Association
www.VisitTheOregonCoast.com
P.O. Box 74
313 S.W. 2nd Street, Suite B
Newport, OR 97365
541/574-2679 or 888/628-2101

Oregon's Mt. Hood Territory
www.MtHoodTerritory.com
> 619 High Street
> Oregon City, OR 97045
> 503/655-5511

Portland Oregon Visitors Association
www.travelportland.com
> 1000 S.W. Broadway, Suite 2300
> Portland, OR 97205
> 503/222-2223 or 877/678-5263

Southern Oregon Visitors Association
www.sova.org
> P.O. Box 1645
> Medford, OR 97504
> 541/779-4691 or 800/448-4856

Willamette Valley Visitors Association
www.willamettevalley.org
> P.O. Box 965
> 300 2nd Avenue S.W.
> Albany, OR 97321
> 541/928-0911 or 800/526-2256

Accommodations and Food
Oregon Bed and Breakfast Guild
www.obbg.org/index.htm
> Lists links to Oregon bed-and-breakfasts by region.

Oregon Lodging
www.oregon.com
> All-Oregon lodging and travel guide.

Oregon Restaurants Network
www.oregonrestaurants.net/ar_oregon.html

Events and Entertainment
Oregon Arts Commission
www.oregonartscommission.org/main.php
> A guide to public art, events, and galleries throughout the state.

Oregon Beer
www.oregonbeer.org/index.html
> Proffers merchandise and features a calendar of statewide beer-related events and an extremely useful map of Oregon's microbreweries.

Oregon Endowment for the Humanities
www.oregonhum.org/index.html
> Includes an amazingly thorough calendar of talks and lectures throughout the state.

Oregon Wine
www.oregonwine.org
> Everything you ever wanted to know about Oregon wines, wineries, and events.

Wines Northwest
www.winesnw.com/orhome.html
> A guide to the world of wine in the great Pacific Northwest (and a useful link to guides and driving services).

History
Haunted Places
www.ghostsandcritters.com
> An eerie look into Oregon's underworld. Offers advice for novice ghost hunters and info about haunted places in the state.

Oregon Historical Society
www.ohs.org

Lewis and Clark Information
**Lewis and Clark Oregon
Bicentennial Association**
www.lewisandclarkcoast.com

Lewis and Clark Bicentennial Oregon
www.lcbo.net

Lewis and Clark Oregon
www.lewisandclarkoregon.com

Lewis and Clark Re-enactors
www.lewisandclark.net

**Lewis and Clark Trail Heritage Foundation
Oregon Chapter**
www.lcarchive.org/or_lcthf.html

National Council of the Lewis and Clark Bicentennial
www.lewisandclark200.org

Outdoor Recreation and Camping
Bureau of Land Management
www.or.blm.gov/
Info on BLM-administered public lands including site locations, recreation opportunities, news, brochures, and maps.

GORP
www.gorp.away.com/gorp/activity/hiking/hik_or.htm
An online magazine focusing on outdoor recreational pursuits in Oregon.

Hiking and Backbacking
www.hikingandbackpacking.com/oregon.html
An online magazine about hiking and backpacking in the state.

National Forest Service
www.fs.fed.us
Links to national forests, camping information and reservation, ranger station contact info, maps and brochures, fees, passes and permit info.

Oregon Cycling Magazine Online
www.efn.org/~ocycling
Useful information for Oregon cyclists including events, trails, safety tips, and more.

Oregon Department of Fish and Wildlife
www.dfw.state.or.us

Oregon Hiking
www.oregonhiking.com
Information on outdoor adventures such as hiking, snowshoeing, rafting, and climbing.

Oregon Parks and Recreation Department
www.pr.state.or.us
Covers Oregon's state parks, historic preservation efforts, ATV information, and more.

Oregon Road Runners Club
www.orrc.net
A community resource for runners and walkers listing info about events, training opportunities, and courses.

Ski Resorts
web.pdx.edu/~cyjh/orresorts.html
Administered by Portland State University, this comprehensive website lists links to all major ski areas in the state.

State Parks
www.oregonstateparks.org
Find a state park or a campsite, make a reservation, or download brochures.

Windsor Nature Discovery, LLC
www.nature-discovery.com
An Oregon company specializing in marine life identification charts and posters of all the wildlife you will see on your trip to the coast.

Transportation
Amtrak
www.amtrak.com
Train schedules, fares, and booking information.

Greyhound
www.greyhound.com
Schedules, fares, and booking information.

PDX
www.portlandairportpdx.com
Portland International Airport's website provides a list of carriers, ground transport, and other useful information on the area.

Weather
Oregon Climate Service
www.ocs.orst.edu
Weather information including forecasts, road conditions, ski conditions and reports, marine conditions, watches and warnings.

Index

Index

Acknowledgments

Oregon Handbook, first penned by Stuart Warren and Ted Long Ishikawa and maintained by them through five editions, forms the solid foundation for this edition of *Moon Handbooks Oregon.* The loving care, hard work, and dedication they put into creating the original book comes through on every page.

The bulk of the information in this new edition of the book was diligently fact-checked by Troy Montserrat-Gonzales, who painstakingly phoned each and every deli, state park, museum, and truck stop from Ashland to Imnaha and who wrote several of the callouts. Thanks also go to Niki "Pickle" Tucker for helping us out, just days after escaping from Bakersfield, California. We also could not have completed this work without the help of Oregon's chamber of commerce and visitor center volunteers and employees, who are some of the most passionate and informed experts on the state.

For assistance with photos and illustrations, thanks go to Patti Kileen at the Oregon Tourism Commission, Mark Simon of Image Perfect & Design, Lynsey Turek of Windsor Nature Discovery, Bob Ward of the Drake in Oregon Society, Angel Crane of National Scenic Byways Online, Jane Kirby of the Salem Public Library, Karen Stevens of Independence National Historical Park, Tim Backer of the Oregon State Archives, Christine Campbell of the British Library, Joanne Holland-Bak of CVALCO, Lillian Toong of POVA, Leigh Rhudy, and Michael Lishinsky.

The following Avalon folks were especially helpful during the editing and production: Krista Lyons-Gould, Mia Lipman, Naomi Adler Dancis, Susan Snyder, and Deb Dutcher. Thanks especially to Marisa Solís, our editor, for showing mercy when *both* of our computers simultaneously crashed.

And while they're too young to read this now, we also want to thank our children, Eamon and Fiona, for their help preparing the maps (color highlighters can be such fun!). Thanks, too, to our loyal babysitters: Grandma Suzie, Grandpa Clark, and Sara Hartt. We owe you, big time.

And we have to thank McKinley, for lulling us to sleep with her soulful songs from the attic.

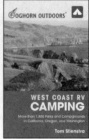
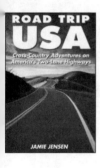

U.S. ~ Metric Conversion

1 inch	=	2.54 centimeters (cm)
1 foot	=	.304 meters (m)
1 yard	=	0.914 meters
1 mile	=	1.6093 kilometers (km)
1 km	=	.6214 miles
1 fathom	=	1.8288 m
1 chain	=	20.1168 m
1 furlong	=	201.168 m
1 acre	=	.4047 hectares
1 sq km	=	100 hectares
1 sq mile	=	2.59 square km
1 ounce	=	28.35 grams
1 pound	=	.4536 kilograms
1 short ton	=	.90718 metric ton
1 short ton	=	2000 pounds
1 long ton	=	1.016 metric tons
1 long ton	=	2240 pounds
1 metric ton	=	1000 kilograms
1 quart	=	.94635 liters
1 US gallon	=	3.7854 liters
1 Imperial gallon	=	4.5459 liters
1 nautical mile	=	1.852 km

To compute Celsius temperatures, subtract 32 from Fahrenheit and divide by 1.8. To go the other way, multiply Celsius by 1.8 and add 32.

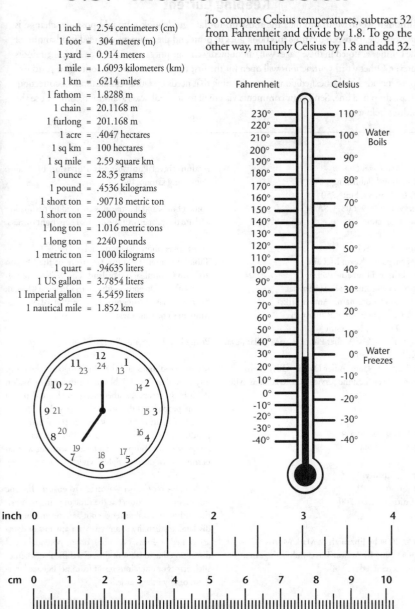

Keeping Current

Although we strive to produce the most up-to-date guidebook humanly possible, change is unavoidable. Between the time this book goes to print and the moment you read it, a handful of the businesses noted in these pages will undoubtedly change prices, move, or even close their doors forever. Other worthy attractions will open for the first time. If you have a favorite gem you'd like to see included in the next edition, or see anything that needs updating, clarification, or correction, please drop us a line. Send your comments via email to atpfeedback@avalonpub.com, or use the address below.

Moon Handbooks Oregon
Avalon Travel Publishing
1400 65th Street, Suite 250
Emeryville, CA 94608, USA
www.moon.com

Editor: Marisa Solís
Series Manager: Kevin McLain
Copy Editor: Elizabeth Wolf
Graphics Coordinator: Susan Snyder
Production Coordinator: Amber Pirker
Freelance Layout: Susan Rimerman
Cover Designer: Kari Gim
Interior Designers: Amber Pirker, Alvaro Villanueva, Kelly Pendragon
Map Editors: Naomi Adler Dancis, Olivia Solís
Cartographers: Suzanne Service, Kat Kalamaras, Mike Morgenfeld
Indexer: Judy Hunt

ISBN: 1-56691-584-8
ISSN: 1080-3394

Printing History
1st Edition—1991
6th Edition—May 2004
5 4 3 2 1

Text © 2004 by Elizabeth & Mark Morris.
Maps © 2004 by Avalon Travel Publishing, Inc.
All rights reserved.

Avalon Travel Publishing is a division of Avalon Publishing Group, Inc.

Some photos and illustrations are used by permission and are the property of the original copyright owners.

Front cover photo: © John Elk III
Table of contents photos: Courtesy of the Oregon Tourism Commission (Portland, The Willamette Valley, Southern Oregon, Southeastern Oregon); © Mark Morris (Coastal Oregon); Courtesy of BLM/Greg Morgan (The Cascades)

Printed in the USA by Worzalla